African Development Indicators 2001

The World Bank
Washington, D.C.

Cover design by Patricia Hord Graphik Design.

ISSN 1020-2927
ISBN 0-8213-4864-7

Contents

6. External Debt and Related Flows   151

7. Government Finance   184

Table des matières

Acknowledgments

This volume was produced by the Operational Quality and Knowledge Services of the Africa Region, in collaboration with the Development Data Group of the Development Economics Vice Presidency.

The volume was prepared by a team led by Ziad Badr and comprising José Delcour, Tosi Mpanu-Mpanu, Rose Mungai, Joan Pandit, and Vildan Verbeek-Demiraydin. Maria Cristina Germany provided valuable guidance. Tariqul Khan prepared the ADI CD-ROM and updated the database. The chapters on national accounts, balance of payments, trade, and government finance draw heavily on the work of World Bank country desks. The chapters on power, communication and transportation, labor force and social indicators tap the World Bank's World Development Indicators database. The chapter on external debt is heavily drawn from DRS (Debt Reporting System) of the World Bank. The chapter on environment was prepared with data from the World Resources Institute. The chapter on privatization of public enterprises was provided by Oliver C. Campbell-White and prepared by Ronnie Hammad. Nicki Marrian provided assistance in editing and production of the volume. Lawrence Mastri desktopped the text.

In addition, many World Bank staff provided information on their countries or related to their economic or sectoral specialties. Other staff aided and advised on the design and content of this volume.

A new milestone in efficiency and technology was reached in preparing this volume. ADI 2001 was produced using the data reporting tool of the 2nd Generation Live Database (2gLDB) system. This tool was programmed to generate automatically all the tables in this volume and can be used for other publications. Using data warehousing technology, the 2gLDB instantly recalculates all indicators and aggregates them once new information is available. This guarantees that the most recent data are reflected in this and future volumes. In the process of reprogramming the system, a major cleanup of the data was performed, which should be reflected in a higher quality product.

Preface

African Development Indicators 2001 continues the data publication series started by the World Bank in 1989 with *African Economic and Financial Data* (published jointly with the United Nations Development Programme), followed by *African Development Indicators 1992, 1994/95, 1996, 1997, 1998/99,* and *2000.* These data volumes are intended to provide Africans and those interested in Africa with a consistent and convenient set of data to monitor development programs and aid flows in the region. Each successive volume provides access to more focused information and represents an improvement in the quality and availability of the data.

The data in this volume derive from a variety of sources. In most cases, the original source is national statistical services in Africa. In addition, many international agencies collect or compile data on Africa and organize national data in a standardized framework. This volume draws heavily from such sources. The data have been supplemented by World Bank staff estimates to help address problems of missing or inconsistent data from standard sources. Some of the estimation methods used here differ from methods used in other sources. This volume addresses these differences in methodologies in the chapter introductions and in the technical notes.

In the tradition of the first seven volumes, this data collection is intended to serve as a prime source of information on Africa. Its wide dissemination to African and non-African analysts and policymakers will contribute to a better understanding of Africa and to development on that continent.

John Roome
Director, Operational Quality
and Knowledge Services
Africa Region

Acronyms and Abbreviations

ADB	African Development Bank	DDG	Development Data Group, World Bank
ADI	*African Development Indicators*	DRS	Debtor Reporting System (World Bank)
AEFD	*African Economic and Financial Data* (UNDP/World Bank 1989)	ECA	Economic Commission for Africa
AFESD	Arab Fund for Economic and Social Development	FAO	UN Food and Agriculture Organization
		f.o.b.	Free on board
BADEA	Arab Bank for Economic Development in Africa	GDF	Global Development Finance (formerly World Debt Tables-WDT
BIS	Bank for International Settlements	GDI	Gross domestic investment
CDIAC	Carbon Dioxide Information Analysis Center	GDP	Gross domestic product
		GDS	Gross domestic savings
CFA	Communauté Financière Africane (franc zone)	*GFS*	*Government Finance Statistics* (IMF)
		GNFS	Goods and nonfactor services
CIDA	Canadian International Development Agency	GNP	Gross national product
		GNS	Gross national savings
c.i.f.	Cost, insurance, freight	IBRD	International Bank for Reconstruction and Development
CITES	Convention on International Trade in Endangered Species of Wild Flora and Fauna	ICP	International Comparison Project
		IDA	International Development Association
CMEA	Council for Mutual Economic Assistance	IEA	International Energy Agency
		IFAD	International Fund for Agricultural Development
COMTRADE	Commodity Trade database (United Nations)	*IFS*	*International Financial Statistics* (IMF)
CPI	Consumer price index	ILO	International Labour Organization
DAC	Development Assistance Committee of the OECD	IMF	International Monetary Fund
		ISIC	UN International Standard Industrial Classification

ITU	International Telecommunications Union	UNCTAD	United Nations Conference on Trade and Development
IUCN	International Union for Conservation of Nature and Natural Resources	UNDP	United Nations Development Programme
LIBOR	London interbank offered rate	UNECE	United Nations Economic Commission for Europe
LIMIC	Low-income and middle-income countries	UNEP	United Nations Environment Programme
MBO	Management employee buyout	UNESCO	United Nations Education, Scientific, and Cultural Organization
METMIN	Metals and minerals database (World Bank)	UNHCR	United Nations High Commissioner for Refugees
ODA	Official development assistance		
OECD	Organization for Economic Cooperation and Development	UNICEF	United Nations Children's Fund
OPEC	Organization of Petroleum Exporting Countries	UNIDO	United Nations Industrial Development Organization
ORT	Oral rehydration therapy	UNSO	United Nations Statistical Office
PE	Public enterprise	UNSTAT	United Nations Statistical Department
SAF	Structural adjustment facility	UNTA	United Nations Technical Assistance
SDA	Social dimensions of adjustment	WFP	World Food Programme
SDR	Special drawing right	WHO	World Health Organization
SIMA	Statistical Information Management and Analysis Database (World Bank)	WRI	World Resources Institute
SITC	UN Standard International Trade Classification	ZIMCO	Zambia Industrial and Mining Corporation
SNA	System of national accounts		

Introduction

The task of monitoring Africa's development progress and aid flows requires basic empirical data that can be readily used by analysts. This publication—which is the seventh in a series that began with the African Economic and Financial Data (AEFD), and was followed by African Development Indicators (ADI) 1992, 1994, 1995, 1996, 1997, 1998/99, and 2000—is meant to provide a starting point to fulfill that task.

This volume has been able to extend the work of the previous volumes in this series. In particular:

- Most macroeconomic data (in particular, national accounts, balance of payments, government finance statistics, and trade) reflect data maintained by World Bank country desks, often referred to as operational data. These data are often more up to date and offer better country coverage than the data stored in the Bank's central files, SIMA, which were used in publications before 1998. SIMA is a large database that contains some, but not all, data produced by Bank staff—operational and other—and some, but not all, data produced by UN agencies.

- The coverage of many of the data series has been improved, reflecting improvements in the underlying data series, as well as estimates made by Bank staff.

However, substantial data gaps remain, notably in areas such as public enterprises, gender, and labor. Strengthening the statistical capacity in African countries is an ongoing process and greater efforts and institutional support will be required if substantial improvements are to be made.

This volume presents the available relevant data for 1970–99, grouped into 14 chapters: background data; national accounts; prices and exchange rates; money and banking; external sector; external debt and related flows; government finance; agriculture; power, communications, and transportation; public enterprises; labor force and employment; aid flows; social indicators; and environmental indicators. Chapter 14 (environmental indicators) was once again taken from the World Resources Institute's World Resources 2000.

Each chapter begins with a brief introduction on the nature of the data, followed by a set of charts, statistical tables, and technical notes. These define the indicators and identify specific sources.

A companion CD-Rom, known as World Bank Africa Database 2001, provides year-by-year time series of most chapters back to 1970. These series will provide analysts with data needed to help place the most recent years in an historical context.

The data in this volume incorporate numerous revisions to those published previously in the series. There are several reasons for this.

- Many of the data that were based on estimates in the earlier volumes have been replaced with updated actual data or improved estimates. In most cases, these reflect revisions made by the original reporting authorities or sources, but it also includes corrections of errors in previous volumes.
- Data series expressed in constant U.S. dollars and exchange rates use a base year of 1995; previous ADIs were based on 1987 exchange rates and prices; and AEFD used 1980 exchange rate and prices.
- Some series expressed in constant prices have been revised as a result of updated or revised deflators.
- As in the 2000 volume, macroeconomic data reflect country desk information. The difference is most noticeable in the chapter on government finance, as figures reflect consolidated government data instead of only central government data.

Considerable effort has been made to standardize and to harmonize related data sets drawn from diverse sources. Because statistical methods, coverage, practices, and definitions differ widely among sources, full comparability cannot be assured, and the indicators must be interpreted with care. In addition, the statistical systems in many developing economies are still weak, and this affects the availability and reliability of the data they report. Moreover, intercountry and intertemporal comparisons always involve complex technical problems, which have no full and unequivocal solution.

The data are drawn from sources thought to be the most authoritative, but many data sources are subject to considerable margins of error. To provide reasonably timely data required for meaningful monitoring, the World Bank, the International Monetary Fund (IMF), and other agencies sometimes make estimates on the basis of available secondary information to fill critical gaps in national reporting, especially for the most recent years, when data cannot be readily produced by national statistical sources. Nonetheless, data gaps exist for many indicators, and some countries are covered only sporadically.

Readers are urged to take these limitations into account in using the data and interpreting the indicators, particularly when making comparisons across economies. Weaknesses in the data point to the need for strengthened statistical systems throughout the region.

As a visual aid to data interpretation and cross-country comparisons, figures for selected indicators are included. As with time series, the figures should also be interpreted with caution, in particular in cross-country analysis, because countries with missing data are excluded from the charts.

Throughout this volume (except when otherwise stated), the symbol ".." indicates that data are not available or not applicable. A zero (0) indicates either zero value or an insignificant value, that is, less than one-half of the smallest unit shown. The symbol "MR" indicates "most recent year available." In chapter 13, columns headed by a period (for example, 1992–95) show data for the latest available year in the period.

To facilitate cross-country comparisons, values of many national series have been converted from the national currencies to U.S. dollars, using the World Bank Atlas methodology.

Indicators in this volume generally follow standard definitions as far as possible and cover years through 1999, depending on the chapter. Data for 1999 are preliminary and therefore may not be internally consistent within and across accounts, and may not be available for all countries. Because data are continually updated, the statistics here may be different from those in other publications.

Shares and ratios are always calculated using current price series; when gross domestic product GDP is used as the denominator for these calculations, it is always expressed at market prices (except in Figure 2-3).

In all but the last chapter, the data are arranged by indicator to facilitate cross-country comparisons. For country-specific work, data can be arranged to show all indicators together for each country.

In this volume, the statistical tables are usually arranged as time series, by country and by country groups. The largest country group is All Africa, consisting of two subgroups: North Africa and Sub-Saharan Africa (including South Africa). In turn, the Sub-Saharan Africa group is shown excluding South Africa and Nigeria. These two subgroups correspond to the Sub-Saharan Africa and Sub-Saharan Africa excluding Nigeria groups shown in the *AEFD* and *ADI 1992*, where South Africa was listed separately.

Annual data shown for country groups are totals, averages, or medians for the countries included in the group, as indicated on the table. These group aggregates can be either simple arithmetic)—where missing data are not imputed-or gap-filled—where weights are used to adjust group totals for missing countries. In the latter case, when values are missing for a country or a year, estimates are made to maintain the same country composition of the groups through time. However, the implicit estimated values for the countries with missing data are not shown separately in the tables. These gap-fill estimates are made, and the aggregate statistics shown, only if the countries for which data are available for a given year account for at least two-thirds of the full group, as defined by benchmarks in 1995. This procedure is standard for many World Bank statistical publications.

Most group averages are weighted according to the relative importance of the countries in the group total for that indicator, based on simple addition across countries when the indicator is expressed in reasonably comparable units. Group averages for analytical ratios (for example, imports to GDP) can be either weighted or simple (arithmetic). Usually they are calculated from the group totals for both the numerator and the denominator, which is analytically equivalent to calculating weighted averages, where the weight for each country is its share in the group total for the denominator. Sometimes, however, when it is appropriate to treat the experiences of different countries equally in determining a representative value for the group, these group averages are arithmetic—that is, each country has equal weight.

Period averages—shown for 1975–84, 1985–89, and 1990 to most recent year—are calculated from time series (levels, ratios, growth rates, or medians) for both countries and country groups. They are either simple averages or average annual percentage growth rates. These growth rates always use the least-squares method and are usually computed from real-term series. In this publication, the least-squares growth rates are computed using the level for the year before the first year shown in the label. The least-squares growth rate, r, is estimated by fitting a least-squares linear regression trend line to the logarithmic annual values of the variable in the relevant period. More specifically, the regression equation takes the form: $\log X = a + bt + e$, where this is equivalent to the logarithmic transformation of the compound growth rate equation, $X = X_t(1 + r)^t$. In these equations X is the variable, t is time, and $a = \log X_o$ and $b = \log(1 + r)$ are the parameters to be estimated; e is the error term. If $b*$ is the least-squares estimate of b, then the annual average growth rate, r, is obtained as [anti log $(b*)$] − 1 and multiplied by 100 to express it in percentage terms. The least-squares growth rate dampens the influence of exceptional values, particularly at the end points. Least-square growth rates are calculated only if more than two-thirds of consecutive data—carrying the same sign—are present in the time series.

Throughout this volume, data for Ethiopia include Eritrea up to 1992, except when otherwise indicated.

1

Selected Background Data

The first two tables of the volume provide selected indicators, including a series on population, as background to the data in the rest of the volume.

Table 1-1 provides a comparative view, across indicators, of some of the more important indicators for all countries in the most recent year for which relatively complete information is available

1-1. Basic indicators

	Population mid-1999 (millions)	Land area (thousands of square km.)	GNP per capita		Life expectancy at birth (years)	School enrollment				Total net ODA per capita
			Atlas dollars	Av. annual percentage growth		Primary		Secondary		
			1999	1988-99	1998	1980	1994-97	1980	1994-97	1999
SUB-SAHARAN AFRICA	642.9	23,628	492	-0.7	50	81	78	15	27	18
excluding South Africa	600.8	22,407	306	-0.4	49	80	74	15	21	18
excl. S.Africa & Nigeria	476.9	21,497	318	-0.6	48	72	67	14	17	23
Angola	12.4	1,247	270	-9.7	47	175	..	21	..	31
Benin	6.1	111	380	1.3	53	67	78	16	17	34
Botswana	1.6	567	3,240	2.2	46	91	108	19	65	38
Burkina Faso	11.0	274	240	1.0	44	18	40	3	..	36
Burundi	6.7	26	120	-4.2	42	26	51	3	7	11
Cameroon	14.7	465	600	-3.0	54	98	85	18	27	30
Cape Verde	0.4	4	1,330	2.5	68	114	148	8	..	318
Central African Republic	3.5	623	290	-1.0	44	71	..	14	..	33
Chad	7.5	1,259	210	-1.1	48	..	58	..	10	25
Comoros	0.5	2	350	-2.8	60	86	75	22	21	39
Congo, Democratic Rep. of	49.8	2,267	..	-8.0	51	92	72	24	26	3
Congo, Republic of	2.9	342	550	-6.0	48	141	114	74	53	49
Côte d'Ivoire	14.7	318	710	0.6	46	75	71	19	24	30
Djibouti	0.6	23	790	..	50	37	39	12	14	116
Equatorial Guinea	0.4	28	1,170	11.0	50	160	..	..	..	46
Eritrea	4.0	101	200	..	51	..	53	..	20	37
Ethiopia	62.8	1,000	100	1.3	43	37	43	9	12	10
Gabon	1.2	258	3,300	0.2	53	174	162	..	..	39
Gambia, The	1.3	10	330	-0.5	53	53	77	11	25	26
Ghana	18.9	228	390	1.5	60	79	79	41	..	32
Guinea	7.2	246	510	1.8	47	36	54	17	12	33
Guinea-Bissau	1.2	28	160	-1.0	44	68	62	6	..	44
Kenya	29.4	569	360	0.0	51	115	85	20	24	10
Lesotho	2.1	30	550	-0.2	55	104	108	18	31	15
Liberia	3.0	96	..	..	47	48	..	22	..	31
Madagascar	15.1	582	250	-1.0	58	130	92	..	16	24
Malawi	10.8	94	180	0.4	42	60	134	5	17	41
Mali	10.9	1,220	240	0.4	50	26	49	8	10	32
Mauritania	2.6	1,025	390	1.0	54	37	79	11	16	84
Mauritius	1.2	2	3,550	4.0	71	93	106	50	65	35
Mozambique	17.3	784	220	3.1	45	99	60	5	7	7
Namibia	1.7	823	1,890	1.8	54	..	131	..	61	104
Niger	10.5	1,267	190	-1.7	46	25	29	5	7	18
Nigeria	123.9	911	260	0.7	53	109	98	18	33	1
Rwanda	8.3	25	250	-3.7	41	63	..	3	..	45
São Tomé and Principe	0.1	1	270	-1.1	64	..	..	..	..	190
Senegal	9.3	193	510	0.4	52	46	71	11	16	58
Seychelles	0.1	0	6,540	2.5	72	..	..	..	..	162
Sierra Leone	4.9	72	130	-5.6	37	52	..	14	..	15
Somalia	9.4	627	..	..	48	22	..	9	..	12
South Africa	42.1	1,221	3,170	-0.4	63	90	133	..	94	13
Sudan	29.0	2,376	330	..	55	50	51	16	21	8
Swaziland	1.0	17	1,360	0.8	56	103	117	38	54	28
Tanzania	32.9	884	260	0.4	47	93	67	3	5	30
Togo	4.6	54	310	-1.2	49	118	120	33	27	16
Uganda	21.5	200	320	3.9	42	50	74	5	12	27
Zambia	9.9	743	330	-2.4	43	90	89	16	27	63
Zimbabwe	11.9	387	530	0.2	51	85	112	8	49	21
NORTH AFRICA	135.5	5,738	1,569	1.2	68	84	100	41	64	19
Algeria	30.0	2,382	1,550	-0.9	71	95	108	33	63	3
Egypt, Arab Republic	62.4	995	1,390	2.5	67	73	101	51	75	25
Libya	5.4	1,760	..	..	70	125	..	76	..	1
Morocco	28.2	446	1,190	0.6	67	83	86	26	39	24
Tunisia	9.5	155	2,090	2.9	72	102	118	27	65	26
ALL AFRICA	778.4	29,367	677	-0.2	54	81	80	20	34	18

Note: 1999 data are preliminary (see page 2).

Selected Background Data

1-2. Population

					Millions of people							Average annual percentage growth		
	1980	*1990*	*1991*	*1992*	*1993*	*1994*	*1995*	*1996*	*1997*	*1998*	*1999*	*75-84*	*85-89*	*90-MR*
SUB-SAHARAN AFRICA	380.74	508.34	523.12	538.14	549.99	563.62	578.88	594.88	611.59	627.27	642.94	2.9	2.9	2.7
excluding South Africa	353.16	473.14	487.19	501.45	512.51	525.34	539.76	554.97	570.92	585.86	600.84	3.0	3.0	2.7
excl. S.Africa & Nigeria	282.01	376.93	388.21	399.57	407.62	417.33	428.49	440.48	453.23	465.05	476.94	3.0	2.9	2.7
Angola	7.02	9.23	9.59	9.94	10.29	10.63	10.97	11.32	11.66	12.00	12.35	2.7	2.8	3.3
Benin	3.46	4.74	4.88	5.03	5.18	5.33	5.48	5.63	5.79	5.95	6.11	2.9	3.2	2.9
Botswana	0.91	1.28	1.31	1.35	1.39	1.43	1.46	1.50	1.53	1.56	1.59	3.6	3.5	2.6
Burkina Faso	6.96	8.88	9.09	9.31	9.53	9.76	9.99	10.23	10.47	10.73	11.00	2.4	2.4	2.4
Burundi	4.13	5.46	5.60	5.75	5.89	6.02	6.16	6.29	6.42	6.55	6.68	2.5	2.9	2.3
Cameroon	8.66	11.47	11.80	12.13	12.47	12.82	13.18	13.55	13.92	14.30	14.69	2.8	2.9	2.8
Cape Verde	0.29	0.34	0.35	0.35	0.36	0.37	0.38	0.39	0.40	0.42	0.43	1.0	1.9	2.5
Central African Republic	2.31	2.94	3.01	3.08	3.15	3.22	3.29	3.35	3.42	3.48	3.54	2.4	2.4	2.1
Chad	4.48	5.75	5.89	6.06	6.25	6.46	6.71	6.89	7.09	7.28	7.49	2.4	2.4	3.0
Comoros	0.34	0.43	0.44	0.46	0.47	0.48	0.49	0.50	0.52	0.53	0.54	..	2.6	2.6
Congo, Democratic Rep. of	27.01	37.36	38.60	39.87	41.16	42.49	43.85	45.25	46.71	48.22	49.78	3.1	3.4	3.2
Congo, Republic of	1.67	2.22	2.28	2.35	2.42	2.49	2.56	2.63	2.71	2.78	2.86	2.9	2.9	2.9
Côte d'Ivoire	8.19	11.64	12.00	12.37	12.75	13.13	13.53	13.89	14.21	14.49	14.73	3.9	3.4	2.8
Djibouti	0.28	0.52	0.53	0.55	0.57	0.58	0.60	0.61	0.62	0.64	0.65	6.7	6.1	2.7
Equatorial Guinea	0.22	0.35	0.36	0.37	0.38	0.39	0.40	0.41	0.42	0.43	0.44	2.4	3.4	2.5
Eritrea	2.38	3.14	3.22	3.31	3.39	3.48	3.57	3.67	3.77	3.88	3.99	2.6	3.0	2.7
Ethiopia	37.72	51.18	52.95	54.79	53.30	54.89	56.53	58.23	59.75	61.27	62.78	2.8	3.2	2.3
Gabon	0.69	0.96	0.99	1.02	1.05	1.07	1.10	1.13	1.15	1.18	1.21	3.2	3.4	2.6
Gambia, The	0.64	0.92	0.96	1.00	1.04	1.08	1.11	1.15	1.18	1.22	1.25	3.1	4.1	3.6
Ghana	10.74	14.87	15.31	15.76	16.20	16.64	17.08	17.52	17.98	18.46	18.95	2.3	3.5	2.7
Guinea	4.46	5.76	5.93	6.10	6.26	6.43	6.59	6.76	6.92	7.08	7.25	1.7	2.8	2.6
Guinea-Bissau	0.80	0.97	0.99	1.01	1.03	1.06	1.09	1.11	1.14	1.16	1.18	3.7	2.3	2.2
Kenya	16.63	23.55	24.28	24.98	25.66	26.31	26.92	27.54	28.16	28.79	29.41	3.8	3.7	2.5
Lesotho	1.35	1.72	1.76	1.80	1.84	1.89	1.93	1.97	2.01	2.06	2.11	2.5	2.5	2.3
Liberia	1.88	2.44	2.48	2.54	2.60	2.66	2.73	2.81	2.88	2.96	3.04	3.2	2.3	2.5
Madagascar	8.87	11.63	11.89	12.20	12.55	12.92	13.30	13.72	14.15	14.59	15.05	2.6	2.8	2.9
Malawi	6.18	8.51	8.74	8.99	9.24	9.49	9.76	10.02	10.28	10.53	10.79	3.2	3.4	2.7
Mali	6.59	8.46	8.70	8.95	9.20	9.45	9.71	9.99	10.29	10.60	10.91	2.2	2.7	2.9
Mauritania	1.55	2.03	2.08	2.14	2.20	2.26	2.33	2.39	2.46	2.53	2.60	2.5	2.8	2.8
Mauritius	0.97	1.06	1.07	1.08	1.10	1.11	1.12	1.13	1.15	1.16	1.17	1.4	0.8	1.1
Mozambique	12.10	14.15	14.42	14.69	15.01	15.42	15.82	16.23	16.63	16.95	17.26	2.7	1.0	2.2
Namibia	1.03	1.35	1.39	1.42	1.46	1.50	1.54	1.58	1.62	1.66	1.70	2.7	2.8	2.6
Niger	5.59	7.73	7.99	8.26	8.54	8.84	9.15	9.47	9.80	10.14	10.49	3.3	3.2	3.4
Nigeria	71.15	96.20	98.98	101.88	104.89	108.01	111.27	114.50	117.68	120.82	123.90	3.1	3.0	2.9
Rwanda	5.16	6.95	7.15	7.35	7.54	6.23	6.40	6.73	7.90	8.11	8.31	3.3	3.0	1.4
São Tomé and Principe	0.09	0.12	0.12	0.12	0.13	0.13	0.13	0.14	0.14	0.14	0.14	1.5	2.8	2.6
Senegal	5.54	7.33	7.50	7.69	7.90	8.11	8.33	8.56	8.79	9.04	9.29	2.9	2.8	2.7
Seychelles	0.06	0.07	0.07	0.07	0.07	0.07	0.08	0.08	0.08	0.08	0.08	1.4	0.7	1.5
Sierra Leone	3.24	4.00	4.09	4.19	4.29	4.40	4.51	4.63	4.75	4.85	4.95	2.0	2.2	2.4
Somalia	5.85	7.77	8.15	8.38	8.47	8.41	8.20	8.48	8.77	9.08	9.39	5.5	2.3	1.9
South Africa	27.58	35.20	35.93	36.69	37.47	38.28	39.12	39.91	40.67	41.40	42.11	2.3	2.5	2.0
Sudan	18.68	24.06	24.57	25.08	25.59	26.10	26.62	27.16	27.74	28.35	28.99	3.1	2.4	2.1
Swaziland	0.57	0.77	0.79	0.82	0.85	0.87	0.90	0.93	0.96	0.99	1.02	3.2	3.2	3.2
Tanzania	18.58	25.47	26.28	27.10	27.94	28.79	29.65	30.49	31.32	32.13	32.92	3.2	3.2	2.9
Togo	2.62	3.51	3.64	3.75	3.87	3.99	4.11	4.23	4.35	4.46	4.57	2.8	3.0	3.0
Uganda	12.81	16.33	16.89	17.46	18.03	18.60	19.17	19.74	20.32	20.90	21.48	2.4	2.6	3.1
Zambia	5.74	7.78	8.02	8.26	8.50	8.74	8.98	9.21	9.44	9.67	9.88	3.4	3.0	2.7
Zimbabwe	7.01	9.75	10.02	10.28	10.53	10.78	11.01	11.24	11.47	11.69	11.90	3.1	3.3	2.3
NORTH AFRICA	88.35	114.07	116.64	119.19	121.68	124.13	126.55	128.85	131.11	133.32	135.49	2.7	2.5	2.0
Algeria	18.67	25.01	25.63	26.25	26.85	27.45	28.06	28.57	29.05	29.51	29.95	3.1	2.8	2.1
Egypt, Arab Republic	40.88	52.44	53.62	54.78	55.93	57.06	58.18	59.27	60.35	61.40	62.43	2.5	2.5	2.0
Libya	3.04	4.42	4.53	4.64	4.75	4.86	4.97	5.08	5.19	5.30	5.42	4.5	3.4	2.3
Morocco	19.38	24.04	24.52	25.00	25.47	25.93	26.39	26.85	27.31	27.78	28.24	2.3	2.2	1.8
Tunisia	6.38	8.16	8.34	8.51	8.68	8.82	8.96	9.09	9.22	9.34	9.46	2.6	2.5	1.7
ALL AFRICA	469.09	622.40	639.77	657.33	671.67	687.75	705.43	723.73	742.69	760.59	778.44	2.9	2.8	2.5

Note: 1999 data are preliminary (see page 2).

Figure 1-1. Development diamonds for all African countries, 1999*

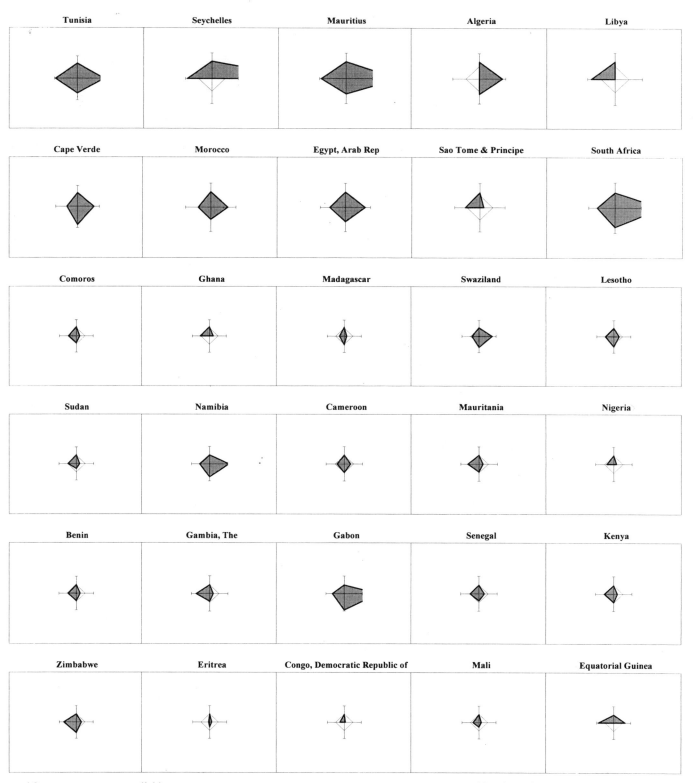

(Graph continued on the following page)

Figure 1-1. *(continued)*

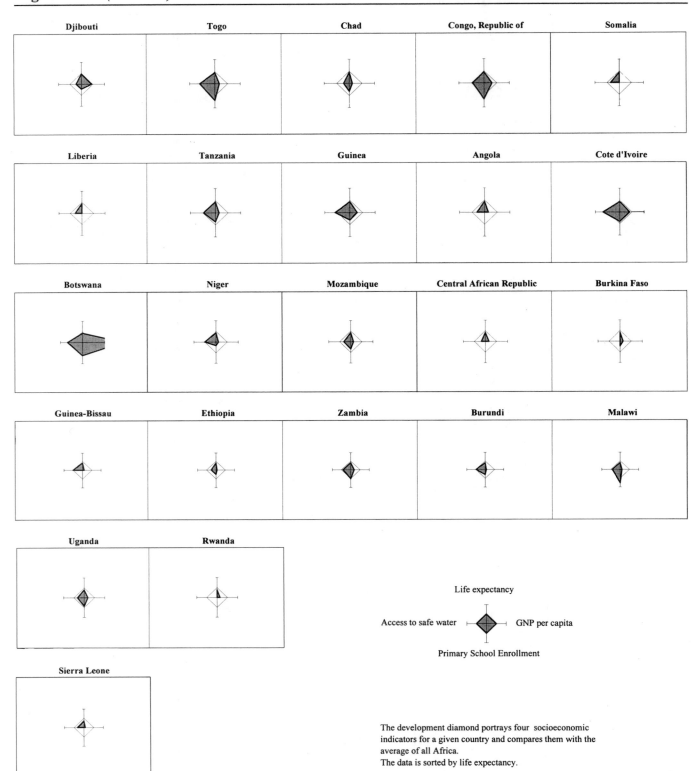

The development diamond portrays four socioeconomic indicators for a given country and compares them with the average of all Africa.
The data is sorted by life expectancy.

Figure 1-2. Selected basic indicators, 1999*

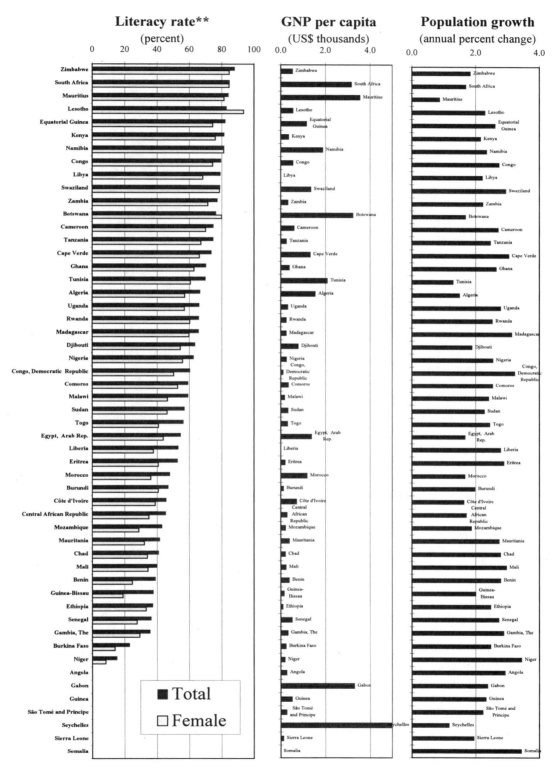

* Or most recent year available.

** Sorted by total literacy rate.

Technical notes

Tables

Table 1-1. Basic indicators. The data for this table are from the World Bank's Statistical Information Management and Analysis Database (SIMA), except for official development assistance (ODA), which are from the OECD, Geographical Distribution of Financial Flows to Developing Countries database (see technical notes to Chapter 12). Regional aggregates for GNP per capita, life expectancy, and education are weighted by population.

Population estimates for mid-1999 are World Bank estimates. These are usually projections from the most recent population censuses or surveys (mostly from 1980–99). Refugees not permanently settled in the country of asylum are generally considered to be part of the population of their country of origin (see technical notes to Tables 13-1, 13-4, and 13-5).

Land area refers to the land surface area of a country, excluding inland waters.

GNP per capita figures in U.S. dollars are calculated according to the World Bank Atlas method described below. GNP measures the total domestic and foreign value added claimed by residents. It comprises GDP (defined in the note for Table 2-5) plus net factor income from abroad, which is the income residents receive from abroad for factor services (labor and capital) less similar payments made to nonresidents who contributed to the domestic economy. The data are from the Food and Agriculture Organization (FAO).

The *World Bank Atlas* method uses a three-year average of conversion factors to convert GNP data, expressed in different national currencies, to a common denomination, conventionally U.S. dollars. The *Atlas* conversion factor for any year is the average of the official exchange rate (Table 3-4) or alternative conversion factor (Table 3-6) for that year and for the two preceding years, after adjusting them for differences in relative inflation between that country and the United States. This three-year average smoothes fluctuations in prices and exchange rates for each country. The resulting GNP in U.S. dollars is divided by the midyear population for the latest of the three years to derive GNP per capita.

The following formulas describe the procedures for computing the conversion factor for year *t*:

$$e^*_{t-2,t} = \frac{1}{3}\left[e_{t-2}\left(\frac{P_t}{P_{t-2}} \Big/ \frac{P^\$_t}{P^\$_{t-2}}\right) + e_{t-1}\left(\frac{P_t}{P_{t-1}} \Big/ \frac{P^\$_t}{P^\$_{t-1}}\right) + e_t \right]$$

and for calculating per capita GNP in U.S. dollars for year *t*:

$$Y^\$_t = (Y_t / N_t) + e^*_{t-2,t}$$

where Y_t = current GNP (local currency) for year *t*, P_{t-2} = GNP deflator for year *t*, N_t midyear population for year *t*, and $P^\$_t$ = US GNP deflator for year *t*.

Growth rates of GNP per capita for this table are shown in real terms. They have been calculated by the least-squares method using constant GNP per capita series in 1995 prices in national currency (World Bank, SIMA). See also technical notes for Table 2-19.

Life expectancy at birth indicates the number of years a newborn infant would live if prevailing patterns of mortality at the time of its birth were to remain the same throughout its life. Figures are World Bank estimates based on data from the UN Population Division, the UN Statistical Office, and national statistical offices.

Primary school enrollment is the ratio of children of all ages enrolled in primary school to the population of children of primary school age. While many countries consider the primary school age to be 6 to 11 years, others use different age groups. These different country practices are also reflected in the ratios. Gross enrollment may be reported in excess of 100 percent if some pupils are younger or older than the country's standard range of primary school age. In practice, enrollment does not necessarily equal attendance, nor does it remain constant throughout the year. Data are from the United Nations Education, Scientific, and Cultural Organization (UNESCO).

Secondary school enrollment is the ratio of children of all ages enrolled in secondary schools to the population of children of secondary school age. The definition of secondary school age differs among countries. It is most commonly considered to be 12 to 17 years. Data are from UNESCO.

Total net ODA per capita consists of net disbursements of loans and grants from all official sources on concessional financial terms, divided by the midyear population for the corresponding year (see the technical notes to Chapter 12).

Table 1-2. Population. Average annual percentage growth shown in this table was calculated using the least-squares method.

Statistical background for the population estimates is available in the UN Population and Vital Statistics Report and the World Bank's World Population Projections (World Bank 1994–95) (see also the technical notes to Chapter 13).

Figures

The following indicators have been used to derive the figures in this chapter.

Figure 1-1. Life expectancy (Table 1-1); access to safe water (Table 13-10); GNP per capita (Table 2-19); primary school enrollment (Table 1-1).

Figure 1-2. Literacy rate (Table 13-13); GNP per capita (Table 2-19); population growth (Table 1-2).

Methodology used for regional aggregations and period averages in chapter 1

Table	Aggregations[a] (1)	(2)	(3)	(4)	(5)	(6)	Period averages[b] (2)	(3)
Table 1-1								
Column 1	x							
Column 2	x							
Column 3				x				
Column 4				x				x
Column 5					x			
Column 6					x			
Column 7					x			
Column 8					x			
Column 9					x			
Column 10		x						
Table 1-2	x						x	

Note: Regional aggregations are shown in the rows for Sub-Saharan Africa, North Africa, and All Africa. Period averages are shown in column 4 for Table 1-1 and in the last three columns for Table 1-2. This table shows only the methodologies used in this chapter.

   a. Regional aggregations: (1) simple total; (2) simple total of the first indicator divided by the simple total of the second indicator (same country coverage); (3) simple total of the gap-filled indicator; (4) simple total of the gap-filled main indicator divided by the simple total of the gap-filled secondary indicator; (5) simple total of the first gap-filled main indicator less the simple total of the second gap-filled main indicator, all divided by the simple total of the secondary indicator; (6) weighted total (by population); (7) median; (8) no aggregation; (9) simple arithmetic mean.

   b. Period averages: (i) arithmetic mean (using the same series as shown in the table i.e., ratio if the rest of the table is shown as ratio, level if the rest of the table is shown as level, growth rate if the rest is shown as growth rate); (2) least-squares growth rate (using main indicator); (3) least-squares growth rate (using main indicator in constant terms, with the rest of the table in current terms).

2

National Accounts

National accounts data provide the broadest picture of a nation's economic performance. National accounts give information on the structure of production in the form of gross domestic product (GDP) and its components by industrial origin, GDP and its components by expenditure, and information on a nation's economic relations with the outside world. These are the key statistics for assessing a nation's economic condition at a given time or the trends in a nation's economic performance over time. National accounts data also provide a quantitative basis for forecasting and policymaking and as such are used widely both by analysts and policymakers.

GDP and its components by industrial origin are compiled following the widely used System of National Accounts (SNA). The SNA methodology accounts for virtually all activities pertinent to the production of goods and the provision of services in an economy by residents and nonresidents, regardless of the allocation to domestic and foreign claims. GDP does not account for the depreciation of fixed capital.

There are three methods of compiling GDP figures: income, expenditure, and production methods. Because of technical and resource constraints, the income method is not used in most developing countries. In this volume, GDP and its components by industrial origin are compiled using the production method. The three components of GDP by industrial origin are value added in agriculture, value added in industry, and value added in services. (See the technical notes at the end of this chapter.) The national accounts are constructed in national currencies and in current prices. Figures reported in this chapter are, however, in U.S. dollars, usually converted from national currency series at the official exchange rate. If the official exchange rate is significantly different from the prevailing market rate or shows extreme volatility, the local currency is converted into U.S. dollars by using an alternative conversion factor. The conversion factors used for this purpose are presented in Table 3-6. Reporting currencies in a common denominator facilitates cross-country comparisons and aggregations in country groups.

In addition, estimates of GDP and its components by industrial origin are converted into constant prices. Reporting figures in constant prices is essential for monitoring real changes in the structure of production and for analyzing relations among prices, production, employment, and so forth.

Constant price series in U.S. dollars use a 1995 base year and are converted from national currency series using 1995 exchange rates. To establish a common base year for all countries, national accounts in national currencies at constant prices based on years other than 1995 have been partly rebased to 1995 by rescaling constant price series of components of GDP.

Using a single base year raises problems when there are profound structural changes or significant changes in relative prices. For example, values expressed in constant U.S. dollars necessarily reflect the exchange rates prevailing during the base year. Where subsequent exchange rate changes have been substantial, as they have for many African countries since 1980, comparisons among countries and aggregate trends will be affected. For this reason alone, the data should be used with considerable caution.

Monitoring resource allocations across sectors in any given point in time requires the use of current prices. Accordingly, in addition to GDP in constant prices, GDP in current prices is provided. Following GDP in current prices are components of GDP by expenditure. Data on consumption, investment, and savings are constructed using the SNA's convention. Conceptually, all income is either consumed or saved, and as such the sum of total consumption and gross domestic saving equals GDP.

When viewed from a production point of view, by definition savings equals investment. Investment measures additions to fixed assets of an economy, whether it represents additions to the stock of capital or merely replenishes depreciated capital stock, plus net changes in the level of inventories. It is financed either through domestic savings or by drawing on the savings of foreigners. Data on gross domestic investment and gross domestic savings thus shed light not only on the nature of the domestic inter-temporal resource allocation but also on the size of the resource gap. Gross national savings, however, indicates the amount of savings generated by a nation's residents.

Although this volume includes a chapter on international trade, the fact that balance of payments is an integral part of the national accounts warrants the inclusion of the resource balance and its components in this chapter. Moreover, a closer examination of the fifth edition of the IMF's Balance of Payments Manual

(1993) reflects differences in concepts, definitions, and classifications from the UN's SNA guidelines. For instance, in the SNA, factor services rendered by residents of another country are excluded from goods and services, but this practice is not universally followed. The tables on resource balance, and on values of exports (f.o.b.) and imports (c.i.f.) of goods and nonfactor services in current U.S. dollars provide a comprehensive and systematic framework for macroeconomic analysis in general. Those interested in a more specialized and rigorous study of international trade transactions should use the data provided in Chapter 5.

The rate of growth of real domestic product is an important indicator of economic progress and as such is widely monitored. Because these growth rates are calculated from national series, they are suitable for both cross-country comparisons and trend analysis for individual countries. Aggregate values and trends, however, reflect the choice of the base year, as explained above.

Gross national income per capita, which is GDP per capita adjusted for changes in international terms of trade and which include net factor income from abroad, and total consumption per capita are also widely monitored indicators of economic progress. When expressed in current U.S. dollars to facilitate comparison and aggregation, however, the values for these indicators necessarily reflect exchange rate fluctuations as well as underlying economic and demographic changes. These indicators may be used with caution for cross-country comparison during any single year. They require special attention when used for trend analysis.

Data for Chapter 2 are from the World Bank's country desks. Estimates are based on data obtained from national sources, usually collected by World Bank staff who review the quality of national accounts data and, in some instances, help adjust national series.

2-1. Gross domestic product, real

	Millions of U.S. dollars, constant 1995 prices											Average annual percentage growth		
	1980	1990	1991	1992	1993	1994	1995	1996	1997	1998	1999	75-84	85-89	90-MR
SUB-SAHARAN AFRICA	252,412	300,100	301,495	298,045	299,889	306,135	318,402	333,583	344,743	352,089	359,810	2.2	2.3	2.1
excluding South Africa	124,817	155,200	158,117	157,759	157,859	159,486	167,204	176,123	183,328	189,700	195,452	1.9	3.3	2.6
excl. S.Africa & Nigeria	101,828	130,343	132,058	130,920	130,420	132,024	139,067	146,781	153,202	159,040	164,500	2.5	3.0	2.5
Angola	5,074	6,371	6,412	6,083	4,638	4,703	5,187	5,706	6,060	6,253	6,422	..	4.5	-0.2
Benin	1,253	1,632	1,709	1,778	1,840	1,921	2,009	2,121	2,242	2,343	2,458	3.8	1.5	4.6
Botswana	1,521	3,986	4,285	4,413	4,501	4,662	4,899	5,239	5,449	5,639	5,893	11.5	10.6	4.5
Burkina Faso	1,445	2,002	2,201	2,256	2,238	2,265	2,355	2,496	2,614	2,776	2,936	3.6	4.4	3.6
Burundi	728	1,126	1,182	1,190	1,122	1,079	1,000	917	920	964	955	3.8	5.1	-2.4
Cameroon	6,319	8,765	8,431	8,170	7,909	7,711	7,965	8,364	8,790	9,233	9,640	8.5	-0.1	0.5
Cape Verde	171	381	386	399	427	456	491	510	536	579	625	13.8	4.5	5.4
Central African Republic	964	1,069	1,063	994	998	1,047	1,122	1,077	1,134	1,187	1,228	0.4	0.7	1.4
Chad	787	1,308	1,420	1,533	1,292	1,424	1,438	1,473	1,539	1,642	1,631	-1.3	5.4	1.9
Comoros	167	223	211	229	236	223	215	214	215	214	211	..	1.3	-0.3
Congo, Democratic Rep. of	8,458	9,234	8,457	7,569	6,549	6,294	6,338	6,281	5,923	6,101	6,589	-0.3	1.7	-4.6
Congo, Republic of	1,536	2,456	2,515	2,580	2,554	2,414	2,510	2,402	2,388	2,476	2,402	9.2	-1.0	-0.3
Côte d'Ivoire	8,556	9,187	9,191	9,168	9,151	9,332	9,992	10,682	11,389	11,903	12,235	2.2	2.0	3.2
Djibouti	..	..	550	548	527	511	491	466	468	471	..	..	..	-2.7
Equatorial Guinea	..	117	116	128	137	144	164	212	363	442	509	..	1.4	17.1
Eritrea	..	..	..	521	508	558	574	612	661	686	692	..	..	5.0
Ethiopia	..	5,134	4,893	4,642	5,262	5,446	5,779	6,393	6,725	6,633	7,045	..	2.9	4.1
Gabon	3,565	4,263	4,524	4,377	4,481	4,635	4,958	5,213	5,514	5,628	5,279	-0.2	-1.4	3.2
Gambia, The	241	344	355	367	378	379	382	390	410	430	457	4.3	3.3	2.8
Ghana	4,231	5,236	5,512	5,726	6,011	6,209	6,457	6,754	7,038	7,369	7,693	-1.1	5.2	4.3
Guinea	..	3,106	3,181	3,277	3,433	3,571	3,729	3,901	4,088	4,269	4,406	..	4.7	4.1
Guinea-Bissau	134	217	228	231	236	243	254	266	280	201	217	2.1	3.1	0.9
Kenya	5,612	8,360	8,481	8,413	8,443	8,665	9,047	9,422	9,620	9,773	9,900	4.7	5.9	2.2
Lesotho	490	764	793	832	863	892	933	1,026	1,108	1,053	1,079	5.2	5.6	4.5
Liberia	..	..	..	..	..	..	..	..	..	..	..	..	..	..
Madagascar	3,048	3,212	3,009	3,045	3,109	3,108	3,160	3,228	3,347	3,479	3,641	-0.2	2.3	1.4
Malawi	992	1,234	1,341	1,243	1,363	1,224	1,429	1,533	1,591	1,623	1,688	3.2	1.9	3.6
Mali	2,013	2,136	2,170	2,351	2,301	2,322	2,466	2,546	2,718	2,811	2,964	2.3	0.8	3.3
Mauritania	753	887	910	925	976	1,021	1,068	1,127	1,163	1,201	1,252	1.6	3.3	3.8
Mauritius	1,741	3,123	3,256	3,459	3,647	3,795	3,973	4,199	4,430	4,679	4,838	3.6	7.7	5.2
Mozambique	2,006	2,036	2,136	1,963	2,134	2,294	2,392	2,562	2,846	3,185	3,417	..	6.0	5.5
Namibia	2,280	2,566	2,776	2,974	2,923	3,109	3,224	3,293	3,380	3,461	3,568	..	2.5	3.6
Niger	1,833	1,813	1,858	1,737	1,762	1,833	1,881	1,945	1,999	2,207	2,194	2.0	4.2	2.0
Nigeria	22,357	24,864	26,046	26,806	27,396	27,423	28,109	29,318	30,109	30,651	30,958	-0.7	5.0	2.7
Rwanda	1,660	2,029	1,978	2,094	1,921	957	1,286	1,489	1,680	1,839	1,952	6.8	2.9	-2.1
São Tomé and Principe	..	42	43	44	44	45	45	46	47	48	49	..	1.8	1.7
Senegal	3,057	4,150	4,133	4,225	4,131	4,253	4,476	4,704	4,939	5,220	5,487	2.1	3.5	3.1
Seychelles	314	441	453	485	515	511	508	532	555	566	574	3.6	5.2	3.3
Sierra Leone	1,145	1,370	1,261	1,139	1,140	1,179	866	1,114	918	911	837	2.3	1.8	-4.6
Somalia	..	..	..	..	..	..	..	..	..	..	..	..	..	..
South Africa	127,410	144,762	143,288	140,226	141,956	146,547	151,113	157,386	161,359	162,371	164,369	2.4	1.4	1.6
Sudan	4,271	4,763	5,049	5,298	5,525	5,748	7,194	7,482	8,208	8,709	9,161	2.6	0.9	7.6
Swaziland	591	1,113	1,141	1,155	1,193	1,234	1,267	1,317	1,366	1,393	1,421	3.3	9.9	3.1
Tanzania	..	4,808	4,908	4,936	4,996	5,074	5,255	5,494	5,687	5,917	6,197	..	..	2.9
Togo	1,175	1,304	1,295	1,244	1,056	1,214	1,309	1,436	1,496	1,463	1,493	2.1	3.4	1.9
Uganda	..	4,102	4,330	4,478	4,851	5,161	5,756	6,278	6,576	6,944	7,458	..	3.4	7.1
Zambia	3,351	3,716	3,715	3,650	3,898	3,559	3,471	3,699	3,821	3,750	3,841	0.2	2.3	0.2
Zimbabwe	4,347	6,689	7,178	6,576	6,736	7,102	7,120	7,843	8,065	8,362	8,366	3.0	4.2	2.9
NORTH AFRICA	106,581	157,526	160,731	163,896	164,673	171,042	173,657	184,917	189,662	200,327	208,087	6.0	3.0	3.1
Algeria	31,561	40,937	40,446	41,093	40,189	39,720	41,248	42,815	43,286	45,494	46,995	5.5	0.8	1.2
Egypt, Arab Republic	29,896	50,915	51,464	53,746	55,295	57,478	60,159	63,173	66,643	70,361	74,610	8.3	4.1	4.3
Libya	..	..	..	..	..	..	..	..	..	..	..	..	..	..
Morocco	21,590	31,507	33,680	32,322	31,995	35,309	32,986	37,016	36,191	38,657	38,387	4.1	4.7	2.3
Tunisia	10,475	14,867	15,448	16,653	17,018	17,579	17,987	19,256	20,304	21,271	22,600	5.3	2.4	4.7
ALL AFRICA	361,709	459,075	463,499	462,827	465,472	477,884	493,114	519,380	535,423	552,957	568,198	3.3	2.5	2.4

Note: 1999 data are preliminary (see page 2).

2-2. Value added in agriculture

	Millions of U.S. dollars, constant 1995 prices											Average annual percentage growth		
	1980	1990	1991	1992	1993	1994	1995	1996	1997	1998	1999	75-84	85-89	90-MR
SUB-SAHARAN AFRICA	42,894	51,715	53,154	50,825	52,898	53,836	54,865	59,263	61,048	62,037	64,484	0.7	4.2	2.4
excluding South Africa	37,334	45,015	46,148	45,831	46,620	47,036	49,519	52,562	54,195	55,422	57,584	0.7	3.6	2.8
excl. S.Africa & Nigeria	..	37,409	38,262	37,754	38,437	38,640	40,833	43,546	44,784	45,880	47,810	..	3.0	2.7
Angola	..	758	748	544	290	318	388	445	490	516	521	..	0.5	-4.3
Benin	361	534	581	601	617	673	684	732	774	826	864	3.0	4.6	5.2
Botswana	159	203	208	209	206	201	195	195	203	210	219	-3.8	13.2	0.4
Burkina Faso	458	594	717	725	735	733	754	810	800	844	870	1.0	4.6	3.3
Burundi	358	494	505	520	499	448	421	427	429	452	438	2.0	4.1	-1.6
Cameroon	2,131	2,702	2,594	2,749	2,782	2,868	3,119	3,350	3,603	3,847	4,078	4.5	0.6	4.6
Cape Verde	31	70	65	60	65	63	67	92	88	90	101	12.7	22.8	3.7
Central African Republic	388	433	443	447	459	464	491	512	546	568	595	0.6	1.1	3.4
Chad	319	336	451	520	406	515	505	519	546	607	567	-1.0	5.1	4.6
Comoros	58	86	86	86	88	84	83	83	83	83	82	..	3.7	-0.3
Congo, Democratic Rep. of	2,332	2,998	3,082	3,178	3,238	3,211	3,584	3,659	3,622	3,688	3,872	1.7	2.5	2.9
Congo, Republic of	159	224	205	219	200	207	221	232	234	242	246	3.4	4.8	1.3
Côte d'Ivoire	2,365	2,550	2,587	2,627	2,629	2,639	2,880	3,011	3,095	3,228	3,251	2.7	3.0	3.0
Djibouti	..	..	..	..	..	..	..	..	..	..	..	..	..	..
Equatorial Guinea	..	70	66	64	64	73	83	95	115	102	112	..	0.1	6.1
Eritrea	..	..	..	..	..	..	..	..	..	..	..	..	..	..
Ethiopia	..	2,599	2,733	2,658	2,819	2,716	2,809	3,221	3,331	2,972	3,084	..	3.4	2.4
Gabon	431	460	464	461	455	448	398	397	417	395	413	..	0.8	-1.8
Gambia, The	95	97	98	96	91	97	99	96	103	106	124	3.0	-2.4	1.5
Ghana	2,143	2,217	2,345	2,316	2,370	2,415	2,504	2,634	2,748	2,888	3,029	0.2	2.3	3.0
Guinea	..	621	643	667	700	735	761	795	835	879	924	..	3.1	4.4
Guinea-Bissau	59	104	109	110	117	123	132	141	152	126	135	-2.6	3.4	3.5
Kenya	1,660	2,377	2,360	2,281	2,207	2,275	2,384	2,490	2,520	2,560	2,593	4.1	4.4	1.2
Lesotho	136	180	145	142	156	152	145	170	171	178	192	-4.5	4.6	1.4
Liberia	..	..	..	..	..	..	..	..	..	..	..	..	..	..
Madagascar	729	900	905	920	950	946	963	987	1,006	1,008	1,022	0.2	2.8	1.5
Malawi	296	340	383	287	439	310	400	516	542	567	606	2.2	1.2	6.6
Mali	823	994	940	1,083	991	1,057	1,082	1,117	1,168	1,175	1,277	3.2	8.9	2.4
Mauritania	160	190	203	208	235	246	251	251	264	281	306	2.9	4.5	4.5
Mauritius	230	345	338	360	336	311	337	351	364	366	274	-2.5	1.3	-0.2
Mozambique	..	798	766	626	760	710	833	923	1,001	1,081	1,164	..	7.3	4.5
Namibia	220	273	305	281	302	348	352	373	348	358	392	..	3.3	4.2
Niger	577	646	728	673	678	747	756	757	777	941	894	1.1	5.4	3.3
Nigeria	6,432	7,748	8,022	8,187	8,298	8,498	8,809	9,169	9,556	9,699	9,951	-3.0	6.4	2.9
Rwanda	908	948	1,003	1,055	897	529	568	658	681	755	799	5.6	1.1	-4.0
São Tomé and Principe	..	10	11	11	12	12	12	13	13	14	14	..	3.5	3.9
Senegal	652	861	817	831	788	861	881	934	911	882	935	-1.2	4.5	1.5
Seychelles	28	27	26	22	20	22	21	21	22	22	22	-2.8	-2.5	-1.4
Sierra Leone	317	419	394	333	335	356	363	444	444	405	462	7.9	0.9	1.2
Somalia	..	..	..	..	..	..	..	..	..	..	..	..	..	..
South Africa	5,448	6,544	6,836	4,973	6,166	6,651	5,326	6,603	6,756	6,545	6,826	0.2	7.6	0.2
Sudan	..	..	..	..	..	..	..	..	..	..	..	..	..	..
Swaziland	161	197	209	168	158	165	157	194	182	187	191	-1.4	2.5	-0.6
Tanzania	..	1,964	2,034	2,059	2,123	2,167	2,294	2,383	2,441	2,488	2,604	..	..	3.4
Togo	285	442	437	442	469	468	494	575	601	582	620	2.8	4.3	4.2
Uganda	..	2,173	2,235	2,213	2,419	2,462	2,607	2,718	2,748	2,800	2,992	..	2.7	3.7
Zambia	253	323	339	227	382	423	564	560	531	541	615	0.5	5.6	7.9
Zimbabwe	686	983	993	763	970	1,040	962	1,152	1,196	1,275	1,360	-0.1	1.2	4.3
NORTH AFRICA	16,202	22,284	25,039	22,008	21,631	24,702	21,322	27,099	24,467	26,972	26,188	2.0	5.4	1.7
Algeria	2,593	3,462	3,996	4,080	3,900	3,468	3,986	4,833	4,183	4,660	4,786	3.6	7.2	2.6
Egypt, Arab Republic	6,302	8,263	8,465	8,631	8,846	9,185	9,451	9,742	10,076	10,452	10,839	2.8	2.7	3.0
Libya	..	..	..	..	..	..	..	..	..	..	..	..	..	..
Morocco	5,032	7,282	8,862	5,588	5,328	8,599	4,820	8,580	6,309	7,870	6,309	0.4	10.0	-0.8
Tunisia	1,504	2,215	2,524	2,661	2,527	2,275	2,049	2,655	2,734	2,706	3,007	1.2	-1.2	3.4
ALL AFRICA	59,036	74,051	78,293	72,887	74,557	78,624	76,192	86,456	85,537	89,077	90,702	1.1	4.6	2.2

Note: 1999 data are preliminary (see page 2).

2-3. Value added in industry

	Millions of U.S. dollars, constant 1995 prices											Average annual percentage growth		
	1980	1990	1991	1992	1993	1994	1995	1996	1997	1998	1999	75-84	85-89	90-MR
SUB-SAHARAN AFRICA	83,391	94,117	92,869	91,565	90,144	91,530	94,458	97,737	101,275	102,965	104,878	2.2	1.7	1.2
excluding South Africa	39,598	46,221	46,708	46,437	44,941	45,171	46,367	48,999	51,330	53,546	55,615	1.7	3.0	1.9
excl. S.Africa & Nigeria	25,052	34,139	33,521	33,197	31,776	32,400	33,445	35,510	37,447	39,270	40,846	..	3.4	1.8
Angola	..	3,446	3,423	3,495	2,669	3,052	3,339	3,638	3,837	4,002	4,182	..	8.1	2.0
Benin	134	237	248	269	272	285	293	306	320	322	333	5.4	-1.9	4.1
Botswana	749	2,041	2,140	2,120	2,108	2,149	2,234	2,385	2,480	2,542	2,593	15.9	8.3	2.7
Burkina Faso	415	548	550	577	566	579	581	600	664	736	815	1.6	4.8	3.5
Burundi	142	230	251	259	217	203	168	146	145	147	158	8.9	3.7	-5.6
Cameroon	1,478	2,773	2,590	2,321	2,221	1,901	1,855	1,939	2,088	2,248	2,360	18.2	0.7	-2.9
Cape Verde	28	74	76	79	85	88	96	99	96	105	112	6.3	17.1	4.4
Central African Republic	189	202	198	188	190	215	224	199	191	198	211	1.4	0.6	0.3
Chad	88	242	209	206	181	172	206	201	223	243	233	-2.0	2.5	0.4
Comoros	25	20	19	28	31	30	27	27	27	27	27	..	-9.0	3.7
Congo, Democratic Rep. of	2,768	2,537	2,032	1,424	1,218	1,192	1,069	1,069	1,022	1,042	1,105	-2.0	0.3	-10.0
Congo, Republic of	483	874	870	894	929	901	949	965	849	878	852	11.5	-0.3	0.2
Côte d'Ivoire	1,406	1,805	1,821	1,878	1,891	1,909	1,999	2,325	2,627	2,896	3,039	6.5	6.5	5.3
Djibouti	..	..	..	..	..	..	..	..	..	..	..	..	..	..
Equatorial Guinea	..	15	17	29	35	35	44	84	237	338	399	..	6.4	43.8
Eritrea	..	..	..	..	..	..	..	..	..	..	..	..	..	..
Ethiopia	..	535	433	402	516	552	597	629	673	679	726	..	-0.1	4.2
Gabon	1,859	2,410	2,215	2,173	2,264	2,469	2,597	2,655	2,679	2,714	2,752	..	-1.7	2.8
Gambia, The	31	45	46	47	48	46	44	46	48	48	50	3.1	10.6	0.9
Ghana	1,356	1,507	1,563	1,661	1,456	1,508	1,568	1,642	1,747	1,803	1,927	-7.5	9.1	2.5
Guinea	..	1,006	998	1,010	1,081	1,102	1,169	1,271	1,328	1,376	1,431	..	3.1	4.3
Guinea-Bissau	18	26	26	26	28	28	29	30	31	19	46	3.2	-3.5	2.6
Kenya	769	1,132	1,161	1,160	1,162	1,184	1,226	1,268	1,294	1,312	1,325	4.7	5.2	2.0
Lesotho	129	216	263	287	280	294	319	348	403	346	377	14.7	8.7	6.5
Liberia	..	..	..	..	..	..	..	..	..	..	..	..	..	..
Madagascar	455	393	391	387	400	396	402	410	429	450	469	-2.9	2.8	1.6
Malawi	185	250	260	266	246	252	259	261	271	277	288	2.7	3.7	1.6
Mali	217	324	365	383	398	382	408	435	532	569	580	1.6	1.4	6.5
Mauritania	169	237	236	234	281	288	298	302	287	286	284	0.6	3.7	2.3
Mauritius	361	882	932	997	1,052	1,106	1,154	1,222	1,277	1,350	1,419	3.6	13.0	5.5
Mozambique	..	369	381	359	352	373	425	483	649	943	1,020	..	-4.5	10.3
Namibia	849	750	808	910	808	879	921	916	940	949	971	..	2.1	2.6
Niger	368	331	328	310	315	317	325	346	358	368	376	10.4	-4.1	1.6
Nigeria	13,605	12,217	13,265	13,309	13,210	12,845	13,009	13,591	14,005	14,416	14,918	0.0	2.1	2.0
Rwanda	267	330	254	291	255	128	212	246	302	336	356	7.4	0.3	0.5
São Tomé and Principe	..	8	8	9	9	9	9	9	9	9	10	..	0.9	1.3
Senegal	541	854	844	887	865	861	961	1,014	1,071	1,162	1,235	3.7	4.9	4.1
Seychelles	49	72	85	81	91	94	115	126	153	156	159	2.0	3.4	10.0
Sierra Leone	245	320	238	243	238	241	193	235	134	156	231	-3.1	2.2	-4.7
Somalia	..	..	..	..	..	..	..	..	..	..	..	..	..	..
South Africa	43,794	47,832	46,143	45,127	45,169	46,305	48,025	48,713	49,942	49,472	49,363	2.6	0.7	0.6
Sudan	..	..	..	..	..	..	..	..	..	..	..	..	..	..
Swaziland	128	360	356	377	387	408	428	437	464	477	490	4.4	23.3	4.3
Tanzania	..	735	736	736	708	719	705	753	803	886	928	..	..	2.6
Togo	277	273	292	270	190	241	290	306	313	316	309	1.5	6.2	1.7
Uganda	..	437	472	512	555	627	754	879	979	1,092	1,191	..	6.4	12.1
Zambia	1,188	1,366	1,349	1,479	1,360	1,274	1,096	1,102	1,181	1,047	996	-0.4	2.7	-3.2
Zimbabwe	1,341	1,861	2,004	1,923	1,893	1,951	1,829	2,004	2,022	2,043	2,005	-1.0	5.4	0.9
NORTH AFRICA	42,479	59,079	60,675	61,607	60,969	62,242	64,250	66,992	70,318	73,825	77,581	6.3	1.8	2.8
Algeria	16,056	20,059	20,394	20,395	19,468	19,073	19,134	19,830	20,767	21,585	22,618	5.3	-0.4	0.8
Egypt, Arab Republic	9,157	15,038	15,835	16,073	16,431	17,327	18,195	19,089	19,967	21,565	23,006	11.0	4.2	4.6
Libya	..	..	..	..	..	..	..	..	..	..	..	..	..	..
Morocco	7,171	9,827	9,884	10,119	10,016	10,416	10,882	11,406	12,038	12,257	12,600	3.4	3.1	3.2
Tunisia	2,945	4,211	4,348	4,650	4,791	4,949	5,224	5,390	5,709	5,991	6,297	7.1	2.6	4.4
ALL AFRICA	126,569	153,270	153,385	152,841	150,756	153,377	158,299	164,255	171,014	175,974	181,395	3.5	1.8	1.8

Note: 1999 data are preliminary (see page 2).

2-4. Value added in services

	\multicolumn{11}{c}{Millions of U.S. dollars, constant 1995 prices}	\multicolumn{3}{c}{Average annual percentage growth}
	1980	1990	1991	1992	1993	1994	1995	1996	1997	1998	1999	75-84	85-89	90-MR
SUB-SAHARAN AFRICA	108,481	139,349	140,563	140,329	140,817	143,687	150,016	156,458	161,425	165,237	168,522	3.1	2.4	2.2
excluding South Africa	46,372	60,579	61,682	61,558	61,459	61,984	64,652	67,390	70,182	72,304	73,786	3.0	3.1	2.2
excl. S.Africa & Nigeria	42,940	55,605	56,604	56,084	55,647	56,149	58,694	61,166	63,754	65,891	67,541	3.1	2.8	2.1
Angola	..	2,092	2,162	2,001	1,652	1,337	1,460	1,619	1,725	1,731	1,722	..	1.7	-2.6
Benin	783	867	881	907	953	958	1,033	1,080	1,148	1,192	1,259	3.8	0.4	4.2
Botswana	609	1,736	1,931	2,081	2,184	2,312	2,469	2,660	2,766	2,888	3,084	10.8	13.8	6.8
Burkina Faso	493	795	834	863	846	860	877	934	1,008	1,049	1,119	8.9	4.0	3.5
Burundi	166	303	310	315	308	298	285	252	253	259	267	6.2	4.1	-1.7
Cameroon	2,365	2,844	2,780	2,473	2,332	2,637	2,793	2,714	2,689	2,669	2,716	8.6	-1.4	-0.6
Cape Verde	114	242	248	261	279	306	328	326	356	387	417	10.5	8.2	6.1
Central African Republic	363	391	366	304	292	314	347	301	324	344	342	0.3	1.0	-1.6
Chad	391	671	723	764	662	712	696	725	733	767	799	-0.7	6.3	1.1
Comoros	85	117	105	115	117	109	104	104	105	104	102	..	2.0	-1.1
Congo, Democratic Rep. of	3,690	3,957	3,512	3,031	2,131	1,926	1,685	1,551	1,274	1,137	1,242	-0.5	2.1	-13.3
Congo, Republic of	912	1,371	1,477	1,500	1,454	1,312	1,340	1,174	1,308	1,361	1,302	9.3	-2.7	-1.2
Côte d'Ivoire	4,847	4,864	4,803	4,663	4,628	4,795	5,113	5,345	5,685	5,785	5,964	1.0	-0.2	2.3
Djibouti	..	..	..	..	..	..	..	..	..	..	..	..	..	..
Equatorial Guinea	..	24	26	30	32	32	34	38	43	52	59	..	6.5	9.3
Eritrea	..	..	..	..	..	..	..	..	..	..	..	..	..	..
Ethiopia	..	1,693	1,478	1,416	1,663	1,794	1,962	2,098	2,246	2,480	2,693	..	4.1	5.8
Gabon	1,326	1,475	1,848	1,756	1,778	1,755	1,963	2,137	2,362	2,447	2,108	..	-1.7	4.4
Gambia, The	119	161	160	171	190	186	188	197	212	221	226	4.7	1.9	4.1
Ghana	1,015	1,685	1,775	1,929	2,189	2,288	2,385	2,482	2,570	2,691	2,780	0.1	7.8	6.1
Guinea	..	1,419	1,454	1,490	1,534	1,596	1,641	1,694	1,756	1,839	1,876	..	5.3	3.3
Guinea-Bissau	47	73	77	79	76	77	78	80	82	53	23	10.0	4.7	-5.6
Kenya	2,112	3,409	3,531	3,635	3,714	3,842	4,046	4,256	4,387	4,475	4,548	5.9	5.6	3.5
Lesotho	187	274	284	295	315	332	348	371	394	399	401	7.6	4.5	4.8
Liberia	..	..	..	..	..	..	..	..	..	..	..	..	..	..
Madagascar	1,605	1,602	1,489	1,506	1,539	1,547	1,571	1,604	1,680	1,770	1,846	0.1	1.8	1.7
Malawi	411	548	585	570	574	541	657	676	697	715	729	3.1	3.3	3.5
Mali	552	661	657	677	699	695	695	754	770	806	833	1.6	0.0	2.4
Mauritania	353	364	367	378	384	398	402	437	487	507	535	2.1	3.6	4.3
Mauritius	880	1,472	1,545	1,644	1,755	1,887	2,000	2,128	2,256	2,387	2,520	5.4	7.4	6.3
Mozambique	..	705	822	796	801	1,025	939	962	967	895	911	..	10.0	3.3
Namibia	969	1,285	1,386	1,454	1,458	1,496	1,529	1,619	1,685	1,736	1,774	..	0.5	3.4
Niger	888	837	803	754	769	769	800	842	864	898	924	-0.1	7.6	1.1
Nigeria	3,488	5,117	5,222	5,580	5,884	5,910	6,049	6,317	6,530	6,538	6,401	1.5	7.6	3.5
Rwanda	334	611	632	643	659	278	434	478	537	578	612	11.2	6.7	-1.7
São Tomé and Principe	..	24	24	23	23	24	25	24	24	25	25	..	1.4	0.6
Senegal	1,850	2,430	2,467	2,504	2,476	2,525	2,634	2,756	2,958	3,182	3,324	3.1	2.8	3.3
Seychelles	241	343	344	382	403	395	372	384	380	388	250	-1.1	6.1	-0.4
Sierra Leone	391	349	335	299	294	298	254	169	247	269	209	2.5	-3.3	-5.5
Somalia	..	..	..	..	..	..	..	..	..	..	..	..	..	..
South Africa	61,526	78,104	78,259	78,147	78,705	80,975	84,598	88,266	90,472	92,182	93,974	3.2	2.0	2.2
Sudan	..	..	..	..	..	..	..	..	..	..	..	..	..	..
Swaziland	187	340	357	370	390	396	409	412	425	453	457	5.7	4.3	3.4
Tanzania	..	1,722	1,773	1,834	1,810	1,816	1,866	1,934	1,994	2,077	2,177	..	..	2.5
Togo	619	593	568	533	396	506	524	554	582	564	563	2.0	1.5	-0.1
Uganda	..	1,268	1,367	1,467	1,571	1,693	1,917	2,082	2,200	2,345	2,513	..	3.2	8.1
Zambia	1,750	1,672	1,761	1,647	1,818	1,429	1,396	1,606	1,670	1,744	1,834	0.0	3.2	-0.2
Zimbabwe	2,078	3,016	3,166	3,180	3,198	3,303	3,503	3,779	3,832	3,941	4,019	5.4	3.7	3.6
NORTH AFRICA	42,543	68,917	70,651	73,680	74,678	77,070	80,271	83,639	87,254	91,635	95,936	7.5	3.5	3.6
Algeria	9,061	12,950	12,849	13,290	13,130	13,452	14,330	14,723	14,999	15,693	16,060	5.7	1.8	2.4
Egypt, Arab Republic	12,642	24,548	25,279	25,826	26,520	27,307	28,682	30,279	32,202	33,726	35,862	11.0	4.3	4.2
Libya	..	..	..	..	..	..	..	..	..	..	..	..	..	..
Morocco	9,925	15,066	15,856	16,776	16,753	17,075	17,285	17,801	18,147	19,081	19,666	5.9	4.0	2.8
Tunisia	6,006	8,402	8,516	9,287	9,659	10,344	10,714	11,186	11,839	12,564	13,279	5.7	3.2	5.3
ALL AFRICA	151,844	208,941	211,839	214,476	215,927	221,154	230,712	240,544	249,093	257,180	264,649	4.3	2.8	2.7

Note: 1999 data are preliminary (see page 2).

2-5. Gross domestic product, nominal

	Millions of U.S. dollars, current prices											Annual average		
	1980	*1990*	*1991*	*1992*	*1993*	*1994*	*1995*	*1996*	*1997*	*1998*	*1999*	*75-84*	*85-89*	*90-MR*
SUB-SAHARAN AFRICA	270,870	297,085	302,800	304,333	287,379	281,425	318,402	330,946	343,399	323,644	326,115	209,481	240,765	311,553
excluding South Africa	191,028	185,517	182,880	173,943	156,993	145,536	167,204	187,232	195,177	189,913	195,284	149,285	161,927	177,968
excl. S.Africa & Nigeria	123,925	157,086	155,624	141,136	135,711	121,864	139,067	151,827	158,848	157,626	160,163	106,433	138,213	147,895
Angola	..	10,260	12,194	5,779	5,286	4,060	5,187	7,522	7,690	6,449	8,545	..	7,560	7,297
Benin	1,405	1,845	1,878	1,624	2,106	1,497	2,009	2,208	2,141	2,306	2,414	1,035	1,413	2,003
Botswana	1,130	3,766	3,920	4,147	4,177	4,404	4,899	4,910	5,054	4,876	5,996	865	2,110	4,615
Burkina Faso	1,709	2,765	2,788	1,996	2,049	1,854	2,355	2,538	2,382	2,580	2,580	1,311	2,038	2,389
Burundi	920	1,132	1,167	1,083	939	925	1,000	900	957	878	714	778	1,136	970
Cameroon	6,741	11,152	12,434	11,396	11,891	7,854	7,965	9,109	9,115	8,703	9,187	5,630	10,942	9,881
Cape Verde	107	339	351	394	363	411	491	502	506	540	581	86	233	448
Central African Republic	797	1,488	1,404	1,434	1,299	853	1,122	1,070	997	1,049	1,053	619	1,150	1,177
Chad	1,033	1,739	1,877	1,882	1,463	1,179	1,438	1,605	1,508	1,682	1,530	928	1,236	1,590
Comoros	124	250	247	266	264	186	215	213	194	197	193	113	176	222
Congo, Democratic Rep. of	14,391	9,348	9,086	8,206	8,975	7,158	6,338	5,869	6,101	6,964	7,752	12,212	8,165	7,580
Congo, Republic of	1,706	2,799	2,725	2,933	1,919	1,769	2,510	2,541	2,323	1,949	2,217	1,452	2,182	2,369
Côte d'Ivoire	10,175	10,796	10,493	11,153	10,405	7,666	9,992	10,700	10,582	11,236	11,206	7,172	9,247	10,423
Djibouti	..	418	456	470	471	487	491	496	504	513	531	..	393	484
Equatorial Guinea	..	132	131	154	152	126	164	259	498	456	696	104	107	277
Eritrea	..	..	..	437	409	510	574	631	655	680	645	..	..	568
Ethiopia	..	6,842	5,321	5,568	6,249	4,894	5,779	6,010	6,383	6,564	6,439	5,603	7,356	6,005
Gabon	4,279	5,952	5,403	5,592	4,381	4,191	4,958	5,741	5,428	4,619	4,352	3,211	3,609	5,062
Gambia, The	241	317	317	347	366	363	382	392	410	417	393	181	236	370
Ghana	4,445	5,886	6,600	6,413	5,966	5,440	6,457	6,988	6,946	7,474	7,774	3,762	5,150	6,594
Guinea	..	2,818	3,015	3,285	3,279	3,435	3,729	3,959	3,895	3,782	3,733	..	2,230	3,493
Guinea-Bissau	111	244	257	226	237	236	254	271	269	206	218	131	165	242
Kenya	7,265	8,533	8,043	8,002	4,977	7,148	9,047	9,206	10,625	11,465	10,638	5,550	7,641	8,769
Lesotho	432	622	680	827	818	837	933	940	1,023	878	874	328	416	843
Liberia	1,117	..	..	..	..	..	..	..	..	..	..	987	1,143	..
Madagascar	4,042	3,081	2,677	3,001	3,371	2,977	3,160	3,995	3,546	3,739	3,721	3,057	2,724	3,327
Malawi	1,238	1,803	2,204	1,800	2,071	1,182	1,429	2,432	2,534	1,737	1,810	1,018	1,266	1,900
Mali	1,787	2,421	2,423	2,846	2,678	1,763	2,466	2,619	2,475	2,634	2,608	1,285	1,776	2,493
Mauritania	709	1,020	1,130	1,191	944	1,027	1,068	1,113	1,096	1,000	960	645	867	1,055
Mauritius	1,132	2,642	2,831	3,189	3,195	3,503	3,973	4,301	4,079	4,073	4,244	990	1,747	3,603
Mozambique	3,526	2,512	2,496	1,955	2,103	2,267	2,392	2,897	3,513	3,910	4,142	3,457	3,293	2,819
Namibia	2,169	2,340	2,483	2,823	2,628	2,978	3,224	3,122	3,234	3,044	3,075	1,903	1,833	2,895
Niger	2,509	2,481	2,328	2,345	1,607	1,563	1,881	1,988	1,846	2,077	2,018	1,725	2,008	2,013
Nigeria	64,202	28,472	27,313	32,710	21,353	23,663	28,109	35,299	36,229	32,249	35,045	42,093	23,750	30,044
Rwanda	1,163	2,584	1,912	2,047	1,956	754	1,286	1,406	1,865	2,024	1,956	1,091	2,123	1,779
São Tomé and Principe	43	50	57	46	48	50	45	45	44	41	47	32	50	47
Senegal	2,987	5,698	5,500	6,027	5,431	3,642	4,476	4,651	4,379	4,666	4,801	2,364	4,110	4,927
Seychelles	147	369	375	434	469	483	508	508	539	535	545	112	244	476
Sierra Leone	1,166	897	807	691	771	927	866	942	850	672	669	1,030	1,081	809
Somalia	604	917	..	..	..	..	..	..	..	..	..	677	989	917
South Africa	80,544	111,997	120,243	130,533	130,406	135,778	151,113	143,840	148,366	133,962	131,127	61,201	79,315	133,736
Sudan	7,617	13,167	11,410	6,402	7,895	8,170	7,194	7,208	10,275	10,018	9,718	7,964	15,971	9,146
Swaziland	582	860	881	969	988	1,062	1,267	1,228	1,313	1,221	1,223	435	563	1,101
Tanzania	..	4,259	4,957	4,601	4,258	4,511	5,255	6,496	7,684	8,591	8,760	5,569	4,561	5,937
Togo	1,136	1,628	1,602	1,693	1,234	983	1,309	1,473	1,501	1,414	1,405	813	1,161	1,424
Uganda	1,245	4,304	3,322	2,858	3,220	3,997	5,756	6,049	6,298	6,777	6,411	4,108	5,097	4,899
Zambia	3,884	3,288	3,377	3,183	3,274	3,347	3,471	3,271	3,911	3,240	3,150	3,159	2,781	3,351
Zimbabwe	6,679	8,784	8,642	6,752	6,564	6,891	7,120	8,632	8,679	6,769	5,608	5,993	6,939	7,444
NORTH AFRICA	124,881	163,130	141,522	153,758	157,689	159,477	173,657	194,565	200,303	211,499	219,904	97,313	144,086	177,550
Algeria	42,345	61,902	46,301	49,116	49,762	42,063	41,248	46,850	47,845	47,362	47,872	34,782	59,855	48,032
Egypt, Arab Republic	22,912	43,130	36,971	41,856	47,197	51,898	60,159	67,651	75,605	82,710	89,148	20,312	37,154	59,632
Libya	35,545	..	..	..	..	..	..	..	..	..	..	24,534	22,902	..
Morocco	18,821	25,821	27,837	28,451	26,801	30,351	32,986	36,639	33,415	35,668	34,998	13,499	18,731	31,297
Tunisia	8,743	12,291	13,075	15,497	14,609	15,626	17,987	19,587	18,897	19,847	20,944	6,901	9,465	16,836
ALL AFRICA	394,807	461,130	447,099	460,023	445,949	441,384	493,114	525,546	543,857	533,575	543,926	305,883	386,104	489,560

Note: 1999 data are preliminary (see page 2).

2-6. Total consumption

	Percentage of GDP											Annual average		
	1980	*1990*	*1991*	*1992*	*1993*	*1994*	*1995*	*1996*	*1997*	*1998*	*1999*	*75-84*	*85-89*	*90-MR*
SUB-SAHARAN AFRICA	74.1	82.1	83.9	87.1	86.0	83.5	83.7	81.9	83.3	84.0	84.2	77.1	81.0	84.0
excluding South Africa	77.0	82.6	85.0	89.9	89.3	84.6	86.3	82.2	83.9	85.4	86.4	78.4	83.1	85.6
excl. S.Africa & Nigeria	83.6	85.0	87.8	93.1	91.1	85.7	87.3	86.4	85.9	87.3	87.4	79.7	83.5	87.7
Angola	..	70.3	83.8	98.3	90.1	73.9	85.3	76.5	59.0	67.5	46.7	..	76.0	75.1
Benin	105.1	94.5	94.1	95.8	94.8	90.5	90.0	92.0	90.2	91.7	91.8	100.0	97.0	92.5
Botswana	65.6	62.9	62.3	64.8	63.9	61.1	59.4	56.6	68.2	78.2	85.8	69.8	50.8	66.3
Burkina Faso	105.8	92.3	93.9	93.0	94.1	92.5	91.4	90.9	89.1	87.3	90.2	101.7	97.6	91.5
Burundi	100.6	105.4	104.2	105.1	104.7	107.6	104.8	97.5	96.1	102.9	100.4	95.9	96.7	102.9
Cameroon	78.3	79.3	78.0	83.5	82.4	82.1	80.5	82.7	80.9	80.1	81.1	76.9	77.1	81.0
Cape Verde	124.0	108.1	104.2	103.5	96.3	97.2	97.6	94.2	91.9	92.4	89.6	119.8	102.9	97.5
Central African Republic	108.9	100.6	97.4	100.4	98.2	94.0	93.8	99.4	96.4	95.5	92.8	101.6	99.2	96.8
Chad	..	99.5	105.9	106.3	106.2	101.5	101.7	96.7	97.7	95.7	103.0	97.6	111.1	101.4
Comoros	110.1	103.2	97.9	101.6	97.1	105.9	109.2	111.4	112.1	98.4	100.0	106.5	102.5	103.7
Congo, Democratic Rep. of	89.9	90.7	98.2	93.9	96.0	89.4	85.9	86.6	91.0	90.2	88.9	89.5	86.7	91.1
Congo, Republic of	64.3	76.2	81.4	75.6	76.4	73.4	57.5	21.0	50.9	63.9	70.3	73.9	76.8	64.7
Côte d'Ivoire	79.6	88.7	89.6	89.3	90.6	77.6	81.1	78.8	77.5	75.2	76.9	75.7	81.6	82.5
Djibouti	..	..	110.2	118.6	111.0	111.3	108.7	105.3	105.4	..	..	..	..	110.1
Equatorial Guinea	..	120.1	107.2	97.8	101.0	74.9	72.7	69.3	56.9	80.1	42.1	92.4	133.3	82.2
Eritrea	..	..	..	131.3	124.6	135.4	138.6	131.0	117.4	124.5	121.3	..	..	128.0
Ethiopia	..	92.8	97.3	97.0	94.4	94.6	92.0	97.5	93.5	94.7	97.3	93.6	92.8	95.1
Gabon	39.4	63.1	59.5	65.3	63.3	54.7	52.7	49.0	49.0	61.0	65.2	41.9	67.7	58.3
Gambia, The	94.2	89.3	89.4	90.7	96.0	97.7	99.1	97.9	95.5	97.2	98.3	95.7	92.4	95.1
Ghana	95.1	94.5	92.7	98.7	93.4	87.4	88.3	85.7	95.6	89.3	93.8	93.7	94.5	91.9
Guinea	..	82.3	82.0	88.8	88.9	87.9	87.3	87.1	85.0	84.7	84.8	..	83.6	85.9
Guinea-Bissau	101.0	97.2	96.8	96.8	93.0	96.1	101.2	98.2	97.2	109.3	102.2	103.0	100.1	98.8
Kenya	86.6	85.6	83.1	86.3	76.2	80.4	88.7	86.9	92.2	93.2	93.2	83.0	83.1	86.6
Lesotho	152.0	151.3	149.1	133.9	145.0	135.7	138.4	136.0	130.9	134.6	133.5	164.3	162.3	138.8
Liberia	72.7	..	..	..	..	..	..	..	..	..	..	76.7	83.6	..
Madagascar	101.4	93.7	99.3	96.6	97.5	96.6	96.4	93.7	96.3	95.4	95.4	98.0	94.2	96.1
Malawi	89.2	90.3	85.8	99.3	100.9	103.0	100.3	97.0	99.1	93.9	100.6	84.4	90.0	97.0
Mali	98.9	93.6	93.6	95.6	93.6	92.5	92.2	92.8	90.0	88.8	89.9	99.8	99.9	92.3
Mauritania	103.5	95.1	90.3	95.2	95.3	83.1	91.1	92.8	92.1	94.9	92.8	105.6	89.7	92.3
Mauritius	89.5	76.4	75.1	73.9	75.5	76.6	76.7	76.2	75.8	76.4	77.3	81.5	74.5	76.0
Mozambique	110.6	112.3	111.2	117.2	122.4	113.9	101.9	101.8	99.1	92.8	93.6	110.4	110.2	106.6
Namibia	61.6	81.8	96.0	92.8	94.6	86.0	90.1	89.0	95.3	90.1	90.7	90.3	88.1	90.7
Niger	85.4	98.8	97.2	94.2	96.1	100.0	99.8	96.9	96.8	97.3	96.2	91.6	92.1	97.3
Nigeria	68.6	70.6	70.7	76.5	79.8	79.4	81.6	65.1	75.4	76.6	81.6	78.5	82.3	75.7
Rwanda	95.8	93.8	96.7	98.4	100.9	146.8	105.8	104.3	102.8	101.8	101.3	93.2	94.7	105.3
São Tomé and Principe	114.9	129.2	121.7	128.1	127.6	121.4	137.9	125.8	126.6	98.0	109.3	109.0	114.8	122.5
Senegal	105.0	91.1	94.1	92.6	94.5	88.1	88.9	87.2	87.7	87.2	87.6	98.9	96.2	89.9
Seychelles	72.9	79.7	81.3	82.4	81.6	77.9	76.5	60.4	77.7	79.7	80.1	68.1	69.9	77.7
Sierra Leone	97.1	91.7	91.9	93.7	96.7	96.6	101.8	103.7	104.3	101.9	106.0	95.3	94.3	98.8
Somalia	112.9	112.5	..	..	..	..	..	..	..	..	..	111.4	94.4	112.5
South Africa	68.6	82.4	83.1	83.9	82.4	82.1	80.9	81.7	82.9	82.6	81.8	75.6	78.0	82.4
Sudan	97.9	..	..	..	..	..	..	..	..	..	..	94.2	92.0	..
Swaziland	93.5	79.6	81.8	81.4	73.7	74.0	71.0	81.2	80.5	80.8	78.9	84.0	82.3	78.3
Tanzania	..	98.7	97.0	99.7	104.6	98.4	97.6	95.7	95.0	97.6	97.8	89.0	89.4	98.2
Togo	76.8	85.3	91.0	93.5	100.2	88.7	88.8	92.2	93.4	97.5	96.4	78.6	92.4	92.7
Uganda	..	99.4	99.3	99.6	98.9	95.7	92.6	95.4	92.0	94.4	95.1	97.0	97.0	96.2
Zambia	80.7	83.4	91.6	100.0	91.0	92.6	87.8	94.7	90.6	96.1	101.1	81.1	85.1	92.9
Zimbabwe	86.2	82.6	84.2	89.0	83.7	72.8	79.1	80.7	88.0	81.9	89.0	84.8	81.0	83.1
NORTH AFRICA	59.7	78.2	76.3	77.5	80.6	82.6	82.7	81.8	80.5	81.6	80.0	64.6	76.0	80.2
Algeria	56.9	72.5	63.3	67.6	72.2	73.0	71.6	68.6	67.8	72.9	68.3	61.1	69.2	69.8
Egypt, Arab Republic	84.8	83.9	86.8	84.6	86.8	88.6	87.8	89.2	87.0	86.0	85.6	84.6	84.3	86.6
Libya	43.1	..	..	..	..	..	..	..	..	..	..	53.5	..	..
Morocco	87.1	84.3	85.3	86.9	86.6	87.7	89.0	88.0	86.5	85.8	84.7	87.0	85.5	86.5
Tunisia	76.0	74.5	72.9	72.6	78.3	78.5	79.3	76.5	76.0	76.3	75.6	75.8	78.4	76.1
ALL AFRICA	70.1	80.8	81.5	84.0	84.1	83.2	83.3	81.9	82.3	83.1	82.7	73.7	78.8	82.7

Note: 1999 data are preliminary (see page 2). Since 1994, Nigeria's ratios are distorted because the official exchange rate used by the Government for oil exports and oil value added is significantly over-valued.

2-7. General government consumption

					Percentage of GDP							Annual average		
	1980	1990	1991	1992	1993	1994	1995	1996	1997	1998	1999	75-84	85-89	90-MR
SUB-SAHARAN AFRICA	14.4	17.4	18.0	19.0	18.4	17.6	16.3	16.2	16.3	16.4	16.7	14.9	16.3	17.2
excluding South Africa	14.6	16.0	16.9	18.0	16.8	15.0	14.3	13.5	13.5	13.9	15.0	14.8	15.1	15.3
excl. S.Africa & Nigeria	15.9	16.2	17.8	17.9	16.8	15.2	15.0	14.9	14.5	14.0	15.0	14.9	15.6	15.7
Angola	..	34.5	45.3	41.9	41.5	40.1	46.7	40.8	41.8	31.9	39.5	..	31.5	40.4
Benin	8.6	11.0	10.8	10.7	10.3	10.1	11.2	10.7	10.4	9.7	10.6	9.9	14.1	10.6
Botswana	19.6	23.8	24.7	26.4	28.5	28.2	28.1	27.4	23.6	26.4	27.7	20.5	22.3	26.5
Burkina Faso	10.4	14.9	14.6	15.8	15.2	17.1	15.6	14.8	14.2	14.3	13.6	12.8	14.2	15.0
Burundi	9.2	10.8	10.8	10.1	13.3	12.7	13.4	12.6	14.5	13.3	16.1	10.3	9.7	12.8
Cameroon	9.7	12.8	13.3	12.8	12.8	10.0	8.6	8.4	8.2	9.2	10.0	9.7	10.8	10.6
Cape Verde	8.2	14.7	15.7	15.7	17.6	18.3	19.8	17.4	16.2	14.8	15.5	10.0	12.3	16.6
Central African Republic	15.1	14.9	16.3	16.9	15.0	17.5	15.2	9.6	11.0	11.7	11.5	15.0	15.9	14.0
Chad	..	10.0	8.9	9.2	10.0	12.7	11.8	8.7	7.9	6.9	8.0	13.0	13.8	9.4
Comoros	30.9	16.5	17.5	15.8	15.1	16.7	17.2	15.2	14.0	11.8	12.4	29.7	27.4	15.2
Congo, Democratic Rep. of	8.4	11.5	13.3	21.7	15.4	4.4	4.9	5.7	8.5	8.8	9.2	9.1	9.7	10.3
Congo, Republic of	17.6	13.8	21.0	21.1	21.2	16.2	10.9	10.5	19.0	14.4	10.8	17.3	20.5	15.9
Côte d'Ivoire	16.9	16.8	16.4	17.4	16.4	13.0	11.9	12.1	11.3	10.4	10.9	16.5	16.2	13.7
Djibouti	..	..	32.0	44.2	44.1	40.1	38.3	32.8	27.7	..	..	..	..	37.0
Equatorial Guinea	..	39.7	34.2	29.4	39.3	15.3	16.4	19.8	11.0	21.0	11.4	28.3	27.4	23.8
Eritrea	..	..	..	32.9	36.6	43.2	46.7	45.0	32.6	49.0	50.6	..	..	42.1
Ethiopia	..	18.5	15.5	10.1	10.6	12.5	11.8	11.7	11.4	14.3	16.4	15.3	16.0	13.3
Gabon	13.2	13.4	14.3	15.5	15.3	12.0	14.1	13.6	13.7	16.9	16.6	14.5	20.9	14.5
Gambia, The	31.2	13.7	13.3	13.9	14.1	14.5	14.1	15.3	13.9	12.7	14.3	36.6	17.7	14.0
Ghana	11.2	9.3	9.5	12.1	14.4	13.7	12.1	11.9	12.2	10.3	10.8	9.9	10.1	11.6
Guinea	..	11.9	9.7	11.4	11.1	8.7	8.4	8.2	8.1	7.2	7.1	..	11.4	9.2
Guinea-Bissau	27.6	10.3	10.6	9.0	7.1	7.1	6.4	6.6	7.0	9.3	11.1	23.6	12.5	8.4
Kenya	19.8	18.7	17.0	16.1	16.7	15.2	14.8	16.1	16.1	16.4	17.5	18.4	18.1	16.5
Lesotho	21.8	13.9	15.5	14.7	15.1	16.4	17.9	16.3	17.0	20.0	22.2	17.7	18.9	16.9
Liberia	16.3	..	..	..	..	..	..	..	..	..	..	15.8	19.0	..
Madagascar	12.1	8.0	8.7	8.3	7.9	6.9	6.7	6.1	7.6	7.5	7.9	11.1	8.9	7.6
Malawi	19.3	15.7	12.0	14.1	13.0	31.6	18.6	12.5	12.6	13.3	12.4	16.4	18.0	15.6
Mali	9.8	13.8	13.5	13.2	12.8	11.3	9.7	10.2	12.0	11.3	12.6	9.4	13.5	12.0
Mauritania	45.3	25.9	18.2	16.4	20.7	16.5	14.1	14.3	13.8	14.5	15.2	45.2	25.3	17.0
Mauritius	14.1	11.8	11.7	11.5	12.1	12.5	12.1	12.2	11.9	11.7	11.3	13.5	11.7	11.9
Mozambique	12.2	11.6	10.6	12.6	11.7	12.9	7.8	8.0	9.0	9.6	10.6	14.2	11.3	10.4
Namibia	17.4	30.7	33.6	35.6	35.0	31.3	32.1	33.0	32.8	31.5	26.3	26.0	29.8	32.2
Niger	10.4	15.0	14.8	17.5	15.8	16.0	14.1	11.3	13.8	13.1	14.9	11.5	12.9	14.6
Nigeria	12.1	15.1	12.2	18.4	17.5	14.3	11.1	8.0	9.4	13.5	14.9	14.4	12.5	13.4
Rwanda	12.5	10.1	12.1	12.9	11.7	10.5	11.3	12.0	10.6	11.3	12.7	14.7	12.6	11.5
São Tomé and Principe	23.6	51.2	35.3	31.5	34.5	31.9	27.6	25.2	31.9	25.6	29.8	20.6	39.2	32.5
Senegal	20.3	14.7	13.5	15.4	14.7	12.8	12.4	12.0	10.4	10.3	10.8	17.2	15.6	12.7
Seychelles	28.7	27.7	28.2	30.4	29.8	29.6	29.3	29.1	27.9	33.2	28.7	28.5	34.5	29.4
Sierra Leone	7.7	9.9	9.4	10.3	11.2	11.1	14.0	10.9	9.0	8.9	11.5	8.8	9.1	10.6
Somalia	15.6	..	..	..	..	..	..	..	..	..	..	19.8	..	..
South Africa	14.3	19.7	19.8	20.2	20.1	20.0	18.3	19.4	19.8	19.8	19.2	15.7	18.8	19.6
Sudan	16.0	..	..	..	..	..	..	..	..	..	..	12.1	11.9	..
Swaziland	19.1	18.5	19.6	17.7	24.2	23.2	20.7	22.6	27.1	20.0	20.0	20.6	18.4	21.4
Tanzania	..	17.8	18.9	19.6	19.4	17.1	11.5	11.6	8.8	11.1	11.6	13.5	14.6	14.7
Togo	22.4	14.2	17.5	12.4	16.1	13.2	12.1	11.7	10.2	12.1	10.9	20.0	15.2	13.0
Uganda	..	7.5	8.8	9.7	9.8	10.3	9.8	10.3	10.4	9.6	9.9	10.8	9.3	9.6
Zambia	25.5	19.0	31.8	15.0	18.4	13.1	12.5	11.4	10.9	11.2	9.6	25.7	19.9	15.3
Zimbabwe	18.5	19.4	16.1	24.2	14.9	16.7	18.0	16.9	16.1	16.4	14.9	16.9	22.1	17.4
NORTH AFRICA	12.0	14.6	14.2	14.9	14.9	14.4	14.2	14.0	14.0	14.3	14.1	13.8	16.3	14.4
Algeria	13.8	16.2	15.0	17.2	17.4	16.8	15.8	16.4	16.7	18.1	17.0	13.8	17.5	16.7
Egypt, Arab Republic	15.7	11.3	11.2	10.4	10.2	10.3	10.5	10.4	10.2	10.1	10.1	19.5	14.9	10.5
Libya	21.8	..	..	..	..	..	..	..	..	..	..	27.8	..	..
Morocco	18.3	15.5	15.6	16.8	18.1	17.1	17.4	16.9	17.8	18.1	19.3	18.9	15.6	17.3
Tunisia	14.5	16.4	16.6	16.0	16.3	16.5	16.9	15.6	15.8	15.7	15.5	15.7	17.1	16.1
ALL AFRICA	13.3	16.5	16.8	17.7	17.2	16.5	15.6	15.4	15.5	15.6	15.7	14.4	16.2	16.3

Note: 1999 data are preliminary (see page 2). Since 1994, Nigeria's ratios are distorted because the official exchange rate used by the Government for oil exports and oil value added is significantly over-valued.

2-8. Gross domestic investment

	Percentage of GDP											Annual average		
	1980	1990	1991	1992	1993	1994	1995	1996	1997	1998	1999	75-84	85-89	90-MR
SUB-SAHARAN AFRICA	20.4	14.2	14.9	14.8	15.7	17.5	18.1	17.1	17.3	18.8	18.4	20.1	15.3	16.7
excluding South Africa	19.3	15.9	17.1	17.0	17.3	19.4	18.0	17.2	18.5	20.8	20.3	19.5	15.6	18.2
excl. S.Africa & Nigeria	17.9	16.2	15.9	15.8	16.3	19.3	18.4	17.9	18.7	19.2	19.4	17.8	15.8	17.7
Angola	..	11.7	12.9	3.6	11.2	16.6	4.1	-5.6	25.3	24.0	32.3	..	14.8	13.6
Benin	15.2	14.2	14.5	13.8	15.4	15.8	19.6	17.1	18.5	17.1	17.8	17.7	12.6	16.4
Botswana	36.8	31.7	30.4	28.6	26.6	26.9	26.9	25.8	23.0	20.6	19.7	32.9	25.0	26.0
Burkina Faso	17.0	20.6	20.6	21.1	20.7	20.6	23.9	26.8	27.3	29.6	27.8	20.2	21.7	23.9
Burundi	13.9	14.5	14.4	15.0	16.3	10.6	9.6	12.1	8.1	8.8	9.1	14.3	15.9	11.8
Cameroon	21.0	17.8	16.7	14.3	16.5	15.3	14.5	15.4	16.2	18.4	19.5	25.1	22.6	16.5
Cape Verde	51.6	22.9	26.2	34.5	39.7	43.4	42.4	38.0	37.4	37.0	37.6	49.1	32.3	35.9
Central African Republic	7.0	12.3	12.4	12.2	10.2	11.7	13.5	4.4	9.0	13.5	14.3	10.5	12.5	11.3
Chad	..	15.9	6.5	7.5	9.8	16.6	10.3	14.9	14.8	16.0	10.3	11.9	7.9	12.3
Comoros	33.2	19.7	20.3	22.2	20.6	21.0	17.6	13.5	15.5	16.6	14.6	33.4	24.2	18.2
Congo, Democratic Rep. of	10.0	9.1	5.6	6.9	1.8	7.9	9.4	7.1	7.1	8.1	10.6	12.7	13.7	7.4
Congo, Republic of	35.8	15.9	20.5	21.6	29.5	54.5	30.8	60.1	22.4	26.7	22.3	36.2	22.4	30.4
Côte d'Ivoire	26.5	6.7	7.4	6.9	8.3	12.5	13.5	13.4	16.0	18.2	16.3	23.6	11.8	11.9
Djibouti	..	..	14.4	19.1	17.3	11.7	8.6	9.7	9.4	..	..	..	..	12.8
Equatorial Guinea	..	17.4	50.7	24.2	22.0	74.1	76.3	113.6	65.7	91.6	41.4	13.9	0.0	57.7
Eritrea	..	..	..	5.4	15.1	17.8	19.3	29.3	40.9	47.2	47.3	..	..	27.8
Ethiopia	..	11.8	9.9	9.2	14.2	15.2	16.4	16.9	17.0	17.2	18.1	13.7	14.7	14.6
Gabon	27.5	21.7	26.5	22.4	22.4	21.9	23.7	23.3	29.6	37.3	28.0	42.9	35.7	25.7
Gambia, The	26.7	22.3	21.9	22.2	21.0	18.1	20.2	21.6	17.2	18.4	17.8	19.7	17.1	20.1
Ghana	5.6	14.4	15.9	12.8	22.2	24.0	20.0	22.2	24.8	23.6	23.2	6.9	10.8	20.3
Guinea	..	17.5	18.1	17.4	17.8	15.4	16.4	16.9	17.1	17.1	17.0	..	16.1	17.1
Guinea-Bissau	28.2	29.9	31.0	48.4	30.9	21.8	22.3	23.0	21.7	11.3	16.3	23.8	35.6	25.7
Kenya	24.5	19.7	17.9	13.7	17.7	16.4	17.5	16.9	15.4	14.6	13.5	21.1	20.3	16.3
Lesotho	37.0	53.2	65.0	66.6	55.0	55.7	60.5	58.3	53.7	47.0	78.6	30.5	43.3	59.4
Liberia	27.3	..	..	..	..	..	..	..	..	..	..	23.8	9.2	..
Madagascar	15.0	17.0	8.2	11.3	11.4	10.9	10.9	11.6	11.9	12.5	12.9	10.2	10.9	11.9
Malawi	24.7	19.7	20.2	19.9	15.2	29.1	17.0	11.6	12.2	13.5	14.8	25.3	17.3	17.3
Mali	15.5	23.0	22.8	21.9	21.8	27.3	22.9	22.9	20.6	20.9	21.2	14.8	20.1	22.5
Mauritania	26.3	20.0	17.9	19.3	20.6	20.7	19.3	18.6	17.6	19.0	17.8	26.7	26.6	19.1
Mauritius	20.7	30.9	28.7	29.3	30.7	32.3	25.8	24.7	28.0	24.4	27.7	25.3	26.6	28.3
Mozambique	5.9	15.6	16.0	15.6	12.7	19.8	22.8	20.9	18.3	23.5	31.3	5.8	10.3	19.7
Namibia	30.5	33.8	18.8	22.0	16.7	23.9	21.2	22.8	17.8	19.9	20.1	23.1	13.6	21.7
Niger	28.1	8.1	7.5	6.9	6.4	10.4	7.3	9.7	10.9	11.3	10.2	18.2	13.7	8.9
Nigeria	21.3	14.7	23.4	21.8	23.3	19.6	16.3	14.2	17.4	28.3	24.2	22.3	15.1	20.3
Rwanda	16.1	14.6	14.0	14.3	14.5	11.7	15.0	15.5	14.9	15.7	14.3	14.8	15.4	14.5
São Tomé and Principe	34.2	36.0	37.0	38.9	39.3	37.6	38.1	44.2	39.1	44.8	40.0	33.4	30.6	39.5
Senegal	11.7	13.8	12.9	14.8	14.1	18.6	16.7	18.5	18.0	18.6	18.8	13.1	11.8	16.5
Seychelles	38.3	24.6	22.3	21.2	28.7	26.2	30.3	50.9	36.0	37.5	37.5	30.1	23.6	31.5
Sierra Leone	17.7	9.4	10.5	8.2	7.7	8.5	5.6	11.0	-2.4	5.3	0.3	14.5	9.3	6.4
Somalia	42.4	15.5	..	..	..	..	..	..	..	..	..	27.1	28.5	15.5
South Africa	23.4	11.8	11.9	12.0	14.0	15.6	18.2	16.9	16.0	16.2	15.7	21.3	14.9	14.8
Sudan	14.7	..	..	..	..	..	..	..	16.5	17.6	16.7	16.0	13.2	16.9
Swaziland	30.3	19.6	20.6	26.1	26.6	32.1	34.1	30.1	33.9	12.3	12.9	31.6	21.6	24.8
Tanzania	..	26.1	26.3	27.2	25.1	24.6	19.8	16.3	14.9	16.5	17.0	..	16.8	21.4
Togo	28.4	26.6	17.1	15.7	7.5	15.0	16.1	16.4	14.9	13.6	13.4	29.8	17.1	15.6
Uganda	6.2	12.7	15.2	15.9	15.2	14.7	16.4	16.1	16.1	15.0	16.4	7.2	9.8	15.4
Zambia	23.3	17.3	11.0	11.9	15.0	8.2	15.9	12.8	14.6	16.3	17.5	22.3	14.7	14.1
Zimbabwe	16.9	17.4	19.1	20.2	18.0	29.1	23.6	19.1	19.0	19.8	11.5	16.7	16.9	19.7
NORTH AFRICA	28.2	28.7	26.3	25.4	23.5	23.0	22.9	20.5	20.9	23.4	24.6	31.1	28.2	23.9
Algeria	39.1	29.3	31.0	30.0	29.2	31.7	32.1	25.1	23.8	27.7	27.4	41.5	30.6	28.9
Egypt, Arab Republic	27.5	28.8	21.2	18.2	16.2	16.6	17.2	16.6	17.7	20.5	22.8	29.9	28.6	19.6
Libya	22.1	..	..	..	..	..	..	..	..	..	..	26.3	..	..
Morocco	24.2	25.3	22.6	23.2	22.5	21.3	20.7	19.6	20.7	22.5	24.2	26.5	23.1	22.3
Tunisia	29.4	32.5	32.1	34.3	29.2	24.5	24.8	25.1	26.5	26.9	26.6	31.2	25.0	28.2
ALL AFRICA	22.3	19.1	18.3	18.1	18.3	19.4	19.7	18.3	18.6	20.5	20.7	23.0	19.8	19.1

Note: 1999 data are preliminary (see page 2). Since 1994, Nigeria's ratios are distorted because the official exchange rate used by the Government for oil exports and oil value added is significantly over-valued.

2-9. Gross public investment

	Percentage of GDP											Annual average		
	1980	1990	1991	1992	1993	1994	1995	1996	1997	1998	1999	75-84	85-89	90-MR
SUB-SAHARAN AFRICA	8.9	6.9	6.4	6.7	5.6	5.1	5.3	5.3	5.5	7.9	6.7	8.7	7.1	6.2
excluding South Africa	..	6.9	6.7	8.1	6.8	6.1	6.4	6.2	6.4	9.9	8.3	..	6.9	7.2
excl. S.Africa & Nigeria	..	6.1	5.8	6.6	6.1	6.7	6.6	6.4	6.2	6.5	6.0	6.2	6.0	6.3
Angola	..	..	..	..	..	..	..	..	..	..	..	..	..	..
Benin	..	7.4	7.4	6.6	7.1	9.3	10.4	7.5	7.5	6.4	6.9	..	9.1	7.6
Botswana	12.5	..	..	..	..	..	..	..	14.2	14.3	14.4	12.1	..	14.3
Burkina Faso	..	4.4	6.3	10.1	8.8	7.8	10.2	12.0	13.9	13.6	15.9	..	7.6	10.3
Burundi	12.8	12.5	12.0	11.7	12.9	9.0	8.3	10.4	5.0	5.6	6.2	14.0	13.6	9.4
Cameroon	4.4	5.5	4.0	2.7	1.8	1.3	1.2	0.5	1.0	2.0	2.3	4.7	9.0	2.2
Cape Verde	..	10.3	12.5	26.2	28.2	32.0	27.1	25.0	18.0	15.7	20.3	..	19.3	21.5
Central African Republic	3.7	4.7	7.2	7.5	6.2	7.2	9.8	1.8	4.0	7.2	6.8	4.7	6.3	6.2
Chad	..	10.0	4.0	4.5	5.8	7.3	6.3	3.5	5.6	6.4	6.4	2.2	4.8	6.0
Comoros	23.2	5.2	4.6	10.9	7.2	10.4	6.9	6.2	6.6	8.5	7.2	23.3	14.2	7.4
Congo, Democratic Rep. of	5.1	4.0	2.6	2.8	0.9	0.6	4.4	2.5	2.5	2.8	4.0	3.9	4.9	2.7
Congo, Republic of	35.8	5.6	4.7	4.7	7.1	12.8	7.8	10.8	3.4	4.7	6.5	35.5	11.1	6.8
Côte d'Ivoire	11.4	3.6	3.4	3.8	3.7	4.1	4.2	4.3	4.6	5.3	3.6	10.5	4.4	4.1
Djibouti	..	..	9.2	9.3	8.2	5.6	3.7	3.9	4.3	..	..	..	..	6.3
Equatorial Guinea	..	10.5	13.4	10.1	8.9	4.1	1.9	1.2	4.4	7.5	1.6	..	0.0	6.3
Eritrea	..	..	..	3.6	14.1	10.5	11.1	15.4	18.9	23.2	28.2	..	..	15.6
Ethiopia	..	5.7	4.3	3.2	5.0	7.1	7.5	7.5	8.3	7.4	7.1	..	6.9	6.3
Gabon	5.3	3.9	5.2	5.3	5.1	5.6	5.1	5.9	9.2	13.4	7.3	15.8	5.9	6.6
Gambia, The	..	7.4	7.7	7.8	7.5	7.0	10.0	12.9	8.4	5.9	5.8	13.8	7.6	8.0
Ghana	..	7.5	8.3	10.3	11.1	13.3	14.0	13.2	12.3	11.3	9.8	2.5	7.0	11.1
Guinea	..	9.2	7.0	6.7	6.2	5.9	6.2	5.3	5.9	3.9	4.0	..	7.4	6.0
Guinea-Bissau	..	21.5	23.2	28.4	24.6	20.4	15.2	14.8	15.6	6.2	11.1	..	29.6	18.1
Kenya	10.1	9.4	8.3	7.1	8.0	8.5	7.4	7.1	6.4	5.6	5.0	8.8	7.6	7.3
Lesotho	31.6	45.3	53.7	55.4	58.0	58.6	52.8	55.7	63.3	71.5	15.6	25.9	36.9	53.0
Liberia	..	..	..	..	..	..	..	..	..	..	..	..	..	..
Madagascar	..	7.9	5.9	7.6	7.8	6.2	6.0	6.7	5.6	5.6	6.1	6.4	7.0	6.5
Malawi	17.5	8.0	8.3	10.2	8.4	15.1	9.4	6.1	7.1	8.7	10.6	13.6	8.2	9.2
Mali	..	10.5	12.1	9.5	9.3	13.7	9.4	9.2	8.2	9.5	9.4	..	10.2	10.1
Mauritania	..	6.2	3.8	3.4	4.3	4.3	3.8	6.1	5.6	5.6	6.0	..	7.6	4.9
Mauritius	8.4	11.4	8.2	9.6	7.9	9.1	8.0	9.3	6.5	6.1	5.9	7.9	7.9	8.2
Mozambique	7.6	12.0	11.4	12.8	12.3	14.0	12.0	10.3	10.5	9.1	10.4	10.4	8.6	11.5
Namibia	15.7	8.2	7.6	10.1	8.5	8.6	7.9	8.2	8.7	9.3	4.5	13.9	7.5	8.1
Niger	20.4	7.4	3.7	5.4	4.9	6.6	5.2	4.6	5.8	6.4	6.4	13.8	8.5	5.6
Nigeria	..	10.8	11.4	13.4	10.7	3.6	5.3	5.2	7.1	25.1	17.8	..	..	11.0
Rwanda	12.2	5.9	7.0	10.1	8.5	2.7	8.1	9.1	8.2	6.7	6.2	13.7	10.2	7.3
São Tomé and Principe	..	34.0	27.0	23.9	20.3	26.6	33.1	29.2	22.1	19.8	26.0	..	27.9	26.2
Senegal	5.5	4.1	4.6	5.2	4.2	5.0	4.4	6.4	6.4	6.4	6.5	4.1	4.0	5.3
Seychelles	..	8.2	12.9	9.4	11.2	7.5	6.8	10.2	10.0	15.0	15.0	16.3	7.6	10.6
Sierra Leone	6.0	3.5	4.4	4.7	5.3	4.4	3.0	3.3	1.5	4.9	2.4	4.9	3.0	3.7
Somalia	..	..	..	..	..	..	..	..	..	..	..	..	..	..
South Africa	13.0	7.0	6.1	5.2	4.4	4.1	4.3	4.4	4.5	5.4	4.6	13.0	8.1	5.0
Sudan	6.9	..	..	..	..	..	..	..	0.6	0.8	1.3	5.6	3.0	0.9
Swaziland	11.8	7.2	12.1	12.2	10.3	9.3	6.3	5.6	4.9	5.5	5.7	13.1	8.8	7.9
Tanzania	..	10.5	8.8	9.2	7.5	6.0	3.4	3.2	2.9	3.1	2.8	..	3.5	5.7
Togo	20.2	7.3	4.5	3.5	2.3	2.3	3.5	2.8	2.0	4.3	3.1	12.2	10.2	3.6
Uganda	..	6.2	7.4	7.4	6.7	5.4	5.4	5.3	4.7	4.6	4.7	..	4.4	5.8
Zambia	4.0	6.2	7.8	6.7	4.5	4.0	5.1	6.0	5.4	9.6	10.5	4.1	4.7	6.6
Zimbabwe	1.8	3.4	3.5	3.8	3.6	3.1	2.9	2.3	2.8	1.7	4.0	2.9	3.3	3.1
NORTH AFRICA	..	9.1	8.2	8.5	9.4	8.4	7.6	6.8	7.0	7.7	..	..	11.0	8.1
Algeria	..	8.2	6.1	6.8	8.7	7.9	7.4	6.8	7.3	7.6	5.9	..	11.2	7.3
Egypt, Arab Republic	..	10.2	9.2	8.5	7.1	6.1	5.5	5.5	5.6	7.2	7.0	..	12.6	7.2
Libya	19.4	..	..	..	..	..	..	..	..	..	..	21.1	..	..
Morocco	9.8	8.6	9.6	9.5	11.8	10.1	8.9	6.8	7.1	6.5	..	13.5	8.8	8.8
Tunisia	15.0	11.0	10.2	12.0	15.3	13.7	12.3	11.3	11.9	11.6	12.0	17.2	11.4	12.1
ALL AFRICA	..	7.6	6.9	7.3	6.9	6.2	6.1	5.8	6.0	7.8	6.8	..	8.4	6.8

Note: 1999 data are preliminary (see page 2). Since 1994, Nigeria's ratios are distorted because the official exchange rate used by the Government for oil exports and oil value added is significantly over-valued.

2-10. Gross private investment

	Percentage of GDP											Annual average		
	1980	*1990*	*1991*	*1992*	*1993*	*1994*	*1995*	*1996*	*1997*	*1998*	*1999*	*75-84*	*85-89*	*90-MR*
SUB-SAHARAN AFRICA	8.3	9.6	10.4	9.5	10.6	11.9	11.7	11.8	11.7	10.9	11.1	9.4	9.2	10.9
excluding South Africa	..	8.0	10.1	8.8	10.9	12.7	11.7	11.9	11.7	10.8	11.6	7.2	7.9	10.8
excl. S.Africa & Nigeria	..	8.9	9.7	8.8	10.6	12.0	11.9	12.7	12.0	12.4	12.8	8.5	8.3	11.2
Angola	..	1.7	10.5	0.1	19.8	28.4	21.3	21.7	20.7	22.7	28.2	..	9.2	17.5
Benin	..	6.0	6.1	6.7	7.9	6.2	6.9	9.1	11.0	10.7	10.9	..	4.5	8.2
Botswana	19.1	..	..	..	..	..	..	..	7.1	4.6	3.5	14.1	..	5.1
Burkina Faso	..	15.3	14.2	13.2	10.7	14.1	13.0	13.6	13.8	16.0	11.9	..	13.0	13.6
Burundi	1.1	2.7	2.9	2.8	3.0	1.6	1.4	1.8	2.2	2.3	1.8	1.5	2.7	2.3
Cameroon	15.6	11.9	12.7	11.6	14.7	14.0	13.3	14.9	15.2	16.4	17.1	24.2	12.1	14.2
Cape Verde	..	12.6	14.0	8.2	11.5	11.3	15.3	13.0	19.4	21.3	17.3	..	7.7	14.4
Central African Republic	3.2	6.7	4.7	4.4	3.3	4.5	3.4	1.6	5.0	6.3	7.5	4.1	5.3	4.8
Chad	..	1.3	0.7	0.8	1.1	4.4	5.3	5.9	7.0	6.6	7.0	0.3	0.8	4.0
Comoros	5.3	6.7	14.3	9.2	9.8	9.5	9.2	7.3	8.9	8.1	13.5	5.4	5.7	9.6
Congo, Democratic Rep. of	3.7	8.9	3.5	4.3	1.4	7.0	5.3	4.6	4.6	5.3	6.6	5.8	8.3	5.1
Congo, Republic of	0.0	11.6	15.0	15.9	21.8	40.1	21.1	48.2	17.9	20.7	15.0	0.0	11.4	22.7
Côte d'Ivoire	13.0	4.9	5.1	4.7	4.1	7.0	8.7	9.6	11.4	12.9	12.7	12.3	7.1	8.1
Djibouti	..	..	5.1	9.7	9.1	6.2	4.9	5.1	5.1	..	..	..	..	6.5
Equatorial Guinea	..	6.9	37.3	14.1	13.1	70.0	74.4	112.4	61.3	84.1	39.8	..	0.0	51.3
Eritrea	..	..	..	1.8	1.0	7.3	8.2	13.9	22.0	24.0	19.1	..	..	12.2
Ethiopia	..	6.2	5.6	6.0	9.2	8.0	9.0	9.4	8.7	9.8	11.0	..	8.9	8.3
Gabon	21.4	17.6	20.9	16.7	17.8	15.4	17.6	17.3	20.4	23.9	20.8	24.0	29.8	18.8
Gambia, The	..	14.9	14.2	14.4	13.5	11.1	10.2	8.6	8.8	12.5	12.0	7.4	9.5	12.0
Ghana	..	6.9	7.5	2.4	12.7	9.3	7.1	8.1	11.6	11.3	12.1	4.4	3.7	8.9
Guinea	..	8.3	10.0	9.8	10.6	11.1	10.2	11.6	11.2	13.1	13.0	..	8.7	10.9
Guinea-Bissau	..	8.4	7.8	20.0	6.3	1.4	7.1	8.3	6.1	5.2	5.2	..	10.0	7.6
Kenya	8.2	6.8	7.7	6.2	8.9	7.5	9.7	9.2	8.1	8.1	7.6	8.1	7.8	8.0
Lesotho	4.1	8.0	12.0	10.2	-2.4	-1.5	8.4	2.4	-8.6	-22.1	39.5	5.3	6.2	4.6
Liberia	..	..	..	..	..	..	..	..	..	..	..	..	..	..
Madagascar	..	6.9	4.6	3.7	3.7	4.7	4.9	5.0	6.3	6.9	6.2	2.2	3.9	5.3
Malawi	4.7	8.6	8.7	6.9	4.6	11.6	5.1	3.0	2.7	2.4	2.3	7.0	6.0	5.6
Mali	..	12.4	10.7	12.4	12.5	13.7	13.5	13.7	12.4	11.4	11.8	..	9.9	12.4
Mauritania	..	13.7	14.1	15.9	16.4	16.4	15.5	12.5	12.0	13.3	11.8	..	19.0	14.1
Mauritius	14.9	19.2	20.4	18.3	20.6	21.7	16.3	16.7	20.8	18.3	21.0	15.3	15.0	19.3
Mozambique	-1.7	3.6	4.7	2.8	0.4	5.8	10.8	10.7	7.8	14.4	20.9	-4.5	1.7	8.2
Namibia	11.4	13.1	8.6	10.9	13.9	13.1	14.3	15.7	9.7	8.8	16.1	8.3	7.3	12.4
Niger	5.1	4.0	4.1	1.9	1.9	2.3	1.8	4.7	4.8	4.6	3.6	3.6	2.4	3.4
Nigeria	..	3.8	12.0	8.3	12.5	16.0	11.1	8.9	10.3	3.2	6.4	5.2	6.1	9.3
Rwanda	0.0	8.7	7.0	4.2	6.1	9.0	6.9	6.4	6.7	9.0	8.0	0.0	4.7	7.2
São Tomé and Principe	..	2.1	10.0	15.0	19.1	11.0	5.0	15.0	17.0	25.0	14.0	..	1.1	13.3
Senegal	7.7	8.8	9.3	9.2	9.7	11.1	10.2	9.9	11.6	11.7	12.3	7.9	8.4	10.4
Seychelles	..	14.8	8.4	11.5	15.6	17.9	23.6	40.6	25.8	22.5	22.5	5.4	14.9	20.3
Sierra Leone	10.7	5.2	4.0	2.9	2.5	4.0	2.4	7.0	-2.6	0.4	-1.7	8.6	5.9	2.4
Somalia	..	..	..	..	..	..	..	..	..	..	..	..	..	..
South Africa	12.9	12.2	11.0	10.4	10.3	11.0	11.6	11.7	11.8	11.1	10.3	13.9	11.8	11.1
Sudan	3.8	..	..	..	..	..	..	..	15.9	16.8	15.4	8.0	8.3	16.0
Swaziland	13.3	11.7	7.5	13.0	15.5	21.9	27.0	23.6	28.2	6.2	6.6	17.2	11.5	16.1
Tanzania	..	15.3	17.2	17.8	17.4	18.5	16.2	12.8	11.8	13.3	14.0	8.6	11.7	15.4
Togo	8.0	18.0	13.5	12.5	8.6	9.7	10.1	12.2	11.4	9.5	10.1	8.0	7.6	11.6
Uganda	..	6.5	7.8	8.5	8.5	9.2	10.2	11.3	11.6	10.5	11.7	..	5.4	9.6
Zambia	17.2	7.2	3.5	3.8	7.0	7.3	7.3	5.2	7.7	5.2	5.4	12.6	4.1	6.0
Zimbabwe	12.3	14.8	17.1	18.6	19.9	18.3	21.9	15.7	15.1	17.9	6.2	13.3	11.7	16.6
NORTH AFRICA	..	17.1	15.9	15.4	13.2	14.0	14.3	13.2	13.9	14.8	15.6	12.2	14.7	14.7
Algeria	22.8	17.6	19.0	19.4	18.4	21.0	22.1	18.1	17.4	19.0	20.0	25.3	16.8	19.2
Egypt, Arab Republic	..	16.7	13.1	10.5	9.2	10.5	10.7	10.5	12.1	12.3	13.0	7.1	13.3	11.9
Libya	1.8	..	..	..	..	..	..	..	..	..	..	3.6	..	..
Morocco	12.4	15.4	12.7	12.8	11.0	10.6	12.5	12.6	13.6	15.8	..	12.3	12.7	13.0
Tunisia	13.3	19.7	19.9	20.3	12.8	13.3	11.9	11.9	12.7	13.2	13.1	13.2	12.2	14.9
ALL AFRICA	10.1	12.1	12.1	11.3	11.5	12.6	12.6	12.3	12.5	12.3	12.7	11.0	11.1	12.2

Note: 1999 data are preliminary (see page 2). Since 1994, Nigeria's ratios are distorted because the official exchange rate used by the Government for oil exports and oil value added is significantly over-valued.

2-11. Gross domestic savings

	Percentage of GDP											Annual average		
	1980	1990	1991	1992	1993	1994	1995	1996	1997	1998	1999	75-84	85-89	90-MR
SUB-SAHARAN AFRICA	25.9	17.9	16.1	12.9	14.0	16.5	16.3	18.1	16.7	16.0	15.8	22.9	19.0	16.0
excluding South Africa	23.0	17.4	15.0	10.1	10.7	15.4	13.7	17.8	16.1	14.6	13.6	21.6	16.9	14.4
excl. S.Africa & Nigeria	16.4	15.0	12.2	6.9	8.9	14.3	12.7	13.6	14.1	12.7	12.6	20.3	16.5	12.3
Angola	..	29.7	16.2	1.7	9.9	26.1	14.7	23.5	41.0	32.5	53.3	..	24.0	24.9
Benin	-5.1	5.5	5.9	4.2	5.2	9.5	10.0	8.0	9.8	8.3	7.5	0.0	3.0	7.4
Botswana	34.4	37.1	37.7	35.2	36.1	38.9	40.6	43.4	31.8	21.8	14.2	30.2	49.2	33.7
Burkina Faso	-5.8	7.7	6.1	7.0	5.9	7.5	8.6	9.1	10.9	12.7	9.8	-1.7	2.4	8.5
Burundi	-0.6	-5.4	-4.2	-5.1	-4.7	-7.6	-4.8	2.5	3.9	-2.9	-0.4	4.1	3.3	-2.9
Cameroon	21.7	20.7	22.0	16.5	17.6	17.9	19.5	17.3	19.1	19.9	18.9	23.1	22.9	19.0
Cape Verde	-24.0	-8.1	-4.2	-3.5	3.7	2.8	2.4	5.8	8.1	7.6	10.4	-19.8	-2.9	2.5
Central African Republic	-8.9	-0.6	2.6	-0.4	1.8	6.0	6.2	0.6	3.6	4.5	7.2	-1.6	0.8	3.2
Chad	..	-1.1	-5.9	-6.3	-6.2	-1.4	-1.7	3.3	2.3	4.3	-3.0	2.4	-11.1	-1.6
Comoros	-10.1	-3.2	2.1	-1.6	2.9	-5.9	-9.2	-11.4	-12.1	1.6	-5.6	-6.5	-2.5	-4.2
Congo, Democratic Rep. of	10.1	9.3	1.8	6.1	4.0	10.6	14.1	13.4	9.0	9.8	11.1	10.5	13.3	8.9
Congo, Republic of	35.7	23.8	18.6	24.4	23.6	26.6	42.5	79.0	49.1	36.1	48.3	26.1	23.2	37.2
Côte d'Ivoire	20.4	11.3	10.4	10.7	9.4	22.4	18.9	21.2	22.5	24.8	23.1	24.3	18.4	17.5
Djibouti	..	..	-10.2	-18.6	-11.0	-11.3	-8.7	-7.5	-6.2	..	..	..	..	-10.5
Equatorial Guinea	..	-20.1	-7.2	2.2	-1.0	25.1	27.3	30.7	43.1	19.9	57.9	7.6	-15.0	17.8
Eritrea	..	..	..	-31.3	-24.6	-35.4	-38.6	-31.0	-17.4	-24.5	-21.3	..	..	-28.0
Ethiopia	..	7.2	2.7	3.0	5.6	5.4	8.0	2.5	6.5	5.3	2.7	6.4	7.2	4.9
Gabon	60.6	36.9	40.5	34.7	36.7	45.3	47.3	51.0	51.0	39.0	34.8	58.1	32.3	41.7
Gambia, The	5.8	10.7	10.6	9.3	4.0	2.3	0.9	2.1	4.5	2.8	1.7	4.3	7.6	4.9
Ghana	4.9	5.5	7.3	1.3	6.6	12.6	11.7	14.3	4.4	10.7	6.2	6.3	5.5	8.1
Guinea	..	17.7	18.0	11.2	11.1	12.1	12.7	12.9	15.0	15.3	15.2	..	16.4	14.1
Guinea-Bissau	-1.0	2.8	3.2	3.2	7.0	3.9	-1.2	1.8	2.8	-9.3	-2.2	-3.0	-0.1	1.2
Kenya	13.4	14.4	16.9	13.7	23.8	19.6	11.3	13.1	7.8	6.8	6.8	17.0	16.9	13.4
Lesotho	-52.0	-51.3	-49.1	-33.9	-45.0	-35.7	-38.4	-36.0	-30.9	-34.6	-28.0	-64.3	-62.3	-38.3
Liberia	27.3	..	..	..	..	..	..	..	..	..	..	23.3	16.4	..
Madagascar	-1.4	6.3	0.7	3.4	2.5	3.4	3.6	6.3	3.7	4.6	4.6	2.0	5.8	3.9
Malawi	10.8	9.7	14.2	0.7	-0.9	-3.0	-0.3	3.0	0.9	6.1	-0.6	15.6	10.0	3.0
Mali	1.1	6.4	6.4	4.4	6.4	7.5	7.8	7.2	10.0	11.2	10.1	0.2	0.1	7.7
Mauritania	-3.5	4.9	9.7	4.8	4.7	16.9	8.9	7.2	7.9	5.1	7.2	-5.6	10.3	7.7
Mauritius	10.5	23.6	24.9	26.1	24.5	23.4	23.3	23.8	24.2	23.6	22.7	18.5	25.5	24.0
Mozambique	-10.6	-12.3	-11.2	-17.2	-22.4	-13.9	-1.9	-1.8	0.9	7.2	6.4	-10.4	-10.2	-6.6
Namibia	38.4	18.2	4.0	7.2	5.4	14.0	9.9	11.0	4.7	9.9	9.3	9.7	11.9	9.3
Niger	14.6	1.2	2.8	5.8	3.9	0.0	0.2	3.1	3.2	2.7	3.8	8.4	7.9	2.7
Nigeria	31.4	29.4	29.3	23.5	20.2	20.6	18.4	34.9	24.6	23.4	18.4	21.5	17.7	24.3
Rwanda	4.2	6.2	3.3	1.6	-0.9	-46.8	-5.8	-4.3	-2.8	-1.8	-0.1	6.8	5.3	-5.1
São Tomé and Principe	-14.9	-29.2	-21.7	-28.1	-27.6	-21.4	-37.9	-25.8	-26.6	2.0	-9.3	-9.0	-14.8	-22.5
Senegal	-5.0	8.9	5.9	7.4	5.5	11.9	11.1	12.8	12.3	12.8	12.4	1.1	3.8	10.1
Seychelles	27.1	20.3	18.7	17.6	18.4	22.1	23.5	39.6	22.3	20.3	19.9	21.9	30.1	22.3
Sierra Leone	2.9	8.3	8.1	6.3	3.3	3.4	-1.8	-3.7	-4.3	-1.9	-6.0	4.7	5.7	1.2
Somalia	-12.9	-12.5	..	..	..	..	..	..	..	..	..	-11.4	5.6	-12.5
South Africa	31.4	17.6	16.9	16.1	17.6	17.9	19.1	18.3	17.1	17.4	18.2	24.4	22.0	17.6
Sudan	2.1	..	..	..	..	..	..	..	..	..	..	5.8	7.9	..
Swaziland	6.5	20.4	18.2	18.6	26.3	26.0	29.0	18.8	19.5	19.2	21.1	16.0	17.7	21.7
Tanzania	..	1.3	3.0	0.3	-4.6	1.6	2.4	4.3	5.0	2.4	2.2	11.0	7.1	1.8
Togo	23.2	14.7	9.0	6.5	-0.2	11.3	11.2	7.8	6.6	2.5	3.6	21.4	7.6	7.3
Uganda	-0.4	0.6	0.7	0.4	1.1	4.3	7.4	4.6	8.0	5.6	4.9	4.1	3.0	3.8
Zambia	19.3	16.6	8.4	0.0	9.0	7.4	12.2	5.3	9.4	3.9	-1.1	18.9	14.9	7.1
Zimbabwe	13.8	17.4	15.8	11.0	16.3	27.2	20.9	19.3	12.0	18.1	11.0	15.2	19.0	16.9
NORTH AFRICA	40.3	21.8	23.7	22.5	19.4	17.4	17.3	18.2	19.5	18.4	20.0	35.4	24.0	19.8
Algeria	43.1	27.5	36.7	32.4	27.8	27.0	28.4	31.4	32.2	27.1	31.7	38.9	30.8	30.2
Egypt, Arab Republic	15.2	16.1	13.2	15.4	13.2	11.4	12.2	10.8	13.0	14.0	14.4	15.4	15.7	13.4
Libya	56.9	..	..	..	..	..	..	..	..	..	..	46.5	..	..
Morocco	12.9	15.7	14.7	13.1	13.4	12.3	11.0	12.0	13.5	14.2	15.3	13.0	14.5	13.5
Tunisia	24.0	20.0	21.0	22.3	21.3	22.2	20.4	..	..	..	..	22.1	19.1	21.2
ALL AFRICA	29.9	19.2	18.5	16.0	15.9	16.8	16.7	18.1	17.7	16.9	17.3	26.3	21.2	17.3

Note: 1999 data are preliminary (see page 2). Since 1994, Nigeria's ratios are distorted because the official exchange rate used by the Government for oil exports and oil value added is significantly over-valued.

2-12. Gross national savings

					Percentage of GDP							Annual average		
	1980	1990	1991	1992	1993	1994	1995	1996	1997	1998	1999	75-84	85-89	90-MR
SUB-SAHARAN AFRICA	22.0	13.5	12.3	9.7	10.7	13.5	12.9	14.7	13.8	13.3	12.1	19.8	15.7	12.6
excluding South Africa	18.6	12.8	10.7	6.3	6.8	11.5	9.3	13.8	13.0	11.9	9.2	19.0	13.8	10.5
excl. S.Africa & Nigeria	12.4	11.4	8.7	3.8	5.5	11.2	8.6	9.6	10.6	10.4	8.5	17.5	14.0	8.8
Angola	..	9.0	-2.8	-35.8	-25.6	-20.0	-35.5	-20.2	-0.4	-17.5	-9.2	..	13.7	-15.8
Benin	0.0	0.0	0.0	0.0	0.0	0.0	0.0	0.0	0.0	0.0	10.5	0.0	0.0	1.1
Botswana	36.3	37.7	43.9	40.7	45.0	35.5	39.3	44.4	33.6	24.0	15.0	34.0	44.4	35.9
Burkina Faso	..	16.9	13.9	14.9	14.8	18.7	18.2	16.9	17.2	19.5	15.2	..	..	16.6
Burundi	4.6	3.4	6.3	4.2	7.9	9.0	9.2	7.7	8.8	2.6	4.0	5.6	7.9	6.3
Cameroon	6.3	16.1	16.3	12.4	11.3	11.2	13.6	11.2	13.4	15.7	15.1	13.4	20.6	13.6
Cape Verde	16.4	17.6	21.4	29.3	31.7	31.4	25.6	25.3	23.8	24.1	26.9	4.7	21.6	25.7
Central African Republic	1.6	-0.4	4.5	0.1	1.8	6.1	6.3	-1.5	3.3	5.2	7.1	6.5	4.2	3.3
Chad	..	-7.7	-0.1	-0.1	-4.6	6.1	1.9	6.5	5.4	6.7	-2.6	6.9	-3.7	1.2
Comoros	0.0	0.0	0.0	0.0	0.0	0.0	0.0	0.0	0.0	0.0	156.2	0.0	0.0	15.6
Congo, Democratic Rep. of	6.1	0.3	-7.4	4.9	-4.5	-2.6	-1.4	-1.3	-4.6	-0.3	5.1	7.2	4.6	-1.2
Congo, Republic of	26.2	6.8	2.2	11.5	9.7	16.6	5.6	33.8	5.1	7.9	12.6	19.8	16.4	11.2
Côte d'Ivoire	..	-6.0	-5.5	-4.9	-6.2	8.5	4.4	7.9	10.7	13.6	13.2	15.7	5.1	3.6
Djibouti	..	..	-4.9	-16.1	-3.4	-5.6	-1.5	-0.5	-0.5	..	..	..	..	-4.6
Equatorial Guinea	..	-22.0	-13.6	-3.4	-3.5	22.5	23.6	10.1	27.6	9.5	41.8	..	-12.3	9.3
Eritrea	..	..	..	27.6	43.3	57.8	22.9	32.5	63.2	29.8	34.4	..	..	38.9
Ethiopia	..	9.6	6.3	8.8	9.7	10.7	14.9	9.2	9.0	9.7	6.6	7.9	9.5	9.5
Gabon	47.8	24.2	28.2	18.4	21.4	29.9	29.0	32.3	34.5	24.0	19.0	48.1	21.8	26.1
Gambia, The	..	5.3	9.5	11.4	..	4.8	3.9	4.9	8.6	8.5	7.0	7.5	3.4	7.1
Ghana	4.5	7.0	8.8	3.6	-1.6	15.5	13.7	16.2	10.5	18.8	12.5	5.9	5.8	10.5
Guinea	..	10.4	10.6	4.7	6.1	7.6	7.9	9.3	10.9	11.0	11.0	..	8.7	9.0
Guinea-Bissau	..	15.3	6.8	10.6	9.8	9.4	4.7	6.6	7.0	-4.3	3.3	-635.9	-108.1	6.9
Kenya	10.7	11.1	13.0	9.7	18.3	16.2	11.8	15.0	10.3	10.2	10.6	13.9	14.0	12.6
Lesotho	-11.4	-8.8	2.0	15.6	1.4	27.8	29.5	29.9	29.7	16.9	21.9	-34.1	-19.0	16.6
Liberia	..	..	..	..	..	..	..	..	..	..	..	..	..	..
Madagascar	-2.4	9.2	0.1	3.9	3.6	1.4	1.2	5.4	6.4	5.3	6.9	1.7	5.6	4.4
Malawi	6.6	16.0	10.6	-0.7	-1.5	-5.0	-4.0	0.4	-1.4	2.2	-3.9	14.4	10.4	1.3
Mali	1.9	15.1	16.6	14.3	14.9	19.1	13.7	12.8	13.0	13.6	12.7	1.0	7.5	14.6
Mauritania	-12.8	11.0	4.3	5.7	0.4	13.1	6.8	5.7	8.1	6.6	8.5	-15.5	20.4	7.0
Mauritius	8.4	26.1	28.2	29.3	27.7	25.6	25.5	25.6	26.5	25.2	23.6	17.4	26.7	26.3
Mozambique	-9.9	-18.1	-17.5	-26.6	-30.9	-22.8	-9.6	-7.7	-4.3	1.7	-3.5	-10.9	-15.5	-13.9
Namibia	26.9	35.0	23.0	23.7	20.9	26.7	26.7	26.5	20.6	25.3	24.5	20.4	16.5	25.3
Niger	13.0	-1.2	1.1	4.5	2.5	-1.9	-2.5	1.7	1.9	1.3	2.2	6.1	3.9	1.0
Nigeria	27.4	22.5	23.2	20.1	10.0	11.1	28.4	29.6	12.0	18.6	12.8	19.1	11.4	18.8
Rwanda	13.3	11.3	12.3	6.6	3.4	4.7	13.9	10.5	7.0	7.4	6.8	15.5	8.8	8.4
São Tomé and Principe	-8.1	-39.2	-31.5	-36.5	-35.9	-25.6	-48.7	-35.1	-35.8	-9.0	-18.0	-5.7	-20.8	-31.5
Senegal	-7.4	6.0	2.9	5.8	2.3	11.7	10.1	12.2	11.6	12.4	11.5	-2.8	-0.6	8.6
Seychelles	..	21.7	20.2	19.5	19.6	21.8	21.6	40.1	23.3	19.0	18.2	0.0	..	22.5
Sierra Leone	2.6	-2.3	-1.5	-10.5	-7.6	-7.9	-4.6	-3.9	-4.9	-3.3	-6.0	4.2	3.3	-5.2
Somalia	..	..	..	..	..	..	..	..	..	..	..	..	..	..
South Africa	27.3	13.7	13.8	13.5	15.1	15.6	16.8	15.6	14.5	14.6	15.3	20.2	18.1	14.8
Sudan	4.6	..	..	..	..	..	..	..	..	..	..	8.0	8.0	..
Swaziland	20.9	39.1	38.4	41.3	46.9	39.2	46.3	39.0	41.1	39.8	43.5	27.7	31.5	41.5
Tanzania	..	5.9	3.9	4.2	4.9	6.6	-1.2	4.2	4.0	6.1	2.2	13.8	21.5	4.1
Togo	27.2	18.2	12.2	8.7	0.6	8.6	10.7	8.3	7.3	3.3	4.3	24.8	9.4	8.2
Uganda	-1.0	0.6	1.4	2.1	3.0	10.4	12.1	10.8	12.8	13.4	10.5	-13.4	3.8	7.7
Zambia	9.3	6.9	-4.2	-10.6	0.7	-0.2	4.6	-1.5	3.7	-3.6	-1.7	9.5	0.3	-0.6
Zimbabwe	10.3	15.7	13.8	11.3	15.9	27.1	20.7	18.6	10.0	15.5	6.7	11.2	17.0	15.5
NORTH AFRICA	36.9	19.3	20.2	19.6	16.5	14.4	14.5	19.8	21.7	21.1	22.5	31.8	20.3	19.0
Algeria	40.8	26.6	34.6	31.0	26.6	26.3	25.8	28.3	30.4	25.7	29.1	37.4	30.6	28.4
Egypt, Arab Republic	..	30.9	14.7	26.2	21.4	17.2	18.8	16.3	19.7	16.8	20.3	..	..	20.2
Libya	53.5	..	..	..	..	..	..	..	..	..	..	39.8	..	..
Morocco	16.6	21.1	19.2	18.5	18.0	15.9	14.2	14.9	16.2	17.7	22.0	17.2	18.2	17.8
Tunisia	25.0	22.2	21.5	21.4	19.3	20.4	19.3	..	..	..	..	22.5	18.9	20.7
ALL AFRICA	26.6	16.8	17.1	14.5	14.6	15.3	14.9	16.5	16.6	16.2	16.0	23.5	19.0	15.9

Note: 1999 data are preliminary (see page 2). Since 1994, Nigeria's ratios are distorted because the official exchange rate used by the Government for oil exports and oil value added is significantly over-valued.

2-13. Resource balance

					Percentage of GDP								*Annual average*		
	1980	1990	1991	1992	1993	1994	1995	1996	1997	1998	1999	75-84	85-89	90-MR
SUB-SAHARAN AFRICA	2.7	1.9	0.2	-1.1	-1.6	-1.1	-1.3	1.6	-0.9	-3.0	-2.6	-1.7	0.5	-0.8
excluding South Africa	0.5	-0.5	-3.1	-5.1	-6.1	-4.3	-3.3	1.8	-2.5	-6.1	-6.2	-3.6	-2.7	-3.6
excl. S.Africa & Nigeria	-5.5	-3.3	-4.6	-6.7	-6.6	-5.3	-4.4	-2.7	-4.7	-6.3	-6.3	-4.8	-3.7	-5.1
Angola	..	18.0	3.2	-1.9	-1.3	9.5	10.7	29.1	15.7	8.4	21.0	..	9.1	11.2
Benin	-20.3	-8.7	-8.6	-9.5	-10.1	-6.2	-9.6	-9.1	-8.7	-8.8	-9.6	-17.8	-9.5	-8.9
Botswana	-2.4	5.3	7.3	6.6	9.5	12.0	13.7	17.6	8.8	1.2	-5.5	-2.8	24.2	7.6
Burkina Faso	-22.9	-12.9	-14.5	-14.1	-14.8	-13.1	-15.3	-17.7	-16.5	-16.9	-18.1	-21.8	-19.3	-15.4
Burundi	-14.5	-19.9	-18.6	-20.1	-21.0	-18.2	-14.4	-9.6	-4.2	-11.6	-9.6	-10.2	-12.6	-14.7
Cameroon	0.8	2.9	5.4	2.2	1.1	2.6	5.0	2.0	2.9	1.5	-0.5	-2.0	0.3	2.5
Cape Verde	-75.6	-31.0	-30.4	-38.0	-36.0	-40.5	-40.0	-32.2	-29.4	-29.4	-27.1	-68.9	-35.2	-33.4
Central African Republic	-15.9	-12.9	-9.8	-12.6	-8.3	-5.7	-7.3	-3.7	-5.4	-9.0	-7.1	-12.0	-11.7	-8.2
Chad	-11.9	-15.5	-12.4	-13.7	-16.0	-18.2	-12.0	-11.6	-12.5	-11.7	-13.4	-10.3	-19.0	-13.7
Comoros	-43.2	-22.9	-18.2	-23.8	-17.7	-26.9	-26.8	-24.9	-27.6	-15.0	-14.6	-39.8	-26.7	-21.8
Congo, Democratic Rep. of	0.1	0.3	-3.7	-0.8	2.2	2.7	4.8	6.3	1.9	1.8	0.5	-2.2	-0.4	1.6
Congo, Republic of	-0.1	7.9	-1.9	2.8	-5.9	-27.9	11.6	18.9	26.7	9.4	7.4	-10.2	0.8	4.9
Côte d'Ivoire	-6.2	4.6	3.0	3.8	1.1	9.8	5.4	7.7	6.5	6.6	6.8	0.7	6.6	5.5
Djibouti	..	..	-24.6	-37.6	-28.2	-23.0	-17.2	-16.5	-15.6	..	..	..	..	-23.3
Equatorial Guinea	..	-37.4	-57.9	-22.0	-23.0	-49.0	-49.0	-82.8	-22.5	-71.7	16.5	-6.3	-28.6	-39.9
Eritrea	..	..	..	-36,6	-39.7	-53.1	-57.8	-60.3	-58.3	-71.7	-68.7	..	..	-55.8
Ethiopia	..	-4.6	-7.2	-6.2	-8.6	-9.8	-8.5	-14.4	-10.5	-11.9	-15.4	-7.4	-7.5	-9.7
Gabon	33.1	15.2	14.0	12.3	14.2	23.4	23.6	27.6	21.4	1.7	6.8	15.2	-3.4	16.0
Gambia, The	-20.9	-11.7	-11.3	-12.9	-17.0	-15.9	-19.2	-19.5	-12.7	-15.6	-16.1	-15.4	-9.5	-15.2
Ghana	-0.7	-9.0	-8.6	-11.5	-15.6	-11.3	-8.3	-7.9	-20.4	-12.8	-16.9	-0.6	-5.3	-12.2
Guinea	..	0.2	-0.1	-6.2	-6.7	-3.3	-3.7	-4.0	-2.2	-1.8	-1.8	..	0.2	-3.0
Guinea-Bissau	-29.2	-27.1	-27.8	-45.2	-23.8	-17.9	-23.5	-21.3	-18.8	-20.6	-18.5	-27.2	-35.6	-24.5
Kenya	-11.1	-5.3	-1.0	0.0	6.0	3.2	-6.2	-3.8	-7.5	-7.7	-6.7	-4.1	-3.5	-2.9
Lesotho	-89.1	-104.5	-114.1	-100.5	-100.0	-91.4	-98.9	-94.3	-84.5	-81.6	-76.5	-94.8	-105.6	-94.6
Liberia	0.0	..	..	..	..	..	..	..	..	..	..	-0.5	7.2	..
Madagascar	-16.4	-10.7	-7.5	-7.9	-8.9	-7.5	-7.3	-5.3	-8.2	-7.9	-7.9	-8.2	-5.1	-7.9
Malawi	-14.0	-10.1	-6.0	-19.2	-16.1	-32.1	-17.4	-8.6	-11.3	-7.4	-15.4	-9.7	-7.2	-14.4
Mali	-14.4	-16.6	-16.4	-17.4	-15.4	-19.9	-15.1	-15.7	-10.6	-9.7	-11.1	-14.6	-20.0	-14.8
Mauritania	-29.8	-15.1	-8.2	-14.5	-15.9	-3.8	-10.4	-11.5	-9.7	-13.9	-10.6	-32.3	-16.2	-11.3
Mauritius	-10.3	-7.2	-3.8	-3.3	-6.2	-8.9	-2.5	-0.9	-3.9	-0.9	-5.0	-6.8	-1.1	-4.2
Mozambique	-16.5	-27.9	-27.3	-32.8	-35.1	-33.7	-24.7	-22.7	-17.4	-16.3	-24.9	-16.2	-20.5	-26.3
Namibia	7.8	-15.6	-14.8	-14.8	-11.4	-9.9	-11.3	-11.9	-13.1	-9.9	-10.8	-13.4	-1.7	-12.4
Niger	-13.5	-6.9	-4.7	-1.1	-2.5	-10.3	-7.2	-6.5	-7.6	-8.6	-6.4	-9.8	-5.8	-6.2
Nigeria	10.2	14.6	5.9	1.7	-3.1	1.0	2.1	20.7	7.2	-4.9	-5.8	-0.8	2.6	3.9
Rwanda	-11.9	-8.5	-10.7	-12.6	-15.4	-58.5	-20.8	-19.8	-17.7	-17.5	-15.6	-8.0	-10.1	-19.7
São Tomé and Principe	-49.1	-65.3	-58.6	-67.0	-66.9	-59.1	-76.0	-70.0	-65.7	-42.8	-49.3	-42.4	-45.3	-62.1
Senegal	-16.7	-4.9	-6.9	-7.4	-8.6	-6.7	-5.7	-5.7	-5.7	-5.7	-6.4	-12.0	-8.0	-6.4
Seychelles	-11.2	-4.3	-3.6	-3.6	-10.3	-4.0	-6.8	-11.3	-13.7	-17.2	-17.6	-8.3	6.5	-9.2
Sierra Leone	-14.8	-1.2	-2.4	-1.9	-4.5	-5.1	-7.4	-14.7	-1.9	-7.2	-6.3	-11.5	-3.6	-5.3
Somalia	-55.3	-28.0	..	..	..	..	..	..	..	..	..	-38.5	-22.9	-28.0
South Africa	8.0	5.8	5.0	4.0	3.7	2.3	0.9	1.4	1.1	1.2	2.5	3.0	7.1	2.8
Sudan	-12.6	..	..	..	..	..	..	..	..	..	..	-10.2	-5.0	..
Swaziland	-23.8	0.8	-2.4	-7.5	-0.3	-6.1	-5.2	-11.3	-14.5	6.9	8.2	-15.6	-3.9	-3.1
Tanzania	..	-24.8	-23.4	-26.9	-29.7	-23.0	-17.4	-12.0	-9.9	-14.1	-14.8	-8.5	-15.3	-19.6
Togo	-5.3	-11.9	-8.1	-9.2	-7.7	-3.7	-5.0	-8.6	-8.4	-11.1	-9.8	-8.4	-9.6	-8.3
Uganda	-6.6	-12.1	-14.5	-15.5	-14.1	-10.4	-9.0	-11.5	-8.1	-9.4	-11.5	-3.1	-6.8	-11.6
Zambia	-4.0	-0.7	-2.6	-11.9	-6.0	-0.8	-3.8	-7.5	-5.2	-12.5	-18.6	-3.4	0.3	-7.0
Zimbabwe	-3.2	0.1	-3.3	-9.3	-1.7	-1.9	-2.7	0.2	-6.9	-1.7	-0.4	-1.5	2.1	-2.8
NORTH AFRICA	7.9	-2.0	3.2	2.6	1.2	-0.5	-0.2	2.8	3.9	-0.5	0.0	0.7	-1.3	1.1
Algeria	4.0	-1.8	5.6	2.3	-1.4	-4.7	-3.7	6.3	8.4	-0.6	4.3	-2.7	0.2	1.5
Egypt, Arab Republic	-12.4	-12.7	-8.0	-2.8	-3.0	-5.2	-5.0	-5.8	-4.7	-6.5	-8.4	-14.5	-12.9	-6.2
Libya	34.8	..	..	..	..	..	..	..	..	..	..	20.1	..	..
Morocco	-11.3	-9.6	-7.9	-10.1	-9.0	-9.1	-9.7	-7.6	-7.2	-8.3	-8.9	-13.5	-8.7	-8.7
Tunisia	-5.4	-7.0	-5.0	-6.9	-7.5	-3.0	-4.1	-1.6	-2.5	-3.2	-2.2	-7.0	-3.4	-4.3
ALL AFRICA	3.7	0.3	0.7	-0.4	-1.1	-1.3	-1.3	1.7	0.4	-2.4	-2.0	-1.5	-0.3	-0.5

Note: 1999 data are preliminary (see page 2). Since 1994, Nigeria's ratios are distorted because the official exchange rate used by the Government for oil exports and oil value added is significantly over-valued.

2-14. Exports of goods and nonfactor services, nominal

| | Millions of U.S. dollars, current prices | | | | | | | | | | | Annual average | | |
	1980	1990	1991	1992	1993	1994	1995	1996	1997	1998	1999	75-84	85-89	90-MR
SUB-SAHARAN AFRICA	81,096	78,795	74,434	78,628	72,020	77,864	91,668	103,195	102,607	91,104	96,521	51,982	58,812	86,684
excluding South Africa	52,934	51,579	47,507	50,875	44,022	47,808	57,021	68,033	66,171	56,771	63,333	34,400	36,372	55,312
excl. S.Africa & Nigeria	32,811	39,241	37,416	37,042	34,003	38,005	44,645	51,062	49,915	46,186	50,661	25,324	30,948	42,818
Angola	..	3,992	3,690	3,976	2,849	3,465	3,652	6,288	5,237	3,666	8,334	..	2,613	4,515
Benin	323	402	459	388	478	411	544	559	532	537	516	244	395	483
Botswana	562	2,087	2,091	1,998	1,960	2,124	2,435	2,657	2,210	1,705	1,650	432	1,371	2,092
Burkina Faso	173	352	337	202	237	244	306	276	267	361	292	126	214	287
Burundi	81	89	116	95	88	95	129	51	96	71	63	86	125	89
Cameroon	1,898	2,251	2,487	2,342	2,032	1,734	2,045	2,048	2,306	2,306	2,243	1,615	2,226	2,179
Cape Verde	19	43	39	43	48	61	94	112	132	124	135	18	39	83
Central African Republic	201	220	176	165	182	205	229	185	196	170	178	145	194	191
Chad	175	234	224	209	195	189	321	281	286	314	260	143	173	251
Comoros	11	36	49	48	53	38	46	42	38	49	50	15	29	45
Congo, Democratic Rep. of	2,371	2,758	1,852	1,369	1,017	1,620	1,805	1,650	1,463	1,656	1,937	1,691	2,105	1,713
Congo, Republic of	1,024	1,502	1,228	1,257	849	1,115	1,366	1,737	1,738	1,442	1,728	782	996	1,396
Côte d'Ivoire	3,561	3,421	3,149	3,559	2,991	3,291	4,109	5,014	4,777	4,901	4,967	2,701	3,301	4,018
Djibouti	..	..	249	201	233	215	200	200	207	..	..	..	..	215
Equatorial Guinea	..	42	42	58	58	70	91	201	502	464	712	34	39	224
Eritrea	..	..	..	88	139	144	171	200	203	109	66	..	..	140
Ethiopia	..	535	304	251	521	489	786	785	1,012	1,037	894	560	640	661
Gabon	2,770	2,740	2,554	2,577	2,136	2,585	2,851	3,489	3,199	2,119	1,964	1,877	1,603	2,621
Gambia, The	103	190	202	219	213	182	172	183	185	213	199	77	117	196
Ghana	376	993	1,120	1,105	1,068	1,225	1,582	2,224	2,231	2,531˙	2,606	336	850	1,668
Guinea	..	870	694	637	640	763	766	737	771	820	763	..	660	746
Guinea-Bissau	14	24	26	11	21	39	30	28	56	30	56	12	16	32
Kenya	2,030	2,206	2,227	2,149	2,244	2,647	2,948	3,019	2,972	2,849	2,600	1,533	1,779	2,586
Lesotho	91	103	107	151	171	181	199	231	283	239	222	55	70	189
Liberia	614	..	..	..	..	..	..	..	..	..	..	508	466	..
Madagascar	539	512	480	496	516	656	762	819	773	801	921	415	406	674
Malawi	307	447	513	418	334	350	424	518	586	578	490	258	293	466
Mali	263	415	442	439	424	406	521	525	646	644	650	175	290	511
Mauritania	261	465	498	448	413	431	525	516	430	399	370	255	455	449
Mauritius	579	1,724	1,780	1,912	1,899	2,018	2,370	2,801	2,588	2,739	2,708	471	1,092	2,254
Mozambique	383	205	279	271	278	317	363	345	383	410	465	275	155	332
Namibia	1,712	1,220	1,324	1,481	1,522	1,579	1,734	1,741	1,724	1,605	1,620	1,210	1,078	1,555
Niger	617	372	327	393	251	258	323	337	303	369	322	397	385	326
Nigeria	18,859	12,366	10,165	13,816	10,062	9,881	12,449	16,995	16,286	10,722	12,796	8,898	5,563	12,554
Rwanda	168	145	140	113	102	47	67	83	144	110	109	144	179	106
São Tomé and Principe	20	9	11	10	11	12	11	11	12	12	16	13	11	11
Senegal	803	1,450	1,358	1,404	1,204	1,272	1,544	1,588	1,488	1,538	1,534	775	1,035	1,438
Seychelles	100	230	219	243	257	250	271	317	365	376	386	77	157	291
Sierra Leone	276	215	213	215	187	166	163	164	112	95	93	203	175	162
Somalia	200	90	..	..	..	..	..	..	..	..	..	142	64	90
South Africa	28,267	27,327	26,997	27,844	28,025	30,090	34,702	35,307	36,549	34,384	33,321	17,752	22,450	31,454
Sudan	806	..	..	..	..	..	..	..	..	..	..	782	838	..
Swaziland	404	660	709	761	838	837	1,052	999	1,075	1,239	1,305	290	444	947
Tanzania	..	538	509	573	766	930	1,265	1,295	1,211	1,099	1,163	581	395	935
Togo	580	545	536	456	301	300	425	453	494	453	425	401	498	439
Uganda	242	312	248	250	227	349	679	724	826	697	726	563	483	504
Zambia	1,608	1,180	1,169	1,149	1,046	1,205	1,252	1,024	1,178	865	701	1,138	946	1,077
Zimbabwe	1,561	2,009	2,064	1,838	2,016	2,384	2,721	3,116	3,227	2,911	2,537	1,211	1,631	2,482
NORTH AFRICA	46,358	45,643	46,420	48,382	47,310	46,567	53,417	57,850	60,743	54,028	58,554	31,029	31,483	51,891
Algeria	14,541	14,425	13,346	12,195	10,880	9,966	11,330	14,156	14,660	10,828	13,233	10,568	9,996	12,502
Egypt, Arab Republic	6,992	8,647	10,284	12,150	13,071	11,904	13,506	13,650	15,251	13,932	14,285	5,294	6,161	12,668
Libya	23,523	..	..	..	..	..	..	..	..	..	..	13,757	..	..
Morocco	2,827	5,005	5,092	4,964	4,791	5,227	6,257	6,316	6,274	6,348	6,588	2,398	3,399	5,686
Tunisia	3,518	5,353	5,278	6,127	5,909	7,010	8,031	8,249	8,304	8,464	8,780	2,441	3,504	7,150
ALL AFRICA	123,355	122,839	118,721	124,881	116,808	122,579	143,173	159,329	161,028	143,052	152,622	80,473	89,580	136,503

Note: 1999 data are preliminary (see page 2).

2-15. Imports of goods and nonfactor services, nominal

	Millions of U.S. dollars, current prices											Annual average		
	1980	1990	1991	1992	1993	1994	1995	1996	1997	1998	1999	75-84	85-89	90-MR
SUB-SAHARAN AFRICA	73,736	73,199	73,840	82,011	76,626	80,910	95,814	97,813	105,634	100,909	105,133	55,273	57,744	89,189
excluding South Africa	52,019	52,581	53,098	59,758	53,630	54,110	62,573	64,646	70,981	68,414	75,533	39,624	40,830	61,532
excl. S.Africa & Nigeria	39,574	44,494	44,640	46,444	42,902	44,507	50,735	55,090	57,316	56,178	60,699	30,493	36,097	50,300
Angola	..	2,147	3,299	4,088	2,915	3,079	3,099	4,099	4,032	3,121	6,540	..	1,895	3,642
Benin	608	563	621	543	692	505	736	761	719	740	748	433	531	663
Botswana	589	1,887	1,805	1,724	1,562	1,597	1,765	1,792	1,766	1,646	1,982	439	876	1,753
Burkina Faso	564	709	743	483	540	488	666	725	660	797	759	413	596	657
Burundi	214	314	333	312	285	263	273	137	136	174	131	175	267	236
Cameroon	1,847	1,931	1,820	2,087	1,904	1,532	1,646	1,867	2,041	2,176	2,289	1,696	2,209	1,929
Cape Verde	100	148	146	192	179	227	290	273	281	282	292	77	113	231
Central African Republic	327	411	314	346	290	253	311	225	250	264	253	220	327	292
Chad	298	503	458	467	429	403	493	467	475	510	465	240	404	467
Comoros	64	93	94	111	99	88	103	95	91	79	78	60	75	93
Congo, Democratic Rep. of	2,353	2,730	2,192	1,438	818	1,424	1,504	1,281	1,350	1,533	1,902	1,916	2,141	1,617
Congo, Republic of	1,026	1,282	1,280	1,176	962	1,609	1,074	1,257	1,118	1,258	1,563	872	963	1,258
Côte d'Ivoire	4,190	2,927	2,832	3,136	2,874	2,538	3,570	4,188	4,086	4,161	4,204	2,714	2,742	3,452
Djibouti	..	..	361	378	366	327	284	282	285	..	..	..	..	326
Equatorial Guinea	..	92	118	92	93	132	171	416	614	791	597	49	72	312
Eritrea	..	..	..	248	301	415	503	580	585	596	509	..	..	467
Ethiopia	..	851	686	595	1,059	969	1,276	1,652	1,683	1,815	1,883	973	1,191	1,247
Gabon	1,354	1,837	1,798	1,890	1,513	1,603	1,679	1,904	2,037	2,041	1,669	1,338	1,717	1,797
Gambia, The	153	227	237	263	275	239	246	260	237	278	262	108	140	252
Ghana	407	1,522	1,685	1,845	2,000	1,842	2,119	2,776	3,648	3,490	3,923	360	1,124	2,485
Guinea	..	864	697	841	860	875	906	895	855	887	828	..	658	851
Guinea-Bissau	46	90	97	113	78	81	89	86	107	72	96	48	75	91
Kenya	2,837	2,661	2,307	2,152	1,943	2,420	3,512	3,366	3,770	3,737	3,313	1,791	2,063	2,918
Lesotho	475	754	883	982	989	946	1,121	1,117	1,148	956	891	371	508	979
Liberia	614	..	..	..	..	..	..	..	..	..	..	514	387	..
Madagascar	1,202	842	681	733	817	878	994	1,031	1,064	1,097	1,215	691	542	935
Malawi	480	629	646	764	667	730	672	727	873	706	770	352	392	718
Mali	520	817	838	935	836	756	894	936	910	901	939	364	635	876
Mauritania	473	619	591	620	563	470	636	643	536	538	471	463	591	569
Mauritius	695	1,915	1,887	2,017	2,098	2,330	2,468	2,839	2,745	2,773	2,923	541	1,122	2,399
Mozambique	965	906	959	913	1,017	1,080	955	1,004	994	1,047	1,494	836	711	1,037
Namibia	1,542	1,584	1,691	1,899	1,820	1,875	2,100	2,112	2,149	1,908	1,954	1,452	1,127	1,909
Niger	957	545	436	418	291	420	457	466	444	547	452	569	495	448
Nigeria	12,324	8,203	8,559	13,248	10,719	9,646	11,858	9,688	13,677	12,291	14,832	8,996	4,898	11,272
Rwanda	307	364	345	372	404	488	334	362	475	464	414	237	397	402
São Tomé and Principe	41	42	44	41	42	41	46	42	41	30	40	27	33	41
Senegal	1,302	1,728	1,740	1,851	1,668	1,515	1,797	1,852	1,737	1,804	1,842	1,070	1,340	1,753
Seychelles	117	246	233	259	306	270	306	375	438	468	483	89	141	338
Sierra Leone	449	225	232	228	222	213	228	303	128	143	135	319	215	206
Somalia	534	346	..	..	..	..	..	..	..	..	..	400	296	346
South Africa	21,838	20,886	21,014	22,585	23,232	26,965	33,385	33,340	34,879	32,733	30,009	15,866	17,053	27,903
Sudan	1,763	..	..	..	..	..	..	..	..	..	..	1,606	1,637	..
Swaziland	543	653	730	834	840	901	1,117	1,138	1,265	1,155	1,205	371	458	984
Tanzania	..	1,595	1,667	1,811	2,031	1,968	2,181	2,075	1,974	2,314	2,457	1,058	1,061	2,007
Togo	640	738	665	612	396	337	490	579	619	610	563	471	609	561
Uganda	324	834	729	694	682	763	1,199	1,417	1,335	1,335	1,467	625	873	1,046
Zambia	1,764	1,203	1,258	1,527	1,244	1,232	1,383	1,271	1,381	1,268	1,287	1,249	941	1,305
Zimbabwe	1,771	2,002	2,348	2,463	2,130	2,516	2,912	3,100	3,829	3,027	2,560	1,342	1,481	2,689
NORTH AFRICA	36,512	48,884	41,933	44,430	45,400	47,363	53,714	52,348	52,882	55,037	58,464	29,786	33,350	50,046
Algeria	12,847	15,529	10,738	11,048	11,557	11,940	12,861	11,197	10,640	11,117	11,176	10,816	9,883	11,780
Egypt, Arab Republic	9,822	14,109	13,234	13,325	14,488	14,604	16,544	17,562	18,820	19,274	21,734	8,159	10,934	16,369
Libya	11,167	..	..	..	..	..	..	..	..	..	..	8,634	..	..
Morocco	4,951	7,492	7,289	7,827	7,208	7,978	9,463	9,110	8,665	9,312	9,699	4,196	4,945	8,404
Tunisia	3,987	6,220	5,926	7,201	7,007	7,480	8,766	8,553	8,771	9,104	9,237	2,950	3,813	7,826
ALL AFRICA	108,622	121,606	115,719	126,512	121,847	128,121	149,497	150,286	158,881	156,018	163,603	84,104	91,008	139,209

Note: 1999 data are preliminary (see page 2).

2-16. Exports of goods and nonfactor services, real

	Millions of U.S. dollars, constant 1995 prices											Average annual percentage growth		
	1980	1990	1991	1992	1993	1994	1995	1996	1997	1998	1999	75-84	85-89	90-MR
SUB-SAHARAN AFRICA	66,576	77,669	77,144	79,360	80,072	85,091	91,487	101,789	105,490	107,428	108,003	0.9	2.8	4.4
excluding South Africa	42,559	49,693	49,178	50,689	49,984	53,713	56,840	63,953	65,550	66,573	67,137	1.0	2.8	4.1
excl. S.Africa & Nigeria	28,974	40,227	39,260	40,440	40,140	43,160	44,464	50,125	51,561	51,880	54,307	2.3	2.9	3.8
Angola	1,969	2,614	2,052	4,425	2,643	3,878	3,652	4,658	4,081	3,045	3,203	..	1.1	4.5
Benin	730	484	602	726	733	579	544	638	652	646	724	4.0	-4.2	2.8
Botswana	..	2,217	2,295	2,140	2,112	2,253	2,435	2,835	2,785	2,610	2,448	..	10.7	2.2
Burkina Faso	335	375	387	333	398	287	306	290	307	444	395	4.7	-0.2	1.2
Burundi	51	89	114	146	131	101	129	82	159	153	208	4.7	0.2	6.1
Cameroon	1,337	2,464	2,363	2,489	2,078	1,976	2,045	2,270	2,590	2,878	3,249	14.0	-1.5	1.4
Cape Verde	31	53	47	47	57	68	94	113	140	133	145	11.5	-5.0	14.0
Central African Republic	144	124	123	108	126	239	229	211	293	298	367	-0.4	0.0	13.0
Chad	190	255	246	237	253	258	321	275	346	388	337	-0.3	5.2	3.7
Comoros	8	24	37	33	44	40	46	49	53	67	53	..	10.2	9.6
Congo, Democratic Rep. of	2,009	3,685	3,054	1,779	1,621	1,499	1,805	2,083	1,834	2,096	2,404	4.2	1.0	-4.9
Congo, Republic of	784	1,425	1,141	1,215	1,219	1,329	1,366	1,557	1,727	1,451	1,726	10.1	2.2	3.0
Côte d'Ivoire	3,073	4,116	3,796	3,787	3,386	4,093	4,109	5,031	5,262	5,227	5,351	8.5	0.7	4.2
Djibouti	..	..	..	..	..	..	..	..	..	..	..	..	..	..
Equatorial Guinea	..	25	27	32	44	80	91	164	365	449	520	..	-1.8	41.2
Eritrea	..	..	..	105	173	158	171	194	205	110	70	..	..	-4.8
Ethiopia	..	812	619	329	605	708	786	824	1,169	1,056	1,029	..	1.6	5.7
Gabon	1,593	2,347	2,415	2,477	2,787	2,913	2,851	2,969	3,060	2,889	2,698	0.7	0.4	2.9
Gambia, The	113	207	214	218	213	185	172	179	183	214	198	7.3	-1.2	-0.6
Ghana	967	1,139	1,245	1,279	1,497	1,554	1,582	2,267	2,360	2,557	2,885	-9.4	11.3	10.8
Guinea	..	669	690	643	652	673	766	791	818	923	953	..	6.6	4.0
Guinea-Bissau	24	20	25	13	19	38	30	28	55	35	58	-1.8	5.8	13.2
Kenya	1,562	2,507	2,475	2,456	3,230	3,193	2,948	3,083	2,666	2,512	2,382	-0.2	5.6	1.2
Lesotho	86	122	132	160	184	193	199	252	299	276	313	9.9	12.3	10.5
Liberia	..	..	..	..	..	..	..	..	..	..	..	..	..	..
Madagascar	889	704	734	707	746	821	762	798	852	870	1,037	-4.1	0.3	3.9
Malawi	353	398	419	407	386	426	424	494	533	649	529	2.7	-1.7	5.3
Mali	243	369	416	444	458	490	521	536	777	768	880	8.9	2.7	9.5
Mauritania	366	445	452	371	323	456	525	522	427	447	469	5.8	-0.3	0.6
Mauritius	802	1,851	1,930	1,996	2,156	2,220	2,370	2,658	2,788	3,070	3,113	3.8	15.5	6.4
Mozambique	269	146	187	233	322	383	363	430	476	527	614	..	2.7	16.4
Namibia	1,313	1,143	1,473	1,566	1,733	1,562	1,734	1,815	1,838	1,821	1,871	..	2.5	4.4
Niger	388	323	312	356	326	291	323	382	376	439	394	-1.3	-1.3	2.7
Nigeria	12,962	9,571	10,005	10,337	9,940	10,656	12,449	13,913	14,082	14,773	12,969	-2.9	2.3	5.1
Rwanda	175	215	199	182	158	61	67	95	123	126	144	6.5	1.8	-6.9
São Tomé and Principe	..	11	14	14	13	12	11	10	11	14	19	..	13.6	0.7
Senegal	956	1,485	1,493	1,386	1,353	1,378	1,544	1,568	1,589	1,681	1,782	0.5	2.8	2.0
Seychelles	..	299	318	300	318	339	271	341	368	386	394	..	21.7	2.8
Sierra Leone	481	514	525	493	427	326	163	304	189	200	187	-11.1	-2.5	-11.1
Somalia	..	..	..	..	..	..	..	..	..	..	..	..	..	..
South Africa	24,198	28,055	28,039	28,749	30,141	31,447	34,702	37,913	40,004	40,916	40,933	0.7	2.8	4.9
Sudan	..	..	..	..	..	..	..	..	..	..	..	..	..	..
Swaziland	468	1,010	1,018	972	997	1,023	1,052	1,104	1,140	1,175	1,213	2.6	20.3	2.0
Tanzania	..	598	535	658	855	954	1,265	1,270	954	1,048	1,098	..	..	8.9
Togo	608	505	509	438	326	360	425	437	473	446	438	4.6	4.2	-1.4
Uganda	..	385	363	420	401	528	679	863	1,118	952	1,265	..	1.2	14.8
Zambia	1,787	1,230	1,286	1,333	1,379	1,500	1,252	1,336	1,593	1,671	1,754	-2.9	-2.9	2.9
Zimbabwe	965	1,530	1,714	1,790	2,069	2,457	2,721	2,831	2,999	3,596	3,785	5.4	5.5	10.6
NORTH AFRICA	28,088	45,165	45,849	48,731	50,212	50,722	53,417	54,488	57,825	57,294	61,136	3.3	6.0	3.5
Algeria	7,241	10,923	10,825	11,247	11,033	10,658	11,330	12,134	12,898	13,105	13,917	1.9	3.0	2.6
Egypt, Arab Republic	6,537	10,481	10,830	12,228	13,113	12,477	13,506	13,718	14,051	12,964	14,152	5.5	7.1	3.5
Libya	..	..	..	..	..	..	..	..	..	..	..	..	..	..
Morocco	2,938	5,365	5,671	5,460	5,645	6,120	6,257	6,081	6,586	6,733	7,060	1.4	5.5	3.5
Tunisia	3,855	6,311	6,255	6,757	6,985	7,895	8,031	7,975	8,816	9,161	9,648	5.6	10.5	5.0
ALL AFRICA	95,164	121,232	121,213	125,963	127,937	133,823	142,977	155,077	161,813	163,497	167,232	1.5	3.7	4.1

Note: 1999 data are preliminary (see page 2).

2-17. Imports of goods and nonfactor services, real

	Millions of U.S. dollars, constant 1995 prices											Average annual percentage growth		
	1980	1990	1991	1992	1993	1994	1995	1996	1997	1998	1999	75-84	85-89	90-MR
SUB-SAHARAN AFRICA	95,803	78,471	79,919	83,333	83,698	86,829	95,810	103,136	109,536	111,144	113,503	1.5	-0.8	4.3
excluding South Africa	74,091	57,712	58,711	60,977	59,425	58,489	62,590	67,006	71,473	72,284	77,531	3.0	-2.0	3.0
excl. S.Africa & Nigeria	44,495	47,517	47,340	49,363	47,978	47,892	50,754	54,591	57,437	58,675	61,308	..	2.4	2.6
Angola	2,366	1,936	1,720	4,474	2,435	3,449	3,099	3,037	3,142	2,606	3,465	..	-3.6	4.2
Benin	1,119	678	720	814	819	539	736	767	795	850	864	2.8	-5.3	3.3
Botswana	..	2,213	2,046	1,885	1,716	1,705	1,765	1,927	1,945	1,971	2,044	..	14.0	-0.6
Burkina Faso	547	687	740	706	763	545	666	709	702	927	875	3.2	4.3	2.6
Burundi	190	247	274	287	313	294	273	162	152	275	311	8.4	-4.1	-0.7
Cameroon	1,207	1,896	1,960	1,580	1,593	1,628	1,646	1,891	2,203	2,493	2,571	10.5	-3.7	3.6
Cape Verde	160	183	176	214	210	252	290	277	297	303	314	11.9	-3.1	6.4
Central African Republic	319	287	306	329	286	305	311	222	292	298	289	3.0	2.8	-0.8
Chad	379	638	592	584	559	460	493	524	572	578	602	-4.0	7.9	-1.3
Comoros	102	104	106	121	115	98	103	99	102	100	101	..	-3.2	-0.9
Congo, Democratic Rep. of	2,102	3,948	3,677	2,270	1,473	1,101	1,504	1,421	1,386	1,515	1,838	4.3	9.5	-11.1
Congo, Republic of	938	1,014	1,039	926	1,166	1,334	1,074	1,851	1,314	1,146	1,312	8.0	-11.9	4.0
Côte d'Ivoire	4,160	2,877	3,013	3,089	3,030	3,077	3,570	3,927	4,193	4,137	4,299	3.2	-0.1	4.3
Djibouti	..	..	..	..	..	..	..	..	..	..	..	..	..	..
Equatorial Guinea	..	54	68	52	60	151	171	340	447	767	437	..	12.6	31.6
Eritrea	..	..	..	277	338	449	503	607	645	670	587	..	..	12.6
Ethiopia	..	1,158	1,250	1,088	1,333	1,174	1,276	1,545	1,573	1,729	2,047	..	3.0	4.4
Gabon	1,900	1,977	1,939	1,960	2,048	1,723	1,679	1,918	2,295	2,297	1,920	4.0	-9.2	0.4
Gambia, The	337	251	264	274	273	242	246	256	237	274	257	5.3	0.1	0.4
Ghana	2,210	1,803	1,984	2,115	2,472	2,124	2,119	2,747	3,725	3,810	4,267	-9.8	9.9	9.3
Guinea	..	898	901	879	837	858	906	881	883	959	949	..	4.9	0.9
Guinea-Bissau	98	104	117	130	98	96	89	84	104	79	100	0.1	-5.9	-3.1
Kenya	2,115	2,050	1,958	1,912	2,558	2,989	3,512	3,576	3,670	3,507	3,279	-3.9	9.4	7.7
Lesotho	592	866	948	983	1,047	1,018	1,121	1,207	1,220	1,135	1,211	7.7	4.1	3.7
Liberia	..	..	..	..	..	..	..	..	..	..	..	..	..	..
Madagascar	1,892	1,008	820	841	960	970	994	1,035	1,125	1,143	1,319	-3.2	-5.1	4.3
Malawi	854	790	787	904	834	757	672	737	884	775	838	-2.1	2.2	0.1
Mali	506	882	907	971	895	835	894	963	1,062	1,084	1,145	7.0	2.6	2.8
Mauritania	471	568	547	553	517	473	636	609	538	612	605	2.9	-3.4	1.1
Mauritius	952	2,224	2,188	2,252	2,416	2,546	2,468	2,717	2,967	3,073	3,216	-1.1	20.6	4.6
Mozambique	1,501	1,036	1,058	1,139	1,390	1,134	955	976	945	1,041	1,492	..	1.2	0.4
Namibia	1,646	1,710	1,770	1,866	1,847	1,846	2,100	2,261	2,102	2,107	2,081	..	4.0	2.5
Niger	1,151	644	521	447	453	465	457	461	452	529	428	4.9	-3.1	-3.1
Nigeria	27,928	10,254	11,378	11,631	11,458	10,640	11,858	12,451	14,036	13,637	16,176	5.8	-15.1	4.4
Rwanda	175	207	381	392	456	515	334	352	503	544	483	10.4	-0.1	7.1
São Tomé and Principe	..	48	50	45	47	43	46	41	43	35	44	..	5.3	-2.3
Senegal	1,548	1,928	1,826	1,901	1,816	1,736	1,797	1,851	1,891	2,096	2,188	2.3	1.3	1.1
Seychelles	..	228	222	249	325	279	306	388	448	512	521	..	14.2	10.6
Sierra Leone	502	339	299	273	264	253	228	352	136	190	181	-7.8	4.3	-6.3
Somalia	..	..	..	..	..	..	..	..	..	..	..	..	..	..
South Africa	22,394	21,144	21,597	22,752	24,599	28,557	33,385	36,294	38,248	39,040	36,298	-1.4	2.8	7.4
Sudan	..	..	..	..	..	..	..	..	..	..	..	..	..	..
Swaziland	716	1,160	1,185	1,240	1,328	1,091	1,117	1,164	1,220	899	898	8.8	7.9	-2.2
Tanzania	..	1,812	1,848	1,927	2,149	2,055	2,181	2,006	1,440	1,435	1,503	..	..	-2.1
Togo	760	863	783	688	467	386	490	585	732	739	718	6.0	5.7	-1.7
Uganda	..	763	727	716	692	772	1,199	1,355	1,382	1,425	1,465	..	7.3	9.0
Zambia	2,287	1,364	1,108	1,166	1,080	1,217	1,383	1,322	1,385	1,449	1,473	-10.7	3.8	1.3
Zimbabwe	960	1,528	1,977	2,477	2,200	2,613	2,912	2,826	3,537	3,746	3,833	3.7	3.1	10.6
NORTH AFRICA	51,854	50,503	47,764	49,497	49,478	50,887	53,714	51,222	53,480	57,293	61,511	4.9	-5.3	1.9
Algeria	18,597	14,832	12,177	12,737	11,884	12,609	12,861	11,151	11,418	12,160	12,379	5.1	-10.1	-2.3
Egypt, Arab Republic	16,885	14,775	14,948	14,253	15,385	15,675	16,544	16,801	17,123	17,311	19,520	4.5	-5.9	2.8
Libya	..	..	..	..	..	..	..	..	..	..	..	..	..	..
Morocco	5,185	7,595	8,074	8,905	8,391	8,339	9,463	8,964	9,621	11,682	12,236	2.2	4.6	4.9
Tunisia	5,316	7,584	7,157	7,998	8,217	8,504	8,766	8,507	9,263	9,654	10,412	8.5	2.0	3.7
ALL AFRICA	147,489	128,559	127,477	132,634	132,993	137,554	149,494	154,729	163,465	168,709	175,108	2.7	-2.6	3.5

Note: 1999 data are preliminary (see page 2).

2-18. GDP growth

	Percent annual change											Average annual percentage growth		
	1980	1990	1991	1992	1993	1994	1995	1996	1997	1998	1999	75-84	85-89	90-MR
SUB-SAHARAN AFRICA	5.7	1.0	0.5	-1.1	0.6	2.1	4.0	4.8	3.3	2.1	2.2	2.2	2.3	2.1
excluding South Africa	1.5	2.4	1.9	-0.2	0.1	1.0	4.8	5.3	4.1	3.5	3.0	1.9	3.3	2.6
excl. S.Africa & Nigeria	0.7	1.3	1.3	-0.9	-0.4	1.2	5.3	5.5	4.4	3.8	3.4	2.5	3.0	2.5
Angola	..	-0.3	0.7	-5.1	-23.8	1.4	10.3	10.0	6.2	3.2	2.7	..	4.5	-0.2
Benin	6.8	3.2	4.7	4.0	3.5	4.4	4.6	5.5	5.7	4.5	4.9	3.8	1.5	4.6
Botswana	11.7	7.2	7.5	3.0	2.0	3.6	5.1	6.9	4.0	3.5	4.5	11.5	10.6	4.5
Burkina Faso	0.8	-1.5	10.0	2.5	-0.8	1.2	4.0	6.0	4.8	6.2	5.8	3.6	4.4	3.6
Burundi	1.0	3.5	5.0	0.7	-5.7	-3.9	-7.3	-8.4	0.4	4.8	-1.0	3.8	5.1	-2.4
Cameroon	-2.0	-6.1	-3.8	-3.1	-3.2	-2.5	3.3	5.0	5.1	5.0	4.4	8.5	-0.1	0.5
Cape Verde	37.7	0.7	1.4	3.3	7.1	6.9	7.5	4.0	5.0	8.0	8.0	13.8	4.5	5.4
Central African Republic	-4.5	-2.1	-0.6	-6.4	0.3	4.9	7.2	-4.0	5.3	4.7	3.4	0.4	0.7	1.4
Chad	-6.0	-4.2	8.5	8.0	-15.7	10.2	1.0	2.4	4.5	6.7	-0.7	-1.3	5.4	1.9
Comoros	..	5.1	-5.4	8.5	3.0	-5.3	-3.9	-0.1	0.5	-0.5	-1.4	..	1.3	-0.3
Congo, Democratic Rep. of	2.2	-6.6	-8.4	-10.5	-13.5	-3.9	0.7	-0.9	-5.7	3.0	8.0	-0.3	1.7	-4.6
Congo, Republic of	17.6	0.9	2.4	2.6	-1.0	-5.5	4.0	-4.3	-0.6	3.7	-3.0	9.2	-1.0	-0.3
Côte d'Ivoire	-11.0	-1.1	0.0	-0.2	-0.2	2.0	7.1	6.9	6.6	4.5	2.8	2.2	2.0	3.2
Djibouti	..	..	..	-0.3	-3.9	-2.9	-4.0	-5.1	0.5	0.7	..	..	..	-2.7
Equatorial Guinea	..	3.3	-1.1	10.7	6.3	5.1	14.3	29.1	71.2	21.9	15.1	..	1.4	17.1
Eritrea	..	..	..	..	-2.5	9.8	2.9	6.8	7.9	3.9	0.8	..	..	5.0
Ethiopia	..	2.5	-4.7	-5.1	13.4	3.5	6.1	10.6	5.2	-1.4	6.2	..	2.9	4.1
Gabon	2.6	5.2	6.1	-3.3	2.4	3.4	7.0	5.2	5.8	2.1	-6.2	-0.2	-1.4	3.2
Gambia, The	6.3	3.6	3.1	3.4	3.0	0.2	0.9	2.2	4.9	4.9	6.4	4.3	3.3	2.8
Ghana	0.5	3.3	5.3	3.9	5.0	3.3	4.0	4.6	4.2	4.7	4.4	-1.1	5.2	4.3
Guinea	..	4.4	2.4	3.0	4.7	4.0	4.4	4.6	4.8	4.4	3.2	..	4.7	4.1
Guinea-Bissau	-16.0	6.1	5.1	1.1	2.1	3.2	4.4	4.6	5.4	-28.1	7.8	2.1	3.1	0.9
Kenya	5.6	4.2	1.4	-0.8	0.4	2.6	4.4	4.1	2.1	1.6	1.3	4.7	5.9	2.2
Lesotho	-2.7	6.2	3.8	4.8	3.8	3.4	4.5	10.0	8.0	-5.0	2.5	5.2	5.6	4.5
Liberia	..	..	..	..	..	..	..	..	..	..	..	..	..	..
Madagascar	0.8	3.1	-6.3	1.2	2.1	0.0	1.7	2.1	3.7	3.9	4.7	-0.2	2.3	1.4
Malawi	0.4	5.7	8.7	-7.3	9.7	-10.2	16.7	7.3	3.8	2.0	4.0	3.2	1.9	3.6
Mali	-4.3	-1.9	1.6	8.3	-2.1	0.9	6.2	3.2	6.8	3.4	5.5	2.3	0.8	3.3
Mauritania	3.4	-1.8	2.6	1.7	5.5	4.6	4.6	5.5	3.2	3.2	4.3	1.6	3.3	3.8
Mauritius	-10.1	7.2	4.3	6.2	5.4	4.1	4.7	5.7	5.5	5.6	3.4	3.6	7.7	5.2
Mozambique	..	1.0	4.9	-8.1	8.7	7.5	4.3	7.1	11.1	11.9	7.3	..	6.0	5.5
Namibia	..	2.0	8.2	7.1	-1.7	6.4	3.7	2.1	2.6	2.4	3.1	..	2.5	3.6
Niger	-2.2	-1.3	2.5	-6.5	1.4	4.0	2.6	3.4	2.8	10.4	-0.6	2.0	4.2	2.0
Nigeria	4.2	8.2	4.8	2.9	2.2	0.1	2.5	4.3	2.7	1.8	1.0	-0.7	5.0	2.7
Rwanda	9.0	-2.4	-2.5	5.9	-8.3	-50.2	34.4	15.8	12.8	9.5	6.1	6.8	2.9	-2.1
São Tomé and Principe	..	1.8	2.2	0.7	1.1	2.2	2.0	1.5	1.0	2.5	2.5	..	1.8	1.7
Senegal	-3.3	3.9	-0.4	2.2	-2.2	2.9	5.2	5.1	5.0	5.7	5.1	2.1	3.5	3.1
Seychelles	-4.2	9.0	2.8	7.2	6.2	-0.8	-0.6	4.7	4.3	2.0	1.5	3.6	5.2	3.3
Sierra Leone	4.8	4.8	-8.0	-9.6	0.1	3.5	-26.6	28.7	-17.6	-0.8	-8.1	2.3	1.8	-4.6
Somalia	..	..	..	..	..	..	..	..	..	..	..	..	..	..
South Africa	9.2	-0.3	-1.0	-2.1	1.2	3.2	3.1	4.2	2.5	0.6	1.2	2.4	1.4	1.6
Sudan	1.5	-0.4	6.0	4.9	4.3	4.0	25.2	4.0	9.7	6.1	5.2	2.6	0.9	7.6
Swaziland	10.7	8.9	2.5	1.3	3.3	3.5	2.7	3.9	3.7	2.0	2.0	3.3	9.9	3.1
Tanzania	..	7.0	2.1	0.6	1.2	1.6	3.6	4.5	3.5	4.0	4.7	..	..	2.9
Togo	14.6	-0.2	-0.7	-4.0	-15.1	15.0	7.8	9.6	4.2	-2.2	2.1	2.1	3.4	1.9
Uganda	..	6.5	5.6	3.4	8.3	6.4	11.5	9.1	4.7	5.6	7.4	..	3.4	7.1
Zambia	3.0	-0.5	0.0	-1.7	6.8	-8.7	-2.5	6.6	3.3	-1.9	2.4	0.2	2.3	0.2
Zimbabwe	14.4	7.0	7.3	-8.4	2.4	5.4	0.3	10.2	2.8	3.7	0.1	3.0	4.2	2.9
NORTH AFRICA	5.0	3.4	2.0	2.0	0.5	3.9	1.5	6.5	2.6	5.6	3.9	6.0	3.0	3.1
Algeria	0.9	-1.3	-1.2	1.6	-2.2	-1.2	3.8	3.8	1.1	5.1	3.3	5.5	0.8	1.2
Egypt, Arab Republic	10.0	5.7	1.1	4.4	2.9	3.9	4.7	5.0	5.5	5.6	6.0	8.3	4.1	4.3
Libya	..	..	..	..	..	..	..	..	..	..	..	..	..	..
Morocco	3.6	4.0	6.9	-4.0	-1.0	10.4	-6.6	12.2	-2.2	6.8	-0.7	4.1	4.7	2.3
Tunisia	7.4	8.0	3.9	7.8	2.2	3.3	2.3	7.1	5.4	4.8	6.2	5.3	2.4	4.7
ALL AFRICA	5.5	1.8	1.0	-0.1	0.6	2.7	3.2	5.3	3.1	3.3	2.8	3.3	2.5	2.4

Note: 1999 data are preliminary (see page 2).

2-19. GNP per capita

	U.S. dollars, Atlas method											Annual average		
	1980	*1990*	*1991*	*1992*	*1993*	*1994*	*1995*	*1996*	*1997*	*1998*	*1999*	*75-84*	*85-89*	*90-MR*
SUB-SAHARAN AFRICA	648	553	552	551	533	512	522	536	543	509	492	540	510	530
excluding South Africa	509	381	369	349	319	286	288	303	319	312	306	423	371	323
excl. S.Africa & Nigeria	446	409	395	365	339	303	307	319	331	323	318	367	390	341
Angola	..	840	930	600	370	150	240	270	340	320	270	..	867	433
Benin	410	360	380	370	380	340	350	360	380	380	380	313	326	368
Botswana	1,230	2,730	3,050	3,300	3,200	3,100	3,360	3,410	3,270	3,070	3,240	996	1,604	3,173
Burkina Faso	260	290	320	290	240	210	220	240	240	240	240	198	242	253
Burundi	220	220	220	210	180	160	150	140	140	140	120	186	246	168
Cameroon	650	970	910	920	900	730	660	620	620	610	600	599	996	754
Cape Verde	..	980	1,000	1,100	1,110	1,150	1,210	1,270	1,290	1,290	1,330	..	940	1,173
Central African Republic	340	470	470	460	440	360	350	300	310	300	290	271	392	375
Chad	240	280	310	350	260	230	210	210	220	230	210	221	238	251
Comoros	370	540	530	620	610	490	440	410	400	370	350	348	420	476
Congo, Democratic Rep. of	630	220	210	200	190	160	150	130	110	110	..	480	238	164
Congo, Republic of	880	980	1,020	1,120	900	720	510	460	500	580	550	831	1,052	734
Côte d'Ivoire	1,140	800	780	800	760	680	670	680	730	720	710	856	798	733
Djibouti	..	..	..	..	..	..	..	..	..	..	790	..	..	790
Equatorial Guinea	..	350	340	400	420	370	390	430	860	1,060	1,170	..	340	579
Eritrea	..	..	..	..	..	180	180	200	230	210	200	..	..	200
Ethiopia	..	160	120	110	120	110	110	110	110	100	100	135	162	115
Gabon	4,750	4,750	5,100	5,050	4,480	4,060	3,850	4,020	4,330	4,000	3,300	4,301	3,980	4,294
Gambia, The	380	320	330	350	350	340	350	340	340	340	330	297	284	339
Ghana	430	390	410	430	420	370	370	380	390	390	390	356	404	394
Guinea	..	460	470	520	540	550	560	580	580	540	510	..	445	531
Guinea-Bissau	150	220	250	240	230	220	220	230	230	160	160	179	182	216
Kenya	450	370	340	330	250	240	260	320	340	350	360	340	366	316
Lesotho	490	590	590	650	680	680	690	720	730	590	550	437	470	647
Liberia	620	..	..	..	..	..	..	..	..	..	..	523	470	..
Madagascar	450	240	220	230	240	240	240	250	250	260	250	353	270	242
Malawi	190	190	230	220	230	160	160	180	210	200	180	162	164	196
Mali	270	270	270	320	300	250	240	240	260	240	240	201	226	263
Mauritania	460	540	540	540	490	470	450	460	440	410	390	404	482	473
Mauritius	1,240	2,430	2,610	2,960	3,080	3,180	3,420	3,720	3,800	3,590	3,550	1,071	1,646	3,234
Mozambique	..	170	170	140	140	140	140	160	180	210	220	240	246	167
Namibia	..	1,800	1,930	2,030	1,940	2,040	2,160	2,130	2,080	1,930	1,890	1,570	1,342	1,993
Niger	440	310	300	290	240	210	190	200	200	200	190	318	288	233
Nigeria	710	270	270	290	240	220	210	240	270	260	260	599	292	253
Rwanda	250	370	320	310	260	140	190	200	220	230	250	207	330	249
São Tomé and Principe	..	410	410	390	370	350	340	320	290	270	270	..	495	342
Senegal	530	720	710	780	710	590	550	530	530	510	510	436	558	614
Seychelles	2,110	5,070	5,240	5,930	6,330	6,440	6,460	6,750	6,910	6,710	6,540	1,646	3,344	6,238
Sierra Leone	360	260	200	150	160	170	180	200	160	150	130	313	296	176
Somalia	110	120	..	..	..	..	..	..	..	..	..	133	140	120
South Africa	2,540	2,890	3,050	3,320	3,460	3,610	3,740	3,770	3,700	3,320	3,170	2,133	2,376	3,403
Sudan	480	610	560	350	300	270	..	..	..	290	330	427	656	387
Swaziland	970	1,200	1,210	1,290	1,260	1,220	1,380	1,470	1,520	1,400	1,360	817	868	1,331
Tanzania	..	190	180	170	170	160	160	190	210	240	260	..	..	193
Togo	440	430	430	440	340	320	310	320	350	320	310	325	340	357
Uganda	..	340	260	200	190	190	250	290	320	310	320	150	324	267
Zambia	630	490	390	360	380	340	340	370	370	330	330	563	332	370
Zimbabwe	950	920	920	750	680	650	630	710	720	640	530	865	808	715
NORTH AFRICA	1,312	1,388	1,305	1,319	1,261	1,295	1,333	1,435	1,481	1,528	1,569	1,078	1,385	1,391
Algeria	2,080	2,400	2,050	1,980	1,790	1,660	1,530	1,540	1,520	1,570	1,550	1,771	2,670	1,759
Egypt, Arab Republic	520	810	780	800	800	870	990	1,100	1,200	1,280	1,390	483	782	1,002
Libya	10,460	..	..	..	..	..	..	..	..	..	..	7,927	6,034	..
Morocco	970	1,030	1,100	1,100	1,060	1,170	1,120	1,300	1,250	1,250	1,190	733	794	1,157
Tunisia	1,360	1,430	1,490	1,700	1,690	1,740	1,820	2,000	2,080	2,050	2,090	1,092	1,244	1,809
ALL AFRICA	769	707	691	692	667	654	668	696	709	687	677	638	674	685

Note: 1999 data are preliminary (see page 2).

2-20. Total consumption per capita

	Current U.S. dollars											Annual average		
	1980	1990	1991	1992	1993	1994	1995	1996	1997	1998	1999	75-84	85-89	90-MR
SUB-SAHARAN AFRICA	527	480	486	493	449	417	461	456	468	433	427	426	417	457
excluding South Africa	417	324	319	312	274	234	267	277	287	277	281	334	310	285
excl. S.Africa & Nigeria	367	354	352	329	303	250	283	298	301	296	293	304	334	306
Angola	..	781	1,066	571	463	282	403	509	389	363	323	..	676	515
Benin	426	368	362	309	386	254	330	361	334	356	362	300	316	342
Botswana	818	1,858	1,856	1,986	1,921	1,888	1,994	1,856	2,249	2,441	3,241	643	900	2,129
Burkina Faso	260	287	288	199	202	176	216	226	203	210	212	193	239	222
Burundi	224	219	217	198	167	165	170	140	143	138	107	179	219	166
Cameroon	609	771	822	784	786	503	486	556	530	488	507	491	799	623
Cape Verde	458	1,072	1,056	1,153	965	1,073	1,253	1,205	1,153	1,199	1,213	349	741	1,134
Central African Republic	375	508	454	467	405	249	320	317	281	288	276	274	416	357
Chad	..	301	337	330	249	185	218	225	208	221	211	200	254	249
Comoros	406	597	545	594	548	410	476	471	419	365	354	343	450	478
Congo, Democratic Rep. of	479	227	231	193	209	151	124	112	119	130	138	411	209	164
Congo, Republic of	658	961	971	943	606	522	564	203	437	447	545	587	818	620
Côte d'Ivoire	989	823	784	805	740	453	599	607	577	583	585	671	715	656
Djibouti	..	..	943	1,015	924	930	888	853	852	..	..	..	..	915
Equatorial Guinea	..	451	388	408	405	242	299	438	673	847	662	446	452	481
Eritrea	..	..	..	173	150	198	222	225	204	218	196	..	..	198
Ethiopia	..	124	98	99	111	84	94	101	100	101	100	130	148	101
Gabon	2,438	3,915	3,249	3,584	2,655	2,141	2,379	2,503	2,309	2,388	2,348	1,944	2,794	2,747
Gambia, The	354	308	295	315	338	330	341	335	331	333	309	272	269	323
Ghana	393	374	399	402	344	286	334	342	369	361	385	326	360	360
Guinea	..	403	417	478	466	470	494	510	479	452	436	..	348	461
Guinea-Bissau	141	244	251	216	213	214	237	239	229	193	188	180	179	222
Kenya	378	310	275	277	148	218	298	291	348	371	337	280	296	287
Lesotho	487	547	576	614	643	602	670	649	665	575	554	397	417	610
Liberia	433	..	..	..	..	..	..	..	..	..	..	408	411	..
Madagascar	462	248	224	238	262	223	229	273	241	245	236	340	241	242
Malawi	179	191	216	199	226	128	147	236	244	155	169	140	148	191
Mali	268	268	261	304	272	173	234	243	217	221	215	196	225	241
Mauritania	473	479	490	529	408	376	418	432	410	375	343	440	414	426
Mauritius	1,049	1,909	1,993	2,181	2,198	2,412	2,716	2,888	2,695	2,685	2,805	847	1,254	2,448
Mozambique	322	199	192	156	172	167	154	182	209	214	224	300	259	187
Namibia	1,298	1,417	1,718	1,839	1,699	1,705	1,883	1,756	1,899	1,649	1,640	1,560	1,296	1,721
Niger	384	317	283	267	181	177	205	203	182	199	185	281	260	220
Nigeria	619	209	195	245	162	174	206	201	232	204	231	464	223	206
Rwanda	216	349	259	274	262	178	213	218	243	254	239	196	312	249
São Tomé and Principe	556	562	585	479	485	468	475	417	402	282	354	394	536	451
Senegal	566	708	690	725	650	396	478	474	437	450	453	428	579	546
Seychelles	1,667	4,196	4,308	4,986	5,267	5,086	5,163	4,006	5,392	5,424	5,489	1,285	2,480	4,932
Sierra Leone	350	206	181	154	174	204	195	211	187	141	143	365	272	180
Somalia	116	133	..	..	..	..	..	..	..	..	..	136	137	133
South Africa	2,004	2,622	2,782	2,986	2,866	2,913	3,125	2,945	3,024	2,672	2,548	1,655	1,873	2,848
Sudan	399	..	..	..	..	..	..	..	..	..	..	405	659	..
Swaziland	964	889	907	963	861	901	1,000	1,074	1,103	997	948	662	645	964
Tanzania	..	165	183	169	159	154	173	204	233	261	260	246	178	196
Togo	334	395	401	422	319	218	283	321	323	309	296	246	332	329
Uganda	..	262	195	163	177	206	278	292	285	306	284	189	333	245
Zambia	546	352	386	385	350	355	339	336	375	322	322	455	334	352
Zimbabwe	822	744	726	585	522	465	512	620	666	474	419	724	629	573
NORTH AFRICA	844	1,119	925	1,000	1,044	1,061	1,135	1,236	1,230	1,294	1,299	705	1,030	1,134
Algeria	1,291	1,795	1,144	1,265	1,337	1,118	1,052	1,125	1,117	1,171	1,092	1,115	1,792	1,222
Egypt, Arab Republic	476	690	599	647	732	806	908	1,018	1,090	1,158	1,222	417	641	887
Libya	5,040	..	..	..	..	..	..	..	..	..	..	4,325	..	..
Morocco	846	906	968	988	911	1,027	1,112	1,202	1,058	1,102	1,050	610	705	1,032
Tunisia	1,041	1,123	1,143	1,322	1,318	1,390	1,593	1,648	1,559	1,623	1,674	820	969	1,439
ALL AFRICA	590	599	570	588	559	534	583	595	603	583	578	481	530	579

Note: 1999 data are preliminary (see page 2).

Figure 2-1. Gross domestic product, 1999*

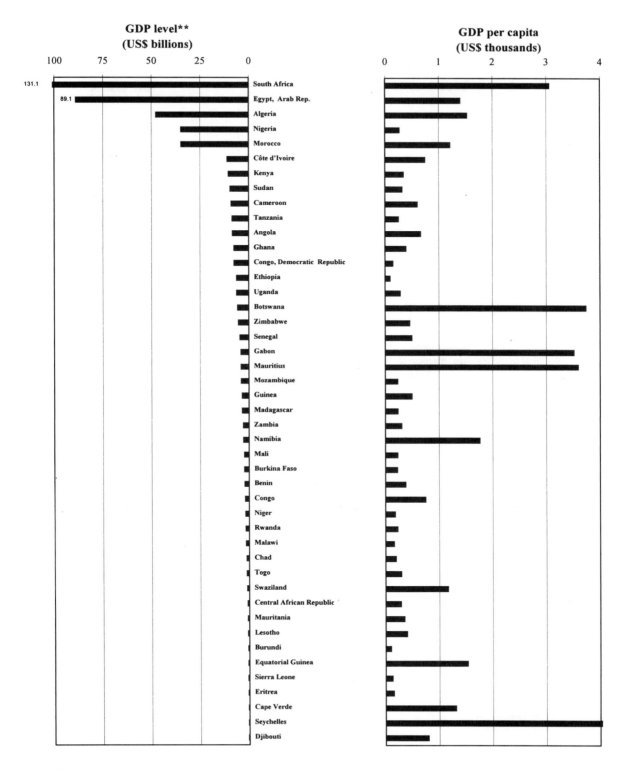

* Or most recent year available.
** Sorted by GDP level.

Figure 2-2. GDP and export growth rates, average 1995-99*

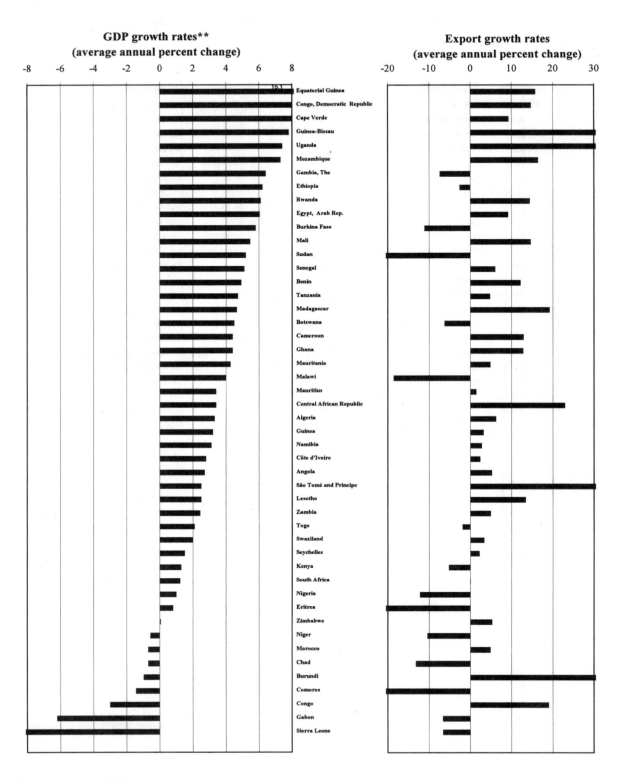

GDP growth rates**
(average annual percent change)

Export growth rates
(average annual percent change)

* Or most recent year available.
** Sorted by GDP.

Figure 2-3. Composition of GDP, 1999*

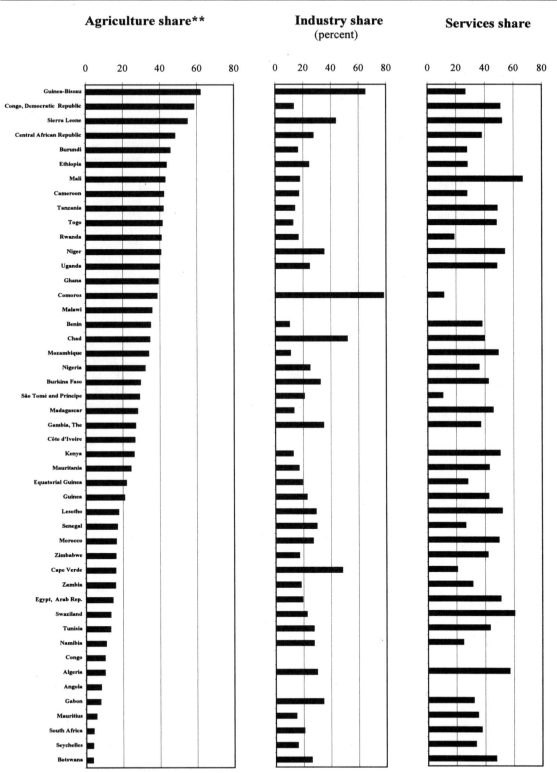

Agriculture share**

Industry share
(percent)

Services share

* Or most recent year available.

** Sorted by agriculture share.

Technical notes

Tables

Table 2-1. Gross domestic product, real.
Gross domestic product (GDP) measures the total output of goods and services for final use produced by residents and nonresidents, regardless of the allocation to domestic and foreign claims (World Bank country desks). It is calculated without making deductions for depreciation of "manmade" assets or depletion and degradation of natural resources. In this table, GDP figures are shown at market prices (also known as purchaser values) and have been converted to U.S. dollars using constant (1995) exchange rates. For a few countries where the official exchange rate does not reflect effectively the rate applied to actual foreign exchange transactions, an alternative currency conversion factor has been used (Table 3-6). The sum of the components of GDP by industrial origin (presented in this volume in the form of value added) will not normally equal total GDP for several reasons. First, components of GDP by expenditure are individually rescaled and summed to provide a partially rebased series for total GDP. Second, total GDP is shown at purchaser value, while value added components are conventionally reported at producer prices. As explained above, the former excludes net indirect taxes, while the latter includes indirect taxes. Third, certain items, such as imputed bank charges, are added in total GDP.

Table 2-2. Value added in agriculture.
Value added in agriculture is shown at factor cost (World Bank country desks). It comprises the gross output of forestry, hunting, and fishing less the value of their intermediate inputs. However, for Botswana, Cameroon, Chad, Congo, Gabon, Guinea, Madagascar, Mali, Morocco, Niger, Rwanda, Senegal, Togo, Zaire, and Zambia it is shown at market prices, that is, including intermediate inputs.

Table 2-3. Value added in industry.
Value added in industry is shown at factor cost (World Bank country desks). It comprises the gross output of mining, manufacturing, construction, electricity, water, and gas, less the value of their intermediate inputs. However, for Botswana, Cameroon, Chad, Congo, Gabon, Guinea, Madagascar, Mali, Morocco, Niger, Rwanda, Senegal, Togo, Zaire, and Zambia it is shown at market prices, that is, including intermediate inputs.

Table 2-4. Value added in services.
Also shown at factor cost, this table consists of the gross output of all other branches of economic activity, including government, less the value of their intermediate inputs (World Bank country desks). However, for Botswana, Cameroon, Chad, Congo, Gabon, Guinea, Madagascar, Mali, Morocco, Niger, Rwanda, Senegal, Togo, Zaire, and Zambia it is shown at market prices, that is, including intermediate inputs. Other items, such as imputed bank service charges (which are difficult to assess in the same fashion for all countries) and any corrections for statistical discrepancies, are not included.

Table 2-5. Gross domestic product, nominal.
This table, presented at market prices, is obtained by converting national currency GDP series in current prices (World Bank country desks) to U.S. dollars at official annual exchange rates (Table 3-4; see also the note for Table 2-1). GDP growth rates are presented in real terms.

Table 2-6. Total consumption.
Total consumption is the sum of private consumption (World Bank country desks) and general government consumption (Table 2-7). Private consumption, not separately shown here, is the value of all goods and services purchased or received as income in kind by households and nonprofit institutions. It excludes purchases

of dwellings, but includes imputed rent for owner-occupied dwellings. In practice, it includes any statistical discrepancy in the use of resources.

Table 2-7. General government consumption. This indicator includes all current expenditure for purchases of goods and services by all levels of government, including capital expenditure on national defense and security (World Bank country desks). Other capital expenditure by government is included in investment.

Tables 2-8, 2-9, and 2-10. Gross domestic, public, and private investment. Gross domestic investment (GDI) consists of gross domestic fixed capital formation plus net changes in the level of inventories (World Bank country desks). GDI comprises outlays by the public sector (Table 2-9) and the private sector (Table 2-10). Examples include improvements in land, dwellings, machinery, and other equipment. For some countries the sum of gross private investment and gross public investment does not add up to gross domestic investment due to statistical discrepancies.

Table 2-11. Gross domestic savings. Gross domestic savings (GDS) is calculated by deducting total consumption (Table 2-6) from gross domestic product in current prices (Table 2-5).

Table 2-12. Gross national savings. Gross national savings (GNS) is the sum of gross domestic savings (Table 2-11), net factor income from abroad (World Bank country desks) and net private transfers from abroad (Table 5-5). The estimate here also includes net public transfers from abroad (Table 5-6).

Table 2-13. Resource balance. The table indicates the difference between exports f.o.b. (Table 2-14) and imports c.i.f. (Table 2-15) of goods and nonfactor services (or the difference between GDS and GDI). The resource balance is shown as a share of GDP in U.S. dollars at current prices (Table 2-5).

Tables 2-14 and 2-15. Exports and imports of goods and nonfactor services, nominal. Data for exports and imports of goods and nonfactor services are from the World Bank country desks and refer to all goods

and nonfactor services (GNFS) provided to, or by, the rest of the world, including merchandise, freight, insurance, travel, and other nonfactor services. The value of factor services, such as investment income, interest, and labor income, is not included. These series are generally estimated on the basis of foreign trade statistics from customs declarations. They are not fully comparable with the series from the balance of payments, which are based on changes in ownership between residents of a country and the rest of the world. Exports, as well as imports of GNFS, are shown in current U.S. dollars.

Tables 2-16 and 2-17. Exports and imports of goods and nonfactor services, real. These are defined as in Tables 2-14 and 2-15, but expressed in constant 1995 U.S. dollars.

Table 2-18. GDP growth. This table (World Bank country desks) provides average annual growth rates calculated from GDP at constant 1995 prices (Table 2-1).

Table 2-19. GNP per capita. Figures presented here (World Bank country desks) are calculated using the *World Bank Atlas* method, as described in the technical notes for Table 1-1; they are similar in concept to GNP per capita in current prices, except that the use of three-year averages of exchange rates smoothes out sharp fluctuations from year to year.

Table 2-20. Total consumption per capita. This table is obtained by dividing total consumption at current U.S. dollars (Table 2-6) by the corresponding midyear population (Table 1-2).

Figures

The following indicators have been used to derive the figures in this chapter.

Figure 2-1. Gross domestic product (Table 2-5); GDP per capita (Tables 1-2 and 2-5).
Figure 2-2. GDP growth (Table 2-1); export growth (Table 2-16).
Figure 2-3. Value added in agriculture (Table 2-2); value added in industry (Table 2-3); value added in services (Table 2-4); gross domestic product (Table 2-1).

Methodology used for regional aggregations and period averages in chapter 2

Table	Aggregations[a]			Period averages[b]	
	(3)	(4)	(5)	(1)	(2)
2-1	x				x
2-2	x				x
2-3	x				x
2-4	x				x
2-5	x			x	
2-6		x		x	
2-7		x		x	
2-8		x		x	
2-9		x		x	
2-10		x		x	
2-11		x		x	
2-12		x		x	
2-13			x	x	
2-14	x			x	
2-15	x			x	
2-16	x				x
2-17	x				x
2-18	x				x
2-19		x		x	
2-20		x		x	

Note: Regional aggregations are shown in the rows for Sub-Saharan Africa, North Africa, and All Africa. Period averages are shown in the last three columns. This table shows only the methodologies used in this chapter.

a. Regional aggregations: (1) simple total; (2) simple total of the first indicator divided by the simple total of the second indicator (same country coverage); (3) simple total of the gap-filled indicator; (4) simple total of the gap-filled main indicator divided by the simple total of the gap-filled secondary indicator; (5) simple total of the first gap-filled main indicator less the simple total of the second gap-filled main indicator, all divided by the simple total of the secondary indicator; (6) weighted total (by population); (7) median; (8) no aggregation; (9) simple arithmetic mean.

b. Period averages: (i) arithmetic mean (using the same series as shown in the table i.e., ratio if the rest of the table is shown as ratio, level if the rest of the table is shown as level, growth rate if the rest is shown as growth rate); (2) least-squares growth rate (using main indicator); (3) least-squares growth rate (using main indicator in constant terms, with the rest of the table in current terms).

n as ratio, level if the rest of the table is shown as level, growth rate if the rest is shown as growth rate); (2) least-squares growth rate (using main indicator); (3) least-squares growth rate (using main indicator in constant terms, with the rest of the table in current terms).

3

Prices and Exchange Rates

Information on prices and exchange rates are important in monitoring national economic performance. This chapter provides three sets of price deflators and six exchange rate indicators. The GDP deflator for national currency series shows changes in domestic prices only. The US dollar series GDP deflator includes the effects of both domestic price changes, as reflected in the national currency series GDP implicit deflator, and changes in the exchange rate between national currencies and U.S. dollars. The consumer price index measures the price changes of a selected bundle of consumer goods, which differs among countries.

The US dollar exchange rate (units of national currency per US dollar) is reported because of extensive use of U.S. dollars to denominate international transactions; U.S. dollars are also widely used for statistical comparisons across countries. The SDR exchange rate index (based on SDRs per unit of national currency) is a broader measure of the changes in the international value of domestic currencies because it is based on five major currencies. For Sub-Saharan Africa, it may be more representative of movements in non-dual exchange rates than that expressed in U.S. dollars alone because a large share of the region's foreign trade and debt is not denominated in U.S. dollars. A decrease in the index shows that the currency has depreciated, which indicates that foreign goods have become relatively more expensive than domestic goods. We have included information on the parallel market exchange rate and the ratio of the parallel to the official exchange rates to provide a measure of the premium on the official rate. It is tempting to view the divergence between the official and parallel rates as a measure of the disequilibrium in the official exchange rate. However, this is not necessarily true. Conversion factors are sometimes used in place of official exchange rates when the latter are considered to be especially unrepresentative of rates effectively applied to international transactions.

3-1. GDP deflator (local currency series)

	Index 1995=100											*Annual average*		
	1980	*1990*	*1991*	*1992*	*1993*	*1994*	*1995*	*1996*	*1997*	*1998*	*1999*	*75-84*	*85-89*	*90-MR*
SUB-SAHARAN AFRICA	24.8	60.9	63.9	65.4	69.9	90.0	100.0	108.5	117.1	121.6	127.7	24.2	46.6	92.5
excluding South Africa	26.8	61.4	64.1	65.1	68.5	89.9	100.0	108.5	117.3	121.3	127.4	26.1	48.7	92.3
excl. S.Africa & Nigeria	28.7	61.5	64.5	65.4	69.9	90.0	100.0	108.5	116.2	121.2	127.1	28.1	50.5	92.4
Angola	..	0.0	0.0	0.0	0.2	4.9	100.0	5,398.2	10,684.4	14,942.3	89,854.9	..	0.0	12,098.5
Benin	47.5	61.7	62.1	64.2	64.9	86.7	100.0	106.7	111.7	116.3	121.1	45.9	59.6	89.5
Botswana	20.8	63.4	66.7	71.5	81.1	91.5	100.0	112.4	122.2	131.8	141.7	18.6	45.2	98.2
Burkina Faso	50.1	75.3	71.6	70.3	71.3	91.0	100.0	104.2	106.5	109.9	108.4	49.1	70.8	90.9
Burundi	45.5	69.0	71.8	75.9	81.3	86.7	100.0	119.0	146.8	163.2	168.8	38.2	58.5	108.3
Cameroon	43.0	73.8	76.4	75.4	77.0	85.4	100.0	105.4	108.2	109.5	108.2	42.9	74.0	91.9
Cape Verde	32.6	81.1	84.5	87.4	89.1	95.9	100.0	105.8	114.5	119.1	124.2	30.1	67.1	100.2
Central African Republic	35.0	75.9	74.7	76.5	73.9	90.7	100.0	101.8	102.6	104.4	105.8	35.1	71.6	90.6
Chad	55.6	72.5	74.7	65.1	64.2	92.1	100.0	111.7	114.5	121.0	115.8	54.6	67.7	93.2
Comoros	41.7	81.6	88.2	82.3	84.6	92.6	100.0	102.0	105.1	108.7	112.5	52.3	73.5	95.8
Congo, Democratic Rep. of	0.0	0.0	0.0	0.0	0.1	17.7	100.0	713.1	2,049.0	2,356.3	2,639.1	0.0	0.0	787.5
Congo, Republic of	47.0	62.2	61.2	60.3	59.6	81.5	100.0	108.4	113.7	93.1	113.9	47.7	62.2	85.4
Côte d'Ivoire	50.3	64.1	64.5	64.5	64.5	91.4	100.0	102.7	108.6	111.6	113.0	45.9	69.3	88.5
Djibouti	..	..	82.9	85.7	89.5	95.3	100.0	104.1	106.8	110.0	..	..	..	96.8
Equatorial Guinea	..	61.4	63.6	63.7	63.2	97.5	100.0	125.4	160.5	121.9	168.7	..	64.5	102.6
Eritrea	..	..	..	57.0	73.6	89.8	100.0	102.9	105.7	108.5	117.4	..	..	94.4
Ethiopia	..	59.1	68.6	76.4	86.4	88.7	100.0	101.2	105.2	115.8	117.3	41.8	56.4	91.9
Gabon	50.8	76.2	67.5	67.8	68.5	100.6	100.0	112.8	115.1	97.0	101.7	46.6	64.2	90.7
Gambia, The	18.0	76.0	82.3	88.2	92.7	96.2	100.0	102.9	106.9	108.1	102.6	17.6	52.1	95.6
Ghana	0.8	30.6	36.7	40.8	53.7	69.8	100.0	141.1	168.6	195.5	222.8	1.6	14.4	106.0
Guinea	..	60.4	72.1	91.2	92.1	94.7	100.0	102.8	105.2	110.5	114.8	..	37.4	94.4
Guinea-Bissau	0.2	13.6	22.8	37.6	56.1	69.1	100.0	148.6	201.3	216.7	222.8	0.3	4.2	108.9
Kenya	18.7	45.5	50.7	59.6	66.5	89.9	100.0	108.5	126.1	137.7	147.1	19.0	35.9	93.2
Lesotho	18.9	58.1	66.2	78.2	85.4	91.8	100.0	108.6	117.3	127.2	136.4	18.5	41.6	96.9
Liberia	..	..	..	..	..	..	..	..	..	..	..	..	..	..
Madagascar	6.6	33.6	38.3	43.1	48.6	68.9	100.0	117.8	126.4	137.1	150.5	7.7	22.6	86.4
Malawi	6.6	26.1	30.1	34.1	43.7	55.2	100.0	158.9	171.3	217.5	309.3	6.9	16.5	114.6
Mali	37.6	61.8	63.1	64.3	66.0	84.4	100.0	105.4	106.5	110.8	108.5	37.1	59.6	87.1
Mauritania	33.3	71.4	78.4	86.3	90.0	95.7	100.0	104.4	110.3	121.3	123.6	33.3	60.4	98.1
Mauritius	28.7	72.3	78.3	82.5	88.9	95.4	100.0	105.7	111.5	120.1	127.1	26.5	53.8	98.2
Mozambique	0.6	12.9	18.9	27.3	41.3	65.8	100.0	143.6	160.3	164.0	174.2	0.8	4.7	90.8
Namibia	20.4	65.1	68.1	74.6	81.0	93.8	100.0	112.4	121.5	134.1	145.1	24.0	47.7	99.6
Niger	57.9	74.6	70.8	71.6	71.5	94.9	100.0	104.7	108.0	111.2	113.4	55.9	77.7	92.1
Nigeria	3.2	14.9	17.9	32.9	50.2	64.1	100.0	136.9	138.8	131.6	148.6	3.2	8.4	83.6
Rwanda	24.8	40.1	46.1	49.7	56.0	66.1	100.0	110.5	127.7	131.1	127.7	25.0	33.9	85.5
São Tomé and Principe	..	12.0	18.9	23.8	33.0	57.3	100.0	150.8	302.0	413.9	480.1	..	6.7	159.2
Senegal	41.4	74.9	75.2	75.7	74.6	95.3	100.0	101.3	103.7	105.7	107.9	40.8	71.0	91.4
Seychelles	62.9	93.7	91.8	96.1	99.1	100.2	100.0	99.6	102.5	104.5	106.6	55.2	83.4	99.4
Sierra Leone	0.1	13.1	25.0	40.1	50.8	61.1	100.0	103.0	120.3	152.8	191.1	0.2	3.4	85.8
Somalia	..	..	..	..	..	..	..	..	..	..	..	..	..	..
South Africa	13.6	55.2	63.9	73.2	82.8	90.7	100.0	108.3	116.8	125.7	134.4	13.1	36.3	95.1
Sudan	0.2	5.8	10.5	20.3	39.2	70.9	100.0	207.4	339.6	397.7	461.2	0.2	1.8	165.3
Swaziland	21.2	55.1	58.7	66.0	74.6	84.2	100.0	109.8	122.0	132.4	145.0	20.1	40.8	94.8
Tanzania	..	30.1	38.5	48.3	60.1	78.8	100.0	119.3	143.9	167.9	183.2	..	22.5	97.0
Togo	41.0	68.1	69.9	72.2	66.3	90.0	100.0	105.2	117.3	114.3	116.1	42.2	63.5	91.9
Uganda	..	36.0	45.3	65.8	85.6	91.4	100.0	104.6	108.7	120.3	125.6	0.2	8.5	88.3
Zambia	0.1	3.5	6.8	18.1	44.0	72.9	100.0	123.6	155.7	186.2	226.6	0.1	0.8	93.7
Zimbabwe	11.4	37.1	47.7	60.4	72.8	91.3	100.0	126.1	147.8	200.2	296.6	11.9	24.9	118.0
NORTH AFRICA	26.0	66.3	73.0	81.7	87.5	91.2	100.0	105.9	111.1	114.9	117.9	25.4	49.3	94.9
Algeria	10.8	28.4	44.4	54.8	60.6	77.9	100.0	125.7	133.8	128.3	142.3	9.8	17.2	89.6
Egypt, Arab Republic	16.3	55.7	63.7	76.3	83.9	89.8	100.0	107.1	113.4	117.4	119.5	14.4	34.4	92.7
Libya	..	..	..	..	..	..	..	..	..	..	..	..	..	..
Morocco	40.2	79.1	84.3	88.0	91.2	92.6	100.0	101.0	103.0	103.8	104.7	38.8	68.2	94.8
Tunisia	35.7	76.9	82.3	87.0	91.1	95.1	100.0	104.7	108.8	112.3	116.2	36.5	64.3	97.5
ALL AFRICA	24.8	60.9	63.9	65.9	71.4	90.0	100.0	108.4	116.0	121.2	127.1	24.2	46.6	92.5

Note: 1999 data are preliminary (see page 2). Group data are medians of individual country values for each year.

3-2. GDP deflator (U.S. dollar series)

	Index 1995=100											Annual average		
	1980	*1990*	*1991*	*1992*	*1993*	*1994*	*1995*	*1996*	*1997*	*1998*	*1999*	*75-84*	*85-89*	*90-MR*
SUB-SAHARAN AFRICA	107.3	99.0	100.4	102.1	95.8	91.9	100.0	99.2	99.6	91.9	90.6	84.9	85.8	97.1
excluding South Africa	153.0	119.5	115.7	110.3	99.5	91.3	100.0	106.3	106.5	100.1	99.9	122.1	114.0	104.9
excl. S.Africa & Nigeria	121.7	120.5	117.8	107.8	104.1	92.3	100.0	103.4	103.7	99.1	97.4	104.3	113.6	104.6
Angola	..	166.8	196.9	98.3	118.0	89.3	100.0	135.0	123.2	113.8	90.7	..	131.1	123.2
Benin	112.1	113.0	109.9	91.4	114.5	77.9	100.0	104.1	95.5	98.4	98.1	83.7	88.8	100.3
Botswana	71.7	89.8	96.1	92.6	99.6	97.1	100.0	103.6	94.0	94.4	100.3	57.9	68.3	96.7
Burkina Faso	118.3	138.1	126.7	88.5	91.6	81.9	100.0	101.7	91.1	93.0	99.1	89.5	105.4	101.1
Burundi	127.7	101.7	99.8	92.2	87.8	85.8	100.0	98.5	104.3	99.0	105.6	104.0	113.4	97.5
Cameroon	106.7	127.2	147.5	139.5	150.4	101.9	100.0	108.9	103.7	94.6	99.2	83.4	110.7	117.3
Cape Verde		86.1	89.0	96.6	85.7	86.6	100.0	97.2	94.4	96.5	99.1	..	77.4	93.1
Central African Republic	82.6	139.2	132.2	144.2	130.2	81.5	100.0	99.5	88.7	89.2	91.1	62.5	106.6	109.6
Chad	131.2	149.9	138.7	126.8	117.2	82.6	100.0	109.8	100.9	103.3	106.2	100.2	112.0	113.5
Comoros	73.9	112.2	117.1	116.3	111.8	83.2	100.0	99.8	90.6	91.0	92.7	61.8	82.7	101.5
Congo, Democratic Rep. of		101.2	107.4	108.4	137.0	113.7	100.0	93.4	103.0	114.2	117.7	85.5	83.5	109.6
Congo, Republic of	131.8	135.2	128.5	134.9	89.1	87.0	100.0	112.3	104.4	85.4	93.3	101.1	108.2	107.0
Côte d'Ivoire	118.8	117.4	114.0	121.5	113.6	82.1	100.0	100.2	90.6	92.3	99.6	82.9	102.8	103.1
Djibouti	..	..	82.9	85.7	89.5	95.3	100.0	104.1	106.8	..	..	..	68.5	94.9
Equatorial Guinea	..	112.6	112.5	120.0	111.4	87.6	100.0	122.3	130.3	..	128.3	..	96.1	113.9
Eritrea	..	..	..	83.9	80.5	91.5	100.0	103.0	99.1	95.5	..	..	..	93.4
Ethiopia	..	133.3	108.7	120.1	118.9	89.9	100.0	93.8	94.0	97.4	90.0	118.4	159.2	104.6
Gabon	120.0	139.6	119.4	127.8	97.7	90.4	100.0	112.3	96.2	101.0	..	82.9	94.7	109.4
Gambia, The	99.9	92.1	89.2	94.7	96.9	95.9	100.0	100.4	99.4	98.8	99.0	75.8	77.4	96.6
Ghana	105.0	112.4	119.7	111.9	99.2	87.6	100.0	102.5	97.8	101.9	103.9	93.9	112.5	103.7
Guinea	..	96.9	101.0	105.5	100.9	97.7	100.0	103.1	97.4	85.9	83.9	..	84.0	97.2
Guinea-Bissau	82.8	112.3	112.6	98.0	100.5	96.9	100.0	101.8	95.5	101.7	105.5	85.3	87.1	102.5
Kenya	129.5	102.1	94.8	95.1	59.0	82.5	100.0	97.9	109.9	118.3	113.6	104.1	105.7	97.3
Lesotho	88.0	97.5	91.0	99.4	101.3	97.2	100.0	89.6	91.7	79.3	81.4	71.1	71.6	92.8
Liberia	..	..	..	..	..	..	..	..	..	..	..	..	..	..
Madagascar	132.6	95.9	89.0	98.5	108.4	95.8	100.0	123.8	106.1	107.9	113.7	108.3	93.2	103.9
Malawi	119.5	140.0	157.4	138.7	145.5	91.9	100.0	140.0	147.9	96.1	98.6	103.2	107.4	125.6
Mali	90.0	114.8	113.1	122.6	117.7	79.9	100.0	103.7	91.9	95.3	100.2	67.8	90.1	103.9
Mauritania	94.1	127.9	124.1	128.5	96.6	100.5	100.0	97.8	93.9	81.8	78.6	87.4	111.9	103.0
Mauritius	65.1	84.7	87.1	92.4	87.8	92.5	100.0	102.8	95.0	90.8	92.5	54.3	66.8	92.5
Mozambique	175.8	123.4	116.8	99.6	98.6	98.8	100.0	110.9	120.5	121.9	118.3	188.4	197.9	110.9
Namibia	92.1	92.9	88.8	95.0	90.3	95.3	100.0	92.9	93.9	87.6	81.9	81.8	73.8	91.9
Niger	136.8	136.8	125.2	134.9	91.1	85.3	100.0	102.3	92.3	94.0	101.8	100.7	115.4	106.4
Nigeria	287.2	114.5	104.9	122.0	77.9	86.3	100.0	120.4	131.2	133.7	146.3	210.6	116.3	113.7
Rwanda	70.3	127.7	96.9	97.6	102.7	77.4	100.0	93.6	113.0	114.8	114.4	69.8	105.8	103.8
São Tomé and Principe	..	118.5	132.7	105.4	109.1	111.1	100.0	97.2	94.2	85.4	94.8	..	131.1	104.8
Senegal	96.8	136.1	131.9	141.4	130.2	84.9	100.0	101.3	90.8	91.7	93.7	73.8	105.5	110.2
Seychelles	46.9	83.6	82.8	89.3	91.1	94.4	100.0	95.4	97.1	94.6	82.6	39.3	67.4	91.1
Sierra Leone	115.8	80.2	78.5	74.4	83.0	96.4	100.0	103.6	113.4	88.5	..	103.1	104.2	90.9
Somalia	..	..	..	..	..	..	..	..	..	..	..	..	..	..
South Africa	70.8	83.2	88.4	96.5	93.0	94.0	100.0	91.5	92.0	83.2	79.8	54.3	61.9	90.2
Sudan	178.4	276.4	226.0	120.8	142.9	142.1	100.0	96.3	126.1	123.7	..	177.1	344.5	150.5
Swaziland	98.5	77.2	77.2	84.0	82.8	86.1	100.0	93.2	96.1	86.9	82.2	75.8	64.6	86.6
Tanzania	..	94.5	101.8	115.4	95.4	87.2	100.0	113.1	131.6	142.6	144.7	..	108.4	112.6
Togo	95.8	123.6	122.5	134.8	117.5	80.2	100.0	102.5	100.1	101.7	108.2	76.6	94.2	109.1
Uganda	..	104.9	76.7	63.8	66.4	77.4	100.0	96.4	95.8	97.6	85.0	72.9	147.1	86.4
Zambia	122.9	93.8	96.4	92.5	89.0	94.3	100.0	88.9	102.9	89.5	81.5	98.8	81.3	92.9
Zimbabwe	148.7	127.1	118.5	101.8	97.7	96.0	100.0	111.6	106.2	73.6	68.6	130.8	117.2	100.1
NORTH AFRICA	117.2	103.6	88.0	93.8	95.8	93.2	100.0	105.2	105.6	105.6	105.7	92.5	100.4	99.7
Algeria	134.1	151.1	114.4	119.4	123.7	105.8	100.0	107.6	108.5	108.9	..	108.5	147.7	115.5
Egypt, Arab Republic	78.0	86.2	73.1	79.3	86.9	91.9	100.0	109.0	115.5	113.6	..	70.4	85.5	95.1
Libya	..	..	..	..	..	..	..	..	..	..	..	..	..	..
Morocco	87.2	82.0	82.6	88.0	83.8	86.0	100.0	99.2	92.5	..	..	66.2	66.6	89.3
Tunisia	83.5	82.7	84.6	93.5	86.2	89.0	100.0	101.7	93.3	103.3	..	68.3	71.2	92.7
ALL AFRICA	109.2	100.4	96.5	99.4	95.8	92.4	100.0	101.2	101.6	96.5	95.7	86.3	90.7	97.9

Note: 1999 data are preliminary (see page 2). Group data are obtained by dividing GDP in current US$ by GDP in constant US$ series for each group.

3-3. Consumer price index

	Index 1995=100											Average annual percentage growth		
	1980	*1990*	*1991*	*1992*	*1993*	*1994*	*1995*	*1996*	*1997*	*1998*	*1999*	*75-84*	*85-89*	*90-MR*
SUB-SAHARAN AFRICA	20.7	57.4	63.9	68.9	70.5	89.0	100.0	108.0	117.1	127.3	134.1	9.8	12.6	10.6
excluding South Africa	21.9	57.0	63.8	68.7	70.4	88.6	100.0	108.5	117.6	127.8	133.9	9.4	11.4	10.7
excl. S.Africa & Nigeria	23.0	57.4	63.9	68.9	70.5	89.0	100.0	108.0	116.7	126.5	133.7	9.8	10.6	10.5
Angola	..	0.0	0.0	0.0	0.2	2.7	100.0	1,751.3	2,872.2	5,957.7	13,396.5	..	3.9	631.5
Benin	..	..	..	..	..	..	..	..	..	..	..	..	..	..
Botswana	20.7	56.6	63.3	73.5	81.8	90.5	100.0	110.1	120.6	131.3	142.3	12.1	9.5	11.0
Burkina Faso	59.6	73.6	75.4	73.9	74.4	92.8	100.0	106.1	108.5	111.3	114.0	..	-0.9	5.5
Burundi	28.9	60.0	65.4	66.5	73.0	83.8	100.0	126.4	165.8	186.6	201.6	13.4	5.4	15.0
Cameroon	33.6	73.2	73.3	73.2	70.5	79.5	100.0	106.6	112.1	115.3	117.6	11.5	6.4	6.2
Cape Verde	..	..	..	..	..	..	..	..	..	..	..	..	..	..
Central African Republic	..	72.0	69.9	69.4	67.4	83.9	100.0	104.4	106.1	104.1	106.6	..	-0.8	5.5
Chad	..	..	..	..	..	..	..	..	..	..	..	..	..	..
Comoros	..	75.5	77.7	95.4	96.1	98.2	100.0	103.7	108.0	112.8	108.0	..	3.9	3.9
Congo, Democratic Rep. of	..	..	..	..	..	..	..	..	..	..	..	..	..	..
Congo, Republic of	32.0	58.5	63.9	61.4	64.4	92.0	100.0	110.2	..	..	..	11.1	3.3	9.9
Côte d'Ivoire	40.2	64.7	65.7	68.5	70.2	92.9	100.0	103.5	106.6	109.8	112.5	13.3	5.3	7.0
Djibouti	..	77.6	82.9	85.7	89.5	95.3	100.0	104.2	106.3	..	..	..	7.1	5.0
Equatorial Guinea	..	..	..	..	..	..	..	..	..	..	..	..	..	..
Eritrea	..	..	..	..	..	..	..	..	..	..	..	..	..	..
Ethiopia	34.6	54.2	65.5	79.3	87.2	88.2	100.0	100.9	94.4	97.9	101.4	10.6	2.4	7.0
Gabon	41.0	72.2	76.1	72.4	65.9	96.7	100.0	106.2	108.3	116.0	107.5	12.5	1.0	6.1
Gambia, The	15.6	76.7	83.3	88.2	91.7	95.4	100.0	102.1	105.0	106.1	108.8	10.5	24.3	4.4
Ghana	0.8	28.3	33.4	36.8	45.9	57.4	100.0	146.6	187.5	223.7	246.1	67.9	27.7	30.6
Guinea	..	60.8	72.8	84.8	90.9	94.7	100.0	103.0	106.3	111.1	115.6	..	30.5	7.7
Guinea-Bissau	..	15.1	23.8	40.2	59.7	68.8	100.0	156.6	233.5	252.2	267.3	..	..	40.2
Kenya	..	34.4	41.2	52.4	76.5	98.5	100.0	109.0	121.2	134.1	141.3	..	10.0	18.0
Lesotho	15.5	54.2	63.8	74.7	84.6	91.5	100.0	109.3	118.7	129.1	138.4	14.2	13.7	11.0
Liberia	..	..	..	..	..	..	..	..	..	..	..	..	..	..
Madagascar	..	35.3	38.3	44.2	48.2	67.1	100.0	119.8	125.1	132.9	140.3	..	17.7	18.9
Malawi	5.5	24.5	27.6	33.9	40.5	54.5	100.0	137.6	150.1	183.3	267.9	..	20.4	30.6
Mali	..	75.2	76.6	71.8	71.3	89.0	100.0	106.5	105.8	110.1	111.1	..	1.3	5.2
Mauritania	..	70.9	74.9	82.5	90.2	93.9	100.0	104.7	109.4	118.2	122.9	..	6.8	6.4
Mauritius	32.3	71.0	76.0	79.5	87.9	94.3	100.0	106.5	113.8	119.4	125.3	14.9	5.3	7.0
Mozambique	0.4	14.4	19.2	27.9	39.7	64.8	100.0	144.6	153.8	154.7	157.0	..	68.4	35.8
Namibia	17.0	57.4	64.2	75.6	82.1	90.9	100.0	108.0	117.6	126.5	134.1	..	13.1	10.2
Niger	..	..	..	..	..	..	..	..	..	..	..	..	..	..
Nigeria	2.0	14.1	15.9	23.0	36.8	57.8	100.0	129.3	140.0	154.5	169.1	17.7	23.2	35.4
Rwanda	23.0	35.1	42.0	46.0	50.0	82.0	100.0	108.9	122.0	130.3	136.8	11.1	1.9	17.6
São Tomé and Principe	..	22.4	32.8	41.7	52.3	66.3	100.0	145.5	246.5	350.7	403.0	..	27.4	39.3
Senegal	40.7	71.8	70.6	70.6	69.9	92.2	100.0	102.7	104.6	106.7	108.8	9.7	1.7	5.6
Seychelles	68.5	92.3	94.2	97.2	98.5	100.3	100.0	98.9	99.5	97.0	104.6	10.6	1.5	1.1
Sierra Leone	..	13.4	26.9	53.4	71.7	84.6	100.0	133.5	146.4	154.9	..	..	92.4	39.3
Somalia	..	..	..	..	..	..	..	..	..	..	..	..	..	..
South Africa	14.9	58.6	67.6	77.0	84.5	92.1	100.0	107.4	116.6	127.3	136.1	12.8	15.7	10.0
Sudan	0.1	2.7	6.0	13.0	28.5	58.5	100.0	214.3	282.9	305.5	..	22.9	39.8	88.6
Swaziland	16.7	58.7	65.0	70.4	78.2	89.0	100.0	106.4	114.1	123.8	133.7	14.4	13.5	9.9
Tanzania	2.0	29.2	37.5	45.8	57.3	74.6	100.0	125.7	147.2	162.5	176.1	19.6	30.7	24.5
Togo	43.1	62.7	62.9	63.9	63.8	86.4	100.0	104.6	112.0	113.1	116.0	11.1	0.7	8.2
Uganda	..	38.9	48.5	68.9	88.5	94.3	100.0	107.5	115.9	122.6	128.7	..	158.9	15.7
Zambia	0.1	3.2	6.3	16.8	48.5	74.5	100.0	146.3	182.6	234.9	297.1	14.7	57.0	70.6
Zimbabwe	..	29.8	36.8	52.3	66.7	81.6	100.0	121.4	144.5	196.1	282.5	..	11.2	26.4
NORTH AFRICA	22.8	52.9	64.7	77.3	85.3	92.3	100.0	107.9	116.5	125.2	136.5	8.2	19.3	9.2
Algeria	12.1	30.6	37.6	49.5	59.7	77.1	100.0	118.7	125.4	131.7	137.0	10.9	8.9	19.9
Egypt, Arab Republic	..	52.9	64.7	77.3	85.3	92.3	100.0	107.9	116.5	125.2	136.5	..	19.3	9.2
Libya	..	..	..	..	..	..	..	..	..	..	..	..	..	..
Morocco	..	..	..	..	..	..	..	..	..	..	..	..	..	..
Tunisia	33.5	75.5	81.7	86.5	90.0	94.1	100.0	103.7	107.4	111.4	115.6	8.5	7.3	4.9
ALL AFRICA	20.7	57.0	64.1	69.2	70.9	89.0	100.0	108.0	116.6	126.9	135.1	9.8	12.7	10.6

Note: 1999 data are preliminary (see page 2).   Group data are medians of individual country values for each year. Some numbers for Angola are shown in scientific notation.

3-4. Official exchange rate

	National currency per U.S. dollar											Annual average		
	1980	*1990*	*1991*	*1992*	*1993*	*1994*	*1995*	*1996*	*1997*	*1998*	*1999*	*75-84*	*85-89*	*90-MR*
SUB-SAHARAN AFRICA	..	..	..	..	..	..	..	..	..	..	..	..	..	..
excluding South Africa	..	..	..	..	..	..	..	..	..	..	..	..	..	..
excl. S.Africa & Nigeria	..	..	..	..	..	..	..	..	..	..	..	..	..	..
Angola	0.0	0.0	0.0	0.0	0.0	0.0	0.0	0.1	0.2	0.4	2.8	0.0	0.0	0.4
Benin	211.3	272.3	282.1	264.7	283.2	555.2	499.1	511.6	583.7	590.0	615.7	276.7	342.6	445.7
Botswana	0.8	1.9	2.0	2.1	2.4	2.7	2.8	3.3	3.7	4.2	4.6	0.9	1.9	3.0
Burkina Faso	211.3	272.3	282.1	264.7	283.2	555.2	499.1	511.6	583.7	590.0	615.7	276.7	342.6	445.7
Burundi	90.0	171.3	181.5	208.3	242.8	252.7	249.8	302.7	352.4	447.8	563.6	91.8	131.5	297.3
Cameroon	211.3	272.3	282.1	264.7	283.2	555.2	499.1	511.6	583.7	590.0	615.7	276.7	342.6	445.7
Cape Verde	40.2	70.0	71.4	68.0	80.4	81.9	76.9	82.6	93.2	98.2	102.7	46.6	78.9	82.5
Central African Republic	211.3	272.3	282.1	264.7	283.2	555.2	499.1	511.6	583.7	590.0	615.7	276.7	342.6	445.7
Chad	211.3	272.3	282.1	264.7	283.2	555.2	499.1	511.6	583.7	590.0	615.7	276.7	342.6	445.7
Comoros	211.3	272.3	282.1	264.7	283.2	416.4	374.4	383.7	437.7	442.5	461.8	276.7	342.6	361.9
Congo, Democratic Rep. of	0.0	0.0	0.0	0.0	0.0	0.0	0.1	0.5	1.3	1.6	140,286.1	0.0	0.0	14,029.0
Congo, Republic of	211.3	272.3	282.1	264.7	283.2	555.2	499.1	511.6	583.7	590.0	615.7	276.7	342.6	445.7
Côte d'Ivoire	211.3	272.3	282.1	264.7	283.2	555.2	499.1	511.6	583.7	590.0	615.7	276.7	342.6	445.7
Djibouti	177.7	177.7	177.7	177.7	177.7	177.7	177.7	177.7	177.7	177.7	177.7	177.7	177.7	177.7
Equatorial Guinea	211.3	272.3	282.1	264.7	283.2	555.2	499.1	511.6	583.7	590.0	615.7	276.7	342.6	445.7
Eritrea	..	..	..	4.6	6.2	6.6	6.8	6.7	7.2	7.4	..	..	..	6.5
Ethiopia	2.1	2.1	2.1	2.8	5.0	5.5	6.2	6.4	6.7	7.1	7.9	2.1	2.1	5.2
Gabon	211.3	272.3	282.1	264.7	283.2	555.2	499.1	511.6	583.7	590.0	615.7	276.7	342.6	445.7
Gambia, The	1.7	7.9	8.8	8.9	9.1	9.6	9.5	9.8	10.2	10.6	11.4	2.3	6.4	9.6
Ghana	2.8	326.3	367.8	437.1	649.1	956.7	1,200.4	1,637.2	2,050.2	2,314.1	2,647.3	6.1	153.9	1,258.6
Guinea	19.0	660.2	753.9	902.0	955.5	976.6	991.4	1,004.0	1,095.3	1,236.8	..	21.1	370.4	952.9
Guinea-Bissau	0.5	33.6	56.3	106.7	155.1	198.3	278.0	405.7	583.7	590.0	615.7	0.6	11.8	302.3
Kenya	7.4	22.9	27.5	32.2	58.0	56.1	51.4	57.1	58.7	60.4	70.3	9.4	17.5	49.5
Lesotho	0.8	2.6	2.8	2.9	3.3	3.6	3.6	4.3	4.6	5.5	6.1	1.0	2.3	3.9
Liberia	1.0	1.0	1.0	1.0	1.0	1.0	1.0	1.0	1.0	41.5	41.9	1.0	1.0	9.1
Madagascar	211.3	1,494.1	1,835.4	1,864.0	1,913.8	3,067.3	4,265.6	4,061.3	5,090.9	5,441.4	6,283.8	297.7	1,083.7	3,531.8
Malawi	0.8	2.7	2.8	3.6	4.4	8.7	15.3	15.3	16.4	31.1	44.1	1.0	2.2	14.4
Mali	211.3	272.3	282.1	264.7	283.2	555.2	499.1	511.6	583.7	590.0	615.7	276.7	342.6	445.7
Mauritania	45.9	80.6	81.9	87.0	120.8	123.6	129.8	137.2	151.9	188.5	209.5	49.0	76.7	131.1
Mauritius	7.7	14.9	15.7	15.6	17.6	18.0	17.4	17.9	21.1	24.0	25.2	8.5	14.1	18.7
Mozambique	32.4	929.1	1,434.5	2,516.5	3,874.2	6,038.6	9,024.3	11,293.8	11,543.6	11,874.6	12,775.1	34.3	328.8	7,130.4
Namibia	0.8	2.6	2.8	2.9	3.3	3.6	3.6	4.3	4.6	5.5	6.1	1.0	2.3	3.9
Niger	211.3	272.3	282.1	264.7	283.2	555.2	499.1	511.6	583.7	590.0	615.7	276.7	342.6	445.7
Nigeria	0.5	8.0	9.9	17.3	22.1	22.0	21.9	21.9	21.9	21.9	92.3	0.6	3.7	25.9
Rwanda	92.8	82.6	125.1	133.4	144.3	220.0	262.2	306.8	301.5	312.3	333.9	93.7	85.0	222.2
São Tomé and Principe	34.8	143.3	201.8	321.3	429.9	732.6	1,420.3	2,203.2	4,552.5	6,883.2	7,119.0	36.5	69.7	2,400.7
Senegal	211.3	272.3	282.1	264.7	283.2	555.2	499.1	511.6	583.7	590.0	615.7	276.7	342.6	445.7
Seychelles	6.4	5.3	5.3	5.1	5.2	5.1	4.8	5.0	5.0	5.3	5.3	6.7	6.0	5.1
Sierra Leone	1.0	151.4	295.3	499.4	567.5	586.7	755.2	920.7	981.5	1,563.6	1,804.2	1.3	29.5	812.6
Somalia	6.3	..	..	..	..	..	..	..	..	..	..	9.1	175.6	..
South Africa	0.8	2.6	2.8	2.9	3.3	3.6	3.6	4.3	4.6	5.5	6.1	1.0	2.3	3.9
Sudan	0.1	0.4	0.7	9.7	15.9	29.0	58.1	125.1	157.6	200.8	252.6	0.1	0.3	85.0
Swaziland	0.8	2.6	2.8	2.9	3.3	3.6	3.6	4.3	4.6	5.5	6.1	1.0	2.3	3.9
Tanzania	8.2	195.1	219.2	297.7	405.3	509.6	574.8	580.0	612.1	664.7	744.8	9.2	71.4	480.3
Togo	211.3	272.3	282.1	264.7	283.2	555.2	499.1	511.6	583.7	590.0	615.7	276.7	342.6	445.7
Uganda	0.1	428.9	734.0	1,133.8	1,195.0	979.4	968.9	1,046.1	1,083.0	1,240.3	1,454.8	0.7	78.6	1,026.4
Zambia	0.8	30.3	64.6	172.2	452.8	669.4	864.1	1,207.9	1,314.5	1,862.1	2,388.0	0.9	8.5	902.6
Zimbabwe	0.6	2.5	3.6	5.1	6.5	8.2	8.7	10.0	12.1	23.7	38.3	0.8	1.8	11.9
NORTH AFRICA	..	..	..	..	..	..	..	..	..	..	..	..	..	..
Algeria	3.8	9.0	18.5	21.8	23.3	35.1	47.7	54.7	57.7	58.7	66.6	4.3	5.6	39.3
Egypt, Arab Republic	0.7	1.5	3.1	3.3	3.4	3.4	3.4	3.4	3.4	3.4	3.4	0.6	0.7	3.2
Libya	0.3	0.3	0.3	0.3	0.3	0.3	0.3	0.4	0.4	0.4	0.5	0.3	0.3	0.3
Morocco	3.9	8.2	8.7	8.5	9.3	9.2	8.5	8.7	9.5	9.6	9.8	5.2	8.8	9.0
Tunisia	0.4	0.9	0.9	0.9	1.0	1.0	0.9	1.0	1.1	1.1	1.2	0.5	0.9	1.0
ALL AFRICA	..	..	..	..	..	..	..	..	..	..	..	..	..	..

Note: 1999 data are preliminary. Uganda changed its currency in 1987 and Congo Dem. Rep. in 1993. Angola and Congo Dem. Rep. again changed their currency in 1998. Guinea-Bissau joined W.A.M.U. in 1997.

Prices and Exchange Rates

3-5. SDR exchange rate index

	SDRs per unit of national currency, index 1995=100											Annual average		
	1980	1989	1990	1991	1992	1993	1994	1995	1996	1997	1998	75-84	85-89	90-MR
SUB-SAHARAN AFRICA	..	..	..	..	..	..	..	..	..	..	..	..	..	..
excluding South Africa	..	..	..	..	..	..	..	..	..	..	..	..	..	..
excl. S.Africa & Nigeria	..	..	..	..	..	..	..	..	..	..	..	..	..	..
Angola	5.E+06	5.E+06	5.E+06	3.E+06	773,107	77,622	6,952	100	4	1	0	5,637,729	5,353,748	929,677
Benin	275	185	205	197	203	192	95	100	102	94	95	245	185	143
Botswana	416	163	167	152	140	124	109	100	88	84	74	402	188	115
Burkina Faso	275	185	205	197	203	192	95	100	102	94	95	245	185	143
Burundi	323	186	163	153	129	112	105	100	86	78	63	354	244	110
Cameroon	275	185	205	197	203	192	95	100	102	94	95	245	185	143
Cape Verde	223	117	123	120	122	104	99	100	97	91	88	240	122	105
Central African Republic	275	185	205	197	203	192	95	100	102	94	95	245	185	143
Chad	275	185	205	197	203	192	95	100	102	94	95	245	185	143
Comoros	207	139	154	148	153	144	95	100	102	94	95	184	139	120
Congo, Democratic Rep. of	7.E+11	5.E+09	3.E+09	3.E+08	8,131,608	422,108	3,010	100	..	..	..	1.E+12	2.E+10	5.E+08
Congo, Republic of	275	185	205	197	203	192	95	100	102	94	95	245	185	143
Côte d'Ivoire	275	185	205	197	203	192	95	100	102	94	95	245	185	143
Djibouti	117	118	112	111	108	109	106	100	104	110	112	130	125	108
Equatorial Guinea	275	185	205	197	203	192	95	100	102	94	95	245	185	143
Eritrea	..	..	..	..	..	..	..	..	..	..	..	..	..	..
Ethiopia	347	352	333	330	274	134	120	100	101	101	97	386	373	177
Gabon	275	185	205	197	203	192	95	100	102	94	95	245	185	143
Gambia, The	647	150	136	121	115	114	106	100	102	103	100	568	204	111
Ghana	50,406	524	408	359	296	201	132	100	76	64	57	76,474	1,429	188
Guinea	6,092	199	168	146	119	113	108	100	103	171	..	6,082	1,435	128
Guinea-Bissau	61,655	1,173	909	551	281	193	148	100	73	52	52	62,731	7,181	262
Kenya	796	292	247	205	170	100	98	100	93	96	94	727	369	134
Lesotho	543	164	157	146	137	121	108	100	89	87	74	510	202	113
Liberia	117	118	112	111	108	109	106	100	104	110	112	130	125	108
Madagascar	2,349	314	318	258	246	241	160	100	110	92	87	2,029	587	179
Malawi	2,199	656	627	605	470	377	211	100	104	103	59	2,087	910	295
Mali	275	185	205	197	203	192	95	100	102	94	95	245	185	143
Mauritania	330	182	180	175	164	119	112	100	99	95	77	347	212	124
Mauritius	264	135	131	123	120	107	103	100	101	93	85	284	155	107
Mozambique	31,524	1,404	1,057	704	385	259	154	100	81	84	83	33,628	13,389	323
Namibia	543	164	157	146	137	121	108	100	89	87	74	510	202	113
Niger	275	185	205	197	203	192	95	100	102	94	95	245	185	143
Nigeria	4,669	352	305	246	145	108	106	100	105	110	112	4,415	1,462	148
Rwanda	302	356	324	213	195	181	115	100	82	88	86	333	356	154
São Tomé and Principe	4,681	1,337	1,090	824	477	355	210	100	67	36	23	5,055	3,204	354
Senegal	275	185	205	197	203	192	95	100	102	94	95	245	185	143
Seychelles	87	100	100	100	100	100	100	100	100	104	101	92	100	101
Sierra Leone	81,552	1,495	569	297	159	141	133	100	84	85	53	78,935	8,296	180
Somalia	..	..	..	..	..	..	..	..	..	..	..	..	..	..
South Africa	543	164	157	146	137	121	108	100	89	87	74	510	202	113
Sudan	129,985	14,664	13,854	11,388	865	392	214	100	49	39	31	142,261	23,432	2,992
Swaziland	543	164	157	146	137	121	108	100	89	87	74	510	202	113
Tanzania	8,149	477	329	291	210	156	119	100	103	103	96	8,361	1,975	168
Togo	275	185	205	197	203	192	95	100	102	94	95	245	185	143
Uganda	1,520,277	545	256	150	92	88	105	100	97	99	88	1,025,920	7,512	119
Zambia	126,813	7,855	3,302	1,535	590	210	121	100	75	72	52	127,103	18,640	673
Zimbabwe	1,570	485	395	280	183	145	113	100	91	80	45	1,556	622	159
NORTH AFRICA	..	..	..	..	..	..	..	..	..	..	..	..	..	..
Algeria	1,441	741	600	290	234	221	150	100	91	91	90	1,447	1,103	207
Egypt, Arab Republic	565	493	267	127	110	110	106	100	105	110	112	823	592	127
Libya	136	137	137	137	131	123	115	100	100	100	..	152	147	118
Morocco	253	119	116	109	108	100	98	100	102	99	99	225	121	104
Tunisia	272	118	120	114	115	102	99	100	101	94	93	254	140	104
ALL AFRICA	..	..	..	..	..	..	..	..	..	..	..	..	..	..

Note: 1999 data are preliminary (see page 2). Guinea-Bissau joined the Western African Monetary Union (W.A.M.U) in May, 1997. Some values for Angola and Congo, Dem, Rep. are in scientific notation.

3-6. Currency conversion factor

	Units of national currency per US dollar											Annual average		
	1980	1990	1991	1992	1993	1994	1995	1996	1997	1998	1999	75-84	85-89	90-MR
SUB-SAHARAN AFRICA	..	..	..	..	..	..	..	..	..	..	..	..	..	..
excluding South Africa	..	..	..	..	..	..	..	..	..	..	..	..	..	..
excl. S.Africa & Nigeria	..	..	..	..	..	..	..	..	..	..	..	..	..	..
Angola	..	0.0	0.1	0.5	5.1	152.8	2,711.0	111,008	228,233	392,814	1,830,830	..	0.0	256,575.4
Benin	211.3	272.3	282.1	350.6	283.2	555.2	499.1	511.6	583.7	590.0	615.7	276.7	342.6	454.3
Botswana	0.8	1.9	2.0	2.1	2.4	2.7	2.8	3.3	3.7	4.2	3.9	0.9	1.9	2.9
Burkina Faso	211.3	272.3	282.1	396.6	388.5	555.2	499.1	511.5	583.7	590.0	615.7	276.7	342.6	469.5
Burundi	90.0	171.3	181.5	208.3	242.8	252.7	249.8	302.8	352.4	447.8	563.6	91.8	131.5	297.3
Cameroon	209.2	300.7	268.6	280.4	265.4	435.0	518.5	501.8	541.1	602.1	588.4	265.6	356.7	430.2
Cape Verde	40.2	70.0	71.4	68.0	80.4	81.9	76.9	82.6	93.1	98.2	102.7	46.6	78.9	82.5
Central African Republic	211.3	272.3	282.1	264.7	283.2	555.2	499.1	511.6	582.4	590.0	615.7	276.7	342.6	445.6
Chad	211.3	272.3	282.1	264.7	283.2	555.2	499.1	511.6	583.7	590.0	615.7	276.7	342.6	445.7
Comoros	211.3	272.3	282.1	264.7	283.2	416.4	374.4	383.7	437.8	442.5	461.8	274.7	342.6	361.9
Congo, Democratic Rep. of	0.0	0.0	0.0	0.2	3.0	970.9	6,254.7	47,729	124,416	129,101	140,286	0.0	0.0	44,876.1
Congo, Republic of	211.3	272.3	282.1	264.7	396.1	555.2	499.1	511.6	583.7	590.0	615.7	276.7	342.6	457.0
Côte d'Ivoire	211.3	272.3	282.1	264.7	283.2	555.2	499.1	511.5	583.7	590.0	615.7	276.7	342.6	445.7
Djibouti	177.7	177.7	177.7	177.7	177.7	177.7	177.7	177.7	177.7	177.7	177.7	177.7	177.7	177.7
Equatorial Guinea	110.6	272.3	282.1	264.7	283.2	555.2	499.1	511.6	583.7	590.0	615.7	146.9	342.6	445.7
Eritrea	..	..	..	4.6	6.2	6.6	6.8	6.7	7.2	7.4	8.5	..	..	6.7
Ethiopia	..	2.6	3.7	3.7	4.3	5.8	5.9	6.3	6.5	6.9	7.5	2.1	2.1	5.3
Gabon	211.3	272.3	282.1	264.7	349.6	555.2	499.1	511.5	583.7	590.0	615.7	276.7	342.6	452.4
Gambia, The	1.7	7.9	8.8	8.9	9.1	9.6	9.5	9.8	10.2	10.6	11.4	2.3	6.4	9.6
Ghana	9.6	326.3	367.8	437.1	649.1	956.7	1,200.4	1,637.2	2,050.2	2,314.1	2,647.3	17.5	157.0	1,258.6
Guinea	19.0	660.2	753.9	902.0	955.5	976.6	991.4	1,004.0	1,095.3	1,236.8	1,343.6	21.1	373.0	991.9
Guinea-Bissau	0.8	33.6	56.3	106.7	155.1	198.3	278.0	405.7	583.7	590.0	615.7	0.8	12.3	302.3
Kenya	7.4	22.9	27.5	32.2	58.0	56.1	51.4	57.1	58.7	60.4	70.4	9.4	17.5	49.5
Lesotho	0.8	2.6	2.8	2.9	3.3	3.6	3.6	4.3	4.6	5.5	6.1	1.0	2.3	3.9
Liberia	1.0	1.0	1.0	..	..	..	..	..	..	..	..	1.0	1.0	1.0
Madagascar	211.3	1,494.2	1,835.4	1,864.0	1,913.8	3,067.3	4,265.6	4,061.3	5,090.9	5,441.4	6,283.8	297.7	1,083.7	3,531.8
Malawi	0.8	2.7	2.8	3.6	4.4	8.7	15.3	15.3	16.4	31.1	44.1	1.0	2.2	14.4
Mali	211.3	272.3	282.1	265.3	283.2	555.2	499.1	511.5	583.7	590.0	615.7	276.7	342.6	445.8
Mauritania	45.9	80.6	81.9	87.0	120.8	123.6	129.8	137.2	151.9	189.0	209.2	49.0	76.7	131.1
Mauritius	7.7	14.9	15.7	15.6	17.6	18.0	17.4	17.9	21.1	24.0	25.2	8.5	14.1	18.7
Mozambique	32.4	929.1	1,434.5	2,432.7	3,722.7	5,918.1	8,889.8	11,293.8	11,543.6	11,874.6	12,775.1	34.3	328.8	7,081.4
Namibia	0.8	2.6	2.8	2.9	3.3	3.6	3.6	4.3	4.6	5.5	6.1	0.9	2.3	3.9
Niger	211.3	272.3	282.1	264.7	391.4	555.2	499.1	511.5	583.7	590.0	615.7	276.7	342.6	456.6
Nigeria	0.8	9.2	12.0	19.0	45.3	52.3	70.4	80.0	81.1	88.0	92.3	1.1	5.3	55.0
Rwanda	92.8	82.6	125.1	133.4	144.3	220.0	262.2	306.8	301.5	312.3	333.9	93.7	85.0	222.2
São Tomé and Principe	34.8	143.3	201.8	320.0	429.9	732.6	1,420.3	2,203.2	4,552.5	6,883.2	7,119.0	36.5	69.7	2,400.6
Senegal	211.3	272.3	282.1	264.7	283.2	555.2	499.1	511.6	583.7	590.0	615.7	276.7	342.6	445.7
Seychelles	6.4	5.3	5.3	5.1	5.2	5.1	4.8	5.0	5.0	5.3	5.3	6.7	6.0	5.1
Sierra Leone	1.0	151.4	295.3	499.4	567.5	586.7	755.2	920.7	981.5	1,563.6	1,804.2	1.3	29.1	812.6
Somalia	28.8	1,896.1	..	..	..	..	..	..	..	..	..	28.1	236.3	1,896.1
South Africa	0.8	2.6	2.8	2.9	3.3	3.6	3.6	4.3	4.6	5.5	6.1	1.0	2.3	3.9
Sudan	0.6	12.2	27.0	97.4	159.3	289.6	580.9	1,250.8	1,575.7	2,008.0	2,525.5	0.7	3.1	852.6
Swaziland	0.8	2.6	2.8	2.9	3.3	3.5	3.6	4.3	4.6	5.5	6.1	1.0	2.3	3.9
Tanzania	8.2	195.1	219.2	297.7	405.3	509.6	574.8	580.0	612.1	664.7	744.8	9.2	71.4	480.3
Togo	211.3	272.3	282.1	264.7	283.2	555.2	499.1	511.6	583.7	590.0	615.7	276.7	342.6	445.7
Uganda	1.0	319.6	550.9	960.8	1,201.8	1,101.0	932.5	1,012.0	1,058.1	1,149.7	1,362.1	2.1	53.2	964.8
Zambia	0.8	34.5	64.6	178.9	452.8	669.4	864.1	1,207.9	1,314.5	1,862.1	2,388.0	0.9	8.5	903.7
Zimbabwe	0.6	2.4	3.4	5.1	6.5	8.1	8.7	9.9	11.9	21.4	38.3	0.8	1.8	11.6
NORTH AFRICA	..	..	..	..	..	..	..	..	..	..	..	..	..	..
Algeria	3.8	9.0	18.5	21.8	23.3	35.1	47.7	54.7	57.7	58.7	66.6	4.3	5.6	39.3
Egypt, Arab Republic	0.7	2.2	3.0	3.3	3.3	3.4	3.4	3.4	3.4	3.4	3.4	0.7	1.4	3.2
Libya	0.3	0.3	0.3	..	..	..	..	0.4	..	..	..	0.3	0.3	0.3
Morocco	3.9	8.2	8.7	8.5	9.3	9.2	8.5	8.7	9.5	9.6	9.8	5.2	8.8	9.0
Tunisia	0.4	0.9	0.9	0.9	1.0	1.0	0.9	1.0	1.1	1.1	1.2	0.5	0.9	1.0
ALL AFRICA	..	..	..	..	..	..	..	..	..	..	..	..	..	..

Note: Off. exch. rate adjusted for some countries to better reflect the rate at which intl. transactions are carried out. G. Bissau joined W.A.M.U. in 1997.

3-7. Parallel market exchange rate

	National currency per U.S. dollar											Annual average		
	1980	1988	1989	1990	1991	1992	1993	1994	1995	1996	1997	75-84	85-89	90-MR
SUB-SAHARAN AFRICA	..	..	..	..	..	..	..	..	..	..	..	..	..	..
excluding South Africa	..	..	..	..	..	..	..	..	..	..	..	..	..	..
excl. S.Africa & Nigeria	..	..	..	..	..	..	..	..	..	..	..	..	..	..
Angola	..	1,850.0	..	..	1,266.7	1,087.5	31,740	203,138	569,574	163,370	283,139	900.0	1,837.5	179,045
Benin	209.5	302.1	324.8	281.8	289.0	270.1 '	288.0	586.4	499.3	516.4	593.3	304.2	343.9	415.5
Botswana	0.8	2.1	2.3	1.9	2.4	2.5	2.8	2.9	2.8	3.4	3.7	1.2	2.4	2.8
Burkina Faso	209.5	302.1	324.8	281.8	17.1	16.8	288.0	586.4	499.3	516.4	593.3	304.2	343.9	349.9
Burundi	106.0	169.6	214.0	186.1	269.3	310.9	370.7	409.4	340.8	369.6	459.2	122.3	161.7	339.5
Cameroon	209.5	302.1	324.8	281.8	289.0	270.1	288.0	586.4	499.3	516.4	593.3	304.2	343.9	415.5
Cape Verde	..	..	..	..	88.0	79.5	87.0	92.0	89.3	89.5	99.5	..	..	89.3
Central African Republic	209.5	302.1	324.8	281.8	289.0	270.1	288.0	586.4	499.3	516.4	593.3	304.2	343.9	415.5
Chad	209.5	302.1	324.8	281.8	289.0	270.1	288.0	586.4	499.3	516.4	593.3	304.2	343.9	415.5
Comoros	209.5	302.1	324.8	281.8	289.0	270.1	288.0	446.0	390.6	415.6	467.6	304.2	343.9	356.1
Congo, Democratic Rep. of	6.4	235.8	469.4	738.1	19,318.8	756,558	3,112,921	1,210	7,452	52,429	160,358	14.3	182.6	513,873
Congo, Republic of	209.5	302.1	324.8	281.8	289.0	270.1	288.0	586.4	499.3	516.4	593.3	304.2	343.9	415.5
Côte d'Ivoire	209.5	302.1	324.8	281.8	289.0	270.1	288.0	586.4	499.3	516.4	593.3	304.2	343.9	415.5
Djibouti	..	213.5	217.9	191.8	213.8	205.8	212.0	208.6	198.5	192.1	183.9	..	207.8	200.8
Equatorial Guinea	209.5	302.1	324.8	281.8	289.0	270.1	288.0	586.4	586.4	516.4	593.3	304.2	343.9	426.4
Eritrea	..	..	..	..	..	..	..	..	..	..	..	..	..	..
Ethiopia	2.8	6.6	5.9	6.0	6.7	9.5	13.3	12.0	10.7	10.2	7.5	3.5	5.1	9.5
Gabon	209.5	302.1	324.8	281.8	289.0	270.1	288.0	586.4	499.3	516.4	593.3	334.6	343.9	415.5
Gambia, The	1.7	8.6	7.4	8.3	8.8	11.5	9.1	9.0	10.4	10.8	10.8	2.5	7.1	9.8
Ghana	15.9	252.2	328.8	360.8	382.2	451.6	665.7	976.4	1,224.3	1,663.4	2,080.7	41.7	222.1	975.6
Guinea	41.7	538.9	580.1	693.3	793.0	1,608.1	1,156.9	1,074.1	1,017.9	1,025.9	1,125.3	102.9	453.8	1,061.8
Guinea-Bissau	..	1,800.0	..	..	4,173	6,075	9,883	14,013	19,167	26,855	..	..	1,800	13,361
Kenya	8.2	21.8	22.4	23.3	30.0	44.4	91.7	66.8	53.4	59.5	62.1	11.9	19.0	53.9
Lesotho	..	2.4	2.7	2.7	2.9	3.0	3.5	3.8	3.7	4.5	4.7	1.4	2.5	3.6
Liberia	..	1.5	..	..	..	..	40.0	45.0	42.3	45.8	48.5	..	1.5	44.3
Madagascar	265.0	1,671.7	1,639.1	1,589.2	2,071.3	2,239.2	2,217.9	3,122.9	4,397.5	4,551.7	5,582.1	521.1	1,133.5	3,221.5
Malawi	1.6	3.1	3.6	3.3	3.9	4.6	5.9	9.2	16.7	16.5	17.6	1.7	2.8	9.7
Mali	209.5	302.1	324.8	281.8	289.0	270.1	288.0	586.4	499.3	516.4	593.3	304.2	343.9	415.5
Mauritania	65.0	200.0	..	..	213.3	221.7	247.5	145.0	139.3	144.0	158.9	93.2	178.0	181.4
Mauritius	..	14.1	16.0	15.7	17.1	16.8	18.3	18.4	18.2	19.4	21.4	..	14.5	18.2
Mozambique	80.0	..	1,250.0	..	2,100.0	2,800.0	3,950.0	6,875.0	9,865.7	12,172.5	12,533.7	322.2	1,793.8	7,185.3
Namibia	..	..	..	..	..	..	..	..	..	..	4.9	..	..	4.9
Niger	209.5	302.1	324.8	281.8	289.0	270.1	288.0	586.4	499.3	516.4	593.3	304.2	343.9	415.5
Nigeria	0.9	6.7	10.7	9.3	6.7	21.9	56.8	71.7	78.3	81.8	84.7	1.4	6.4	51.4
Rwanda	115.0	98.7	109.8	104.2	209.1	238.9	297.4	286.5	268.1	331.8	360.5	135.4	111.4	262.1
São Tomé and Principe	..	..	..	..	222.5	360.0	432.5	810.0	1,503.3	2,407.5	7,300.0	..	..	1,862.3
Senegal	209.5	302.1	324.8	281.8	289.0	270.1	288.0	586.4	499.3	516.4	593.3	304.2	343.9	415.5
Seychelles	..	..	..	5.9	5.7	5.5	5.4	5.5	5.5	5.4	5.5	..	..	5.6
Sierra Leone	1.4	131.6	180.9	470.6	535.7	845.1	647.5	618.7	741.3	942.1	1,137.9	2.1	86.5	742.4
Somalia	9.9	319.2	398.8	1,982.1	4,675.0	6,095.0	7,456.3	6,961.3	6,549.2	7,789.8	5,919.3	14.7	224.0	5,928.5
South Africa	0.9	2.4	2.7	2.7	2.9	3.0	3.5	3.8	3.7	4.5	4.7	1.2	2.5	3.6
Sudan	1.0	11.2	15.9	43.6	105.3	62.4	31.6	45.3	77.5	147.2	171.2	1.3	8.4	85.5
Swaziland	..	2.4	3.0	2.7	3.1	3.3	3.8	3.9	3.9	4.7	4.9	..	2.5	3.8
Tanzania	21.0	211.0	263.5	292.4	348.5	405.9	443.5	523.2	587.3	604.7	656.9	30.5	175.4	482.8
Togo	209.5	302.1	324.8	281.8	289.0	270.1	288.0	586.4	499.3	516.4	593.3	304.2	343.9	415.5
Uganda	75.7	470.8	597.5	685.8	859.2	1,365.4	1,515.8	1,289.2	1,076.2	1,135.2	1,178.1	203.8	3,681.6	1,138.1
Zambia	1.3	30.3	107.8	121.2	133.3	104.2	531.0	805.4	935.6	1,281.8	1,583.0	1.7	33.5	686.9
Zimbabwe	1.1	3.1	3.5	3.3	5.3	6.7	7.7	9.4	8.9	10.8	13.9	1.7	2.8	8.2
NORTH AFRICA	..	..	..	..	..	..	..	..	..	..	..	..	..	..
Algeria	10.9	29.7	37.1	29.8	33.8	87.4	106.8	128.7	131.9	127.6	129.8	13.6	27.2	97.0
Egypt, Arab Republic	0.8	2.2	2.6	2.6	3.4	3.4	3.4	3.4	3.4	3.6	3.4	0.9	2.0	3.3
Libya	0.5	1.0	0.9	1.0	1.2	1.6	1.7	1.6	1.3	2.0	2.2	0.5	1.0	1.6
Morocco	4.1	8.5	9.2	9.3	9.2	8.9	9.4	9.4	8.6	8.8	9.7	6.0	9.1	9.2
Tunisia	0.4	0.9	1.0	0.9	1.0	1.0	1.0	1.1	0.9	1.0	1.1	0.6	0.9	1.0
ALL AFRICA	..	..	..	..	..	..	..	..	..	..	..	..	..	..

Note: Rates are annual avg. of month-end est., based on a sample of transactions. G. Bissau joined the W.A.M.U. in 97. New Ugandan shilling introduced in 1987.

3-8. Ratio of parallel market to official exchange rates

| | Ratio of parallel market to official exchange rates | | | | | | | | | | | Annual average | | |
	1980	1988	1989	1990	1991	1992	1993	1994	1995	1996	1997	75-84	85-89	90-MR
SUB-SAHARAN AFRICA	..	..	..	..	..	..	..	..	..	..	..	..	..	..
excluding South Africa	..	..	..	..	..	..	..	..	..	..	..	..	..	..
excl. S.Africa & Nigeria	..	..	..	..	..	..	..	..	..	..	..	..	..	..
Angola	..	6.18E+10	..	..	2.30E+10	4.33E+09	1.19E+10	3.41E+09	2.07E+08	1.28E+06	1.24E+06	3.01E+10	6.14E+10	6.12E+09
Benin	0.99	1.01	1.02	1.04	1.02	1.02	1.02	1.06	1.00	1.01	1.02	1.03	1.01	1.02
Botswana	1.03	1.15	1.14	1.02	1.19	1.18	1.16	1.08	1.01	1.02	1.01	1.23	1.27	1.08
Burkina Faso	0.99	1.01	1.02	1.04	0.06	0.06	1.02	1.06	1.00	1.01	1.02	1.03	1.01	0.78
Burundi	1.18	1.21	1.35	1.09	1.48	1.49	1.53	1.62	1.36	1.22	1.30	1.28	1.22	1.39
Cameroon	0.99	1.01	1.02	1.04	1.02	1.02	1.02	1.06	1.00	1.01	1.02	1.03	1.01	1.02
Cape Verde	..	..	..	..	1.23	1.17	1.08	1.12	1.16	1.08	1.07	..	..	1.13
Central African Republic	0.99	1.01	1.02	1.04	1.02	1.02	1.02	1.06	1.00	1.01	1.02	1.03	1.01	1.02
Chad	0.99	1.01	1.02	1.04	1.02	1.02	1.02	1.06	1.00	1.01	1.02	1.03	1.01	1.02
Comoros	0.99	1.01	1.02	1.04	1.02	1.02	1.02	1.07	1.04	1.08	1.07	1.03	1.01	1.05
Congo, Democratic Rep. of	6.86E+11	3.78E+11	3.69E+11	3.08E+11	3.72E+11	3.52E+11	1.24E+11	1.01E+05	1.06E+05	1.04E+05	1.22E+05	6.49E+11	3.25E+11	1.44E+11
Congo, Republic of	0.99	1.01	1.02	1.04	1.02	1.02	1.02	1.06	1.00	1.01	1.02	1.03	1.01	1.02
Côte d'Ivoire	0.99	1.01	1.02	1.04	1.02	1.02	1.02	1.06	1.00	1.01	1.02	1.03	1.01	1.02
Djibouti	..	1.20	1.23	1.08	1.20	1.16	1.19	1.17	1.12	1.08	1.03	:.	1.17	1.13
Equatorial Guinea	0.99	1.01	1.02	1.04	1.02	1.02	1.02	1.06	1.17	1.01	1.02	1.03	1.01	1.04
Eritrea	..	..	..	..	..	..	..	..	..	..	..	..	..	..
Ethiopia	1.35	3.19	2.85	2.90	3.24	3.39	2.66	2.20	1.74	1.61	1.12	1.70	2.48	2.36
Gabon	0.99	1.01	1.02	1.04	1.02	1.02	1.02	1.06	1.00	1.01	1.02	1.02	1.01	1.02
Gambia, The	0.99	1.28	0.98	1.05	1.00	1.29	1.00	0.94	1.09	1.10	1.06	1.06	1.10	1.07
Ghana	5.78	1.25	1.22	1.11	1.04	1.03	1.03	1.02	1.02	1.02	1.01	7.98	1.67	1.03
Guinea	2.20	1.14	0.98	1.05	1.05	1.78	1.21	1.10	1.03	1.02	1.03	4.62	3.42	1.16
Guinea-Bissau	..	105.43	..	..	74.13	56.95	63.72	70.65	68.94	66.19	..	..	105.43	66.76
Kenya	1.11	1.23	1.09	1.02	1.09	1.38	1.58	1.19	1.04	1.04	1.06	1.18	1.08	1.17
Lesotho	..	1.06	1.03	1.04	1.05	1.05	1.07	1.07	1.02	1.05	1.02	1.09	1.09	1.05
Liberia	..	1.50	..	..	..	..	40.00	45.00	42.30	45.80	48.50	..	1.50	44.32
Madagascar	1.25	1.19	1.02	1.06	1.13	1.20	1.16	1.02	1.03	1.12	1.10	1.53	1.05	1.10
Malawi	1.97	1.21	1.30	1.21	1.39	1.28	1.34	1.05	1.09	1.08	1.07	1.77	1.25	1.19
Mali	0.99	1.01	1.02	1.04	1.02	1.02	1.02	1.06	1.00	1.01	1.02	1.03	1.01	1.02
Mauritania	1.42	2.66	..	..	2.60	2.55	2.05	1.17	1.07	1.05	1.05	1.79	2.37	1.65
Mauritius	..	1.05	1.05	1.06	1.09	1.08	1.04	1.02	1.05	1.08	1.02	..	1.03	1.05
Mozambique	2.47	..	1.68	..	1.46	1.11	1.02	1.14	1.09	1.08	1.09	8.19	24.52	1.14
Namibia	..	..	..	..	..	..	..	..	..	..	1.06	..	..	1.06
Niger	0.99	1.01	1.02	1.04	1.02	1.02	1.02	1.06	1.00	1.01	1.02	1.03	1.01	1.02
Nigeria	1.65	1.48	1.45	1.16	0.68	1.27	2.57	3.26	3.58	3.74	3.87	2.09	2.24	2.51
Rwanda	1.24	1.29	1.37	1.26	1.67	1.79	2.06	1.30	1.02	1.08	1.20	1.44	1.31	1.42
São Tomé and Principe	..	..	..	..	1.10	1.12	1.01	1.11	1.06	1.09	1.60	..	..	1.16
Senegal	0.99	1.01	1.02	1.04	1.02	1.02	1.02	1.06	1.00	1.01	1.02	1.03	1.01	1.02
Seychelles	..	..	..	1.11	1.08	1.07	1.04	1.09	1.15	1.09	1.09	..	..	1.09
Sierra Leone	1.33	4.05	3.02	3.11	1.81	1.69	1.14	1.05	0.98	1.02	1.16	1.42	2.46	1.50
Somalia	1.57	1.87	0.81	..	..	..	..	..	..	..	..	1.45	1.76	..
South Africa	1.16	1.06	1.03	1.04	1.05	1.05	1.07	1.07	1.02	1.05	1.02	1.12	1.09	1.05
Sudan	20.00	24.89	35.33	96.89	151.39	6.40	1.98	1.56	1.33	1.18	1.09	16.25	23.50	32.73
Swaziland	..	1.06	1.14	1.04	1.12	1.16	1.16	1.10	1.08	1.09	1.06	..	1.11	1.10
Tanzania	2.56	2.13	1.84	1.50	1.59	1.36	1.09	1.03	1.02	1.04	1.07	3.02	3.08	1.21
Togo	0.99	1.01	1.02	1.04	1.02	1.02	1.02	1.06	1.00	1.01	1.02	1.03	1.01	1.02
Uganda	1,020.63	4.44	2.68	1.60	1.17	1.20	1.27	1.32	1.11	1.09	1.09	535.92	151.70	1.23
Zambia	1.65	3.67	7.80	4.00	2.06	0.61	1.17	1.20	1.08	1.06	1.20	1.69	3.17	1.55
Zimbabwe	1.71	1.72	1.65	1.35	1.46	1.31	1.19	1.15	1.03	1.08	1.15	2.09	1.55	1.21
NORTH AFRICA	..	..	..	..	..	..	..	..	..	..	..	..	..	..
Algeria	2.84	5.02	4.88	3.33	1.83	4.00	4.57	3.67	2.77	2.33	2.25	3.08	4.82	3.09
Egypt, Arab Republic	1.14	3.14	3.00	1.68	1.08	1.02	1.01	1.00	1.00	1.06	1.00	1.42	2.74	1.11
Libya	1.69	3.50	3.00	3.53	4.27	5.62	5.57	4.99	3.76	5.53	5.77	1.64	3.47	4.88
Morocco	1.04	1.04	1.08	1.13	1.06	1.04	1.01	1.02	1.01	1.01	1.02	1.07	1.03	1.04
Tunisia	0.99	1.05	1.05	1.02	1.08	1.13	1.00	1.09	0.95	1.03	0.99	1.02	1.03	1.04
ALL AFRICA	..	..	..	..	..	..	..	..	..	..	..	..	..	..

Note: 1999 data are preliminary (see page 2). New Ugandan shilling = 100 old Ugandan shilling was introduced in 1987. Some values for Angola and Congo, Dem, Rep. are in scientific notation.

Prices and Exchange Rates

3-9. Real effective exchange rate index

	Index 1990=100											Annual average		
	1980	1990	1991	1992	1993	1994	1995	1996	1997	1998	1999	75-84	85-89	90-MR
SUB-SAHARAN AFRICA	115.3	100.0	96.3	93.3	91.0	79.9	79.0	82.5	79.9	83.6	82.7	70.3	106.8	86.8
excluding South Africa	113.4	100.0	96.0	93.1	90.4	79.9	78.9	82.3	79.1	82.7	81.9	69.4	107.3	86.4
excl. S.Africa & Nigeria	112.0	100.0	96.3	93.3	91.0	75.8	78.4	82.3	78.2	82.5	80.8	68.6	106.8	85.9
Angola	..	..	..	..	..	..	..	..	..	..	..	..	..	..
Benin	..	100.0	98.7	102.5	102.3	65.7	75.2	76.0	76.4	82.2	..	..	93.1	86.6
Botswana	117.1	100.0	98.0	101.5	104.2	102.7	104.3	99.0	99.0	99.0	99.0	114.2	92.4	100.7
Burkina Faso	..	..	..	..	..	..	..	..	..	..	..	..	..	..
Burundi	129.8	100.0	100.4	84.5	81.7	85.1	92.2	97.9	85.6	87.9	90.1	159.6	137.1	90.5
Cameroon	88.2	100.0	95.7	96.4	89.8	57.6	66.4	67.3	66.1	65.7	71.3	84.0	98.8	77.6
Cape Verde	88.7	100.0	89.0	90.2	87.6	88.0	89.6	89.0	92.1	88.4	..	97.2	100.1	90.4
Central African Republic	105.9	100.0	94.4	94.4	89.7	56.0	66.0	67.5	65.2	64.0	64.9	100.7	101.7	76.2
Chad	102.3	100.0	100.6	108.6	111.6	58.7	64.4	66.8	66.9	66.9	66.9	114.4	108.5	81.1
Comoros		100.0	93.6	96.3	97.3		..	..	..	..	..	..	104.9	96.8
Congo, Democratic Rep. of	332.2	100.0	96.3	93.5	123.3	89.1	83.5	82.6	..	..	..	335.1	126.8	95.5
Congo, Republic of	102.2	100.0	89.5	90.0	89.2	69.3	79.0	75.2	77.6	79.9	80.8	102.2	102.1	83.0
Côte d'Ivoire	106.1	100.0	96.7	100.8	99.2	60.9	70.3	70.7	69.5	74.1	72.7	90.0	94.5	81.5
Djibouti	..	..	..	..	..	..	..	..	..	..	..	..	..	..
Equatorial Guinea	..	..	..	..	..	..	..	..	..	..	..	..	..	..
Eritrea	..	..	..	..	..	..	..	..	..	..	..	..	..	..
Ethiopia	92.5	100.0	108.6	98.9	44.5	37.9	38.5	35.4	35.8	35.8	35.3	92.5	109.5	57.1
Gabon	113.4	100.0	87.1	87.2	84.1	56.5	62.5	63.9	62.4	67.8	68.7	102.5	98.7	74.0
Gambia, The	100.8	100.0	97.1	103.2	103.1	95.9	95.3	94.8	99.6	98.2	96.0	97.0	81.0	98.3
Ghana	..	100.0	101.7	92.1	77.5	63.9	73.4	82.3	88.3	95.4	102.6	312.6	128.9	87.7
Guinea	..	100.0	104.5	96.9	100.6	98.5	92.8	95.1	94.4	93.7	80.6	..	116.2	95.7
Guinea-Bissau	..	100.0	91.2	75.8	80.8	71.8	66.4	69.6	78.2	81.3	..	..	100.0	79.5
Kenya	142.5	100.0	98.1	102.5	87.2	113.1	117.8	113.4	124.4	129.5	144.6	141.2	120.5	113.1
Lesotho	118.4	100.0	66.2	92.2	86.9	79.9	85.9	88.5	72.8	73.8	73.8	116.8	109.9	82.0
Liberia	..	..	..	..	..	..	..	..	..	..	..	..	..	..
Madagascar	193.1	100.0	87.3	92.9	102.7	90.2	81.9	104.1	96.3	96.7	96.1	200.0	130.3	94.8
Malawi	110.6	100.0	103.5	95.2	97.0	68.6	59.6	82.3	91.9	126.2	126.1	108.1	97.5	95.0
Mali	..	..	..	..	..	..	..	..	..	..	..	..	..	..
Mauritania	120.7	100.0	101.8	102.6	93.8	86.3	78.9	79.6	79.9	..	..	139.8	115.1	90.4
Mauritius	..	..	..	..	..	..	..	..	..	..	..	..	..	..
Mozambique	117.6	100.0	85.0	65.5	63.5	61.4	58.7	67.4	73.4	75.6	75.6	150.1	205.2	72.6
Namibia	129.0	100.0	98.3	103.3	103.5	103.8	104.4	96.5	99.6	84.6	83.0	133.6	105.3	97.7
Niger	..	100.0	87.4	82.8	79.3	55.2	62.1	63.2	62.1	67.8	70.1	..	108.0	73.0
Nigeria	350.6	100.0	85.0	70.5	77.2	142.8	122.1	167.7	193.1	203.6	193.3	431.4	282.8	135.5
Rwanda	83.3	100.0	76.0	73.4	85.1	128.7	78.0	85.2	102.2	103.2	104.8	60.9	112.9	93.7
São Tomé and Principe	..	..	..	..	..	..	..	..	..	..	..	..	..	..
Senegal	108.2	100.0	93.7	93.3	91.0	58.8	63.7	64.2	59.9	62.2	60.7	98.2	106.9	74.7
Seychelles	90.6	100.0	99.2	99.5	106.0	104.5	102.1	97.3	101.1	101.1	101.1	103.8	109.4	101.2
Sierra Leone	122.8	100.0	101.1	92.1	102.5	116.6	105.4	106.0	122.8	104.3	121.6	173.7	166.9	107.2
Somalia	..	..	..	..	..	..	..	..	..	..	..	..	..	..
South Africa	133.9	100.0	104.2	107.7	105.5	100.8	97.8	90.2	96.5	87.4	82.7	134.6	97.3	97.3
Sudan	45.0	100.0	176.9	28.2	27.9	33.0	25.4	25.3	26.2	19.9	21.5	43.4	47.1	48.4
Swaziland	..	..	..	..	..	..	..	..	..	..	..	..	..	..
Tanzania	..	100.0	98.8	86.8	94.0	93.6	97.7	118.3	125.6	135.5	135.5	..	138.3	108.6
Togo	..	100.0	95.0	96.5	93.1	61.9	71.8	73.6	75.6	82.7	..	117.5	104.9	83.3
Uganda	..	100.0	61.2	49.2	50.4	61.0	65.9	64.8	66.2	67.7	58.9	..	133.2	64.5
Zambia	135.0	100.0	93.2	89.3	101.4	97.5	93.4	97.7	117.0	127.4	134.4	143.7	85.3	105.1
Zimbabwe	165.4	100.0	66.2	92.2	86.9	79.9	85.9	88.5	72.8	73.8	..	167.1	127.3	82.9
NORTH AFRICA	151.6	100.0	98.2	101.6	103.8	106.2	107.6	108.9	109.3	110.7	118.7	147.8	120.2	106.5
Algeria	133.2	100.0	62.2	60.7	72.3	61.7	51.7	53.0	58.3	61.1	56.2	152.2	152.2	63.7
Egypt, Arab Republic	..	100.0	95.4	100.1	107.6	112.0	116.9	123.2	129.6	148.2	159.2	..	103.4	119.2
Libya	..	..	..	..	..	..	..	..	..	..	..	..	..	..
Morocco	156.8	100.0	102.4	103.1	105.9	108.3	111.9	113.7	114.7	117.5	118.7	139.6	109.3	109.6
Tunisia	151.6	100.0	101.0	103.1	101.7	104.0	103.4	104.1	103.9	103.9	..	149.8	117.0	102.8
ALL AFRICA	117.6	100.0	96.3	93.5	93.1	82.5	80.4	83.9	85.6	86.0	82.9	72.9	107.8	88.4

Note: 1999 data are preliminary (see page 2).

Figure 3-1. Real effective exchange rate, 1999*

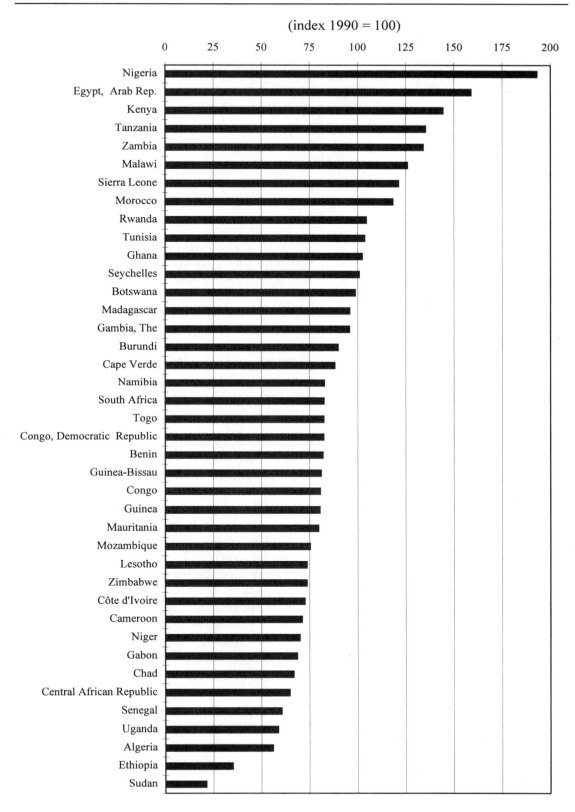

(index 1990 = 100)

* Or most recent year available.

Technical notes

Tables

Table 3-1. GDP deflator (local currency series). The implicit GDP deflator for national currency series is obtained by dividing, for each year of the time series, the value of GDP at current prices (World Bank country desks) by the value of GDP at constant 1995 prices (World Bank country desks), both in national currency.

Table 3-2. GDP deflator (US dollar series). The GDP deflator for US dollar series (with base year 1995 = 100) (World Bank country desks) is obtained by dividing, for each year of the time series, the value of GDP at current U.S. dollars (Table 2-5) by the value of GDP at constant 1995 dollars (Table 2-1). GDP at current U.S. dollars was obtained by converting current national series at single-year exchange rates, while GDP at constant 1995 dollars was obtained by converting constant national series at 1995 prices at a fixed (1995) exchange rate. As a result, the GDP deflator for US dollar series includes both the effects of domestic price changes and the effects of exchange rate variations.

Table 3-3. Consumer price index. Consumer price indexes (IMF, *IFS*, line 64) are generally compiled using the Laspeyres formula: goods in the consumption basket selected according to consumption patterns in the base year, derived from household expenditure surveys, are weighted by their relative prices in the base year. The data often relate only to selected representative income groups in capital cities or ma-

jor urban areas. Thus, the consumer price indexes shown for some countries may not accurately represent price movements because the underlying consumption basket may not be representative of overall national consumption patterns, and the weights assigned to prices may be outdated.

Table 3-4. Official exchange rate. The official exchange rate (IMF, *IFS*, line rf) is expressed as the annual average of the official market exchange rate in national currency per US dollar.

Table 3-5. SDR exchange rate index. This index is based on the average annual exchange rate for SDRs per unit of national currency (IMF, *IFS*, line rd-zf).

Table 3-6. Currency conversion factor. These are the annual exchange rates used by the World Bank (World Bank country desks) to convert national currency series into U.S. dollars. For most countries, in most years, the conversion factor is identical to the average annual official exchange rate. However, where the official exchange rate is judged to diverge by an exceptionally large margin from the rate effectively applied to international transactions, a more appropriate conversion factor is estimated. An alternative conversion factor is used when there are egregious differences between the official and effective transaction rates, when officially recognized multiple exchange rates have analytically significant spreads, or when exchange rates need to be adjusted to a fiscal year base. The objective in estimating alternative conversion factors is to approximate as closely as possible exchange rates actually used. For example, where multiple exchange rates are maintained, a transaction-weighted rate is calculated.

Note that national statistical compilers sometimes use an official exchange rate to assign a national currency value to international transactions originally denominated in foreign currencies. In these cases, the official rate must be used to convert the same items back to dollars, regardless of whether it was the rate actually applied to the international transactions, even if an alternative conversion factor is used for other components of GDP.

Table 3-7. Parallel market exchange rate. Data reported here are from *Pick's Currency Yearbooks* and *Currency Alerts* (now discontinued) and *Global Currency Report*. They are averages of month-end rates for the period covered, based on a sample of transactions, usually in a capital city or a financial center of the country. They include the rates at the *Bureaux de Change* that have been established in some countries with auction markets as semi-official foreign exchange windows for small transactions. The current table corrects some errors contained in *ADI 1994-95*.

Table 3-8. Ratio of parallel market to official exchange rates. This ratio is obtained by dividing parallel market exchange rates (Table 3-7) by official exchange rates (Table 3-4), to measure the premium on the official exchange rate. The premium is usually high in the presence of an overvalued exchange rate. This table reflects the corrected series for Table 3-7.

Table 3-9. Real effective exchange rate index. This index (IMF, *IFS* Database) gives a measure of price competitiveness of the country's exports relative to its trading partners. A decline (increase) in the index indicates real depreciation (appreciation) of the exchange rate. The data have been rebased to 1990. The year 1987 coincided with the early period of massive devaluations in the process of adjustment by several Sub-Saharan African countries. As a result, the substantial devaluations that continued to take place after 1987 may not be very pronounced in the data. Relative movements in the inflation rates between a country and the trading partner(s) may diminish the real impact of a devaluation, particularly if inflationary tendencies are stronger domestically than abroad.

Figure

The following indicator has been used to derive the figure in this chapter.

Figure 3-1. Real effective exchange rate (Table 3-9).

Methodology used for regional aggregations and period averages in chapter 3

Table	Aggregations[a]			Period averages[b]	
	(4)	(7)	(8)	(1)	(2)
3-1		x		x	
3-2	x			x	
3-3		x			x
3-4			x	x	
3-5			x	x	
3-6			x	x	
3-7			x	x	
3-8			x	x	
3-9		x		x	

Note: Regional aggregations are shown in the rows for Sub-Saharan Africa, North Africa, and All Africa. Period averages are shown in the last three columns. This table shows only the methodologies used in this chapter.

a. Regional aggregations: (1) simple total; (2) simple total of the first indicator divided by the simple total of the second indicator (same country coverage); (3) simple total of the gap-filled indicator; (4) simple total of the gap-filled main indicator divided by the simple total of the gap-filled secondary indicator; (5) simple total of the first gap-filled main indicator less the simple total of the second gap-filled main indicator, all divided by the simple total of the secondary indicator; (6) weighted total (by population); (7) median; (8) no aggregation; (9) simple arithmetic mean.

b. Period averages: (i) arithmetic mean (using the same series as shown in the table i.e., ratio if the rest of the table is shown as ratio, level if the rest of the table is shown as level, growth rate if the rest is shown as growth rate); (2) least-squares growth rate (using main indicator); (3) least-squares growth rate (using main indicator in constant terms, with the rest of the table in current terms).

4

Money and Banking

Monetary variables directly affect prices and exchange rates and indirectly affect real economic performance. Money plays a vital role in any modern economy. Data in this chapter are concerned with the creation of the types of assets that transactors in the economy wish to hold from the types of liabilities that debtors are willing to incur. However, emphasis here is on the creation of the means of payment, that is, on the more liquid end of the liquidity spectrum for assets.

Money and the institutions that deal in money provide cover against credit risks, limit transactions costs, help mobilize savings, allocate credit, and facilitate investment and hence growth of the economy. Data on money and banking help to assess the prevailing financial conditions of a country and to arrive at a proper evaluation of the financial policy options open to a country for achieving its macroeconomic objectives. The government usually intervenes in finance to control the supply of money and credit. The primary objective of such intervention is to maintain price stability. However, the government may also intervene to finance a budget deficit that in turn may threaten price stability. The government also ensures that financial institutions are properly supervised to ensure continued confidence in the financial system and to avoid destabilizing runs on the banking system. Time series are provided for nine indicators in this section.

4-1. Domestic Credit

	Level	Percentage annual change											Average annual percentage growth		
	1995	1980	1990	1991	1992	1993	1994	1995	1996	1997	1998	1999	75-84	85-89	90-MR
SUB-SAHARAN AFRICA	..	20	11	11	11	6	20	11	11	14	9	9	21	14	11
excluding South Africa	..	19	11	11	11	5	20	11	10	13	9	10	21	14	11
excl. S.Africa & Nigeria	..	18	11	10	10	4	20	11	11	14	9	9	21	14	10
Angola	8	..	..	..	..	..	..	..	404	340	156	-451	..	..	..
Benin	117,710	49	11	-30	-4	-26	74	21	4	-24	2	6	9	..	-20
Botswana	-4,747	-26	28	0	14	10	20	-3	16	146	19	0	..	-54	20
Burkina Faso	66,293	3	1	-10	-16	-5	4	-14	30	116	9	5	-32	68	9
Burundi	39,933	20	7	16	-6	4	16	-14	52	20	25	34	-12	..	18
Cameroon	791,344	28	-2	21	-34	-3	-1	-1	-4	6	9	9	-11	13	..
Cape Verde	21,027	39	15	27	17	19	23	19	11	21	6	11	-17	-4	-8
Central African Republic	63,333	39	1	18	-18	0	31	-4	-4	-2	11	14	-11	..	16
Chad	71,325	-1	-17	17	12	-15	30	-10	28	0	2	6	-11	..	-23
Comoros	12,449	..	18	11	8	-20	9	0	-18	3	-2	20	..	2	-8
Congo, Democratic Rep. of	7	22	341	1,404	2,862	1,648	5,299	182	..	..	..	..	3	84	26
Congo, Republic of	183,036	17	-4	3	4	-32	3	10	8	14	11	9	-2	-13	7
Côte d'Ivoire	1,540,052	23	-5	0	2	-3	6	12	3	8	5	-1	-20	35	11
Djibouti	45,598	..	-2	3	8	-2	10	17	7	-3	-4	-31	..	-36	23
Equatorial Guinea	20,829	..	-7	91	-10	-28	47	1	11	16	-15	36	..	..	6
Eritrea	..	..	..	..	..	..	..	..	..	..	..	..	..	..	..
Ethiopia	14,361	18	19	10	14	6	9	11	19	7	9	26	-3	7	0
Gabon	453,735	11	-14	3	-7	1	25	15	-4	14	26	-4	-13	-27	29
Gambia, The	281	23	-61	..	..	-17	-13	41	9	35	17	31	-3	..	..
Ghana	1,850,561	28	4	82	45	52	19	53	20	73	23	54	1	-12	9
Guinea	282,366	..	..	..	24	9	18	29	17	-7	-7	..	..	..	..
Guinea-Bissau	2,171	..	265	-70	30	52	14	-50	58	234	15	44	..	..	-11
Kenya	198,876	13	26	19	18	-2	50	37	19	21	9	10	-6	-13	-1
Lesotho	-212	..	-12	-4	-44	-45	-98	..	112	119	0	-99	..	25	..
Liberia	1,692	2	..	..	14	11	6	14	11	5	1,783	-9	7	30	28
Madagascar	2,506,189	50	6	12	28	16	29	-3	-2	2	29	10	1	-27	-3
Malawi	2,644	12	3	21	65	14	36	-3	16	12	-3	75	-16	31	12
Mali	136,883	5	-17	-3	2	12	20	15	0	29	29	18	-9	..	12
Mauritania	32,877	13	11	10	0	7	-1	-37	-36	-38	-66	-87	-16	44	..
Mauritius	46,369	14	16	25	19	25	23	13	6	26	22	9	-9	2	-3
Mozambique	887,600	..	25	38	-3	-39	131	28	-40	107	4	192	..	1	8
Namibia	5,595	..	..	10	91	29	28	31	22	-1	9	9	..	..	-14
Niger	81,241	45	-4	-10	-4	-17	25	-17	10	23	3	3	-3	..	..
Nigeria	444,710	23	34	15	128	64	57	7	-23	-3	-32	180	-21	31	14
Rwanda	44,016	12	16	-15	33	23	-7	-7	-2	61	13	13	4	10	0
São Tomé and Principe	22,360	..	..	..	..	..	..	..	22	-110	-783	-30	..	..	..
Senegal	538,122	16	-9	-2	-1	-2	7	2	7	2	6	8	-13	-13	9
Seychelles	1,615	12	11	10	11	25	20	15	16	23	31	15	-3	15	4
Sierra Leone	426,184	35	204	24	-8	1	1,076	-12	6	11	7	13	-3	1	-19
Somalia	..	31	..	..	..	..	..	..	..	..	..	..	-6	16	..
South Africa	333,490	21	16	..	..	12	21	12	18	16	17	9	3	1	-2
Sudan	46,238	22	39	56	153	65	48	47	114	18	24	23	-6	16	-9
Swaziland	328	0	38	-67	68	109	163	-36	-45	-15	-269	6	-17	..	..
Tanzania	693,880	24	72	13	23	40	11	11	-15	-1	17	23	-6	14	-8
Togo	169,769	13	14	10	-7	2	21	44	10	7	11	-7	-20	..	2
Uganda	234,994	64	..	..	..	-4	-13	-42	34	38	31	15	19	..	..
Zambia	1,921,138	17	90	137	..	..	123	63	21	0	71	13	-8	62	-15
Zimbabwe	20,496	28	19	29	43	59	20	19	27	83	41	7	..	15	-3
NORTH AFRICA	..	18	10	9	11	7	10	15	6	15	9	12	20	11	10
Algeria	968,930	17	13	17	32	17	4	25	10	10	9	25	-3	-13	1
Egypt, Arab Republic	157,300	42	26	8	4	7	13	17	14	16	19	12	-3	3	1
Libya	11,529	-11	10	9	1	4	10	8	-4	-16	2	-9	-11	8	-22
Morocco	166,721	18	-1	19	11	9	11	15	6	49	9	3	-7	-3	-6
Tunisia	9,746	19	6	8	11	5	6	7	0	15	8	14	-2	-5	0
ALL AFRICA	..	18	11	10	11	6	20	11	10	14	9	10	20	14	11

Note: 1999 data are preliminary (see page 2). Levels for 1995 are expressed in millions of units of national currency. Group data are medians of individual country values in each year or period.

4-2. Credit to the private sector

	Level	Percentage annual change											Average annual percentage growth		
	1995	1980	1990	1991	1992	1993	1994	1995	1996	1997	1998	1999	75-84	85-89	90-MR
SUB-SAHARAN AFRICA	..	15	14	12	7	11	14	17	13	16	14	11	16	14	14
excluding South Africa	..	15	14	12	7	11	14	17	13	16	14	11	15	13	13
excl. S.Africa & Nigeria	..	15	14	12	6	10	13	17	13	16	13	11	15	13	13
Angola	1	..	..	..	..	..	..	..	3,595	241	-1	381	..	..	..
Benin	80,447	34	-1	-16	-20	-2	11	7	27	-30	40	61	-17	..	..
Botswana	1,560	10	52	43	36	12	12	-3	4	9	39	43	-2	1	-8
Burkina Faso	80,590	4	4	-23	-12	-9	-17	9	13	80	10	3	-27	5	1
Burundi	30,648	14	35	39	7	35	8	-15	31	7	26	29	-9	57	-4
Cameroon	371,390	29	1	0	-55	-8	0	1	4	-10	23	12	-5	..	54
Cape Verde	10,391	-14	20	15	20	59	1	37	17	20	12	12	-10	3	-6
Central African Republic	23,159	50	-4	-9	-37	-5	17	24	0	4	16	-1	-24	..	-7
Chad	27,790	-2	3	-8	-1	-33	14	17	8	-3	17	0	-7	..	..
Comoros	9,525	..	43	7	3	-12	-3	10	-29	25	-17	23	..	-3	7
Congo, Democratic Rep. of	4	32	77	744	4,696	1,889	22,432	474	..	..	..	..	1	13	89
Congo, Republic of	85,683	23	6	3	-1	-46	15	13	14	9	5	41	6	-22	15
Côte d'Ivoire	1,016,035	12	-3	-1	-11	-5	-5	19	2	13	1	-7	-18	..	..
Djibouti	37,901	..	-5	-3	-1	-6	2	13	3	-1	9	-35	..	-32	..
Equatorial Guinea	3,397	..	1	58	-36	-75	13	51	82	94	18	51	..	..	30
Eritrea	..	..	..	..	..	..	..	..	..	..	..	..	..	..	..
Ethiopia	5,336	-1	-5	-1	22	98	26	47	54	16	7	17	7	..	-18
Gabon	196,080	16	1	7	-28	-3	0	25	-2	41	6	0	-12	-8	-2
Gambia, The	363	19	16	14	-24	59	7	-10	0	23	14	20	-7	-11	-6
Ghana	393,289	18	14	-6	56	35	46	44	73	70	42	50	9	-4	1
Guinea	181,518	..	..	..	34	22	11	26	4	-1	-13	..	..	..	..
Guinea-Bissau	6,129	..	72	7	27	78	53	-8	20	51	13	-22	..	..	-10
Kenya	118,189	20	12	22	31	5	28	50	24	25	1	11	-8	5	-11
Lesotho	739	-10	22	31	16	59	39	6	-10	10	7	3	-5	-1	-16
Liberia	191	-39	..	..	53	-12	64	-20	-60	36	1,040	-21	-10	79	..
Madagascar	1,563,020	26	28	12	6	15	26	16	2	14	1	7	14	-22	-15
Malawi	1,264	8	35	28	34	-12	54	5	12	15	98	6	-13	..	-10
Mali	131,787	8	0	2	7	3	-9	52	31	16	27	14	-22	..	34
Mauritania	31,417	13	13	11	2	3	3	-27	13	8	6	18	-10	30	-4
Mauritius	32,879	9	20	17	23	28	20	15	5	26	31	10	-3	-1	-4
Mozambique	2,374,200	..	32	44	45	14	58	54	46	50	27	32	..	40	-1
Namibia	4,743	..	..	17	30	30	31	34	19	16	9	4	..	..	-17
Niger	42,004	20	-8	-9	-4	-10	10	-41	3	-18	39	-3	-21	..	..
Nigeria	172,628	38	16	26	79	17	77	50	24	25	25	35	-19	12	6
Rwanda	28,538	46	-17	-17	26	17	-9	74	1	56	20	11	-20	-13	2
São Tomé and Principe	6,694	..	..	..	..	..	..	..	32	36	88	24	..	..	..
Senegal	357,834	16	-7	-4	6	2	-17	2	16	4	2	11	-20	9	9
Seychelles	245	3	8	9	5	10	21	17	10	44	19	9	-6	..	4
Sierra Leone	17,600	28	19	154	28	44	12	5	23	25	6	-13	4	31	-22
Somalia	..	-5	..	..	..	..	..	..	..	..	..	..	17	64	..
South Africa	327,114	26	14	..	..	11	18	16	17	14	16	10	7	4	-3
Sudan	13,068	29	55	83	90	69	96	48	144	23	13	-2	-2	-7	-1
Swaziland	928	15	39	40	3	9	22	2	6	12	6	6	-13	63	-16
Tanzania	201,015	11	30	32	-12	40	20	-10	-42	43	44	26	-1	78	-14
Togo	131,241	13	3	12	0	-8	-1	28	7	10	4	-10	-18	-6	5
Uganda	246,361	85	..	..	..	56	12	28	31	-1	33	22	5	..	-3
Zambia	253,971	10	61	57	..	..	98	81	47	10	3	31	-10	74	-20
Zimbabwe	15,276	18	28	70	42	44	29	28	21	49	37	13	..	116	-6
NORTH AFRICA	..	13	12	9	14	10	11	9	10	12	12	20	18	9	11
Algeria	103,499	14	18	32	-77	1	25	7	33	-21	19	35	-4	-13	8
Egypt, Arab Republic	66,777	-9	20	1	25	19	32	37	26	26	27	20	-3	-6	10
Libya	3,475	8	4	2	7	10	7	8	-17	8	0	28	-1	..	2
Morocco	90,906	13	..	34	15	11	11	15	10	54	12	9	-4	..	-5
Tunisia	9,274	22	5	9	14	7	8	9	1	12	10	10	-1	1	-6
ALL AFRICA	..	14	14	12	7	10	14	16	13	16	14	11	17	13	13

Note: 1999 data are preliminary (see page 2). Levels for 1995 are expressed in millions of units of national currency. Group data are medians of individual country values in each year or period.

4-3. Credit to the government

	Level	Percentage annual change											Average annual percentage growth		
	1995	1980	1990	1991	1992	1993	1994	1995	1996	1997	1998	1999	75-84	85-89	90-MR
SUB-SAHARAN AFRICA	..	21	8	8	21	8	35	3	7	4	16	9	25	11	8
excluding South Africa	..	23	7	8	21	8	35	4	7	2	15	9	26	12	8
excl. S.Africa & Nigeria	..	24	6	8	19	7	34	4	7	4	16	10	28	11	8
Angola	4	..	..	..	..	..	..	..	153	652	338	-673	..	..	..
Benin	36,262	-9	-511	-178	-172	-308	-274	73	-45	8	-125	1,037	..	..	..
Botswana	-6,521	17	31	7	19	11	19	-3	12	111	24	6	-11	-24	-1
Burkina Faso	-14,605	46	6	-51	4	-25	-115	-704	-63	-500	-7	27	..	-60	..
Burundi	6,347	3	-28	8	-42	-55	176	10	130	80	23	45	10	-50	15
Cameroon	368,878	40	73	-675	79	8	1	-4	-10	22	-5	9	..	..	-17
Cape Verde	10,069	-54	29	84	33	27	120	5	6	25	0	8	..	-37	-17
Central African Republic	32,521	26	-21	112	15	2	39	-22	-6	-5	5	7	-6	..	-20
Chad	36,281	0	-119	-766	510	22	45	-24	21	-9	-11	33	-10	..	..
Comoros	2,924	..	-24	25	23	-41	49	-23	17	-41	62	11	..	..	-13
Congo, Democratic Rep. of	1	19	396	1,399	2,945	1,629	3,724	-30	..	..	..	..	3	141	82
Congo, Republic of	82,754	7	-18	7	36	-6	-4	4	3	24	17	-17	8	..	-13
Côte d'Ivoire	510,099	-52	-11	6	70	2	35	1	6	0	13	11	-8	..	-22
Djibouti	7,233	..	-15	-48	-132	192	140	40	30	-16	-83	30	..	..	30
Equatorial Guinea	16,715	..	-29	230	23	4	52	-5	-5	-13	-44	21	..	..	..
Eritrea	..	..	..	..	..	..	..	..	..	..	..	..	..	..	..
Ethiopia	8,286	18	26	14	15	-1	5	-4	-6	-1	11	38	-26	16	1
Gabon	237,064	-3	-39	-9	75	7	54	9	-6	-13	61	-10	..	..	..
Gambia, The	-82	28	797	65	-113	-453	38	-60	-30	-43	-22	-194	-9	..	..
Ghana	1,223,690	33	9	165	44	63	3	61	10	85	18	50	-7	52	1
Guinea	96,400	..	..	..	11	-14	35	36	43	-16	-19	..	..	..	..
Guinea-Bissau	-3,959	..	557	-100	988	-979	324	72	-1	-108	85	1,383	..	..	-2
Kenya	64,657	8	57	14	0	-11	97	18	7	14	12	-8	-9	64	5
Lesotho	-962	329	-29	-36	-156	364	84	36	17	53	3	-53	-19	-9	-16
Liberia	1,473	63	..	..	10	13	1	25	21	4	1,837	-8	-29	28	36
Madagascar	943,169	81	-20	11	68	16	33	-24	-7	-21	102	14	-17	-23	7
Malawi	1,070	31	-34	-22	300	31	43	-20	3	12	-120	-408	-10	-27	-1
Mali	5,096	2	-77	-80	-374	-239	639	-84	-799	-37	16	-15	0	..	..
Mauritania	1,351	13	4	5	-6	25	-17	-85	-1,167	76	43	31	1	53	12
Mauritius	13,358	18	4	49	10	20	32	11	9	26	-1	-2	-25	..	8
Mozambique	-1,647,500	..	38	35	171	105	28	62	84	39	33	-6	..	..	-4
Namibia	724	..	..	57	-255	29	4	17	54	-91	46	228	..	..	22
Niger	39,237	-59	8	-13	-6	-39	102	50	17	62	-14	8	-12	16	-6
Nigeria	270,389	6	54	3	201	88	53	-9	-54	-54	-324	-240	-12	38	..
Rwanda	15,365	132	63	-13	41	28	-7	-50	-7	70	-1	19	..	-15	-4
São Tomé and Principe	7,829	..	..	..	..	..	..	..	137	-178	-68	231	..	..	..
Senegal	179,488	53	-15	2	-26	-23	174	3	-10	-5	18	4	-18	-25	..
Seychelles	1,277	52	13	8	15	26	17	19	20	20	35	17	-9	-15	5
Sierra Leone	408,563	37	260	11	-16	-14	1,691	-12	5	10	7	14	-5	-8	-20
Somalia	..	38	..	..	..	..	..	..	..	..	..	..	-28	-12	..
South Africa	6,376	0	51	..	..	51	112	-60	81	79	50	-7	-25	..	3
Sudan	31,507	13	40	62	174	68	34	49	105	16	30	29	1	29	-11
Swaziland	-600	27	39	102	-3	-6	-28	50	34	19	50	6	..	..	-18
Tanzania	492,865	25	121	1	55	40	7	23	-4	-12	6	21	-7	12	-7
Togo	38,278	14	-60	59	66	-57	-278	177	20	-3	32	0	..	..	-48
Uganda	-92,176	59	..	..	..	-25	-43	-166	7	-124	130	18	18	..	..
Zambia	1,630,301	23	99	154	..	..	147	61	17	-2	83	8	-29	67	-18
Zimbabwe	4,290	48	35	-32	117	103	17	-2	43	194	50	-8	..	39	13
NORTH AFRICA	..	14	10	6	5	1	2	2	-4	12	7	2	20	15	4
Algeria	403,286	24	6	-5	43	133	-11	-14	-29	49	28	21	-5	-17	12
Egypt, Arab Republic	52,820	14	26	4	5	-7	7	2	-1	9	17	2	-7	12	-12
Libya	5,693	-88	10	6	5	1	2	5	-4	-44	7	-73	23	19	-24
Morocco	74,178	21	-9	6	8	7	10	14	3	12	-1	-11	-10	3	0
Tunisia	473	2	13	6	-13	-14	-12	-16	-22	81	-17	97	-1	-26	..
ALL AFRICA	..	19	8	6	15	7	33	3	6	9	15	8	21	12	8

Note: 1999 data are preliminary (see page 2). Levels for 1995 are expressed in millions of units of national currency. Group data are medians of individual country values in each year or period.

4-4. Net foreign assets

	Billions of units of national currency											Annual average		
	1980	1990	1991	1992	1993	1994	1995	1996	1997	1998	1999	75-84	85-89	90-MR
SUB-SAHARAN AFRICA	..	..	..	..	..	..	..	..	..	..	..	..	..	..
excluding South Africa	..	..	..	..	..	..	..	..	..	..	..	..	..	..
excl. S.Africa & Nigeria	..	..	..	..	..	..	..	..	..	..	..	..	..	..
Angola	..	..	..	..	..	..	0	0	0	0	4	..	..	1
Benin	-23	4	41	65	70	160	146	173	215	206	298	-17	-43	138
Botswana	0	6	8	9	11	11	12	19	22	28	30	0	3	16
Burkina Faso	0	66	76	90	106	164	236	220	204	183	170	6	58	151
Burundi	5	10	18	30	35	45	54	47	46	32	33	3	6	35
Cameroon	-14	-185	-182	-182	-236	-318	-343	-302	-204	-195	-191	13	-60	-234
Cape Verde	2	5	4	5	6	6	5	7	6	6	8	2	5	6
Central African Republic	3	19	14	13	21	85	92	101	90	66	66	1	14	57
Chad	-4	32	20	11	-1	14	48	55	47	35	24	0	12	28
Comoros	..	7	7	7	11	16	16	19	19	15	20	4	6	14
Congo, Democratic Rep. of	0	0	0	0	0	0	0	..	..	..	..	0	0	0
Congo, Republic of	8	-8	-20	-19	-4	4	15	25	18	-44	-11	-3	-22	-4
Côte d'Ivoire	-223	-495	-474	-511	-515	-72	58	62	100	114	25	-211	-409	-171
Djibouti	..	42	45	35	37	36	34	28	26	24	34	21	32	34
Equatorial Guinea	..	-7	-9	-10	-7	-14	-10	-7	-7	-6	1	..	-5	-8
Eritrea	..	..	..	..	..	..	..	..	..	..	..	..	..	..
Ethiopia	0	0	0	1	2	5	5	4	5	6	5	0	0	3
Gabon	16	2	18	-29	-33	52	9	86	69	-64	-74	35	-20	4
Gambia, The	0	0	0	1	1	1	1	1	1	1	1	0	0	1
Ghana	0	-152	-11	-126	-146	14	181	206	244	311	-744	-2	-111	-22
Guinea	..	..	76	105	159	112	97	80	·151	176	..	..	..	120
Guinea-Bissau	..	-1	-2	-4	-5	-6	-4	-3	16	15	14	..	-1	2
Kenya	2	-5	-8	-6	30	16	24	47	56	54	55	1	-2	26
Lesotho	0	0	0	1	1	1	2	2	3	4	3	0	0	2
Liberia	0	..	-1	-1	-1	-1	-1	-1	-1	-28	-25	0	0	-6
Madagascar	-110	-2,202	-2,807	-133	-11	1	309	860	1,486	911	1,473	-150	-1,458	-11
Malawi	0	0	0	-1	0	-2	0	2	1	8	9	0	0	2
Mali	-8	27	65	69	74	107	120	184	205	172	126	-29	-33	115
Mauritania	-2	-16	-24	-32	-30	-33	-25	-11	-2	0	7	-3	-11	-16
Mauritius	0	12	15	16	17	16	19	20	22	20	26	0	3	18
Mozambique	..	-922	-2,002	-2,708	-5,674	-3,167	-3,541	-1,634	-869	-252	725	-26	-354	-2,005
Namibia	..	0	1	0	0	0	0	0	1	1	2	..	..	1
Niger	5	26	26	28	24	23	22	12	0	-9	-17	5	16	13
Nigeria	6	41	54	36	63	56	109	149	222	661	666	3	8	206
Rwanda	14	3	12	10	5	3	28	38	46	40	45	8	9	23
São Tomé and Principe	..	..	..	..	..	..	9	19	101	139	149	..	..	83
Senegal	-97	-188	-179	-172	-207	-130	-70	-46	36	78	119	-102	-233	-76
Seychelles	0	0	0	0	0	0	0	0	0	0	0	0	0	0
Sierra Leone	0	-64	-145	-188	-204	-339	-396	-159	-169	-220	-322	0	-11	-221
Somalia	0	..	..	..	..	..	..	..	..	..	..	0	-63	..
South Africa	6	1	..	-11	-16	-21	-18	-31	-23	-32	2	2	1	-16
Sudan	0	-1	-2	-37	-59	-122	-202	-444	-494	-687	-724	0	-1	-277
Swaziland	0	1	1	1	1	1	1	2	2	2	3	0	0	1
Tanzania	0	-131	-159	-295	-384	-278	-207	-68	245	275	374	0	-79	-63
Togo	0	70	74	54	23	43	33	13	14	8	23	21	62	35
Uganda	0	..	..	-243	-104	64	177	252	392	655	790	0	-3	248
Zambia	-1	-51	-102	..	-496	-788	-1,022	-1,287	-1,228	-2,397	-2,572	-1	-12	-1,105
Zimbabwe	0	0	-2	-3	-3	-2	-3	-3	-13	-30	-12	0	0	-7
NORTH AFRICA	..	..	..	..	..	..	..	..	..	..	..	..	..	..
Algeria	17	7	24	23	20	60	26	134	350	281	170	12	10	109
Egypt, Arab Republic	-1	-1	17	34	46	51	49	54	49	36	25	-1	1	36
Libya	4	2	2	2	2	2	3	3	2	2	3	2	2	2
Morocco	0	15	23	30	35	40	34	36	40	43	59	-1	-3	35
Tunisia	0	1	1	1	1	1	1	1	2	1	2	0	0	1
ALL AFRICA	..	..	..	..	..	..	..	..	..	..	..	..	..	..

Note: 1999 data are preliminary (see page 2).

4-5. Growth of money supply

	Level	Percentage annual change											Average annual percentage growth		
	1995	1980	1990	1991	1992	1993	1994	1995	1996	1997	1998	1999	75-84	85-89	90-MR
SUB-SAHARAN AFRICA	..	19	11	13	11	12	32	15	14	15	9	16	14	15	13
excluding South Africa	..	16	10	12	11	12	33	15	14	14	9	16	14	14	13
excl. S.Africa & Nigeria	..	14	9	11	11	12	32	15	14	14	9	16	14	15	13
Angola	3	..	..	..	..	..	..	..	3,393	108	40	326	..	..	..
Benin	161,730	32	24	12	10	-13	67	-13	17	2	-5	47	-5	..	-1
Botswana	829	10	16	5	-1	15	11	7	15	9	46	17	-10	16	4
Burkina Faso	213,703	20	-2	6	1	12	39	25	7	18	-3	-2	-8	-8	28
Burundi	38,802	3	9	11	10	12	28	-3	12	10	1	42	-11	-23	4
Cameroon	319,242	13	-7	3	-28	-14	35	-12	-2	35	14	11	-1	3	14
Cape Verde	11,867	26	8	9	31	7	8	3	11	22	-2	17	-11	-14	7
Central African Republic	111,237	32	-4	-3	-4	16	74	8	5	-8	-18	13	-10	15	-6
Chad	85,330	-16	0	4	-9	-28	32	43	33	-5	-8	-3	0	-26	..
Comoros	12,040	..	6	-7	9	5	10	-5	8	-19	-6	16	..	-4	4
Congo, Democratic Rep. of	19	73	176	2,387	4,114	2,461	5,635	407	..	..	..	..	31	30	54
Congo, Republic of	134,845	37	25	-7	6	-20	40	0	14	9	-14	28	1	..	-1
Côte d'Ivoire	944,519	1	3	-3	-4	1	62	18	2	12	13	-2	-15	..	20
Djibouti	36,998	..	9	16	11	4	3	-2	-3	-10	-10	4	..	23	-14
Equatorial Guinea	9,509	..	-57	-16	35	-29	135	58	50	-4	10	90	..	..	-2
Eritrea	..	..	..	..	..	..	..	..	..	..	..	..	..	..	..
Ethiopia	9,280	0	22	18	15	4	21	3	0	9	-8	13	-3	0	-8
Gabon	219,087	10	6	8	-27	-3	42	12	26	8	-5	-5	-17	-6	16
Gambia, The	471	6	14	33	11	6	-12	16	-4	39	0	14	5	-10	1
Ghana	925,287	30	11	14	53	28	50	33	31	45	17	3	1	-1	-9
Guinea	274,125	..	..	..	20	19	-3	9	0	21	9	..	..	..	..
Guinea-Bissau	7,211	..	729	-75	83	27	58	47	51	236	-12	22	..	..	-9
Kenya	69,333	-8	27	15	47	27	13	4	14	15	3	16	-2	-23	-10
Lesotho	521	..	8	18	12	23	12	7	22	20	27	-3	..	-13	8
Liberia	653	-4	..	..	-6	60	8	42	7	-1	129	15	1	-9	2
Madagascar	1,848,007	22	-4	31	22	12	57	15	17	23	11	20	8	4	-6
Malawi	2,211	7	6	31	19	35	51	44	24	17	56	33	14	-9	18
Mali	198,195	5	-11	9	1	9	48	14	21	6	5	-1	-7	-34	8
Mauritania	18,202	12	3	10	4	4	-5	-8	-11	8	33	-16	-4	-12	9
Mauritius	9,573	21	24	20	8	3	19	8	3	8	9	4	-13	5	-13
Mozambique	3,264,000	..	36	47	45	52	51	35	20	25	15	25	..	44	-10
Namibia	1,822	..	..	34	22	46	15	8	54	4	27	22	..	..	-8
Niger	100,238	13	-12	3	-10	11	15	9	-10	-19	-18	15	-4	3	13
Nigeria	204,415	50	30	41	59	55	46	16	14	18	20	20	-24	36	-8
Rwanda	40,658	7	5	8	25	11	16	41	12	23	-1	7	-11	-28	6
São Tomé and Principe	14,225	..	..	..	..	..	..	..	66	108	-3	4	..	..	..
Senegal	316,756	14	-12	4	2	-9	54	4	8	0	16	11	-30	7	11
Seychelles	335	38	-1	23	10	14	-3	3	34	44	20	37	-7	22	8
Sierra Leone	49,902	20	64	76	25	12	10	29	7	57	7	49	15	9	-12
Somalia	..	19	..	..	..	..	..	..	..	..	..	..	-8	38	..
South Africa	111,844	36	16	37	3	7	25	18	32	17	23	22	19	-18	9
Sudan	40,464	31	46	60	101	76	55	67	86	32	29	28	-3	19	-8
Swaziland	363	22	14	10	20	14	7	17	16	16	2	32	-15	2	-4
Tanzania	428,284	28	35	23	34	33	33	30	5	10	10	16	-21	109	-12
Togo	131,199	5	19	4	-27	-18	105	38	-8	2	7	10	-19	..	-9
Uganda	408,701	32	50	50	61	26	36	15	10	14	19	13	9	-10	-16
Zambia	227,058	0	61	78	..	..	45	61	19	31	17	24	4	29	-11
Zimbabwe	11,270	37	28	23	6	95	18	52	23	54	24	35	12	8	7
NORTH AFRICA	..	21	17	8	9	5	11	7	7	13	8	9	19	9	8
Algeria	520,286	17	8	20	16	19	8	7	13	15	21	9	-4	-9	0
Egypt, Arab Republic	41,540	56	17	8	9	12	11	9	7	9	20	1	-5	-7	-10
Libya	6,251	29	26	-4	16	4	13	6	1	5	0	5	-3	..	-24
Morocco	135,964	8	37	14	6	5	11	6	6	16	8	12	-11	7	-5
Tunisia	3,637	21	6	1	7	4	11	10	13	13	8	16	-2	-23	25
ALL AFRICA	..	19	12	12	10	12	25	12	13	14	9	15	15	14	12

Note: 1999 data are preliminary (see page 2). Levels for 1995 are expressed in millions of units of national currency. Group data are medians of individual country values in each year or period.

4-6. Discount rate

					Percentage						Annual average		
	1980	1990	1991	1992	1993	1994	1995	1996	1997	1998	75-84	85-89	90-MR
SUB-SAHARAN AFRICA	8.5	11.0	11.3	12.5	11.8	12.5	13.3	13.5	11.6	11.4	8.4	9.8	12.1
excluding South Africa	8.5	11.0	11.1	12.5	11.5	12.0	13.1	13.3	10.8	10.2	8.2	9.7	11.7
excl. S.Africa & Nigeria	8.5	11.0	11.0	12.5	11.5	12.0	13.0	13.0	10.6	9.1	8.4	9.7	11.5
Angola	..	..	..	..	..	..	160.0	2.0	48.0	58.0	..	..	67.0
Benin	10.5	11.0	11.0	12.5	10.5	10.0	7.5	6.5	6.0	6.3	9.5	9.6	9.0
Botswana	5.8	8.5	12.0	14.3	14.3	13.5	13.0	13.0	12.5	12.5	8.3	7.9	12.6
Burkina Faso	10.5	11.0	11.0	12.5	10.5	10.0	7.5	6.5	6.0	6.3	9.5	9.6	9.0
Burundi	7.0	8.0	10.7	9.8	9.8	9.4	9.9	..	..	..	6.4	6.6	9.6
Cameroon	8.5	11.0	10.8	12.0	11.5	7.8	8.6	7.8	7.5	7.0	7.6	8.9	9.3
Cape Verde	..	..	..	..	..	..	..	..	..	..	..	..	..
Central African Republic	8.5	11.0	10.8	12.0	11.5	7.8	8.6	7.8	7.5	7.5	7.6	8.9	9.4
Chad	8.5	11.0	10.8	12.0	11.5	7.8	8.6	7.8	7.5	7.0	7.7	8.9	9.3
Comoros	..	..	..	..	..	..	..	..	..	..	10.0	9.3	..
Congo, Democratic Rep. of	12.0	45.0	55.0	55.0	95.0	145.0	125.0	238.0	..	..	14.7	33.6	108.3
Congo, Republic of	8.5	11.0	10.8	12.0	11.5	7.8	8.6	7.8	7.5	7.0	7.6	8.9	9.3
Côte d'Ivoire	10.5	11.0	11.0	12.5	10.5	10.0	7.5	6.5	6.0	6.3	9.5	9.6	9.0
Djibouti	..	..	..	..	..	..	..	..	..	..	..	..	..
Equatorial Guinea	..	11.0	10.8	12.0	11.5	7.8	8.6	7.8	7.5	7.0	..	8.9	9.3
Eritrea	..	..	..	..	..	..	..	..	..	..	..	..	..
Ethiopia	..	3.0	3.0	5.3	12.0	12.0	12.0	..	..	..	..	4.2	7.9
Gabon	8.5	11.0	10.8	12.0	11.5	7.8	8.6	7.8	7.5	7.0	7.6	8.9	9.3
Gambia, The	8.0	16.5	15.5	17.5	13.5	13.5	14.0	14.0	14.0	13.0	7.6	18.0	14.6
Ghana	13.5	33.0	20.0	30.0	35.0	33.0	45.0	45.0	45.0	37.0	12.7	22.9	35.9
Guinea	..	15.0	19.0	19.0	17.0	17.0	18.0	18.0	15.0	..	..	10.5	17.3
Guinea-Bissau	..	42.0	42.0	45.5	41.0	26.0	39.0	54.0	6.0	..	..	..	36.9
Kenya	8.0	19.4	20.3	20.5	45.5	21.5	24.5	26.9	32.3	17.1	9.9	14.0	25.3
Lesotho	8.0	15.8	18.0	15.0	13.5	13.5	15.5	17.0	15.6	19.5	11.8	12.6	15.9
Liberia	..	..	..	..	..	..	..	..	..	..	..	..	..
Madagascar	5.5	..	..	..	..	..	..	..	..	..	8.0	11.5	..
Malawi	10.0	14.0	13.0	20.0	25.0	40.0	50.0	27.0	23.0	43.0	8.5	11.6	28.3
Mali	10.5	11.0	11.0	12.5	10.5	10.0	7.5	6.5	6.0	6.3	9.5	9.6	9.0
Mauritania	6.0	7.0	7.0	7.0	..	..	..	..	..	..	5.5	6.6	7.0
Mauritius	10.5	12.0	11.3	8.3	8.3	13.8	11.4	11.8	10.5	17.2	9.5	10.8	11.6
Mozambique	..	..	..	..	..	..	..	..	..	..	..	..	..
Namibia	..	..	20.5	16.5	14.5	15.5	17.5	17.8	16.0	18.8	..	..	17.1
Niger	10.5	11.0	11.0	12.5	10.5	10.0	7.5	6.5	6.0	6.3	9.5	9.4	9.0
Nigeria	6.0	18.5	15.5	17.5	26.0	13.5	13.5	13.5	13.5	13.5	5.9	12.8	16.1
Rwanda	9.0	14.0	14.0	11.0	11.0	11.0	16.0	16.0	10.8	11.4	7.4	9.0	12.8
São Tomé and Principe	..	25.0	45.0	45.0	30.0	32.0	50.0	35.0	55.0	38.5	..	25.0	39.5
Senegal	10.5	11.0	11.0	12.5	10.5	10.0	7.5	6.5	6.0	6.3	9.5	9.6	9.0
Seychelles	..	1.0	1.0	1.0	1.0	1.0	1.0	1.0	1.0	1.0	6.0	6.0	1.0
Sierra Leone	12.0	55.0	..	..	..	..	..	..	..	..	10.2	15.6	55.0
Somalia	4.0	..	..	..	..	..	..	..	..	..	5.2	25.2	..
South Africa	6.5	18.0	17.0	14.0	12.0	13.0	15.0	17.0	16.0	19.3	11.1	12.9	15.7
Sudan	..	..	..	..	..	..	..	..	..	..	..	..	..
Swaziland	7.0	12.0	13.0	12.0	11.0	12.0	15.0	16.8	15.8	18.0	11.1	10.8	13.9
Tanzania	4.8	..	..	14.5	14.5	67.5	47.9	19.0	16.2	17.6	4.5	11.1	28.2
Togo	10.5	11.0	11.0	12.5	10.5	10.0	7.5	6.5	6.0	6.3	9.5	9.6	9.0
Uganda	8.0	50.0	46.0	41.0	24.0	15.0	13.3	15.9	14.1	9.1	13.7	38.2	25.4
Zambia	6.5	..	..	47.0	72.5	20.5	40.2	47.0	17.7	..	7.5	21.3	40.8
Zimbabwe	4.5	10.3	20.0	29.5	28.5	29.5	29.5	27.0	31.5	39.5	6.3	9.0	27.3
NORTH AFRICA	5.9	11.9	11.9	11.4	8.9	8.9	11.2	10.4	12.3	12.0	6.0	9.4	11.0
Algeria	..	..	..	..	..	..	..	..	..	..	..	..	..
Egypt, Arab Republic	11.0	14.0	20.0	18.4	16.5	14.0	13.5	13.0	12.3	12.0	9.7	13.2	14.8
Libya	5.0	5.0	5.0	5.0	5.0	..	..	..	..	..	5.0	5.0	5.0
Morocco	6.0	..	..	..	..	7.0	..	..	..	..	5.6	8.5	7.0
Tunisia	5.8	11.9	11.9	11.4	8.9	8.9	8.9	7.9	..	..	6.1	9.7	10.0
ALL AFRICA	8.5	11.0	11.6	12.5	11.5	12.0	13.3	13.0	12.3	11.7	8.1	9.8	12.1

Note: Group data are medians of individual country values in each year or period.

4-7. Real discount rate

	Percentage										Annual average		
	1980	1990	1991	1992	1993	1994	1995	1996	1997	1998	75-84	85-89	90-MR
SUB-SAHARAN AFRICA	-4.1	3.1	1.6	1.7	2.6	-0.8	-0.1	2.4	4.8	4.2	-3.5	1.2	2.2
excluding South Africa	-3.6	3.1	1.6	2.1	3.1	-1.2	-0.2	2.1	4.5	4.2	-3.9	1.3	2.1
excl. S.Africa & Nigeria	-3.9	3.1	1.6	2.8	3.6	-0.8	-0.1	2.4	4.2	4.2	-3.4	1.3	2.3
Angola	..	..	..	..	..	..	-93.1	-94.2	-9.8	-23.8	..	..	-55.2
Benin	..	..	..	..	..	..	..	..	..	..	..	..	..
Botswana	-6.9	-2.6	0.2	-1.6	2.6	2.6	2.3	2.6	2.7	3.3	-3.1	-1.5	1.3
Burkina Faso	..	11.9	8.3	14.8	9.8	-11.8	-0.3	0.4	3.6	3.7	3.9	10.6	4.5
Burundi	-2.3	0.9	1.6	7.9	0.1	-4.7	-7.9	..	..	..	-5.6	0.9	-0.4
Cameroon	-1.0	9.8	10.6	12.1	15.8	-4.4	-13.7	1.1	2.2	4.1	-3.8	3.1	4.2
Cape Verde	..	..	..	..	..	..	..	..	..	..	..	..	..
Central African Republic	..	11.2	14.0	12.9	14.8	-13.5	-8.9	3.2	5.8	9.6	-1.3	8.7	5.5
Chad	..	..	..	..	..	..	..	..	..	..	..	..	..
Comoros	..	..	..	..	..	..	..	..	..	..	2.4	6.2	..
Congo, Democratic Rep. of	..	..	..	..	..	..	..	..	..	..	..	..	..
Congo, Republic of	1.2	16.5	1.5	16.5	6.3	-24.5	0.0	-2.2	..	..	-3.4	5.1	2.0
Côte d'Ivoire	-6.3	11.7	9.3	8.0	7.7	-16.8	-0.2	2.9	2.9	3.2	-2.3	4.8	3.2
Djibouti	..	..	..	..	..	..	..	..	..	..	..	..	..
Equatorial Guinea	..	..	..	..	..	..	..	..	..	..	..	..	..
Eritrea	..	..	..	..	..	..	..	..	..	..	..	..	..
Ethiopia	..	-2.1	-14.8	-13.0	1.8	10.7	-1.2	..	..	..	..	0.5	-3.1
Gabon	-3.3	3.0	5.1	17.8	22.4	-26.6	5.0	1.5	5.4	0.0	-4.9	7.0	3.7
Gambia, The	1.1	3.8	6.4	11.0	9.1	9.1	8.8	11.7	10.9	11.8	-4.2	-3.1	9.2
Ghana	-24.4	-3.1	1.6	18.2	8.0	6.5	-16.8	-1.1	13.4	14.8	-30.2	-2.2	4.6
Guinea	..	-3.6	-0.6	2.1	9.2	12.3	11.8	14.6	11.4	..	..	-15.1	7.1
Guinea-Bissau	..	6.8	-9.9	-14.1	-5.0	9.4	-4.4	-1.7	-28.9	..	..	..	-6.0
Kenya	..	3.2	0.6	-5.4	-0.3	-5.7	22.7	16.4	18.9	5.8	..	3.3	6.2
Lesotho	-6.6	3.7	0.3	-1.9	0.3	4.9	5.7	7.0	6.4	9.9	-1.6	-1.0	4.0
Liberia	..	..	..	..	..	..	..	..	..	..	..	..	..
Madagascar	..	..	..	..	..	..	..	..	..	..	..	-6.3	..
Malawi	..	2.0	0.3	-2.2	4.5	4.0	-18.2	-7.7	12.7	17.1	-3.2	-5.9	1.4
Mali	..	10.3	9.0	20.0	11.2	-11.8	-4.3	0.0	6.7	2.1	..	8.4	4.8
Mauritania	..	0.4	1.3	-2.8	..	..	..	..	..	..	..	-0.6	-0.4
Mauritius	-22.3	-1.3	4.0	3.5	-2.0	6.0	5.1	5.0	3.4	11.7	-3.4	4.6	3.9
Mozambique	..	..	..	..	..	..	..	..	..	..	..	..	..
Namibia	..	..	7.7	-1.0	5.5	4.3	6.8	9.0	6.6	10.3	..	..	6.1
Niger	..	..	..	..	..	..	...	..	..	..	..	..	..
Nigeria	-3.6	10.4	2.2	-18.7	-21.4	-27.7	-34.4	-12.2	4.8	2.9	-11.7	-8.1	-10.5
Rwanda	1.6	9.4	-4.7	1.3	2.2	-32.3	-4.9	6.5	-1.1	4.3	-3.6	7.2	-2.1
São Tomé and Principe	..	-12.1	-1.0	13.9	3.6	4.3	-0.6	-7.2	-8.5	-2.7	..	-14.4	-1.1
Senegal	1.6	10.6	13.0	12.5	11.6	-16.7	-0.9	3.7	4.2	4.2	-1.2	7.1	4.7
Seychelles	..	-2.8	-1.0	-2.2	-0.3	-0.8	1.3	2.1	0.4	3.7	1.2	4.5	0.0
Sierra Leone	..	-18.8	..	..	..	..	..	..	..	..	..	-37.0	-18.8
Somalia	..	..	..	..	..	..	..	..	..	..	..	..	..
South Africa	-6.4	3.1	1.5	0.1	2.1	3.7	5.9	8.9	6.8	9.3	-1.4	-2.4	4.6
Sudan	..	..	..	..	..	..	..	..	..	..	..	..	..
Swaziland	-9.6	0.9	2.0	3.5	-0.2	-1.6	2.4	9.7	8.0	8.8	-2.4	-2.4	3.7
Tanzania	-19.5	..	..	-6.0	-8.6	28.6	10.4	-5.3	-0.8	6.5	-13.2	-14.8	3.5
Togo	-1.6	9.8	10.7	10.7	10.6	-18.7	-7.2	1.8	-1.0	5.2	-0.8	9.1	2.4
Uganda	..	3.1	17.2	-0.7	-3.4	8.0	6.8	7.8	5.8	3.1	..	-44.4	5.3
Zambia	-4.6	..	..	-45.4	-40.1	-21.6	4.5	0.5	-5.7	..	-6.7	-17.2	-18.0
Zimbabwe	..	-6.1	-2.7	-8.9	0.7	6.0	5.6	4.6	10.5	2.8	-7.4	-1.8	1.4
NORTH AFRICA	-2.1	23.9	0.7	2.2	5.1	4.7	3.6	4.4	4.0	4.2	-2.3	-1.3	5.9
Algeria	..	..	..	..	..	..	..	..	0.0	0.0	..	..	0.0
Egypt, Arab Republic	..	11.7	18.2	16.4	15.4	14.2	12.5	6.0	6.0	8.4	..	7.3	11.9
Libya	..	..	..	..	..	..	..	..	..	..	..	..	..
Morocco	..	..	..	..	..	..	..	..	..	..	..	..	0.0
Tunisia	..	..	..	..	..	..	..	..	-4.0	-3.1	..	..	-3.6
ALL AFRICA	-3.6	3.2	1.6	1.7	3.6	2.6	0.6	2.8	4.5	4.2	-3.4	1.2	2.7

Note: Real discount rate in each year is the nominal discount rate deflated by the annual change in the CPI.

4-8. Commercial bank lending rate

	Percentage										Annual average		
	1980	*1990*	*1991*	*1992*	*1993*	*1994*	*1995*	*1996*	*1997*	*1998*	*75-84*	*85-89*	*90-MR*
SUB-SAHARAN AFRICA	12.0	18.5	18.1	17.8	17.5	17.5	19.3	22.0	22.0	22.0	12.1	14.0	19.4
excluding South Africa	12.0	18.5	18.1	17.8	17.5	17.5	20.2	22.0	22.0	22.0	12.0	14.0	19.5
excl. S.Africa & Nigeria	12.3	18.3	18.1	17.8	17.5	17.5	19.3	22.0	22.0	22.0	12.2	14.0	19.4
Angola	..	..	..	..	..	..	206.3	217.9	37.8	45.0	..	..	126.7
Benin	14.5	16.0	16.0	16.8	..	..	..	..	..	..	13.8	14.0	16.3
Botswana	8.5	7.9	11.8	14.0	14.9	13.9	14.3	14.5	14.1	13.5	13.5	9.6	13.2
Burkina Faso	14.5	16.0	16.0	16.8	..	..	..	..	..	..	13.8	14.0	16.3
Burundi	12.0	12.3	12.8	13.7	13.8	14.2	15.3	..	..	..	12.0	12.0	13.7
Cameroon	13.0	18.5	18.1	17.8	17.5	17.5	16.0	22.0	22.0	22.0	13.0	13.9	19.0
Cape Verde	6.5	10.0	10.0	10.0	10.0	10.7	12.0	12.0	12.1	12.5	6.5	10.0	11.0
Central African Republic	10.5	18.5	18.1	17.8	17.5	17.5	16.0	22.0	22.0	22.0	11.1	12.2	19.0
Chad	11.0	18.5	18.1	17.8	17.5	17.5	16.0	22.0	22.0	22.0	10.7	11.1	19.0
Comoros	..	..	..	..	..	..	..	..	..	..	15.0	14.0	..
Congo, Democratic Rep. of	..	..	..	..	..	..	..	..	..	..	..	..	..
Congo, Republic of	11.0	18.5	18.1	17.8	17.5	17.5	16.0	22.0	22.0	22.0	11.3	11.8	19.0
Côte d'Ivoire	14.5	16.0	16.0	16.8	..	..	..	..	..	..	13.8	14.0	16.3
Djibouti	..	..	..	..	..	..	..	..	..	..	..	..	..
Equatorial Guinea	..	18.5	18.1	17.8	17.5	17.5	16.0	22.0	22.0	22.0	..	14.8	19.0
Eritrea	..	..	..	..	..	..	..	..	..	..	..	..	..
Ethiopia	..	6.0	6.0	8.0	14.0	14.3	15.1	13.9	10.5	10.5	..	6.8	10.9
Gabon	12.5	18.5	18.1	17.8	17.5	17.5	16.0	22.0	22.0	22.0	11.8	11.9	19.0
Gambia, The	15.0	26.5	26.5	26.8	26.1	25.0	25.0	25.5	25.5	25.4	16.7	25.4	25.8
Ghana	19.0	..	..	..	..	..	..	..	..	..	19.3	23.1	..
Guinea	..	21.2	24.5	27.0	24.5	22.0	21.5	..	..	..	..	15.8	23.4
Guinea-Bissau	..	45.8	47.0	50.3	63.6	36.3	32.9	51.8	..	..	..	26.1	46.8
Kenya	10.6	18.8	19.0	21.1	30.0	36.2	28.8	33.8	30.2	29.5	11.8	14.9	27.5
Lesotho	11.0	20.4	20.0	18.3	15.8	14.3	16.4	17.7	18.0	20.1	15.2	15.3	17.9
Liberia	18.4	..	..	..	..	14.5	..	..	16.8	..	19.9	14.9	15.7
Madagascar	..	25.8	24.5	25.0	26.0	30.5	37.5	32.8	30.0	..	..	22.3	29.0
Malawi	16.7	21.0	20.0	22.0	29.5	31.0	47.3	45.3	28.3	37.7	17.7	20.4	31.3
Mali	14.5	16.0	16.0	16.8	..	..	..	..	..	..	13.8	14.0	16.3
Mauritania	12.0	10.0	10.0	10.0	..	..	..	..	..	..	12.0	11.6	10.0
Mauritius	..	18.0	17.8	17.1	16.6	18.9	20.8	20.8	18.9	19.9	13.5	14.7	18.8
Mozambique	..	..	..	..	..	..	..	..	..	..	..	..	..
Namibia	..	..	23.4	20.2	18.0	17.1	18.5	19.2	20.2	20.7	..	..	19.7
Niger	14.5	16.0	16.0	16.8	..	..	..	..	..	..	13.8	14.0	16.3
Nigeria	8.4	25.3	20.0	24.8	31.6	20.5	20.2	20.3	20.4	..	8.0	14.1	22.9
Rwanda	13.5	13.2	19.0	16.7	15.0	..	..	..	..	..	13.3	13.0	16.0
São Tomé and Principe	..	20.0	37.0	37.0	37.0	30.0	52.0	38.0	51.5	55.6	..	20.0	39.8
Senegal	14.5	16.0	16.0	16.8	..	..	..	..	..	..	13.8	14.0	16.3
Seychelles	..	15.6	15.6	15.6	15.7	15.7	15.8	16.2	14.9	14.4	..	15.5	15.5
Sierra Leone	11.0	52.5	56.3	62.8	50.5	27.3	28.8	32.1	23.9	23.8	12.7	24.1	39.8
Somalia	7.5	..	..	..	..	..	..	..	..	..	8.9	23.8	..
South Africa	9.5	21.0	20.3	18.9	16.2	15.6	17.9	19.5	20.0	21.8	14.1	16.7	19.0
Sudan	..	..	..	..	..	..	..	..	..	..	..	..	..
Swaziland	9.5	14.5	16.3	15.0	14.0	15.0	18.0	19.8	18.8	21.0	13.2	14.2	16.9
Tanzania	11.5	..	..	..	31.0	39.0	42.8	37.2	29.2	26.7	11.4	23.8	34.3
Togo	14.5	16.0	16.0	17.5	..	..	..	..	..	..	13.8	14.4	16.5
Uganda	10.8	38.7	34.4	..	..	..	20.2	20.3	21.4	20.9	15.2	33.4	26.0
Zambia	9.5	35.1	..	54.6	113.3	70.6	45.5	53.8	46.7	31.8	9.7	20.8	56.4
Zimbabwe	17.5	11.7	15.5	19.8	36.3	34.9	34.7	34.2	32.5	42.1	20.3	13.8	29.1
NORTH AFRICA	7.1	9.0	8.0	13.7	12.6	13.3	16.5	15.6	13.8	13.0	7.5	9.0	12.8
Algeria	..	..	..	..	..	..	..	..	..	..	..	..	..
Egypt, Arab Republic	13.3	19.0	..	20.3	18.3	16.5	16.5	15.6	13.8	13.0	12.5	16.3	16.6
Libya	7.0	7.0	7.0	7.0	7.0	..	..	..	..	..	7.0	7.0	7.0
Morocco	7.0	9.0	9.0	..	..	10.0	..	..	..	..	7.0	8.7	9.3
Tunisia	7.3	..	..	..	..	..	..	..	..	..	7.9	8.9	..
ALL AFRICA	11.8	18.5	18.1	17.8	17.5	17.5	18.5	22.0	22.0	22.0	11.6	14.0	19.3

Note: Group data are medians of individual country values in each year or period.

4-9. Commercial bank deposit rate

	Percentage										Annual average		
	_1980_	_1990_	_1991_	_1992_	_1993_	_1994_	_1995_	_1996_	_1997_	_1998_	_75-84_	_85-89_	_90-MR_
SUB-SAHARAN AFRICA	6.2	7.5	9.6	9.0	10.6	10.7	12.4	12.5	9.5	7.6	6.6	7.9	9.9
excluding South Africa	6.2	7.5	9.2	8.4	9.6	10.4	12.2	12.5	9.4	7.5	6.6	7.8	9.6
excl. S.Africa & Nigeria	6.2	7.5	8.8	7.8	9.6	10.2	11.8	12.4	9.5	7.5	6.6	7.6	9.4
Angola	..	..	..	..	..	..	125.9	147.1	29.3	36.9	..	..	84.8
Benin	6.2	7.0	7.0	7.8	..	..	..	..	..	3.5	6.5	6.1	6.3
Botswana	5.0	6.1	11.4	12.5	13.5	10.4	10.0	10.4	9.3	8.7	9.3	7.2	10.3
Burkina Faso	6.2	7.0	7.0	7.8	..	..	..	..	..	3.5	6.5	6.1	6.3
Burundi	2.5	..	..	..	..	..	..	..	..	..	3.4	4.9	..
Cameroon	7.5	7.5	7.5	7.5	7.8	8.1	5.5	5.4	5.0	5.0	7.3	7.3	6.6
Cape Verde	..	4.0	4.0	4.0	4.0	4.0	5.0	5.0	5.0	5.3	..	4.0	4.5
Central African Republic	5.5	7.5	7.5	7.5	7.8	8.1	5.5	5.5	5.0	5.0	6.4	7.4	6.6
Chad	5.5	7.5	7.5	7.5	7.8	8.1	5.5	5.5	5.0	5.0	5.3	5.0	6.6
Comoros	..	..	..	..	..	..	..	..	..	..	7.5	7.0	..
Congo, Democratic Rep. of													
Congo, Republic of	6.5	7.5	7.5	7.5	7.8	8.1	5.5	5.5	5.0	5.0	6.5	8.0	6.6
Côte d'Ivoire	6.2	7.0	7.0	7.8	..	..	..	..	..	3.5	6.5	6.1	6.3
Djibouti	..	..	..	3.0	2.6	..	..	..	..	..	..	..	2.8
Equatorial Guinea	..	7.5	7.5	7.5	7.8	8.1	5.5	5.5	5.0	5.0	..	7.3	6.6
Eritrea	..	..	..	..	..	..	..	..	..	..	..	..	..
Ethiopia	..	2.4	5.0	3.6	11.5	11.5	11.5	9.4	7.0	6.0	..	6.5	7.5
Gabon	7.5	7.5	7.5	7.5	7.8	8.1	5.5	5.5	5.0	5.0	7.4	8.1	6.6
Gambia, The	5.0	11.3	12.7	13.8	13.0	12.6	12.5	12.5	12.5	12.5	7.1	13.9	12.6
Ghana	11.5	..	21.3	16.3	23.6	23.1	28.7	34.5	35.8	32.0	12.0	16.7	26.9
Guinea	..	21.0	22.0	23.0	19.8	18.0	17.5	..	..	..	..	17.1	20.2
Guinea-Bissau	..	32.7	36.0	39.3	53.9	28.7	26.5	47.3	4.6	..	..	25.5	33.6
Kenya	5.8	13.7	..	..	..	..	13.6	17.6	16.7	18.4	7.7	11.0	16.0
Lesotho	..	13.0	13.0	10.6	8.1	8.4	13.3	12.7	11.8	10.7	10.2	10.0	11.3
Liberia	10.3	..	..	..	..	6.3	..	..	..	6.5	10.4	6.9	6.4
Madagascar	..	20.5	20.5	20.5	19.5	19.5	18.5	19.0	14.4	..	..	17.8	19.0
Malawi	7.9	12.1	12.5	16.5	21.8	25.0	37.3	26.3	10.2	19.1	9.8	13.2	20.1
Mali	6.2	7.0	7.0	7.8	..	..	..	..	..	3.5	6.5	6.1	6.3
Mauritania	..	5.0	5.0	5.0	..	..	..	..	..	..	5.5	6.2	5.0
Mauritius	..	12.6	12.3	10.1	8.4	11.0	12.2	10.8	9.1	9.3	10.7	9.9	10.6
Mozambique	..	..	..	..	..	..	..	..	..	..	..	..	..
Namibia	..	..	12.8	11.4	9.6	9.2	10.8	12.6	12.7	12.9	..	..	11.5
Niger	6.2	7.0	7.0	7.8	..	..	..	..	..	3.5	6.5	6.1	6.3
Nigeria	5.3	19.8	14.9	18.0	23.2	13.1	13.5	13.0	7.3	..	5.1	11.8	15.4
Rwanda	6.3	6.9	8.8	7.7	5.0	..	..	10.9	9.5	8.5	5.1	6.3	8.2
São Tomé and Principe	..	16.0	35.0	35.0	35.0	35.0	35.0	31.0	36.8	38.3	..	16.0	33.0
Senegal	6.2	7.0	7.0	7.8	..	..	..	..	..	3.5	6.5	6.1	6.3
Seychelles	..	9.5	9.6	9.6	9.5	8.9	9.2	9.9	9.2	7.5	9.1	9.8	9.2
Sierra Leone	9.2	40.5	47.8	54.7	27.0	11.6	7.0	14.0	9.9	7.1	9.2	14.9	24.4
Somalia	4.5	..	..	..	..	..	..	..	..	..	5.5	18.2	..
South Africa	5.5	18.9	17.3	13.8	11.5	11.1	13.5	14.9	15.4	16.5	10.0	13.7	14.8
Sudan	6.0	..	..	..	..	..	..	..	..	..	9.2	..	..
Swaziland	4.5	8.9	10.9	9.0	7.4	8.0	10.3	12.3	11.3	13.4	9.0	7.8	10.1
Tanzania	4.0	..	..	..	..	..	24.6	13.6	7.8	7.8	4.0	12.6	13.5
Togo	6.2	7.0	7.0	7.8	..	..	..	..	..	3.5	6.5	6.1	6.3
Uganda	6.8	31.3	31.2	35.8	16.3	10.0	7.6	10.6	11.8	11.4	9.9	23.4	18.4
Zambia	7.0	25.7	..	48.5	..	46.1	30.2	42.1	34.5	13.1	6.2	13.8	34.3
Zimbabwe	3.5	8.8	14.2	28.6	29.4	26.8	25.9	21.6	18.6	29.1	6.6	9.7	22.6
NORTH AFRICA	5.0	8.5	8.5	8.8	8.8	11.8	10.9	10.5	9.8	9.4	4.9	7.7	9.7
Algeria	..	..	..	..	..	..	..	..	..	..	..	..	..
Egypt, Arab Republic	8.3	12.0	12.0	12.0	12.0	11.8	10.9	10.5	9.8	9.4	8.0	11.1	11.2
Libya	5.1	5.5	5.5	5.5	5.5	..	..	..	..	..	4.7	5.5	5.5
Morocco	4.9	8.5	8.5	..	..	..	..	..	..	..	5.6	8.4	8.5
Tunisia	2.5	..	..	..	..	..	..	..	..	..	3.4	6.7	..
ALL AFRICA	6.2	8.0	9.2	9.0	10.6	11.0	12.2	12.5	9.6	7.8	6.4	7.9	10.0

Note: Group data are medians of individual country values in each year or period.

Figure 4-1. Credit to private and public sectors as a share of GDP, 1999*

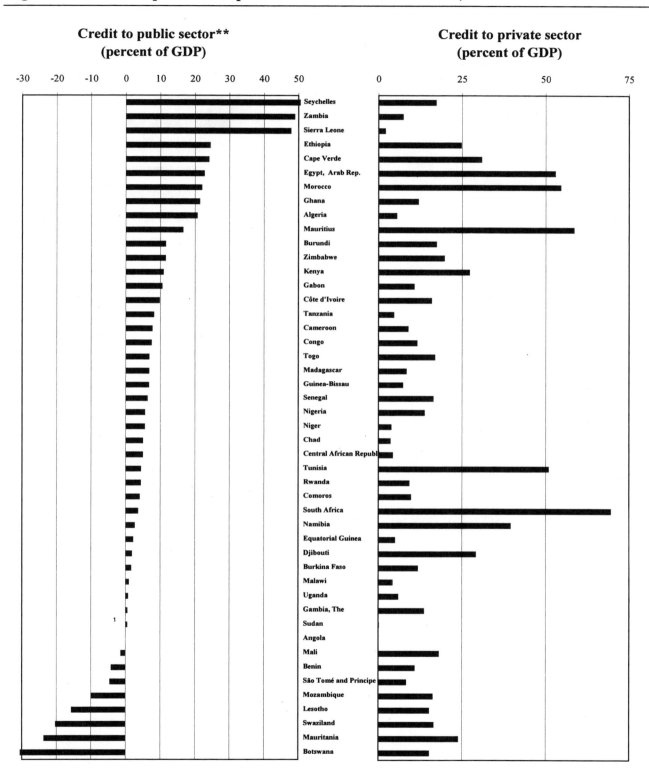

* Or most recent year available.
** Sorted by credit to public sector.

Figure 4-2. Real discount rate, average 1992-99*

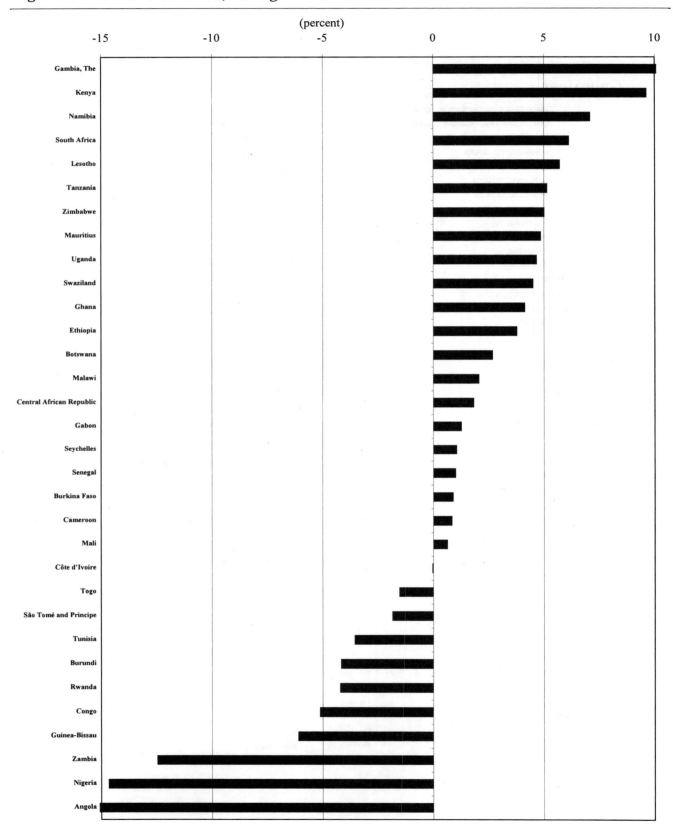

* Or most recent year available.

Technical notes

Tables

Table 4-1. Domestic credit. Domestic credit (IMF, IFS, line 32) includes all domestic assets of the banking system. It is the sum of the claims on the central government (net), on official entities, and on the private sector. Domestic credit comprises credit to the private sector (Table 4-2) and credit to the government (Table 4-3).

Table 4-2. Credit to the private sector. Credit to the private sector is taken from IMF, *IFS*, line 32d.

Table 4-3. Credit to the government. Credit to the government sector is taken from IMF, *IFS*, line 32an. Negative numbers for net claims on the central government indicate that government is a net depositor to the banking system. The government's financial position with the monetary system is always presented on a net basis because its recourse to the monetary system cannot always be analyzed meaningfully in terms of liquidity preferences or by considering debtor and creditor positions separately. Movements in net claims on the central government (that is, claims or credits less government deposits) indicate the impact of government operations on the liquidity of the rest of the economy.

Table 4-4. Net foreign assets. Data for net foreign assets are from the IMF, *IFS*, line 31n. As for credit to the government, the financial position of the foreign sector with the monetary system is presented on a net basis for the same reason as noted above. Movements in net for-

eign assets (that is, foreign assets less foreign liabilities) indicate the direct monetary impact of a country's transactions with the rest of the world.

Table 4-5. Growth of money supply. This table shows the annual percentage change in money (M1), defined as the sum of currency outside of banks and demand deposits other than those of the central government (IMF, *IFS*, line 34). The presentation of the money supply in the form of growth rates rather than levels reflects the importance from the point of view of macroeconomic stability of the rate of growth rather than the stock of money.

Table 4-6. Discount rate. The discount rate reported here is the nominal interest rate at which the monetary authorities lend to (or discount eligible paper from) deposit money banks (IMF, *IFS*, line 60).

Table 4-7. Real discount rate. The real discount rate in each year is the nominal discount rate (Table 4-6) deflated by the annual change in inflation as reflected by the consumer price index (CPI) (Table 3-3). It has been calculated using the formula:

$$\{[l + (i/100)] / [(\pi_t / \pi_{t-1})] - 1\} \times 100$$

where i is nominal interest rate and π is inflation rate based on the CPI.

Table 4-8. Commercial bank lending rate. The commercial bank lending rate (IMF, *IFS*, line 60p) is the rate charged to borrowers by commercial banks for short- and medium-term use of funds.

Table 4-9. Commercial bank deposit rate. The deposit rate (IMF, IFS, line 60l) is the rate paid to depositors on time savings and demand deposits by deposit money banks and similar financial institutions.

Figures

The following indicators have been used to derive the figures in this chapter.

Figure 4-1. Credit to the private sector (Table 4-2); credit to the public sector (Table 4-3); gross domestic product (Table 2-5).

Figure 4-2. Real discount rate (Table 4-7).

Methodology used for regional aggregations and period averages in chapter 4

Table	Aggregations[a]		Period averages[b]	
	(4)	(8)	(1)	(2)
4-1	x			x
4-2	x			x
4-3	x			x
4-4		x	x	
4-5	x			x
4-6	x		x	
4-7	x		x	
4-8	x		x	
4-9	x		x	

Note: Regional aggregations are shown in the rows for Sub-Saharan Africa, North Africa, and All Africa. Period averages are shown in the last three columns. This table shows only the methodologies used in this chapter. The definitions of the methodologies used throughout the book are given below.

a. Regional aggregations: (1) simple total; (2) simple total of the first indicator divided by the simple total of the second indicator (same country coverage); (3) simple total of the gap-filled indicator; (4) simple total of the gap-filled main indicator divided by the simple total of the gap-filled secondary indicator; (5) simple total of the first gap-filled main indicator less the simple total of the second gap-filled main indicator, all divided by the simple total of the secondary indicator; (6) weighted total (by population); (7) median; (8) no aggregation; (9) simple arithmetic mean.

b. Period averages: (i) arithmetic mean (using the same series as shown in the table i.e., ratio if the rest of the table is shown as ratio, level if the rest of the table is shown as level, growth rate if the rest is shown as growth rate); (2) least-squares growth rate (using main indicator); (3) least-squares growth rate (using main indicator in constant terms, with the rest of the table in current terms).

5

External Sector

The external sector provides data on economic and financial relations between African countries and the rest of the world, with detailed accounting of commodity trade, one of the principal components of the current account within the balance of payments framework. Commodity trade and price data can also provide a partial basis for analyzing Africa's constraints and performance in the international marketplace, including its terms of trade. Commodity exports are a major source of foreign exchange. Other sources of foreign exchange include receipts from factor and nonfactor services, borrowing from abroad, incoming foreign investment, and foreign transfers and grants.

The balance of payments is a system of accounts, covering a given period, that is intended to record systematically: flows of real resources, including the services of the original factors of production, between the domestic economy of a country and the rest of the world; changes in the country's foreign assets and liabilities that arise from economic transactions; and transfer payments, which are the counterpart of real resources or financial claims provided to, or received from, the rest of the world that carry no provision for repayment.

The tables provide gross entries for goods and services and net entries for unrequited transfers (official and private) and other financial flows; a table for current account balance as traditionally defined (with transfers above the line) is also shown. The information is presented for broad aggregates; fuller detail can be found in the IMF's *Balance of Payments Manual (1993) and Balance of Payments Year books*.

Unit values for exports (f.o.b.) and imports (c.i.f.) measure changes in the aggregate price level of a country's exports and imports of goods and nonfactor services over time. Unit values reflect average price changes for broad groups of commodities, rather than for any single commodity. The terms of trade indicate relative movements in export and import unit values (here, they are based on goods and nonfactor services from the national accounts). If the prices of exports rise while the prices of imports rise more slowly, stay constant, or decline, the same quantity of exports "buys" a bigger quantity of imports. The effect of such price changes is equivalent to an increase in the real value of output (or increased productivity in value terms) of the export sector. Were import prices to rise more quickly than export prices, the reverse would be true. Export figures for specific commodities show physical quantities rather than value in either current or constant prices. Most of the key nonagricultural primary commodities are exported from a few countries with substantial mineral resources. Variations in export prices and earnings for the five major oil-exporting countries in Sub-Saharan Africa (which in the 1980s have accounted for about half of Sub-Saharan export earnings) have dominated trends in this region as a whole.

5-1. Merchandise exports, f.o.b.

	Millions of U.S. dollars (current prices)											Average annual percentage growth		
	1980	1990	1991	1992	1993	1994	1995	1996	1997	1998	1999	75-84	85-89	90-MR
SUB-SAHARAN AFRICA	78,665	69,260	66,425	66,500	62,922	65,897	78,545	86,808	87,205	75,695	79,206	6.9	2.9	3.0
excluding South Africa	53,049	45,738	42,645	42,033	38,178	39,558	48,476	56,563	56,025	46,590	50,875	5.3	0.6	2.8
excl. S.Africa & Nigeria	26,406	31,800	30,508	30,137	28,255	30,153	36,752	40,431	40,477	36,501	38,964	5.9	3.9	3.5
Angola	..	3,884	3,449	3,833	2,900	3,017	3,723	5,169	5,007	3,543	5,344	..	7.0	4.1
Benin	222	287	337	371	341	308	405	424	400	393	375	7.1	6.0	4.6
Botswana	544	1,795	1,871	1,744	1,722	1,874	2,160	2,233	2,069	1,711	1,388	20.0	24.5	-0.5
Burkina Faso	161	283	269	238	260	191	237	233	229	325	255	8.1	11.1	0.9
Burundi	66	73	90	77	74	81	113	40	87	64	56	9.9	-1.0	-3.6
Cameroon	1,506	1,882	2,159	1,937	1,652	1,433	1,655	1,605	1,816	1,800	1,684	18.2	-5.5	-1.4
Cape Verde	9	5	4	4	4	20	25	30	40	33	36	15.2	-8.8	29.3
Central African Republic	147	151	126	116	132	162	179	142	155	138	136	8.6	3.9	0.5
Chad	71	193	194	182	152	135	243	238	237	261	211	0.8	10.0	4.0
Comoros	11	18	24	21	22	11	12	6	6	6	8	..	15.7	-13.3
Congo, Democratic Rep. of	2,269	2,326	1,649	1,246	1,144	1,256	1,612	1,727	1,395	1,598	1,872	·5.9	5.8	-2.1
Congo, Republic of	911	1,388	1,110	1,179	1,119	959	1,287	1,655	1,662	1,368	1,662	22.9	-3.2	3.5
Côte d'Ivoire	3,013	3,070	2,810	3,189	2,695	3,026	4,304	4,281	4,076	4,045	4,233	6.4	0.8	4.9
Djibouti	..	..	72	53	71	56	38	40	43	..	..	..	..	-9.5
Equatorial Guinea	..	37	35	52	52	65	86	197	498	460	707	..	12.7	39.3
Eritrea	0	0	0	15	36	65	81	95	54	28	20	..	..	0.3
Ethiopia	459	366	276	154	222	280	454	412	599	602	484	6.3	-0.1	7.0
Gabon	2,531	2,490	2,230	2,257	2,326	2,365	2,643	3,190	3,043	2,209	2,526	8.9	-6.5	3.2
Gambia, The	51	108	132	151	141	124	121	115	108	130	120	3.2	7.9	1.1
Ghana	1,104	897	997	986	1,064	1,227	1,431	1,810	1,810	2,091	2,099	-3.8	8.5	11.0
Guinea	500	671	764	651	672	610	649	613	660	709	717	4.7	2.5	0.5
Guinea-Bissau	..	19	20	6	16	33	24	22	48	26	51	..	1.3	12.5
Kenya	1,363	997	1,056	1,013	1,103	1,484	1,924	2,083	2,060	2,012	1,755	5.8	-2.1	9.6
Lesotho	58	59	67	109	134	143	154	180	195	183	179	10.4	25.7	13.4
Liberia	600	..	..	..	..	..	..	..	..	..	..	1.4	-5.6	..
Madagascar	437	318	334	324	332	447	523	524	505	519	582	2.0	-1.1	7.2
Malawi	281	412	476	397	321	327	404	483	567	476	502	8.8	-0.4	4.5
Mali	205	330	371	362	349	336	442	433	561	561	566	10.9	8.9	7.2
Mauritania	196	414	434	400	380	393	479	484	408	360	333	6.8	7.1	-1.4
Mauritius	434	1,201	1,213	1,303	1,334	1,386	1,530	1,703	1,642	1,741	1,619	2.9	24.5	5.1
Mozambique	281	126	162	139	132	164	174	226	230	245	271	..	4.5	9.2
Namibia	1,534	1,088	1,179	1,311	1,293	1,320	1,418	1,403	1,343	1,288	1,289	..	8.3	1.7
Niger	576	313	270	344	301	225	287	302	271	301	256	14.6	3.9	-1.2
Nigeria	25,956	13,914	12,127	11,886	9,924	9,415	11,734	16,117	15,539	10,114	11,927	3.8	-7.1	1.1
Rwanda	134	103	96	69	68	32	50	62	93	64	61	5.6	-6.0	-4.3
São Tomé and Principe	17	4	6	5	5	6	5	5	5	5	4	-3.0	-7.7	-2.0
Senegal	480	912	904	828	719	791	968	986	932	966	960	2.1	6.0	2.0
Seychelles	6	57	49	48	49	52	53	78	115	77	80	-1.8	32.2	12.9
Sierra Leone	214	155	176	150	118	194	102	105	88	65	61	-1.0	0.0	-9.2
Somalia	133	58	..	..	..	..	..	..	..	..	..	3.6	-2.7	..
South Africa	25,698	23,560	23,805	24,487	24,750	26,342	30,084	30,285	31,213	29,116	28,362	10.3	7.4	3.2
Sudan	566	393	346	350	427	462	556	620	594	596	780	2.8	-4.4	6.5
Swaziland	368	550	594	639	685	791	868	896	961	914	1,100	6.3	22.6	7.9
Tanzania	508	389	394	414	411	486	593	696	794	577	541	0.1	1.6	5.9
Togo	476	395	393	327	215	226	355	376	425	386	360	7.1	10.1	0.3
Uganda	319	210	176	172	157	254	595	590	671	458	549	1.3	-6.1	13.9
Zambia	1,457	1,264	1,085	1,120	994	1,067	1,186	993	1,119	816	755	-0.9	10.2	-4.3
Zimbabwe	281	1,753	1,785	1,530	1,610	1,947	2,216	2,496	2,424	1,925	1,924	0.0	9.3	3.0
NORTH AFRICA	41,264	33,432	34,726	33,255	31,134	30,611	37,625	41,279	43,368	38,416	41,015	9.7	-5.0	4.1
Algeria	13,652	12,889	12,387	11,439	10,410	8,899	10,260	13,220	13,820	10,140	12,320	14.3	-7.7	0.8
Egypt, Arab Republic	3,854	3,145	4,250	3,880	3,725	3,337	4,957	4,609	5,345	5,128	4,445	9.4	-8.0	5.4
Libya	21,919	11,352	..	..	..	..	..	..	..	..	..	6.7	-10.5	..
Morocco	2,414	4,936	5,089	5,024	4,922	5,541	6,871	6,886	7,039	7,144	7,402	5.1	14.5	6.3
Tunisia	2,395	3,516	3,708	4,014	3,746	4,643	5,470	5,519	5,559	5,724	5,873	12.0	10.7	7.2
ALL AFRICA	119,816	102,566	100,511	99,409	93,793	96,625	116,086	128,053	130,167	113,607	119,535	7.9	0.2	3.3

Note: 1999 data are preliminary (see page 2).

5-2. Merchandise imports, f.o.b.

	Millions of U.S. dollars (current prices)											Average annual percentage growth		
	1980	1990	1991	1992	1993	1994	1995	1996	1997	1998	1999	75-84	85-89	90-MR
SUB-SAHARAN AFRICA	61,043	55,739	56,467	59,460	57,382	59,190	71,865	74,226	79,875	77,249	77,381	8.3	4.0	4.7
excluding South Africa	42,766	39,007	39,320	41,281	38,899	37,327	44,459	46,640	51,020	50,010	52,831	8.3	2.7	4.0
excl. S.Africa & Nigeria	28,042	31,950	31,426	32,381	30,599	30,866	36,282	38,435	41,395	40,740	41,820	6.5	6.3	3.9
Angola	..	1,578	1,347	1,988	1,463	1,454	1,852	2,040	2,477	2,079	3,267	..	-1.8	7.2
Benin	499	428	482	561	539	374	561	563	535	550	572	8.3	6.9	4.0
Botswana	602	1,611	1,604	1,557	1,455	1,350	1,579	1,436	1,449	1,486	1,559	17.4	18.4	0.6
Burkina Faso	368	542	490	516	534	355	485	562	511	639	600	8.1	10.3	2.2
Burundi	165	189	196	182	173	173	176	100	96	124	97	17.1	-1.8	-6.4
Cameroon	1,452	1,453	1,251	1,023	1,021	1,017	1,074	1,200	1,347	1,452	1,498	12.5	5.5	1.0
Cape Verde	80	119	128	167	152	191	234	206	211	218	236	10.1	6.2	8.1
Central African Republic	185	242	179	189	158	151	179	125	145	150	139	8.7	4.6	-4.2
Chad	55	259	250	243	205	212	277	243	246	272	246	-1.8	12.5	0.5
Comoros	22	45	49	58	50	45	54	48	48	41	43	..	6.1	0.3
Congo, Democratic Rep. of	1,519	1,739	1,304	935	614	667	997	923	834	936	1,211	0.0	10.7	-5.0
Congo, Republic of	545	513	494	438	500	613	653	586	649	559	615	15.2	-5.0	2.8
Côte d'Ivoire	2,614	2,236	2,186	1,984	1,784	1,608	2,474	2,763	2,712	2,777	2,778	6.1	10.4	3.3
Djibouti	..	..	258	259	255	237	205	200	203	..	..	..	..	-5.0
Equatorial Guinea	..	52	90	62	52	67	97	248	353	434	304	..	10.6	26.2
Eritrea	0	0	0	278	275	396	404	514	495	527	495	..	..	10.2
Ethiopia	692	881	1,029	875	1,052	915	1,063	1,144	1,309	1,357	1,558	16.4	1.0	4.8
Gabon	829	805	861	887	845	777	898	969	1,018	987	841	4.6	0.0	1.6
Gambia, The	116	134	174	204	205	179	184	196	176	207	194	11.0	7.8	4.1
Ghana	908	1,200	1,313	1,457	1,728	1,580	1,684	2,295	3,042	2,897	3,258	-1.6	11.2	12.3
Guinea	339	586	566	589	602	583	583	584	573	572	580	5.0	5.7	0.3
Guinea-Bissau	..	68	67	84	54	54	59	57	73	51	66	..	1.5	-1.6
Kenya	2,585	1,992	1,686	1,608	1,385	1,761	2,636	2,512	2,944	3,028	2,626	8.1	4.3	6.6
Lesotho	424	673	804	933	868	810	1,013	1,003	1,012	873	758	14.2	10.5	3.0
Liberia	478	..	..	..	..	..	..	..	..	..	..	1.8	-1.5	..
Madagascar	764	566	440	465	510	546	628	645	682	672	743	5.4	-3.1	6.6
Malawi	308	491	616	712	628	536	474	624	783	646	595	2.7	8.7	3.0
Mali	308	464	505	532	502	466	556	552	556	558	592	9.7	8.3	3.3
Mauritania	321	405	385	424	375	304	395	403	355	358	305	7.0	2.6	-1.4
Mauritius	516	1,469	1,419	1,473	1,576	1,784	1,756	2,004	2,071	2,057	1,942	4.6	27.6	5.2
Mozambique	720	780	791	745	830	881	727	783	760	817	1,200	..	11.4	2.4
Namibia	1,094	1,230	1,228	1,389	1,335	1,406	1,548	1,531	1,615	1,462	1,479	..	8.0	3.5
Niger	677	337	281	266	259	263	297	306	298	340	290	11.0	-14.5	3.3
Nigeria	14,735	7,070	7,892	8,891	8,293	6,470	8,183	8,216	9,630	9,276	10,999	12.7	-8.9	4.3
Rwanda	196	228	228	241	268	367	194	213	277	256	225	12.3	6.8	0.0
São Tomé and Principe	15	21	24	22	26	24	23	20	19	17	22	12.5	2.1	-2.7
Senegal	973	1,176	1,186	1,192	1,102	1,022	1,217	1,268	1,196	1,239	1,280	4.9	4.7	1.6
Seychelles	84	166	162	180	216	188	214	263	310	317	325	12.4	14.2	9.0
Sierra Leone	334	136	139	136	130	131	120	185	81	85	71	1.4	2.6	-6.8
Somalia	402	211	..	..	..	..	..	..	..	..	..	15.0	-6.3	..
South Africa	18,268	16,778	17,190	18,224	18,518	21,875	27,412	27,599	28,876	27,269	24,614	8.7	7.0	6.2
Sudan	1,440	1,092	1,201	1,002	975	957	1,036	1,315	1,343	1,636	1,200	5.6	-0.7	3.4
Swaziland	538	589	635	780	789	832	1,009	1,076	1,173	1,049	1,360	16.6	10.0	9.4
Tanzania	1,089	1,346	1,381	1,444	1,472	1,591	1,510	1,370	1,388	1,519	1,631	3.6	9.0	2.0
Togo	524	511	452	409	251	212	350	418	455	446	436	9.4	13.8	-0.4
Uganda	318	584	545	451	523	672	1,085	1,218	1,246	1,411	1,376	4.5	9.9	12.8
Zambia	1,114	889	952	1,302	1,019	1,003	1,194	1,056	1,218	971	871	0.3	6.9	0.6
Zimbabwe	308	1,511	1,700	1,781	1,512	1,778	2,128	2,247	2,654	2,020	1,675	1.4	6.5	4.2
NORTH AFRICA	30,995	36,035	37,098	37,012	37,896	37,656	45,426	44,783	46,533	46,560	49,504	8.0	2.0	4.2
Algeria	9,596	9,659	7,747	8,541	7,990	9,158	10,100	9,090	8,130	8,630	8,960	5.6	-3.1	-0.2
Egypt, Arab Republic	6,814	10,298	13,410	10,753	12,879	10,377	13,372	14,263	16,718	15,321	16,969	10.2	-3.7	5.5
Libya	10,368	7,575	..	..	..	..	..	..	..	..	..	12.0	-3.1	..
Morocco	3,770	6,805	6,848	7,450	6,981	7,648	9,353	9,080	8,903	9,463	9,956	7.3	8.7	5.5
Tunisia	3,453	5,193	4,895	6,079	5,757	6,210	7,458	7,280	7,514	7,875	8,015	13.2	7.2	6.2
ALL AFRICA	91,096	91,405	93,149	96,183	94,842	96,500	116,891	118,752	126,252	123,547	126,419	7.8	2.0	4.5

Note: 1999 data are preliminary (see page 2).

5-3. Exports of total services

	Millions of U.S. dollars (current prices)											Average annual percentage growth		
	1980	1990	1991	1992	1993	1994	1995	1996	1997	1998	1999	75-84	85-89	90-MR
SUB-SAHARAN AFRICA	12,220	13,471	13,381	13,677	13,277	13,661	16,242	17,794	18,626	19,124	19,586	6.3	6.1	5.4
excluding South Africa	8,691	9,091	9,330	9,406	9,313	8,947	10,493	11,697	11,993	12,547	13,229	7.7	6.8	4.8
excl. S.Africa & Nigeria	6,238	8,728	8,872	9,171	9,167	8,783	10,281	11,298	11,617	11,450	12,041	8.8	8.3	4.3
Angola	..	119	186	159	117	163	129	311	251	158	160	..	3.4	3.5
Benin	84	115	123	143	137	108	145	142	140	151	151	11.3	8.9	3.9
Botswana	203	626	693	731	746	417	744	669	788	851	917	14.8	16.5	5.8
Burkina Faso	65	86	85	83	80	67	80	71	55	53	52	9.2	5.8	-1.9
Burundi	26	25	35	31	25	23	27	17	13	11	8	21.0	7.4	-11.1
Cameroon	395	378	334	436	394	310	405	456	507	521	575	21.7	-1.7	3.2
Cape Verde	14	46	41	46	46	53	73	85	99	92	107	43.2	11.5	12.1
Central African Republic	58	70	56	56	54	45	53	47	43	32	43	7.0	10.9	-5.7
Chad	0	44	40	44	47	28	79	55	54	57	54	-13.0	10.2	3.7
Comoros	3	21	28	33	35	30	38	38	26	27	28	..	48.4	2.3
Congo, Democratic Rep. of	135	258	226	135	151	66	159	66	63	65	83	3.1	13.3	-13.4
Congo, Republic of	119	114	118	79	68	159	82	84	77	74	69	7.6	-28.9	8.3
Côte d'Ivoire	587	396	358	404	337	380	328	774	741	814	835	8.4	-3.5	10.3
Djibouti	..	..	194	178	192	182	188	184	188	..	..	..	..	-0.1
Equatorial Guinea	..	8	10	7	8	7	5	5	5	7	7	..	137.4	-4.7
Eritrea	0	0	0	73	103	80	99	113	160	93	61	..	..	0.5
Ethiopia	131	311	271	305	291	283	354	413	442	458	460	5.0	11.5	5.3
Gabon	350	270	352	369	344	231	286	298	263	249	261	12.2	10.1	-2.4
Gambia, The	21	43	58	70	77	62	55	71	80	86	82	10.0	19.7	5.8
Ghana	110	87	103	137	156	159	164	438	448	468	483	-5.8	14.7	23.3
Guinea	54	158	145	160	187	153	118	124	111	111	112	..	20.3	-2.5
Guinea-Bissau	..	5	5	5	5	6	6	7	8	4	5	..	-13.6	1.0
Kenya	835	1,230	1,177	1,144	1,152	1,184	1,050	958	952	879	873	7.1	9.9	-2.8
Lesotho	305	496	518	538	481	407	476	456	511	449	357	14.8	6.8	-1.4
Liberia	13	..	..	..	..	..	..	..	..	..	..	18.0	17.0	..
Madagascar	82	209	151	177	187	208	246	306	276	295	335	2.6	24.1	7.7
Malawi	34	45	45	27	19	29	22	42	61	47	53	-5.4	5.5	3.3
Mali	58	107	96	106	99	78	88	103	102	111	99	10.7	14.1	1.6
Mauritania	73	55	66	53	34	40	48	33	23	41	42	9.6	9.8	-5.6
Mauritius	150	589	643	691	632	677	786	930	942	1,048	1,132	8.1	31.6	8.4
Mozambique	171	173	203	223	240	246	292	314	342	333	353	..	9.0	8.3
Namibia	205	315	388	372	441	473	689	656	632	558	565	..	8.8	8.0
Niger	68	71	58	56	49	37	41	39	35	39	38	7.4	10.5	-7.0
Nigeria	2,164	379	478	259	171	187	239	427	405	1,129	1,219	2.7	-11.0	11.4
Rwanda	49	47	47	50	37	22	38	27	60	57	56	27.2	8.4	0.0
São Tomé and Principe	6	5	5	5	5	6	6	6	7	7	13	20.0	17.7	7.8
Senegal	416	602	599	616	577	504	604	630	582	600	600	9.0	10.8	0.7
Seychelles	97	176	173	198	211	201	224	245	256	302	306	15.4	14.2	5.8
Sierra Leone	21	16	18	15	25	18	59	57	16	27	28	42.5	-4.0	3.2
Somalia	71	33	..	..	..	..	..	..	..	..	..	13.9	-15.9	..
South Africa	3,560	4,391	4,062	4,281	3,975	4,720	5,756	6,106	6,640	6,581	6,371	8.5	4.5	6.7
Sudan	228	139	54	74	111	96	134	57	47	29	101	12.6	-3.4	-9.1
Swaziland	82	269	356	296	248	265	324	276	296	206	394	15.4	18.4	0.9
Tanzania	179	134	141	141	206	369	511	472	520	567	672	-1.1	1.8	21.6
Togo	95	180	172	161	121	162	136	158	158	156	161	17.7	10.9	-0.4
Uganda	11	36	27	27	85	90	87	157	192	218	227	9.2	1.4	29.5
Zambia	168	79	87	94	107	123	152	143	228	142	116	3.7	1.6	6.6
Zimbabwe	34	287	297	330	401	443	542	646	696	660	656	5.2	8.4	11.3
NORTH AFRICA	11,110	15,196	14,999	18,333	18,444	19,234	21,076	23,518	24,448	23,803	24,968	12.2	7.5	6.6
Algeria	978	587	504	729	746	808	800	960	1,330	1,110	940	7.4	3.1	7.2
Egypt, Arab Republic	2,662	6,783	7,153	8,189	8,332	8,677	9,556	10,636	11,241	10,455	11,015	19.9	11.9	6.2
Libya	1,446	783	..	..	..	..	..	..	..	..	..	12.8	1.9	..
Morocco	896	1,977	1,821	2,402	2,288	2,238	2,425	2,932	2,643	3,020	3,323	8.1	14.5	6.5
Tunisia	1,214	1,783	1,507	2,107	2,143	2,364	2,657	2,697	2,692	2,848	3,009	11.3	14.5	6.7
ALL AFRICA	21,245	26,936	26,683	29,688	29,339	30,394	34,696	38,355	40,012	40,039	41,482	11.5	7.8	5.9

Note: 1999 data are preliminary (see page 2).

5-4. Imports of total services

	Millions of U.S. dollars (current prices)										Average annual percentage growth		
	1980	1990	1991	1992	1993	1994	1995	1996	1997	1998	1999	75-84	85-89	90-MR
SUB-SAHARAN AFRICA	32,207	37,758	36,849	38,108	36,094	35,633	40,779	42,539	43,284	43,212	45,564	7.8	5.1	2.8
excluding South Africa	24,559	28,634	29,003	29,937	28,071	27,197	30,845	32,661	32,823	33,484	35,983	8.9	5.5	2.9
excl. S.Africa & Nigeria	15,873	22,860	23,260	24,615	23,273	21,948	25,432	27,423	27,520	26,881	28,348	10.1	7.2	2.9
Angola	..	2,584	2,967	2,980	2,568	2,534	3,149	3,913	3,756	3,804	4,197	..	20.3	6.4
Benin	112	174	170	219	192	171	226	252	221	224	229	11.2	4.1	4.0
Botswana	351	898	803	790	587	777	960	893	1,214	1,289	1,369	18.6	18.7	6.3
Burkina Faso	228	192	279	238	230	165	204	198	180	191	187	9.1	5.1	-0.9
Burundi	58	149	158	158	133	110	120	57	61	62	44	20.4	14.1	-11.9
Cameroon	1,026	964	1,350	1,741	1,626	1,071	1,115	1,270	1,320	1,208	1,274	19.0	-12.1	0.6
Cape Verde	8	35	24	31	36	40	66	77	84	103	119	29.4	15.8	16.8
Central African Republic	144	192	157	179	155	126	156	124	123	134	133	7.0	12.3	-3.7
Chad	28	260	219	239	240	188	235	246	250	257	237	-7.6	16.6	0.7
Comoros	12	51	48	55	52	45	53	48	30	21	21	..	2.8	-7.7
Congo, Democratic Rep. of	1,160	1,556	1,552	1,223	1,092	1,186	1,266	1,192	1,315	1,359	1,257	8.5	11.3	-1.8
Congo, Republic of	650	1,244	1,232	1,115	1,219	1,253	1,393	1,851	1,497	1,243	1,507	16.3	6.0	5.2
Côte d'Ivoire	2,110	2,321	2,035	2,725	2,484	1,638	2,359	2,383	2,192	2,251	2,197	11.6	7.4	0.2
Djibouti	..	..	110	117	118	97	88	90	92	..	..	..	..	-4.8
Equatorial Guinea	..	49	36	41	51	82	95	224	345	411	410	..	69.2	32.4
Eritrea	0	0	0	0	1	7	44	70	108	78	112	..	..	105.9
Ethiopia	105	260	274	292	314	273	293	318	406	386	398	-1.9	16.5	4.5
Gabon	1,414	1,668	1,519	1,781	1,688	1,336	1,679	1,985	1,833	1,511	1,663	10.8	-3.3	2.0
Gambia, The	44	66	72	80	80	70	70	73	73	82	79	14.3	15.0	1.8
Ghana	355	417	461	513	568	543	588	648	767	757	760	0.4	8.9	7.3
Guinea	238	454	484	408	403	365	407	406	406	443	470	..	12.3	0.0
Guinea-Bissau	..	33	47	43	39	41	48	48	48	37	45	..	10.7	1.2
Kenya	872	1,057	999	906	930	1,041	1,222	1,101	1,036	910	894	4.9	4.3	-0.2
Lesotho	58	103	104	115	93	104	144	137	189	161	144	12.9	14.1	6.2
Liberia	97	..	..	..	..	..	..	..	..	..	..	28.2	7.5	..
Madagascar	368	436	439	421	457	480	539	555	492	523	524	10.2	8.7	2.5
Malawi	330	100	121	96	84	111	125	149	142	147	140	11.5	-0.9	4.5
Mali	221	391	360	440	356	322	395	446	424	432	417	7.9	8.8	2.2
Mauritania	172	277	270	267	258	221	295	298	233	222	205	13.2	4.2	-2.1
Mauritius	207	519	542	619	591	609	681	691	687	884	1,091	8.7	22.1	7.4
Mozambique	155	286	312	355	366	393	416	404	423	509	628	..	7.0	6.7
Namibia	787	500	609	696	640	628	787	830	714	628	644	..	5.2	1.8
Niger	339	198	155	152	143	193	215	193	173	180	165	10.7	3.6	0.0
Nigeria	8,498	5,770	5,743	5,328	4,806	5,250	5,420	5,251	5,315	6,598	7,622	5.3	-0.8	2.7
Rwanda	139	152	131	147	154	132	156	169	222	223	207	13.4	8.8	3.6
São Tomé and Principe	7	26	26	23	22	22	28	27	27	18	23	14.7	11.0	0.2
Senegal	475	808	803	832	787	657	763	743	682	670	660	12.0	9.6	-1.9
Seychelles	43	96	84	91	104	94	116	131	144	173	178	14.6	19.7	8.9
Sierra Leone	95	155	148	154	130	161	133	139	57	73	78	3.4	1.0	-6.2
Somalia	139	-211	..	..	..	..	..	..	..	..	..	9.9	6.1	..
South Africa	7,720	9,168	7,904	8,231	8,077	8,485	9,987	9,937	10,518	9,794	9,659	10.5	4.0	2.6
Sudan	416	1,145	1,097	1,091	1,146	1,183	1,236	1,271	1,391	1,493	1,692	19.8	5.6	3.6
Swaziland	121	247	344	282	364	347	291	268	283	121	347	9.8	18.1	-1.6
Tanzania	160	402	379	635	723	805	659	759	793	898	911	5.7	19.5	7.3
Togo	227	288	273	249	202	264	259	281	289	289	289	14.0	9.9	1.1
Uganda	132	169	187	222	223	241	371	450	460	511	521	6.2	11.9	13.0
Zambia	872	799	693	623	530	566	588	490	622	536	483	3.1	7.5	-4.3
Zimbabwe	330	784	931	961	836	1,016	1,120	1,224	1,415	1,048	993	8.8	7.5	4.6
NORTH AFRICA	8,015	14,795	11,294	13,233	12,612	16,131	16,894	16,860	15,468	19,536	17,503	12.7	4.3	3.8
Algeria	5,035	3,984	4,211	4,065	3,507	3,769	4,320	4,710	4,630	4,590	5,070	16.1	-3.1	2.4
Egypt, Arab Republic	2,931	5,100	1,592	3,027	2,620	5,273	4,952	4,688	3,894	7,342	5,069	20.4	2.5	6.0
Libya	-10,368	-7,575	..	..	..	..	..	..	..	..	..	..	..	..
Morocco	2,076	2,637	2,752	2,943	3,045	3,124	3,459	3,280	3,072	3,190	3,171	9.0	11.8	2.4
Tunisia	918	1,399	1,461	1,701	2,012	2,138	2,250	2,274	2,121	2,203	2,212	11.5	6.6	6.8
ALL AFRICA	41,911	53,008	48,809	51,917	49,245	52,030	58,090	59,890	59,374	63,078	63,634	11.6	5.3	3.0

Note: 1999 data are preliminary (see page 2).

5-5. Net private transfers

	Millions of U.S. dollars (current prices)											Annual average		
	1980	*1990*	*1991*	*1992*	*1993*	*1994*	*1995*	*1996*	*1997*	*1998*	*1999*	*75-84*	*85-89*	*90-MR*
SUB-SAHARAN AFRICA	-319	350	617	1,937	1,850	2,329	2,437	2,895	4,533	4,691	4,529	19	948	2,617
excluding South Africa	-413	395	624	1,934	1,857	2,341	2,454	2,918	4,530	4,681	4,526	-11	857	2,626
excl. S.Africa & Nigeria	-413	369	596	1,150	1,065	1,792	1,655	1,974	2,663	3,111	2,884	7	864	1,726
Angola	..	-142	-32	11	-14	-4	31	31	32	68	70	26	-19	5
Benin	107	86	84	95	94	50	68	67	77	89	95	60	77	81
Botswana	-11	-41	-39	-19	-65	-85	103	-23	220	220	220	-5	-9	49
Burkina Faso	112	105	98	169	153	98	106	84	75	75	67	75	164	103
Burundi	3	10	13	13	17	21	16	11	9	6	6	6	9	12
Cameroon	19	-67	-59	-72	-95	-41	-23	7	86	80	100	11	-69	-8
Cape Verde	40	55	58	70	71	81	100	96	71	90	96	30	34	79
Central African Republic	0	-31	-30	-27	-31	-10	-11	-10	-10	-9	-6	0	-14	-17
Chad	-4	-1	-9	-15	-23	-8	2	4	4	3	3	-6	-5	-4
Comoros	2	6	4	5	11	7	9	12	11	11	13	2	6	9
Congo, Democratic Rep. of	-79	-81	-82	-97	-123	-98	-124	-138	-35	-37	-38	-47	-72	-85
Congo, Republic of	-1	-16	-15	-19	-9	60	-1	-4	-4	-11	-13	-44	-64	-3
Côte d'Ivoire	-706	-501	-368	-379	-305	-259	-439	-470	-417	-450	-475	-403	-413	-406
Djibouti	..	..	-8	-9	-10	-11	-11	-10	-9	..	..	..	..	-10
Equatorial Guinea	..	-2	-2	-4	-3	0	-3	-3	-1	0	0	0	-1	-2
Eritrea	0	0	0	128	165	276	215	244	352	246	244	0	0	187
Ethiopia	20	171	203	316	248	247	311	313	258	317	289	37	162	267
Gabon	-124	-158	-125	-190	-209	-163	-192	-216	-218	-160	-170	-58	-143	-180
Gambia, The	2	9	10	12	13	15	16	17	17	24	20	2	3	15
Ghana	-3	202	220	255	261	271	263	276	400	454	472	7	136	307
Guinea	-3	-53	-57	-73	-79	-82	-92	-49	-37	-32	-31	-3	-26	-59
Guinea-Bissau	..	1	1	1	1	1	3	2	2	16	5	-10	-1	3
Kenya	27	167	144	68	147	148	408	433	497	474	566	41	76	305
Lesotho	2	19	14	16	13	13	3	2	2	1	2	29	20	8
Liberia	-29	..	..	..	..	..	..	..	..	..	..	-32	-25	..
Madagascar	-21	77	67	109	114	46	75	88	116	83	104	-14	54	88
Malawi	..	-11	-33	14	30	20	-4	-24	-19	-22	-23	15	13	-7
Mali	40	102	70	74	93	85	96	90	73	68	68	24	53	82
Mauritania	-28	6	1	77	28	14	30	39	54	56	46	-25	69	35
Mauritius	0	74	71	79	92	94	90	101	77	182	110	4	47	97
Mozambique	0	0	0	0	0	0	0	0	0	0	0	0	0	0
Namibia	0	25	27	50	23	16	24	26	21	10	12	0	0	24
Niger	-57	-50	-38	-40	-34	-41	-23	-23	-22	-22	-15	-40	-26	-31
Nigeria	..	26	28	784	792	549	799	945	1,867	1,570	1,642	-137	-18	900
Rwanda	0	6	21	20	22	45	16	27	25	18	18	1	7	22
São Tomé and Principe	1	0	1	1	2	3	1	1	1	1	1	1	0	1
Senegal	0	29	28	26	40	39	40	40	36	37	36	-1	7	35
Seychelles	0	-3	-2	-3	-6	-7	-5	-6	-6	-6	-6	0	5	-5
Sierra Leone	0	0	0	0	0	0	0	0	6	5	7	1	1	2
Somalia	57	..	..	..	..	..	..	..	..	..	..	43	..	..
South Africa	94	-44	-7	3	-7	-12	-17	-23	3	10	3	79	91	-9
Sudan	257	134	124	138	81	68	60	321	429	490	446	267	330	229
Swaziland	0	4	9	4	27	40	37	32	21	50	24	1	3	25
Tanzania	22	196	172	194	197	465	18	20	26	31	34	22	364	135
Togo	1	10	14	9	10	8	13	13	12	13	14	-1	8	12
Uganda	-2	78	81	136	108	304	330	421	322	539	375	7	95	269
Zambia	-176	-43	-40	-33	-19	-19	-20	-17	-16	-27	-16	-86	-35	-25
Zimbabwe	120	-2	2	40	26	86	120	149	126	128	115	87	23	79
NORTH AFRICA	..	..	..	..	..	..	..	7,170	7,224	7,887	7,870	..	..	7,538
Algeria	..	..	..	..	..	..	..	1,045	1,075	1,104	1,108	..	..	1,083
Egypt, Arab Republic	2,791	3,743	2,569	3,029	3,835	3,232	3,279	2,798	3,256	3,718	3,772	2,091	3,289	3,323
Libya	-1,089	-446	..	..	..	..	..	..	..	..	..	-1,075	-571	-446
Morocco	1,070	2,151	2,157	2,325	2,141	2,096	2,261	2,526	2,158	2,293	2,148	822	1,419	2,226
Tunisia	348	613	563	570	597	688	753	801	736	772	842	255	435	693
ALL AFRICA	2,802	6,411	5,906	7,860	8,423	8,346	8,729	10,065	11,757	12,578	12,399	2,308	5,520	9,247

Note: 1999 data are preliminary (see page 2). Nigeria's series shows a data break between 1991 and 1992.

5-6. Net official current transfers

	Millions of U.S. dollars (current prices)											Annual average		
	1980	1990	1991	1992	1993	1994	1995	1996	1997	1998	1999	75-84	85-89	90-MR
SUB-SAHARAN AFRICA	1,229	2,808	2,184	2,184	1,755	1,973	1,509	1,478	1,303	1,354	1,071	1,365	1,958	1,762
excluding South Africa	..	2,704	2,689	2,553	2,389	2,569	2,137	2,201	2,028	2,102	2,001	1,330	1,903	2,337
excl. S.Africa & Nigeria	..	2,656	2,667	2,562	2,335	2,618	2,203	2,269	2,053	2,156	1,981	1,358	1,895	2,350
Angola	..	65	60	91	179	249	125	194	74	92	87	..	67	122
Benin	0	19	19	20	64	5	6	4	0	0	3	0	3	14
Botswana	65	171	218	135	142	160	-131	113	129	129	129	31	135	119
Burkina Faso	0	158	128	79	108	129	133	121	90	115	88	0	0	115
Burundi	42	105	120	102	111	144	136	50	51	50	46	45	65	91
Cameroon	64	28	118	248	76	61	80	28	0	25	17	40	115	68
Cape Verde	0	30	32	58	35	40	19	9	16	5	5	0	28	25
Central African Republic	0	56	73	50	50	32	33	8	23	34	31	27	41	39
Chad	0	105	102	108	49	129	78	57	59	50	21	0	95	76
Comoros	11	36	33	24	38	21	24	21	15	12	4	20	38	23
Congo, Democratic Rep. of	267	54	25	8	7	99	153	112	68	170	240	137	113	93
Congo, Republic of	0	10	5	0	0	19	44	35	6	6	10	0	3	14
Côte d'Ivoire	0	226	74	-20	46	-31	-27	-28	-22	-21	-20	23	92	18
Djibouti	..	..	34	26	49	42	50	48	41	..	..	..	..	41
Equatorial Guinea	..	8	2	1	1	7	7	4	6	4	3	0	6	4
Eritrea	0	0	0	43	17	44	22	27	0	0	0	0	0	15
Ethiopia	60	49	26	57	108	87	148	133	1	32	13	40	57	65
Gabon	33	21	14	6	14	15	0	0	0	17	17	30	16	10
Gambia, The	..	..	..	..	0	0	0	0	0	0	0	1	0	0
Ghana	0	0	0	0	0	0	0	0	160	287	148	0	0	60
Guinea	0	0	0	0	0	0	0	0	0	0	0	0	0	0
Guinea-Bissau	..	40	25	29	21	26	30	30	23	8	22	6	24	25
Kenya	0	0	0	0	0	0	0	0	0	83	-2	0	0	8
Lesotho	-90	-161	-45	-33	-39	139	241	225	225	165	137	-174	-166	86
Liberia	36	..	..	..	..	..	..	..	..	..	..	57	78	..
Madagascar	0	161	113	54	70	44	17	33	80	17	35	37	106	62
Malawi	0	0	0	0	0	0	0	0	0	0	0	0	0	0
Mali	-6	124	179	214	132	143	97	106	56	47	39	2	98	114
Mauritania	118	67	61	72	86	41	32	104	105	87	118	119	111	77
Mauritius	0	13	17	14	6	7	17	13	35	5	2	3	19	13
Mozambique	0	0	0	0	0	0	0	0	0	0	0	0	0	0
Namibia	101	329	348	401	328	310	379	390	424	396	393	360	294	370
Niger	154	25	18	34	61	0	0	0	0	0	-5	127	104	13
Nigeria	-167	48	22	-9	54	-49	-66	-68	-26	-54	20	-44	8	-13
Rwanda	104	138	162	92	78	347	231	196	176	172	206	92	74	180
São Tomé and Principe	0	12	9	3	2	3	5	1	10	9	6	0	6	6
Senegal	28	3	3	8	-26	95	70	18	5	16	-8	-10	-4	19
Seychelles	15	21	19	20	22	15	13	22	21	21	21	13	23	19
Sierra Leone	26	30	34	0	0	10	0	21	7	3	11	11	13	12
Somalia	143	265	..	..	..	..	..	..	..	..	..	111	291	265
South Africa	145	104	-505	-369	-634	-596	-628	-723	-725	-748	-930	96	55	-575
Sudan	84	274	237	177	77	55	44	41	23	17	11	124	335	95
Swaziland	79	98	100	124	128	116	102	110	128	79	129	46	60	111
Tanzania	0	264	235	262	266	0	0	0	0	0	0	42	0	103
Togo	86	77	68	56	28	16	26	24	21	22	..	55	56	37
Uganda	0	0	0	0	0	0	0	0	0	0	0	6	0	0
Zambia	0	0	0	0	0	0	0	0	0	0	0	10	0	0
Zimbabwe	0	0	0	0	0	0	0	0	0	0	0	0	0	0
NORTH AFRICA	..	1,233	..	..	..	..	..	798	962	952	1,101	..	..	1,009
Algeria	0	0	0	0	0	0	0	0	0	0	0	0	0	0
Egypt, Arab Republic	..	1,094	4,851	1,352	1,902	814	919	724	890	883	1,097	..	584	1,452
Libya	-46	-35	..	..	..	..	..	..	..	..	..	-85	-39	-35
Morocco	47	174	118	208	154	173	70	50	48	52	-11	15	95	104
Tunisia	42	0	0	0	0	0	0	25	25	18	16	36	7	8
ALL AFRICA	..	4,041	7,153	3,745	3,811	2,959	2,498	2,276	2,265	2,306	2,173	1,339	2,365	3,323

Note: 1999 data are preliminary (see page 2).

5-7. Current account balance, excluding net capital grants

	Millions of U.S. dollars (current prices)											Annual average		
	1980	1990	1991	1992	1993	1994	1995	1996	1997	1998	1999	75-84	85-89	90-MR
SUB-SAHARAN AFRICA	-717	-7,484	-10,584	-13,137	-13,541	-10,817	-13,731	-7,636	-11,285	-19,126	-18,345	-8,867	-7,728	-12,569
excluding South Africa	-4,226	-9,550	-12,845	-15,084	-15,030	-10,911	-11,527	-5,745	-9,022	-17,022	-17,878	-8,526	-10,025	-12,461
excl. S.Africa & Nigeria	-8,536	-11,077	-11,865	-13,786	-12,872	-9,293	-10,630	-9,698	-11,862	-13,907	-14,065	-6,759	-8,184	-11,906
Angola	..	-236	-651	-874	-848	-563	-993	-249	-869	-2,023	-1,803	..	-49	-911
Benin	-197	-95	-89	-151	-95	-73	-163	-177	-140	-141	-177	-174	-84	-130
Botswana	-152	42	337	244	503	239	338	663	542	136	-275	-101	301	277
Burkina Faso	-259	-101	-188	-186	-163	-35	-133	-251	-243	-261	-326	-203	-227	-189
Burundi	-86	-126	-95	-117	-79	-15	-4	-39	2	-55	-26	-98	-90	-55
Cameroon	-495	-196	-50	-216	-620	-324	-71	-375	-258	-235	-396	-389	-356	-274
Cape Verde	-25	-18	-17	-20	-33	-38	-83	-64	-69	-100	-110	-38	-14	-55
Central African Republic	-43	-189	-111	-173	-108	-48	-81	-63	-57	-87	-67	-24	-96	-98
Chad	-16	-178	-143	-162	-219	-115	-110	-134	-143	-158	-195	-80	-150	-156
Comoros	-9	-22	-12	-35	-7	-22	-25	-20	-20	-6	-11	-14	-9	-18
Congo, Democratic Rep. of	-87	-738	-1,037	-866	-528	-530	-465	-348	-658	-583	-432	-366	-514	-618
Congo, Republic of	-167	-261	-508	-315	-541	-670	-634	-667	-406	-366	-393	-258	-230	-476
Côte d'Ivoire	..	-1,368	-1,347	-1,515	-1,496	-131	-668	-588	-527	-639	-401	-594	-686	-868
Djibouti	..	..	-77	-130	-71	-64	-28	-29	-32	..	..	..	..	-62
Equatorial Guinea	..	-49	-81	-47	-45	-71	-96	-268	-189	-375	3	-15	-35	-122
Eritrea	0	0	0	-19	46	62	-31	-104	-37	-238	-282	0	0	-60
Ethiopia	-126	-244	-528	-335	-497	-291	-90	-191	-417	-333	-709	-176	-376	-363
Gabon	514	150	91	-226	-58	336	159	317	237	-183	131	157	-490	95
Gambia, The	-86	-41	-46	-51	-54	-48	-62	-65	-43	-49	-50	-47	-33	-51
Ghana	-54	-432	-454	-592	-815	-456	-414	-420	-991	-353	-816	-154	-254	-574
Guinea	-26	-264	-198	-260	-225	-267	-316	-302	-244	-227	-253	-62	-227	-256
Guinea-Bissau	..	-36	-62	-86	-50	-29	-45	-45	-39	-34	-28	..	-49	-45
Kenya	-1,233	-655	-309	-290	88	14	-475	-140	-472	-490	-329	-493	-572	-306
Lesotho	-207	-363	-354	-418	-371	-212	-283	-276	-269	-235	-226	-222	-270	-301
Liberia	46	..	..	..	..	..	..	..	..	..	..	15	-15	..
Madagascar	-635	-238	-216	-222	-263	-280	-307	-249	-198	-281	-211	-264	-142	-247
Malawi	-310	-145	-250	-371	-342	-271	-177	-272	-317	-292	-203	-163	-110	-264
Mali	-232	-191	-150	-216	-185	-146	-228	-265	-187	-203	-232	-168	-216	-200
Mauritania	-133	-139	-93	-90	-105	-37	-102	-40	1	-36	29	-133	-22	-61
Mauritius	-139	-111	-16	-6	-103	-228	-14	52	-62	35	-171	-81	-6	-63
Mozambique	-423	-766	-738	-738	-825	-864	-677	-647	-611	-749	-1,204	-489	-635	-782
Namibia	-40	28	105	50	110	85	176	116	91	163	136	-13	39	106
Niger	-429	-177	-128	-24	-24	-233	-208	-183	-187	-202	-181	-247	-33	-155
Nigeria	4,310	1,527	-980	-1,298	-2,158	-1,618	-897	3,953	2,840	-3,115	-3,813	-1,767	-1,841	-556
Rwanda	-48	-86	-33	-157	-218	-53	-15	-70	-146	-167	-90	-23	-157	-103
São Tomé and Principe	1	-26	-30	-31	-33	-28	-35	-34	-23	-12	-21	-6	-19	-28
Senegal	-524	-438	-455	-545	-578	-251	-298	-336	-322	-289	-352	-392	-488	-386
Seychelles	-23	-11	-8	-8	-42	-21	-44	-55	-68	-98	-103	-17	6	-46
Sierra Leone	-168	-90	-60	-125	-117	-69	-93	-140	-21	-58	-42	-128	-56	-82
Somalia	-136	-81	..	..	..	..	..	..	..	..	..	-117	-121	-81
South Africa	3,508	2,065	2,261	1,947	1,489	94	-2,204	-1,891	-2,263	-2,104	-467	-341	2,297	-107
Sudan	-721	-1,299	-1,538	-1,354	-1,426	-1,459	-1,479	-1,548	-1,641	-1,997	-1,555	-555	-603	-1,529
Swaziland	-130	85	80	1	-64	34	30	-30	-49	280	-61	-61	42	31
Tanzania	-540	-764	-818	-1,068	-1,115	-1,076	-1,047	-942	-842	-1,242	-1,295	-424	-586	-1,021
Togo	-95	-137	-79	-119	-84	-64	-63	-112	-88	-89	-120	-101	-90	-95
Uganda	-121	-429	-449	-338	-396	-265	-444	-500	-521	-706	-746	-57	-177	-479
Zambia	-538	-388	-513	-743	-467	-398	-464	-427	-509	-576	-499	-377	-308	-498
Zimbabwe	-444	-257	-547	-842	-311	-318	-370	-180	-823	-355	28	-283	-46	-398
NORTH AFRICA	6,271	2,071	5,053	2,168	1,293	-2,787	-3,870	597	2,858	-4,248	-2,441	-3,616	-3,798	69
Algeria	242	1,352	2,223	1,020	802	-1,820	-2,240	1,260	3,450	-910	20	-1,008	-1,123	516
Egypt, Arab Republic	-438	-634	3,821	2,670	2,295	410	386	-185	119	-2,479	-1,709	-1,765	-1,701	469
Libya	8,259	2,236	..	..	..	..	..	..	..	..	..	1,034	-408	2,236
Morocco	-1,420	-204	-413	-433	-521	-723	-1,186	35	-87	-144	-265	-1,369	-251	-394
Tunisia	-373	-679	-577	-1,089	-1,283	-654	-830	-513	-623	-716	-487	-507	-314	-745
ALL AFRICA	5,553	-5,413	-5,531	-10,970	-12,248	-13,603	-17,601	-7,039	-8,427	-23,374	-20,786	-12,483	-11,526	-12,499

Note: 1999 data are preliminary (see page 2).

5-8. Current account balance, excluding net capital grants/GDP

	Percentage of GDP											*Annual average*		
	1980	*1990*	*1991*	*1992*	*1993*	*1994*	*1995*	*1996*	*1997*	*1998*	*1999*	*75-84*	*85-89*	*90-MR*
SUB-SAHARAN AFRICA	0.0	-2.5	-3.5	-4.4	-4.8	-3.9	-4.4	-2.3	-3.3	-6.0	-5.7	-4.4	-3.2	-4.1
excluding South Africa	-2.3	-5.2	-7.2	-8.8	-9.7	-7.6	-7.0	-3.1	-4.7	-9.1	-9.3	-6.2	-6.2	-7.2
excl. S.Africa & Nigeria	-8.5	-7.2	-7.8	-10.0	-9.7	-7.8	-7.8	-6.5	-7.6	-9.0	-9.0	-7.5	-6.0	-8.2
Angola	..	-2.3	-5.3	-15.1	-16.0	-13.9	-19.1	-3.3	-11.3	-31.4	-21.1	..	-0.6	-13.9
Benin	-14.0	-5.1	-4.8	-9.3	-4.5	-4.9	-8.1	-8.0	-6.5	-6.1	-7.3	-16.6	-5.8	-6.5
Botswana	-13.4	1.1	8.6	5.9	12.1	5.4	6.9	13.5	10.7	2.8	-4.6	-11.4	13.5	6.2
Burkina Faso	-15.2	-3.7	-6.8	-9.3	-7.9	-1.9	-5.7	-9.9	-10.2	-10.1	-12.6	-15.6	-11.4	-7.8
Burundi	-9.3	-11.1	-8.2	-10.8	-8.4	-1.6	-0.4	-4.4	0.3	-6.2	-3.6	-9.8	-8.0	-5.4
Cameroon	-7.3	-1.8	-0.4	-1.9	-5.2	-4.1	-0.9	-4.1	-2.8	-2.7	-4.3	-7.5	-3.2	-2.8
Cape Verde	-23.5	-5.3	-4.8	-5.2	-9.0	-9.1	-16.9	-12.7	-13.6	-18.6	-19.0	-42.3	-9.4	-11.4
Central African Republic	-5.4	-12.7	-7.9	-12.1	-8.3	-5.6	-7.2	-5.9	-5.7	-8.3	-6.4	-4.0	-8.2	-8.0
Chad	-1.5	-10.3	-7.6	-8.6	-15.0	-9.8	-7.7	-8.4	-9.5	-9.4	-12.7	-8.6	-12.3	-9.9
Comoros	-7.2	-8.7	-5.0	-13.3	-2.5	-11.7	-11.5	-9.2	-10.2	-3.1	-5.7	-13.0	-6.0	-8.1
Congo, Democratic Rep. of	-0.6	-7.9	-11.4	-10.6	-5.9	-7.4	-7.3	-5.9	-10.8	-8.4	-5.6	-3.4	-6.2	-8.1
Congo, Republic of	-9.8	-9.3	-18.7	-10.7	-28.2	-37.8	-25.3	-26.3	-17.5	-18.8	-17.7	-21.5	-11.1	-21.0
Côte d'Ivoire	..	-12.7	-12.8	-13.6	-14.4	-1.7	-6.7	-5.5	-5.0	-5.7	-3.6	-8.6	-6.8	-8.2
Djibouti	..	..	-16.8	-27.6	-15.1	-13.2	-5.7	-6.1	-6.4	..	..	..	..	-13.0
Equatorial Guinea	..	-37.1	-61.8	-30.6	-29.7	-56.4	-58.3	-103.5	-38.1	-82.2	0.4	..	-30.6	-49.7
Eritrea	..	..	..	-4.4	11.2	12.1	-5.4	-16.5	-5.6	-35.0	-43.7	..	..	-10.9
Ethiopia	..	-3.6	-9.9	-6.0	-8.0	-5.9	-1.6	-3.2	-6.5	-5.1	-11.0	-5.8	-5.1	-6.1
Gabon	12.0	2.5	1.7	-4.0	-1.3	8.0	3.2	5.5	4.4	-4.0	3.0	4.2	-13.9	1.9
Gambia, The	-35.7	-12.8	-14.4	-14.7	-14.6	-13.3	-16.3	-16.6	-10.6	-11.7	-12.8	-22.5	-15.1	-13.8
Ghana	-1.2	-7.3	-6.9	-9.2	-13.7	-8.4	-6.4	-6.0	-14.3	-4.7	-10.5	-3.9	-5.0	-8.7
Guinea	..	-9.4	-6.6	-7.9	-6.9	-7.8	-8.5	-7.6	-6.3	-6.0	-6.8	..	-10.1	-7.4
Guinea-Bissau	..	-14.6	-24.2	-37.8	-21.0	-12.4	-17.6	-16.5	-14.7	-16.5	-13.0	..	-26.6	-18.8
Kenya	-17.0	-7.7	-3.8	-3.6	1.8	0.2	-5.3	-1.5	-4.4	-4.3	-3.1	-8.4	-7.4	-3.2
Lesotho	-47.9	-58.3	-52.0	-50.5	-45.4	-25.3	-30.4	-29.4	-26.3	-26.8	-25.8	-66.6	-61.1	-37.0
Liberia	4.1	..	..	..	..	..	..	..	..	..	..	1.9	-1.2	..
Madagascar	-15.7	-7.7	-8.1	-7.4	-7.8	-9.4	-9.7	-6.2	-5.6	-7.5	-5.7	-7.6	-5.3	-7.5
Malawi	-25.0	-8.0	-11.3	-20.6	-16.5	-22.9	-12.4	-11.2	-12.5	-16.8	-11.2	-15.6	-8.4	-14.4
Mali	-13.0	-7.9	-6.2	-7.6	-6.9	-8.3	-9.2	-10.1	-7.6	-7.7	-8.9	-12.9	-12.6	-8.0
Mauritania	-18.8	-13.7	-8.2	-7.6	-11.1	-3.6	-9.5	-3.6	0.1	-3.6	3.1	-19.9	-3.0	-5.8
Mauritius	-12.3	-4.2	-0.6	-0.2	-3.2	-6.5	-0.4	1.2	-1.5	0.9	-4.0	-7.6	0.0	-1.9
Mozambique	-12.0	-30.5	-29.6	-37.8	-39.2	-38.1	-28.3	-22.3	-17.4	-19.2	-29.1	-14.2	-23.1	-29.1
Namibia	-1.8	1.2	4.2	1.8	4.2	2.9	5.5	3.7	2.8	5.4	4.4	-0.6	2.9	3.6
Niger	-17.1	-7.1	-5.5	-1.0	-1.5	-14.9	-11.0	-9.2	-10.1	-9.7	-9.0	-13.6	-3.1	-7.9
Nigeria	6.7	5.4	-3.6	-4.0	-10.1	-6.8	-3.2	11.2	7.8	-9.7	-10.9	-4.5	-8.5	-2.4
Rwanda	-4.1	-3.3	-1.7	-7.7	-11.1	-7.0	-1.2	-5.0	-7.8	-8.2	-4.6	-1.6	-7.0	-5.8
São Tomé and Príncipe	2.3	-51.8	-53.3	-67.9	-70.1	-57.4	-76.7	-76.0	-53.1	-30.5	-45.8	-18.5	-40.7	-58.3
Senegal	-17.5	-7.7	-8.3	-9.0	-10.6	-6.9	-6.7	-7.2	-7.4	-6.2	-7.3	-16.1	-12.4	-7.7
Seychelles	-15.9	-2.9	-2.1	-1.7	-9.0	-4.4	-8.7	-10.8	-12.7	-18.3	-18.9	-15.8	2.8	-9.0
Sierra Leone	-14.4	-10.0	-7.5	-18.1	-15.2	-7.5	-10.7	-14.9	-2.4	-8.6	-6.3	-10.1	-5.1	-10.1
Somalia	-22.6	-8.8	..	..	..	..	..	..	..	..	..	-17.3	-12.2	-8.8
South Africa	4.4	1.8	1.9	1.5	1.1	0.1	-1.5	-1.3	-1.5	-1.6	-0.4	-0.5	3.2	0.0
Sudan	-9.5	-9.9	-13.5	-21.1	-18.1	-17.9	-20.6	-21.5	-16.0	-19.9	-16.0	-7.0	-3.8	-17.4
Swaziland	-22.3	9.8	9.1	0.1	-6.4	3.2	2.4	-2.5	-3.7	22.9	-5.0	-11.0	5.4	3.0
Tanzania	..	-17.9	-16.5	-23.2	-26.2	-23.8	-19.9	-14.5	-11.0	-14.5	-14.8	-10.0	-13.5	-18.2
Togo	-8.4	-8.4	-4.9	-7.0	-6.8	-6.5	-4.8	-7.6	-5.8	-6.3	-8.5	-12.2	-7.8	-6.7
Uganda	-9.7	-10.0	-13.5	-11.8	-12.3	-6.6	-7.7	-8.3	-8.3	-10.4	-11.6	-3.1	-3.2	-10.1
Zambia	-13.8	-11.8	-15.2	-23.4	-14.3	-11.9	-13.4	-13.1	-13.0	-17.8	-15.8	-11.9	-13.0	-15.0
Zimbabwe	-6.6	-2.9	-6.3	-12.5	-4.7	-4.6	-5.2	-2.1	-9.5	-5.2	0.5	-4.0	-0.8	-5.3
NORTH AFRICA	4.9	-0.1	4.1	1.6	0.9	-2.0	-2.5	0.3	1.6	-2.3	-1.3	-4.0	-2.6	0.0
Algeria	0.6	2.2	4.8	2.1	1.6	-4.3	-5.4	2.7	7.2	-1.9	0.0	-4.5	-1.9	0.9
Egypt, Arab Republic	-1.9	-1.5	10.3	6.4	4.9	0.8	0.6	-0.3	0.2	-3.0	-1.9	-9.6	-4.7	1.7
Libya	23.2	..	..	..	..	..	..	..	..	..	..	4.8	-2.2	..
Morocco	-7.5	-0.8	-1.5	-1.5	-1.9	-2.4	-3.6	0.1	-0.3	-0.4	-0.8	-10.3	-1.7	-1.3
Tunisia	-4.3	-5.5	-4.4	-7.0	-8.8	-4.2	-4.6	-2.6	-3.3	-3.6	-2.3	-7.4	-3.5	-4.6
ALL AFRICA	1.7	-1.7	-1.3	-2.5	-2.9	-3.2	-3.8	-1.4	-1.6	-4.6	-4.0	-4.3	-3.0	-2.7

Note: 1999 data are preliminary (see page 2). Since 1994, Nigeria's ratios are distorted because the official exchange rate used by the Government for oil exports and oil value added is significantly over-valued.

5-9. Net capital grants

	Millions of U.S. dollars (current prices)											Annual average		
	1980	1990	1991	1992	1993	1994	1995	1996	1997	1998	1999	75-84	85-89	90-MR
SUB-SAHARAN AFRICA	1,130	3,573	4,040	5,076	4,332	3,932	4,118	3,745	3,459	3,854	3,739	1,095	2,656	3,987
excluding South Africa	1,130	3,561	4,076	5,118	4,390	3,866	4,158	3,792	3,653	3,910	3,782	1,110	2,652	4,031
excl. S.Africa & Nigeria	1,130	3,561	4,076	5,118	4,390	3,866	4,158	3,792	3,653	3,910	3,782	1,110	2,652	4,031
Angola	0	0	0	0	0	0	0	0	0	0	0	0	0	0
Benin	63	59	45	59	63	54	70	56	84	62	76	63	63	63
Botswana	8	3	4	7	9	6	3	5	5	5	5	6	4	5
Burkina Faso	211	68	98	142	98	65	103	159	139	144	191	151	193	121
Burundi	34	59	66	63	53	0	0	0	0	0	0	38	37	24
Cameroon	0	0	0	0	0	0	0	0	0	0	0	0	0	0
Cape Verde	29	2	8	9	19	20	51	53	39	48	57	20	10	31
Central African Republic	0	62	65	82	69	63	56	39	38	70	66	0	43	61
Chad	28	88	77	76	95	70	53	49	53	70	49	76	107	68
Comoros	0	14	11	21	14	0	0	6	8	11	11	0	0	10
Congo, Democratic Rep. of	0	163	76	24	19	41	204	110	1	50	50	0	108	74
Congo, Republic of	0	0	0	0	0	0	0	0	0	·0	28	0	0	3
Côte d'Ivoire	..	0	53	86	95	53	70	79	69	68	65	0	0	64
Djibouti	0	0	56	58	42	24	10	9	13	0	0	0	0	21
Equatorial Guinea	..	35	35	26	29	5	3	2	3	3	2	7	20	14
Eritrea	0	0	0	125	52	36	49	55	51	63	77	0	0	51
Ethiopia	0	113	266	375	293	199	280	259	225	229	200	26	183	244
Gabon	0	0	0	0	0	0	0	0	0	0	0	0	0	0
Gambia, The	..	44	38	36	40	35	28	26	28	36	31	17	41	34
Ghana	83	214	202	216	256	201	260	206	159	288	149	69	144	215
Guinea	17	95	114	131	124	124	150	130	125	128	101	13	56	122
Guinea-Bissau	..	30	33	28	37	44	56	41	32	0	21	16	32	32
Kenya	118	205	204	214	94	87	90	125	82	83	62	84	174	125
Lesotho	..	69	58	50	42	40	41	40	43	30	20	6	25	43
Liberia	..	..	..	..	..	..	..	..	..	..	..	..	..	..
Madagascar	0	0	0	72	87	72	85	99	113	100	108	16	0	74
Malawi	50	81	59	147	120	111	152	97	83	157	140	33	50	115
Mali	78	45	63	36	30	57	99	94	92	76	78	95	62	67
Mauritania	0	21	22	21	20	26	30	10	16	25	12	0	42	20
Mauritius	11	25	15	19	2	1	13	13	13	13	13	5	18	13
Mozambique	56	448	502	499	503	565	339	225	313	313	434	90	293	414
Namibia	0	42	29	32	27	43	40	42	33	24	22	0	0	34
Niger	0	159	140	95	94	134	120	117	113	127	105	0	55	120
Nigeria	0	0	0	0	0	0	0	0	0	0	0	0	0	0
Rwanda	0	0	0	79	87	7	69	68	87	71	53	10	0	52
São Tomé and Principe	0	8	7	4	8	8	18	20	22	4	9	0	3	11
Senegal	92	262	262	328	266	256	272	273	251	209	177	138	226	256
Seychelles	15	21	19	20	22	15	13	22	21	15	16	10	23	18
Sierra Leone	11	0	0	0	0	0	0	3	0	1	4	5	5	1
Somalia	0	0	0	0	0	0	0	0	0	..	..	0	0	0
South Africa	0	12	-36	-42	-58	66	-40	-47	-194	-56	-43	-16	4	-44
Sudan	0	0	0	20	29	15	11	8	4	0	23	4	0	11
Swaziland	-2	2	0	0	0	0	0	0	0	0	0	-1	0	0
Tanzania	108	530	549	809	759	634	525	581	690	695	737	115	378	651
Togo	..	37	24	26	4	7	8	7	13	15	..	24	34	16
Uganda	38	153	262	206	277	228	303	277	307	380	277	47	72	267
Zambia	23	296	521	635	340	338	318	304	198	221	214	13	95	338
Zimbabwe	58	108	95	242	173	181	167	85	85	77	101	39	68	131
NORTH AFRICA	43	210	122	81	104	103	70	46	95	82	73	195	537	98
Algeria	0	0	0	0	0	0	0	0	0	0	0	0	0	0
Egypt, Arab Republic	2	0	0	0	0	0	0	0	0	0	0	182	461	0
Libya	0	0	0	0	0	0	0	0	0	..	..	0	0	0
Morocco	0	0	0	0	0	0	0	0	0	0	0	0	0	0
Tunisia	42	210	122	81	104	103	70	46	95	82	73	27	75	98
ALL AFRICA	1,173	3,782	4,162	5,158	4,435	4,035	4,189	3,791	3,554	3,936	3,812	1,290	3,193	4,085

Note: 1999 data are preliminary (see page 2).

5-10. Net foreign direct investment

	Millions of U.S. dollars (current prices)											Annual average		
	1980	1990	1991	1992	1993	1994	1995	1996	1997	1998	1999	75-84	85-89	90-MR
SUB-SAHARAN AFRICA	-728	756	1,667	793	999	2,105	2,458	4,012	4,701	5,214	..	690	1,800	2,523
excluding South Africa	37	760	1,656	1,571	1,311	1,921	2,683	3,868	4,017	4,814	..	878	1,934	2,511
excl. S.Africa & Nigeria	776	158	1,068	857	730	1,333	2,006	3,109	2,871	3,462	..	796	1,077	1,733
Angola	..	-336	665	288	302	327	303	588	492	1,115	2,520	346	192	626
Benin	4	2	4	26	-7	8	4	-6	19	18	31	2	1	10
Botswana	109	89	-17	-12	-296	-24	30	89	100	100	100	46	64	16
Burkina Faso	0	-11	22	9	9	25	20	16	11	-13	13	1	0	10
Burundi	1	1	1	1	0	0	1	0	0	0	0	1	1	0
Cameroon	105	110	147	206	134	-228	-154	92	100	-50	25	58	322	38
Cape Verde	..	0	1	-1	3	2	26	28	12	6	69	..	1	15
Central African Republic	5	1	-8	4	-15	-13	4	12	-5	7	2	6	4	-1
Chad	0	25	5	3	21	35	37	43	37	46	45	11	21	30
Comoros	0	-1	3	-1	0	0	1	1	0	0	0	0	3	0
Congo, Democratic Rep. of	0	13	0	0	0	0	0	0	0	20	100	91	9	13
Congo, Republic of	40	-60	-65	49	254	285	181	35	296	42	85	24	18	110
Côte d'Ivoire	83	26	45	35	24	-25	234	223	314	247	196	51	53	132
Djibouti	..	..	2	2	1	1	3	3	2	..	..	..	..	2
Equatorial Guinea	..	12	43	-3	-10	65	93	264	185	366	30	0	1	105
Eritrea	0	0	0	0	0	0	0	37	39	52	83	0	0	21
Ethiopia	0	0	0	0	0	0	0	0	60	7	136	3	0	20
Gabon	24	80	-150	-87	-114	-100	-109	-146	-63	-62	129	59	219	-62
Gambia, The	..	6	10	11	9	6	6	8	9	12	7	..	5	8
Ghana	16	15	20	22	106	128	83	70	36	45	46	13	7	57
Guinea	34	10	46	56	6	11	25	17	45	29	39	12	25	28
Guinea-Bissau	..	0	0	0	0	0	0	0	0	0	0	..	0	0
Kenya	78	23	19	6	2	4	33	13	40	40	42	25	27	22
Lesotho	4	17	7	3	185	249	295	278	290	193	180	2	9	170
Liberia	..	..	..	..	..	..	..	..	..	..	..	47	2	..
Madagascar	0	22	14	21	15	6	10	10	14	16	58	-1	3	19
Malawi	10	0	0	0	0	0	0	30	24	34	39	4	0	13
Mali	2	-14	-8	-9	-7	38	30	60	-14	16	16	0	1	11
Mauritania	27	6	4	5	12	3	7	0	-3	0	0	1	2	3
Mauritius	1	35	14	-16	-18	10	26	18	26	-2	25	2	19	12
Mozambique	0	9	23	25	32	35	45	73	64	213	382	0	3	90
Namibia	..	28	114	120	47	104	157	150	90	99	95	..	..	100
Niger	44	-12	0	0	0	0	0	0	0	0	2	17	-5	-1
Nigeria	-739	602	588	714	581	588	677	760	1,539	1,220	1,494	206	857	876
Rwanda	16	7	5	6	6	0	2	2	3	7	2	11	19	4
São Tomé and Principe	..	1	3	1	4	2	2	2	0	4	3	..	1	2
Senegal	61	-13	-4	-53	-48	48	-10	-5	92	10	157	34	-25	17
Seychelles	6	9	8	-3	6	17	27	17	45	28	20	5	11	17
Sierra Leone	10	3	3	5	18	17	-5	0	0	4	2	4	1	5
Somalia	..	..	..	..	..	..	..	..	..	..	..	-1	..	..
South Africa	-765	-5	40	-1,933	-288	-856	-1,256	-226	1,466	-1,171	262	-178	-134	-397
Sudan	0	0	0	0	0	0	0	70	300	700	224	0	0	129
Swaziland	18	23	58	50	44	-1	10	23	34	10	30	15	35	28
Tanzania	..	0	10	15	62	63	104	134	150	172	183	..	..	89
Togo	42	8	12	19	2	6	5	24	19	1	..	23	13	11
Uganda	0	6	1	2	4	5	2	110	160	190	230	1	22	71
Zambia	62	0	0	0	3	40	97	117	207	198	163	20	0	83
Zimbabwe	-26	-12	3	15	32	30	98	35	107	436	50	-18	-5	79
NORTH AFRICA	-78	336	..	..	..	..	1,350	1,465	2,409	2,517	3,571	72	199	1,941
Algeria	281	-39	-34	3	-2	0	0	270	260	500	460	-2	-67	142
Egypt, Arab Republic	541	136	1,094	1,032	1,021	1,285	735	612	723	967	655	456	171	826
Libya	-1,136	54	..	..	..	..	..	..	..	..	..	-564	-33	54
Morocco	..	..	..	..	..	..	320	327	1,071	313	839	..	..	574
Tunisia	236	185	166	487	545	442	295	261	355	697	337	182	128	377
ALL AFRICA	-664	1,319	2,314	2,145	2,585	4,387	3,766	5,409	7,398	7,913	..	809	2,121	4,137

Note: 1999 data are preliminary (see page 2).

5-11. Net long-term borrowing

	Millions of U.S. dollars (current prices)											Annual average		
	1980	*1990*	*1991*	*1992*	*1993*	*1994*	*1995*	*1996*	*1997*	*1998*	*1999*	*75-84*	*85-89*	*90-MR*
SUB-SAHARAN AFRICA	7,741	5,091	4,351	3,850	4,971	4,427	3,983	765	2,097	-279	261	6,163	5,672	2,952
excluding South Africa	7,741	5,091	4,351	3,850	4,971	2,903	2,505	1,244	2,202	107	959	6,163	5,672	2,818
excl. S.Africa & Nigeria	6,231	5,344	4,427	5,193	5,006	3,051	2,990	2,346	2,727	594	1,379	5,148	5,469	3,306
Angola	..	679	96	501	622	263	215	124	385	-122	-672	234	758	209
Benin	56	102	84	65	63	85	77	83	23	32	35	77	57	65
Botswana	21	-37	49	23	45	-10	1	-45	-52	-33	75	28	37	2
Burkina Faso	55	61	121	128	119	80	83	73	39	56	68	48	73	83
Burundi	35	68	60	86	58	31	27	23	7	18	50	37	85	43
Cameroon	500	449	219	520	264	249	-102	-41	-11	-89	-24	313	237	144
Cape Verde	..	8	-1	10	6	23	16	19	12	31	28	18	8	15
Central African Republic	24	105	94	41	48	36	30	25	3	-4	-2	17	68	38
Chad	3	100	88	139	52	61	56	91	68	29	123	21	41	81
Comoros	13	5	-3	15	4	6	9	6	3	-1	-5	11	14	4
Congo, Democratic Rep. of	271	267	263	55	54	1	0	3	0	0	198	281	239	84
Congo, Republic of	488	-43	-167	33	383	30	-67	-136	-30	-7	-315	222	141	-32
Côte d'Ivoire	1,017	521	389	351	284	524	204	64	-580	-225	-213	636	141	132
Djibouti	8	18	46	36	19	17	9	15	7	2	1	8	17	17
Equatorial Guinea	18	9	7	13	9	4	2	0	1	0	3	8	17	5
Eritrea	..	..	..	..	..	27	7	7	33	67	106	..	..	41
Ethiopia	93	222	357	263	314	170	141	3	127	82	-281	426	448	140
Gabon	-109	170	68	8	58	38	57	-42	-23	-66	-264	52	207	0
Gambia, The	51	3	13	37	7	3	9	43	11	1	2	18	21	13
Ghana	143	294	388	354	324	302	405	690	417	273	117	69	244	357
Guinea	47	100	145	149	245	122	49	85	143	54	-35	44	132	105
Guinea-Bissau	72	34	38	37	22	25	13	23	25	12	13	22	40	24
Kenya	424	290	544	175	111	-276	137	-76	-163	-128	229	251	340	84
Lesotho	10	43	47	59	50	44	44	33	34	26	215	15	32	59
Liberia	61	-1	-13	0	20	-14	0	0	0	0	0	61	22	-1
Madagascar	333	144	150	77	91	51	66	93	217	45	61	171	153	100
Malawi	120	69	120	106	151	74	149	121	129	121	109	75	72	115
Mali	89	141	128	131	58	69	138	110	76	50	88	78	125	99
Mauritania	108	54	23	81	92	82	42	83	26	-7	-35	100	77	44
Mauritius	79	101	77	-1	22	83	255	32	691	-102	349	37	58	151
Mozambique	..	189	73	168	153	176	196	222	221	181	217	300	281	180
Namibia	..	..	..	..	..	..	..	..	..	5	..	..	..	5
Niger	223	92	-31	56	44	36	-3	8	54	49	8	107	105	31
Nigeria	1,510	-253	-76	-1,343	-35	-148	-486	-1,102	-525	-487	-421	1,015	203	-488
Rwanda	25	53	77	71	50	20	43	53	62	79	99	27	71	61
São Tomé and Principe	9	14	29	23	14	14	13	10	3	4	10	6	11	13
Senegal	171	81	33	225	100	7	4	66	124	50	143	166	215	83
Seychelles	12	-4	9	13	6	8	-7	2	2	9	23	7	7	6
Sierra Leone	50	17	14	41	95	47	40	31	33	35	44	25	14	40
Somalia	106	43	13	0	0	0	0	0	0	0	0	136	83	6
South Africa	..	..	..	..	..	1,524	1,478	-478	-105	-386	-698	..	..	223
Sudan	658	171	116	94	91	9	36	17	5	-1	-6	495	164	53
Swaziland	21	-21	-6	-10	-9	-4	3	8	8	3	3	22	0	-2
Tanzania	318	209	162	222	139	158	131	63	166	120	459	290	183	183
Togo	78	56	47	35	11	34	19	77	25	48	16	88	30	37
Uganda	51	227	119	202	301	183	161	169	235	109	208	62	197	191
Zambia	388	63	102	136	99	109	110	80	108	-49	46	205	161	81
Zimbabwe	93	177	239	426	322	57	171	33	63	-165	86	164	44	141
NORTH AFRICA	4,953	1,527	384	1,214	207	1,407	1,376	781	-672	-2,310	-2,143	5,088	3,328	177
Algeria	869	156	-692	475	-446	1,447	1,466	947	-369	-1,541	-1,855	1,435	808	-41
Egypt, Arab Republic	2,337	261	297	-105	180	122	-372	-437	-163	-452	-358	2,162	1,483	-103
Libya	..	..	..	..	..	..	..	..	..	..	..	..	..	..
Morocco	1,394	965	428	491	196	-293	-183	-202	-794	-148	-441	1,118	825	2
Tunisia	352	144	352	352	277	131	465	473	655	-170	510	373	212	319
ALL AFRICA	12,694	6,618	4,735	5,064	5,178	5,834	5,360	1,546	1,425	-2,589	-1,882	11,251	8,999	3,129

5-12. Other capital flows

	Millions of U.S. dollars (current prices)											Annual average		
	1980	1990	1991	1992	1993	1994	1995	1996	1997	1998	1999	75-84	85-89	90-MR
SUB-SAHARAN AFRICA	1,210	-743	-5,746	-5,129	-3,687	-6,325	-3,798	-3,717	-11,061	-4,047	-10,660	1,140	-1,949	-5,491
excluding South Africa	2,749	-136	-1,741	-3,222	-4,533	-3,257	-2,445	-4,842	-3,060	-1,177	-1,585	870	88	-2,600
excl. S.Africa & Nigeria	2,966	-999	-2,531	-3,979	-2,012	-3,394	-3,036	-3,318	-2,283	-2,010	-2,204	1,496	666	-2,577
Angola	0	-155	-7	193	-648	-574	199	-379	-700	502	-252	0	342	-182
Benin	116	158	48	89	-109	-120	-77	-49	-89	-95	-32	95	83	-28
Botswana	125	168	50	162	180	-91	-157	-208	-5	-5	0	104	47	9
Burkina Faso	..	-63	-190	-144	-24	-29	-44	-148	-124	-130	-183	83	46	-108
Burundi	-22	1	-4	-25	-22	34	-1	-55	-29	-16	-9	-24	-27	-13
Cameroon	665	-235	-336	-1,143	241	-345	-455	76	147	0	10	475	-141	-204
Cape Verde	..	3	-1	5	-24	-40	-72	-66	-29	-40	-97	4	-7	-36
Central African Republic	24	-27	-67	-67	-10	-47	-75	-31	-44	-99	-64	5	-58	-53
Chad	-24	7	-40	-32	-48	-103	-102	-87	-91	-79	-63	-27	-21	-64
Comoros	-11	-5	24	6	16	12	-10	11	-5	-26	-11	-3	0	1
Congo, Democratic Rep. of	652	-81	188	191	-159	-221	-512	-486	-70	30	30	175	-18	-109
Congo, Republic of	219	1,209	604	170	463	96	608	458	245	416	538	317	389	481
Côte d'Ivoire	626	-51	227	144	521	-94	-103	-125	3	546	-214	355	680	85
Djibouti	..	..	10	16	-14	13	3	2	-26	..	..	..	..	1
Equatorial Guinea	..	-9	-9	25	4	-10	5	-8	3	9	11	12	-8	2
Eritrea	0	0	0	-139	-43	-84	-133	-125	-194	-72	-43	0	0	-83
Ethiopia	-7	-442	-981	-1,277	-856	-55	-416	-461	-521	-149	-47	-4	-148	-521
Gabon	-337	-340	33	187	26	-245	-153	-217	-126	-128	-83	-259	-169	-105
Gambia, The	..	-24	-17	-10	1	-6	27	33	-26	-30	-21	..	-27	-7
Ghana	-189	7	46	-157	249	63	-78	-428	265	-219	268	-25	-15	2
Guinea	-8	-3	-176	-115	-176	-84	-75	-91	-164	-145	-151	6	28	-118
Guinea-Bissau	..	-44	-60	-9	-66	-97	-67	-58	-48	10	-36	-8	-21	-47
Kenya	482	157	-317	-37	54	122	190	419	438	425	400	128	259	185
Lesotho	..	356	400	484	-17	13	21	33	15	-15	13	115	245	130
Liberia	..	..	..	..	..	..	..	..	..	..	..	..	..	..
Madagascar	399	-38	13	-61	-30	45	53	79	1,087	22	146	68	-4	131
Malawi	62	-95	27	14	38	-6	19	105	-5	-85	-171	31	-9	-16
Mali	34	-106	-138	-144	-106	-109	-169	-101	-102	-188	-126	38	-109	-129
Mauritania	-5	-39	-66	-75	27	-107	98	40	-16	8	-34	15	-145	-16
Mauritius	74	-10	-78	2	97	86	-181	-70	-8	-80	-17	14	-60	-26
Mozambique	-85	-471	-498	-540	-551	-554	-316	-113	-322	-360	-500	-90	-325	-423
Namibia	..	-72	-235	-224	-168	-205	-426	-308	-158	-215	-130	..	..	-214
Niger	0	-70	-37	-185	-125	-63	16	-40	-132	-106	-78	0	-115	-82
Nigeria	-217	863	790	757	-2,521	137	591	-1,524	-777	832	619	-783	-578	-23
Rwanda	1	-18	8	-11	13	27	-46	-40	24	3	-2	-14	49	-4
São Tomé and Principe	-22	-26	-17	0	-1	-9	-15	-23	-22	-8	-11	0	-2	-13
Senegal	-136	-258	-276	-328	-266	-241	-286	-273	-251	-209	-177	-134	-218	-257
Seychelles	3	-17	-19	9	12	-8	18	13	-7	44	0	-4	-54	4
Sierra Leone	28	56	29	25	-12	-66	7	66	-21	-9	-4	31	-3	7
Somalia	..	..	..	..	..	..	..	..	..	..	..	..	..	..
South Africa	-1,538	-606	-4,005	-1,907	846	-3,068	-1,353	1,125	-8,001	-2,869	-9,076	300	-2,038	-2,891
Sudan	-71	107	351	252	394	501	591	614	274	206	151	65	460	344
Swaziland	131	-104	-129	53	-10	-64	-59	-60	43	-268	55	31	-65	-54
Tanzania	..	-14	19	-68	-14	-289	-279	-490	-711	-563	-576	..	..	-299
Togo	..	..	..	..	..	..	..	..	..	..	..	..	..	..
Uganda	..	24	-352	-269	-361	-199	-429	-348	-432	-362	-256	-27	-17	-298
Zambia	-123	-405	-600	-895	-552	-295	-380	-331	-229	-437	-406	12	-124	-453
Zimbabwe	365	-28	39	-51	67	55	225	-50	-118	-94	-34	66	-54	1
NORTH AFRICA	-573	-598	-2,860	-2,170	968	2,129	-646	3	117	1,635	149	152	384	-127
Algeria	201	-1,473	-798	-1,413	-373	180	-180	-220	-40	0	-950	-19	133	-527
Egypt, Arab Republic	0	1,076	-1,221	-333	333	318	-525	237	-138	1,673	-575	0	-595	85
Libya	-481	-142	..	..	..	..	..	..	..	..	..	161	1,348	-142
Morocco	-101	-100	-636	-673	610	1,377	43	-144	268	38	1,398	97	-457	218
Tunisia	-192	42	-206	249	398	255	16	130	27	-76	275	-22	-45	111
ALL AFRICA	637	-1,340	-8,606	-7,299	-2,719	-4,196	-4,444	-3,714	-10,945	-2,411	-10,512	1,283	-1,565	-5,619

Note: Includes all capital account flows, except changes in reserves, that are not included in the tables on foreign investment or long-term borrowing.

5-13. Use of reserves

	Millions of U.S. dollars (current prices)											Annual average		
	1980	*1990*	*1991*	*1992*	*1993*	*1994*	*1995*	*1996*	*1997*	*1998*	*1999*	*75-84*	*85-89*	*90-MR*
SUB-SAHARAN AFRICA	-4,655	-4,225	-6	1,768	-2,356	-1,431	1,706	-7,269	-1,741	-264	4,505	1,262	-1,397	-931
excluding South Africa	-3,840	-2,809	-1,505	1,569	373	-2,376	-660	-6,081	-4,097	463	532	1,074	-1,422	-1,459
excl. S.Africa & Nigeria	705	-711	-1,218	-446	-352	-2,377	-261	-3,728	-1,036	348	-1,134	638	-1,280	-1,091
Angola	0	0	0	-115	900	35	626	-1,520	184	317	-534	33	-40	-11
Benin	19	-110	-113	-92	-30	-75	18	-58	-14	-9	-7	10	-5	-49
Botswana	-91	-307	-374	-405	-397	-135	-213	-548	-606	-192	100	-55	-416	-308
Burkina Faso	-11	-2	-43	-61	-72	-119	-143	4	35	33	15	-13	-14	-35
Burundi	8	2	-26	-13	0	-48	-11	62	19	39	14	-1	-37	4
Cameroon	-162	-55	-41	-112	-291	333	-13	-81	-142	39	-4	-38	-108	-37
Cape Verde	0	7	10	-15	4	3	9	-22	10	0	-9	-1	-4	0
Central African Republic	-10	4	10	-4	-27	-72	-11	-20	18	41	-6	-4	3	-7
Chad	5	-3	8	33	32	-19	-58	13	14	20	31	-3	-9	7
Comoros	4	3	4	0	-14	-10	4	-9	4	3	-4	0	-3	-2
Congo, Democratic Rep. of	-35	1	43	-1	14	17	39	-15	21	-188	-137	76	-60	-21
Congo, Republic of	-59	0	45	27	5	-56	-6	-37	20	28	2	1	2	3
Côte d'Ivoire	112	150	-50	235	-88	-794	-222	-39	-82	3	115	92	-75	-77
Djibouti	..	..	-6	17	8	-3	7	-1	12	..	..	..	..	5
Equatorial Guinea	13	-2	-3	8	2	-1	-8	-4	-7	2	-29	2	3	-4
Eritrea	0	0	0	-91	-109	-78	58	76	61	179	-20	0	0	8
Ethiopia	40	46	-154	-46	-112	-256	-253	-83	-163	-130	50	27	2	-110
Gabon	-93	-51	-67	222	79	-137	42	-83	-39	107	59	-9	-180	13
Gambia, The	..	8	5	1	-6	5	-4	-13	-7	-10	-3	5	-4	-2
Ghana	96	-118	-171	124	-41	-164	-211	14	-25	-100	94	25	-44	-60
Guinea	-25	-51	-18	-3	-49	34	-13	27	-47	5	42	-5	-12	-7
Guinea-Bissau	0	-15	9	-5	9	6	1	-12	-25	-1	10	5	-6	-2
Kenya	131	115	91	-76	-331	-104	133	-417	-5	26	-49	7	-194	-62
Lesotho	-41	-17	-42	-50	120	-121	-108	-112	-143	-6	10	-8	-1	-47
Liberia	41	-1	..	0	-1	-3	..	..	..	..	..	27	-3	-1
Madagascar	-83	137	-17	-17	-20	8	-46	-117	-24	116	-38	6	-44	-2
Malawi	17	-29	-11	93	-7	29	-87	-109	53	-74	2	16	-1	-14
Mali	-9	-84	-178	-89	-28	-87	-68	-128	3	61	56	-6	-38	-54
Mauritania	2	32	-28	3	-26	11	-131	-67	-61	-19	-23	9	32	-31
Mauritius	-25	-42	-22	0	-8	43	-105	-44	-41	-36	-201	24	-28	-46
Mozambique	32	-6	-13	-40	46	-52	-60	-159	-115	-62	-71	46	-17	-53
Namibia	..	-37	12	7	-91	-75	-24	-23	-68	-56	-94	..	..	-45
Niger	53	-22	-4	10	-6	5	0	16	21	-7	32	6	5	5
Nigeria	-4,545	-2,098	-287	2,015	725	1	-399	-2,353	-3,061	115	1,666	436	-142	-368
Rwanda	33	58	-66	41	31	-4	-35	-8	-29	3	11	19	91	0
São Tomé and Principe	12	0	0	0	0	0	-5	0	-8	3	-1	0	0	-1
Senegal	135	-66	-16	-20	112	-240	-82	-55	-133	-25	-25	56	-5	-55
Seychelles	-8	-3	-10	-4	-3	6	1	4	-5	6	-9	-1	-1	-2
Sierra Leone	32	7	1	-26	-17	7	18	20	-5	11	15	19	-4	3
Somalia	18	-51	..	..	..	..	..	..	..	..	..	5	-12	-51
South Africa	-815	-1,416	1,499	199	-2,729	945	2,366	-1,188	2,356	-726	3,973	188	25	528
Sudan	177	-52	-23	35	2	1	-23	-13	-23	-25	-36	85	135	-16
Swaziland	-34	-11	-14	-92	64	13	-30	-15	-25	-20	-24	-8	-17	-16
Tanzania	66	-57	-63	-102	123	-107	-46	-81	-208	-34	-129	9	-2	-70
Togo	2	-3	-15	86	125	11	-12	12	-35	19	..	-18	-21	21
Uganda	55	10	37	-2	-29	-90	-146	-73	-132	-134	-33	25	-10	-59
Zambia	162	-116	-31	-76	-17	-77	1,210	-52	-33	211	-19	152	-85	100
Zimbabwe	125	19	126	171	-207	-17	-255	43	739	205	-286	46	-52	54
NORTH AFRICA	-7,615	-908	-4,899	-5,350	-4,622	-3,311	865	-3,638	-6,982	1,164	2,139	434	143	-2,554
Algeria	-1,341	85	-527	-67	48	-489	740	-2,380	-4,180	1,090	2,350	-39	237	-333
Egypt, Arab Republic	168	1,722	-3,843	-3,999	-4,312	-2,106	-754	-570	-1,912	135	2,117	421	161	-1,352
Libya	-6,407	-1,158	150	-520	-35	..	..	..	..	..	..	73	-81	-391
Morocco	30	-1,641	-782	-683	-284	-361	982	-292	-553	-247	-1,638	0	-117	-550
Tunisia	-65	83	103	-82	-39	-355	-103	-397	-336	187	-690	-20	-57	-163
ALL AFRICA	-12,270	-5,133	-4,905	-3,582	-6,977	-4,742	2,571	-10,907	-8,723	901	6,644	1,696	-1,254	-3,485

Note: Excludes IMF credit transactions, which appear in the table on long-term borrowing.

5-14. Import coverage ratio of reserves

	Reserves in months of imports of goods and services											Annual average		
	1980	*1990*	*1991*	*1992*	*1993*	*1994*	*1995*	*1996*	*1997*	*1998*	*1999*	*75-84*	*85-89*	*90-MR*
SUB-SAHARAN AFRICA	4	6	6	7	8	8	7	8	8	8	9	3	5	8
excluding South Africa	5	7	7	9	10	10	9	9	10	10	12	3	6	9
excl. S.Africa & Nigeria	3	8	9	10	11	11	9	10	11	12	12	3	7	10
Angola	..	..	..	..	..	..	1	1	1	0	1	..	..	1
Benin	0	1	4	4	4	6	3	4	4	4	6	1	0	4
Botswana	4	16	19	19	24	25	22	26	26	26	26	4	15	23
Burkina Faso	2	5	5	5	6	6	6	5	6	5	5	2	5	6
Burundi	6	4	5	6	7	9	9	11	9	5	5	5	3	7
Cameroon	1	0	0	0	0	0	0	0	0	0	0	1	1	0
Cape Verde	6	6	5	5	4	2	2	2	2	1	2	6	7	3
Central African Republic	2	3	4	3	4	9	9	11	8	6	6	2	3	6
Chad	2	3	3	2	1	2	3	4	3	3	2	1	2	3
Comoros	2	4	4	3	5	6	5	6	6	8	7	2	3	5
Congo, Democratic Rep. of	2	1	1	1	0	1	1	0	..	..	..	1	2	1
Congo, Republic of	1	0	0	0	0	0	0	0	0	0	0	0	0	0
Côte d'Ivoire	0	0	0	0	0	1	1	1	2	2	2	0	0	1
Djibouti	..	..	3	3	2	3	3	3	3	..	..	..	..	3
Equatorial Guinea	..	0	1	2	0	0	0	0	0	0	0	0	1	0
Eritrea	..	..	..	..	..	..	..	..	..	..	..	..	..	..
Ethiopia	4	1	1	3	4	6	7	6	4	4	3	5	2	4
Gabon	1	1	2	0	0	1	1	1	1	0	0	1	1	1
Gambia, The	0	3	3	4	..	5	5	5	5	4	5	2	2	4
Ghana	3	2	4	3	3	4	4	4	..	2	2	3	5	3
Guinea	..	..	1	1	2	1	1	1	1	3	..	..	..	1
Guinea-Bissau	..	2	2	2	2	2	2	1	3	5	4	..	1	3
Kenya	2	1	1	0	2	3	1	3	2	2	3	2	2	2
Lesotho	1	1	2	2	3	5	5	5	6	7	7	1	1	4
Liberia	0	..	..	..	..	..	..	..	..	..	..	0	0	..
Madagascar	0	1	1	..	..	1	1	2	3	2	2	1	3	2
Malawi	1	3	3	1	1	1	2	4	2	4	4	2	2	2
Mali	1	3	5	4	5	3	4	5	5	5	4	1	1	4
Mauritania	4	1	1	1	1	1	2	2	4	4	5	3	1	2
Mauritius	2	5	6	5	4	4	4	4	3	2	3	2	3	4
Mozambique	..	3	3	3	2	2	2	3	5	6	4	1	2	3
Namibia	..	..	..	0	1	1	1	1	1	1	2	..	..	1
Niger	2	5	6	7	6	3	2	2	1	1	1	2	6	3
Nigeria	5	4	4	1	2	2	2	4	6	5	..	3	2	3
Rwanda	7	1	4	2	1	1	3	3	4	4	5	5	4	3
São Tomé and Principe	..	..	..	..	..	..	1	1	3	3	3	..	..	2
Senegal	0	0	0	0	0	1	2	2	3	3	3	0	0	1
Seychelles	2	1	1	1	1	1	1	1	1	1	1	1	1	1
Sierra Leone	1	0	0	1	1	2	2	1	3	3	3	1	0	2
Somalia	1	..	..	..	..	..	..	..	..	..	..	2	0	..
South Africa	4	1	2	1	1	1	1	1	2	2	3	2	1	2
Sudan	0	0	0	0	0	0	1	0	0	0	1	0	0	0
Swaziland	3	3	2	3	3	3	3	2	2	4	3	3	3	3
Tanzania	0	1	1	2	1	2	1	2	3	3	4	1	0	2
Togo	1	5	6	5	4	3	3	2	2	2	2	3	6	3
Uganda	0	1	1	2	2	4	4	4	4	5	5	1	1	3
Zambia	1	1	1	..	1	2	1	2	2	1	0	1	1	1
Zimbabwe	8	2	1	2	3	3	3	3	1	1	2	3	2	2
NORTH AFRICA	..	..	..	7	8	8	8	9	9	8	7	..	..	8
Algeria	6	2	3	3	4	4	3	5	9	8	5	4	4	5
Egypt, Arab Republic	3	3	5	10	11	11	11	12	11	10	8	2	2	9
Libya	..	..	..	..	..	..	..	..	..	..	..	..	..	..
Morocco	2	3	4	4	5	5	4	4	4	4	5	1	1	4
Tunisia	2	2	2	1	1	2	2	2	3	2	3	2	2	2
ALL AFRICA	4	5	5	7	8	8	8	8	9	8	8	3	4	7

Note: 1999 data are preliminary (see page 2). Based on total reserves, excluding gold, at year-end and on imports of all goods and services at current prices and exchange rates.

5-15. Export unit values

					Index 1995=100							Average annual percentage growth		
	1980	1990	1991	1992	1993	1994	1995	1996	1997	1998	1999	75-84	85-89	90-MR
SUB-SAHARAN AFRICA	121.8	101.4	96.5	99.1	89.9	91.5	100.2	101.4	97.3	84.8	89.4	6.0	3.6	-0.5
excluding South Africa	124.4	103.8	96.6	100.4	88.1	89.0	100.3	106.4	100.9	85.3	94.3	4.2	2.8	-0.1
excl. S.Africa & Nigeria	113.2	97.5	95.3	91.6	84.7	88.1	100.4	101.9	96.8	89.0	93.3	2.4	1.4	0.2
Angola	..	152.7	179.9	89.9	107.8	89.3	100.0	135.0	128.3	120.4	260.2	..	4.1	1.8
Benin	44.2	83.0	76.3	53.5	65.3	71.0	100.0	87.6	81.6	83.2	71.3	5.9	7.6	1.9
Botswana	..	94.1	91.1	93.3	92.8	94.3	100.0	93.7	79.4	65.3	67.4	..	12.4	-2.5
Burkina Faso	51.6	93.9	87.2	60.5	59.6	85.0	100.0	95.3	87.0	81.4	73.9	5.1	12.3	-0.1
Burundi	159.5	100.0	101.3	64.9	67.1	93.8	100.0	61.4	60.0	46.8	30.1	6.3	-0.9	-10.0
Cameroon	142.0	91.3	105.2	94.1	97.8	87.8	100.0	90.2	89.0	80.1	69.0	4.8	-3.4	-1.9
Cape Verde	62.3	80.9	82.7	89.8	85.1	90.0	100.0	98.4	94.5	93.2	92.9	7.1	11.8	2.4
Central African Republic	139.5	176.8	143.7	153.5	144.1	85.7	100.0	87.8	66.8	57.1	48.5	8.4	6.4	-12.4
Chad	92.3	91.9	91.2	88.2	77.1	73.3	100.0	102.4	82.7	80.8	77.2	-0.7	3.2	0.4
Comoros	135.7	149.8	135.2	144.4	120.8	95.4	100.0	86.9	71.5	72.9	95.7	..	12.8	-6.5
Congo, Democratic Rep. of	118.1	74.8	60.6	76.9	62.7	108.0	100.0	79.2	79.8	79.0	80.6	0.9	1.8	2.7
Congo, Republic of	130.7	105.4	107.6	103.4	69.6	83.9	100.0	111.5	100.6	99.4	100.1	9.7	-6.1	0.7
Côte d'Ivoire	115.9	83.1	83.0	94.0	88.3	80.4	100.0	99.7	90.8	93.8	92.8	-1.1	-1.1	1.4
Djibouti	..	..	..	..	..	..	..	..	..	..	..	..	..	..
Equatorial Guinea	..	173.2	159.6	180.0	133.3	87.6	100.0	122.4	137.5	103.2	136.9	..	17.8	-3.4
Eritrea	..	..	..	83.9	80.5	91.5	100.0	103.0	99.1	99.1	93.3	..	..	2.5
Ethiopia	..	65.9	49.1	76.3	86.1	69.1	100.0	95.3	86.5	98.2	86.9	..	2.0	3.5
Gabon	173.9	116.8	105.7	104.0	76.6	88.7	100.0	117.5	104.5	73.3	72.8	8.8	-4.5	-2.3
Gambia, The	91.0	91.8	94.4	100.3	99.8	98.2	100.0	102.2	100.8	99.5	100.3	3.4	13.0	1.3
Ghana	38.9	87.2	89.9	86.4	71.4	78.8	100.0	98.1	94.5	99.0	90.3	0.9	8.5	1.6
Guinea	..	129.9	100.6	99.0	98.1	113.3	100.0	93.2	94.2	88.8	80.1	..	0.6	-3.4
Guinea-Bissau	57.5	124.1	102.6	88.7	109.8	102.2	100.0	102.1	102.3	84.1	96.3	14.0	0.9	-2.5
Kenya	130.0	88.0	90.0	87.5	69.5	82.9	100.0	97.9	111.5	113.4	109.1	5.5	-1.8	2.8
Lesotho	105.8	84.5	81.0	94.4	93.1	93.7	100.0	91.7	94.5	86.5	70.9	1.9	5.9	0.3
Liberia	..	..	..	..	..	..	..	..	..	..	..	..	..	..
Madagascar	60.6	72.7	65.5	70.1	69.2	79.9	100.0	102.7	90.8	92.1	88.8	6.5	3.4	3.6
Malawi	87.1	112.5	122.4	102.7	86.5	82.3	100.0	104.9	110.0	89.0	92.8	3.8	1.4	-1.0
Mali	108.3	112.6	106.3	99.0	92.6	82.7	100.0	97.8	83.2	83.9	73.9	3.5	6.5	-2.8
Mauritania	71.4	104.5	110.1	120.5	127.8	94.6	100.0	98.7	100.8	89.2	78.8	1.7	7.5	-2.4
Mauritius	72.2	93.1	92.2	95.8	88.1	90.9	100.0	105.4	92.8	89.2	87.0	0.5	8.9	0.4
Mozambique	142.6	140.9	149.2	116.5	86.4	82.6	100.0	80.3	80.4	77.8	75.7	..	4.8	-6.9
Namibia	130.4	106.8	89.9	94.6	87.8	101.1	100.0	95.9	93.8	88.2	86.6	..	5.2	-1.0
Niger	158.9	115.3	105.0	110.5	77.0	88.7	100.0	88.2	80.6	84.0	81.8	12.0	6.0	-3.5
Nigeria	145.5	129.2	101.6	133.7	101.2	92.7	100.0	122.2	115.6	72.6	98.7	3.1	10.3	-1.4
Rwanda	95.9	67.6	70.5	62.5	64.7	77.4	100.0	88.1	116.9	87.4	75.7	8.0	-8.3	4.0
São Tomé and Principe	..	81.3	77.5	73.1	80.7	94.0	100.0	108.5	111.4	88.5	87.6	..	-12.4	2.9
Senegal	84.0	97.7	91.0	101.3	89.0	92.3	100.0	101.2	93.6	91.5	86.1	2.5	6.8	-0.1
Seychelles	..	77.0	68.9	81.0	80.9	73.8	100.0	93.1	99.2	97.4	98.0	..	-5.3	4.0
Sierra Leone	57.4	41.9	40.5	43.6	43.8	50.9	100.0	54.1	59.2	47.2	49.8	11.7	2.1	3.4
Somalia	..	..	..	..	..	..	..	..	..	..	..	..	..	..
South Africa	116.8	97.4	96.3	96.9	93.0	95.7	100.0	93.1	91.4	84.0	81.4	9.1	5.0	-1.2
Sudan	..	..	..	..	..	..	..	..	..	..	..	..	..	..
Swaziland	86.4	65.4	69.6	78.2	84.0	81.8	100.0	90.5	94.3	105.5	107.6	3.8	4.5	5.1
Tanzania	..	89.8	95.0	87.0	89.5	97.5	100.0	102.0	126.9	104.8	105.9	..	..	2.2
Togo	95.4	108.0	105.3	104.2	92.3	83.4	100.0	103.6	104.4	101.4	97.1	-1.9	5.9	-0.2
Uganda	..	81.0	68.2	59.6	56.7	66.2	100.0	83.8	73.9	73.3	57.4	..	-2.1	-2.1
Zambia	90.0	95.9	90.9	86.2	75.8	80.3	100.0	76.7	74.0	51.7	40.0	2.4	9.3	-5.8
Zimbabwe	161.6	131.3	120.4	102.7	97.5	97.0	100.0	110.1	107.6	81.0	67.0	0.3	3.9	-4.9
NORTH AFRICA	165.0	101.1	101.2	99.3	94.2	91.8	100.0	106.2	105.0	94.3	95.8	6.8	-6.3	0.7
Algeria	200.8	132.1	123.3	108.4	98.6	93.5	100.0	116.7	113.7	82.6	95.1	11.3	-10.2	-1.8
Egypt, Arab Republic	106.9	82.5	95.0	99.4	99.7	95.4	100.0	99.5	108.5	107.5	100.9	9.8	-7.5	2.9
Libya	..	..	..	..	..	..	..	..	..	..	..	..	..	..
Morocco	96.2	93.3	89.8	90.9	84.9	85.4	100.0	103.9	95.3	94.3	93.3	1.8	6.0	0.9
Tunisia	91.3	84.8	84.4	90.7	84.6	88.8	100.0	103.4	94.2	92.4	91.0	5.3	1.6	2.0
ALL AFRICA	129.6	101.3	97.9	99.1	91.3	91.6	100.1	102.7	99.5	87.5	91.3	6.7	0.6	-0.2

Note: 1999 data are preliminary (see page 2).

5-16. Import unit values

	Index 1995=100											Average annual percentage growth		
	1980	1990	1991	1992	1993	1994	1995	1996	1997	1998	1999	75-84	85-89	90-MR
SUB-SAHARAN AFRICA	77.0	93.3	92.4	98.4	91.6	93.2	100.0	94.8	96.4	90.8	92.6	5.3	7.7	0.5
excluding South Africa	70.2	91.1	90.4	98.0	90.2	92.5	100.0	96.5	99.3	94.6	97.4	3.0	9.2	1.4
excl. S.Africa & Nigeria	88.9	93.6	94.3	94.1	89.4	92.9	100.0	100.9	99.8	95.7	99.0	..	3.9	1.3
Angola	..	110.9	191.8	91.4	119.7	89.3	100.0	135.0	128.3	119.8	188.7	..	1.4	3.8
Benin	54.3	83.0	86.2	66.7	84.4	93.6	100.0	99.3	90.4	87.1	86.6	6.3	11.7	1.4
Botswana		85.2	88.2	91.5	91.0	93.7	100.0	93.0	90.8	83.5	97.0	..	7.8	1.7
Burkina Faso	103.1	103.2	100.4	68.5	70.8	89.5	100.0	102.2	93.9	86.0	86.7	5.8	4.3	-0.4
Burundi	112.9	127.5	121.5	108.6	91.2	89.7	100.0	84.5	89.5	63.1	42.1	8.9	7.4	-8.1
Cameroon	153.0	101.8	92.9	132.1	119.5	94.1	100.0	98.8	92.7	87.3	89.1	6.9	-1.1	-2.4
Cape Verde	62.3	80.9	82.7	89.8	85.1	90.0	100.0	98.4	94.5	93.2	92.9	-0.5	11.8	2.4
Central African Republic	102.6	143.1	102.8	105.1	101.4	83.0	100.0	101.7	85.8	88.6	87.5	4.4	4.1	-3.3
Chad	78.6	78.9	77.3	80.0	76.8	87.7	100.0	89.2	83.0	88.2	77.2	2.2	5.8	1.7
Comoros	62.8	89.6	89.1	91.9	86.3	89.3	100.0	96.1	89.7	78.5	77.4	..	11.9	0.0
Congo, Democratic Rep. of	111.9	69.1	59.6	63.4	55.5	129.3	100.0	90.1	97.4	101.2	103.5	-2.6	-4.9	8.2
Congo, Republic of	109.4	126.4	123.3	127.0	82.5	120.6	100.0	68.0	85.1	109.8	119.2	5.8	7.4	-1.3
Côte d'Ivoire	100.7	101.8	94.0	101.5	94.9	82.5	100.0	106.7	97.5	100.6	97.8	4.4	6.3	0.6
Djibouti	..	..	..	..	..	..	..	..	..	..	..	..	..	..
Equatorial Guinea	..	169.7	173.3	177.3	156.1	87.7	100.0	122.4	137.3	103.1	136.7	..	12.9	-2.5
Eritrea	..	..	..	89.5	89.2	92.4	100.0	95.6	90.8	89.0	86.6	..	..	-0.4
Ethiopia	..	73.5	54.9	54.7	79.5	82.5	100.0	106.9	107.0	105.0	92.0	..	-0.9	5.2
Gabon	71.2	92.9	92.7	96.4	73.9	93.0	100.0	99.3	88.8	88.8	86.9	1.3	10.7	0.3
Gambia, The	45.5	90.3	90.0	96.0	100.7	99.0	100.0	101.5	100.1	101.3	102.0	7.6	10.0	1.8
Ghana	18.4	84.4	84.9	87.2	80.9	86.7	100.0	101.1	97.9	91.6	91.9	2.0	11.9	2.1
Guinea	..	96.2	77.4	95.7	102.8	101.9	100.0	101.6	96.9	92.5	87.3	..	5.8	0.5
Guinea-Bissau	47.0	86.8	82.9	87.1	79.3	84.3	100.0	102.6	102.7	91.9	96.3	8.1	13.0	2.1
Kenya	134.1	129.8	117.9	112.6	75.9	81.0	100.0	94.1	102.7	106.6	101.0	9.6	-0.6	-2.0
Lesotho	80.3	87.0	93.1	99.8	94.5	92.9	100.0	92.5	94.1	84.2	73.6	6.8	6.4	-0.3
Liberia	..	..	..	..	..	..	..	..	..	..	..	..	..	..
Madagascar	63.5	83.5	83.0	87.1	85.1	90.6	100.0	99.6	94.6	96.0	92.1	9.1	6.5	2.4
Malawi	56.3	79.5	82.1	84.5	80.0	96.4	100.0	98.6	98.7	91.2	91.9	6.4	8.7	2.7
Mali	102.9	92.6	92.5	96.3	93.4	90.5	100.0	97.2	85.7	83.1	82.1	1.7	4.9	-0.5
Mauritania	100.4	109.1	108.1	112.0	109.0	99.4	100.0	105.7	99.6	87.9	77.9	5.6	4.9	-2.4
Mauritius	73.0	86.1	86.2	89.6	86.8	91.5	100.0	104.5	92.5	90.3	90.9	6.1	5.5	1.5
Mozambique	64.3	87.5	90.7	80.1	73.2	95.3	100.0	103.0	105.3	100.6	100.1	..	8.4	2.7
Namibia	93.7	92.7	95.5	101.8	98.5	101.6	100.0	93.4	102.2	90.6	93.9	..	3.7	0.9
Niger	83.1	84.6	83.7	93.6	64.1	90.4	100.0	101.1	98.1	103.3	105.6	1.8	9.3	3.3
Nigeria	44.1	80.0	75.2	113.9	93.6	90.7	100.0	77.8	97.4	90.1	91.7	-3.4	31.6	2.1
Rwanda	175.5	175.8	90.5	95.0	88.7	94.9	100.0	102.9	94.4	85.4	85.7	5.9	6.4	-5.2
São Tomé and Principe	..	87.0	87.8	91.0	90.3	94.4	100.0	102.0	95.6	84.6	90.0	..	4.6	0.8
Senegal	84.1	89.6	95.3	97.4	91.9	87.3	100.0	100.1	91.9	86.1	84.2	3.8	5.6	0.1
Seychelles	..	107.7	105.1	103.8	94.1	96.5	100.0	96.6	97.8	91.4	92.6	..	1.8	-1.1
Sierra Leone	89.4	66.6	77.6	83.6	84.0	84.2	100.0	86.0	94.2	75.1	74.8	9.3	-2.9	1.4
Somalia	..	..	..	..	..	..	..	..	..	..	..	..	..	..
South Africa	97.5	98.8	97.3	99.3	94.4	94.4	100.0	91.9	91.2	83.8	82.7	10.3	4.2	-1.3
Sudan	..	..	..	..	..	..	..	..	..	..	..	..	..	..
Swaziland	75.8	56.3	61.6	67.2	63.3	82.6	100.0	97.8	103.7	128.4	134.2	4.6	8.4	8.9
Tanzania	..	88.0	90.2	94.0	94.5	95.8	100.0	103.4	137.1	161.2	163.5	..	..	6.8
Togo	84.2	85.6	84.9	89.0	84.8	87.1	100.0	99.0	84.6	82.5	78.5	0.2	7.0	0.2
Uganda	..	109.2	100.2	96.9	98.6	98.9	100.0	104.5	96.6	93.7	100.1	..	10.9	-1.4
Zambia	77.1	88.2	113.5	130.9	115.2	101.3	100.0	96.2	99.7	87.5	87.4	11.9	3.7	-1.3
Zimbabwe	184.6	131.0	118.7	99.4	96.8	96.3	100.0	109.7	108.3	80.8	66.8	5.7	3.7	-4.8
NORTH AFRICA	70.4	96.8	87.8	89.8	91.8	93.1	100.0	102.2	98.9	96.1	95.0	5.1	6.6	1.7
Algeria	69.1	104.7	88.2	86.7	97.2	94.7	100.0	100.4	93.2	91.4	90.3	4.7	4.2	1.7
Egypt, Arab Republic	58.2	95.5	88.5	93.5	94.2	93.2	100.0	104.5	109.9	111.3	111.3	8.6	9.7	2.4
Libya	..	..	..	..	..	..	..	..	..	..	..	..	..	..
Morocco	95.5	98.6	90.3	87.9	85.9	95.7	100.0	101.6	90.1	79.7	79.3	3.7	2.8	-0.8
Tunisia	75.0	82.0	82.8	90.0	85.3	88.0	100.0	100.5	94.7	94.3	88.7	5.1	4.4	2.3
ALL AFRICA	73.6	94.6	90.8	95.4	91.6	93.1	100.0	97.1	97.2	92.5	93.4	5.4	7.5	0.9

Note: 1999 data are preliminary (see page 2).

5-17. Terms of trade

	Index 1995=100											Average annual percentage growth		
	1980	*1990*	*1991*	*1992*	*1993*	*1994*	*1995*	*1996*	*1997*	*1998*	*1999*	*75-84*	*85-89*	*90-MR*
SUB-SAHARAN AFRICA	158.3	108.8	104.4	100.7	98.2	98.2	100.0	106.9	100.9	93.4	96.5	0.6	-3.8	-1.0
excluding South Africa	177.1	113.9	106.8	102.4	97.6	96.2	100.0	110.3	101.6	90.1	96.8	1.1	-5.8	-1.5
excl. S.Africa & Nigeria	127.3	104.2	101.1	97.4	94.7	94.8	100.0	100.9	97.0	93.0	94.2	..	-2.4	-1.0
Angola	..	137.7	93.8	98.4	90.0	100.1	100.0	100.0	100.0	100.5	137.9	..	2.6	-2.0
Benin	81.4	100.0	88.5	80.1	77.3	75.9	100.0	88.2	90.3	95.4	82.3	-0.3	-3.7	0.6
Botswana	..	110.4	103.2	102.1	101.9	100.6	100.0	100.7	87.4	78.2	69.5	..	4.3	-4.1
Burkina Faso	50.0	91.0	86.8	88.4	84.2	94.9	100.0	93.2	92.7	94.7	85.2	-0.7	7.7	0.3
Burundi	141.3	78.5	83.3	59.7	73.6	104.6	100.0	72.7	67.1	74.1	71.6	-2.4	-7.8	-2.0
Cameroon	92.8	89.7	113.3	71.2	81.8	93.2	100.0	91.4	96.1	91.8	77.5	-1.9	-2.4	0.5
Cape Verde	100.0	100.0	100.0	100.0	100.0	100.0	100.0	100.0	100.0	100.0	100.0	7.6	0.0	0.0
Central African Republic	136.0	123.6	139.8	146.0	142.1	103.3	100.0	86.4	77.9	64.4	55.4	3.9	2.1	-9.4
Chad	117.5	116.4	118.0	110.3	100.4	83.6	100.0	114.8	99.7	91.6	100.0	-2.8	-2.4	-1.3
Comoros	216.1	167.2	151.8	157.1	140.0	106.7	100.0	90.4	79.8	92.8	123.6	..	0.8	-6.5
Congo, Democratic Rep. of	105.5	108.2	101.7	121.4	113.0	83.5	100.0	87.9	81.9	78.1	77.9	3.6	7.0	-5.1
Congo, Republic of	119.5	83.4	87.3	81.4	84.4	69.6	100.0	164.1	118.3	90.5	84.0	3.7	-12.6	2.0
Côte d'Ivoire	115.1	81.7	88.3	92.6	93.1	97.5	100.0	93.4	93.2	93.2	94.9	-5.2	-7.0	0.8
Djibouti	..	..	..	..	..	..	..	..	..	..	..	..	..	..
Equatorial Guinea	..	102.1	92.1	101.6	85.4	100.0	100.0	100.0	100.2	100.2	100.1	..	4.3	-0.9
Eritrea	..	..	..	93.8	90.3	98.9	100.0	107.8	109.2	111.4	107.7	..	..	2.9
Ethiopia	..	89.7	89.5	139.4	108.3	83.8	100.0	89.1	80.9	93.6	94.5	..	2.9	-1.6
Gabon	244.0	125.7	114.0	107.9	103.7	95.4	100.0	118.4	117.7	82.5	83.7	7.5	-13.7	-2.5
Gambia, The	199.9	101.7	104.9	104.4	99.1	99.3	100.0	100.7	100.7	98.2	98.4	-3.9	2.7	-0.4
Ghana	211.3	103.3	105.9	99.1	88.2	90.9	100.0	97.1	96.5	108.1	98.2	-1.1	-3.0	-0.5
Guinea	..	135.0	130.0	103.4	95.4	111.2	100.0	91.7	97.2	96.0	91.8	..	-5.0	-3.8
Guinea-Bissau	122.2	143.0	123.8	101.8	138.4	121.3	100.0	99.6	99.6	91.5	100.0	5.3	-10.7	-4.5
Kenya	96.9	67.8	76.3	77.7	91.5	102.4	100.0	104.0	108.5	106.4	108.0	-3.8	-1.2	4.9
Lesotho	131.8	97.1	87.0	94.5	98.5	100.9	100.0	99.1	100.5	102.7	96.4	-4.6	-0.4	0.6
Liberia	..	..	..	..	..	..	..	..	..	..	..	..	..	..
Madagascar	95.4	87.1	78.9	80.4	81.4	88.3	100.0	103.1	95.9	95.9	96.4	-2.4	-2.9	1.2
Malawi	154.7	141.4	149.1	121.5	108.2	85.3	100.0	106.3	111.5	97.6	100.9	-2.4	-6.7	-3.6
Mali	105.3	121.6	115.0	102.8	99.1	91.4	100.0	100.7	97.1	101.0	90.1	1.8	1.5	-2.4
Mauritania	71.1	95.8	101.8	107.6	117.2	95.1	100.0	93.4	101.2	101.4	101.1	-3.6	2.5	0.1
Mauritius	98.8	108.2	106.9	107.0	101.5	99.4	100.0	100.8	100.3	98.8	95.7	-5.3	3.2	-1.0
Mozambique	221.8	161.1	164.5	145.4	118.1	86.7	100.0	77.9	76.4	77.4	75.6	..	-3.4	-9.3
Namibia	139.1	115.2	94.1	92.9	89.1	99.6	100.0	102.7	91.8	97.4	92.2	..	1.5	-1.9
Niger	191.1	136.4	125.5	118.1	120.1	98.1	100.0	87.2	82.1	81.3	77.5	10.1	-3.0	-6.6
Nigeria	329.7	161.5	135.1	117.3	108.2	102.3	100.0	157.0	118.7	80.5	107.6	6.7	-16.2	-3.4
Rwanda	54.7	38.4	77.8	65.7	73.0	81.6	100.0	85.6	123.9	102.3	88.4	2.0	-13.8	9.8
São Tomé and Principe	..	93.4	88.3	80.3	89.3	99.5	100.0	106.3	116.6	104.6	97.4	..	-16.3	2.1
Senegal	99.9	109.0	95.5	104.0	96.9	105.8	100.0	101.2	102.0	106.3	102.3	-1.2	1.1	-0.2
Seychelles	..	71.5	65.6	78.0	86.0	76.5	100.0	96.3	101.4	106.6	105.9	..	-7.0	5.2
Sierra Leone	64.2	62.9	52.2	52.1	52.2	60.5	100.0	62.9	62.9	62.9	66.5	2.1	5.1	2.0
Somalia	..	..	..	..	..	..	..	..	..	..	..	..	..	..
South Africa	119.8	98.6	99.0	97.6	98.5	101.3	100.0	101.4	100.2	100.2	98.5	-1.2	0.8	0.1
Sudan	..	..	..	..	..	..	..	..	..	..	..	..	..	..
Swaziland	113.9	116.1	113.1	116.3	132.8	99.1	100.0	92.6	90.9	82.2	80.2	-0.7	-3.5	-3.5
Tanzania	..	102.0	105.3	92.6	94.7	101.8	100.0	98.6	92.6	65.0	64.8	..	..	-4.3
Togo	113.2	126.2	124.0	117.1	108.8	95.7	100.0	104.6	123.4	122.9	123.8	-2.1	-1.0	-0.4
Uganda	..	74.2	68.1	61.5	57.5	66.9	100.0	80.2	76.5	78.2	57.3	..	-11.7	-0.7
Zambia	116.6	108.7	80.0	65.9	65.8	79.3	100.0	79.7	74.2	59.1	45.7	-8.5	5.4	-4.5
Zimbabwe	87.6	100.2	101.4	103.3	100.7	100.7	100.0	100.3	99.4	100.2	100.3	-5.1	0.1	-0.1
NORTH AFRICA	234.4	104.4	115.3	110.6	102.7	98.6	100.0	103.9	106.2	98.2	100.8	1.5	-12.1	-1.0
Algeria	290.7	126.1	139.8	125.0	101.4	98.7	100.0	116.2	122.0	90.4	105.3	6.2	-13.8	-3.5
Egypt, Arab Republic	183.9	86.4	107.3	106.3	105.9	102.4	100.0	95.2	98.7	96.5	90.7	1.0	-15.6	0.5
Libya	..	..	..	..	..	..	..	..	..	..	..	..	..	..
Morocco	100.8	94.6	99.5	103.4	98.8	89.3	100.0	102.2	105.8	118.3	117.7	-1.8	3.1	1.7
Tunisia	121.7	103.4	101.9	100.7	99.2	100.9	100.0	102.9	99.5	98.0	102.6	0.2	-2.7	-0.3
ALL AFRICA	176.0	107.1	107.9	103.9	99.7	98.3	100.0	105.8	102.4	94.6	97.7	1.3	-6.4	-1.1

Note: 1999 data are preliminary (see page 2).

5-18. Forest products exports

	Thousands of cubic meters											Average annual percentage growth		
	1980	1987	1988	1989	1990	1991	1992	1993	1994	1995	1996	75-84	85-89	90-MR
SUB-SAHARAN AFRICA	8,169	6,803	8,821	7,032	6,931	6,824	7,170	4,764	4,364	3,788	4,289	149.9	2.4	-9.3
excluding South Africa	7,413	5,283	6,044	5,855	5,794	5,632	5,478	4,339	3,960	3,300	3,748	149.8	-1.3	-8.2
excl. S.Africa & Nigeria	7,402	5,266	6,028	5,844	5,757	5,583	5,444	3,908	3,672	3,030	3,499	150.2	-1.1	-9.5
Angola	..	0	0	3	0	..	2	..	..	..	..	..	56.3	..
Benin	..	..	..	..	..	0	0	..	..	..	..	..	..	..
Botswana	..	..	..	..	..	..	..	..	..	..	..	..	..	..
Burkina Faso	..	..	..	..	..	..	..	..	..	..	..	..	..	..
Burundi	..	..	..	..	..	..	..	..	..	..	..	..	..	..
Cameroon	934	521	652	539	837	1,049	816	..	..	..	..	151.6	-4.7	..
Cape Verde	..	..	..	..	..	..	..	..	..	..	..	..	..	..
Central African Republic	177	74	80	113	67	37	36	..	..	..	..	150.6	-5.5	..
Chad	..	..	..	..	..	..	..	..	..	..	..	..	..	..
Comoros	..	..	..	..	1	..	0	..	..	..	..	..	..	..
Congo, Democratic Rep. of	116	147	163	143	142	172	136	113	101	74	91	171.2	0.4	-9.3
Congo, Republic of	385	643	941	937	816	609	530	..	..	..	..	163.8	28.3	..
Côte d'Ivoire	3,394	1,175	1,138	1,084	1,127	967	878	..	..	..	..	150.4	-16.9	..
Djibouti	..	..	..	..	..	..	..	..	..	..	..	..	..	..
Equatorial Guinea	16	133	133	142	129	126	143	400	380	..	5	218.1	12.4	-24.1
Eritrea	..	..	..	..	..	..	..	..	..	..	..	..	..	..
Ethiopia	..	..	..	..	..	..	..	..	..	..	..	..	..	..
Gabon	1,150	1,353	1,343	1,460	1,244	1,392	1,447	1,685	1,729	1,359	1,632	154.9	0.8	2.4
Gambia, The	..	..	..	..	..	0	0	..	..	..	..	..	..	..
Ghana	183	514	531	371	361	390	426	936	735	754	1,018	107.8	26.0	17.3
Guinea	..	8	8	8	13	15	17	45	45	45	45	112.1	-7.6	31.0
Guinea-Bissau	6	5	4	4	6	12	9	5	5	6	8	117.7	22.1	1.3
Kenya	33	4	4	3	4	3	0	82	94	95	27	138.6	-26.5	78.3
Lesotho	..	..	..	..	..	..	..	..	..	..	..	..	..	..
Liberia	524	255	701	729	663	429	642	149	145	206	225	147.3	30.0	-20.0
Madagascar	0	2	1	2	3	26	6	6	10	8	4	111.7	21.2	10.2
Malawi	..	..	1	0	0	0	1	1	1	1	1	153.8	..	20.3
Mali	..	..	..	..	..	0	..	..	..	..	..	..	..	..
Mauritania	..	..	..	..	1	..	..	..	..	..	..	..	..	..
Mauritius	..	..	..	..	..	..	2	..	..	..	..	..	..	..
Mozambique	31	5	10	2	5	4	1	149	137	140	158	68.8	-3.8	115.9
Namibia	..	..	..	..	..	..	..	..	..	..	..	..	..	..
Niger	..	..	..	..	..	..	..	..	..	..	..	..	..	..
Nigeria	11	17	16	11	37	49	34	431	288	269	248	143.7	-32.2	59.9
Rwanda	..	..	..	..	..	0	..	..	..	..	..	..	..	..
São Tomé and Principe	..	..	..	..	0	..	..	0	..	..	..	..	..	..
Senegal	..	..	..	..	..	..	..	..	..	..	..	..	..	..
Seychelles	..	..	..	..	0	..	..	..	..	..	..	..	..	..
Sierra Leone	..	1	1	0	0	0	0	..	..	..	..	..	-8.8	..
Somalia	..	..	..	..	..	..	..	48	..	..	..	..	..	..
South Africa	756	1,520	2,777	1,177	1,137	1,191	1,692	425	405	488	541	150.9	24.9	-15.6
Sudan	..	..	..	..	..	0	..	..	..	..	..	..	..	..
Swaziland	421	355	293	285	254	254	254	241	239	299	270	163.6	-13.1	0.2
Tanzania	5	5	6	3	25	14	8	40	40	37	9	115.7	3.0	16.4
Togo	..	..	..	..	0	..	..	0	0	1	0	..	..	..
Uganda	0	..	..	..	..	..	..	9	11	7	7	45.4	..	..
Zambia	..	..	..	..	0	0	..	..	..	..	..	..	..	..
Zimbabwe	26	65	17	17	56	83	89	..	..	..	..	214.2	-14.1	..
NORTH AFRICA	88	94	117	95	95	77	105	78	84	71	60	160.0	6.1	-5.4
Algeria	..	..	..	..	1	..	..	..	..	..	..	..	..	..
Egypt, Arab Republic	..	..	..	..	0	0	..	3	6	0	..	..	..	..
Libya	..	..	..	..	..	0	0	..	..	..	..	..	..	..
Morocco	74	85	102	88	84	70	98	43	48	50	39	169.1	6.3	-11.4
Tunisia	14	10	16	7	10	8	7	32	29	20	21	135.1	3.4	22.6
ALL AFRICA	8,258	6,897	8,938	7,127	7,026	6,901	7,275	4,842	4,448	3,859	4,349	150.0	2.5	-9.3

5-19. Petroleum exports

| | Thousands of metric tons | | | | | | | | | | Average annual percentage growth | | |
	1980	1990	1991	1992	1993	1994	1995	1996	1997	1998	75-84	85-89	90-MR
SUB-SAHARAN AFRICA	116,952	127,608	132,770	137,869	147,511	145,809	147,326	160,589	172,724	172,919	-4.6	4.9	4.0
excluding South Africa	116,952	127,608	132,770	137,869	147,208	145,613	147,242	160,589	172,724	172,434	-4.6	4.9	4.0
excl. S.Africa & Nigeria	20,221	50,465	52,602	54,862	55,014	56,355	59,925	64,854	69,896	72,217	3.2	9.9	4.8
Angola	6,334	22,198	23,255	25,706	23,497	25,315	28,654	31,441	33,410	35,108	-0.2	21.6	5.9
Benin	..	210	200	138	157	131	97	76	65	53	..	63.1	-14.6
Botswana													
Burkina Faso	..	..	..	..	..	..	..	..	..	..	..	..	..
Burundi	..	..	..	..	..	..	..	..	..	..	..	..	..
Cameroon	3,407	7,166	6,456	6,097	6,091	5,278	5,014	5,354	5,532	6,200	81.7	-0.7	-3.0
Cape Verde													
Central African Republic	..	..	..	..	..	..	..	..	..	..	..	..	..
Chad	..	..	..	..	..	..	..	..	..	..	..	..	..
Comoros	..	..	..	..	..	..	..	..	..	..	..	..	..
Congo, Democratic Rep. of	859	1,158	1,125	995	1,019	1,085	1,087	1,087	1,021	963	0.3	-0.8	-1.9
Congo, Republic of	3,383	7,611	7,498	8,136	9,227	8,837	8,001	9,221	12,013	12,811	12.3	3.5	6.1
Côte d'Ivoire	122	..	..	..	..	..	..	..	..	..	..	-34.8	..
Djibouti	..	..	..	..	..	..	..	..	..	..	..	..	..
Equatorial Guinea	..	..	..	..	..	..	..	..	..	..	..	..	..
Eritrea	..	..	..	..	..	..	..	..	..	..	..	..	..
Ethiopia	0	0	0	0	0	0	0	0	0	0	..	..	..
Gabon	7,637	12,123	14,068	13,790	15,023	15,710	17,072	17,676	17,855	17,083	-4.5	1.9	6.6
Gambia, The	..	..	..	..	..	..	..	..	..	..	..	..	..
Ghana	0	0	0	0	0	0	0	0	0	0	..	..	..
Guinea	..	..	..	..	..	..	..	..	..	..	..	..	..
Guinea-Bissau	..	..	..	..	..	..	..	..	..	..	..	..	..
Kenya	..	..	..	..	..	..	..	..	..	..	..	..	..
Lesotho	..	..	..	..	..	..	..	..	..	..	..	..	..
Liberia	..	..	..	..	..	..	..	..	..	..	..	..	..
Madagascar	..	..	..	..	..	..	..	..	..	..	..	..	..
Malawi	..	..	..	..	..	..	..	..	..	..	..	..	..
Mali	..	..	..	..	..	..	..	..	..	..	..	..	..
Mauritania	..	..	..	..	..	..	..	..	..	..	..	..	..
Mauritius	..	..	..	..	..	..	..	..	..	..	..	..	..
Mozambique	..	..	..	..	..	..	..	..	..	..	..	..	..
Namibia													
Niger	..	..	..	..	..	..	..	..	..	..	..	..	..
Nigeria	96,731	77,143	80,168	83,006	92,194	89,258	87,317	95,735	102,828	100,217	-6.8	2.2	3.4
Rwanda	..	..	..	..	..	..	..	..	..	..	..	..	..
São Tomé and Principe	..	..	..	..	..	..	..	..	..	..	..	..	..
Senegal	..	..	..	..	..	..	..	..	..	..	..	..	..
Seychelles	..	..	..	..	..	..	..	..	..	..	..	..	..
Sierra Leone	..	..	..	..	..	..	..	..	..	..	..	..	..
Somalia	..	..	..	..	..	..	..	..	..	..	..	..	..
South Africa	..	..	..	..	303	196	84	..	..	485	..	..	..
Sudan	..	..	..	..	..	..	..	..	..	..	..	..	..
Swaziland	..	..	..	..	..	..	..	..	..	..	..	..	..
Tanzania	..	..	..	..	..	..	..	..	..	..	..	..	..
Togo	..	..	..	..	..	..	..	..	..	..	..	..	..
Uganda	..	..	..	..	..	..	..	..	..	..	..	..	..
Zambia	..	..	..	..	..	..	..	..	..	..	..	..	..
Zimbabwe	..	..	..	..	..	..	..	..	..	..	..	..	..
NORTH AFRICA	145,865	111,371	114,024	113,950	110,186	99,427	98,517	101,031	96,971	97,430	-3.7	-0.6	-1.5
Algeria	38,918	32,303	31,648	30,966	31,920	32,015	31,875	35,434	34,234	35,813	-5.7	1.1	1.5
Egypt, Arab Republic	17,146	19,929	18,461	20,413	19,924	8,480	8,503	6,836	6,241	2,836	20.7	-2.8	-18.8
Libya	85,054	55,766	60,403	58,463	54,893	55,661	54,573	55,365	53,633	55,854	-6.4	-0.4	0.4
Morocco	..	..	..	..	..	..	..	..	..	..	..	..	..
Tunisia	4,747	3,373	3,512	4,109	3,449	3,271	3,566	3,397	2,863	2,927	-0.5	-3.9	-1.7
ALL AFRICA	262,817	238,979	246,794	251,819	257,697	245,236	245,842	261,620	269,696	270,349	-4.2	55.7	1.7

5-20. Copper exports

	Thousands of metric tons										Average annual percentage growth		
	1980	*1990*	*1991*	*1992*	*1993*	*1994*	*1995*	*1996*	*1997*	*1998*	*75-84*	*85-89*	*90-MR*
SUB-SAHARAN AFRICA	1,286	973	792	714	598	495	418	392	393	316	5.2	-3.1	-12.8
excluding South Africa	1,164	883	688	581	517	421	339	318	322	248	4.6	-3.4	-14.0
excl. S.Africa & Nigeria	1,164	883	688	581	517	421	339	318	322	248	4.6	-3.4	-14.0
Angola	0	0	0	0	0	0	0	0	0	0	..	..	..
Benin	0	0	0	0	0	0	0	0	0	0		..	..
Botswana	20	19	20	19	22	20	18	23	18	20	..	1.0	0.4
Burkina Faso	0	0	0	0	0	0	0	0	0	0	..	..	..
Burundi	0	0	0	0	0	0	0	0	0	0	..		..
Cameroon	0	0	0	0	0	0	0	0	0	0	..	..	
Cape Verde	0	0	0	0	0	0	0	0	0	0		..	..
Central African Republic	0	0	0	0	0	0	0	0	0	0	..	..	..
Chad	0	0	0	0	0	0	0	0	0	0	..	..	..
Comoros	0	0	0	0	0	0	0	0	0	0		..	..
Congo, Democratic Rep. of	461	374	252	116	28	14	5	0	..	..	16.8	-2.7	-55.3
Congo, Republic of	1	0	0	0	0	0	0	0	..	..	..	..	..
Côte d'Ivoire	0	0	0	0	0	0	0	0	0	0	..	..	..
Djibouti	0	0	0	0	0	0	0	0	0	0	..	..	..
Equatorial Guinea	0	0	0	0	0	0	0	0	0	0	..	..	..
Eritrea	0	0	0	0	0	0	0	0	0	0	..		..
Ethiopia	0	0	0	0	0	0	0	0	0	0	..	..	..
Gabon	0	0	0	0	0	0	0	0	0	0	..	..	..
Gambia, The	0	0	0	0	0	0	0	0	0	0	..	..	..
Ghana	0	0	0	0	0	0	0	0	0	0	..	..	..
Guinea	0	0	0	0	0	0	0	0	0	0	..	..	..
Guinea-Bissau	0	0	0	0	0	0	0	0	0	0	..	..	..
Kenya	0	0	0	0	0	0	0	0	0	0	..	..	..
Lesotho	0	0	0	0	0	0	0	0	0	.0	..	..	..
Liberia	0	0	0	0	0	0	0	0	0	0	..	..	..
Madagascar	0	0	0	0	0	0	0	0	0	0	..	..	..
Malawi	0	0	0	0	0	0	0	0	0	0	..	..	..
Mali	0	0	0	0	0	0	0	0	0	0	..	..	..
Mauritania	1	0	0	0	0	0	0	0	..	..	..	..	..
Mauritius	0	0	0	0	0	0	0	0	0	0	..	..	..
Mozambique	0	0	0	0	0	0	0	0	0	0	..	..	..
Namibia	41	30	34	35	30	26	25	18	..	..	1.9	-7.0	-6.8
Niger	0	0	0	0	0	0	0	0	0	0	..	..	..
Nigeria	0	0	0	0	0	0	0	0	0	0	..	..	..
Rwanda	0	0	0	0	0	0	0	0	0	0	..	..	..
São Tomé and Principe	0	0	0	0	0	0	0	0	0	0	..	..	..
Senegal	0	0	0	0	0	0	0	0	0	0	..	..	..
Seychelles	0	0	0	0	0	0	0	0	0	0	..	..	..
Sierra Leone	0	0	0	0	0	0	0	0	0	0	..	..	..
Somalia	0	0	0	0	0	0	0	0	0	0	..	..	..
South Africa	121	90	104	132	81	74	79	74	71	68	13.2	-0.8	-5.7
Sudan	0	0	0	0	0	0	0	0	0	0	..	..	..
Swaziland	0	0	0	0	0	0	0	0	0	0	..	..	..
Tanzania	0	0	0	0	0	0	0	0	0	0	..	..	..
Togo	0	0	0	0	0	0	0	0	0	0	..	..	..
Uganda	0	0	0	0	0	0	0	0	..	..	..	..	..
Zambia	617	460	382	412	437	361	292	276	304	228	-1.8	-3.4	-7.0
Zimbabwe	23	0	0	0	0	0	0	0	..	..	3.8	-16.6	..
NORTH AFRICA	6	16	16	17	13	19	16	16	0	0	..	-13.1	2.5
Algeria	0	0	0	0	0	0	0	0	..	..	..	..	..
Egypt, Arab Republic	0	0	0	0	0	0	0	0	0	0	..	..	..
Libya	0	0	0	0	0	0	0	0	0	0	..	..	..
Morocco	6	16	16	17	13	19	16	16	..	..	..	-12.9	2.5
Tunisia	0	0	0	0	0	0	0	0	0	0	..	..	..
ALL AFRICA	1,292	989	807	730	611	514	434	408	393	316	5.4	-3.3	-12.9

External Sector

5-21. Iron exports

	Thousands of metric tons										Average annual percentage growth		
	1980	*1988*	*1989*	*1990*	*1991*	*1992*	*1993*	*1994*	*1995*	*1996*	*75-84*	*85-89*	*90-MR*
SUB-SAHARAN AFRICA	28,215	22,981	24,956	21,057	17,509	15,778	18,986	19,465	21,397	19,545	..	-0.4	-1.3
excluding South Africa	17,482	15,734	15,780	9,988	7,474	6,114	6,276	6,722	7,196	7,000	..	-2.3	-8.7
excl. S.Africa & Nigeria	17,482	15,734	15,780	9,988	7,474	6,114	6,276	6,722	7,196	7,000	..	-2.3	-8.7
Angola	0	0	0	0	0	0	0	0	0	0	..	..	..
Benin	0	0	0	0	0	0	0	0	0	0	..	..	..
Botswana	0	0	0	0	0	0	0	0	0	0	..	..	..
Burkina Faso	0	0	0	0	0	0	0	0	0	0	..	..	..
Burundi	0	0	0	0	0	0	0	0	0	0	..	..	..
Cameroon	0	0	0	0	0	0	0	0	0	0	..	..	..
Cape Verde	0	0	0	0	0	0	0	0	0	0	..	..	..
Central African Republic	0	0	0	0	0	0	0	0	0	0	..	..	..
Chad	0	0	0	0	0	0	0	0	0	0	..	..	..
Comoros	0	0	0	0	0	0	0	0	0	0	..	..	..
Congo, Democratic Rep. of	0	0	0	0	0	0	0	0	0	0	..	..	..
Congo, Republic of	0	0	0	0	0	0	0	0	0	0	..	..	..
Côte d'Ivoire	0	0	0	0	0	0	0	0	0	0	..	..	..
Djibouti	0	0	0	0	0	0	0	0	0	0	..	..	..
Equatorial Guinea	0	0	0	0	0	0	0	0	0	0	..	..	..
Eritrea	0	0	0	0	0	0	0	0	0	0	..	..	..
Ethiopia	0	0	0	0	0	0	0	0	0	0	..	..	..
Gabon	0	0	0	0	0	0	0	0	0	0	..	..	..
Gambia, The	0	0	0	0	0	0	0	0	0	0	..	..	..
Ghana	0	0	0	0	0	0	0	0	0	0	..	..	..
Guinea	0	0	0	0	0	0	0	0	0	0	..	..	..
Guinea-Bissau	0	0	0	0	0	0	0	0	0	0	..	..	..
Kenya	0	0	0	0	0	0	0	0	0	0	..	..	..
Lesotho	0	0	0	0	0	0	0	0	0	0	..	..	..
Liberia	11,695	9,231	8,540	2,607	670	853	0	0	0	0	..	-5.4	..
Madagascar	0	0	0	0	0	0	0	0	0	0	..	..	..
Malawi	0	0	0	0	0	0	0	0	0	0	..	..	..
Mali	0	0	0	0	0	0	0	0	0	0	..	..	..
Mauritania	5,673	6,503	7,240	7,381	6,804	5,261	6,276	6,722	7,196	7,000	..	3.0	-0.3
Mauritius	0	0	0	0	0	0	0	0	0	0	..	..	..
Mozambique	0	0	0	0	0	0	0	0	0	0	..	..	..
Namibia	0	0	0	0	0	0	0	0	0	0	..	..	..
Niger	0	0	0	0	0	0	0	0	0	0	..	..	..
Nigeria	0	0	0	0	0	0	0	0	0	0	..	..	..
Rwanda	0	0	0	0	0	0	0	0	0	0	..	..	..
São Tomé and Principe	0	0	0	0	0	0	0	0	0	0	..	..	..
Senegal	0	0	0	0	0	0	0	0	0	0	..	..	..
Seychelles	0	0	0	0	0	0	0	0	0	0	..	..	..
Sierra Leone	0	0	0	0	0	0	0	0	0	0	..	..	..
Somalia	0	0	0	0	0	0	0	0	0	0	..	..	..
South Africa	10,733	7,247	9,176	11,069	10,035	9,664	12,710	12,743	14,201	12,545	..	4.0	5.4
Sudan	0	0	0	0	0	0	0	0	0	0	..	..	..
Swaziland	114	0	0	0	0	0	0	0	0	0	..	..	..
Tanzania	0	0	0	0	0	0	0	0	0	0	..	..	..
Togo	0	0	0	0	0	0	0	0	0	0	..	..	..
Uganda	0	0	0	0	0	0	0	0	0	0	..	..	..
Zambia	0	0	0	0	0	0	0	0	0	0	..	..	..
Zimbabwe	0	0	0	0	0	0	0	0	0	0	..	..	..
NORTH AFRICA	784	48	62	47	50	55	58	42	21	4	..	-11.3	-24.3
Algeria	699	0	10	9	10	20	25	25	5	4	..	-41.9	-6.9
Egypt, Arab Republic	0	0	0	0	0	0	0	0	0	0	..	..	..
Libya	0	0	0	0	0	0	0	0	0	0	..	..	..
Morocco	85	48	52	38	40	35	33	17	16	0	..	..	-17.4
Tunisia	0	0	0	0	0	0	0	0	0	0	..	..	..
ALL AFRICA	28,999	23,029	25,018	21,104	17,559	15,833	19,044	19,507	21,418	19,549	..	-0.6	-1.4

5-22. Phosphate exports

	1980	1988	1989	1990	1991	1992	1993	1994	1995	1996	1997	75-84	85-89	90-MR
	Thousands of metric tons											*Average annual percentage growth*		
SUB-SAHARAN AFRICA	4,277	5,983	5,877	4,995	5,544	4,617	3,747	4,154	4,919	4,496	4,290	0.4	6.9	-3.1
excluding South Africa	4,274	4,715	4,783	3,778	4,378	3,272	2,550	2,881	3,511	3,522	2,990	-0.6	4.6	-4.3
excl. S.Africa & Nigeria	4,274	4,715	4,783	3,778	4,378	3,272	2,550	2,881	3,511	3,522	2,990	-0.6	4.6	-4.3
Angola	0	0	0	0	0	0	0	0	0	0	0	..	..	..
Benin	0	0	0	0	0	0	0	0	0	0	0	..	..	..
Botswana	0	0	0	0	0	0	0	0	0	0	0	..	..	..
Burkina Faso	0	0	0	0	0	0	0	0	0	0	0	..	..	..
Burundi	0	0	0	0	0	0	0	0	0	0	0	..	..	..
Cameroon	0	0	0	0	0	0	0	0	0	0	0	..	..	..
Cape Verde	0	0	0	0	0	0	0	0	0	0	0	..	..	..
Central African Republic	0	0	0	0	0	0	0	0	0	0	0	..	..	..
Chad	0	0	0	0	0	0	0	0	0	0	0	..	..	..
Comoros	0	0	0	0	0	0	0	0	0	0	0	..	..	..
Congo, Democratic Rep. of	0	0	0	0	0	0	0	0	0	0	0	..	..	..
Congo, Republic of	0	0	0	0	0	0	0	0	0	0	0	..	..	..
Côte d'Ivoire	0	0	0	0	0	0	0	0	0	0	0	..	..	..
Djibouti	0	0	0	0	0	0	0	0	0	0	0	..	..	..
Equatorial Guinea	0	0	0	0	0	0	0	0	0	0	0	..	..	..
Eritrea	0	0	0	0	0	0	0	0	0	0	0	..	..	..
Ethiopia	0	0	0	0	0	0	0	0	0	0	0	..	..	..
Gabon	0	0	0	0	0	0	0	0	0	0	0	..	..	..
Gambia, The	0	0	0	0	0	0	0	0	0	0	0	..	..	..
Ghana	0	0	0	0	0	0	0	0	0	0	0	..	..	..
Guinea	0	0	0	0	0	0	0	0	0	0	0	..	..	..
Guinea-Bissau	0	0	0	0	0	0	0	0	0	0	0	..	..	..
Kenya	0	0	0	0	0	0	0	0	0	0	0	..	..	..
Lesotho	0	0	0	0	0	0	0	0	0	0	0	..	..	..
Liberia	0	0	0	0	0	0	0	0	0	0	0	..	..	..
Madagascar	0	0	0	0	0	0	0	0	0	0	0	..	..	..
Malawi	0	0	0	0	0	0	0	0	0	0	0	..	..	..
Mali	0	0	0	0	0	0	0	0	0	0	0	..	..	..
Mauritania	0	0	0	0	0	0	0	0	0	0	0	..	..	..
Mauritius	0	0	0	0	0	0	0	0	0	0	0	..	..	..
Mozambique	0	0	0	0	0	0	0	0	0	0	0	..	..	..
Namibia	0	0	0	0	0	0	0	0	0	0	0	..	..	..
Niger	0	0	0	0	0	0	0	0	0	0	0	..	..	..
Nigeria	0	0	0	0	0	0	0	0	0	0	0	..	..	..
Rwanda	0	0	0	0	0	0	0	0	0	0	0	..	..	..
São Tomé and Principe	0	0	0	0	0	0	0	0	0	0	0	..	..	..
Senegal	1,378	1,847	1,435	1,356	1,304	1,187	983	648	859	836	598	-3.9	4.4	-10.1
Seychelles	0	0	0	0	0	0	0	0	0	0	0	..	..	..
Sierra Leone	0	0	0	0	0	0	0	0	0	0	0	..	..	..
Somalia	0	0	0	0	0	0	0	0	0	0	0	..	..	..
South Africa	4	1,268	1,094	1,217	1,166	1,344	1,197	1,273	1,408	1,350	1,300	39.6	20.6	2.2
Sudan	0	0	0	0	0	0	0	0	0	0	0	..	..	..
Swaziland	0	0	0	0	0	0	0	0	0	0	0	..	..	..
Tanzania	0	0	0	0	0	0	0	0	0	0	0	..	..	..
Togo	2,896	2,868	3,347	2,422	3,074	2,086	1,567	2,234	2,652	2,686	2,392	1.9	4.5	-2.1
Uganda	0	0	0	0	0	0	0	0	0	0	0	..	..	..
Zambia	0	0	0	0	0	0	0	0	0	0	0	..	..	..
Zimbabwe	0	0	0	0	0	0	0	0	0	0	0	..	..	..
NORTH AFRICA	18,932	16,560	14,700	13,297	10,537	11,068	10,096	11,523	11,466	12,422	13,398	-1.1	-2.3	-0.6
Algeria	768	877	970	735	804	800	449	575	671	993	474	5.6	8.5	-4.3
Egypt, Arab Republic	258	268	246	297	164	180	134	114	48	65	..	12.4	3.8	-21.0
Libya	0	0	0	0	0	0	0	0	0	0	0	..	..	..
Morocco	16,457	14,260	12,407	11,672	9,143	9,132	8,398	9,527	9,420	10,141	11,669	-0.8	-3.1	-0.9
Tunisia	1,449	1,156	1,077	593	426	956	1,114	1,308	1,327	1,224	1,247	-6.9	-0.8	9.3
ALL AFRICA	23,210	22,543	20,576	18,292	16,080	15,684	13,843	15,678	16,385	16,918	17,688	-0.8	-0.2	-1.3

5-23. Cocoa exports

	\multicolumn{11}{c}{Thousands of metric tons}										Average annual percentage growth		
	1980	1990	1991	1992	1993	1994	1995	1996	1997	1998	1999	75-84	85-89	90-MR
SUB-SAHARAN AFRICA	869	1,352	1,369	1,190	1,469	1,271	1,340	1,995	1,633	1,749	1,975	0.4	5.3	4.0
excluding South Africa	869	1,349	1,364	1,180	1,456	1,260	1,332	1,985	1,623	1,740	1,967	0.4	5.3	4.0
excl. S.Africa & Nigeria	718	1,196	1,203	1,069	1,296	1,113	1,193	1,803	1,469	1,605	1,759	1.1	5.2	4.3
Angola	..	..	..	..	..	..	..	..	..	..	..	-20.0	..	..
Benin	5	0	0	..	..	..	..	..	..	0	..	6.2	-63.8	..
Botswana	0	0	0	0	0	0	0	0	0	0	0	..	128.8	-15.0
Burkina Faso	..	..	..	..	..	..	..	..	..	..	..	..	..	..
Burundi	..	..	..	..	..	..	..	..	..	..	..	..	..	..
Cameroon	105	119	98	68	112	82	120	142	110	122	121	0.1	3.8	2.4
Cape Verde	..	..	..	..	..	..	..	..	..	..	..	..	..	..
Central African Republic	0	..	..	..	..	..	..	..	..	..	..	-21.8	..	..
Chad	..	..	..	..	..	..	..	..	..	..	..	..	..	..
Comoros	0	..	..	..	..	..	..	..	..	..	..	-14.3	..	..
Congo, Democratic Rep. of	4	5	4	3	3	6	2	3	3	3	2	-0.2	2.8	-6.7
Congo, Republic of	2	1	0	0	0	0	0	1	1	1	1	-5.1	-18.7	7.4
Côte d'Ivoire	332	767	793	724	872	744	795	1,138	1,028	1,103	1,277	9.1	5.4	5.0
Djibouti	..	..	..	..	..	..	..	..	..	..	..	..	..	..
Equatorial Guinea	7	6	6	5	3	3	3	6	4	6	3	-0.2	0.4	-4.1
Eritrea	..	..	..	..	..	..	..	..	..	..	..	..	..	..
Ethiopia	..	..	..	..	..	..	..	..	..	..	..	..	..	..
Gabon	4	2	1	2	1	1	1	1	1	1	1	-4.2	2.6	-12.0
Gambia, The	..	..	..	..	..	..	..	..	..	..	..	..	..	..
Ghana	218	270	265	243	278	252	253	478	288	333	321	-7.7	9.0	3.0
Guinea	4	2	2	2	4	4	3	6	7	8	4	4.3	-6.2	11.9
Guinea-Bissau	..	..	..	..	..	..	..	..	..	..	..	..	..	..
Kenya	0	0	0	1	1	1	0	0	0	0	0	-8.2	46.3	19.8
Lesotho	..	..	..	..	..	..	..	..	..	..	..	..	..	..
Liberia	4	3	2	0	0	0	0	1	1	2	2	9.1	-15.1	-7.1
Madagascar	2	3	4	3	4	3	2	2	1	1	1	5.8	7.6	-12.9
Malawi	..	..	..	..	..	..	..	..	..	..	..	-21.2	..	..
Mali	..	..	..	..	..	..	..	..	..	..	..	..	..	..
Mauritania	..	..	..	..	..	..	..	..	..	..	..	..	..	..
Mauritius	..	..	..	0	0	0	0	0	0	0	0	..	..	-5.5
Mozambique	..	..	..	..	..	..	..	..	..	..	..	..	..	..
Namibia	..	..	..	..	..	..	..	..	..	..	..	..	..	..
Niger	0	..	..	..	..	..	..	..	..	..	..	..	..	..
Nigeria	151	154	161	111	161	148	139	182	155	135	208	-2.6	4.2	1.7
Rwanda	..	..	..	..	..	..	..	..	..	..	..	..	..	..
São Tomé and Principe	7	3	5	4	4	3	3	4	3	5	4	-4.3	0.4	0.3
Senegal	0	0	0	0	0	0	0	0	0	0	0	65.7	-28.8	51.4
Seychelles	..	..	0	0	..	0	0	0	..	0	0	..	..	3.4
Sierra Leone	8	5	13	5	4	3	3	4	3	3	3	6.0	-4.6	-11.0
Somalia	..	..	..	..	..	..	..	..	..	..	..	..	..	..
South Africa	0	3	6	10	13	11	8	10	10	9	8	-8.5	34.0	11.3
Sudan	..	..	..	..	..	..	..	..	..	..	..	..	..	..
Swaziland	..	..	..	..	..	..	..	..	6	8	7	..	..	..
Tanzania	1	3	2	2	2	2	3	3	3	3	2	9.0	9.7	2.6
Togo	15	8	6	6	5	6	4	11	10	6	8	-1.7	-11.9	1.7
Uganda	0	0	1	1	1	1	1	1	1	2	1	2.5	5.5	16.2
Zambia	..	..	..	..	..	..	..	..	..	..	..	..	..	..
Zimbabwe	0	0	0	0	0	0	0	0	0	0	0	-14.6	-4.1	17.2
NORTH AFRICA	..	1	2	1	0	0	1	1	1	1	1	6.1	25.6	-2.7
Algeria	..	..	..	..	..	..	0	..	0	..	..	..	..	..
Egypt, Arab Republic	..	1	2	0	0	0	0	1	1	0	1	-22.9	81.9	-0.7
Libya	..	..	..	..	..	..	..	..	..	..	..	..	..	..
Morocco	..	0	0	0	0	0	0	0	0	0	0	..	-17.2	0.0
Tunisia	..	0	0	0	0	0	0	0	0	0	0	..	17.4	-4.7
ALL AFRICA	869	1,353	1,372	1,191	1,469	1,272	1,341	1,996	1,634	1,750	1,976	0.4	5.3	4.0

5-24. Coffee exports

	1980	1990	1991	1992	1993	1994	1995	1996	1997	1998	1999	75-84	85-89	90-MR
					Thousands of metric tons							*Average annual percentage growth*		
SUB-SAHARAN AFRICA	819	1,032	828	847	830	751	788	949	937	841	791	-2.3	0.0	-0.9
excluding South Africa	818	1,030	827	846	830	750	787	948	933	835	789	-2.4	-0.1	-0.9
excl. S.Africa & Nigeria	816	1,030	827	846	829	750	786	947	932	834	788	-2.4	-0.1	-0.9
Angola	47	5	5	5	2	0	2	3	3	3	3	-17.7	-19.0	-7.1
Benin	0	..	0	0	0	..	..	..	..	..	..	18.1	-21.6	..
Botswana	0	0	0	0	0	0	..	0	0	0	0	3.8	56.4	-23.1
Burkina Faso	..	..	..	..	..	..	..	..	..	..	..	..	..	..
Burundi	19	34	41	40	23	29	29	13	32	22	24	3.0	-0.2	-4.8
Cameroon	92	158	113	104	67	54	63	74	59	53	69	0.0	4.4	-9.5
Cape Verde	..	..	..	..	0	..	..	..	0	..	..	..	..	..
Central African Republic	11	13	9	6	8	8	14	5	12	6	12	2.2	10.4	-5.2
Chad	..	..	..	..	..	..	..	..	..	..	..	..	..	..
Comoros	0	..	..	..	..	..	..	..	..	..	..	-17.4	..	..
Congo, Democratic Rep. of	74	104	84	104	55	63	61	49	23	38	23	0.3	2.7	-14.0
Congo, Republic of	2	0	0	0	0	0	2	1	0	..	..	8.4	-28.7	17.2
Côte d'Ivoire	207	232	199	203	226	122	135	145	254	239	132	-2.6	-7.4	-0.2
Djibouti	..	..	..	..	..	..	..	..	..	..	..	..	..	..
Equatorial Guinea	0	0	0	0	0	0	0	0	0	..	..	-10.7	-18.2	-19.1
Eritrea	..	..	..	..	..	..	..	..	..	..	..	..	..	..
Ethiopia	..	..	..	..	70	89	77	110	119	115	109	..	..	8.5
Gabon	1	0	0	0	0	0	0	0	..	0	0	26.9	12.9	-13.2
Gambia, The	..	..	..	..	..	..	0	..	..	..	..	..	..	..
Ghana	0	1	1	2	3	1	2	1	3	6	6	-21.1	12.5	23.0
Guinea	3	7	4	5	6	12	19	8	20	22	7	0.4	105.1	9.1
Guinea-Bissau	..	..	..	..	..	..	..	..	..	..	..	..	..	..
Kenya	80	112	83	78	88	80	89	114	68	51	70	2.9	-2.7	-4.0
Lesotho	..	..	..	..	..	..	..	..	..	..	..	..	..	..
Liberia	13	2	..	..	..	..	..	..	..	..	..	6.3	-10.9	..
Madagascar	69	48	41	50	51	37	35	40	26	30	13	-2.5	2.6	-10.0
Malawi	0	7	6	9	6	5	5	5	4	4	4	25.2	12.9	-3.7
Mali	..	..	..	..	..	..	..	..	..	..	..	..	..	..
Mauritania	..	..	..	..	..	..	..	..	..	..	..	..	..	..
Mauritius	0	0	..	0	..	..	..	..	0	..	0	..	..	..
Mozambique	..	..	..	..	..	..	..	..	..	..	..	..	..	..
Namibia	..	..	..	..	..	..	..	..	..	..	..	..	..	..
Niger	0	..	..	..	..	..	..	..	..	..	..	..	..	..
Nigeria	2	0	0	0	1	0	1	1	1	1	1	-1.8	41.6	20.6
Rwanda	22	46	38	34	30	2	8	18	14	14	17	1.4	1.4	-11.9
São Tomé and Principe	0	..	0	..	0	0	0	0	0	0	0	-6.1	-41.0	32.0
Senegal	1	0	..	0	0	..	..	..	..	..	0	0.9	-2.6	..
Seychelles	..	..	..	..	..	0	..	..	..	..	..	..	..	..
Sierra Leone	10	8	6	4	3	4	5	2	3	3	1	-0.7	12.2	-13.1
Somalia	..	..	..	..	..	..	..	..	..	..	..	..	..	..
South Africa	0	1	1	1	0	0	1	1	4	6	2	24.9	26.1	18.7
Sudan	..	..	..	..	..	..	..	..	..	..	..	..	..	..
Swaziland	..	..	..	..	..	..	..	..	0	0	0	..	..	..
Tanzania	43	61	52	51	59	37	48	62	47	45	38	0.8	-2.2	-2.4
Togo	9	14	9	19	13	9	13	5	19	10	19	-6.2	28.6	0.0
Uganda	110	141	127	119	114	194	169	279	210	163	230	-2.8	3.8	5.1
Zambia	..	1	0	1	1	0	1	2	2	2	3	..	59.2	16.4
Zimbabwe	3	35	9	10	4	4	10	11	12	8	7	13.2	-9.3	-3.3
NORTH AFRICA	..	2	0	0	0	0	0	0	0	0	0	-34.0	..	-25.4
Algeria	..	1	..	..	..	..	..	..	..	..	..	..	..	..
Egypt, Arab Republic	..	1	0	0	0	0	0	0	..	0	0	..	..	-47.1
Libya	..	..	..	..	..	..	..	..	..	..	..	..	..	..
Morocco	..	..	0	..	0	0	0	0	0	0	0	..	..	-4.2
Tunisia	..	0	0	0	0	0	0	0	0	0	0	..	..	11.5
ALL AFRICA	819	1,033	828	847	830	751	788	949	937	841	791	-2.4	0.0	-0.9

External Sector

5-25. Cotton exports

	Thousands of metric tons											Average annual percentage growth		
	1980	1990	1991	1992	1993	1994	1995	1996	1997	1998	1999	75-84	85-89	90-MR
SUB-SAHARAN AFRICA	459	700	661	693	695	699	786	833	973	943	792	1.2	7.6	2.5
excluding South Africa	459	694	658	689	695	698	786	833	969	936	787	1.3	7.4	2.5
excl. S.Africa & Nigeria	459	691	657	688	691	696	784	811	937	927	778	1.3	7.4	2.3
Angola	..	..	..	..	..	..	..	..	..	..	..	-27.7	10.4	..
Benin	8	41	43	58	60	74	99	89	112	107	84	-0.6	13.3	9.6
Botswana	..	..	..	0	1	1	1	1	1	1	1	..	..	20.7
Burkina Faso	28	59	55	55	60	40	55	42	61	96	69	10.8	14.3	3.7
Burundi	1	0	..	..	2	2	1	0	..	..	..	-0.4	2.0	24.7
Cameroon	26	38	23	42	51	59	54	66	51	61	65	15.1	19.5	3.5
Cape Verde	0	0	0	0	0	0	0	..	..	..	..	..	..	..
Central African Republic	14	9	13	6	8	5	12	15	9	15	10	-4.0	-12.8	4.4
Chad	35	57	65	85	40	32	62	50	72	68	37	-2.4	-0.4	-0.9
Comoros	0	0	0	0	0	0	0	..	..	..	..	..	..	..
Congo, Democratic Rep. of	2	..	..	..	..	1	1	1	0	0	0	..	..	-29.7
Congo, Republic of	0	0	0	0	0	0	0	..	..	..	..	..	..	..
Côte d'Ivoire	39	89	97	67	96	100	88	75	86	117	122	14.7	15.3	2.2
Djibouti	0	0	0	0	0	0	0	..	..	..	..	..	..	..
Equatorial Guinea	0	0	0	0	0	0	0	..	..	..	..	..	..	..
Eritrea	0	0	0	0	0	0	0	..	..	..	..	..	..	..
Ethiopia	..	..	..	..	0	0	8	1	0	1	5	..	..	43.8
Gabon	0	0	0	0	0	0	0	..	..	..	..	..	..	..
Gambia, The	..	1	2	1	1	1	1	1	0	0	0	..	10.6	-17.5
Ghana	..	..	..	..	2	7	1	..	0	1	7	..	..	-19.5
Guinea	..	2	1	4	10	6	7	5	4	5	9	..	..	18.6
Guinea-Bissau	..	0	1	0	1	1	1	1	1	1	1	..	25.4	7.2
Kenya	4	..	1	6	8	7	1	..	0	0	0	-18.6	-73.2	-47.6
Lesotho	0	0	0	0	0	0	0	..	..	..	..	..	..	..
Liberia	0	0	0	0	..	..	..	..	..	..	..	..	..	..
Madagascar	1	0	3	..	..	1	1	1	0	..	0	22.2	-16.8	-6.9
Malawi	3	3	6	3	0	..	..	..	9	5	3	-20.5	-0.6	6.0
Mali	53	93	114	113	133	90	105	130	140	160	138	9.9	14.2	4.2
Mauritania	0	0	0	0	0	0	0	..	..	..	..	..	..	..
Mauritius	..	..	0	..	0	..	..	0	..	..	0	..	..	..
Mozambique	6	6	6	11	13	16	13	16	16	17	10	-8.0	1.1	10.8
Namibia	0	0	0	0	0	0	0	..	..	..	..	..	..	..
Niger	0	1	0	1	1	1	0	2	3	1	1	-12.4	80.4	0.8
Nigeria	..	3	1	0	3	3	2	22	32	9	9	..	..	36.2
Rwanda	0	0	0	0	0	0	0	..	..	..	..	..	..	..
São Tomé and Principe	0	0	0	0	0	0	0	..	..	..	..	..	..	..
Senegal	6	5	12	16	20	15	9	11	15	14	5	2.1	-6.4	0.4
Seychelles	0	0	0	0	0	0	0	..	..	..	..	..	..	..
Sierra Leone	0	0	0	0	0	0	0	..	..	..	..	..	..	..
Somalia	..	..	..	..	..	..	..	..	..	..	..	..	..	..
South Africa	0	6	3	5	0	0	0	0	4	7	5	-30.6	269.4	-7.9
Sudan	132	126	87	76	48	78	96	104	94	62	24	0.0	1.2	-9.7
Swaziland	4	19	10	6	7	4	3	4	2	0	0	4.8	40.8	-29.1
Tanzania	31	46	39	73	61	60	71	82	86	37	28	-3.9	17.8	-1.2
Togo	5	33	36	39	42	43	61	56	48	67	53	27.3	22.1	6.6
Uganda	2	4	8	8	8	4	6	10	19	1	10	-21.5	-25.3	5.6
Zambia	5	3	2	2	1	1	3	5	17	12	16	15.9	12.7	18.9
Zimbabwe	54	54	34	16	18	47	27	44	91	78	80	4.2	-0.2	7.5
NORTH AFRICA	167	41	16	16	20	114	68	23	42	67	112	0.1	-17.0	9.0
Algeria	..	..	..	..	..	..	..	..	..	..	..	..	..	..
Egypt, Arab Republic	164	39	13	16	18	113	67	23	42	66	112	0.2	-18.9	10.4
Libya	0	0	0	0	0	0	0	..	..	..	..	..	..	..
Morocco	3	1	3	1	2	1	0	..	0	1	0	3.4	..	-25.6
Tunisia	..	..	..	..	..	0	0	..	..	0	0	..	..	..
ALL AFRICA	627	740	677	710	715	813	854	857	1,015	1,010	904	0.9	3.6	2.9

5-26. Groundnut exports

	1980	1990	1991	1992	1993	1994	1995	1996	1997	1998	1999	75-84	85-89	90-MR
					Thousands of metric tons							*Average annual percentage growth*		
SUB-SAHARAN AFRICA	605	574	342	336	276	397	280	390	392	405	229	-8.9	15.7	-4.7
excluding South Africa	560	535	309	312	249	337	244	351	334	372	203	-8.7	15.2	-4.9
excl. S.Africa & Nigeria	559	535	309	310	249	330	243	347	312	359	190	-8.2	15.1	-5.5
Angola	1	..	..	..	..	..	..	..	..	..	..	-4.9	..	..
Benin	2	..	0	..	..	..	..	..	..	..	..	-27.0	..	..
Botswana	0	0	..	0	0	0	0	0	0	0	0	-10.2	29.0	2.8
Burkina Faso	1	1	1	1	0	0	0	0	0	0	0	-43.9	152.2	-8.8
Burundi	..	..	..	..	..	..	..	..	..	..	..	..	..	..
Cameroon	1	0	0	0	0	0	0	0	0	0	0	-39.5	15.8	17.9
Cape Verde	..	..	..	..	..	..	..	..	..	..	..	..	..	..
Central African Republic	..	..	..	..	..	1	1	0	1	1	1	..	..	-8.1
Chad	..	..	..	0	1	2	..	1	0	0	0	..	..	13.7
Comoros	..	..	..	..	..	..	..	..	..	..	..	..	..	..
Congo, Democratic Rep. of	..	..	..	..	..	..	..	..	..	..	..	..	..	..
Congo, Republic of	0	..	..	..	..	..	..	..	..	..	..	-10.6	..	..
Côte d'Ivoire	0	..	..	..	..	..	1	0	1	1	1	-8.4	..	..
Djibouti	..	..	..	..	..	..	..	..	..	..	..	..	..	..
Equatorial Guinea	..	..	..	..	..	..	..	..	..	..	..	..	..	..
Eritrea	..	..	..	..	..	..	..	..	..	..	..	..	..	..
Ethiopia	..	..	..	..	..	..	0	..	..	..	..	..	..	..
Gabon	..	..	..	..	..	..	..	..	..	..	..	..	..	..
Gambia, The	67	24	17	18	28	26	38	32	38	37	33	-7.7	-11.7	6.7
Ghana	2	..	..	..	..	..	..	0	0	0	0	..	..	..
Guinea	0	..	..	..	..	..	..	..	..	..	..	..	..	..
Guinea-Bissau	8	2	0	0	..	0	0	0	0	0	0	-4.4	-17.9	-14.2
Kenya	0	..	0	0	1	0	0	0	0	0	0	-24.6	23.1	14.5
Lesotho	..	..	..	..	..	..	..	..	..	..	..	..	..	..
Liberia	..	..	..	..	..	..	..	..	..	..	..	..	..	..
Madagascar	4	0	1	0	0	0	0	0	1	0	0	-44.9	..	-1.3
Malawi	28	0	1	..	0	1	1	1	3	4	1	-17.8	23.7	22.8
Mali	15	12	10	11	12	17	16	15	15	12	12	-11.7	9.3	2.4
Mauritania	..	..	..	0	..	..	..	..	..	..	..	..	..	..
Mauritius	..	0	0	0	0	..	..	..	..	0	0	..	..	37.1
Mozambique	10	2	0	0	0	0	1	0	0	0	0	-8.5	22.4	-15.3
Namibia	..	..	..	..	..	..	..	..	..	..	..	..	..	..
Niger	1	1	1	1	0	0	0	0	0	5	5	-38.0	182.2	-2.0
Nigeria	1	..	0	1	0	7	1	4	22	13	13	-37.9	..	73.1
Rwanda	..	..	..	..	..	..	..	..	..	..	..	..	..	..
São Tomé and Principe	..	..	..	..	..	..	..	..	..	..	..	..	..	..
Senegal	175	360	215	219	119	164	98	207	88	103	54	-9.1	21.2	-14.6
Seychelles	..	..	..	..	..	..	..	..	..	..	..	..	..	..
Sierra Leone	..	..	..	..	..	..	..	..	..	..	..	..	..	..
Somalia	..	..	..	..	..	..	..	..	..	..	..	..	..	..
South Africa	45	39	32	24	27	59	36	38	58	33	26	-12.5	23.7	-2.9
Sudan	238	109	39	51	84	110	82	84	156	167	71	-6.0	15.7	5.0
Swaziland	..	..	..	..	..	..	..	..	3	11	8	..	..	..
Tanzania	1	7	16	7	..	..	0	1	1	1	0	..	181.1	-23.1
Togo	..	..	0	..	..	0	0	2	0	0	0	-36.2	296.1	28.6
Uganda	..	0	0	0	1	0	0	0	0	0	0	..	..	-1.9
Zambia	0	0	5	1	0	0	0	0	0	0	0	-26.0	..	-7.7
Zimbabwe	3	16	3	1	3	7	3	1	5	15	2	-19.6	107.4	-3.7
NORTH AFRICA	13	7	5	5	21	16	15	10	19	23	13	-7.3	-19.9	16.9
Algeria	..	..	..	..	..	..	0	..	..	..	..	..	..	..
Egypt, Arab Republic	13	4	2	4	12	9	10	6	11	15	4	-7.3	-19.9	13.1
Libya	..	3	4	1	8	4	5	5	8	8	8	..	..	15.8
Morocco	..	0	0	0	0	..	..	..	0	..	..	..	..	..
Tunisia	..	0	..	..	0	3	0	..	..	..	..	..	..	..
ALL AFRICA	618	581	347	341	297	413	296	400	411	428	241	-8.9	15.5	-4.3

5-27. Oil palm products exports

	Thousands of metric tons											Average annual percentage growth		
	1980	1990	1991	1992	1993	1994	1995	1996	1997	1998	1999	75-84	85-89	90-MR
SUB-SAHARAN AFRICA	280	233	194	269	319	247	187	221	180	207	191	-12.2	9.5	-1.9
excluding South Africa	280	232	194	267	317	244	187	220	179	205	189	-12.2	9.4	-2.0
excl. S.Africa & Nigeria	184	223	186	264	315	237	175	203	169	194	179	-9.3	6.3	-0.9
Angola	..	..	..	..	..	..	..	..	..	..	..			
Benin	13	6	1	2	3	7	9	8	13	17	15	-12.5	8.9	22.6
Botswana	..	..	0	0	..	..	0	..	..	..	..			
Burkina Faso	..	..	..	..	..	..	..	..	..	..	..			
Burundi	..	..	..	..	..	..	1	1	0	0	0	..	..	..
Cameroon	21	28	10	27	27	30	8	41	13	15	15	-7.7	12.3	-4.9
Cape Verde	..	..	..	..	..	..	..	..	..	..	..			
Central African Republic	..	..	..	..	..	..	0	0	0	0	0			
Chad	..	..	..	..	..	..	..	..	..	..	..			
Comoros	..	..	..	..	..	..	..	..	..	..	..			
Congo, Democratic Rep. of	10	4	1	1	1	3	1	1	1	1	..	-23.7	-21.9	-17.6
Congo, Republic of	0	..	..	..	..	..	..	..	..	..	..	-17.6	..	..
Côte d'Ivoire	99	166	158	186	207	153	121	103	76	103	106	-7.9	9.5	-3.9
Djibouti	..	..	0	..	..	..	..	..	..	..	..			
Equatorial Guinea	..	..	..	..	..	..	..	..	..	..	..			
Eritrea	..	..	..	..	..	..	..	..	..	..	..			
Ethiopia	..	..	..	..	..	..	..	..	..	..	..			
Gabon	..	4	2	5	1	..	3	6	9	3	6	..	9.6	4.2
Gambia, The	1		..	..	..	..	..	..	..	..	..	-19.8	..	..
Ghana	..	7	3	8	9	11	12	21	19	10	11	..	39.0	10.7
Guinea	15	1	1	1	7	1	0	4	4	1	1	-3.6	1.5	1.0
Guinea-Bissau	6	2	5	3	2	3	1	3	1	2	2	2.0	5.1	-7.6
Kenya	0	..	1	25	53	14	13	10	26	31	12	-52.7	..	43.8
Lesotho	..	..	..	..	..	..	..	..	..	..	..			
Liberia	6	5	4	5	5	5	5	5	5	6	6	24.9	12.7	-0.6
Madagascar	..	..	..	0	0	0	0	0	0	0	0	..	..	44.3
Malawi	..	..	..	..	..	..	..	..	..	..	..			
Mali	..	..	..	..	..	..	..	..	..	..	..			
Mauritania	..	..	..	..	..	..	..	..	..	..	..			
Mauritius	..	..	0	0	0	0	0	0	0	0	..	..	..	29.1
Mozambique	..	..	..	..	..	..	..	..	..	..	..			
Namibia	..	..	..	..	..	..	..	..	..	..	..			
Niger	..	..	..	..	..	..	..	..	..	0	0			
Nigeria	96	9	8	3	2	6	11	17	10	11	11	-16.9	17.5	-2.0
Rwanda	..	..	..	..	..	..	..	..	..	..	..			
São Tomé and Principe	0	..	..	..	..	..	..	..	..	..	..	-19.1		
Senegal	0	..	..	..	0	0	0	0	2	2	2	-55.4	18.6	62.6
Seychelles	..	0	0	..	..	..	..	..	..	..	..			
Sierra Leone	1	0	0	0	..	11	0	0	0	0	0	-11.4	-48.9	-15.4
Somalia	..	..	..	..	..	..	..	..	..	..	..			
South Africa	..	0	1	2	2	3	0	1	1	3	1	..	..	43.1
Sudan	..	..	..	..	..	..	..	..	..	..	..			
Swaziland	..	..	..	..	..	..	..	..	..	0	..	..	..	..
Tanzania	1	..	0	..	..	..	..	..	1	0	0	..	..	..
Togo	10	0	0	2	0	0	..	..	..	..	..	-13.6	-15.9	65.0
Uganda	..	..	..	..	..	..	..	..	..	3	2	..	..	..
Zambia	..	..	..	0	..	..	..	..	..	..	..			
Zimbabwe	..	0	0	0	..	..	..	..	..	..	..			
NORTH AFRICA	..	0	0	..	0	0	0	0	0	0	0	..	..	-12.9
Algeria	..	..	..	..	..	..	..	..	..	..	..	..	..	..
Egypt, Arab Republic	..	..	0	..	0	0	0	0	0	0	0	..	..	-15.1
Libya	..	..	..	..	..	..	..	..	..	..	..			
Morocco	..	0	..	..	..	..	0	..	..	0	0	..	..	..
Tunisia	..	..	..	..	..	..	..	0	0	0	..	..	..	..
ALL AFRICA	280	233	195	269	319	247	187	221	181	207	191	-12.2	9.5	-1.9

5-28. Sisal exports

	Thousands of metric tons											Average annual percentage growth		
	1980	1990	1991	1992	1993	1994	1995	1996	1997	1998	1999	75-84	85-89	90-MR
SUB-SAHARAN AFRICA	109	50	42	44	42	41	47	36	38	32	37	-9.6	-8.7	-3.4
excluding South Africa	109	50	42	43	42	41	47	36	38	32	37	-9.7	-8.7	-3.4
excl. S.Africa & Nigeria	109	50	42	43	42	41	47	36	38	32	37	-9.7	-8.7	-3.4
Angola	3	..	..	..	..	..	..	..	..	..	..	-30.8	..	..
Benin	0	0	0	0	0	0	0	0	0	..	..	..	..	..
Botswana	..	..	..	..	..	..	0	..	..	..	..	..	..	..
Burkina Faso	0	0	0	0	0	0	0	0	0	..	..	..	..	..
Burundi	0	0	0	0	0	0	0	0	0	..	..	..	..	..
Cameroon	0	0	0	0	0	0	0	0	0	..	..	..	..	..
Cape Verde	0	0	0	0	0	0	0	0	0	..	..	..	..	..
Central African Republic	..	..	..	..	..	..	..	..	..	..	..	..	..	..
Chad	0	0	0	0	0	0	0	0	0	..	..	..	..	..
Comoros	..	..	..	..	..	..	..	..	..	..	..	..	..	..
Congo, Democratic Rep. of	..	..	..	..	..	..	..	..	..	..	..	..	..	..
Congo, Republic of	0	0	0	0	0	0	0	0	0	..	..	..	..	..
Côte d'Ivoire	..	..	..	..	..	0	0	0	0	0	0	..	..	-4.8
Djibouti	0	0	0	0	0	0	0	0	0	..	..	..	..	..
Equatorial Guinea	0	0	0	0	0	0	0	0	0	..	..	..	..	..
Eritrea	0	0	0	0	0	0	0	0	0	..	..	..	..	..
Ethiopia	0	0	0	0	0	0	0	0	0	..	..	..	..	..
Gabon	0	0	0	0	0	0	0	0	0	..	..	..	..	..
Gambia, The	0	0	0	0	0	0	0	0	0	..	..	..	..	..
Ghana	0	0	0	0	0	0	0	0	0	..	..	..	..	..
Guinea	0	0	0	0	0	0	0	0	0	..	..	..	..	..
Guinea-Bissau	0	0	0	0	0	0	0	0	0	..	..	..	..	..
Kenya	40	30	28	32	27	26	25	17	19	18	17	-1.3	-4.8	-7.0
Lesotho	0	0	0	0	0	0	0	0	0	..	..	..	..	..
Liberia	0	0	0	0	0	0	0	0	0	..	..	..	..	..
Madagascar	10	12	10	7	9	8	10	10	4	3	5	-5.9	-8.1	-9.0
Malawi	..	..	..	..	0	..	..	..	..	..	..	..	..	..
Mali	0	0	0	0	0	0	0	0	0	..	..	..	..	..
Mauritania	0	0	0	0	0	0	0	0	0	..	..	..	..	..
Mauritius	0	0	0	0	0	0	0	0	0	..	..	..	..	..
Mozambique	7	..	0	0	0	0	0	0	0	0	0	-14.5	1.7	-11.4
Namibia	0	0	0	0	0	0	0	0	0	..	..	..	..	..
Niger	0	0	0	0	0	0	0	0	0	..	..	..	..	..
Nigeria	0	0	0	0	0	0	0	0	0	..	..	..	..	..
Rwanda	0	0	0	0	0	0	0	0	0	..	..	..	..	..
São Tomé and Principe	0	0	0	0	0	0	0	0	0	..	..	..	..	..
Senegal	0	..	..	..	..	..	..	..	..	..	..	38.6	..	..
Seychelles	0	0	0	0	0	0	0	0	0	..	..	..	..	..
Sierra Leone	0	0	0	0	0	0	0	0	0	..	..	..	..	..
Somalia	..	..	..	..	..	..	..	..	..	..	..	..	..	..
South Africa	0	0	0	0	0	0	0	0	0	0	0	-4.4	-7.3	-24.5
Sudan	0	0	0	0	0	0	0	0	0	..	..	..	..	..
Swaziland	..	..	..	..	..	..	..	..	0	..	..	..	..	..
Tanzania	48	8	5	4	5	7	11	9	15	12	15	-12.1	-16.9	10.0
Togo	0	0	0	0	0	0	0	0	0	..	..	..	..	..
Uganda	..	..	..	..	..	..	..	..	..	0	..	..	..	..
Zambia	0	0	0	0	0	0	0	0	0	..	..	..	..	..
Zimbabwe	0	0	0	0	0	0	0	0	0	..	..	..	..	..
NORTH AFRICA	0	0	0	0	0	0	0	0	0	0	0	..	..	24.4
Algeria	0	0	0	0	0	0	0	0	0	..	..	..	..	..
Egypt, Arab Republic	..	..	..	..	..	0	0	..	..	0	0	..	..	..
Libya	0	0	0	0	0	0	0	0	0	..	..	..	..	..
Morocco	..	..	..	0	0	0	0	0	0	0	0	..	..	43.3
Tunisia	..	..	0	..	0	..	0	0	0	0	0	..	..	-8.5
ALL AFRICA	109	50	42	44	42	41	47	36	38	32	37	-9.6	-8.7	-3.4

5-29. Tea exports

	Thousands of metric tons											Average annual percentage growth		
	1980	1990	1991	1992	1993	1994	1995	1996	1997	1998	1999	75-84	85-89	90-MR
SUB-SAHARAN AFRICA	182	267	277	271	298	274	347	354	312	380	359	3.8	4.9	3.8
excluding South Africa	180	266	275	270	297	273	346	353	311	377	354	3.7	4.8	3.7
excl. S.Africa & Nigeria	180	266	275	270	297	273	346	353	311	377	354	3.7	4.8	3.7
Angola	..	..	..	..	..	..	..	..	..	..	..	..	..	..
Benin	0	0	0	0	0	0	0	0	0	..	..	..	..	..
Botswana	0	0	0	0	0	0	0	0	0	0	0	21.8	-48.8	27.5
Burkina Faso	..	..	..	..	..	..	..	..	..	..	..	-6.7	..	..
Burundi	1	4	5	6	5	7	7	4	6	6	6	12.3	2.6	4.0
Cameroon	1	3	0	..	0	..	0	0	..	..	..	23.2	-32.4	-18.7
Cape Verde	0	0	0	0	0	0	0	0	0	..	..	..	..	..
Central African Republic	..	..	..	..	..	..	..	..	..	..	..	..	..	..
Chad	..	..	..	..	..	..	..	..	..	..	..	..	..	..
Comoros	0	0	0	0	0	0	0	0	0	..	..	..	..	..
Congo, Democratic Rep. of	1	3	2	1	2	2	1	2	1	1	1	-8.5	-4.9	-7.0
Congo, Republic of	..	..	..	..	..	..	..	..	..	..	..	..	..	..
Côte d'Ivoire	0	..	..	..	..	..	0	0	0	0	0	..	..	..
Djibouti	..	..	0	..	..	..	..	..	..	..	..	..	..	..
Equatorial Guinea	0	0	0	0	0	0	0	0	0	..	..	..	..	..
Eritrea	0	0	0	0	0	0	0	0	0	..	..	..	..	..
Ethiopia	..	..	..	..	..	0	0	0	0	0	0	..	..	-5.3
Gabon	0	0	0	0	0	0	0	0	0	..	..	..	..	..
Gambia, The	..	..	..	..	..	..	0	0	0	0	0	..	..	..
Ghana	..	..	..	..	..	..	..	0	..	0	0	..	..	..
Guinea	0	0	0	0	0	0	0	0	0	..	..	..	..	..
Guinea-Bissau	0	0	0	0	0	0	0	0	0	..	..	..	..	..
Kenya	84	166	176	172	199	177	259	261	199	264	246	6.7	8.4	4.9
Lesotho	0	0	0	0	0	0	0	0	0	..	..	..	..	..
Liberia	..	..	..	..	0	0	..	..	..	..	..	..	..	..
Madagascar	0	0	0	0	0	0	0	0	0	0	0	..	-54.8	42.4
Malawi	31	41	37	37	35	35	32	32	40	41	30	3.8	-0.2	-1.3
Mali	..	..	..	..	..	..	..	..	..	..	..	..	..	..
Mauritania	0	0	0	0	0	0	0	0	0	..	..	..	..	..
Mauritius	4	4	4	5	4	4	3	1	0	0	0	8.2	-7.0	-33.8
Mozambique	30	1	1	1	0	0	0	0	0	0	0	-0.2	-48.5	-8.1
Namibia	0	0	0	0	0	0	0	0	0	..	..	..	..	..
Niger	..	..	..	..	..	..	..	..	..	0	0	..	..	..
Nigeria	..	0	0	0	..	..	0	0	0	0	0	..	..	16.7
Rwanda	7	12	13	13	12	5	3	3	10	12	10	8.5	8.0	-5.8
São Tomé and Principe	0	0	0	0	0	0	0	0	0	..	..	..	..	..
Senegal	0	1	..	..	..	..	..	..	..	..	0	-8.6	281.6	..
Seychelles	0	..	0	..	0	0	0	0	0	0	0	-7.6	..	-1.9
Sierra Leone	0	0	0	0	0	0	0	0	0	..	..	..	..	..
Somalia	0	..	..	..	..	..	..	..	..	..	..	..	..	..
South Africa	2	1	1	1	1	1	1	1	1	3	5	44.8	13.6	11.0
Sudan	0	0	0	0	0	0	0	0	0	..	..	..	..	..
Swaziland	..	..	..	..	..	..	..	..	0	0	0	..	..	..
Tanzania	13	15	18	20	20	22	22	22	22	22	21	2.6	1.2	5.0
Togo	..	0	0	..	..	0	..	..	..	..	..	..	..	..
Uganda	1	5	7	8	10	11	11	15	18	19	22	-28.0	11.3	19.3
Zambia	..	0	0	0	..	..	0	0	0	0	0	..	..	28.0
Zimbabwe	6	12	11	6	8	10	9	12	13	11	16	10.5	5.4	2.5
NORTH AFRICA	..	0	0	0	0	0	0	0	0	0	0	..	87.0	16.4
Algeria	..	..	..	..	..	..	..	..	..	..	..	..	..	..
Egypt, Arab Republic	..	0	0	0	0	0	0	0	0	0	0	..	..	29.6
Libya	..	..	..	..	..	..	..	..	..	..	..	..	..	..
Morocco	..	0	0	0	0	0	0	0	0	0	0	..	..	48.0
Tunisia	..	..	..	..	..	0	0	0	0	0	0	..	..	-34.2
ALL AFRICA	182	267	277	271	298	274	348	354	312	380	359	3.8	4.9	3.8

5-30. Sugar exports

	Thousands of metric tons											Average annual percentage growth		
	1980	1990	1991	1992	1993	1994	1995	1996	1997	1998	1999	75-84	85-89	90-MR
SUB-SAHARAN AFRICA	2,148	2,441	2,068	1,627	1,259	1,741	1,604	2,356	2,614	2,760	2,476	0.8	2.6	1.9
excluding South Africa	1,362	1,469	1,356	1,343	1,118	1,422	1,215	1,523	1,610	1,527	1,338	3.1	0.5	0.7
excl. S.Africa & Nigeria	1,362	1,469	1,356	1,343	1,118	1,422	1,215	1,523	1,610	1,527	1,338	3.1	0.3	0.7
Angola	..	..	..	..	..	..	..	..	..	..	..	..	..	..
Benin	..	..	..	..	..	..	..	..	..	..	..	..	..	..
Botswana	0	0	0	0	0	0	0	1	1	1	1	-14.0	65.9	33.4
Burkina Faso	2	..	..	..	..	..	..	..	..	..	..	91.6	..	..
Burundi	..	0	0	10	..	0	0	4	0	1	2	..	..	27.3
Cameroon	9	0	2	..	1	0	1	7	1	1	1	42.1	-24.4	3.7
Cape Verde	..	..	..	..	..	..	..	..	..	..	..	..	..	..
Central African Republic	..	..	0	..	..	0	0	0	0	0	0	..	..	-5.5
Chad	..	..	..	..	..	..	..	..	..	..	..	..	..	..
Comoros	0	0	0	0	0	0	0	0	0	..	..	..	..	..
Congo, Democratic Rep. of	..	..	..	..	..	..	..	..	..	..	..	..	..	..
Congo, Republic of	0	26	23	29	18	11	14	7	37	21	25	-1.3	-14.0	0.3
Côte d'Ivoire	11	23	40	23	39	33	12	29	31	6	18	142.4	-18.9	-6.3
Djibouti	..	..	0	..	..	..	..	..	..	10	10	..	..	..
Equatorial Guinea	0	0	0	0	0	0	0	0	0	..	..	..	..	..
Eritrea	..	..	..	..	..	0	..	..	..	..	..	..	..	..
Ethiopia	..	..	..	..	15	5	..	..	..	..	..	..	..	..
Gabon	2	..	8	7	0	..	..	..	..	..	..	9.3	..	..
Gambia, The	..	..	..	..	..	..	..	..	..	..	..	..	..	..
Ghana	..	..	..	..	..	..	..	1	0	0	2	..	..	..
Guinea	0	0	0	0	0	0	0	0	0	..	..	..	..	..
Guinea-Bissau	..	..	..	..	..	..	..	..	..	..	..	..	..	..
Kenya	56	0	0	104	50	112	13	52	31	2	5	19.0	-15.5	61.9
Lesotho	0	0	0	0	0	0	0	0	0	..	..	..	..	..
Liberia	0	..	..	..	..	..	..	..	..	..	..	8.1	..	..
Madagascar	26	47	21	17	11	24	15	7	1	1	7	-1.1	19.9	-29.6
Malawi	92	62	51	22	26	34	66	55	30	72	30	13.9	-5.4	-1.0
Mali	..	..	..	..	..	..	..	..	..	..	..	..	..	..
Mauritania	0	0	0	0	0	0	0	0	0	..	..	..	..	..
Mauritius	618	578	551	598	535	519	524	773	575	602	534	-0.7	4.4	-0.1
Mozambique	64	18	25	52	..	52	54	25	59	20	..	-12.8	-8.1	8.3
Namibia	0	0	0	0	0	0	0	0	0	..	..	..	..	..
Niger	..	1	..	..	..	..	..	..	..	1	1	..	..	..
Nigeria	..	0	0	0	0	..	0	0	0	0	0	..	..	3.6
Rwanda	0	0	0	0	0	0	0	0	0	..	..	..	..	..
São Tomé and Principe	0	0	0	0	0	0	0	0	0	..	..	..	..	..
Senegal	0	3	0	0	0	0	0	..	0	0	0	-34.3	244.7	-19.9
Seychelles	..	..	..	..	..	0	..	..	..	0	0	..	..	..
Sierra Leone	..	..	..	..	..	..	..	..	..	..	..	..	..	..
Somalia	0	..	..	..	..	..	..	..	..	..	..	..	..	..
South Africa	786	971	712	284	141	318	390	833	1,005	1,233	1,138	-2.7	6.2	5.0
Sudan	..	65	49	54	39	136	20	49	80	127	76	..	..	5.5
Swaziland	300	425	492	379	363	279	275	241	466	345	395	9.2	1.5	-2.2
Tanzania	13	22	..	11	11	11	11	12	13	22	12	33.4	0.9	0.5
Togo	..	..	0	0	0	..	0	0	0	0	0	..	..	-1.0
Uganda	..	..	..	..	..	..	..	..	..	1	5	..	..	..
Zambia	..	2	4	26	11	7	50	69	63	87	50	60.8	-21.0	47.4
Zimbabwe	169	197	89	12	0	201	160	192	219	207	165	3.9	-7.3	14.0
NORTH AFRICA	23	6	25	1	1	7	6	4	1	2	0	-29.0	53.1	-23.8
Algeria	..	..	13	..	..	..	..	0	..	..	..	..	..	..
Egypt, Arab Republic	10	2	8	1	1	7	6	4	0	2	0	-12.4	134.0	-26.8
Libya	0	0	0	0	0	0	0	0	0	..	..	..	..	..
Morocco	..	0	0	0	0	0	..	0	0	0	..	..	-17.5	39.7
Tunisia	13	3	4	0	0	0	0	..	0	0	0	-28.6	-44.5	-11.2
ALL AFRICA	2,171	2,446	2,093	1,628	1,260	1,748	1,610	2,360	2,615	2,762	2,477	0.4	2.7	1.9

5-31. Tobacco exports

	Hundreds of metric tons											Average annual percentage growth		
	1980	*1990*	*1991*	*1992*	*1993*	*1994*	*1995*	*1996*	*1997*	*1998*	*1999*	*75-84*	*85-89*	*90-MR*
SUB-SAHARAN AFRICA	1,777	2,259	2,494	2,817	3,164	4,414	3,116	3,669	3,364	3,823	3,089	3.0	0.4	5.8
excluding South Africa	1,705	2,179	2,404	2,736	3,070	4,244	3,004	3,581	3,243	3,678	2,930	3.2	0.2	5.8
excl. S.Africa & Nigeria	1,705	2,178	2,403	2,731	3,068	4,241	3,003	3,573	3,240	3,677	2,928	3.2	0.2	5.8
Angola	16	..	..	..	..	..	..	..	..	..	..	-4.7	..	..
Benin	0	..	..	..	..	..	..	..	..	..	..	-36.9	..	..
Botswana	1	0	0	0	0	0	0	1	1	1	1	32.5	-1.9	21.7
Burkina Faso	..	..	..	..	..	..	..	..	..	..	..	..	..	..
Burundi	..	7	11	11	10	4	0	2	0	1	0	..	89.6	-43.2
Cameroon	21	8	7	7	6	1	3	..	1	1	2	-7.9	-11.6	-19.5
Cape Verde	0	0	0	0	0	0	0	0	0	..	..	..	..	..
Central African Republic	8	0	1	1	1	1	2	1	1	1	1	-8.6	-2.0	4.3
Chad	..	..	..	..	..	..	..	..	..	..	..	..	..	..
Comoros	0	0	0	0	0	0	0	0	0	..	..	..	..	..
Congo, Democratic Rep. of	..	..	..	..	..	..	..	..	..	..	..	..	..	..
Congo, Republic of	1	..	..	..	..	..	..	..	..	..	..	-23.6	-46.4	..
Côte d'Ivoire	0	1	..	0	..	..	2	2	1	1	1	-2.6	..	10.4
Djibouti	0	0	0	0	0	0	0	0	0	..	..	..	..	..
Equatorial Guinea	0	0	0	0	0	0	0	0	0	..	..	..	..	..
Eritrea	0	0	0	0	0	0	0	0	0	..	..	..	..	..
Ethiopia	0	0	0	0	0	0	0	0	0	..	..	..	..	..
Gabon	0	0	0	0	0	0	0	0	0	..	..	..	..	..
Gambia, The	..	..	..	..	..	..	1	1	1	1	1	..	..	..
Ghana	..	3	3	2	3	5	2	7	4	2	3	-33.6	-12.6	5.6
Guinea	0	0	0	0	0	0	0	0	0	..	..	..	..	..
Guinea-Bissau	..	..	..	..	..	..	..	..	..	..	..	..	..	..
Kenya	0	0	19	48	56	29	30	76	51	50	44	9.8	31.8	35.0
Lesotho	0	0	0	0	0	0	0	0	0	..	..	..	..	..
Liberia	0	..	..	..	..	..	..	..	..	..	..	3.3	..	..
Madagascar	1	..	0	0	0	0	4	4	1	..	0	-11.2	-6.9	-0.1
Malawi	611	874	982	973	957	983	980	1,121	1,168	1,296	930	8.4	-3.3	4.7
Mali	..	..	..	0	..	..	..	..	..	..	..	-53.9	..	..
Mauritania	0	0	0	0	0	0	0	0	0	..	..	..	..	..
Mauritius	..	..	..	..	..	0	0	..	..	..	..	..	..	..
Mozambique	..	..	..	..	..	..	..	..	..	..	..	..	..	..
Namibia	0	0	0	0	0	0	0	0	0	..	..	..	..	..
Niger	3	9	..	..	..	..	..	..	..	4	4	39.9	..	..
Nigeria	..	1	1	5	2	4	2	9	3	2	2	..	..	14.9
Rwanda	0	0	0	0	0	0	0	0	0	..	..	..	..	..
São Tomé and Principe	0	0	0	0	0	0	0	0	0	..	..	..	..	..
Senegal	..	3	0	0	1	1	1	1	2	2	4	..	..	8.6
Seychelles	0	0	0	0	0	0	0	0	0	..	..	..	..	..
Sierra Leone	..	1	2	7	2	2	2	2	2	2	1	..	23.3	-1.8
Somalia	..	..	..	..	..	..	..	..	..	..	..	..	..	..
South Africa	72	80	90	81	94	169	112	88	121	145	159	-1.8	7.0	5.8
Sudan	..	..	..	..	..	..	..	..	..	..	..	..	..	..
Swaziland	2	0	0	0	1	1	1	1	0	0	0	-17.4	-22.6	-25.9
Tanzania	83	71	80	127	106	154	171	249	279	264	214	-7.4	6.4	16.0
Togo	..	..	..	..	..	..	..	..	..	..	..	4.7	..	..
Uganda	3	23	25	23	41	41	35	31	48	72	47	-8.6	-20.7	18.1
Zambia	26	20	13	25	41	30	9	34	31	38	36	-13.6	0.0	10.0
Zimbabwe	930	1,158	1,261	1,505	1,843	2,989	1,760	2,042	1,650	1,941	1,639	3.9	2.3	5.3
NORTH AFRICA	15	10	11	7	7	9	12	4	6	5	3	6.5	-7.2	-8.5
Algeria	..	..	..	..	..	..	..	..	..	..	..	..	..	..
Egypt, Arab Republic	..	1	..	0	0	0	..	0	..	..	..	..	..	-48.4
Libya	..	..	..	..	..	..	..	..	..	..	..	..	..	..
Morocco	..	..	..	3	3	1	0	..	..	0	..	..	..	..
Tunisia	15	9	11	4	4	8	12	4	6	5	3	26.9	-5.4	-5.5
ALL AFRICA	1,792	2,269	2,505	2,825	3,171	4,423	3,128	3,674	3,371	3,828	3,092	3.0	0.4	5.7

5-32. Meat exports

	1980	1990	1991	1992	1993	1994	1995	1996	1997	1998	1999	75-84	85-89	90-MR
	Hundreds of metric tons											Average annual percentage growth		
SUB-SAHARAN AFRICA	1,436	730	839	928	1,281	1,153	1,417	1,320	1,046	1,158	833	-6.8	-8.8	3.8
excluding South Africa	895	648	754	837	1,133	1,068	1,113	978	905	965	641	-7.2	-8.8	2.2
excl. S.Africa & Nigeria	895	647	754	836	1,133	1,068	1,113	978	905	965	641	-7.2	-8.8	2.2
Angola	..	..	..	..	..	..	..	..	..	..	..	..	..	..
Benin	..	..	..	0	..	..	..	..	..	..	..	..	..	..
Botswana	249	209	256	240	279	250	241	201	228	217	168	-0.8	-8.6	-2.2
Burkina Faso	3	..	..	..	..	..	..	..	..	..	..	-4.6	-52.2	..
Burundi	0	0	0	0	0	0	0	0	0	..	..	..	..	..
Cameroon	0	0	..	..	..	0	..	0	..	..	..	-53.6	-61.3	..
Cape Verde	..	..	..	..	..	..	..	..	..	..	..	..	..	..
Central African Republic	20	..	..	..	..	..	..	..	..	..	..	-19.8	..	..
Chad	..	4	2	2	2	2	2	2	2	2	2	-37.5	14.5	-1.9
Comoros	0	0	0	0	0	0	0	0	0	..	..	..	..	..
Congo, Democratic Rep. of	..	..	..	..	..	..	..	..	..	..	..	..	..	..
Congo, Republic of	0	..	..	..	0	1	0	0	0	0	0	..	..	10.0
Côte d'Ivoire	2	..	..	..	..	0	0	0	0	0	0	11.9	..	16.3
Djibouti	..	..	0	..	..	..	..	..	..	..	..	..	..	..
Equatorial Guinea	0	0	0	0	0	0	0	0	0	..	..	..	..	..
Eritrea	0	0	0	0	0	0	0	0	0	..	..	..	..	..
Ethiopia	..	..	..	..	0	2	6	6	6	6	6	..	..	42.4
Gabon	..	..	..	..	..	0	0	0	0	0	0	..	..	67.3
Gambia, The	..	..	..	..	..	..	..	..	..	..	..	..	..	..
Ghana	..	..	..	..	..	..	..	0	..	0	..	..	..	..
Guinea	0	0	0	0	0	0	0	0	0	..	..	..	..	..
Guinea-Bissau	..	..	..	..	..	..	..	..	..	..	..	..	..	..
Kenya	16	20	28	6	10	11	8	11	12	12	12	-11.6	-54.6	0.7
Lesotho	..	..	..	..	..	..	..	..	..	..	..	..	..	..
Liberia	0	..	..	..	..	..	..	..	..	..	..	..	..	..
Madagascar	72	1	5	17	22	30	49	24	8	1	0	-16.0	-61.1	-5.5
Malawi	..	..	..	..	..	0	..	..	0	0	0	..	-61.0	..
Mali	0	..	..	..	..	..	..	..	..	..	..	-24.4	..	..
Mauritania	..	..	..	..	..	0	..	..	..	..	..	..	..	..
Mauritius	0	6	4	16	32	65	69	45	52	32	11	13.7	44.6	19.2
Mozambique	..	..	..	..	..	..	..	..	..	..	..	9.6	..	..
Namibia	306	286	350	360	438	459	425	391	265	372	132	5.1	5.8	-3.6
Niger	0	0	..	..	..	..	..	..	..	0	0	-20.1	..	..
Nigeria	..	0	..	1	0	..	..	..	..	..	..	..	..	..
Rwanda	0	0	0	0	0	0	0	0	0	..	..	..	..	..
São Tomé and Principe	0	0	0	0	0	0	0	0	0	..	..	..	..	..
Senegal	3	1	0	1	1	1	0	0	1	1	1	3.1	-18.2	-6.1
Seychelles	..	..	..	..	..	..	..	0	0	..	..	..	..	..
Sierra Leone	..	..	..	..	..	..	..	..	..	..	..	..	..	..
Somalia	10	..	..	..	..	..	..	..	..	..	..	-40.8	..	..
South Africa	542	82	85	91	148	84	304	342	141	193	192	-7.0	-9.2	13.3
Sudan	0	..	..	7	61	40	65	134	169	134	78	-12.0	..	36.8
Swaziland	35	10	15	4	10	10	9	10	16	21	22	-5.1	-53.1	23.7
Tanzania	2	43	..	..	..	..	..	..	1	1	1	-37.0	..	..
Togo	..	..	0	0	..	..	0	0	0	0	0	..	..	10.4
Uganda	..	..	..	..	..	..	..	..	..	0	0	..	..	..
Zambia	0	0	1	0	1	1	1	1	1	1	1	-11.8	51.9	6.2
Zimbabwe	175	66	91	183	275	195	238	151	143	164	205	-16.5	-19.4	9.2
NORTH AFRICA	34	59	12	45	39	24	17	13	18	19	18	-2.2	19.8	-5.6
Algeria	0	..	0	..	..	..	..	0	..	..	..	-58.2	..	..
Egypt, Arab Republic	1	56	11	43	37	21	14	10	14	11	7	-0.4	60.4	-11.8
Libya	..	2	0	..	..	..	..	..	..	..	..	..	..	..
Morocco	32	0	0	0	1	2	2	2	3	3	5	-2.5	-19.9	64.8
Tunisia	1	1	1	2	1	2	1	1	2	5	6	-6.5	-9.8	18.1
ALL AFRICA	1,471	789	851	973	1,320	1,177	1,434	1,333	1,064	1,177	851	-6.7	-8.5	3.5

5-33. Manufactured goods exports

	Millions of U.S. dollars (current prices)											Annual average		
	1980	1990	1991	1992	1993	1994	1995	1996	1997	1998	1999	75-84	85-89	90-MR
SUB-SAHARAN AFRICA	4,207	10,000	9,789	9,461	9,840	10,990	13,532	13,452	14,587	15,857	10,506	3,212	6,958	11,801
excluding South Africa	658	3,899	3,768	3,808	3,867	4,196	5,027	5,247	5,131	5,687	5,884	612	2,600	4,652
excl. S.Africa & Nigeria	658	3,830	3,683	3,773	3,828	4,149	4,957	5,200	5,092	5,548	5,858	612	2,586	4,592
Angola	..	56	56	66	63	72	78	105	101	62	75	..	89	73
Benin	..	0	0	0	0	0	0	0	0	0	0	0	0	0
Botswana	..	..	..	..	..	..	..	..	0	0	0	..	..	0
Burkina Faso	..	..	..	..	..	..	..	..	..	..	..	..	..	..
Burundi	1	4	4	11	9	5	7	4	1	0	1	3	8	5
Cameroon	96	359	268	241	227	204	259	302	291	423	281	81	232	285
Cape Verde	..	1	1	1	1	2	6	0	0	0	0	..	1	1
Central African Republic	..	0	0	0	0	0	0	0	0	0	0	..	0	0
Chad	..	2	0	1	0	0	1	2	1	27	29	5	4	6
Comoros	..	0	0	0	0	0	0	0	0	0	0	0	0	0
Congo, Democratic Rep. of	..	0	0	0	0	0	0	0	..	63	67	0	5	15
Congo, Republic of	0	35	26	25	20	13	23	17	16	10	12	6	40	20
Côte d'Ivoire	..	1,149	988	1,037	956	1,012	1,294	1,329	1,210	1,184	1,309	672	841	1,147
Djibouti	..	..	..	..	..	..	..	..	..	..	..	..	..	..
Equatorial Guinea	..	0	0	0	0	0	0	0	0	0	0	0	0	0
Eritrea	..	..	..	1	16	21	31	41	21	7	..	..	..	20
Ethiopia	..	0	0	0	0	0	0	0	0	0	0	..	0	0
Gabon	..	0	0	0	0	0	0	0	0	0	0	0	0	0
Gambia, The	..	..	..	..	..	..	..	..	..	..	..	..	..	..
Ghana	..	..	..	..	..	..	..	..	..	..	..	..	..	..
Guinea	..	0	0	0	0	0	0	0	0	0	0	..	0	0
Guinea-Bissau	..	..	..	..	..	..	..	..	..	..	..	..	..	..
Kenya	177	140	171	144	230	224	298	290	283	220	238	128	127	224
Lesotho	..	..	..	..	..	..	..	5	..	..	169	..	..	87
Liberia	..	..	..	..	..	..	..	..	..	..	..	..	..	..
Madagascar	..	146	159	180	183	237	335	356	342	402	443	44	72	278
Malawi	..	36	51	46	45	62	79	112	125	138	102	..	40	80
Mali	..	..	..	..	..	..	..	..	..	..	..	..	..	..
Mauritania	..	..	..	..	..	..	..	..	..	..	..	0	..	..
Mauritius	..	410	419	439	417	440	477	576	507	941	1,004	156	76	563
Mozambique	..	27	40	14	7	3	5	8	20	14	14	0	0	15
Namibia	158	344	367	471	480	502	529	461	471	602	649	169	161	488
Niger	..	0	0	0	0	0	0	0	0	0	..	0	0	0
Nigeria	..	70	85	36	40	47	70	47	40	140	27	..	34	60
Rwanda	..	2	2	2	7	2	4	5	18	10	15	4	4	7
São Tomé and Principe	..	..	..	..	..	..	..	..	..	..	..	..	..	..
Senegal	136	181	213	190	164	201	254	250	254	258	244	145	157	221
Seychelles	..	10	12	13	11	17	18	34	57	60	63	0	5	30
Sierra Leone	..	0	0	0	0	0	0	0	0	0	0	0	0	0
Somalia	..	..	..	..	..	..	..	..	..	..	..	..	..	..
South Africa	3,548	6,100	6,021	5,653	5,972	6,794	8,504	8,205	9,455	10,170	4,622	2,600	4,358	7,150
Sudan	..	11	..	..	..	..	..	..	..	..	..	31	30	11
Swaziland	..	25	42	54	103	117	120	94	114	127	139	..	20	94
Tanzania	90	104	87	67	59	76	69	117	102	68	84	55	55	83
Togo	..	150	145	128	75	60	86	78	76	81	91	66	92	97
Uganda	..	..	..	..	..	..	..	..	..	..	..	..	..	..
Zambia	..	67	46	62	103	129	155	168	180	194	188	101	47	129
Zimbabwe	..	571	587	579	652	750	829	846	900	655	640	319	495	701
NORTH AFRICA	1,292	6,426	6,642	7,389	6,958	7,178	9,189	8,761	8,903	10,788	11,454	1,039	3,192	8,369
Algeria	..	258	226	213	68	28	30	31	40	42	46	7	105	98
Egypt, Arab Republic	..	1,302	1,163	1,461	1,167	1,127	1,655	1,314	1,302	1,685	2,080	..	868	1,426
Libya	..	..	..	..	..	..	..	..	..	..	..	..	..	..
Morocco	387	2,246	2,374	2,612	2,710	3,010	3,754	3,673	3,802	3,932	4,085	320	1,093	3,220
Tunisia	905	2,621	2,880	3,102	3,012	3,012	3,749	3,742	3,759	5,128	5,244	718	1,473	3,625
ALL AFRICA	5,498	16,426	16,430	16,850	16,797	18,168	22,721	22,213	23,490	26,645	21,960	4,251	10,150	20,170

5-34. Manufactured goods exports, growth

					Percent							Average annual percentage growth		
	1980	1990	1991	1992	1993	1994	1995	1996	1997	1998	1999	75-84	85-89	90-MR
SUB-SAHARAN AFRICA	..	14.4	2.5	-0.4	1.5	8.1	2.9	10.3	3.8	2.4	4.5	40.2	33.1	4.6
excluding South Africa		14.4	2.5	-0.4	1.5	8.1	2.9	10.3	3.8	2.4	4.5	40.2	29.3	4.6
excl. S.Africa & Nigeria	..	13.8	2.2	0.8	1.4	8.0	2.6	10.8	3.9	0.6	6.6	40.2	28.9	4.6
Angola	..	-54.9	12.6	-6.3	28.3	12.0	-4.9	4.7	-0.6	-20.1	-15.7	..	9.4	-1.4
Benin	..	..	..	..	..	..	..	..	..	..	..	..	..	..
Botswana	..	..	..	..	..	..	..	..	..	..	..	..	..	..
Burkina Faso	..	..	..	..	..	..	..	..	..	..	..	..	..	..
Burundi	..	-5.8	-15.1	185.4	-19.2	-39.1	19.1	-36.3	-87.7	3.0	2.2	..	0.3	-22.5
Cameroon	21.3	4.2	-16.0	1.1	-0.4	-4.6	-5.5	21.1	5.6	2.7	9.6	13.0	0.7	1.1
Cape Verde	..	..	..	..	..	..	..	..	..	..	..	..	..	..
Central African Republic	..	..	..	..	..	..	..	..	..	..	..	..	..	..
Chad	..	9.9	1.1	-2.9	-4.5	-0.8	22.6	14.0	0.0	5.0	6.1	..	..	4.7
Comoros	..	..	..	..	..	..	..	..	..	..	..	..	..	..
Congo, Democratic Rep. of	..	..	..	..	..	..	..	..	..	..	..	..	..	..
Congo, Republic of	..	0.3	0.3	0.3	-33.3	0.0	0.0	0.0	0.0	0.0	0.0	..	..	-5.0
Côte d'Ivoire	..	15.1	-7.4	5.5	-7.3	19.7	1.2	11.5	2.0	6.0	7.1	..	0.7	4.7
Djibouti	..	..	..	..	..	..	..	..	..	..	..	..	..	..
Equatorial Guinea	..	..	..	..	..	..	..	..	..	..	..	..	..	..
Eritrea	..	..	..	..	..	..	..	..	..	..	..	..	..	..
Ethiopia	..	..	..	..	..	..	..	..	..	..	..	..	..	..
Gabon	..	..	..	..	..	..	..	..	..	..	..	..	..	..
Gambia, The	..	..	..	..	..	..	..	..	..	..	..	..	..	..
Ghana	..	..	..	..	..	..	..	..	..	..	..	..	..	..
Guinea	..	..	..	..	..	..	..	..	..	..	..	..	..	..
Guinea-Bissau	..	..	..	..	..	..	..	..	..	..	..	..	..	..
Kenya	..	27.9	10.3	-8.3	7.0	10.2	9.4	18.8	5.2	2.9	7.7	..	-9.1	8.0
Lesotho	..	..	..	..	..	..	..	..	..	..	..	..	..	..
Liberia	..	..	..	..	..	..	..	..	..	..	..	..	..	..
Madagascar	..	25.9	5.6	12.2	5.3	23.6	42.0	12.8	11.2	17.9	10.5	..	11.3	16.8
Malawi	..	..	..	..	..	..	..	..	..	..	..	..	..	..
Mali	..	..	..	..	..	..	..	..	..	..	..	..	..	..
Mauritania	..	..	..	..	..	..	..	..	..	..	..	..	..	..
Mauritius	..	23.2	6.1	7.4	9.5	1.0	5.0	5.0	5.0	0.1	2.5	..	14.9	5.6
Mozambique	..	..	45.1	-66.6	-49.5	-55.5	43.4	67.8	159.7	-28.3	-2.2	..	..	28.8
Namibia	..	70.7	3.1	27.2	10.9	-7.6	1.8	-2.6	1.6	28.2	3.8	..	3.0	8.1
Niger	..	..	..	..	..	..	..	..	..	..	..	..	..	..
Nigeria	..	67.9	19.4	-59.7	11.6	14.4	38.3	-30.6	-10.0	260.3	-81.2	..	..	-1.4
Rwanda	..	-28.0	-23.9	16.5	-25.9	-38.8	175.0	-15.5	2.8	2.3	2.5	..	-22.1	-0.3
São Tomé and Principe	..	..	..	..	..	..	..	..	..	..	..	..	..	..
Senegal	..	27.5	13.1	-4.8	-19.1	-37.5	40.2	-4.0	-10.7	0.5	-9.4	..	8.8	-5.0
Seychelles	..	-34.3	18.2	47.0	27.7	-61.0	33.2	-55.0	-100.0	..	..	..	..	-8.6
Sierra Leone	..	..	..	..	..	..	..	..	..	..	..	..	..	..
Somalia	..	..	..	..	..	..	..	..	..	..	..	..	..	..
South Africa	..	..	..	..	..	..	..	..	..	..	..	..	..	..
Sudan	..	..	..	..	..	..	..	..	..	..	..	..	..	..
Swaziland	..	..	..	..	..	..	..	..	..	..	..	..	..	..
Tanzania	..	..	..	-100.0	-22.7	-6.0	30.6	-10.3	70.4	-12.6	-33.1	..	..	-58.8
Togo	..	10.6	-1.9	-164.5	192.4	-22.7	88.5	-94.3	1,063.5	29.6	..	..	..	..
Uganda	..	..	..	..	..	..	..	..	..	..	..	..	..	..
Zambia	..	74.4	-32.4	28.9	67.3	19.9	11.3	13.5	12.5	12.2	-2.2	..	-10.8	17.7
Zimbabwe	..	-6.7	2.8	1.3	8.8	20.2	-4.6	5.1	14.9	-25.1	0.2	..	..	2.8
NORTH AFRICA	2.2	18.7	-0.5	6.2	-3.7	-9.0	21.1	-6.1	1.1	12.2	-28.1	11.8	29.9	1.0
Algeria	..	-9.6	-34.0	8.7	-23.6	-57.6	-1.5	7.6	27.3	4.6	9.2	..	100.0	-13.0
Egypt, Arab Republic	..	30.0	-14.0	21.6	-21.6	-5.0	38.6	-21.9	-1.6	43.0	26.3	..	..	3.5
Libya	..	..	..	..	..	..	..	..	..	..	..	..	..	..
Morocco	2.2	29.4	3.4	5.5	4.0	7.1	15.3	2.1	9.1	7.6	4.5	5.5	23.6	7.7
Tunisia	..	10.5	6.8	0.0	1.7	-19.3	18.3	-4.5	-5.4	2.5	..	..	16.5	-0.4
ALL AFRICA	..	17.0	0.6	3.7	-1.8	-2.5	13.4	0.2	2.2	7.9	-14.7	22.5	31.6	2.5

5-35. Food Imports

	Millions of U.S. dollars (current prices)											Annual average		
	1980	1990	1991	1992	1993	1994	1995	1996	1997	1998	1999	75-84	85-89	90-MR
SUB-SAHARAN AFRICA	5,290	5,276	5,417	5,569	5,380	5,882	7,727	7,606	7,630	7,653	7,571	3,634	4,895	6,571
excluding South Africa	4,357	4,331	4,452	4,621	4,431	4,466	5,771	5,765	5,980	6,021	5,986	2,800	3,922	5,182
excl. S.Africa & Nigeria	1,196	3,686	3,692	3,814	3,660	3,728	4,712	4,836	4,761	4,625	4,403	893	3,020	4,192
Angola	..	286	57	244	203	215	205	275	365	..	..	..	263	231
Benin	..	78	99	116	111	80	119	120	114	117	121	..	141	107
Botswana	109	227	265	347	316	289	305	293	307	322	340	121	140	301
Burkina Faso	..	97	104	90	0	0	70	86	71	111	..	..	..	70
Burundi	18	12	15	11	19	30	29	11	11	10	11	19	14	16
Cameroon	82	190	199	189	161	189	123	138	155	173	194	70	134	171
Cape Verde	0	38	41	75	53	65	85	75	78	73	53	0	25	64
Central African Republic	..	34	28	30	25	23	29	22	20	23	23	20	26	26
Chad	..	18	7	0	6	25	22	21	18	4	4	..	16	12
Comoros	..	10	12	13	10	9	19	12	20	21	22	8	8	15
Congo, Democratic Rep. of	..	0	0	0	0	0	0	0	210	216	234	0	0	66
Congo, Republic of	0	30	31	34	36	15	16	18	19	20	21	10	23	24
Côte d'Ivoire	435	471	490	377	431	317	523	563	538	541	544	389	441	479
Djibouti	..	..	..	..	..	..	..	..	..	..	..	..	..	..
Equatorial Guinea	..													
Eritrea	..	..	..	25	35	76	69	92	94	75	..	..	..	67
Ethiopia	..	73	152	131	167	126	181	103	17	28	100	126	219	108
Gabon	..	143	157	174	166	166	181	191	189	166	138	142	151	167
Gambia, The	..	10	12	14	13	7	8	8	8	9	9	..	7	10
Ghana	..	39	39	38	..	..	..	..	..	..	..	39	48	39
Guinea	..	12	8	49	53	76	77	76	77	79	82	..	12	59
Guinea-Bissau	..	15	21	32	25	17	26	25	31	17	31	16	14	24
Kenya	109	125	149	156	145	173	117	199	401	312	189	89	123	197
Lesotho	..	..	..	..	..	..	..	..	..	..	75	..	..	75
Liberia	..	..	..	..	..	..	..	..	..	..	..	..	..	..
Madagascar	89	49	35	58	51	79	67	60	49	54	46	87	42	55
Malawi	..	5	14	63	6	68	92	51	33	47	23	..	3	40
Mali	103	114	117	97	97	86	111	113	111	123	105	113	88	107
Mauritania	..	127	121	137	104	95	128	103	117	103	98	76	107	113
Mauritius	..	197	195	213	237	270	295	340	359	368	276	93	118	275
Mozambique	..	..	..	..	..	..	44	29	30	32	39	..	..	35
Namibia	..	..	..	..	..	..	396	413	..	..	360	..	..	390
Niger	..	40	31	22	22	16	18	19	27	36	..	..	30	26
Nigeria	3,161	644	760	807	771	738	1,060	929	1,219	1,397	1,583	1,906	902	991
Rwanda	..	32	35	29	59	218	56	51	54	49	47	27	31	63
São Tomé and Principe	..	8	6	6	7	7	7	6	5	5	6	8	7	6
Senegal	210	361	362	..	348	310	393	395	336	344	345	237	243	355
Seychelles	..	34	33	40	46	42	47	63	88	85	75	17	25	55
Sierra Leone	..	37	53	58	57	52	66	110	41	36	28	39	49	54
Somalia	..	..	..	..	..	..	..	..	..	..	..	..	..	..
South Africa	933	945	965	948	950	1,416	1,956	1,842	1,650	1,632	1,585	835	972	1,389
Sudan	..	231	275	166	205	181	215	232	238	264	276	219	189	228
Swaziland	42	98	97	110	134	136	202	172	169	182	199	32	49	150
Tanzania	..	59	32	25	58	97	97	54	57	169	200	96	86	85
Togo	..	160	156	131	82	75	96	149	209	212	..	118	137	141
Uganda	..	..	..	..	..	..	..	..	..	..	..	..	..	..
Zambia	..	9	..	258	50	55	98	25	12	108	0	24	16	68
Zimbabwe	..	218	245	257	121	43	78	119	84	90	88	77	28	134
NORTH AFRICA	1,108	5,551	4,626	5,431	5,364	5,541	7,709	7,124	7,246	7,923	6,890	1,102	4,242	6,340
Algeria	..	2,134	1,894	2,127	2,092	2,206	2,762	2,601	2,544	2,657	2,609	1,757	2,102	2,363
Egypt, Arab Republic	..	2,328	1,802	1,979	1,878	1,982	2,760	2,513	2,885	3,194	2,374	..	1,999	2,369
Libya	..	..	..	..	..	..	..	..	..	..	..	..	..	..
Morocco	720	584	594	895	978	817	1,373	1,298	1,072	1,191	1,177	594	512	998
Tunisia	388	506	336	430	417	536	815	712	745	882	730	333	428	611
ALL AFRICA	6,398	10,827	10,043	10,999	10,745	11,423	15,437	14,730	14,876	15,577	14,461	4,736	9,136	12,912

5-36. Food imports, growth

	1980	1990	1991	1992	1993	1994	1995	1996	1997	1998	1999	75-84	85-89	90-MR
							Percent						*Average annual percentage growth*	
SUB-SAHARAN AFRICA	74.2	20.9	-4.4	4.7	-3.8	-5.3	10.9	-0.8	16.9	-35.8	-3.5	22.4	-2.0	-1.0
excluding South Africa	74.2	20.9	-4.4	4.7	-3.8	-5.3	10.9	-0.8	16.9	-35.8	-3.5	22.4	-2.8	-1.0
excl. S.Africa & Nigeria	181.3	13.9	-9.9	4.5	-4.0	-3.2	5.0	5.1	10.4	-12.8	-3.5	28.6	9.8	0.4
Angola	..	25.1	-79.9	340.6	-12.6	2.5	-13.2	34.2	47.1	..	..	..	-12.7	7.3
Benin	..	..	..	..	..	..	..	..	..	..	..	..	..	..
Botswana	..	..	..	..	..	..	..	..	..	..	..	..	..	..
Burkina Faso	..	..	..	..	..	..	..	..	..	..	..	..	..	..
Burundi	..	0.3	0.2	-0.3	75.5	61.3	-4.0	-62.2	2.8	-9.6	4.0	..	3.3	0.4
Cameroon	0.8	11.8	35.3	-6.8	-17.2	9.5	-27.6	-3.8	20.6	9.5	5.0	-0.9	20.2	-0.8
Cape Verde	..	13.8	9.8	78.5	-27.7	11.9	19.8	-14.1	11.0	-5.5	3.5	..	..	6.7
Central African Republic	..	19.6	-19.1	1.4	-16.9	-11.4	19.4	-26.5	-7.7	9.4	-3.9	..	..	-6.4
Chad	..	3.0	2.0	-89.5	500.0	25.0	-12.8	-0.3	-1.9	2.8	1.2	..	..	-0.3
Comoros	..	-22.4	17.4	1.5	-12.6	32.7	77.9	-30.5	1.0	1.5	2.0	..	5.3	6.2
Congo, Democratic Rep. of	..	..	..	..	..	..	..	..	..	..	..	..	..	..
Congo, Republic of	..	-7.9	-1.9	-16.5	32.2	10.9	-1.1	-0.7	9.6	7.6	3.0	..	-6.5	4.0
Côte d'Ivoire	..	-13.3	2.5	-25.8	13.0	-26.1	52.6	1.5	7.1	5.0	4.5	..	..	1.0
Djibouti	..	..	..	..	..	..	..	..	..	..	..	..	..	..
Equatorial Guinea	..	..	..	..	..	..	..	..	..	..	..	..	..	..
Eritrea	..	..	..	..	..	..	..	..	..	..	..	..	..	..
Ethiopia	..	..	..	..	..	..	..	..	..	..	..	..	-11.2	..
Gabon	..	..	..	..	..	..	..	..	..	..	..	..	..	..
Gambia, The	..	28.6	23.0	8.0	-11.6	-41.9	3.6	-1.8	-1.7	1.3	1.6	..	..	-4.9
Ghana	..	1.7	2.7	4.3	5.5	4.2	5.4	7.7	-0.7	7.3	6.0	..	8.4	4.5
Guinea	..	-9.6	-34.3	513.8	12.8	38.7	-7.4	0.0	-2.0	5.3	5.8	..	7.8	23.8
Guinea-Bissau	..	-13.9	37.2	43.8	-21.4	-15.6	61.3	-7.9	20.2	-44.9	87.3	..	..	6.1
Kenya	..	1.7	-37.6	112.6	-41.6	186.6	-59.6	66.3	97.6	-20.7	-3.2	..	22.4	12.1
Lesotho	..	..	..	..	..	..	..	..	..	..	..	..	..	..
Liberia	..	..	..	..	..	..	..	..	..	..	..	..	..	..
Madagascar	..	28.1	-40.6	61.7	-17.5	53.4	-26.2	-19.9	-8.8	22.0	-22.2	..	-17.0	-2.0
Malawi	..	30.7	161.0	354.3	-90.5	967.9	23.5	-47.9	-30.5	56.2	-8.6	..	..	24.2
Mali	2.1	45.4	11.1	-20.9	1.9	-8.7	13.3	11.3	7.5	17.5	-3.3	6.7	-17.6	4.1
Mauritania	..	19.6	-4.5	12.3	-22.4	-5.1	-19.4	4.6	-6.1	11.9	-9.0	..	-3.0	-4.7
Mauritius	..	9.3	5.8	6.9	8.0	6.0	2.5	8.0	7.5	3.5	3.0	..	-11.1	6.1
Mozambique	..	..	..	..	..	..	..	-39.4	4.3	..	..	..	..	..
Namibia	..	..	..	..	..	..	..	..	..	..	..	..	..	..
Niger	..	..	..	..	..	..	..	..	..	..	..	..	..	..
Nigeria	59.2	63.5	19.0	5.3	-3.0	-11.7	31.3	-17.1	39.8	..	..	20.0	-27.0	7.9
Rwanda	..	5.5	5.4	1.5	0.9	5.1	8.1	12.2	-10.8	-12.7	-2.9	..	-11.6	1.7
São Tomé and Principe	..	-3.0	-22.1	-1.9	23.6	-14.2	2.9	-24.9	-14.6	25.7	22.5	..	20.0	-3.9
Senegal	..	26.7	-3.2	..	27.2	-54.6	41.0	-2.0	-25.4	1.3	-4.0	..	17.0	-8.5
Seychelles	..	9.3	-1.5	14.4	27.2	-16.4	10.4	38.5	40.6	3.0	1.5	..	6.3	12.6
Sierra Leone	..	..	45.9	6.9	5.4	-11.6	16.3	64.9	-60.1	-5.5	-25.8	..	..	-2.7
Somalia	..	..	..	..	..	..	..	..	..	..	..	..	..	..
South Africa	..	..	..	..	..	..	..	..	..	..	..	..	..	..
Sudan	..	..	..	..	..	..	..	..	..	..	..	..	10.1	..
Swaziland	..	..	..	..	..	..	..	..	..	..	..	..	..	..
Tanzania	..	..	..	..	..	..	..	-64.1	..	..	..	..	..	..
Togo	..	-2.2	..	..	..	..	..	..	..	..	..	..	2.6	..
Uganda	..	..	..	..	..	..	..	..	..	..	..	..	..	..
Zambia	..	-33.1	-100.0	..	-80.3	0.7	64.0	-75.9	-47.3	864.4	-100.0	..	-14.5	-75.1
Zimbabwe	..	773.2	13.1	3.2	-51.0	-65.7	71.9	59.4	-26.4	13.5	0.8	..	-12.7	-1.4
NORTH AFRICA	5.8	-14.5	-8.9	16.4	-3.4	-0.5	17.0	-12.9	-2.1	18.4	-9.8	9.9	17.7	0.7
Algeria	..	-29.4	3.5	8.6	-10.5	7.5	-12.0	-7.0	-10.6	12.4	-2.5	..	10.0	-3.8
Egypt, Arab Republic	..	0.2	-19.2	9.8	-4.8	2.0	27.8	-15.3	14.0	21.3	-14.6	..	..	2.5
Libya	..	..	..	..	..	..	..	..	..	..	..	..	..	..
Morocco	5.8	6.9	2.6	49.5	10.9	-22.9	53.6	-10.6	-12.2	23.1	18.4	3.6	-3.8	8.5
Tunisia	..	-19.1	-35.5	21.9	2.3	21.1	35.1	-28.5	-6.9	12.2	..	..	6.6	0.4
ALL AFRICA	51.7	-5.3	-7.4	12.4	-3.6	-2.0	15.1	-9.3	4.1	-1.4	-8.3	16.9	10.0	0.3

5-37. Nonfood consumer goods imports

	Millions of U.S. dollars (current prices)											Annual average		
	1980	1990	1991	1992	1993	1994	1995	1996	1997	1998	1999	75-84	85-89	90-MR
SUB-SAHARAN AFRICA	9,783	11,994	12,146	12,721	11,845	14,267	18,396	17,966	17,091	15,816	10,014	7,286	10,173	14,226
excluding South Africa	1,577	5,153	5,162	5,862	4,974	5,212	7,066	7,083	7,360	6,191	6,695	1,101	4,386	6,076
excl. S.Africa & Nigeria	1,577	5,153	5,162	5,862	4,974	5,212	7,066	7,083	7,360	6,191	6,695	1,101	4,386	6,076
Angola	..	551	676	1,009	778	712	1,069	1,119	1,263	..	..	..	328	897
Benin	..	102	107	124	119	85	128	128	122	125	130	..	97	117
Botswana	146	406	426	394	355	363	367	350	375	403	436	158	197	387
Burkina Faso	..	214	168	215	0	0	170	192	176	160	..	..	..	144
Burundi	53	44	36	45	33	28	28	8	19	49	-4	43	38	28
Cameroon	136	109	131	68	89	76	64	74	179	244	317	222	262	135
Cape Verde	..	46	57	60	57	65	90	91	81	87	48	0	43	68
Central African Republic	..	62	20	27	26	29	11	32	51	15	-13	30	45	26
Chad	..	120	117	102	131	85	103	109	116	120	117	..	108	112
Comoros	..	36	40	49	41	36	36	41	25	26	27	25	29	36
Congo, Democratic Rep. of	..	0	0	0	0	0	0	0	220	231	256	0	0	71
Congo, Republic of	0	3	2	3	3	5	5	7	9	28	36	26	212	10
Côte d'Ivoire	629	438	398	534	491	454	743	793	771	786	789	466	475	620
Djibouti	..	..	..	..	..	..	..	..	..	..	..	..	..	..
Equatorial Guinea	..	25	28	33	25	22	29	50	43	39	49	21	27	34
Eritrea	..	..	..	198	109	95	28	59	69	162	..	..	..	103
Ethiopia	..	176	168	174	189	183	176	187	177	67	299	116	140	180
Gabon	..	202	224	252	241	71	77	78	79	67	61	330	236	135
Gambia, The	..	0	1	0	0	0	0	0	0	0	0	..	0	0
Ghana	..	160	228	306	..	..	..	..	..	..	..	80	125	231
Guinea	..	339	334	313	318	320	389	313	355	378	405	..	259	346
Guinea-Bissau	..	12	10	7	5	6	7	7	9	9	10	11	9	8
Kenya	152	727	550	537	376	689	1,008	980	987	1,123	1,035	130	599	801
Lesotho	..	..	..	..	..	..	..	..	..	..	113	..	..	113
Liberia	..	..	..	..	..	..	..	..	..	..	..	..	..	..
Madagascar	..	159	155	188	209	236	299	309	353	363	417	89	90	269
Malawi	..	65	51	57	53	37	26	42	58	45	40	..	42	47
Mali	181	118	151	182	188	176	159	182	168	171	186	163	95	168
Mauritania	..	38	27	29	16	12	18	17	23	22	25	23	32	23
Mauritius	..	126	138	152	163	173	179	169	166	174	229	49	91	167
Mozambique	..	..	..	..	..	..	140	137	137	164	175	..	..	151
Namibia	..	..	..	..	..	..	318	326	..	..	444	..	..	363
Niger	..	93	87	94	92	117	112	154	130	147	..	..	113	114
Nigeria	..	..	..	..	..	..	..	..	..	..	..	..	..	..
Rwanda	..	83	46	92	88	158	69	71	125	110	106	31	46	95
São Tomé and Principe	..	4	9	10	11	9	7	8	8	3	5	15	9	7
Senegal	151	223	216	..	192	169	199	203	191	199	218	139	166	201
Seychelles	..	26	23	29	39	32	33	40	51	50	51	8	16	38
Sierra Leone	..	15	15	15	19	16	11	11	4	7	6	18	34	12
Somalia	..	..	..	..	..	..	..	..	..	..	..	..	..	..
South Africa	8,206	6,841	6,984	6,859	6,872	9,055	11,330	10,884	9,731	9,625	3,319	6,185	5,787	8,150
Sudan	..	98	126	3	8	15	17	15	32	20	..	120	88	37
Swaziland	127	64	85	143	81	136	163	101	109	111	120	86	75	111
Tanzania	..	144	179	274	293	237	355	268	323	272	357	71	117	270
Togo	..	22	19	27	16	22	27	29	28	14	..	61	89	23
Uganda	..	..	..	..	..	..	..	..	..	..	..	..	..	..
Zambia	..	..	..	..	..	167	199	200	125	121	128	..	..	157
Zimbabwe	..	103	115	121	119	173	205	183	203	77	76	303	198	138
NORTH AFRICA	929	5,275	5,144	5,738	6,125	7,612	7,455	5,366	6,894	7,509	4,483	959	4,160	6,160
Algeria	..	2,206	1,485	1,617	1,373	2,027	1,757	1,037	1,095	1,314	1,422	2,086	2,029	1,533
Egypt, Arab Republic	..	267	799	813	1,448	2,159	1,531	121	1,167	785	582	..	1,252	967
Libya	..	..	..	..	..	..	..	..	..	..	..	..	..	..
Morocco	334	1,232	1,337	1,414	1,366	1,525	1,853	2,037	2,134	2,418	2,479	288	580	1,779
Tunisia	595	1,570	1,523	1,895	1,939	1,901	2,315	2,171	2,498	2,992	..	462	799	2,089
ALL AFRICA	10,712	17,269	17,290	18,459	17,971	21,879	25,851	23,332	23,985	23,325	14,497	8,244	14,333	20,386

5-38. Nonfood consumer goods imports, growth

	1980	1990	1991	1992	1993	1994	1995	1996	1997	1998	1999	75-84	85-89	90-MR
						Percent							Average annual percentage growth	
SUB-SAHARAN AFRICA	2.5	12.7	-1.3	10.5	-3.3	12.1	9.2	9.6	10.6	-16.4	-0.6	..	21.4	4.7
excluding South Africa	2.5	12.7	-1.3	10.5	-3.3	12.1	9.2	9.6	10.6	-16.4	-0.6	..	18.3	4.7
excl. S.Africa & Nigeria	2.5	12.7	-1.3	10.5	-3.3	12.1	9.2	9.6	10.6	-16.4	-0.6	..	18.3	4.7
Angola	..	24.9	23.4	54.2	-19.0	-11.5	36.7	4.7	25.1	..	..	..	52.1	12.3
Benin	..	..	..	..	..	..	..	..	..	..	..	..	..	..
Botswana	..	..	..	..	..	..	..	..	..	..	..	..	..	..
Burkina Faso	..	..	..	..	..	..	..	..	..	..	..	..	..	..
Burundi	..	14.2	-18.4	9.2	-33.2	-46.6	0.2	-101.6	-5,796.8	259.1	-130.0	..	-9.7	-7.8
Cameroon	-40.2	-10.6	28.4	58.8	-25.5	69.5	-22.2	40.4	21.7	16.6	3.4	-3.7	-3.0	15.6
Cape Verde	..	16.2	30.1	8.2	-4.5	-6.5	27.9	7.6	-8.7	7.3	1.5	..	..	6.3
Central African Republic	..	69.6	-69.0	29.9	-1.4	8.2	-64.1	166.4	66.9	-72.7	-186.3	..	..	-8.3
Chad	..	-8.7	-23.3	9.5	-20.4	-96.4	-313.0	183.6	-5.4	4.2	1.9	..	..	-43.9
Comoros	..	15.3	13.9	14.6	-9.5	27.5	-11.0	20.0	1.0	1.5	2.0	..	-6.6	6.5
Congo, Democratic Rep. of	..	..	..	..	..	..	..	..	..	..	..	..	..	..
Congo, Republic of	..	-7.9	-1.9	-16.5	32.2	10.9	-1.1	140.8	-22.9	-22.1	8.7	..	2.9	9.4
Côte d'Ivoire	..	-13.3	2.5	22.8	-8.2	-8.4	48.7	5.0	4.7	4.5	4.5	..	..	6.8
Djibouti	..	..	..	..	..	..	..	..	..	..	..	..	..	..
Equatorial Guinea	..	6.0	38.1	-6.6	13.5	-8.5	18.6	71.3	57.6	157.1	-59.7	..	1.5	22.5
Eritrea	..	..	..	..	..	..	..	..	..	..	..	..	..	..
Ethiopia	..	..	..	..	..	..	..	..	..	..	..	..	..	..
Gabon	..	..	..	..	..	..	..	..	..	..	..	..	..	..
Gambia, The	..	-5.3	144.8	-60.9	-1.7	-5.2	-17.0	-6.2	4.9	-4.5	0.4	..	..	-7.1
Ghana	..	10.0	40.0	28.6	69.6	-30.7	4.8	10.3	0.9	7.3	6.1	..	11.8	11.0
Guinea	..	4.0	-3.8	-9.3	6.2	-3.0	10.6	-20.2	18.6	4.0	4.4	..	12.1	0.0
Guinea-Bissau	..	11.7	-25.7	-32.3	-36.5	15.8	13.8	10.9	12.2	2.8	9.3	..	..	-4.9
Kenya	..	67.3	-23.5	20.9	-25.3	70.4	-0.9	-19.5	7.1	4.6	0.3	..	9.0	4.1
Lesotho	..	..	..	..	..	..	..	..	..	..	..	..	..	..
Liberia	..	..	..	..	..	..	..	..	..	..	..	..	..	..
Madagascar	..	66.0	-0.5	15.5	17.1	8.2	15.9	6.6	23.8	3.8	17.1	..	-9.3	14.0
Malawi	..	12.4	-23.7	7.3	-5.4	-32.3	-35.3	66.0	45.9	-19.2	-8.9	..	..	-4.4
Mali	2.5	-21.2	29.3	9.6	7.7	-9.5	-19.0	17.8	10.4	3.4	1.0	-3.4	9.9	2.2
Mauritania	..	31.1	-31.1	2.8	-46.9	-12.1	23.2	7.7	-7.1	4.3	-42.3	..	-10.9	-10.0
Mauritius	..	-7.8	17.3	-3.3	-1.7	6.0	-1.8	5.0	4.0	3.0	4.0	..	33.0	2.4
Mozambique	..	..	..	..	..	..	..	-1.5	4.3	..	..	..	..	..
Namibia	..	..	..	..	..	..	..	..	..	..	..	..	..	..
Niger	..	..	..	..	..	..	..	..	..	..	..	..	..	..
Nigeria	..	..	..	..	..	..	..	..	..	..	..	..	..	..
Rwanda	..	21.7	11.5	3.9	-6.3	3.3	11.8	12.5	177.7	-20.5	-8.2	..	0.1	14.7
São Tomé and Principe	..	-47.4	111.2	7.8	13.3	-20.2	-31.9	17.6	5.1	-57.9	64.2	..	-9.4	-4.8
Senegal	..	28.2	-6.4	..	-55.1	30.4	-0.2	-17.6	3.0	4.9	..	26.6	-8.9
Seychelles	..	14.8	-10.0	18.3	47.0	-25.4	-1.6	34.6	24.0	3.0	1.5	..	21.0	9.1
Sierra Leone	..	..	4.6	-4.8	34.3	-17.7	-38.2	4.1	-58.2	66.6	-8.0	..	..	-11.8
Somalia	..	..	..	..	..	..	..	..	..	..	..	..	..	..
South Africa	..	..	..	..	..	..	..	..	..	..	..	..	..	..
Sudan	..	..	..	..	..	..	..	..	..	..	..	..	..	..
Swaziland	..	..	..	..	..	..	..	..	..	..	..	..	..	..
Tanzania	..	..	..	..	..	..	..	13.1	..	..	..	..	..	..
Togo	..	-14.9	..	..	..	..	..	..	..	..	..	..	10.7	..
Uganda	..	..	..	..	..	..	..	..	..	..	..	..	..	..
Zambia	..	..	..	..	..	..	10.2	4.9	-33.9	0.0	7.0	..	..	-7.0
Zimbabwe	..	-15.1	13.1	3.2	2.2	40.9	11.7	-6.2	15.5	-59.5	0.8	..	-19.5	0.5
NORTH AFRICA	1.5	24.0	13.5	-7.9	16.7	31.2	-5.5	-25.0	11.1	1.4	-38.9	..	-2.9	1.4
Algeria	..	-8.5	-1.4	-21.9	-9.3	73.2	17.3	-16.7	-27.0	5.5	7.7	..	-20.3	0.2
Egypt, Arab Republic	..	563.1	146.3	-15.0	60.7	50.8	-38.4	-99.9	68,113.8	-66.3	-9.5	..	..	-5.2
Libya	..	..	..	..	..	..	..	..	..	..	..	..	..	..
Morocco	1.5	41.0	6.2	1.3	-3.1	7.7	12.3	14.7	10.4	17.9	3.1	-4.9	21.0	9.1
Tunisia	..	21.0	-5.0	0.9	19.9	11.6	3.1	-8.7	-12.0	23.1	..	..	9.7	4.2
ALL AFRICA	2.2	17.7	5.5	1.4	5.7	21.6	1.3	-7.7	10.8	-9.1	-18.1	..	7.2	3.3

5-39. Fuel imports

	Millions of U.S. dollars (current prices)											Annual average		
	1980	1990	1991	1992	1993	1994	1995	1996	1997	1998	1999	75-84	85-89	90-MR
SUB-SAHARAN AFRICA	10,260	10,166	10,192	9,539	9,672	11,474	13,354	14,765	16,028	15,572	7,485	7,148	8,261	11,825
excluding South Africa	2,705	3,793	3,686	3,149	3,270	3,326	3,895	4,768	4,978	4,643	4,608	1,687	2,784	4,012
excl. S.Africa & Nigeria	2,365	3,739	3,642	3,100	3,225	3,240	3,777	4,679	4,835	4,520	4,450	1,417	2,726	3,921
Angola	..	0	0	0	0	0	0	0	0	..	..	..	0	0
Benin	..	54	63	74	71	51	76	76	73	75	78	..	38	69
Botswana	90	100	123	102	113	98	98	111	112	116	121	91	68	109
Burkina Faso	..	83	80	53	0	0	52	73	69	72	..	..	..	54
Burundi	25	30	29	26	24	29	27	18	14	14	19	30	27	23
Cameroon	187	16	9	8	7	7	139	151	136	149	86	96	13	71
Cape Verde	0	10	8	8	6	5	11	9	9	7	13	0	3	9
Central African Republic	..	23	16	16	15	11	17	13	15	14	13	17	18	15
Chad	..	37	11	4	4	12	12	14	18	22	24	20	28	16
Comoros	..	6	6	7	6	6	8	4	8	8	8	5	4	7
Congo, Democratic Rep. of	..	157	133	60	61	45	52	82	82	85	97	0	89	85
Congo, Republic of	0	129	196	104	162	367	187	215	225	216	221	2	9	202
Côte d'Ivoire	557	569	530	511	459	396	470	589	624	530	576	433	355	525
Djibouti	..	..	..	..	..	..	..	..	..	..	..	..	..	..
Equatorial Guinea	..	7	3	4	3	3	3	5	11	11	13	5	5	6
Eritrea	..	..	..	1	1	2	7	6	7	6	..	..	..	4
Ethiopia	..	109	102	120	198	222	169	215	241	332	177	183	125	188
Gabon	..	11	10	12	11	161	173	221	217	216	162	44	33	119
Gambia, The	..	19	1	16	15	9	9	10	10	10	10	..	9	11
Ghana	..	205	175	162	158	176	194	266	240	220	342	168	156	214
Guinea	..	65	68	69	73	69	82	87	90	86	93	..	55	78
Guinea-Bissau	..	8	10	5	3	6	8	9	9	6	7	9	7	7
Kenya	852	466	385	412	407	333	401	448	519	532	527	456	343	443
Lesotho	..	..	..	..	..	..	..	..	..	..	167	..	..	167
Liberia	..	..	..	..	..	..	..	..	..	..	..	..	..	..
Madagascar	159	113	71	72	85	72	81	106	117	102	124	123	60	94
Malawi	..	50	54	47	40	25	49	59	79	76	82	..	38	56
Mali	120	69	79	84	74	52	85	102	105	88	112	99	67	85
Mauritania	..	46	39	36	37	36	51	43	69	50	61	43	34	47
Mauritius	..	131	131	125	120	119	133	166	165	139	184	78	75	141
Mozambique	..	..	..	..	..	..	68	78	78	84	86	..	..	79
Namibia	..	..	..	..	..	..	116	122	..	..	77	..	..	105
Niger	..	27	19	22	23	20	35	32	28	23	..	..	19	25
Nigeria	340	54	44	49	46	86	118	89	143	123	158	270	58	91
Rwanda	..	45	39	37	35	24	22	27	32	35	47	49	52	34
São Tomé and Principe	..	3	2	3	2	2	3	4	5	2	3	..	0	3
Senegal	276	159	148	..	124	142	138	176	191	153	202	235	170	159
Seychelles	..	36	38	33	34	32	30	43	50	47	45	26	23	39
Sierra Leone	..	38	26	24	22	29	24	23	15	25	21	45	25	25
Somalia	..	..	..	..	..	..	..	..	..	..	..	..	..	..
South Africa	7,555	6,373	6,506	6,390	6,401	8,148	9,460	9,997	11,050	10,929	2,877	5,461	5,478	7,813
Sudan	..	244	356	225	249	230	225	355	324	308	..	351	230	280
Swaziland	99	79	95	108	91	42	17	135	184	141	154	57	71	105
Tanzania	..	174	189	142	101	124	186	189	194	129	104	247	175	153
Togo	..	48	35	37	26	22	41	34	42	38	..	33	25	36
Uganda	..	78	83	72	58	55	64	90	92	84	65	91	69	74
Zambia	..	119	83	53	47	56	41	51	87	42	115	144	85	69
Zimbabwe	..	176	197	207	260	150	176	222	250	229	216	213	143	208
NORTH AFRICA	1,806	2,580	2,580	2,679	2,820	2,270	2,555	2,856	3,981	3,616	3,317	1,153	2,014	2,925
Algeria	..	141	130	147	141	150	115	110	132	110	127	211	183	130
Egypt, Arab Republic	..	781	1,062	959	1,267	542	721	854	1,909	2,188	1,319	..	1,237	1,160
Libya	..	..	..	..	..	..	..	..	..	..	..	..	..	..
Morocco	1,006	1,171	991	1,124	957	1,113	1,177	1,285	1,296	922	1,330	745	776	1,137
Tunisia	799	487	396	449	455	466	541	607	644	396	541	387	313	498
ALL AFRICA	12,066	12,746	12,772	12,218	12,492	13,744	15,909	17,621	20,009	19,188	10,802	8,301	10,275	14,750

5-40. Fuel imports, growth

					Percent							Average annual percentage growth		
	1980	1990	1991	1992	1993	1994	1995	1996	1997	1998	1999	75-84	85-89	90-MR
SUB-SAHARAN AFRICA	60.7	-2.0	15.5	-18.7	27.0	-21.8	17.2	9.1	12.9	5.4	5.8	10.9	4.5	3.9
excluding South Africa	60.7	-2.0	15.5	-18.7	27.0	-21.8	17.2	9.1	12.9	5.4	5.8	10.9	0.7	3.9
excl. S.Africa & Nigeria	145.4	-1.9	15.9	-19.3	27.5	-24.2	16.7	11.7	11.1	10.7	5.8	26.1	1.1	3.9
Angola	..	-14.3	-16.7	-20.0	-25.0	-33.3	-50.0	-100.0	..	..	..	..	..	..
Benin	..	..	..	..	..	..	..	..	..	..	..	..	..	..
Botswana	..	..	..	..	..	..	..	..	..	..	..	..	..	..
Burkina Faso	..	..	..	..	..	..	..	..	..	..	..	..	..	..
Burundi	..	15.5	15.3	-8.5	2.4	29.0	-15.1	-42.3	-19.8	50.0	20.0	..	-0.3	-2.8
Cameroon	9.7	17.2	-14.3	-63.5	379.3	-38.3	40.6	-12.9	101.9	-4.4	28.3	-42.7	10.1	14.0
Cape Verde	..	45.9	-9.3	-0.6	-10.2	-15.1	104.1	-15.5	-1.1	-18.2	13.5	..	..	3.7
Central African Republic	..	9.3	-33.5	-3.7	-5.9	-28.1	46.2	-25.4	18.6	-12.5	-9.0	..	..	-6.6
Chad	..	-7.0	-19.2	-61.0	-21.0	190.0	35.4	20.5	9.3	124.3	135.4	..	..	18.7
Comoros	..	111.5	6.2	8.2	-5.7	42.0	13.8	-47.9	2.0	2.5	2.9	..	-14.2	2.8
Congo, Democratic Rep. of	..	..	..	..	..	..	..	..	..	..	..	..	..	..
Congo, Republic of	..	-7.9	-1.9	-16.5	32.2	10.9	-1.1	-3.6	12.7	9.4	2.1	..	-2.6	4.1
Côte d'Ivoire	..	-13.3	2.5	-3.1	1.8	27.1	9.8	26.7	6.2	4.8	4.4	..	..	8.6
Djibouti	..	..	..	..	..	..	..	..	..	..	..	..	..	..
Equatorial Guinea	..	-14.0	-50.3	24.3	-2.4	-4.5	15.8	23.9	126.9	5.3	24.7	..	22.7	10.6
Eritrea	..	..	..	..	..	..	..	..	..	..	..	..	..	..
Ethiopia	..	4.9	46.5	20.0	119.9	..	..	..	..	..	..	..	-10.4	..
Gabon	..	..	..	..	..	..	..	..	..	..	..	..	..	..
Gambia, The	..	39.1	-94.9	1,470.5	-11.6	-40.3	0.8	-1.8	-1.7	1.3	1.6	..	..	-1.5
Ghana	..	-13.3	4.2	-7.1	3.2	19.0	3.9	9.9	17.9	22.7	11.9	..	9.3	7.6
Guinea	..	-3.6	26.1	1.4	14.1	0.1	10.2	11.1	1.5	7.7	5.4	..	-3.4	7.5
Guinea-Bissau	..	-10.9	16.4	-49.1	-39.3	137.1	44.3	14.9	4.0	-33.1	15.0	..	..	3.4
Kenya	..	6.5	29.8	-9.5	2.8	-18.7	12.8	11.7	16.0	2.5	-2.4	..	-10.2	3.7
Lesotho	..	..	..	..	..	..	..	..	..	..	..	..	..	..
Liberia	..	..	..	..	..	..	..	..	..	..	..	..	..	..
Madagascar	..	123.9	-24.4	1.2	33.7	-14.4	3.8	11.6	16.9	27.3	-12.1	..	-4.5	8.4
Malawi	..	-5.5	27.4	-12.6	-2.8	-33.5	78.2	2.7	41.8	31.5	1.2	..	..	9.1
Mali	3.0	28.2	-9.4	2.5	-14.1	12.9	28.3	14.8	20.2	9.8	4.0	0.7	2.7	8.8
Mauritania	..	-12.3	1.3	-7.3	17.2	-2.6	158.8	3.3	-6.1	15.0	17.1	..	6.2	16.1
Mauritius	..	25.6	9.1	-7.9	1.7	4.8	2.3	5.1	5.0	3.3	4.0	..	-16.9	3.7
Mozambique	..	..	..	..	..	..	..	5.4	-62.5	..	..	..	..	..
Namibia	..	..	..	..	..	..	..	..	..	..	..	..	..	..
Niger	..	..	..	..	..	..	..	..	..	..	..	..	..	..
Nigeria	-35.3	-7.5	-5.1	14.8	5.3	98.6	26.6	-36.1	70.8	..	..	-10.6	-9.8	16.3
Rwanda	..	-12.1	-14.1	0.0	-8.2	-5.4	8.0	18.4	-5.4	-14.2	-8.3	..	-6.9	-2.7
São Tomé and Principe	..	..	-26.0	16.7	-21.7	-1.9	36.5	6.2	40.8	-12.3	-12.1	..	..	4.5
Senegal	..	19.8	-9.9	..	-41.4	8.1	24.6	-5.1	-20.6	26.3	..	0.8	-6.6	
Seychelles	..	-5.9	6.3	0.8	8.2	-3.4	-14.2	44.7	17.7	11.1	1.8	..	3.2	6.4
Sierra Leone	..	..	-30.5	-10.4	-0.6	27.3	-25.5	-1.1	-28.4	69.4	-18.4	..	..	-4.4
Somalia	..	..	..	..	..	..	..	..	..	..	..	..	..	..
South Africa	..	..	..	..	..	..	..	..	..	..	..	..	..	..
Sudan	..	..	..	..	..	..	..	..	..	..	..	..	-15.0	..
Swaziland	..	..	..	..	..	..	..	..	..	..	..	..	..	..
Tanzania	..	..	..	..	..	..	..	-5.2	..	..	..	..	..	..
Togo	..	57.7	-22.8	..	..	..	..	..	..	..	..	..	5.3	..
Uganda	..	..	..	..	..	..	..	..	..	..	..	..	..	..
Zambia	..	-9.9	-17.5	-35.0	0.1	25.2	-31.7	4.6	82.1	-29.5	98.0	..	0.5	-1.5
Zimbabwe	..	28.9	28.3	6.4	42.3	-39.1	8.5	6.3	19.4	34.8	-31.3	..	-0.9	6.4
NORTH AFRICA	19.0	4.9	4.5	10.6	9.8	-4.1	4.8	-6.8	30.2	18.5	-25.2	5.3	18.1	5.1
Algeria	..	87.6	-10.0	8.0	-13.6	5.9	1.3	-12.8	-9.9	30.0	3.6	..	-8.7	1.4
Egypt, Arab Republic	..	-8.1	31.1	-0.7	41.4	-53.2	31.9	4.1	116.1	38.3	-37.6	..	..	9.4
Libya	..	..	..	..	..	..	..	..	..	..	..	..	..	..
Morocco	19.0	8.3	0.0	15.5	-3.9	23.3	-2.1	-8.2	7.4	4.4	4.3	3.8	4.7	4.3
Tunisia	..	-0.7	-13.2	15.0	16.5	9.8	7.1	-14.0	1.2	12.7	..	..	9.4	3.9
ALL AFRICA	35.5	2.1	8.8	-1.6	15.7	-10.7	8.9	-1.2	23.5	13.8	-14.9	7.5	12.3	4.7

5-41. Primary intermediate goods imports

	Millions of U.S. dollars (current prices)											Annual average		
	1980	*1990*	*1991*	*1992*	*1993*	*1994*	*1995*	*1996*	*1997*	*1998*	*1999*	*75-84*	*85-89*	*90-MR*
SUB-SAHARAN AFRICA	4,325	4,218	4,004	3,792	3,624	4,269	5,207	5,050	6,096	5,869	5,913	2,853	3,361	4,804
excluding South Africa	141	1,990	1,730	1,559	1,387	1,616	2,321	2,562	2,589	2,400	2,317	174	1,392	2,047
excl. S.Africa & Nigeria	141	1,990	1,730	1,559	1,387	1,616	2,321	2,562	2,589	2,400	2,317	174	1,392	2,047
Angola	..	357	254	223	89	129	157	0	0	..	..	..	292	151
Benin	..	..	..	..	..	..	..	..	..	..	..	..	..	..
Botswana	22	102	103	106	97	95	145	127	126	125	124	25	41	115
Burkina Faso	..	19	28	28	0	0	42	42	40	68	..	..	..	30
Burundi	0	0	0	0	0	0	0	0	0	0	0	0	0	0
Cameroon	55	85	65	72	61	60	69	77	94	76	69	61	76	73
Cape Verde	..	..	..	..	..	..	..	16	16	17	18	..	..	17
Central African Republic	..	63	55	53	40	44	58	44	39	45	54	..	53	49
Chad	..	0	0	0	0	0	0	0	0	0	0	..	0	0
Comoros	..	4	3	3	4	4	4	2	0	0	0	2	2	2
Congo, Democratic Rep. of	..	0	0	0	0	0	0	0	190	201	225	0	0	62
Congo, Republic of	0	32	23	28	28	72	78	98	89	101	108	0	6	66
Côte d'Ivoire	..	..	..	..	..	..	..	..	..	..	..	..	..	..
Djibouti	..	..	..	..	..	..	..	..	..	..	..	..	..	..
Equatorial Guinea	..	..	..	..	..	..	..	..	..	..	..	..	..	..
Eritrea	..	..	..	1	5	7	10	17	9	6	..	..	..	8
Ethiopia	..	28	28	17	21	15	21	29	27	28	27	35	28	24
Gabon	..	9	10	10	10	10	10	10	11	5	5	..	10	9
Gambia, The	..	51	79	85	88	79	76	82	73	87	80	..	45	78
Ghana	..	..	..	..	..	..	..	..	..	..	..	..	..	..
Guinea	..	0	0	0	0	0	0	0	0	0	0	..	0	0
Guinea-Bissau	..	..	..	..	..	..	..	12	15	4	19	..	..	12
Kenya	..	56	57	59	47	51	71	75	67	60	54	42	47	60
Lesotho	..	..	..	..	..	..	..	..	..	..	188	..	..	188
Liberia	..	..	..	..	..	..	..	..	..	..	..	..	..	..
Madagascar	..	..	..	..	..	..	..	..	46	41	44	..	..	44
Malawi	..	184	76	85	80	56	39	62	86	68	59	..	119	80
Mali	..	..	..	..	..	..	..	..	..	..	..	..	..	..
Mauritania	..	0	0	0	0	0	0	0	0	0	0	..	0	0
Mauritius	..	169	162	170	179	192	215	245	252	239	251	16	49	208
Mozambique	..	..	..	..	..	..	124	140	140	167	178	..	..	150
Namibia	..	..	..	..	..	..	159	163	..	..	0	..	..	107
Niger	..	..	..	..	..	..	..	..	..	..	..	..	..	..
Nigeria	..	..	..	..	..	..	..	..	..	..	..	..	..	..
Rwanda	..	0	0	0	0	0	0	0	0	0	0	0	0	0
São Tomé and Principe	..	0	0	0	0	0	0	0	0	0	0	..	0	0
Senegal	..	..	..	..	..	..	..	..	..	..	..	..	..	..
Seychelles	..	0	0	0	0	0	0	0	0	29	29	..	0	6
Sierra Leone	..	12	10	14	13	11	18	29	14	12	12	..	..	15
Somalia	..	..	..	..	..	..	..	..	..	..	..	..	..	..
South Africa	4,184	2,227	2,274	2,233	2,237	2,653	2,886	2,487	3,507	3,469	3,596	2,678	1,970	2,757
Sudan	..	81	154	57	113	117	134	234	190	157	..	172	195	137
Swaziland	64	64	66	67	86	110	152	172	209	213	230	41	34	137
Tanzania	..	371	236	132	116	113	255	381	284	123	207	134	232	222
Togo	..	..	..	..	..	..	..	..	..	..	..	..	..	..
Uganda	..	..	..	..	..	..	..	..	..	..	..	..	..	..
Zambia	..	49	34	48	20	72	80	80	50	54	2	..	45	49
Zimbabwe	..	255	287	300	292	379	404	424	522	476	332	39	163	367
NORTH AFRICA	501	1,777	1,681	1,796	1,601	1,818	1,072	1,384	1,378	1,452	761	458	1,308	1,472
Algeria	..	939	870	981	942	999	..	..	..	..	..	638	652	946
Egypt, Arab Republic	..	..	..	..	..	..	..	..	..	..	..	..	..	..
Libya	..	..	..	..	..	..	..	..	..	..	..	..	..	..
Morocco	501	838	811	816	659	819	1,072	893	871	799	761	395	656	834
Tunisia	..	..	..	..	..	..	..	491	507	653	..	..	..	550
ALL AFRICA	4,826	5,995	5,685	5,588	5,225	6,087	6,279	6,433	7,475	7,322	6,674	3,311	4,670	6,276

5-42. Primary intermediate goods imports, growth

					Percent							Average annual percentage growth		
	1980	1990	1991	1992	1993	1994	1995	1996	1997	1998	1999	75-84	85-89	90-MR
SUB-SAHARAN AFRICA	17.2	13.8	6.3	-18.5	-19.2	17.1	14.8	-10.0	12.2	-9.3	-20.9	35.9	36.3	-1.7
excluding South Africa	17.2	13.8	6.3	-18.5	-19.2	17.1	14.8	-10.0	12.2	-9.3	-20.9	35.9	31.9	-1.7
excl. S.Africa & Nigeria	17.2	13.8	6.3	-18.5	-19.2	17.1	14.8	-10.0	12.2	-9.3	-20.9	35.9	31.9	-1.7
Angola	..	24.7	-28.4	-9.4	-58.0	40.2	10.8	-100.0	..	..	..	..	-3.2	-15.8
Benin	..	..	..	..	..	..	..	..	..	..	..	..	..	..
Botswana	..	..	..	..	..	..	..	..	..	..	..	..	..	..
Burkina Faso	..	..	..	..	..	..	..	..	..	..	..	..	..	..
Burundi	..	..	..	..	..	..	..	..	..	..	..	..	..	..
Cameroon	17.2	39.5	-21.1	15.9	-16.5	-19.4	2.6	-8.7	12.6	-7.3	-4.0	15.3	0.6	-4.3
Cape Verde	..	..	..	..	..	..	..	..	..	..	..	..	..	..
Central African Republic	..	12.6	-14.4	-8.3	-25.0	8.5	19.4	-26.5	-7.7	9.4	17.5	..	..	-5.0
Chad	..	..	..	..	..	..	..	..	..	..	..	..	..	..
Comoros	..	208.2	-4.2	-5.0	16.6	64.2	-1.4	-46.7	..	..	..	..	-12.8	15.2
Congo, Democratic Rep. of	..	..	..	..	..	..	..	..	..	..	..	..	..	..
Congo, Republic of	..	..	..	..	..	..	..	..	..	..	..	..	..	..
Côte d'Ivoire	..	..	..	..	..	..	..	..	..	..	..	..	..	..
Djibouti	..	..	..	..	..	..	..	..	..	..	..	..	..	..
Equatorial Guinea	..	..	..	..	..	..	..	..	..	..	..	..	..	..
Eritrea	..	..	..	..	..	..	..	..	..	..	..	..	..	..
Ethiopia	..	..	..	..	..	..	..	..	..	..	..	..	..	..
Gabon	..	..	..	..	..	..	..	..	..	..	..	..	..	..
Gambia, The	..	16.0	51.3	4.7	0.5	-10.8	-8.0	4.2	-13.8	16.9	-9.5	..	..	1.7
Ghana	..	..	..	..	..	..	..	..	..	..	..	..	..	..
Guinea	..	..	..	..	..	..	..	..	..	..	..	..	..	..
Guinea-Bissau	..	..	..	..	..	..	..	..	..	..	..	..	..	..
Kenya	..	-11.1	9.4	1.6	-17.6	5.1	50.3	-10.8	14.7	38.5	0.5	..	0.8	7.1
Lesotho	..	..	..	..	..	..	..	..	..	..	..	..	..	..
Liberia	..	..	..	..	..	..	..	..	..	..	..	..	..	..
Madagascar	..	..	..	..	..	..	..	..	..	..	..	..	..	..
Malawi	..	12.4	-59.6	7.3	-5.4	-32.3	-35.3	66.0	45.9	-19.2	-8.9	..	..	-9.2
Mali	..	..	..	..	..	..	..	..	..	..	..	..	..	..
Mauritania	..	..	..	..	..	..	..	..	..	..	..	..	..	..
Mauritius	..	40.3	5.2	2.4	10.8	5.1	2.4	4.1	4.5	3.0	4.0	..	-8.4	6.1
Mozambique	..	..	..	..	..	..	..	3.7	4.3	..	..	..	..	..
Namibia	..	..	..	..	..	..	..	..	..	..	..	..	..	..
Niger	..	..	..	..	..	..	..	..	..	..	..	..	..	..
Nigeria	..	..	..	..	..	..	..	..	..	..	..	..	..	..
Rwanda	..	..	..	..	..	..	..	..	..	..	..	..	..	..
São Tomé and Principe	..	..	..	..	..	..	..	..	..	..	..	..	..	..
Senegal	..	..	..	..	..	..	..	..	..	..	..	..	..	..
Seychelles	..	..	..	..	..	..	..	..	..	..	..	..	..	..
Sierra Leone	..	..	-8.1	35.4	-6.4	-14.1	52.7	54.4	-45.4	-8.3	-7.1	..	..	3.3
Somalia	..	..	..	..	..	..	..	..	..	..	..	..	..	..
South Africa	..	..	..	..	..	..	..	..	..	..	..	..	..	..
Sudan	..	..	..	..	..	..	..	..	..	..	..	..	..	..
Swaziland	..	..	..	..	..	..	..	..	..	..	..	..	..	..
Tanzania	..	..	..	..	..	..	..	43.8	..	..	..	..	..	..
Togo	..	..	..	..	..	..	..	..	..	..	..	..	..	..
Uganda	..	..	..	..	..	..	..	..	..	..	..	..	..	..
Zambia	..	-27.7	-32.5	51.0	-52.3	222.6	0.1	-13.5	-37.5	5.1	-95.8	..	52.5	-13.6
Zimbabwe	..	4.7	13.1	3.2	1.1	25.6	0.2	10.4	28.2	-2.9	-28.8	..	42.1	7.3
NORTH AFRICA	4.3	3.4	-5.1	3.7	-22.7	9.4	13.5	17.9	1.1	22.9	-26.8	8.1	-0.7	2.3
Algeria	..	-23.3	-10.0	8.0	-13.6	10.1	1.3	-10.8	-10.6	25.6	4.9	..	-2.7	-2.2
Egypt, Arab Republic	..	..	..	..	..	..	..	..	..	..	..	..	..	..
Libya	..	..	..	..	..	..	..	..	..	..	..	..	..	..
Morocco	4.3	29.0	-2.4	1.4	-27.9	8.9	21.8	-11.4	9.0	19.5	-6.1	4.7	0.9	1.4
Tunisia	..	..	..	..	..	..	..	..	-1.3	27.5	..	..	..	..
ALL AFRICA	5.1	7.7	-0.1	-6.7	-21.3	12.6	14.1	5.7	5.3	10.0	-24.9	9.7	9.5	0.7

5-43. Manufactured goods imports

	Millions of U.S. dollars (current prices)											Annual average		
	1980	1990	1991	1992	1993	1994	1995	1996	1997	1998	1999	75-84	85-89	90-MR
SUB-SAHARAN AFRICA	2,016	5,876	4,565	4,712	4,681	4,803	5,933	6,847	7,876	7,917	8,849	1,423	3,506	6,206
excluding South Africa	1,057	4,995	3,666	3,829	3,796	3,647	4,556	5,310	5,740	5,805	5,013	715	2,856	4,636
excl. S.Africa & Nigeria	1,057	4,995	3,666	3,829	3,796	3,647	4,556	5,310	5,740	5,805	5,013	715	2,856	4,636
Angola	..	151	91	135	72	71	94	343	400	..	..	..	154	170
Benin	..	..	..	..	..	..	..	..	..	..	..	..	..	..
Botswana	54	1,588	174	175	163	159	177	178	188	198	211	59	86	321
Burkina Faso	..	..	..	..	..	..	..	..	..	..	..	..	..	..
Burundi	40	60	68	55	57	55	62	38	33	35	41	46	49	50
Cameroon	605	603	455	367	378	370	363	398	385	407	424	511	569	415
Cape Verde	..	..	..	..	..	..	..	10	10	12	13	..	..	11
Central African Republic	..	..	..	..	..	..	..	..	..	..	..	..	..	..
Chad	..	96	108	127	156	136	92	108	109	82	81	..	87	110
Comoros	..	1	2	2	2	2	2	2	3	3	3	0	2	2
Congo, Democratic Rep. of	..	0	0	0	0	0	0	0	170	182	208	0	0	56
Congo, Republic of	0	149	116	142	141	86	94	118	141	148	156	14	128	129
Côte d'Ivoire	..	..	..	..	..	..	..	..	..	..	..	..	..	..
Djibouti	..	..	..	..	..	..	..	..	..	..	..	..	..	..
Equatorial Guinea	..	..	..	..	..	..	..	..	..	..	..	..	..	..
Eritrea	..	..	..	41	63	102	117	177	153	139	..	..	..	113
Ethiopia	..	156	115	113	95	129	183	200	332	321	312	117	140	195
Gabon	..	85	100	103	89	30	32	286	289	388	401	..	85	180
Gambia, The	..	51	79	85	88	79	76	82	73	87	80	..	45	78
Ghana	..	..	..	..	..	..	..	..	..	..	..	..	..	..
Guinea	..	211	223	211	196	151	173	159	174	194	215	..	140	191
Guinea-Bissau	..	..	..	..	..	..	..	5	6	2	8	..	..	5
Kenya	..	265	289	291	307	293	487	443	465	413	402	186	268	366
Lesotho	..	..	..	..	..	..	..	..	..	..	113	..	..	113
Liberia	..	..	..	..	..	..	..	..	..	..	..	..	..	..
Madagascar	..	..	..	..	..	..	..	..	92	83	89	..	..	88
Malawi	..	43	126	170	163	138	86	133	187	149	128	..	29	132
Mali	193	131	148	156	136	122	150	150	148	159	189	174	93	149
Mauritania	..	139	151	137	133	113	138	200	97	148	86	..	101	134
Mauritius	..	554	551	587	626	659	695	707	700	735	708	181	412	652
Mozambique	..	..	..	..	..	..	185	229	221	307	417	..	..	272
Namibia	..	..	..	..	..	..	159	164	..	..	0	..	..	108
Niger	..	..	..	..	..	..	..	..	..	..	..	..	..	..
Nigeria	..	..	..	..	..	..	..	..	..	..	..	..	..	..
Rwanda	..	97	128	92	91	23	41	55	71	69	37	82	100	70
São Tomé and Principe	..	0	0	0	0	0	0	0	0	0	0	..	0	0
Senegal	..	..	..	..	..	..	..	..	..	..	..	..	..	..
Seychelles	..	0	0	0	0	0	0	0	0	44	63	..	0	11
Sierra Leone	..	20	16	19	15	15	7	15	6	8	6	..	..	13
Somalia	..	..	..	..	..	..	..	..	..	..	..	..	..	..
South Africa	959	880	899	883	884	1,156	1,377	1,536	2,136	2,112	3,836	707	650	1,570
Sudan	..	77	175	200	293	255	307	324	353	636	..	160	122	291
Swaziland	165	176	174	241	249	271	322	275	282	290	315	91	104	260
Tanzania	..	7	17	21	12	10	15	17	27	18	15	6	7	16
Togo	..	120	116	102	60	48	80	72	63	75	..	67	74	82
Uganda	..	..	..	..	..	..	..	..	..	..	..	..	..	..
Zambia	..	..	..	..	..	40	54	55	116	108	103	..	..	79
Zimbabwe	..	217	244	256	212	290	364	369	447	365	189	166	184	295
NORTH AFRICA	899	3,968	3,887	4,151	3,882	4,342	2,350	3,986	4,061	3,973	2,227	1,021	3,154	3,683
Algeria	..	2,225	2,045	2,306	2,212	2,347	..	..	..	..	..	3,053	2,073	2,227
Egypt, Arab Republic	..	..	..	..	..	..	..	..	..	..	..	..	..	..
Libya	..	..	..	..	..	..	..	..	..	..	..	..	..	..
Morocco	899	1,743	1,842	1,846	1,670	1,994	2,350	2,247	2,210	2,376	2,227	716	1,081	2,050
Tunisia	..	..	..	..	..	..	..	1,738	1,851	1,597	..	..	..	1,729
ALL AFRICA	2,916	9,844	8,452	8,863	8,563	9,144	8,282	10,832	11,937	11,890	11,075	2,443	6,659	9,888

5-44. Manufactured goods imports, growth

					Percent							Average annual percentage growth		
	1980	1990	1991	1992	1993	1994	1995	1996	1997	1998	1999	75-84	85-89	90-MR
SUB-SAHARAN AFRICA	18.5	6.1	-5.4	-1.6	5.6	-1.9	19.0	11.1	10.6	-16.3	-4.8	31.4	10.3	3.2
excluding South Africa	18.5	6.1	-5.4	-1.6	5.6	-1.9	19.0	11.1	10.6	-16.3	-4.8	31.4	9.6	3.2
excl. S.Africa & Nigeria	18.5	6.1	-5.4	-1.6	5.6	-1.9	19.0	11.1	10.6	-16.3	-4.8	31.4	9.6	3.2
Angola	..	24.9	-39.4	53.5	-43.9	-5.0	20.5	264.7	29.4	..	..	..	-15.4	11.9
Benin	..	..	..	..	..	..	..	..	..	..	..	..	..	..
Botswana	..	..	..	..	..	..	..	..	..	..	..	..	..	..
Burkina Faso	..	..	..	..	..	..	..	..	..	..	..	..	..	..
Burundi	..	17.2	9.7	-21.6	1.9	-6.4	4.3	-36.1	-7.9	9.0	15.7	..	-4.2	-6.3
Cameroon	16.5	-4.1	-5.0	-17.1	31.5	-12.3	10.6	2.4	0.8	8.1	2.3	-3.9	3.5	1.6
Cape Verde	..	..	..	..	..	..	..	..	..	..	..	..	..	..
Central African Republic	..	..	..	..	..	..	..	..	..	..	..	..	..	..
Chad	..	-7.0	-19.2	19.2	-13.0	27.0	21.5	18.3	-0.6	7.0	3.6	..	..	7.0
Comoros	..	-11.9	60.8	31.2	-1.4	24.3	3.3	6.7	2.0	2.0	2.0	..	17.6	11.4
Congo, Democratic Rep. of	..	..	..	..	..	..	..	..	..	..	..	..	..	..
Congo, Republic of	..	-7.9	-1.9	-16.5	32.2	10.9	-1.1	35.9	35.9	-31.0	8.5	..	4.7	7.1
Côte d'Ivoire	..	..	..	..	..	..	..	..	..	..	..	..	..	..
Djibouti	..	..	..	..	..	..	..	..	..	..	..	..	..	..
Equatorial Guinea	..	..	..	..	..	..	..	..	..	..	..	..	..	..
Eritrea	..	..	..	..	..	..	..	..	..	..	..	..	..	..
Ethiopia	..	..	..	..	..	..	..	..	..	..	..	..	..	..
Gabon	..	..	..	..	..	..	..	..	..	..	..	..	..	..
Gambia, The	..	16.0	51.3	4.7	0.5	-10.8	-8.0	4.2	-13.8	16.9	-9.5	..	..	1.7
Ghana	..	..	..	..	..	..	..	..	..	..	..	..	..	..
Guinea	..	31.5	2.1	-8.6	-2.0	-25.6	3.2	-7.5	8.1	9.4	7.9	..	2.8	-2.5
Guinea-Bissau	..	..	..	..	..	..	..	..	..	..	..	..	..	..
Kenya	..	-20.6	17.1	-1.5	9.6	-7.7	86.9	-12.3	0.5	-9.8	-2.1	..	1.3	6.3
Lesotho	..	..	..	..	..	..	..	..	..	..	..	..	..	..
Liberia	..	..	..	..	..	..	..	..	..	..	..	..	..	..
Madagascar	..	..	..	..	..	..	..	..	..	..	..	..	..	..
Malawi	..	12.4	187.3	29.2	-3.9	-18.3	-42.3	60.6	48.2	-18.4	-8.9	..	..	9.9
Mali	4.5	13.7	18.6	4.7	-5.0	-13.6	10.2	3.5	4.7	3.8	3.6	4.6	0.0	2.6
Mauritania	..	5.0	6.4	-13.4	-2.2	-6.3	-20.3	-3.8	0.8	26.6	-23.3	..	-2.7	-4.7
Mauritius	..	8.3	6.1	3.7	13.1	5.0	2.5	5.6	4.5	3.0	4.0	..	3.3	5.6
Mozambique	..	..	..	..	..	..	..	13.5	-3.3	..	..	..	..	..
Namibia	..	..	..	..	..	..	..	..	..	..	..	..	..	..
Niger	..	..	..	..	..	..	..	..	..	..	..	..	..	..
Nigeria	..	..	..	..	..	..	..	..	..	..	..	..	..	..
Rwanda	..	-12.0	-19.8	3.9	-6.3	3.3	11.2	-3.0	-8.2	-1.4	3.4	..	-0.3	-2.2
São Tomé and Principe	..	..	..	..	..	..	..	..	..	..	..	..	..	..
Senegal	..	..	..	..	..	..	..	..	..	..	..	..	..	..
Seychelles	..	..	..	..	..	..	..	..	..	..	..	..	..	..
Sierra Leone	..	..	-15.7	12.0	-14.2	-2.4	-59.6	120.8	-54.9	47.5	-33.2	..	..	-12.1
Somalia	..	..	..	..	..	..	..	..	..	..	..	..	..	..
South Africa	..	..	..	..	..	..	..	..	..	..	..	..	..	..
Sudan	..	..	..	..	..	..	..	..	..	..	..	..	..	..
Swaziland	..	..	..	..	..	..	..	..	..	..	..	..	..	..
Tanzania	..	..	..	..	..	..	..	-29.3	..	..	..	..	..	..
Togo	..	..	..	..	..	..	..	..	..	..	..	..	..	..
Uganda	..	..	..	..	..	..	..	..	..	..	..	..	..	..
Zambia	..	47.1	..	..	..	..	54.3	55.7	130.3	-0.1	-8.5	..	..	-9.7
Zimbabwe	..	7.1	13.1	3.2	-13.7	32.5	18.1	6.4	26.2	-13.1	-47.0	..	-2.9	5.3
NORTH AFRICA	-2.7	-9.1	-4.2	2.5	-11.7	10.5	4.9	40.0	-1.2	8.8	-34.5	6.6	-6.9	2.9
Algeria	..	-19.9	-10.0	8.1	-13.6	6.7	1.3	-11.1	-10.6	5.5	5.8	..	-12.3	-3.8
Egypt, Arab Republic	..	..	..	..	..	..	..	..	..	..	..	..	..	..
Libya	..	..	..	..	..	..	..	..	..	..	..	..	..	..
Morocco	-2.7	10.5	3.4	-3.9	-9.3	15.2	8.9	-0.2	3.6	11.8	-5.7	-1.2	8.0	3.2
Tunisia	..	..	..	..	..	..	..	..	2.9	8.5	..	..	..	..
ALL AFRICA	7.2	-2.3	-4.8	0.5	-3.5	4.1	11.8	25.0	4.2	-3.5	-21.9	12.7	-0.3	3.1

5-45. Capital goods imports

	Millions of U.S. dollars (current prices)											Annual average		
	1980	*1990*	*1991*	*1992*	*1993*	*1994*	*1995*	*1996*	*1997*	*1998*	*1999*	*75-84*	*85-89*	*90-MR*
SUB-SAHARAN AFRICA	2,968	8,276	8,255	7,906	7,264	7,228	9,932	11,044	10,704	10,172	21,660	1,828	6,450	10,244
excluding South Africa	2,968	8,276	8,255	7,906	7,264	7,228	9,932	11,044	10,704	10,172	9,830	1,828	6,450	9,061
excl. S.Africa & Nigeria	2,968	8,276	8,255	7,906	7,264	7,228	9,932	11,044	10,704	10,172	9,830	1,828	6,450	9,061
Angola	..	233	269	378	322	327	327	303	354	..	..	..	263	314
Benin	..	157	182	212	203	146	218	219	208	214	223	..	120	198
Botswana	195	674	642	536	542	485	657	523	502	487	500	197	348	555
Burkina Faso	..	129	111	131	0	0	151	169	155	196	..	..	..	116
Burundi	33	80	91	78	78	81	88	49	45	49	52	45	67	69
Cameroon	388	452	392	319	325	314	315	362	399	403	407	359	480	369
Cape Verde	0	52	65	98	71	98	129	114	117	125	99	0	29	97
Central African Republic	..	59	60	64	53	43	63	14	20	54	62	73	67	49
Chad	..	88	100	97	125	124	126	149	158	174	154	52	67	129
Comoros	..	..	..	..	..	..	..	..	13	13	14	..	..	13
Congo, Democratic Rep. of	..	394	296	192	90	68	111	167	150	231	439	0	217	214
Congo, Republic of	0	237	180	188	203	113	336	1,105	510	371	412	20	249	366
Côte d'Ivoire	1,102	397	404	481	417	410	584	734	740	776	801	663	512	574
Djibouti	..	..	..	..	..	..	..	..	..	..	..	..	..	..
Equatorial Guinea	..	20	60	26	24	42	64	192	300	384	205	10	15	132
Eritrea	..	..	..	12	62	114	173	162	161	139	..	..	..	117
Ethiopia	..	340	466	320	382	239	334	411	516	582	643	449	396	423
Gabon	..	354	360	335	320	320	339	355	388	343	311	188	245	342
Gambia, The	..	2	1	3	3	3	14	13	12	14	13	..	4	8
Ghana	..	226	247	277	..	..	..	..	..	..	..	200	171	250
Guinea	..	96	101	98	92	72	88	78	83	85	106	..	62	90
Guinea-Bissau	..	22	15	24	14	15	15	10	18	26	26	12	13	19
Kenya	409	673	527	411	328	503	995	869	844	896	708	287	455	676
Lesotho	..	..	..	..	..	..	..	..	..	..	103	..	..	103
Liberia	..	..	..	..	..	..	..	..	..	..	..	..	..	..
Madagascar	333	186	165	129	140	143	141	164	146	149	154	160	109	152
Malawi	..	143	294	291	285	210	181	277	340	305	314	..	91	264
Mali	225	194	188	201	182	193	246	226	221	218	231	214	146	210
Mauritania	..	88	78	121	114	73	93	72	79	64	59	85	115	84
Mauritius	..	439	380	377	394	511	381	481	486	510	497	54	224	446
Mozambique	..	..	..	..	..	..	166	170	154	211	307	..	..	202
Namibia	..	..	..	..	..	..	318	322	..	..	598	..	..	413
Niger	..	148	102	85	80	67	87	56	68	87	..	..	107	87
Nigeria	..	..	..	..	..	..	..	..	..	..	..	..	..	..
Rwanda	..	58	54	69	72	36	50	54	62	61	44	50	84	56
São Tomé and Principe	..	12	13	9	11	12	12	7	7	10	12	1	10	11
Senegal	158	195	197	..	159	154	180	186	184	218	243	136	141	191
Seychelles	..	49	40	40	60	48	67	166	75	90	91	16	35	73
Sierra Leone	..	33	38	25	23	27	11	24	12	9	8	54	40	21
Somalia	..	..	..	..	..	..	..	..	..	..	..	..	..	..
South Africa	..	..	..	..	..	..	..	..	..	..	11,830	..	..	11,830
Sudan	..	304	348	355	336	259	322	387	443	541	..	348	266	366
Swaziland	126	181	200	196	231	232	249	312	321	-13	-11	95	107	190
Tanzania	..	540	579	639	628	597	602	461	503	733	710	458	472	599
Togo	..	132	113	102	58	41	75	105	101	97	..	51	95	92
Uganda	..	..	..	..	..	..	..	..	..	..	..	..	..	..
Zambia	..	346	285	349	328	365	722	645	665	539	523	118	243	477
Zimbabwe	..	543	611	640	508	743	901	930	1,148	784	773	345	440	758
NORTH AFRICA	1,548	9,353	8,411	8,100	7,895	7,904	9,743	10,633	10,743	12,089	11,560	1,840	5,295	9,643
Algeria	..	3,092	1,888	1,894	1,835	2,118	2,934	3,023	2,831	2,907	3,155	3,129	2,444	2,568
Egypt, Arab Republic	..	3,151	3,340	2,610	2,545	2,349	3,108	4,101	4,114	4,801	5,575	..	2,001	3,569
Libya	..	..	..	..	..	..	..	..	..	..	..	..	..	..
Morocco	806	1,875	1,880	2,019	1,946	2,003	2,186	1,948	1,939	2,567	2,830	808	1,009	2,119
Tunisia	742	1,235	1,304	1,578	1,569	1,433	1,516	1,561	1,860	1,814	..	719	642	1,541
ALL AFRICA	4,516	17,629	16,666	16,006	15,159	15,132	19,675	21,677	21,447	22,262	33,220	3,668	11,745	19,887

5-46. Capital goods imports, growth

						Percent							Average annual percentage growth		
	1980	1990	1991	1992	1993	1994	1995	1996	1997	1998	1999	75-84	85-89	90-MR
SUB-SAHARAN AFRICA	44.8	-1.8	11.9	-11.0	-1.8	4.2	27.1	11.7	3.5	-6.8	0.9	24.7	14.0	4.5
excluding South Africa	44.8	-1.8	11.9	-11.0	-1.8	4.2	27.1	11.7	3.5	-6.8	0.9	24.7	14.0	4.5
excl. S.Africa & Nigeria	44.8	-1.8	11.9	-11.0	-1.8	4.2	27.1	11.7	3.5	-6.8	0.9	24.7	14.0	4.5
Angola	..	24.6	16.2	45.1	-10.5	-1.7	-9.0	-7.3	29.4	..	..	..	-19.2	6.3
Benin	..	..	..	..	..	..	..	..	..	..	..	..	..	..
Botswana	..	..	..	..	..	..	..	..	..	..	..	..	..	..
Burkina Faso	..	..	..	..	..	..	..	..	..	..	..	..	..	..
Burundi	..	16.1	8.9	-16.8	6.9	0.2	-3.3	-42.7	2.8	12.0	7.0	..	-3.0	-5.6
Cameroon	-7.4	3.9	12.2	-1.9	2.3	-15.3	13.2	21.9	6.3	6.0	4.0	-5.6	8.2	4.6
Cape Verde	..	0.1	24.4	49.3	-27.7	36.1	29.4	-14.0	0.1	3.6	4.3	..	..	8.7
Central African Republic	..	9.0	-1.0	2.9	-17.2	-21.1	34.1	-79.1	47.6	162.6	11.9	..	..	-7.9
Chad	..	-7.0	-19.2	-7.0	-8.0	-2.0	29.6	18.9	5.9	0.4	1.1	..	..	2.3
Comoros	..	..	..	..	..	..	..	..	..	..	..	..	..	..
Congo, Democratic Rep. of	..	..	..	..	..	..	..	..	..	..	..	..	..	..
Congo, Republic of	..	-7.9	-1.9	-16.5	32.2	10.9	-1.1	199.4	-58.4	19.1	2.6	..	7.6	8.6
Côte d'Ivoire	..	-13.3	2.5	52.6	-13.5	-2.6	29.4	23.7	8.5	7.5	8.0	..	..	10.5
Djibouti	..	..	..	..	..	..	..	..	..	..	..	..	..	..
Equatorial Guinea	..	35.3	194.2	-58.9	-4.3	67.5	39.0	189.2	62.3	22.4	-48.3	..	3.3	33.5
Eritrea	..	..	..	..	..	..	..	..	..	..	..	..	..	..
Ethiopia	..	..	..	..	..	..	..	..	..	..	..	..	..	..
Gabon	..	..	..	..	..	..	..	..	..	..	..	..	..	..
Gambia, The	..	-68.4	-43.2	177.2	-10.8	24.4	322.4	-11.8	-12.6	15.1	-8.5	..	..	22.3
Ghana	..	12.2	7.5	7.2	14.7	6.0	9.1	24.8	-17.1	13.8	9.8	..	-3.1	8.2
Guinea	..	37.3	2.2	-6.7	-0.5	-24.3	9.4	5.2	7.2	23.5	21.2	..	1.9	2.2
Guinea-Bissau	..	3.7	-35.9	58.5	-40.9	26.2	13.8	-37.4	74.0	38.2	3.8	..	..	2.7
Kenya	..	72.9	-19.2	-23.4	-15.9	50.3	102.4	-12.6	-2.9	8.9	-2.0	..	-3.7	9.8
Lesotho	..	..	..	..	..	..	..	..	..	..	..	..	..	..
Liberia	..	..	..	..	..	..	..	..	..	..	..	..	..	..
Madagascar	..	41.3	-9.8	-25.4	13.9	-2.1	-9.9	20.1	-3.3	2.8	5.5	..	3.4	-0.1
Malawi	..	12.4	101.3	-5.4	-1.8	-28.7	-20.4	59.8	29.5	-8.1	1.6	..	..	6.1
Mali	3.0	11.1	0.7	3.0	-5.0	2.2	15.5	-8.0	8.9	-0.9	1.0	-1.1	3.2	2.3
Mauritania	..	8.6	-13.8	48.8	-4.9	-31.0	46.9	-26.3	-15.9	-0.1	-24.0	..	-14.3	-3.9
Mauritius	..	33.1	-4.5	-4.0	6.7	4.0	-20.0	7.0	7.0	3.0	5.5	..	19.8	0.9
Mozambique	..	..	..	..	..	..	..	-14.2	-9.6	..	..	..	..	..
Namibia	..	..	..	..	..	..	..	..	..	..	..	..	..	..
Niger	..	..	..	..	..	..	..	..	..	..	..	..	..	..
Nigeria	..	..	..	..	..	..	..	..	..	..	..	..	..	..
Rwanda	..	6.9	-10.2	3.9	-6.3	3.3	11.2	-3.0	-8.2	-1.4	3.4	..	6.4	-0.4
São Tomé and Principe	..	-39.5	12.6	-32.4	20.8	3.9	-6.4	-38.0	0.2	51.7	22.9	..	18.8	-5.1
Senegal	..	32.1	-2.1	..	..	-50.7	30.4	0.8	-13.5	17.3	6.8	..	22.7	-6.8
Seychelles	..	-3.9	-9.4	8.8	52.2	-12.7	32.7	125.5	-46.4	25.0	2.0	..	23.4	13.6
Sierra Leone	..	..	16.2	-35.1	-3.2	16.1	-61.4	106.6	-47.0	-21.1	-15.7	..	..	-15.5
Somalia	..	..	..	..	..	..	..	..	..	..	..	..	..	..
South Africa	..	..	..	..	..	..	..	..	..	..	..	..	..	..
Sudan	..	..	..	..	..	..	..	..	..	..	..	..	20.1	..
Swaziland	..	..	..	..	..	..	..	..	..	..	..	..	..	..
Tanzania	..	..	..	..	..	..	..	-22.7	..	..	..	..	..	..
Togo	..	15.6	..	..	..	..	..	..	..	..	..	..	6.7	..
Uganda	..	..	..	..	..	..	..	..	..	..	..	..	..	..
Zambia	..	-11.9	-19.4	17.4	-5.8	7.3	82.9	-6.8	8.6	-15.7	-2.4	..	16.6	6.6
Zimbabwe	..	4.7	13.1	3.2	-17.3	41.4	14.0	8.5	28.5	-27.2	0.8	..	3.4	7.1
NORTH AFRICA	-13.0	45.2	-12.0	-9.9	-3.1	-7.0	9.7	10.8	3.3	25.9	-3.6	8.6	-2.7	2.8
Algeria	..	60.1	-35.2	-13.1	-10.5	7.6	7.0	8.9	-1.0	25.3	-1.0	..	-20.6	0.3
Egypt, Arab Republic	..	50.0	2.0	-24.3	-4.4	-9.2	24.8	29.8	-0.4	28.9	18.8	..	..	6.4
Libya	..	..	..	..	..	..	..	..	..	..	..	..	..	..
Morocco	-13.0	21.8	-1.9	3.0	-3.4	-0.7	0.9	-7.0	4.8	37.7	10.9	-2.0	6.8	3.4
Tunisia	..	27.8	3.4	21.2	8.7	-23.7	-4.1	-10.7	22.4	7.1	..	..	-9.2	1.5
ALL AFRICA	8.0	25.6	-4.2	-10.3	-2.6	-2.7	16.8	11.2	3.4	11.3	-1.9	12.6	2.8	3.5

5-47. Direction of trade matrix, imports, 1987

		Importers								*Percentage of total imports*											
Exporters		DZA	AGO	BEN	BFA	BDI	CMR	CPV	CAF	TCD	COM	ZAR	COG	CIV	DJI	EGY	GNQ	ETH	GAB	GMB	GHA
Algeria	DZA	**	0.00	0.00	0.29	0.00	0.41	53.78	0.00	0.05	0.00	0.01	0.34	0.17	0.00	0.42	0.02	0.55	0.45	0.00	0.00
Angola	AGO	..	**	..	..	..	..	..	..	..	..	..	..	..	..	..	..	..	..	..	..
Benin	BEN	..	..	**	..	..	..	..	..	..	..	..	..	..	..	..	..	..	..	..	..
Burkina Faso	BFA	..	..	..	**	..	..	..	..	..	..	..	..	..	..	..	..	..	..	..	..
Burundi	BDI	..	..	..	..	**	..	..	..	..	..	..	..	..	..	..	..	..	..	..	..
Cameroon	CMR	0.00	0.03	0.60	0.00	0.00	**	0.00	0.10	3.92	0.00	0.00	0.08	0.25	0.00	0.03	0.02	0.00	0.22	0.02	0.00
Cape Verde	CPV	..	..	..	..	..	..	**	..	..	..	..	..	..	..	..	..	..	..	..	..
Central African	CAF	..	..	..	..	..	..	..	**	..	..	..	..	..	..	..	..	..	..	..	..
Chad	TCD	0.00	0.00	0.00	0.00	0.00	0.00	0.00	0.00	**	0.00	0.00	0.00	0.00	0.00	0.00	0.00	0.00	0.00	0.00	0.00
Comoros	COM	..	..	..	..	..	..	..	..	..	**	..	..	..	..	..	..	..	..	..	..
Congo, Dem. Rep	ZAR	..	..	..	..	..	..	..	..	..	..	**	..	..	..	..	..	..	..	..	..
Congo, Rep.	COG	..	..	..	..	..	..	..	..	..	..	..	**	..	..	..	..	..	..	..	..
Côte d'Ivoire	CIV	..	..	..	..	..	..	..	..	..	..	..	..	**	..	..	..	..	..	..	..
Djibouti	DJI	0.00	0.00	0.00	0.00	0.00	0.00	0.00	0.00	0.00	0.00	0.00	0.00	0.00	**	0.02	0.00	4.90	0.00	0.00	0.00
Egypt, Arab Rep	EGY	0.00	0.00	0.00	0.00	0.00	0.05	0.00	0.00	0.00	0.00	0.25	0.00	0.14	0.00	**	1.06	0.07	0.00	0.00	0.00
Equatorial Guinea	GNQ	..	..	..	..	..	..	..	..	..	..	..	..	..	..	..	**	..	..	..	..
Ethiopia	ETH	0.00	0.00	0.02	0.00	0.01	0.00	0.00	0.09	0.36	0.66	0.00	0.00	0.00	56.02	0.03	0.00	**	0.00	0.00	0.01
Gabon	GAB	..	..	..	..	..	..	..	..	..	..	..	..	..	..	..	..	..	**	..	..
Gambia, The	GMB	..	..	..	..	..	..	..	..	..	..	..	..	..	..	..	..	..	..	**	..
Ghana	GHA	..	..	..	..	..	..	..	..	..	..	..	..	..	..	..	..	..	..	..	**
Guinea	GIN	..	..	..	..	..	..	..	..	..	..	..	..	..	..	..	..	..	..	..	..
Guinea-Bissau	GNB	..	..	..	..	..	..	..	..	..	..	..	..	..	..	..	..	..	..	..	..
Kenya	KEN	0.00	0.00	0.00	0.00	3.37	0.00	0.00	0.00	0.00	0.00	0.07	0.00	0.01	3.40	0.01	0.00	0.82	0.01	0.00	0.00
Liberia	LBR	..	..	..	..	..	..	..	..	..	..	..	..	..	..	..	..	..	..	..	..
Libya	LBY	0.11	0.00	0.00	0.00	0.00	0.00	0.00	0.00	0.00	0.00	0.00	0.00	0.00	0.00	0.00	0.00	0.00	0.00	0.00	0.00
Madagascar	MDG	..	..	..	..	..	..	..	..	..	..	..	..	..	..	..	..	..	..	..	..
Malawi	MWI	0.00	0.00	0.00	0.00	0.00	0.00	0.00	0.00	0.00	0.00	0.00	0.00	0.00	0.00	0.00	0.00	0.00	0.00	0.00	0.00
Mali	MLI	0.02	0.02	0.32	0.16	0.00	0.01	0.00	0.00	0.00	0.00	0.00	0.01	2.41	0.00	0.00	0.00	0.00	0.00	0.00	0.01
Mauritania	MRT	..	..	..	..	..	..	..	..	..	..	..	..	..	..	..	..	..	..	..	..
Mauritius	MUS	0.00	0.00	0.00	0.00	0.00	0.00	0.00	0.00	0.00	0.00	0.00	0.00	0.00	0.00	0.00	0.00	0.00	0.00	0.00	0.00
Morocco	MAR	0.00	0.00	0.42	2.94	0.00	0.02	0.00	0.00	1.07	0.18	0.00	0.21	0.75	0.00	0.11	0.00	0.01	0.89	0.00	0.08
Mozambique	MOZ	..	..	..	..	..	..	..	..	..	..	..	..	..	..	..	..	..	..	..	..
Niger	NER	..	..	..	..	..	..	..	..	..	..	..	..	..	..	..	..	..	..	..	..
Nigeria	NGA	0.00	0.10	1.93	0.01	0.00	0.01	0.00	0.00	0.01	0.00	0.00	0.00	0.17	0.00	0.05	0.02	0.01	0.00	0.03	0.03
Reunion	REU	0.00	0.00	0.00	0.00	0.00	0.01	0.00	0.11	0.00	0.13	0.00	0.60	0.03	0.43	0.01	0.00	0.00	0.02	0.00	0.00
Rwanda	RWA	..	..	..	..	..	..	..	..	..	..	..	..	..	..	..	..	..	..	..	..
São Tomé and Principe	STP	..	..	..	..	..	..	..	..	..	..	..	..	..	..	..	..	..	..	..	..
Senegal	SEN	0.09	1.76	0.09	0.02	0.00	0.03	0.39	0.00	0.00	0.00	0.00	0.01	1.58	0.00	0.00	0.00	0.00	0.05	0.06	0.00
Seychelles	SYC	..	..	..	..	..	..	..	..	..	..	..	..	..	..	..	..	..	..	..	..
Sierra Leone	SLE	..	..	..	..	..	..	..	..	..	..	..	..	..	..	..	..	..	..	..	..
Somalia	SOM	..	..	..	..	..	..	..	..	..	..	..	..	..	..	..	..	..	..	..	..
South Africa	ZAF	..	..	..	..	..	..	..	..	..	..	..	..	..	..	..	..	..	..	..	..
Sudan	SDN	..	..	..	..	..	..	..	..	..	..	..	..	..	..	..	..	..	..	..	..
Tanzania	TZA	1.09	0.00	1.14	5.68	0.05	0.09	0.00	0.00	0.32	0.00	0.27	0.29	0.22	0.00	0.21	0.00	0.00	0.11	0.01	0.00
Togo	TGO	..	..	..	..	..	..	..	..	..	..	..	..	..	..	..	..	..	..	..	..
Tunisia	TUN	0.00	0.01	1.04	2.45	0.00	0.06	0.00	0.00	0.01	0.00	0.01	0.00	0.82	0.00	0.00	0.00	0.00	0.30	0.02	0.37
Uganda	UGA	0.00	0.00	0.00	0.00	3.83	0.00	0.00	0.00	0.00	0.00	0.06	0.00	0.00	0.00	0.01	0.00	0.00	0.00	0.00	0.00
Zambia	ZMB	..	..	..	..	..	..	..	..	..	..	..	..	..	..	..	..	..	..	..	..
Zimbabwe	ZWE	..	..	..	..	..	..	..	..	..	..	..	..	..	..	..	..	..	..	..	..
Sub-Saharan Africa	SSA	1.20	1.91	4.10	5.87	7.26	0.15	0.39	0.30	4.61	0.80	0.40	1.00	4.67	59.86	0.37	0.04	5.74	0.42	0.12	0.05
European Community	EEC	66.89	26.38	65.65	38.71	79.92	70.48	44.98	84.30	90.45	35.16	69.44	49.81	71.99	31.49	64.75	96.96	50.17	61.70	64.58	48.29
North America	NNA	23.00	58.10	12.85	0.45	4.83	22.95	0.00	5.08	0.08	56.05	19.17	45.18	14.75	1.08	13.45	0.11	19.95	27.68	0.61	27.71
Rest of World	ROW	10.02	13.62	17.83	58.36	8.05	6.46	54.63	10.42	5.16	8.13	11.25	4.92	10.42	8.01	21.65	2.89	24.14	10.04	34.68	23.58
World	WLD	100.00	100.00	100.00	100.00	100.00	100.00	100.00	100.00	100.00	100.00	100.00	100.00	100.00	100.00	100.00	100.00	100.00	100.00	100.00	100.00

Note: ** means "not applicable."

(Table continues on the following page)

5-47. Direction of trade matrix, imports, 1987 *(continued)*

Exporters		GIN	GNB	KEN	LBR	LBY	MDG	MWI	MLI	MRT	MUS	MAR	MOZ	NER	NGA	REU	RWA	STP	SEN	SYC	SLE
		Importers				*Percentage of total imports*															
Algeria	DZA	0.00	0.00	0.03	0.00	0.01	0.85	0.00	19.53	1.75	0.00	0.00	0.11	0.01	0.00	0.00	0.00	0.00	0.00	0.28	0.88
Angola	AGO	..	..	..	..	..	..	..	..	..	..	..	..	..	..	..	..	..	..	..	..
Benin	BEN	..	..	..	..	..	..	..	..	..	..	..	..	..	..	..	..	..	..	..	..
Burkina Faso	BFA	..	..	..	..	..	..	..	..	..	..	..	..	..	..	..	..	..	..	..	..
Burundi	BDI	..	..	..	..	..	..	..	..	..	..	..	..	..	..	..	..	..	..	..	..
Cameroon	CMR	5.10	0.00	0.00	0.00	0.00	0.00	0.19	0.03	1.52	0.01	0.15	0.26	0.00	0.05	0.00	0.00	0.00	3.77	0.00	0.20
Cape Verde	CPV	..	..	..	..	..	..	..	..	..	..	..	..	..	..	..	..	..	..	..	..
Central African	CAF	..	..	..	..	..	..	..	..	..	..	..	..	..	..	..	..	..	..	..	..
Chad	TCD	0.00	0.00	0.22	0.00	0.00	0.04	0.01	0.00	0.00	0.11	0.00	0.00	0.00	0.00	0.34	0.00	0.00	0.00	0.00	0.00
Comoros	COM	..	..	..	..	..	..	..	..	..	..	..	..	..	..	..	..	..	..	..	..
Congo, Dem. Rep	ZAR	..	..	..	..	..	..	..	..	..	..	..	..	..	..	..	..	..	..	..	..
Congo, Rep.	COG	..	..	..	..	..	..	..	..	..	..	..	..	..	..	..	..	..	..	..	..
Côte d'Ivoire	CIV	..	..	..	..	..	..	..	..	..	..	..	..	..	..	..	..	..	..	..	..
Djibouti	DJI	0.00	0.00	0.13	0.00	0.00	0.02	0.00	0.01	0.00	0.00	0.00	0.00	0.00	0.00	0.02	0.00	0.00	0.00	0.01	0.00
Egypt, Arab Rep	EGY	0.02	2.28	1.03	0.00	0.00	0.08	1.95	0.00	0.13	0.00	0.08	0.03	0.00	0.00	0.00	0.00	0.00	0.00	0.00	0.00
Equatorial Guinea	GNQ	..	..	..	..	..	..	..	..	..	..	..	..	..	..	..	..	..	..	..	..
Ethiopia	ETH	0.03	0.00	1.19	0.00	0.00	0.00	0.00	0.00	0.00	0.00	0.00	0.00	0.00	0.00	0.00	0.00	0.00	0.00	0.00	0.00
Gabon	GAB	..	..	..	..	..	..	..	..	..	..	..	..	..	..	..	..	..	..	..	..
Gambia, The	GMB	..	..	..	..	..	..	..	..	..	..	..	..	..	..	..	..	..	..	..	..
Ghana	GHA	..	..	..	..	..	..	..	..	..	..	..	..	..	..	..	..	..	..	..	..
Guinea	GIN	**	..	..	..	..	..	..	..	..	..	..	..	..	..	..	..	..	:	..	..
Guinea-Bissau	GNB	..	**	..	..	..	..	..	..	..	..	..	..	..	..	..	..	..	..	..	..
Kenya	KEN	0.00	0.00	**	0.00	0.00	0.57	0.03	0.00	0.00	0.05	0.00	1.15	0.00	0.00	0.00	6.77	0.00	0.06	0.02	0.00
Liberia	LBR	..	..	..	**	..	..	..	..	..	..	..	..	..	..	..	..	..	..	..	..
Libya	LBY	0.00	0.00	0.00	0.00	**	0.00	0.00	0.00	0.00	0.00	2.57	0.00	0.00	0.00	0.00	0.00	0.00	0.00	0.00	0.00
Madagascar	MDG	..	..	..	..	..	**	..	..	..	..	..	..	..	..	..	..	..	..	..	..
Malawi	MWI	0.00	0.00	0.05	0.00	0.00	0.00	**	0.00	0.00	0.00	0.00	0.30	0.00	0.00	0.00	0.00	0.00	0.00	0.00	0.00
Mali	MLI	0.02	0.00	0.01	0.00	0.00	0.00	0.00	**	0.24	0.00	0.01	0.02	0.02	0.05	0.00	0.00	0.00	6.42	0.00	0.01
Mauritania	MRT	..	..	..	..	..	..	..	..	**	..	..	..	..	..	..	..	..	..	..	..
Mauritius	MUS	0.00	0.00	0.32	0.00	0.00	0.00	0.00	0.00	0.00	**	0.00	0.00	0.00	0.00	0.00	0.00	0.00	0.00	0.00	0.00
Morocco	MAR	0.03	0.00	0.03	0.01	0.60	0.04	0.02	7.60	0.00	0.00	**	0.00	0.22	0.01	0.00	0.00	0.00	0.21	0.04	0.01
Mozambique	MOZ	..	..	..	..	..	..	..	..	..	..	..	**	..	..	..	..	..	..	..	..
Niger	NER	..	..	..	..	..	..	..	..	..	..	..	..	**	..	..	..	..	..	..	..
Nigeria	NGA	0.00	0.22	0.01	0.22	0.00	0.00	0.00	0.00	0.85	0.10	0.14	0.00	5.35	**	0.00	0.00	0.00	0.22	0.00	0.01
Reunion	REU	0.00	0.00	0.84	0.00	0.00	3.16	0.02	0.00	0.00	2.13	0.06	0.00	0.00	0.00	**	0.00	0.00	0.10	1.85	0.00
Rwanda	RWA	..	..	..	..	..	..	..	..	..	..	..	..	..	..	..	**	..	..	..	..
São Tomé and Principe	STP	..	..	..	..	..	..	..	..	..	..	..	..	..	..	..	..	**	..	..	..
Senegal	SEN	0.00	0.29	0.00	0.02	0.00	0.02	0.14	0.79	0.29	0.00	0.10	0.00	0.01	0.33	0.00	0.00	0.00	**	0.00	0.01
Seychelles	SYC	..	..	..	..	..	..	..	..	..	..	..	..	..	..	..	..	..	..	**	..
Sierra Leone	SLE	..	..	..	..	..	..	..	..	..	..	..	..	..	..	..	..	..	..	..	**
Somalia	SOM	..	..	..	..	..	..	..	..	..	..	..	..	..	..	..	..	..	..	..	..
South Africa	ZAF	..	..	..	..	..	..	..	..	..	..	..	..	..	..	..	..	..	..	..	..
Sudan	SDN	..	..	..	..	..	..	..	..	..	..	..	..	..	..	..	..	..	..	..	..
Tanzania	TZA	0.00	0.00	0.09	0.00	0.00	0.03	0.00	2.90	0.00	0.00	0.85	0.00	0.00	0.00	0.00	0.00	0.00	0.42	0.26	0.00
Togo	TGO	..	..	..	..	..	..	..	..	..	..	..	..	..	..	..	..	..	..	..	..
Tunisia	TUN	0.09	0.02	0.01	0.02	0.00	0.01	0.00	0.02	0.56	0.00	0.04	0.01	0.17	0.04	0.00	0.00	0.09	0.95	0.00	0.04
Uganda	UGA	0.00	0.00	3.19	0.00	0.00	0.06	0.09	0.00	0.00	0.00	0.00	0.71	0.00	0.01	0.00	0.02	0.00	0.00	0.00	0.00
Zambia	ZMB	..	..	..	..	..	..	..	..	..	..	..	..	..	..	..	..	..	..	..	..
Zimbabwe	ZWE	..	..	..	..	..	..	..	..	..	..	..	..	..	..	..	..	..	..	..	..
Sub-Saharan Africa	SSA	5.15	0.51	6.06	0.24	0.00	3.88	0.49	3.73	2.91	2.39	1.30	2.42	5.37	0.44	0.36	6.80	0.00	10.98	2.13	0.24
European Community	EEC	66.59	24.14	63.55	68.37	84.41	54.38	71.00	48.08	54.39	75.40	70.26	24.89	92.26	42.20	94.54	82.13	50.89	72.39	46.39	80.46
North America	NNA	25.43	15.44	9.81	10.07	0.00	17.85	9.19	3.84	4.78	19.78	2.30	12.71	1.71	46.03	1.51	8.18	0.00	1.55	19.38	16.72
Rest of World	ROW	2.76	59.88	21.88	21.30	15.58	27.07	19.34	47.22	37.59	4.56	27.02	60.28	0.50	11.35	3.60	2.90	49.02	21.06	34.20	2.55
World	WLD	100.00	100.00	100.00	100.00	100.00	100.00	100.00	100.00	100.00	100.00	100.00	100.00	100.00	100.00	100.00	100.00	100.00	100.00	100.00	100.00

Note: ** means "not applicable."

(Table continues on the following page)

5-47. Direction of trade matrix, imports, 1987

Exporters		SOM	ZAF	SDN	TZA	TGO	TUN	UGA	ZMB	ZWE	SSA	EEC	NNA	ROW	WLD
Algeria	DZA	0.00	0.01	0.00	2.87	0.00	4.03	1.21	0.00	..	0.26	0.47	0.18	0.18	0.30
Angola	AGO	..	..	..	..	..	..	..	..	..	..	..	..	..	..
Benin	BEN	..	..	..	..	..	..	..	..	..	..	..	..	..	..
Burkina Faso	BFA	..	..	..	..	..	..	..	..	..	..	..	..	..	..
Burundi	BDI	..	..	..	..	..	..	..	..	..	..	..	..	..	..
Cameroon	CMR	0.00	0.00	0.00	0.00	0.11	0.88	0.00	0.00	..	0.24	0.12	0.02	0.05	0.08
Cape Verde	CPV	..	..	..	..	..	..	..	..	..	..	..	..	..	..
Central African	CAF	..	..	..	..	..	..	..	..	..	..	..	..	..	..
Chad	TCD	0.00	0.14	0.00	0.00	0.00	0.00	0.00	0.00	..	0.01	0.01	0.00	0.01	0.00
Comoros	COM	..	..	..	..	..	..	..	..	..	..	..	..	..	..
Congo, Dem. Rep	ZAR	..	..	..	..	..	..	..	..	..	..	..	..	..	..
Congo, Rep.	COG	..	..	..	..	..	..	..	..	..	..	..	..	..	..
Côte d'Ivoire	CIV	..	..	..	..	..	..	..	..	..	..	..	..	..	..
Djibouti	DJI	1.41	0.00	0.02	0.05	0.00	0.00	0.00	0.00	..	0.01	0.01	0.00	0.01	0.01
Egypt, Arab Rep	EGY	1.83	0.01	6.05	0.37	0.00	0.04	0.15	0.08	..	0.23	0.36	0.32	0.30	0.33
Equatorial Guinea	GNQ	..	..	..	..	..	..	..	..	..	..	..	..	..	..
Ethiopia	ETH	0.00	0.00	0.01	0.00	0.00	0.00	0.00	0.00	..	0.08	0.05	0.04	0.04	0.05
Gabon	GAB	..	..	..	..	..	..	..	..	..	..	..	..	..	..
Gambia, The	GMB	..	..	..	..	..	..	..	..	..	..	..	..	..	..
Ghana	GHA	..	..	..	..	..	..	..	..	..	..	..	..	..	..
Guinea	GIN	..	..	..	..	..	..	..	..	..	..	..	..	..	..
Guinea-Bissau	GNB	..	..	..	..	..	..	..	..	..	..	..	..	..	..
Kenya	KEN	0.04	0.03	0.07	1.07	0.00	0.07	0.33	0.40	..	0.14	0.08	0.04	0.08	0.07
Liberia	LBR	..	..	..	..	..	..	..	..	..	..	..	..	..	..
Libya	LBY	0.00	0.00	0.27	0.00	0.00	0.13	1.30	0.00	..	0.03	0.31	0.02	0.16	0.20
Madagascar	MDG	..	..	..	..	..	..	..	..	..	..	..	..	..	..
Malawi	MWI	0.01	1.00	0.00	0.09	0.00	0.00	0.00	0.77	..	0.08	0.01	0.00	0.01	0.01
Mali	MLI	0.00	0.00	0.00	0.00	0.61	0.01	0.00	0.00	..	0.34	0.02	0.01	0.01	0.02
Mauritania	MRT	..	..	..	..	..	..	..	..	..	..	..	..	..	..
Mauritius	MUS	0.00	0.19	0.00	0.00	0.00	0.00	0.00	0.00	..	0.01	0.01	0.00	0.09	0.04
Morocco	MAR	0.00	0.00	0.02	0.00	0.57	1.29	0.00	0.00	..	0.18	0.24	0.17	0.13	0.18
Mozambique	MOZ	..	..	..	..	..	..	..	..	..	..	..	..	..	..
Niger	NER	..	..	..	..	..	..	..	..	..	..	..	..	..	..
Nigeria	NGA	0.00	0.00	0.01	0.04	1.48	0.00	0.00	0.00	..	0.14	0.24	0.10	0.13	0.17
Reunion	REU	0.00	0.41	0.00	0.29	0.00	0.00	0.01	0.00	..	0.18	0.12	0.00	0.03	0.06
Rwanda	RWA	..	..	..	..	..	..	..	..	..	..	..	..	..	..
São Tomé and Principe	STP	..	..	..	..	..	..	..	..	..	..	..	..	..	..
Senegal	SEN	0.00	0.00	0.00	0.00	0.00	0.10	0.00	0.00	..	0.38	0.06	0.02	0.03	0.04
Seychelles	SYC	..	..	..	..	..	..	..	..	..	..	..	..	..	..
Sierra Leone	SLE	..	..	..	..	..	..	..	..	..	..	..	..	..	..
Somalia	SOM	**	..	..	..	..	..	..	..	..	..	..	..	..	..
South Africa	ZAF	..	**	..	..	..	..	..	..	..	..	..	..	..	..
Sudan	SDN	..	..	**	..	..	..	..	..	..	..	..	..	..	..
Tanzania	TZA	0.00	0.00	0.55	**	0.65	0.00	0.00	0.00	..	0.13	0.22	0.07	0.06	0.13
Togo	TGO	..	..	..	..	**	..	..	..	..	..	..	..	..	..
Tunisia	TUN	0.00	0.00	0.00	0.00	0.00	**	0.00	0.00	..	0.16	0.03	0.01	0.01	0.02
Uganda	UGA	0.05	0.01	0.02	0.00	0.00	0.00	**	0.69	..	0.16	0.05	0.01	0.04	0.04
Zambia	ZMB	..	..	..	..	..	..	..	**	..	..	..	..	..	..
Zimbabwe	ZWE	..	..	..	..	..	..	..	..	**	..	..	..	..	..
Sub-Saharan Africa	SSA	1.51	1.79	0.69	1.90	2.86	1.07	0.40	1.86	..	1.90	0.99	0.32	0.57	0.73
European Community	EEC	35.19	44.00	46.35	61.24	56.62	80.54	61.83	32.46	..	54.17	67.73	23.20	29.34	44.94
North America	NNA	3.54	14.36	4.43	4.10	15.54	3.25	25.62	5.45	..	27.71	10.50	37.79	27.68	21.94
Rest of World	ROW	59.77	41.46	49.08	33.49	26.24	15.15	12.15	60.99	..	16.80	21.12	38.77	42.60	32.64
World	WLD	100.00	100.00	100.00	100.00	100.00	100.00	100.00	100.00	..	100.00	100.00	100.00	100.00	100.00

Note: ** means "not applicable."

5-48. Direction of trade matrix, imports, 1991

Exporters		**Importers** DZA	AGO	BEN	BFA	BDI	CMR	CPV	CAF	**Percentage of total imports** TCD	COM	ZAR	COG	CIV	DJI	EGY	GNQ	ETH	GAB	GMB	GHA
Algeria	DZA	**	0.00	0.00	0.99	0.00	0.26	0.00	0.00	0.03	0.00	0.01	0.00	1.08	0.00	0.13	0.00	0.00	0.10	0.00	0.00
Angola	AGO	..	**	..	..																
Benin	BEN	..	..	**	..																
Burkina Faso	BFA	..	..	..	**	..	..	..	..												
Burundi	BDI					**	..	..	..												
Cameroon	CMR	..	..	..	..	..	**	..	..												
Cape Verde	CPV	..	..	..	..	..	..	**	..												
Central African	CAF	..	..	..	..	..	..	..	**	..											
Chad	TCD	0.00	0.00	0.00	0.00	0.00	0.00	0.00	0.00	**	0.00	0.00	0.00	0.00	0.00	0.00	0.00	0.00	0.00	0.00	0.00
Comoros	COM	..	..	..	..					..	**	..									
Congo, Dem. Rep	ZAR	..	..	..	..					..	..	**	..								
Congo, Rep.	COG	..	..	..	..					..	..	..	**	..							
Côte d'Ivoire	CIV	..	..	..	..	..	..	..	..	..	..	..	..	**	..			..	..	..	..
Djibouti	DJI	0.00	0.00	0.00	0.00	0.00	0.00	0.00	0.00	0.00	0.01	0.00	0.00	0.00	**	0.02	0.00	7.32	0.00	0.00	0.00
Egypt, Arab Rep	EGY	0.04	0.00	0.00	0.00	0.00	0.03	0.00	0.00	0.00	0.00	0.27	0.00	0.05	0.70	**	0.00	0.00	0.02	0.00	0.03
Equatorial Guinea	GNQ	..	..	..	..	..	..	..	..	..	..	..	..	..	..	..	**	..	..	..	..
Ethiopia	ETH	0.00	0.00	0.10	0.00	0.00	0.00	0.00	0.00	0.00	0.00	0.00	0.00	0.00	56.03	0.03	0.00	**	0.00	0.01	0.00
Gabon	GAB	..	..	..	..													..	**	..	..
Gambia, The	GMB	..	..	..	..													..	..	**	..
Ghana	GHA	..	..	..	..													..	..	..	**
Guinea	GIN	..	..	..	..																
Guinea-Bissau	GNB	..	..	..	..	..	..	..	..									..			
Kenya	KEN	0.00	0.00	0.00	0.00	0.14	0.00	0.00	0.00	0.00	0.00	0.13	0.00	0.00	0.34	0.15	0.02	0.04	0.00	0.00	0.01
Liberia	LBR	..	..	..	..													..			
Libya	LBY	0.07	0.00	0.00	0.00	0.00	0.00	0.00	0.00	0.00	0.00	0.00	0.00	0.14	0.03	1.77	0.59	0.00	0.00	0.00	0.09
Madagascar	MDG	0.00	0.00	0.03	0.00	0.00	0.00	0.00	0.00	0.00	0.99	0.00	0.00	0.14	0.01	0.00	0.00	0.00	0.00	0.00	0.00
Malawi	MWI	0.00	0.00	0.00	0.00	0.00	0.00	0.00	0.00	0.00	0.00	0.00	0.00	0.00	0.00	0.00	0.00	0.00	0.00	0.00	0.00
Mali	MLI	..	..	..	..	..	..	..	..	..	..	..	..	..	..	..	..	..	..	..	..
Mauritania	MRT	..	..	..	..	..	..	..	..	..								..	..	..	..
Mauritius	MUS	0.00	0.00	0.00	0.64	0.02	0.00	0.00	0.22	0.00	0.17	0.01	0.00	0.81	1.18	0.01	0.00	0.05	0.00	0.00	0.00
Morocco	MAR	0.43	0.00	13.51	0.28	0.00	2.24	0.00	0.55	4.40	0.51	0.03	1.36	0.71	0.00	0.78	0.00	0.00	0.68	0.00	0.12
Mozambique	MOZ	..	..	..	..	..	..	..	..	..	..	..	..	..	..	..	..	..	..	..	..
Niger	NER	..	..	..	..	..	..	..	..	..	..	..	..	..	..	..	..	..	..	..	..
Nigeria	NGA	0.00	0.00	1.65	0.20	0.02	0.14	0.00	0.01	1.92	0.00	0.00	0.00	0.20	0.01	0.02	0.00	0.00	0.03	0.03	0.02
Reunion	REU	0.00	0.00	0.00	0.00	0.00	0.07	0.00	0.04	0.00	1.39	0.00	0.49	0.31	0.58	0.00	0.00	0.00	0.22	0.00	0.00
Rwanda	RWA	..	..	..	..	..	..	..	..	..	..	..	..	..	..	..	..	..	..	..	..
São Tomé and Principe	STP	..	..	..	..	..	..	..	..	..	..	..	..	..	..	..	..	..	..	..	..
Senegal	SEN	0.00	0.00	0.19	0.01	0.00	0.19	0.03	0.00	0.00	0.00	0.00	0.03	2.30	0.00	0.00	0.00	0.00	0.86	0.50	0.00
Seychelles	SYC	..	..	..	..	..	..	..	..	..	..	..	..	..	..	..	..	..	..	..	..
Sierra Leone	SLE	..	..	..	..	..	..	..	..	..	..	..	..	..	..	..	..	..	..	..	..
Somalia	SOM	..	..	..	..	..	..	..	..	..	..	..	..	..	..	..	..	..	..	..	..
South Africa	ZAF	0.00	0.00	0.00	0.00	0.00	0.00	0.00	0.00	0.00	0.00	0.00	0.00	0.00	0.00	0.00	0.00	0.00	0.00	0.00	0.00
Sudan	SDN	..	..	..	..	..	..	..	..	..	..	..	..	..	..	..	..	..	..	..	..
Tanzania	TZA	0.78	0.00	0.00	0.64	0.00	0.10	0.00	0.36	0.00	0.56	0.10	0.01	0.22	0.00	0.49	0.00	0.09	0.03	0.00	0.00
Togo	TGO	..	..	..	..	..	..	..	..	..	..	..	..	..	..	..	..	..	..	..	..
Tunisia	TUN	0.00	0.04	3.30	1.05	0.00	0.71	0.02	0.02	0.01	0.00	0.00	0.04	0.63	0.00	0.00	0.02	0.01	0.13	0.00	0.57
Uganda	UGA	..	..	..	..	..	..	..	..	..	..	..	..	..	..	..	..	..	..	..	..
Zambia	ZMB	..	..	..	..	..	..	..	..	..	..	..	..	..	..	..	..	..	..	..	..
Zimbabwe	ZWE	..	..	..	..	..	..	..	..	..	..	..	..	..	..	..	..	..	..	..	..
Sub-Saharan Africa	SSA	0.78	0.00	1.97	1.49	0.17	0.50	0.03	0.64	1.92	3.12	0.25	0.53	3.98	58.16	0.72	0.02	7.50	1.14	0.55	0.04
European Community	EEC	75.05	33.86	40.27	41.02	79.28	81.56	95.47	81.04	61.19	61.79	67.03	58.97	73.27	16.25	66.52	98.38	56.46	50.15	69.46	63.99
North America	NNA	18.12	59.32	20.46	0.40	12.05	8.14	0.11	0.73	0.24	30.25	19.90	37.68	9.91	0.14	5.64	0.68	8.42	28.01	1.23	18.11
Rest of World	ROW	6.83	6.78	34.04	57.32	7.97	9.26	4.37	18.20	36.64	7.95	12.90	3.26	13.68	27.22	27.62	0.90	27.73	20.82	28.76	17.29
World	WLD	100.00	100.00	100.00	100.00	100.00	100.00	100.00	100.00	100.00	100.00	100.00	100.00	100.00	100.00	100.00	100.00	100.00	100.00	100.00	100.00

Note: ** means "not applicable."

(Table continues on the following page)

5-48. Direction of trade matrix, imports, 1991 *(continued)*

Exporters		*Importers* GIN	GNB	KEN	LBR	LBY	*Percentage of total imports* MDG	MWI	MLI	MRT	MUS	MAR	MOZ	NER	NGA	REU	RWA	STP	SEN	SYC	SLE
Algeria	DZA	0.00	0.00	0.03	0.00	0.00	0.32	0.00	6.99	0.00	0.00	1.13	0.00	0.21	0.00	0.02	0.00	0.00	0.00	0.00	0.00
Angola	AGO	..	..	..	..	..	..	..	..	..	..	..	..	..	..	..	..	..	..	..	..
Benin	BEN	..	..	..	..	..	..	..	..	..	..	..	..	..	..	..	..	..	..	..	..
Burkina Faso	BFA	..	..	..	..	..	..	..	..	..	..	..	..	..	..	..	..	..	..	..	..
Burundi	BDI	..	..	..	..	..	..	..	..	..	..	..	..	..	..	..	..	..	..	..	..
Cameroon	CMR	..	..	..	..	..	..	..	..	..	..	..	..	..	..	..	..	..	..	..	..
Cape Verde	CPV	..	..	..	..	..	..	..	..	..	..	..	..	..	..	..	..	..	..	..	..
Central African	CAF	..	..	..	..	..	..	..	..	..	..	..	..	..	..	..	..	..	..	..	..
Chad	TCD	0.00	0.00	0.21	0.00	0.00	0.00	0.03	0.00	0.00	0.26	0.00	0.16	0.00	0.00	0.37	0.00	0.00	0.00	0.00	0.00
Comoros	COM	..	..	..	..	..	..	..	..	..	..	..	..	..	..	..	..	..	..	..	..
Congo, Dem. Rep	ZAR	..	..	..	..	..	..	..	..	..	..	..	..	..	..	..	..	..	..	..	..
Congo, Rep.	COG	..	..	..	..	..	..	..	..	..	..	..	..	..	..	..	..	..	..	..	..
Côte d'Ivoire	CIV	..	..	..	..	..	..	..	..	..	..	..	..	..	..	..	..	..	..	..	..
Djibouti	DJI	0.00	0.00	0.13	0.00	0.00	0.02	0.00	0.00	0.00	0.00	0.00	0.00	0.00	0.00	0.02	0.04	0.00	0.00	0.00	0.00
Egypt, Arab Rep	EGY	0.02	0.00	3.43	0.00	0.19	0.02	2.32	0.00	0.27	0.00	0.06	0.00	0.05	0.00	0.00	0.00	0.00	0.01	0.00	0.18
Equatorial Guinea	GNQ	..	..	..	..	..	..	..	..	..	..	..	..	..	..	..	..	..	..	..	..
Ethiopia	ETH	0.00	0.00	1.79	0.00	0.00	0.00	0.00	0.00	0.00	0.00	0.00	0.00	0.00	0.01	0.00	0.00	0.00	0.00	0.00	0.00
Gabon	GAB	..	..	..	..	..	..	..	..	..	..	..	..	..	..	..	..	..	..	..	..
Gambia, The	GMB	..	..	..	..	..	..	..	..	..	..	..	..	..	..	..	..	..	..	..	..
Ghana	GHA	..	..	..	..	..	..	..	..	..	..	..	..	..	..	..	..	..	..	..	..
Guinea	GIN	**	..	..	..	..	..	..	..	..	..	..	..	..	..	..	..	..	..	..	..
Guinea-Bissau	GNB	..	**	..	..	..	..	..	..	..	..	..	..	..	..	..	..	..	..	..	..
Kenya	KEN	0.00	0.03	**	0.13	0.00	0.04	0.01	0.00	0.00	0.11	0.00	0.22	0.00	0.00	0.00	0.01	0.00	0.11	0.01	0.00
Liberia	LBR	..	..	..	**	..	..	..	..	..	..	..	..	..	..	..	..	..	..	..	..
Libya	LBY	0.00	0.00	0.00	0.00	**	0.00	0.00	0.00	0.00	0.00	3.32	0.00	0.01	0.00	0.00	0.00	0.00	0.00	0.00	0.38
Madagascar	MDG	0.00	0.00	0.16	0.00	0.00	**	0.00	0.00	0.00	0.07	0.01	0.01	0.00	0.00	0.39	0.00	0.00	0.01	0.00	0.00
Malawi	MWI	0.00	0.00	0.18	0.00	0.00	0.00	**	0.00	0.00	0.00	0.00	0.40	0.00	0.00	0.00	0.00	0.00	0.01	0.00	0.00
Mali	MLI	..	..	..	..	..	..	..	**	..	..	..	..	..	..	..	..	..	..	..	..
Mauritania	MRT	..	..	..	..	..	..	..	..	**	..	..	..	..	..	..	..	..	..	..	..
Mauritius	MUS	0.01	0.01	1.10	0.00	0.00	4.26	0.05	0.00	0.00	**	0.04	0.32	0.00	0.00	0.77	0.00	0.00	0.00	1.92	0.00
Morocco	MAR	0.06	0.00	0.03	0.00	1.25	0.20	0.82	0.04	0.11	0.00	**	0.06	0.00	0.11	0.00	0.00	0.00	0.01	0.00	0.00
Mozambique	MOZ	..	..	..	..	..	..	..	..	..	..	..	**	..	..	..	..	..	..	..	..
Niger	NER	..	..	..	..	..	..	..	..	..	..	..	..	**	..	..	..	..	..	..	..
Nigeria	NGA	0.06	2.00	0.05	0.01	0.00	0.10	0.05	0.65	0.01	0.00	0.18	0.02	1.89	**	0.00	0.03	0.01	0.19	0.00	0.03
Reunion	REU	0.00	0.00	1.01	0.00	0.00	4.00	0.00	0.00	0.00	1.64	0.04	0.00	0.00	0.00	**	0.00	0.00	0.01	1.91	0.00
Rwanda	RWA	..	..	..	..	..	..	..	..	..	..	..	..	..	..	..	**	..	..	..	..
São Tomé and Principe	STP	..	..	..	..	..	..	..	..	..	..	..	..	..	..	..	..	**	..	..	..
Senegal	SEN	0.06	0.13	0.01	0.00	0.00	0.00	0.08	0.19	0.00	0.00	0.09	0.00	0.03	0.60	0.00	0.00	0.00	**	0.00	0.10
Seychelles	SYC	..	..	..	..	..	..	..	..	..	..	..	..	..	..	..	..	..	..	**	..
Sierra Leone	SLE	..	..	..	..	..	..	..	..	..	..	..	..	..	..	..	..	..	..	..	**
Somalia	SOM	..	..	..	..	..	..	..	..	..	..	..	..	..	..	..	..	..	..	..	..
South Africa	ZAF	0.00	0.00	0.00	0.00	0.00	0.00	0.00	0.00	0.00	0.00	0.00	0.00	0.00	0.00	0.00	0.00	0.00	0.00	0.00	0.00
Sudan	SDN	..	..	..	..	..	..	..	..	..	..	..	..	..	..	..	..	..	..	..	..
Tanzania	TZA	0.00	0.00	0.13	0.00	0.28	0.10	0.00	1.62	0.12	0.00	1.17	0.01	0.01	0.00	0.00	0.00	0.00	0.43	0.00	0.00
Togo	TGO	..	..	..	..	..	..	..	..	..	..	..	..	..	..	..	..	..	..	..	..
Tunisia	TUN	0.00	0.24	0.01	0.03	0.00	0.01	0.00	0.07	0.66	0.21	0.02	0.00	0.16	0.10	0.00	0.01	0.00	0.25	0.00	0.01
Uganda	UGA	..	..	..	..	..	..	..	..	..	..	..	..	..	..	..	..	..	..	..	..
Zambia	ZMB	..	..	..	..	..	..	..	..	..	..	..	..	..	..	..	..	..	..	..	..
Zimbabwe	ZWE	..	..	..	..	..	..	..	..	..	..	..	..	..	..	..	..	..	..	..	..
Sub-Saharan Africa	SSA	0.12	2.16	4.77	0.15	0.29	8.51	0.22	2.46	0.13	2.10	1.53	1.14	1.94	0.62	1.54	0.09	0.01	0.78	3.83	0.13
European Community	EEC	59.43	25.80	63.43	38.34	89.39	54.90	49.84	37.82	69.00	81.44	68.84	21.51	90.39	47.66	95.59	79.97	81.15	69.46	57.24	71.02
North America	NNA	27.76	0.28	7.44	1.12	0.00	12.55	18.44	3.75	2.69	12.25	3.94	8.51	6.07	44.89	0.93	7.60	0.02	2.32	0.83	21.94
Rest of World	ROW	12.70	71.53	26.41	60.36	10.60	32.32	30.89	57.49	27.59	5.13	26.92	68.96	1.42	6.74	3.10	12.32	18.78	27.61	41.86	6.87
World	WLD	100.00	100.00	100.00	100.00	100.00	100.00	100.00	100.00	100.00	100.00	100.00	100.00	100.00	100.00	100.00	100.00	100.00	100.00	100.00	100.00

Note: ** means "not applicable."

(Table continues on the following page)

5-48. Direction of trade matrix, imports, 1991

Exporters		*Importers* SOM	ZAF	SDN	TZA	TGO	TUN	UGA	ZMB	ZWE	*Percentage of total imports* SSA	EEC	NNA	ROW	WLD
Algeria	DZA	1.42	0.06	0.16	0.03	0.18	2.75	0.00	0.00	..	0.15	0.36	0.18	0.12	0.23
Angola	AGO	..	..	..	..	..	..	..	..		..	..	..	..	..
Benin	BEN	..	..	..	..	..	..	..	..		..	..	..	..	..
Burkina Faso	BFA	..	..	..	..	..	..	..	..		..	..	..	..	..
Burundi	BDI	..	..	..	..	..	..	..	..		..	..	..	..	..
Cameroon	CMR	..	..	..	..	..	..	..	..		..	..	..	..	..
Cape Verde	CPV	..	..	..	..	..	..	..	..		..	..	..	..	..
Central African	CAF	..	..	..	..	..	..	..	..		..	..	..	..	..
Chad	TCD	0.00	0.15	0.00	0.00	0.00	0.00	0.00	0.00	..	0.02	0.00	0.00	0.01	0.01
Comoros	COM	..	..	..	..	..	..	..	..		..	..	..	..	..
Congo, Dem. Rep	ZAR	..	..	..	..	..	..	..	..		..	..	..	..	..
Congo, Rep.	COG	..	..	..	..	..	..	..	..		..	..	..	..	..
Côte d'Ivoire	CIV	..	..	..	..	..	..	..	..		..	..	..	..	..
Djibouti	DJI	0.14	0.00	0.00	0.07	0.00	0.00	0.02	0.00	..	0.01	0.01	0.00	0.01	0.01
Egypt, Arab Rep	EGY	0.85	0.01	0.89	0.35	0.00	0.15	1.46	0.00	..	0.27	0.24	0.25	0.21	0.23
Equatorial Guinea	GNQ	..	..	..	..	..	..	..	..		..	..	..	..	..
Ethiopia	ETH	0.26	0.00	0.00	0.00	0.00	0.00	0.02	0.00	..	0.11	0.01	0.01	0.01	0.01
Gabon	GAB	..	..	..	..	..	..	..	..		..	..	..	..	..
Gambia, The	GMB	..	..	..	..	..	..	..	..		..	..	..	..	..
Ghana	GHA	..	..	..	..	..	..	..	..		..	..	..	..	..
Guinea	GIN	..	..	..	..	..	..	..	..		..	..	..	..	..
Guinea-Bissau	GNB	..	..	..	..	..	..	..	..		..	..	..	..	..
Kenya	KEN	0.06	0.07	0.02	1.99	0.00	0.00	0.99	0.51	..	0.10	0.06	0.02	0.06	0.05
Liberia	LBR	..	..	..	..	..	..	..	..		..	..	..	..	..
Libya	LBY	0.01	0.00	1.28	0.00	0.00	3.20	0.00	0.00	..	0.04	0.24	0.02	0.13	0.16
Madagascar	MDG	0.00	0.12	0.00	0.04	0.02	0.00	0.00	0.00	..	0.03	0.02	0.00	0.01	0.01
Malawi	MWI	0.00	1.58	0.00	0.12	0.00	0.00	0.00	0.45	..	0.10	0.02	0.01	0.02	0.02
Mali	MLI	..	..	..	..	..	..	..	..		..	..	..	..	..
Mauritania	MRT	..	..	..	..	..	..	..	..		..	..	..	..	..
Mauritius	MUS	0.00	1.38	0.26	1.68	0.00	0.00	0.00	0.00	..	0.17	0.04	0.01	0.07	0.05
Morocco	MAR	0.00	0.04	0.00	0.00	0.97	0.99	0.00	0.07	..	0.37	0.29	0.12	0.14	0.20
Mozambique	MOZ	..	..	..	..	..	..	..	..		..	..	..	..	..
Niger	NER	..	..	..	..	..	..	..	..		..	..	..	..	..
Nigeria	NGA	0.00	0.05	0.00	0.00	4.83	0.00	0.00	0.01	..	0.09	0.33	0.11	0.13	0.21
Reunion	REU	0.00	0.42	0.00	0.52	0.00	0.00	0.00	0.00	..	0.20	0.11	0.02	0.03	0.06
Rwanda	RWA	..	..	..	..	..	..	..	..		..	..	..	..	..
São Tomé and Principe	STP	..	..	..	..	..	..	..	..		..	..	..	..	..
Senegal	SEN	0.00	0.00	0.00	0.00	0.12	0.03	0.00	0.00	..	0.44	0.04	0.02	0.01	0.03
Seychelles	SYC	..	..	..	..	..	..	..	..		..	..	..	..	..
Sierra Leone	SLE	..	..	..	..	..	..	..	..		..	..	..	..	..
Somalia	SOM	**	..	..	..	..	..	..	..		..	..	..	..	..
South Africa	ZAF	0.00	**	0.00	0.00	0.00	0.00	0.00	0.00	..	0.00	0.00	0.00	1.21	0.51
Sudan	SDN	..	..	**	..	..	..	..	..		..	..	..	..	..
Tanzania	TZA	0.01	0.00	0.42	**	0.74	0.00	0.01	0.00	..	0.08	0.27	0.06	0.07	0.15
Togo	TGO	..	..	..	..	**	..	..	..		..	..	..	..	..
Tunisia	TUN	0.00	0.00	0.00	0.00	0.00	**	0.00	0.00	..	0.17	0.02	0.01	0.01	0.01
Uganda	UGA	..	..	..	..	..	..	**	..		..	..	..	..	..
Zambia	ZMB	..	..	..	..	..	..	..	**		..	..	..	..	..
Zimbabwe	ZWE	..	..	..	..	..	..	..	..	**	..	..	..	..	..
Sub-Saharan Africa	SSA	0.47	3.79	0.70	4.44	5.71	0.03	1.05	0.97	..	1.34	0.92	0.26	1.63	1.12
European Community	EEC	22.35	47.60	35.49	54.47	41.27	83.43	76.76	28.88	..	53.87	70.69	24.37	29.84	45.96
North America	NNA	3.31	13.92	5.14	4.21	12.21	1.00	11.77	3.56	..	28.04	7.88	31.03	23.34	18.29
Rest of World	ROW	73.88	34.16	59.34	38.57	41.56	15.52	10.29	66.09	..	17.07	20.90	44.42	46.51	35.36
World	WLD	100.00	100.00	100.00	100.00	100.00	100.00	100.00	100.00	..	100.00	100.00	100.00	100.00	100.00

Note: ** means "not applicable."

Table 5-49. Direction of trade matrix, imports, 1997

Exporters		Importers				*Percentage of total imports*															
		DZA	AGO	BEN	BFA	BDI	CMR	CPV	CAF	TCD	COM	ZAR	COG	CIV	DJI	EGY	GNQ	ERI	ETH	GAB	GMB
Algeria	DZA	**	0.00	0.11	0.00	0.00	0.47	0.00	0.00	0.00	0.00	0.01	0.02	1.50	0.00	0.40	0.00	0.00	1.22	0.02	0.00
Angola	AGO	..	**	..	..	..	..	..	..	..	..	..	..	..	..	..	..	..	..	..	..
Benin	BEN	..	..	**	..	..	..	..	..	..	..	..	..	..	..	..	..	..	..	..	..
Burkina Faso	BFA	..	..	..	**	..	..	..	..	..	..	..	..	..	..	..	..	..	..	..	..
Burundi	BDI	..	..	..	..	**	..	..	..	..	..	..	..	..	..	..	..	..	..	..	..
Cameroon	CMR	..	..	..	..	..	**	..	..	..	..	..	..	..	..	..	..	..	..	..	..
Cape Verde	CPV	..	..	..	..	..	..	**	..	..	..	..	..	..	..	..	..	..	..	..	..
Central African	CAF	..	..	..	..	..	..	..	**	..	..	..	..	..	..	..	..	..	..	..	..
Chad	TCD	..	..	..	..	..	..	..	..	**	..	..	..	..	..	..	..	..	..	..	..
Comoros	COM	..	..	..	..	..	..	..	..	..	**	..	..	..	..	..	..	..	..	..	..
Congo, Dem. Rep	ZAR	0.10	0.09	0.51	0.61	0.52	0.27	0.03	0.03	0.02	0.79	**	0.05	0.75	0.00	0.13	0.00	0.00	0.18	0.24	0.05
Congo, Rep.	COG	..	..	..	..	..	..	..	..	..	..	..	**	..	..	..	..	..	..	..	..
Côte d'Ivoire	CIV	..	..	..	..	..	..	..	..	..	..	..	..	**	..	..	..	..	..	..	..
Djibouti	DJI	..	..	..	..	..	..	..	..	..	..	..	..	..	**	..	..	..	..	..	..
Egypt, Arab Rep	EGY	0.01	0.00	0.00	0.02	0.00	0.01	0.00	3.95	0.13	0.00	0.02	0.00	0.02	0.00	**	0.01	4.86	3.21	0.00	0.00
Equatorial Guinea	GNQ	..	..	..	..	..	..	..	..	..	..	..	..	..	..	..	**	..	..	..	..
Ethiopia	ETH	..	..	..	..	..	..	..	..	..	..	..	..	..	..	..	..	..	**	..	..
Gabon	GAB	..	..	..	..	..	..	..	..	..	..	..	..	..	..	..	..	..	..	**	..
Gambia, The	GMB	..	..	..	..	..	..	..	..	..	..	..	..	..	..	..	..	..	..	..	**
Ghana	GHA	..	..	..	..	..	..	..	..	..	..	..	..	..	..	..	..	..	..	..	..
Guinea	GIN	..	..	..	..	..	..	..	..	..	..	..	..	..	..	..	..	..	..	..	..
Guinea-Bissau	GNB	..	..	..	..	..	..	..	..	..	..	..	..	..	..	..	..	..	..	..	..
Kenya	KEN	0.00	0.00	0.00	0.00	0.00	0.01	0.00	0.00	0.00	0.00	0.25	0.00	0.00	1.27	0.08	0.00	0.07	1.91	0.00	0.00
Liberia	LBR	..	..	..	..	..	..	..	..	..	..	..	..	..	..	..	..	..	..	..	..
Libya	LBY	0.01	0.00	0.00	0.00	0.00	0.00	0.00	0.00	0.00	0.00	0.00	0.00	0.03	0.00	2.24	0.00	0.00	0.02	0.00	0.00
Madagascar	MDG	0.00	0.00	0.00	0.00	0.00	0.00	0.00	0.00	0.00	0.01	0.00	0.00	0.00	0.38	0.01	0.00	0.00	0.02	0.00	0.00
Malawi	MWI	..	..	..	..	..	..	..	..	..	..	..	..	..	..	..	..	..	..	..	..
Mali	MLI	..	..	..	..	..	..	..	..	..	..	..	..	..	..	..	..	..	..	..	..
Mauritania	MRT	..	..	..	..	..	..	..	..	..	..	..	..	..	..	..	..	..	..	..	..
Mauritius	MUS	0.00	0.00	0.00	5.14	0.00	0.20	0.12	0.69	0.02	0.00	0.01	0.01	0.04	0.00	0.01	0.00	0.00	0.00	0.00	0.00
Morocco	MAR	0.76	0.00	7.27	2.08	0.00	0.29	0.00	0.33	1.67	0.00	0.08	0.24	0.77	0.00	0.28	0.00	0.00	0.06	0.66	0.00
Mozambique	MOZ	..	..	..	..	..	..	..	..	..	..	..	..	..	..	..	..	..	..	..	..
Niger	NER	..	..	..	..	..	..	..	..	..	..	..	..	..	..	..	..	..	..	..	..
Nigeria	NGA	0.01	0.04	6.81	0.01	0.06	0.02	29.05	0.67	0.00	0.00	0.03	0.00	0.32	2.37	0.02	0.01	0.00	0.00	0.01	0.03
Reunion	REU	..	..	..	..	..	..	..	..	..	..	..	..	..	..	..	..	..	..	..	..
Rwanda	RWA	..	..	..	..	..	..	..	..	..	..	..	..	..	..	..	..	..	..	..	..
São Tomé and Principe	STP	..	..	..	..	..	..	..	..	..	..	..	..	..	..	..	..	..	..	..	..
Senegal	SEN	..	..	..	..	..	..	..	..	..	..	..	..	..	..	..	..	..	..	..	..
Seychelles	SYC	..	..	..	..	..	..	..	..	..	..	..	..	..	..	..	..	..	..	..	..
Sierra Leone	SLE	..	..	..	..	..	..	..	..	..	..	..	..	..	..	..	..	..	..	..	..
Somalia	SOM	..	..	..	..	..	..	..	..	..	..	..	..	..	..	..	..	..	..	..	..
South Africa	ZAF	..	..	..	..	..	..	..	..	..	..	..	..	..	..	..	..	..	..	..	..
Sudan	SDN	..	..	..	..	..	..	..	..	..	..	..	..	..	..	..	..	..	..	..	..
Tanzania	TZA	0.51	0.00	0.00	0.72	0.00	0.45	0.33	2.61	1.89	0.26	0.02	0.06	0.47	0.00	0.70	0.00	0.00	0.01	0.08	0.08
Togo	TGO	..	..	..	..	..	..	..	..	..	..	..	..	..	..	..	..	..	..	..	..
Tunisia	TUN	..	..	..	..	..	..	..	..	..	..	..	..	..	..	..	..	..	..	..	..
Uganda	UGA	0.00	0.00	0.00	0.01	0.16	0.02	0.00	0.00	0.01	0.00	0.01	0.00	0.01	0.04	0.04	0.02	0.00	0.05	0.01	0.03
Zambia	ZMB	..	..	..	..	..	..	..	..	..	..	..	..	..	..	..	..	..	..	..	..
Zimbabwe	ZWE	..	..	..	..	..	..	..	..	..	..	..	..	..	..	..	..	..	..	..	..
Sub-Saharan Africa	SSA	0.61	0.14	7.32	6.49	0.74	0.98	29.52	4.00	1.94	1.06	7.31	0.12	1.59	4.07	0.98	0.03	0.07	2.16	0.35	0.18
European Community	EEC	62.36	14.39	23.43	41.47	70.37	78.30	54.51	77.81	66.02	71.41	59.62	32.90	67.67	79.21	53.62	34.55	72.76	56.11	12.36	86.49
North America	NNA	20.42	62.57	2.97	0.70	15.67	3.04	1.80	0.84	2.30	19.86	23.72	20.72	9.81	0.05	12.44	9.18	13.67	14.11	68.49	1.84
Rest of World	ROW	17.22	23.00	66.79	57.81	13.72	18.62	14.64	20.68	31.67	8.73	16.34	46.35	22.19	17.06	33.79	56.24	13.50	27.81	19.12	11.55
World	WLD	100.00	100.00	100.00	100.00	100.00	100.00	100.00	100.00	100.00	100.00	100.00	100.00	100.00	100.00	100.00	100.00	100.00	100.00	100.00	100.00

Note: ** means "not applicable."

(Table continues on the following page)

Table 5-49. Direction of trade matrix, imports, 1997 *(continued)*

Exporters		GHA	GIN	GNB	KEN	LBR	LBY	MDG	MWI	MLI	MRT	MUS	MAR	MOZ	NER	NGA	REU	RWA	STP	SEN	SYC
		Importers								*Percentage of total imports*											
Algeria	DZA	0.01	0.34	0.00	0.03	0.00	0.02	1.97	0.00	0.29	0.02	0.00	0.09	0.00	0.24	0.01	..	0.00	0.00	0.29	0.00
Angola	AGO	..	..	..	..	..	..	..	..	..	..	..	..	..	..	..	..	..	..	..	..
Benin	BEN	..	..	..	..	..	..	..	..	..	..	..	..	..	..	..	..	..	..	..	..
Burkina Faso	BFA	..	..	..	..	..	..	..	..	..	..	..	..	..	..	..	..	..	..	..	..
Burundi	BDI	..	..	..	..	..	..	..	..	..	..	..	..	..	..	..	..	..	..	..	..
Cameroon	CMR	..	..	..	..	..	..	..	..	..	..	..	..	..	..	..	..	..	..	..	..
Cape Verde	CPV	..	..	..	..	..	..	..	..	..	..	..	..	..	..	..	..	..	..	..	..
Central African	CAF	..	..	..	..	..	..	..	..	..	..	..	..	..	..	..	..	..	..	..	..
Chad	TCD	..	..	..	..	..	..	..	..	..	..	..	..	..	..	..	..	..	..	..	..
Comoros	COM	..	..	..	..	..	..	..	..	..	..	..	..	..	..	..	..	..	..	..	..
Congo, Dem. Rep	ZAR	0.24	0.01	0.23	0.80	0.80	0.00	0.56	14.46	1.24	0.06	0.33	0.09	12.36	0.42	0.05	..	0.83	0.87	0.13	1.33
Congo, Rep.	COG	..	..	..	..	..	..	..	..	..	..	..	..	..	..	..	..	..	..	..	..
Côte d'Ivoire	CIV	..	..	..	..	..	..	..	..	..	..	..	..	..	..	..	..	..	..	..	..
Djibouti	DJI	..	..	..	..	..	..	..	..	..	..	..	..	..	..	..	..	..	..	..	..
Egypt, Arab Rep	EGY	0.06	0.02	0.29	4.63	0.01	0.73	0.02	2.27	0.06	0.29	0.07	0.09	0.00	0.00	0.01	..	0.00	0.01	0.00	0.00
Equatorial Guinea	GNQ	..	..	..	..	..	..	..	..	..	..	..	..	..	..	..	..	..	..	..	..
Ethiopia	ETH	..	..	..	..	..	..	..	..	..	..	..	..	..	..	..	..	..	..	..	..
Gabon	GAB	..	..	..	..	..	..	..	..	..	..	..	..	..	..	..	..	..	..	..	..
Gambia, The	GMB	..	..	..	..	..	..	..	..	..	..	..	..	..	..	..	..	..	..	..	..
Ghana	GHA	**	..	..	..	..	..	..	..	..	..	..	..	..	..	..	..	..	..	..	..
Guinea	GIN	..	**	..	..	..	..	..	..	..	..	..	..	..	..	..	..	..	..	..	..
Guinea-Bissau	GNB	..	..	**	..	..	..	..	..	..	..	..	..	..	..	..	..	..	..	..	..
Kenya	KEN	0.04	0.00	0.00	**	0.00	0.00	0.02	0.02	0.00	0.00	0.28	0.00	0.80	0.03	0.01	..	4.85	0.00	0.04	0.14
Liberia	LBR	..	..	..	..	**	..	..	..	..	..	..	..	..	..	..	..	..	..	..	..
Libya	LBY	0.00	0.00	0.00	0.00	0.00	**	0.00	0.00	0.00	0.21	0.00	1.57	0.00	0.00	0.00	..	0.06	0.00	0.00	0.00
Madagascar	MDG	0.00	0.00	0.00	0.09	0.00	0.00	**	0.00	0.00	0.00	0.32	0.01	0.00	0.00	0.00	..	0.00	0.00	0.01	1.53
Malawi	MWI	..	..	..	..	..	..	..	**	..	..	..	..	..	..	..	..	..	..	..	..
Mali	MLI	..	..	..	..	..	..	..	..	**	..	..	..	..	..	..	..	..	..	..	..
Mauritania	MRT	..	..	..	..	..	..	..	..	..	**	..	..	..	..	..	..	..	..	..	..
Mauritius	MUS	0.01	0.00	0.00	0.72	0.00	0.01	4.51	0.01	0.72	0.00	**	0.02	0.32	0.00	0.01	..	0.00	0.00	0.00	0.25
Morocco	MAR	0.18	2.09	0.00	0.00	0.00	0.31	0.14	0.44	1.65	0.10	0.00	**	0.66	0.00	1.26	..	0.00	0.00	0.46	0.01
Mozambique	MOZ	..	..	..	..	..	..	..	..	..	..	..	..	**	..	..	..	..	..	..	..
Niger	NER	..	..	..	..	..	..	..	..	..	..	..	..	..	**	..	..	..	..	..	..
Nigeria	NGA	0.17	0.01	0.01	0.05	0.02	0.02	0.00	0.00	0.00	13.70	0.00	0.06	0.04	0.02	**	..	0.02	0.17	0.82	0.03
Reunion	REU	..	..	..	..	..	..	..	..	..	..	..	..	..	..	..	**	..	..	..	..
Rwanda	RWA	..	..	..	..	..	..	..	..	..	..	..	..	..	..	..	..	**	..	..	..
São Tomé and Principe	STP	..	..	..	..	..	..	..	..	..	..	..	..	..	..	..	..	..	**	..	..
Senegal	SEN	..	..	..	..	..	..	..	..	..	..	..	..	..	..	..	..	..	..	**	..
Seychelles	SYC	..	..	..	..	..	..	..	..	..	..	..	..	..	..	..	..	..	..	..	**
Sierra Leone	SLE	..	..	..	..	..	..	..	..	..	..	..	..	..	..	..	..	..	..	..	..
Somalia	SOM	..	..	..	..	..	..	..	..	..	..	..	..	..	..	..	..	..	..	..	..
South Africa	ZAF	..	..	..	..	..	..	..	..	..	..	..	..	..	..	..	..	..	..	..	..
Sudan	SDN	..	..	..	..	..	..	..	..	..	..	..	..	..	..	..	..	..	..	..	..
Tanzania	TZA	0.03	0.29	0.25	0.10	0.00	2.35	0.06	0.20	0.96	0.16	0.01	0.65	0.00	0.00	0.00	..	0.00	0.00	0.37	0.66
Togo	TGO	..	..	..	..	..	..	..	..	..	..	..	..	..	..	..	..	..	..	..	..
Tunisia	TUN	..	..	..	..	..	..	..	..	..	..	..	..	..	..	..	..	..	..	..	..
Uganda	UGA	0.00	0.01	0.12	6.07	0.00	0.00	0.00	0.47	0.09	0.00	0.03	0.00	1.69	0.00	0.00	..	1.33	0.00	0.01	0.00
Zambia	ZMB	..	..	..	..	..	..	..	..	..	..	..	..	..	..	..	..	..	..	..	..
Zimbabwe	ZWE	..	..	..	..	..	..	..	..	..	..	..	..	..	..	..	..	..	..	..	..
Sub-Saharan Africa	SSA	0.49	0.31	0.60	7.83	0.82	2.39	5.15	15.16	3.00	13.93	0.97	0.84	15.21	0.47	0.07	..	7.04	1.05	1.39	3.93
European Community	EEC	66.09	56.58	21.21	59.38	42.68	83.76	70.33	38.79	31.55	56.59	75.16	72.08	42.29	15.94	30.98	..	61.53	75.80	75.89	76.45
North America	NNA	11.75	20.23	0.38	8.34	0.43	0.00	10.21	15.29	4.38	0.05	16.14	4.88	11.06	17.82	43.09	..	6.82	2.46	2.15	3.53
Rest of World	ROW	21.94	23.17	78.28	25.15	56.86	16.21	19.41	42.71	63.93	29.66	7.46	22.98	36.51	66.15	25.92	..	25.45	11.60	21.06	19.85
World	WLD	100.00	100.00	100.00	100.00	100.00	100.00	100.00	100.00	100.00	100.00	100.00	100.00	100.00	100.00	100.00	..	100.00	100.00	100.00	100.00

Note: ** means "not applicable."

(Table continues on the following page)

External Sector

Table 5-49. Direction of trade matrix, imports, 1997

Exporters		*Importers* SLE	SOM	ZAF	SDN	TZA	TGO	TUN	UGA	ZMB	ZWE	*Percentage of total imports* SSA	EEC	NNA	ROW	WLD
Algeria	DZA	0.02	0.02	0.09	0.04	0.01	0.26	0.28	0.40	0.00	..	0.19	0.26	0.15	0.09	0.16
Angola	AGO	..	..	..	..	..	..	..	..	..		..	..	..	..	..
Benin	BEN	..	..	..	..	..	..	..	..	..		..	..	..	..	..
Burkina Faso	BFA	..	..	..	..		..	..	..	..		..	..	..	..	..
Burundi	BDI	..	..	..	..	..	..	..	..	..		..	..	..	..	..
Cameroon	CMR	..	..	..	..	..	..	..	..	..		..	..	..	..	..
Cape Verde	CPV	..	..	..	..	..	..	..	..	..		..	..	..	..	..
Central African	CAF	..	..	..	..	..	..	..	..	..		..	..	..	..	..
Chad	TCD	..	..	..	..	..	..	..	..	..		..	..	..	..	..
Comoros	COM	..	..	..	..	..	..	..	..	..		..	..	..	..	..
Congo, Dem. Rep	ZAR	0.19	0.00	0.00	0.12	0.64	7.25	0.13	0.12	4.11	..	1.12	0.60	0.41	0.62	0.58
Congo, Rep.	COG	..	..	..	..	..	..	..	..	..		..	..	..	..	..
Côte d'Ivoire	CIV	..	..	..	..	..	..	..	..	..		..	..	..	..	..
Djibouti	DJI	..	..	..	..	..	..	..	..	..		..	..	..	..	..
Egypt, Arab Rep	EGY	0.01	0.45	0.06	5.29	0.25	0.00	0.25	0.15	0.00	..	0.30	0.26	0.20	0.25	0.25
Equatorial Guinea	GNQ	..	..	..	..	..	..	..	..	..		..	..	..	..	..
Ethiopia	ETH	..	..	..	..	..	..	..	..	..		..	..	..	..	..
Gabon	GAB	..	..	..	..	..	..	..	..	..		..	..	..	..	..
Gambia, The	GMB	..	..	..	..	..	..	..	..	..		..	..	..	..	..
Ghana	GHA	..	..	..	..	..	..	..	..	..		..	..	..	..	..
Guinea	GIN	..	..	..	..	..	..	..	..	..		..	..	..	..	..
Guinea-Bissau	GNB	..	..	..	..	..	..	..	..	..		..	..	..	..	..
Kenya	KEN	0.00	0.02	1.55	1.36	2.23	0.00	0.00	1.35	0.28	..	0.22	0.06	0.03	0.08	0.06
Liberia	LBR	..	..	..	..	..	..	..	..	..		..	..	..	..	..
Libya	LBY	0.00	0.50	0.00	0.00	0.00	0.00	3.96	0.00	0.00	..	0.01	0.16	0.02	0.09	0.10
Madagascar	MDG	0.00	0.00	0.23	0.00	0.08	0.00	0.00	0.00	0.00	..	0.02	0.01	0.00	0.01	0.01
Malawi	MWI	..	..	..	..	..	..	..	..	..		..	..	..	..	..
Mali	MLI	..	..	..	..	..	..	..	..	..		..	..	..	..	..
Mauritania	MRT	..	..	..	..	..	..	..	..	..		..	..	..	..	..
Mauritius	MUS	0.01	0.00	1.15	0.22	0.14	0.05	0.00	0.00	0.16	..	0.14	0.04	0.01	0.06	0.04
Morocco	MAR	0.88	0.00	0.36	0.01	0.08	0.56	0.69	0.03	0.00	..	0.66	0.22	0.07	0.11	0.15
Mozambique	MOZ	..	..	..	..	..	..	..	..	..		..	..	..	..	..
Niger	NER	..	..	..	..	..	..	..	..	..		..	..	..	..	..
Nigeria	NGA	0.31	0.00	0.18	0.01	0.00	0.97	0.00	0.00	0.02	..	0.29	0.14	0.12	0.10	0.12
Reunion	REU	..	..	..	..	..	..	..	..	..		..	..	..	..	..
Rwanda	RWA	..	..	..	..	..	..	..	..	..		..	..	..	..	..
São Tomé and Principe	STP	..	..	..	..	..	..	..	..	..		..	..	..	..	..
Senegal	SEN	..	..	..	..	..	..	..	..	..		..	..	..	..	..
Seychelles	SYC	..	..	..	..	..	..	..	..	..		..	..	..	..	..
Sierra Leone	SLE	**	..	..	..	..	..	..	..	..		..	..	..	..	..
Somalia	SOM	..	**	..	..	..	..	..	..	..		..	..	..	..	..
South Africa	ZAF	..	..	**	..	..	..	..	..	..		..	..	..	..	..
Sudan	SDN	..	..	..	**	..	..	..	..	..		..	..	..	..	..
Tanzania	TZA	0.01	0.04	0.00	0.99	**	0.00	0.00	0.21	0.00	..	0.12	0.30	0.04	0.07	0.15
Togo	TGO	..	..	..	..	..	**	..	..	..		..	..	..	..	..
Tunisia	TUN	..	..	..	..	..	..	**	..	..		..	..	..	..	..
Uganda	UGA	0.00	0.09	0.44	0.01	0.00	0.01	0.00	**	0.46	..	0.24	0.02	0.01	0.03	0.02
Zambia	ZMB	..	..	..	..	..	..	..	..	**		..	..	..	..	..
Zimbabwe	ZWE	..	..	..	..	..	..	..	..	..	**	..	..	..	..	..
Sub-Saharan Africa	SSA	0.52	0.15	3.55	2.70	3.10	8.29	0.14	2.59	5.04	..	2.15	1.17	0.61	0.97	0.99
European Community	EEC	81.71	63.89	35.64	44.63	40.34	23.82	85.36	68.67	26.89	..	41.23	62.05	19.16	24.09	36.94
North America	NNA	12.57	0.94	13.14	3.03	4.55	15.94	1.32	7.86	8.86	..	29.51	9.54	32.35	24.27	20.48
Rest of World	ROW	5.41	35.06	44.04	50.96	50.55	59.25	13.32	21.19	60.54	..	28.28	28.16	48.32	51.35	42.32
World	WLD	100.00	100.00	100.00	100.00	100.00	100.00	100.00	100.00	100.00	..	100.00	100.00	100.00	100.00	100.00

Note: ** means "not applicable."

5-50. Direction of trade matrix, exports, 1987

Exporters		DZA	AGO	BEN	BFA	BDI	CMR	CPV	CAF	TCD	COM	ZAR	COG	CIV	DJI	EGY	GNQ	ETH	GAB	GMB	GHA
		Importers															*Percentage of total exports*				
Algeria	DZA	**	0.00	0.00	0.00	0.00	0.00	0.00	0.00	0.00	0.00	0.00	0.00	0.00	0.00	0.00	0.00	0.00	0.00	0.00	0.00
Angola	AGO	..	**	..	..	..	..	..	..	..	..	..	..	..	..	..	..	..	..	..	..
Benin	BEN	..	..	**	..	..	..	..	..	..	..	..	..	..	..	..	..	..	..	..	..
Burkina Faso	BFA	..	..	..	**	..	..	..	..	..	..	..	..	..	..	..	..	..	..	..	..
Burundi	BDI	..	..	..	..	**	..	..	..	..	..	..	..	..	..	..	..	..	..	..	..
Cameroon	CMR	0.06	0.01	0.04	0.00	0.00	**	0.00	1.50	2.18	0.00	0.01	2.16	0.71	0.00	0.03	1.14	0.00	5.75	0.00	0.04
Cape Verde	CPV	..	..	..	..	..	..	**	..	..	..	..	..	..	..	..	..	..	..	..	..
Central African	CAF	..	..	..	..	..	..	..	**	..	..	..	..	..	..	..	..	..	..	..	..
Chad	TCD	0.00	0.00	0.00	0.00	0.00	0.00	0.00	0.00	**	0.00	0.00	0.03	0.00	0.00	0.00	0.00	0.00	0.00	0.00	0.00
Comoros	COM	..	..	..	..	..	..	..	..	..	**	..	..	..	..	..	..	..	..	..	..
Congo, Dem. Rep	ZAR	..	..	..	..	..	..	..	..	..	..	**	..	..	..	..	..	..	..	..	..
Congo, Rep.	COG	..	..	..	..	..	..	..	..	..	..	..	**	..	..	..	..	..	..	..	..
Côte d'Ivoire	CIV	..	..	..	..	..	..	..	..	..	..	..	..	**	..	..	..	..	..	..	..
Djibouti	DJI	0.00	0.00	0.02	0.00	0.00	0.00	0.00	0.00	0.00	0.00	0.00	0.00	0.05	**	0.05	0.00	5.44	0.00	0.00	0.00
Egypt, Arab Rep	EGY	0.18	0.00	0.00	0.00	0.00	0.00	0.00	0.00	0.00	0.00	0.00	0.00	0.00	0.00	**	0.00	0.01	0.00	0.00	0.00
Equatorial Guinea	GNQ	..	..	..	..	..	..	..	..	..	..	..	..	..	..	..	**	..	..	..	..
Ethiopia	ETH	0.41	0.00	0.00	0.00	0.00	0.00	0.00	0.00	0.00	0.00	0.00	0.00	0.00	8.47	0.00	0.00	**	0.00	0.00	0.00
Gabon	GAB	..	..	..	..	..	..	..	..	..	..	..	..	..	..	..	..	..	**	..	..
Gambia, The	GMB	..	..	..	..	..	..	..	..	..	..	..	..	..	..	..	..	..	..	**	..
Ghana	GHA	..	..	..	..	..	..	..	..	..	..	..	..	..	..	..	..	..	..	..	**
Guinea	GIN	..	..	..	..	..	..	..	..	..	..	..	..	..	..	..	..	..	..	..	..
Guinea-Bissau	GNB	..	..	..	..	..	..	..	..	..	..	..	..	..	..	..	..	..	..	..	..
Kenya	KEN	0.00	0.51	0.00	0.00	1.50	0.01	0.00	0.00	0.00	0.12	1.37	0.03	0.06	0.19	0.86	0.00	0.96	0.00	0.00	0.00
Liberia	LBR	..	..	..	..	..	..	..	..	..	..	..	..	..	..	..	..	..	..	..	..
Libya	LBY	0.02	0.00	0.00	0.00	0.00	0.00	0.00	0.00	0.00	0.00	0.00	0.00	0.01	0.00	0.00	0.00	0.00	0.00	0.00	0.00
Madagascar	MDG	..	..	..	..	..	..	..	..	..	..	..	..	..	..	..	..	..	..	..	..
Malawi	MWI	0.00	0.02	0.06	0.00	0.18	0.04	0.00	0.00	0.00	0.00	1.47	0.00	0.01	0.00	0.57	0.00	0.00	0.05	0.45	0.00
Mali	MLI	0.27	0.00	0.01	0.54	0.00	0.02	0.00	0.00	0.04	0.00	0.00	0.00	58.50	0.00	0.00	0.00	0.00	0.00	0.00	0.00
Mauritania	MRT	..	..	..	..	..	..	..	..	..	..	..	..	..	..	..	..	..	..	..	..
Mauritius	MUS	0.00	0.00	0.00	0.00	0.00	0.00	0.00	0.00	0.00	0.00	0.00	0.00	0.00	0.00	0.00	0.00	0.00	0.00	0.00	0.00
Morocco	MAR	0.00	0.02	0.05	0.01	0.00	0.36	0.00	0.03	0.00	0.00	0.16	0.12	0.35	0.00	0.20	0.00	0.00	0.20	0.00	0.00
Mozambique	MOZ	..	..	..	..	..	..	..	..	..	..	..	..	..	..	..	..	..	..	..	..
Niger	NER	..	..	..	..	..	..	..	..	..	..	..	..	..	..	..	..	..	..	..	..
Nigeria	NGA	0.00	0.00	0.04	0.00	0.00	0.06	0.00	0.00	0.04	0.00	0.23	0.06	2.96	0.00	0.00	0.00	0.00	0.13	0.00	1.44
Reunion	REU	0.00	0.00	0.00	0.00	0.00	0.00	0.00	0.00	0.00	3.65	0.00	0.00	0.00	0.02	0.00	0.00	0.00	0.00	0.00	0.00
Rwanda	RWA	..	..	..	..	..	..	..	..	..	..	..	..	..	..	..	..	..	..	..	..
São Tomé and Principe	STP	..	..	..	..	..	..	..	..	..	..	..	..	..	..	..	..	..	..	..	..
Senegal	SEN	0.03	0.00	0.56	0.53	0.00	2.65	0.00	0.03	0.06	0.00	0.15	0.48	3.83	0.00	0.00	0.00	0.00	0.20	0.70	0.02
Seychelles	SYC	..	..	..	..	..	..	..	..	..	..	..	..	..	..	..	..	..	..	..	..
Sierra Leone	SLE	..	..	..	..	..	..	..	..	..	..	..	..	..	..	..	..	..	..	..	..
Somalia	SOM	..	..	..	..	..	..	..	..	..	..	..	..	..	..	..	..	..	..	..	..
South Africa	ZAF	..	..	..	..	..	..	..	..	..	..	..	..	..	..	..	..	..	..	..	..
Sudan	SDN	..	..	..	..	..	..	..	..	..	..	..	..	..	..	..	..	..	..	..	..
Tanzania	TZA	3.13	0.02	0.00	0.00	0.30	0.00	0.00	0.00	0.00	0.00	0.38	0.00	0.06	0.00	0.75	0.00	0.31	0.00	0.00	0.00
Togo	TGO	..	..	..	..	..	..	..	..	..	..	..	..	..	..	..	..	..	..	..	..
Tunisia	TUN	3.12	0.01	0.06	0.01	0.00	0.34	0.00	0.00	0.00	0.00	0.00	0.02	0.08	0.00	0.04	0.00	0.00	0.03	0.00	0.00
Uganda	UGA	..	..	..	..	..	..	..	..	..	..	..	..	..	..	..	..	..	..	..	..
Zambia	ZMB	..	..	..	..	..	..	..	..	..	..	..	..	..	..	..	..	..	..	..	..
Zimbabwe	ZWE	..	..	..	..	..	..	..	..	..	..	..	..	..	..	..	..	..	..	..	..
Sub-Saharan Africa	SSA	0.10	0.04	0.06	0.03	0.13	0.17	0.00	0.11	0.18	0.05	0.30	0.21	2.70	0.28	0.10	0.08	0.10	0.49	0.05	0.90
European Community	EEC	0.45	0.06	0.02	0.02	0.01	0.10	0.01	0.01	0.01	0.01	0.08	0.03	0.11	0.01	0.45	0.00	0.05	0.05	0.01	0.05
North America	NNA	0.17	0.03	0.01	0.00	0.00	0.02	0.00	0.00	0.00	0.01	0.03	0.00	0.03	0.00	0.47	0.00	0.05	0.02	0.00	0.04
Rest of World	ROW	0.13	0.05	0.02	0.00	0.00	0.04	0.00	0.00	0.00	0.00	0.03	0.01	0.05	0.01	0.30	0.00	0.03	0.01	0.00	0.02
World	WLD	0.29	0.05	0.02	0.01	0.01	0.07	0.00	0.00	0.01	0.00	0.05	0.02	0.09	0.01	0.40	0.00	0.04	0.03	0.01	0.04

Note: ** means "not applicable."

(Table continues on the following page)

5-50. Direction of trade matrix, exports, 1987 (continued)

Exporters		GIN	GNB	KEN	LBR	LBY	MDG	MWI	MLI	MRT	MUS	MAR	MOZ	NER	NGA	REU	RWA	STP	SEN	SYC	SLE
		Importers								*Percentage of total exports*											
Algeria	DZA	0.00	0.00	0.00	0.00	0.21	0.00	0.00	0.01	0.56	0.00	0.00	0.00	0.00	0.00	0.00	0.00	0.00	0.06	0.00	0.00
Angola	AGO	..	..	..	..	..	..	..	..	..	..	..	..	..	..	..	..	..	..	..	..
Benin	BEN	..	..	..	..	..	..	..	..	..	..	..	..	..	..	..	..	..	..	..	..
Burkina Faso	BFA	..	..	..	..	..	..	..	..	..	..	..	..	..	..	..	..	..	..	..	..
Burundi	BDI	..	..	..	..	..	..	..	..	..	..	..	..	..	..	..	..	..	..	..	..
Cameroon	CMR	0.37	0.00	0.00	0.00	0.00	0.00	0.00	0.00	0.00	0.00	0.02	0.07	0.03	3.13	0.00	0.00	0.00	0.30	0.00	0.01
Cape Verde	CPV	..	..	..	..	..	..	..	..	..	..	..	..	..	..	..	..	..	..	..	..
Central African	CAF	..	..	..	..	..	..	..	..	..	..	..	..	..	..	..	..	..	..	..	..
Chad	TCD	0.00	0.00	0.00	0.00	0.00	0.00	0.00	0.00	0.00	0.36	0.00	0.00	0.00	0.00	10.17	0.00	0.00	0.00	0.00	0.00
Comoros	COM	..	..	..	..	..	..	/	..	..	..	..	..	..	..	..	..	..	..	..	..
Congo, Dem. Rep	ZAR	..	..	..	..	..	..	..	..	..	..	..	..	..	..	..	..	..	..	..	..
Congo, Rep.	COG	..	..	..	..	..	..	..	..	..	..	..	..	..	..	..	..	..	..	..	..
Côte d'Ivoire	CIV	..	..	..	..	..	..	..	..	..	..	..	..	..	..	..	..	..	..	..	..
Djibouti	DJI	0.00	0.00	0.07	0.00	0.00	0.29	0.00	0.00	0.00	0.00	0.00	0.00	0.00	0.00	0.35	0.00	0.00	0.01	0.01	0.00
Egypt, Arab Rep	EGY	0.00	0.00	0.00	0.00	0.01	0.00	0.00	0.00	0.00	0.00	0.23	0.02	0.00	0.02	0.00	0.00	0.00	0.00	0.00	0.00
Equatorial Guinea	GNQ	..	..	..	..	..	..	..	..	..	..	..	..	..	..	..	..	..	..	..	..
Ethiopia	ETH	0.00	0.00	0.20	0.00	0.00	0.00	0.00	0.00	0.00	0.04	0.00	0.00	0.00	0.00	0.00	0.00	0.00	0.00	0.00	0.00
Gabon	GAB	..	..	..	..	..	..	..	..	..	..	..	..	..	..	..	..	..	..	..	..
Gambia, The	GMB	..	..	..	..	..	..	..	..	..	..	..	..	..	..	..	..	..	..	..	..
Ghana	GHA	..	..	..	..	..	..	..	..	..	..	..	..	..	..	..	..	..	..	..	..
Guinea	GIN	**	..	..	..	..	..	..	..	..	..	..	..	..	..	..	..	..	..	..	..
Guinea-Bissau	GNB	..	**	..	..	..	..	..	..	..	..	..	..	..	..	..	..	..	..	..	..
Kenya	KEN	0.01	0.00	**	0.00	0.03	0.04	0.05	0.00	0.02	0.28	0.02	1.36	0.01	0.12	0.41	3.05	0.00	0.00	0.11	0.00
Liberia	LBR	..	..	..	**	..	..	..	..	..	..	..	..	..	..	..	..	..	..	..	..
Libya	LBY	0.00	0.00	0.00	0.00	**	0.00	0.00	0.00	0.00	0.00	0.59	0.00	0.00	0.00	0.00	0.00	0.00	0.00	0.00	0.00
Madagascar	MDG	..	..	..	..	..	**	..	..	..	..	..	..	..	..	..	..	..	..	..	..
Malawi	MWI	0.05	0.00	0.04	0.15	0.00	0.00	**	0.00	0.00	0.07	0.00	0.70	0.00	0.00	0.00	0.01	0.00	0.01	0.00	0.01
Mali	MLI	0.07	0.00	0.00	0.08	0.01	0.00	0.00	**	0.18	0.00	0.00	0.00	0.17	0.00	0.00	0.00	0.00	37.59	0.00	0.00
Mauritania	MRT	..	..	..	..	..	..	..	..	**	..	..	..	..	..	..	..	..	..	..	..
Mauritius	MUS	0.00	0.00	0.00	0.00	0.00	0.00	0.00	0.00	0.00	**	0.00	0.00	0.00	0.00	0.33	0.00	0.00	0.00	0.00	0.00
Morocco	MAR	0.17	0.00	0.00	0.03	3.25	0.00	0.00	0.06	0.07	0.04	**	0.00	0.01	0.15	0.06	0.00	0.00	0.42	0.00	0.00
Mozambique	MOZ	..	..	..	..	..	..	..	..	..	..	..	**	..	..	..	..	..	..	..	..
Niger	NER	..	..	..	..	..	..	..	..	..	..	..	..	**	..	..	..	..	..	..	..
Nigeria	NGA	0.01	0.00	0.00	0.03	0.00	0.00	0.00	0.01	0.00	0.00	0.01	0.00	0.07	**	0.00	0.00	0.00	0.54	0.00	0.42
Reunion	REU	0.00	0.00	0.00	0.00	0.00	2.29	0.00	0.00	0.00	0.84	0.00	0.00	0.00	0.00	**	0.00	0.00	0.00	0.10	0.00
Rwanda	RWA	..	..	..	..	..	..	..	..	..	..	..	..	..	..	..	**	..	..	..	..
São Tomé and Principe	STP	..	..	..	..	..	..	..	..	..	..	..	..	..	..	..	..	**	..	..	..
Senegal	SEN	1.06	0.37	0.03	0.01	0.00	0.00	0.00	2.94	3.83	0.00	0.11	0.00	0.23	0.33	0.03	0.00	0.00	**	0.00	0.03
Seychelles	SYC	..	..	..	..	..	..	..	..	..	..	..	..	..	..	..	..	..	..	**	..
Sierra Leone	SLE	..	..	..	..	..	..	..	..	..	..	..	..	..	..	..	..	..	..	..	**
Somalia	SOM	..	..	..	..	..	..	..	..	..	..	..	..	..	..	..	..	..	..	..	..
South Africa	ZAF	..	..	..	..	..	..	..	..	..	..	..	..	..	..	..	..	..	..	..	..
Sudan	SDN	..	..	..	..	..	..	..	..	..	..	..	..	..	..	..	..	..	..	..	..
Tanzania	TZA	0.00	0.00	2.81	0.00	0.00	0.00	0.12	0.00	0.00	0.03	0.00	1.31	0.00	0.01	0.00	0.08	0.00	0.00	0.00	0.00
Togo	TGO	..	..	..	..	..	..	..	..	..	..	..	..	..	..	..	..	..	..	..	..
Tunisia	TUN	0.03	0.00	0.00	0.00	0.36	0.00	0.00	0.00	0.00	0.00	0.79	0.00	0.00	0.00	0.00	0.00	0.00	0.15	0.00	0.01
Uganda	UGA	..	..	..	..	..	..	..	..	..	..	..	..	..	..	..	..	..	..	..	..
Zambia	ZMB	..	..	..	..	..	..	..	..	..	..	..	..	..	..	..	..	..	..	..	..
Zimbabwe	ZWE	..	..	..	..	..	..	..	..	..	..	..	..	..	..	..	..	..	..	..	..
Sub-Saharan Africa	SSA	0.09	0.02	0.08	0.02	0.00	0.03	0.01	0.16	0.20	0.04	0.01	0.16	0.06	0.24	0.07	0.24	0.00	0.75	0.01	0.26
European Community	EEC	0.03	0.00	0.08	0.04	0.27	0.02	0.01	0.02	0.03	0.03	0.26	0.03	0.02	0.27	0.10	0.01	0.00	0.06	0.00	0.01
North America	NNA	0.01	0.01	0.03	0.02	0.01	0.01	0.00	0.00	0.00	0.01	0.15	0.02	0.00	0.09	0.00	0.00	0.00	0.02	0.00	0.01
Rest of World	ROW	0.01	0.00	0.06	0.20	0.19	0.01	0.00	0.00	0.01	0.05	0.06	0.02	0.01	0.15	0.01	0.01	0.00	0.02	0.00	0.00
World	WLD	0.02	0.00	0.06	0.10	0.20	0.01	0.01	0.01	0.02	0.03	0.17	0.03	0.01	0.20	0.05	0.01	0.00	0.04	0.00	0.01

Note: ** means "not applicable."

(Table continues on the following page)

5-50. Direction of trade matrix, exports, 1987

Exporters		SOM	ZAF	SDN	TZA	TGO	TUN	UGA	ZMB	ZWE	SSA	EEC	NNA	ROW	WLD
		Importers					*Percentage of total exports*								
Algeria	DZA	0.00	0.00	0.00	0.00	0.00	0.89	0.00	0.00	..	0.64	72.31	19.42	8.20	100.00
Angola	AGO	..	..	..	..	..	..	..	..	..	..	..	..	..	..
Benin	BEN	..	..	..	..	..	..	..	..	..	..	..	..	..	..
Burkina Faso	BFA	..	..	..	..	..	..	..	..	..	..	..	..	..	..
Burundi	BDI	..	..	..	..	..	..	..	..	..	..	..	..	..	..
Cameroon	CMR	0.00	0.00	0.01	0.00	0.01	0.04	0.00	0.00	..	17.47	68.37	7.36	6.88	100.00
Cape Verde	CPV	..	..	..	..	..	..	..	..	..	..	..	..	..	..
Central African	CAF	..	..	..	..	..	..	..	..	..	..	..	..	..	..
Chad	TCD	0.00	0.27	0.00	0.00	0.00	0.00	0.00	0.00	..	0.40	70.61	0.44	28.92	100.00
Comoros	COM	..	..	..	..	..	..	..	..	..	..	..	..	..	..
Congo, Dem. Rep	ZAR	..	..	..	..	..	..	..	..	..	..	..	..	..	..
Congo, Rep.	COG	..	..	..	..	..	..	..	..	..	..	..	..	..	..
Côte d'Ivoire	CIV	..	..	..	..	..	..	..	..	..	..	..	..	..	..
Djibouti	DJI	9.40	0.00	0.01	0.01	0.00	0.02	0.00	0.00	..	9.87	59.10	0.39	25.50	100.00
Egypt, Arab Rep	EGY	0.00	0.00	2.81	0.00	0.00	0.39	0.01	0.00	..	2.89	39.46	8.42	49.25	100.00
Equatorial Guinea	GNQ	..	..	..	..	..	..	..	..	..	..	..	..	..	..
Ethiopia	ETH	0.00	0.00	0.10	0.00	0.00	0.00	0.01	0.00	..	8.83	39.25	18.35	33.62	100.00
Gabon	GAB	..	..	..	..	..	..	..	..	..	..	..	..	..	..
Gambia, The	GMB	..	..	..	..	..	..	..	..	..	..	..	..	..	..
Ghana	GHA	..	..	..	..	..	..	..	..	..	..	..	..	..	..
Guinea	GIN	..	..	..	..	..	..	..	..	..	..	..	..	..	..
Guinea-Bissau	GNB	..	..	..	..	..	..	..	..	..	..	..	..	..	..
Kenya	KEN	1.01	0.42	2.66	2.54	0.01	0.03	7.69	0.27	..	23.74	45.92	6.39	24.74	100.00
Liberia	LBR	..	..	..	..	..	..	..	..	..	..	..	..	..	..
Libya	LBY	0.00	0.00	0.00	0.00	0.00	0.00	0.00	0.00	..	0.01	80.65	0.00	19.34	100.00
Madagascar	MDG	..	..	..	..	..	..	..	..	..	..	..	..	..	..
Malawi	MWI	0.00	11.13	0.00	0.14	0.00	0.00	0.01	0.44	..	5.31	55.59	11.03	28.97	100.00
Mali	MLI	0.00	0.00	0.00	0.00	0.00	0.00	0.00	0.00	..	97.21	1.46	0.04	1.55	100.00
Mauritania	MRT	..	..	..	..	..	..	..	..	..	..	..	..	..	..
Mauritius	MUS	0.00	0.04	0.00	0.00	0.00	0.00	0.00	0.00	..	0.00	67.74	14.69	17.57	100.00
Morocco	MAR	0.00	0.00	0.00	0.04	0.09	1.03	0.00	0.00	..	2.40	62.93	2.16	32.71	100.00
Mozambique	MOZ	..	..	..	..	..	..	..	..	..	..	..	..	..	..
Niger	NER	..	..	..	..	..	..	..	..	..	..	..	..	..	..
Nigeria	NGA	0.00	0.02	0.00	0.00	0.01	0.02	0.00	0.00	..	6.04	41.94	49.33	2.73	100.00
Reunion	REU	0.00	0.07	0.00	0.00	0.00	0.00	0.00	0.00	..	6.89	89.31	0.17	6.75	100.00
Rwanda	RWA	..	..	..	..	..	..	..	..	..	..	..	..	..	..
São Tomé and Principe	STP	..	..	..	..	..	..	..	..	..	..	..	..	..	..
Senegal	SEN	0.00	0.00	0.00	0.00	0.44	0.26	0.00	0.00	..	18.48	45.09	0.37	42.84	100.00
Seychelles	SYC	..	..	..	..	..	..	..	..	..	..	..	..	..	..
Sierra Leone	SLE	..	..	..	..	..	..	..	..	..	..	..	..	..	..
Somalia	SOM	**	..	..	..	..	..	..	..	..	..	..	..	..	..
South Africa	ZAF	..	**	..	..	..	..	..	..	..	..	..	..	..	..
Sudan	SDN	..	..	**	..	..	..	..	..	..	..	..	..	..	..
Tanzania	TZA	0.08	0.16	0.25	**	0.00	0.00	0.95	0.58	..	7.16	53.43	2.47	38.09	100.00
Togo	TGO	..	..	..	..	**	..	..	..	..	..	..	..	..	..
Tunisia	TUN	0.00	0.00	0.00	0.01	0.04	**	0.00	0.18	..	0.98	78.42	1.90	18.70	100.00
Uganda	UGA	..	..	..	..	..	..	**	..	..	..	..	..	..	..
Zambia	ZMB	..	..	..	..	..	..	..	**	..	..	..	..	..	..
Zimbabwe	ZWE	..	..	..	..	..	..	..	..	**	..	..	..	..	..
Sub-Saharan Africa	SSA	0.10	0.31	0.22	0.20	0.03	0.03	0.62	0.05	0.00	9.44	46.98	33.66	10.44	100.00
European Community	EEC	0.03	0.58	0.05	0.05	0.03	0.20	0.02	0.03	..	1.47	64.19	9.70	24.77	100.00
North America	NNA	0.01	0.41	0.05	0.02	0.01	0.05	0.01	0.01	..	0.54	19.84	37.82	41.81	100.00
Rest of World	ROW	0.01	0.42	0.04	0.03	0.02	0.04	0.02	0.01	..	0.94	24.58	27.76	46.98	100.00
World	WLD	0.02	0.49	0.05	0.04	0.02	0.12	0.02	0.02	..	1.17	42.82	20.75	35.42	100.00

Note: ** means "not applicable."

5-51. Direction of trade matrix, exports, 1991

Exporters		*Importers* DZA	AGO	BEN	BFA	BDI	CMR	CPV	CAF	TCD	COM	ZAR	COG	CIV	DJI	EGY	GNQ	ETH	GAB	GMB	GHA *Percentage of total exports*
Algeria	DZA	**	0.00	0.00	0.00	0.00	0.00	0.00	0.00	0.00	0.00	0.00	0.00	0.00	0.00	0.09	0.00	0.00	0.00	0.00	0.00
Angola	AGO	0.00	**	0.00	0.00	0.00	0.26	0.00	0.00	0.00	0.00	0.03	0.00	0.00	0.00	0.00	0.00	0.00	0.00	0.00	0.00
Benin	BEN	..	..	**	..	..	..	..	..	..	..	..	..	..	..	..	..	..	..	..	..
Burkina Faso	BFA	..	..	..	**	..	..	..	..	..	..	..	..	..	..	..	..	..	..	..	..
Burundi	BDI	..	..	..	..	**	..	..	..	..	..	..	..	..	..	..	..	..	..	..	..
Cameroon	CMR	..	..	..	..	..	**	..	..	..	..	..	..	..	..	..	..	..	..	..	..
Cape Verde	CPV	..	..	..	..	..	..	**	..	..	..	..	..	..	..	..	..	..	..	..	..
Central African	CAF	..	..	..	..	..	..	..	**	..	..	..	..	..	..	..	..	..	..	..	..
Chad	TCD	0.00	0.00	0.00	0.00	0.00	0.00	0.00	0.00	**	0.25	0.00	0.00	0.00	0.00	0.00	0.00	0.00	0.00	0.00	0.00
Comoros	COM	..	..	..	..	..	..	..	..	..	**	..	..	..	..	..	..	..	..	..	..
Congo, Dem. Rep	ZAR	..	..	..	..	..	..	..	..	..	..	**	..	..	..	..	..	..	..	..	..
Congo, Rep.	COG	..	..	..	..	..	..	..	..	..	..	..	**	..	..	..	..	..	..	..	..
Côte d'Ivoire	CIV	..	..	..	..	..	..	..	..	..	..	..	..	**	..	..	..	..	..	..	..
Djibouti	DJI	0.02	0.00	0.00	0.13	0.02	0.00	0.00	0.00	0.00	0.14	0.00	0.06	0.05	**	0.01	0.00	1.78	0.00	0.00	0.00
Egypt, Arab Rep	EGY	0.20	0.00	0.00	0.00	0.00	0.00	0.00	0.00	0.00	0.00	0.00	0.00	0.02	0.05	**	0.00	0.05	0.00	0.00	0.01
Equatorial Guinea	GNQ	..	..	..	..	..	..	..	..	..	..	..	..	..	..	..	**	..	..	..	..
Ethiopia	ETH	0.00	0.00	0.00	0.00	0.00	0.00	0.00	0.00	0.00	0.00	0.00	0.00	0.00	4.36	0.00	0.00	**	0.00	0.00	0.00
Gabon	GAB	..	..	..	..	..	..	..	..	..	..	..	..	..	..	..	..	..	**	..	..
Gambia, The	GMB	..	..	..	..	..	..	..	..	..	..	..	..	..	..	..	..	..	..	**	..
Ghana	GHA	..	..	..	..	..	..	..	..	..	..	..	..	..	..	..	..	..	..	..	**
Guinea	GIN	..	..	..	..	..	..	..	..	..	..	..	..	..	..	..	..	..	..	..	..
Guinea-Bissau	GNB	..	..	..	..	..	..	..	..	..	..	..	..	..	..	..	..	..	..	..	..
Kenya	KEN	0.02	0.00	0.00	0.01	0.92	0.05	0.03	0.00	0.00	0.38	1.01	0.00	0.04	0.30	2.96	0.00	0.86	0.00	0.00	0.02
Liberia	LBR	..	..	..	..	..	..	..	..	..	..	..	..	..	..	..	..	..	..	..	..
Libya	LBY	0.01	0.00	0.00	0.00	0.00	0.00	0.00	0.00	0.00	0.00	0.00	0.00	0.00	0.00	0.17	0.00	0.00	0.00	0.00	0.00
Madagascar	MDG	0.14	0.00	0.00	0.00	0.00	0.00	0.00	0.00	0.00	0.60	0.01	0.05	0.01	0.01	0.03	0.00	0.01	0.02	0.00	0.00
Malawi	MWI	0.02	0.06	0.00	0.00	0.42	0.01	0.00	0.00	0.00	0.00	0.19	0.00	0.00	0.00	0.80	0.00	0.00	0.04	0.00	0.00
Mali	MLI	..	..	..	..	..	..	..	..	..	..	..	..	..	..	..	..	..	..	..	..
Mauritania	MRT	..	..	..	..	..	..	..	..	..	..	..	..	..	..	..	..	..	..	..	..
Mauritius	MUS	0.00	0.00	0.00	0.00	0.05	0.00	0.00	0.00	0.00	0.14	0.00	0.01	0.06	0.00	0.01	0.00	0.00	0.01	0.00	0.00
Morocco	MAR	1.72	0.12	0.05	0.01	0.00	0.17	0.00	0.01	0.00	0.01	0.08	0.11	0.17	0.00	0.07	0.00	0.00	0.19	0.01	0.04
Mozambique	MOZ	..	..	..	..	..	..	..	..	..	..	..	..	..	..	..	..	..	..	..	..
Niger	NER	..	..	..	..	..	..	..	..	..	..	..	..	..	..	..	..	..	..	..	..
Nigeria	NGA	0.00	0.00	0.01	0.00	0.00	0.61	0.00	0.00	0.06	0.00	0.29	0.00	2.32	0.00	0.00	0.01	0.00	0.16	0.00	1.48
Reunion	REU	0.00	0.03	0.00	0.00	0.00	0.00	0.00	0.00	0.00	5.82	0.00	0.00	0.03	0.14	0.00	0.00	0.00	0.00	0.00	0.00
Rwanda	RWA	..	..	..	..	..	..	..	..	..	..	..	..	..	..	..	..	..	..	..	..
São Tomé and Principe	STP	..	..	..	..	..	..	..	..	..	..	..	..	..	..	..	..	..	..	..	..
Senegal	SEN	0.00	0.01	0.77	0.33	0.00	1.59	0.01	0.05	0.10	0.00	0.08	0.78	2.73	0.00	0.00	0.00	0.00	0.34	1.46	0.00
Seychelles	SYC	..	..	..	..	..	..	..	..	..	..	..	..	..	..	..	..	..	..	..	..
Sierra Leone	SLE	..	..	..	..	..	..	..	..	..	..	..	..	..	..	..	..	..	..	..	..
Somalia	SOM	..	..	..	..	..	..	..	..	..	..	..	..	..	..	..	..	..	..	..	..
South Africa	ZAF	0.00	0.00	0.00	0.00	0.00	0.00	0.00	0.00	0.00	0.00	0.00	0.00	0.00	0.00	0.00	0.00	0.00	0.00	0.00	0.00
Sudan	SDN	..	..	..	..	..	..	..	..	..	..	..	..	..	..	..	..	..	..	..	..
Tanzania	TZA	2.13	0.00	0.01	0.00	0.00	0.07	0.00	0.00	0.00	0.00	0.00	0.00	0.13	0.00	0.30	0.00	0.11	0.00	0.00	0.13
Togo	TGO	..	..	..	..	..	..	..	..	..	..	..	..	..	..	..	..	..	..	..	..
Tunisia	TUN	0.00	0.00	2.02	2.25	0.00	0.01	0.00	0.02	0.00	0.00	0.00	0.36	0.22	0.00	0.01	0.00	0.00	0.21	0.00	1.13
Uganda	UGA	..	..	..	..	..	..	..	..	..	..	..	..	..	..	..	..	..	..	..	..
Zambia	ZMB	..	..	..	..	..	..	..	..	..	..	..	..	..	..	..	..	..	..	..	..
Zimbabwe	ZWE	..	..	..	..	..	..	..	..	..	..	..	..	..	..	..	..	..	..	..	..
Sub-Saharan Africa	SSA	0.18	0.00	0.01	0.01	0.03	0.23	0.00	0.00	0.02	0.04	0.12	0.01	0.73	0.02	0.11	0.00	0.03	0.05	0.02	0.44
European Community	EEC	0.37	0.08	0.02	0.02	0.01	0.05	0.01	0.01	0.01	0.01	0.04	0.03	0.07	0.01	0.36	0.00	0.03	0.04	0.01	0.05
North America	NNA	0.18	0.04	0.01	0.01	0.00	0.01	0.00	0.00	0.00	0.00	0.01	0.01	0.02	0.00	0.53	0.00	0.04	0.02	0.00	0.03
Rest of World	ROW	0.11	0.03	0.01	0.00	0.00	0.01	0.00	0.00	0.00	0.00	0.01	0.01	0.03	0.01	0.24	0.00	0.01	0.01	0.01	0.03
World	WLD	0.24	0.05	0.01	0.01	0.00	0.03	0.00	0.00	0.00	0.00	0.02	0.02	0.06	0.01	0.34	0.00	0.02	0.02	0.01	0.04

Note: ** means "not applicable."

(Table continues on the following page)

5-51. Direction of trade matrix, exports, 1991 *(continued)*

Exporters		GIN	GNB	KEN	LBR	LBY	MDG	MWI	MLI	MRT	MUS	MAR	MOZ	NER	NGA	REU	RWA	STP	SEN	SYC	SLE
		Importers									*Percentage of total exports*										
Algeria	DZA	0.00	0.00	0.00	0.00	0.06	0.00	0.00	0.00	0.25	0.00	0.43	0.01	0.00	0.00	0.00	0.00	0.00	0.01	0.00	0.00
Angola	AGO	0.00	0.00	0.00	0.00	0.00	0.00	0.00	0.00	0.00	0.00	0.02	0.00	0.00	0.53	0.00	0.00	0.03	0.00	0.00	0.00
Benin	BEN	..	..	..	..	..	..	..	..	..	..	..	..	..	..	..	..	..	..	..	..
Burkina Faso	BFA	..	..	..	..	..	..	..	..	..	..	..	..	..	..	..	..	..	..	..	..
Burundi	BDI	..	..	..	..	..	..	..	..	..	..	..	..	..	..	..	..	..	..	..	..
Cameroon	CMR	..	..	..	..	..	..	..	..	..	..	..	..	..	..	..	..	..	..	..	..
Cape Verde	CPV	..	..	..	..	..	..	..	..	..	..	..	..	..	..	..	..	..	..	..	..
Central African	CAF	..	..	..	..	..	..	..	..	..	..	..	..	..	..	..	..	..	..	..	..
Chad	TCD	0.00	0.00	0.00	0.00	0.00	0.00	0.18	0.00	0.00	2.44	0.00	0.00	0.00	0.00	13.64	0.00	0.00	0.00	0.00	0.00
Comoros	COM	..	..	..	..	..	..	..	..	..	..	..	..	..	..	..	..	..	..	..	..
Congo, Dem. Rep	ZAR	..	..	..	..	..	..	..	..	..	..	..	..	..	..	..	..	..	..	..	..
Congo, Rep.	COG	..	..	..	..	..	..	..	..	..	..	..	..	..	..	..	..	..	..	..	..
Côte d'Ivoire	CIV	..	..	..	..	..	..	..	..	..	..	..	..	..	..	..	..	..	..	..	..
Djibouti	DJI	0.02	0.00	0.26	0.00	0.09	0.97	0.00	0.00	0.00	0.00	0.01	0.00	0.02	0.01	1.18	0.09	0.00	0.00	0.00	0.00
Egypt, Arab Rep	EGY	0.00	0.00	0.08	0.21	3.26	0.00	0.00	0.00	0.00	0.00	0.54	0.00	0.00	0.05	0.00	0.00	0.00	0.01	0.00	0.00
Equatorial Guinea	GNQ	..	..	..	..	..	..	..	..	..	..	..	..	..	..	..	..	..	..	..	..
Ethiopia	ETH	0.00	0.00	0.42	0.00	0.00	0.00	0.00	0.00	0.00	0.03	0.00	0.00	0.00	0.00	0.00	0.00	0.00	0.01	0.00	0.00
Gabon	GAB	..	..	..	..	..	..	..	..	..	..	..	..	..	..	..	..	..	..	..	..
Gambia, The	GMB	..	..	..	..	..	..	..	..	..	..	..	..	..	..	..	..	..	..	..	..
Ghana	GHA	..	..	..	..	..	..	..	..	..	..	..	..	..	..	..	..	..	..	..	..
Guinea	GIN	**																			
Guinea-Bissau	GNB	..	**																		
Kenya	KEN	0.01	0.00	**	0.00	0.00	0.09	0.13	0.00	0.00	0.40	0.02	0.14	0.00	0.19	0.35	1.83	0.00	0.00	0.07	0.02
Liberia	LBR	..	..	..	**																
Libya	LBY	0.00	0.00	0.00	0.00	**	0.00	0.00	0.00	0.00	0.00	1.09	0.00	0.00	0.00	0.00	0.00	0.00	0.00	0.00	0.00
Madagascar	MDG	0.00	0.00	0.12	0.00	0.00	**	0.00	0.00	0.00	3.00	0.05	0.09	0.00	0.06	5.19	0.00	0.00	0.01	0.11	0.00
Malawi	MWI	0.03	0.00	0.04	0.00	0.00	0.00	**	0.00	0.00	0.02	0.00	0.21	0.00	0.04	0.00	0.10	0.00	0.02	0.00	0.00
Mali	MLI	..	..	..	..	..	..	..	**												
Mauritania	MRT	..	..	..	..	..	..	..	..	**											
Mauritius	MUS	0.00	0.00	0.11	0.03	0.00	0.59	0.00	0.00	0.00	**	0.00	0.00	0.00	0.00	1.91	0.14	0.00	0.00	0.94	0.00
Morocco	MAR	0.15	0.00	0.00	0.00	4.59	0.01	0.00	0.12	0.13	0.04	**	0.01	0.01	0.30	0.05	0.00	0.00	0.12	0.00	0.01
Mozambique	MOZ	..	..	..	..	..	..	..	..	..	..	..	**								
Niger	NER	..	..	..	..	..	..	..	..	..	..	..	..	**							
Nigeria	NGA	0.10	0.00	0.02	0.01	0.00	0.00	0.00	0.00	0.00	0.00	0.04	0.00	0.02	**	0.00	0.00	0.00	0.00	0.00	0.05
Reunion	REU	0.00	0.00	0.00	0.00	0.00	3.53	0.00	0.00	0.00	2.36	0.00	0.00	0.00	0.00	**	0.00	0.00	0.00	0.21	0.00
Rwanda	RWA	..	..	..	..	..	..	..	..	..	..	..	..	..	..	..	**				
São Tomé and Principe	STP	..	..	..	..	..	..	..	..	..	..	..	..	..	..	..	..	**			
Senegal	SEN	0.83	0.43	0.00	0.01	0.00	0.01	0.00	3.71	0.00	0.00	0.03	0.33	0.02	0.18	0.00	0.00	0.00	**	0.00	0.06
Seychelles	SYC	..	..	..	..	..	..	..	..	..	..	..	..	..	..	..	..	..	..	**	
Sierra Leone	SLE	..	..	..	..	..	..	..	..	..	..	..	..	..	..	..	..	..	..	..	**
Somalia	SOM	..	..	..	..	..	..	..	..	..	..	..	..	..	..	..	..	..	..	..	..
South Africa	ZAF	0.00	0.00	0.00	0.00	0.00	0.00	0.00	0.00	0.00	0.00	0.00	0.00	0.00	0.00	0.00	0.00	0.00	0.00	0.00	0.00
Sudan	SDN	..	..	..	..	..	..	..	..	..	..	..	..	..	..	..	..	..	..	..	..
Tanzania	TZA	0.01	0.05	0.00	0.00	5.47	0.00	0.00	0.00	0.05	0.00	0.72	0.00	0.00	0.00	0.00	0.00	0.00	0.03	0.00	0.00
Togo	TGO	..	..	..	..	..	..	..	..	..	..	..	..	..	..	..	..	..	..	..	..
Tunisia	TUN	0.07	0.00	0.00	0.03	0.01	0.00	0.00	0.30	0.00	0.00	0.69	0.03	1.31	7.67	0.00	0.00	0.00	0.10	0.00	0.03
Uganda	UGA	..	..	..	..	..	..	..	..	..	..	..	..	..	..	..	..	..	..	..	..
Zambia	ZMB	..	..	..	..	..	..	..	..	..	..	..	..	..	..	..	..	..	..	..	..
Zimbabwe	ZWE	..	..	..	..	..	..	..	..	..	..	..	..	..	..	..	..	..	..	..	..
Sub-Saharan Africa	SSA	0.04	0.01	0.01	0.00	0.46	0.03	0.00	0.06	0.00	0.04	0.08	0.01	0.01	0.05	0.10	0.05	0.00	0.00	0.03	0.01
European Community	EEC	0.02	0.00	0.06	0.04	0.24	0.01	0.01	0.02	0.02	0.03	0.31	0.02	0.01	0.25	0.11	0.01	0.00	0.05	0.00	0.01
North America	NNA	0.02	0.00	0.02	0.01	0.01	0.00	0.01	0.00	0.01	0.00	0.11	0.02	0.00	0.16	0.00	0.00	0.00	0.02	0.00	0.00
Rest of World	ROW	0.01	0.00	0.05	0.32	0.14	0.01	0.01	0.00	0.01	0.04	0.09	0.02	0.00	0.15	0.01	0.00	0.00	0.02	0.00	0.00
World	WLD	0.02	0.00	0.05	0.14	0.16	0.01	0.01	0.01	0.01	0.03	0.19	0.02	0.01	0.20	0.05	0.00	0.00	0.03	0.00	0.01

Note: ** means "not applicable."

(Table continues on the following page)

5-51. Direction of trade matrix, exports, 1991

Exporters		SOM	ZAF	SDN	TZA	TGO	TUN	UGA	ZMB	ZWE	SSA	EEC	NNA	ROW	WLD
		Importers							*Percentage of total exports*						
Algeria	DZA	0.00	0.00	0.00	0.11	0.00	0.86	0.02	0.00	..	0.40	74.07	17.28	8.51	100.00
Angola	AGO	0.00	0.00	0.00	0.27	0.00	0.00	0.00	0.00	..	1.12	26.95	62.52	9.41	100.00
Benin	BEN	..	..	..	..	..	..	..	..	..	..	..	..	..	..
Burkina Faso	BFA	..	..	..	..	..	..	..	..	..	..	..	..	..	..
Burundi	BDI	..	..	..	..	..	..	..	..	..	..	..	..	..	..
Cameroon	CMR	..	..	..	..	..	..	..	..	..	..	..	..	..	..
Cape Verde	CPV	..	..	..	..	..	..	..	..	..	..	..	..	..	..
Central African	CAF	..	..	..	..	..	..	..	..	..	..	..	..	..	..
Chad	TCD	0.00	0.38	0.00	0.00	0.00	0.00	0.00	0.00	..	2.87	78.65	0.06	21.04	100.00
Comoros	COM	..	..	..	..	..	..	..	..	..	..	..	..	..	..
Congo, Dem. Rep	ZAR	..	..	..	..	..	..	..	..	..	..	..	..	..	..
Congo, Rep.	COG	..	..	..	..	..	..	..	..	..	..	..	..	..	..
Côte d'Ivoire	CIV	..	..	..	..	..	..	..	..	..	..	..	..	..	..
Djibouti	DJI	4.12	0.00	0.00	0.00	0.00	0.15	0.06	0.00	..	5.95	62.65	0.88	29.71	100.00
Egypt, Arab Rep	EGY	0.00	0.00	0.70	0.06	0.00	0.42	0.00	0.00	..	1.22	43.14	7.79	48.02	100.00
Equatorial Guinea	GNQ	..	..	..	..	..	..	..	..	..	..	..	..	..	..
Ethiopia	ETH	0.00	0.33	0.00	0.00	0.00	0.00	0.07	0.00	..	4.88	53.93	6.04	35.18	100.00
Gabon	GAB	..	..	..	..	..	..	..	..	..	..	..	..	..	..
Gambia, The	GMB	..	..	..	..	..	..	..	..	..	..	..	..	..	..
Ghana	GHA	..	..	..	..	..	..	..	..	..	..	..	..	..	..
Guinea	GIN	..	..	..	..	..	..	..	..	..	..	..	..	..	..
Guinea-Bissau	GNB	..	..	..	..	..	..	..	..	..	..	..	..	..	..
Kenya	KEN	1.11	0.31	1.81	3.27	0.00	0.09	6.64	0.23	..	19.08	40.76	4.17	35.90	100.00
Liberia	LBR	..	..	..	..	..	..	..	..	..	..	..	..	..	..
Libya	LBY	0.00	0.00	1.36	0.00	0.00	0.86	0.00	0.00	..	1.37	86.23	0.00	12.40	100.00
Madagascar	MDG	0.00	0.27	0.00	0.03	0.00	0.16	0.00	0.00	..	4.14	50.91	14.68	33.35	100.00
Malawi	MWI	0.00	8.83	0.00	0.42	0.00	0.00	0.01	0.59	..	2.82	47.29	15.16	34.95	100.00
Mali	MLI	..	..	..	..	..	..	..	..	..	..	..	..	..	..
Mauritania	MRT	..	..	..	..	..	..	..	..	..	..	..	..	..	..
Mauritius	MUS	0.00	0.42	0.00	0.02	0.00	0.00	0.03	0.11	..	2.54	77.63	12.09	8.36	100.00
Morocco	MAR	0.00	0.00	0.00	0.08	0.08	1.46	0.00	0.00	..	2.03	63.23	3.09	31.97	100.00
Mozambique	MOZ	..	..	..	..	..	..	..	..	..	..	..	..	..	..
Niger	NER	..	..	..	..	..	..	..	..	..	..	..	..	..	..
Nigeria	NGA	0.00	0.00	0.00	0.00	0.02	0.00	0.00	0.00	..	5.17	43.76	48.04	3.04	100.00
Reunion	REU	0.00	0.27	0.00	0.00	0.00	0.00	0.00	0.00	..	12.13	80.02	0.15	13.59	100.00
Rwanda	RWA	..	..	..	..	..	..	..	..	..	..	..	..	..	..
São Tomé and Principe	STP	..	..	..	..	..	..	..	..	..	..	..	..	..	..
Senegal	SEN	0.00	0.00	0.00	0.00	0.21	0.24	0.00	0.00	..	14.08	51.15	1.79	37.05	100.00
Seychelles	SYC	..	..	..	..	..	..	..	..	..	..	..	..	..	..
Sierra Leone	SLE	..	..	..	..	..	..	..	..	..	..	..	..	..	..
Somalia	SOM	**	..	..	..	..	..	..	..	..	..	..	..	..	..
South Africa	ZAF	0.00	**	0.00	0.00	0.00	0.00	0.00	0.00	..	0.00	0.00	0.00	100.00	100.00
Sudan	SDN	..	..	**	..	..	..	..	..	..	..	..	..	..	..
Tanzania	TZA	0.00	0.00	0.11	**	0.07	0.00	0.00	0.00	..	0.68	76.91	0.77	21.64	100.00
Togo	TGO	..	..	..	..	**	..	..	..	..	..	..	..	..	..
Tunisia	TUN	0.00	0.02	0.04	0.00	0.00	**	0.00	0.00	..	15.81	29.45	11.40	43.69	100.00
Uganda	UGA	..	..	..	..	..	..	**	..	..	..	..	..	..	..
Zambia	ZMB	..	..	..	..	..	..	..	**	..	..	..	..	..	..
Zimbabwe	ZWE	..	..	..	..	..	..	..	..	**	..	..	..	..	..
Sub-Saharan Africa	SSA	0.03	0.12	0.06	0.11	0.01	0.01	0.17	0.02	..	2.54	26.65	19.67	51.26	100.00
European Community	EEC	0.00	0.51	0.04	0.03	0.02	0.26	0.01	0.02	..	1.18	66.46	7.20	25.29	100.00
North America	NNA	0.00	0.43	0.02	0.01	0.00	0.04	0.00	0.00	..	0.50	21.45	33.11	44.96	100.00
Rest of World	ROW	0.00	0.28	0.04	0.03	0.02	0.06	0.01	0.01	..	0.93	24.91	23.17	51.39	100.00
World	WLD	0.00	0.41	0.04	0.03	0.02	0.15	0.01	0.01	..	1.01	43.58	17.55	38.08	100.00

Note: ** means "not applicable."

5-52. Direction of trade matrix, exports, 1997

Exporters		**Importers** DZA	AGO	BEN	BFA	BDI	CMR	CPV	CAF	TCD	COM	ZAR	COG	CIV	DJI	EGY	GNQ	ERI	ETH	GAB	*Percentage of total exports* GMB
Algeria	DZA	**	0.00	0.00	0.00	0.00	0.00	0.00	0.00	0.00	0.00	0.00	0.00	0.00	0.00	0.03	0.00	0.00	0.00	0.00	0.00
Angola	AGO	..	**	..	..	..	..	..	..	..	..	..	..	..	..	..	..	..	..	..	..
Benin	BEN	..	..	**	..	..	..	..	..	..	..	..	..	..	..	..	..	..	..	..	..
Burkina Faso	BFA	..	..	..	**	..	..	..	..	..	..	..	..	..	..	..	..	..	..	..	..
Burundi	BDI	..	..	..	..	**	..	..	..	..	..	..	..	..	..	..	..	..	..	..	..
Cameroon	CMR	..	..	..	..	..	**	..	..	..	..	..	..	..	..	..	..	..	..	..	..
Cape Verde	CPV	..	..	..	..	..	..	**	..	..	..	..	..	..	..	..	..	..	..	..	..
Central African	CAF	..	..	..	..	..	..	..	**	..	..	..	..	..	..	..	..	..	..	..	..
Chad	TCD	..	..	..	..	..	..	..	..	**	..	..	..	..	..	..	..	..	..	..	..
Comoros	COM	..	..	..	..	..	..	..	..	..	**	..	..	..	..	..	..	..	..	..	..
Congo, Dem. Rep	ZAR	..	..	..	..	..	..	..	..	..	..	**	..	..	..	..	..	..	..	..	..
Congo, Rep.	COG	..	..	..	..	..	..	..	..	..	..	..	**	..	..	..	..	..	..	..	..
Côte d'Ivoire	CIV	..	..	..	..	..	..	..	..	..	..	..	..	**	..	..	..	..	..	..	..
Djibouti	DJI	..	..	..	..	..	..	..	..	..	..	..	..	..	**	..	..	..	..	..	..
Egypt, Arab Rep	EGY	0.18	0.01	0.01	0.00	0.00	0.01	0.00	0.00	0.01	0.00	0.02	0.00	0.04	0.02	**	0.00	0.00	0.06	0.01	0.00
Equatorial Guinea	GNQ	..	..	..	..	..	..	..	..	..	..	..	..	..	..	..	**	..	..	..	..
Ethiopia	ETH	..	..	..	..	..	..	..	..	..	..	..	..	..	..	..	..	..	**	..	..
Gabon	GAB	..	..	..	..	..	..	..	..	..	..	..	..	..	..	..	..	..	..	**	..
Gambia, The	GMB	..	..	..	..	..	..	..	..	..	..	..	..	..	..	..	..	..	..	..	**
Ghana	GHA	..	..	..	..	..	..	..	..	..	..	..	..	..	..	..	..	..	..	..	..
Guinea	GIN	..	..	..	..	..	..	..	..	..	..	..	..	..	..	..	..	..	..	..	..
Guinea-Bissau	GNB	..	..	..	..	..	..	..	..	..	..	..	..	..	..	..	..	..	..	..	..
Kenya	KEN	0.05	0.01	0.01	0.02	0.23	0.04	0.00	0.00	0.00	0.17	1.97	0.08	0.02	0.18	2.69	0.01	0.05	1.82	0.02	0.00
Liberia	LBR	..	..	..	..	..	..	..	..	..	..	..	..	..	..	..	..	..	..	..	..
Libya	LBY	0.01	0.00	0.00	0.00	0.00	0.00	0.00	0.00	0.00	0.00	0.00	0.00	0.00	0.00	0.94	0.00	0.00	0.00	0.00	0.00
Madagascar	MDG	0.75	0.00	0.00	0.00	0.00	0.04	0.00	0.00	0.00	0.27	0.00	0.00	0.01	0.00	0.01	0.00	0.00	0.01	0.02	0.00
Malawi	MWI	..	..	..	..	..	..	..	..	..	..	..	..	..	..	..	..	..	..	..	..
Mali	MLI	..	..	..	..	..	..	..	..	..	..	..	..	..	..	..	..	..	..	..	..
Mauritania	MRT	..	..	..	..	..	..	..	..	..	..	..	..	..	..	..	..	..	..	..	..
Mauritius	MUS	0.00	0.00	0.00	0.00	0.06	0.00	0.00	0.00	0.00	0.07	0.00	0.00	0.01	0.01	0.01	0.00	0.00	0.00	0.00	0.00
Morocco	MAR	0.07	0.13	0.09	0.02	0.00	0.07	0.00	0.00	0.00	0.01	0.06	0.14	0.46	0.00	0.26	0.03	0.00	0.01	0.39	0.03
Mozambique	MOZ	..	..	..	..	..	..	..	..	..	..	..	..	..	..	..	..	..	..	..	..
Niger	NER	..	..	..	..	..	..	..	..	..	..	..	..	..	..	..	..	..	..	..	..
Nigeria	NGA	0.00	0.00	0.12	0.00	0.00	0.54	0.00	0.00	0.00	0.00	0.00	0.01	5.10	0.00	0.00	0.00	0.00	0.00	0.00	0.01
Reunion	REU	..	..	..	..	..	..	..	..	..	..	..	..	..	..	..	..	..	..	..	..
Rwanda	RWA	..	..	..	..	..	..	..	..	..	..	..	..	..	..	..	..	..	..	..	..
São Tomé and Principe	STP	..	..	..	..	..	..	..	..	..	..	..	..	..	..	..	..	..	..	..	..
Senegal	SEN	..	..	..	..	..	..	..	..	..	..	..	..	..	..	..	..	..	..	..	..
Seychelles	SYC	..	..	..	..	..	..	..	..	..	..	..	..	..	..	..	..	..	..	..	..
Sierra Leone	SLE	..	..	..	..	..	..	..	..	..	..	..	..	..	..	..	..	..	..	..	..
Somalia	SOM	..	..	..	..	..	..	..	..	..	..	..	..	..	..	..	..	..	..	..	..
South Africa	ZAF	0.12	0.80	0.02	0.01	0.03	0.13	0.02	0.00	0.00	0.06	0.79	0.14	0.11	0.00	0.14	0.00	0.00	0.05	0.04	0.03
Sudan	SDN	..	..	..	..	..	..	..	..	..	..	..	..	..	..	..	..	..	..	..	..
Tanzania	TZA	0.00	0.02	0.00	0.00	0.14	0.00	0.00	0.00	0.00	0.00	1.47	0.02	0.02	0.00	0.22	0.00	0.07	0.63	0.00	0.00
Togo	TGO	..	..	..	..	..	..	..	..	..	..	..	..	..	..	..	..	..	..	..	..
Tunisia	TUN	0.68	0.00	0.06	0.01	0.00	0.10	0.01	0.00	0.00	0.00	0.00	0.00	0.11	0.00	0.43	0.01	0.00	0.00	0.02	0.00
Uganda	UGA	..	..	..	..	..	..	..	..	..	..	..	..	..	..	..	..	..	..	..	..
Zambia	ZMB	..	..	..	..	..	..	..	..	..	..	..	..	..	..	..	..	..	..	..	..
Zimbabwe	ZWE	..	..	..	..	..	..	..	..	..	..	..	..	..	..	..	..	..	..	..	..
Sub-Saharan Africa	SSA	0.04	0.24	0.02	0.00	0.02	0.12	0.00	0.00	0.00	0.02	0.30	0.04	0.79	0.01	0.11	0.00	0.00	0.07	0.01	0.01
European Community	EEC	0.23	0.06	0.02	0.01	0.00	0.04	0.01	0.00	0.00	0.01	0.02	0.02	0.07	0.01	0.36	0.00	0.01	0.02	0.03	0.01
North America	NNA	0.13	0.03	0.01	0.00	0.00	0.01	0.00	0.00	0.00	0.00	0.01	0.01	0.02	0.00	0.46	0.01	0.00	0.02	0.01	0.00
Rest of World	ROW	0.07	0.04	0.01	0.00	0.00	0.01	0.00	0.00	0.00	0.00	0.02	0.01	0.02	0.00	0.30	0.00	0.00	0.02	0.01	0.01
World	WLD	0.15	0.04	0.02	0.01	0.00	0.02	0.00	0.00	0.00	0.00	0.01	0.01	0.05	0.01	0.35	0.00	0.00	0.02	0.02	0.00

Note: ** means "not applicable."

(Table continues on the following page)

5-52. Direction of trade matrix, exports, 1997 *(continued)*

Exporters		GHA	GIN	GNB	KEN	LBR	LBY	MDG	MWI	MLI	MRT	MUS	MAR	MOZ	NER	NGA	REU	RWA	STP	SEN	SYC
Algeria	DZA	0.00	0.00	0.00	0.00	0.00	0.02	0.00	0.00	0.00	0.37	0.00	0.68	0.00	0.00	0.01	0.00	0.00	0.00	0.07	0.00
Angola	AGO	..	..	..	..	..	..	..	..	..	..	..	..	..	..	..	..	..	..	..	..
Benin	BEN	..	..	..	..	..	..	..	..	..	..	..	..	..	..	..	..	..	..	..	..
Burkina Faso	BFA	..	..	..	..	..	..	..	..	..	..	..	..	..	..	..	..	..	..	..	..
Burundi	BDI	..	..	..	..	..	..	..	..	..	..	..	..	..	..	..	..	..	..	..	..
Cameroon	CMR	..	..	..	..	..	..	..	..	..	..	..	..	..	..	..	..	..	..	..	..
Cape Verde	CPV	..	..	..	..	..	..	..	..	..	..	..	..	..	..	..	..	..	..	..	..
Central African	CAF	..	..	..	..	..	..	..	..	..	..	..	..	..	..	..	..	..	..	..	..
Chad	TCD	..	..	..	..	..	..	..	..	..	..	..	..	..	..	..	..	..	..	..	..
Comoros	COM	..	..	..	..	..	..	..	..	..	..	..	..	..	..	..	..	..	..	..	..
Congo, Dem. Rep	ZAR	..	..	..	..	..	..	..	..	..	..	..	..	..	..	..	..	..	..	..	..
Congo, Rep.	COG	..	..	..	..	..	..	..	..	..	..	..	..	..	..	..	.	..	..	..	..
Côte d'Ivoire	CIV	..	..	..	..	..	..	..	..	..	..	..	..	..	..	..	..	..	..	..	..
Djibouti	DJI	..	..	..	..	..	..	..	..	..	..	..	..	..	..	..	..	..	..	..	..
Egypt, Arab Rep	EGY	0.01	0.01	0.00	0.07	0.00	1.78	0.00	0.00	0.00	0.00	0.00	0.29	0.00	0.00	0.05	0.00	0.00	0.00	0.02	0.00
Equatorial Guinea	GNQ	..	..	..	..	..	..	..	..	..	..	..	..	..	..	..	..	..	..	..	..
Ethiopia	ETH	..	..	..	..	..	..	..	..	..	..	..	..	..	..	..	..	..	..	..	..
Gabon	GAB	..	..	..	..	..	..	..	..	..	..	..	..	..	..	..	..	..	..	..	..
Gambia, The	GMB	..	..	..	..	..	..	..	..	..	..	..	..	..	..	..	..	..	..	..	..
Ghana	GHA	**	..	..	..	..	..	..	..	..	..	..	..	..	..	..	..	..	..	..	..
Guinea	GIN	..	**	..	..	..	..	..	..	..	..	..	..	..	..	..	..	..	..	..	..
Guinea-Bissau	GNB	..	..	**	..	..	..	..	..	..	..	..	..	..	..	..	..	..	..	..	..
Kenya	KEN	0.02	0.00	0.00	**	0.00	0.00	0.14	0.30	0.01	0.01	0.71	0.00	0.08	0.00	0.14	0.00	3.03	0.00	0.04	0.20
Liberia	LBR	..	..	..	..	**	..	..	..	..	..	..	..	..	..	..	..	..	..	..	..
Libya	LBY	0.02	0.00	0.00	0.01	0.00	**	0.00	0.00	0.00	0.00	0.00	0.44	0.00	0.00	0.03	0.00	0.00	0.00	0.05	0.00
Madagascar	MDG	0.00	0.01	0.00	0.03	0.00	0.00	**	0.00	0.01	0.01	3.94	0.04	0.08	0.00	0.01	0.00	0.00	0.00	0.01	0.07
Malawi	MWI	..	..	..	..	..	..	..	**	..	..	..	..	..	..	..	..	..	..	..	..
Mali	MLI	..	..	..	..	..	..	..	..	**	..	..	..	..	..	..	..	..	..	..	..
Mauritania	MRT	..	..	..	..	..	..	..	..	..	**	..	..	..	..	..	..	..	..	..	..
Mauritius	MUS	0.00	0.00	0.00	0.25	0.00	0.00	3.61	0.21	0.00	0.00	**	0.00	0.00	0.00	0.00	0.00	0.10	0.00	0.00	0.22
Morocco	MAR	0.11	0.17	0.00	0.01	0.02	2.79	0.02	0.00	0.17	0.21	0.03	**	0.00	0.02	0.10	0.00	0.00	0.00	0.23	0.00
Mozambique	MOZ	..	..	..	..	..	..	..	..	..	..	..	..	**	..	..	..	..	..	..	..
Niger	NER	..	..	..	..	..	..	..	..	..	..	..	..	..	**	..	..	..	..	..	..
Nigeria	NGA	1.28	0.04	0.00	0.00	0.01	0.00	0.00	0.00	0.00	0.00	0.00	0.98	0.00	0.00	**	0.00	0.00	0.00	0.68	0.00
Reunion	REU	..	..	..	..	..	..	..	..	..	..	..	..	..	..	..	**	..	..	..	..
Rwanda	RWA	..	..	..	..	..	..	..	..	..	..	..	..	..	..	..	..	**	..	..	..
São Tomé and Principe	STP	..	..	..	..	..	..	..	..	..	..	..	..	..	..	..	..	..	**	..	..
Senegal	SEN	..	..	..	..	..	..	..	..	..	..	..	..	..	..	..	..	..	..	**	..
Seychelles	SYC	..	..	..	..	..	..	..	..	..	..	..	..	..	..	..	..	..	..	..	**
Sierra Leone	SLE	..	..	..	..	..	..	..	..	..	..	..	..	..	..	..	..	..	..	..	..
Somalia	SOM	..	..	..	..	..	..	..	..	..	..	..	..	..	..	..	..	..	..	..	..
South Africa	ZAF	0.38	0.04	0.00	1.43	0.02	0.02	0.24	1.03	0.07	0.01	0.85	0.12	1.86	0.01	0.19	0.00	0.02	0.01	0.01	0.18
Sudan	SDN	..	..	..	..	..	..	..	..	..	..	..	..	..	..	..	..	..	..	..	..
Tanzania	TZA	0.09	0.01	0.00	4.03	0.00	0.00	0.01	0.90	0.06	0.02	0.23	0.00	0.05	0.00	0.01	0.00	1.02	0.00	0.00	0.00
Togo	TGO	..	..	..	..	..	..	..	..	..	..	..	..	..	..	..	..	..	..	..	..
Tunisia	TUN	0.07	0.00	0.00	0.00	0.00	4.63	0.00	0.00	0.02	0.02	0.00	0.59	0.00	0.03	0.01	0.00	0.00	0.00	0.06	0.00
Uganda	UGA	..	..	..	..	..	..	..	..	..	..	..	..	..	..	..	..	..	..	..	..
Zambia	ZMB	..	..	..	..	..	..	..	..	..	..	..	..	..	..	..	..	..	..	..	..
Zimbabwe	ZWE	..	..	..	..	..	..	..	..	..	..	..	..	..	..	..	..	..	..	..	..
Sub-Saharan Africa	SSA	0.31	0.02	0.00	0.47	0.01	0.01	0.15	0.33	0.02	0.00	0.29	0.18	0.56	0.00	0.06	0.00	0.10	0.00	0.11	0.06
European Community	EEC	0.06	0.02	0.00	0.05	0.03	0.15	0.02	0.00	0.02	0.02	0.03	0.28	0.01	0.01	0.14	0.00	0.00	0.00	0.04	0.01
North America	NNA	0.04	0.01	0.00	0.03	0.01	0.02	0.00	0.00	0.00	0.00	0.00	0.07	0.01	0.00	0.10	0.00	0.00	0.00	0.01	0.00
Rest of World	ROW	0.03	0.01	0.00	0.06	0.14	0.08	0.01	0.01	0.00	0.01	0.05	0.07	0.03	0.00	0.10	0.00	0.00	0.00	0.01	0.01
World	WLD	0.05	0.01	0.00	0.05	0.07	0.10	0.01	0.01	0.01	0.01	0.03	0.16	0.02	0.00	0.12	0.00	0.01	0.00	0.03	0.00

Note: ** means "not applicable."

(Table continues on the following page)

5-52. Direction of trade matrix, exports, 1997

Exporters		SLE	SOM	ZAF	SDN	TZA	TGO	TUN	UGA	ZMB	ZWE	SSA	EEC	NNA	ROW	WLD
		Importers						*Percentage of total exports*								
Algeria	DZA	0.00	0.00	0.00	0.03	0.00	0.00	0.43	0.00	0.00	..	0.49	63.46	19.38	17.04	100.00
Angola	AGO	..	..	..	..	..	..	..	..	..		..	..	..	..	..
Benin	BEN	..	..	..	..	..	..	..	..	..		..	..	..	..	..
Burkina Faso	BFA	..	..	..	..	..	..	..	..	..		..	..	..	..	..
Burundi	BDI	..	..	..	..	..	..	..	..	..		..	..	..	..	..
Cameroon	CMR	..	..	..	..	..	..	..	..	..		..	..	..	..	..
Cape Verde	CPV	..	..	..	..	..	..	..	..	..		..	..	..	..	..
Central African	CAF	..	..	..	..	..	..	..	..	..		..	..	..	..	..
Chad	TCD	..	..	..	..	..	..	..	..	..		..	..	..	..	..
Comoros	COM	..	..	..	..	..	..	..	..	..		..	..	..	..	..
Congo, Dem. Rep	ZAR	..	..	..	..	..	..	..	..	..		..	..	..	..	..
Congo, Rep.	COG	..	..	..	..	..	..	..	..	..		..	..	..	..	..
Côte d'Ivoire	CIV	..	..	..	..	..	..	..	..	..		..	..	..	..	..
Djibouti	DJI	..	..	..	..	..	..	..	..	..		..	..	..	..	..
Egypt, Arab Rep	EGY	0.01	0.01	1.03	0.65	0.03	0.01	0.48	0.01	0.05	..	1.16	41.49	11.60	45.78	100.00
Equatorial Guinea	GNQ	..	..	..	..	..	..	..	..	..		..	..	..	..	..
Ethiopia	ETH	..	..	..	..	..	..	..	..	..		..	..	..	..	..
Gabon	GAB	..	..	..	..	..	..	..	..	..		..	..	..	..	..
Gambia, The	GMB	..	..	..	..	..	..	..	..	..		..	..	..	..	..
Ghana	GHA	..	..	..	..	..	..	..	..	..		..	..	..	..	..
Guinea	GIN	..	..	..	..	..	..	..	..	..		..	..	..	..	..
Guinea-Bissau	GNB	..	..	..	..	..	..	..	..	..		..	..	..	..	..
Kenya	KEN	0.01	1.66	0.89	1.64	12.22	0.00	0.04	14.33	0.21	..	39.64	34.65	3.67	23.42	100.00
Liberia	LBR	..	..	..	..	..	..	..	..	..		..	..	..	..	..
Libya	LBY	0.00	0.00	0.00	0.01	0.00	0.00	4.26	0.00	0.00	..	0.12	77.67	0.03	22.18	100.00
Madagascar	MDG	0.00	0.00	1.19	0.00	0.02	0.00	0.02	0.02	0.00	..	4.63	65.80	3.99	29.62	100.00
Malawi	MWI	..	..	..	..	..	..	..	..	..		..	..	..	..	..
Mali	MLI	..	..	..	..	..	..	..	..	..		..	..	..	..	..
Mauritania	MRT	..	..	..	..	..	..	..	..	..		..	..	..	..	..
Mauritius	MUS	0.00	0.00	0.58	0.00	0.06	0.00	0.00	0.04	0.05	..	5.48	74.19	14.77	9.38	100.00
Morocco	MAR	0.01	0.00	0.09	0.00	0.01	0.04	0.85	0.00	0.00	..	2.64	60.70	4.18	32.95	100.00
Mozambique	MOZ	..	..	..	..	..	..	..	..	..		..	..	..	..	..
Niger	NER	..	..	..	..	..	..	..	..	..		..	..	..	..	..
Nigeria	NGA	0.00	0.00	0.59	0.00	0.00	0.01	0.00	0.00	0.00	..	7.80	29.80	42.85	19.55	100.00
Reunion	REU	..	..	..	..	..	..	..	..	..		..	..	..	..	..
Rwanda	RWA	..	..	..	..	..	..	..	..	..		..	..	..	..	..
São Tomé and Principe	STP	..	..	..	..	..	..	..	..	..		..	..	..	..	..
Senegal	SEN	..	..	..	..	..	..	..	..	..		..	..	..	..	..
Seychelles	SYC	..	..	..	..	..	..	..	..	..		..	..	..	..	..
Sierra Leone	SLE	**	..	..	..	..	..	..	..	..		..	..	..	..	..
Somalia	SOM	..	**	..	..	..	..	..	..	..		..	..	..	..	..
South Africa	ZAF	0.03	0.00	**	0.02	0.49	0.03	0.01	0.15	1.97	..	15.87	26.24	10.36	51.61	100.00
Sudan	SDN	..	..	..	**	..	..	..	..	..		..	..	..	..	..
Tanzania	TZA	0.00	0.01	1.16	0.26	**	0.00	0.00	1.24	0.28	..	13.31	37.28	2.21	48.68	100.00
Togo	TGO	..	..	..	..	..	**	..	..	..		..	..	..	..	..
Tunisia	TUN	0.00	0.00	0.08	0.01	0.00	0.02	**	0.00	0.00	..	0.57	78.40	0.73	20.35	100.00
Uganda	UGA	..	..	..	..	..	..	..	**	..		..	..	..	..	..
Zambia	ZMB	..	..	..	..	..	..	..	..	**		..	..	..	..	..
Zimbabwe	ZWE	..	..	..	..	..	..	..	..	..	**	..	..	..	..	..
Sub-Saharan Africa	SSA	0.01	0.04	0.14	0.05	0.47	0.01	0.00	0.43	0.60	..	**	48.10	14.41	31.40	100.00
European Community	EEC	0.01	0.00	0.53	0.02	0.02	0.01	0.28	0.01	0.01	..	0.89	61.01	8.32	29.93	100.00
North America	NNA	0.00	0.00	0.39	0.01	0.01	0.00	0.04	0.00	0.00	..	0.40	16.66	36.33	46.64	100.00
Rest of World	ROW	0.00	0.00	0.40	0.02	0.03	0.01	0.06	0.01	0.03	..	0.80	22.63	23.22	**	100.00
World	WLD	0.00	0.00	0.46	0.02	0.03	0.01	0.15	0.01	0.02	..	0.81	37.56	19.28	42.53	100.00

Note: ** means "not applicable."

5-53. Direction of trade matrix, current U.S. dollars, 1987

Importers   *Millions of current US dollars*

Exporters		DZA	AGO	BEN	BFA	BDI	CMR	CPV	CAF	TCD	COM	ZAR	COG	CIV	DJI	EGY	GNQ	ETH	GAB	GMB	GHA
Algeria	DZA	**	..	0	0	0	..	..	..	..	..	..	0	..	..	..	..	..	..	..	..
Angola	AGO	..	**	..	..	..	..	..	..	..	..	..	..	..	..	..	..	..	..	..	..
Benin	BEN	..	..	**	..	..	..	..	..	..	..	..	..	..	..	..	..	..	..	..	..
Burkina Faso	BFA	..	..	..	**	..	..	..	..	..	..	..	..	..	..	..	..	..	..	..	..
Burundi	BDI	..	..	..	..	**	..	..	..	..	..	..	..	..	..	..	..	..	..	..	..
Cameroon	CMR	0	0	0	0	..	**	..	12	18	..	0	18	6	0	0	9	0	48	0	0
Cape Verde	CPV	..	..	..	..	..	..	**	..	..	..	..	..	..	..	..	..	..	..	..	..
Central African	CAF	..	..	..	..	..	..	..	**	..	..	..	..	..	..	..	..	..	..	..	..
Chad	TCD	..	..	..	..	..	..	..	..	**	..	..	0	..	..	..	..	..	..	..	..
Comoros	COM	..	..	..	..	..	..	..	..	..	**	..	..	..	..	..	..	..	..	..	..
Congo, Dem. Rep	ZAR	..	..	..	..	..	..	..	..	..	..	**	..	..	..	..	..	..	..	..	..
Congo, Rep.	COG	..	..	..	..	..	..	..	..	..	..	..	**	..	..	..	..	..	..	..	..
Côte d'Ivoire	CIV	..	..	..	..	..	..	..	..	..	..	..	..	**	..	..	..	..	..	..	..
Djibouti	DJI	..	..	0	..	..	..	..	..	..	0	0	..	0	**	0	..	2	..	..	..
Egypt, Arab Rep	EGY	4	..	..	..	..	0	..	..	0	..	0	0	0	0	**	..	0	..	0	0
Equatorial Guin	GNQ	..	..	..	..	..	..	..	..	..	..	..	..	..	..	..	**	..	..	..	..
Ethiopia	ETH	2	..	..	..	0	..	..	..	..	..	..	..	0	31	0	..	**	..	..	0
Gabon	GAB	..	..	..	..	..	..	..	..	..	..	..	..	..	..	..	..	..	**	..	..
Gambia, The	GMB	..	..	..	..	..	..	..	..	..	..	..	..	..	..	..	..	..	..	**	..
Ghana	GHA	..	..	..	..	..	..	..	..	..	..	..	..	..	..	..	..	..	..	..	**
Guinea	GIN	..	..	..	..	..	..	..	..	..	..	..	..	..	..	..	..	..	..	..	..
Guinea-Bissau	GNB	..	..	..	..	..	..	..	..	..	..	..	..	..	..	..	..	..	..	..	..
Kenya	KEN	0	5	0	0	14	0	..	0	..	1	13	0	1	2	8	0	9	0	0	0
Liberia	LBR	..	..	..	..	..	..	..	..	..	..	..	..	..	..	..	..	..	..	..	..
Libya	LBY	1	..	..	..	..	..	..	..	..	..	..	..	1	..	..	..	..	..	..	..
Madagascar	MDG	..	..	..	..	..	..	..	..	..	..	..	..	..	..	..	..	..	..	..	..
Malawi	MWI	..	0	0	..	0	0	..	..	..	..	4	0	0	..	2	..	0	0	1	0
Mali	MLI	0	..	0	1	..	0	..	..	0	..	0	..	73	..	..	..	..	..	0	0
Mauritania	MRT	..	..	..	..	..	..	..	..	..	..	..	..	..	..	..	..	..	..	..	..
Mauritius	MUS	..	..	..	..	..	..	..	..	..	..	..	..	..	..	..	..	..	..	..	..
Morocco	MAR	0	0	2	0	0	10	..	1	..	0	5	3	10	0	6	0	..	6	0	0
Mozambique	MOZ	..	..	..	..	..	..	..	..	..	..	..	..	..	..	..	..	..	..	..	..
Niger	NER	..	..	..	..	..	..	..	..	..	..	..	..	..	..	..	..	..	..	..	..
Nigeria	NGA	0	0	3	..	..	4	..	..	3	0	17	4	219	0	0	0	0	9	0	107
Reunion	REU	..	..	..	..	..	..	..	..	..	5	..	..	..	0	..	..	..	..	..	..
Rwanda	RWA	..	..	..	..	..	..	..	..	..	..	..	..	..	..	..	..	..	..	..	..
São Tomé and Principe	STP	..	..	..	..	..	..	..	..	..	..	..	..	..	..	..	..	..	..	..	..
Senegal	SEN	0	0	3	3	0	16	0	0	0	..	1	3	23	..	0	0	0	1	4	0
Seychelles	SYC	..	..	..	..	..	..	..	..	..	..	..	..	..	..	..	..	..	..	..	..
Sierra Leone	SLE	..	..	..	..	..	..	..	..	..	..	..	..	..	..	..	..	..	..	..	..
Somalia	SOM	..	..	..	..	..	..	..	..	..	..	..	..	..	..	..	..	..	..	..	..
South Africa	ZAF	..	..	..	..	..	..	..	..	..	..	..	..	..	..	..	..	..	..	..	..
Sudan	SDN	..	..	..	..	..	..	..	..	..	..	..	..	..	..	..	..	..	..	..	..
Tanzania	TZA	9	0	..	..	1	..	..	..	..	..	1	..	0	..	2	..	1	..	..	..
Togo	TGO	..	..	..	..	..	..	..	..	..	..	..	..	..	..	..	..	..	..	..	..
Tunisia	TUN	67	0	1	0	..	7	..	..	0	0	0	0	2	0	1	0	..	1	0	0
Uganda	UGA	..	..	..	..	..	..	..	..	..	..	..	..	..	..	..	..	..	..	..	..
Zambia	ZMB	..	..	..	..	..	..	..	..	..	..	..	..	..	..	..	..	..	..	..	..
Zimbabwe	ZWE	..	..	..	..	..	..	..	..	..	..	..	..	..	..	..	..	..	..	..	..
Sub-Saharan Africa	SSA	12	5	7	4	15	20	0	13	21	7	36	25	321	33	12	10	11	58	5	107
European Community	EEC	4,717	601	222	195	110	1,091	87	78	87	52	803	355	1,159	119	4,723	36	511	493	94	473
North America	NNA	578	98	20	10	2	57	..	2	4	22	116	9	90	4	1,573	0	164	53	12	133
Rest of World	ROW	1,059	370	198	23	19	297	14	12	4	15	210	68	388	91	2,398	14	255	82	37	194
World	WLD	6,366	1,074	452	240	145	1,467	101	104	116	90	1,161	458	1,886	246	8,704	60	941	686	148	912

Note: ** means "not applicable."

(Table continues on the following page)

5-53. Direction of trade matrix, current U.S. dollars, 1987 *(continued)*

Importers — *Millions of current US dollars*

Exporters		GIN	GNB	KEN	LBR	LBY	MDG	MWI	MLI	MRT	MUS	MAR	MOZ	NER	NGA	REU	RWA	STP	SEN	SYC	SLE
Algeria	DZA	..	..	..	0	17	..	..	1	46	..	..	..	0	0	..	..	..	5	..	..
Angola	AGO	..	..	..	..	..	..	..	..	..	..	..	..	..	..	..	..	..	..	..	..
Benin	BEN	..	..	..	..	..	..	..	..	..	..	..	..	..	..	..	..	..	..	..	..
Burkina Faso	BFA	..	..	..	..	..	..	..	..	..	..	..	..	..	..	..	..	..	..	..	..
Burundi	BDI	..	..	..	..	..	..	..	..	..	..	..	..	..	..	..	..	..	..	..	..
Cameroon	CMR	3	..	0	0	..	0	..	0	0	..	0	1	0	26	0	0	..	2	..	0
Cape Verde	CPV	..	..	..	..	..	..	..	..	..	..	..	..	..	..	..	..	..	..	..	..
Central African	CAF	..	..	..	..	..	..	..	..	..	..	..	..	..	..	..	..	..	..	..	..
Chad	TCD	..	..	..	..	..	0	..	..	..	0	..	..	..	..	1	..	..	..	..	..
Comoros	COM	..	..	..	..	..	..	..	..	..	..	..	..	..	..	..	..	..	..	..	..
Congo, Dem. Rep	ZAR	..	..	..	..	..	..	..	..	..	..	..	..	..	..	..	..	..	..	..	..
Congo, Rep.	COG	..	..	..	..	..	..	..	..	..	..	..	..	..	..	..	..	..	..	..	..
Côte d'Ivoire	CIV	..	..	..	..	..	..	..	..	..	..	..	..	..	..	..	..	..	..	..	..
Djibouti	DJI	..	..	0	..	..	0	..	..	..	0	..	..	0	0	..	..	..	0	0	..
Egypt, Arab Rep	EGY	..	..	0	..	0	..	..	..	0	..	5	0	0	..	..	..	..	0	..	..
Equatorial Guin	GNQ	..	..	..	..	..	..	..	..	..	..	..	..	..	..	..	..	..	..	..	..
Ethiopia	ETH	0	..	1	..	..	..	..	..	..	0	..	..	..	0	0	0	..	0	..	..
Gabon	GAB	..	..	..	..	..	..	..	..	..	..	..	..	..	..	..	..	..	..	..	..
Gambia, The	GMB	..	..	..	..	..	..	..	..	..	..	..	..	..	..	..	..	..	..	..	..
Ghana	GHA	..	..	..	..	..	..	..	..	..	..	..	..	..	..	..	..	..	..	..	..
Guinea	GIN	**	..	..	..	..	..	..	..	..	..	..	..	..	..	..	..	..	..	..	..
Guinea-Bissau	GNB	..	**	..	..	..	..	..	..	..	..	..	..	..	..	..	..	..	..	..	..
Kenya	KEN	0	..	**	0	0	0	0	..	0	3	0	12	0	1	4	28	..	..	1	0
Liberia	LBR	..	..	..	**	..	..	..	..	..	..	..	..	..	..	..	..	..	..	..	..
Libya	LBY	..	..	..	..	**	..	..	..	..	..	52	..	..	..	..	..	..	..	..	..
Madagascar	MDG	..	..	..	..	..	**	..	..	..	..	..	..	..	..	..	..	..	..	..	..
Malawi	MWI	0	..	0	0	..	..	**	..	..	0	..	2	..	..	0	0	..	0	..	0
Mali	MLI	0	..	..	0	0	..	..	**	0	..	0	..	0	0	..	..	..	47	..	..
Mauritania	MRT	..	..	..	..	..	..	..	..	**	..	..	..	..	..	..	..	..	..	..	..
Mauritius	MUS	..	..	..	..	..	..	..	..	..	**	..	..	..	..	3	..	..	..	..	..
Morocco	MAR	5	0	0	1	91	..	..	2	2	1	**	..	0	4	2	..	..	12	..	0
Mozambique	MOZ	..	..	..	..	..	..	..	..	..	..	..	**	..	..	..	..	..	..	..	..
Niger	NER	..	..	..	..	..	..	..	..	..	..	..	..	**	..	..	..	..	..	..	..
Nigeria	NGA	1	0	0	2	0	..	..	1	0	..	1	..	5	**	0	0	..	40	..	31
Reunion	REU	..	..	..	..	..	3	..	..	..	1	..	..	..	..	**	..	..	..	0	..
Rwanda	RWA	..	..	..	..	..	..	..	..	..	..	..	..	..	..	..	**	..	..	..	..
São Tomé and Principe	STP	..	..	..	..	..	..	..	..	..	..	..	..	..	..	..	..	**	..	..	..
Senegal	SEN	6	2	0	0	..	0	..	18	23	0	1	0	1	2	0	..	..	**	0	0
Seychelles	SYC	..	..	..	..	..	..	..	..	..	..	..	..	..	..	..	..	..	..	**	..
Sierra Leone	SLE	..	..	..	..	..	..	..	..	..	..	..	..	..	..	..	..	..	..	..	**
Somalia	SOM	..	..	..	..	..	..	..	..	..	..	..	..	..	..	..	..	..	..	..	..
South Africa	ZAF	..	..	..	..	..	..	..	..	..	..	..	..	..	..	..	..	..	..	..	..
Sudan	SDN	..	..	..	..	..	..	..	..	..	..	..	..	..	..	..	..	..	..	..	..
Tanzania	TZA	..	..	8	..	..	..	..	0	..	0	..	4	..	0	..	0	..	..	..	..
Togo	TGO	..	..	..	..	..	..	..	..	..	..	..	..	..	..	..	..	..	..	..	..
Tunisia	TUN	1	0	..	..	8	..	..	0	0	..	17	..	0	0	..	..	..	3	..	0
Uganda	UGA	..	..	..	..	..	..	..	..	..	..	..	..	..	..	..	..	..	..	..	..
Zambia	ZMB	..	..	..	..	..	..	..	..	..	..	..	..	..	..	..	..	..	..	..	..
Zimbabwe	ZWE	..	..	..	..	..	..	..	..	..	..	..	..	..	..	..	..	..	..	..	..
Sub-Saharan Africa	SSA	10	2	9	3	0	4	1	19	24	4	2	19	7	29	8	28	..	89	1	31
European Community	EEC	271	43	865	434	2,849	202	86	222	299	318	2,714	309	175	2,764	1,045	124	12	665	52	87
North America	NNA	38	26	95	70	23	23	8	10	9	27	489	64	2	310	3	4	..	55	1	26
Rest of World	ROW	48	12	451	1,573	1,494	58	24	26	107	379	502	172	41	1,167	81	55	2	190	27	31
World	WLD	367	83	1,421	2,080	4,366	284	118	277	439	727	3,708	562	227	4,273	1,134	212	14	953	81	176

Note: ** means "not applicable."

(Table continues on the following page)

5-53. Direction of trade matrix, current U.S. dollars, 1987

Exporters		SOM	ZAF	SDN	TZA	TGO	TUN	UGA	ZMB	ZWE	SSA	EEC	NNA	ROW	WLD
Algeria	DZA	..	..	..	0	..	73	..	..	..	53	5,919	1,590	672	8,186
Angola	AGO	..	..	..	..	..	..	..	..	..	..	..	..	..	..
Benin	BEN	..	..	..	..	..	..	..	..	..	..	..	..	..	..
Burkina Faso	BFA	..	..	..	..	..	..	..	..	..	..	..	..	..	..
Burundi	BDI	..	..	..	..	..	..	..	..	..	..	..	..	..	..
Cameroon	CMR	..	0	0	0	0	0	..	0	..	145	567	61	57	829
Cape Verde	CPV	..	..	..	..	..	..	..	..	..	..	..	..	..	..
Central African	CAF	..	..	..	..	..	..	..	..	..	..	..	..	..	..
Chad	TCD	..	0	..	..	..	..	..	..	..	0	5	0	2	6
Comoros	COM	..	..	..	..	..	..	..	..	..	..	..	..	..	..
Congo, Dem. Rep	ZAR	..	..	..	..	..	..	..	..	..	..	..	..	..	..
Congo, Rep.	COG	..	..	..	..	..	..	..	..	..	..	..	..	..	..
Côte d'Ivoire	CIV	..	..	..	..	..	..	..	..	..	..	..	..	..	..
Djibouti	DJI	3	..	0	0	..	0	..	..	..	3	16	0	7	28
Egypt, Arab Rep	EGY	0	..	57	0	..	8	0	..	..	59	804	172	1,003	2,037
Equatorial Guin	GNQ	..	..	..	..	..	..	..	..	..	..	..	..	..	..
Ethiopia	ETH	..	..	0	0	..	..	0	0	..	33	145	68	125	371
Gabon	GAB	..	..	..	..	..	..	..	..	..	..	..	..	..	..
Gambia, The	GMB	..	..	..	..	..	..	..	..	..	..	..	..	..	..
Ghana	GHA	..	..	..	..	..	..	..	..	..	..	..	..	..	..
Guinea	GIN	..	..	..	..	..	..	..	..	..	..	..	..	..	..
Guinea-Bissau	GNB	..	..	..	..	..	..	..	..	..	..	..	..	..	..
Kenya	KEN	9	4	24	23	0	0	70	2	..	217	421	59	227	916
Liberia	LBR	..	..	..	..	..	..	..	..	..	..	..	..	..	..
Libya	LBY	..	..	..	..	..	..	..	..	..	1	7,070	..	1,696	8,766
Madagascar	MDG	..	..	..	..	..	..	..	..	..	..	..	..	..	..
Malawi	MWI	..	30	0	0	0	0	0	1	..	14	151	30	79	272
Mali	MLI	..	..	..	..	0	..	..	..	..	121	2	0	2	125
Mauritania	MRT	..	..	..	..	..	..	..	..	..	..	..	..	..	..
Mauritius	MUS	..	0	..	..	..	..	..	..	..	..	624	135	162	921
Morocco	MAR	..	0	0	1	3	29	..	..	..	67	1,766	61	918	2,807
Mozambique	MOZ	..	..	..	..	..	..	..	..	..	..	..	..	..	..
Niger	NER	..	..	..	..	..	..	..	..	..	..	..	..	..	..
Nigeria	NGA	..	1	0	0	1	1	..	..	..	446	3,096	3,642	202	7,383
Reunion	REU	..	0	..	..	..	..	..	0	..	10	132	0	10	148
Rwanda	RWA	..	..	..	..	..	..	..	..	..	..	..	..	..	..
São Tomé and Principe	STP	..	..	..	..	..	..	..	..	..	..	..	..	..	..
Senegal	SEN	0	0	0	0	3	2	0	0	..	112	273	2	259	605
Seychelles	SYC	..	..	..	..	..	..	..	..	..	..	..	..	..	..
Sierra Leone	SLE	..	..	..	..	..	..	..	..	..	..	..	..	..	..
Somalia	SOM	**													
South Africa	ZAF	..	**												
Sudan	SDN	..	..	**											
Tanzania	TZA	0	0	1	**	..	..	3	2	..	21	155	7	111	291
Togo	TGO	..	..	..	..	**	..	..	..	..	..	..	..	..	..
Tunisia	TUN	0	..	0	0	1	**	0	4	..	21	1,688	41	403	2,152
Uganda	UGA	..	..	..	..	..	..	**	..	..	..	..	..	..	..
Zambia	ZMB	..	..	..	..	..	..	..	**	..	..	..	..	..	..
Zimbabwe	ZWE	..	..	..	..	..	..	..	..	**	..	..	..	..	..
Sub-Saharan Africa	SSA	12	37	26	24	3	3	73	5	..	1,122	5,588	4,005	1,242	11,896
European Community	EEC	263	6,092	495	474	311	2,126	193	275	..	15,317	669,044	101,155	258,189	1,042,347
North America	NNA	37	1,383	155	52	20	159	19	48	..	1,816	66,781	127,288	140,729	336,567
Rest of World	ROW	51	3,323	325	273	143	333	147	88	..	7,513	196,168	221,510	374,862	797,968
World	WLD	363	10,804	1,001	821	477	2,623	432	415	..	25,648	936,799	453,824	774,830	2,187,555

Note: ** means "not applicable."

5-54. Direction of trade matrix, current U.S. dollars, 1991

Exporters		DZA	AGO	BEN	BFA	BDI	CMR	CPV	CAF	TCD	COM	ZAR	COG	CIV	DJI	EGY	GNQ	ETH	GAB	GMB	GHA
		Importers									*Percentage of total exports*										
Algeria	DZA	**	..	..	..	..	0	..	..	..	..	..	0	0	..	11	..	..	..	..	0
Angola	AGO	..	**	..	..	..	9	..	..	..	..	1	..	..	..	..	..	..	..	..	..
Benin	BEN	..	..	**	..	..	..	..	..	..	..	..	..	..	..	..	..	..	..	..	..
Burkina Faso	BFA	..	..	..	**	..	..	..	..	..	..	..	..	..	..	..	..	..	..	..	..
Burundi	BDI	..	..	..	..	**	..	..	..	..	..	..	..	..	..	..	..	..	..	..	..
Cameroon	CMR	..	..	..	..	..	**	..	..	..	..	..	..	..	..	..	..	..	..	..	..
Cape Verde	CPV	..	..	..	..	..	..	**	..	..	..	..	..	..	..	..	..	..	..	..	..
Central African	CAF	..	..	..	..	..	..	..	**	..	..	..	..	..	..	..	..	..	..	..	..
Chad	TCD	..	..	..	..	..	..	..	..	**	0	..	..	..	..	..	..	..	..	..	..
Comoros	COM	..	..	..	..	..	..	..	..	..	**	..	..	..	..	..	..	..	..	..	..
Congo, Dem. Rep	ZAR	..	..	..	..	..	..	..	..	..	..	**	..	..	..	..	..	..	..	..	..
Congo, Rep.	COG	..	..	..	..	..	..	..	..	..	..	..	**	..	..	..	..	..	..	..	..
Côte d'Ivoire	CIV	..	..	..	..	..	..	..	..	..	..	..	..	**	..	..	..	..	..	..	..
Djibouti	DJI	0	..	..	0	0	..	..	0	..	0	..	0	0	**	0	..	0	..	..	..
Egypt, Arab Rep	EGY	7	..	0	..	0	0	..	0	0	..	0	0	1	2	**	..	2	0	0	0
Equatorial Guin	GNQ	..	..	..	..	..	..	..	..	..	..	..	..	..	..	..	**	..	..	..	..
Ethiopia	ETH	..	..	..	..	..	..	..	..	0	..	0	0	0	7	..	..	**	..	..	0
Gabon	GAB	..	..	..	..	..	..	..	..	..	..	..	..	..	..	..	..	..	**	..	..
Gambia, The	GMB	..	..	..	..	..	..	..	..	..	..	..	..	..	..	..	..	..	..	**	..
Ghana	GHA	..	..	..	..	..	..	..	..	..	..	..	..	..	..	..	..	..	..	..	**
Guinea	GIN	..	..	..	..	..	..	..	..	..	..	..	..	..	..	..	..	..	..	..	..
Guinea-Bissau	GNB	..	..	..	..	..	..	..	..	..	..	..	..	..	..	..	..	..	..	..	..
Kenya	KEN	0	0	..	0	10	1	0	0	..	4	11	0	0	3	34	..	10	0	..	0
Liberia	LBR	..	..	..	..	..	..	..	..	..	..	..	..	..	..	..	..	..	..	..	..
Libya	LBY	1	..	..	..	..	..	..	..	..	..	..	..	..	..	19	..	..	..	..	0
Madagascar	MDG	0	0	..	..	0	0	0	..	..	2	0	0	0	0	0	..	0	0	..	0
Malawi	MWI	0	0	..	..	2	0	..	..	..	..	1	0	0	..	4	..	0	0	..	0
Mali	MLI	..	..	..	..	..	..	..	..	..	..	..	..	..	..	..	..	..	..	..	..
Mauritania	MRT	..	..	..	..	..	..	..	..	..	..	..	..	..	..	..	..	..	..	..	..
Mauritius	MUS	0	..	0	..	1	0	0	0	0	2	0	0	1	0	0	..	0	0	..	0
Morocco	MAR	74	5	2	0	..	7	..	0	0	1	3	5	7	0	3	0	..	8	0	2
Mozambique	MOZ	..	..	..	..	..	..	..	..	..	..	..	..	..	..	..	..	..	..	..	..
Niger	NER	..	..	..	..	..	..	..	..	..	..	..	..	..	..	..	..	..	..	..	..
Nigeria	NGA	0	0	1	0	0	78	..	..	8	0	38	0	298	..	0	1	0	21	0	190
Reunion	REU	..	0	..	..	..	..	..	..	..	9	..	..	0	0	..	..	..	..	..	..
Rwanda	RWA	..	..	..	..	..	..	..	..	..	..	..	..	..	..	..	..	..	..	..	..
São Tomé and Principe	STP	..	..	..	..	..	..	..	..	..	..	..	..	..	..	..	..	..	..	..	..
Senegal	SEN	0	0	5	2	0	10	0	0	1	..	1	5	18	..	0	..	..	2	10	0
Seychelles	SYC	..	..	..	..	..	..	..	..	..	..	..	..	..	..	..	..	..	..	..	..
Sierra Leone	SLE	..	..	..	..	..	..	..	..	..	..	..	..	..	..	..	..	..	..	..	..
Somalia	SOM	..	..	..	..	..	..	..	..	..	..	..	..	..	..	..	..	..	..	..	..
South Africa	ZAF	..	..	..	..	..	..	..	..	..	..	..	..	..	..	..	..	..	..	..	..
Sudan	SDN	..	..	..	..	..	..	..	..	..	..	..	..	..	..	..	..	..	..	..	..
Tanzania	TZA	79	..	0	..	..	2	..	..	0	..	..	0	5	0	11	0	4	0	..	5
Togo	TGO	..	..	..	..	..	..	..	..	..	..	..	..	..	..	..	..	..	..	..	..
Tunisia	TUN	..	..	5	6	..	0	..	0	0	..	0	1	1	..	0	0	..	1	0	3
Uganda	UGA	..	..	..	..	..	..	..	..	..	..	..	..	..	..	..	..	..	..	..	..
Zambia	ZMB	..	..	..	..	..	..	..	..	..	..	..	..	..	..	..	..	..	..	..	..
Zimbabwe	ZWE	..	..	..	..	..	..	..	..	..	..	..	..	..	..	..	..	..	..	..	..
Sub-Saharan Africa	SSA	79	1	7	2	13	101	0	0	9	17	52	6	322	11	49	1	14	23	10	195
European Community	EEC	5,552	1,194	259	230	104	767	103	94	107	94	552	414	1,075	158	5,360	38	388	574	125	685
North America	NNA	934	193	29	28	2	62	4	1	15	0	67	44	84	13	2,785	13	230	90	11	173
Rest of World	ROW	1,266	329	136	29	38	139	16	20	10	28	119	107	327	136	2,841	2	135	114	84	303
World	WLD	7,753	1,723	436	294	157	1,067	124	116	141	126	797	571	1,804	318	11,026	55	763	801	229	1,356

Note: ** means "not applicable."

(Table continues on the following page)

5-54. Direction of trade matrix, current U.S. dollars, 1991 *(continued)*

Exporters		GIN	GNB	KEN	LBR	LBY	MDG	MWI	MLI	MRT	MUS	MAR	MOZ	NER	NGA	REU	RWA	STP	SEN	SYC	SLE
Algeria	DZA	..	..	..	0	7	..	..	0	30	0	51	1	0	..	..	..		1	..	..
Angola	AGO	..	..	..	..	..	..	..	..	..	..	1	..	..	18	..	..		1	..	..
Benin	BEN	..	..	..	..	..	..	..	..	..	..	..	..	..	..	..	..	..	..	..	..
Burkina Faso	BFA	..	..	..	..	..	..	..	..	..	..	..	..	..	..	..	..	..	..	..	..
Burundi	BDI	..	..	..	..	..	..	..	..	..	..	..	..	..	..	..	..	..	..	..	..
Cameroon	CMR	..	..	..	..	..	..	..	..	..	..	..	..	..	..	..	..	..	..	..	..
Cape Verde	CPV	..	..	..	..	..	..	..	..	..	..	..	..	..	..	..	..	..	..	..	..
Central African	CAF	..	..	..	..	..	..	..	..	..	..	..	..	..	..	..	..	..	..	..	..
Chad	TCD	..	..	..	..	..	..	..	0	..	0	..	..	..	..	2	..	..	..	..	..
Comoros	COM	..	..	..	..	..	..	..	..	..	..	..	..	..	..	..	..	..	..	..	..
Congo, Dem. Rep	ZAR	..	..	..	..	..	..	..	..	..	..	..	..	..	..	..	..	..	..	..	..
Congo, Rep.	COG	..	..	..	..	..	..	..	..	..	..	..	..	..	..	..	..	..	..	..	..
Côte d'Ivoire	CIV	..	..	..	..	..	..	..	..	..	..	..	..	..	..	..	..	..	..	..	..
Djibouti	DJI	0	..	0	..	0	0	..	..	0	0	0	..	0	0	0	0	..	0	..	..
Egypt, Arab Rep	EGY	0	..	3	8	120	0	0	0	..	0	20	0	0	2	..	0	..	0	..	0
Equatorial Guin	GNQ	..	..	..	..	..	..	..	..	..	..	..	..	..	..	..	..	..	..	..	..
Ethiopia	ETH	..	..	1	..	0	..	0	..	0	0	..	0	0	0	..	..	..	0	..	..
Gabon	GAB	..	..	..	..	..	..	..	..	..	..	..	..	..	..	..	..	..	..	..	..
Gambia, The	GMB	..	..	..	..	..	..	..	..	..	..	..	..	..	..	..	..	..	..	..	..
Ghana	GHA	..	..	..	..	..	..	..	..	..	..	..	..	..	..	..	..	..	..	..	..
Guinea	GIN	**	..	..	..	..	..	..	..	..	..	..	..	..	..	..	..	..	..	..	..
Guinea-Bissau	GNB	..	**	..	..	..	..	..	..	..	..	..	..	..	..	..	..	..	..	..	..
Kenya	KEN	0	0	**	0	0	1	2	..	0	5	0	2	..	2	4	21	..	..	1	0
Liberia	LBR	..	..	..	**	..	..	..	..	..	..	..	..	..	..	..	..	..	..	..	..
Libya	LBY	0	..	..	..	**	..	..	..	0	..	122	..	0	0	..	..	..	0	..	..
Madagascar	MDG	..	0	0	..	..	**	..	..	..	9	0	0	..	0	15	0	..	0	0	..
Malawi	MWI	0	..	0	..	..	..	**	..	..	0	..	1	..	0	..	0	..	0	..	..
Mali	MLI	..	..	..	..	..	..	..	**	..	..	..	..	..	..	..	..	..	..	..	..
Mauritania	MRT	..	..	..	..	..	..	..	..	**	..	..	..	..	..	..	..	..	..	..	..
Mauritius	MUS	0	..	1	0	..	7	0	..	0	**	0	0	..	0	23	2	..	..	11	0
Morocco	MAR	6	0	0	0	197	0	..	5	6	2	**	1	0	13	2	..	..	5	..	0
Mozambique	MOZ	..	..	..	..	..	..	..	..	..	..	..	**	..	..	..	..	..	..	..	..
Niger	NER	..	..	..	..	..	..	..	..	..	..	..	..	**	..	..	..	..	..	..	..
Nigeria	NGA	13	..	2	1	..	0	0	0	..	..	5	..	3	**	..	0	..	0	..	6
Reunion	REU	..	..	..	..	5	..	..	..	..	4	..	0	..	..	**	..	..	..	0	..
Rwanda	RWA	..	..	..	..	..	..	..	..	..	..	..	..	..	..	..	**	..	..	..	..
São Tomé and Principe	STP	..	..	..	..	..	..	..	..	..	..	..	..	..	..	..	..	**	..	..	..
Senegal	SEN	5	3	..	0	..	0	0	24	0	..	0	2	0	1	..	..	..	**	..	0
Seychelles	SYC	..	..	..	..	..	..	..	..	..	..	..	..	..	..	..	..	..	..	**	..
Sierra Leone	SLE	..	..	..	..	..	..	..	..	..	..	..	..	..	..	..	..	..	..	..	**
Somalia	SOM	..	..	..	..	..	..	..	..	..	..	..	..	..	..	..	..	..	..	..	..
South Africa	ZAF	..	..	..	..	..	..	..	..	..	..	..	..	..	..	..	..	..	..	..	..
Sudan	SDN	..	..	..	..	..	..	..	..	..	..	..	..	..	..	..	..	..	..	..	..
Tanzania	TZA	0	2	0	0	202	0	..	0	2	..	27	0	0	0	..	..	..	1	..	0
Togo	TGO	..	..	..	..	..	..	..	..	..	..	..	..	..	..	..	..	..	..	..	..
Tunisia	TUN	0	..	..	0	0	..	..	1	..	..	2	0	3	19	..	..	..	0	..	0
Uganda	UGA	..	..	..	..	..	..	..	..	..	..	..	..	..	..	..	..	..	..	..	..
Zambia	ZMB	..	..	..	..	..	..	..	..	..	..	..	..	..	..	..	..	..	..	..	..
Zimbabwe	ZWE	..	..	..	..	..	..	..	..	..	..	..	..	..	..	..	..	..	..	..	..
Sub-Saharan Africa	SSA	19	5	5	1	202	14	2	25	2	17	33	5	3	22	45	23	1	2	13	6
European Community	EEC	324	61	949	582	3,531	207	150	227	303	446	4,619	295	169	3,738	1,561	88	24	695	53	101
North America	NNA	87	1	101	49	50	15	56	21	29	15	565	116	12	848	2	4	5	92	2	24
Rest of World	ROW	76	26	604	3,874	1,653	83	61	43	82	515	1,059	226	26	1,772	152	23	3	181	54	35
World	WLD	506	91	1,670	4,506	5,236	306	311	315	414	981	6,251	675	213	6,399	1,723	136	33	970	111	166

Note: ** means "not applicable."   (Table continues on the following page)

5-54. Direction of trade matrix, current U.S. dollars, 1991

Exporters		**Importers** SOM	ZAF	SDN	TZA	TGO	TUN	UGA	ZMB	ZWE	*Percentage of total exports* SSA	EEC	NNA	ROW	WLD
Algeria	DZA	..	..	..	13	0	101	2	..	..	47	8,733	2,038	1,003	11,790
Angola	AGO	..	..	..	9	..	..	..	..	..	38	919	2,132	321	3,410
Benin	BEN	..	..	..	..	..	..	..	..	..	..	..	..	..	..
Burkina Faso	BFA	..	..	..	..	..	..	..	..	..	..	..	..	..	..
Burundi	BDI	..	..	..	..	..	..	..	..	..	..	..	..	..	..
Cameroon	CMR	..	..	..	..	..	..	..	..	..	..	..	..	..	..
Cape Verde	CPV	..	..	..	..	..	..	..	..	..	..	..	..	..	..
Central African	CAF	..	..	..	..	..	..	..	..	..	..	..	..	..	..
Chad	TCD	..	0	..	..	..	..	..	..	..	0	13	0	3	16
Comoros	COM	..	..	..	..	..	..	..	..	..	..	..	..	..	..
Congo, Dem. Rep	ZAR	..	..	..	..	..	..	..	..	..	..	..	..	..	..
Congo, Rep.	COG	..	..	..	..	..	..	..	..	..	..	..	..	..	..
Côte d'Ivoire	CIV	..	..	..	..	..	..	..	..	..	..	..	..	..	..
Djibouti	DJI	1	..	..	..	..	0	0	..	..	1	11	0	5	17
Egypt, Arab Rep	EGY	0	0	26	2	0	15	0	0	..	45	1,593	288	1,773	3,693
Equatorial Guin	GNQ	..	..	..	..	..	..	..	..	..	..	..	..	..	..
Ethiopia	ETH	..	1	0	..	..	..	0	0	..	8	90	10	59	167
Gabon	GAB	..	..	..	..	..	..	..	..	..	..	..	..	..	..
Gambia, The	GMB	..	..	..	..	..	..	..	..	..	..	..	..	..	..
Ghana	GHA	..	..	..	..	..	..	..	..	..	..	..	..	..	..
Guinea	GIN	..	..	..	..	..	..	..	..	..	..	..	..	..	..
Guinea-Bissau	GNB	..	..	..	..	..	..	..	..	..	..	..	..	..	..
Kenya	KEN	13	3	21	37	0	1	75	3	..	216	463	47	407	1,135
Liberia	LBR	..	..	..	..	..	..	..	..	..	..	..	..	..	..
Libya	LBY	..	..	153	..	..	96	..	..	..	154	9,668	0	1,390	11,212
Madagascar	MDG	..	1	..	0	..	0	..	..	..	12	150	43	98	294
Malawi	MWI	..	42	0	2	..	..	0	3	..	13	223	72	165	472
Mali	MLI	..	..	..	..	..	..	..	..	..	..	..	..	..	..
Mauritania	MRT	..	..	..	..	..	..	..	..	..	..	..	..	..	..
Mauritius	MUS	..	5	..	0	0	0	0	1	..	31	946	147	102	1,218
Morocco	MAR	..	0	0	3	4	62	..	..	..	87	2,710	132	1,370	4,287
Mozambique	MOZ	..	..	..	..	..	..	..	..	..	..	..	..	..	..
Niger	NER	..	..	..	..	..	..	..	..	..	..	..	..	..	..
Nigeria	NGA	..	0	0	0	2	..	..	0	..	664	5,613	6,163	390	12,828
Reunion	REU	..	0	..	0	..	..	..	..	..	18	120	0	20	150
Rwanda	RWA	..	..	..	..	..	..	..	..	..	..	..	..	..	..
São Tomé and Principe	STP	..	..	..	..	..	..	..	..	..	..	..	..	..	..
Senegal	SEN	..	..	..	..	1	2	..	..	..	92	334	12	242	652
Seychelles	SYC	..	..	..	..	..	..	..	..	..	..	..	..	..	..
Sierra Leone	SLE	..	..	..	..	..	..	..	..	..	..	..	..	..	..
Somalia	SOM	**	..	..	..	..	..	..	..	..	..	..	..	..	..
South Africa	ZAF	..	**	..	..	..	..	..	..	..	..	..	..	19,944	19,944
Sudan	SDN	..	..	**	..	..	..	..	..	..	..	..	..	..	..
Tanzania	TZA	..	..	4	**	3	..	0	..	..	25	2,845	28	801	3,700
Togo	TGO	..	..	..	..	**	..	..	..	..	..	..	..	..	..
Tunisia	TUN	..	0	0	..	..	**	..	..	..	40	75	29	111	253
Uganda	UGA	..	..	..	..	..	..	**	..	..	..	..	..	..	..
Zambia	ZMB	..	..	..	..	..	..	..	**	..	..	..	..	..	..
Zimbabwe	ZWE	..	..	..	..	..	..	..	..	**	..	..	..	..	..
Sub-Saharan Africa	SSA	13	52	25	48	6	3	76	7	..	1,119	11,727	8,654	22,558	44,005
European Community	EEC	55	7,541	533	470	352	3,891	176	255	..	17,466	987,386	106,985	375,677	1,485,693
North America	NNA	7	2,240	104	49	25	220	15	25	..	2,595	112,072	172,994	234,930	522,523
Rest of World	ROW	20	3,371	504	361	216	680	115	152	..	11,187	298,666	277,751	616,084	1,198,937
World	WLD	96	13,376	1,163	931	597	4,794	383	481	..	32,476	1,406,187	566,202	1,228,801	3,226,919

Note: ** means "not applicable."

5-55. Direction of trade matrix, current U.S. dollars, 1997

Exporters		Importers DZA	AGO	BEN	BFA	BDI	CMR	CPV	CAF	TCD	COM	ZAR	COG	CIV	DJI	EGY	GNQ	ERI	ETH	GAB	GMB
Algeria	DZA	**	0	0	0	..	0	..	..	..	..	..	0	..	..	5	..	..	..	0	..
Angola	AGO	..	**	..	..	..	..	..	..	..	..	..	..	..	..	..	..	..	..	..	..
Benin	BEN	..	..	**	..	..	..	..	..	..	..	..	..	..	..	..	..	..	..	..	..
Burkina Faso	BFA	..	..	..	**	..	..	..	..	..	..	..	..	..	..	..	..	..	..	..	..
Burundi	BDI	..	..	..	..	**	..	..	..	..	..	..	..	..	..	..	..	..	..	..	..
Cameroon	CMR	..	..	..	..	..	**	..	..	..	..	..	..	..	..	..	..	..	..	..	..
Cape Verde	CPV	..	..	..	..	..	..	**	..	..	..	..	..	..	..	..	..	..	..	..	..
Central African	CAF	..	..	..	..	..	..	..	**	..	..	..	..	..	..	..	..	..	..	..	..
Chad	TCD	..	..	..	..	..	..	..	..	**	..	..	..	..	..	..	..	..	..	..	..
Comoros	COM	..	..	..	..	..	..	..	..	..	**	..	..	..	..	..	..	..	..	..	..
Congo, Dem. Rep	ZAR	..	..	..	..	..	..	..	..	..	..	**	..	..	..	..	..	..	..	..	..
Congo, Rep.	COG	..	..	..	..	..	..	..	..	..	..	..	**	..	..	..	..	..	..	..	..
Côte d'Ivoire	CIV	..	..	..	..	..	..	..	..	..	..	..	..	**	..	..	..	..	..	..	..
Djibouti	DJI	..	..	..	..	..	..	..	..	..	..	..	..	..	**	..	..	..	..	..	..
Egypt, Arab Rep	EGY	7	1	0	0	0	0	..	..	0	0	1	0	2	1	**	0	0	2	0	0
Equatorial Guinea	GNQ	..	..	..	..	..	..	..	..	..	..	..	..	..	..	..	**	..	..	..	..
Ethiopia	ETH	..	..	..	..	..	..	..	..	..	..	..	..	..	..	..	..	..	**	..	..
Gabon	GAB	..	..	..	..	..	..	..	..	..	..	..	..	..	..	..	..	..	..	**	..
Gambia, The	GMB	..	..	..	..	..	..	..	..	..	..	..	..	..	..	..	..	..	..	..	**
Ghana	GHA	..	..	..	..	..	..	..	..	..	..	..	..	..	..	..	..	..	..	..	..
Guinea	GIN	..	..	..	..	..	..	..	..	..	..	..	..	..	..	..	..	..	..	..	..
Guinea-Bissau	GNB	..	..	..	..	..	..	..	..	..	..	..	..	..	..	..	..	..	..	..	..
Kenya	KEN	1	0	0	0	5	1	..	0	0	3	38	2	0	3	52	0	1	35	0	0
Liberia	LBR	..	..	..	..	..	..	..	..	..	..	..	..	..	..	..	..	..	..	..	..
Libya	LBY	0	..	..	..	..	..	..	..	0	..	..	..	..	..	85	..	..	..	..	..
Madagascar	MDG	2	0	0	0	..	0	..	..	..	1	0	..	0	0	0	0	..	0	0	..
Malawi	MWI	..	..	..	..	..	..	..	..	..	..	..	..	..	..	..	..	..	..	..	..
Mali	MLI	..	..	..	..	..	..	..	..	..	..	..	..	..	..	..	..	..	..	..	..
Mauritania	MRT	..	..	..	..	..	..	..	..	..	..	..	..	..	..	..	..	..	..	..	..
Mauritius	MUS	..	..	0	0	1	0	..	0	0	1	0	0	0	0	0	..	..	..	0	..
Morocco	MAR	3	6	4	1	..	3	0	0	0	0	3	6	22	0	12	2	..	0	18	1
Mozambique	MOZ	..	..	..	..	..	..	..	..	..	..	..	..	..	..	..	..	..	..	..	..
Niger	NER	..	..	..	..	..	..	..	..	..	..	..	..	..	..	..	..	..	..	..	..
Nigeria	NGA	..	0	14	0	..	61	..	..	0	..	0	1	569	..	0	..	..	..	0	1
Reunion	REU	..	..	..	..	..	..	..	..	..	..	..	..	..	..	..	..	..	..	..	..
Rwanda	RWA	..	..	..	..	..	..	..	..	..	..	..	..	..	..	..	..	..	..	..	..
São Tomé and Principe	STP	..	..	..	..	..	..	..	..	..	..	..	..	..	..	..	..	..	..	..	..
Senegal	SEN	..	..	..	..	..	..	..	..	..	..	..	..	..	..	..	..	..	..	..	..
Seychelles	SYC	..	..	..	..	..	..	..	..	..	..	..	..	..	..	..	..	..	..	..	..
Sierra Leone	SLE	..	..	..	..	..	..	..	..	..	..	..	..	..	..	..	..	..	..	..	..
Somalia	SOM	..	..	..	..	..	..	..	..	..	..	..	..	..	..	..	..	..	..	..	..
South Africa	ZAF	26	180	4	1	8	28	4	0	0	13	178	30	24	0	31	0	..	12	9	6
Sudan	SDN	..	..	..	..	..	..	..	..	..	..	..	..	..	..	..	..	..	..	..	..
Tanzania	TZA	..	0	..	..	1	0	..	..	..	0	9	0	0	..	1	..	0	4	..	..
Togo	TGO	..	..	..	..	..	..	..	..	..	..	..	..	..	..	..	..	..	..	..	..
Tunisia	TUN	38	0	3	1	..	6	0	0	0	..	0	0	6	..	24	0	..	0	1	0
Uganda	UGA	..	..	..	..	..	..	..	..	..	..	..	..	..	..	..	..	..	..	..	..
Zambia	ZMB	..	..	..	..	..	..	..	..	..	..	..	..	..	..	..	..	..	..	..	..
Zimbabwe	ZWE	..	..	..	..	..	..	..	..	..	..	..	..	..	..	..	..	..	..	..	..
Sub-Saharan Africa	SSA	29	181	18	2	14	90	4	0	0	18	226	33	594	4	85	0	1	52	10	8
European Community	EEC	4,906	1,176	439	234	46	820	195	65	78	121	319	473	1,449	148	7,548	95	143	517	671	113
North America	NNA	1,143	288	60	19	1	124	10	4	3	0	43	78	155	8	3,951	47	16	128	89	10
Rest of World	ROW	1,453	746	301	69	15	187	21	7	11	29	319	116	463	99	6,172	12	50	426	152	105
World	WLD	7,504	2,217	813	322	68	1,195	226	76	92	153	738	674	2,637	258	17,730	153	210	1,110	913	228

Note: ** means "not applicable."

(Table continues on the following page)

5-55. Direction of trade matrix, current U.S. dollars, 1997 *(continued)*

Exporters		GHA	GIN	GNB	KEN	LBR	LBY	MDG	MWI	MLI	MRT	MUS	MAR	MOZ	NER	NGA	REU	RWA	STP	SEN	SYC
Importers → *Percentage of total exports*																					
Algeria	DZA	..	..	..	..	0	3	0	..	0	52	..	94	..	1	2	..	..	..	10	..
Angola	AGO	..	..	..	..	..	..	..	..	..	..	..	..	..	..	..	..	..	..	..	..
Benin	BEN	..	..	..	..	..	..	..	..	..	..	..	..	..	..	..	..	..	..	..	..
Burkina Faso	BFA	..	..	..	..	..	..	..	..	..	..	..	..	..	..	..	..	..	..	..	..
Burundi	BDI	..	..	..	..	..	..	..	..	..	..	..	..	..	..	..	..	..	..	..	..
Cameroon	CMR	..	..	..	..	..	..	..	..	..	..	..	..	..	..	..	..	..	..	..	..
Cape Verde	CPV	..	..	..	..	..	..	..	..	..	..	..	..	..	..	..	..	..	..	..	..
Central African	CAF	..	..	..	..	..	..	..	..	..	..	..	..	..	..	..	..	..	..	..	..
Chad	TCD	..	..	..	..	..	..	..	..	..	..	..	..	..	..	..	..	..	..	..	..
Comoros	COM	..	..	..	..	..	..	..	..	..	..	..	..	..	..	..	..	..	..	..	..
Congo, Dem. Rep	ZAR	..	..	..	..	..	..	..	..	..	..	..	..	..	..	..	..	..	..	..	..
Congo, Rep.	COG	..	..	..	..	..	..	..	..	..	..	..	..	..	..	..	..	..	..	..	..
Côte d'Ivoire	CIV	..	..	..	..	..	..	..	..	..	..	..	..	..	..	..	..	..	..	..	..
Djibouti	DJI	..	..	..	..	..	..	..	..	..	..	..	..	..	..	..	..	..	..	..	..
Egypt, Arab Rep	EGY	0	0	0	3	0	70	0	0	0	0	0	11	0	0	2	..	0	..	1	..
Equatorial Guinea	GNQ	..	..	..	..	..	..	..	..	..	..	..	..	..	..	..	..	..	..	..	..
Ethiopia	ETH	..	..	..	..	..	..	..	..	..	..	..	..	..	..	..	..	..	..	..	..
Gabon	GAB	..	..	..	..	..	..	..	..	..	..	..	..	..	..	..	..	..	..	..	..
Gambia, The	GMB	..	..	..	..	..	..	..	..	..	..	..	..	..	..	..	..	..	..	..	..
Ghana	GHA	**	..	..	..	..	..	..	..	..	..	..	..	..	..	..	..	..	..	..	..
Guinea	GIN	..	**	..	..	..	..	..	..	..	..	..	..	..	..	..	..	..	..	..	..
Guinea-Bissau	GNB	..	..	**	..	..	..	..	..	..	..	..	..	..	..	..	..	..	..	..	..
Kenya	KEN	0	0	..	**	0	0	3	6	0	0	14	0	2	..	3	..	59	0	1	4
Liberia	LBR	..	..	..	..	**	..	..	..	..	..	..	..	..	..	..	..	..	..	..	..
Libya	LBY	2	..	..	1	..	**	..	..	..	..	..	39	..	0	3	..	..	..	4	..
Madagascar	MDG	0	0	..	0	0	..	**	..	0	0	11	0	0	0	0	..	..	..	0	0
Malawi	MWI	..	..	..	..	..	..	..	**	..	..	..	..	..	..	..	..	..	..	..	..
Mali	MLI	..	..	..	..	..	..	..	..	**	..	..	..	..	..	..	..	..	..	..	..
Mauritania	MRT	..	..	..	..	..	..	..	..	..	**	..	..	..	..	..	..	..	..	..	..
Mauritius	MUS	0	0	..	4	..	0	58	3	0	0	**	0	0	0	0	..	2	..	0	4
Morocco	MAR	5	8	..	0	1	130	1	..	8	10	1	**	..	1	5	..	..	..	11	..
Mozambique	MOZ	..	..	..	..	..	..	..	..	..	..	..	..	**	..	..	..	..	..	..	..
Niger	NER	..	..	..	..	..	..	..	..	..	..	..	..	..	**	..	..	..	..	..	..
Nigeria	NGA	143	4	..	0	1	0	..	..	..	..	..	109	..	0	**	..	..	..	76	..
Reunion	REU	..	..	..	..	..	..	..	..	..	..	..	..	..	..	..	**	..	..	..	..
Rwanda	RWA	..	..	..	..	..	..	..	..	..	..	..	..	..	..	..	..	**	..	..	..
São Tomé and Principe	STP	..	..	..	..	..	..	..	..	..	..	..	..	..	..	..	..	..	**	..	..
Senegal	SEN	..	..	..	..	..	..	..	..	..	..	..	..	..	..	..	..	..	..	**	..
Seychelles	SYC	..	..	..	..	..	..	..	..	..	..	..	..	..	..	..	..	..	..	..	**
Sierra Leone	SLE	..	..	..	..	..	..	..	..	..	..	..	..	..	..	..	..	..	..	..	..
Somalia	SOM	..	..	..	..	..	..	..	..	..	..	..	..	..	..	..	..	..	..	..	..
South Africa	ZAF	86	10	0	321	5	4	53	231	15	2	192	26	419	2	44	..	5	3	3	40
Sudan	SDN	..	..	..	..	..	..	..	..	..	..	..	..	..	..	..	..	..	..	..	..
Tanzania	TZA	1	0	..	24	..	..	0	5	0	0	1	..	0	..	0	..	6	..	..	0
Togo	TGO	..	..	..	..	..	..	..	..	..	..	..	..	..	..	..	..	..	..	..	..
Tunisia	TUN	4	0	0	0	0	257	0	0	1	1	0	33	..	1	0	..	..	0	4	..
Uganda	UGA	..	..	..	..	..	..	..	..	..	..	..	..	..	..	..	..	..	..	..	..
Zambia	ZMB	..	..	..	..	..	..	..	..	..	..	..	..	..	..	..	..	..	..	..	..
Zimbabwe	ZWE	..	..	..	..	..	..	..	..	..	..	..	..	..	..	..	..	..	..	..	..
Sub-Saharan Africa	SSA	230	14	0	349	5	4	114	246	15	2	218	135	421	2	46	..	72	3	79	47
European Community	EEC	1,257	353	59	1,019	603	3,124	359	81	338	315	725	5,830	159	168	2,979	..	91	24	899	112
North America	NNA	366	88	3	250	44	158	12	24	35	21	30	576	62	33	886	..	38	13	65	6
Rest of World	ROW	730	152	22	1,300	2,825	1,676	265	299	78	177	975	1,506	584	36	2,050	..	57	5	238	121
World	WLD	2,500	598	84	2,613	3,472	4,959	638	494	451	513	1,748	8,022	878	237	5,920	..	253	42	1,277	246

Note: ** means "not applicable."

(Table continues on the following page)

5-55. Direction of trade matrix, current U.S. dollars, 1997

Exporters		*Importers*													*Percentage of total exports*		
		SLE	SOM	ZAF	SDN	TZA	TGO	TUN	UGA	ZMB	ZWE	SSA	EEC	NNA	ROW	WLD
Algeria	DZA	..	..	0	4	..	..	60	..	..	..	69	8,817	2,692	2,368	13,894
Angola	AGO	..	..	..	..	..	..	..	..	..	..	..	..	..	..	..
Benin	BEN	..	..	..	..	..	..	..	..	..	..	..	..	..	..	..
Burkina Faso	BFA	..	..	..	..	..	..	..	..	..	..	..	..	..	..	..
Burundi	BDI	..	..	..	..	..	..	..	..	..	..	..	..	..	..	..
Cameroon	CMR	..	..	..	..	..	..	..	..	..	..	..	..	..	..	..
Cape Verde	CPV	..	..	..	..	..	..	..	..	..	..	..	..	..	..	..
Central African	CAF	..	..	..	..	..	..	..	..	..	..	..	..	..	..	..
Chad	TCD	..	..	..	..	..	..	..	..	..	..	..	..	..	..	..
Comoros	COM	..	..	..	..	..	..	..	..	..	..	..	..	..	..	..
Congo, Dem. Rep	ZAR	..	..	..	..	..	..	..	..	..	..	..	..	..	..	..
Congo, Rep.	COG	..	..	..	..	..	..	..	..	..	..	..	..	..	..	..
Côte d'Ivoire	CIV	..	..	..	..	..	..	..	..	..	..	..	..	..	..	..
Djibouti	DJI	..	..	..	..	..	..	..	..	..	..	..	..	..	..	..
Egypt, Arab Rep	EGY	0	0	40	25	1	0	19	1	2	..	45	1,621	453	1,789	3,908
Equatorial Guinea	GNQ	..	..	..	..	..	..	..	..	..	..	..	..	..	..	..
Ethiopia	ETH	..	..	..	..	..	..	..	..	..	..	..	..	..	..	..
Gabon	GAB	..	..	..	..	..	..	..	..	..	..	..	..	..	..	..
Gambia, The	GMB	..	..	..	..	..	..	..	..	..	..	..	..	..	..	..
Ghana	GHA	..	..	..	..	..	..	..	..	..	..	..	..	..	..	..
Guinea	GIN	..	..	..	..	..	..	..	..	..	..	..	..	..	..	..
Guinea-Bissau	GNB	..	..	..	..	..	..	..	..	..	..	..	..	..	..	..
Kenya	KEN	0	32	17	32	239	0	1	280	4	..	774	676	72	457	1,952
Liberia	LBR	..	..	..	..	..	..	..	..	..	..	..	..	..	..	..
Libya	LBY	..	..	..	1	..	..	385	..	..	..	11	7,012	3	2,003	9,029
Madagascar	MDG	..	..	3	0	0	..	0	0	0	..	13	183	11	82	278
Malawi	MWI	..	..	..	..	..	..	..	..	..	..	..	..	..	..	..
Mali	MLI	..	..	..	..	..	..	..	..	..	..	..	..	..	..	..
Mauritania	MRT	..	..	..	..	..	..	..	..	..	..	..	..	..	..	..
Mauritius	MUS	..	..	9	0	1	0	..	1	1	..	88	1,187	236	150	1,600
Morocco	MAR	1	0	4	..	1	2	40	0	..	..	123	2,837	195	1,540	4,674
Mozambique	MOZ	..	..	..	..	..	..	..	..	..	..	..	..	..	..	..
Niger	NER	..	..	..	..	..	..	..	..	..	..	..	..	..	..	..
Nigeria	NGA	..	..	66	..	..	1	..	..	..	..	871	3,327	4,784	2,183	11,164
Reunion	REU	..	..	..	..	..	..	..	..	..	..	..	..	..	..	..
Rwanda	RWA	..	..	..	..	..	..	..	..	..	..	..	..	..	..	..
São Tomé and Principe	STP	..	..	..	..	..	..	..	..	..	..	..	..	..	..	..
Senegal	SEN	..	..	..	..	..	..	..	..	..	..	..	..	..	..	..
Seychelles	SYC	..	..	..	..	..	..	..	..	..	..	..	..	..	..	..
Sierra Leone	SLE	**	..	..	..	..	..	..	..	..	..	..	..	..	..	..
Somalia	SOM	..	**	..	..	..	..	..	..	..	..	..	..	..	..	..
South Africa	ZAF	7	0	**	5	111	6	3	33	444	..	3,566	5,898	2,329	11,598	22,474
Sudan	SDN	..	..	..	**	..	..	..	..	..	..	..	..	..	..	..
Tanzania	TZA	..	0	7	2	**	..	0	7	2	..	79	222	13	290	597
Togo	TGO	..	..	..	..	..	**	..	..	..	..	..	..	..	..	..
Tunisia	TUN	0	..	4	1	..	1	**	..	0	..	31	4,358	41	1,131	5,559
Uganda	UGA	..	..	..	..	..	..	..	**	..	..	..	..	..	..	..
Zambia	ZMB	..	..	..	..	..	..	..	..	**	..	..	..	..	..	..
Zimbabwe	ZWE	..	..	..	..	..	..	..	..	..	**	..	..	..	..	..
Sub-Saharan Africa	SSA	7	32	103	39	350	7	4	321	450	..	5,670	36,140	10,828	23,593	75,128
European Community	EEC	111	17	11,157	396	457	281	5,879	213	161	..	18,633	1,275,384	173,841	625,576	2,090,426
North America	NNA	17	4	3,287	56	75	31	312	42	34	..	3,391	141,823	309,207	397,026	851,173
Rest of World	ROW	32	62	8,274	466	662	240	1,343	175	580	..	16,660	472,199	484,394	1,118,426	2,086,327
World	WLD	161	114	23,182	956	1,446	553	7,535	719	898	..	40,753	1,894,397	972,440	2,144,992	5,043,758

Note: ** means "not applicable."

Figure 5-1. Terms of trade gains and losses, average 1992-99*

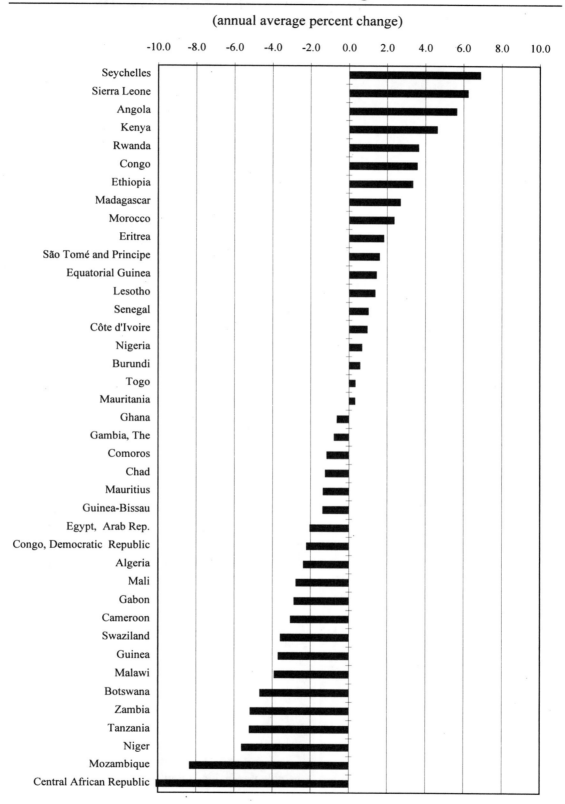

(annual average percent change)

*Or most recent year available

Technical notes

Tables

Tables 5-1 and 5-2. Merchandise exports and merchandise imports, f.o.b. Merchandise exports and imports (World Bank country desks) are both valued f.o.b. and comprise all transactions involving a change of ownership of goods, including nonmonetary gold, between residents of a country and the rest of the world. These transactions include those in which ownership changes even though goods do not cross customs borders. The few types of goods not covered by the merchandise account include travelers' purchases abroad, which are included in travel, and purchases of goods by diplomatic and military personnel, which are classified under other official goods, services, and income.

Tables 5-3 and 5-4. Exports and imports of total services. Service exports and imports (World Bank country desks) include total nonfactor and factor services, based on transactions involving ownership changes as explained above for goods. Nonfactor services comprise shipment, passenger and other transport services, and travel, as well as current account transactions not separately reported (that is, not classified as merchandise, nonfactor services, or transfers). These include transactions with nonresidents by government agencies and their personnel abroad, as well as transactions by private residents with foreign governments and government personnel stationed in the reporting country. Factor services comprise services of labor and capital, thus covering income from direct investment abroad, interest, dividends, and

property and labor income. Net interest is recorded on an accrual basis; that is, interest obligations are included whether payments are made or not.

Table 5-5. Net private transfers. Net private transfers (World Bank country desks) are inflows (from private sources to either private or public recipients) less outflows from private sources to either private or public recipients that carry no provisions for repayments. They include workers' remittances; transfers by migrants; gifts, dowries, and inheritances; and alimony and other support remittances.

Table 5-6. Net current official transfers. Net official transfers (World Bank country desks) are the official sources counterpart of Table 5-5. They include transfers on both current and capital accounts, including government grants of real resources and financial items such as subsidies to current budgets, grants of technical assistance, and government contributions to international organizations for administrative expenses.

Table 5-7. Current account balance, excluding net capital grants. Current account balance (World Bank country desks), as presented here, is the difference between exports of goods and all services plus inflows of unrequited current transfers (official and private) and imports of goods and all services plus outflows of unrequited transfers to the rest of the world. Other common presentations exclude or include both current and capital official transfers. Data in previous volumes included both.

Table 5-8. Current account balance, excluding net capital grants, as a percentage of GDP. It is defined as the ratio of figures presented in Table 5-7 to GDP in current prices (Table 2-5).

Table 5-9. Net capital grants. These grants (World Bank country desks) are unrequited transfers, often used to finance balance of payments deficits.

Table 5-10. Net foreign direct investment. Net foreign direct investment (World Bank country desks) is the net amount invested or reinvested by nonresidents to acquire a lasting interest in enterprises in which they exercise significant managerial control. Investment includes equity capital, reinvested earnings, and other capital. The net figures subtract the value of direct investment abroad by residents of the reporting country.

Table 5-11. Net long-term borrowing. Net long-term borrowing is calculated as disbursements less the repayment of principal (amortization) of public, publicly guaranteed, and private nonguaranteed borrowings that have an original or extended maturity of more than one year and that are repayable in foreign currencies, goods, or services. These data are as reported in the World Bank's Debtor Reporting System (DRS) and are in accord with the data on external debt discussed in Chapter 6.

Table 5-12. Other capital flows. Other capital flows comprise the net balance of inflows and outflows of capital not elsewhere included. It covers, for example, changes in the stock of short-term debt, arrears, and other liabilities (all adjusted for valuation changes resulting from exchange rate changes and other factors), and errors and omissions. This table incorporates corrections to data in *ADI 1992*.

Table 5-13. Use of reserves. This table (World Bank country desks) shows the variation from year to year of the net balance of international reserve assets and is valued throughout at year-end London prices (for example, US$37.37 an ounce in 1970 and US$484.10 an ounce in 1987). Positive numbers represent a decrease or use of reserves; negative numbers represent an increase in reserves. This table incorporates corrections to data in ADI 1996.

Table 5-14. Import coverage ratio of reserves. This ratio gives the number of months, at current import levels, that can adequately be covered by available foreign exchange reserves (World Bank country desks). It is obtained by dividing the stock of reserves by imports divided by 12.

Tables 5-15 and 5-16. Export and import unit values. The indexes for total export and import unit values (World Bank country desks) are based on exports and imports of goods and nonfactor services from the national accounts. These indexes are calculated by dividing the values of exports and imports expressed in current U.S. dollars (Tables 2-14 and 2-15) by the volume of exports (f.o.b.) and imports (c.i.f.) expressed in constant 1995 U.S. dollars (Tables 2-16 and 2-17). Because of the way these trade unit value indexes are calculated (Paasche indexes, with changing weights), they reflect the composition of exports and imports in each year and may not give a reliable trend in unit values when trade composition changes dramatically. By contrast, this index reflects more accurately shifts in a country's actual composition of trade than would an index using weights based on trade shares in a single year. Data may differ from those in ADI 1992 and ADI 1994–95 because a different source was used for this volume.

Table 5-17. Terms of trade. Terms of trade measure the relative movement of export and import prices. This series is calculated as the ratio of a country's export unit values or prices (Table 5-15) to its import unit values or prices (Table 5-16). It shows changes over a base year (1995) in the level of export unit values as a percentage of import unit values. Data may differ from those in *ADI 1992* and *ADI 1994–95* because a different source was used for this volume.

Table 5-18. Forest products exports. Exports of forest production (FAO data) is given as an aggregate including all wood from trees and forests (coniferous and nonconiferous), whether in natural form or partially processed (SITC 245, 246, and 247);

sawwood and sleepers (SITC 248); and wood-based panels and fiberwood, compressed or noncompressed (SITC 634 and 641).

Table 5-19. Petroleum exports. This table contains the volumes of crude petroleum exported (World Bank, IEABAL). Data may differ from *ADI 1992* and *ADI 1994–95* because a different source was used for this volume.

Table 5-20. Copper exports. The table presents the unweighted sum of the metal content weights of copper ore and concentrate and of unrefined plus refined copper, metal, and alloys, unwrought (World Bank, METMIN). Data may differ from ADI 1992 and ADI 1994–95 because a different source was used for this volume.

Table 5-21. Iron exports. These are exports measured in metal content weight of iron ore (World Bank, METMIN).

Table 5-22. Phosphates exports. These are the volume of phosphates exports, expressed as the weight of mineral content in phosphate rock (World Bank, METMIN).

Table 5-23. Cocoa exports. Cocoa exports include cocoa beans, cocoa powder and cake, cocoa paste, cocoa butter, and chocolate products not elsewhere specified (FAO data).

Table 5-24. Coffee exports. Coffee exports are shown for green and roasted beans (FAO data).

Table 5-25. Cotton exports. Cotton exports refer to cotton lint only (FAO data).

Table 5-26. Groundnut exports. Groundnut exports include the weight of groundnuts in shelled equivalent (using a conversion factor of 70 percent), groundnut oil, and groundnut cake (FAO data).

Table 5-27. Oil palm products exports. Exports of oil palm products consist of palm oil and palm kernels (FAO data).

Table 5-28. Sisal exports. Only sisal fiber exports are included (FAO data).

Table 5-29. Tea exports. Tea exports figures are for processed tea (FAO data).

Table 5-30. Sugar exports. Sugar exports are shown in terms of raw sugar equivalent. The conversion factor to express refined sugar in raw sugar equivalent is 1.087 for all countries (FAO data).

Table 5-31. Tobacco exports. Only tobacco leaves are included (FAO data).

Table 5-32. Meat exports. Meat exports are defined as fresh, chilled, or frozen meat (SITC category 011) (FAO data).

Tables 5-33 and 5-34. Manufactured goods exports. Data reported in these tables follow the classification of manufacturing industries as reported in the UN *International Standard Industrial Classification of All Economic Activities* (ISIC), Revision 2 (World Bank country desks). First table is expressed in current prices; second table shows growth.

Tables 5-35 and 5-36. Food imports. Data refer to the sum of food, beverages, tobacco, oilseeds and oleaginous fruits, animal and vegetable oils, and fats (SITC sections 0, 1, and 4 and division 22) (World Bank country desks). First table is expressed in current prices; second table shows growth.

Tables 5-37 and 5-38. Nonfood consumer goods imports. Data reported in these tables show consumer goods imports other than food. Data are calculated as total merchandise imports less food, fuel, intermediate goods, and capital goods imports (World Bank country desks). First table is expressed in current prices; second table shows growth.

Tables 5-39 and 5-40. Fuel imports. Figures are defined as SITC section 3 (sum of Canada, Mexico, and United States) (World Bank country desks). First table presents data in current prices; second table shows growth.

Tables 5-41 and 5-42. Primary intermediate goods imports. Data on these tables comprise minerals, ores, and metals imports (the sum of SITC divisions 27, 28, and 68 and item 522.56) and agricultural raw materials imports (the sum of SITC section 2, less divisions 22, 27, and 28 and groups 233, 244, 266, and 267). Synthetics are excluded (World Bank country desks). First table presents data in current prices; second table shows growth.

Tables 5-43 and 5-44. Manufactured goods imports. Data reported on these tables follow the classification of manufacturing industries as reported in the UN *International Standard Industrial Classification of All Economic Activities* (ISIC), Revision 2 (World Bank country desks). First table presents data in current prices; second table shows growth.

Tables 5-45 and 5-46. Capital goods imports. Data shown here are for machinery and transport equipment (SITC section 7) (World Bank country desks). First table presents data in current prices; second table shows growth.

Tables 5-47, 5-48, and 5-49. Direction of trade matrix, imports. These tables show, for each importing country, the percentage of the value of its total imports that originates from each of the exporting countries for 1987, 1991, and 1997, respectively. They are calculated from Tables 5-53 to 5-55, below.

In these tables data posted under South Africa are for South Africa Customs Union, which comprises Botswana, Lesotho, Namibia, South Africa, and Swaziland.

Tables 5-50, 5-51, and 5-52. Direction of trade matrix, exports. As with the foregoing, for each exporter, these tables show the percentage of the value of total exports, f.o.b., that goes to each of its trade partners for 1987, 1991, and 1997, respectively. These are calculated from Tables 5-53 to 5-55, below.

In these tables data posted under South Africa are for South Africa Customs Union, which comprises Botswana, Lesotho, Namibia, South Africa, and Swaziland.

Tables 5-53, 5-54, and 5-55. Direction of trade matrix, current U.S. dollars. These are the value of trade in goods and services to or from the countries indicated. Matrices are shown for 1987, 1991, and 1997. They form the basis for the calculations in the previous six tables (UNSTAT, COMTRADE). Data for South Africa are for the South Africa Customs Union, which comprises Botswana, Lesotho, Namibia, South Africa, and Swaziland.

Figure

The following indicator has been used to derive the figures in this chapter.

Figure 5-1. Terms of trade gains or losses (Table 5-17).

Methodology used for regional aggregations and period averages in chapter 5

Table	Aggregations[a] (1)	(3)	(4)	(6)	Period averages[b] (2)	(3)
5-1		X				X
5-2		X				X
5-3		X				X
5-4		X				X
5-5	X				X	
5-6	X				X	
5-7	X				X	
5-8				X	X	
5-9	X				X	
5-10	X				X	
5-11	X				X	
5-12	X				X	
5-13	X				X	
5-14				X	X	
5-15			X		X	
5-16			X		X	
5-17			X		X	
5-18	X					X
5-19	X					X
5-20	X					X
5-21	X					X
5-22	X					X
5-23	X					X
5-24	X					X
5-25	X					X
5-26	X					X
5-27	X					X
5-28	X					X
5-29	X					X
5-30	X					X
5-31	X					X
5-32	X				X	
5-33	X				X	
5-34	X					X
5-35	X				X	
5-36	X					X
5-37	X				X	
5-38	X					X
5-39	X				X	
5-40	X					X
5-41	X				X	
5-42	X					X
5-43	X				X	
5-44	X					X
5-45	X				X	
5-46	X					X
5-47	X					
5-48	X					
5-49	X					
5-50	X					
5-51	X					
5-52	X					
5-53	X					
5-54	X					
5-55	X					

Note: Regional aggregations are shown in the rows for Sub-Saharan Africa, North Africa, and All Africa. Period averages are shown in the last three columns. This table shows only the methodologies used in this chapter.

a. Regional aggregations: (1) simple total; (2) simple total of the first indicator divided by the simple total of the second indicator (same country coverage); (3) simple total of the gap-filled indicator; (4) simple total of the gap-filled main indicator divided by the simple total of the gap-filled secondary indicator; (5) simple total of the first gap-filled main indicator less the simple total of the second gap-filled main indicator, all divided by the simple total of the secondary indicator; (6) weighted total (by population); (7) median; (8) no aggregation; (9) simple arithmetic mean.

b. Period averages: (i) arithmetic mean (using the same series as shown in the table i.e., ratio if the rest of the table is shown as ratio, level if the rest of the table is shown as level, growth rate if the rest is shown as growth rate); (2) least-squares growth rate (using main indicator); (3) least-squares growth rate (using main indicator in constant terms, with the rest of the table in current terms).

6

External Debt and Related Flows

The tables in this chapter provide a consistent presentation of the structure and terms of external debt and debt servicing. No data are presented on debt owed to domestic lenders. The aggregates and ratios provide various measures of a country's external debt situation. These measures include the size of debt and its servicing requirements, the amount of debt relative to GDP, the ratio of debt-servicing payments to exports, and the interest rate and terms of the stock of debt (including grace period, maturity, and grant element).

Unlike the presentation in the *ADI 1992*, these tables follow the presentation in the *Global Development Finance (GDF—formerly World Debt Tables)* and therefore show IMF purchases, repurchases, charges, and net purchases separately from long- and short-term lending, repayments, interests, or net lending. While IMF purchases and repurchases are not strictly lending (they are swaps of currency), they do add to, or subtract from, the resources available for consumption or investment and do impose a liability against future income streams. For this reason, IMF transactions are included here.

Data on debt and related flows are drawn largely from the World Bank's Debtor Reporting System (DRS), to which member countries submit detailed accounts on the annual status, transactions, and terms of debt and related flows. World Bank and IMF staff

estimates based on other sources of data supplement DRS data, especially for recent years, on debt not guaranteed by debtor governments and on short-term debt. The figures in this chapter are based mostly on data supplied by debtor countries. Other data series on debt, on which the World Bank may base some of its estimates, are maintained by the Organization for Economic Cooperation and Development (OECD) and the Bank for International Settlements (BIS) from data provided by creditor governments and agencies. No figures are given for Libya and Namibia, which do not report debt information to the DRS. However, totals do include estimates for these countries.

The following definitions apply throughout the chapter. Long-term loans have an original or extended maturity of more than one year, while the maturity on short-term loans is one year or less. Official and private refer to the source of the foreign loans. Official loans are from multilateral organizations (excluding the IMF) and from foreign governments; these loans are either made directly to the government of the borrowing country or guaranteed by it, or its agencies, when made to a third party. Private loans are from the private sector, including foreign parent companies and their affiliates, suppliers, financial markets (such as commercial banks), and other sources. These private loans may or may not be guaranteed by creditor or debtor governments and agencies. "Public and publicly guaranteed" loans, as defined by the DRS, refer to loans from both official and private foreign sources that are made to, or guaranteed by, the debtor government or its agencies. Almost all loans from foreign official sources are public or publicly guaranteed. Some loans from foreign private sources are made to, or guaranteed by, the debtor government or its agencies (these are labeled *private guaranteed* by the DRS). Some loans from foreign private sources are not public or publicly guaranteed (these are labeled *private nonguaranteed* by DRS).

Concessional loans carry a grant element of 25 percent or more (based on a standard 10 percent discount rate), which is consistent with the Development Assistance Committee of the OECD (DAC) definition of ODA (see Chapter 12). Nonconcessional loans carry a grant element of less than 25 percent. In this chapter, private loans are shown separately from official nonconcessional loans.

Additional information, definitions, and methodology are available in the World Bank, *Global Development Finance 2000* (formerly *World Debt Tables*).

6-1. Gross disbursements: official concessional long-term loans

	Millions of U.S. dollars (current prices)									Annual average		
	1980	1990	1991	1992	1993	1994	1995	1996	1997	75-84	85-89	90-MR
SUB-SAHARAN AFRICA	2,557	4,920	4,508	4,836	4,869	4,830	4,646	4,186	3,970	2,657	4,433	4,596
excluding South Africa	2,557	4,920	4,508	4,836	4,869	4,830	4,646	4,186	3,970	2,657	4,433	4,596
excl. S.Africa & Nigeria	2,509	4,813	4,464	4,800	4,802	4,753	4,547	4,092	3,873	2,632	4,411	4,518
Angola	4	61	78	40	31	73	63	43	34	4	38	53
Benin	35	111	94	76	79	101	96	104	49	33	66	89
Botswana	9	18	47	21	40	33	57	15	13	11	18	30
Burkina Faso	41	68	137	133	131	105	110	102	70	36	75	107
Burundi	38	91	84	105	76	52	45	34	19	32	95	63
Cameroon	143	108	91	380	311	372	64	155	220	118	115	213
Cape Verde	3	7	5	14	6	28	16	17	21	5	11	14
Central African Republic	19	110	95	45	50	44	32	27	5	15	65	51
Chad	5	95	91	69	58	69	60	99	80	16	43	77
Comoros	13	5	3	18	6	8	10	7	5	11	13	8
Congo, Democratic Rep. of	131	214	116	66	58	1	0	3	0	125	234	57
Congo, Republic of	49	116	29	17	8	194	14	2	3	61	71	48
Côte d'Ivoire	42	304	231	366	466	766	546	395	150	62	91	403
Djibouti	1	27	54	43	26	26	18	24	12	7	23	29
Equatorial Guinea	4	9	7	15	10	4	2	2	3	3	17	6
Eritrea	0	0	0	0	2	27	7	5	32	0	0	9
Ethiopia	70	259	155	184	348	213	199	224	96	395	438	210
Gabon	16	67	71	10	19	54	64	27	96	11	36	51
Gambia, The	27	22	26	48	22	24	19	63	26	13	26	31
Ghana	114	309	362	318	342	324	389	353	374	66	251	346
Guinea	56	190	185	156	228	125	123	84	177	57	176	158
Guinea-Bissau	49	37	40	40	23	26	21	28	30	16	32	30
Kenya	160	398	389	229	299	169	523	285	151	117	222	305
Lesotho	8	44	45	54	28	43	28	21	28	11	27	36
Liberia	39	0	2	0	33	0	0	0	0	34	20	4
Madagascar	153	197	186	102	104	72	88	116	214	97	169	135
Malawi	45	119	172	137	187	107	211	157	138	44	86	154
Mali	75	163	142	162	79	120	188	153	118	73	139	141
Mauritania	96	89	58	73	142	111	101	114	77	82	106	96
Mauritius	16	72	64	48	42	25	22	13	30	14	34	39
Mozambique	1	180	98	187	155	221	219	272	239	79	255	197
Namibia	0	0	0	0	0	0	0	0	0	0	0	0
Niger	59	90	30	81	67	68	28	40	85	39	108	61
Nigeria	49	107	44	36	67	77	99	94	97	25	21	78
Rwanda	27	62	89	80	61	22	54	62	70	27	80	62
São Tomé and Principe	8	15	19	25	15	15	14	11	5	4	11	15
Senegal	113	198	135	241	84	98	150	183	212	88	279	163
Seychelles	6	5	9	4	3	1	1	4	6	4	6	4
Sierra Leone	33	20	16	42	96	61	94	76	44	18	19	56
Somalia	74	46	13	0	0	0	0	0	0	101	82	7
South Africa	0	0	0	0	0	0	0	0	0	0	0	0
Sudan	270	180	129	93	95	10	27	2	0	313	203	67
Swaziland	9	10	7	6	2	16	15	6	6	9	10	8
Tanzania	159	239	255	336	187	230	201	198	245	186	196	236
Togo	35	82	61	43	15	40	26	95	54	35	70	52
Uganda	13	246	175	229	327	267	221	212	275	33	148	244
Zambia	243	50	282	223	254	211	296	211	220	100	122	218
Zimbabwe	1	83	89	243	190	183	85	49	141	29	85	133
NORTH AFRICA	2,079	1,561	1,661	1,480	1,625	1,545	1,703	1,386	1,044	1,742	1,087	1,500
Algeria	79	292	164	222	352	392	683	344	148	78	69	324
Egypt, Arab Republic	1,064	721	963	524	534	437	337	408	373	1,085	566	537
Libya	0	0	0	0	0	0	0	0	0	0	0	0
Morocco	731	326	296	433	497	439	405	471	360	406	265	403
Tunisia	205	222	239	301	242	277	278	164	163	173	186	236
ALL AFRICA	4,636	6,481	6,169	6,316	6,494	6,375	6,349	5,572	5,014	4,398	5,519	6,096

External Debt and Related Flows

6-2. Gross disbursements: official nonconcessional long-term loans

	Millions of U.S. dollars (current prices)											Annual average		
	1980	1990	1991	1992	1993	1994	1995	1996	1997	1998	1999	75-84	85-89	90-MR
SUB-SAHARAN AFRICA	1,684	2,280	2,165	2,045	1,664	1,488	1,222	1,112	966	4,289	5,788	1,459	2,030	2,302
excluding South Africa	1,684	2,280	2,165	2,045	1,664	1,488	1,222	1,112	966	4,289	5,778	1,459	2,030	2,301
excl. S.Africa & Nigeria	1,611	1,745	1,615	1,550	1,187	966	888	891	749	4,013	5,603	1,280	1,490	1,921
Angola	0	109	60	54	5	0	56	12	2	81	563	6	103	94
Benin	23	9	5	5	2	5	5	5	2	62	71	8	7	17
Botswana	17	12	56	64	31	19	9	13	9	20	130	16	46	36
Burkina Faso	18	11	9	10	7	2	2	1	1	88	105	11	14	24
Burundi	1	2	1	2	1	1	0	1	0	30	33	4	8	7
Cameroon	107	450	227	148	84	68	45	21	25	182	240	71	142	149
Cape Verde	0	5	0	4	4	1	1	1	0	47	43	5	0	11
Central African Republic	6	3	3	1	0	0	1	0	2	3	6	3	9	2
Chad	0	9	1	74	0	0	1	2	0	40	149	3	2	28
Comoros	0	0	0	0	0	0	0	0	0	4	3	1	1	1
Congo, Democratic Rep. of	70	99	188	18	0	0	0	0	0	0	0	64	82	30
Congo, Republic of	60	11	3	0	0	137	1	2	22	0	0	38	54	18
Côte d'Ivoire	189	454	435	285	163	152	123	70	35	389	421	178	234	253
Djibouti	4	0	0	0	0	0	0	0	0	5	12	1	0	2
Equatorial Guinea	11	1	2	0	0	0	0	0	0	1	0	3	2	0
Eritrea	0	0	0	0	0	0	0	2	1	67	110	0	0	18
Ethiopia	7	65	28	30	21	21	33	51	54	136	232	11	62	67
Gabon	20	91	71	99	71	79	158	62	29	36	114	36	71	81
Gambia, The	3	2	3	7	3	0	5	0	0	16	16	2	2	5
Ghana	106	70	57	67	26	21	39	163	67	438	491	38	40	144
Guinea	8	6	44	42	47	44	46	42	35	142	108	12	11	56
Guinea-Bissau	5	0	16	1	0	2	0	0	0	14	19	3	6	5
Kenya	73	7	76	100	31	87	43	74	20	194	320	101	134	95
Lesotho	1	8	11	23	42	17	24	18	14	34	42	3	9	23
Liberia	26	0	0	0	0	0	0	0	0	0	0	23	11	0
Madagascar	59	15	14	16	21	10	1	20	103	103	130	47	50	43
Malawi	60	9	9	8	6	3	4	4	28	156	141	26	22	37
Mali	10	4	4	1	5	2	5	3	0	94	116	5	7	23
Mauritania	16	47	13	60	25	28	10	16	12	55	49	24	26	31
Mauritius	20	24	33	16	23	12	17	37	45	49	35	18	37	29
Mozambique	0	6	10	10	27	8	12	10	20	222	134	23	18	46
Namibia	0	0	0	0	0	0	0	0	0	0	..	0	0	0
Niger	33	0	2	1	33	6	0	1	0	85	41	27	10	17
Nigeria	73	535	550	495	477	522	334	222	217	276	175	180	540	380
Rwanda	0	0	1	1	0	0	0	0	2	88	82	0	0	17
São Tomé and Principe	2	1	11	0	0	0	0	0	0	6	10	2	1	3
Senegal	73	9	29	73	68	34	7	0	0	204	279	63	28	70
Seychelles	6	3	1	6	7	8	7	7	5	13	17	2	3	7
Sierra Leone	9	0	0	10	4	3	1	0	0	46	65	4	2	13
Somalia	13	0	0	0	0	0	0	0	0	0	0	19	2	0
South Africa	0	0	0	0	0	0	0	0	0	0	11	0	0	1
Sudan	296	5	0	15	6	2	24	15	5	0	0	138	23	7
Swaziland	20	6	8	1	7	0	4	23	19	18	15	15	7	10
Tanzania	86	43	21	16	9	12	15	5	8	216	459	82	26	80
Togo	12	1	6	1	2	0	0	2	0	65	33	15	4	11
Uganda	5	8	7	18	65	2	10	14	19	175	260	15	42	58
Zambia	68	67	29	27	0	48	31	13	2	64	208	91	67	49
Zimbabwe	76	75	126	240	370	130	149	189	188	325	301	31	64	209
NORTH AFRICA	1,580	3,309	3,371	2,947	2,626	2,665	2,339	2,766	2,265	2,557	3,197	1,555	2,408	2,804
Algeria	487	1,461	1,540	1,196	792	1,138	911	1,238	1,066	768	661	489	644	1,077
Egypt, Arab Republic	840	477	307	427	450	343	145	148	216	437	500	703	825	345
Libya	0	0	0	0	0	0	0	0	0	..	0	0	0	0
Morocco	135	895	860	882	785	602	950	858	491	894	912	229	616	813
Tunisia	119	477	663	442	599	583	333	522	493	458	1,123	135	323	569
ALL AFRICA	3,264	5,589	5,535	4,992	4,290	4,153	3,561	3,878	3,231	6,846	8,985	3,015	4,438	5,106

6-3. Gross disbursements: private long-term loans

	Millions of U.S. dollars (current prices)											Annual average		
	1980	1990	1991	1992	1993	1994	1995	1996	1997	1998	1999	75-84	85-89	90-MR
SUB-SAHARAN AFRICA	6,289	2,532	1,975	1,915	1,913	4,662	5,195	4,303	7,136	3,252	7,728	4,468	3,511	4,061
excluding South Africa	6,289	2,532	1,975	1,915	1,913	1,144	1,646	2,012	2,560	1,206	1,383	4,468	3,511	1,829
excl. S.Africa & Nigeria	4,659	2,247	1,782	1,911	1,913	1,144	1,646	2,012	2,560	1,206	1,372	3,069	2,729	1,779
Angola	..	693	191	553	649	344	431	723	1,154	709	29	233	712	548
Benin	4	0	0	0	0	0	0	0	0	0	0	44	1	0
Botswana	3	0	0	0	30	0	0	0	0	0	0	6	4	3
Burkina Faso	6	0	0	0	0	0	0	0	0	0	0	8	1	0
Burundi	0	2	0	0	0	0	0	0	0	1	53	5	2	6
Cameroon	364	160	103	141	104	8	0	25	14	10	136	230	354	70
Cape Verde	..	0	0	0	0	0	4	5	2	0	0	0	0	1
Central African Republic	0	0	0	0	0	0	0	0	0	0	11	2	1	1
Chad	0	0	0	0	0	0	0	0	0	0	0	5	1	0
Comoros	0	0	0	0	0	0	0	0	0	0	34	0	0	3
Congo, Democratic Rep. of	263	3	0	0	0	0	0	0	0	0	0	176	16	0
Congo, Republic of	412	185	6	114	451	1	0	0	0	0	49	207	272	81
Côte d'Ivoire	1,508	261	236	202	190	317	75	411	52	56	184	791	219	198
Djibouti	5	0	0	0	0	0	0	0	0	0	2	1	0	0
Equatorial Guinea	5	0	0	0	0	0	0	0	0	0	0	3	0	0
Eritrea	..	..	..	..	..	0	0	0	0	0	0	..	..	0
Ethiopia	33	51	261	113	10	4	0	22	30	10	4	45	98	50
Gabon	135	37	16	0	3	2	0	0	20	10	-78	174	174	1
Gambia, The	22	0	0	0	0	0	0	0	0	0	0	5	0	0
Ghana	0	59	82	103	77	123	178	381	208	85	0	12	64	130
Guinea	57	0	0	0	11	0	0	17	20	7	1	29	13	6
Guinea-Bissau	21	0	0	0	0	0	0	0	0	0	0	5	5	0
Kenya	387	237	438	173	87	6	132	72	48	36	427	224	284	165
Lesotho	5	7	6	2	0	0	13	12	15	18	8	4	8	8
Liberia	11	0	0	0	0	0	0	0	0	0	0	23	0	0
Madagascar	163	1	0	0	0	0	1	0	0	0	0	64	10	0
Malawi	48	7	1	14	1	10	0	0	1	0	2	29	7	4
Mali	10	0	0	0	0	0	0	0	0	0	-21	6	1	-2
Mauritania	14	0	0	0	0	0	0	25	0	0	0	24	4	2
Mauritius	61	65	76	63	39	150	369	91	752	7	416	28	45	203
Mozambique	..	44	6	4	8	4	36	0	6	0	360	61	46	47
Namibia	..	..	..	..	..	..	..	..	..	0	0	..	..	0
Niger	190	48	0	0	0	0	0	0	0	0	0	91	45	5
Nigeria	1,630	285	193	4	0	0	0	0	0	0	11	1,399	782	49
Rwanda	0	0	0	0	0	0	0	0	0	0	72	3	1	7
São Tomé and Principe	0	0	0	0	0	0	0	0	0	0	0	1	0	0
Senegal	141	15	11	8	1	1	1	0	21	2	0	74	29	6
Seychelles	0	2	10	15	8	9	0	1	0	10	18	1	6	7
Sierra Leone	42	4	0	0	0	0	0	0	0	0	0	24	1	0
Somalia	27	0	0	0	0	0	0	0	0	0	0	25	1	0
South Africa	..	..	..	..	..	3,518	3,549	2,291	4,575	2,046	6,345	..	..	3,721
Sudan	145	0	0	0	0	0	0	0	0	0	0	100	0	0
Swaziland	0	0	0	0	0	0	0	0	0	0	-518	3	3	-52
Tanzania	122	16	3	38	41	17	42	6	0	0	0	62	47	16
Togo	50	0	0	0	0	0	0	0	0	0	0	63	0	0
Uganda	65	38	5	6	18	0	0	0	0	0	7	36	60	7
Zambia	289	48	47	33	11	35	25	13	50	20	0	154	62	28
Zimbabwe	55	266	284	329	172	115	338	209	167	225	177	167	128	228
NORTH AFRICA	5,015	6,680	6,067	7,529	6,566	4,488	3,644	2,417	1,912	1,343	2,199	4,733	6,358	4,284
Algeria	2,832	5,182	4,824	6,118	5,363	3,268	2,092	1,308	438	400	1,039	2,743	4,206	3,003
Egypt, Arab Republic	776	754	673	375	168	260	40	33	188	22	101	778	1,316	261
Libya	..	..	..	..	..	..	..	..	..	..	0	..	..	0
Morocco	1,119	426	327	569	755	762	734	428	462	732	582	906	519	578
Tunisia	288	318	244	467	281	199	777	648	824	189	477	306	318	442
ALL AFRICA	11,304	9,212	8,042	9,444	8,479	9,150	8,838	6,719	9,048	4,595	9,926	9,201	9,869	8,345

External Debt and Related Flows

6-4. Disbursements: long-term loans and IMF purchases

	Millions of U.S. dollars (current prices)											Annual average		
	1980	1990	1991	1992	1993	1994	1995	1996	1997	1998	1999	75-84	85-89	90-MR
SUB-SAHARAN AFRICA	11,748	10,394	9,230	9,323	9,593	11,895	14,056	10,253	12,596	8,342	15,466	9,551	10,784	11,115
excluding South Africa	11,748	10,394	9,230	9,323	8,735	8,377	10,508	7,962	8,020	6,297	9,110	9,551	10,784	8,796
excl. S.Africa & Nigeria	9,995	9,467	8,443	8,789	8,191	7,778	10,075	7,646	7,706	6,021	8,974	7,948	9,440	8,309
Angola	0	862	328	647	685	417	550	778	1,190	790	592	102	853	684
Benin	71	120	112	81	103	131	115	128	57	62	175	86	76	108
Botswana	28	30	103	85	102	52	66	28	22	20	130	34	69	64
Burkina Faso	70	79	155	143	151	132	139	112	89	106	344	56	90	145
Burundi	45	96	91	126	77	53	45	35	19	31	86	44	113	66
Cameroon	626	718	433	669	499	479	122	230	296	266	376	427	634	409
Cape Verde	0	12	5	18	10	29	21	24	22	47	43	8	12	23
Central African Republic	40	121	98	46	50	59	33	27	7	15	39	27	82	49
Chad	5	112	92	143	58	83	72	125	92	52	100	26	51	93
Comoros	13	5	4	18	6	10	10	7	5	4	37	12	14	11
Congo, Democratic Rep. of	603	315	304	84	58	1	0	3	0	0	576	482	461	134
Congo, Republic of	526	318	38	132	459	350	15	24	24	10	84	310	399	145
Côte d'Ivoire	1,777	1,172	948	853	819	1,405	924	1,014	236	613	716	1,114	599	870
Djibouti	10	27	54	43	26	26	18	28	14	8	19	9	24	26
Equatorial Guinea	38	10	16	15	14	7	2	2	3	1	0	12	21	7
Eritrea	..	..	..	..	..	27	7	7	33	67	107	..	..	41
Ethiopia	119	374	443	346	409	258	233	317	179	167	229	470	606	295
Gabon	171	204	162	108	93	198	279	121	168	46	36	222	308	141
Gambia, The	56	33	31	55	26	23	24	58	24	21	13	26	35	31
Ghana	249	503	660	488	509	468	648	936	649	635	528	184	495	602
Guinea	129	196	241	210	286	182	200	143	265	180	109	103	212	201
Guinea-Bissau	75	37	55	41	23	28	24	31	36	18	24	24	44	32
Kenya	714	778	952	502	447	294	698	467	219	231	747	515	722	533
Lesotho	15	62	66	86	80	66	66	51	57	52	56	19	47	64
Liberia	109	0	2	0	33	0	0	0	0	0	0	113	31	4
Madagascar	444	231	217	117	125	82	90	156	336	103	112	234	264	157
Malawi	190	161	203	159	194	147	227	184	178	173	172	120	129	180
Mali	109	194	146	177	98	164	238	186	147	108	173	95	157	163
Mauritania	155	148	71	145	179	163	133	176	108	55	47	141	150	123
Mauritius	143	161	173	127	105	186	409	140	827	56	481	87	128	266
Mozambique	0	242	156	265	211	254	267	300	300	254	501	122	331	275
Namibia	..	..	..	..	..	..	..	..	..	..	4	..	..	4
Niger	290	148	32	83	100	90	28	55	111	111	97	164	180	85
Nigeria	1,752	927	787	535	544	599	433	316	314	276	136	1,603	1,344	487
Rwanda	34	62	101	81	61	22	68	62	92	104	125	31	81	78
São Tomé and Principe	10	16	30	24	15	15	14	11	5	6	10	7	13	15
Senegal	395	252	233	322	154	201	241	216	268	254	327	261	399	247
Seychelles	12	9	20	25	18	18	8	12	11	23	35	7	16	18
Sierra Leone	104	24	16	52	100	200	115	90	48	62	65	62	26	77
Somalia	135	46	13	0	0	0	0	0	0	0	0	158	101	6
South Africa	0	0	0	0	858	3,518	3,549	2,291	4,575	2,046	6,356	0	0	2,319
Sudan	921	185	129	108	101	12	51	17	5	0	42	655	226	65
Swaziland	31	15	15	7	8	16	19	29	25	18	20	29	21	17
Tanzania	433	327	309	479	238	259	258	246	337	264	539	353	294	326
Togo	119	104	67	55	17	55	59	97	69	80	33	122	89	63
Uganda	161	372	267	308	410	321	287	290	353	225	290	135	287	312
Zambia	690	164	358	283	241	294	2,606	236	286	84	222	482	276	477
Zimbabwe	132	424	499	1,034	799	504	652	447	496	604	513	257	277	597
NORTH AFRICA	9,014	11,614	11,702	12,175	10,817	9,539	8,161	7,312	5,685	4,243	6,377	8,255	10,211	8,762
Algeria	3,398	6,935	6,835	7,536	6,507	5,639	4,160	3,633	2,116	1,511	2,682	3,310	5,040	4,755
Egypt, Arab Republic	2,743	1,951	2,025	1,445	1,152	1,039	523	588	776	459	689	2,625	2,737	1,065
Libya	..	..	..	..	..	..	..	..	..	..	..	..	..	..
Morocco	2,262	1,711	1,483	1,910	2,037	1,802	2,089	1,757	1,313	1,625	1,887	1,704	1,557	1,761
Tunisia	611	1,017	1,358	1,283	1,122	1,059	1,389	1,334	1,480	648	1,119	616	877	1,181
ALL AFRICA	20,762	22,007	20,932	21,498	20,410	21,434	22,217	17,565	18,281	12,585	21,843	17,807	20,996	19,877

Note: In 1995, Zambia was able to clear its arrears to the IMF after completing a 3 year Rights Arrangement Program.

6-5. Amortization: official concessional long-term loans

	Millions of U.S. dollars (current prices)										Annual average		
	1980	1990	1991	1992	1993	1994	1995	1996	1997	1998	75-84	85-89	90-MR
SUB-SAHARAN AFRICA	243	587	619	589	773	718	877	885	1,021	1,375	232	533	827
excluding South Africa	243	587	619	589	773	718	877	885	1,021	1,375	232	533	827
excl. S.Africa & Nigeria	229	580	616	588	611	716	875	884	949	1,054	219	523	764
Angola	0	1	5	3	2	9	3	8	8	13	0	2	6
Benin	1	7	9	8	12	12	15	14	18	19	2	4	13
Botswana	0	6	7	9	13	14	11	15	30	14	1	5	13
Burkina Faso	4	13	14	9	11	18	20	23	25	27	2	8	18
Burundi	1	14	17	14	15	16	14	6	8	9	1	10	12
Cameroon	13	24	23	20	37	12	12	14	49	75	12	23	30
Cape Verde	0	1	3	6	2	3	4	3	6	6	0	1	4
Central African Republic	0	3	2	2	1	5	2	2	4	6	1	2	3
Chad	3	2	2	3	1	6	2	7	6	7	1	2	4
Comoros	0	0	1	2	2	2	0	1	3	5	0	0	2
Congo, Democratic Rep. of	3	8	4	5	4	0	0	0	0	0	4	9	2
Congo, Republic of	11	2	0	0	1	8	7	22	0	0	10	4	5
Côte d'Ivoire	18	75	77	88	78	56	65	81	68	106	15	35	77
Djibouti	2	8	8	7	6	9	9	9	5	3	1	5	7
Equatorial Guinea	0	1	1	0	0	0	0	1	1	1	0	0	0
Eritrea	0	0	0	0	0	0	0	0	0	0	0	0	0
Ethiopia	7	19	21	14	16	19	25	35	27	38	9	53	24
Gabon	4	1	7	23	7	8	12	9	39	28	5	4	15
Gambia, The	0	11	9	9	8	9	7	9	10	13	1	5	9
Ghana	14	40	29	33	32	56	55	56	54	83	20	33	49
Guinea	44	53	51	19	16	26	86	44	29	31	36	42	39
Guinea-Bissau	0	1	15	1	1	2	4	3	5	2	0	2	4
Kenya	6	34	42	33	39	67	69	68	59	64	8	25	53
Lesotho	0	4	4	5	9	6	11	11	13	13	1	3	8
Liberia	1	0	11	0	1	1	0	0	0	0	4	2	1
Madagascar	18	17	12	20	12	13	10	21	55	39	19	13	22
Malawi	2	7	14	10	9	10	16	19	21	19	2	4	14
Mali	4	22	14	22	23	39	45	41	38	40	4	17	31
Mauritania	3	26	20	26	40	33	37	37	39	41	3	28	33
Mauritius	2	14	19	31	23	22	24	27	47	23	2	10	25
Mozambique	0	9	10	13	12	17	24	29	27	25	2	18	18
Namibia	..	..	..	..	..	..	..	..	..	..	..	..	..
Niger	16	5	5	4	12	6	6	7	14	12	5	8	8
Nigeria	14	7	2	1	162	1	2	1	72	321	13	10	63
Rwanda	0	7	10	8	11	2	11	8	9	8	1	7	8
São Tomé and Principe	0	0	1	1	0	0	1	1	1	1	0	1	1
Senegal	7	54	44	32	31	68	72	64	47	89	5	28	56
Seychelles	0	2	3	4	4	3	4	2	2	4	0	1	3
Sierra Leone	2	3	2	5	3	9	7	6	7	10	3	3	6
Somalia	2	2	0	0	0	0	0	0	0	0	2	2	0
South Africa	0	0	0	0	0	0	0	0	0	0	0	0	0
Sudan	14	4	6	8	5	3	9	0	0	0	16	48	4
Swaziland	1	6	8	7	7	7	8	11	8	8	1	3	8
Tanzania	19	36	41	36	38	40	38	54	34	48	14	32	41
Togo	2	6	8	5	4	4	7	15	13	13	2	6	8
Uganda	2	8	12	10	16	23	22	24	38	38	2	5	21
Zambia	3	2	4	4	10	21	47	34	33	27	2	3	20
Zimbabwe	2	21	25	31	38	35	58	46	51	48	1	9	39
NORTH AFRICA	294	569	435	512	576	739	701	781	990	1,105	264	374	712
Algeria	73	103	85	86	84	62	54	114	130	179	72	97	100
Egypt, Arab Republic	119	270	149	99	56	68	151	225	288	432	111	120	193
Libya	..	..	..	..	..	..	..	..	..	..	..	..	..
Morocco	62	47	55	168	282	343	289	227	361	269	41	48	227
Tunisia	41	150	146	158	154	266	207	216	211	225	39	109	192
ALL AFRICA	537	1,156	1,054	1,101	1,348	1,456	1,578	1,666	2,010	2,479	496	907	1,539

6-6. Amortization: official nonconcessional long-term loans

	Millions of U.S. dollars (current prices)										Annual average		
	1980	1990	1991	1992	1993	1994	1995	1996	1997	1998	75-84	85-89	90-MR
SUB-SAHARAN AFRICA	424	1,972	1,835	1,448	1,432	1,925	2,118	2,446	1,942	1,699	337	1,128	1,868
excluding South Africa	424	1,972	1,835	1,448	1,432	1,925	2,118	2,446	1,942	1,699	337	1,128	1,868
excl. S.Africa & Nigeria	392	1,205	1,288	1,117	1,104	1,495	1,650	1,719	1,432	1,281	303	860	1,366
Angola	..	58	62	38	21	25	21	26	29	49	1	31	36
Benin	1	11	7	7	6	9	10	11	10	10	2	5	9
Botswana	6	42	45	50	43	46	48	49	40	35	3	22	44
Burkina Faso	4	5	11	6	9	9	10	7	7	5	2	4	8
Burundi	1	6	6	6	3	5	3	6	4	4	0	4	5
Cameroon	16	74	86	61	101	119	134	180	177	147	18	60	120
Cape Verde	..	2	3	3	2	3	2	2	3	8	1	2	3
Central African Republic	0	4	1	2	1	2	0	0	0	2	1	4	1
Chad	0	1	1	1	4	2	1	3	7	5	0	1	3
Comoros	0	0	5	1	0	0	0	0	0	0	0	0	1
Congo, Democratic Rep. of	100	26	24	19	0	0	0	0	0	0	37	53	8
Congo, Republic of	10	68	4	1	0	137	25	104	53	7	11	16	44
Côte d'Ivoire	37	172	196	202	216	299	414	429	261	248	30	103	271
Djibouti	1	0	0	0	0	0	0	0	0	0	0	0	0
Equatorial Guinea	1	0	1	2	1	0	0	2	0	0	1	2	1
Eritrea	..	..	..	..	..	0	0	0	0	0	..	..	0
Ethiopia	4	26	17	15	13	13	19	26	18	19	6	30	18
Gabon	15	16	34	61	24	55	78	71	105	67	14	16	57
Gambia, The	0	2	4	6	6	6	7	5	3	2	0	1	5
Ghana	22	25	35	44	36	45	62	45	55	56	15	22	45
Guinea	20	24	22	23	17	12	20	14	21	46	9	18	22
Guinea-Bissau	0	1	2	2	0	1	4	3	1	1	0	1	2
Kenya	25	146	148	141	139	183	201	195	170	142	22	96	163
Lesotho	0	4	7	8	6	6	7	5	8	11	1	4	7
Liberia	2	1	5	0	12	13	0	0	0	0	6	6	3
Madagascar	1	36	27	12	14	14	9	18	43	18	8	36	21
Malawi	3	54	37	26	21	23	27	18	15	14	5	20	26
Mali	0	2	4	7	3	13	11	5	4	5	0	2	6
Mauritania	1	55	26	25	36	24	32	36	22	19	6	25	30
Mauritius	4	25	31	53	34	37	36	31	31	30	4	19	34
Mozambique	..	14	10	13	15	35	34	25	12	10	1	7	19
Namibia	..	..	..	..	..	..	..	..	..	..	..	..	..
Niger	2	4	3	3	20	8	1	2	2	0	5	12	5
Nigeria	31	767	547	331	328	429	468	727	510	418	34	269	503
Rwanda	0	0	1	0	0	0	0	1	1	1	0	0	0
São Tomé and Principe	1	1	0	1	1	1	0	1	0	1	1	1	1
Senegal	12	57	54	27	19	47	55	41	42	49	8	45	43
Seychelles	0	3	3	4	3	3	3	3	5	5	0	2	3
Sierra Leone	2	5	1	7	2	8	20	38	0	1	2	2	9
Somalia	5	0	0	0	- 0	0	0	0	0	0	3	1	0
South Africa	..	..	..	..	..	0	0	0	0	0	..	..	0
Sudan	32	11	6	6	4	0	6	0	0	1	24	14	4
Swaziland	4	28	12	9	9	12	8	10	8	6	3	13	11
Tanzania	7	41	65	50	50	45	62	74	34	33	8	47	51
Togo	8	21	11	4	2	2	0	6	9	3	8	28	6
Uganda	9	35	26	27	61	49	38	25	20	26	6	21	34
Zambia	34	42	198	97	80	105	132	83	74	53	28	37	96
Zimbabwe	3	57	50	50	71	81	109	121	139	142	5	30	91
NORTH AFRICA	287	2,276	2,526	2,484	2,507	2,367	2,766	2,370	2,932	2,512	312	1,655	2,527
Algeria	171	1,069	1,162	1,092	1,054	591	589	532	917	802	157	760	868
Egypt, Arab Republic	32	615	610	409	336	306	391	346	350	272	54	357	404
Libya	..	..	..	..	..	..	..	..	..	..	..	..	..
Morocco	52	384	517	677	806	1,128	1,354	1,115	1,293	1,053	57	353	925
Tunisia	32	208	236	307	312	342	432	376	373	386	44	185	330
ALL AFRICA	711	4,248	4,361	3,933	3,939	4,291	4,883	4,816	4,874	4,210	649	2,784	4,395

6-7. Amortization: private long-term loans

	Millions of U.S. dollars (current prices)											Annual average		
	1980	1990	1991	1992	1993	1994	1995	1996	1997	1998	1999	75-84	85-89	90-MR
SUB-SAHARAN AFRICA	2,123	2,084	1,845	2,909	1,271	3,909	4,084	5,505	7,012	4,748	6,375	1,852	2,642	3,974
excluding South Africa	2,123	2,084	1,845	2,909	1,271	1,914	2,014	2,735	2,332	2,317	2,069	1,852	2,642	2,149
excl. S.Africa & Nigeria	1,926	1,678	1,533	1,364	1,182	1,599	1,565	2,045	2,074	2,292	1,680	1,312	1,779	1,701
Angola	..	123	166	106	39	120	312	621	768	850	478	19	62	358
Benin	3	0	0	0	0	0	0	0	0	0	0	4	8	0
Botswana	0	19	3	3	1	2	6	9	5	5	5	2	6	6
Burkina Faso	2	1	1	0	0	0	0	0	0	0	0	2	5	0
Burundi	3	8	3	2	1	1	1	1	0	0	0	2	6	2
Cameroon	85	171	93	67	98	67	65	49	43	59	28	76	292	74
Cape Verde	..	0	0	0	0	0	0	0	1	1	0	0	0	0
Central African Republic	1	1	0	1	0	0	0	0	0	0	0	1	1	0
Chad	0	1	1	0	1	0	0	0	0	0	1	1	1	0
Comoros	0	0	0	0	0	0	0	0	0	0	0	0	0	0
Congo, Democratic Rep. of	90	15	13	5	0	0	0	0	0	0	3	42	32	4
Congo, Republic of	12	285	200	97	75	157	50	15	0	0	228	62	236	111
Côte d'Ivoire	667	252	240	212	242	356	60	302	487	316	286	350	264	275
Djibouti	0	1	0	0	0	0	0	0	0	0	1	1	2	0
Equatorial Guinea	0	0	0	0	0	0	0	0	0	0	0	1	0	0
Eritrea	..	..	..	..	..	0	0	0	0	0	0	..	..	0
Ethiopia	7	107	49	33	37	36	48	231	8	8	10	10	68	57
Gabon	260	8	48	17	4	33	75	51	25	17	17	149	55	29
Gambia, The	0	8	5	5	4	4	0	0	0	0	0	1	1	3
Ghana	42	79	48	58	52	66	85	105	124	110	75	11	56	80
Guinea	11	19	10	8	8	9	15	0	40	17	12	8	9	14
Guinea-Bissau	3	0	0	0	0	0	0	0	0	0	0	1	0	0
Kenya	165	172	170	153	126	287	290	243	153	154	165	161	181	191
Lesotho	3	7	5	7	6	5	4	2	2	2	3	2	5	4
Liberia	12	0	0	0	0	0	0	0	0	0	0	9	0	0
Madagascar	23	16	11	8	8	5	5	5	2	1	2	10	28	6
Malawi	28	6	11	16	13	14	23	4	3	1	2	17	19	9
Mali	2	1	1	3	1	1	0	0	0	0	0	1	3	1
Mauritania	13	1	2	2	0	0	0	0	2	2	2	21	5	1
Mauritius	14	21	46	43	26	45	93	50	58	105	74	17	28	56
Mozambique	..	18	21	7	10	5	13	6	5	4	37	0	14	13
Namibia	..	..	..	..	..	..	..	..	..	0	0	..	..	0
Niger	40	39	55	20	24	24	24	24	14	24	23	40	38	27
Nigeria	197	406	313	1,546	89	316	448	690	258	25	389	540	863	448
Rwanda	2	2	1	1	0	0	0	0	0	0	0	1	4	0
São Tomé and Principe	0	0	0	0	0	0	0	0	0	0	0	0	0	0
Senegal	137	30	45	39	4	10	27	11	7	17	28	46	49	22
Seychelles	0	8	5	4	5	4	9	5	3	5	3	0	5	5
Sierra Leone	29	0	0	0	0	0	28	0	0	0	0	16	2	3
Somalia	0	0	0	0	0	0	0	0	0	0	0	3	0	0
South Africa	..	..	..	..	..	1,994	2,070	2,770	4,680	2,432	4,306	..	..	3,042
Sudan	7	0	0	0	0	0	0	0	0	0	0	16	1	0
Swaziland	3	2	2	2	2	2	0	0	0	0	0	2	5	1
Tanzania	23	12	12	80	11	16	27	18	19	15	4	18	7	21
Togo	9	0	0	0	0	0	0	0	6	0	0	16	10	1
Uganda	21	22	30	14	32	15	10	7	1	2	3	15	27	14
Zambia	175	57	54	46	51	60	62	39	57	52	20	111	51	50
Zimbabwe	34	169	185	305	301	256	234	247	244	525	170	58	195	264
NORTH AFRICA	3,139	7,177	7,753	7,746	7,527	4,185	2,843	2,636	1,971	2,593	3,485	2,367	4,495	4,792
Algeria	2,284	5,606	5,972	5,883	5,816	2,698	1,577	1,297	975	1,728	2,041	1,646	3,255	3,359
Egypt, Arab Republic	192	806	885	921	579	544	352	454	302	207	266	238	746	531
Libya	..	..	..	..	..	..	..	..	..	..	..	..	..	..
Morocco	477	250	484	548	754	624	630	617	453	451	847	325	174	566
Tunisia	186	515	411	393	378	320	285	268	241	208	332	157	320	335
ALL AFRICA	5,262	9,261	9,598	10,655	8,798	8,094	6,927	8,141	8,983	7,341	9,861	4,219	7,137	8,766

6-8. Amortization: long-term loans and IMF repurchases

	Millions of U.S. dollars (current prices)											Annual average		
	1980	*1990*	*1991*	*1992*	*1993*	*1994*	*1995*	*1996*	*1997*	*1998*	*1999*	*75-84*	*85-89*	*90-MR*
SUB-SAHARAN AFRICA	3,174	5,593	4,912	5,476	3,930	7,017	9,451	9,432	11,040	8,933	12,108	2,706	5,448	7,789
excluding South Africa	3,174	5,593	4,912	5,476	3,930	5,023	7,380	6,663	5,937	6,085	7,802	2,706	5,448	5,880
excl. S.Africa & Nigeria	2,932	4,413	4,050	3,598	3,351	4,276	6,462	5,245	5,097	5,321	7,207	2,118	4,307	4,902
Angola	0	183	233	146	63	153	335	654	806	912	767	8	95	425
Benin	6	21	16	15	18	21	26	27	32	35	45	7	20	26
Botswana	6	67	54	62	57	62	65	73	75	53	55	6	32	62
Burkina Faso	11	19	25	15	20	27	29	31	34	34	42	7	20	28
Burundi	4	28	25	24	23	28	27	21	20	21	43	5	24	26
Cameroon	131	270	214	203	282	204	217	248	281	297	556	112	381	277
Cape Verde	0	4	6	8	4	6	6	5	10	15	15	0	3	8
Central African Republic	7	17	7	7	3	13	10	8	12	21	30	6	17	13
Chad	5	7	4	4	8	10	10	16	24	23	31	4	7	14
Comoros	0	0	6	3	2	2	0	1	3	5	9	0	0	3
Congo, Democratic Rep. of	277	200	91	29	4	5	1	37	0	1	391	123	279	76
Congo, Republic of	41	362	209	98	77	305	84	140	56	18	391	86	259	174
Côte d'Ivoire	722	621	618	594	585	787	625	860	838	670	826	405	550	702
Djibouti	2	9	8	8	6	9	9	9	5	3	14	2	7	8
Equatorial Guinea	2	4	2	2	1	1	1	3	4	4	3	2	6	2
Eritrea	..	..	..	..	..	0	0	0	0	0	1	..	..	0
Ethiopia	17	177	92	62	66	68	91	292	52	69	496	30	177	147
Gabon	279	40	114	137	71	119	216	137	172	135	324	169	75	146
Gambia, The	0	26	23	22	21	24	21	22	20	20	11	4	15	21
Ghana	106	260	189	198	186	248	308	331	398	389	449	57	248	296
Guinea	76	110	93	51	44	54	129	67	100	104	151	56	77	90
Guinea-Bissau	3	2	16	3	1	4	9	7	6	3	6	2	4	6
Kenya	205	458	399	410	366	552	600	567	449	421	580	217	411	480
Lesotho	3	15	16	20	20	18	25	22	27	30	37	4	13	23
Liberia	18	2	15	0	13	15	0	0	0	1	1	23	10	5
Madagascar	44	121	84	56	48	43	38	60	118	72	121	43	123	76
Malawi	35	86	83	72	49	53	76	56	55	60	74	30	70	66
Mali	9	44	27	38	35	63	62	54	49	55	23	8	43	45
Mauritania	26	99	62	61	82	63	79	82	70	69	70	35	72	73
Mauritius	19	104	117	128	83	103	154	108	136	158	132	30	99	122
Mozambique	0	41	41	34	44	67	85	92	59	63	286	2	39	81
Namibia	..	..	..	..	..	..	..	..	..	0	0	..	..	0
Niger	58	63	74	36	66	48	41	44	45	50	39	50	74	51
Nigeria	242	1,180	862	1,878	579	746	918	1,418	840	763	596	588	1,141	978
Rwanda	3	10	12	10	11	2	11	10	13	11	36	3	13	12
São Tomé and Principe	1	1	1	1	1	1	1	2	2	2	0	1	2	1
Senegal	165	197	190	142	81	154	195	160	158	215	169	67	183	166
Seychelles	0	13	11	12	12	10	16	10	10	14	12	1	8	12
Sierra Leone	50	12	10	16	13	98	59	47	7	11	33	28	16	31
Somalia	11	5	0	0	0	0	0	0	0	0	0	9	20	1
South Africa	0	0	0	0	0	1,994	2,070	2,769	5,103	2,848	4,306	0	0	1,909
Sudan	131	16	12	14	9	3	54	36	42	59	44	90	63	29
Swaziland	8	36	21	17	17	20	16	21	16	14	17	6	24	20
Tanzania	81	118	145	172	104	116	146	168	118	134	101	59	101	132
Togo	19	43	27	19	14	13	18	32	40	28	27	27	61	26
Uganda	45	109	102	79	120	111	98	106	116	128	134	35	129	110
Zambia	269	126	290	183	211	206	2,067	156	164	132	162	193	130	370
Zimbabwe	40	270	266	387	410	372	401	423	459	763	454	67	306	420
NORTH AFRICA	3,942	10,407	11,102	11,120	11,100	7,660	6,691	6,103	6,312	6,694	8,475	3,022	6,849	8,566
Algeria	2,528	6,779	7,220	7,227	7,282	3,546	2,391	2,079	2,372	3,143	3,850	1,875	4,111	4,589
Egypt, Arab Republic	446	1,737	1,726	1,470	971	939	989	1,111	955	910	1,047	450	1,273	1,186
Libya	..	..	..	..	..	..	..	..	..	..	..	..	..	..
Morocco	678	908	1,227	1,535	1,998	2,246	2,373	2,006	2,110	1,773	2,327	454	849	1,850
Tunisia	290	984	929	887	850	928	939	907	875	867	1,251	243	615	942
ALL AFRICA	7,116	16,000	16,015	16,596	15,030	14,677	16,142	15,536	17,352	15,627	20,583	5,728	12,297	16,356

Note: In 1995, Zambia was able to clear its arrears to the IMF after completing a 3 year Rights Arrangement Program.

6-9. Interest payments: official concessional long-term loans

	Millions of U.S. dollars (current prices)										Annual average		
	1980	1990	1991	1992	1993	1994	1995	1996	1997	1998	75-84	85-89	90-MR
SUB-SAHARAN AFRICA	238	725	525	804	762	600	613	793	741	934	172	354	722
excluding South Africa	238	725	525	804	762	600	613	793	741	934	172	354	722
excl. S.Africa & Nigeria	229	413	491	443	506	598	611	791	673	798	164	349	592
Angola	0	1	4	3	3	7	7	3	6	4	0	1	4
Benin	1	7	9	7	8	9	10	9	11	12	1	5	9
Botswana	1	4	5	5	6	3	3	8	7	6	1	2	5
Burkina Faso	2	7	6	6	6	7	9	11	13	12	2	6	8
Burundi	1	7	8	9	9	10	9	6	7	7	1	8	8
Cameroon	15	32	29	16	24	19	54	36	61	62	13	24	37
Cape Verde	0	1	1	1	1	2	2	1	2	2	0	1	1
Central African Republic	0	5	3	6	2	6	3	3	2	5	0	4	4
Chad	0	3	4	4	4	5	3	7	5	6	0	2	5
Comoros	0	1	2	1	1	1	1	1	1	1	0	1	1
Congo, Democratic Rep. of	47	16	14	10	7	0	0	0	0	0	11	12	5
Congo, Republic of	12	30	8	5	4	93	9	35	1	1	6	7	21
Côte d'Ivoire	14	5	52	29	30	32	47	77	75	145	13	13	54
Djibouti	1	2	2	2	2	2	2	3	2	2	1	2	2
Equatorial Guinea	0	0	1	1	0	1	0	1	1	1	0	0	1
Eritrea	0	0	0	0	0	0	0	0	0	4	0	0	0
Ethiopia	7	16	13	10	12	16	19	19	21	25	7	26	17
Gabon	3	2	9	20	4	15	40	39	36	24	2	2	21
Gambia, The	0	4	3	3	4	4	3	3	5	5	0	2	4
Ghana	11	23	25	32	38	39	28	51	43	64	13	19	38
Guinea	12	29	26	20	23	27	29	22	23	24	10	12	25
Guinea-Bissau	0	2	4	1	2	2	3	3	3	4	0	2	3
Kenya	9	23	54	28	39	47	59	57	47	50	10	23	45
Lesotho	0	3	4	6	5	4	5	5	5	5	0	2	5
Liberia	2	0	1	0	1	0	0	0	0	0	2	2	0
Madagascar	4	19	18	19	14	11	11	12	42	36	7	11	20
Malawi	4	9	12	11	13	13	19	17	18	16	4	6	14
Mali	2	14	10	14	38	19	19	57	18	16	3	11	23
Mauritania	8	13	12	11	20	22	18	18	19	18	8	13	17
Mauritius	1	10	11	16	15	16	18	17	15	15	1	6	15
Mozambique	0	9	15	22	31	16	19	25	27	23	0	14	21
Namibia	..	..	..	..	..	..	..	..	..	..	..	..	..
Niger	2	5	5	4	7	6	7	5	8	8	2	7	6
Nigeria	9	312	34	361	256	2	2	3	68	136	8	4	130
Rwanda	1	6	6	5	4	2	8	6	7	6	1	6	6
São Tomé and Principe	0	0	1	1	1	1	1	1	2	1	0	0	1
Senegal	7	29	31	19	7	25	22	79	29	37	4	30	31
Seychelles	0	1	2	2	1	1	2	1	1	1	0	1	1
Sierra Leone	0	2	1	7	3	4	5	4	6	5	1	1	4
Somalia	2	4	0	0	0	0	0	0	0	0	2	3	0
South Africa	0	0	0	0	0	0	0	0	0	0	0	0	0
Sudan	28	7	8	10	6	0	1	0	0	0	13	17	3
Swaziland	1	2	2	2	2	2	2	3	2	2	1	2	2
Tanzania	15	20	24	22	49	28	28	55	27	76	14	15	37
Togo	1	8	8	7	6	5	5	13	8	8	1	6	7
Uganda	1	6	10	10	13	18	23	25	25	22	1	6	17
Zambia	14	12	14	19	22	36	32	29	20	23	5	8	23
Zimbabwe	1	17	16	18	19	23	26	23	22	20	2	12	20
NORTH AFRICA	289	375	251	577	671	782	907	948	804	781	237	261	677
Algeria	35	22	23	26	26	56	90	144	119	125	32	20	70
Egypt, Arab Republic	153	210	82	392	422	467	567	553	417	381	121	131	388
Libya	..	..	..	..	..	..	..	..	..	..	..	..	..
Morocco	70	64	69	81	145	153	161	166	190	200	55	44	137
Tunisia	30	79	76	78	78	107	89	84	78	75	29	66	82
ALL AFRICA	526	1,100	775	1,381	1,434	1,382	1,520	1,741	1,545	1,714	409	614	1,399

6-10. Interest payments: official nonconcessional long-term loans

| | Millions of U.S. dollars (current prices) | | | | | | | | | | Annual average | | |
	1980	1990	1991	1992	1993	1994	1995	1996	1997	1998	75-84	85-89	90-MR
SUB-SAHARAN AFRICA	453	1,988	2,363	1,427	1,190	1,430	1,402	1,864	1,342	1,100	384	1,312	1,567
excluding South Africa	453	1,988	2,363	1,427	1,190	1,430	1,402	1,864	1,342	1,100	384	1,312	1,567
excl. S.Africa & Nigeria	399	1,000	1,147	961	877	1,095	1,081	1,351	1,044	861	325	911	1,046
Angola	..	18	22	12	5	3	5	15	6	4	1	16	10
Benin	1	7	4	4	4	10	11	7	7	9	1	3	7
Botswana	6	32	28	28	26	26	22	61	19	15	6	26	29
Burkina Faso	2	3	9	9	10	8	9	4	3	3	2	6	6
Burundi	0	4	4	4	3	3	2	3	2	1	0	4	3
Cameroon	27	93	100	71	106	116	99	185	113	98	22	59	109
Cape Verde	..	1	2	2	1	1	1	1	1	1	1	2	1
Central African Republic	0	3	2	1	1	2	0	0	0	1	1	4	1
Chad	0	1	1	2	4	2	1	6	4	5	0	0	3
Comoros	0	0	1	1	0	0	0	0	0	0	0	0	0
Congo, Democratic Rep. of	59	60	36	16	1	0	0	0	0	0	33	75	12
Congo, Republic of	13	39	6	1	0	89	11	141	40	6	8	25	37
Côte d'Ivoire	64	182	220	210	188	236	206	252	194	224	48	160	212
Djibouti	0	0	0	0	0	0	0	0	0	0	0	0	0
Equatorial Guinea	0	0	1	1	0	0	0	0	0	0	0	1	0
Eritrea	..	..	..	..	..	0	0	0	0	0	..	..	0
Ethiopia	8	8	9	10	9	15	13	19	21	20	6	10	14
Gabon	17	66	76	182	25	60	134	181	192	110	11	28	114
Gambia, The	0	1	2	3	2	2	2	1	1	1	0	1	2
Ghana	13	22	27	30	31	24	24	27	36	26	10	19	27
Guinea	9	19	12	13	13	12	14	21	19	19	7	13	16
Guinea-Bissau	0	1	1	2	0	1	2	1	0	0	0	1	1
Kenya	45	111	100	83	87	114	108	106	70	46	37	99	92
Lesotho	0	3	5	6	6	7	8	7	8	8	1	3	6
Liberia	5	1	1	0	8	0	0	0	0	0	6	7	1
Madagascar	3	53	41	11	10	7	4	5	51	15	6	50	22
Malawi	6	22	18	15	12	10	16	9	7	6	8	17	13
Mali	1	3	3	2	2	5	4	3	2	2	1	2	3
Mauritania	1	22	13	8	23	16	14	11	14	12	4	15	15
Mauritius	6	23	25	24	19	18	18	16	14	13	5	18	19
Mozambique	..	7	13	17	40	36	52	21	14	5	0	8	23
Namibia	..	..	..	..	..	..	..	..	..	..	..	..	..
Niger	5	2	6	1	7	3	0	1	2	2	5	19	3
Nigeria	54	988	1,216	466	314	335	322	512	297	238	59	401	521
Rwanda	0	0	0	0	0	0	0	0	0	0	0	0	0
São Tomé and Principe	0	1	0	0	0	0	0	0	0	0	0	1	0
Senegal	15	42	44	20	14	36	43	36	44	51	13	57	37
Seychelles	0	2	2	2	2	2	3	2	3	3	0	2	2
Sierra Leone	2	2	1	4	10	16	14	6	1	3	2	1	6
Somalia	0	0	0	0	0	0	0	3	0	0	0	2	0
South Africa	..	..	..	..	..	0	0	0	0	0	..	..	0
Sudan	16	2	2	1	2	0	2	0	0	2	13	9	1
Swaziland	6	7	5	5	4	4	3	9	5	5	4	9	5
Tanzania	19	25	27	30	49	33	49	36	12	25	15	24	32
Togo	11	21	11	3	1	1	2	11	5	2	8	30	6
Uganda	1	11	17	11	17	14	9	13	12	7	2	14	12
Zambia	39	31	203	59	54	75	83	39	33	25	31	34	67
Zimbabwe	1	50	49	58	79	90	95	95	93	85	6	40	77
NORTH AFRICA	301	1,485	1,486	1,704	1,812	2,004	2,289	2,499	2,155	2,132	369	1,240	1,952
Algeria	124	290	321	345	339	342	714	1,090	1,007	1,071	104	284	613
Egypt, Arab Republic	68	509	318	448	462	540	534	401	248	229	162	480	410
Libya	..	..	..	..	..	..	..	..	..	..	..	..	..
Morocco	66	517	661	700	780	865	762	722	639	579	66	352	692
Tunisia	44	170	187	211	231	256	279	286	261	253	37	124	237
ALL AFRICA	754	3,473	3,849	3,131	3,003	3,434	3,691	4,363	3,497	3,231	753	2,553	3,519

6-11. Interest payments: private long-term loans

	Millions of U.S. dollars (current prices)											Annual average		
	1980	1990	1991	1992	1993	1994	1995	1996	1997	1998	1999	75-84	85-89	90-MR
SUB-SAHARAN AFRICA	1,685	1,650	1,541	1,623	749	1,942	1,982	2,160	1,640	1,787	1,999	1,257	1,641	1,707
excluding South Africa	1,685	1,650	1,541	1,623	749	1,325	1,127	1,237	790	895	1,129	1,257	1,641	1,207
excl. S.Africa & Nigeria	1,219	827	737	620	457	586	592	709	612	750	853	848	974	674
Angola	..	81	78	34	18	41	67	266	127	163	171	7	52	105
Benin	1	0	0	0	0	0	0	0	0	0	0	3	7	0
Botswana	1	3	3	2	1	1	3	9	2	2	2	1	3	3
Burkina Faso	3	0	0	0	0	0	0	0	0	0	0	1	1	0
Burundi	1	1	1	0	0	0	0	0	0	0	3	1	2	1
Cameroon	78	73	41	65	26	21	21	14	16	19	..	56	93	33
Cape Verde	..	0	0	0	0	0	0	0	1	1	0	0	0	0
Central African Republic	0	1	1	0	0	0	0	0	0	0	2	1	0	0
Chad	0	0	0	0	0	0	0	0	0	0	0	0	0	0
Comoros	0	0	0	0	0	0	0	0	0	0	6	0	0	1
Congo, Democratic Rep. of	99	12	7	1	0	0	0	0	0	0	0	61	40	2
Congo, Republic of	13	52	36	22	17	50	40	3	0	0	176	36	64	40
Côte d'Ivoire	513	256	220	171	163	159	138	145	145	246	212	343	341	185
Djibouti	0	0	0	0	0	0	0	0	0	0	0	0	0	0
Equatorial Guinea	0	0	0	0	0	0	0	0	0	0	0	0	0	0
Eritrea	..	..	..	..	..	0	0	0	0	0	0	..	..	0
Ethiopia	2	24	16	22	3	9	29	15	4	3	6	4	25	13
Gabon	100	11	51	36	6	29	44	12	10	8	22	52	26	23
Gambia, The	0	5	2	1	0	0	0	0	0	0	0	0	1	1
Ghana	7	14	14	19	17	21	8	31	48	59	31	4	16	26
Guinea	2	6	1	0	1	2	1	0	3	0	1	2	2	1
Guinea-Bissau	1	0	0	0	0	0	0	0	0	0	0	0	0	0
Kenya	110	96	93	90	82	129	97	82	73	55	34	69	82	83
Lesotho	1	2	1	1	1	1	3	3	5	7	7	1	1	3
Liberia	16	0	0	0	0	0	0	0	0	0	0	5	0	0
Madagascar	19	13	7	3	1	1	1	2	0	0	0	12	12	3
Malawi	25	6	7	4	2	2	4	2	1	0	1	13	7	3
Mali	1	1	0	0	0	0	0	0	0	0	0	1	1	0
Mauritania	4	1	1	0	0	0	0	0	2	2	0	3	2	1
Mauritius	15	10	13	13	8	11	21	38	94	100	110	11	11	42
Mozambique	..	6	5	5	4	2	4	1	1	8	8	1	6	4
Namibia	..	..	..	..	..	..	..	..	..	1	40	..	..	21
Niger	58	16	10	8	7	6	6	5	3	2	1	30	26	6
Nigeria	466	823	805	1,004	292	739	535	528	178	145	276	409	667	533
Rwanda	0	0	0	0	0	0	0	0	0	0	0	0	1	0
São Tomé and Principe	0	0	0	0	0	0	0	0	0	0	0	0	0	0
Senegal	46	13	18	8	2	2	4	2	1	1	8	22	22	6
Seychelles	0	2	1	1	2	3	2	1	1	2	1	0	2	2
Sierra Leone	5	0	0	0	0	0	0	0	0	0	0	4	0	0
Somalia	0	0	0	0	0	0	0	0	0	0	0	1	0	0
South Africa	..	..	..	..	..	617	855	923	850	892	870	..	..	835
Sudan	5	0	0	0	0	0	0	0	0	0	0	15	9	0
Swaziland	2	1	1	1	0	0	0	0	0	0	-31	1	1	-3
Tanzania	13	3	4	6	5	1	5	5	2	3	2	9	3	3
Togo	8	5	0	0	0	0	0	0	0	0	0	7	6	1
Uganda	1	1	7	5	3	1	2	0	0	2	0	2	4	2
Zambia	63	29	20	20	15	15	20	8	12	7	4	43	23	15
Zimbabwe	9	83	81	81	72	80	75	65	59	60	32	30	83	69
NORTH AFRICA	2,078	2,111	2,176	3,257	1,972	1,678	1,604	1,452	1,260	1,153	1,282	1,372	2,060	1,794
Algeria	1,280	1,472	1,445	1,443	1,338	1,098	918	771	818	683	612	837	1,283	1,060
Egypt, Arab Republic	129	280	258	189	170	137	130	97	71	63	67	128	267	146
Libya	..	..	..	..	..	..	..	..	..	..	..	..	..	..
Morocco	515	213	352	1,516	354	345	437	447	232	239	411	319	370	455
Tunisia	154	146	122	109	109	99	118	137	140	168	192	88	141	134
ALL AFRICA	3,763	3,760	3,717	4,880	2,720	3,620	3,586	3,613	2,900	2,940	3,280	2,629	3,701	3,502

6-12. Interest payments: long-term loans and IMF charges

	Millions of U.S. dollars (current prices)											Annual average		
	1980	*1990*	*1991*	*1992*	*1993*	*1994*	*1995*	*1996*	*1997*	*1998*	*1999*	*75-84*	*85-89*	*90-MR*
SUB-SAHARAN AFRICA	2,479	4,601	4,657	4,041	2,839	4,142	4,556	4,940	3,823	3,885	4,565	1,942	3,661	4,205
excluding South Africa	2,479	4,601	4,657	4,041	2,839	3,487	3,651	3,978	2,940	2,978	3,693	1,942	3,661	3,686
excl. S.Africa & Nigeria	1,950	2,478	2,602	2,210	1,977	2,411	2,792	2,935	2,396	2,459	3,405	1,466	2,589	2,567
Angola	0	100	103	48	26	51	80	284	140	171	214	3	69	122
Benin	3	14	13	11	13	19	22	17	19	22	21	5	14	17
Botswana	8	39	35	36	33	31	28	78	28	23	21	8	31	35
Burkina Faso	6	10	15	14	16	15	18	16	16	16	17	5	13	15
Burundi	3	12	13	14	12	13	11	9	9	8	14	2	14	12
Cameroon	121	209	180	160	159	157	176	238	192	181	..	92	177	184
Cape Verde	0	2	3	3	2	3	3	3	4	4	3	1	3	3
Central African Republic	1	10	7	7	4	9	5	4	3	7	23	3	10	8
Chad	1	4	5	6	8	8	5	14	11	11	15	1	3	9
Comoros	0	1	2	3	1	1	1	1	1	1	7	0	1	2
Congo, Democratic Rep. of	220	127	67	35	10	2	16	5	0	0	204	118	179	47
Congo, Republic of	38	121	51	29	21	232	62	181	41	7	489	50	97	123
Côte d'Ivoire	590	474	524	436	399	437	398	478	416	618	614	417	560	479
Djibouti	1	2	2	2	2	2	2	3	2	2	4	1	3	2
Equatorial Guinea	0	1	2	1	1	1	1	1	1	1	1	0	2	1
Eritrea	..	..	..	..	..	0	0	0	1	4	2	..	..	1
Ethiopia	19	51	38	42	24	40	61	54	46	49	82	20	65	49
Gabon	120	91	148	246	41	106	223	236	244	148	272	66	60	175
Gambia, The	1	12	7	7	6	6	5	5	6	6	5	2	6	6
Ghana	35	96	96	102	100	95	69	116	132	151	123	30	100	108
Guinea	24	55	40	33	37	41	44	44	45	44	60	20	29	44
Guinea-Bissau	1	3	5	3	2	4	6	4	3	5	14	1	3	5
Kenya	171	256	266	212	212	292	265	247	191	152	147	126	237	224
Lesotho	2	8	10	13	12	11	15	15	18	21	22	2	6	15
Liberia	24	1	2	1	9	0	2	2	0	0	2	17	11	2
Madagascar	28	95	72	37	27	20	17	19	93	51	44	29	85	47
Malawi	37	42	42	33	28	26	40	29	27	23	28	28	39	32
Mali	4	21	16	18	42	25	23	60	21	19	26	5	19	27
Mauritania	15	38	27	20	43	38	33	30	36	33	37	16	33	34
Mauritius	26	48	51	53	42	45	56	71	123	127	136	24	47	75
Mozambique	0	23	34	43	76	55	76	48	42	37	130	1	27	57
Namibia	..	..	..	..	..	..	..	..	..	1	40	..	..	21
Niger	65	27	24	15	23	16	14	11	14	11	11	37	57	16
Nigeria	529	2,123	2,054	1,831	862	1,075	859	1,043	544	519	288	476	1,072	1,120
Rwanda	2	6	6	6	5	2	8	7	8	7	12	1	7	7
São Tomé and Principe	0	1	1	1	1	1	1	1	2	1	2	0	1	1
Senegal	70	99	103	53	26	66	72	121	78	91	89	45	126	80
Seychelles	0	6	4	5	5	6	7	5	5	6	6	0	5	5
Sierra Leone	10	4	2	14	14	58	19	11	8	9	19	8	5	16
Somalia	2	5	0	0	0	0	1	3	0	0	1	5	11	1
South Africa	0	0	0	0	0	656	905	962	884	908	871	0	0	519
Sudan	63	9	10	13	11	1	15	12	15	3	13	57	52	10
Swaziland	9	10	8	8	7	6	5	12	7	8	24	5	12	9
Tanzania	54	53	57	59	103	62	83	98	42	105	37	41	46	70
Togo	19	37	22	12	9	6	8	24	14	10	10	17	47	15
Uganda	7	31	41	29	35	35	36	40	39	33	45	14	44	36
Zambia	141	74	302	167	151	167	555	86	71	60	169	102	85	180
Zimbabwe	10	152	147	163	179	203	209	194	184	175	151	41	150	176
NORTH AFRICA	2,698	4,143	4,064	5,684	4,558	4,532	4,902	4,991	4,322	4,172	4,480	2,015	3,662	4,585
Algeria	1,440	1,846	1,848	1,883	1,746	1,527	1,791	2,081	2,037	1,978	1,965	972	1,591	1,870
Egypt, Arab Republic	367	1,014	669	1,042	1,066	1,153	1,241	1,054	736	673	745	422	885	939
Libya	..	..	..	..	..	..	..	..	..	..	..	..	..	..
Morocco	663	866	1,145	2,341	1,311	1,375	1,367	1,337	1,062	1,018	1,175	466	844	1,300
Tunisia	229	418	402	417	436	477	503	519	488	503	595	155	341	476
ALL AFRICA	5,177	8,743	8,720	9,725	7,396	8,675	9,458	9,932	8,146	8,057	9,045	3,957	7,323	8,790

6-13. Total external debt service payments: long-term loans and IMF credits

	Millions of U.S. dollars (current prices)										Annual average		
	1980	1990	1991	1992	1993	1994	1995	1996	1997	1998	75-84	85-89	90-MR
SUB-SAHARAN AFRICA	5,658	10,192	9,566	9,511	6,756	11,150	13,984	14,212	12,912	12,388	4,638	9,109	11,186
excluding South Africa	5,658	10,192	9,566	9,511	6,756	8,500	11,009	10,480	8,693	12,388	4,638	9,109	9,677
excl. S.Africa & Nigeria	4,887	6,888	6,650	5,803	5,316	6,678	9,232	8,019	7,310	8,695	3,575	6,896	7,177
Angola	0	283	336	191	87	203	410	783	795	1,118	0	164	467
Benin	9	35	29	26	31	40	48	44	51	..	13	34	38
Botswana	14	106	89	98	90	93	92	151	102	..	13	64	103
Burkina Faso	17	29	40	29	36	42	47	47	49	4	11	33	36
Burundi	7	41	38	38	35	41	38	30	29	54	8	38	38
Cameroon	252	479	394	363	441	361	393	486	473	18	203	559	379
Cape Verde	0	6	9	11	5	6	5	6	12	17	1	6	9
Central African Republic	8	28	14	14	7	21	15	12	12	61	9	27	20
Chad	6	10	9	10	16	18	15	30	35	45	5	10	21
Comoros	0	1	8	6	2	3	1	1	2	..	1	1	3
Congo, Democratic Rep. of	497	327	158	64	15	6	18	42	0	..	241	458	79
Congo, Republic of	78	483	260	127	98	538	146	321	96	1,117	136	355	354
Côte d'Ivoire	1,312	1,095	1,142	1,030	984	1,224	1,023	1,338	1,254	1,502	822	1,110	1,177
Djibouti	3	11	10	10	9	11	11	12	7	16	3	10	11
Equatorial Guinea	2	5	4	3	1	2	2	5	5	3	3	7	3
Eritrea	..	..	..	..	..	0	0	0	1	1	..	..	0
Ethiopia	36	228	131	104	90	107	153	346	98	457	51	242	190
Gabon	399	131	261	383	112	225	439	373	415	494	235	134	315
Gambia, The	1	37	30	29	27	30	26	27	26	22	5	21	28
Ghana	141	356	285	300	286	343	378	442	476	618	87	348	387
Guinea	100	165	133	84	81	94	173	110	151	0	76	105	110
Guinea-Bissau	4	6	22	6	3	7	15	11	9	5	2	8	9
Kenya	376	708	660	616	574	839	859	810	618	644	342	646	703
Lesotho	5	23	26	34	33	29	40	37	45	71	6	19	37
Liberia	43	3	17	1	22	15	2	2	0	..	41	21	8
Madagascar	76	215	156	93	75	63	55	79	211	168	76	208	124
Malawi	71	128	126	105	78	79	116	84	75	101	57	109	99
Mali	13	64	42	55	76	87	84	114	75	121	13	62	80
Mauritania	40	137	89	81	124	102	112	112	106	155	51	104	113
Mauritius	44	151	168	180	125	148	210	179	259	212	54	146	181
Mozambique	0	64	75	78	119	122	161	140	101	34	0	66	99
Namibia	..	..	..	..	..	..	..	..	..	1	..	..	1
Niger	122	90	98	51	88	64	55	56	59	14	87	130	64
Nigeria	772	3,304	2,917	3,709	1,441	1,822	1,777	2,461	1,383	3,693	1,064	2,213	2,501
Rwanda	4	16	18	15	16	3	20	17	20	41	4	20	18
São Tomé and Principe	1	2	2	2	2	2	2	3	6	3	1	3	3
Senegal	235	296	293	196	108	220	267	282	236	284	112	309	242
Seychelles	0	18	15	17	17	16	23	15	14	17	1	13	17
Sierra Leone	60	16	12	30	27	155	78	58	19	48	36	21	49
Somalia	13	10	0	0	0	0	1	3	0	..	14	31	2
South Africa	0	0	0	0	0	2,650	2,976	3,732	4,219	..	0	0	1,697
Sudan	194	25	22	27	20	3	69	48	58	..	147	115	34
Swaziland	17	46	29	25	24	26	21	33	24	30	12	36	29
Tanzania	135	171	202	231	208	179	228	264	155	152	100	147	199
Togo	38	80	50	32	23	19	26	56	52	..	44	108	42
Uganda	52	143	143	109	154	148	135	147	187	63	49	172	136
Zambia	411	200	596	352	363	371	2,611	245	258	244	296	219	582
Zimbabwe	50	422	413	550	585	575	613	620	633	740	107	456	572
NORTH AFRICA	6,640	14,569	15,155	16,824	15,638	12,210	11,609	10,934	10,512	3,315	5,037	10,513	12,307
Algeria	3,968	8,624	9,067	9,110	9,027	5,073	4,179	4,148	4,408	..	2,848	5,703	6,705
Egypt, Arab Republic	813	2,770	2,385	2,532	2,017	2,109	2,248	2,149	1,665	..	871	2,160	2,234
Libya		..	..				..			..			..
Morocco	1,341	1,774	2,372	3,876	3,308	3,622	3,740	3,210	3,075	3,315	921	1,693	3,144
Tunisia	518	1,402	1,331	1,305	1,285	1,405	1,442	1,427	1,363	..	398	956	1,370
ALL AFRICA	12,298	24,761	24,721	26,335	22,394	23,359	25,593	25,146	23,424	15,703	9,676	19,622	23,493

Note: In 1995, Zambia was able to clear its arrears to the IMF after completing a 3 year Rights Arrangement Program.

6-14. Interest payments: short-term loans

	Millions of U.S. dollars (current prices)											Annual average		
	1980	*1990*	*1991*	*1992*	*1993*	*1994*	*1995*	*1996*	*1997*	*1998*	*1999*	*75-84*	*85-89*	*90-MR*
SUB-SAHARAN AFRICA	1,029	715	603	558	527	636	819	884	1,051	1,155	995	542	691	794
excluding South Africa	1,029	715	603	558	527	384	404	379	496	533	115	542	691	472
excl. S.Africa & Nigeria	650	683	575	518	477	334	348	332	463	496	115	306	522	434
Angola	..	43	53	54	66	55	53	49	46	45	0	6	35	46
Benin	11	4	3	2	1	1	2	2	4	5	5	5	7	3
Botswana	2	0	0	0	0	0	0	0	1	0	0	0	0	0
Burkina Faso	5	6	6	5	2	2	2	2	3	3	4	2	4	3
Burundi	2	2	1	1	1	1	1	0	0	1	0	1	2	1
Cameroon	28	43	33	31	30	24	39	24	40	55	..	17	54	35
Cape Verde	..	0	0	0	0	0	1	0	0	0	0	0	0	0
Central African Republic	2	2	2	2	2	2	1	1	1	1	2	1	2	1
Chad	0	2	2	1	1	0	1	0	1	1	0	0	0	1
Comoros	0	0	0	0	0	0	0	0	0	0	0	0	0	0
Congo, Democratic Rep. of	45	21	20	13	13	9	8	7	12	18	0	18	27	12
Congo, Republic of	31	48	40	35	30	20	35	18	16	16	0	12	45	26
Côte d'Ivoire	95	167	138	130	110	20	23	37	105	96	10	47	80	84
Djibouti	1	4	4	2	2	1	1	0	1	0	0	1	2	1
Equatorial Guinea	1	0	0	0	0	1	0	0	1	2	1	1	0	0
Eritrea	..	..	..	..	..	0	0	0	0	0	0	..	..	0
Ethiopia	9	8	7	5	5	4	1	1	1	1	0	4	7	3
Gabon	33	45	48	50	45	43	17	11	18	25	0	13	31	30
Gambia, The	3	1	1	1	1	2	1	1	1	1	0	1	2	1
Ghana	18	12	17	19	22	26	28	36	29	38	16	12	12	24
Guinea	9	4	4	4	3	3	5	3	10	12	0	4	5	5
Guinea-Bissau	1	3	1	0	0	0	0	1	1	0	0	1	2	1
Kenya	58	78	55	49	53	38	36	30	30	39	0	24	39	41
Lesotho	1	0	0	0	0	0	0	0	0	0	0	0	0	0
Liberia	11	0	0	0	0	0	0	0	0	0	0	4	3	0
Madagascar	29	7	5	3	3	2	3	4	1	2	0	9	4	3
Malawi	16	4	4	4	1	1	3	4	3	1	0	5	5	2
Mali	3	3	3	2	2	1	2	2	15	8	0	2	4	4
Mauritania	7	9	10	6	4	4	5	4	8	8	0	5	7	6
Mauritius	8	5	5	3	4	10	16	19	23	27	0	3	3	11
Mozambique	..	15	7	5	3	1	1	1	3	4	0	0	8	4
Namibia	..	..	..	..	..	..	..	..	..	0	19	..	..	9
Niger	19	9	10	2	2	2	1	1	2	1	1	7	7	3
Nigeria	379	32	28	40	50	50	56	48	33	38	1	236	169	38
Rwanda	3	5	6	6	6	1	1	1	2	2	0	1	3	3
São Tomé and Principe	0	1	0	0	1	0	0	0	0	0	0	0	0	0
Senegal	24	29	21	15	15	14	14	7	11	15	6	13	21	15
Seychelles	37	4	3	2	1	1	1	1	1	1	0	5	2	1
Sierra Leone	6	5	4	5	4	5	1	1	1	0	0	3	4	3
Somalia	0	0	0	0	0	0	0	0	0	0	0	0	0	0
South Africa	..	..	..	..	..	251	415	504	555	622	880	..	..	538
Sudan	70	25	0	0	0	0	0	0	0	0	0	39	38	3
Swaziland	2	0	0	0	0	0	0	0	8	2	0	1	1	1
Tanzania	26	9	5	5	4	5	4	6	6	7	6	12	19	6
Togo	14	6	5	5	4	4	3	2	2	2	4	6	6	4
Uganda	5	5	5	5	3	3	2	3	4	4	0	2	3	3
Zambia	0	3	3	1	1	2	1	9	10	10	0	0	0	4
Zimbabwe	15	49	48	45	33	28	35	44	44	43	41	22	25	41
NORTH AFRICA	669	530	377	420	285	233	216	194	330	305	127	462	569	302
Algeria	116	179	100	200	36	33	22	13	13	15	10	150	125	62
Egypt, Arab Republic	422	301	220	168	164	130	132	133	262	227	40	246	351	178
Libya	..	..	..	..	..	..	..	..	..	..	..	..	..	..
Morocco	105	20	18	15	18	18	24	9	6	3	0	57	71	13
Tunisia	26	30	39	37	67	52	38	39	49	60	77	9	21	49
ALL AFRICA	1,699	1,245	980	978	812	869	1,035	1,078	1,381	1,460	1,123	1,004	1,260	1,096

6-15. Net flows: long- and short-term loans, including IMF

	Millions of U.S. dollars (current prices)											Annual average		
	1980	1990	1991	1992	1993	1994	1995	1996	1997	1998	1999	75-84	85-89	90-MR
SUB-SAHARAN AFRICA	9,996	7,081	3,860	5,028	5,038	10,307	7,383	3,192	5,021	-1,060	1,933	7,831	5,215	4,778
excluding South Africa	9,996	7,081	3,860	5,028	5,038	1,044	3,970	2,511	5,453	-774	294	7,831	5,215	3,351
excl. S.Africa & Nigeria	7,215	7,115	4,021	5,736	4,566	1,704	4,529	3,838	6,115	-505	992	6,307	6,101	3,811
Angola	..	977	227	905	294	305	-93	74	429	58	-672	316	1,029	250
Benin	42	92	106	39	87	113	105	101	114	-24	72	85	52	80
Botswana	8	-37	49	23	45	-10	2	-43	-18	-66	130	29	37	8
Burkina Faso	56	70	131	105	109	117	124	81	71	64	125	52	76	100
Burundi	0	65	66	101	45	25	26	4	3	10	-9	0	19	34
Cameroon	538	685	70	380	134	305	65	-188	672	65	48	354	283	224
Cape Verde	..	11	-1	12	6	25	35	-5	14	31	28	18	8	16
Central African Republic	31	107	94	39	54	32	25	14	-3	-8	25	22	67	38
Chad	-8	107	97	120	51	72	63	110	77	24	118	22	47	84
Comoros	13	2	-2	15	5	7	11	4	8	-5	1	12	14	5
Congo, Democratic Rep. of	278	88	125	-26	0	-140	61	-91	242	-13	185	368	234	43
Congo, Republic of	541	93	-266	-35	310	79	166	-451	96	-66	183	241	189	11
Côte d'Ivoire	1,257	1,189	561	627	731	-1,002	935	2,117	413	-1,064	-110	741	351	440
Djibouti	9	21	17	30	36	-10	13	18	11	3	3	10	22	14
Equatorial Guinea	41	10	8	13	13	17	-8	0	19	12	-7	12	12	8
Eritrea	..	..	..	..	..	27	7	7	33	73	106	..	..	42
Ethiopia	94	204	358	233	314	190	134	23	130	97	-267	446	435	142
Gabon	-122	164	87	-193	19	-18	14	-84	260	-172	-288	72	295	-21
Gambia, The	58	16	13	35	26	-20	-6	44	-5	3	4	26	15	11
Ghana	75	341	563	306	370	323	410	654	273	288	40	150	242	357
Guinea	23	86	122	143	228	120	98	72	403	-43	64	52	149	129
Guinea-Bissau	73	46	34	23	19	27	13	30	27	11	6	28	33	24
Kenya	718	615	280	114	154	-322	104	-185	21	-183	167	318	346	76
Lesotho	20	47	51	67	59	47	41	30	30	22	209	16	33	60
Liberia	95	-1	-15	-1	10	-14	0	11	-21	3	1	93	23	-3
Madagascar	476	194	119	51	67	22	59	60	210	100	-28	199	128	85
Malawi	154	88	96	106	107	95	183	181	48	112	174	95	66	119
Mali	99	158	116	119	63	92	200	135	283	-36	118	93	111	125
Mauritania	139	102	60	-49	85	96	68	103	158	-84	-48	115	86	49
Mauritius	104	76	56	56	22	260	312	110	768	-25	349	60	27	198
Mozambique	..	173	58	235	99	189	193	197	341	189	382	320	309	206
Namibia	..	..	..	..	..	..	..	..	..	5	..	..	..	5
Niger	286	123	-128	48	26	28	-9	13	102	33	-55	120	110	18
Nigeria	2,780	-34	-162	-708	472	-660	-559	-1,327	-663	-269	-698	1,524	-886	-461
Rwanda	36	55	91	73	50	-11	53	52	114	79	89	32	70	64
São Tomé and Principe	7	9	28	26	15	8	14	5	5	5	14	6	14	13
Senegal	246	222	-69	177	70	-29	74	-14	141	98	181	221	214	85
Seychelles	-390	7	10	-1	-3	6	-17	-2	9	33	23	8	10	6
Sierra Leone	62	11	19	112	161	90	-136	41	24	58	32	53	40	41
Somalia	138	58	13	0	0	0	0	0	-7	5	0	154	74	7
South Africa	..	..	..	..	..	9,263	3,412	681	-432	-287	1,638	..	..	2,379
Sudan	839	169	116	272	91	9	0	-119	-157	-14	-191	642	243	18
Swaziland	31	-38	-7	-9	-8	-3	7	-1	164	-127	3	24	-1	-2
Tanzania	405	225	131	309	109	162	90	147	231	140	-692	341	157	85
Togo	108	10	44	27	-60	56	39	68	9	49	88	101	48	33
Uganda	130	269	169	236	246	224	184	206	248	100	227	103	164	211
Zambia	360	-127	123	82	29	88	435	169	-83	25	60	305	236	80
Zimbabwe	148	335	202	793	283	28	437	142	213	-369	102	225	-16	217
NORTH AFRICA	5,618	-1,000	1,044	386	-1,014	1,973	1,712	1,598	-251	-1,773	-1,740	5,935	3,180	93
Algeria	1,261	-892	64	-137	-868	2,029	1,392	1,624	-421	-1,609	-1,900	1,611	945	-72
Egypt, Arab Republic	2,465	-1,288	385	-608	-333	28	-28	-547	465	820	-358	2,596	1,411	-146
Libya	..	..	..	..	..	..	..	..	..	..	..	..	..	..
Morocco	1,624	889	140	555	-35	-532	-306	-172	-863	-266	-441	1,346	521	-103
Tunisia	267	292	455	576	221	448	654	693	568	-718	958	382	303	414
ALL AFRICA	15,614	6,081	4,903	5,414	4,024	12,280	9,095	4,791	4,770	-2,834	192	13,766	8,395	4,872

6-16. Net flows: long-term loans, including IMF

	Millions of U.S. dollars (current prices)										Annual average		
	1980	*1990*	*1991*	*1992*	*1993*	*1994*	*1995*	*1996*	*1997*	*1998*	*75-84*	*85-89*	*90-MR*
SUB-SAHARAN AFRICA	7,742	5,139	4,362	3,872	5,003	4,354	3,880	-43	1,769	-1,072	5,954	5,678	3,029
excluding South Africa	7,742	5,139	4,362	3,872	5,003	2,831	2,402	435	1,278	-1,072	5,954	5,678	2,694
excl. S.Africa & Nigeria	6,231	5,392	4,437	5,216	5,038	2,979	2,888	1,545	1,803	714	4,938	5,475	3,334
Angola	..	679	95	503	624	264	219	-463	-401	-673	..	758	94
Benin	56	102	84	65	63	84	77	83	23	..	77	57	72
Botswana	21	-37	49	22	45	-10	1	-45	-52	0	28	37	-3
Burkina Faso	55	61	121	128	119	80	83	73	39	..	48	73	88
Burundi	35	69	60	86	58	31	27	23	7	57	37	85	46
Cameroon	500	449	220	520	264	249	-103	-41	-11	..	313	237	193
Cape Verde	3	8	-1	10	7	24	18	20	16	48	10	8	17
Central African Republic	24	105	94	41	48	36	30	25	4	..	17	68	48
Chad	3	100	88	139	52	61	56	89	68	107	21	41	85
Comoros	13	5	-3	15	4	6	9	6	4	..	11	14	6
Congo, Democratic Rep. of	271	267	263	54	53	1	0	3	0	..	281	239	80
Congo, Republic of	488	-42	-167	33	383	30	-67	-136	-30	-267	222	141	-29
Côte d'Ivoire	1,017	521	389	351	278	524	204	64	-580	172	636	141	214
Djibouti	8	18	46	36	19	17	9	15	7	1	8	17	19
Equatorial Guinea	18	9	7	13	9	4	2	0	1	..	8	17	6
Eritrea	..	..	..	..	..	27	7	7	33	40	..	..	23
Ethiopia	93	225	357	263	314	170	140	1	128	-153	425	448	161
Gabon	-109	170	68	8	58	38	57	-42	-23	62	52	207	44
Gambia, The	51	3	13	37	7	5	5	48	13	19	18	21	17
Ghana	143	293	388	353	324	302	338	493	336	224	69	243	339
Guinea	47	100	145	149	245	122	49	85	141	0	44	132	115
Guinea-Bissau	72	34	38	37	22	25	13	23	25	8	22	40	25
Kenya	424	317	545	179	103	-301	138	-66	-165	-173	250	335	64
Lesotho	10	43	47	59	50	44	44	33	34	173	15	32	58
Liberia	61	-1	-13	0	20	-14	0	0	0	..	61	22	-1
Madagascar	329	144	150	77	89	51	66	93	216	..	170	153	111
Malawi	120	69	120	106	151	74	149	117	106	82	75	72	108
Mali	88	141	127	130	58	69	138	110	71	70	78	123	101
Mauritania	108	54	23	81	91	82	42	83	23	-24	100	77	50
Mauritius	79	102	77	-1	22	83	255	32	691	223	37	58	165
Mozambique	..	190	73	168	135	176	196	222	221	91	..	281	164
Namibia	..	..	..	..	..	..	..	..	..	5	..	..	5
Niger	223	92	-32	56	44	35	-3	8	54	..	107	105	32
Nigeria	1,510	-253	-76	-1,343	-35	-148	-486	-1,110	-525	-1,786	1,015	203	-640
Rwanda	25	53	77	71	50	20	43	53	62	191	27	71	69
São Tomé and Principe	9	15	19	24	14	14	14	10	1	5	6	11	13
Senegal	171	81	33	225	100	7	4	67	141	79	166	215	82
Seychelles	12	-4	9	13	6	8	-7	2	2	5	7	7	4
Sierra Leone	50	17	14	41	95	47	40	34	34	6	25	14	36
Somalia	106	43	13	0	0	0	0	0	0	..	136	83	7
South Africa	..	..	..	..	..	1,524	1,478	-478	492	..	..	..	754
Sudan	658	171	116	94	91	9	36	17	5	..	495	164	67
Swaziland	21	-21	-6	-10	-9	-4	3	8	8	195	22	0	18
Tanzania	318	215	162	220	151	164	136	65	171	228	290	184	168
Togo	78	56	47	35	11	34	19	77	27	..	88	30	38
Uganda	51	234	118	204	298	182	162	168	196	-5	62	197	173
Zambia	391	64	127	146	148	57	93	62	76	42	210	175	90
Zimbabwe	93	177	239	437	325	55	144	20	82	-125	164	44	150
NORTH AFRICA	4,953	1,567	385	1,228	200	1,408	1,499	891	-799	2,129	5,087	3,328	945
Algeria	869	156	-692	474	-453	1,446	1,496	922	-436	3,369	1,435	808	698
Egypt, Arab Republic	2,337	301	299	-89	180	123	-382	-438	-161	..	2,162	1,483	-21
Libya	..	..	..	..	..	..	..	..	..	..	..	..	..
Morocco	1,394	965	427	491	196	-293	-180	-66	-894	-1,240	1,118	825	-66
Tunisia	352	145	352	352	277	131	565	473	691	..	373	212	373
ALL AFRICA	12,695	6,706	4,747	5,100	5,203	5,762	5,380	848	971	1,056	11,041	9,006	3,975

6-17. Net transfers: long- and short-term loans, including IMF

	Millions of U.S. dollars (current prices)											*Annual average*		
	1980	1990	1991	1992	1993	1994	1995	1996	1997	1998	1999	75-84	85-89	90-MR
SUB-SAHARAN AFRICA	6,527	1,767	-1,401	430	2,530	5,529	2,007	-2,632	146	-5,674	-3,788	5,384	756	-109
excluding South Africa	6,527	1,767	-1,401	430	1,672	-2,826	-85	-1,846	2,017	-4,274	-1,339	5,384	756	-589
excl. S.Africa & Nigeria	4,656	3,957	843	3,009	2,112	-1,041	1,389	572	3,256	-3,448	-631	4,573	2,883	1,002
Angola	0	834	71	802	202	200	-226	-259	243	-157	-886	121	926	82
Benin	27	74	91	26	73	92	81	82	91	-44	37	75	31	60
Botswana	-1	-76	13	-13	12	-41	-26	-122	-48	-89	54	21	5	-33
Burkina Faso	45	54	110	86	91	100	104	63	53	31	47	46	59	74
Burundi	36	51	52	85	32	12	15	-5	-6	2	29	37	74	27
Cameroon	389	433	-143	189	-55	124	-150	-450	440	-228	24	245	51	19
Cape Verde	0	9	-3	9	4	21	30	-8	10	27	36	7	5	13
Central African Republic	28	95	85	31	49	21	19	9	-7	-14	-26	18	55	26
Chad	-9	102	91	113	42	63	57	96	65	1	93	21	44	72
Comoros	13	1	-4	12	4	6	11	4	7	-5	-12	11	13	2
Congo, Democratic Rep. of	13	-60	38	-74	-23	-151	38	-103	229	-31	-18	232	29	-16
Congo, Republic of	473	-75	-357	-99	258	-174	69	-650	39	-76	-306	180	47	-137
Côte d'Ivoire	572	549	-100	61	222	-1,459	514	1,602	-109	-1,764	-66	277	-290	-55
Djibouti	7	15	11	26	31	-13	11	15	9	-3	-5	8	16	10
Equatorial Guinea	40	9	6	11	12	15	-9	-1	17	13	1	11	10	8
Eritrea	..	..	..	..	..	27	7	7	33	69	104	..	..	41
Ethiopia	67	145	313	186	285	146	71	-33	82	27	-349	422	363	87
Gabon	-275	28	-109	-489	-67	-167	-226	-331	-2	-343	-559	-7	205	-227
Gambia, The	55	3	5	27	18	-27	-12	39	-12	1	-2	24	7	4
Ghana	22	234	451	185	248	202	312	503	111	98	-98	108	130	225
Guinea	-11	27	79	106	188	76	49	25	348	-121	-102	28	116	68
Guinea-Bissau	71	40	27	20	17	23	7	26	23	7	7	26	28	20
Kenya	489	281	-41	-147	-111	-651	-197	-462	-199	-373	20	168	70	-188
Lesotho	18	39	40	54	47	36	26	14	11	-1	187	13	27	45
Liberia	60	-2	-17	-1	1	-14	-2	10	-21	3	-1	72	9	-4
Madagascar	419	92	42	11	36	0	39	37	116	60	21	161	38	45
Malawi	101	41	49	70	78	69	141	148	18	87	146	62	14	85
Mali	92	134	97	99	19	67	175	73	247	-63	92	86	87	94
Mauritania	117	55	24	-74	39	54	30	69	114	-126	-85	94	47	10
Mauritius	70	23	0	-1	-24	205	241	21	621	-179	213	34	-23	112
Mozambique	0	136	16	187	20	133	116	148	295	173	84	127	274	131
Namibia	0	0	0	0	0	0	0	0	0	4	-59	0	0	-5
Niger	202	88	-161	31	1	10	-24	1	87	8	36	75	46	8
Nigeria	1,872	-2,190	-2,244	-2,579	-440	-1,785	-1,474	-2,418	-1,239	-826	-709	811	-2,127	-1,590
Rwanda	31	43	79	61	39	-14	44	45	104	52	78	29	60	53
São Tomé and Principe	7	7	27	25	13	7	13	3	3	4	8	6	12	11
Senegal	151	94	-193	109	28	-110	-13	-143	52	-8	54	162	67	-13
Seychelles	-427	-2	3	-7	-10	-2	-25	-7	4	25	17	3	3	0
Sierra Leone	47	2	14	94	143	28	-156	29	15	33	13	41	31	21
Somalia	135	53	13	0	0	0	-1	-3	-7	5	-1	149	62	6
South Africa	0	0	0	0	858	8,356	2,092	-786	-1,870	-1,400	-2,449	0	0	480
Sudan	707	136	106	259	81	9	-15	-131	-173	41	89	544	-17	40
Swaziland	20	-49	-15	-17	-15	-9	2	-13	149	-136	-21	17	-14	-12
Tanzania	325	163	69	245	2	95	4	43	184	71	496	288	92	137
Togo	74	-33	17	11	-72	46	28	42	-7	33	83	78	-5	15
Uganda	118	234	123	202	208	186	147	163	205	71	140	87	117	168
Zambia	219	-203	-182	-86	-124	-81	-121	74	-165	-45	-109	203	151	-104
Zimbabwe	122	135	7	585	70	-202	193	-96	-15	-586	-133	163	-191	-4
NORTH AFRICA	2,250	-5,672	-3,398	-5,716	-5,856	-2,792	-3,406	-3,586	-4,904	-6,570	-7,033	3,458	-1,051	-4,893
Algeria	-294	-2,917	-1,884	-2,220	-2,649	468	-422	-470	-2,470	-3,971	-3,831	489	-772	-2,036
Egypt, Arab Republic	1,676	-2,603	-505	-1,816	-1,562	-1,255	-1,401	-1,734	-533	-80	-1,143	1,928	174	-1,263
Libya	..	..	..	..	..	..	..	..	..	..	..	..	..	..
Morocco	857	3	-1,023	-1,801	-1,363	-1,925	-1,696	-1,517	-1,931	-1,287	-1,616	822	-394	-1,416
Tunisia	12	-156	14	122	-282	-81	113	134	30	-1,232	-444	218	-59	-178
ALL AFRICA	8,778	-3,906	-4,798	-5,286	-3,326	2,737	-1,399	-6,218	-4,757	-12,244	-10,822	8,842	-295	-5,002

6-18. Net transfers: long-term loans, including IMF

	Millions of U.S. dollars (current prices)											Annual average		
	1980	1990	1991	1992	1993	1994	1995	1996	1997	1998	1999	75-84	85-89	90-MR
SUB-SAHARAN AFRICA	6,095	201	-340	-194	2,824	736	49	-4,120	-2,268	-4,045	-4,293	4,904	1,676	-1,145
excluding South Africa	6,095	201	-340	-194	1,966	-132	-524	-2,679	-857	-2,751	-2,724	4,904	1,676	-803
excl. S.Africa & Nigeria	5,114	2,577	1,790	2,981	2,863	1,091	820	-533	212	-1,745	-2,016	4,364	2,544	804
Angola	0	579	-7	452	597	213	135	-161	245	-292	-886	90	689	87
Benin	63	86	84	54	72	91	67	84	6	11	14	74	42	57
Botswana	14	-76	14	-12	12	-41	-26	-123	-80	-56	54	20	6	-34
Burkina Faso	53	50	115	114	115	90	92	66	40	41	51	45	57	77
Burundi	38	55	53	87	41	12	7	5	-10	2	29	36	75	28
Cameroon	374	239	38	306	58	118	-271	-256	-177	-270	-24	224	75	-24
Cape Verde	0	6	-3	7	4	20	13	16	8	28	25	7	6	12
Central African Republic	32	94	84	32	43	38	18	15	-8	-12	-25	18	55	28
Chad	-1	101	83	134	42	66	57	95	57	6	103	21	40	74
Comoros	13	5	-4	12	3	7	9	6	2	-1	-12	11	13	3
Congo, Democratic Rep. of	106	-12	146	20	43	-5	-18	-39	0	0	-18	241	3	12
Congo, Republic of	448	-166	-223	4	362	-188	-131	-296	-73	-2	-797	174	44	-151
Côte d'Ivoire	465	77	-194	-177	-165	181	-99	-323	-1,018	-662	-724	292	-511	-310
Djibouti	7	16	44	33	17	15	7	16	7	0	-3	7	14	15
Equatorial Guinea	36	5	12	11	12	5	0	-2	-3	-1	2	9	13	4
Eritrea	..	..	..	..	..	27	7	7	33	64	104	..	..	40
Ethiopia	83	146	313	241	319	150	80	-29	81	29	-349	419	364	98
Gabon	-228	73	-99	-275	-19	-27	-160	-252	-247	-236	-559	-13	174	-180
Gambia, The	54	-4	1	27	-2	-7	-2	31	-2	-1	-2	21	14	4
Ghana	108	147	375	188	223	125	270	489	120	95	-45	96	147	199
Guinea	30	31	108	127	205	88	27	32	119	10	-102	27	107	64
Guinea-Bissau	71	31	33	35	20	21	9	21	27	11	3	22	37	21
Kenya	338	65	287	-119	-132	-549	-168	-347	-421	-342	20	172	74	-171
Lesotho	10	39	40	53	47	37	26	15	11	0	187	13	28	45
Liberia	67	-3	-15	-1	11	-15	-2	-2	0	0	-2	72	10	-3
Madagascar	373	16	62	24	49	19	35	77	125	-7	17	162	56	42
Malawi	119	33	77	54	117	68	111	99	96	90	70	63	20	81
Mali	96	129	103	121	22	76	153	72	76	34	92	82	94	88
Mauritania	115	11	-17	64	55	62	22	63	3	-47	-71	90	46	14
Mauritius	98	10	5	-53	-21	38	199	-39	568	-229	213	33	-19	69
Mozambique	0	178	81	188	92	132	106	160	199	178	84	119	265	140
Namibia	0	0	0	0	0	0	0	0	0	4	-40	0	0	-4
Niger	168	58	-66	32	12	25	-26	0	52	37	-3	77	49	12
Nigeria	981	-2,377	-2,130	-3,174	-897	-1,223	-1,344	-2,146	-1,069	-1,007	-709	540	-869	-1,607
Rwanda	29	47	83	65	45	19	48	45	72	68	78	27	62	57
São Tomé and Principe	9	13	28	22	13	12	12	8	2	3	8	6	10	12
Senegal	160	-44	-59	127	46	-19	-26	-65	32	-53	70	150	90	1
Seychelles	12	-9	5	8	0	2	-14	-3	-3	3	17	6	3	1
Sierra Leone	45	8	5	22	72	45	37	32	32	26	13	27	5	29
Somalia	122	35	13	0	0	0	-1	-3	0	0	-1	144	70	4
South Africa	0	0	0	0	858	868	573	-1,441	-1,411	-1,294	-1,569	0	0	-342
Sudan	727	161	106	81	81	9	-18	-31	-53	-4	-19	509	111	31
Swaziland	15	-31	-14	-17	-16	-10	-2	-4	1	-4	-21	17	-16	-12
Tanzania	298	157	107	248	30	80	29	-19	178	68	502	253	148	138
Togo	81	24	17	23	-6	36	33	41	15	38	6	78	-19	23
Uganda	109	233	123	200	256	175	153	143	198	72	128	87	115	168
Zambia	280	-35	-235	-67	-122	-80	-16	-6	51	-109	-109	187	60	-73
Zimbabwe	82	2	85	484	209	-70	42	-170	-147	-335	-92	150	-179	1
NORTH AFRICA	2,374	-2,936	-3,464	-4,627	-4,841	-2,653	-3,432	-3,782	-4,948	-6,944	-6,675	3,218	-300	-4,430
Algeria	-570	-1,689	-2,232	-1,574	-2,521	566	-22	-526	-2,292	-3,981	-3,821	463	-663	-1,809
Egypt, Arab Republic	1,930	-800	-371	-1,065	-886	-1,053	-1,708	-1,577	-914	-1,124	-1,103	1,754	578	-1,060
Libya	..	..	..	..	..	..	..	..	..	..	..	..	..	..
Morocco	922	-63	-889	-1,966	-1,271	-1,820	-1,650	-1,586	-1,859	-1,166	-1,616	784	-136	-1,389
Tunisia	92	-385	27	-22	-163	-346	-53	-92	117	-673	-136	218	-79	-173
ALL AFRICA	8,469	-2,736	-3,804	-4,820	-2,017	-1,917	-3,384	-7,901	-7,216	-10,989	-10,969	8,122	1,376	-5,575

6-19. Long-term debt: official concessional

| | Millions of U.S. dollars (current prices) | | | | | | | | | | | Annual average | | |
	1980	1990	1991	1992	1993	1994	1995	1996	1997	1998	1999	75-84	85-89	90-MR
SUB-SAHARAN AFRICA	16,310	58,608	63,233	66,199	69,819	76,110	80,989	82,970	83,247	90,223	85,163	16,398	42,892	75,656
excluding South Africa	16,310	58,608	63,233	66,199	69,819	76,110	80,989	82,970	83,247	90,223	85,163	16,398	42,892	75,656
excl. S.Africa & Nigeria	15,872	58,087	62,271	65,227	68,725	74,820	79,612	81,616	81,925	88,641	83,439	16,030	42,475	74,436
Angola	..	1,197	1,280	1,302	1,315	1,405	1,490	2,152	2,212	2,739	2,754	18	423	1,785
Benin	166	1,009	1,036	1,105	1,165	1,270	1,253	1,293	1,265	1,333	1,359	166	539	1,209
Botswana	59	185	229	233	264	293	340	322	290	296	268	86	126	272
Burkina Faso	221	597	724	820	914	906	1,001	1,085	1,077	1,175	1,249	177	493	955
Burundi	104	779	836	890	946	1,012	1,047	1,040	989	1,048	1,023	107	570	961
Cameroon	873	1,826	1,868	2,350	2,490	3,510	4,108	4,158	4,231	4,559	4,268	690	1,335	3,337
Cape Verde	..	96	98	105	107	133	147	154	162	194	233	32	80	143
Central African Republic	59	511	609	629	674	723	765	768	724	750	745	64	354	690
Chad	171	402	495	538	592	674	694	763	807	873	928	141	218	677
Comoros	43	159	158	168	163	172	183	184	181	179	171	44	152	172
Congo, Democratic Rep. of	862	3,136	3,269	3,207	3,217	3,403	3,511	3,361	3,127	3,406	3,206	820	1,947	3,284
Congo, Republic of	404	1,739	1,816	1,756	1,690	1,884	1,984	2,003	1,854	1,886	1,730	373	885	1,834
Côte d'Ivoire	438	3,096	3,398	3,504	3,696	3,883	4,563	4,806	4,503	4,943	4,418	411	1,770	4,081
Djibouti	15	152	202	217	229	253	267	278	252	263	252	19	123	236
Equatorial Guinea	32	118	125	132	139	142	148	145	139	144	142	31	84	137
Eritrea	..	..	..	..	..	29	37	42	73	140	237	..	..	93
Ethiopia	562	7,533	7,677	7,858	8,184	8,485	8,717	8,695	8,633	8,812	4,795	1,352	5,913	7,939
Gabon	113	422	488	448	408	573	702	742	893	948	821	87	230	645
Gambia, The	68	250	269	298	310	336	362	395	389	417	413	59	185	344
Ghana	775	2,120	2,382	2,574	2,895	3,343	3,741	4,006	4,077	4,620	4,822	683	1,447	3,458
Guinea	678	1,675	1,804	1,977	2,157	2,329	2,457	2,426	2,479	2,649	2,614	734	1,256	2,257
Guinea-Bissau	87	393	415	439	475	534	565	675	666	702	666	63	238	553
Kenya	684	2,380	2,713	2,788	3,090	3,394	3,879	3,938	3,762	4,123	4,140	650	1,741	3,421
Lesotho	44	292	335	371	382	440	469	465	456	484	472	48	183	417
Liberia	211	594	585	573	599	622	635	610	585	598	582	221	540	598
Madagascar	467	1,723	1,944	1,958	1,952	2,118	2,242	2,132	2,681	2,913	2,919	499	1,249	2,258
Malawi	258	1,051	1,227	1,310	1,502	1,681	1,897	1,946	1,973	2,184	2,475	275	743	1,725
Mali	613	2,247	2,379	2,690	2,692	2,464	2,660	2,687	2,626	2,763	2,744	592	1,652	2,595
Mauritania	526	1,280	1,328	1,327	1,521	1,598	1,688	1,739	1,700	1,842	1,809	507	1,174	1,583
Mauritius	65	349	393	383	383	416	439	402	345	354	316	65	207	378
Mozambique	..	2,083	2,394	2,634	2,864	3,239	2,936	3,204	3,190	4,066	3,485	269	1,910	3,010
Namibia	..	..	..	..	..	..	..	..	..	..	..	..	..	..
Niger	155	826	833	879	932	978	1,017	1,031	1,056	1,169	1,173	173	611	989
Nigeria	439	521	961	972	1,094	1,290	1,377	1,354	1,322	1,582	1,724	368	417	1,220
Rwanda	141	659	743	787	835	903	961	977	985	1,114	1,158	126	487	912
São Tomé and Principe	20	108	124	144	157	177	221	219	219	236	230	16	65	184
Senegal	400	1,968	1,947	2,080	2,111	2,104	2,239	2,286	2,391	2,600	2,521	412	1,598	2,225
Seychelles	19	71	76	70	66	67	68	67	67	70	68	13	55	69
Sierra Leone	175	312	329	384	492	590	700	736	729	780	774	157	266	583
Somalia	546	1,557	1,577	1,540	1,546	1,576	1,596	1,557	1,503	1,531	1,516	564	1,304	1,550
South Africa	..	..	..	..	..	0	0	0	0	0	0	..	..	0
Sudan	1,730	4,452	4,599	4,597	4,671	4,775	4,838	4,750	4,636	4,704	4,654	1,697	3,727	4,667
Swaziland	86	160	157	146	135	153	167	154	141	143	131	63	122	149
Tanzania	2,692	3,458	3,577	3,848	4,016	4,372	4,454	4,482	5,096	5,528	5,774	2,556	3,034	4,461
Togo	245	699	760	788	795	880	901	955	943	1,028	1,021	186	456	877
Uganda	254	1,451	1,625	1,806	2,130	2,456	2,767	2,878	2,977	3,192	3,277	222	792	2,456
Zambia	797	2,066	2,494	2,484	2,616	3,087	3,294	3,502	3,488	3,648	3,531	672	1,561	3,021
Zimbabwe	15	906	955	1,089	1,206	1,440	1,462	1,405	1,354	1,492	1,555	81	628	1,286
NORTH AFRICA	13,487	24,145	25,824	26,570	27,751	30,679	32,775	36,810	34,547	35,660	34,438	11,995	22,082	30,920
Algeria	1,269	860	955	1,056	1,313	2,053	3,082	3,285	3,137	3,277	3,287	1,031	599	2,231
Egypt, Arab Republic	8,115	12,520	16,621	17,151	17,996	19,531	20,285	24,030	22,585	23,467	22,533	7,116	13,200	19,672
Libya	..	..	..	..	..	..	..	..	..	..	..	..	..	..
Morocco	2,717	7,984	5,374	5,467	5,532	6,012	6,371	6,659	6,285	6,419	6,046	2,597	5,982	6,215
Tunisia	1,386	2,782	2,874	2,896	2,910	3,082	3,039	2,836	2,539	2,497	2,572	1,251	2,301	2,803
ALL AFRICA	29,798	82,753	89,057	92,769	97,571	106,789	113,765	119,780	117,794	125,884	119,601	28,393	64,974	106,576

6-20. Long-term debt: official nonconcessional

	Millions of U.S. dollars (current prices)									Annual average		
	1980	1990	1991	1992	1993	1994	1995	1996	1997	75-84	85-89	90-MR
SUB-SAHARAN AFRICA	9,328	50,395	52,656	51,765	50,461	54,655	56,269	52,184	47,166	8,369	34,401	51,944
excluding South Africa	9,328	50,395	52,656	51,765	50,461	54,655	56,269	52,184	47,166	8,369	34,401	51,944
excl. S.Africa & Nigeria	8,774	33,908	34,465	34,410	33,308	36,133	37,153	34,894	31,477	7,635	25,324	34,469
Angola	14	666	654	656	648	712	762	726	661	18	409	686
Benin	50	193	196	215	203	213	226	152	125	30	85	190
Botswana	76	345	360	351	340	334	306	249	205	76	309	311
Burkina Faso	39	115	152	154	148	130	130	70	58	34	111	120
Burundi	6	63	59	52	49	48	47	40	33	9	55	49
Cameroon	364	2,056	2,201	2,658	2,555	2,785	3,007	3,026	3,154	299	961	2,680
Cape Verde	1	33	30	30	31	31	32	30	26	12	32	30
Central African Republic	40	92	87	81	78	62	71	68	64	37	106	75
Chad	34	53	57	126	116	78	137	134	118	24	28	102
Comoros	0	14	9	7	7	7	8	8	8	2	13	9
Congo, Democratic Rep. of	1,747	5,003	5,157	4,915	4,741	5,044	5,261	5,067	4,681	1,336	3,793	4,984
Congo, Republic of	200	1,318	1,332	1,236	1,192	1,949	2,059	1,797	1,598	158	815	1,560
Côte d'Ivoire	809	4,590	5,030	5,086	4,904	4,756	4,652	3,978	3,399	694	3,117	4,549
Djibouti	7	3	3	3	2	2	2	1	1	4	5	2
Equatorial Guinea	14	74	75	67	61	63	66	62	56	13	62	65
Eritrea	0	0	0	0	0	0	0	2	3	0	0	1
Ethiopia	76	368	381	380	399	432	462	435	440	82	208	412
Gabon	204	2,013	2,060	1,976	1,929	2,853	2,988	3,004	2,569	173	807	2,424
Gambia, The	5	40	39	39	35	32	24	18	13	5	34	30
Ghana	259	431	442	439	426	417	387	320	279	181	307	393
Guinea	183	469	497	382	398	460	448	458	453	149	378	445
Guinea-Bissau	10	205	230	224	212	200	201	180	172	15	146	203
Kenya	522	1,330	1,261	1,167	1,055	1,436	1,351	1,151	918	490	1,311	1,209
Lesotho	2	52	56	66	97	115	133	129	125	5	38	97
Liberia	148	330	326	314	303	306	318	301	285	131	299	310
Madagascar	105	1,472	1,450	1,398	1,277	1,333	1,380	1,344	1,148	253	1,408	1,350
Malawi	184	253	225	193	177	170	157	126	106	132	256	176
Mali	15	73	71	81	89	79	77	75	66	13	44	76
Mauritania	57	411	398	410	363	383	385	361	316	73	343	378
Mauritius	89	300	304	254	242	234	224	213	210	74	244	248
Mozambique	0	1,478	1,468	1,857	1,832	1,888	2,227	2,132	2,027	61	796	1,864
Namibia	0	0	0	0	0	0	0	0	0	0	0	0
Niger	101	288	302	285	277	289	312	298	274	90	302	291
Nigeria	554	16,487	18,191	17,355	17,153	18,521	19,115	17,291	15,689	733	9,077	17,475
Rwanda	2	2	1	1	1	1	7	6	7	1	2	3
São Tomé and Principe	4	24	24	23	23	23	11	5	4	5	21	17
Senegal	253	791	789	800	829	840	868	817	705	272	916	805
Seychelles	6	27	26	28	31	38	42	41	39	6	24	34
Sierra Leone	71	193	189	257	245	233	198	159	154	52	152	204
Somalia	.21	333	332	322	316	323	329	325	315	60	299	324
South Africa	0	0	0	0	0	0	0	0	0	0	0	0
Sudan	1,564	3,048	3,038	2,911	2,870	2,990	3,083	3,026	2,886	1,201	2,537	2,981
Swaziland	79	83	79	66	63	57	56	66	70	57	113	67
Tanzania	349	1,836	1,766	1,618	1,417	1,391	1,376	1,256	715	343	1,385	1,422
Togo	236	324	319	283	267	287	322	289	253	180	423	293
Uganda	39	375	357	367	354	320	212	196	177	65	311	295
Zambia	704	2,139	1,945	1,782	1,564	1,518	1,475	1,430	1,294	635	1,854	1,643
Zimbabwe	86	602	689	852	1,142	1,271	1,338	1,322	1,272	86	464	1,061
NORTH AFRICA	8,111	24,941	25,793	25,910	25,705	30,746	35,345	32,201	30,667	8,070	26,647	28,914
Algeria	2,226	4,735	5,313	5,212	4,946	8,610	12,314	14,657	15,165	1,739	3,838	8,869
Egypt, Arab Republic	4,507	8,669	7,848	7,525	7,448	8,201	8,509	3,486	3,142	4,824	15,536	6,854
Libya	0	0	0	0	0	0	0	0	0	0	0	0
Morocco	802	9,007	9,608	10,121	9,955	10,114	10,149	9,408	7,908	983	5,535	9,534
Tunisia	575	2,531	3,023	3,052	3,356	3,821	4,373	4,650	4,452	524	1,738	3,657
ALL AFRICA	17,439	75,336	78,449	77,675	76,166	85,401	91,613	84,385	77,833	16,439	61,048	80,857

6-21. Long-term debt: private

	Millions of U.S. dollars (current prices)											Annual average		
	1980	1990	1991	1992	1993	1994	1995	1996	1997	1998	1999	75-84	85-89	90-MR
SUB-SAHARAN AFRICA	20,778	40,631	38,945	32,663	32,673	46,461	48,579	44,747	42,270	40,779	43,293	17,542	37,420	41,104
excluding South Africa	20,778	40,631	38,945	32,663	32,673	33,426	33,807	30,412	28,391	27,512	29,331	17,542	37,420	32,779
excl. S.Africa & Nigeria	16,402	25,703	25,429	24,181	24,177	24,971	25,858	23,326	22,476	21,451	23,502	13,046	23,441	24,107
Angola	..	5,767	5,788	6,200	6,781	7,031	7,320	6,511	5,813	5,696	5,886	557	3,853	6,279
Benin	118	17	8	5	4	4	4	4	3	4	0	142	295	5
Botswana	8	27	25	21	48	50	47	36	28	24	18	15	43	32
Burkina Faso	20	38	6	5	4	4	5	4	4	4	4	18	34	8
Burundi	8	9	6	4	3	2	2	1	1	1	95	10	22	12
Cameroon	1,014	1,713	1,716	1,525	1,467	1,245	1,238	1,119	777	659	508	727	1,386	1,197
Cape Verde	..	3	2	2	2	2	6	12	12	11	9	0	3	6
Central African Republic	48	22	21	20	21	18	18	14	14	33	265	40	23	45
Chad	54	9	8	7	6	6	2	17	17	17	14	42	31	10
Comoros	0	0	0	0	0	0	0	0	0	0	113	0	0	11
Congo, Democratic Rep. of	1,462	889	872	852	836	860	878	861	834	899	826	1,393	879	861
Congo, Republic of	652	1,145	893	883	1,232	941	913	866	832	814	555	546	1,408	907
Côte d'Ivoire	5,091	5,537	5,436	5,263	5,125	5,210	5,345	4,429	4,592	4,330	6,558	3,507	5,570	5,183
Djibouti	5	0	0	0	0	0	0	0	0	0	0	3	3	0
Equatorial Guinea	7	18	17	16	15	16	17	16	14	15	0	9	18	14
Eritrea	..	..	..	..	..	0	0	0	0	0	0	..	..	0
Ethiopia	49	577	786	765	704	654	596	354	353	350	333	103	565	547
Gabon	955	715	676	626	596	268	199	143	131	125	207	766	850	369
Gambia, The	24	18	14	9	5	1	0	0	0	0	0	16	25	5
Ghana	131	257	319	332	345	419	525	795	850	838	758	132	291	544
Guinea	159	108	98	91	104	98	82	98	76	30	70	133	133	85
Guinea-Bissau	36	33	32	30	25	28	32	1	1	1	1	17	45	18
Kenya	1,286	1,927	2,273	1,769	1,696	1,266	1,153	953	805	834	857	898	1,235	1,353
Lesotho	11	34	35	28	21	17	28	34	44	55	60	9	19	36
Liberia	156	192	196	195	200	208	208	199	192	199	205	115	186	199
Madagascar	346	140	125	112	87	86	84	77	45	41	5	256	272	80
Malawi	192	80	69	64	50	49	28	24	21	20	234	128	72	64
Mali	36	16	12	6	4	2	2	0	0	0	3	30	37	4
Mauritania	131	97	94	88	19	9	8	25	24	22	20	118	125	40
Mauritius	165	262	292	306	275	448	751	783	1,421	1,327	1,669	94	148	754
Mozambique	..	670	491	227	162	1,743	1,815	1,872	1,930	1,770	2,153	70	768	1,283
Namibia	..	..	..	..	..	..	..	..	..	..	27	..	..	27
Niger	432	372	226	206	182	157	133	110	96	72	49	267	368	160
Nigeria	4,376	14,928	13,516	8,482	8,496	8,455	7,949	7,086	5,915	6,061	5,829	4,496	13,979	8,672
Rwanda	8	4	3	2	1	2	2	2	1	1	16	7	9	3
São Tomé and Principe	0	1	1	1	1	1	0	0	0	0	0	1	2	1
Senegal	461	241	202	162	156	153	127	53	66	33	63	301	303	126
Seychelles	0	19	23	33	35	43	36	30	25	31	32	2	27	31
Sierra Leone	111	99	98	36	26	26	8	8	6	7	6	91	84	32
Somalia	28	37	36	35	34	36	37	36	34	35	34	86	58	35
South Africa	..	..	..	..	..	13,035	14,772	14,334	13,878	13,268	13,962	..	..	13,875
Sudan	854	2,151	2,079	1,972	1,949	2,131	2,355	2,090	1,973	2,055	1,843	872	1,730	2,060
Swaziland	24	7	5	4	2	1	0	0	0	0	0	14	15	2
Tanzania	339	478	462	400	400	397	442	418	277	263	136	259	472	367
Togo	415	52	52	51	50	51	52	50	0	0	0	247	64	36
Uganda	244	335	301	260	115	93	84	77	76	74	58	149	301	147
Zambia	726	446	400	372	333	259	224	193	183	141	121	671	559	267
Zimbabwe	594	1,141	1,233	1,196	1,054	938	1,054	1,011	908	619	603	561	1,113	976
NORTH AFRICA	21,549	35,954	32,033	30,040	28,191	26,952	25,363	22,230	19,871	18,788	18,109	16,616	31,599	25,753
Algeria	13,545	20,822	19,701	19,221	18,588	17,514	15,647	13,124	10,465	9,054	7,437	9,882	17,164	15,157
Egypt, Arab Republic	2,070	7,184	4,847	3,671	2,859	2,457	1,998	1,420	1,130	957	723	2,131	6,539	2,725
Libya	..	..	..	..	..	..	..	..	..	..	..	..	..	..
Morocco	4,505	6,310	6,010	5,646	5,373	5,661	5,901	5,600	5,745	6,155	6,089	3,534	6,064	5,849
Tunisia	1,429	1,638	1,475	1,502	1,372	1,319	1,817	2,086	2,531	2,621	3,859	1,069	1,832	2,022
ALL AFRICA	42,327	76,585	70,978	62,703	60,864	73,413	73,942	66,977	62,140	59,567	61,401	34,159	69,019	66,857

6-22. Total external debt

	1980	1990	1991	1992	1993	1994	1995	1996	1997	1998	1999	75-84	85-89	90-MR
	Millions of U.S. dollars (current prices)											*Annual average*		
SUB-SAHARAN AFRICA	60,612	177,052	183,248	182,281	188,412	221,424	235,514	231,319	221,371	229,983	227,558	54,892	136,754	209,816
excluding South Africa	60,612	177,052	183,248	182,281	188,412	199,753	210,156	205,269	196,150	205,271	202,657	54,892	136,754	195,025
excl. S.Africa & Nigeria	51,691	143,613	149,721	153,263	157,677	166,660	176,063	173,862	167,695	174,957	171,040	46,377	110,830	163,455
Angola	..	8,594	9,004	10,070	10,586	11,172	11,382	10,425	9,838	11,223	10,915	695	5,137	10,321
Benin	424	1,292	1,333	1,373	1,447	1,589	1,614	1,594	1,628	1,651	1,419	408	1,078	1,494
Botswana	147	561	620	612	660	689	703	614	562	516	649	182	481	618
Burkina Faso	330	834	967	1,040	1,117	1,129	1,267	1,294	1,297	1,405	1,452	269	708	1,180
Burundi	166	907	964	1,022	1,062	1,123	1,158	1,127	1,066	1,119	1,126	153	697	1,067
Cameroon	2,588	6,676	6,901	7,426	7,463	8,333	9,444	9,640	9,368	9,930	8,142	1,976	4,445	8,332
Cape Verde	..	135	135	142	148	176	214	202	207	244	258	62	120	186
Central African Republic	195	698	794	814	875	888	946	933	883	924	878	181	557	863
Chad	284	524	629	723	768	828	902	997	1,026	1,092	944	227	323	843
Comoros	44	185	180	188	185	192	204	206	206	203	210	48	175	196
Congo, Democratic Rep. of	4,773	10,274	10,840	10,977	11,282	12,336	13,256	12,840	12,341	13,187	13,358	4,319	7,993	12,069
Congo, Republic of	1,526	4,947	4,832	4,770	5,081	5,413	6,004	5,241	5,071	5,119	5,460	1,227	3,849	5,194
Côte d'Ivoire	7,462	17,251	18,174	18,546	19,071	17,395	18,898	19,524	15,609	14,852	14,816	5,644	12,570	17,414
Djibouti	32	205	226	235	264	263	282	296	274	288	280	33	163	261
Equatorial Guinea	76	241	254	255	264	288	292	282	283	306	201	71	185	267
Eritrea	..	..	..	..	..	29	37	44	76	151	242	..	..	97
Ethiopia	824	8,630	9,119	9,341	9,703	10,067	10,310	10,079	10,079	10,351	9,286	1,656	6,850	9,696
Gabon	1,514	3,983	4,223	3,850	3,861	4,171	4,360	4,310	4,278	4,425	3,204	1,231	2,393	4,067
Gambia, The	137	369	383	403	426	423	427	453	425	459	432	116	301	420
Ghana	1,402	3,881	4,380	4,508	4,887	5,469	5,936	6,439	6,346	6,883	6,297	1,313	2,974	5,503
Guinea	1,134	2,476	2,622	2,634	2,848	3,110	3,242	3,240	3,519	3,546	3,017	1,119	1,949	3,025
Guinea-Bissau	140	692	745	761	787	852	898	937	921	970	844	110	465	841
Kenya	3,387	7,058	7,453	6,898	7,111	7,202	7,412	6,931	6,603	6,943	6,894	2,646	5,254	7,051
Lesotho	72	396	448	495	541	620	677	670	660	692	712	69	249	591
Liberia	686	1,849	1,954	1,922	1,956	2,056	2,154	2,107	2,012	2,103	2,077	620	1,550	2,019
Madagascar	1,248	3,704	3,908	3,911	3,805	4,096	4,322	4,146	4,109	4,394	4,354	1,187	3,267	4,075
Malawi	830	1,558	1,665	1,709	1,826	2,025	2,243	2,315	2,228	2,444	2,594	659	1,263	2,061
Mali	727	2,467	2,596	2,898	2,902	2,694	2,957	3,006	3,142	3,201	3,018	699	1,879	2,888
Mauritania	840	2,096	2,188	2,088	2,141	2,223	2,349	2,412	2,456	2,589	2,035	805	1,844	2,258
Mauritius	467	984	1,043	1,051	1,008	1,382	1,757	1,818	2,472	2,482	2,392	359	768	1,639
Mozambique	..	4,650	4,718	5,130	5,212	7,272	7,458	7,566	7,638	8,315	6,322	513	3,803	6,428
Namibia	..	..	..	..	..	..	..	..	..	123	178	..	..	151
Niger	863	1,726	1,494	1,517	1,542	1,525	1,587	1,536	1,576	1,663	1,643	640	1,481	1,581
Nigeria	8,921	33,439	33,527	29,019	30,736	33,092	34,093	31,407	28,455	30,315	31,617	8,515	25,924	31,570
Rwanda	190	712	810	857	909	952	1,028	1,043	1,111	1,226	1,253	158	540	990
São Tomé and Principe	24	150	167	189	209	222	246	230	233	252	296	22	97	219
Senegal	1,473	3,736	3,570	3,666	3,764	3,658	3,841	3,663	3,661	3,847	3,138	1,269	3,396	3,654
Seychelles	84	163	173	164	157	171	159	148	149	187	169	127	140	164
Sierra Leone	469	1,151	1,206	1,245	1,396	1,492	1,178	1,179	1,144	1,256	1,263	442	942	1,251
Somalia	660	2,370	2,449	2,447	2,500	2,616	2,678	2,643	2,561	2,635	2,606	785	1,939	2,551
South Africa	..	..	..	..	..	21,671	25,358	26,050	25,221	24,711	24,901	..	..	24,652
Sudan	5,177	14,762	15,227	15,450	15,836	16,918	17,603	16,972	16,326	16,843	23,700	4,807	10,945	16,964
Swaziland	210	254	245	222	208	220	235	222	368	251	437	149	272	266
Tanzania	5,322	6,451	6,558	6,678	6,791	7,235	7,406	7,362	7,129	7,633	6,385	4,881	6,275	6,963
Togo	1,049	1,275	1,342	1,339	1,278	1,444	1,464	1,472	1,327	1,448	1,382	715	1,127	1,377
Uganda	689	2,583	2,777	2,928	3,029	3,372	3,572	3,675	3,913	4,016	3,480	611	1,733	3,334
Zambia	3,244	6,916	6,968	6,709	6,485	6,804	6,952	7,054	6,654	6,865	6,717	2,954	5,982	6,813
Zimbabwe	786	3,247	3,437	4,060	4,285	4,524	5,007	4,976	4,919	4,707	4,566	982	2,671	4,373
NORTH AFRICA	51,281	92,974	90,884	88,748	86,681	94,059	99,533	97,950	92,131	93,971	91,460	43,825	91,656	92,839
Algeria	19,365	27,877	28,203	27,078	26,020	29,973	32,781	33,421	30,890	30,665	29,381	14,323	23,682	29,629
Egypt, Arab Republic	19,131	32,949	32,564	31,066	30,509	32,314	33,266	31,300	29,850	31,965	29,955	18,165	42,351	31,574
Libya	..	..	..	..	..	..	..	..	..	..	..	..	..	..
Morocco	9,259	24,458	21,866	22,061	21,459	22,158	22,665	21,851	20,162	20,491	20,247	8,335	19,338	21,742
Tunisia	3,527	7,690	8,251	8,543	8,694	9,614	10,820	11,379	11,230	10,850	11,877	3,002	6,284	9,895
ALL AFRICA	111,893	270,026	274,133	271,029	275,093	315,483	335,046	329,269	313,502	323,954	319,017	98,717	228,409	302,655

6-23. Structure of external debt

| | Bilateral | | | | Multilateral | | | | Private | | Short-term | | IMF | |
| | Concessional | | Nonconcessional | | Concessional | | Nonconcessional | | | | | | | |
	1980	1998	1980	1998	1980	1998	1980	1998	1980	1998	1980	1998	1980	1998
SUB-SAHARAN AFRICA	12,374	45,208	5,695	36,680	3,936	45,015	3,601	12,188	20,778	40,779	11,195	42,593	3,033	7,396
excluding South Africa	12,374	45,208	5,695	36,680	3,936	45,015	3,601	12,188	20,778	27,512	11,195	31,149	3,033	7,396
excluding South Africa & Nigeria	11,973	44,289	5,674	24,003	3,899	44,352	3,068	8,769	16,402	21,451	7,642	24,574	3,033	7,396
Angola	..	2,527	..	1,011	..	212	..	67	..	5,696	..	1,710	0	0
Benin	82	429	31	106	84	904	20	28	118	4	73	86	16	94
Botswana	28	102	23	11	32	194	53	178	8	24	4	7	0	0
Burkina Faso	89	122	30	8	133	1,053	9	47	20	4	35	59	15	112
Burundi	49	157	1	0	55	891	5	30	8	1	12	20	36	20
Cameroon	663	3,724	142	2,506	210	835	222	652	1,014	659	278	1,398	59	156
Cape Verde	..	29	..	17	..	164	..	16	..	11	..	6	0	0
Central African Republic	17	138	28	48	42	613	12	15	48	33	25	60	24	18
Chad	97	95	34	78	75	778	0	37	54	17	12	23	14	64
Comoros	21	28	0	0	21	152	0	9	0	0	1	12	0	3
Congo, Democratic Rep. of	667	1,806	1,620	4,213	194	1,601	127	681	1,462	899	329	3,565	373	423
Congo, Republic of	355	1,643	132	1,169	49	243	69	382	652	814	247	834	22	34
Côte d'Ivoire	369	3,232	355	1,579	69	1,711	454	1,780	5,091	4,330	1,059	1,576	65	644
Djibouti	14	119	5	0	1	144	1	1	5	0	6	15	0	9
Equatorial Guinea	30	56	13	47	2	88	1	10	7	15	7	79	16	11
Eritrea	..	68	..	2	..	72	..	5	..	0	..	5	..	0
Ethiopia	281	6,422	18	216	282	2,391	58	239	49	350	57	626	79	107
Gabon	103	916	173	2,238	10	32	30	522	955	125	228	478	15	113
Gambia, The	33	86	0	0	36	331	5	16	24	0	23	15	16	10
Ghana	636	1,275	119	157	139	3,345	140	218	131	838	131	716	105	334
Guinea	615	1,200	116	208	63	1,448	67	240	159	30	80	293	35	127
Guinea-Bissau	58	303	5	161	29	399	5	15	36	1	5	76	1	15
Kenya	414	1,539	159	516	270	2,584	364	415	1,286	834	640	858	254	197
Lesotho	4	83	2	24	40	401	0	98	11	55	8	8	6	24
Liberia	179	398	50	77	33	200	98	218	156	199	81	694	89	317
Madagascar	319	1,221	71	1,062	148	1,692	34	89	346	41	244	230	87	58
Malawi	111	284	112	16	147	1,900	72	90	192	20	116	32	80	102
Mali	451	1,218	6	37	163	1,545	9	28	36	0	24	188	39	187
Mauritania	420	1,008	38	189	106	835	18	161	131	22	65	265	62	110
Mauritius	39	294	37	27	25	60	53	201	165	1,327	47	573	102	0
Mozambique	..	2,268	..	1,810	..	1,798	..	96	..	1,770	..	365	0	207
Namibia	..	..	..	..	..	..	..	..	..	..	..	..	..	..
Niger	42	238	70	247	112	930	30	36	432	72	159	63	16	76
Nigeria	401	919	21	12,677	38	663	533	3,419	4,376	6,061	3,553	6,575	0	0
Rwanda	51	155	1	4	91	959	0	0	8	1	26	50	14	56
São Tomé and Principe	9	70	4	2	11	166	0	1	0	0	0	12	0	0
Senegal	221	838	169	454	179	1,762	84	194	461	33	219	273	140	293
Seychelles	16	49	4	7	3	22	2	37	0	31	59	42	0	0
Sierra Leone	136	276	47	139	39	504	23	32	111	7	53	108	59	191
Somalia	400	808	9	302	147	723	13	18	28	35	47	591	18	158
South Africa	..	0	..	0	..	0	..	0	..	13,268	..	11,444	0	0
Sudan	1,361	2,865	1,298	2,750	368	1,839	266	212	854	2,055	598	6,349	431	772
Swaziland	69	74	34	0	17	69	45	79	24	0	15	28	6	0
Tanzania	2,388	2,480	88	581	305	3,049	261	93	339	263	1,770	900	171	268
Togo	155	253	210	250	90	775	26	24	415	0	120	52	33	95
Uganda	191	815	23	149	63	2,377	16	67	244	74	63	135	89	398
Zambia	778	1,617	314	1,348	19	2,031	374	211	726	141	586	329	447	1,188
Zimbabwe	15	961	83	238	0	532	3	1,183	594	619	90	768	0	407
NORTH AFRICA	11,435	31,809	6,098	17,048	2,053	3,852	2,013	14,733	21,549	18,788	7,266	5,602	868	2,140
Algeria	1,255	2,892	1,956	12,132	14	385	270	4,005	13,545	9,054	2,325	186	0	2,011
Egypt, Arab Republic	6,230	21,300	3,767	1,253	1,885	2,167	741	2,028	2,070	957	4,027	4,260	411	0
Libya	..	..	..	..	..	..	..	..	..	..	..	..	..	..
Morocco	2,638	5,540	158	2,224	79	879	644	5,577	4,505	6,155	778	116	457	0
Tunisia	1,311	2,076	218	1,440	75	421	357	3,123	1,429	2,621	136	1,040	0	129
ALL AFRICA	23,809	77,017	11,793	53,729	5,989	48,867	5,613	26,921	42,327	59,567	18,461	48,195	3,901	9,536

6-24. Structure of external debt service payments

| | Bilateral | | | | Multilateral | | | | Private | | Short-term | | IMF | |
| | Concessional | | Nonconcessional | | Concessional | | Nonconcessional | | | | | | | |
	1980	1998	1980	1998	1980	1998	1980	1998	1980	1998	1980	1998	1980	1998
SUB-SAHARAN AFRICA	422	1,502	453	825	59	806	425	2,418	3,809	6,535	1,029	115	487	1,177
excluding South Africa	422	1,502	453	825	59	806	425	2,418	3,809	3,211	1,029	115	487	745
excluding South Africa & Nigeria	400	1,051	438	760	58	801	354	1,675	3,145	3,041	650	114	487	745
Angola	..	16	0	61	..	1	0	1	..	1,013	0	0	0	0
Benin	1	9	1	11	1	23	1	6	4	0	11	..	0	6
Botswana	1	7	2	6	0	13	10	53	1	6	2	0	0	0
Burkina Faso	3	8	4	1	3	31	2	8	5	0	5	..	0	3
Burundi	1	1	0	0	0	14	1	6	4	0	2	0	1	9
Cameroon	25	117	18	76	4	19	24	214	163	78	28	..	19	19
Cape Verde	..	2	0	1	..	7	0	3	..	2	0	0	0	0
Central African Republic	0	0	0	0	0	11	0	0	1	0	2	40	7	13
Chad	1	0	0	6	2	12	0	5	0	0	0	0	3	12
Comoros	0	3	0	0	0	3	0	0	0	0	0	..	0	0
Congo, Democratic Rep. of	48	0	136	0	2	0	22	0	189	0	45	..	101	1
Congo, Republic of	22	0	13	19	1	1	11	74	25	0	31	0	8	11
Côte d'Ivoire	29	198	55	80	3	52	46	376	1,180	562	95	10	0	3
Djibouti	2	2	1	0	0	3	0	0	0	0	1	0	0	0
Equatorial Guinea	0	0	1	0	0	1	0	1	0	0	1	..	0	3
Eritrea	..	3	0	0	..	1	0	0	..	0	0	0	..	0
Ethiopia	11	19	1	5	2	44	10	34	9	12	9	0	2	5
Gabon	6	50	28	199	0	1	4	82	359	25	33	0	1	29
Gambia, The	0	9	0	0	0	9	0	3	0	0	3	0	1	5
Ghana	24	98	22	12	1	49	13	50	48	169	18	17	33	141
Guinea	55	29	7	7	0	26	21	32	14	17	9	0	2	10
Guinea-Bissau	0	3	0	0	0	3	0	1	4	0	1	0	0	1
Kenya	13	73	22	81	2	40	47	139	274	209	58	33	17	64
Lesotho	0	7	0	5	0	11	0	11	4	9	1	0	0	5
Liberia	3	0	0	0	0	0	7	0	27	0	11	..	5	1
Madagascar	21	42	2	28	1	33	3	66	42	1	29	0	3	14
Malawi	4	6	7	1	2	29	3	18	53	1	16	0	3	26
Mali	4	18	0	3	1	37	0	4	3	0	3	0	4	12
Mauritania	8	27	0	7	3	33	2	29	17	4	7	0	11	8
Mauritius	2	33	4	6	0	4	6	39	29	205	8	0	3	0
Mozambique	..	24	0	13	..	24	0	12	..	12	0	0	0	25
Namibia	..	..	0	0	..	..	0	0	..	1	..	..	..	0
Niger	3	4	5	3	16	15	2	2	98	25	19	..	0	15
Nigeria	22	451	15	65	1	5	70	743	663	170	379	1	0	0
Rwanda	0	1	0	1	1	13	0	0	3	0	3	0	0	4
São Tomé and Principe	0	0	1	0	0	2	0	0	0	0	0	0	0	0
Senegal	13	67	19	50	1	59	8	33	183	18	24	8	12	63
Seychelles	0	4	0	2	0	1	0	6	0	6	37	0	0	0
Sierra Leone	2	1	2	1	0	13	2	1	35	0	6	0	19	1
Somalia	3	0	0	0	1	0	5	0	0	0	0	..	4	0
South Africa	..	0	0	0	..	0	0	0	..	3,324	0	0	0	432
Sudan	37	0	30	0	5	0	18	0	12	0	70	..	92	58
Swaziland	2	8	6	0	0	3	4	13	5	0	2	0	0	0
Tanzania	32	63	2	1	2	61	23	44	36	18	26	6	39	39
Togo	2	9	17	6	1	12	2	8	16	0	14	..	0	12
Uganda	3	16	8	18	1	44	2	14	22	4	5	..	16	64
Zambia	16	17	22	20	0	33	51	88	238	59	0	..	84	6
Zimbabwe	3	59	0	33	0	8	3	200	43	59	15	0	0	58
NORTH AFRICA	571	1,635	328	2,106	11	250	261	2,955	5,216	3,746	669	0	253	591
Algeria	107	255	226	1,004	2	48	69	936	3,564	2,411	116	..	0	534
Egypt, Arab Republic	265	730	50	134	7	83	51	457	320	270	422	..	121	0
Libya	..	..	0	0	..	..	0	0	..	..	..	..	..	..
Morocco	130	402	24	879	1	68	94	1,012	992	691	105	0	100	0
Tunisia	70	249	28	89	1	51	47	550	340	375	26	..	33	57
ALL AFRICA	994	3,137	782	2,931	70	1,056	685	5,373	9,025	10,282	1,699	115	739	1,768

Note: In 1995, Zambia was able to clear its arrears to the IMF after completing a 3 year Rights Arrangement Program.

6-25. Terms of long-term external financing, 1998

	Concessional terms				Nonconcessional terms				Structure of financing (percentage of total)		
	Interest (percent)	Grace period (years)	Maturity (years)	Grant element (percent)	Interest (percent)	Grace period (years)	Maturity (years)	Grant element (percent)	Grants	Conces-sional loans	Noncon-cessional loans
SUB-SAHARAN AFRICA	1.2	9.3	35.9	73.1	6.6	3.7	13.9	14.7	29.9	64.8	5.3
excluding South Africa	1.2	9.3	35.9	73.1	6.6	3.7	13.9	14.7	29.3	65.5	5.1
excl. S. Africa & Nigeria	1.2	9.3	35.9	73.1	6.6	3.7	13.9	14.7	29.2	65.6	5.1
Angola	1.8	4.1	29.0	58.7	7.2	0.6	9.0	9.0	61.4	34.4	4.2
Benin	1.3	8.8	33.2	70.2	6.8	5.8	17.3	19.7	23.7	74.1	2.2
Botswana	2.9	4.1	15.5	40.5	8.3	5.0	9.5	7.5	82.7	15.7	1.6
Burkina Faso	1.3	8.5	33.7	70.2	7.5	7.4	24.1	17.0	40.1	57.8	2.1
Burundi	0.8	9.9	38.0	78.4	..	..	..	..	56.7	43.3	0.0
Cameroon	1.3	9.1	34.7	71.9	8.8	1.2	10.7	4.2	23.1	76.3	0.7
Cape Verde	1.3	8.5	35.4	70.9	0.2	0.9	0.9	9.0	34.1	53.4	12.5
Central African Republic	0.8	10.0	42.0	80.4	..	..	..	..	82.6	17.4	0.0
Chad	0.7	9.4	41.8	79.8	1.3	1.6	5.0	21.2	24.3	75.1	0.5
Comoros	0.7	10.3	39.8	81.3	..	..	..	..	45.9	54.1	0.0
Congo, Democratic Rep. of	2.5	4.4	19.9	48.7	..	..	..	..	87.5	12.5	0.0
Congo, Republic of	2.2	9.0	31.8	63.7	..	..	..	..	63.6	36.4	0.0
Côte d'Ivoire	1.5	8.9	32.8	69.1	6.3	5.3	15.2	21.4	21.9	77.6	0.6
Djibouti	1.0	7.0	36.9	72.0	9.0	3.0	8.0	3.1	63.4	33.3	3.3
Equatorial Guinea	0.0	10.2	49.7	90.0	..	..	..	..	82.5	17.5	0.0
Eritrea	1.3	8.6	33.1	69.6	4.0	2.3	6.3	19.6	15.7	82.2	2.1
Ethiopia	0.7	9.9	39.4	79.6	..	..	..	..	22.4	77.6	0.0
Gabon	4.5	5.5	11.9	30.5	7.2	4.9	19.3	16.7	11.8	60.0	28.3
Gambia, The	1.8	8.0	31.8	64.5	..	..	..	..	15.9	84.1	0.0
Ghana	1.4	9.7	36.7	72.2	6.3	2.1	8.3	11.5	13.0	76.9	10.1
Guinea	1.4	9.2	33.1	70.3	8.5	3.9	13.0	5.7	27.2	69.8	3.0
Guinea-Bissau	0.7	10.4	43.8	81.8	..	..	..	..	39.3	60.7	0.0
Kenya	1.2	9.8	37.1	74.7	3.9	0.5	4.1	9.7	15.3	80.1	4.6
Lesotho	1.0	9.3	37.8	76.3	7.6	4.5	15.6	12.5	19.3	47.5	33.3
Liberia	..	..	..	..	..	..	..	..	100.0	0.0	0.0
Madagascar	0.8	9.7	38.8	78.5	7.1	7.2	23.5	20.7	34.3	55.4	10.3
Malawi	0.9	10.1	40.3	79.6	10.0	0.5	9.0	-0.8	26.3	73.4	0.3
Mali	1.3	9.2	35.7	72.5	..	..	..	..	25.8	74.2	0.0
Mauritania	1.4	8.7	35.0	71.3	6.0	3.3	10.2	17.9	27.9	66.7	5.3
Mauritius	3.2	5.6	20.1	45.7	6.6	5.1	15.8	19.9	4.0	51.7	44.3
Mozambique	0.8	9.8	40.6	78.7	8.8	7.8	32.3	9.2	56.6	40.9	2.4
Namibia	..	..	..	..	..	..	..	..	..	..	..
Niger	0.8	9.4	37.9	77.1	6.0	1.0	6.0	11.0	32.4	67.5	0.1
Nigeria	..	..	..	..	..	..	..	..	100.0	0.0	0.0
Rwanda	0.6	10.3	41.3	82.8	..	..	..	..	51.4	48.6	0.0
São Tomé and Principe	0.8	10.5	50.0	82.2	..	..	..	..	65.1	34.9	0.0
Senegal	1.2	9.7	37.9	75.0	6.9	7.6	28.3	20.4	23.5	73.9	2.6
Seychelles	3.6	4.2	14.9	36.2	7.3	5.1	18.1	15.0	13.1	58.8	28.1
Sierra Leone	0.7	8.3	34.9	72.4	5.0	0.6	12.1	20.6	31.6	62.7	5.7
Somalia	..	..	..	..	..	..	..	..	100.0	0.0	0.0
South Africa	..	..	..	..	6.3	2.8	14.3	19.2	84.3	0.0	15.7
Sudan	..	..	..	..	..	..	..	..	100.0	0.0	0.0
Swaziland	..	..	..	..	7.2	5.1	19.6	17.4	19.3	0.0	80.7
Tanzania	1.0	9.4	37.8	75.5	5.3	0.8	6.4	12.7	47.2	50.9	1.9
Togo	1.0	9.2	36.3	75.4	5.6	4.9	15.0	19.8	15.8	80.9	3.3
Uganda	0.7	10.2	41.5	81.4	4.3	2.3	9.8	22.0	44.2	54.5	1.3
Zambia	1.0	9.9	38.1	76.0	10.6	2.7	7.9	-2.5	24.4	73.7	1.8
Zimbabwe	1.0	8.5	30.7	70.6	6.8	2.6	10.1	12.6	14.5	60.4	25.1
NORTH AFRICA*	3.4	6.4	21.1	46.1	6.1	3.7	13.8	17.2	0.0	38.9	61.1
Algeria	2.7	5.6	19.3	48.6	5.6	3.5	11.5	16.5	0.0	0.7	99.3
Egypt, Arab Republic	0.7	9.9	33.0	77.6	7.5	3.8	13.8	12.8	0.7	63.5	35.8
Libya	..	..	..	..	..	..	..	..	..	..	..
Morocco	2.9	7.0	21.0	49.8	6.1	2.9	15.8	20.1	0.0	54.1	45.9
Tunisia	4.2	5.4	19.7	38.2	7.4	5.8	18.6	16.1	0.0	65.0	35.0
ALL AFRICA	1.5	8.5	33.9	69.1	6.6	3.6	13.3	14.0	26.4	61.7	11.9

*North Africa's data are from 1997.

6-26. External debt and debt service ratios, 1998

	Debt-GDP ratio		Total external debt per capita (US dollars)	Percentage of debt disbursed	Debt-export ratio		Present value of debt-export ratio	Debt service-export ratio (Ex post)
	Concessional	*Non-concessional*			*Concessional*	*Non-concessional*		
SUB-SAHARAN AFRICA	28	43	367	88	96	146	418	15
excluding South Africa	48	60	350	89	156	192	427	15
excl. S. Africa & Nigeria	57	54	376	88	190	178	432	16
Angola	42	9	935	88	71	220	298	29
Benin	58	6	277	81	211	50	165	10
Botswana	6	4	330	91	12	9	..	3
Burkina Faso	46	2	131	74	249	49	175	11
Burundi	119	3	171	88	1,395	94	833	40
Cameroon	52	35	694	91	196	231	353	23
Cape Verde	36	5	586	62	96	25	76	9
Central African Republic	72	6	265	92	440	102	..	17
Chad	52	8	150	77	263	66	190	10
Comoros	91	4	383	90	408	54	305	14
Congo, Democratic Rep. of	49	77	273	96	205	588	..	1
Congo, Republic of	97	69	1,840	95	131	224	325	3
Côte d'Ivoire	44	32	1,025	92	102	204	262	28
Djibouti	51	0	453	84	..	..	..	..
Equatorial Guinea	32	11	710	88	31	35	54	1
Eritrea	21	0	39	21	57	5	36	2
Ethiopia	134	7	169	91	831	145	824	11
Gabon	21	47	3,749	90	39	141	181	12
Gambia, The	100	3	378	85	172	17	111	11
Ghana	62	4	373	84	179	88	156	22
Guinea	70	12	501	85	321	109	305	19
Guinea-Bissau	341	64	835	91	2,436	932	2,412	27
Kenya	36	9	241	86	143	98	179	21
Lesotho	55	12	336	76	77	33	78	8
Liberia	..	..	710	99	..	..	..	..
Madagascar	78	32	301	89	325	165	365	14
Malawi	126	4	232	81	416	50	261	16
Mali	105	3	302	82	373	59	295	11
Mauritania	184	29	1,024	88	400	162	309	24
Mauritius	9	5	2,140	80	12	69	82	10
Mozambique	104	58	491	82	705	736	..	18
Namibia	..	0	74	..	0	7	..	4
Niger	56	15	164	81	338	143	322	18
Nigeria	5	43	251	94	14	256	262	12
Rwanda	55	0	151	80	921	92	564	17
São Tomé and Principe	579	9	1,781	82	1,965	133	1,198	32
Senegal	56	16	426	81	155	74	162	19
Seychelles	13	7	2,372	73	18	30	43	6
Sierra Leone	116	18	259	84	849	517	896	22
Somalia	..	..	290	89	..	..	..	..
South Africa	0	0	597	88	0	69	68	12
Sudan	47	28	594	94	753	1,942	2,538	10
Swaziland	12	5	254	67	12	9	17	2
Tanzania	64	9	238	83	483	184	497	22
Togo	73	17	325	85	186	76	181	7
Uganda	47	3	192	88	472	122	351	24
Zambia	113	33	710	92	381	336	576	21
Zimbabwe	22	15	403	75	58	124	..	38
NORTH AFRICA	19	31	734	85	67	110	159	22
Algeria	7	32	1,039	82	27	222	242	42
Egypt, Arab Republic	28	4	521	94	122	44	127	9
Libya	..	..	..	..	..	..	..	..
Morocco	18	24	738	83	53	116	153	23
Tunisia	13	24	1,162	73	27	89	114	15
ALL AFRICA	25	39	429	87	86	133	394	16

Figure 6-1. Debt service ratio (ex post), 1998

(percent of exports of goods and services)

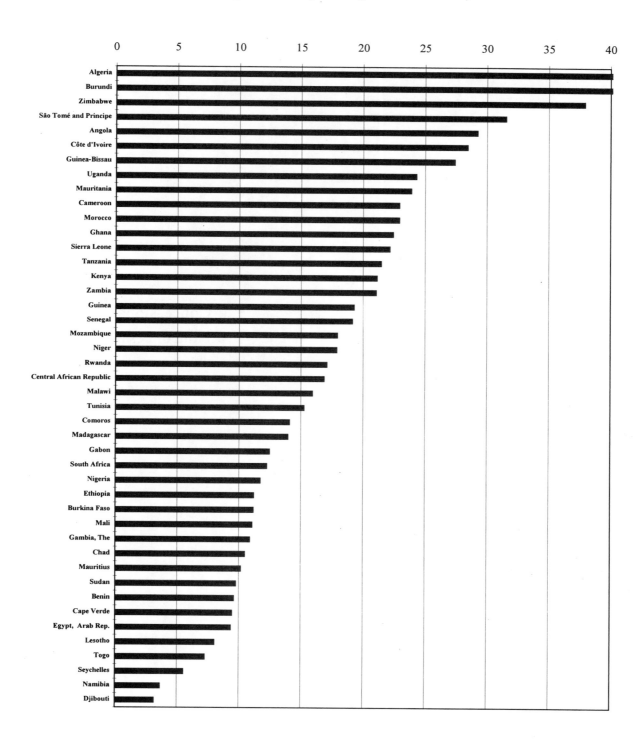

Figure 6-2. Debt to GDP ratio, 1998

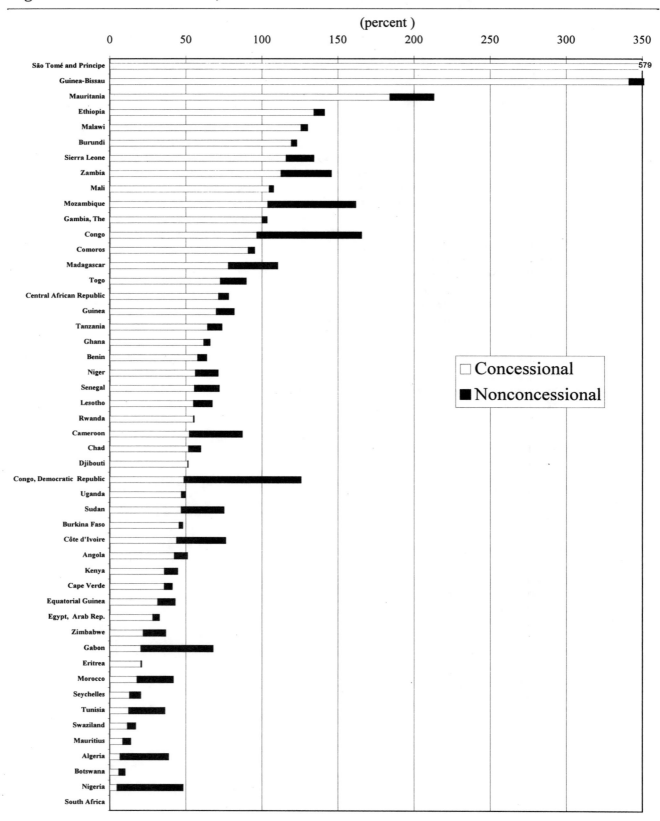

* Sorted by concessional debt.

Technical notes

Tables

Tables 6-1, 6-2, and 6-3. Gross disbursements: official concessional, official nonconcessional, and private long-term loans. Gross disbursements are from commitments of long-term external loans by official concessional, official nonconcessional, and private sources, respectively (World Bank, DRS).

Table 6-4. Disbursements: long-term loans and IMF purchases. This is the sum of tables 6-1 through 6-3, plus IMF purchases.

Tables 6-5, 6-6, and 6-7. Amortization: official concessional, official nonconcessional, and private long-term loans. Amortization is the actual repayment of principal made in foreign currencies, goods, or services on outstanding long-term official concessional, official nonconcessional, and private long-term loans as described above (World Bank, DRS).

Table 6-8. Amortization: long-term loans and IMF repurchases. This is the sum of Tables 6-5 to 6-7, plus repurchases of drawings from the IMF.

Tables 6-9, 6-10, and 6-11. Interest payments: official concessional, official nonconcessional, and private long-term loans. These are actual payments made in foreign currencies, goods, and services to various lenders described above on interest obligations, including IMF charges on drawings due on disbursed debt and on commitment charges due on undisbursed debt (where information is available), that is, on long-term official concessional, official nonconcessional, and private loans (World Bank, DRS).

Table 6-12. Interest payments: long-term loans and IMF charges. This is the sum of Tables 6-9 through 6-11, plus IMF charges on drawings.

Table 6-13. Total external debt service payments: long-term loans and IMF credit. Total external debt service payments include the sum of amortization on long-term loans and IMF credit and interest payments on long-term loans and IMF credit (World Bank, DRS).

Table 6-14. Interest payments: short-term loans. These are estimated for the respective year based on the estimated year-end stock of short-term debt (which may include interest arrears on long-term debt) and the annual average six-month London interbank offered rate (LIBOR) on notes denominated in U.S. dollars as reported in the IFS (with no adjustment for spreads). Actual payments may be different because the LIBOR only approximates actual interest rates on short-term loans, and because not all interest due on short-term loans is actually paid (World Bank, DRS).

Table 6-15. Net flows: long- and short-term loans, including IMF. These flows represent all disbursements of long- and short-term loans net of all repayments of principal on long- and short-term loans and IMF credit (World Bank, DRS).

Table 6-16. Net flows: long-term loans, including IMF. Net flows of long-term loans are as defined above for Table 6-15, but excluding short-term loans (World Bank, DRS).

Table 6-17. Net transfers: long- and short-term loans, including IMF. Net transfers are net flows (Table 6-15) less interest payments (Tables 6-12 and 6-14).

Table 6-18. Net transfers: long-term loans, including IMF. Net transfers include long-term loans and IMF credit only (Table 6-16 less Table 6-12).

Tables 6-19, 6-20, and 6-21. Long-term debt: official concessional, official nonconcessional, and private. This series reflects the total debt outstanding and disbursed of official concessional, official nonconcessional, and private loans (World Bank, DRS). The time series reflects changes in the valuation of year-end debt stocks (because of US dollar exchange rate fluctuation) and debt cancellation, as well as net disbursements. Therefore changes in debt stocks from year to year cannot be used as a measure of net borrowing or vice versa.

Table 6-22. Total external debt. When Tables 6-19 to 6-21 are supplemented with IMF credit and estimates of total short-term debt (which includes interest in arrears on public and publicly guaranteed long-term loans), they sum up to total external debt (World Bank, DRS).

Table 6-23. Structure of external debt. This table summarizes debt structure for 1980 and 1997 (World Bank, DRS). The columns cover the type of creditor and concessionality. The private debt shown includes both the private guaranteed (by an entity of the debtor government) and the private nonguaranteed debt. For each year, all components shown add to the total in Table 6-22.

Table 6-24. Structure of external debt service payments. This summary table compares debt service payments for all types of creditors in 1980 and 1997 (World Bank, DRS). Debt service payments on short-term loans are excluded, to be consistent with Table 6-13. Debt service payments are actual repayments of principal (amortization) and actual payments of interest. The column headings have the same definitions as given above for Table 6-23.

Table 6-25. Terms of long-term external financing, 1997. This table presents the average interest rates, grace periods, maturities, and grant elements shown separately for concessional and nonconcessional long-term loans (official and private); short-term loans are excluded (World Bank, DRS). Grant elements are calculated using a standard 10 percent discount rate. The indicators are weighted averages (based on amount of commitments) across all loans in each category. For the column on structure of financing (that is, total flows), grants are based on sources for Chapter 12 (Aid Flows) and are not comparable with net official transfers shown in Chapter 5.

Table 6-26. External debt and debt service ratios, 1997. This table includes the ratio of debt outstanding and disbursed to GDP; per capita debt; the ratio of debt outstanding and disbursed to debt outstanding, including undisbursed; the ratio of debt outstanding and disbursed and the ratio of the present value of debt to exports of goods and all services, including receipts of workers' remittances; and the ratio of total debt service paid to exports of goods and all services, more commonly called the debt service ratio (World Bank, DRS). Ratios are shown separately for concessional debt and for all nonconcessional (including private) debt. Both the stock of external debt and debt service payments include short- and long-term loans and IMF credit, except for the ratio of debt outstanding to debt outstanding including undisbursed, which is calculated for public and publicly guaranteed debt only. The data for exports of goods and all services, plus receipts of workers' remittances, are taken from balance of payments data in Chapter 5. The present value of debt is the sum of all future payments discounted to the present (usually with a commercial discount rate similar to LIBOR. The debt service ratio is shown for the ex post category, depicting the amount paid after debt relief and/or arrears.

Figures

The following indicators have been used to derive the figures in this chapter.

Figure 6-1. Debt service ratio (Table 6-26).
Figure 6-2. Debt to GDP ratio (Table 6-26).

Methodology used for regional aggregations and period averages in chapter 6

Table	Aggregations [a] (1)	(2)	(6)	Period averages [b] (1)
6-1	x			x
6-2	x			x
6-3	x			x
6-4	x			x
6-5	x			x
6-6	x			x
6-7	x			x
6-8	x			x
6-9	x			x
6-10	x			x
6-11	x			x
6-12	x			x
6-13	x			x
6-14	x			x
6-15	x			x
6-16	x			x
6-17	x			x
6-18	x			x
6-19	x			x
6-20	x			x
6-21	x			x
6-22	x			
6-23	x			
6-24	x			
6-25			x	
6-26		x		

Note: Regional aggregations are shown in the rows for Sub-Saharan Africa, North Africa, and All Africa. Period averages are shown in the last three columns. This table shows only the methodologies used in this chapter.

a. Regional aggregations: (1) simple total; (2) simple total of the first indicator divided by the simple total of the second indicator (same country coverage); (3) simple total of the gap-filled indicator; (4) simple total of the gap-filled main indicator divided by the simple total of the gap-filled secondary indicator; (5) simple total of the first gap-filled main indicator less the simple total of the second gap-filled main indicator, all divided by the simple total of the secondary indicator; (6) weighted total (by population); (7) median; (8) no aggregation; (9) simple arithmetic mean.

b. Period averages: (i) arithmetic mean (using the same series as shown in the table i.e., ratio if the rest of the table is shown as ratio, level if the rest of the table is shown as level, growth rate if the rest is shown as growth rate); (2) least-squares growth rate (using main indicator); (3) least-squares growth rate (using main indicator in constant terms, with the rest of the table in current terms).

7

Government Finance

The data in this chapter pertain to consolidated government (except when not available) instead of to central government operations, which were reported in previous volumes.

Definitions have been taken from the IMF's Government Finance Statistics (GFS). For this volume, data are taken from country desks. When not available from country desks, data are taken from the GFS and supplemented with data from IMF, World Bank, or staff reports, or from other national government sources. Data from various sources have been harmonized to produce a consistent and comparable time series.

The focus of this chapter is on the principal financial transactions of government—taxing, borrowing, spending, and lending—rather than on the production and consumption of goods and services, the use of labor, or other government activities. Spending covers both current and capital transactions.

The data cover major government finance indicators—fiscal deficit or surplus, expenditure and lending minus repayments, revenue, grants, and domestic and foreign financing—expressed as a percentage of GDP. The chapter also includes information on the major components of revenue and expenditure by economic category, shown as percentages of total revenue and as a percentage of expenditure and lending minus repayments, respectively.

Measures of fiscal deficit or surplus are among the single most important indicators of government fiscal performance. The measure is usually calculated as the difference between total revenue (including grants) and total expenditure (including lending minus repayments). As such, it measures government net financing requirements. *GFS* methodology recommends grouping grants receipt with revenue because they can be spent without incurring an obligation for future payments but lists them separately because grants can sometimes be treated as financing items. Financing includes all government borrowing from others (at home and abroad) minus amortization (government repayment of its borrowing from others and changes in cash balances). Other measures of fiscal balance include the fiscal deficit or surplus without capital grants, which measures the government's ability to operate without foreign capital transfers, and the fiscal deficit or surplus, excluding interest payments from expenditure, referred to as the primary deficit or surplus.

Revenue is divided between taxes—unrequited compulsory payments to government—and nontax revenue. It includes only non- repayable receipts other than grants. Tax revenue is also classified according to the base upon which the tax is levied (for example, income and profits).

Expenditure is classified by economic category (such as wages, purchases, and interest payments). Lending minus repayments—government lending less repayment of past government lending—is grouped with expenditure, except in certain cases (see Technical Notes).

The economic classification of expenditures (for example, on wages) is presented as a percentage of total expenditure and lending minus repayments, because lending minus repayments is itself a separate economic classification.

No attempt was made to reconcile GFS data in this chapter with the System of National Accounts (SNA). The fundamental difference between the two systems is that GFS focuses on government financial transactions, whereas the SNA considers government transactions as part of total demand and value added. (For further discussion, see World Bank 1988b, box 2.1, p. 45.) Indicators calculated as ratios to GDP use GDP at purchaser values or market prices (see Technical Notes to Chapter 1). Because GDP at purchaser values includes import duties (and GDP at market prices includes indirect taxes), ratios for revenues tend to understate tax burdens, especially where such taxes are an important source of government revenue.

Fiscal year data are compared with the calendar year GDP data that correspond either to the second half of the fiscal year or to the calendar year in which most of the fiscal year falls. Fiscal years do not correspond to calendar years in Botswana, Cameroon, Egypt, Ethiopia, the Gambia, and Ghana (before 1982), Kenya, Lesotho, Liberia, Malawi, Mauritius, Niger, Nigeria, Senegal, Sierra Leone, Sudan, Swaziland, Tanzania, Uganda, and Zimbabwe (after 1985).

Tables in this volume contain corrections to mislabeled subtitles in ADI 1992. Thus subtitles in tables 7-1 through 7-8 are now correctly labeled percentage of total GDP (instead of revenues).

7-1. Government deficit/surplus (including grants)

					Percentage of GDP							*Annual average*		
	1980	*1990*	*1991*	*1992*	*1993*	*1994*	*1995*	*1996*	*1997*	*1998*	*1999*	*75-84*	*85-89*	*90-MR*
SUB-SAHARAN AFRICA	..	-4.3	-4.6	-7.3	-7.3	-5.2	-3.3	-3.1	-3.1	-5.2	-4.5	-5.1	-4.8	-4.8
excluding South Africa	..	-5.7	-5.4	-7.0	-5.5	-4.1	-1.6	-1.1	-1.9	-5.3	-4.4	..	-5.3	-4.2
excl. S.Africa & Nigeria	..	-5.7	-5.4	-7.0	-5.5	-5.5	-4.0	-3.2	-2.5	-3.7	-3.8	..	-5.3	-4.6
Angola	..	-26.8	-21.9	-56.9	-21.7	-20.1	-26.6	-14.1	-17.1	-13.9	-18.1	..	-11.1	-23.7
Benin	..	-8.4	-6.9	-7.2	-2.9	-4.4	-4.6	-2.2	-0.8	1.5	2.8	..	-5.8	-3.3
Botswana	..	10.5	9.1	9.5	8.7	3.1	1.8	6.4	3.8	-4.0	-2.6	9.7	14.5	4.6
Burkina Faso	..	-4.6	-3.6	-2.9	-4.6	-3.2	-3.6	-0.6	-3.2	-2.9	-3.4	..	..	-3.3
Burundi	9.8	-2.7	-0.2	-2.7	-3.7	-2.2	-2.2	-7.4	-4.1	-4.7	-6.4	9.5	-4.4	-3.6
Cameroon	0.4	-7.6	-8.2	-6.3	-6.3	-9.2	-3.2	-1.7	-0.9	-2.0	-3.6	0.5	-5.2	-4.9
Cape Verde	..	-3.0	-4.3	-7.9	-9.3	-14.0	-12.9	-13.7	-10.0	-3.9	-7.7	-7.2	-5.1	-8.7
Central African Republic	..	..	..	..	..	-10.0	-5.1	-3.4	-2.3	-0.8	-1.9	..	..	-3.9
Chad	..	-7.7	-4.1	-8.1	-8.6	-4.7	-4.4	-5.1	-3.9	-2.6	-6.0	..	-5.3	-5.5
Comoros	..	-0.5	-2.2	-2.5	2.6	-7.7	-7.9	-15.8	-2.4	-4.2	-0.7	0.0	-4.8	-4.1
Congo, Democratic Rep. of	..	..	..	..	..	..	..	..	..	-9.2	-6.8	..	..	-8.0
Congo, Republic of	..	-6.6	-13.1	-14.1	-12.6	-13.2	-6.9	-5.0	-9.1	-20.0	-6.3	7.1	-7.9	-10.7
Côte d'Ivoire	..	-10.9	-11.1	-9.8	-10.3	-4.1	-1.5	0.4	0.7	0.7	-0.3	..	-7.9	-4.6
Djibouti	..	-21.0	-3.0	-11.7	-13.0	-8.4	-8.1	-3.9	-5.5	-2.3	0.2	..	..	-7.7
Equatorial Guinea	..	..	..	..	..	-5.7	-6.3	-6.3	2.1	-1.4	4.0	..	..	-2.3
Eritrea	..	..	..	-3.2	-6.4	-12.7	-22.4	-19.5	-5.8	-32.3	-47.8	..	..	-18.8
Ethiopia	..	-9.8	-8.5	-7.0	-5.9	-7.7	-3.9	-5.6	-1.5	-3.6	-6.9	-6.6	-5.7	-6.0
Gabon	..	-4.1	-2.2	-5.2	-5.7	-1.6	3.2	2.7	2.5	-14.4	-1.4	-36.9	-7.1	-2.6
Gambia, The	..	-0.1	1.1	1.3	1.3	-1.1	-6.7	-10.0	-6.5	-2.4	-3.6	-14.7	3.8	-2.7
Ghana	..	-3.1	-1.4	-9.4	-9.9	-8.9	-6.4	-9.5	-9.7	-6.5	-7.4	-2.3	-2.7	-7.2
Guinea	..	-5.2	-4.5	-3.1	-3.7	-3.6	-2.7	-3.0	-3.2	-3.3	-3.0	..	-5.4	-3.5
Guinea-Bissau	0.0	-6.3	-17.5	-21.7	-13.0	-8.4	-1.4	-12.2	-18.2	-16.3	-10.0	-8.3	-8.0	-12.5
Kenya	-8.9	-7.8	-6.9	-4.9	-7.7	-4.0	-1.3	-2.7	-2.0	-2.6	-1.5	-7.6	-5.4	-4.1
Lesotho	..	-2.4	-0.6	2.5	4.9	5.3	4.5	3.5	3.4	0.5	-3.5	-4.6.	-5.8	1.8
Liberia	..	..	..	..	..	..	..	..	..	..	..	..	..	..
Madagascar	..	-0.7	-5.5	-6.6	-7.2	-8.4	-6.2	-4.9	-2.4	-4.7	-1.2	-6.0	-3.6	-4.8
Malawi	-11.6	-4.2	-3.3	-11.1	-6.9	-20.0	-7.6	-8.8	-9.5	-2.3	-4.0	-8.3	-6.0	-7.8
Mali	-14.9	-2.7	-4.1	-3.9	-4.1	-4.6	-3.1	-0.9	-2.1	-2.5	-3.8	-11.9	-5.4	-3.2
Mauritania	..	-12.1	-3.8	-0.7	-7.4	-0.5	1.2	7.4	5.1	3.6	4.7	..	-9.7	-0.2
Mauritius	..	-1.9	-2.2	-2.3	-2.2	-3.0	-5.5	-7.4	-5.7	-3.1	-2.2	-6.6	-2.5	-3.5
Mozambique	-2.1	-6.2	-3.1	-2.7	-3.6	-5.3	-3.2	-2.9	-2.5	-2.4	-1.5	-8.6	-8.1	-3.3
Namibia	..	..	..	..	..	..	..	-5.9	-3.9	-3.7	-3.8	..	..	-4.3
Niger	..	-7.0	-3.6	-4.7	-3.8	-6.7	-3.3	-0.2	-2.7	-4.0	-5.9	-4.9	-4.8	-4.2
Nigeria	..	..	..	..	..	1.9	9.9	9.1	1.0	-13.4	-7.4	..	..	0.2
Rwanda	..	-5.0	-5.4	-8.1	-8.3	-11.5	-2.4	-5.7	-2.4	-2.9	-3.8	..	..	-5.5
São Tomé and Principe	..	-25.1	-21.2	-41.8	-33.6	-43.0	-37.6	-32.3	-26.7	-24.9	-25.8	..	-3.8	-31.2
Senegal	-4.6	-3.0	2.0	-1.8	-3.1	-1.9	-0.2	2.2	0.5	-0.3	-1.4	-5.7	-2.0	-0.7
Seychelles	..	0.2	-4.9	-5.8	-11.4	-16.5	-16.1	-10.7	-13.4	-25.0	-14.4	..	..	-11.8
Sierra Leone	..	-10.5	-10.1	-9.0	-7.4	-5.8	-9.8	-5.1	-7.0	-10.4	-9.5	..	-13.4	-8.5
Somalia	..	..	..	..	..	..	..	..	..	..	..	..	..	..
South Africa	-18.0	-3.1	-3.9	-7.4	-8.9	-6.2	-5.2	-5.4	-4.5	-5.1	-4.7	-6.5	-4.3	-5.5
Sudan	..	-9.2	-15.3	-20.1	-1.7	..	-3.2	-3.8	-0.7	-0.7	-0.9	-12.2	-12.1	-6.2
Swaziland	..	..	5.5	-0.1	-3.6	-3.6	-2.5	-2.4	-2.6	-2.4	-2.1	..	..	-1.5
Tanzania	..	2.9	2.5	3.2	-1.4	1.6	-3.4	-1.9	1.8	0.2	0.4	-9.4	-3.7	0.6
Togo	..	-2.9	-6.1	-4.2	-15.6	-11.6	-6.4	-5.8	-2.1	-5.5	-4.7	-2.1	-3.8	-6.5
Uganda	..	-4.4	-3.7	-7.3	-3.2	-3.8	-2.6	-1.9	-1.4	-0.4	-1.2	-2.1	-3.6	-3.0
Zambia	..	-8.3	-7.0	-2.5	-5.6	-6.5	-4.3	-0.5	-0.2	-3.2	-2.0	..	-10.8	-4.0
Zimbabwe	7.6	-6.5	-5.2	-6.8	-6.1	-6.7	-10.1	-7.7	-7.5	-2.4	-9.4	8.0	-7.9	-6.8
NORTH AFRICA	..	-6.1	-5.1	-2.3	-4.4	-2.2	-2.0	-0.6	-0.5	-2.2	-3.0	..	-6.4	-2.9
Algeria	..	3.6	1.7	-1.1	-8.7	-2.9	-1.4	2.9	2.4	-3.9	-0.5	-8.1	-8.0	-0.8
Egypt, Arab Republic	..	-12.1	-12.5	-3.1	-2.3	-0.9	-0.3	-0.7	-0.3	-0.5	-3.9	..	-14.1	-3.7
Libya	..	..	..	..	..	..	..	..	..	..	..	..	..	..
Morocco	6.9	-9.2	-1.1	-2.2	-2.9	-3.6	-5.1	-3.5	-3.6	-2.7	-4.7	8.4	9.1	-3.9
Tunisia	..	..	-5.2	-3.0	-2.8	-2.1	-4.2	-4.9	-3.9	-2.5	-3.5	..	..	-3.6
ALL AFRICA	..	-5.0	-4.8	-5.4	-6.2	-4.1	-2.9	-2.3	-2.2	-4.2	-4.0	..	-4.8	-4.1

Note: 1999 data are preliminary. Nigeria: from 1992 accounts are for consolidated budget; since 1994, ratios are distorted as off. exch. rate used by the Gov. for oil exports oil value added is significantly over-valued.

7-2. Government deficit/surplus (excluding grants)

	1980	1990	1991	1992	1993	1994	1995	1996	1997	1998	1999	75-84	85-89	90-MR
					Percentage of GDP								*Annual average*	
SUB-SAHARAN AFRICA	..	-5.5	-6.0	-8.7	-8.6	-6.5	-4.5	-4.2	-4.1	-6.2	-5.6	-5.7	-5.6	-6.0
excluding South Africa	..	-7.9	-7.8	-9.8	-8.3	-6.8	-3.8	-3.1	-3.7	-7.1	-6.3	..	-7.2	-6.5
excl. S.Africa & Nigeria	..	-7.9	-7.8	-9.8	-8.3	-8.8	-6.6	-5.6	-4.7	-5.9	-6.1	..	-7.2	-7.1
Angola	..	-26.8	-21.9	-56.9	-21.7	-20.1	-26.6	-15.8	-17.9	-15.1	-20.4	..	-11.1	-24.3
Benin	..	-14.2	-10.3	-11.4	-6.8	-9.0	-8.6	-6.1	-5.3	-1.8	-2.2	..	-15.5	-7.6
Botswana	..	9.1	8.1	8.5	7.1	2.2	1.5	6.0	3.7	-4.1	-2.7	7.3	12.6	3.9
Burkina Faso	..	-7.3	-8.2	-9.1	-10.1	-10.6	-10.3	-9.0	-10.2	-9.7	-12.3	..	..	-9.7
Burundi	6.1	-10.8	-8.8	-11.3	-12.7	-4.7	-5.8	-9.7	-7.1	-5.3	-7.6	5.4	-6.0	-8.4
Cameroon	0.4	-7.6	-8.2	-6.3	-6.3	-9.4	-3.3	-1.7	-1.0	-2.3	-3.8	0.5	-5.2	-5.0
Cape Verde	..	-10.8	-14.2	-25.5	-24.6	-29.2	-27.8	-26.7	-20.1	-13.8	-15.0	-45.0	-24.5	-20.8
Central African Republic	..	..	..	..	..	-15.0	-11.4	-5.0	-6.3	-8.6	-8.7	..	..	-9.2
Chad	..	-15.7	-9.0	-13.0	-13.2	-14.2	-11.9	-11.2	-10.3	-7.8	-10.7	..	-16.0	-11.7
Comoros	..	-15.5	-18.5	-17.6	-11.9	-24.0	-19.7	-24.7	-12.1	-12.2	-8.4	-19.1	-24.0	-16.4
Congo, Democratic Rep. of	..	..	..	..	..	..	..	..	..	-11.1	-9.0	..	..	-10.0
Congo, Republic of	..	-7.0	-13.3	-14.1	-12.6	-14.3	-7.8	-5.3	-9.2	-20.3	-6.7	6.2	-8.0	-11.1
Côte d'Ivoire	..	-10.9	-11.6	-10.3	-10.8	-4.8	-2.2	-0.4	-0.7	-0.7	-1.4	..	-7.9	-5.4
Djibouti	..	-21.0	-15.2	-24.1	-21.8	-13.4	-10.1	-5.7	-8.1	-4.5	-2.0	..	..	-12.6
Equatorial Guinea	..	..	..	..	..	-9.9	-8.9	-7.2	1.4	-2.1	3.7	..	..	-3.8
Eritrea	..	..	..	-12.3	-26.5	-31.2	-35.1	-30.7	-12.0	-41.4	-54.3	..	..	-30.4
Ethiopia	..	-12.0	-10.9	-9.6	-7.6	-11.1	-7.3	-8.5	-5.2	-6.5	-10.5	-8.7	-9.4	-8.9
Gabon	..	-4.4	-2.4	-5.3	-6.0	-2.0	3.2	2.7	2.5	-14.4	-1.4	-37.3	-7.6	-2.8
Gambia, The	..	-6.0	-4.3	-3.3	-2.4	-4.2	-9.1	-12.2	-7.8	-4.4	-5.3	-14.7	-10.5	-5.9
Ghana	..	-5.7	-4.5	-12.7	-14.1	-12.4	-10.0	-12.0	-11.0	-8.6	-9.8	-3.1	-5.1	-10.1
Guinea	..	-8.8	-8.2	-7.1	-7.3	-7.1	-6.6	-6.1	-6.1	-6.0	-5.2	..	-8.5	-6.8
Guinea-Bissau	0.0	-24.4	-33.1	-37.4	-29.9	-23.1	-17.7	-21.2	-30.9	-19.5	-14.4	-10.1	-38.4	-25.2
Kenya	-11.4	-10.0	-8.9	-7.5	-10.8	-6.7	-3.4	-4.0	-3.0	-3.2	-1.7	-9.3	-7.4	-5.9
Lesotho	..	-13.5	-8.9	-3.6	-0.3	0.6	0.1	-0.8	-0.8	-2.8	-5.8	-7.6	-11.3	-3.6
Liberia	..	..	..	..	..	..	..	..	..	..	..	..	..	..
Madagascar	..	-5.1	-7.7	-10.1	-10.7	-11.4	-9.1	-9.1	-7.7	-8.1	-4.8	-6.4	-4.9	-8.4
Malawi	-15.9	-7.0	-6.3	-13.9	-9.7	-31.6	-16.1	-13.6	-13.3	-10.7	-11.1	-11.1	-10.0	-13.3
Mali	-35.4	-8.7	-12.3	-11.0	-9.6	-14.6	-10.7	-8.1	-7.9	-8.3	-9.0	-38.2	-10.5	-10.0
Mauritania	..	-14.6	-6.1	-2.5	-9.6	-3.1	-0.8	5.3	4.3	2.2	2.1	..	-14.8	-2.3
Mauritius	..	-2.1	-2.3	-2.4	-2.4	-3.3	-5.8	-7.6	-5.9	-3.2	-2.5	-7.0	-3.3	-3.8
Mozambique	-3.9	-15.9	-14.2	-16.5	-15.5	-19.2	-13.0	-9.9	-11.7	-10.6	-12.9	-10.4	-13.4	-13.9
Namibia	..	..	..	..	..	..	..	-6.2	-4.2	-3.9	-4.2	..	..	-4.6
Niger	..	-12.4	-8.4	-8.6	-9.4	-12.5	-7.4	-5.1	-7.3	-8.5	-9.7	-8.3	-9.4	-8.9
Nigeria	..	..	..	..	..	1.9	9.9	9.1	1.0	-13.4	-7.4	..	..	0.2
Rwanda	..	-9.6	-12.8	-14.2	-14.7	-12.4	-13.8	-13.0	-9.2	-8.1	-9.8	..	..	-11.7
São Tomé and Principe	..	-56.1	-46.5	-50.8	-50.3	-60.5	-60.9	-55.8	-54.5	-34.6	-50.4	..	-19.1	-52.0
Senegal	-5.3	-4.3	0.3	-3.1	-4.2	-6.1	-3.5	-4.4	-2.0	-3.3	-3.5	-6.6	-3.4	-3.4
Seychelles	..	-1.7	-6.4	-7.1	-13.0	-17.2	-16.7	-11.3	-13.8	-25.5	-15.0	..	..	-12.8
Sierra Leone	..	-10.5	-10.1	-9.0	-7.4	-5.8	-9.8	-6.8	-7.5	-12.8	-14.9	..	-14.0	-9.5
Somalia	..	..	..	..	..	..	..	..	..	..	..	..	..	..
South Africa	-2.5	-3.3	-4.3	-7.8	-9.0	-6.2	-5.2	-5.4	-4.5	-5.1	-4.7	-4.6	-4.4	-5.5
Sudan	..	-9.2	-15.3	-20.1	-1.7	..	-3.2	-3.8	-0.7	-0.7	-0.9	-12.2	-12.1	-6.2
Swaziland	..	..	4.7	-1.5	-4.7	-4.6	-3.3	-3.2	-3.4	-3.3	-3.0	..	..	-2.5
Tanzania	..	-0.5	0.4	0.8	-4.8	-1.7	-5.2	-3.9	-1.4	-2.6	-3.3	-12.2	-6.7	-2.2
Togo	..	-6.2	-8.0	-5.9	-15.9	-13.0	-7.8	-6.3	-3.5	-7.2	-5.8	-5.6	-6.9	-7.9
Uganda	..	-5.9	-7.6	-14.4	-11.3	-10.3	-6.9	-5.9	-5.8	-5.6	-5.9	-2.7	-4.7	-7.9
Zambia	..	-12.7	-16.0	-12.6	-13.6	-11.8	-9.5	-6.6	-5.3	-9.8	-10.0	..	-12.0	-10.8
Zimbabwe	6.9	-7.3	-6.3	-8.4	-8.1	-8.6	-11.9	-9.0	-8.5	-4.0	-10.4	7.0	-9.0	-8.3
NORTH AFRICA	..	-8.1	-6.6	-3.2	-4.9	-2.7	-2.4	-0.9	-0.8	-2.4	-3.2	..	-7.2	-3.5
Algeria		3.6	1.7	-1.1	-8.7	-2.9	-1.4	2.9	2.4	-3.9	-0.6	-8.1	-8.0	-0.8
Egypt, Arab Republic	..	-15.1	-15.2	-5.5	-3.5	-2.1	-1.2	-1.3	-0.9	-1.0	-4.2	..	-16.0	-5.0
Libya	..	..	..	..	..	..	..	..	..	..	..	..	..	..
Morocco	6.4	-12.2	-3.1	-2.2	-3.2	-3.8	-5.2	-3.5	-3.6	-2.7	-4.7	6.7	9.1	-4.4
Tunisia	..	..	-5.2	-3.0	-2.8	-2.5	-4.5	-5.1	-4.2	-2.8	-3.9	..	..	-3.8
ALL AFRICA	..	-6.4	-6.2	-6.7	-7.3	-5.2	-3.8	-3.0	-3.0	-4.9	-4.8	..	-5.6	-5.1

Note: 1999 data are preliminary. Nigeria: from 1992 accounts are for consolidated budget; since 1994, ratios are distorted as off. exch. rate used by the Gov. for oil exports oil value added is significantly over-valued.

7-3. Government primary deficit/surplus (-/+)

	Percentage of GDP											Annual average		
	1980	1990	1991	1992	1993	1994	1995	1996	1997	1998	1999	75-84	85-89	90-MR
SUB-SAHARAN AFRICA	..	..	..	..	..	..	..	..	..	-10.7	-9.8	..	..	-10.2
excluding South Africa	..	..	..	..	..	-14.0	-6.2	-5.1	-5.4	-9.6	-8.9	..	..	-8.2
excl. S.Africa & Nigeria	..	-10.4	-9.9	-11.5	-11.6	-16.5	-9.2	-7.8	-6.2	-7.4	-7.6	..	-9.3	-9.8
Angola	..	-21.7	-15.9	-48.7	-12.2	219.0	-19.5	-2.4	-11.3	-6.8	-12.0	..	-8.6	6.8
Benin	..	-5.3	-4.3	-3.6	-0.2	-1.2	-1.8	0.2	0.9	2.8	4.0	..	-2.7	-0.9
Botswana	..	..	..	..	..	..	..	..	3.7	-4.5	-2.6	..	..	-1.1
Burkina Faso	..	-3.5	-2.2	-1.5	-3.1	-1.8	-2.2	0.3	-2.3	-2.1	-2.6	..	..	-2.1
Burundi	10.1	-0.9	1.4	-0.8	-2.2	-0.7	-0.4	-5.6	-2.1	-2.3	-3.2	10.1	-1.7	-1.7
Cameroon	0.7	-5.5	-4.1	-1.2	-1.5	-2.2	3.2	5.0	5.1	3.7	1.6	1.6	-3.9	0.4
Cape Verde	..	-1.1	-0.9	-4.5	-2.9	-13.0	-9.7	-10.1	-6.1	-0.4	-6.0	-7.2	-4.2	-5.5
Central African Republic	..	..	..	..	..	-7.6	-2.8	-1.5	-0.9	0.5	-0.5	..	..	-2.1
Chad	..	-7.3	-3.5	-7.4	-7.4	-3.5	-3.4	-4.0	-2.9	-1.8	-5.1	..	-5.1	-4.6
Comoros	..	0.9	-1.0	-1.6	3.6	-6.5	-6.9	-14.9	-1.4	-3.1	0.4	-22.0	-7.3	-3.0
Congo, Democratic Rep. of	..	..	..	..	..	..	..	..	..	0.4	0.8	..	..	0.6
Congo, Republic of	..	3.6	-4.4	-6.2	-5.2	-1.1	5.0	7.0	3.0	-5.4	6.0	7.1	-3.2	0.2
Côte d'Ivoire	..	-1.1	-0.2	0.6	-1.7	3.7	5.4	6.3	5.6	5.0	4.1	..	0.2	2.8
Djibouti	..	-20.3	..	-11.1	-12.5	-8.1	-7.5	-3.3	-5.0	..	..	..	..	-9.7
Equatorial Guinea	..	..	..	..	..	1.4	-0.4	-2.4	3.6	0.3	5.7	..	..	1.3
Eritrea	..	..	..	-3.2	-6.4	-12.6	-22.0	-18.6	-4.8	-31.0	-45.8	..	..	-18.0
Ethiopia	..	-8.5	-7.2	-5.5	-3.9	-4.3	-1.4	-3.2	0.7	-1.8	-5.0	-5.7	-4.2	-4.0
Gabon	..	1.5	3.9	1.1	1.3	5.1	11.3	8.6	8.3	-7.1	5.8	-34.5	-2.4	4.0
Gambia, The	..	3.9	4.7	4.7	5.1	2.6	-2.9	-5.6	-1.3	2.9	1.9	..	8.0	1.6
Ghana	..	-1.6	0.4	-7.3	-6.4	-4.4	-2.1	-4.4	-3.5	-1.3	-1.9	-1.1	-1.2	-3.3
Guinea	..	-2.6	-2.2	-1.5	-2.4	-2.0	-1.3	-1.7	-1.6	-1.9	-1.5	..	-2.7	-1.9
Guinea-Bissau	0.0	-2.2	-12.2	-17.0	-7.2	-3.0	5.2	-5.6	-12.7	-9.5	-3.4	-3.2	-4.1	-6.8
Kenya	-3.7	1.1	2.7	5.1	8.8	8.3	7.3	6.2	6.2	6.2	4.8	-3.0	0.0	5.7
Lesotho	..	..	..	..	..	7.3	6.2	5.1	5.0	2.6	-0.6	..	..	4.3
Liberia	..	..	..	..	..	..	..	..	..	..	..	..	..	..
Madagascar	..	0.8	-3.5	-3.2	-3.2	-3.0	-1.1	-0.2	0.6	-1.9	0.9	-5.0	-1.9	-1.4
Malawi	-8.3	-0.3	-0.5	-7.9	-3.8	-14.0	-1.1	-3.9	-4.5	1.8	-0.5	-5.2	0.5	-3.5
Mali	-10.5	-0.3	-2.3	-2.2	-2.5	-2.1	-1.7	0.2	-1.1	-1.7	-3.0	-7.7	-3.7	-1.7
Mauritania	..	-9.5	-1.2	2.3	-3.3	2.4	4.4	10.6	8.0	7.1	8.3	..	-6.5	2.9
Mauritius	..	2.5	1.9	1.1	0.6	0.0	-2.3	-4.1	-2.0	1.0	1.7	-0.6	2.2	0.0
Mozambique	-2.1	-4.3	-1.8	-0.4	-1.1	-4.2	-1.6	-1.4	-1.2	-1.4	-0.9	-8.5	-7.1	-1.8
Namibia	..	..	..	..	..	..	..	-4.2	-1.7	-1.0	-0.8	..	..	-1.9
Niger	..	-4.7	-1.7	-3.1	-2.1	-4.4	-1.0	1.4	-1.2	-2.5	-4.4	-2.8	-2.1	-2.4
Nigeria	..	..	..	..	..	7.5	13.6	11.4	3.5	-5.7	0.8	..	..	5.2
Rwanda	..	-4.0	-3.6	-6.2	-6.1	-7.0	0.0	-4.1	-1.2	-2.0	-2.8	..	..	-3.7
São Tomé and Principe	..	-14.9	-10.2	-30.8	-22.2	-32.0	-25.5	-22.3	-15.4	-12.5	-14.5	..	2.5	-20.0
Senegal	-2.5	-0.3	4.5	0.2	-0.8	1.6	2.7	4.6	2.8	0.9	0.0	-4.3	1.2	1.6
Seychelles	..	8.2	3.0	2.0	-3.5	-8.1	-6.5	-2.2	-4.0	-15.9	-3.1	..	..	-3.0
Sierra Leone	..	-4.9	-3.8	-3.2	-3.3	-3.3	-7.8	-3.0	-4.9	-5.6	-3.7	..	-8.7	-4.3
Somalia	..	..	..	..	..	..	..	..	..	..	..	..	..	..
South Africa	..	..	..	..	..	..	..	..	..	1.7	1.4	..	..	1.6
Sudan	..	..	..	..	..	..	..	..	..	0.0	-0.1	..	..	0.0
Swaziland	..	..	..	..	..	..	..	..	..	..	-1.2	..	..	-1.2
Tanzania	..	1.5	2.2	2.6	-2.5	0.5	-0.4	1.1	4.2	2.2	1.8	-7.0	-1.2	1.3
Togo	..	0.3	-2.9	-1.4	-11.4	-6.1	-3.0	-3.0	0.2	-3.2	-2.2	4.0	1.0	-3.3
Uganda	..	-3.8	-2.4	-4.0	-1.4	-2.3	-1.6	-0.9	-0.4	0.5	-0.3	-0.1	-2.7	-1.7
Zambia	..	-0.5	1.5	6.1	6.7	5.2	3.8	4.2	3.9	0.1	0.8	..	-1.3	3.2
Zimbabwe	-2.2	-1.7	-0.7	-1.1	0.1	0.0	-0.7	0.7	-0.4	6.9	0.6	-3.2	-3.2	0.4
NORTH AFRICA	..	-9.7	-9.6	-7.1	-10.0	-8.7	-7.4	-6.0	-5.5	-6.8	..	-15.4	-14.6	-7.9
Algeria	..	5.3	3.5	1.0	-6.3	-1.6	1.7	6.4	6.4	0.1	..	-7.0	-6.4	1.8
Egypt, Arab Republic	..	-8.3	-6.1	3.7	6.1	8.6	6.9	6.2	5.7	4.8	1.5	-22.6	-14.3	2.9
Libya	..	..	..	..	..	..	..	..	..	..	..	..	..	..
Morocco	-0.7	-3.0	4.4	3.4	3.0	2.1	0.9	2.0	1.8	2.4	0.7	4.4	-2.6	1.8
Tunisia	..	-3.2	-3.0	0.1	0.3	1.6	-0.2	-0.6	-0.4	0.6	-0.2	-4.5	-1.9	-0.5
ALL AFRICA	..	..	..	..	..	..	..	..	..	-9.4	-9.6	..	..	-9.5

Note: 1999 data are preliminary. Nigeria: from 1992 data are for consolidated budget; since 1994 ratios are distorted as off. exch. rt. used by Gov. for oil sector is significantly over-valued.

7-4. Government expenditure and lending minus repayments

	1980	1990	1991	1992	1993	1994	1995	1996	1997	1998	1999	75-84	85-89	90-MR
						Percentage of GDP							*Annual average*	
SUB-SAHARAN AFRICA	..	28.0	27.8	29.8	31.5	29.7	27.9	27.6	28.0	30.6	31.1	26.4	28.4	29.2
excluding South Africa	..	26.4	26.2	28.3	27.1	25.6	23.2	22.5	23.7	28.0	27.5	..	27.3	25.9
excl. S.Africa & Nigeria	..	26.4	26.2	28.3	27.1	27.6	25.4	24.9	24.7	25.2	25.5	24.9	27.3	26.1
Angola	..	52.5	40.2	92.5	60.7	62.1	55.9	60.8	56.6	42.1	68.6	..	43.4	59.2
Benin	..	19.9	19.0	20.8	17.8	19.8	22.1	19.5	18.8	16.6	16.9	..	20.0	19.1
Botswana	..	39.4	41.2	42.0	42.5	36.6	36.6	36.0	41.2	43.4	45.1	33.5	33.4	40.4
Burkina Faso	..	19.6	21.5	20.9	22.6	21.6	21.1	21.3	23.3	22.8	27.3	..	..	22.2
Burundi	11.9	25.9	25.8	28.5	30.1	24.7	25.9	27.4	22.2	23.3	27.0	12.6	23.9	26.1
Cameroon	16.0	21.8	23.4	22.1	20.0	19.3	16.2	16.0	16.1	17.9	18.9	10.6	23.9	19.2
Cape Verde	..	27.5	30.3	44.2	48.0	52.6	51.7	47.4	40.4	35.9	37.2	67.4	42.2	41.5
Central African Republic	..	..	..	..	..	22.4	20.6	11.0	14.1	17.7	17.9	..	..	17.3
Chad	..	22.4	15.1	19.3	20.2	19.1	18.1	18.5	18.1	15.4	19.0	..	21.8	18.5
Comoros	..	32.5	32.4	33.4	26.4	38.3	34.0	28.5	27.2	24.1	22.1	36.8	36.9	29.9
Congo, Democratic Rep. of	..	..	..	..	..	..	..	..	..	22.0	21.8	..	..	21.9
Congo, Republic of	..	34.3	38.6	36.6	36.7	36.7	27.7	32.8	37.7	42.9	34.9	28.4	33.9	35.9
Côte d'Ivoire	..	32.3	31.1	30.5	28.4	24.7	24.3	22.9	22.2	21.7	19.8	..	35.6	25.8
Djibouti	..	48.9	41.0	51.0	50.1	43.0	39.2	34.5	35.3	31.5	28.8	..	..	40.3
Equatorial Guinea	..	56.8	54.5	47.6	55.9	27.1	24.6	24.9	16.6	30.0	16.6	..	38.0	35.4
Eritrea	..	..	..	36.7	61.8	59.3	69.2	63.3	54.9	76.2	91.4	..	..	64.1
Ethiopia	..	29.7	24.6	20.2	19.6	25.0	24.7	26.9	24.2	25.2	30.0	26.1	29.5	25.0
Gabon	..	24.1	26.7	28.3	28.6	25.5	26.3	23.0	28.8	46.2	27.0	36.9	37.6	28.4
Gambia, The	..	26.9	25.7	26.4	25.4	25.1	27.6	31.1	26.9	23.2	25.0	35.9	31.8	26.3
Ghana	18.7	18.2	19.1	24.6	29.0	31.2	30.4	29.5	28.7	28.6	26.2	13.1	18.3	26.5
Guinea	..	24.6	22.7	19.3	18.5	17.3	17.5	16.1	17.3	16.6	15.5	..	23.0	18.5
Guinea-Bissau	0.0	43.1	45.4	48.1	40.3	35.5	30.4	33.7	46.3	25.0	32.2	10.8	52.0	38.0
Kenya	34.3	33.6	33.3	32.4	40.7	34.7	31.8	31.4	29.1	29.2	25.9	28.0	29.8	32.2
Lesotho	..	50.9	49.5	44.2	45.3	46.4	44.2	44.7	45.1	48.7	49.3	32.1	44.7	46.8
Liberia	..	..	..	..	..	..	..	..	..	..	..	..	..	..
Madagascar	..	17.0	16.4	20.0	20.6	19.8	17.6	17.8	17.4	18.8	16.2	18.8	17.8	18.2
Malawi	35.7	28.0	24.8	34.6	27.0	51.8	33.9	22.2	26.2	30.3	27.6	29.2	32.9	30.6
Mali	108.2	26.3	28.4	24.4	23.4	27.2	23.5	23.5	23.9	24.7	26.0	106.8	25.6	25.1
Mauritania	..	39.2	28.3	24.8	36.8	27.7	24.8	24.0	22.7	24.9	25.8	..	39.5	27.9
Mauritius	..	24.9	25.0	24.5	23.8	23.8	24.4	26.4	26.1	23.6	24.1	29.4	26.1	24.7
Mozambique	17.4	28.7	26.7	30.3	29.5	30.9	24.4	20.5	23.1	22.0	24.6	26.5	24.5	26.1
Namibia	..	..	..	..	..	..	..	39.5	40.1	39.4	40.3	..	..	39.8
Niger	..	22.7	16.9	16.8	16.7	18.6	14.6	12.9	15.7	17.3	18.2	19.2	20.1	17.0
Nigeria	..	..	..	..	..	16.6	12.7	10.6	19.0	42.0	37.9	..	..	23.1
Rwanda	..	19.7	23.2	24.3	23.9	16.0	20.6	22.1	19.5	18.6	19.5	..	..	20.7
São Tomé and Principe	..	74.1	62.7	71.1	68.3	73.8	77.5	69.3	70.1	59.6	69.8	..	43.6	69.6
Senegal	27.4	21.0	19.1	21.5	20.8	21.0	19.9	20.9	18.9	20.0	20.6	25.6	20.6	20.4
Seychelles	..	49.4	50.6	51.6	64.9	70.0	63.8	55.9	59.8	69.8	65.2	..	..	60.1
Sierra Leone	..	19.8	20.9	21.4	21.2	18.5	19.4	16.9	13.0	20.1	22.0	..	20.5	19.3
Somalia	..	..	..	..	..	..	..	..	..	..	..	..	..	..
South Africa	24.1	29.3	29.2	31.1	35.5	34.0	33.0	33.3	32.7	33.7	35.4	26.4	29.3	32.7
Sudan	..	15.5	22.5	29.0	10.0	..	12.0	10.8	7.4	8.5	9.3	23.1	20.8	13.9
Swaziland	..	..	27.6	31.6	49.5	47.5	42.3	40.4	37.5	35.1	32.0	..	..	38.2
Tanzania	..	15.2	14.0	14.2	17.7	15.6	16.2	15.8	13.6	13.4	13.9	30.9	20.5	15.0
Togo	40.5	28.8	25.4	22.1	26.9	25.1	22.5	20.9	18.2	22.5	21.1	34.9	32.4	23.3
Uganda	..	12.7	15.0	21.2	18.6	18.6	16.7	16.2	16.8	15.8	16.8	13.7	11.0	16.8
Zambia	38.1	32.9	34.7	31.0	29.4	31.9	29.4	27.3	25.2	28.6	27.6	35.1	32.1	29.8
Zimbabwe	4.2	34.3	33.0	36.1	34.8	33.1	38.6	34.4	37.0	33.4	38.7	11.4	35.6	35.3
NORTH AFRICA	..	31.2	33.7	32.5	33.1	32.0	30.4	29.1	29.1	28.9	29.6	..	31.7	31.0
Algeria	..	25.2	30.2	30.7	36.2	33.9	32.0	29.2	31.2	31.7	30.3	46.3	39.3	31.1
Egypt, Arab Republic	..	37.9	40.9	36.6	33.2	32.2	28.6	27.8	26.1	25.3	28.5	..	41.3	31.7
Libya	..	..	..	..	..	..	..	..	..	..	..	..	..	..
Morocco	9.3	27.5	26.1	28.4	29.8	28.1	29.1	27.7	30.0	30.1	31.6	13.0	6.8	28.8
Tunisia	..	..	31.8	30.2	30.7	33.8	34.5	35.5	32.6	32.0	27.6	..	..	32.1
ALL AFRICA	..	29.1	30.0	30.8	32.1	30.6	28.8	28.1	28.4	30.0	30.6	..	29.2	29.8

Note: 1999 data are preliminary. Nigeria: from 1992 accounts are for consolidated budget; since 1994, ratios are distorted as off. exch. rate used by the Gov. for oil exports oil value added is significantly over-valued.

7-5. Government interest payments

					Percentage of GDP							Annual average		
	1980	1990	1991	1992	1993	1994	1995	1996	1997	1998	1999	75-84	85-89	90-MR
SUB-SAHARAN AFRICA	..	..	..	..	..	..	..	..	..	5.6	5.2	..	..	5.4
excluding South Africa	..	5.5	5.4	5.5	5.6	9.4	4.9	4.4	3.9	4.5	4.5	3.3	4.4	5.3
excl. S.Africa & Nigeria	..	4.2	4.3	4.6	5.0	10.2	5.1	4.8	4.2	3.8	3.8	3.1	3.6	5.0
Angola	..	5.2	6.0	8.2	9.4	239.1	7.1	11.7	5.8	7.0	6.1	..	2.5	30.6
Benin	..	3.0	2.6	3.7	2.7	3.2	2.8	2.4	1.7	1.3	1.2	..	2.0	2.5
Botswana	..	..	..	..	..	..	..	..	-0.1	-0.5	0.0	..	..	-0.2
Burkina Faso	..	1.1	1.4	1.4	1.6	1.5	1.4	0.9	0.8	0.8	0.9	0.7	1.2	1.2
Burundi	0.2	1.8	1.6	1.8	1.5	1.5	1.8	1.8	2.0	2.4	3.2	0.7	2.0	1.9
Cameroon	0.3	2.1	4.1	5.2	4.8	7.0	6.4	6.7	6.1	5.7	5.2	0.6	1.3	5.3
Cape Verde	..	1.4	1.1	1.1	1.2	1.0	3.2	3.6	3.9	3.6	1.7	0.0	1.1	2.2
Central African Republic	..	1.2	1.4	1.9	2.1	2.4	2.3	1.9	1.3	1.3	1.4	..	1.4	1.7
Chad	..	0.4	0.6	0.7	1.2	1.2	1.0	1.0	1.0	0.8	0.9	..	0.2	0.9
Comoros	..	1.4	1.2	1.0	1.0	1.2	1.0	0.9	1.0	1.1	1.1	0.0	0.3	1.1
Congo, Democratic Rep. of	..	10.0	6.4	8.3	6.4	11.0	12.3	11.9	11.9	9.5	7.5	2.1	4.6	9.5
Congo, Republic of	..	10.2	8.7	7.9	7.4	12.1	11.9	12.0	12.1	14.6	12.3	0.0	4.8	10.9
Côte d'Ivoire	0.0	9.8	10.9	10.4	8.7	7.9	6.9	5.9	4.9	4.3	4.3	1.6	8.1	7.4
Djibouti	..	0.7	..	0.6	0.4	0.3	0.6	0.6	0.5	..	..	..	..	0.5
Equatorial Guinea	..	6.6	6.9	8.0	7.6	7.1	5.9	3.9	1.4	1.7	1.7	..	5.8	5.1
Eritrea	..	..	..	0.0	0.0	0.1	0.4	0.9	1.0	1.3	2.0	..	..	0.7
Ethiopia	..	1.3	1.3	1.5	2.0	3.4	2.5	2.4	2.2	1.9	1.9	0.9	1.5	2.0
Gabon	..	5.6	6.0	6.4	7.0	6.7	8.1	5.9	5.8	7.3	7.2	2.4	4.8	6.6
Gambia, The	..	4.0	3.5	3.4	3.8	3.7	3.8	4.4	5.1	5.3	5.5	..	4.2	4.3
Ghana	..	1.4	1.8	2.2	3.5	4.4	4.2	5.1	6.2	5.1	5.6	1.3	1.5	3.9
Guinea	..	2.6	2.3	1.6	1.3	1.6	1.4	1.3	1.6	1.4	1.5	..	2.7	1.7
Guinea-Bissau	0.0	4.1	5.3	4.6	5.8	5.4	6.7	6.6	5.5	6.8	6.5	0.1	3.9	5.7
Kenya	3.5	8.9	9.1	8.4	14.3	11.2	8.1	7.0	5.9	5.5	6.4	3.7	5.1	8.5
Lesotho	..	..	..	..	..	..	2.0	1.7	1.6	1.6	2.1	2.9	..	..	2.0
Liberia	..	..	..	..	..	..	..	..	..	..	..	..	..	..
Madagascar	..	1.5	2.0	3.4	4.0	5.4	5.1	4.7	3.0	2.7	2.1	1.0	1.8	3.4
Malawi	3.2	3.9	2.7	3.2	3.1	5.9	6.5	4.9	5.0	4.1	3.5	4.2	6.1	4.3
Mali	4.4	2.4	1.8	1.8	1.6	2.4	1.4	1.1	1.0	0.8	0.9	5.9	1.7	1.5
Mauritania	..	2.6	2.6	3.0	4.1	2.9	3.2	3.2	3.0	3.5	3.6	..	3.2	3.2
Mauritius	..	4.4	4.1	3.4	2.8	2.9	3.1	3.4	3.7	4.1	3.9	6.0	4.8	3.6
Mozambique	0.0	1.9	1.3	2.4	2.5	1.1	1.6	1.4	1.3	1.0	0.6	0.0	1.0	1.5
Namibia	..	0.9	0.3	0.3	0.7	1.0	1.2	1.7	2.2	2.7	3.0	2.8	2.9	1.4
Niger	..	2.3	1.9	1.6	1.7	2.3	2.3	1.7	1.5	1.5	1.5	2.1	2.7	1.8
Nigeria	1.4	11.3	10.1	9.8	8.2	5.6	3.7	2.3	2.4	7.8	8.2	1.7	8.0	6.9
Rwanda	0.2	1.0	1.8	1.9	2.2	4.5	2.3	1.6	1.2	0.9	1.0	0.4	1.0	1.8
São Tomé and Principe	..	10.2	11.0	11.0	11.5	11.0	12.0	10.0	11.3	12.4	11.3	..	6.3	11.2
Senegal	2.0	2.7	2.5	2.0	2.3	3.5	2.9	2.3	2.3	1.3	1.4	2.5	3.2	2.3
Seychelles	1.8	8.0	7.9	7.9	8.0	8.4	9.7	8.6	9.4	9.0	11.3	1.9	6.6	8.8
Sierra Leone	1.9	5.7	6.3	5.8	4.0	2.6	2.0	2.1	2.1	4.8	5.8	2.0	4.7	4.1
Somalia	..	..	..	..	..	..	..	..	..	..	..	..	..	..
South Africa	..	..	..	..	..	..	..	..	..	6.8	6.1	..	..	6.5
Sudan	..	..	..	..	..	..	..	..	..	0.7	0.8	..	..	0.8
Swaziland	..	..	..	..	..	..	..	..	..	0.3	0.9	..	..	0.6
Tanzania	..	2.0	1.9	1.7	2.3	2.2	3.0	3.0	2.4	2.0	1.5	2.4	2.4	2.2
Togo	..	3.3	3.2	2.8	4.2	5.5	3.5	2.7	2.3	2.3	2.5	7.2	4.8	3.2
Uganda	..	0.6	1.3	3.3	1.8	1.4	1.0	1.0	0.9	1.0	0.9	2.0	0.9	1.3
Zambia	4.1	7.8	8.5	8.5	12.3	11.6	8.1	4.8	4.1	3.4	2.8	4.2	9.5	7.2
Zimbabwe	1.2	4.8	4.6	5.7	6.2	6.7	9.4	8.4	7.0	9.3	10.1	2.6	4.8	7.2
NORTH AFRICA	..	3.5	4.4	4.8	5.6	6.0	5.4	5.3	5.0	4.6	..	1.8	3.2	5.0
Algeria	..	1.6	1.8	2.2	2.3	2.8	3.2	3.5	4.0	4.0	..	1.2	1.6	2.8
Egypt, Arab Republic	..	3.8	6.3	6.8	8.5	9.4	7.3	7.0	6.0	5.3	5.4	0.0	3.0	6.6
Libya	..	..	..	..	..	..	..	..	..	..	..	..	..	..
Morocco	5.3	6.2	5.5	5.6	5.9	5.7	6.0	5.4	5.4	5.2	5.4	4.4	6.1	5.6
Tunisia	1.6	3.0	2.9	3.2	3.5	3.7	4.0	4.3	3.4	3.1	3.4	1.8	2.8	3.5
ALL AFRICA	..	..	..	..	..	..	..	..	..	5.2	5.2	..	..	5.2

Note: 1999 data are preliminary. Nigeria: from 1992 accounts are for consolidated budget; since 1994, ratios are distorted as off. exch. rate used by the Gov. for oil exports oil value added is significantly over-valued.

7-6. Government revenue (excluding grants)

					Percentage of GDP							Annual average		
	1980	1990	1991	1992	1993	1994	1995	1996	1997	1998	1999	75-84	85-89	90-MR
SUB-SAHARAN AFRICA	..	22.5	21.5	22.4	23.2	22.6	23.3	23.2	23.6	24.5	25.6	21.0	21.9	23.2
excluding South Africa	..	19.2	18.5	21.6	20.2	18.0	19.5	19.1	19.8	20.9	21.3	18.5	19.1	19.8
excl. S.Africa & Nigeria	..	18.8	18.7	18.9	19.1	17.9	18.9	19.0	19.7	19.4	19.5	18.5	20.2	19.0
Angola	..	25.6	18.3	35.6	39.1	42.0	29.3	45.1	38.7	27.0	48.2	..	32.3	34.9
Benin	..	5.7	8.7	9.5	11.0	10.8	13.5	13.4	13.4	14.9	14.8	14.2	4.5	11.6
Botswana	..	48.5	49.3	50.5	49.6	38.8	38.1	41.9	44.8	39.3	42.4	40.8	46.0	44.3
Burkina Faso	..	12.3	13.3	11.7	12.6	11.0	10.8	12.3	13.0	13.1	16.5	9.7	10.6	12.7
Burundi	18.1	15.1	16.9	17.2	17.4	20.1	20.1	17.7	15.1	16.4	17.9	18.0	17.9	17.4
Cameroon	16.3	14.3	15.2	15.7	13.7	9.9	12.9	14.3	15.1	15.9	15.3	11.1	18.6	14.2
Cape Verde	..	24.1	13.7	18.7	23.5	23.4	17.8	13.2	11.6	14.2	16.1	22.4	27.6	17.6
Central African Republic	..	10.7	9.2	8.9	7.7	7.5	9.2	6.1	7.7	9.1	9.2	..	..	8.5
Chad	..	6.7	6.1	6.3	7.0	4.9	6.2	7.3	7.8	9.0	8.4	3.6	5.4	7.0
Comoros	..	17.0	13.9	15.8	14.5	16.1	17.4	6.8	15.0	12.4	10.9	17.6	12.9	14.0
Congo, Democratic Rep. of	..	..	..	..	..	6.0	13.2	11.6	13.6	12.1	12.8	..	..	11.6
Congo, Republic of	..	27.4	25.3	22.5	24.1	22.4	19.9	27.5	28.5	22.6	27.0	34.6	25.9	24.7
Côte d'Ivoire	..	21.5	19.5	20.1	17.6	19.9	22.1	22.5	22.2	21.7	19.0	30.0	27.7	20.6
Djibouti	..	27.9	25.8	26.9	28.4	29.5	29.1	28.8	27.2	27.0	26.8	..	..	27.8
Equatorial Guinea	..	..	..	..	..	17.3	15.7	17.7	18.0	28.0	20.2	..	..	19.5
Eritrea	..	..	..	24.4	35.3	28.1	34.1	32.6	42.9	34.8	37.0	..	..	33.7
Ethiopia	..	17.7	13.7	10.6	12.0	13.9	17.4	18.4	19.0	18.7	19.5	17.4	20.0	16.1
Gabon	..	19.6	24.3	22.9	22.6	23.5	29.5	25.7	31.3	31.8	25.6	-0.3	30.0	25.7
Gambia, The	..	20.8	21.5	23.2	23.0	20.9	18.5	18.8	19.1	18.8	19.9	21.2	21.3	20.4
Ghana	..	12.5	14.6	11.9	14.9	18.7	20.4	17.5	17.7	20.0	17.6	8.0	13.2	16.6
Guinea	..	15.8	14.5	12.2	11.2	10.2	10.9	10.0	11.2	10.6	10.3	..	14.4	11.7
Guinea-Bissau	0.0	18.7	12.4	10.7	10.4	12.4	12.7	12.5	15.3	5.4	18.4	0.6	13.2	12.9
Kenya	24.6	23.6	24.4	24.9	29.9	28.0	28.5	27.4	26.1	25.9	24.1	19.5	22.7	26.3
Lesotho	..	37.4	40.5	40.6	45.0	47.0	44.3	43.9	44.3	45.9	43.6	29.2	33.5	43.2
Liberia	..	..	..	..	..	..	..	..	..	..	..	..	..	..
Madagascar	..	12.0	8.7	10.0	9.9	8.3	8.5	8.7	9.7	10.6	11.9	12.4	12.8	9.8
Malawi	19.8	21.0	18.6	20.7	17.3	20.1	17.8	8.7	12.9	19.6	16.6	18.1	22.9	17.3
Mali	74.7	17.6	16.0	13.3	13.8	12.7	12.9	15.4	16.0	16.4	17.8	74.9	15.1	15.2
Mauritania	..	24.6	22.3	21.2	25.5	23.2	22.7	27.4	27.0	26.7	27.9	..	24.7	24.9
Mauritius	..	22.8	22.7	22.1	21.4	20.6	18.6	18.8	20.2	20.4	21.5	22.4	22.8	20.9
Mozambique	13.5	12.8	12.5	13.9	14.0	11.8	11.3	10.6	11.4	11.5	10.5	16.1	11.1	12.0
Namibia	0.0	31.9	34.7	34.3	34.8	32.8	33.6	33.3	35.9	35.5	36.1	14.2	29.8	34.3
Niger	..	10.2	8.5	8.2	7.3	6.0	7.2	7.8	8.4	8.7	6.8	11.0	10.7	7.9
Nigeria	..	21.5	17.7	35.1	25.5	18.5	22.6	19.6	20.0	28.5	30.5	..	13.6	24.0
Rwanda	..	10.1	10.4	10.1	9.2	3.6	6.9	9.1	10.3	10.4	9.2	9.0	10.5	8.9
São Tomé and Principe	..	33.8	29.6	20.2	18.0	13.3	16.5	13.4	15.6	25.0	20.5	..	33.0	20.6
Senegal	22.1	16.8	19.4	18.4	16.6	14.9	16.4	16.6	16.9	16.7	17.1	18.8	17.2	17.0
Seychelles	..	47.7	44.2	44.5	51.9	52.7	47.1	44.6	46.1	44.3	50.2	40.2	47.0	47.3
Sierra Leone	..	9.2	10.8	12.4	13.9	12.7	9.5	9.8	5.4	7.4	10.6	..	6.6	10.2
Somalia	..	..	..	..	..	..	..	..	..	..	..	..	..	..
South Africa	6.0	26.1	24.9	23.4	26.5	27.8	27.8	27.9	28.2	28.6	30.7	19.9	24.9	27.2
Sudan	.	6.3	7.2	8.8	8.3	8.8	8.7	7.0	6.6	7.8	8.4	10.9	8.7	7.8
Swaziland	..	..	32.3	30.1	44.8	43.0	39.0	37.2	34.1	31.9	29.1	..	..	35.7
Tanzania	..	14.7	14.4	15.1	12.9	13.9	11.0	11.9	12.2	10.8	10.6	18.6	13.8	12.7
Togo	..	22.6	17.5	16.2	10.7	12.1	14.7	14.6	14.7	15.3	15.3	28.1	25.5	15.4
Uganda	..	6.8	7.5	6.8	7.3	8.3	9.8	10.2	11.0	10.3	10.9	11.1	6.3	8.9
Zambia	..	20.3	18.7	18.4	15.9	20.1	19.9	20.7	19.9	18.7	17.6	..	20.1	19.0
Zimbabwe	11.1	27.0	26.6	27.7	26.8	24.5	26.7	25.4	28.4	29.4	28.3	18.5	26.6	27.1
NORTH AFRICA	..	23.4	27.0	29.2	28.2	29.3	27.9	28.2	28.3	26.5	26.4	..	24.8	27.4
Algeria	..	28.9	31.8	29.5	27.6	31.0	30.6	32.2	33.6	27.8	29.8	38.2	31.3	30.3
Egypt, Arab Republic	..	22.8	25.7	31.2	29.7	30.0	27.3	26.5	25.2	24.2	24.2	..	25.3	26.7
Libya	..	..	..	..	..	..	..	..	..	..	..	..	..	..
Morocco	15.2	14.4	22.3	25.8	26.3	23.9	23.6	24.1	26.4	27.4	26.9	19.4	15.2	24.1
Tunisia	..	27.1	26.7	27.2	27.8	31.7	30.3	30.6	28.7	29.5	24.0	32.8	29.5	28.4
ALL AFRICA	..	22.8	23.4	24.8	24.9	24.9	24.9	24.9	25.3	25.2	25.9	23.4	23.1	24.7

Note: 1999 data are preliminary. Nigeria: from 1992 accounts are for consolidated budget; since 1994, ratios are distorted as off. exch. rate used by the Gov. for oil exports oil value added is significantly over-valued.

7-7. Grants to government

	Percentage of GDP											Annual average		
	1980	1990	1991	1992	1993	1994	1995	1996	1997	1998	1999	75-84	85-89	90-MR
SUB-SAHARAN AFRICA	0.1	1.1	1.2	1.3	1.2	1.3	1.2	1.1	1.0	1.0	1.0	0.2	0.9	1.2
excluding South Africa	0.7	1.8	2.0	2.2	2.2	2.5	2.3	2.1	1.8	1.9	1.9	0.8	1.6	2.1
excl. S.Africa & Nigeria	0.9	2.2	2.4	2.6	2.7	2.9	2.7	2.5	2.2	2.3	2.3	1.0	2.0	2.5
Angola	..	0.0	0.0	0.0	0.0	0.0	0.0	1.7	0.8	1.2	2.2	..	0.0	0.6
Benin	0.0	5.9	3.4	4.1	3.9	4.6	4.0	3.9	4.5	3.3	5.1	1.1	5.0	4.3
Botswana	0.0	1.4	1.0	1.1	1.6	0.9	0.3	0.4	0.1	0.1	0.1	0.2	2.0	0.7
Burkina Faso	0.0	2.7	4.6	6.2	5.4	7.3	6.7	8.4	7.0	6.8	8.9	0.7	5.5	6.4
Burundi	3.7	8.1	8.7	8.6	9.1	2.4	3.6	2.2	3.1	0.6	1.2	2.0	1.6	4.8
Cameroon	0.0	0.0	0.0	0.0	0.0	0.1	0.0	0.0	0.0	0.3	0.2	0.0	0.0	0.1
Cape Verde	0.0	7.8	9.9	17.5	15.3	15.2	14.9	13.0	10.1	9.9	7.3	3.8	19.3	12.1
Central African Republic	4.4	4.2	4.6	5.7	5.3	4.9	6.3	1.5	4.1	7.8	6.8	1.6	5.1	5.1
Chad	0.0	8.0	5.0	4.9	4.6	9.5	7.5	6.2	6.4	5.1	4.7	0.8	9.8	6.2
Comoros	0.0	15.1	16.3	15.0	14.4	16.3	11.8	8.9	9.7	8.0	7.6	3.8	19.2	12.3
Congo, Democratic Rep. of	0.0	2.5	1.2	0.4	0.4	2.4	6.3	3.9	1.2	1.9	2.2	0.0	1.7	2.3
Congo, Republic of	0.0	0.3	0.2	0.0	0.0	1.1	0.9	0.3	0.1	0.3	0.5	0.2	0.1	0.4
Côte d'Ivoire	0.0	0.0	0.5	0.5	0.5	0.7	0.7	0.7	1.4	1.5	1.2	0.0	0.0	0.8
Djibouti	..	0.0	12.2	12.4	8.8	5.0	2.0	1.8	2.6	2.2	2.1	..	0.0	4.9
Equatorial Guinea	..	30.4	27.7	17.1	19.3	4.2	2.6	0.9	0.7	0.7	0.3	0.0	4.6	10.4
Eritrea	..	..	..	9.1	20.1	18.5	12.7	11.3	6.1	9.1	6.5	..	..	11.7
Ethiopia	..	2.3	2.4	2.6	1.7	3.5	3.3	2.9	3.6	2.8	3.6	2.1	3.7	2.9
Gabon	0.0	0.4	0.3	0.1	0.3	0.4	0.0	0.0	0.0	0.0	0.0	0.0	0.5	0.1
Gambia, The	0.0	5.9	5.4	4.5	3.7	3.1	2.4	2.2	1.3	2.0	1.7	0.0	14.2	3.2
Ghana	0.1	2.7	3.1	3.3	4.3	3.5	3.6	2.5	1.3	2.2	2.4	0.1	2.3	2.9
Guinea	..	3.7	3.6	4.0	3.6	3.5	4.0	3.1	3.0	2.7	2.2	..	3.1	3.3
Guinea-Bissau	0.0	18.1	15.5	15.8	16.9	14.7	16.3	9.0	12.8	3.2	4.5	1.8	30.4	12.7
Kenya	2.5	2.2	2.0	2.6	3.1	2.7	2.0	1.3	1.0	0.6	0.2	1.1	2.0	1.8
Lesotho	0.0	11.1	8.3	6.1	5.2	4.8	4.4	4.3	4.2	3.4	2.3	0.9	5.5	5.4
Liberia	0.0	..	..	..	..	..	..	..	..	..	..	0.0	0.0	..
Madagascar	0.0	4.4	2.1	3.5	3.5	3.0	2.9	4.2	5.3	3.5	3.6	0.2	1.3	3.6
Malawi	4.3	2.8	3.0	2.8	2.8	11.7	8.6	4.8	3.8	8.4	7.0	2.2	4.0	5.6
Mali	20.5	6.0	8.2	7.1	5.5	10.0	7.5	7.2	5.8	5.8	5.2	26.3	5.1	6.8
Mauritania	0.0	2.6	2.3	1.7	2.2	2.6	2.0	2.2	0.8	1.4	2.6	0.0	5.1	2.0
Mauritius	0.0	0.2	0.1	0.1	0.2	0.3	0.3	0.2	0.2	0.2	0.3	0.0	0.8	0.2
Mozambique	1.8	9.7	11.1	13.7	11.9	13.8	9.8	7.0	9.1	8.2	11.4	1.9	5.4	10.6
Namibia	0.0	1.3	1.1	0.9	0.7	0.4	0.4	0.4	0.4	0.2	0.4	0.0	0.0	0.6
Niger	0.0	5.4	4.8	3.9	5.6	5.8	4.1	4.9	4.6	4.4	3.8	0.3	4.6	4.7
Nigeria	0.0	0.0	0.0	0.0	0.0	0.0	0.0	0.0	0.0	0.0	0.0	0.0	0.0	0.0
Rwanda	0.0	4.6	7.4	6.1	6.4	0.9	11.4	7.3	6.7	5.2	6.0	1.6	3.5	6.2
São Tomé and Principe	0.0	31.0	25.3	9.0	16.6	17.5	23.4	23.5	27.8	9.7	24.6	0.0	12.2	20.8
Senegal	0.7	1.3	1.7	1.3	1.1	4.2	3.3	6.6	2.6	3.0	2.1	0.6	1.4	2.7
Seychelles	0.0	1.9	1.5	1.3	1.6	0.8	0.5	0.5	0.4	0.6	0.6	1.0	2.2	1.0
Sierra Leone	1.0	0.0	0.0	0.0	0.0	0.0	0.0	1.7	0.6	2.4	5.4	0.4	0.5	1.0
Somalia	0.0	0.0	..	..	..	..	..	..	..	..	..	0.0	0.0	0.0
South Africa	0.0	0.2	0.4	0.3	0.1	0.0	0.0	0.0	0.0	0.0	0.0	-0.4	0.1	0.1
Sudan	0.0	0.0	0.0	0.0	0.0	0.0	0.0	0.0	0.0	0.0	0.0	0.0	0.0	0.0
Swaziland	0.0	0.0	0.8	1.4	1.2	0.9	0.8	0.7	0.8	0.9	0.8	0.0	0.0	0.8
Tanzania	..	3.3	2.1	2.4	3.4	3.3	1.8	2.0	3.2	2.7	3.7	2.8	3.0	2.8
Togo	1.5	3.2	1.9	1.6	0.3	1.4	1.4	0.5	1.4	1.8	1.1	1.4	3.1	1.5
Uganda	0.0	1.5	3.8	7.1	8.1	6.5	4.4	4.1	4.4	5.1	4.7	0.1	1.1	5.0
Zambia	0.0	4.3	9.0	10.2	8.0	5.3	5.2	6.1	5.1	6.6	7.9	0.0	1.2	6.8
Zimbabwe	0.7	0.9	1.1	1.7	2.0	1.9	1.8	1.3	1.1	1.6	1.0	0.5	1.0	1.4
NORTH AFRICA	0.1	1.7	1.5	0.9	0.5	0.6	0.4	0.2	0.3	0.2	0.2	0.3	0.4	0.7
Algeria	0.0	0.0	0.0	0.0	0.0	0.0	0.0	0.0	0.0	0.0	0.1	0.0	0.0	0.0
Egypt, Arab Republic	0.0	3.0	2.8	2.3	1.2	1.3	0.9	0.6	0.6	0.5	0.3	0.0	1.2	1.3
Libya	0.0	..	..	..	..	..	..	..	..	..	..	0.0	0.0	..
Morocco	0.5	2.9	2.1	0.0	0.3	0.2	0.1	0.0	0.0	0.0	0.0	1.7	0.0	0.6
Tunisia	0.0	0.0	0.0	0.0	0.0	0.4	0.3	0.2	0.3	0.4	0.3	0.0	0.0	0.2
ALL AFRICA	0.2	1.3	1.3	1.2	1.0	1.1	0.9	0.8	0.7	0.8	0.8	0.2	0.7	1.0

Note: 1999 data are preliminary. Nigeria: from 1992 accounts are for consolidated budget; since 1994, ratios are distorted as off. exch. rate used by the Gov. for oil exports oil value added is significantly over-valued.

7-8. Foreign financing

						Percentage of GDP							Annual average		
	1980	1990	1991	1992	1993	1994	1995	1996	1997	1998	1999	75-84	85-89	90-MR
SUB-SAHARAN AFRICA	1.0	1.6	1.2	0.0	0.7	2.0	0.7	1.4	0.7	1.0	-0.1	1.0	1.5	0.9
excluding South Africa	..	3.3	2.1	-0.2	1.2	3.3	0.9	2.4	1.0	1.6	0.7	1.6	3.1	1.6
excl. S.Africa & Nigeria	..	4.0	2.5	2.9	2.4	4.7	1.7	3.3	1.4	1.2	0.7	2.1	3.3	2.5
Angola	..	3.9	1.6	1.2	-8.7	7.3	-10.0	0.0	9.0	-2.6	-4.2	..	0.6	-0.2
Benin	..	9.3	11.3	7.9	6.9	10.3	8.3	7.6	5.1	6.9	4.7	..	27.9	7.8
Botswana	..	..	0.3	0.8	0.5	0.0	-0.3	-0.3	-0.7	0.4	2.0	..	..	0.3
Burkina Faso	..	3.5	8.4	9.4	10.0	10.0	12.1	10.9	9.3	9.8	9.1	3.0	1.1	9.2
Burundi	3.3	8.1	10.6	14.2	10.6	7.4	2.9	3.0	1.6	2.3	0.0	5.6	7.5	6.1
Cameroon	2.2	5.3	1.9	8.4	0.1	20.5	0.1	8.2	-4.0	9.0	3.3	1.6	3.0	5.3
Cape Verde	..	1.6	0.6	2.2	3.2	3.7	2.0	3.3	5.1	3.8	4.7	11.5	4.8	3.0
Central African Republic	0.4	1.2	1.6	0.8	0.3	2.3	0.6	-1.6	-1.6	-1.6	-1.9	1.0	1.9	0.0
Chad	..	6.2	2.7	2.0	2.8	2.6	2.8	6.7	5.6	2.7	5.4	0.5	4.1	4.0
Comoros	..	2.0	3.2	-2.5	2.4	4.8	4.5	3.8	2.1	2.8	0.0	0.0	0.7	2.3
Congo, Democratic Rep. of	..	2.9	-4.0	-6.0	-4.8	0.0	0.0	0.0	0.0	-3.9	-3.6	0.0	6.2	-1.9
Congo, Republic of	11.2	24.8	8.3	7.0	8.1	5.4	-11.9	75.4	11.0	-13.3	-13.0	5.7	6.9	10.2
Côte d'Ivoire	7.9	11.5	10.9	9.8	7.5	11.0	4.2	3.0	1.0	0.7	0.2	6.8	6.1	6.0
Djibouti	..	..	0.4	0.1	3.0	2.4	1.6	3.3	1.7	..	..	..	..	1.8
Equatorial Guinea	..	0.1	-7.0	0.4	0.6	-8.5	-8.0	-0.4	-0.7	-0.9	-0.7	..	-0.8	-2.5
Eritrea	..	..	..	0.0	0.1	4.6	1.2	1.3	4.3	9.7	15.9	..	..	4.6
Ethiopia	..	2.8	2.1	1.4	2.7	6.0	3.7	3.7	1.8	1.7	2.6	2.6	3.1	2.9
Gabon	..	-3.1	-2.8	-4.2	-5.1	-3.2	-5.7	-3.1	-4.9	-6.2	-6.9	..	6.8	-4.5
Gambia, The	0.0	4.2	4.6	4.1	2.0	0.7	2.9	6.6	4.1	1.2	0.7	1.3	5.6	3.1
Ghana	0.9	4.5	3.5	3.5	6.2	4.5	4.3	3.7	4.6	3.1	0.9	0.7	2.7	3.9
Guinea	..	2.0	1.3	1.5	3.1	-0.3	1.7	1.1	3.1	2.5	2.3	..	4.7	1.8
Guinea-Bissau	0.0	4.9	2.1	18.9	14.0	9.8	3.3	9.0	20.8	7.8	5.3	0.0	16.0	9.6
Kenya	0.3	2.6	1.0	1.3	1.2	-0.5	-0.5	-0.6	-1.1	-1.7	-1.5	0.2	1.0	0.0
Lesotho	..	-3.4	-1.7	0.7	0.7	-0.9	3.8	5.9	7.4	5.4	0.3	-0.4	-4.9	1.8
Liberia	..	..	..	..	..	..	..	..	..	..	..	..	..	..
Madagascar	5.6	2.1	3.9	2.7	2.9	1.7	1.9	5.0	3.8	0.0	-0.1	4.1	3.4	2.4
Malawi	4.0	4.7	3.5	4.9	6.4	9.2	2.9	3.9	3.5	7.9	5.6	4.8	3.5	5.3
Mali	15.2	5.4	6.2	4.3	3.4	7.8	7.4	6.1	3.4	3.7	3.8	20.5	8.1	5.2
Mauritania	..	0.5	-1.6	0.7	23.5	6.8	2.7	3.4	0.1	-3.2	-2.0	0.0	6.8	3.1
Mauritius	..	-0.7	-0.8	-0.7	-0.4	-0.4	1.5	1.7	0.0	-0.8	0.1	-1.0	0.6	0.0
Mozambique	2.1	6.1	3.6	2.1	2.6	5.9	3.8	4.2	5.7	4.7	1.7	3.7	4.1	4.0
Namibia	..	0.0	0.0	0.4	0.7	0.4	0.8	0.9	0.7	0.1	0.6	0.0	0.0	0.4
Niger	..	6.8	0.6	1.5	-0.1	12.5	-0.6	4.1	3.5	4.3	..	5.4	4.2	3.6
Nigeria	0.5	-0.1	-0.1	-15.1	-4.7	-3.7	-2.9	-2.1	-1.4	3.9	1.1	0.6	1.9	-2.5
Rwanda	-0.3	3.0	4.0	4.2	3.0	-1.4	2.2	2.5	2.1	6.3	5.5	0.9	3.4	3.1
São Tomé and Principe	..	18.8	19.1	40.7	23.4	29.8	29.6	24.9	26.7	5.3	16.9	..	8.1	23.5
Senegal	2.7	3.5	0.5	0.8	0.6	9.2	3.6	0.4	1.8	1.8	0.8	3.3	3.2	2.3
Seychelles	..	-1.8	3.1	-1.5	0.9	-1.4	-2.0	-1.2	-0.7	1.9	1.1	6.6	3.2	-0.2
Sierra Leone	7.3	0.1	6.5	5.4	8.6	5.2	7.4	3.7	1.4	1.4	-1.2	4.9	-2.5	3.9
Somalia	..	..	..	..	..	..	..	..	..	..	..	..	..	..
South Africa	-0.1	-0.1	0.2	0.2	0.0	0.4	0.4	0.2	0.5	0.2	-1.1	0.1	-0.1	0.1
Sudan	..	..	..	..	2.0	1.1	1.0	0.2	0.2	0.2	0.3	..	..	0.7
Swaziland	..	..	-0.5	-0.4	..	..	..	..	..	4.0	3.5	..	..	1.6
Tanzania	..	0.2	0.8	1.7	1.7	2.1	0.8	-1.1	-0.4	0.9	0.4	1.5	0.7	0.7
Togo	..	4.9	4.0	2.4	0.8	4.9	11.7	5.9	5.4	4.6	-0.5	..	7.3	4.4
Uganda	..	6.7	3.9	5.2	5.2	5.5	4.5	3.4	3.2	2.7	3.0	0.4	1.3	4.3
Zambia	..	6.3	2.2	2.3	6.4	4.1	4.1	2.3	2.0	0.8	3.0	..	4.5	3.3
Zimbabwe	0.4	1.1	2.1	3.5	2.0	0.5	0.2	0.2	0.3	-2.4	-0.8	1.8	1.9	0.7
NORTH AFRICA	..	-0.1	4.0	-0.3	-0.4	1.8	2.0	0.8	0.1	-0.8	-1.1	2.1	2.3	0.6
Algeria	..	0.6	0.6	-0.3	0.1	7.9	7.7	4.1	2.3	-0.3	-2.3	0.0	0.6	2.0
Egypt, Arab Republic	..	0.3	10.2	-0.2	-1.0	-1.0	-1.1	-1.2	-1.2	-1.0	-1.0	3.7	3.8	0.3
Libya	..	..	..	..	..	..	..	..	..	..	..	..	..	..
Morocco	4.8	-3.1	-1.8	-1.3	-0.7	-1.8	-0.8	-1.5	-1.9	-1.7	-1.1	4.7	-2.0	-1.6
Tunisia	..	2.1	2.4	1.0	1.2	1.4	2.9	2.8	2.4	0.0	1.4	2.4	2.8	1.8
ALL AFRICA	..	1.0	2.2	-0.1	0.3	1.9	1.1	1.2	0.5	0.4	-0.5	1.3	1.7	0.8

Note: 1999 data are preliminary. Nigeria: from 1992 accounts are for consolidated budget; since 1994, ratios are distorted as off. exch. rate used by the Gov. for oil exports oil value added is significantly over-valued.

7-9. Taxes on income and profits

	1980	1990	1991	1992	1993	1994	1995	1996	1997	1998	1999	75-84	85-89	90-MR
					Percentage of total revenue								*Annual average*	
SUB-SAHARAN AFRICA	..	36.2	36.4	36.4	32.6	31.5	32.4	33.6	35.0	35.6	35.6	40.9	36.6	34.5
excluding South Africa	..	21.3	19.3	18.9	18.4	18.5	20.2	21.2	22.3	22.3	24.2	22.9	20.6	20.7
excl. S.Africa & Nigeria	..	25.7	23.2	22.8	22.2	22.1	24.1	25.3	24.7	25.0	25.9	22.9	25.0	24.1
Angola	..	64.6	46.1	65.5	66.4	72.9	71.2	92.9	89.7	81.3	92.1	..	47.6	74.3
Benin	..	32.0	23.6	28.4	29.6	36.7	31.3	30.6	25.5	24.5	22.8	26.3	34.1	28.5
Botswana	..	8.2	8.7	8.3	8.1	8.6	7.0	5.5	4.0	3.8	4.8	12.1	8.1	6.7
Burkina Faso	..	21.5	20.4	22.0	18.9	18.7	23.4	24.7	21.9	21.8	22.6	19.7	19.1	21.6
Burundi	18.9	23.1	23.7	23.4	27.3	18.3	19.1	22.3	23.8	26.2	24.4	21.0	17.7	23.2
Cameroon	21.7	44.3	17.3	18.0	10.9	12.6	10.9	10.0	13.6	16.0	21.3	26.9	49.7	17.5
Cape Verde	..	20.7	21.2	20.4	22.2	25.1	24.4	29.4	29.7	26.2	29.6	29.5	23.6	24.9
Central African Republic	..	24.0	23.9	22.7	23.0	24.4	20.6	24.3	19.4	14.0	19.9	..	..	21.6
Chad	..	18.7	26.7	27.6	23.5	28.7	38.9	37.6	32.7	30.5	32.2	7.6	18.1	29.7
Comoros	..	19.8	13.5	11.1	9.0	12.6	12.2	46.0	11.2	15.3	17.0	0.0	12.2	16.8
Congo, Democratic Rep. of	..	..	..	..	..	13.2	18.0	14.8	15.9	24.0	22.8	..	..	18.1
Congo, Republic of	..	51.6	62.7	52.0	51.3	67.7	53.4	62.2	79.1	55.0	72.1	15.1	29.4	60.7
Côte d'Ivoire	..	22.5	20.9	20.3	19.4	14.9	18.3	20.5	22.9	23.6	25.3	15.8	18.3	20.9
Djibouti	..	30.9	32.6	38.9	38.7	38.5	37.2	41.0	39.2	..	..	..	..	37.1
Equatorial Guinea	..	..	..	..	..	19.6	20.5	52.9	63.1	74.2	73.5	..	..	50.6
Eritrea	..	..	..	13.1	20.1	33.2	25.7	27.4	22.1	29.3	25.5	..	..	24.6
Ethiopia	..	29.4	30.7	30.1	23.1	24.0	22.2	25.2	24.2	22.2	21.3	28.6	28.9	25.2
Gabon	..	14.2	13.0	13.4	12.8	10.7	10.5	10.6	10.1	13.0	17.0	..	23.7	12.5
Gambia, The	..	13.1	13.2	14.8	16.2	17.7	19.4	19.9	21.1	22.3	23.0	14.2	13.8	18.1
Ghana	..	23.0	17.6	18.6	19.1	17.5	17.4	21.7	24.1	22.0	27.3	18.7	22.9	20.8
Guinea	..	2.1	4.2	6.8	6.9	8.8	9.1	10.9	9.7	9.7	11.2	..	1.6	7.9
Guinea-Bissau	..	7.4	6.0	6.8	7.2	6.7	7.9	7.8	8.3	15.2	3.8	21.9	9.7	7.7
Kenya	30.1	29.3	29.0	28.8	32.9	35.7	34.6	33.5	31.9	30.8	31.8	28.3	29.6	31.8
Lesotho	..	11.4	15.8	16.7	13.8	15.2	16.0	15.9	14.8	15.8	16.3	14.2	11.6	15.2
Liberia	..	..	..	..	..	..	..	..	..	..	..	..	..	..
Madagascar	..	12.7	15.0	12.9	16.2	19.8	14.6	18.3	18.9	16.3	14.8	16.9	12.2	16.0
Malawi	83.8	52.6	51.5	49.2	54.4	38.7	32.5	69.0	47.4	38.2	34.2	83.4	70.2	46.8
Mali	15.2	13.2	12.8	14.3	13.1	15.2	18.4	18.5	18.0	18.6	14.5	17.4	12.7	15.6
Mauritania	..	28.5	26.6	26.5	24.8	24.5	25.3	17.3	19.2	18.5	18.3	..	27.0	22.9
Mauritius	..	20.6	20.5	19.7	18.4	18.9	21.4	21.1	19.5	18.6	19.3	13.2	16.3	19.8
Mozambique	12.4	17.8	17.7	15.6	14.3	17.3	16.6	18.2	19.0	18.1	14.0	15.5	21.4	16.8
Namibia	..	35.8	24.6	26.4	29.9	29.0	27.4	28.8	34.1	33.8	30.5	19.3	34.3	30.0
Niger	..	23.6	28.8	33.8	33.7	30.0	30.5	25.4	21.1	22.1	24.8	22.0	25.9	27.4
Nigeria	..	..	..	..	..	..	..	..	10.0	8.5	15.6	..	..	11.4
Rwanda	..	25.3	21.2	23.4	24.8	25.8	12.5	26.2	25.1	27.7	24.8	26.0	25.3	23.7
São Tomé and Principe	..	11.8	10.2	6.7	8.9	10.7	14.1	21.1	29.3	16.4	18.5	..	9.8	14.8
Senegal	26.2	24.6	23.0	24.2	23.4	21.1	21.9	21.6	21.8	23.3	21.8	25.4	23.7	22.7
Seychelles	..	22.9	21.0	16.9	26.8	30.0	35.3	26.8	28.0	25.7	25.3	22.6	18.4	25.9
Sierra Leone	..	24.4	23.6	23.9	21.7	21.4	15.9	16.5	13.2	17.3	25.8	..	25.8	20.4
Somalia	..	..	..	..	..	..	..	..	..	..	..	..	..	..
South Africa	58.2	52.7	55.4	56.0	48.3	46.6	46.5	48.0	49.8	51.1	48.9	57.8	53.8	50.3
Sudan	..	18.7	18.4	..	..	..	28.7	28.3	20.2	19.9	17.5	18.9	14.9	21.7
Swaziland	..	..	32.1	34.9	..	..	..	..	..	31.1	33.5	..	..	32.9
Tanzania	..	22.0	26.8	27.6	30.9	31.2	41.1	37.4	34.7	39.6	34.3	33.6	31.5	32.5
Togo	..	31.8	30.4	30.5	31.5	40.6	41.8	30.9	26.7	23.6	22.5	35.0	34.3	31.0
Uganda	..	10.0	10.1	12.7	14.5	14.6	14.7	13.2	14.0	15.6	17.9	6.7	7.8	13.7
Zambia	..	23.1	27.0	33.0	28.6	28.7	28.9	30.0	32.0	35.2	36.5	..	27.5	30.3
Zimbabwe	0.0	47.0	44.1	46.0	48.7	47.7	45.9	45.7	47.6	48.0	48.9	8.6	45.4	47.0
NORTH AFRICA	..	20.4	17.8	18.6	18.8	19.6	19.6	20.3	20.8	22.6	19.6	..	20.9	19.8
Algeria	..	13.5	8.3	8.9	10.9	9.4	8.9	8.2	8.8	11.4	7.6	14.1	19.5	9.6
Egypt, Arab Republic	..	19.4	22.4	23.0	23.8	22.9	21.8	22.5	22.6	22.5	22.6	..	18.0	22.4
Libya	..	..	..	..	..	..	..	..	..	..	..	..	..	..
Morocco	30.3	36.3	24.2	26.6	21.7	22.4	24.0	25.9	25.8	30.5	27.7	25.9	30.5	26.5
Tunisia	..	13.7	15.7	15.1	17.2	31.0	33.3	35.1	38.1	38.9	26.7	13.7	14.2	26.5
ALL AFRICA	..	30.7	29.9	30.2	27.8	27.4	28.0	29.0	30.1	31.1	30.1	34.8	31.8	29.4

Note: 1999 data are preliminary (see page 2). Total revenue does not include grants. Nigeria's fiscal data are for consolidated government starting from 1992.

7-10. Taxes on international trade and transactions

	Percentage of total revenue											Annual average		
	1980	1990	1991	1992	1993	1994	1995	1996	1997	1998	1999	75-84	85-89	90-MR
SUB-SAHARAN AFRICA	..	11.8	11.6	11.2	11.4	12.9	13.6	13.9	14.5	13.8	14.6	7.8	10.7	12.9
excluding South Africa	..	18.0	18.7	18.7	19.1	21.4	22.5	22.7	24.0	23.1	24.2	14.2	16.2	21.2
excl. S.Africa & Nigeria	..	21.7	22.5	22.5	22.9	25.5	26.9	27.1	26.4	26.1	27.1	14.2	19.6	24.9
Angola	..	0.9	1.0	13.9	6.5	4.6	4.9	4.3	5.0	8.2	3.0	..	3.0	5.2
Benin	..	74.9	56.1	52.8	50.8	47.1	44.5	46.5	49.3	45.1	48.4	52.7	80.6	51.6
Botswana	..	13.2	17.7	21.3	17.3	16.1	15.5	12.9	10.2	9.8	10.2	22.3	13.3	14.4
Burkina Faso	..	38.3	36.8	33.3	36.4	54.0	48.4	28.2	27.6	26.2	25.3	35.3	45.7	35.5
Burundi	30.5	21.0	23.7	21.8	21.0	26.6	25.4	15.5	17.5	25.9	21.7	22.5	28.3	22.0
Cameroon	..	15.4	13.1	18.0	16.6	18.3	19.5	19.3	17.1	17.5	16.9	..	17.7	17.2
Cape Verde	..	43.8	48.4	49.0	41.2	40.5	41.6	45.7	43.3	41.9	43.5	..	42.1	43.9
Central African Republic	..	39.8	37.6	34.6	33.0	32.5	42.5	38.7	38.1	44.7	38.0	..	..	37.9
Chad	..	24.4	15.3	15.6	13.6	19.4	27.1	31.1	30.3	36.0	29.5	..	26.1	24.2
Comoros	..	41.8	38.6	32.2	36.6	36.6	32.3	122.5	43.1	34.6	31.3	..	48.4	44.9
Congo, Democratic Rep. of	..	..	..	..	27.5	21.2	17.8	16.7	18.7	19.2		..		20.2
Congo, Republic of	..	16.0	17.4	21.2	20.0	13.9	19.2	16.3	9.1	13.4	5.6	0.0	4.3	15.2
Côte d'Ivoire	..	26.2	31.0	25.3	26.3	39.0	38.9	39.6	36.5	34.3	38.4	..	34.9	33.6
Djibouti	..	..	..	13.9	16.8	19.3	19.2	17.2	17.2	..	..	..	..	17.3
Equatorial Guinea	..	..	..	..	..	26.9	30.8	19.0	18.1	6.7	8.0	..	..	18.2
Eritrea	..	..	..	25.5	21.9	20.9	17.0	19.5	14.8	15.2	13.0	..	..	18.5
Ethiopia	..	15.1	17.2	19.0	22.6	32.9	27.4	26.0	27.5	26.4	25.2	24.3	17.9	23.9
Gabon	..	19.2	21.1	19.4	21.1	16.0	17.6	19.6	17.7	19.6	25.6	..	..	19.7
Gambia, The	..	54.0	53.9	50.4	44.3	37.6	49.4	61.8	0.0	0.0	56.3	..	55.2	40.8
Ghana	..	38.8	23.8	22.6	21.0	28.2	22.7	27.3	25.0	25.2	23.3	..	39.1	25.8
Guinea	..	8.7	11.6	12.8	14.6	15.7	14.4	14.1	15.5	14.5	15.6	..	6.4	13.8
Guinea-Bissau	..	25.2	28.7	18.6	29.5	35.8	27.4	32.9	36.7	34.8	29.3	0.0	21.0	29.9
Kenya	0.0	0.0	4.6	9.5	12.7	14.9	15.0	15.2	14.5	14.7	16.0	0.0	0.0	11.7
Lesotho	..	55.3	52.8	54.0	58.0	58.6	..	..	..	..	46.1	57.9	57.3	54.1
Liberia	..	..	..	..	..	..	..	..	..	..	..	..	..	
Madagascar	..	46.2	43.4	44.7	42.2	44.0	55.1	53.3	53.9	57.3	55.6	32.4	40.5	49.6
Malawi	0.0	32.5	34.7	32.8	30.5	51.5	55.0	18.8	43.9	7.5	13.3	0.0	11.7	32.0
Mali	51.6	26.4	41.1	42.9	45.3	44.4	46.1	45.8	48.7	50.1	49.7	46.8	27.2	44.0
Mauritania	..	28.7	32.9	34.1	33.7	32.4	22.5	16.5	12.0	10.9	9.6	..	33.0	23.3
Mauritius	..	49.4	46.5	44.6	45.2	41.5	38.5	36.1	33.8	30.5	28.5	49.8	52.9	39.4
Mozambique	18.5	21.9	24.4	25.5	25.5	21.8	24.0	19.9	17.6	17.6	16.9	11.7	12.6	21.5
Namibia	..	26.5	38.0	31.9	29.4	26.0	27.8	29.1	28.2	29.2	30.1	47.3	33.5	29.6
Niger	..	39.5	39.0	35.4	41.3	41.5	43.2	46.7	47.7	52.4	48.8	36.9	34.7	43.5
Nigeria	..	..	..	..	..	..	..	..	11.6	7.9	9.3	..	..	9.6
Rwanda	..	27.5	30.9	31.0	27.8	35.8	38.5	29.2	31.8	23.9	17.3	54.7	45.0	29.4
São Tomé and Principe	..	27.9	26.5	29.0	28.2	30.8	24.1	25.5	21.0	18.6	31.0	..	0.0	26.3
Senegal	..	..	..	27.6	31.5	31.1	33.7	30.0	26.5	23.7		45.0	..	29.2
Seychelles	..	51.7	50.7	54.2	37.7	31.0	26.6	23.9	25.8	33.8	30.4	0.0	0.0	36.6
Sierra Leone	..	40.4	37.8	37.3	39.2	38.1	45.7	47.2	39.3	52.9	47.7	..	46.8	42.5
Somalia	..	..	..	..	..	..	..	..	..	..	..	..	..	
South Africa	3.6	4.9	3.7	2.7	2.9	3.0	3.2	3.6	3.4	2.9	3.4	4.8	4.8	3.4
Sudan	..	..	..	..	..	..	31.2	44.0	44.9	44.2	40.8	..	..	41.0
Swaziland	..	..	46.0	43.3	..	..	..	..	..	36.7	40.4	..	..	41.6
Tanzania	..	18.8	20.2	18.7	14.2	15.7	27.6	27.0	30.5	29.2	31.7	17.4	19.9	23.4
Togo	..	37.9	41.0	34.8	35.9	41.2	37.7	41.2	44.3	45.0	42.9	35.2	34.4	40.2
Uganda	..	49.2	54.6	50.3	50.8	53.0	48.6	50.6	51.4	47.7	44.1	58.1	57.3	50.1
Zambia	..	36.1	32.4	32.9	33.3	30.8	27.4	29.7	28.2	25.2	25.5	..	29.8	30.2
Zimbabwe	..	..	..	..	..	..	..	..	..	..	14.0	..	..	14.0
NORTH AFRICA	..	22.5	19.2	17.0	16.6	17.2	16.5	15.4	11.6	12.0	12.2	..	18.7	16.0
Algeria	..	16.6	19.9	15.6	15.6	16.3	12.2	10.2	7.9	9.7	8.5	4.6	7.9	13.3
Egypt, Arab Republic	..	13.3	11.4	10.6	10.7	11.6	12.6	13.0	12.6	13.1	13.8	..	14.9	12.3
Libya	..	..	..	..	..	..	..	..	..	..	..	..	..	
Morocco	45.2	52.4	34.8	32.4	30.6	30.2	30.8	28.8	14.9	13.6	13.1	39.0	41.1	28.2
Tunisia	..	16.9	16.6	15.3	14.9	15.6	16.0	13.5	12.4	11.4	14.7	14.4	15.3	14.7
ALL AFRICA	..	15.5	14.3	13.2	13.2	14.4	14.6	14.4	13.5	13.2	13.7	11.1	13.1	14.0

Note: 1999 data are preliminary (see page 2). Total revenue does not include grants. Nigeria's fiscal data are for consolidated government starting from 1992.

7-11. Indirect taxes

				Percentage of total revenue							Annual average		
	1980	1990	1991	1992	1993	1994	1995	1996	1997	1998	1999	75-84	85-89	90-MR
SUB-SAHARAN AFRICA	..	43.8	43.7	40.9	41.6	43.3	44.0	43.5	45.2	45.8	47.1	44.1	42.6	43.9
excluding South Africa		47.6	48.4	44.7	44.4	46.5	48.3	48.1	51.9	51.5	52.2	54.7	46.8	48.4
excl. S.Africa & Nigeria	..	57.4	58.3	53.8	53.4	55.5	57.6	57.4	58.6	59.0	59.1	54.7	56.7	57.0
Angola	..	23.1	34.5	32.7	31.9	25.5	27.8	6.6	9.0	17.1	7.3	..	19.5	21.5
Benin		92.9	72.8	74.8	72.0	66.1	59.6	63.7	69.2	65.7	69.5	67.4	94.7	70.6
Botswana		71.1	68.6	66.5	63.6	70.8	68.8	66.1	63.7	65.7	63.3	70.8	72.4	66.8
Burkina Faso	..	57.7	53.1	49.8	51.2	71.2	66.8	65.6	67.4	67.3	68.5	61.9	68.6	61.9
Burundi	53.8	62.5	63.4	60.1	59.6	64.4	63.3	50.4	60.7	61.8	64.9	50.3	58.7	61.1
Cameroon	61.6	52.0	46.0	46.5	52.7	59.5	61.0	58.9	79.1	77.8	73.5	40.4	39.9	60.7
Cape Verde	..	51.2	56.0	55.4	47.3	45.9	46.6	51.8	48.4	45.6	48.0	45.4	46.9	49.6
Central African Republic		73.8	68.1	69.4	70.4	66.4	75.1	74.8	74.8	75.2	68.1	..	..	71.6
Chad	..	77.2	53.2	53.6	54.0	67.5	49.7	49.7	55.0	54.9	49.7	71.0	71.5	56.5
Comoros	..	50.9	65.0	71.5	78.5	75.9	74.0	272.1	82.1	73.7	70.1	62.7	71.1	91.4
Congo, Democratic Rep. of	..	..	..	..	..	70.7	60.1	57.6	56.5	69.4	72.2	..	..	64.4
Congo, Republic of	..	44.9	35.6	46.1	45.7	30.7	41.7	35.7	20.1	43.5	25.5	13.8	36.2	37.0
Côte d'Ivoire	..	59.3	65.7	63.8	64.6	65.2	63.0	64.0	60.9	58.6	65.0	48.6	56.2	63.0
Djibouti	..	54.3	61.1	49.8	50.7	51.2	50.1	46.5	46.4	..	..	..	..	51.3
Equatorial Guinea	..	..	..	..	..	61.2	62.4	35.1	31.1	16.4	17.7	..	..	37.3
Eritrea	..	..	..	47.9	38.0	35.9	28.5	32.5	25.3	26.6	24.6	..	..	32.4
Ethiopia	..	39.3	45.2	43.2	46.0	54.1	43.4	42.6	43.8	40.4	37.9	46.7	38.8	43.6
Gabon	..	35.5	35.9	35.1	37.0	26.7	26.1	25.3	24.2	27.5	37.2	..	73.4	31.0
Gambia, The	..	80.8	80.7	76.5	74.0	70.7	70.6	71.2	68.3	68.1	65.1	75.9	77.8	72.6
Ghana	..	68.7	72.5	71.9	69.0	68.7	54.5	63.9	58.1	57.0	40.2	63.8	66.0	62.5
Guinea	..	90.2	89.9	85.9	86.2	84.1	84.6	82.6	83.5	83.7	82.5	..	92.1	85.3
Guinea-Bissau	..	34.0	42.4	29.0	41.3	48.5	46.8	47.0	43.8	53.0	49.8	78.1	46.5	43.6
Kenya	60.9	55.1	55.7	57.7	57.3	54.2	52.6	53.2	51.7	52.8	63.4	60.7	59.4	55.4
Lesotho	..	76.5	70.3	70.6	73.0	72.6	71.0	65.8	62.5	63.7	59.2	63.6	77.1	68.5
Liberia	..	..	..	..	..	..	..	..	..	..	..	..	..	..
Madagascar	..	66.2	63.3	73.9	66.2	72.4	82.9	79.3	77.8	78.3	75.3	60.6	65.2	73.6
Malawi	0.0	32.5	34.7	32.8	30.5	51.5	55.0	18.8	43.9	7.5	54.5	0.0	11.7	36.2
Mali	71.7	43.6	62.4	63.3	66.9	68.0	64.6	65.3	66.9	68.2	71.8	67.3	50.0	64.1
Mauritania	..	45.9	47.8	47.0	45.3	48.1	45.8	41.3	38.9	39.2	38.2	..	49.7	43.8
Mauritius	..	72.3	70.5	69.6	71.1	68.6	67.2	66.6	66.0	66.9	65.7	73.8	73.3	68.5
Mozambique	65.7	71.6	67.3	71.3	76.7	71.3	74.7	73.6	72.6	74.5	78.4	53.8	58.1	73.2
Namibia	..	51.6	62.1	59.7	60.1	58.8	61.6	60.5	56.7	56.7	57.2	69.9	53.4	58.5
Niger	..	53.6	54.1	47.9	56.1	59.1	60.9	61.4	64.9	67.8	70.0	65.3	54.9	59.6
Nigeria	..	..	..	..	..	..	..	..	17.0	12.6	16.6	..	..	15.4
Rwanda	..	61.7	66.0	64.3	67.5	73.5	81.4	65.8	69.5	67.1	70.1	86.9	83.5	68.7
São Tomé and Principe	..	48.2	52.9	59.3	63.4	64.5	45.1	46.0	38.6	35.7	65.2	..	38.7	51.9
Senegal	67.7	59.7	57.2	60.0	73.0	76.7	74.3	77.2	72.5	72.5	75.2	69.5	59.8	69.8
Seychelles	..	57.4	56.5	60.6	56.7	49.5	46.8	48.6	49.8	51.9	52.3	49.1	52.0	53.0
Sierra Leone	..	75.6	76.4	76.1	69.0	70.7	76.9	76.0	73.1	74.2	66.1	..	74.2	73.4
Somalia	..	..	..	..	..	..	..	..	..	..	..	..	..	..
South Africa	29.0	39.5	38.4	36.6	38.6	39.5	39.1	38.1	37.4	39.3	41.1	30.7	38.1	38.8
Sudan	..	52.5	51.7	..	..	..	50.3	56.4	64.5	60.7	56.7	66.7	63.0	56.1
Swaziland	..	..	58.5	56.4	..	..	..	..	..	54.6	60.0	..	..	57.4
Tanzania	..	44.6	49.0	46.8	35.0	37.8	49.5	48.2	55.2	51.9	55.1	59.6	61.1	47.3
Togo	..	50.4	56.8	45.0	50.7	51.0	50.5	58.0	63.3	66.9	65.7	43.4	46.1	55.8
Uganda	..	81.5	83.6	80.2	77.5	78.5	77.7	80.7	80.1	78.5	75.5	86.8	82.5	79.4
Zambia	..	75.1	70.9	62.5	68.0	64.4	62.7	62.1	62.6	61.5	61.0	..	63.9	65.1
Zimbabwe	0.0	41.4	46.1	44.0	39.1	40.3	42.7	44.6	44.2	44.6	42.7	9.2	42.6	43.0
NORTH AFRICA	..	64.9	59.5	59.2	58.7	57.7	61.2	60.3	60.0	58.8	61.4	..	58.7	60.2
Algeria	..	83.3	90.0	89.1	86.3	82.7	89.6	90.1	89.0	86.2	87.8	75.1	68.4	87.4
Egypt, Arab Republic	..	34.3	31.8	32.9	34.7	36.8	39.7	40.3	40.2	42.2	43.0	..	34.0	37.6
Libya	..	..	..	..	..	..	..	..	..	..	..	..	..	..
Morocco	88.8	100.0	66.3	64.4	64.2	65.1	66.3	61.7	60.5	54.4	57.5	73.4	91.8	66.0
Tunisia	..	58.8	61.1	60.2	58.2	49.1	50.2	47.4	49.9	50.5	61.7	42.3	52.0	54.7
ALL AFRICA	..	51.1	49.2	47.2	47.6	48.2	49.9	49.2	50.3	50.3	52.0	52.1	48.8	49.5

Note: 1999 data are preliminary (see page 2). Total revenue does not include grants. Nigeria's fiscal data are for consolidated government starting from 1992.

7-12. Nontax revenue, excluding grants

	Percentage of total revenue											Annual average		
	1980	1990	1991	1992	1993	1994	1995	1996	1997	1998	1999	75-84	85-89	90-MR
SUB-SAHARAN AFRICA	..	4.8	4.5	8.6	10.7	25.6	15.4	13.8	11.1	23.1	20.7	..	10.5	13.8
excluding South Africa		9.1	8.5	11.0	9.0	47.6	28.6	25.6	20.7	22.4	21.4	..	20.1	20.4
excl. S.Africa & Nigeria	..	0.6	-1.0	13.3	10.8	50.9	31.0	28.3	22.3	21.5	20.4	..	12.0	19.8
Angola	..	12.4	19.3	1.8	1.8	1.7	1.0	0.5	1.3	1.6	0.6	..	32.9	4.2
Benin	..	..	..	..	..	..	9.1	5.7	5.3	9.8	7.7	6.3	..	7.5
Botswana	..	17.8	20.3	24.8	28.2	20.6	24.2	28.3	32.1	30.3	31.7	11.1	15.3	25.8
Burkina Faso	..	6.0	15.3	13.4	11.5	..	..	..	2.1	..	..	18.4	12.3	9.7
Burundi	6.7	13.0	12.0	13.9	13.1	7.0	5.4	14.5	5.1	8.5	4.7	7.2	8.4	9.7
Cameroon	16.7	3.8	36.7	35.5	10.5	6.0	7.9	9.3	7.3	6.2	5.3	32.7	10.4	12.8
Cape Verde	..	20.8	16.1	16.6	15.9	16.4	18.9	15.7	10.5	14.4	22.4	25.1	23.1	16.8
Central African Republic	..	2.2	8.0	7.9	6.6	9.2	4.3	0.9	5.7	10.7	12.0	..	..	6.8
Chad	..	4.1	20.2	18.8	22.4	3.8	11.5	12.6	12.3	14.6	18.1	21.4	10.5	13.8
Comoros	..	..	..	..	..	..	..	..	6.7	11.0	12.8	..	..	10.2
Congo, Democratic Rep. of	..	..	..	..	..	..	..	..	..	..	..	..	..	..
Congo, Republic of	..	1.0	0.9	1.9	2.9	-3.2	0.6	0.8	0.5	0.2	0.7	68.5	34.0	0.6
Côte d'Ivoire	..	18.2	13.4	15.9	16.0	19.9	18.7	15.5	16.2	17.8	9.6	33.6	24.2	16.1
Djibouti	..	9.0	6.3	5.7	5.4	5.0	7.2	7.5	10.4		..	..	..	7.1
Equatorial Guinea	..	..	..	..	..	19.2	17.1	12.0	5.8	9.4	8.8	..	..	12.1
Eritrea	..	..	..	39.1	41.9	30.8	45.8	40.0	52.6	34.2	29.8	..	..	39.3
Ethiopia	..	31.3	24.1	26.7	30.9	21.9	34.4	32.2	27.6	33.7	32.4	24.7	32.4	29.5
Gabon	..	2.7	1.7	4.9	3.7	1.6	2.9	4.6	4.3	6.7	4.6	..	2.9	3.8
Gambia, The	..	3.9	4.9	8.6	9.5	11.1	9.8	8.9	10.6	9.7	12.0	9.5	7.7	8.9
Ghana	..	8.3	..	..	0.4	8.7	22.2	10.4	15.2	10.1	..	17.5	11.0	10.8
Guinea	..	7.7	5.9	7.3	6.8	7.1	6.3	6.5	6.8	6.6	6.3	..	6.3	6.7
Guinea-Bissau	..	58.6	51.7	64.2	51.5	44.8	45.3	45.2	47.9	31.8	46.4	0.0	27.8	48.7
Kenya	5.7	6.4	9.3	7.7	3.1	2.9	7.3	10.1	13.8	14.6	4.1	6.0	3.5	7.9
Lesotho	..	12.0	13.8	12.6	13.2	12.2	13.0	18.3	22.7	20.6	19.3	21.8	10.9	15.8
Liberia	..	..	..	..	..	..	..	..	..	..	..	..	..	..
Madagascar	..	5.7	4.1	3.5	4.6	6.1	2.4	2.2	3.4	2.7	3.4	14.0	2.4	3.8
Malawi	16.2	14.9	13.8	18.0	14.8	9.8	12.5	12.2	8.7	14.1	11.3	16.6	18.0	13.0
Mali	10.3	33.9	3.9	0.0	8.6	-19.1	-2.4	3.1	5.5	4.1	4.6	6.4	32.2	4.2
Mauritania	..	20.3	21.3	22.5	27.9	25.9	24.0	38.9	39.6	39.4	41.8	..	16.3	30.2
Mauritius	..	6.7	8.7	10.5	10.3	12.4	11.4	12.2	14.4	14.4	13.5	0.0	10.1	11.5
Mozambique	21.8	10.6	15.0	13.2	8.9	11.4	8.7	8.2	8.4	7.4	7.6	30.7	20.5	9.9
Namibia	..	12.3	13.1	13.9	9.9	12.2	11.0	10.7	9.1	9.5	10.8	10.8	12.2	11.3
Niger	..	22.8	17.1	18.3	10.2	10.9	8.5	13.3	14.0	10.0	5.2	12.7	19.2	13.0
Nigeria	..	..	..	..	..	..	..	..	73.0	78.9	67.8	..	..	73.2
Rwanda	..	13.0	12.9	12.3	7.7	0.6	6.0	8.1	5.4	5.2	5.0	-13.0	-8.8	7.6
São Tomé and Principe	..	40.1	36.9	34.0	27.7	24.7	40.8	32.9	32.0	25.4	16.3	..	51.5	31.1
Senegal	6.0	13.2	15.5	13.2	-15.7	-8.1	-3.2	2.9	0.1	2.3	5.5	12.2	2.3
Seychelles	..	7.7	9.0	13.5	8.6	14.7	9.0	11.7	12.3	11.3	12.0	28.3	29.6	11.0
Sierra Leone	..	0.0	0.0	0.0	9.3	7.9	7.2	7.6	13.8	8.6	8.1	..	0.0	6.2
Somalia	..	..	..	..	..	..	..	..	..	..	..	..	..	..
South Africa	84.4	6.6	4.6	5.9	12.5	13.6	13.9	13.6	12.6	9.4	9.8	20.3	7.5	10.2
Sudan	..	28.9	29.9	28.1	22.5	23.6	21.0	15.4	15.3	19.4	25.8	14.4	22.1	23.0
Swaziland	..	..	6.5	3.5	5.1	4.1	4.1	4.3	4.8	5.1	4.7	..	..	4.7
Tanzania	..	10.8	9.6	9.8	8.0	6.9	9.5	14.4	10.1	8.6	10.6	6.8	7.4	9.8
Togo	..	12.7	10.2	23.8	17.8	3.0	2.8	11.0	6.7	4.9	11.8	18.0	15.8	10.5
Uganda	..	8.5	6.3	7.1	8.0	6.9	7.7	6.1	5.9	5.9	6.6	6.6	9.7	6.9
Zambia	..	1.8	2.1	4.5	3.4	6.8	8.4	8.0	5.4	3.4	2.6	..	8.6	4.6
Zimbabwe	0.0	11.6	9.8	10.0	12.2	12.0	11.4	9.7	8.2	7.4	4.9	2.2	11.9	9.7
NORTH AFRICA	..	17.5	17.3	16.3	19.5	20.9	19.9	19.5	18.3	17.8	14.3	..	16.3	18.1
Algeria	..	3.2	1.7	2.0	2.8	2.9	1.5	1.8	2.2	2.4	4.2	10.8	12.2	2.5
Egypt, Arab Republic	..	24.2	35.4	31.2	35.0	34.3	33.5	32.0	31.4	29.3	28.0	..	26.7	31.4
Libya	..	..	..	..	..	..	..	..	..	..	..	..	..	..
Morocco	11.2	20.3	9.5	9.0	12.6	12.1	7.9	9.7	8.9	10.1	9.5	12.8	10.5	11.0
Tunisia	..	21.0	22.2	23.2	23.8	18.5	15.6	16.4	10.7	9.2	10.1	25.7	25.9	17.1
ALL AFRICA	..	9.2	8.9	11.4	13.6	24.0	16.9	15.7	13.6	21.3	18.5	..	12.3	15.3

Note: 1999 data are preliminary (see page 2). Total revenue does not include grants. Nigeria's fiscal data are for consolidated government starting from 1992.

7-13. Government expenditure: wages and salaries

	1980	1990	1991	1992	1993	1994	1995	1996	1997	1998	1999	75-84	85-89	90-MR
	Percentage of total expenditure and lending minus repayments											Annual average		
SUB-SAHARAN AFRICA	..	..	..	..	..	..	..	..	..	..	..	..	..	..
excluding South Africa	..	..	..	..	..	..	..	..	..	..	..	..	..	..
excl. S.Africa & Nigeria	..	..	..	..	..	..	..	..	..	..	..	..	..	..
Angola	..	45.8	52.7	24.4	21.5	8.7	13.0	14.3	16.9	24.7	8.8	..	45.5	23.1
Benin	..	36.3	37.1	33.0	35.5	27.8	24.3	26.4	26.5	28.5	26.4	..	38.5	30.2
Botswana	..	..	..	22.8	25.0	24.1	22.8	20.1	21.3	21.5	..	..	..	22.5
Burkina Faso	..	38.8	31.9	30.8	29.0	26.2	24.9	23.4	20.9	20.7	19.0	..	..	26.6
Burundi	49.1	24.6	26.1	23.0	23.7	30.0	28.0	28.7	32.2	29.7	27.6	49.0	27.7	27.4
Cameroon	31.4	39.2	38.4	42.0	43.7	31.4	29.1	25.8	26.9	27.7	26.9	24.8	29.0	33.1
Cape Verde	..	26.7	28.3	20.0	22.1	19.2	20.2	21.8	23.8	25.7	34.0	0.0	14.8	24.2
Central African Republic	..	..	..	..	..	24.2	22.5	41.8	32.6	24.2	23.3	..	..	28.1
Chad	..	19.4	25.1	21.1	27.1	28.0	28.6	20.3	19.4	20.6	19.0	..	15.0	22.9
Comoros	..	30.8	32.0	27.7	30.8	23.2	28.3	35.5	37.1	34.2	32.7	0.0	5.8	31.2
Congo, Democratic Rep. of	..	..	..	..	..	..	..	..	..	6.4	6.8	..	..	6.6
Congo, Republic of	..	30.3	43.8	47.5	48.8	36.3	32.1	24.8	20.4	20.8	21.2	0.0	33.3	32.6
Côte d'Ivoire	..	35.8	36.3	37.2	37.6	31.2	28.6	31.1	29.7	28.9	31.1	..	28.4	32.7
Djibouti	..	41.6	46.0	46.6	48.0	56.4	61.6	60.3	62.2	..	..	..	..	52.8
Equatorial Guinea	..	10.5	11.6	12.7	10.8	16.4	17.9	17.3	15.3	11.3	15.5	..	15.4	13.9
Eritrea	..	..	..	18.6	15.0	23.0	24.3	29.6	27.3	22.4	19.6	..	..	22.5
Ethiopia	..	27.5	33.8	28.0	28.3	24.8	22.6	20.6	21.7	23.4	20.1	25.1	22.5	25.1
Gabon	..	32.2	32.4	34.4	34.0	27.9	27.4	27.3	21.4	16.1	29.8	16.2	25.1	28.3
Gambia, The	..	20.7	21.0	19.5	21.1	23.3	21.5	20.3	24.0	27.5	27.0	..	17.6	22.6
Ghana	..	23.5	22.8	24.8	20.2	18.3	18.3	18.2	18.4	19.4	21.3	17.6	25.6	20.5
Guinea	..	17.1	20.0	23.1	24.2	25.1	23.9	27.1	23.3	23.3	25.0	..	14.3	23.2
Guinea-Bissau	..	9.4	10.3	8.0	8.1	7.5	9.2	9.5	6.8	18.8	15.9	10.4	13.1	10.3
Kenya	16.8	..	..	29.0	24.9	26.7	30.0	28.5	30.4	31.0	32.7	55.1	22.6	29.1
Lesotho	..	21.9	27.2	29.1	29.2	31.3	..	..	..	..	31.7	32.1	32.7	28.4
Liberia	..	..	..	..	..	..	..	..	..	..	..	..	..	..
Madagascar	..	23.1	26.5	19.7	18.0	17.0	18.1	17.7	20.3	21.6	25.5	32.5	27.0	20.8
Malawi	14.3	17.0	18.0	18.3	22.1	17.0	20.3	21.1	21.3	18.0	16.9	16.4	16.3	19.0
Mali	16.5	22.0	21.9	22.6	23.0	16.7	16.6	16.1	16.4	15.8	15.6	19.8	25.0	18.7
Mauritania	..	16.0	20.7	23.2	15.4	19.0	20.3	20.3	21.2	19.3	18.6	..	16.4	19.4
Mauritius	..	29.6	28.1	28.3	30.4	32.0	30.4	27.1	27.2	29.8	30.5	29.2	29.7	29.3
Mozambique	25.8	9.7	10.6	9.9	10.4	7.9	9.6	10.8	10.1	12.7	23.0	19.2	12.2	11.5
Namibia	..	..	..	..	..	..	..	47.3	46.7	46.4	45.4	..	..	46.5
Niger	..	24.0	34.9	37.4	38.3	29.4	36.1	25.5	26.1	22.9	22.5	18.8	21.2	29.7
Nigeria	..	..	..	..	..	10.8	12.2	13.7	8.2	4.7	11.2	..	..	10.1
Rwanda	..	27.8	23.9	22.1	24.1	25.0	19.5	20.1	26.2	24.6	27.0	..	..	24.0
São Tomé and Principe	..	12.9	11.6	10.1	7.8	7.0	4.3	6.0	8.4	11.3	10.8	..	12.0	9.0
Senegal	39.7	39.7	46.8	40.4	41.4	35.0	35.4	32.7	33.1	29.5	27.3	39.2	41.9	36.1
Seychelles	..	25.2	25.7	27.2	20.9	19.6	23.4	28.0	26.2	27.1	25.1	..	..	24.8
Sierra Leone	..	7.3	8.2	10.1	18.5	20.9	17.3	20.2	25.4	23.8	27.5	..	8.6	17.9
Somalia	..	..	..	..	..	..	..	..	..	..	..	..	..	..
South Africa	17.2	22.8	23.5	36.3	33.4	33.7	33.8	33.1	33.4	325.1	31.1	17.7	21.2	60.6
Sudan	..	..	..	..	17.1	..	12.0	22.6	31.5	33.5	35.2	..	..	25.3
Swaziland	..	..	..	30.9	37.5	37.4	37.0	36.7	36.5	36.4	37.4	..	..	36.2
Tanzania	..	21.3	20.0	19.3	19.0	21.7	22.8	26.2	31.2	28.6	24.4	20.9	21.3	23.4
Togo	..	28.6	36.5	39.0	41.4	36.1	35.6	34.0	35.8	31.4	33.3	27.1	25.7	35.2
Uganda	..	7.4	8.8	8.2	8.7	10.3	15.1	16.9	20.3	20.7	23.3	10.9	11.9	14.0
Zambia	..	23.3	21.3	25.4	17.7	16.1	20.2	20.5	25.1	19.0	19.4	..	..	20.8
Zimbabwe	103.4	34.2	32.3	30.0	29.5	29.1	29.2	32.0	35.5	35.5	34.3	75.2	29.0	32.2
NORTH AFRICA	..	..	..	..	..	..	..	..	..	..	..	..	..	..
Algeria	..	36.7	27.5	31.8	28.9	30.2	29.8	29.7	28.5	30.4	29.6	19.1	27.8	30.3
Egypt, Arab Republic	..	16.7	15.6	15.8	18.8	19.7	21.5	22.0	23.0	24.1	21.9	..	17.2	19.9
Libya	..	..	..	..	..	..	..	..	..	..	..	..	..	..
Morocco	48.6	37.1	39.4	38.1	36.0	37.0	38.4	38.6	39.4	39.1	38.8	64.6	142.6	38.2
Tunisia	..	..	34.2	35.7	35.5	30.1	30.3	29.1	34.1	35.1	39.2	..	..	33.7
ALL AFRICA	..	..	..	..	..	..	..	..	..	..	..	..	..	..

Note: 1999 data are preliminary (see page 2). Nigeria's fiscal data are for consolidated government starting from 1992.

7-14. Government expenditure: trends in real wages and salaries

					Index 1987=100						Annual average		
	1980	1990	1991	1992	1993	1994	1995	1996	1997	1998	75-84	85-89	90-MR
SUB-SAHARAN AFRICA	..	119	128	121	132	137	134	114	118	142	..	106	131
excluding South Africa	..	120	129	115	126	136	122	106	106	130	..	106	123
excl. S.Africa & Nigeria	..	113	122	114	117	116	126	93	88	117	..	107	111
Angola	..	127	106	62	19	39	43	72	78	59	..	89	67
Benin	..	..	..	..	..	..	..	..	..	..	..	..	..
Botswana	..	..	..	..	..	..	..	..	..	..	..	..	..
Burkina Faso	..	132	121	117	119	106	104	103	108	114	..	103	115
Burundi	..	116	124	125	126	117	102	96	82	83	99	101	106
Cameroon	..	101	106	105	101	67	50	47	51	60	70	98	75
Cape Verde	..	104	125	121	149	158	170	174	169	175	..	98	160
Central African Republic	..	97	106	103	100	90	76	71	74	75	..	102	87
Chad	..	164	154	162	195	212	206	153	144	141	..	112	170
Comoros	..	..	..	..	..	..	..	..	..	..	..	..	..
Congo, Democratic Rep. of	..	186	310	88	108	44	56	19	94	98	..	110	111
Congo, Republic of	..	92	138	149	144	97	76	65	57	55	..	94	92
Côte d'Ivoire	..	94	91	87	80	63	62	67	67	67	0	99	74
Djibouti	..	..	..	..	..	..	..	..	..	..	..	..	..
Equatorial Guinea	..	108	121	126	131	113	118	176	220	266	..	103	169
Eritrea	..	..	..	..	..	..	..	..	..	..	..	..	..
Ethiopia	..	123	114	68	77	91	86	95	105	124	106	103	101
Gabon	..	114	113	130	148	111	116	114	118	120	86	101	121
Gambia, The	..	..	..	..	..	..	..	..	..	..	..	..	..
Ghana	..	101	110	162	173	181	164	159	153	163	..	82	154
Guinea	..	219	234	227	247	246	248	269	262	263	..	165	249
Guinea-Bissau	..	104	134	108	95	85	93	105	99	106	..	104	106
Kenya	..	..	..	..	..	..	..	..	..	..	..	100	..
Lesotho	..	..	..	..	..	..	..	..	..	..	..	..	..
Liberia	..	..	..	..	..	..	..	..	..	..	..	..	..
Madagascar	..	89	97	87	87	80	75	74	88	106	..	98	90
Malawi	..	91	96	116	129	159	144	121	148	147	92	91	128
Mali	..	90	98	102	102	89	85	84	95	98	..	93	95
Mauritania	..	99	99	99	97	97	95	97	100	105	..	102	100
Mauritius	..	119	119	126	135	148	149	151	155	167	..	107	144
Mozambique	..	134	156	152	179	151	147	149	182	249	240	126	206
Namibia	..	153	198	209	208	205	218	252	258	268	74	95	225
Niger	..	..	..	..	..	..	..	..	..	..	..	..	..
Nigeria	..	213	209	180	289	224	180	185	192	212	..	131	237
Rwanda	..	107	101	102	104	26	43	56	76	71	..	97	77
São Tomé and Principe	..	84	70	69	57	78	65	91	154	165	..	84	102
Senegal	..	109	119	119	115	98	95	96	93	93	115	104	103
Seychelles	..	..	..	..	..	..	..	..	..	..	..	..	..
Sierra Leone	..	110	113	124	234	232	191	209	169	228	409	142	186
Somalia	..	..	..	..	..	..	..	..	..	..	..	..	..
South Africa	..	..	..	..	..	..	..	..	..	..	..	..	..
Sudan	..	..	..	..	..	..	..	..	..	..	..	..	..
Swaziland	..	..	..	..	..	..	..	..	..	..	..	..	..
Tanzania	..	133	117	119	146	148	163	178	188	183	136	110	154
Togo	..	111	121	114	111	96	96	93	93	97	98	100	103
Uganda	..	120	179	250	255	322	488	560	705	751	..	133	463
Zambia	..	..	..	..	..	..	..	..	..	..	..	..	..
Zimbabwe	..	138	139	116	106	108	113	126	152	147	95	104	130
NORTH AFRICA	..	116	122	120	120	124	127	133	143	150	..	108	129
Algeria	..	103	116	130	125	121	115	116	120	125	..	99	120
Egypt, Arab Republic	..	98	100	93	103	106	110	115	118	126	..	102	103
Libya	..	..	..	..	..	..	..	..	..	..	..	..	..
Morocco	36	125	133	132	128	132	135	142	155	162	55	105	141
Tunisia	..	111	117	125	130	125	130	139	158	167	84	101	138
ALL AFRICA	..	126	128	119	132	131	120	120	125	141	..	103	129

Note: 1999 data are preliminary (see page 2). Nigeria's fiscal data are for consolidated government starting from 1992.

7-15. Government expenditure: other goods and services

	Percentage of total expenditure and lending minus repayments											*Annual average*		
	1980	1990	1991	1992	1993	1994	1995	1996	1997	1998	1999	75-84	85-89	90-MR
SUB-SAHARAN AFRICA	..	-3.0	-3.6	-10.9	-7.6	25.1	23.7	24.4	25.9	27.0	26.0	-8.0	4.8	12.7
excluding South Africa	..	19.4	18.8	17.6	21.2	25.1	21.8	20.7	23.3	21.9	21.6	..	20.8	21.1
excl. S.Africa & Nigeria	..	19.4	18.8	17.6	21.2	20.0	22.6	21.9	23.3	23.5	22.2	11.5	20.8	21.0
Angola	..	20.0	17.1	10.9	43.1	41.0	53.3	48.5	55.7	50.4	43.6	..	26.4	38.4
Benin	..	7.1	8.2	7.6	8.4	6.3	5.2	7.7	6.9	7.4	7.1	..	7.4	7.2
Botswana	..	..	..	..	36.0	41.0	42.3	42.3	37.3	39.5	39.8	..	..	39.7
Burkina Faso	..	7.1	7.7	8.6	10.7	12.0	10.8	9.8	8.7	9.9	8.7	..	..	9.4
Burundi	28.0	17.2	15.6	12.4	20.4	21.3	24.0	20.9	33.2	27.4	31.9	22.6	16.9	22.4
Cameroon	22.9	17.5	12.5	10.5	10.7	7.5	15.8	16.0	16.4	14.5	16.3	20.3	13.7	13.8
Cape Verde	..	4.3	3.7	2.5	1.8	1.6	1.5	1.4	3.3	1.8	7.6	23.4	8.8	2.9
Central African Republic	..	..	..	..	..	13.9	10.0	12.6	15.7	10.3	11.4	..	..	12.3
Chad	..	21.0	34.4	26.4	26.3	14.4	11.7	22.1	19.2	22.3	25.2	..	18.5	22.3
Comoros	..	20.0	22.2	19.7	26.4	20.3	22.4	17.8	14.3	14.8	23.6	0.0	4.1	20.1
Congo, Democratic Rep. of	..	..	..	..	..	..	..	..	..	33.7	35.6	..	..	34.7
Congo, Republic of	..	8.3	10.7	10.4	9.1	8.1	7.7	7.2	24.4	36.1	19.1	24.5	10.3	14.1
Côte d'Ivoire	..	25.8	24.7	23.4	23.5	23.7	24.0	25.8	25.2	22.9	28.0	..	31.8	24.7
Djibouti	..	26.7	31.5	29.2	29.2	24.2	22.4	19.9	16.2	..	..	..	..	24.9
Equatorial Guinea	..	9.7	10.1	14.6	10.1	20.3	25.2	23.8	30.6	16.0	18.1	..	18.8	17.9
Eritrea	..	..	..	71.0	44.1	49.8	43.2	41.4	32.0	41.9	35.8	..	..	44.9
Ethiopia	..	34.9	29.1	22.1	25.7	25.0	25.3	23.1	25.5	33.4	34.4	30.5	32.0	27.8
Gabon	..	23.5	21.0	20.5	19.4	19.2	17.3	21.1	24.5	36.8	21.9	13.8	20.4	22.5
Gambia, The	..	19.0	21.1	23.5	25.5	25.1	20.1	21.1	17.9	16.0	18.5	..	19.5	20.8
Ghana	..	12.9	13.1	10.0	12.6	10.5	8.1	7.2	6.9	9.6	-5.4	34.5	15.4	8.5
Guinea	..	18.9	18.7	15.6	13.9	13.2	11.3	11.7	11.4	11.5	11.5	..	24.7	13.8
Guinea-Bissau	..	14.4	13.1	10.7	9.4	12.6	11.9	10.0	8.4	18.5	18.5	0.0	13.8	12.7
Kenya	27.6	..	..	19.4	17.1	17.6	21.6	26.8	27.5	30.1	27.8	-7.4	30.5	23.5
Lesotho	..	17.0	19.0	23.7	7.9	26.4	..	..	..	..	0.0	19.9	23.6	15.7
Liberia	..	..	..	..	..	..	..	..	..	..	..	..	..	..
Madagascar	..	11.8	10.3	15.9	11.5	12.9	10.0	7.2	15.8	9.5	11.6	18.9	15.0	11.7
Malawi	0.0	45.3	50.5	49.1	45.3	47.5	38.7	36.2	44.9	38.4	29.0	0.0	0.0	42.5
Mali	13.0	2.1	8.3	9.8	10.2	10.6	12.2	11.7	13.0	12.4	13.2	15.8	4.7	10.4
Mauritania	..	12.3	17.7	18.9	14.4	17.6	20.1	20.0	21.8	20.8	22.5	..	8.8	18.6
Mauritius	..	8.3	9.5	10.1	9.7	9.5	9.1	8.4	8.4	9.5	16.4	7.2	8.1	9.9
Mozambique	44.2	30.7	29.0	31.5	29.3	33.8	22.4	28.3	29.0	31.0	20.1	36.0	34.2	28.5
Namibia	..	..	..	..	..	..	..	21.4	20.8	20.0	19.9	..	..	20.5
Niger	..	17.4	12.5	21.3	15.3	18.8	17.9	21.3	22.9	21.5	25.1	13.8	14.9	19.4
Nigeria	..	..	..	..	..	48.1	17.7	15.1	23.1	13.4	18.4	..	..	22.6
Rwanda	..	23.7	28.0	30.9	24.8	26.4	25.0	26.3	19.4	21.7	21.0	..	..	24.7
São Tomé and Principe	..	3.5	3.2	4.7	3.7	5.0	4.6	5.0	5.0	5.5	5.5	..	16.6	4.6
Senegal	22.9	15.2	9.8	21.1	11.9	11.8	11.4	11.0	10.8	13.0	14.6	19.6	15.5	13.0
Seychelles	..	30.2	30.9	31.5	25.1	22.3	18.1	19.5	20.4	20.4	18.9	..	..	23.7
Sierra Leone	..	44.3	38.0	38.8	31.2	35.4	51.6	35.9	44.1	19.3	23.6	..	35.5	36.2
Somalia	..	..	..	..	..	..	..	..	..	..	..	..	..	..
South Africa	..	..	..	..	..	25.1	25.7	28.5	28.9	26.0	31.1	..	..	27.6
Sudan	..	..	..	..	37.4	..	47.5	36.0	48.3	38.4	32.9	..	..	40.1
Swaziland	..	..	..	15.3	26.5	25.7	26.0	24.3	23.6	20.5	24.9	..	..	23.3
Tanzania	..	28.6	40.2	36.2	30.7	30.4	28.9	24.2	23.7	21.1	26.0	30.5	31.5	29.0
Togo	..	20.7	19.2	17.1	19.1	16.3	18.2	21.7	20.2	22.4	25.1	20.7	21.3	20.0
Uganda	..	43.9	31.9	31.8	26.6	29.7	33.9	33.1	33.8	32.2	31.0	35.0	45.2	32.8
Zambia	..	15.4	19.1	24.5	20.3	22.3	22.5	21.2	18.3	20.3	15.4	..	..	19.9
Zimbabwe	-103.4	16.3	15.1	16.9	19.4	18.1	16.9	16.5	14.1	13.2	14.6	-69.3	16.7	16.1
NORTH AFRICA	..	9.4	9.2	9.3	10.5	10.8	11.1	11.3	11.6	11.8	11.4	..	17.3	10.6
Algeria	..	2.7	3.1	2.3	4.0	3.6	4.7	4.6	5.1	5.4	5.5	2.3	2.3	4.1
Egypt, Arab Republic	..	14.1	12.4	13.0	15.3	15.5	16.1	15.9	16.3	16.3	14.2	..	15.1	14.9
Libya	..	..	..	..	..	..	..	..	..	..	..	..	..	..
Morocco	103.8	10.4	11.3	11.7	10.9	14.9	13.8	14.7	15.5	16.0	16.4	56.8	43.1	13.6
Tunisia	..	..	11.0	10.9	10.7	6.5	6.1	6.9	5.9	5.7	8.3	..	..	8.0
ALL AFRICA	..	1.3	1.2	-3.3	-0.8	20.0	19.3	19.8	21.0	-68.9	21.0	..	8.6	3.0

Note: 1999 data are preliminary (see page 2). Nigeria's fiscal data are for consolidated government starting from 1992.

7-16. Government expenditure: interest payments

	Percentage of total expenditure and lending minus repayments											Annual average		
	1980	1990	1991	1992	1993	1994	1995	1996	1997	1998	1999	75-84	85-89	90-MR
SUB-SAHARAN AFRICA	..	6.3	7.3	6.7	7.2	14.2	10.1	9.2	7.6	17.8	16.6	4.4	5.7	10.3
excluding South Africa	..	13.6	15.6	14.2	15.3	28.0	19.4	17.4	14.5	15.8	16.2	..	12.7	17.0
excl. S.Africa & Nigeria	..	13.6	15.6	14.2	15.3	26.7	17.5	16.5	14.8	15.3	15.1	11.0	12.7	16.4
Angola	..	9.9	15.0	8.9	15.5	384.9	12.7	19.2	10.2	16.7	8.9	..	5.4	50.2
Benin	..	15.3	13.8	17.5	15.0	15.9	12.6	12.4	9.0	7.6	7.2	..	15.6	12.6
Botswana	..	..	..	..	..	..	..	..	-0.2	-1.1	0.0	..	..	-0.4
Burkina Faso	..	5.7	6.5	6.9	6.9	6.9	6.6	4.2	3.6	3.7	3.2	..	..	5.4
Burundi	2.0	7.1	6.1	6.4	5.0	6.0	6.9	6.7	8.9	10.4	11.9	5.3	8.9	7.5
Cameroon	2.0	9.6	17.6	23.4	24.1	36.5	39.5	41.8	37.8	32.0	27.6	2.9	5.7	29.0
Cape Verde	..	5.0	3.8	2.6	2.5	1.9	6.2	7.6	9.6	9.9	4.5	0.0	3.1	5.4
Central African Republic	..	..	..	..	..	10.8	11.1	17.2	9.6	7.6	7.8	..	..	10.7
Chad	..	1.8	4.1	3.8	5.8	6.1	5.6	5.6	5.3	5.5	4.8	..	1.0	4.8
Comoros	..	4.2	3.7	2.9	3.7	3.1	3.0	3.3	3.8	4.6	4.8	0.0	0.8	3.7
Congo, Democratic Rep. of	..	..	..	..	..	..	..	..	..	43.5	34.6	..	..	39.1
Congo, Republic of	..	29.7	22.5	21.6	20.1	33.0	43.0	36.5	32.2	34.0	35.3	0.0	13.0	30.8
Côte d'Ivoire	..	30.3	35.1	34.2	30.6	31.8	28.3	25.7	22.1	19.9	21.8	..	22.8	28.0
Djibouti	..	1.4	..	1.1	0.8	0.8	1.5	1.6	1.4	..	..	..	..	1.2
Equatorial Guinea	..	11.6	12.7	16.7	13.7	26.0	24.0	15.6	8.7	5.5	10.3	..	17.8	14.5
Eritrea	..	..	..	0.0	0.1	0.2	0.6	1.3	1.9	1.8	2.2	..	..	1.0
Ethiopia	..	4.3	5.4	7.3	10.2	13.5	10.0	9.0	9.2	7.4	6.4	3.4	5.1	8.3
Gabon	..	23.2	22.6	22.5	24.4	26.4	30.9	25.6	20.1	15.9	26.8	6.6	14.1	23.8
Gambia, The	..	14.9	13.8	12.9	14.8	14.8	13.9	14.2	19.1	23.0	22.2	..	13.4	16.4
Ghana	..	7.8	9.2	8.9	12.0	14.2	13.9	17.2	21.7	17.9	21.2	11.4	8.3	14.4
Guinea	..	10.4	10.3	8.5	7.2	9.0	8.1	8.1	9.1	8.3	9.6	..	11.6	8.9
Guinea-Bissau	..	9.5	11.7	9.7	14.3	15.2	21.9	19.7	11.9	27.4	20.3	1.1	7.5	16.2
Kenya	10.1	26.5	27.5	26.1	35.2	32.4	25.4	22.3	20.2	18.7	24.6	13.4	17.3	25.9
Lesotho	..	..	..	..	..	4.2	3.8	3.5	3.6	4.2	5.9	..	..	4.2
Liberia	..	..	..	..	..	..	..	..	..	..	..	..	..	..
Madagascar	..	8.9	12.3	17.1	19.4	27.3	29.0	26.3	17.5	14.5	13.0	5.6	9.9	18.5
Malawi	9.1	14.1	11.0	9.3	11.4	11.5	19.2	22.0	19.0	13.5	12.7	12.9	18.6	14.4
Mali	4.1	9.1	6.3	7.3	6.9	9.0	6.1	4.8	4.1	3.1	3.4	4.8	6.6	6.0
Mauritania	..	6.6	9.2	12.2	11.1	10.4	13.0	13.4	13.0	14.0	13.9	..	8.2	11.7
Mauritius	..	17.7	16.4	13.7	11.9	12.3	12.9	12.8	14.2	17.3	16.2	20.4	18.3	14.5
Mozambique	0.0	6.7	4.8	7.9	8.6	3.6	6.6	7.0	5.7	4.5	2.5	0.1	3.8	5.8
Namibia	..	..	..	..	..	..	..	4.2	5.4	6.8	7.6	..	..	6.0
Niger	..	10.1	11.5	9.8	10.2	12.3	16.0	12.8	9.7	8.9	8.4	11.1	13.6	11.0
Nigeria	..	..	..	..	..	33.9	28.9	21.8	12.8	18.5	21.6	..	..	22.9
Rwanda	..	5.1	7.7	7.8	9.1	27.9	11.3	7.2	6.2	4.9	5.0	..	..	9.2
São Tomé and Principe	..	13.7	17.5	15.5	16.8	14.9	15.6	14.4	16.1	20.8	16.2	..	22.4	16.1
Senegal	7.5	12.6	12.9	9.3	10.9	16.8	14.5	11.2	12.1	6.3	7.0	9.4	15.7	11.4
Seychelles	..	16.2	15.7	15.2	12.3	12.0	15.2	15.4	15.7	12.9	17.4	..	..	14.8
Sierra Leone	..	28.7	30.0	26.9	18.9	14.0	10.5	12.5	16.3	23.9	26.4	..	23.7	20.8
Somalia	..	..	..	..	..	..	..	..	..	..	..	..	..	..
South Africa	..	..	..	..	..	..	..	..	..	20.2	17.2	..	..	18.7
Sudan	..	..	..	..	..	..	..	..	..	8.6	8.9	..	..	8.7
Swaziland	..	..	..	..	..	..	..	..	..	0.7	2.9	..	..	1.8
Tanzania	..	13.2	13.2	12.2	12.9	14.4	18.4	18.9	17.4	15.2	10.6	8.0	12.3	14.6
Togo	..	11.3	12.6	12.9	15.8	21.9	15.4	13.0	12.7	10.2	11.7	20.9	14.8	13.8
Uganda	..	4.9	8.9	15.5	9.7	7.8	5.9	6.0	5.6	6.1	5.1	14.4	7.8	7.6
Zambia	10.9	23.7	24.4	27.5	41.8	36.5	27.7	17.4	16.4	11.8	10.2	12.2	28.6	23.8
Zimbabwe	27.7	14.1	13.9	15.6	17.9	20.4	24.2	24.5	19.1	27.8	26.0	24.8	13.5	20.4
NORTH AFRICA	..	11.6	13.1	14.5	17.1	19.1	18.2	18.6	17.6	16.5	12.2	..	26.6	15.8
Algeria	..	6.4	6.0	7.0	6.4	8.2	9.9	11.9	12.7	12.6	..	2.5	4.2	9.0
Egypt, Arab Republic	..	10.0	15.5	18.7	25.5	29.3	25.4	25.1	23.1	21.1	19.1	..	9.1	21.3
Libya	..	..	..	..	..	..	..	..	..	..	..	..	..	..
Morocco	56.9	22.6	21.1	19.6	19.8	20.2	20.5	19.5	18.1	17.2	17.2	38.5	90.1	19.6
Tunisia	..	..	9.2	10.7	11.5	11.0	11.7	12.2	10.6	9.6	12.2	..	..	11.0
ALL AFRICA	..	8.2	9.5	9.6	10.9	15.9	13.0	12.4	11.1	17.4	15.1	..	13.1	12.3

Note: 1999 data are preliminary (see page 2). Nigeria's fiscal data are for consolidated government starting from 1992.

7-17. Government expenditure: subsidies and current transfers

| | 1980 | *Percentage of total expenditure and lending minus repayments* | | | | | | | | | | *Annual average* | | |
		1990	1991	1992	1993	1994	1995	1996	1997	1998	1999	75-84	85-89	90-MR
SUB-SAHARAN AFRICA	..	1.4	1.2	1.2	1.2	3.2	2.8	2.5	2.6	2.7	2.2	1.5	1.5	2.1
excluding South Africa		3.1	2.6	2.4	2.6	1.9	2.1	1.9	2.3	2.3	2.1	..	3.4	2.3
excl. S.Africa & Nigeria	..	3.1	2.6	2.4	2.6	2.3	2.5	2.3	2.7	2.8	2.5	3.6	3.4	2.6
Angola	..	6.3	5.0	8.1	9.1	0.0	0.0	0.0	0.0	0.0	..	..	5.3	3.2
Benin	..	..	..	..	..	..	..	..	..	..	..	..	..	..
Botswana	..	..	..	..	..	..	..	..	0.0	0.0	0.0	..	..	0.0
Burkina Faso	..	..	..	..	..	..	..	..	..	..	..	..	..	..
Burundi	10.9	6.7	6.0	8.0	5.7	7.5	6.7	5.9	7.6	7.8	7.4	10.1	5.8	6.9
Cameroon	11.1	0.0	0.0	0.0	0.0	0.0	0.0	0.0	4.3	4.8	5.4	8.6	0.0	1.5
Cape Verde	..	0.6	0.5	0.2	0.1	0.0	0.1	0.0	0.0	0.0	0.0	1.2	0.9	0.1
Central African Republic	..	..	..	..	..	..	..	..	..	..	..	..	..	..
Chad	..	0.0	0.0	0.0	0.0	0.0	0.0	0.0	0.0	0.0	0.0	..	0.0	0.0
Comoros	..	0.0	0.0	0.0	0.0	0.0	0.0	0.0	0.0	0.0	0.0	0.0	0.0	0.0
Congo, Democratic Rep. of	..	..	..	..	..	..	..	..	..	2.3	2.3	..	..	2.3
Congo, Republic of	..	1.9	0.0	0.0	0.0	0.0	0.0	0.0	0.0	0.0	0.0	0.0	2.4	0.2
Côte d'Ivoire	..	3.7	0.2	0.0	3.1	4.0	4.3	3.2	4.0	3.9	4.3	..	5.5	3.1
Djibouti	..	..	..	0.6	0.6	0.3	0.4	0.5	1.3	..	..	..	..	0.6
Equatorial Guinea	..	6.0	4.9	4.1	3.5	4.4	4.4	4.0	4.1	9.0	7.0	..	5.3	5.2
Eritrea	..	..	..	0.0	0.0	0.0	0.0	0.0	0.0	0.0	0.0	..	..	0.0
Ethiopia	..	1.7	1.3	1.4	0.1	1.2	1.8	1.7	1.3	0.0	0.0	3.5	1.4	1.1
Gabon	..	0.0	0.0	0.0	0.0	0.0	0.0	0.0	0.0	0.0	0.0	0.0	0.0	0.0
Gambia, The	..	3.0	0.0	0.5	0.6	0.1	0.0	0.0	0.0	0.0	0.0	..	10.4	0.4
Ghana	..	0.0	0.0	0.0	0.0	0.0	7.9	5.6	4.9	9.3	0.0	..	..	2.8
Guinea	..	3.8	3.5	4.0	3.6	4.3	6.2	6.0	7.4	6.8	8.1	..	6.8	5.4
Guinea-Bissau	..	0.0	0.0	0.0	0.0	0.0	0.0	0.0	..	..	..	0.0	0.0	0.0
Kenya	0.1	1.6	0.8	0.0	0.0	0.0	0.0	0.0	0.0	0.0	0.0	0.2	1.4	0.2
Lesotho	..	4.0	4.9	4.9	..	..	0.0	0.0	0.0	0.0	0.0	..	3.8	1.7
Liberia	..	..	..	..	..	..	..	..	..	..	..	..	..	..
Madagascar	..	..	..	..	..	..	..	..	..	..	..	0.0	..	..
Malawi	0.0	0.0	0.0	0.0	0.0	0.0	0.0	0.0	0.0	0.0	0.0	0.0	0.0	0.0
Mali	6.0	1.8	2.3	2.7	2.7	1.6	1.3	1.4	1.2	5.7	5.6	3.7	1.6	2.6
Mauritania	..	..	..	..	..	..	..	..	..	..	..	..	..	..
Mauritius	..	19.1	20.2	21.0	21.3	21.8	22.7	23.3	24.8	10.0	13.6	19.9	18.3	19.8
Mozambique	1.4	3.6	2.2	2.2	1.2	0.9	1.3	1.2	1.0	1.0	0.5	7.1	14.3	1.5
Namibia	..	..	..	..	..	..	..	3.8	2.7	2.3	2.4	..	..	2.8
Niger	..	7.4	6.7	6.9	12.9	6.6	4.4	6.0	7.6	5.3	4.9	9.4	6.6	6.9
Nigeria	..	..	..	..	..	0.0	0.0	0.0	0.0	0.0	0.0	..	..	0.0
Rwanda	..	17.2	8.3	8.1	5.0	3.8	4.8	3.3	5.7	7.9	9.0	..	..	7.3
São Tomé and Principe	..	..	..	..	..	..	..	..	..	..	..	..	..	..
Senegal	13.9	10.5	8.9	8.2	13.9	11.4	9.9	7.9	9.6	7.5	9.2	12.1	10.1	9.7
Seychelles	..	7.4	5.8	5.4	4.6	4.6	9.7	-3.7	1.3	2.1	1.5	..	..	3.9
Sierra Leone	..	1.9	2.6	2.4	4.3	5.9	4.6	9.6	3.0	7.0	10.3	..	0.5	5.2
Somalia	..	..	..	..	..	..	..	..	..	..	..	..	..	..
South Africa	..	..	..	..	..	4.5	3.5	3.2	3.0	3.0	2.3	..	..	3.3
Sudan	..	..	..	..	..	..	..	..	..	5.1	3.3	..	..	4.2
Swaziland	..	..	..	..	..	..	..	..	..	0.0	0.0	..	..	0.0
Tanzania	..	0.0	0.0	0.0	0.0	0.0	0.0	0.0	0.0	0.0	0.0	0.0	0.0	0.0
Togo	..	4.4	5.1	5.8	4.7	9.0	6.7	5.1	6.9	6.4	8.7	2.3	0.7	6.3
Uganda	..	0.0	0.0	0.0	0.0	0.0	0.0	0.0	0.0	0.0	0.0	0.0	0.0	0.0
Zambia	13.7	10.9	11.6	2.5	0.6	0.0	0.0	0.0	0.2	0.9	0.8	9.9	11.9	2.7
Zimbabwe	29.3	5.9	7.7	8.3	4.9	1.4	0.5	0.3	0.1	0.0	0.0	23.2	8.5	2.9
NORTH AFRICA	..	5.5	7.1	10.6	7.8	6.1	5.7	5.4	4.9	4.7	4.1	..	6.7	6.2
Algeria	..	0.4	1.0	10.4	9.1	7.8	6.2	4.4	2.1	2.2	2.0	..	0.0	4.6
Egypt, Arab Republic	..	11.4	12.2	14.2	7.7	5.8	6.6	6.8	6.2	5.9	5.2	..	10.2	8.2
Libya	..	..	..	..	..	..	..	..	..	..	..	..	..	..
Morocco	12.5	1.7	1.9	2.3	2.6	4.1	3.3	3.7	6.4	6.0	4.4	13.3	14.5	3.6
Tunisia	..	..	14.6	13.3	13.9	6.0	5.9	6.2	5.6	4.8	5.2	..	..	8.4
ALL AFRICA	..	2.8	3.4	4.7	3.7	4.2	3.8	3.5	3.4	3.3	2.8	..	3.3	3.6

Note: 1999 data are preliminary (see page 2). Nigeria's fiscal data are for consolidated government starting from 1992.

7-18. Government expenditure: capital and net lending

		Percentage of total expenditure and lending minus repayments										Annual average		
	1980	1990	1991	1992	1993	1994	1995	1996	1997	1998	1999	75-84	85-89	90-MR
SUB-SAHARAN AFRICA	..	18.1	16.6	16.6	18.7	19.6	19.2	19.8	20.1	21.5	22.5	20.6	18.1	19.3
excluding South Africa	..	26.3	25.1	24.5	25.9	29.3	28.4	29.9	31.1	32.7	29.5	..	27.5	28.3
excl. S.Africa & Nigeria	..	26.3	25.1	24.5	25.9	26.7	25.7	25.9	26.1	26.8	25.8	29.4	27.5	25.9
Angola	..	18.0	10.1	6.4	10.7	5.7	12.1	8.1	8.1	3.3	6.1	..	17.3	8.9
Benin	..	26.9	28.1	21.1	26.8	32.9	36.6	32.9	35.4	34.2	34.9	..	27.0	31.0
Botswana	..	50.5	47.3	42.4	39.5	32.0	31.8	33.4	34.4	32.8	31.9	43.3	45.1	37.6
Burkina Faso	..	27.8	44.5	43.4	34.4	40.8	45.9	51.3	56.5	54.6	58.6	..	..	45.8
Burundi	113.6	41.9	43.7	47.9	43.4	32.6	30.3	35.8	18.0	24.7	21.2	119.7	61.9	34.0
Cameroon	32.6	26.2	23.2	15.5	13.8	17.3	7.1	5.9	9.3	16.3	19.1	40.3	43.0	15.4
Cape Verde	..	37.2	41.3	59.4	58.7	60.9	52.4	52.8	44.7	43.7	49.5	67.8	54.3	50.1
Central African Republic	..	..	..	..	..	46.0	50.2	21.9	37.5	54.2	50.9	..	..	43.4
Chad	..	54.9	32.3	45.1	38.0	47.5	50.4	49.1	53.8	51.1	50.8	..	63.1	47.3
Comoros	..	16.4	14.2	32.3	15.6	32.1	21.4	21.9	24.1	35.1	28.1	0.0	60.0	24.1
Congo, Democratic Rep. of	..	..	..	..	..	..	..	..	..	12.7	18.4	..	..	15.6
Congo, Republic of	..	7.9	2.3	2.1	4.6	7.6	9.1	24.4	9.1	11.1	18.9	61.7	27.2	9.7
Côte d'Ivoire	..	4.4	3.7	5.2	5.3	9.3	13.1	13.2	17.6	21.2	14.8	..	11.4	10.8
Djibouti	..	27.5	22.5	18.3	16.4	12.9	9.4	11.3	12.1	13.9	..	..	..	16.0
Equatorial Guinea	..	62.2	60.7	51.6	49.5	32.9	18.0	9.6	20.9	36.4	47.2	..	34.0	38.9
Eritrea	..	..	..	12.4	29.2	22.6	20.5	30.1	44.1	37.5	45.2	..	..	30.2
Ethiopia	..	27.3	25.0	22.6	34.2	38.0	37.7	45.2	42.9	37.5	30.4	27.2	32.9	34.1
Gabon	..	16.1	19.6	18.9	17.7	22.1	20.9	22.8	31.7	29.2	8.9	58.1	35.4	20.8
Gambia, The	..	34.0	34.4	34.6	29.9	27.4	34.8	35.5	29.3	22.2	20.7	36.5	31.2	30.3
Ghana	17.8	41.0	41.1	41.9	38.3	42.7	46.1	44.8	42.9	39.6	30.9	14.5	38.0	40.9
Guinea	..	49.8	45.6	47.0	49.4	46.3	48.5	45.1	46.2	46.7	44.2	..	42.5	46.9
Guinea-Bissau	..	63.4	61.5	66.8	64.4	59.1	49.6	53.0	66.9	24.4	34.4	32.0	62.2	54.4
Kenya	29.5	22.1	19.6	19.0	18.2	20.0	20.4	17.3	17.2	17.5	12.2	26.0	22.0	18.3
Lesotho	..	45.0	38.4	35.4	34.7	31.7	32.3	37.8	41.1	32.8	24.0	37.9	24.1	35.3
Liberia	..	..	..	..	..	..	..	..	..	..	..	..	..	..
Madagascar	..	42.7	36.4	37.6	38.2	33.3	34.8	39.7	37.5	43.8	42.6	30.4	34.4	38.7
Malawi	48.8	22.4	20.5	23.3	21.1	24.0	21.8	20.7	19.7	30.0	37.5	38.0	27.5	24.1
Mali	53.0	61.7	57.7	53.3	50.4	50.4	53.5	56.2	51.4	50.6	47.8	47.9	59.1	53.3
Mauritania	..	27.2	22.9	24.3	41.3	32.9	27.6	27.8	25.8	29.2	29.3	..	26.7	28.8
Mauritius	..	18.3	18.7	19.6	19.2	17.0	18.0	22.1	18.4	26.0	26.8	13.9	19.4	20.4
Mozambique	44.0	51.9	52.4	50.3	49.3	51.1	57.3	55.1	55.8	47.6	49.7	40.1	35.6	52.0
Namibia	..	..	..	..	..	..	..	13.1	13.3	11.8	12.4	..	..	12.7
Niger	..	39.0	30.4	21.9	21.5	28.6	27.0	29.6	30.6	32.2	30.0	46.9	40.8	29.1
Nigeria	..	..	..	..	..	41.1	41.3	49.4	55.8	63.4	48.8	..	..	50.0
Rwanda	..	30.1	30.2	30.3	32.1	16.6	39.4	41.3	42.1	36.0	32.0	..	..	33.0
São Tomé and Principe	..	56.0	55.4	57.4	52.3	57.9	69.1	60.7	60.3	51.8	61.1	..	43.9	58.2
Senegal	17.6	12.2	15.0	24.1	20.3	23.6	26.5	35.6	32.9	42.2	40.6	16.3	13.5	27.3
Seychelles	..	23.3	22.5	19.7	22.8	22.8	22.6	18.1	20.1	24.0	25.7	..	..	22.2
Sierra Leone	..	17.8	21.2	21.8	25.2	21.8	13.4	19.6	11.3	24.6	11.2	..	24.0	18.8
Somalia	..	..	..	..	..	..	..	..	..	..	..	..	..	..
South Africa	25.8	10.9	9.0	9.6	12.3	9.6	9.2	8.4	7.8	8.5	14.3	23.6	10.3	10.0
Sudan	..	12.0	13.6	16.2	28.7	..	13.4	5.7	7.8	9.1	14.1	16.9	14.0	13.4
Swaziland	..	..	25.6	23.5	20.2	18.5	17.9	16.5	15.4	15.6	17.7	..	..	19.0
Tanzania	..	17.7	10.9	16.7	21.2	20.8	17.6	20.4	17.3	25.8	27.4	26.2	22.1	19.6
Togo	..	25.7	17.8	16.0	8.8	9.1	15.5	13.2	11.1	19.4	12.0	..	26.0	14.9
Uganda	..	43.8	50.4	44.5	55.0	52.2	45.1	44.1	40.2	41.0	40.5	39.7	35.1	45.7
Zambia	10.5	18.9	15.5	12.1	10.7	12.5	17.5	32.0	30.1	39.4	45.4	11.6	2.2	23.4
Zimbabwe	43.1	18.2	20.2	18.0	16.8	17.6	14.5	12.7	12.3	6.7	14.2	42.7	15.7	15.1
NORTH AFRICA	..	33.1	29.4	27.5	25.6	23.4	23.0	22.0	22.0	22.5	25.0	..	53.6	25.4
Algeria	..	30.8	27.3	28.2	31.3	31.0	29.4	26.6	25.2	24.8	19.9	56.9	46.5	27.4
Egypt, Arab Republic	..	38.3	34.8	29.0	20.9	18.1	18.2	18.7	20.0	21.3	29.6	..	39.0	24.9
Libya	..	..	..	..	..	..	..	..	..	..	..	..	..	..
Morocco	100.0	26.5	23.9	24.9	26.3	23.8	24.0	22.4	20.6	21.8	23.1	100.0	100.0	23.7
Tunisia	..	..	26.6	24.8	25.6	21.1	20.9	20.7	22.4	21.9	25.9	..	..	23.3
ALL AFRICA	..	23.3	21.4	20.7	21.3	21.0	20.6	20.5	20.7	21.9	23.3	..	30.8	21.5

Note: 1999 data are preliminary (see page 2). Nigeria's fiscal data are for consolidated government starting from 1992.

7-19. Government expenditure: trends in real defense spending

	Index 1980=100											Annual average		
	1980	*1990*	*1991*	*1992*	*1993*	*1994*	*1995*	*1996*	*1997*	*1998*	*1999*	*75-84*	*85-89*	*90-MR*
SUB-SAHARAN AFRICA	100.0	109.8	167.8	152.1	148.8	124.0	149.7	163.3	154.5	153.0	144.7	110.2	188.4	146.8
excluding South Africa	100.0	109.8	167.8	152.1	148.8	125.7	149.7	163.3	154.5	153.0	144.7	110.2	185.8	146.9
excl. S.Africa & Nigeria	100.0	109.8	167.8	152.1	148.8	127.4	149.7	163.3	154.5	153.0	144.7	110.2	188.4	147.1
Angola	..	..	..	..	..	..	..	..	..	..	..	..	..	..
Benin														
Botswana	..	..	..	..	..	..	..	..	..	..	..	..	..	..
Burkina Faso	100.0	188.2	..	..	..	339.2	..	..	..	..	..	100.0	140.4	263.7
Burundi	..	..	..	..	..	..	..	..	..	..	..	..	..	..
Cameroon	100.0	..	..	..	..	124.0	..	..	..	..	..	100.0	190.6	124.0
Cape Verde	..	..	..	..	..	..	..	..	..	..	..	..	..	..
Central African Republic	..	..	..	..	..	..	..	..	..	..	..	..	..	..
Chad	..	..	..	..	..	..	..	..	..	..	..	..	..	..
Comoros	..	..	..	..	..	..	..	..	..	..	..	..	..	..
Congo, Democratic Rep. of	..	..	..	..	..	..	..	..	..	..	..	..	..	..
Congo, Republic of														
Côte d'Ivoire	100.0	91.6	..	..	..	62.7	..	..	..	..	..	100.0	83.3	77.2
Djibouti	..	..	..	..	..	..	..	..	..	..	..	..	..	..
Equatorial Guinea	..	..	..	..	..	..	..	..	..	..	..	..	..	..
Eritrea	..	..	..	..	..	..	..	..	..	..	..	..	..	..
Ethiopia	..	..	..	..	..	..	..	..	..	..	..	..	..	..
Gabon	100.0	116.9	..	..	..	140.4	..	..	..	..	..	100.0	162.2	128.7
Gambia, The	..	..	..	..	..	..	..	..	..	..	..	..	..	..
Ghana	..	..	..	..	..	..	..	..	..	..	..	..	..	..
Guinea	..	..	..	..	..	..	..	..	..	..	..	..	..	..
Guinea-Bissau	..	..	..	..	..	..	..	..	..	..	..	..	..	..
Kenya	100.0	294.5	230.1	172.2	143.8	119.8	137.6	160.6	152.7	144.0	144.7	110.2	194.5	170.0
Lesotho	..	..	..	..	..	..	..	..	..	..	..	..	..	..
Liberia	..	..	..	..	..	..	..	..	..	..	..	..	..	..
Madagascar	..	..	..	..	..	..	..	..	..	..	..	..	..	..
Malawi	100.0	23.4	..	..	..	21.3	..	..	..	..	..	100.0	59.2	22.3
Mali	..	..	..	..	..	..	..	..	..	..	..	..	..	..
Mauritania	..	..	..	..	..	..	..	..	..	..	..	..	..	..
Mauritius	..	..	..	..	..	..	..	..	..	..	..	..	..	..
Mozambique	..	..	..	..	..	..	..	..	..	..	..	..	..	..
Namibia	..	..	..	..	..	..	..	..	..	..	..	..	..	..
Niger	..	..	..	..	..	..	..	..	..	..	..	..	..	..
Nigeria	100.0	21.0	..	..	..	16.5	..	..	..	..	..	100.0	40.1	18.8
Rwanda	100.0	94.2	..	..	..	234.0	..	..	..	..	..	100.0	98.2	164.1
São Tomé and Principe	..	..	..	..	..	..	..	..	..	..	..	..	..	..
Senegal	100.0	109.8	..	..	..	102.8	..	..	..	..	..	100.0	93.6	106.3
Seychelles	..	..	..	..	..	..	..	..	..	..	..	..	..	..
Sierra Leone	100.0	25.6	..	..	..	172.6	..	..	..	..	..	100.0	133.0	99.1
Somalia	..	..	..	..	..	..	..	..	..	..	..	..	..	..
South Africa	100.0	128.4	..	..	..	94.1	..	..	..	..	..	100.0	143.0	111.3
Sudan	..	..	..	..	..	..	..	..	..	..	..	..	..	..
Swaziland	100.0	109.9	105.4	132.0	153.8	159.6	161.9	166.0	156.4	162.0	..	100.0	58.9	145.2
Tanzania	..	..	..	..	..	..	..	..	..	..	..	..	..	..
Togo	100.0	162.3	..	..	..	127.4	..	..	..	..	..	100.0	124.1	144.9
Uganda	..	..	..	..	..	..	..	..	..	..	..	..	..	..
Zambia	..	..	..	..	..	..	..	..	..	..	..	..	..	..
Zimbabwe	..	..	..	..	..	..	..	..	..	..	..	..	..	..
NORTH AFRICA	100.0	86.0	..	..	..	95.5	..	..	..	..	..	100.0	111.1	90.7
Algeria	100.0	148.0	..	..	..	273.1	..	..	..	..	..	100.0	111.1	210.6
Egypt, Arab Republic	..	..	..	..	..	..	..	..	..	..	..	..	..	..
Libya	..	..	..	..	..	..	..	..	..	..	..	..	..	..
Morocco	100.0	86.0	..	..	..	95.5	..	..	..	..	..	100.0	82.3	90.7
Tunisia	100.0	62.1	..	..	..	60.4	..	..	..	..	..	100.0	176.9	61.3
ALL AFRICA	100.0	109.8	167.8	152.1	148.8	121.9	149.7	163.3	154.5	153.0	144.7	110.2	187.1	146.6

Note: Nigeria's fiscal data are for federal level only. Nigeria's fiscal data are for consolidated government starting from 1992.

7-20. Government expenditure: real per capita education spending

	Constant 1995 U.S. dollars											Annual average		
	1980	1990	1991	1992	1993	1994	1995	1996	1997	1998	1999	75-84	85-89	90-MR
SUB-SAHARAN AFRICA	..	..	..	..	..	..	..	..	..	..	..	..	..	..
excluding South Africa	..	..	..	..	..	..	..	..	..	..	..	..	..	..
excl. S.Africa & Nigeria	..	..	..	..	..	..	..	..	..	..	..	..	..	..
Angola	..	..	..	..	..	..	..	..	..	..	..	..	..	..
Benin	..	..	..	..	..	..	..	0.1	0.1	0.1	0.1	0.1	..	0.1
Botswana	..	2.0	2.2	2.4	2.5	2.5	2.7	3.2	..	..	..	..	1.7	2.5
Burkina Faso	0.0	0.1	0.1	0.1	0.1	..	0.1	0.1	0.1	0.1	..	0.0	0.1	0.1
Burundi	..	..	..	0.0	0.0	0.0	0.0	0.0	0.0	0.0	0.0	..	..	0.0
Cameroon	0.1	0.3	0.2	0.2	0.2	0.2	0.1	..	..	..	..	0.2	0.3	0.2
Cape Verde	..	..	..	..	..	..	..	..	..	..	..	..	..	..
Central African Republic	..	..	..	..	..	..	..	..	..	..	..	0.2	..	..
Chad	..	..	..	..	..	..	..	..	..	..	..	..	..	..
Comoros	..	..	..	..	..	..	..	0.2	0.2	0.1	0.1	..	..	0.2
Congo, Democratic Rep. of	0.1	..	..	0.0	0.0	0.0	0.0	..	..	..	..	0.1	..	0.0
Congo, Republic of	..	0.0	0.0	0.0	0.0	0.0	0.0	0.0	0.0	0.0	0.0	0.0	0.0	0.0
Côte d'Ivoire	..	0.6	0.5	0.5	0.5	0.4	0.3	0.3	0.4	0.4	0.4	..	0.6	0.4
Djibouti	..	..	..	..	..	..	..	..	..	..	..	..	..	..
Equatorial Guinea	..	..	..	..	..	..	..	..	..	..	..	..	..	..
Eritrea	..	..	..	0.0	0.0	0.0	0.0	0.0	0.1	0.1	0.0	..	..	0.1
Ethiopia	..	0.0	0.0	0.0	0.0	0.0	0.0	0.0	0.0	0.0	0.0	0.0	0.0	0.0
Gabon	..	..	..	..	..	..	..	..	..	..	..	..	..	..
Gambia, The	..	..	..	0.1	0.1	0.1	0.1	0.1	0.1	0.1	0.1	..	..	0.1
Ghana	..	..	..	..	..	0.1	0.1	0.2	0.1	0.2	..	..	..	0.1
Guinea	..	..	..	..	..	0.1	0.1	0.2	0.1	0.1	0.1	..	..	0.1
Guinea-Bissau	..	0.0	0.0	0.0	0.0	0.0	0.0	0.0	0.0	0.0	0.0	0.0	0.0	0.0
Kenya	0.2	0.2	0.2	0.2	0.2	0.2	0.2	0.2	0.2	0.2	0.2	0.2	0.2	0.2
Lesotho	..	0.2	0.3	0.3	0.3	0.4	..	..	..	..	..	..	0.2	0.3
Liberia	..	..	..	..	..	..	..	..	..	..	..	..	..	..
Madagascar	..	0.1	0.1	0.1	0.1	0.0	0.0	0.0	..	..	..	..	0.1	0.1
Malawi	..	..	..	..	0.1	..	0.1	0.1	0.1	0.1	0.1	..	..	0.1
Mali	..	..	..	..	..	..	0.1	0.1	0.1	0.1	0.1	0.1	0.1	0.1
Mauritania	..	..	..	..	..	..	..	0.0	0.2	0.2	0.2	..	..	0.2
Mauritius	..	1.0	1.1	1.1	1.2	1.3	1.4	1.5	0.8	0.0	..	..	0.8	1.0
Mozambique	..	0.0	0.0	0.0	0.0	0.0	0.0	0.0	0.0	0.0	0.0	0.0	0.0	0.0
Namibia	..	..	..	..	..	..	..	..	..	..	..	..	..	..
Niger	0.1	..	..	..	..	..	..	..	..	..	..	0.1	..	..
Nigeria	..	..	..	..	..	..	..	..	..	..	..	0.1	0.0	..
Rwanda	..	..	..	..	..	..	..	..	..	..	..	..	..	..
São Tomé and Principe	..	..	..	..	..	..	..	..	0.2	0.2	..	..	..	0.2
Senegal	..	..	..	..	0.2	0.2	0.2	0.2	0.2	0.2	0.2	..	..	0.2
Seychelles	..	..	..	..	5.5	5.5	4.3	..	..	..	..	..	..	5.1
Sierra Leone	..	0.0	..	..	..	..	..	..	..	..	..	0.1	..	0.0
Somalia	..	..	..	..	..	..	..	..	..	..	..	..	..	..
South Africa	..	..	..	..	..	..	..	..	..	..	..	..	..	..
Sudan	0.0	..	..	..	..	..	..	..	..	..	..	0.0	..	..
Swaziland	0.7	..	1.1	1.0	1.0	1.1	1.0	0.9	0.9	0.9	..	0.6	0.7	1.0
Tanzania	..	..	..	..	..	..	..	..	..	..	..	..	..	..
Togo	..	..	..	..	..	..	..	..	..	..	..	0.2	0.2	..
Uganda	..	..	..	..	..	0.1	0.1	0.1	0.1	0.1	0.1	..	..	0.1
Zambia	..	0.1	0.1	0.1	0.1	0.1	0.1	0.1	0.1	0.1	0.1	..	..	0.1
Zimbabwe	..	..	..	..	..	..	..	..	..	0.8	0.6	..	..	0.7
NORTH AFRICA	0.5	0.5	0.5	0.5	0.6	0.6	0.6	..	..	..	..	0.5	0.5	0.6
Algeria	..	..	..	..	..	..	..	..	..	..	..	..	..	..
Egypt, Arab Republic	0.3	0.4	0.4	0.4	0.4	0.5	0.5	..	..	..	..	0.3	0.4	0.4
Libya	..	..	..	..	..	..	..	..	..	..	..	..	..	..
Morocco	0.6	0.7	0.7	0.7	0.7	0.7	0.7	..	..	..	..	0.6	0.6	0.7
Tunisia	0.9	1.1	1.0	1.1	1.1	1.1	1.2	1.3	..	..	..	0.9	0.9	1.1
ALL AFRICA	..	..	..	..	..	..	..	..	..	..	..	..	..	..

Note: Nigeria's fiscal data are for consolidated government starting from 1992.

Figure 7-1. Government deficit as percentage of GDP, 1992-99*

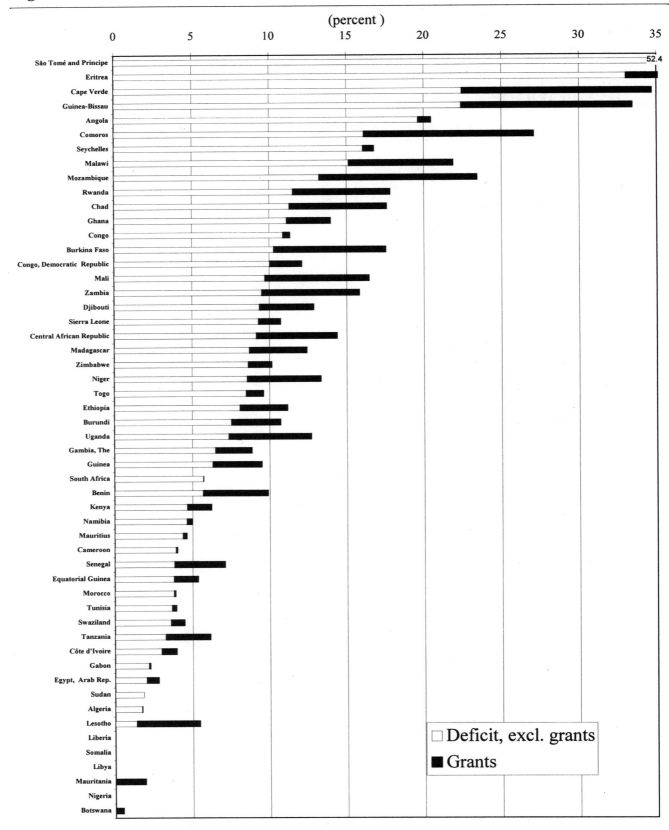

* Or most recent year available.

Technical notes

Tables

Table 7-1. Government deficit/surplus (including grants). Overall surplus/deficit is the difference between total revenue plus grants (as defined in GFS line A-I) and total expenditures and lending minus repayments (as defined in GFS line C-I). It represents the net financing requirement of the consolidated government. This indicator is shown as a percentage of current GDP in national currency (World Bank country desks).

Table 7-2. Government deficit/surplus (excluding grants). This is calculated as above, except that capital grants are excluded from receipts (as defined in *GFS* line A-II, less line C-I). It is a measure of the ability of a government to fund its activities from its own resources. Because some budgetary grants may be tied to certain expenditures that would not otherwise be incurred, excluding grants may overstate the deficit or understate the surplus if no account is taken of the expenditures dependent on these grants. This indicator is shown as a percentage of current GDP in national currency (World Bank country desks).

Table 7-3. Government primary deficit/surplus (−/+). The primary deficit or surplus is the government deficit or surplus including grants (as presented in Table 7-1) excluding interest expenditures on both domestic and foreign debt (Table 7-5). In countries with large government interest payments, this ratio may provide a more reliable indicator for monitoring fiscal stabilization efforts. This indicator is shown as a percentage of current GDP in national currency (World Bank country desks).

Table 7-4. Government expenditure and lending minus repayments. Total expenditure and lending minus repayments (as defined in *GFS* line C-I) represents the government's total outlays for current or capital purposes. Expenditure includes all nonrepayable payments by the government. Lending minus repayments comprises government transactions in debt and equity claims upon others, acquired for purposes of public policy rather than for managing government liquidity or earning a return. It consists of gross lending and acquisition of financial equity minus repayments of past government lending and government sales of equities. (This definition differs from the concept of lending minus repayments adopted in the SNA, which is gross government lending minus repayments of past government lending minus net government borrowing.) In determining a government's deficit or surplus, lending minus repayments is grouped with expenditures rather than with financing. This indicator is shown as a percentage of current GDP in national currency (World Bank country desks).

Table 7-5. Government interest payments. Government interest payments (as defined in *GFS* line C2) include interest on all borrowings, both domestic and foreign, but exclude commission charges paid for assistance in placement of debt (which would be classified as expenditure for the payment of goods and services). This indicator is shown as a percentage of current GDP in national currency (World Bank country desks).

Table 7-6. Government revenue (excluding grants). Government revenue less grants (as defined in *GFS* line A-II) refers to current revenues (tax and nontax) and capital revenues, such as proceeds from the sale of real assets, including land. They do not include grant receipts from other governments or international organizations. This indicator is shown as a percentage of current GDP in national currency (World Bank country desks).

Table 7-7. Grants to government. These are unrequited, nonrepayable, noncompulsory government receipts from other governments or international institutions (as defined in *GFS* line A-II). Grants of goods and services in kind are excluded. This indicator is shown as a percentage of current GDP in national currency (World Bank country desks).

Table 7-8. Foreign financing. Includes all government financing transactions except grants (as defined in *GFS* line D-III) with nonresident individuals, enterprises, governments, international organizations, and other entities. It may be affected by trading in outstanding government securities between residents and nonresidents. The data also reflect changes, resulting from transactions but not revaluations, in government holdings of foreign exchange, deposits in nonresident financial institutions, and securities issued by nonresident entities held by government for liquidity purposes (reserves). This indicator is shown as a percentage of current GDP in national currency (World Bank country desks).

Table 7-9. Taxes on income and profits. These taxes (as defined in *GFS* line A1) are levied on the actual or presumptive net income of individuals and profits of enterprises. Also included are taxes levied on capital gains that are realized on land sales, securities, and other assets. This indicator is shown as a percentage of total revenue (as defined in *GFS* line A-II) (World Bank country desks).

Table 7-10. Taxes on international trade and transactions. Include import duties, export duties, profits of export or import monopolies remitted to government, and monopoly profits of monetary authorities made in foreign exchange transactions as well as taxes levied on the sale of foreign exchange (as defined in *GFS* line A6). This indicator is shown as a percentage of total revenue (as defined in *GFS* line A-II) (World Bank country desks).

Table 7-11. Indirect taxes. These are sales and excise taxes and duties (as defined in GFS line A-IV less A1). This indicator is shown as a percentage of total revenue (as defined in GFS line A-II) (World Bank country desks).

Table 7-12. Nontax revenue, excluding grants. This is all nonrepayable government receipts, other than compulsory unrequited receipts (taxes) and revenue from capital sales or government grants, plus all fines and penalties other than for noncompliance with taxes (as defined in *GFS* line A-V). For some mineral-exporting countries in Africa, this category is quite large, since royalties on the extraction of minerals, such as petroleum in Egypt and Nigeria and bauxite in Guinea, make up significant portions of total government revenues. This indicator is shown as a percentage of total revenue (as defined in *GFS* line A-II) (World Bank country desks).

Table 7-13. Government expenditure: wages and salaries. Are payments in cash, but not in kind, to employees in return for services, before withholding taxes and employee contributions to social security and pension funds are deducted (as defined in GFS line C1.1). Included are basic wages and salaries; pay for overtime, weekends, and nights; cost of living allowances; local allowances and expatriation allowances; and similar compensation. Reimbursement to employees for expenses incurred as part of their employment are excluded. This indicator is shown as a percentage of total expenditure and lending minus repayments (as defined in GFS line C-I) (World Bank country desks).

Table 7-14. Government expenditure: trends in real wages and salaries. Includes expenditure on wages and salaries as discussed above (as defined in *GFS* line C1.1), deflated by the CPI. For most countries the trend is shown in index numbers beginning with 100 in 1987 (World Bank country desks).

Table 7-15. Government expenditure: other goods and services. Includes expenditures for all goods and services (except fixed capital assets and wages and salaries) bought on the market, goods and services to be used to produce fixed capital assets, strategic or emergency stocks, stocks held by market regulatory organizations, and land and intangible assets. This category encompasses purchases of materials, office supplies, fuel and lighting, travel services, and payment of rent, as well as payments in kind to certain civil servants (as defined in *GFS* line C1.3). This indicator is presented as a percentage of total expenditure and lending minus repayments (as defined in *GFS* lines C-I) (World Bank country desks).

Table 7-16. Government expenditure: interest payments. Are payments for the use of all borrowed money, excluding commission charges paid for assistance in placing debt, which would be classified as expenditures for payment of other goods and services (as defined in GFS line C2). This indicator is presented as a percentage of total expenditure and lending minus repayments (as defined in GFS lines C-I) (World Bank country desks).

Table 7-17. Government expenditure: subsidies and current transfers. Are all unrequited, nonrepayable government payments for current purposes (as defined in *GFS* line C3). Transfers for capital purposes (that is, to permit the recipient to acquire capital assets) and transfers in kind are excluded. This indicator is presented as a percentage of total expenditure and lending minus repayments (as defined in *GFS* line C-I) (World Bank country desks).

Table 7-18. Government expenditure: capital and net lending. Represents payments for acquiring land, buildings, and other nonfinancial assets to be used for more than one year in the process of production, including transfers for capital assets as well as net lending (as defined in GFS lines C-IV plus C-V). This indicator is presented as a percentage of total expenditure and lending minus repayments (as defined in GFS line C-I) (World Bank country desks).

Table 7-19. Government expenditure: trends in real defense spending. Real defense spending has been calculated by deflating defense spending in current prices national currency (IMF, as defined in GFS line B2) by the national GDP deflator (Table 3-1). The results are presented in the form of 1980 base indexes.

Table 7-20. Government expenditure: real per capita education spending. Presents education spending (IMF, as defined in *GFS* line B4) deflated by the national GDP deflator (Table 3-1) and divided by total population (Table 2-1). The result is converted into 1995 U.S. dollars by using the 1995 local currency/ US dollar conversion factor (Table 3-6).

Figure

The following indicators have been used to derive the figure in this chapter.

Figure 7-1. Government deficit/surplus (Tables 7-1 and 7-2).

Methodology used for regional aggregations and period averages in chapter 7

Table	Aggregations[a] (6)	(7)	Period averages[b] (1)
7-1	x		x
7-2	x		x
7-3	x		x
7-4	x		x
7-5	x		x
7-6	x		x
7-7	x		x
7-8	x		x
7-9	x		x
7-10	x		x
7-11	x		x
7-12	x		x
7-13	x		x
7-14		x	x
7-15	x		x
7-16	x		x
7-17	x		x
7-18	x		x
7-19		x	x
7-20	x		x

Note: Regional aggregations are shown in the rows for Sub-Saharan Africa, North Africa, and All Africa. Period averages are shown in the last three columns. This table shows only the methodologies used in this chapter. For aggregation purposes, all data used in this chapter were converted to U.S. dollars, using the conversion factors shown in Table 3-6.

a. Regional aggregations: (1) simple total; (2) simple total of the first indicator divided by the simple total of the second indicator (same country coverage); (3) simple total of the gap-filled indicator; (4) simple total of the gap-filled main indicator divided by the simple total of the gap-filled secondary indicator; (5) simple total of the first gap-filled main indicator less the simple total of the second gap-filled main indicator, all divided by the simple total of the secondary indicator; (6) weighted total (by population); (7) median; (8) no aggregation; (9) simple arithmetic mean.

b. Period averages: (i) arithmetic mean (using the same series as shown in the table i.e., ratio if the rest of the table is shown as ratio, level if the rest of the table is shown as level, growth rate if the rest is shown as growth rate); (2) least-squares growth rate (using main indicator); (3) least-squares growth rate (using main indicator in constant terms, with the rest of the table in current terms).

8

Agriculture

Agriculture is one of Africa's important sectors. African agriculture has two major components: food production and export commodities. Food production, including meat, is the livelihood for most Africans. Export crops provide many African countries with their main source of foreign exchange and thus the capacity to import, invest, and develop. The information in this chapter provides a basis for assessing recent trends in producer prices, aggregate agricultural production and trade, cereal imports, and food aid in Africa.

The data in this chapter are estimates based on a variety of sources whose quality and reliability vary from country to country and year to year. Furthermore, production and export data are probably underestimated for two reasons. It is difficult to estimate production levels of staple food crops, especially roots and tubers, when much of the output is consumed directly by farmers, rather than marketed. Moreover, parallel market activity, including trade, may not be fully accounted for.

8-1. Nominal producer prices

	Category	*Local currency per kilogram*										
		1980	*1986*	*1987*	*1988*	*1989*	*1990*	*1991*	*1992*	*1993*	*1994*	*1995*
ALGERIA												
Wheat (hard)	F1	1.2	2.2	2.2	2.7	3.7	4.6	5.4	10.3	10.3	10.3	19.0
Citrus (oranges)	F2	..	..	..	..	..	..	..	..	..	..	..
Dates	F3	4.5	11.3	11.5	..	..	..	..	..	..	..	..
Barley	NT1	0.8	1.4	1.7	1.7	2.3	2.3	2.3	4.7	4.7	6.0	14.0
Potatoes	NT2	1.3	2.6	2.8	2.7	3.0	3.3	3.3	6.5	6.5	6.5	10.0
ANGOLA												
Coffee	X1	..	67.0	67.0	67.0	67.0	135.0	158.0	..	..	..	..
Maize	F1	..	10.0	10.0	11.5	11.5	11.5	100.0	..	..	..	..
Millet	F2	4.0	10.0	10.0	10.0	10.0	10.0	100.0	..	..	..	..
Wheat	F3	4.5	17.5	17.5	17.5	17.5	17.5	200.0	..	..	..	..
Cassava	NT1	..	5.0	5.0	7.7	7.7	7.7	150.0	..	..	..	..
Sweet potatoes	NT2	2.5	7.5	7.5	14.0	14.0	14.0	200.0	..	..	..	..
BENIN												
Cotton (seed cotton)	X1	65.0	110.0	100.0	105.0	95.0	100.0	100.0	100.0	94.8	..	..
Palm kernels	X2	35.0	20.0	20.0	30.0	30.0	30.0	35.0	35.0	..	..	..
Maize	F1	40.0	65.0	68.0	64.0	55.0	85.0	58.0	62.0	53.0	..	..
Sorghum	F2	46.0	65.0	72.0	67.0	60.0	60.0	63.0	65.0	55.0	..	..
Cassava	NT1	30.0	15.0	20.0	16.0	16.0	16.0	17.0	17.5	18.2	..	..
Yams	NT2	32.0	50.0	58.0	49.0	49.0	49.0	49.0	50.0	52.0	..	..
BOTSWANA												
Groundnuts (in shell)	X1	0.2	0.7	0.7	0.7	0.7	0.7	1.1	1.0	1.4	..	..
Sorghum	F1	0.1	0.3	0.3	0.3	0.3	0.3	0.3	0.4	0.4	..	..
Maize	F2	0.1	0.3	0.3	0.3	0.3	0.3	0.3	0.3	0.4	..	..
BURKINA FASO												
Cotton (seed cotton)	X1	55.0	97.2	89.7	94.4	94.6	95.0	..	..	..	..	..
Groundnuts (in shell)	X2	54.0	50.0	60.0	55.0	60.0	60.0	..	..	..	..	..
Sesame seed	X3	70.0	80.0	55.0	65.0	85.0	80.0	..	..	..	..	..
Sorghum	F1	45.0	40.0	45.0	40.0	45.0	60.0	..	..	..	..	..
Millet	F2	45.0	40.0	45.0	40.0	45.0	60.0	..	..	..	..	..
Maize	F3	45.0	45.0	55.0	45.0	50.0	65.0	..	..	..	..	..
BURUNDI												
Coffee (green)	X1	..	..	..	..	..	..	..	..	..	..	..
Tea	X2	..	..	..	..	..	..	..	..	..	..	..
Cotton (seed)	X3	36.1	51.9	52.6	55.3	57.8	60.2	62.4	64.4	..	..	..
Maize	F1	25.0	..	..	..	..	..	..	..	..	..	..
Sorghum	F2	20.0	..	..	..	..	..	..	..	..	..	..
Rice	F3	25.0	..	..	..	..	..	..	..	..	..	..
Millet	F4	20.0	..	..	..	..	..	..	..	..	..	..
Bananas	NT1	..	..	..	..	..	..	..	..	..	..	..
Cassava	NT1	10.9	..	..	..	..	..	..	..	..	..	..
CAMEROON												
Coffee (Arabica)	X1	320.0	475.0	475.0	475.0	458.0	186.0	165.0	..	..	..	..
Cocoa (grade 1, superior)	X2	300.0	420.0	420.0	42.0	250.0	220.0	200.0	200.0	200.0	..	..
Cotton (seed cotton, nonselected)	X3	70.0	130.0	130.0	140.0	95.0	95.0	95.0	85.0	..	..	..
Maize	F1	60.0	83.2	76.8	82.4	57.0	51.7	..	..	..	..	..
Sorghum	F2	40.0	38.9	60.6	47.2	43.0	77.9	..	..	..	..	..
Millet	F3	40.0	38.9	60.6	47.2	43.0	77.9	..	..	..	..	..
Rice (paddy)	F4	105.0	91.0	64.7	77.5	82.7	53.5	..	..	..	..	..
Cassava	NT1	19.0	48.0	46.6	41.7	..	..	..	..	..	..	..
Plantains	NT2	25.0	45.3	46.7	47.3	..	54.0	..	..	..	..	..
CENTRAL AFRICAN REPUBLIC												
Coffee (Robusta, cherries)	X1	120.0	135.0	135.0	190.0	110.0	80.0	40.0	40.0	120.0	120.0	240.0
Cotton (seed cotton)	X2	60.0	100.0	100.0	100.0	100.0	..	68.5	60.0	60.0	87.0	117.0
Sorghum	F1	..	103.5	128.3	107.7	92.5	..	..	..	..	136.7	168.9
Maize	F2	40.0	65.3	67.7	104.3	111.6	..	..	..	..	136.0	271.0
Groundnuts (unshelled)	F3	70.0	..	..	171.7	..	..	..	..	..	217.6	526.3
Cassava	NT1	30.0	76.2	89.5	57.5	103.7	..	..	..	..	119.2	176.6
Yams	NT2	25.0	107.1	91.0	124.5	86.6	..	..	..	..	..	222.5
CHAD												
Cotton (seed cotton, avg. white/yellow)	X1	..	99.0	99.0	97.0	88.0	88.0	88.0	77.0	89.0	..	..
Millet	F2	..	31.0	31.0	48.0	47.0	52.0	62.0	41.0	41.0	..	..
Groundnuts	F3	..	57.0	46.0	44.0	46.0	48.0	70.0	67.0	77.0	..	..

(Table continues on the following page)

8-1. Nominal producer prices *(continued)*

	Category	Local currency per kilogram 1980	1986	1987	1988	1989	1990	1991	1992	1993	1994	1995
COMOROS												
Vanilla	X1	1150.0	..	..	..	..	..	..	..	..	..	..
Cloves	X2	1250.0	..	..	..	..	..	..	..	..	..	..
Ylang Ylang (flower)	X3	45.0	90.0	65.0	65.0	..	..	..	..	..	..	..
Copra	X4	40.0	..	..	..	..	..	..	..	..	..	..
Bananas	F1	50.0	..	..	..	..	..	..	..	..	..	..
Cassava	NT1	40.0	..	..	..	..	..	..	..	..	..	..
CONGO, DEMOCRATIC REPUBLIC OF												
Coffee (Arabica, green beans)	X1	4.0	42.6	69.3	107.5	166.9	440.5	13837.3	..	..	..	..
Palm oil	X2	2.1	23.0	37.6	59.4	93.8	247.7	7778.7	..	..	..	..
Rubber (natural)	X3	..	..	..	..	..	..	..	..	..	..	..
Cocoa (beans)	X4	..	30.0	50.0	..	..	..	..	..	..	..	..
Maize	F1	1.2	7.5	10.1	25.8	40.3	106.4	..	..	..	..	..
Rice (paddy)	F2	2.0	11.5	17.0	28.7	45.2	119.4	..	..	..	..	..
Cassava	NT1	1.3	3.0	3.9	8.4	13.2	34.7	1090.8	..	..	..	..
Plantains	NT2	2.9	..	..	..	..	..	..	..	..	..	..
CONGO, REPUBLIC OF												
Coffee	X1	146.0	215.0	215.0	115.0	115.0	115.0	115.0	115.0	115.0	..	..
Cocoa	X2	134.8	190.0	240.0	108.0	108.0	88.0	88.0	88.0	88.0	88.0	88.0
Maize	F1	43.0	73.0	85.0	60.0	60.0	60.0	60.0	100.0	100.0	100.0	100.0
Cassava	NT1	..	..	..	..	..	..	..	..	..	..	..
Plantains	NT2	..	..	..	..	..	..	..	..	..	..	..
COTE D'IVOIRE												
Coffee (Robusta, green)	X1	310.6	399.5	400.0	400.0	404.0	419.0	390.0	232.0	200.0	530.0	700.0
Cocoa (beans)	X2	300.0	400.0	400.0	400.0	400.0	200.0	200.0	200.0	200.0	315.0	320.0
Palm oil	X3	..	..	..	213.8	213.8	213.8	190.0	190.0	190.0	225.0	225.0
Rice (paddy)	F1	50.0	84.0	84.0	60.0	60.0	60.0	60.0	60.0	75.0	75.0	110.0
Maize	F2	68.0	76.0	45.0	45.0	45.0	45.0	45.0	..	..	..	..
Cassava	NT1	49.0	46.0	..	..	..	..	..	..	..	..	..
Yams	NT2	59.0	99.9	..	..	..	..	..	..	..	..	..
EGYPT												
Cotton	X1	0.3	0.6	0.7	0.9	1.3	1.7	2.0	2.4	2.4	2.1	..
Rice (96% humidity)	X2	0.1	0.2	0.2	0.3	0.4	0.4	0.4	0.5	0.5	0.6	..
Wheat (94% humidity)	F1	0.1	0.2	0.2	0.2	0.4	0.5	0.5	0.5	0.5	0.5	..
Sugarcane	F2	0.0	0.0	0.0	0.0	0.1	0.1	0.1	0.1	0.1	0.1	0.1
Broadbeans	NT1	0.2	0.5	0.6	0.6	0.6	0.7	0.9	1.1	1.0	1.0	..
EQUATORIAL GUINEA												
Cocoa (first grade dried beans)	X1	..	..	..	..	..	..	..	..	..	..	..
Coffee (Robusta, cherry)	X2	..	..	..	..	..	..	..	..	..	..	..
Cassava	NT1	..	..	..	..	..	..	..	..	..	..	..
Plantains	NT2	..	..	..	..	..	..	..	..	..	..	..
ETHIOPIA												
Coffee (Arabica, beans)	X1	2.6	3.7	4.1	4.2	4.2	4.2	3.1	3.1	..	..	..
Sesame seed	X2	..	1.1	1.1	1.3	1.3	1.4	1.7	..	..	..	..
Sorghum (mixed)	F1	..	0.5	0.4	0.5	0.5	0.5	0.8	0.8	..	..	..
Maize	F2	..	0.5	0.4	0.4	0.5	0.4	0.6	0.7	..	..	..
Barley (non-white mixed)	NT1	..	0.5	0.4	0.5	0.5	0.5	0.7	0.9	..	..	..
GABON												
Cocoa (first quality)	X1	320.0	430.0	430.0	370.0	210.0	224.0	224.0	269.0	260.0	..	..
Coffee (merchant, processed)	X2	180.0	0.0	260.0	260.0	130.0	130.0	..	150.0	147.0	..	..
Maize	F1	..	..	..	..	..	..	..	..	..	..	..
Cassava	NT1	139.5	..	..	..	..	..	..	..	..	..	..
Yams	NT3	124.5	..	..	..	..	..	..	..	..	..	..
GAMBIA, THE												
Groundnuts (unshelled)	X1	0.5	1.8	1.5	1.1	1.5	1.8	..	..	..	..	..
Cotton (seed cotton)	X2	0.5	1.3	1.5	1.6	1.8	1.9	1.9	2.0	2.0	2.2	2.2
Palm kernels	X3	0.3	0.3	..	..	..	..	..	..	..	..	..
Millet	F1	0.5	1.1	1.2	1.2	1.5	1.9	1.9	..	..	..	..
Rice (paddy)	F2	..	..	2.1	2.1	3.4	2.8	2.7	..	..	..	..
Maize	F3	..	0.0	1.2	1.2	1.4	2.1	1.9	..	..	..	..
Sorghum	F4	0.3	0.9	0.0	0.0	1.2	0.0	1.9	..	..	..	..

(Table continues on the following page)

8-1. Nominal producer prices *(continued)*

						Local currency per kilogram						
	Category	1980	1986	1987	1988	1989	1990	1991	1992	1993	1994	1995
GHANA												
Cocoa	X1	4.0	80.3	101.3	153.8	..	..	..	..	..	..	..
Maize	F1	4.1	25.0	42.0	48.0	35.8	86.9	69.5	83.5	93.7	..	..
Millet	F2	5.3	24.2	36.0	83.3	89.7	77.9	113.5	141.4	149.9	..	..
Groundnuts	F3	8.4	..	..	..	..	..	..	..	..	..	..
Cassava	NT1	1.5	8.8	10.8	12.9	10.0	10.0	15.8	22.5	25.3	..	..
Plantains	NT2	1.9	15.0	18.6	43.0	45.9	27.8	26.8	35.5	91.4	..	..
GUINEA												
Coffee (Robusta)	X1	49.0	400.0	400.0	..	..	..	..	..	..	..	..
Palm kernels	X2	6.0	60.0	60.0	..	..	..	..	..	..	..	..
Rice (paddy)	F1	9.0	..	..	..	..	168.0	166.0	..	..	..	..
Maize	F2	7.0	..	..	..	..	130.0	144.0	..	..	..	..
Groundnuts (unshelled)	F3	11.0	..	..	..	250.0	213.0	..	..	..	..	..
Cassava	NT1	5.0	..	..	..	..	..	81.0	..	..	..	..
Plantains	NT2	4.5	..	..	..	..	..	..	..	..	..	..
GUINEA-BISSAU												
Cashew nuts	X1	..	38.5	125.0	230.0	350.0	450.0	550.0	1000.0	3500.0	..	..
Groundnuts (unshelled, grade 1)	X2	..	32.5	40.0	80.0	140.0	225.0	275.0	500.0	1000.0	..	..
Palm kernels	X3	..	..	..	..	..	..	..	..	..	..	..
Rice (paddy, grade 1)	F1	8.5	37.5	50.0	85.0	180.0	225.0	400.0	650.0	1100.0	..	..
Sorghum	F2	..	..	..	..	..	..	..	..	..	..	..
Maize (grade 1)	F3	..	..	..	..	..	..	..	..	740.0	..	..
KENYA												
Coffee (Arabica, washed bean, grade 1-6)	X1	26.4	54.8	34.1	43.0	43.1	36.4	46.5	49.4	98.9	..	..
Tea	X2	15.9	33.8	25.0	26.8	27.2	35.2	38.5	47.5	92.4	..	..
Sugar (cane)	X3	0.1	0.3	0.3	0.4	0.4	0.5	0.5	0.6	0.8	..	..
Sisal	X4	4.2	7.4	7.1	7.4	8.9	9.2	9.4	9.8	9.9	..	..
Maize	F1	1.0	2.1	2.1	2.2	2.7	2.6	3.1	4.7	8.1	..	..
Wheat	F2	1.6	2.9	3.0	3.2	3.4	4.5	5.0	5.6	5.7	..	..
LESOTHO												
Wheat	X1	0.2	0.4	0.5	0.5	0.6	..	..	0.8	..	..	..
Beans	X2	0.5	1.1	1.3	1.3	1.4	..	..	..	..	..	..
Peas	X3	0.4	0.9	0.9	1.1	1.2	1.2	..	..	..	..	..
Maize	X4	0.1	0.3	0.3	0.4	0.4	0.4	0.5	0.6	0.6	0.6	..
Sorghum	F1	0.2	0.2	0.3	0.3	0.3	0.3	..	0.5	0.6	..	..
LIBERIA												
Rubber (nonspec. coagul.)	X1	0.8	1.0	1.0	..	..	..	..	..	..	..	..
Coffee (Robusta)	X2	2.1	1.6	1.6	..	..	..	..	..	..	..	..
Cocoa (fair average quality)	X3	2.1	2.3	2.3	..	..	..	..	..	..	..	..
Rice	F1	0.3	0.3	0.3	0.3	..	..	..	..	..	..	..
Cassava	NT1	0.0	0.1	0.1	0.1	..	..	..	..	..	..	..
LIBYA												
Wheat	F1	0.0	..	..	..	..	..	..	..	..	..	..
Olives	F2	..	..	..	..	..	..	..	..	..	..	..
Oranges	F3	..	..	..	..	..	..	..	..	..	..	..
Barley	NT1	..	..	..	..	..	..	..	..	..	..	..
MADAGASCAR												
Coffee (Robusta)	X1	215.0	600.0	800.0	950.0	950.0	950.0	..	..	..	..	..
Vanilla (green)	X2	600.0	1100.0	1200.0	1700.0	2000.0	2000.0	2000.0	..	..	..	..
Cloves	X3	395.0	525.0	600.0	600.0	600.0	600.0	..	..	..	..	..
Rice (paddy)	F1	42.5	100.0	127.5	180.0	250.0	250.0	274.0	..	..	..	..
Cassava	NT1	7.0	55.0	55.0	..	..	..	124.0	..	..	..	..
Sweet potatoes	NT2	..	50.0	60.0	60.0	60.0	..	116.0	..	..	..	..
MALAWI												
Tobacco (flue-cured)	X1	..	..	..	..	..	..	..	..	..	..	..
Tobacco (Northen division dark-fired, G2)	X1	0.4	1.0	1.0	1.1	1.7	2.5	2.8	2.8	2.8	3.5	6.0
Tea (dry leaves)	X2	0.7	1.0	1.0	1.5	1.6	2.0	2.0	2.5	2.5	3.0	5.0
Groundnuts (in shell)	X3	0.3	0.5	0.6	0.6	0.6	0.8	0.7	0.9	1.1	1.6	2.5
Cotton (seed cotton)	X4	..	0.5	0.5	0.7	0.8	0.8	0.8	0.9	0.9	1.0	2.5
Maize	F1	0.1	0.1	0.1	0.2	0.2	0.3	0.3	0.3	0.4	0.5	0.7
Sorghum	F2	0.1	0.2	0.1	0.1	0.2	0.2	0.0	0.0	0.7	0.8	1.1
Rice (paddy, grade 1)	F3	0.1	0.2	0.2	0.3	0.3	0.4	0.4	0.5	0.9	1.5	1.8
Cassava	NT1	0.0	..	..	0.1	0.1	0.1	..	..	..	..	..

(Table continues on the following page)

8-1. Nominal producer prices *(continued)*

		Local currency per kilogram										
	Category	1980	1986	1987	1988	1989	1990	1991	1992	1993	1994	1995
MALI												
Cotton (seed cotton)	X1	55.0	85.0	85.0	85.0	85.0	85.0	85.0	85.0	..	..	..
Groundnuts (unshelled)	X2	40.0	..	..	..	..	..	..	..	..	..	..
Millet	F1	35.0	55.0	55.0	0.0	0.0	77.0	41.5	42.0	..	..	..
Rice (paddy)	F2	37.5	70.0	70.0	70.0	70.0	70.0	70.0	68.0	..	..	..
Sorghum	F3	35.0	55.0	55.0	58.0	60.0	61.0	..	..	..	..	..
Maize	F4	35.0	55.0	55.0	..	..	54.0	35.0	35.0	..	..	..
MAURITANIA												
Sorghum	F1	11.0	15.4	15.4	16.0	16.0	16.0	16.5	16.5	16.8	17.0	17.2
Millet	F2	11.0	..	..	..	..	..	..	..	..	..	..
Rice (paddy)	F3	10.0	..	..	..	..	..	..	..	..	..	..
Maize	F4	15.0	..	..	..	..	..	..	..	..	..	..
MAURITIUS												
Sugarcane	X1	..	..	..	..	..	..	..	..	..	..	..
Tea	X2	..	9.2	7.4	10.3	10.4	13.5	13.4	16.8	16.4	..	..
Maize (12% moisture)	F1	2.0	4.3	4.3	4.8	4.8	4.8	4.8	5.0	5.0	..	..
Rice (paddy, 14% moisture)	F2	1.4	4.9	4.9	5.0	7.0	..	..	..	..	..	..
Potatoes	NT1	2.2	1.9	2.5	2.5	2.8	3.1	3.7	4.1	4.7	..	..
Onions	NT2	4.2	4.2	4.8	5.8	5.7	7.1	7.8	7.7	7.6	..	..
MOROCCO												
Citrus (oranges)	X1	1.3	1.6	1.6	1.7	1.8	1.9	2.0	2.1	2.2	2.3	2.4
Cotton	X3	3.2	6.0	6.0	6.0	6.7	0.0	6.7	5.7	5.7	..	..
Wheat (hard)	F1	1.5	2.2	2.2	2.1	2.3	2.5	2.5	2.9	2.9	2.5	..
Sugarbeet (16.5% sugar)	F2	0.1	0.2	0.2	0.2	0.2	0.2	0.3	0.3	0.3	..	..
Barley	NT1	1.3	1.3	1.3	1.2	1.3	1.5	1.5	2.0	2.0	2.1	..
MOZAMBIQUE												
Cashew nuts	X1	7.5	13.2	86.0	..	..	..	..	..	..	..	..
Cotton (seed, prime grade)	X2	11.0	16.0	65.0	..	..	..	..	..	..	..	..
Tea	X3	25.6	..	..	..	..	..	..	..	..	..	..
Maize	F1	..	..	..	..	..	..	..	..	..	..	..
Rice	F2	6.2	16.0	48.0	..	..	..	..	..	..	..	..
Cassava	NT1	2.0	..	..	..	..	..	..	..	..	..	..
NAMIBIA												
Wheat	F1	..	0.4	0.4	0.4	0.5	0.6	0.6	0.7	0.7	0.7	..
Maize (white)	F2	..	0.3	0.3	0.4	0.4	0.4	0.5	0.5	0.6	0.7	..
NIGER												
Cowpeas	X1	45.0	80.0	80.0	..	..	..	..	..	..	..	..
Cotton (unginned, top grade)	X2	62.0	120.0	120.0	120.0	130.0	110.0	70.0	70.0	77.0	..	..
Groundnuts (in shell)	X3	50.0	130.0	130.0	130.0	132.0	133.0	134.0	135.0	140.0	143.8	146.4
Millet	F1	50.0	..	..	..	..	..	..	..	..	..	..
Sorghum (red)	F2	50.0	..	..	..	..	..	..	..	..	..	..
NIGERIA												
Cocoa (bean)	X1	1.3	3.5	7.5	11.0	10.1	8.5	10.2	12.7	..	..	..
Palm kernels	X2	0.2	0.4	0.9	1.0	1.3	1.2	..	..	..	..	..
Cotton (seed cotton)	X3	0.4	1.0	4.0	4.5	2.4	2.6	4.2	3.8	..	..	..
Groundnuts (in shell)	X4	0.4	1.0	2.3	2.3	4.8	4.3	6.3	6.8	19.7	10.6	..
Sorghum	F1	0.2	0.6	0.8	1.6	2.0	1.7	3.6	4.7	7.0	5.3	..
Millet	F2	0.2	0.6	0.6	1.3	2.1	1.7	3.4	5.7	6.6	6.2	..
Maize	F3	0.2	0.5	0.6	1.6	2.7	2.1	3.3	5.5	7.5	5.6	..
Rice (paddy)	F4	0.3	1.0	2.3	3.8	6.3	6.3	7.5	12.6	18.8	12.3	..
Yams	NT1	..	1.0	0.9	2.0	2.4	2.3	2.6	5.9	11.7	14.4	..
Cassava (gari)	NT2	..	0.3	0.4	0.8	1.2	2.2	2.1	2.3	4.6	4.5	..
RWANDA												
Coffee	X1	120.0	122.5	125.0	125.0	125.0	99.7	107.4	115.0	..	..	427.0
Tea	X2	75.0	75.0	75.0	..	..	..	..	..	..	..	..
Beans (dry)	F1	20.3	22.3	28.6	30.5	38.4	37.9	40.8	40.2	..	..	90.0
Sorghum	F2	12.7	20.2	20.2	19.3	23.3	24.5	29.3	33.6	..	..	141.0
Maize	F3	11.9	15.6	15.4	13.6	24.7	26.9	32.4	29.0	..	..	45.0
Bananas	NT1	..	..	..	10.6	10.7	12.7	15.9	14.9	..	..	..
Sweet potatoes	NT2	5.7	6.1	6.2	5.5	9.4	9.8	9.9	6.8	..	..	24.0

(Table continues on the following page)

8-1. Nominal producer prices *(continued)*

		Local currency per kilogram										
	Category	1980	1986	1987	1988	1989	1990	1991	1992	1993	1994	1995
SAO TOME & PRINCIPE												
Cocoa	X1	16.5	24.0	25.0	26.0	27.0	28.0	29.0	30.0	..	..	..
Maize	F1	1.9	2.5	2.6	2.6	2.7	2.7	2.8	2.8	..	..	..
Cassava	NT1	2.1	2.7	2.7	2.8	2.8	2.9	2.9	3.0	..	..	..
SENEGAL												
Groundnuts (in shell)	X1	50.0	90.0	90.0	70.0	70.0	70.0	70.0	70.0	100.0	120.0	125.0
Cotton (seed cotton, first quality)	X2	60.0	100.0	100.0	100.0	100.0	100.0	100.0	100.0	115.0	150.0	170.0
Millet	F1	40.0	70.0	70.0	70.0	70.0	70.0	70.0	70.0	70.0	70.0	70.0
Rice (paddy)	F2	41.5	85.0	85.0	85.0	85.0	85.0	85.0	85.0	90.0	..	..
Maize	F3	37.0	70.0	70.0	70.0	70.0	70.0	70.0	70.0	70.0	70.0	70.0
Sorghum	F4	40.0	70.0	70.0	70.0	70.0	70.0	70.0	70.0	70.0	70.0	70.0
SIERRA LEONE												
Cocoa	X1	2.1	17.8	30.2	30.2	..	..	..	..	..	..	..
Coffee (Robusta)	X2	2.0	25.0	40.3	..	..	..	..	..	..	..	..
Palm kernels	X3	0.2	1.1	1.3	..	..	..	..	..	..	..	..
Rice (paddy)	F1	0.4	2.8	7.4	22.2	29.0	37.0	44.4	..	..	..	..
Cassava	NT1	0.3	4.9	..	..	..	..	..	..	..	..	..
SOMALIA												
Bananas	X1	..	..	..	..	..	..	..	..	..	..	..
Maize	F1	5.5	21.4	34.5	..	..	..	..	..	..	..	..
Sorghum	F2	5.8	18.9	22.7	..	..	..	..	..	..	..	..
Sesame (seed)	NT1	25.2	61.6	76.4	..	..	..	..	..	..	..	..
SOUTH AFRICA												
Maize	X1	0.1	0.2	0.3	0.3	0.3	0.3	0.4	0.5	0.4	0.4	0.6
Wheat	X2	0.2	0.4	0.4	0.4	0.5	0.5	0.6	0.7	0.8	0.8	0.8
Sugar cane	X3	0.0	0.0	0.0	0.0	..	0.1	0.1	0.1	0.1	0.1	0.0
Sorghum	F1	0.1	0.2	0.2	0.2	0.2	0.2	0.3	0.5	0.5	0.4	0.4
Barley	F2	0.2	0.3	0.3	0.3	0.4	0.5	0.5	0.6	0.7	0.7	0.7
SUDAN												
Cotton (seed cotton, long-staple, grade 1)	X1	0.4	1.8	2.5	4.3	4.8	6.7	14.1	37.2	..	..	..
Groundnuts (El-Obeid, in shell)	X2	0.2	1.1	1.2	1.8	4.4	23.5	21.1	22.6	..	..	..
Sesame (El-Obeid, mixed)	X3	0.3	1.3	1.6	5.0	6.5	12.7	30.9	41.6	..	..	..
Gum arabic (El-Obeid)	X4	0.0	6.8	9.0	9.4	10.2	10.3	18.9	17.8	..	..	..
Sorghum	F1	0.1	0.2	0.8	0.9	1.9	11.4	6.6	11.8	..	..	..
Wheat	F2	0.2	0.7	1.0	2.3	2.9	5.7	8.3	11.4	33.3	..	..
SWAZILAND												
Sugarcane (sucrose)	X1	0.0	0.0	0.0	0.0	0.0	..	..	..	..	..	..
Citrus	X2	0.2	0.4	0.2	0.4	0.4	..	..	..	..	..	..
Pineapple	X3	0.0	0.3	0.2	0.2	0.3	0.4	0.5	0.5	0.5	0.6	0.6
Cotton (seed cotton)	X4	0.5	0.9	0.9	1.1	1.1	..	..	..	..	..	..
Maize	F1	0.1	0.3	0.3	0.3	0.4	..	..	..	..	..	..
TANZANIA												
Coffee (Arabica) (parchment)	X1	9.0	50.8	66.0	90.0	..	..	..	..	..	..	..
Cotton (seed cotton, AR)	X2	3.2	16.9	19.5	22.4	28.0	..	..	..	..	..	..
Tea (green leaves)	X3	1.5	7.6	9.9	13.4	..	..	..	..	..	..	..
Maize	F1	1.0	6.3	8.2	9.0	11.0	..	..	..	..	..	..
Sorghum	F2	1.0	4.8	6.0	0.0	0.0	..	..	..	..	..	..
Rice (paddy)	F3	1.8	9.6	14.4	17.3	19.0	..	..	..	..	..	..
Millet	F4	1.5	4.8	6.0	6.6	7.3	..	..	..	..	..	..
Cassava (grade 1, Makopa)	NT1	0.7	3.6	4.5	5.0	5.5	..	..	..	..	..	..
TOGO												
Coffee (Robusta)	X1	200.0	365.0	400.0	350.0	175.0	175.0	185.0	140.0	350.0	650.0	..
Cocoa	X2	220.0	330.0	360.0	300.0	225.0	250.0	250.0	225.0	300.0	550.0	..
Cotton (seed cotton)	X3	52.0	105.0	105.0	95.0	95.0	100.0	100.0	90.0	110.0	145.0	..
Maize	F1	68.4	73.0	72.0	79.0	60.0	61.0	58.0	73.0	43.0	62.0	..
Sorghum	F2	68.0	76.0	66.0	98.0	69.0	68.0	67.0	92.0	64.0	68.0	..
Millet	F3	66.7	59.0	61.0	87.0	72.0	58.0	75.0	87.0	61.0	52.0	..
Cassava	NT1	20.3	30.0	32.0	26.0	30.0	23.0	28.0	29.0	30.0	31.0	..
Yams	NT2	48.5	61.0	63.0	63.0	68.0	68.0	66.0	66.0	63.0	59.0	..

(Table continues on the following page)

8-1. Nominal producer prices *(continued)*

	Category	Local currency per kilogram										
		1980	1986	1987	1988	1989	1990	1991	1992	1993	1994	1995
TUNISIA												
Olives	X1	0.1	0.1	0.2	0.2	0.2	0.2	0.3	0.3	0.3	0.3	0.3
Citrus (oranges)	X2	0.1	0.1	0.2	0.2	0.2	0.3	0.3	..	..	..	..
Wheat	F1	0.1	0.2	0.2	0.2	0.2	0.2	0.2	0.3	0.3	0.3	0.3
Barley	NT1	0.1	0.1	0.1	0.1	0.1	0.2	0.2	0.2	0.2	0.2	0.2
UGANDA												
Coffee	X1	0.1	8.5	24.0	44.5	60.0	97.5	210.0	190.0	..	..	..
Cotton (seed cotton)	X2	0.2	4.0	19.0	56.0	105.0	175.0	286.7	340.0	..	..	..
Tea (greenleaf)	X3	0.0	5.0	10.0	20.0	35.0	38.3	45.0	70.0	..	..	..
Millet	F1	0.2	7.4	17.6	30.7	109.6	134.8	142.6	294.3	..	..	..
Maize	F2	0.1	4.6	11.3	26.0	82.9	72.0	80.0	225.0	..	..	..
Sorghum	F3	0.1	5.4	18.3	30.5	84.6	104.0	115.3	237.3	..	..	..
Cassava	NT1	0.1	2.3	9.3	22.5	35.5	39.5	76.0	163.0	..	..	..
Plantains	NT2	0.1	3.9	7.5	13.6	46.9	51.2	64.5	156.7	..	..	..
ZAMBIA												
Cotton (seed cotton)	X1	0.5	1.0	1.6	3.0	3.6	9.7	..	..	..	..	..
Tobacco (Virginia)	X2	1.6	5.1	6.3	14.0	14.4	60.0	94.5	..	..	..	..
Sunflower (seeds)	X3	0.3	0.8	1.4	1.8	3.2	6.4	11.4	..	..	..	..
Maize	F1	0.1	0.6	0.9	0.9	1.2	3.2	5.6	..	..	..	..
Wheat	F2	0.2	1.0	1.2	2.1	..	5.4	8.6	..	..	..	..
Cassava	NT1	..	0.6	0.7	1.0	1.4	3.2	5.4	..	..	..	..
ZIMBABWE												
Tobacco	X1	0.8	3.1	2.2	3.9	4.0	6.5	11.6	8.1	6.5	..	..
Cotton (seed cotton)	X2	0.4	0.8	0.8	0.9	1.1	1.4	1.6	1.4	2.6	..	..
Sugarcane	X3	0.0	..	..	..	..	..	..	..	..	..	..
Maize	X4	0.1	0.2	0.2	0.2	0.2	0.2	0.3	0.6	0.9	..	..
Wheat	F1	0.2	0.3	0.3	0.4	0.4	0.5	0.5	1.0	1.5	..	..

Notes: The categories of crops are defined in the technical notes.

Categories are mutually exclusive, and ordering is intended to reflect relative importance of these crops as of 1986-88. In many cases official markets operate simultaneously with parallel or open market activites. Where a large majority of marketed production is believed to pass through the official channels, the official price is also reported as the farmgate price. In most cases, only very rough estimates of the share of marketed production passing through each channel is available.

The CPI is based in 1987 rescaled from price index based in 1980.

For each country one to four export crops (X1,...,X4) are presented in order of importance, in terms of value of total producti

Similarly, up to three traded food crops (F1,...,F3) and two nontraded staples (NT1,NT2) are included.

Agriculture

8-2. Food price index

	Index (average 1995 = 100)										Average annual percentage growth		
	1980	*1990*	*1991*	*1992*	*1993*	*1994*	*1995*	*1996*	*1997*	*1998*	*75-84*	*85-89*	*90-MR*
SUB-SAHARAN AFRICA	7	55	62	71	71	90	100	108	124	130	..	13.9	12.1
excluding South Africa	6	57	62	69	70	89	100	109	125	131	..	13.7	12.0
excl. S.Africa & Nigeria	7	59	63	71	71	89	100	108	124	130	..	13.6	11.5
Angola	..	..	0	0	0	4	100	3,954	7,968	..	..	..	1,216.9
Benin	..	62	67	73	78	84	100	100	103	118	..	..	8.2
Botswana	18	55	61	72	83	90	100	113	125	132	..	9.6	12.1
Burkina Faso	..	80	87	81	76	89	100	115	..	..	..	-2.6	4.4
Burundi	35	69	74	73	72	85	100	..	..	..	..	3.3	6.3
Cameroon	..	..	..	..	..	..	..	..	..	..	..	..	..
Cape Verde	..	..	..	..	..	..	..	..	..	..	..	..	..
Central African Republic	0	71	69	68	65	81	100	106	107	..	..	-2.1	6.4
Chad	..	70	71	73	63	95	100	114	124	128	..	..	9.6
Comoros	..	..	..	..	..	..	..	..	..	..	..	..	..
Congo, Democratic Rep. of	..	..	..	..	..	..	..	..	..	..	..	..	..
Congo, Republic of	42	67	65	59	63	94	100	107	..	..	..	-1.0	8.0
Côte d'Ivoire	..	..	..	..	..	..	..	..	..	..	..	..	..
Djibouti	..	..	..	..	..	..	..	..	..	..	..	..	..
Equatorial Guinea	..	..	..	..	..	..	..	..	..	..	..	..	..
Eritrea	..	..	..	..	..	..	..	..	..	..	..	..	..
Ethiopia	34	51	71	80	81	89	100	95	91	93	..	0.4	7.8
Gabon	..	84	83	69	70	93	100	107	..	..	..	0.1	4.5
Gambia, The	14	73	79	86	93	92	100	101	103	..	..	24.8	5.9
Ghana	1	33	36	39	49	62	100	136	..	..	..	23.1	26.6
Guinea	..	60	70	81	88	93	100	101	..	..	..	..	11.2
Guinea-Bissau	..	..	..	..	..	..	..	..	..	..	..	..	..
Kenya	0	32	40	54	78	102	100	108	125	130	..	..	19.4
Lesotho	15	52	61	76	84	89	100	111	..	..	..	12.9	13.4
Liberia	..	..	..	..	..	..	..	..	..	..	..	..	..
Madagascar	7	34	38	44	47	66	100	119	124	131	..	13.8	20.5
Malawi	5	20	23	30	37	52	100	145	157	..	..	21.1	35.0
Mali	..	..	..	..	..	..	..	..	..	..	..	..	..
Mauritania	..	..	..	..	..	..	..	..	..	..	..	..	..
Mauritius	..	71	74	76	87	95	100	105	..	..	..	6.7	7.5
Mozambique	..	..	..	..	..	..	..	..	..	..	..	..	..
Namibia	..	59	62	74	79	90	100	107	115	118	..	14.3	10.3
Niger	..	..	..	..	..	..	..	..	..	..	..	..	..
Nigeria	4	26	29	43	68	100	100	224	243	259	..	23.1	35.0
Rwanda	..	..	..	..	..	..	..	..	..	..	..	..	..
São Tomé and Principe	..	..	..	..	..	..	..	..	..	..	..	..	..
Senegal	43	70	68	67	66	91	100	102	..	..	..	0.6	6.6
Seychelles	..	..	..	..	..	..	..	..	..	..	..	..	..
Sierra Leone	..	..	..	..	..	..	..	..	..	..	..	..	..
Somalia	..	..	..	..	..	..	..	..	..	..	..	..	..
South Africa	12	51	60	76	81	92	100	106	116	123	..	17.3	12.2
Sudan	..	..	..	..	..	..	..	..	..	..	..	..	..
Swaziland	..	..	..	..	..	..	..	..	..	..	..	..	..
Tanzania	3	31	38	46	57	75	100	120	141	162	..	31.3	23.4
Togo	..	..	..	..	..	..	..	..	..	..	..	..	..
Uganda	..	47	58	96	92	96	100	107	..	..	..	..	13.4
Zambia	0	3	5	17	50	75	100	146	176	219	..	57.7	80.1
Zimbabwe	6	23	29	45	62	78	100	127	149	208	..	11.8	30.7
NORTH AFRICA	23	63	71	75	85	92	100	106	110	114	..	10.1	8.3
Algeria	13	29	35	43	54	76	100	120	127	134	..	9.7	23.7
Egypt, Arab Republic	11	61	71	77	83	91	100	108	112	116	..	21.6	9.1
Libya	..	..	..	..	..	..	..	..	..	..	..	..	..
Morocco	32	65	70	74	87	93	100	101	100	103	..	3.7	6.6
Tunisia	34	76	83	86	89	92	100	104	108	111	..	7.4	5.0
ALL AFRICA	12	59	63	73	74	90	100	108	124	129	..	14.2	11.4

8-3. Food production index

	Index (average 1989-91 = 100)											Average annual percentage growth		
	1980	*1990*	*1991*	*1992*	*1993*	*1994*	*1995*	*1996*	*1997*	*1998*	*1999*	*75-84*	*85-89*	*90-MR*
SUB-SAHARAN AFRICA	78	101	108	107	112	115	118	124	123	129	131	0.9	4.1	2.8
excluding South Africa	77	101	109	109	113	116	120	126	125	132	134	0.9	4.1	3.0
excl. S.Africa & Nigeria	81	100	106	104	107	110	114	118	118	123	124	1.0	3.2	2.3
Angola	91	98	104	111	109	125	123	128	123	148	141	-0.7	1.2	4.1
Benin	62	99	106	109	111	116	126	135	142	149	154	3.1	3.7	5.1
Botswana	73	100	107	103	104	90	106	106	102	96	99	0.7	-1.9	0.0
Burkina Faso	59	93	110	115	121	120	121	129	120	136	136	2.4	6.7	3.4
Burundi	79	103	105	108	107	90	97	98	97	92	92	0.3	3.4	-0.9
Cameroon	80	100	104	103	110	113	120	124	119	125	126	0.6	2.0	2.9
Cape Verde	55	103	90	83	133	105	126	125	131	140	139	1.8	21.3	4.1
Central African Republic	80	100	100	107	108	112	115	129	126	129	135	2.0	4.9	3.4
Chad	94	91	112	114	98	119	120	125	135	158	154	1.0	3.9	5.1
Comoros	84	100	104	103	108	109	115	113	113	123	118	0.6	3.9	2.2
Congo, Democratic Rep. of	73	101	103	105	105	107	109	95	98	95	92	2.3	3.3	-0.7
Congo, Republic of	82	101	98	101	103	111	115	116	111	116	119	2.3	1.8	2.0
Côte d'Ivoire	70	101	102	105	109	110	124	128	131	129	130	4.1	3.7	3.4
Djibouti	54	108	78	82	76	82	84	86	83	87	88	10.9	9.2	-1.6
Equatorial Guinea	88	101	100	100	103	96	89	99	92	94	100	0.0	2.1	-0.6
Eritrea	..	..	..	..	89	120	111	102	101	148	127	..	..	5.1
Ethiopia	..	..	..	..	98	98	108	125	126	116	123	..	..	4.3
Gabon	80	98	105	103	101	103	105	108	107	112	115	3.0	3.0	1.4
Gambia, The	72	84	95	73	86	90	88	70	92	91	129	-1.1	3.7	0.4
Ghana	69	82	118	117	125	120	138	149	150	157	167	-1.6	4.1	6.0
Guinea	98	100	108	116	118	122	128	132	137	144	143	0.9	-1.9	4.4
Guinea-Bissau	67	103	99	105	106	111	118	115	118	120	120	3.3	2.2	2.2
Kenya	66	100	100	98	93	102	102	104	106	106	104	2.2	7.3	0.7
Lesotho	88	111	83	89	101	109	90	111	117	97	101	1.0	3.2	0.5
Liberia	..	..	..	..	..	..	..	..	..	..	..	..	..	..
Madagascar	86	100	102	102	106	104	107	109	110	110	112	1.1	1.0	1.3
Malawi	91	98	105	77	112	88	105	120	101	142	160	1.7	1.1	4.3
Mali	74	95	108	100	105	110	109	112	115	123	129	3.2	5.5	2.7
Mauritania	87	100	102	95	94	96	101	107	105	107	106	2.8	3.5	0.9
Mauritius	78	101	101	106	105	99	105	108	117	112	83	-0.3	1.8	0.1
Mozambique	101	107	94	81	93	91	109	123	130	139	140	-1.4	1.1	4.4
Namibia	109	96	103	105	108	114	110	118	129	96	96	-2.6	5.4	0.6
Niger	100	100	108	111	95	119	106	120	124	145	138	2.7	6.4	3.9
Nigeria	58	97	110	117	123	127	132	140	136	149	154	0.6	7.1	4.9
Rwanda	83	96	107	106	79	59	66	70	80	85	91	4.1	0.3	-2.4
São Tomé and Principe	112	97	99	123	127	131	118	137	133	152	163	-2.5	0.5	4.7
Senegal	59	96	100	93	103	105	117	108	98	101	121	-3.6	8.5	1.2
Seychelles	132	96	102	100	93	116	143	138	144	128	135	-0.2	-6.0	4.3
Sierra Leone	85	100	100	93	92	98	92	97	101	94	81	0.8	2.1	-1.1
Somalia	..	..	..	..	..	..	..	..	..	..	..	..	..	..
South Africa	91	98	100	85	96	101	87	103	102	98	103	0.6	4.2	0.4
Sudan	103	92	113	127	116	140	141	155	157	157	154	1.3	1.2	5.7
Swaziland	82	97	105	99	94	98	88	97	96	89	90	3.3	1.2	-1.0
Tanzania	74	100	100	95	97	96	101	103	94	104	106	3.6	2.2	0.4
Togo	76	103	98	101	120	104	117	136	141	133	144	1.2	3.6	4.3
Uganda	67	101	103	104	110	107	111	103	106	114	116	-1.6	3.7	1.4
Zambia	75	94	97	81	117	101	93	113	107	93	103	-1.5	8.3	0.4
Zimbabwe	76	104	96	65	89	100	75	107	108	98	108	-1.6	4.2	1.2
NORTH AFRICA	72	104	115	113	114	116	118	143	131	141	144	1.7	4.9	3.7
Algeria	69	93	113	120	113	105	121	143	116	129	135	0.2	4.1	3.3
Egypt, Arab Republic	68	101	105	111	114	115	126	138	142	144	151	2.1	4.4	4.9
Libya	82	101	103	102	103	111	125	134	126	157	164	4.9	0.8	5.4
Morocco	58	93	107	83	83	108	73	114	97	111	97	2.0	10.3	0.7
Tunisia	73	97	123	105	117	85	83	143	98	123	131	0.5	-0.5	2.8
ALL AFRICA	76	101	109	108	112	115	118	128	124	131	134	1.0	4.2	3.0

8-4. Nonfood production index

	Index (average 1989-91 = 100)											Average annual percentage growth		
	1980	1990	1991	1992	1993	1994	1995	1996	1997	1998	1999	75-84	85-89	90-MR
SUB-SAHARAN AFRICA	83	99	101	97	94	97	100	105	107	106	101	1.8	1.0	0.7
excluding South Africa	82	99	101	100	95	98	100	109	109	109	101	2.2	1.3	0.8
excl. S.Africa & Nigeria	83	99	101	97	95	99	100	105	107	106	101	1.9	1.1	0.7
Angola	209	93	95	89	95	85	90	90	94	97	72	-19.4	-0.8	-1.9
Benin	12	100	126	117	195	174	219	280	261	253	253	8.1	3.9	13.5
Botswana	100	100	100	100	100	100	100	100	81	75	77	0.0	0.0	-2.8
Burkina Faso	35	111	100	100	92	95	91	125	205	194	194	8.9	10.5	8.2
Burundi	59	97	107	113	87	112	79	72	54	58	86	5.3	3.4	-5.0
Cameroon	86	95	105	91	92	91	108	100	99	109	110	3.5	0.9	1.1
Cape Verde	94	95	36	21	21	21	21	21	21	21	21	-3.0	6.1	-15.3
Central African Republic	89	102	92	73	60	94	85	130	137	110	71	-0.5	-0.5	0.9
Chad	51	97	109	76	65	73	99	138	138	166	166	-4.4	11.2	6.9
Comoros	64	114	72	79	65	79	86	79	69	103	93	-5.0	4.6	-1.1
Congo, Democratic Rep. of	105	103	98	94	92	90	87	88	76	67	56	0.6	-3.6	-4.9
Congo, Republic of	156	93	92	93	91	92	94	78	71	69	75	0.0	-5.1	-4.0
Côte d'Ivoire	77	107	91	67	76	81	84	81	114	131	139	0.2	12.5	3.2
Djibouti	..	..	..	..	..	..	..	..	..	..	..	..	..	..
Equatorial Guinea	92	100	93	85	85	78	70	63	54	52	55	2.2	0.4	-7.3
Eritrea	..	..	..	..	96	99	98	101	100	102	101	..	..	0.8
Ethiopia	..	..	..	..	92	101	109	109	109	110	111	..	..	2.6
Gabon	36	69	78	67	93	124	142	209	284	307	307	19.5	21.2	15.7
Gambia, The	55	73	95	123	157	135	84	79	51	25	25	22.5	3.9	-13.7
Ghana	86	90	137	174	239	170	184	244	253	321	321	-6.0	4.4	14.3
Guinea	48	100	111	120	120	117	112	96	105	127	127	0.9	11.1	1.9
Guinea-Bissau	111	109	103	66	83	75	109	109	100	100	100	25.0	-7.5	1.4
Kenya	62	101	101	94	99	98	114	117	104	120	108	6.1	4.5	1.7
Lesotho	87	111	105	176	176	176	180	116	116	78	85	2.0	-9.1	-1.7
Liberia	..	..	..	..	..	..	..	..	..	..	..	..	..	..
Madagascar	90	101	93	86	91	89	83	84	77	83	85	-1.0	0.9	-2.3
Malawi	59	99	110	108	120	93	120	132	141	115	109	6.3	2.0	2.5
Mali	38	105	105	123	92	117	154	172	197	190	190	5.1	11.8	8.7
Mauritania	..	..	..	..	..	..	..	..	..	..	..	..	..	..
Mauritius	84	99	102	103	105	92	73	51	38	33	34	5.0	-5.6	-12.3
Mozambique	251	90	122	116	117	124	123	124	160	192	193	-6.7	-4.4	7.5
Namibia	276	110	75	88	96	123	115	109	121	119	120	-6.7	-1.0	2.4
Niger	84	84	89	131	89	86	86	86	82	82	81	-5.3	4.4	-3.1
Nigeria	41	105	112	117	85	86	101	116	122	126	129	-8.0	23.7	3.1
Rwanda	61	107	94	117	91	25	65	63	73	76	79	6.4	3.6	-4.3
São Tomé and Principe	321	198	59	70	107	118	134	161	214	268	311	1.1	-20.6	16.6
Senegal	51	91	131	124	129	121	83	82	105	87	62	2.1	-2.4	-2.9
Seychelles	21	108	119	110	121	121	111	110	133	123	128	7.6	6.7	3.3
Sierra Leone	44	100	101	101	96	106	97	97	114	114	60	11.2	5.0	-1.5
Somalia	..	..	..	..	..	..	..	..	..	..	..	..	..	..
South Africa	107	98	99	80	69	73	66	66	60	62	67	0.7	0.0	-5.3
Sudan	100	84	99	81	84	114	127	128	113	103	100	-1.6	-7.4	1.6
Swaziland	85	92	93	21	36	27	25	55	63	64	64	-3.4	12.1	-3.6
Tanzania	100	94	124	126	106	97	126	134	132	98	101	-2.2	0.1	1.5
Togo	34	90	123	126	124	121	105	129	148	161	167	5.1	20.5	5.6
Uganda	82	88	104	84	107	141	131	199	159	153	158	-5.8	0.7	6.9
Zambia	49	78	113	60	134	68	100	87	61	62	63	5.1	7.4	-4.5
Zimbabwe	77	90	110	101	117	106	104	129	137	153	129	2.1	1.8	4.1
NORTH AFRICA	84	102	100	98	97	92	91	95	100	94	95	4.1	-0.2	-0.6
Algeria	84	101	97	102	103	98	96	91	91	94	97	5.1	-0.7	-0.9
Egypt, Arab Republic	171	100	101	121	135	86	85	115	114	80	84	0.6	-6.5	-1.8
Libya	105	102	100	98	97	94	100	108	110	112	113	0.2	-1.6	1.4
Morocco	46	102	99	94	89	92	91	95	100	104	95	0.9	6.2	-0.1
Tunisia	73	103	102	92	87	74	75	74	74	76	72	3.8	3.8	-3.7
ALL AFRICA	84	100	101	98	95	95	99	101	105	103	100	2.5	0.7	0.4

8-5. Food production per capita index

					Index (average 1989-91 = 100)							Average annual percentage growth		
	1980	1990	1991	1992	1993	1994	1995	1996	1997	1998	1999	75-84	85-89	90-MR
SUB-SAHARAN AFRICA	105	100	100	97	96	95	97	98	95	96	94	-1.5	0.5	-0.5
excluding South Africa	105	100	100	97	96	96	97	98	95	99	96	-1.5	0.5	-0.4
excl. S.Africa & Nigeria	105	100	100	97	96	95	97	98	95	96	94	-1.6	0.4	-0.6
Angola	120	98	100	103	99	109	104	105	102	113	105	-3.3	-1.6	0.8
Benin	84	99	103	103	102	104	110	115	126	120	121	0.3	0.6	2.5
Botswana	103	100	104	97	95	80	92	89	78	78	79	-2.8	-5.2	-2.7
Burkina Faso	77	93	107	109	111	108	105	109	102	109	106	-0.1	3.8	0.7
Burundi	104	103	102	103	99	81	86	85	83	77	76	-2.1	0.5	-3.0
Cameroon	107	100	101	97	101	101	104	105	100	100	99	-2.1	-0.9	0.1
Cape Verde	65	103	88	79	125	96	113	110	107	117	113	0.8	19.1	1.7
Central African Republic	102	100	98	102	101	102	103	113	108	109	112	-0.4	2.4	1.2
Chad	120	91	109	107	90	105	103	105	110	125	119	-1.3	1.6	2.1
Comoros	113	100	101	97	100	98	100	95	95	99	92	-3.0	1.0	-0.6
Congo, Democratic Rep. of	101	101	99	97	93	91	90	76	74	72	68	-0.8	0.1	-4.1
Congo, Republic of	108	101	95	95	94	99	99	97	93	93	92	-0.5	-1.1	-0.8
Côte d'Ivoire	100	101	99	99	99	97	107	108	108	105	104	0.2	0.3	0.8
Djibouti	98	107	74	76	68	71	72	72	72	72	71	4.0	2.9	-3.8
Equatorial Guinea	142	101	98	96	95	87	78	85	76	77	80	-2.2	-1.0	-3.1
Eritrea	..	..	..	..	85	112	101	89	89	119	99	..	..	1.6
Ethiopia	..	..	..	..	90	87	94	106	104	94	97	..	..	1.7
Gabon	109	98	102	97	93	92	91	91	91	90	90	-0.1	-0.1	-1.3
Gambia, The	102	84	91	67	77	77	72	56	71	68	93	-4.0	-0.5	-3.2
Ghana	97	82	115	110	114	106	118	124	117	125	128	-4.0	0.9	2.9
Guinea	127	100	104	106	102	102	103	105	108	113	112	-0.8	-4.3	1.3
Guinea-Bissau	81	103	97	100	99	102	105	101	101	101	98	-0.5	0.2	0.0
Kenya	94	100	97	92	85	90	89	88	88	86	83	-1.6	3.6	-1.9
Lesotho	112	111	81	84	94	99	80	97	99	81	83	-1.5	0.7	-1.7
Liberia	..	..	..	..	..	..	..	..	..	..	..	..	..	..
Madagascar	113	100	99	96	96	91	91	89	89	85	84	-1.5	-1.7	-1.9
Malawi	137	97	103	75	109	85	100	113	106	127	140	-1.4	-4.2	3.3
Mali	96	95	106	95	98	101	97	97	95	102	104	0.8	3.2	0.2
Mauritania	114	100	99	90	86	86	88	91	87	86	83	0.3	0.7	-1.8
Mauritius	86	101	100	104	101	95	100	102	108	104	77	-1.7	1.0	-0.9
Mozambique	119	107	92	76	83	77	89	98	100	105	104	-4.1	0.3	0.8
Namibia	142	96	100	100	99	103	96	101	71	78	77	-5.2	2.5	-3.1
Niger	139	100	105	104	86	104	89	99	76	112	103	-0.6	3.1	-0.2
Nigeria	77	98	107	111	114	115	116	120	120	122	123	-2.2	4.2	2.5
Rwanda	111	95	110	117	95	75	86	88	90	89	87	0.8	-3.5	-1.8
São Tomé and Principe	142	96	97	118	118	119	105	120	121	128	134	-5.1	-1.8	2.6
Senegal	78	95	97	88	95	95	103	93	85	82	96	-6.3	5.5	-1.3
Seychelles	146	96	101	98	90	110	136	130	133	118	122	-1.3	-7.2	3.2
Sierra Leone	105	99	99	91	90	95	87	90	91	82	69	-1.2	-0.3	-2.7
Somalia	..	..	..	..	..	..	..	..	..	..	..	..	..	..
South Africa	112	98	98	81	91	93	79	92	91	85	88	-1.6	2.1	-1.4
Sudan	132	92	110	122	110	129	128	137	134	133	128	-1.7	-1.2	3.5
Swaziland	110	97	102	94	86	87	76	82	72	71	69	0.3	-1.8	-4.1
Tanzania	102	100	97	89	88	84	86	85	79	83	83	0.4	-0.9	-2.3
Togo	102	103	95	95	109	92	101	114	116	107	112	-1.5	0.6	1.4
Uganda	84	101	100	98	101	96	97	87	87	91	91	-4.5	1.5	-1.4
Zambia	94	94	95	77	109	92	82	98	82	77	83	-4.3	5.7	-2.3
Zimbabwe	105	104	94	62	83	92	68	95	97	85	92	-4.6	0.8	-0.5
NORTH AFRICA	92	97	105	101	105	101	107	122	96	107	113	-1.5	2.0	1.2
Algeria	92	93	110	114	105	96	107	124	96	107	109	-2.9	1.3	0.9
Egypt, Arab Republic	88	101	103	106	107	106	114	122	127	123	127	-0.3	1.8	2.9
Libya	119	100	101	97	96	101	111	116	124	130	132	0.4	-2.5	3.3
Morocco	72	93	105	80	79	102	68	104	86	97	83	-0.3	8.1	-1.0
Tunisia	93	97	121	101	110	79	76	129	87	107	113	-2.1	-2.6	1.0
ALL AFRICA	104	100	100	97	96	96	97	99	95	100	97	-1.4	0.6	-0.3

8-6. Volume of food output, by major food crop

	Thousands of metric tons											* Average annual percentage growth		
	1980	*1990*	*1991*	*1992*	*1993*	*1994*	*1995*	*1996*	*1997*	*1998*	*1999*	*75-84*	*85-89*	*90-MR*
ALGERIA														
Wheat	1,511	750	1,869	1,837	1,017	714	1,500	2,983	662	2,280	1,100	0.1	0.6	0.2
Citrus	422	281	324	362	361	376	323	334	351	418	454	-0.4	0.0	0.2
Dates	201	206	209	261	262	317	285	361	303	387	428	0.6	0.5	0.3
Barley	794	833	1,810	1,398	408	234	585	1,800	191	700	410	0.5	0.7	-0.3
Potatoes	591	809	1,077	1,158	1,065	716	1,200	1,150	948	1,100	996	0.1	1.1	0.0
ANGOLA														
Maize	360	180	299	320	275	201	211	398	370	505	428	-0.3	0.0	0.3
Millet	57	63	67	75	40	60	61	102	62	89	102	-0.3	0.4	0.2
Cassava	1,150	1,600	1,640	1,861	1,861	2,379	2,550	2,500	2,326	3,211	3,130	-0.2	0.3	0.3
Sweet potatoes	165	165	170	180	185	180	185	188	189	190	182	0.0	0.0	0.1
BENIN														
Palm oil	34	20	14	14	14	9	11	10	10	10	10	-0.3	-0.7	-0.3
Maize	271	410	431	460	483	492	576	556	728	662	823	0.5	-0.6	0.3
Sorghum	56	99	115	110	106	113	108	110	120	138	154	-0.3	0.3	0.1
Cassava	583	937	1,046	1,041	1,147	1,146	1,238	1,457	1,926	1,989	2,377	0.1	-0.2	0.4
Yam	694	1,046	1,178	1,125	1,185	1,250	1,286	1,342	1,514	1,584	1,771	0.3	0.1	0.2
BOTSWANA														
Livestock (1,000 head	149	317	349	300	250	238	250	240	250	240	250	-0.5	0.8	-0.1
Onions ,dry	1	1	1	1	1	1	1	1	1	1	1	-5.6	0.0	-0.1
Sorghum	29	38	33	16	38	37	38	78	17	9	13	-2.1	2.3	-0.4
Maize	12	12	15	3	4	11	2	20	12	1	5	-2.3	4.3	-0.5
Millet	2	2	1	1	2	4	1	8	2	1	1	-1.4	-1.7	0.2
BURKINA FASO														
Groundnuts	54	134	99	143	206	203	213	230	152	215	215	0.1	0.2	0.3
Sorghum	547	751	1,238	1,292	1,310	1,232	1,266	1,254	1,094	1,203	1,203	0.1	0.5	0.1
Millet	351	449	849	784	899	831	734	811	737	973	973	0.2	0.7	0.2
Maize	105	258	315	341	271	350	212	294	332	378	378	0.6	1.0	0.1
Rice	40	48	39	47	54	61	84	95	99	89	89	0.1	-1.2	0.4
BURUNDI														
Maize	9	13	13	14	13	11	14	11	17	11	10	0.1	0.4	-0.1
Sorghum	52	64	65	67	65	45	66	66	68	67	60	1.1	0.4	0.0
Rice	10	40	40	40	40	38	27	42	65	41	59	0.3	1.2	0.1
Millet	9	13	13	14	13	11	14	11	17	11	10	0.1	0.4	-0.1
Bananas	1,100	1,547	1,586	1,626	1,586	1,487	1,421	1,545	1,543	1,399	1,511	-0.1	0.4	0.0
Cassava	400	569	584	598	584	527	501	549	603	622	617	0.1	0.2	0.0
CAMEROON														
Maize	414	369	495	430	430	430	650	750	600	550	600	-0.1	0.1	0.2
Sorghum	331	329	400	380	390	350	460	439	400	500	500	0.3	-0.5	0.2
Millets	100	63	63	55	60	50	66	71	71	71	71	0.2	0.0	0.0
Rice	46	55	90	52	79	80	62	54	65	65	65	0.4	-0.3	0.0
Cassava	980	1,588	1,500	1,500	1,550	1,500	1,400	1,700	1,700	1,500	1,500	0.2	-0.2	0.0
Plantains	1,020	870	870	900	930	950	970	1,000	1,030	1,030	1,000	0.3	-0.2	0.0
CENTRAL AFRICAN REP														
Sorghum	36	20	18	21	20	21	22	26	28	29	29	0.2	-0.3	0.1
Maize	41	57	58	59	58	63	71	76	83	88	95	0.1	0.3	0.2
Groundnuts	123	80	63	71	72	79	86	91	97	102	110	0.0	0.0	0.1
Cassava	920	547	586	580	575	518	492	526	579	608	559	0.0	-0.5	0.0
Yam	150	230	230	260	260	280	320	340	340	360	360	0.0	0.1	0.2
CHAD														
Sorghum	250	280	286	387	306	379	437	453	521	637	637	-0.5	0.1	0.4
Millet	200	168	226	293	212	307	228	258	248	366	366	-0.5	0.6	0.3
Groundnuts	99	108	230	224	190	207	293	305	352	471	471	0.0	0.5	0.5
COMOROS														
Bananas	32	50	54	54	55	57	56	57	58	59	59	0.2	0.7	0.1
Cassava	33	45	45	47	48	48	49	50	51	52	53	-0.2	1.3	0.1
CONGO														
Maize	9	5	5	5	5	5	5	5	4	2	2	-0.7	0.5	-0.6
Cassava	628	700	585	600	632	740	790	791	780	791	800	0.2	0.1	0.1
Plantains	56	68	70	73	75	78	77	76	76	77	78	0.4	0.3	0.1
COTE D'IVOIRE														
Palm oil	189	250	264	290	283	285	249	267	249	240	242	0.1	0.4	0.0
Rice	420	660	687	714	890	988	1,045	833	1,287	1,197	1,162	0.0	0.3	0.3
Maize	380	497	515	517	529	517	552	569	576	573	571	0.4	-0.2	0.1
Cassava	1,010	1,393	1,465	1,502	1,509	1,564	1,641	1,653	1,699	1,692	1,673	0	0	0
Yams	2,040	2,528	2,690	2,758	2,771	2,824	2,894	2,924	2,986	2,921	2,923	0	0	0

(Table continues on the following page)

8-6. Volume of food output, by major food crop *(continued)*

					Thousands of metric tons							*Average annual percentage growth*		
	1980	1990	1991	1992	1993	1994	1995	1996	1997	1998	1999	75-84	85-89	90-MR
EGYPT														
Rice	2,382	3,167	3,448	3,910	4,161	4,583	4,788	4,895	5,480	4,450	5,816	0.1	0.2	0.3
Wheat	1,736	4,268	4,483	4,618	4,833	4,437	5,722	5,735	5,849	6,093	6,347	0.1	1.1	0.2
Sugarcane	8,618	11,095	11,624	11,708	12,412	13,822	14,105	13,958	13,726	14,353	15,325	0.1	-0.2	0.1
Dry Broadbeans	213	451	466	382	438	357	392	442	476	523	307	-0.1	0.7	-0.1
EQUATORIAL GUINEA														
Cassava	32	45	46	47	47	47	47	48	45	43	45	0.0	0.1	0.0
Sweet Potatoes	21	30	35	35	35	35	35	36	35	34	36	0.1	0.2	0.1
ETHIOPIA														
Sorghum	-	-	-	-	628	703	1,141	1,808	2,040	1,083	1,340	..	..	0.3
Maize	-	-	-	-	1,456	1,396	1,990	3,164	2,987	2,344	2,840	..	..	0.3
Barley	-	-	-	-	787	875	986	1,125	953	983	970	..	..	0.1
Sugarcane	-	-	-	-	1,700	1,200	1,200	1,582	1,490	1,650	2,200	..	..	0.2
GABON														
Oil palm	2	4	7	7	8	8	7	7	7	6	6	0.0	0.2	0.2
Maize	10	23	24	25	27	28	29	30	31	31	31	0.3	1.0	0.2
Cassava	250	210	222	230	207	211	215	215	218	220	225	0.2	0.2	0.0
Yam	79	110	110	120	110	125	130	135	140	145	150	0.3	0.2	0.2
Plantains	175	220	291	253	238	243	248	260	270	275	280	0.3	0.0	0.1
GAMBIA,THE														
Groundnuts	60	75	84	55	77	81	75	46	78	73	126	-0.3	0.5	0.0
Palm oil	3	3	3	3	3	3	3	3	3	3	3	0.0	0.0	0.0
Millet	15	47	58	46	52	53	54	61	66	65	76	0.7	0.4	0.2
Rice	43	21	21	19	12	20	19	18	17	27	29	0.9	-0.7	0.1
Maize	6	14	20	18	24	13	14	10	8	13	21	0.7	0.1	-0.1
Sorghum	5	8	12	12	9	9	12	14	13	10	18	0.5	-0.3	0.2
GHANA														
Maize	382	553	932	731	961	940	1,034	1,008	996	1,035	1,014	0.2	-0.1	0.2
Millet	82	75	112	133	198	168	201	193	144	172	160	-0.2	1.0	0.2
Groundnuts	142	113	67	100	140	176	168	162	154	212	212	0.2	0.3	0.3
Cassava	1,858	2,717	5,701	5,662	5,973	6,025	6,612	7,111	7,000	7,227	7,845	0.1	0.5	0.3
Plantains	734	799	1,178	1,082	1,322	1,475	1,638	1,823	1,818	1,893	2,046	-0.4	-0.3	0.4
GUINEA														
Palm oil	40	41	43	40	48	50	50	55	55	50	50	0.1	0.0	0.1
Rice	480	424	501	512	531	544	631	673	716	764	750	0.0	-0.3	0.3
Maize	90	74	80	88	85	83	79	82	85	89	89	0.3	-0.6	0.1
Groundnuts	84	78	104	139	128	126	132	145	158	174	174	0.0	-0.6	0.4
Cassava	480	372	437	512	550	525	601	667	732	812	812	-0.3	-0.9	0.4
Plantains	350	385	385	405	410	420	425	435	430	429	429	0.2	0.0	0.1
GUINEA-BISSAU														
Groundnuts	30	18	15	16	18	18	18	17	18	18	18	-0.1	-1.1	0.0
Palm kernels	9	7	10	8	7	8	8	8	8	8	8	0.1	-0.4	0.0
Rice	42	123	123	124	126	131	133	120	125	130	130	-0.1	0.0	0.0
Sorghum	18	11	13	11	14	14	16	22	19	21	21	1.0	-1.3	0.3
Maize	12	14	13	10	13	14	15	9	9	9	9	0.6	0.2	-0.2
KENYA														
Sugarcane	4,532	4,750	4,600	4,180	4,370	3,800	4,550	4,650	4,450	4,900	5,200	0.7	0.2	0.0
Maize	1,620	2,290	2,340	2,430	2,089	3,060	2,699	2,160	2,214	2,450	2,100	-0.3	0.7	0.0
Wheat	216	190	195	126	150	297	313	320	252	315	135	0.2	0.4	0.1
LESOTHO														
Wheat	28	33	7	12	8	12	11	30	34	29	15	-1.0	1.0	0.1
Dry Beans	4	8	2	1	2	3	5	6	14	8	9	-1.3	2.0	0.3
Dry Peas	5	3	1	2	1	1	1	4	3	5	3	-0.5	-1.7	0.5
Maize	106	172	49	61	92	149	63	188	142	119	125	0.3	0.5	0.2
Sorghum	59	36	10	19	52	61	7	36	29	23	33	0.1	-0.4	0.2
LIBERIA														
Rice	243	185	130	110	65	50	56	94	168	210	210	0.0	0.0	0.0
Cassava	300	360	270	280	245	250	175	213	283	313	313	0.1	1.1	-0.1
LIBYA														
Wheat	141	129	130	125	126	120	117	124	156	165	168	0.9	-0.1	0.1
Olives	161	68	80	100	120	140	168	186	186	190	190	0.9	-1.9	0.5
MADAGASCAR														
Rice Paddy	2,109	2,420	2,342	2,450	2,550	2,357	2,450	2,500	2,558	2,447	2,637	0.0	0.1	0.0
Cassava	1,683	2,292	2,307	2,280	2,350	2,360	2,400	2,353	2,418	2,404	2,435	0.3	0.0	0.0
Sweet potatoes	373	486	488	452	500	560	450	500	510	510	520	-0.1	0.0	0.0

(Table continues on the following page)

8-6. Volume of food output, by major food crop *(continued)*

					Thousands of metric tons							* Average annual percentage growth		
	1980	1990	1991	1992	1993	1994	1995	1996	1997	1998	1999	75-84	85-89	90-MR
MALAWI														
Groundnuts	177	37	58	26	55	31	32	40	69	108	100	0.0	-0.1	0.3
Maize	1,186	1,343	1,589	657	2,034	1,040	1,661	1,793	1,226	1,772	2,480	0.1	-0.2	0.2
Sorghum	20	15	19	4	22	17	45	55	40	41	60	-2.4	-0.2	0.6
Cassava	292	145	168	129	216	190	190	190	200	200	200	0.1	-0.9	0.1
MALI														
Groundnuts	144	157	180	184	127	149	215	157	134	144	144	-0.6	1.3	-0.1
Millet	407	842	737	890	582	708	898	707	739	641	641	0.1	0.9	-0.1
Rice	132	338	282	454	410	428	469	463	576	589	589	-0.3	1.4	0.3
Sorghum	356	731	531	770	602	777	746	710	540	559	559	0.2	0.6	0.0
Maize	45	225	197	257	193	283	322	264	290	341	341	-0.3	1.7	0.2
MAURITANIA														
Sorghum	28	45	58	50	92	147	157	145	58	73	75	0.1	2.2	0.2
Millet	3	3	2	2	4	7	8	8	3	3	10	0.2	2.1	0.2
Rice	11	52	42	51	65	45	53	67	81	111	102	1.5	2.1	0.3
Maize	5	2	2	3	7	6	4	14	12	11	8	0.2	-2.6	0.8
MAURITIUS														
Sugarcane	4,564	5,548	5,621	5,781	5,402	4,813	5,159	5,260	5,787	5,781	3,500	-0.1	0.3	-0.1
Potatoes	12	18	16	19	14	18	16	11	18	15	15	0.1	-0.2	-0.1
Dry Onions	2	3	3	3	4	5	6	6	5	7	7	0.8	-0.9	0.4
MOROCCO														
Citrus	1,084	1,039	1,462	1,111	1,230	1,324	997	1,393	1,229	1,597	1,312	0.3	0.0	0.1
Wheat	1,811	3,614	4,939	1,562	1,573	5,523	1,091	5,916	2,316	4,378	2,154	0.1	0.1	0.0
Sugarbeet	2,241	2,984	3,036	2,754	3,062	3,144	2,717	2,750	2,613	2,823	3,223	0.3	0.2	0.0
Barley	2,210	2,138	3,253	1,081	1,027	3,720	608	3,831	1,324	1,970	1,474	0.0	-0.5	0.0
MOZAMBIQUE														
Cashew nuts	71	23	31	54	24	23	33	65	43	52	53	-0.8	1.3	0.3
Maize	380	453	327	132	533	489	734	947	1,042	1,124	1,185	-0.2	-0.8	0.6
Rice	75	96	56	33	66	101	113	139	180	191	200	0.2	0.1	0.5
Cassava	3,600	4,590	3,690	3,239	3,511	3,352	4,178	4,734	5,337	5,639	5,650	0.1	0.0	0.2
NAMIBIA														
Wheat	2	4	6	3	6	6	3	6	6	3	3	0.9	0.3	-0.1
Maize	32	29	51	11	26	41	18	19	50	15	18	0.2	-2.9	-0.2
NIGER														
Cowpeas	266	217	381	402	168	525	184	295	192	775	641	0.4	0.1	0.4
Groundnuts	126	18	46	57	26	67	111	196	88	112	108	0.1	0.0	0.8
Sorghum	368	281	463	387	289	393	266	408	290	501	481	0.2	0.7	0.1
Millet	1,364	1,766	1,833	1,788	1,658	1,968	1,769	1,761	1,352	2,391	2,253	0.2	0.1	0.1
NIGERIA														
Groundnuts	471	992	1,361	1,297	1,323	1,453	1,579	2,278	2,531	2,534	2,783	-0.2	0.3	0.5
Palm oil	650	730	760	792	825	837	860	776	810	845	847	0.1	0.5	0.1
Sorghum	3,690	4,185	5,367	5,909	6,051	6,197	6,184	7,084	7,297	7,103	8,443	0.0	0.2	0.2
Millet	2,450	5,136	4,109	4,501	4,602	4,757	4,952	5,681	5,902	5,956	5,457	-0.2	0.4	0.1
Maize	612	5,768	5,810	5,840	6,290	6,902	7,048	5,667	5,354	5,127	5,777	-0.2	2.5	0.0
Rice	1,090	2,500	3,226	3,260	3,065	2,427	2,920	3,122	3,268	3,275	3,397	1.5	1.2	0.0
Yam	5,248	13,624	16,956	19,781	21,632	23,153	22,818	23,201	19,566	24,768	25,077	-0.3	0.4	0.3
Cassava	11,500	19,043	26,004	29,185	30,128	31,005	31,404	31,418	30,409	32,695	33,060	0.1	0.5	0.2
RWANDA														
Sorghum	179	143	205	113	128	55	77	102	122	121	108	0.2	-0.1	-0.2
Maize	85	101	104	109	74	60	71	67	83	59	55	0.2	-0.3	-0.3
Plantains	2,063	2,777	3,093	3,547	2,136	1,489	2,002	2,105	2,248	2,625	2,897	0.2	0.4	-0.1
Sweet potatoes	871	857	1,000	1,055	997	410	551	665	742	751	863	0.4	0.0	-0.1
SENEGAL														
Groundnuts	523	703	724	578	628	678	791	646	545	579	828	0.0	1.2	0.0
Millet	451	505	593	446	654	548	667	601	426	428	506	0.3	1.3	-0.1
Rice	65	181	170	177	193	162	155	149	174	124	240	0.3	0.1	0.0
Maize	57	133	103	115	138	108	107	89	60	44	66	0.2	0.3	-0.4
Sorghum	102	157	78	117	99	123	127	133	118	120	147	0.3	0.2	0.1
SIERRA LEONE														
Palm oil	47	50	51	48	47	50	45	48	51	51	36	0.1	0.0	-0.1
Palm kernels	30	29	30	31	33	32	29	31	31	31	22	-0.2	-0.2	-0.1
Rice	513	504	504	479	486	405	356	392	411	328	247	-0.2	-0.2	-0.3
Cassava	95	123	123	117	106	244	219	281	310	289	240	0.1	0.2	0.5

(Table continues on the following page)

8-6. Volume of food output, by major food crop *(continued)*

					Thousands of metric tons							* Average annual percentage growth		
	1980	1990	1991	1992	1993	1994	1995	1996	1997	1998	1999	75-84	85-89	90-MR
SOMALIA														
Bananas	60	110	70	70	55	43	50	55	55	53	55	-0.3	1.0	-0.3
Maize	110	315	100	101	79	150	146	142	128	145	150	0.2	-0.1	-0.1
Sorghum	140	250	145	92	80	252	136	145	153	50	55	0.3	0.5	-0.5
Sesame	38	45	35	15	22	22	25	23	24	21	22	0.2	0.3	-0.3
SOUTH AFRICA														
Maize	11,040	9,180	8,614	3,277	9,997	13,275	4,866	10,171	10,136	7,693	7,712	0.1	1.1	0.0
Wheat	1,472	1,709	2,142	1,324	1,984	1,840	1,977	2,712	2,429	1,788	1,561	0.0	0.4	0.0
Sugarcane	14,062	18,084	20,078	12,955	11,244	15,683	16,714	20,951	22,155	22,930	21,248	-0.1	0.0	0.1
Sorghum	711	341	302	118	515	520	291	536	433	358	209	0.2	0.6	0.0
Barley	60	262	170	265	230	275	300	176	182	215	91	0.3	1.4	-0.3
SUDAN														
Groundnuts	712	123	180	380	428	714	738	815	1,104	800	980	-0.4	-0.3	0.8
Sesame	221	80	97	266	175	170	313	416	281	165	220	-0.3	0.7	0.4
Sorghum	2,084	1,180	3,581	4,042	2,386	3,648	2,450	4,179	3,159	4,781	3,045	-0.2	-1.0	0.3
Wheat	231	409	686	895	453	475	448	527	642	597	168	-0.5	0.2	-0.2
SWAZILAND														
Sugarcane	2,782	3,842	3,941	3,885	3,647	3,786	3,440	3,846	3,694	3,887	3,700	0.5	0.1	0.0
Citrus (oranges)	45	35	33	35	23	48	29	33	33	31	31	-0.1	-0.8	0.0
Maize	97	94	139	54	73	99	76	151	108	125	113	-0.1	-1.0	0.1
TANZANIA														
Maize	1,726	2,445	2,332	2,226	2,282	2,159	2,567	2,663	1,879	2,750	2,458	0.2	0.6	0.0
Sorghum	510	368	550	587	719	478	839	872	498	593	561	0.8	0.6	0.1
Rice	291	740	625	392	641	614	723	734	551	811	676	-0.1	1.2	0.1
Millet	340	200	200	263	210	218	411	367	347	206	194	0.7	0.0	0.0
Cassava	4,828	7,792	7,460	7,112	6,833	7,208	5,969	5,992	5,700	6,128	7,182	0.2	-0.3	-0.1
TOGO														
Maize	138	285	231	278	393	348	290	388	452	350	350	0.4	0.2	0.2
Sorghum	95	115	141	112	126	110	172	156	152	137	137	-0.4	-0.3	0.0
Millet	43	58	50	75	75	57	51	55	49	41	41	-1.2	0.1	-0.2
Cassava	408	593	511	452	389	412	602	548	596	579	579	0.1	-0.5	0.1
Yam	484	392	376	368	530	364	531	605	683	696	696	0.2	0.0	0.3
TUNISIA														
Olive oil	115	165	265	120	210	70	60	310	90	150	160	-0.4	0.2	0.0
Citrus	160	237	226	186	298	208	194	224	206	227	210	0.2	0.3	-0.1
Wheat	869	1,122	1,786	1,584	1,413	503	531	2,018	885	1,354	1,400	0.3	1.7	0.2
Barley	296	478	721	570	478	145	80	835	160	303	410	0.9	2.1	0.0
UGANDA														
Millet	459	560	576	634	610	610	632	440	502	642	638	-0.3	1.0	0.0
Maize	286	602	567	657	804	850	913	759	740	770	780	-0.5	0.6	0.1
Sorghum	299	360	363	375	383	390	399	298	294	420	454	-0.2	0.5	0.1
Cassava	2,072	3,420	3,229	2,896	3,139	2,080	2,224	2,245	2,291	3,204	3,400	-0.4	0.3	-0.1
Plantains	5,699	7,842	8,080	7,806	8,222	8,500	9,012	9,144	9,303	9,318	9,400	-0.4	0.3	0.1
ZAIRE														
Palm oil	168	179	180	181	182	183	186	188	166	157	157	-0.1	0.2	-0.1
Maize	594	1,008	1,023	1,053	1,130	1,184	1,225	1,101	1,167	1,215	1,100	0.2	0.4	0.1
Rice	234	392	394	403	430	426	441	357	355	363	350	0.2	0.4	-0.1
Cassava	13,087	18,715	19,366	19,780	18,890	19,102	19,378	16,887	16,973	17,060	16,500	0.1	0.3	-0.1
Plantains	1,563	2,097	2,090	2,117	2,186	2,262	2,424	2,140	1,889	1,850	1,800	0.1	0.1	0.0
ZAMBIA														
Sunflower seeds	28	20	11	1	21	10	21	27	8	6	7	0.5	-2.2	-0.2
Maize	937	1,093	1,096	483	1,598	1,021	738	1,409	960	638	856	-0.7	0.4	-0.2
Wheat	10	55	65	58	71	43	50	58	71	64	90	1.1	2.0	0.1
Cassava	290	520	570	560	620	600	590	620	702	817	850	0.4	0.4	0.2
ZIMBABWE														
Sugarcane	2,528	3,093	3,236	125	538	3,420	3,773	2,826	4,651	4,811	4,657	0.2	-0.2	0.4
Maize	1,511	1,972	1,586	362	2,012	2,326	840	2,609	2,192	1,418	1,520	-0.1	-0.7	0.1
Wheat	191	326	259	58	276	239	83	280	300	280	320	0.3	1.2	0.1

* The standard Bank least square methodology was used to compute the average annual percentage growth.

Notes: Crops shown represent same major food crops as in Table 8-1, Nominal producer prices, excluding beverages (coffee, tea, cocoa), cotton, and tobacco.

The following commodities are in their least-processed form unless otherwise indicated: groundnuts (unshelled), rice (paddy), sunflower (seeds), Citurs (total for country), Sesame (seeds), Livestock (combined total head of cattle, sheep, oats, pigs, horses, asses and mules), Chickens/rabbits (combined total).

For South Africa, barley production is for white areas only.

Countries excluded from listing: Cape Verde, Djibouti, Eritrea, São Tomé and Principe, and Seychelles.

8-7. Value of agricultural exports

	Millions of U.S. dollars (current prices)									Average annual percentage growth		
	1980	1990	1991	1992	1993	1994	1995	1996	1997	75-84	85-89	90-MR
SUB-SAHARAN AFRICA	12,212	10,358	9,563	9,258	9,317	11,506	13,108	14,312	13,368	1.8	2.0	4.6
excluding South Africa	9,695	8,440	7,725	7,467	7,738	9,389	10,823	11,823	10,904	2.0	0.6	4.8
excl. S.Africa & Nigeria	9,249	8,210	7,511	7,277	7,462	9,062	10,420	11,281	10,383	2.4	0.6	4.5
Angola	172	6	5	5	3	1	5	6	6	-12.8	-30.5	-7.6
Benin	55	84	86	93	83	115	201	188	198	3.0	-4.2	14.2
Botswana	51	79	90	91	96	97	132	115	115	5.2	2.7	5.9
Burkina Faso	80	116	94	86	93	80	141	123	119	5.3	5.1	5.6
Burundi	64	69	88	67	53	113	96	32	82	8.8	-4.0	-1.9
Cameroon	699	563	341	364	245	393	565	624	504	2.6	5.1	0.5
Cape Verde	0	0	0	0	0	0	0	0	0	17.7	38.3	-31.8
Central African Republic	60	45	46	33	36	37	51	28	33	6.8	3.3	-6.4
Chad	115	134	136	127	84	118	145	127	135	13.2	-7.4	0.9
Comoros	7	11	20	16	18	8	7	4	4	8.6	13.4	-16.4
Congo, Democratic Rep. of	235	141	78	83	53	93	135	102	95	-1.7	-8.5	-3.9
Congo, Republic of	13	15	14	17	9	7	11	16	15	-1.7	-15.1	2.8
Côte d'Ivoire	2,009	1,615	1,532	1,434	1,605	1,557	2,216	2,421	2,001	7.0	-2.7	4.2
Djibouti	0	0	0	0	0	0	0	0	0	96.6	18.8	-7.8
Equatorial Guinea	12	8	6	6	3	4	4	7	4	-4.0	-10.3	-6.5
Eritrea	..	..	..	..	4	4	2	2	2	..	..	..
Ethiopia	..	..	..	..	193	362	409	426	526	..	..	..
Gabon	14	3	6	7	4	5	8	10	10	13.3	-1.1	8.4
Gambia, The	28	14	12	11	15	15	16	16	12	-5.0	-22.1	2.9
Ghana	744	413	369	319	302	358	393	638	616	-5.1	3.2	5.2
Guinea	33	27	23	31	43	45	61	43	48	5.3	10.7	9.4
Guinea-Bissau	6	13	16	4	14	32	21	22	22	9.0	2.8	12.4
Kenya	693	687	641	812	975	1,044	1,153	1,165	1,157	6.5	-1.8	9.1
Lesotho	16	13	12	13	12	13	12	9	9	7.0	7.7	-7.7
Liberia	151	23	27	23	32	24	13	13	20	5.7	0.6	-16.5
Madagascar	334	176	157	143	133	237	200	138	92	2.6	-4.9	-4.8
Malawi	251	376	462	371	286	288	389	383	359	9.2	-0.6	1.5
Mali	192	251	267	266	251	239	270	312	271	12.3	3.8	1.8
Mauritania	39	44	47	48	49	31	38	40	40	7.3	-0.6	-0.6
Mauritius	302	379	365	402	367	367	420	501	405	-1.1	13.2	2.8
Mozambique	157	41	45	53	26	64	67	50	50	-8.0	1.4	3.4
Namibia	188	147	180	200	185	201	199	202	201	-8.0	18.9	3.1
Niger	86	62	65	55	48	48	45	45	45	8.4	-7.5	-4.1
Nigeria	446	230	214	189	275	327	403	542	522	-4.4	-2.5	12.9
Rwanda	66	95	85	60	52	14	42	39	38	5.5	8.6	-15.1
São Tomé and Principe	19	4	4	4	4	5	2	3	3	0.1	-9.9	-5.5
Senegal	115	219	135	126	91	126	115	87	58	-5.6	7.7	-12.7
Seychelles	3	1	1	1	1	1	2	2	2	-1.8	-16.3	16.3
Sierra Leone	59	18	24	11	9	21	15	16	14	-0.3	-11.6	-3.9
Somalia	125	74	41	62	60	68	75	76	76	4.9	3.6	2.4
South Africa	2,517	1,918	1,838	1,792	1,580	2,118	2,284	2,489	2,464	0.6	10.6	3.7
Sudan	553	550	381	367	455	471	501	565	556	1.9	5.8	0.3
Swaziland	211	347	339	306	265	283	291	311	300	6.7	20.8	0.0
Tanzania	406	279	243	281	303	379	431	496	400	-0.2	-0.6	7.5
Togo	77	120	101	125	75	76	127	133	128	5.4	4.8	2.7
Uganda	344	173	167	134	180	425	469	491	405	1.1	-7.4	13.9
Zambia	13	24	29	36	27	16	32	46	50	-8.1	10.3	8.7
Zimbabwe	453	750	731	584	617	1,177	895	1,207	1,157	4.4	5.0	9.1
NORTH AFRICA	1,544	1,406	1,591	1,396	1,313	1,708	1,892	1,876	1,895	-2.1	1.0	5.0
Algeria	120	50	54	76	97	35	108	137	91	-12.7	-9.2	13.2
Egypt, Arab Republic	677	427	391	401	360	553	536	521	442	-1.9	-6.9	1.4
Libya	0	0	0	0	0	0	0	0	0	-58.1	3.9	26.4
Morocco	606	647	670	581	509	598	780	896	832	0.4	11.9	5.5
Tunisia	140	282	477	338	347	523	468	322	530	-2.7	8.0	7.8
ALL AFRICA	13,756	11,764	11,154	10,654	10,630	13,214	15,000	16,188	15,263	1.2	1.9	4.6

8-8. Cereal production

	Thousands of metric tons										Average annual percentage growth		
	1980	1990	1991	1992	1993	1994	1995	1996	1997	1998	1999	75-84	85-89	90-MR
SUB-SAHARAN AFRICA	49,742	63,780	69,586	60,572	78,464	84,333	77,127	90,204	86,379	86,140	85,396	-0.6	8.0	3.2
excluding South Africa	36,369	52,226	58,296	55,527	65,671	68,366	69,635	76,553	73,149	76,042	75,535	0.0	7.3	4.0
excl. S.Africa & Nigeria	28,581	34,548	39,681	35,930	45,580	47,993	47,122	54,888	51,296	54,002	53,130	-0.3	5.7	4.7
Angola	435	249	372	402	322	285	296	525	457	621	550	-6.0	-1.4	7.8
Benin	346	546	587	609	627	646	725	714	906	867	890	3.0	2.0	5.5
Botswana	44	53	50	20	44	52	42	106	31	12	20	-20.5	60.0	-9.3
Burkina Faso	1,048	1,518	2,455	2,477	2,552	2,492	2,308	2,470	2,274	2,662	2,662	0.3	10.9	3.2
Burundi	217	293	300	306	300	225	269	273	305	261	265	3.9	5.4	-1.2
Cameroon	892	816	1,048	917	959	910	1,238	1,314	1,296	1,425	1,455	-1.6	3.5	6.1
Cape Verde	9	11	8	10	12	8	8	10	10	10	10	2.1	52.9	-0.2
Central African Republic	100	95	92	94	94	101	113	126	138	148	173	1.4	4.0	5.1
Chad	573	601	812	976	683	1,059	907	975	1,079	1,353	1,153	-5.1	8.2	7.1
Comoros	18	19	20	20	21	21	21	21	21	21	21	1.4	1.4	1.2
Congo, Democratic Rep. of	889	1,491	1,507	1,553	1,655	1,708	1,766	1,557	1,633	1,692	1,649	3.9	5.8	1.5
Congo, Republic of	12	6	6	6	7	7	6	5	4	2	2	-6.2	8.1	-14.1
Côte d'Ivoire	860	1,239	1,286	1,319	1,511	1,599	1,690	1,494	1,963	1,870	1,832	2.6	1.7	5.0
Djibouti	0	0	0	0	0	0	0	0	0	0	0	..	-5.1	7.2
Equatorial Guinea	..	..	..	..	..	..	..	..	..	..	..	..	..	..
Eritrea	..	..	..	..	87	259	153	84	99	458	270	..	..	15.8
Ethiopia	..	..	..	..	5,295	5,245	6,740	9,379	9,473	7,197	8,406	..	..	8.8
Gabon	11	24	25	26	27	29	30	31	32	32	32	5.7	12.4	4.2
Gambia, The	70	90	111	96	97	95	98	103	104	114	144	7.0	0.1	2.7
Ghana	674	844	1,436	1,254	1,645	1,594	1,797	1,770	1,669	1,788	1,686	-0.6	3.9	5.6
Guinea	725	627	686	683	711	718	825	879	927	985	971	1.2	-4.6	5.5
Guinea-Bissau	93	167	179	169	181	190	201	174	183	191	191	8.3	-1.6	1.9
Kenya	2,233	2,728	2,773	2,849	2,530	3,663	3,275	2,773	2,767	3,082	2,514	-2.3	9.8	-0.4
Lesotho	194	242	67	94	153	223	81	256	206	171	174	-4.8	9.5	2.4
Liberia	243	185	130	110	65	50	56	94	168	210	210	2.2	0.2	-0.8
Madagascar	2,238	2,581	2,497	2,591	2,724	2,517	2,642	2,685	2,742	2,610	2,829	0.5	1.5	0.8
Malawi	1,252	1,413	1,680	689	2,137	1,109	1,778	1,943	1,349	1,904	2,655	0.6	1.4	4.6
Mali	968	1,771	2,414	1,809	2,228	2,457	2,173	2,219	2,149	2,552	2,952	0.5	12.0	2.8
Mauritania	47	103	105	107	169	207	222	234	154	198	196	1.8	25.5	5.5
Mauritius	1	2	2	2	2	1	0	0	0	0	0	-0.9	-9.5	-24.8
Mozambique	663	734	546	242	765	791	1,127	1,379	1,531	1,688	1,821	-1.0	-4.7	15.4
Namibia	74	98	115	31	75	116	62	89	173	55	76	3.7	3.5	-0.4
Niger	1,775	2,134	2,384	2,253	2,023	2,430	2,096	2,261	1,702	2,958	2,823	3.2	9.7	2.3
Nigeria	7,788	17,678	18,615	19,597	20,091	20,373	22,513	21,665	21,853	22,040	22,405	1.3	11.4	2.6
Rwanda	273	265	341	251	221	126	157	183	223	194	179	4.4	-3.0	-4.8
São Tomé and Principe	0	3	4	4	4	4	3	2	1	2	1	1.5	24.6	-7.2
Senegal	676	977	946	856	1,086	943	1,059	976	783	720	963	-1.6	3.2	-1.9
Seychelles	..	..	..	..	..	..	..	..	..	..	..	..	..	..
Sierra Leone	551	563	560	534	542	466	408	444	467	373	280	-1.0	1.0	-5.7
Somalia	267	581	256	209	165	405	285	290	284	197	207	8.2	5.2	-7.5
South Africa	13,373	11,553	11,290	5,045	12,793	15,967	7,492	13,651	13,230	10,098	9,861	-3.3	10.9	-0.7
Sudan	2,701	1,702	4,637	5,438	3,102	5,146	3,305	5,202	4,261	5,603	3,097	-3.5	4.1	6.3
Swaziland	105	99	142	58	75	101	79	152	110	126	114	-4.2	-6.3	1.1
Tanzania	2,961	3,842	3,777	3,533	3,917	3,550	4,629	4,719	3,390	4,495	3,977	5.8	6.6	0.1
Togo	296	484	465	495	634	559	550	687	744	620	761	4.1	6.4	4.1
Uganda	1,078	1,580	1,576	1,743	1,880	1,936	2,030	1,588	1,625	1,911	1,874	-4.5	10.3	1.3
Zambia	984	1,210	1,225	612	1,758	1,170	882	1,573	1,137	798	1,057	-6.3	16.3	-3.4
Zimbabwe	1,989	2,560	2,060	481	2,498	2,780	987	3,127	2,723	1,829	1,987	-4.1	5.6	1.0
NORTH AFRICA	16,445	22,835	29,152	23,308	21,329	26,440	20,788	34,577	24,302	29,503	26,147	-0.3	5.1	2.0
Algeria	2,419	1,627	3,810	3,330	1,454	965	2,140	4,902	870	3,026	1,540	-2.5	-4.7	-1.9
Egypt, Arab Republic	8,100	13,022	13,864	14,611	14,961	15,012	16,097	16,542	18,071	17,941	18,677	1.0	5.4	4.6
Libya	215	273	258	218	180	165	146	160	206	238	251	4.2	3.8	-2.9
Morocco	4,515	6,276	8,665	2,950	2,818	9,639	1,783	10,104	4,098	6,632	3,860	-2.2	12.2	-3.0
Tunisia	1,197	1,638	2,556	2,199	1,917	660	622	2,869	1,056	1,667	1,819	0.5	-18.7	1.9
ALL AFRICA	66,187	86,615	98,738	83,880	99,793	110,772	97,915	124,780	110,681	115,643	111,542	-0.5	7.3	2.9

8-9. Crop production index

	Index (average 1989-91 = 100)										Average annual percentage growth		
	1980	*1990*	*1991*	*1992*	*1993*	*1994*	*1995*	*1996*	*1997*	*1998*	*1999*	*75-84*	*85-89*	*90-MR*
SUB-SAHARAN AFRICA	76	98	108	106	110	116	118	127	124	132	133	-0.4	4.8	3.2
excluding South Africa	76	99	109	109	112	118	122	129	126	135	136	-0.4	4.6	3.4
excl. S.Africa & Nigeria	82	97	106	103	105	110	114	121	120	126	125	-0.3	3.3	2.7
Angola	107	96	104	111	108	137	132	134	129	158	143	-6.5	0.9	4.7
Benin	52	99	110	111	127	128	144	162	172	172	178	3.2	4.3	7.3
Botswana	91	96	98	68	88	97	80	127	78	64	74	-6.4	13.1	-2.6
Burkina Faso	55	92	110	116	120	119	115	127	126	146	146	2.2	8.1	4.1
Burundi	77	102	106	108	105	90	96	96	96	90	92	0.8	3.3	-1.1
Cameroon	87	100	104	99	107	110	120	123	120	124	125	0.4	0.6	2.9
Cape Verde	79	104	77	73	82	73	70	98	101	97	97	3.0	22.5	-0.1
Central African Republic	103	100	96	98	97	107	111	124	131	131	127	0.0	1.8	3.4
Chad	70	89	116	110	90	110	123	136	147	182	176	-1.1	6.6	6.9
Comoros	79	101	103	102	107	109	116	113	114	126	119	0.8	4.7	2.3
Congo, Democratic Rep. of	74	101	103	105	104	106	108	94	96	92	89	2.4	2.8	-1.1
Congo, Republic of	84	101	97	99	101	110	114	115	109	113	115	2.0	1.5	1.7
Côte d'Ivoire	71	102	99	97	102	104	116	119	128	129	132	3.3	4.8	3.4
Djibouti	71	97	98	99	99	100	100	102	106	106	106	29.6	2.4	0.7
Equatorial Guinea	90	101	98	95	97	90	82	87	92	81	86	0.6	1.5	-2.0
Eritrea	..	..	..	..	93	158	135	110	115	215	154	..	..	7.2
Ethiopia	..	..	..	..	96	96	111	131	138	117	126	..	..	5.3
Gabon	79	96	107	103	100	103	106	110	110	117	119	4.6	4.0	1.9
Gambia, The	66	81	94	69	85	89	84	63	87	84	129	-1.0	4.0	-0.1
Ghana	68	80	121	120	130	123	144	156	159	167	178	-2.5	4.7	6.9
Guinea	92	100	109	118	119	122	126	129	135	143	142	0.9	-1.1	4.2
Guinea-Bissau	63	104	98	104	104	111	119	115	118	119	119	3.7	1.8	2.2
Kenya	72	98	99	98	94	109	112	110	106	116	105	1.6	6.3	1.3
Lesotho	92	127	60	71	90	122	74	136	133	114	117	-3.8	9.5	3.0
Liberia	..	..	..	..	..	..	..	..	..	..	..			
Madagascar	85	100	101	100	106	100	102	104	105	104	109	0.3	1.1	0.7
Malawi	84	98	107	83	115	89	111	127	111	140	154	2.0	1.2	4.4
Mali	51	93	112	99	100	115	117	123	129	139	148	0.1	11.4	4.5
Mauritania	61	82	88	89	111	138	149	152	127	139	147	2.4	17.5	4.8
Mauritius	80	101	102	105	101	92	100	98	104	104	72	0.1	0.1	-1.4
Mozambique	111	108	94	79	93	91	113	130	141	154	155	-2.3	0.5	5.7
Namibia	80	100	104	74	88	103	91	103	127	99	109	1.9	2.2	1.7
Niger	93	100	110	112	86	122	98	122	128	160	148	2.1	9.2	4.7
Nigeria	51	97	111	120	126	130	135	144	135	153	157	-1.0	10.1	5.1
Rwanda	82	96	106	108	78	52	63	67	76	82	87	4.3	0.4	-3.0
São Tomé and Principe	117	97	98	123	127	131	116	137	132	152	164	-2.7	0.4	4.7
Senegal	57	94	97	84	95	96	110	97	86	85	112	-5.1	8.8	-0.2
Seychelles	190	94	107	86	87	103	118	124	116	107	106	-2.8	-11.1	2.0
Sierra Leone	81	100	100	92	91	98	90	95	101	94	75	1.0	2.2	-1.5
Somalia	..	..	..	..	..	..	..	..	..	..	..	..	..	..
South Africa	92	96	96	68	93	106	81	110	107	98	106	-0.5	6.9	1.0
Sudan	125	78	122	145	112	158	149	180	177	171	155	-2.4	-0.9	6.7
Swaziland	77	97	100	84	78	85	73	90	87	89	89	3.6	1.9	-1.3
Tanzania	79	99	101	94	94	92	99	103	89	99	101	3.0	1.3	-0.1
Togo	71	100	102	104	121	105	113	137	146	140	152	1.8	5.2	4.7
Uganda	65	100	102	100	108	108	112	109	108	116	118	-3.2	4.4	1.7
Zambia	66	89	94	64	119	90	84	109	96	81	93	-2.5	10.4	-0.7
Zimbabwe	76	98	100	59	100	106	78	120	123	117	113	-0.6	4.0	2.8
NORTH AFRICA	78	102	117	113	113	111	110	146	122	135	136	1.0	3.7	3.0
Algeria	81	84	118	127	109	93	114	155	103	129	129	-1.6	2.3	2.9
Egypt, Arab Republic	77	102	104	112	116	112	123	135	134	136	143	2.1	3.3	4.1
Libya	79	99	102	100	104	108	116	125	122	131	134	4.1	1.8	3.5
Morocco	59	91	109	73	74	110	62	122	92	110	91	0.6	9.7	0.5
Tunisia	76	98	129	103	115	74	69	146	88	115	122	0.5	-2.5	2.0
ALL AFRICA	77	99	110	107	111	115	116	131	124	133	134	-0.1	4.6	3.2

8-10. Fertilizer use

	Thousands of metric tons										Average annual percentage growth		
	1980	1990	1991	1992	1993	1994	1995	1996	1997	1998	75-84	85-89	90-MR
SUB-SAHARAN AFRICA	1,973	1,972	1,927	1,920	2,170	1,962	1,832	2,099	2,038	2,059	4.4	-0.6	0.7
excluding South Africa	909	1,181	1,187	1,187	1,327	1,210	1,065	1,295	1,250	1,276	5.3	2.2	0.9
excl. S.Africa & Nigeria	735	781	757	747	866	914	882	1,122	1,112	1,088	2.4	0.8	5.1
Angola	17	10	7	9	8	10	8	6	2	5	-0.5	16.0	-14.3
Benin	1	11	12	15	17	17	36	31	39	38	7.5	-15.0	26.0
Botswana	1	1	1	1	1	1	2	3	4	4	-5.7	2.7	22.4
Burkina Faso	4	21	21	21	21	23	24	24	43	50	23.4	11.1	9.0
Burundi	1	2	2	5	4	3	3	3	1	2	11.4	15.1	-7.6
Cameroon	32	17	18	24	22	30	30	34	39	40	12.9	-9.8	8.2
Cape Verde	0	0	0	0	0	0	0	0	0	0	-0.6	22.3	..
Central African Republic	1	1	1	1	1	0	0	0	0	1	-11.1	-17.6	-11.8
Chad	1	6	9	10	5	7	9	12	8	17	-4.9	-7.3	9.3
Comoros	0	0	0	0	0	0	0	0	0	0	..	..	21.7
Congo, Democratic Rep. of	8	6	8	2	4	10	9	6	0	0	0.1	-9.8	1.5
Congo, Republic of	1	2	1	2	2	2	2	4	4	5	4.0	-33.9	21.2
Côte d'Ivoire	53	36	39	37	54	65	66	71	110	113	1.4	-0.6	14.5
Djibouti	1	0	0	0	0	0	0	0	0	0	-44.2	..	..
Equatorial Guinea	0	0	0	0	0	0	0	0	0	0	0.0	..	..
Eritrea	..	..	..	..	1	1	2	5	6	7	..	..	61.9
Ethiopia	..	..	..	..	74	122	131	178	132	164	..	..	13.9
Gabon	0	1	1	1	0	0	0	0	0	0	28.9	-18.8	-15.7
Gambia, The	2	1	1	1	1	1	1	1	1	2	7.9	-13.3	1.0
Ghana	12	13	8	10	8	8	10	17	21	15	-0.9	1.3	7.8
Guinea	0	1	2	1	2	4	5	4	2	3	-15.8	29.7	18.0
Guinea-Bissau	0	1	1	0	0	0	0	0	0	1	9.8	..	-6.0
Kenya	62	116	113	102	103	130	78	161	140	128	6.1	6.4	2.0
Lesotho	5	5	6	6	6	5	6	6	6	6	18.1	2.3	2.4
Liberia	3	0	0	0	0	0	0	0	0	0	-11.1	24.9	..
Madagascar	9	11	9	8	11	11	13	17	10	9	3.1	-1.5	3.9
Malawi	33	48	70	74	74	21	44	58	57	50	12.4	7.4	-2.0
Mali	14	15	15	27	25	25	27	27	48	53	14.3	-16.4	13.4
Mauritania	1	4	5	7	5	4	4	5	2	2	-9.6	28.4	-5.1
Mauritius	27	28	28	27	26	29	32	38	33	33	0.7	3.3	2.3
Mozambique	28	3	5	5	3	6	8	8	7	5	6.5	-13.1	11.2
Namibia	..	..	..	..	..	..	..	..	..	..	..	..	..
Niger	3	2	1	1	2	6	10	9	1	1	23.0	-2.8	2.1
Nigeria	174	400	429	440	461	296	183	174	138	188	23.8	5.5	-12.1
Rwanda	0	3	2	1	1	0	0	0	0	0	11.8	-18.3	-16.6
São Tomé and Principe	..	..	..	..	..	..	..	..	..	..	..	..	..
Senegal	19	12	17	17	24	26	16	22	24	27	-8.9	-3.3	8.1
Seychelles	0	0	0	0	0	0	0	0	0	0	..	..	..
Sierra Leone	2	1	1	1	3	3	3	3	3	3	-3.5	-17.8	14.3
Somalia	1	3	0	0	0	0	0	1	1	1	7.3	-7.4	..
South Africa	1,064	792	740	733	844	752	767	804	788	783	3.6	-3.9	0.3
Sudan	81	89	56	60	53	58	52	95	77	38	-1.5	-3.8	-0.7
Swaziland	20	13	12	12	12	5	5	4	5	6	4.0	11.8	-13.2
Tanzania	36	51	50	48	36	36	27	31	38	28	-1.0	5.7	-6.6
Togo	3	12	12	12	10	11	16	18	17	17	8.6	10.2	5.6
Uganda	1	0	1	1	2	2	1	1	1	2	-16.2	-5.2	13.4
Zambia	79	60	63	85	85	59	55	51	57	40	2.2	6.1	-5.3
Zimbabwe	173	177	164	114	159	171	147	168	175	174	2.0	-0.3	1.4
NORTH AFRICA	1,221	1,589	1,534	1,455	1,660	1,429	1,608	1,645	1,590	1,730	6.5	1.3	0.8
Algeria	236	139	92	97	131	119	46	38	97	96	1.6	-11.9	-6.4
Egypt, Arab Republic	664	965	963	877	988	851	1,113	1,158	1,004	1,113	7.5	3.5	1.9
Libya	53	78	85	86	111	75	89	62	62	50	14.2	0.3	-4.4
Morocco	207	326	296	290	334	295	282	290	327	350	5.4	3.0	0.3
Tunisia	62	83	99	105	95	89	77	97	100	121	6.3	3.2	1.0
ALL AFRICA	3,194	3,562	3,461	3,375	3,830	3,391	3,439	3,744	3,628	3,789	5.3	0.3	0.7

8-11. Fertilizer imports

	Thousands of metric tons										Average annual percentage growth		
	1980	1990	1991	1992	1993	1994	1995	1996	1997	1998	75-84	85-89	90-MR
SUB-SAHARAN AFRICA	971	1,004	1,046	1,157	1,275	1,218	1,011	1,427	1,421	1,485	5.9	-0.4	3.8
excluding South Africa	742	872	860	953	1,077	1,019	827	1,205	1,152	1,198	6.8	0.1	3.3
excl. S.Africa & Nigeria	565	675	653	713	796	728	799	1,128	1,061	1,045	3.7	3.8	6.0
Angola	17	7	7	9	8	10	8	6	2	5	-0.2	19.3	-12.9
Benin	1	11	12	16	18	17	36	30	39	38	6.7	-16.1	25.7
Botswana	1	1	1	1	1	1	3	4	4	4	-5.7	2.7	22.8
Burkina Faso	5	19	21	21	21	23	24	31	44	50	23.7	14.8	9.8
Burundi	1	2	2	6	5	3	3	3	1	2	11.9	13.6	-8.4
Cameroon	32	17	18	24	22	47	32	34	39	40	13.2	-9.4	8.6
Cape Verde	0	0	0	0	0	0	0	0	0	0	-0.6	22.3	..
Central African Republic	1	1	1	1	1	0	0	0	0	1	-11.1	-17.6	-11.8
Chad	1	6	9	10	5	8	8	24	8	17	-4.9	-7.3	11.6
Comoros	0	0	0	0	0	0	0	0	0	0	..	..	21.7
Congo, Democratic Rep. of	8	6	8	2	4	10	9	6	0	0	0.1	-5.6	-1.1
Congo, Republic of	1	2	1	2	2	3	3	4	4	5	34.9	-38.7	22.4
Côte d'Ivoire	45	35	41	68	52	79	87	75	176	157	6.4	-6.9	18.1
Djibouti	1	0	0	0	0	0	0	0	0	0	-44.2	..	..
Equatorial Guinea	0	0	0	0	0	0	0	0	0	0	0.0	..	..
Eritrea	..	..	..	..	1	2	2	6	6	7	..	..	51.0
Ethiopia	..	..	..	..	115	35	151	248	93	176	..	..	17.0
Gabon	0	1	1	1	0	0	0	0	0	0	28.0	-18.8	-15.7
Gambia, The	2	1	1	1	1	1	1	1	1	3	7.9	-15.0	5.6
Ghana	12	7	8	11	7	8	10	17	22	15	-2.3	15.5	4.9
Guinea	0	1	2	1	2	4	5	4	2	3	-16.0	29.7	18.0
Guinea-Bissau	0	1	1	0	0	0	0	0	0	1	9.8	..	-6.0
Kenya	62	116	113	102	100	131	78	161	140	128	5.2	7.7	1.9
Lesotho	5	5	6	6	6	6	6	7	6	6	18.1	2.3	2.7
Liberia	3	0	0	0	0	0	0	0	0	0	-11.1	24.9	..
Madagascar	9	11	9	8	11	11	13	17	10	9	3.1	-1.5	3.9
Malawi	33	48	76	68	74	21	44	58	57	50	13.9	4.8	-2.1
Mali	14	19	13	27	25	25	27	27	48	53	14.3	-16.4	12.9
Mauritania	1	5	7	9	7	4	4	5	2	2	-9.6	28.4	-7.4
Mauritius	17	52	28	28	24	24	25	38	36	34	0.0	5.5	-0.1
Mozambique	20	3	5	5	3	6	9	8	7	5	24.2	-23.1	11.4
Namibia	..	..	..	..	..	..	..	..	..	..	..	..	..
Niger	3	2	1	1	2	5	8	9	1	1	23.0	-2.8	1.3
Nigeria	177	197	207	240	281	290	28	77	92	153	23.0	-9.1	-11.4
Rwanda	0	1	2	1	1	0	0	0	0	0	11.8	1.3	-17.2
São Tomé and Principe	..	..	..	..	..	..	..	..	..	..	..	..	..
Senegal	16	29	31	27	35	14	18	16	34	34	-7.7	6.8	-0.9
Seychelles	0	0	0	0	0	0	0	0	0	0	..	..	..
Sierra Leone	2	1	1	2	3	3	3	3	3	3	-4.1	-17.7	13.7
Somalia	2	3	0	0	0	0	0	1	1	1	0.9	20.5	..
South Africa	229	132	185	204	198	199	185	222	269	287	2.9	-3.2	6.0
Sudan	81	89	56	60	53	60	50	95	77	38	0.0	-6.8	-0.7
Swaziland	18	13	12	12	12	5	5	4	5	6	1.2	11.8	-13.3
Tanzania	20	38	53	40	42	31	27	35	36	30	4.0	14.1	-5.7
Togo	3	12	7	12	13	13	14	22	17	17	7.6	9.6	7.1
Uganda	1	0	1	1	2	2	1	1	1	2	-13.1	-5.2	13.4
Zambia	69	67	63	86	68	53	52	47	53	38	-1.1	42.7	-7.9
Zimbabwe	56	44	39	44	49	63	33	81	87	67	5.9	5.3	7.9
NORTH AFRICA	588	491	394	344	333	392	438	322	430	478	-2.2	-0.1	-0.6
Algeria	189	40	32	19	26	52	19	51	90	90	-1.8	-18.3	8.6
Egypt, Arab Republic	182	184	102	107	59	93	133	68	86	139	-10.2	3.6	-5.1
Libya	53	68	76	87	108	73	102	62	62	42	11.5	4.2	-3.9
Morocco	133	172	169	126	136	167	177	137	188	193	3.3	3.0	1.6
Tunisia	30	28	15	6	4	7	7	4	5	13	-0.7	5.2	-7.5
ALL AFRICA	1,559	1,496	1,439	1,501	1,609	1,610	1,449	1,749	1,851	1,962	3.0	-0.3	2.6

8-12. Area under permanent crops

	Thousands of hectares										Average annual percentage growth		
	1980	1990	1991	1992	1993	1994	1995	1996	1997	1998	75-84	85-89	90-MR
SUB-SAHARAN AFRICA	123,373	132,405	133,371	134,181	149,668	150,902	152,570	152,843	153,340	153,451	0.7	0.9	2.1
excluding South Africa	110,933	118,965	119,641	120,161	135,358	136,302	137,655	137,968	138,530	138,660	0.8	0.8	2.2
excl. S.Africa & Nigeria	83,083	89,426	89,841	90,239	105,314	106,137	107,284	109,268	110,330	110,460	1.0	0.8	3.0
Angola	2,900	2,900	2,950	3,000	3,000	3,000	3,000	3,000	3,000	3,000	0.0	0.0	0.4
Benin	1,500	1,615	1,620	1,630	1,650	1,660	1,670	1,680	1,690	1,700	1.7	0.6	0.6
Botswana	402	418	417	415	407	1,394	343	343	343	343	0.1	0.3	-2.0
Burkina Faso	2,745	3,520	3,495	3,470	3,450	3,381	3,400	3,400	3,400	3,400	1.8	4.4	-0.5
Burundi	920	810	800	800	790	780	770	770	770	770	-0.4	-1.5	-0.8
Cameroon	5,910	5,940	5,950	5,960	5,960	5,960	5,960	5,960	5,960	5,960	0.8	0.1	0.0
Cape Verde	38	41	41	41	41	40	39	39	39	39	0.0	1.2	-0.6
Central African Republic	1,870	1,920	1,920	1,930	1,930	1,930	1,930	1,930	1,930	1,930	0.5	0.2	0.1
Chad	3,137	3,273	3,322	3,342	3,370	3,390	3,420	3,470	3,500	3,520	0.5	0.6	0.9
Comoros	75	78	78	78	78	78	78	78	78	78	0.0	0.7	0.0
Congo, Democratic Rep. of	6,620	6,670	6,680	6,700	6,700	6,700	6,700	6,700	6,700	6,700	0.2	0.1	0.0
Congo, Republic of	138	154	156	155	160	163	165	167	170	173	1.5	1.0	1.5
Côte d'Ivoire	1,955	2,430	2,450	2,600	2,902	2,905	2,920	2,930	2,950	2,950	1.9	0.9	2.7
Djibouti	..	..	..	..	..	..	..	..	..	..	..	..	..
Equatorial Guinea	130	130	130	130	130	130	130	130	130	130	0.0	0.0	0.0
Eritrea	..	..	..	..	498	437	438	369	391	498	..	..	-1.4
Ethiopia	..	..	..	..	11,000	9,822	9,850	9,850	9,900	9,950	..	..	-1.4
Gabon	290	295	295	295	295	295	325	325	325	325	2.5	0.0	1.5
Gambia, The	155	182	191	157	156	175	180	185	195	195	1.0	2.5	1.1
Ghana	1,900	2,700	2,800	2,800	2,800	2,800	2,800	2,800	3,600	3,600	2.5	2.6	3.0
Guinea	702	728	735	755	785	820	883	885	885	885	0.4	0.3	2.8
Guinea-Bissau	255	300	300	300	300	300	300	300	300	300	1.0	1.0	0.0
Kenya	3,800	4,000	4,000	4,000	4,000	4,000	4,000	4,000	4,000	4,000	0.4	0.7	0.0
Lesotho	292	317	319	332	325	325	320	322	325	325	-2.3	1.5	0.5
Liberia	126	170	180	180	180	180	190	190	190	190	0.8	3.3	1.5
Madagascar	2,500	2,502	2,512	2,525	2,555	2,565	2,565	2,565	2,565	2,565	1.3	0.3	0.3
Malawi	1,518	1,815	1,823	1,830	1,837	1,845	1,875	1,875	1,875	1,875	3.0	0.7	0.5
Mali	2,010	2,053	2,063	2,163	3,060	3,160	3,379	4,606	4,606	4,606	1.0	0.4	11.7
Mauritania	210	400	410	420	431	470	498	488	488	488	4.0	6.3	3.1
Mauritius	100	100	100	100	100	100	100	100	100	100	0.0	0.0	0.0
Mozambique	2,870	3,070	3,100	3,120	3,120	3,120	3,120	3,120	3,120	3,120	0.3	0.9	0.2
Namibia	655	660	660	660	698	747	816	816	816	816	0.1	0.0	3.2
Niger	3,549	3,600	3,600	3,600	3,995	4,494	4,994	4,994	4,994	4,994	4.4	0.5	4.9
Nigeria	27,850	29,539	29,800	29,922	30,044	30,165	30,371	28,700	28,200	28,200	0.3	0.7	-0.5
Rwanda	760	880	880	880	850	700	700	750	800	820	2.0	0.8	-1.6
São Tomé and Principe	1	2	2	2	2	2	2	2	2	2	0.0	10.4	0.0
Senegal	2,341	2,325	2,323	2,320	2,318	2,331	2,230	2,230	2,230	2,230	0.0	-0.1	-0.6
Seychelles	1	1	1	1	1	1	1	1	1	1	0.0	0.0	0.0
Sierra Leone	450	486	486	486	486	485	485	485	484	484	1.1	0.7	-0.1
Somalia	984	1,022	1,022	1,023	1,024	1,030	1,035	1,038	1,039	1,040	0.5	0.4	0.2
South Africa	12,440	13,440	13,730	14,020	14,310	14,600	14,915	14,875	14,810	14,791	-0.2	1.3	1.4
Sudan	12,360	13,000	13,000	12,900	14,618	15,000	16,157	16,672	16,700	16,700	0.4	0.6	3.7
Swaziland	185	180	183	179	164	166	168	168	168	168	-0.9	3.1	-1.4
Tanzania	3,100	3,500	3,550	3,600	3,650	3,700	3,748	3,750	3,750	3,750	4.8	1.1	1.0
Togo	1,950	2,100	2,100	2,100	2,200	2,200	2,200	2,300	2,250	2,200	1.2	0.6	1.0
Uganda	4,080	5,000	5,020	5,040	5,040	5,060	5,060	5,060	5,060	5,060	1.5	0.8	0.1
Zambia	5,094	5,249	5,249	5,254	5,254	5,254	5,260	5,260	5,260	5,260	0.4	2.1	-0.6
Zimbabwe	2,505	2,890	2,928	2,966	3,004	3,042	3,080	3,165	3,251	3,220	0.8	1.4	1.5
NORTH AFRICA	21,634	22,786	22,954	23,738	23,951	23,870	23,914	24,152	24,179	24,243	-0.1	0.6	0.8
Algeria	6,875	7,081	7,260	7,562	7,533	7,477	7,519	7,521	7,650	7,661	0.0	0.7	0.8
Egypt, Arab Republic	2,286	2,284	2,267	2,519	2,617	2,624	2,817	2,820	2,834	2,834	-1.8	-0.1	3.0
Libya	1,753	1,805	1,810	1,815	1,815	1,815	1,815	1,815	1,815	1,815	0.2	0.3	0.1
Morocco	7,530	8,707	8,717	8,934	8,999	9,124	8,921	9,096	8,980	9,033	0.8	1.5	0.6
Tunisia	3,190	2,909	2,900	2,908	2,987	2,830	2,842	2,900	2,900	2,900	-1.2	-1.4	-0.1
ALL AFRICA	145,007	155,191	156,325	157,919	173,619	174,772	176,484	176,995	177,519	177,694	0.6	0.8	1.9

8-13. Agricultural yields by major crop

	Thousands of hectograms per hectare											* Average annual percentage growth		
	1980	1990	1991	1992	1993	1994	1995	1996	1997	1998	1999	75-84	85-89	90-MR
ALGERIA														
Wheat	7.3	6.3	10.8	9.9	8.1	8.0	8.9	13.1	8.0	8.8	8.0	3.0	2.0	0.6
Citrus	262.9	74.5	87.2	92.5	87.1	91.4	80.2	86.1	87.2	101.8	111.3	-2.0	2.1	1.8
Dates	30.0	26.2	25.5	31.2	31.0	37.2	32.8	37.3	31.4	39.5	42.7	3.7	3.6	3.1
Barley	8.4	7.6	11.6	9.0	6.3	6.5	7.1	14.0	7.2	7.5	8.7	7.1	0.9	0.1
Potatoes	77.7	78.9	90.7	107.9	111.2	95.1	136.8	134.6	141.0	160.3	153.5	0.2	-2.0	3.2
ANGOLA														
Coffee(green)	2.2	0.3	0.5	0.5	0.5	0.3	0.4	0.3	0.3	0.4	0.4	-9.1	-5.5	-1.3
Maize	6.0	2.7	4.0	3.8	2.6	2.5	3.5	7.0	6.0	7.4	6.4	-2.3	4.8	4.8
Millet	7.1	5.7	4.8	4.8	2.7	5.4	5.1	4.8	3.8	5.0	5.3	-2.8	0.8	0.3
Wheat	5.8	8.0	8.0	8.0	8.6	10.0	16.7	16.7	16.7	17.1	13.3	-6.3	-1.3	4.1
Cassava	33.8	40.0	40.3	42.3	42.3	58.6	51.0	48.1	44.2	55.7	59.8	-0.7	-1.5	2.6
Sweet potatoes	91.7	86.8	89.5	90.0	88.1	85.7	88.1	85.5	85.9	86.4	82.8	0.2	0.1	-0.3
BENIN														
Seed Cotton	6.6	11.9	11.7	12.0	17.9	13.9	13.3	12.3	10.2	9.4	9.7	-0.2	-2.2	-0.9
Maize	7.4	9.0	9.3	9.8	9.8	10.2	11.7	10.8	12.6	11.1	12.7	0.2	-4.1	1.6
Sorghum	6.3	7.3	7.8	7.7	7.6	7.8	7.5	7.6	8.1	8.2	8.5	-1.2	0.0	0.5
Cassava	65.9	79.8	83.0	83.8	84.9	81.5	78.4	87.2	104.1	105.0	108.1	-2.2	-2.5	1.4
Yams	97.2	111.5	114.0	106.0	107.7	108.4	109.7	102.6	116.2	109.5	110.7	0.5	-1.5	-0.3
BOTSWANA														
Sorghum	2.2	2.5	3.7	2.9	2.9	2.2	2.1	4.2	1.7	1.8	1.9	-16.8	-12.7	-2.0
Maize	2.5	2.9	4.0	1.9	1.9	1.7	1.5	2.2	3.9	1.4	2.5	-13.0	10.2	-3.8
Millet	1.6	1.8	1.8	1.3	1.4	3.6	1.0	3.7	2.5	1.7	1.9	-8.9	-22.3	2.2
BURKINA FASO														
Seed Cotton	8.3	11.4	9.3	10.0	9.6	8.9	8.5	9.4	12.4	9.7	9.7	6.9	-2.6	-0.5
Groundnuts	5.1	7.1	5.6	6.3	9.5	8.4	8.2	8.2	6.5	10.0	10.0	3.1	-3.5	2.6
Sorghum	5.7	5.8	9.1	9.1	8.9	8.0	8.0	7.8	7.9	8.5	8.5	1.4	-1.8	0.7
Millet	4.9	4.4	7.0	6.5	7.0	6.3	6.4	6.2	6.4	7.8	7.8	3.0	-2.2	1.9
Maize	9.0	14.6	16.9	13.5	13.7	16.0	13.3	14.0	13.8	13.9	13.9	1.0	-4.9	0.0
BURUNDI														
Coffee	6.3	8.4	9.0	9.3	8.2	9.4	7.3	7.2	6.1	5.9	9.4	0.6	2.2	-0.4
Tea	4.0	7.7	8.8	10.7	9.0	10.4	9.8	7.5	5.6	8.9	9.2	-4.5	2.9	0.7
Maize	10.8	13.5	13.9	14.2	14.3	12.3	12.8	12.6	12.6	11.5	11.2	0.5	-0.9	-1.2
Sorghum	10.0	11.0	11.2	11.5	11.3	9.9	12.2	12.2	12.4	12.5	12.0	0.2	1.5	0.3
Rice, paddy	23.5	33.3	30.9	31.1	30.9	29.4	26.8	27.9	32.6	29.9	32.6	2.2	-6.3	-0.4
Millet	10.0	10.9	11.2	11.0	10.3	11.1	11.1	10.3	12.9	11.1	11.2	0.7	-0.4	0.0
Bananas	..	..	..	..	..	..	..	..	..	..	..	..	..	..
Cassava	90.9	89.0	89.8	92.0	89.9	87.9	83.5	85.8	86.2	88.8	88.2	-0.1	0.6	0.0
CAMEROON														
Coffee	3.0	3.4	4.0	2.6	2.8	2.3	2.5	2.0	1.8	2.3	2.1	5.6	-7.8	-3.6
Cocoa	2.6	3.2	3.0	2.7	3.0	3.1	3.8	3.5	3.5	4.1	4.1	2.9	-0.5	1.7
Seed Cotton	12.9	12.1	12.7	12.7	12.3	11.8	12.3	13.7	10.1	11.0	10.5	7.4	-3.4	-0.6
Maize	8.3	18.5	19.8	11.3	9.6	9.6	16.3	18.8	16.0	13.8	15.0	-0.5	-0.7	-1.6
Sorghum	8.7	8.5	7.7	7.6	7.6	7.3	8.7	8.3	7.3	8.3	8.3	1.0	-5.5	0.4
Millet	7.6	10.5	10.5	10.0	10.3	10.0	10.2	10.1	10.1	10.1	10.1	0.6	-6.2	-0.3
Rice	23.4	50.0	45.0	34.7	43.7	44.4	38.8	47.0	40.6	40.6	40.6	2.7	-2.7	-0.8
Cassava	59.0	164.4	187.5	187.5	193.8	187.5	175.0	170.0	188.9	166.7	166.7	-1.1	0.9	-0.2
Plantains	..	..	..	..	..	..	..	..	..	..	..	..	..	..
CENTRAL AFRICAN REPUBLIC														
Coffee	3.6	5.9	6.9	5.0	4.1	8.2	4.7	7.2	6.0	5.0	4.8	-0.9	-2.5	-0.3
Seed Cotton	3.4	7.9	5.1	6.0	6.6	6.5	7.6	6.9	7.7	7.3	7.6	4.0	3.5	0.9
Sorghum	6.5	7.8	10.1	12.6	11.6	8.0	7.3	7.8	8.4	8.8	8.8	-0.8	-8.5	-1.3
Maize	3.8	8.2	8.1	9.0	9.0	8.5	8.5	8.5	9.2	9.3	9.8	1.1	-3.1	0.5
Groundnuts	10.1	9.2	8.6	9.8	9.8	9.4	9.4	9.3	9.7	10.2	11.0	-0.6	-2.3	0.4
Cassava	30.7	28.4	33.6	34.5	34.5	31.0	28.9	29.2	30.5	30.4	28.0	0.9	-0.3	-0.5
Yams	60.0	65.7	65.7	68.4	65.0	66.7	66.7	68.0	68.0	67.9	67.9	-1.2	-0.6	0.2
CHAD														
Seed Cotton	5.1	7.7	6.2	5.7	6.3	6.8	7.6	7.5	7.3	7.8	7.8	6.0	3.2	0.6
Sorghum	5.1	6.4	5.7	7.4	5.9	6.6	6.5	6.7	6.2	7.5	7.5	0.8	-0.5	1.5
Millet	4.7	3.4	4.0	5.2	3.7	4.9	3.6	4.2	3.8	4.4	4.4	1.9	-1.1	1.4
Groundnuts	5.7	5.9	8.5	8.3	6.9	7.0	9.2	9.6	8.8	11.2	11.2	0.9	-8.2	1.2
COMOROS														
Bananas	..	..	..	..	..	..	..	..	..	..	..	..	..	..
Cassava	48.5	50.5	50.2	52.0	52.8	53.6	53.3	54.0	53.9	54.1	55.2	-2.0	1.0	0.5

(Table continues on the following page)

8-13. Agricultural yields by major crop *(continued)*

	Thousands of hectograms per hectare											* Average annual percentage growth		
	1980	1990	1991	1992	1993	1994	1995	1996	1997	1998	1999	75-84	85-89	90-MR
CONGO														
Coffee	8.0	4.2	4.0	4.2	4.3	4.4	4.6	4.1	4.2	4.1	4.1	-4.7	-6.4	-0.1
Cocoa beans	5.6	4.1	3.8	3.9	3.9	4.0	4.0	3.3	3.2	3.3	3.4	0.1	1.5	-0.8
Maize	8.1	5.8	6.8	7.1	7.3	7.6	7.8	7.0	7.0	6.7	6.7	-1.7	-2.2	0.0
Cassava	68.8	65.0	73.7	73.9	65.6	67.3	71.8	71.9	70.9	71.9	72.7	0.8	0.5	0.4
Plantains	..	..	..	..	..	..	..	..	..	..	..	..	..	..
COTE D'IVOIRE														
Coffee	2.4	2.2	1.6	1.0	1.1	1.1	1.4	1.3	1.7	1.8	1.8	-4.5	1.6	-1.2
Cocoa	5.0	5.2	5.4	5.6	5.5	5.4	5.7	5.8	5.6	5.6	5.8	0.0	0.1	0.3
Oil Palm, fruit	..	..	..	..	..	..	..	..	..	..	..	..	..	..
Rice	11.7	11.5	11.0	11.0	17.6	15.8	16.1	12.8	16.1	16.0	15.5	1.1	0.1	1.9
Maize	8.1	7.2	7.5	7.9	8.0	7.7	8.1	8.2	8.2	8.2	8.2	3.2	0.5	0.7
Cassava	52.3	55.1	52.0	50.1	49.5	50.5	52.9	50.9	50.7	50.5	49.9	0.8	-0.3	-0.4
Yams	90.7	95.0	89.7	89.0	88.0	89.6	99.8	108.3	108.6	108.2	108.3	1.2	0.1	0.9
EGYPT														
Seed Cotton	26.9	20.1	22.8	27.6	29.2	22.4	21.4	24.8	25.5	18.9	23.8	4.2	2.4	0.1
Rice, paddy	58.3	72.7	74.6	76.5	77.2	79.1	81.4	82.9	84.2	86.5	88.8	1.7	-1.0	1.3
Wheat	31.2	52.0	48.2	52.5	53.0	50.0	54.2	56.4	56.0	59.9	63.5	-0.3	0.4	1.2
Sugarcane	812.5	1,003.3	1,036.4	1,029.1	1,061.7	1,093.4	1,095.3	1,107.4	1,122.5	1,172.0	1,190.5	..	-5.0	1.0
Dry Broadbeans	20.7	31.1	34.0	21.4	35.1	22.7	31.7	32.0	31.9	32.3	22.9	-0.1	-0.9	-1.2
EQUATORIAL GUINEA														
Cocoa	1.1	1.0	1.0	0.8	0.9	0.8	0.7	0.8	0.7	0.8	0.9	1.6	2.5	-0.9
Coffee(green)	3.4	3.7	3.7	3.7	3.7	3.7	3.7	3.6	3.6	3.6	3.7	0.7	0.0	-0.1
Cassava	24.6	25.0	25.6	26.1	26.1	26.1	26.1	25.3	25.0	25.3	25.0	-0.2	0.0	-0.3
ETHIOPIA														
Coffee(green)	..	..	..	..	..	..	..	..	..	..	..	..	..	..
Sorghum	..	..	..	..	..	..	..	..	..	..	..	..	..	..
Maize	..	..	..	..	..	..	..	..	..	..	..	..	..	..
Barley	..	..	..	..	..	..	..	..	..	..	..	..	..	..
GABON														
Coffee(green)	2.4	3.6	4.1	3.9	4.3	4.3	2.7	3.7	2.6	2.4	2.4	3.8	0.4	-2.7
Sugarcane	497.5	520.8	517.0	488.9	542.0	568.6	573.3	576.7	583.3	576.7	583.3	16.1	0.3	0.8
Maize	16.6	16.3	16.9	17.6	17.9	17.7	17.6	17.6	17.2	17.2	17.2	1.6	0.9	0.5
Cassava	50.0	50.0	51.6	51.1	49.3	49.1	50.1	50.0	50.7	51.2	52.3	-0.1	-0.1	0.1
Taro (cocoyam)	58.8	56.8	57.8	57.6	60.4	61.7	59.6	60.0	60.5	61.1	61.6	0.1	1.4	0.5
Yams	56.4	64.7	64.7	66.7	64.7	69.4	68.4	67.5	70.0	72.5	75.0	1.0	0.3	0.9
GAMBIA, THE														
Groundnuts	8.7	8.3	10.5	8.5	12.1	10.8	9.6	7.1	11.1	10.4	11.3	0.5	0.5	-0.5
Seed Cotton	6.9	5.3	6.3	7.5	9.4	5.9	4.2	4.7	4.4	4.6	4.6	4.1	-0.2	-2.2
Oil Palm, fruit	..	..	..	..	..	..	..	..	..	..	..	..	..	..
Millet	8.7	9.3	10.3	11.2	10.3	10.6	9.8	11.0	9.0	9.6	9.4	0.4	0.8	0.1
Rice, paddy	19.7	14.7	15.3	17.3	14.6	15.4	12.3	10.7	11.7	15.4	18.3	10.9	-1.8	0.3
Maize	10.7	12.0	11.8	15.1	16.3	12.6	12.9	12.2	11.7	14.3	14.5	3.6	-2.3	0.6
Sorghum	8.0	6.3	9.6	9.5	11.0	10.6	8.5	10.8	9.6	8.1	9.7	2.6	-5.1	0.5
GHANA														
Cocoa	2.3	4.2	3.4	4.3	3.6	4.2	4.0	3.8	3.0	3.0	3.0	-0.1	-6.2	-1.1
Maize	8.7	11.9	15.3	12.0	15.1	14.9	15.1	15.2	15.3	14.9	14.5	-0.3	-4.6	0.8
Millet	5.9	6.0	5.4	6.4	9.7	8.8	9.8	10.2	8.4	9.5	9.1	0.2	1.5	2.9
Groundnuts	17.0	8.9	6.7	7.7	8.8	9.4	9.3	9.0	8.7	10.9	10.9	1.7	-2.3	1.2
Cassava	80.8	84.2	106.6	102.6	112.3	115.8	119.9	120.4	118.8	114.8	120.7	0.7	-1.5	1.8
Plantains	..	..	..	..	..	..	..	..	..	..	..	..	..	..
GUINEA														
Coffee(green)	3.2	5.0	5.2	5.3	5.2	5.5	5.1	4.1	4.0	4.2	4.2	-0.1	-4.0	-1.1
Oil Palm, fruit	..	..	..	..	..	..	..	..	..	..	..	..	..	..
Rice, paddy	9.0	9.7	13.8	13.3	13.8	13.8	14.4	14.7	14.9	15.2	15.0	0.5	-2.9	1.7
Maize	10.0	10.1	10.4	10.7	10.4	10.3	9.7	9.9	10.1	10.4	10.4	-1.6	0.1	0.1
Groundnuts	6.6	7.6	8.8	10.1	8.8	9.2	9.1	9.5	9.8	10.3	10.3	0.2	-0.7	1.7
Cassava	70.0	78.2	74.9	71.7	75.5	71.9	63.0	61.2	59.7	58.0	58.0	0.0	-0.5	-1.7
GUINEA-BISSAU														
Groundnuts	3.5	10.1	7.8	10.1	10.0	11.7	11.3	11.0	11.3	11.3	11.3	-0.6	-6.5	1.6
Rice, paddy	7.0	20.5	20.1	19.0	19.7	20.1	19.1	18.4	18.9	18.6	18.6	-2.7	-1.4	-0.5
Sorghum	6.4	8.8	10.3	8.6	9.0	9.2	9.3	9.1	9.5	9.5	9.5	-2.5	-4.7	0.2
Millet	7.2	8.7	12.2	8.6	8.6	7.7	9.1	8.6	9.1	9.4	9.4	0.6	-4.3	-0.7
Maize	10.0	10.7	11.4	9.5	9.3	9.3	10.0	9.4	10.0	10.0	10.0	1.5	-4.4	-0.5

(Table continues on the following page)

8-13. Agricultural yields by major crop *(continued)*

					Thousands of hectograms per hectare							* Average annual percentage growth		
	1980	1990	1991	1992	1993	1994	1995	1996	1997	1998	1999	75-84	85-89	90-MR
KENYA														
Coffee(green)	8.9	6.8	5.6	5.5	4.7	5.0	5.9	6.0	4.9	3.5	4.0	-2.3	-3.1	-2.8
Tea	11.7	20.3	20.4	18.2	20.1	19.8	22.0	22.6	19.4	25.1	19.3	1.5	-1.2	0.4
Sugarcane	1,211.8	1,173.0	960.7	877.7	841.3	662.1	810.4	815.8	794.6	844.8	866.7	4.2	-2.7	-1.9
Sisal	9.9	12.0	11.4	11.4	11.7	11.3	13.2	13.4	13.4	12.9	12.4	0.5	0.5	0.6
Maize	12.0	15.8	15.9	17.3	16.0	20.4	19.6	16.6	14.7	16.2	14.1	-1.9	-3.5	-0.2
Wheat	21.6	18.6	18.6	12.6	9.7	19.2	19.6	20.0	16.1	23.3	13.5	2.1	-4.6	0.6
LESOTHO														
Wheat	9.7	8.1	2.0	8.6	7.3	4.2	6.2	13.3	11.8	11.6	12.3	-1.8	0.7	5.4
Dry Peas	7.8	2.4	0.7	5.6	5.4	3.1	2.9	9.2	3.5	5.8	7.8	2.0	-6.5	6.8
Dry Beans	5.2	18.8	3.4	2.9	10.7	3.2	12.4	6.3	10.4	8.4	8.0	1.0	-4.9	-0.3
Maize	9.6	11.0	5.4	5.8	8.9	8.6	8.1	12.5	9.9	9.5	9.4	0.6	-5.7	1.3
Sorghum	9.7	10.1	5.4	6.1	13.0	8.8	8.0	8.6	8.1	7.6	11.1	1.5	-8.6	1.5
LIBERIA														
Rubber	7.6	10.0	9.5	10.7	10.0	10.0	9.3	10.0	10.0	10.0	10.0	-2.0	-0.2	0.0
Coffee(green)	4.6	1.1	1.0	1.9	2.0	2.0	2.0	2.0	2.0	2.0	2.0	0.9	-1.6	2.4
Cocoa	2.3	1.4	1.0	0.9	0.8	0.9	1.3	1.1	0.9	0.9	0.9	-1.5	-3.3	-2.2
Rice, paddy	12.3	9.3	9.3	9.2	10.8	11.1	11.2	12.5	12.4	12.9	12.9	0.4	0.4	1.7
Cassava	66.7	69.2	64.3	66.7	61.3	62.5	60.3	65.0	65.1	65.3	65.3	1.0	-0.5	-0.4
LIBYA														
Wheat	5.2	12.3	12.4	11.9	8.4	7.7	7.3	7.3	10.1	10.3	10.2	1.5	0.3	-1.2
MADAGASCAR														
Coffee	3.7	3.5	3.8	3.7	3.7	4.2	3.5	3.5	2.9	3.1	3.4	-1.8	-0.8	-0.5
Vanilla	0.4	0.5	0.6	0.4	0.7	0.6	0.6	0.6	0.6	0.7	0.7	-4.9	7.6	-0.2
Cloves	1.7	1.2	1.8	1.4	2.1	1.8	1.7	1.7	1.9	2.1	1.9	-13.0	-1.6	2.6
Rice	17.6	20.8	20.5	20.9	20.8	20.7	21.3	21.9	21.7	20.3	21.5	-1.2	0.2	0.1
Cassava	60.8	66.5	66.5	67.1	67.7	67.4	68.9	67.4	67.5	66.8	68.0	-1.4	0.6	0.1
Sweet potatoes	48.6	53.4	50.3	53.1	51.1	53.8	59.1	58.1	56.0	54.3	55.9	-3.8	-0.6	0.5
MALAWI														
Tobacco leaves	8.6	10.1	9.7	9.7	10.0	12.5	12.2	12.4	13.8	10.9	10.7	2.1	-1.0	1.0
Tea	17.1	21.0	21.9	15.4	21.3	18.7	18.2	19.8	22.0	22.0	20.5	1.4	-4.2	-0.2
Groundnuts	7.1	7.7	8.2	4.0	9.0	5.4	4.6	5.6	6.9	9.0	8.3	-0.3	0.4	0.8
Seed Cotton	6.9	5.3	6.3	7.5	9.4	5.9	4.2	4.7	4.4	4.6	4.6	4.1	-0.2	-2.2
Maize	12.2	10.0	11.4	4.8	15.2	9.2	13.5	14.4	9.9	12.7	17.7	-0.4	-2.1	2.2
Sorghum	6.7	5.0	6.0	1.4	4.9	3.1	6.1	7.2	4.7	6.1	6.7	-3.7	-7.1	0.9
Cassava	58.4	23.5	23.4	20.1	28.8	27.1	27.1	27.1	27.8	27.8	27.8	0.5	2.4	1.3
MALI														
Seed Cotton	11.3	12.3	13.4	12.7	13.0	12.7	10.9	12.1	10.7	10.5	10.5	-0.6	0.8	-1.1
Groundnuts	8.9	10.7	7.3	10.9	7.5	7.8	8.4	9.4	9.8	9.5	9.5	-1.9	4.3	0.0
Millet	6.2	7.8	6.1	8.3	5.9	5.4	6.4	5.5	7.9	7.3	7.3	6.9	-1.5	-0.7
Rice, paddy	9.7	14.6	14.4	17.3	17.6	17.8	16.5	15.3	17.8	17.8	17.8	-2.2	-5.3	1.4
Sorghum	8.0	9.4	6.6	10.9	6.8	7.5	7.6	8.3	10.0	9.8	9.8	7.2	0.3	0.6
Maize	11.1	12.9	11.6	13.8	10.1	11.0	11.3	12.9	16.0	16.9	16.9	9.2	1.8	1.1
MAURITANIA														
Sorghum	3.2	5.2	4.5	5.0	5.9	5.8	6.4	6.9	4.1	4.7	4.7	-6.7	1.4	-0.3
Rice	32.0	33.3	28.1	39.9	32.9	27.4	39.4	38.3	37.2	43.4	44.3	2.5	1.4	1.2
Millet	2.3	2.8	2.7	2.6	2.6	2.9	3.6	3.4	1.4	1.6	4.1	-2.0	-6.7	-0.2
Maize	6.5	6.8	6.0	7.7	12.3	5.0	8.0	5.9	8.6	8.4	6.4	0.9	-8.6	-0.5
MAURITIUS														
Sugarcane	576.8	727.1	740.0	770.0	729.7	659.2	716.5	732.6	795.4	780.9	538.5	-1.4	1.3	-0.9
Potatoes	165.6	181.1	197.4	192.1	200.9	175.7	198.5	195.9	215.8	176.0	180.7	1.8	0.7	-0.7
Onions	107.6	122.0	137.7	151.4	164.6	176.0	184.4	177.9	171.3	220.6	217.7	4.1	-2.8	3.2
MOROCCO														
Wheat	10.6	13.3	18.7	7.0	6.8	18.1	5.5	18.4	9.3	14.2	8.0	5.7	-10.5	-0.6
Sugarbeet	353.5	464.0	438.7	528.6	490.6	499.8	467.7	487.1	415.4	577.2	619.9	1.5	-1.5	1.6
Barley	10.3	8.9	13.8	4.8	4.8	14.4	3.9	15.8	6.6	8.1	7.1	3.7	-15.6	-0.2
MOZAMBIQUE														
Seed Cotton	4.9	3.7	5.3	5.8	6.1	6.6	6.0	6.8	4.4	4.6	4.8	3.3	4.1	2.1
Tea	10.3	6.9	7.7	5.1	8.4	10.0	7.5	8.0	7.5	7.5	8.0	1.0	9.3	1.7
Maize	5.4	4.5	3.2	1.6	6.3	5.2	6.8	9.4	9.0	9.0	9.4	-5.0	-4.9	6.4
Rice, paddy	8.3	8.7	5.3	3.0	6.2	8.3	8.7	9.7	10.9	10.6	11.0	2.1	-1.2	3.0
Cassava	41.4	48.6	38.0	33.3	41.7	36.9	42.4	47.7	53.8	55.6	55.4	-0.2	0.5	1.4
NAMIBIA														
Wheat	25.0	44.3	59.0	51.9	43.8	52.5	40.0	43.8	46.4	60.3	77.3	3.1	-2.5	1.6
Maize	12.3	14.9	12.0	2.4	7.8	11.5	8.8	6.7	15.9	5.5	5.5	0.5	-10.7	-4.3

(Table continues on the following page)

8-13. Agricultural yields by major crop *(continued)*

	Thousands of hectograms per hectare											* Average annual percentage growth		
	1980	1990	1991	1992	1993	1994	1995	1996	1997	1998	1999	75-84	85-89	90-MR
NIGER														
Cowpeas	2.4	0.8	1.5	1.0	0.5	1.8	0.5	1.0	0.6	2.1	1.7	1.0	-9.4	3.4
Groundnuts	6.7	2.8	3.4	3.3	2.3	4.5	4.1	4.7	3.8	4.9	4.3	-2.0	-2.5	2.5
Millet	4.4	3.8	4.2	3.6	3.5	4.0	3.4	3.5	3.0	4.5	4.2	0.4	-7.4	0.6
Sorghum	4.8	1.3	2.1	1.5	1.3	2.0	1.4	1.9	1.5	2.2	2.3	-1.4	-5.7	1.5
NIGERIA														
Cocoa	3.9	4.0	2.8	3.6	3.4	3.4	3.5	3.7	3.2	3.2	3.2	-1.8	2.0	-0.3
Oil Palm, fruit	..	..	..	..	..	..	..	..	..	..	..	..	..	..
Seed Cotton	1.8	6.7	7.0	6.8	7.9	8.0	8.0	7.5	8.1	7.3	5.7	-8.6	-6.0	0.2
Groundnuts	8.4	14.0	12.1	12.4	11.8	9.2	8.9	10.1	11.2	9.7	10.5	0.8	-4.2	-1.3
Sorghum	11.2	10.0	9.7	10.8	10.8	10.8	10.7	11.4	11.1	10.7	11.1	5.3	1.2	0.7
Millet	8.7	10.7	9.0	10.3	9.5	9.5	9.8	10.6	10.8	10.6	10.1	3.7	0.5	-0.1
Maize	13.2	11.3	11.3	11.2	11.8	12.7	12.9	13.3	12.7	13.2	13.6	2.9	-2.6	0.8
Rice, paddy	19.8	20.7	19.5	19.6	19.6	14.2	16.3	17.5	16.0	16.0	16.6	5.0	3.6	-1.5
Yams	105.4	106.8	103.5	113.5	113.5	114.0	107.7	110.5	90.2	94.4	95.5	0.0	-6.1	-0.3
Cassava	95.8	116.5	101.9	105.9	105.9	105.9	106.8	106.5	112.7	107.5	108.4	0.3	-1.4	0.0
RWANDA														
Coffee(green)	6.9	6.3	5.2	6.8	5.3	2.9	11.0	7.6	7.4	5.7	7.0	0.8	3.0	0.0
Tea	7.4	10.5	11.3	11.1	11.2	4.6	6.0	8.2	11.0	12.2	12.9	-5.1	-1.4	-0.8
Sorghum	12.4	10.7	12.8	7.5	12.8	6.9	11.5	13.6	11.2	10.5	8.3	1.1	2.4	-1.5
Maize	11.8	10.3	11.6	13.6	14.8	15.0	14.1	11.1	10.9	8.2	7.6	0.3	0.1	-1.7
Plantains	..	..	..	..	..	..	..	..	..	..	..	..	..	..
Sweet potatoes	76.3	48.7	62.5	66.0	60.4	34.1	50.0	51.1	49.7	50.5	47.9	1.1	2.6	-1.2
SENEGAL														
Groundnuts	4.9	7.7	8.3	6.0	8.5	7.6	9.4	7.0	6.9	10.4	10.1	3.2	2.8	0.6
Seed Cotton	6.9	10.0	11.8	10.7	11.4	11.0	8.2	7.6	9.7	6.0	9.6	-2.6	2.0	-2.2
Millet	4.7	5.8	6.7	5.8	6.7	5.9	7.5	6.2	5.2	5.4	5.7	2.6	4.0	-0.7
Rice, paddy	9.6	24.8	23.5	24.1	24.8	20.9	22.5	20.2	23.3	27.2	25.0	1.3	-1.2	0.2
Maize	7.3	11.4	11.3	10.9	12.7	10.1	10.9	10.4	9.7	8.7	9.4	-5.0	0.1	-1.7
Sorghum	7.7	9.1	7.8	8.9	7.8	8.7	8.6	8.9	7.7	5.9	6.4	2.0	-0.7	-1.6
SIERRA LEONE														
Cocoa	4.0	4.2	3.8	2.7	2.7	3.7	3.7	3.7	3.7	3.7	3.6	0.1	-0.8	-0.4
Coffee(green)	12.7	23.0	22.6	23.0	23.0	18.5	17.9	17.9	21.9	21.9	11.0	3.2	-1.6	-3.0
Palm oil	..	..	..	..	..	..	..	..	..	..	..	..	..	..
Rice, paddy	12.5	12.8	13.5	13.5	12.7	12.3	13.0	13.5	13.0	11.5	11.6	-1.4	-0.7	-0.6
Cassava	38.0	59.9	54.0	53.3	45.8	58.7	58.5	58.6	49.9	51.6	51.8	-3.1	-3.7	-0.3
SOMALIA														
Bananas	..	..	..	..	..	..	..	..	..	..	..	..	..	..
Maize	10.1	11.5	10.0	10.1	9.9	4.1	7.3	7.1	6.4	7.3	7.5	-0.9	-3.0	-3.4
Sorghum	3.1	5.6	4.1	3.1	2.9	4.1	3.4	3.2	3.1	2.3	2.5	2.1	-2.2	-3.9
Sesame	4.6	4.5	4.1	3.8	3.1	3.0	3.4	3.3	3.4	3.0	3.1	-3.3	-1.6	-2.3
SOUTH AFRICA														
Maize	24.2	22.1	22.6	7.9	22.8	28.5	13.8	27.0	25.2	21.6	22.1	3.5	-5.1	0.5
Wheat	9.0	10.9	14.9	17.7	18.5	17.6	14.5	21.0	17.6	23.9	21.7	-1.3	3.0	3.8
Sugarcane	661.4	683.2	727.4	471.6	422.9	582.4	612.0	699.2	711.4	713.5	683.2	-2.2	2.4	0.1
Sorghum	26.9	17.4	18.2	6.2	21.6	22.9	16.1	30.8	26.9	27.4	21.1	4.1	-0.7	2.3
Barley	8.8	23.8	12.6	19.2	19.8	22.9	24.0	13.9	13.8	19.2	8.9	3.8	7.6	-2.7
SUDAN														
Seed Cotton	8.2	12.6	14.6	11.4	12.1	14.1	12.4	11.6	14.4	14.6	14.6	2.7	3.1	0.3
Groundnuts	8.0	5.5	7.8	7.0	5.5	8.0	6.8	8.6	7.2	5.7	6.8	-2.3	-2.9	1.4
Sesame	2.6	1.7	1.8	2.0	1.4	1.3	2.1	2.2	1.8	1.3	1.5	0.6	5.3	-0.6
Sorghum	7.1	4.3	7.0	6.5	5.1	5.7	4.9	6.4	5.9	7.5	6.9	-3.0	-11.2	2.1
Wheat	12.1	15.9	14.8	23.2	13.8	13.3	16.1	17.7	19.5	21.6	11.9	-0.6	0.1	-0.3
SWAZILAND														
Sugarcane	1,077.2	1,052.5	985.3	971.2	911.8	946.5	908.4	986.0	953.9	1,009.7	966.1	0.3	0.0	-0.2
Seed Cotton	10.2	9.5	9.8	2.9	6.3	5.8	6.2	9.4	5.2	5.2	5.2	-2.1	3.1	-2.5
Maize	13.6	10.3	17.3	9.4	12.2	17.6	12.7	24.5	17.8	19.2	18.2	-2.3	-0.6	3.0
TANZANIA														
Coffee	4.2	4.3	3.9	4.2	4.3	3.9	3.6	4.2	3.9	3.5	4.1	-0.4	4.0	-0.3
Seed Cotton	4.5	3.8	5.3	7.1	3.1	3.8	6.8	5.7	4.7	3.4	4.2	-2.2	1.8	-0.2
Tea	10.9	14.4	10.4	11.8	12.0	13.2	13.1	13.0	13.4	11.8	13.2	3.3	3.4	-0.2
Maize	12.3	15.0	12.6	11.7	12.5	13.3	15.5	16.2	12.0	13.6	13.9	1.3	1.7	0.1
Rice	11.9	19.2	16.9	12.8	18.1	17.4	15.1	15.3	12.5	16.5	14.3	-1.3	-1.5	-0.9
Sorghum	6.9	9.7	9.2	8.6	11.2	7.2	12.2	12.6	8.0	12.1	8.5	10.5	1.3	0.0
Millet	7.6	11.2	7.8	8.5	6.5	6.4	10.9	9.8	9.8	10.1	9.9	3.5	4.6	0.0
Cassava	107.3	132.0	123.5	104.0	104.0	103.9	102.1	103.5	101.1	88.4	102.6	1.6	-0.1	-1.0

(Table continues on the following page)

8-13. Agricultural yields by major crop *(continued)*

					Thousands of hectograms per hectare							* Average annual percentage growth		
	1980	1990	1991	1992	1993	1994	1995	1996	1997	1998	1999	75-84	85-89	90-MR
TOGO														
Coffee(green)	4.9	6.2	6.8	6.8	7.0	6.6	6.7	6.5	6.7	6.5	6.5	2.7	-1.2	0.2
Cocoa	4.5	2.0	1.9	1.8	2.1	2.0	1.9	2.8	2.5	2.9	2.9	-1.8	4.1	2.4
Seed Cotton	7.7	12.5	12.4	11.6	11.2	13.5	10.6	13.3	13.5	13.8	13.8	7.8	5.6	1.1
Maize	9.2	9.7	9.1	10.1	11.6	9.3	8.6	9.4	10.7	9.9	9.9	3.2	-3.3	-0.2
Sorghum	7.5	6.2	7.4	7.8	6.4	7.1	8.7	6.3	7.4	6.7	6.7	1.3	-2.9	-0.5
Millet	2.6	4.1	3.7	5.6	5.0	4.8	4.6	4.7	5.2	4.5	4.5	-7.9	2.4	-0.4
Cassava	103.3	76.9	77.9	69.0	68.6	53.8	59.2	56.9	60.3	51.9	51.9	-8.7	1.6	-2.6
Yams	86.6	90.7	90.3	83.3	103.4	82.2	85.8	87.2	110.3	105.8	105.8	0.1	-2.8	0.2
TUNISIA														
Wheat	10.2	12.7	17.0	17.0	13.7	10.7	12.8	16.2	10.9	14.0	14.7	5.4	12.9	0.9
Barley	7.7	9.4	13.1	12.0	9.3	5.9	6.6	11.9	5.2	11.6	10.8	4.0	20.8	1.2
UGANDA														
Coffee(green)	6.0	4.8	5.5	4.2	5.5	7.5	6.9	10.3	8.1	7.4	7.5	-1.0	1.0	2.7
Seed Cotton	0.4	2.8	2.0	1.3	3.0	3.3	3.3	3.3	3.3	2.6	2.6	-11.8	-1.1	2.4
Millet	16.5	15.0	15.0	16.0	15.1	14.8	16.0	11.0	12.7	16.0	16.0	3.3	1.1	-0.2
Maize	11.1	15.0	13.5	15.0	16.0	15.1	16.0	13.0	12.4	12.5	12.3	0.9	-1.1	-0.8
Sorghum	17.9	15.0	14.8	15.0	15.0	15.0	15.0	11.0	10.7	15.0	16.0	3.8	1.3	-0.1
Cassava	68.6	83.0	83.0	80.0	85.1	65.0	67.0	67.0	67.0	90.0	90.9	-1.0	0.3	-0.2
Plantains	..	..	..	..	..	..	..	..	..	..	..	..	..	..
ZAIRE														
Coffee(green)	3.7	3.5	3.3	3.2	3.6	3.5	3.7	3.7	3.7	3.7	2.9	-1.0	0.9	-0.1
Palm oil	..	..	..	..	..	..	..	..	..	..	..	..	..	..
Maize	8.0	8.2	8.1	8.1	8.3	8.3	8.8	8.0	8.2	8.2	7.9	1.1	1.2	-0.1
Rice	8.0	8.1	8.0	7.3	7.2	7.3	7.5	7.1	7.1	7.3	7.0	0.2	0.3	-0.8
Cassava	70.0	80.7	80.0	80.0	78.1	77.2	77.5	81.1	80.3	79.4	78.6	0.1	-0.3	-0.1
Plantains	..	..	..	..	..	..	..	..	..	..	..	..	..	..
ZAMBIA														
Seed Cotton	5.0	4.8	6.6	4.3	7.3	7.8	6.7	5.6	5.1	4.8	5.1	-5.5	-4.3	-0.3
Tobacco leaves	10.4	8.7	17.8	4.4	5.1	6.7	8.3	10.5	10.8	10.9	10.9	3.6	11.3	0.3
Sunflower	9.2	4.5	2.9	0.5	5.4	6.6	6.5	5.6	3.8	3.6	5.1	-2.5	6.9	3.5
Maize	16.9	14.3	17.1	7.3	25.2	15.0	14.2	20.9	14.8	15.6	14.3	0.8	-6.4	-0.1
Wheat	40.7	43.9	43.8	43.3	40.1	43.0	50.0	55.8	66.2	56.7	74.8	-2.7	-5.1	2.2
Cassava	50.0	50.4	51.8	50.9	51.7	50.0	49.2	51.7	50.1	49.5	50.0	0.5	-0.2	-0.1
ZIMBABWE														
Tobacco leaves	19.5	21.7	24.9	24.3	21.9	24.6	24.2	24.2	22.0	26.3	21.0	1.4	1.2	0.1
Seed Cotton	17.5	8.2	7.8	2.7	8.6	7.8	4.6	9.2	8.9	9.2	8.3	0.8	-3.4	0.6
Sugarcane	1,031.2	955.2	1,027.2	89.3	597.8	1,072.5	1,109.7	905.1	1,081.6	962.2	1,083.0	1.8	-0.8	1.5
Maize	13.4	17.2	14.4	4.1	16.3	16.6	6.0	17.0	13.4	11.6	10.5	-3.4	-14.4	-1.0
Wheat	49.7	58.2	56.4	48.3	70.3	56.1	20.8	54.9	51.7	53.8	56.1	1.9	0.0	-0.2

* The Bank least square methodology was used to compute the average annual percentage growth.

Notes: The following commodities are in their least-processed form unless otherwise indicated:

      Cotton, seed cotton

      Groundnuts, unshelled

      Coffee, green or roasted

      Rice, paddy

      Cloves, whole

      Cocoa, beans

      Tobacco, leaves

      Sunflower, seeds

      1 hectogram = 100 grams = 3.527 oz.

      Countries excluded from listing: Cape Verde, Djibouti, Sao Tome and Principe, and Seychelles.

      For livestock "yield," see Table 8-6. Food Output by Major Crops.

8-14. Incidence of drought

							D=Significant shortage of rain						
	1986	1987	1988	1989	1990	1991	1992	1993	1994	1995	1996	1997	1998
SUB-SAHARAN AFRICA	..	..	..	..	..	..	..	..	..	..	..	..	..
excluding South Africa	..	..	..	..	..	..	..	..	..	..	..	..	..
excluding South Africa & Nigeria	..	..	..	..	..	..	..	..	..	..	..	..	..
Angola	..	..	..	..	..	..	..	..	..	..	..	..	..
Benin	..	..	..	..	..	..	..	..	..	..	..	..	..
Botswana	D	D	..	..	..	..	D	..	..	D	..	..	..
Burkina Faso	..	..	..	..	..	..	..	..	..	..	..	D	..
Burundi	..	..	..	..	..	..	..	..	..	..	..	..	D
Cameroon	..	..	..	..	..	..	..	..	..	..	D	D	..
Cape Verde	..	..	..	..	..	..	..	D	D	..	..	D	D
Central African Republic	..	..	..	..	..	..	..	..	..	..	..	..	..
Chad	..	..	..	..	..	..	..	D	..	D	D	D	..
Comoros	..	..	..	..	..	..	..	..	..	..	..	..	..
Congo, Democratic Rep. of	..	..	..	..	..	..	..	..	..	..	..	..	..
Congo, Republic of	..	..	..	..	..	..	..	..	..	..	..	..	..
Côte d'Ivoire	..	..	..	..	..	..	..	..	..	..	..	D	..
Djibouti	..	..	..	..	..	..	..	..	..	..	..	..	..
Equatorial Guinea	..	..	..	..	..	..	..	..	..	..	..	..	..
Eritrea	..	..	..	..	..	..	..	..	..	..	D	D	..
Ethiopia	..	D	D	..	..	D	D	..	D	..	..	D	..
Gabon	..	..	..	..	..	..	..	..	..	..	..	..	..
Gambia, The	..	..	..	..	..	..	..	..	..	..	..	..	..
Ghana	..	..	..	..	..	..	..	..	..	..	..	..	D
Guinea	..	..	..	..	..	..	..	..	..	..	..	..	..
Guinea-Bissau	..	..	..	..	..	..	..	..	..	..	..	..	..
Kenya	..	..	..	..	..	..	D	D	..	..	..	D	D
Lesotho	..	..	..	..	..	..	D	..	..	D	..	..	..
Liberia	..	..	..	..	..	..	..	..	..	..	..	..	..
Madagascar	..	..	..	..	..	..	..	..	..	..	..	..	..
Malawi	..	..	..	..	..	..	D	..	D	D	..	D	D
Mali	..	..	..	..	..	..	..	..	..	..	..	..	..
Mauritania	..	..	..	..	..	..	..	..	..	..	..	..	..
Mauritius	..	..	..	..	..	..	..	..	..	..	..	..	..
Mozambique	..	..	..	..	..	..	D	..	..	D	..	..	D
Namibia	..	..	..	..	..	..	D	..	..	D	..	..	..
Niger	..	D	..	..	D	..	..	..	..	D	D	D	..
Nigeria	..	..	..	..	..	..	..	..	..	..	..	..	..
Rwanda	..	..	..	..	..	..	..	..	..	D	D	..	D
São Tomé and Principe	..	..	..	..	..	..	..	..	..	..	..	..	..
Senegal	..	..	..	..	..	..	..	..	..	..	..	..	..
Seychelles	..	..	..	..	..	..	..	..	..	..	..	..	..
Sierra Leone	..	..	..	..	..	..	..	..	..	..	..	..	..
Somalia	..	..	..	..	..	..	..	..	..	..	..	..	D
South Africa	..	..	..	..	..	..	D	..	..	D	..	D	..
Sudan	..	D	..	D	D	..	..	..	..	D	..	D	..
Swaziland	..	D	..	..	..	..	D	..	..	D	..	..	..
Tanzania	..	..	..	..	..	..	D	..	..	..	..	D	D
Togo	..	..	..	..	..	..	..	..	..	..	..	..	..
Uganda	..	..	..	..	..	..	..	..	..	..	..	D	..
Zambia	..	..	..	..	..	..	D	..	D	D	..	D	D
Zimbabwe	..	..	..	..	..	..	D	..	D	D	..	..	..
NORTH AFRICA	..	..	..	..	..	..	..	..	..	..	..	..	
Algeria	..	..	D	D	..	..	..	D	D	D	..	D	..
Egypt, Arab Republic	..	..	..	..	..	..	..	..	..	..	..	..	
Libya	..	..	..	..	..	..	..	..	..	..	..	..	
Morocco	..	..	..	..	..	..	..	..	..	D	..	D	..
Tunisia	D	..	D	D	..	..	..	..	..	D	..	..	..
ALL AFRICA	..	..	..	..	..	..	..	..	..	..	..	..	

238

Figure 8-1. Food price index, 1998*

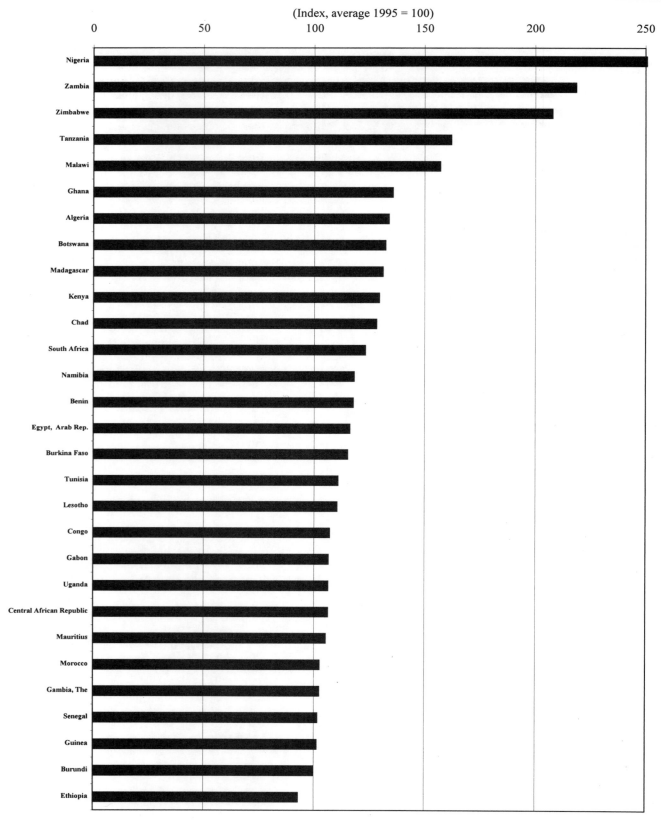

(Index, average 1995 = 100)

* Or most recent year available.

Figure 8-2. Food production per capita index, 1998*

(Index, average 1989-91 = 100)

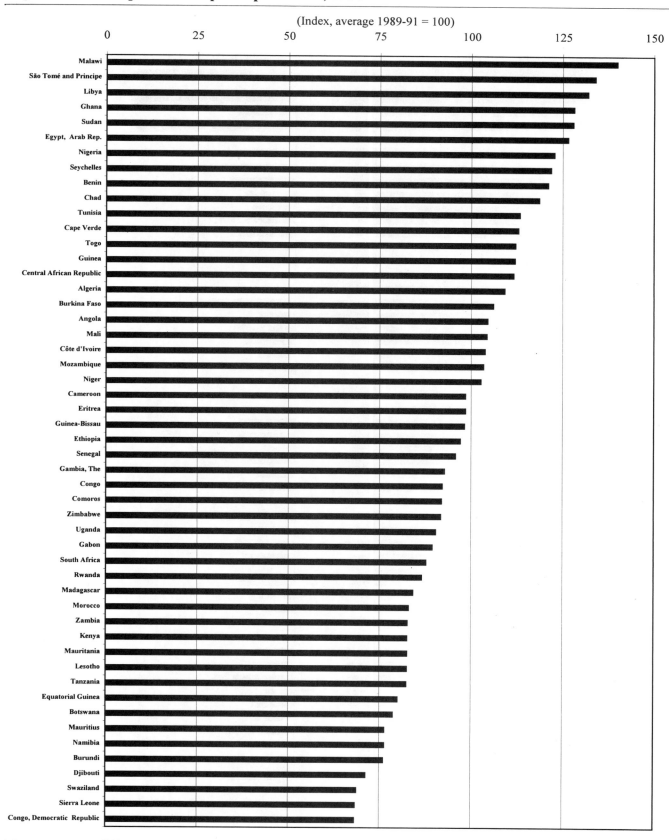

* Or most recent year available.

Figure 8-3. Food and nonfood production index, 1999*

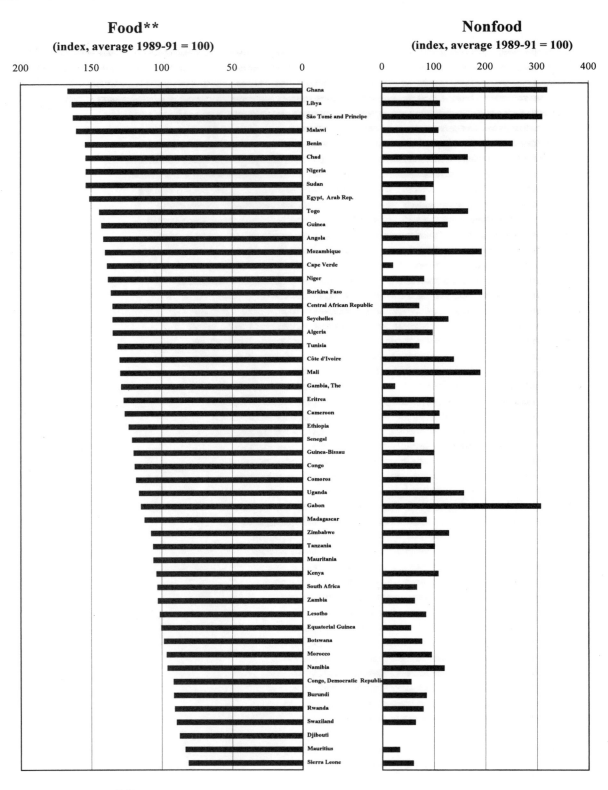

Food**
(index, average 1989-91 = 100)

Nonfood
(index, average 1989-91 = 100)

* Or most recent year available.
** Sorted by food production.

Figure 8-4. Agriculture exports, 1998*

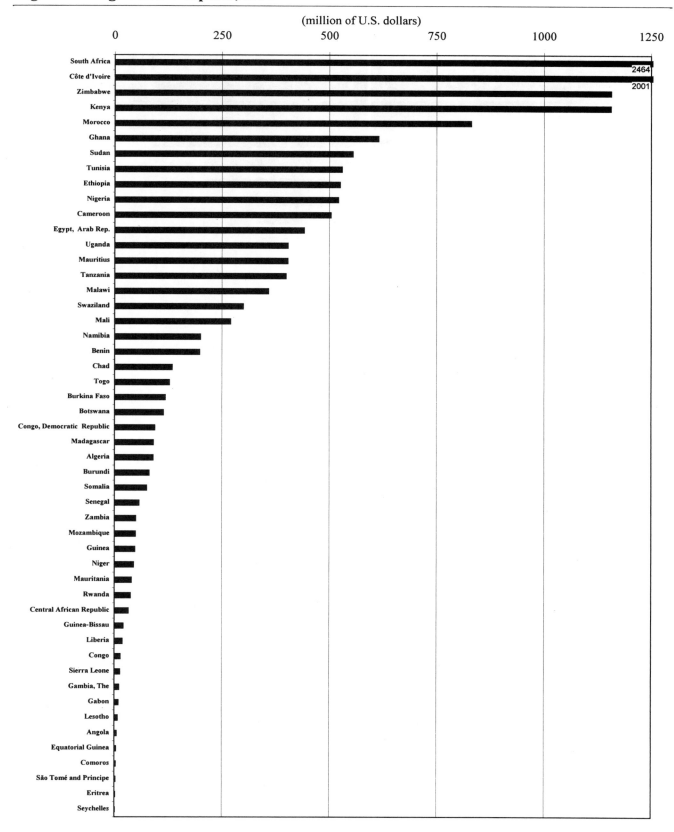

(million of U.S. dollars)

South Africa — 2464
Côte d'Ivoire — 2001
Zimbabwe
Kenya
Morocco
Ghana
Sudan
Tunisia
Ethiopia
Nigeria
Cameroon
Egypt, Arab Rep.
Uganda
Mauritius
Tanzania
Malawi
Swaziland
Mali
Namibia
Benin
Chad
Togo
Burkina Faso
Botswana
Congo, Democratic Republic
Madagascar
Algeria
Burundi
Somalia
Senegal
Zambia
Mozambique
Guinea
Niger
Mauritania
Rwanda
Central African Republic
Guinea-Bissau
Liberia
Congo
Sierra Leone
Gambia, The
Gabon
Lesotho
Angola
Equatorial Guinea
Comoros
São Tomé and Principe
Eritrea
Seychelles

* Or most recent year available.

Figure 8-5. Drought, 1980-1998

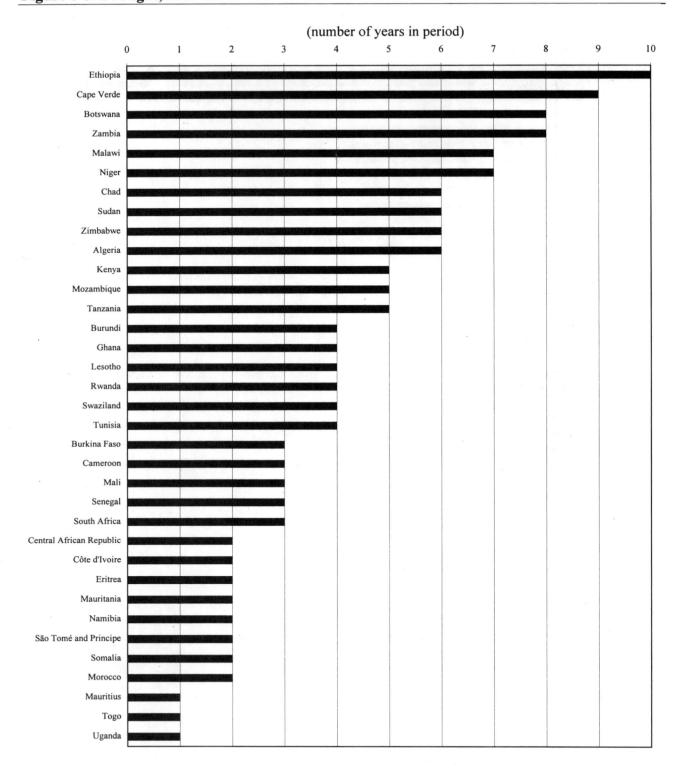

(number of years in period)

Technical notes

Tables

Table 8-1. Nominal producer prices. Data on nominal producer prices are compiled from the FAO. In general, the figures reflect the average annual price received by farmers in the most important producing regions. But given the wide regional and seasonal variation and the lack of precision in recording specifics about prices quoted, the data should be interpreted only as a rough indication of price levels for an entire country during an entire year.

Unlike *ADI 1992*, because of lack of recent information, this volume does not differentiate between official producer prices and farmgate prices. In most cases they happen to be the same.

Crop years for most countries span parts of two calendar years; planting takes place in the first calendar year, while harvest and marketing take place at the end of the first and beginning of the second year. For consistency, producer prices are listed corresponding to the calendar year during which planting decisions are made. For example, producer prices for the crop year 1987/88 are listed as 1987.

For each country, up to four exports crops and five food crops are included, which represent the most important commodities for that country in terms of value of total production during the early 1980s. The food crops include up to three cereals of "traded" grains (those commonly imported or exported) and up to two "nontraded" staples, generally roots and tubers, which are not normally imported or exported by African countries. In the table, these categories of crops are designated by the following symbols: X1

through X4 for export crops; Fl through F3 for traded food crops; and NT1 and NT2 for nontraded staple food crops. The categorization is consistent across countries, but the numbering of crops within categories in each country depends on which crops are most important.

Where commodities may be marketed in several different forms, the form is generally specified (for instance, shelled or unshelled groundnuts). When not specified, the form of the commodity is the most common (for instance, shelled and dried maize). Where commodities are graded, an average grade has been used unless otherwise specified.

Table 8-2. Food price index. This is a subindex of the consumer price index. It reflects the cost to the average consumer of acquiring a fixed basket of food (IMF, IFS).

Table 8-3. Food production index. These indexes are based on 169 commodities that provide calories when consumed (FAO data). Some of these (such as cottonseed, cocoa, and vanilla) are not, however, a significant part of African diets, but are produced primarily for export.

Table 8-4. Nonfood production index. Data in this table are derived from 29 products that are not considered nutritious, including coffee, rubber, cotton lint, and tobacco leaves (FAO data).

Table 8-5. Food production per capita index. These are derived as the ratio of the food production index

(Table 8-3) and estimated total midyear population figures (Table 1-2).

Table 8-6. Volume of food output, by major food crop. The table covers, with only a few differences, the same major food crops as presented in Table 8-1, excluding beverages (coffee, tea, cocoa), cotton, and tobacco. Included also are figures for livestock, which represent the combined total head of cattle, sheep, goats, pigs, horses, asses, and mules, and figures for the total head of rabbits (FAO data).

Table 8-7. Value of agricultural exports. Value of agricultural exports is expressed in current U.S. dollars at f.o.b. prices (FAO data).

Table 8-8. Cereal production. This refers to crops harvested for dry grain only. Cereal crops harvested for hay or harvested green for food, feed, or silage and those used for grazing are excluded (FAO data).

Table 8-9. Crop production index. Shows agricultural production for each year relative to the base period 1989–91. It includes all crops except fodder crops (FAO data).

Tables 8-10 and 8-11. Fertilizer use and imports. Figures are in metric tons and represent the aggregate of nitrogenous, phosphate, and potash fertilizers (FAO database for *Fertilizer Yearbook*).

Table 8-12. Area under permanent crops. Reflects land under permanent crops as defined and reported by THE FAO.

Table 8-13. Agricultural yields, by major crop. This table follows closely the selection of commodities of Table 8-1. Units are in thousands of hectograms (which are equivalent to hundreds of kilograms) per hectare. Most of the data come from the database for the FAO Production Yearbook, with additional information from World Bank agricultural sector reports.

Table 8-14. Incidence of drought. This is the only indicator in this chapter based on subjective considerations. Data on rainfall levels from other sources are usually presented to suit different purposes, without considering seasonal and regional characteristics of the producing regions. A low rainfall level might not harm agricultural production, if it did not adversely affect the regions where the main crops are produced, whereas an average rainfall level might be associated with difficulties in the producing regions, due to delay, for example. Therefore, simply presenting the annual rainfall levels would not necessarily enrich the agricultural data.

For each country, a binary classification was thus created. A "D" was assigned to a country if a significant shortage of rain unfavorably affected its agricultural production. For normal or average rainfall, the standard sign was given, as in the cases of insufficient information or "not applicable." (Specialists who work on the relevant countries were surveyed, as well as World Bank agricultural and environmental experts. In addition, the Federal Early Warning System project of the U.S. Agency for International Development provided information for 1993–94 for about half of the countries listed.)

Figures

The following indicators have been used to derive the figures in this chapter.

Figure 8-1. Food price index (Table 8-2).

Figure 8-2. Food production per capita index (Table 8-5).

Figure 8-3. Food production index (Table 8-3); nonfood production index (Table 8-4).

Figure 8-4. Agricultural exports (Table 8-7).

Figure 8-5. Drought (Table 8-14).

Methodology used for regional aggregations and period averages in chapter 8

Table	Aggregations[a]				Period averages[b]
	(1)	(6)	(7)	(8)	(2)
8-1				x	
8-2			x		x
8-3		x			x
8-4			x		
8-5			x		x
8-6				x	x
8-7	x				x
8-8	x				x
8-9		x			x
8-10	x				x
8-11	x				x
8-12	x				x
8-13				x	x
8-14				x	

Note: Regional aggregations are shown in the rows for Sub-Saharan Africa, North Africa, and All Africa. Period averages are shown in the last three columns. This table shows only the methodologies used in this chapter.

a. Regional aggregations: (1) simple total; (2) simple total of the first indicator divided by the simple total of the second indicator (same country coverage); (3) simple total of the gap-filled indicator; (4) simple total of the gap-filled main indicator divided by the simple total of the gap-filled secondary indicator; (5) simple total of the first gap-filled main indicator less the simple total of the second gap-filled main indicator, all divided by the simple total of the secondary indicator; (6) weighted total (by population); (7) median; (8) no aggregation; (9) simple arithmetic mean.

b. Period averages: (i) arithmetic mean (using the same series as shown in the table i.e., ratio if the rest of the table is shown as ratio, level if the rest of the table is shown as level, growth rate if the rest is shown as growth rate); (2) least-squares growth rate (using main indicator); (3) least-squares growth rate (using main indicator in constant terms, with the rest of the table in current terms).

9

Power, Communications, and Transportation

This chapter provides data on the power, communications, and transportation sectors of the economy.

An adequate and reliable supply of power is a vital ingredient for the economic development of African countries. This chapter presents information on electric power production and distribution losses. Data are from the International Energy Agency's (IEA's) *Energy Statistics and Balances of Non-OECD Countries, 1993–94* (1997).

Telecommunications are also an essential ingredient of a modern economy. In this chapter telephone main lines represent the supply side of the system, which in Africa is well short of demand. In fact, waiting time for telephone lines is the highest of any other geographical region. Data on telecommunications are from the International Telecommunications Union's (ITU) *World Telecommunications Development Report* (1996).

In addition to power and communication, countries must have a solid transportation sector to underpin expansion of their economies and ensure support to the activities of households, producers, and government. This chapter presents data on vehicle use, roads, and railway traffic. Data are from the World Bank databases and from the International World Road Federation's *World Road Statistics* (1996).

9-1. Electric power consumption per capita

	Million KWH									Annual average		
	1980	1990	1991	1992	1993	1994	1995	1996	1997	75-84	85-89	90-MR
SUB-SAHARAN AFRICA	427.7	445.9	441.1	432.5	439.3	430.1	437.9	442.3	446.6	407.6	447.3	439.5
excluding South Africa	133.0	122.8	126.2	126.2	130.1	127.1	125.0	126.1	125.8	128.0	129.9	126.2
excl. S.Africa & Nigeria	157.3	140.1	142.9	141.4	143.4	141.7	140.3	141.7	141.8	151.9	146.9	141.7
Angola	67.2	60.3	65.3	64.1	62.1	60.4	58.8	61.0	63.9	74.9	67.1	62.0
Benin	29.7	36.7	38.7	41.2	41.7	42.3	45.1	48.0	43.2	29.5	34.8	42.1
Botswana	..	..	..	..	..	..	..	..	..	..	..	..
Burkina Faso	..	..	..	..	..	..	..	..	..	..	..	..
Burundi	..	..	..	..	..	..	..	..	..	..	..	..
Cameroon	155.5	204.3	197.9	194.5	196.9	172.6	165.1	170.9	180.7	179.5	215.6	185.4
Cape Verde	..	..	..	..	..	..	..	..	..	..	..	..
Central African Republic	..	..	..	..	..	..	..	..	..	..	..	..
Chad	..	..	..	..	..	..	..	..	..	..	..	..
Comoros	..	..	..	..	..	..	..	..	..	..	..	..
Congo, Democratic Rep. of	147.3	121.8	131.7	130.4	147.4	144.9	132.0	129.6	120.4	138.8	136.1	132.3
Congo, Republic of	94.1	254.1	236.3	224.5	220.3	216.5	212.8	204.7	197.2	100.0	202.1	220.8
Côte d'Ivoire	191.6	158.0	149.6	81.4	139.6	140.3	170.5	174.3	181.3	166.4	164.9	149.4
Djibouti	..	..	..	..	..	..	..	..	..	..	..	..
Equatorial Guinea	..	..	..	..	..	..	..	..	..	..	..	..
Eritrea	..	..	..	..	..	..	..	..	..	..	..	..
Ethiopia	16.2	21.4	21.1	20.4	19.4	22.7	22.1	21.5	21.4	16.3	18.0	21.3
Gabon	617.9	806.3	784.8	762.5	747.4	754.4	736.8	742.2	752.2	603.3	942.4	760.8
Gambia, The	..	..	..	..	..	..	..	..	..	..	..	..
Ghana	423.5	300.5	309.7	323.4	329.9	305.1	283.5	274.9	275.8	335.9	260.7	300.3
Guinea	..	..	..	..	..	..	..	..	..	..	..	..
Guinea-Bissau	..	..	..	..	..	..	..	..	..	..	..	..
Kenya	92.5	114.7	116.2	116.6	119.8	121.8	121.8	127.2	128.7	90.1	105.9	120.9
Lesotho	..	..	..	..	..	..	..	..	..	..	..	..
Liberia	..	..	..	..	..	..	..	..	..	..	..	..
Madagascar	..	..	..	..	..	..	..	..	..	..	..	..
Malawi	..	..	..	..	..	..	..	..	..	..	..	..
Mali	..	..	..	..	..	..	..	..	..	..	..	..
Mauritania	..	..	..	..	..	..	..	..	..	..	..	..
Mauritius	..	..	..	..	..	..	..	..	..	..	..	..
Mozambique	34.0	35.1	48.3	46.2	46.2	41.3	44.1	40.7	46.8	42.4	32.8	43.6
Namibia	..	..	..	..	..	..	..	..	..	..	..	..
Niger	..	..	..	..	..	..	..	..	..	..	..	..
Nigeria	68.2	77.1	81.6	85.5	95.3	88.8	84.8	85.3	84.0	64.6	84.9	85.3
Rwanda	..	..	..	..	..	..	..	..	..	..	..	..
São Tomé and Principe	..	..	..	..	..	..	..	..	..	..	..	..
Senegal	93.7	93.6	96.4	95.7	102.4	97.8	103.8	103.3	107.2	87.4	96.2	100.0
Seychelles	..	..	..	..	..	..	..	..	..	..	..	..
Sierra Leone	..	..	..	..	..	..	..	..	..	..	..	..
Somalia	..	..	..	..	..	..	..	..	..	..	..	..
South Africa	3,212.9	3,676.0	3,618.2	3,548.1	3,581.3	3,530.7	3,659.8	3,723.2	3,800.2	3,037.2	3,555.5	3,642.2
Sudan	35.3	52.3	50.6	50.8	48.8	50.8	50.5	51.4	48.5	37.3	49.4	50.5
Swaziland	..	..	..	..	..	..	..	..	..	..	..	..
Tanzania	36.8	51.2	54.4	53.2	51.4	50.7	54.7	58.8	54.3	35.4	41.7	53.6
Togo	..	..	..	..	..	..	..	..	..	..	..	..
Uganda	..	..	..	..	..	..	..	..	..	..	..	..
Zambia	1,015.7	502.8	651.8	623.4	606.2	589.5	574.3	560.0	562.9	1,058.2	807.9	583.9
Zimbabwe	990.4	932.9	829.6	900.2	787.3	824.0	849.1	893.7	918.8	955.4	929.3	866.9
NORTH AFRICA	362.8	675.9	692.6	696.6	715.8	737.1	752.3	745.7	772.9	352.0	601.0	723.6
Algeria	265.3	449.2	467.6	464.2	508.7	509.8	516.9	526.3	570.8	259.8	399.9	501.7
Egypt, Arab Republic	379.9	697.1	722.7	721.1	743.2	765.5	792.5	772.4	803.4	377.8	606.0	752.2
Libya	1,588.2	3,804.3	3,707.0	3,649.7	3,576.2	3,661.8	3,623.9	3,581.7	3,504.6	1,505.7	3,643.7	3,638.7
Morocco	222.8	339.8	355.4	380.9	377.1	398.1	403.7	408.4	423.3	212.1	299.2	385.8
Tunisia	379.2	531.5	543.1	571.8	607.7	646.2	663.7	673.5	709.2	323.6	459.5	618.3
ALL AFRICA	412.5	498.2	498.1	492.0	501.6	498.9	507.9	509.4	518.3	394.4	482.6	503.0

9-2. Energy production and use

	Energy production (KT oil equivalent)		Commercial energy use (KT oil equivalent)		Electric power transmission and distribution losses (% of output)	
	1980	1997	1980	1997	1980	1997
SUB-SAHARAN AFRICA	319,801	517,698	203,560	324,252	..	..
excluding South Africa	246,632	375,724	138,143	213,266		
excl. S. Africa & Nigeria	98,153	184,417	85,297	126,777	..	..
Angola	11,301	41,616	4,437	7,147	25	28
Benin	1,212	1,909	1,363	2,240	220	76
Botswana	..	..	..	..	..	..
Burkina Faso	..	..	..	..	..	..
Burundi	..	..	..	..	..	..
Cameroon	6,707	12,108	3,676	6,183	7	20
Cape Verde	..	..	..	..	..	..
Central African Republic	..	..	..	..	..	..
Chad	..	..	..	..	..	..
Comoros	..	..	..	..	..	..
Congo, Democratic Rep. of	8,697	14,364	8,706	13,711	8	3
Congo, Republic of	3,970	13,546	845	1,206	1	1
Côte d'Ivoire	0	0	0	0	7	16
Djibouti	..	..	..	..	..	..
Equatorial Guinea	..	..	..	..	..	..
Eritrea					..	..
Ethiopia	10,588	15,610	11,157	17,429	8	1
Gabon	9,441	19,786	1,493	1,668	1	10
Gambia, The	..	..	..	..	..	..
Ghana	3,305	5,545	4,027	7,270	0	0
Guinea	..	..	..	..	..	..
Guinea-Bissau	..	..	..	..	..	..
Kenya	7,891	11,641	9,791	14,527	16	17
Lesotho	..	..	..	..	..	..
Liberia	..	..	..	..	..	..
Madagascar	..	..	..	..	..	..
Malawi	..	..	..	..	..	..
Mali	..	..	..	..	..	..
Mauritania	..	..	..	..	..	..
Mauritius	..	..	..	..	..	..
Mozambique	7,413	6,441	8,074	6,863	39	31
Namibia	..	..	..	..	..	..
Niger	..	..	..	..	..	..
Nigeria	148,479	191,307	52,846	86,489	36	32
Rwanda	..	..	..	..	..	..
São Tomé and Principe	..	..	..	..	..	..
Senegal	1,046	1,655	1,921	2,822	11	17
Seychelles	..	..	..	..	..	..
Sierra Leone	..	..	..	..	..	..
Somalia	..	..	..	..	..	..
South Africa	73,169	141,974	65,417	110,986	8	8
Sudan	7,089	13,057	8,406	14,899	14	31
Swaziland	..	..	..	..	..	..
Tanzania	9,502	13,529	10,280	14,660	14	14
Togo	..	..	..	..	..	..
Uganda	..	..	..	..	..	..
Zambia	4,198	5,556	4,551	6,088	7	11
Zimbabwe	5,793	8,053	6,570	10,065	9	13
NORTH AFRICA	205,303	270,225	43,937	97,650	..	..
Algeria	66,741	126,400	12,089	26,506	11	15
Egypt, Arab Republic	34,168	57,732	15,970	41,798	13	12
Libya	96,550	78,494	7,193	12,420	..	..
Morocco	877	837	4,778	9,344	10	4
Tunisia	6,966	6,761	3,907	7,582	12	11
ALL AFRICA	525,103	787,923	247,497	421,903	..	..

9-3. Telephone, radio, and television availability, 1994-98

	Telephones				Radios	Television
	Mainlines	*Waiting list*	*Average cost of call*	*Mobile phones*		*sets*
	(per 1,000 persons)	*(Thousands)*	*US$ per three minutes*	*(per 1,000 persons)*	*(per 1,000 persons)*	*(per 1,000 persons)*
SUB-SAHARAN AFRICA	11	1,440	..	5	198	52
excluding South Africa	5	1,303	..	1	190	46
excl. S. Africa & Nigeria	5	1,213	..	1	181	41
Angola	5	..	0.14	1	54	14
Benin	5	3	0.12	1	108	10
Botswana	41	12	0.03	15	156	20
Burkina Faso	3	..	0.10	0	33	9
Burundi	3	5	0.03	0	71	4
Cameroon	5	45	0.06	0	163	32
Cape Verde	56	10	0.04	3	180	5
Central African Republic	2	0	0.20	0	83	5
Chad	1	1	0.17	0	242	1
Comoros	9	..	0.17	0	138	4
Congo, Democratic Rep. of	1	6	..	0	375	135
Congo, Republic of	8	1	0.12	1	124	12
Côte d'Ivoire	9	82	0.11	6	164	70
Djibouti	13	0	0.19	0	84	45
Equatorial Guinea	6	..	..	1	429	162
Eritrea	5	42	0.03	0	91	14
Ethiopia	3	207	0.03	0	195	5
Gabon	29	10	0.15	8	183	55
Gambia, The	18	22	0.32	4	168	3
Ghana	4	28	0.09	1	238	99
Guinea	2	2	0.10	3	47	41
Guinea-Bissau	9	1	0.14	0	44	..
Kenya	9	77	0.05	0	104	21
Lesotho	9	9	0.03	5	49	25
Liberia	..	2	..	0	274	24
Madagascar	2	10	0.09	1	192	21
Malawi	3	31	0.03	1	249	2
Mali	2	..	0.14	0	54	12
Mauritania	4	1	0.10	0	151	91
Mauritius	132	23	0.04	53	368	226
Mozambique	4	17	0.04	0	40	5
Namibia	51	7	0.05	12	144	37
Niger	1	1	0.15	0	69	27
Nigeria	4	98	0.26	0	223	66
Rwanda	2	..	0.04	1	102	0
São Tomé and Principe	19	1	0.02	0	275	227
Senegal	10	17	0.13	2	142	41
Seychelles	176	2	0.16	49	545	149
Sierra Leone	4	14	0.04	0	253	13
Somalia	2	..	..	0	46	13
South Africa	100	116	0.07	56	317	125
Sudan	3	320	0.02	0	271	87
Swaziland	22	15	0.14	5	164	111
Tanzania	3	37	0.09	1	279	21
Togo	5	13	0.10	2	218	18
Uganda	2	6	0.18	1	128	27
Zambia	9	12	0.06	1	121	137
Zimbabwe	14	109	0.03	4	93	30
NORTH AFRICA	47	2,187	..	2	278	131
Algeria	42	732	0.02	1	241	105
Egypt, Arab Republic	9	12	0.06	1	121	122
Libya	14	109	0.03	4	93	126
Morocco	42	732	0.02	1	241	160
Tunisia	47	1,310	0.01	1	324	198
ALL AFRICA	18	2,338	..	5	212	66

9-4. Vehicle ownership

	Units per 1000 persons									Annual average		
	1980	1990	1991	1992	1993	1994	1995	1996	1997	75-84	85-89	90-MR
SUB-SAHARAN AFRICA	..	23	24	24	26	22	23	22	..	..	..	23
excluding South Africa	..	9	15	15	16	14	15	15	..	..	..	14
excl. S.Africa & Nigeria	..	9	10	10	11	11	12	12	..	..	..	11
Angola	..	19	20	20	20	20	20	20	..	..	..	20
Benin	..	3	4	5	6	6	7	8	..	..	..	6
Botswana	27	19	23	28	33	36	41	45	..	27	..	32
Burkina Faso	..	4	4	5	5	5	5	5	..	..	..	5
Burundi	..	0	..	..	..	..	..	..	..	..	..	0
Cameroon	8	10	10	10	11	11	12	12	..	8	..	11
Cape Verde	..	8	8	8	8	9	9	10	..	..	..	9
Central African Republic	8	..	1	1	1	1	1	0	1	8	..	1
Chad	..	5	5	6	7	7	8	8	..	..	..	6
Comoros	..	10	12	13	14	17	18	21	..	..	..	15
Congo, Democratic Rep. of	..	22	25	28	28	29	30	31	..	..	..	27
Congo, Republic of	..	18	19	19	20	19	20	20	..	..	..	19
Côte d'Ivoire	24	23	24	26	27	27	28	28	..	24	..	26
Djibouti	..	16	17	18	19	19	20	21	..	..	..	18
Equatorial Guinea	..	3	4	4	4	4	4	5	..	..	..	4
Eritrea	..	1	1	1	1	1	2	2	..	..	..	1
Ethiopia	2	1	1	1	1	1	1	2	2	2	1	1
Gabon	..	26	27	27	28	28	29	29	..	..	..	28
Gambia, The	..	14	14	15	15	16	16	17	..	..	..	15
Ghana	..	..	..	..	..	8	7	7	..	..	..	7
Guinea	..	4	4	5	5	5	5	5	..	..	..	5
Guinea-Bissau	..	7	8	8	8	9	10	10	..	..	..	9
Kenya	8	13	14	14	14	14	14	14	..	8	12	14
Lesotho	10	11	12	13	14	15	16	17	..	10	..	14
Liberia	1	15	14	13	12	13	12	12	..	1	..	13
Madagascar	..	6	5	5	5	5	5	5	..	..	..	5
Malawi	5	4	4	4	5	5	5	5	..	5	..	4
Mali	..	4	4	4	4	5	5	5	..	..	..	4
Mauritania	..	9	10	10	10	11	11	12	..	..	..	11
Mauritius	44	60	63	68	71	75	79	83	84	44	54	75
Mozambique	..	4	4	5	5	3	2	1	..	..	..	3
Namibia	..	71	85	74	79	82	81	82	..	..	..	79
Niger	6	6	6	6	6	6	6	5	..	6	5	6
Nigeria	4	..	33	32	32	24	28	26	..	4	..	29
Rwanda	2	2	3	3	3	3	3	3	..	2	1	3
São Tomé and Principe	..	35	36	36	38	39	41	42	..	..	..	38
Senegal	19	11	11	12	13	13	13	14	..	19	..	13
Seychelles	..	102	103	106	107	116	116	123	..	..	..	110
Sierra Leone	..	10	10	11	11	11	9	6	..	..	10	10
Somalia	..	2	2	1	1	1	1	1	..	..	..	1
South Africa	133	160	132	132	157	134	132	121	..	133	160	138
Sudan	..	9	9	9	10	10	10	10	..	..	..	10
Swaziland	52	72	77	70	64	62	66	68	66	52	63	68
Tanzania	3	5	4	5	5	5	5	5	..	3	..	5
Togo	..	24	24	25	25	26	27	27	..	..	1	25
Uganda	1	2	3	3	3	3	4	4	..	1	..	3
Zambia	..	15	16	18	19	20	22	23	..	..	..	19
Zimbabwe	..	..	..	..	31	31	31	31	..	..	..	31
NORTH AFRICA	..	32	32	33	34	45	49	48	..	..	38	39
Algeria	..	..	..	..	..	54	53	52	..	..	54	53
Egypt, Arab Republic	..	26	27	27	26	28	28	30	..	..	26	27
Libya	..	..	..	..	..	148	259	209	..	..	..	206
Morocco	..	37	38	41	43	46	48	48	..	..	..	43
Tunisia	38	48	50	51	52	60	60	64	..	38	62	55
ALL AFRICA	..	25	25	25	27	26	28	27	..	..	..	26

9-5. Road-to-population ratio

	Road 1000 km/1 million persons									Annual average		
	1980	*1990*	*1991*	*1992*	*1993*	*1994*	*1995*	*1996*	*1997*	*75-84*	*85-89*	*90-MR*
SUB-SAHARAN AFRICA	3.3	2.5	..	..	2.5	2.4	2.9	2.4	..	3.3	3.1	2.5
excluding South Africa	3.1	2.2	..	..	2.5	2.4	2.5	2.4	..	3.1	2.8	2.4
excl. S.Africa & Nigeria	3.5	2.6	..	..	2.8	2.6	2.7	2.6	..	3.5	3.3	2.6
Angola	10.3	7.9	..	7.3	7.1	6.8	6.6	6.4	6.2	11.1	9.0	6.9
Benin	2.1	1.8	1.2	1.2	1.3	1.3	1.2	1.2	..	2.1	1.6	1.3
Botswana	9.1	7.0	..	..	13.2	12.9	12.5	12.4	..	11.7	9.8	11.6
Burkina Faso	1.1	..	..	1.4	1.1	1.1	1.3	1.2	..	1.7	1.2	1.2
Burundi	1.2	1.2	..	2.5	2.5	2.4	2.4	2.3	..	1.8	0.6	2.2
Cameroon	7.2	6.1	..	..	2.7	2.7	2.6	..	..	6.6	5.5	3.5
Cape Verde	..	..	..	..	3.0	3.0	2.9	2.8	..	..	..	2.9
Central African Republic	9.8	8.0	7.9	7.7	7.5	7.4	7.3	7.2	..	9.8	7.9	7.6
Chad	6.0	4.7	..	..	5.0	5.0	4.9	4.8	..	6.6	5.3	4.9
Comoros	..	..	..	..	1.8	1.8	1.8	1.8	..	2.3	..	1.8
Congo, Democratic Rep. of	5.4	..	3.8	3.6	3.6	3.6	3.5	3.5	..	5.4	4.6	3.6
Congo, Republic of	5.0	..	5.6	5.4	5.3	5.1	5.0	4.9	..	5.5	4.5	5.2
Côte d'Ivoire	5.0	4.2	..	..	3.9	3.8	3.7	3.6	..	5.6	4.8	3.9
Djibouti	..	5.6	5.4	..	5.1	5.0	4.8	4.7	..	7.6	6.7	5.1
Equatorial Guinea	..	..	..	..	7.2	7.1	7.1	7.0	..	5.2	..	7.1
Eritrea	..	..	..	..	1.1	1.1	1.1	1.1	..	..	..	1.1
Ethiopia	1.0	0.5	0.5	..	0.5	0.5	0.5	0.5	..	0.9	0.7	0.5
Gabon	10.2	..	7.6	7.4	7.2	7.1	7.0	6.8	..	10.9	9.3	7.2
Gambia, The	3.4	2.6	..	..	2.4	2.4	2.4	2.4	..	3.0	4.2	2.4
Ghana	3.0	2.6	..	..	2.3	2.2	2.2	2.2	..	2.8	2.7	2.3
Guinea	5.4	..	..	2.6	0.0	4.7	4.6	4.5	..	4.2	5.8	3.3
Guinea-Bissau	..	..	..	..	4.1	4.1	4.0	4.0	..	4.7	..	4.0
Kenya	3.1	2.6	2.6	..	2.5	2.4	2.4	2.3	..	3.2	3.0	2.5
Lesotho	3.0	..	..	2.9	2.9	2.8	2.6	2.5	..	2.7	2.7	2.7
Liberia	2.9	2.4	..	..	3.8	3.8	3.8	3.8	..	3.9	3.2	3.5
Madagascar	5.7	..	2.9	2.8	4.0	3.9	3.7	3.6	..	4.8	4.0	3.5
Malawi	1.7	3.2	..	..	1.5	1.5	1.5	1.5	1.6	1.9	1.5	1.8
Mali	2.0	1.7	1.7	..	1.6	1.5	1.5	1.5	..	2.1	1.8	1.6
Mauritania	4.7	3.6	..	..	3.4	3.3	3.3	3.2	..	4.7	4.1	3.4
Mauritius	1.8	1.7	1.7	..	1.8	1.7	1.7	1.7	1.7	2.2	1.7	1.7
Mozambique	2.9	2.5	..	..	1.9	1.9	1.9	1.9	..	3.3	2.0	2.0
Namibia	..	28.7	..	..	42.8	42.2	41.0	39.9	39.0	..	..	38.9
Niger	2.8	1.5	..	..	1.6	1.1	1.1	1.1	..	2.4	2.7	1.3
Nigeria	1.5	1.2	..	..	1.6	1.6	1.7	1.7	..	1.5	1.3	1.5
Rwanda	2.1	1.9	..	..	1.9	2.3	2.3	2.2	..	1.7	1.9	2.1
São Tomé and Principe	..	..	..	..	2.4	2.3	2.3	2.4	..	..	..	2.4
Senegal	2.5	2.0	..	..	1.8	1.8	1.8	1.7	..	2.4	2.2	1.8
Seychelles	..	..	..	..	3.6	3.5	3.6	3.7	..	..	..	3.6
Sierra Leone	2.4	..	..	2.8	2.7	2.7	2.5	2.4	2.4	2.5	2.3	2.6
Somalia	2.9	2.8	..	..	2.6	2.6	2.7	2.6	..	3.5	3.3	2.7
South Africa	6.7	5.3	5.1	..	..	..	8.5	..	..	7.1	5.5	6.3
Sudan	0.5	0.4	..	..	0.4	0.4	0.4	0.4	..	0.7	0.4	0.4
Swaziland	5.8	3.6	3.5	3.6	3.3	3.3	4.1	4.1	..	5.1	4.4	3.7
Tanzania	2.5	..	2.1	2.1	3.1	3.1	3.0	2.9	..	2.5	3.8	2.7
Togo	2.7	2.1	2.1	2.0	1.9	1.9	1.8	1.8	..	2.8	2.3	2.0
Uganda	2.1	1.8	..	1.7	..	..	..	..	..	2.1	2.0	1.7
Zambia	6.3	4.8	4.7	4.5	4.4	4.4	7.4	7.2	7.1	6.4	5.3	5.6
Zimbabwe	12.0	..	..	8.9	8.7	1.8	1.7	1.6	..	12.0	9.4	4.5
NORTH AFRICA	2.1	..	1.9	1.6	2.5	..	..	..	..	2.1	1.6	2.0
Algeria	3.9	..	3.5	3.6	3.7	3.6	3.7	3.6	..	4.1	3.6	3.6
Egypt, Arab Republic	0.7	0.9	0.9	0.9	0.8	..	..	..	..	0.7	0.7	0.9
Libya	..	..	..	..	16.5	16.5	16.4	4.8	..	..	..	13.6
Morocco	3.0	..	2.4	1.1	2.4	2.3	2.3	2.3	2.1	2.9	2.6	2.1
Tunisia	3.7	..	..	..	2.4	2.5	2.5	2.5	..	3.4	3.6	2.5
ALL AFRICA	3.1	2.3	..	..	2.5	2.6	3.0	2.5	..	3.1	2.9	2.6

9-6. Paved primary roads

	Percentage of roads							Percent in good condition
	1992	1993	1994	1995	1996	1997	1998	1989
SUB-SAHARAN AFRICA	16.5	16.4	17.1	16.0	15.8	19.0	11.8	39
excluding South Africa	16.5	16.4	17.1	15.5	15.8	19.0	49.4	39
excl. S. Africa & Nigeria	16.0	15.8	16.1	15.0	15.0	13.7	49.4	41
Angola	25.0	25.0	25.0	25.0	25.0	25.0	..	..
Benin	20.0	20.0	20.0	20.0	20.0	..	..	13
Botswana	19.9	21.1	22.2	23.3	23.5	..	..	94
Burkina Faso	17.6	18.2	18.7	16.0	..	..	..	70
Burundi	7.1	7.1	7.1	7.1	..	..	..	75
Cameroon	11.3	11.7	12.1	12.5	..	..	..	25
Cape Verde	78.0	78.0	78.0	78.0	..	..	..	14
Central African Republic	..	..	2.1	2.1	2.1	2.4	2.7	30
Chad	0.8	0.8	0.8	0.8	..	..	..	..
Comoros	72.1	73.5	75.0	76.5	..	..	..	43
Congo, Democratic Rep. of	..	..	..	..	..	..	..	20
Congo, Republic of	9.7	9.7	9.7	9.7	9.7	..	..	50
Côte d'Ivoire	9.1	9.2	9.4	9.6	9.7	..	..	75
Djibouti	12.6	12.6	12.6	12.6	12.6	..	..	51
Equatorial Guinea	..	..	..	..	..	..	..	27
Eritrea	20.2	20.6	21.0	21.4	21.8	..	..	..
Ethiopia	15.0	15.0	15.0	15.0	15.0	..	..	47
Gabon	8.2	8.2	8.2	8.2	8.2	..	..	30
Gambia, The	33.3	34.0	34.6	35.3	35.4	..	..	22
Ghana	23.5	23.9	24.4	24.9	24.1	..	..	28
Guinea	15.5	15.8	16.1	16.4	16.5	..	..	50
Guinea-Bissau	9.1	9.4	9.8	10.2	10.3	..	..	39
Kenya	13.8	14.3	13.6	13.8	13.9	..	..	32
Lesotho	16.0	15.0	15.0	17.9	17.9	..	..	53
Liberia	5.7	5.9	6.0	6.1	6.2	..	..	85
Madagascar	15.4	11.5	18.7	11.5	11.6	..	..	56
Malawi	17.0	18.0	18.0	20.0	20.0	19.0	..	56
Mali	11.3	11.5	11.8	12.0	12.1	..	..	70
Mauritania	11.1	11.1	11.1	11.2	11.3	..	..	58
Mauritius	93.0	93.0	93.0	93.0	93.0	93.0	96.0	95
Mozambique	17.5	17.8	18.2	18.6	18.7	..	..	19
Namibia	10.9	7.3	7.9	7.9	8.2	8.3	..	..
Niger	..	..	7.9	7.9	7.9	..	..	67
Nigeria	30.0	30.0	21.3	18.8	18.8	30.9	..	34
Rwanda	9.4	9.6	9.7	9.9	9.1	..	..	41
São Tomé and Principe	64.1	65.4	66.7	68.0	68.1	..	..	..
Senegal	28.3	28.3	28.4	28.5	29.3	..	..	28
Seychelles	59.1	60.3	61.5	62.8	62.9	..	..	..
Sierra Leone	11.0	11.0	11.0	8.0	8.0	8.0	..	62
Somalia	11.5	11.8	11.8	11.8	11.8	..	..	52
South Africa	..	..	..	41.5	..	..	11.8	..
Sudan	33.7	34.5	35.4	36.2	36.3	..	..	27
Swaziland	58.6	59.8	28.2	..	..	..	..	35
Tanzania	37.0	4.2	4.2	4.2	4.2	..	..	39
Togo	31.0	31.6	31.6	31.6	31.6	..	..	75
Uganda	..	..	..	..	..	..	..	10
Zambia	17.3	17.6	18.0	..	..	..	..	40
Zimbabwe	16.0	17.0	54.9	48.0	47.4	..	..	70
NORTH AFRICA	66.0	66.7	68.0	68.9	78.1	52.3	52.3	..
Algeria	66.0	66.7	68.0	68.9	..	..	..	..
Egypt, Arab Republic	73.0	72.0	75.0	78.0	78.1	..	..	..
Libya	53.8	54.9	56.0	57.1	..	..	..	..
Morocco	49.5	49.6	50.2	50.2	50.2	52.3	52.3	..
Tunisia	74.6	76.0	77.4	78.8	78.9	..	..	..
ALL AFRICA	17.5	17.8	18.2	18.3	17.9	22.0	32.0	39

9-7. Rail goods traffic-to-$PPP GDP ratio

	Ton-km per million of $PPP GDP									Annual average		
	1980	1990	1991	1992	1993	1994	1995	1996	1997	75-84	85-89	90-MR
SUB-SAHARAN AFRICA	..	..	..	..	..	..	..	..	..	..	..	..
excluding South Africa	..	..	..	..	..	..	..	..	..	..	..	..
excl. S.Africa & Nigeria	..	..	..	..	..	..	..	..	..	..	..	..
Angola	..	..	..	..	..	..	..	..	..	..	..	..
Benin	..	..	..	..	..	..	..	..	..	..	..	..
Botswana	..	..	..	..	..	..	..	..	..	..	..	..
Burkina Faso	..	..	..	..	..	..	..	..	..	..	..	..
Burundi	..	..	..	..	..	..	..	..	..	..	..	..
Cameroon	60,200	37,699	32,480	34,159	29,663	38,283	38,711	27,318	37,719	57,898	37,959	34,504
Cape Verde	..	..	..	..	..	..	..	..	..	..	..	..
Central African Republic	..	..	..	..	..	..	..	..	..	..	..	..
Chad	..	..	..	..	..	..	..	..	..	..	..	..
Comoros	..	..	..	..	..	..	..	..	..	..	..	..
Congo, Democratic Rep. of	52,689	32,460	..	..	..	4,367	..	..	..	48,570	35,919	18,413
Congo, Republic of	..	..	189,871	109,802	82,885	73,671	..	..	..	230,730	221,938	114,057
Côte d'Ivoire	54,623	15,674	14,590	13,648	8,451	8,507	13,829	..	19,827	47,220	33,751	13,504
Djibouti	..	..	..	..	..	..	..	..	..	..	..	..
Equatorial Guinea	..	..	..	..	..	..	..	..	..	..	..	..
Eritrea	..	..	..	..	..	..	..	..	..	..	..	..
Ethiopia	..	..	2,120	..	..	..	..	..	..	8,510	5,540	2,120
Gabon	8,327	..	..	51,885	57,461	55,195	72,779	..	67,137	17,872	41,887	60,892
Gambia, The	..	..	..	..	..	..	..	..	..	..	..	..
Ghana	10,710	6,191	..	..	..	..	..	..	..	8,391	6,675	6,191
Guinea	..	..	..	..	..	..	..	..	..	..	..	..
Guinea-Bissau	..	..	..	..	..	..	..	..	..	..	..	..
Kenya	216,646	80,740	72,062	56,064	48,334	46,797	..	..	41,917	183,062	100,010	57,652
Lesotho	..	..	..	..	..	..	..	..	..	..	..	..
Liberia	..	..	..	..	..	..	..	..	..	..	..	..
Madagascar	..	..	..	..	..	..	..	..	..	..	..	..
Malawi	95,747	15,207	14,848	12,312	10,064	10,949	11,185	..	..	72,219	23,511	12,427
Mali	41,564	53,612	51,060	45,934	..	..	..	..	34,053	44,181	54,124	46,165
Mauritania	..	..	..	..	..	..	..	..	..	..	..	..
Mauritius	..	..	..	..	..	..	..	..	..	..	..	..
Mozambique	..	..	..	..	..	..	..	..	..	..	..	..
Namibia	..	285,327	184,822	169,879	149,047	136,942	129,941	..	..	..	..	175,993
Niger	..	..	..	..	..	..	..	..	..	..	..	..
Nigeria	22,511	3,359	..	608	..	1	..	..	4,834	29,236	8,105	2,201
Rwanda	..	..	..	..	..	..	..	..	..	..	..	..
São Tomé and Principe	..	..	..	..	..	..	..	..	..	..	..	..
Senegal	68,169	61,227	51,331	47,088	38,987	36,421	..	..	35,183	61,461	65,056	45,039
Seychelles	..	..	..	..	..	..	..	..	..	..	..	..
Sierra Leone	..	..	..	..	..	..	..	..	..	..	..	..
Somalia	..	..	..	..	..	..	..	..	..	..	..	..
South Africa	609,747	362,402	328,050	305,387	302,050	293,411	283,262	..	..	518,912	379,497	312,427
Sudan	154,698	..	27,556	..	..	..	43,190	..	41,113	99,855	44,524	37,286
Swaziland	..	..	..	..	..	..	..	..	..	..	..	..
Tanzania	..	..	77,249	79,689	93,304	78,787	94,859	..	71,671	..	62,999	82,593
Togo	..	..	..	..	..	..	..	..	..	..	..	..
Uganda	..	13,470	10,717	8,524	8,743	12,436	12,350	..	4,764	12,184	8,381	9,499
Zambia	351,669	81,810	162,157	148,206	142,220	87,920	62,092	66,938	57,858	325,335	244,573	101,150
Zimbabwe	610,603	215,462	192,362	212,313	198,217	143,980	153,978	148,660	140,231	489,214	299,577	175,650
NORTH AFRICA	..	..	..	..	..	..	..	..	..	..	..	..
Algeria	42,086	23,449	23,288	20,467	18,635	18,339	..	..	..	38,704	28,224	20,836
Egypt, Arab Republic	46,354	21,444	23,448	19,895	23,046	24,774	..	..	20,062	41,780	34,850	22,111
Libya	..	..	..	..	..	..	..	..	..	..	..	..
Morocco	114,590	67,356	53,917	60,804	53,023	49,847	51,939	..	49,613	108,853	79,160	55,214
Tunisia	105,521	52,684	49,112	48,088	45,889	48,270	47,829	..	42,976	90,924	72,243	47,835
ALL AFRICA	..	..	..	..	..	..	..	..	..	..	..	..

9-8. Rail load-to-locomotive ratio

	Million rail ton-km/locomotive									Annual average		
	1980	*1990*	*1991*	*1992*	*1993*	*1994*	*1995*	*1996*	*1997*	*75-84*	*85-89*	*90-MR*
SUB-SAHARAN AFRICA	..	20.5	18.5	16.8	..	19.1	..	..	..	14.9	15.2	18.7
excluding South Africa	..	..	..	..	..	..	..	..	..	..	..	..
excl. S.Africa & Nigeria	..	..	..	..	..	..	..	..	..	..	..	..
Angola	..	..	..	..	..	..	..	..	..	..	..	..
Benin	..	..	..	..	..	..	..	..	..	..	..	..
Botswana	..	..	..	..	..	..	..	..	19.9	..	..	19.9
Burkina Faso	..	..	..	..	..	..	..	18.0	24.9	..	..	21.4
Burundi	..	..	..	..	..	..	..	..	..	..	..	..
Cameroon	10.9	10.1	8.9	9.6	8.6	12.4	13.3	10.0	14.2	9.8	8.4	10.9
Cape Verde	..	..	..	..	..	..	..	..	..	..	..	..
Central African Republic	..	..	..	..	..	..	..	..	..	..	..	..
Chad	..	..	..	..	..	..	..	..	..	..	..	..
Comoros	..	..	..	..	..	..	..	..	..	..	..	..
Congo, Democratic Rep. of	11.7	11.2	..	..	..	1.0	..	..	1.7	12.0	11.5	4.6
Congo, Republic of	..	..	14.8	9.4	..	5.8	..	..	3.0	11.3	9.4	8.3
Côte d'Ivoire	12.8	8.0	6.7	6.8	4.5	4.5	5.7	..	17.4	12.3	12.3	7.7
Djibouti	..	..	..	..	..	..	..	..	..	..	..	..
Equatorial Guinea	..	..	..	..	..	..	..	..	..	..	..	..
Eritrea	..	..	..	..	..	..	..	..	..	..	..	..
Ethiopia	..	..	2.3	..	..	..	..	..	..	..	6.1	2.3
Gabon	2.1	..	..	4.8	5.2	5.3	7.6	..	30.8	4.2	6.6	10.7
Gambia, The	..	..	..	..	..	..	..	..	..	..	..	..
Ghana	..	3.3	..	..	..	..	..	..	..	..	1.6	3.3
Guinea	..	..	..	..	..	..	..	..	..	..	..	..
Guinea-Bissau	..	..	..	..	..	..	..	..	..	..	..	..
Kenya	6.9	8.8	9.0	..	..	..	..	..	..	9.2	8.7	8.9
Lesotho	..	..	..	..	..	..	..	..	..	..	..	..
Liberia	..	..	..	..	..	..	..	..	..	..	..	..
Madagascar	..	..	..	..	..	..	..	..	..	..	..	..
Malawi	..	1.4	1.5	1.1	1.0	0.9	1.1	..	..	3.5	1.9	1.2
Mali	..	7.8	7.8	7.9	..	..	..	..	11.2	6.6	9.0	8.7
Mauritania	..	..	..	..	..	..	..	..	..	..	..	..
Mauritius	..	..	..	..	..	..	..	..	..	..	..	..
Mozambique	..	..	..	..	..	..	..	..	5.9	..	..	5.9
Namibia	..	27.7	21.4	22.3	19.9	20.3	21.6	..	..	..	..	22.2
Niger	..	..	..	..	..	..	..	..	..	..	..	..
Nigeria	3.8	..	..	0.3	..	0.0	..	..	..	5.0	2.5	0.2
Rwanda	..	..	..	..	..	..	..	..	..	..	..	..
São Tomé and Principe	..	..	..	..	..	..	..	..	..	..	..	..
Senegal	13.3	20.9	18.0	16.4	14.6	16.1	..	..	..	14.3	18.0	17.2
Seychelles	..	..	..	..	..	..	..	..	..	..	..	..
Sierra Leone	..	..	..	..	..	..	..	10.8	15.4	..	..	13.1
Somalia	..	..	..	..	..	..	..	..	..	..	..	..
South Africa	..	25.4	23.6	22.6	25.8	26.4	26.9	..	..	18.2	20.5	25.1
Sudan	8.0	..	4.5	..	..	..	11.1	14.2	12.3	7.0	4.8	10.5
Swaziland	..	..	..	..	..	..	..	..	..	..	..	..
Tanzania	..	..	11.7	11.4	13.9	12.2	14.9	..	17.4	7.7	8.1	13.6
Togo	..	..	..	..	..	..	..	..	..	..	..	..
Uganda	..	3.1	2.7	2.0	2.3	3.5	4.1	..	8.3	..	1.5	3.7
Zambia	16.1	7.5	15.4	14.6	15.1	9.9	6.8	..	7.2	17.2	21.1	10.9
Zimbabwe	21.7	13.6	14.0	16.0	17.5	27.9	27.5	..	..	20.7	20.0	19.4
NORTH AFRICA	9.9	10.2	10.6	9.7	10.3	10.4	..	..	10.3	9.9	10.3	10.2
Algeria	9.8	12.2	12.5	10.7	11.1	10.8	..	..	7.7	10.9	13.6	10.8
Egypt, Arab Republic	3.9	3.7	6.1	3.6	4.9	4.9	..	..	5.1	3.7	3.8	4.7
Libya	..	..	..	..	..	..	..	..	..	..	..	..
Morocco	19.5	20.4	17.3	19.6	17.4	19.2	19.8	..	22.3	19.1	20.3	19.4
Tunisia	13.9	9.3	9.3	10.3	14.0	12.7	13.4	..	13.5	12.7	10.4	11.8
ALL AFRICA	..	16.0	15.2	13.9	16.4	15.5	..	..	..	12.9	13.9	15.4

Technical notes

Tables

Table 9-1. Electric power consumption per capita. This table refers to per capita electricity consumption, which means the production of power plants and combined heat and power plants, less distribution losses, and own use by heat and power plants (IEA and UN *Energy Statistics Yearbook*).

Table 9-2. Energy production and use, 1980 and 1996. This table presents three indicators. *Energy production* refers to commercial forms of primary energy—petroleum (crude oil, natural gas liquids, and oil from nonconventional sources), natural gas, solid fuels, and primary electricity—all converted into oil equivalent (IEA and UN *Energy Statistics Yearbook*). *Commercial energy use* is indigenous production plus imports and stock changes, minus exports and international marine bunkers (IEA and UN *Energy Statistics Yearbook*). *Electric power transmission* includes losses in transmission between sources of supply and points of distribution and in the distribution to consumers, including pilferage. Production less transmission and distribution losses, own-use, and transformation losses is equal to end-use electricity consumption (IEA and UN *Energy Statistics Yearbook*).

Table 9-3. Telephone, radio, and television availability, 1994–97. This table presents data for six communication indicators. Telephone mainlines (ITU) refer to telephone lines connecting a customer's equipment to the public switched telephone network, where mainline is normally identified by a unique number. Mainlines are presented for every 1,000 people (Table 1.2). *Waiting list* shows the number of applications (in thousands) for a connection to a mainline that have been held up by a lack of technical capacity (ITU). *Cost of local call* is the cost of a three-minute call within the same exchange area using the subscriber's equipment (that is, not from a public phone) (ITU). *Mobile phones* refer to users of portable telephones who subscribe to an automatic public mobile telephone service using cellular technology that provides access to the public switched-telephone network, per 1,000 people (Table 1.2)(ITU). *Radios* are the estimated number of radio receivers in use for broadcast to the general public, per 1,000 people (Table 1.2) (*UNESCO Statistical Yearbook*). *Television sets* are the estimated number of television sets in use, per 1,000 people (Table 1.2) (ITU).

Table 9-4. Vehicle ownership. Vehicles (International Road Federation) include all forms of road transportation, except buses. They are expressed as a ratio of 1,000 people (Table 1.2).

Table 9-5. Road-to-population ratio. This table presents the ratio of 1,000 kilometers of paved or unpaved road (International Road Federation) per 1 million people (Table 1.2).

Table 9-6. Paved primary roads. This table presents paved primary roads, that is, those that have been sealed with asphalt or similar road-bonding material (International Road Federation) as a ratio to total roads and then shows the percentage that is in good condition (World Bank data).

Table 9-7. Rail goods traffic-to-$ PPP GDP ratio. This measures the tonnage of goods per million dollars of GDP measured in PPP terms (World Bank data).

Table 9-8. Rail load-to-locomotive ratio. This is the volume of rail transported goods (measured in millions of metric tons times kilometers traveled) per single locomotive (World Bank data).

Methodology used for regional aggregations and period averages in chapter 9

Table	Aggregations[a]				Period averages[b]
	(1)	*(6)*	*(7)*	*(8)*	*(1)*
9-1		x			x
9-2					
Columns 1-4	x				
Columns 5-6				x	
9-3					x
Columns 1-2, 4-6		x			
Column 3				x	
9-4		x	x		
9-5		x	x		x
9-6					x
Columns 1-8				x	
Column 9		x			
9-7				x	x
9-8		x	x		

Note: Regional aggregations are shown in the rows for Sub-Saharan Africa, North Africa, and All Africa. Period averages are shown in the last three columns. This table shows only the methodologies used in this chapter.

a. Regional aggregations: (1) simple total; (2) simple total of the first indicator divided by the simple total of the second indicator (same country coverage); (3) simple total of the gap-filled indicator; (4) simple total of the gap-filled main indicator divided by the simple total of the gap-filled secondary indicator; (5) simple total of the first gap-filled main indicator less the simple total of the second gap-filled main indicator, all divided by the simple total of the secondary indicator; (6) weighted total (by population); (7) median; (8) no aggregation; (9) simple arithmetic mean.

b. Period averages: (i) arithmetic mean (using the same series as shown in the table i.e., ratio if the rest of the table is shown as ratio, level if the rest of the table is shown as level, growth rate if the rest is shown as growth rate); (2) least-squares growth rate (using main indicator); (3) least-squares growth rate (using main indicator in constant terms, with the rest of the table in current terms).

10

Privatization of Public Enterprises

In the past, the dominance of the public enterprise sector in most African economies warranted the collection and publication of the sector's performance. With its diminishing size and importance due to privatization, it is no longer informative to produce such data. Instead, as privatization programs advance to maturity, it will become important to track the performance of private sector businesses. In the meantime, measurement of the level of privatization activity is a useful gauge of the decreasing role of governments in commercial business; conversely, it indicates how much of state-owned commercial activity has been transferred to the private sector. To the extent that data is available, it is also possible to measure how privatization has, over time, contributed to government revenues and mobilized savings and investment. However, this measurement is by no means easy or precise, partly because of incomplete and inconsistent data but also because of redefinitions of the public enterprise sector. For example, some enterprises, notably those formerly in a monopolistic position, are being split in order to separate their commercial, social, developmental, and regulatory activities. In some cases, separate operating divisions or geographically distinct assets are sold separately. And in yet other cases, commercial and semi-commercial activities are being separated out from government ministries and other agencies to become redefined as "commercial enterprises."

These include, for example, business centers, media, and some training institutes. So, the public enterprise sector, as defined several years ago, has changed. Nevertheless, the well over 3,000 privatization transactions that were reported across Africa up to the end of 1998 have brought about fundamental changes:

- The fiscal burden of public enterprises has been reduced or eliminated.
- Privatization receipts have contributed to a reduction in fiscal deficits.
- Privatization has attracted foreign direct investment both to acquire enterprises and for post-privatization investment in those businesses.
- The process has stimulated private sector development by making investment opportunities available, spurring capital market development, and contributing to a more competitive business environment.
- Being a politically sensitive subject, the process has highlighted the need for transparency and public accountability.

The tables presented in this chapter summarizes data contained in the World Bank's Africa Privatization Database which is accessible through the internet at:

http://www.worldbank.org/afr/database/ afrpriv/p1query.cfm

10-1. Summary of privatization of public enterprises

	Total no. of trans-actions	Total sales value (US$m)	Transactions completed Before 1995	1995	1996	1997	1998	1999	Agric. prod. & process	Financial	Manu-facturing	Services	Trade	Other
SUB-SAHARAN AFRICA	3,387	7,352	1,538	482	426	241	125	82	715	145	1,025	736	321	445
excluding South Africa	3,374	4,891	1,535	482	425	239	122	79	715	145	1,020	728	321	445
excl. S. Africa & Nigeria	3,293	4,684	1,454	482	426	241	125	82	715	145	997	718	321	445
Angola	331	25	..	..	56	..	..	..	9	..	29	9	9	275
Benin	46	63	39	5	..	..	..	..	7	1	15	18	5	..
Botswana	40	..	..	..	..	..	..	..	..	..	..	..	..	..
Burkina Faso	..	24	17	3	6	..	2	4	9	4	16	9	2	..
Burundi	42	11	26	..	13	3	..	..	21	4	6	9	2	..
Cameroon	48	72	13	3	23	5	4	..	24	4	7	12	1	..
Cape Verde	46	172	13	9	10	9	..	..	8	3	17	14	4	..
Central African Republic	35	0	35	..	..	..	..	..	8	4	9	14	..	..
Chad	31	6	12	13	6	..	..	..	9	5	6	8	3	..
Comoros	4	0	..	..	..	..	..	..	..	..	..	..	..	4
Congo, Dem. Rep. of	61	50	2	44	15	..	..	..	20	5	14	22	..	..
Congo, Rep. of	21	0	16	2	3	..	..	..	3	1	6	10	1	..
Côte d'Ivoire	105	811	21	27	21	15	11	6	40	5	33	25	2	..
Djibouti	..	..	..	..	..	..	..	..	..	..	..	..	..	..
Equatorial Guinea	3	0	..	..	..	..	..	..	..	..	..	..	..	3
Eritrea	..	..	..	..	..	..	..	..	..	..	..	..	..	..
Ethiopia	125	203	..	9	..	..	1	..	..	..	6	3	1	115
Gabon	26	0	..	..	..	1	..	..	..	..	1	..	..	25
Gambia, The	34	10	31	..	..	..	1	1	8	4	9	8	5	..
Ghana	233	674	146	23	20	27	4	8	44	8	101	50	30	..
Guinea	117	9	112	4	..	1	..	..	11	7	56	14	29	..
Guinea-Bissau	29	1	18	11	..	..	..	..	4	..	6	14	5	..
Kenya	188	248	66	69	22	27	4	..	71	12	59	39	7	..
Lesotho	21	24	2	7	..	1	4	6	1	5	2	9	4	..
Liberia	..	..	..	..	..	..	..	..	..	..	..	..	..	..
Madagascar	86	43	60	24	..	..	..	1	31	4	33	14	4	..
Malawi	68	57	35	..	8	5	5	12	37	5	14	9	..	3
Mali	65	32	60	..	..	..	..	..	11	2	21	23	8	..
Mauritania	56	10	29	6	..	..	..	2	21	6	7	18	3	1
Mauritius	..	..	..	..	..	..	..	..	..	..	..	..	..	..
Mozambique	579	217	398	112	38	31	..	..	75	2	256	120	126	..
Namibia	..	..	..	..	..	..	..	..	..	..	..	..	..	..
Niger	34	3	32	2	..	..	..	..	2	2	5	4	3	18
Nigeria	81	207	81	..	..	..	..	..	23	24	23	10	1	..
Rwanda	2	0	..	..	..	..	..	..	1	..	1	..	..	..
São Tomé and Principe	9	0	8	1	..	..	..	..	..	..	5	1	3	..
Senegal	61	412	37	1	11	4	4	1	7	11	13	28	2	..
Seychelles	..	..	..	..	..	..	..	..	..	..	..	..	..	..
Sierra Leone	10	0	7	1	..	1	..	..	..	..	4	6	..	..
Somalia	..	..	..	..	..	..	..	..	..	..	..	..	..	..
South Africa	13	2,461	3	..	1	2	3	3	..	..	5	8	..	..
Sudan	32	0	32	..	..	..	..	..	11	1	8	11	1	..
Swaziland	..	..	..	..	..	..	..	..	..	..	..	..	..	..
Tanzania	283	246	86	22	46	40	64	23	98	3	109	45	27	1
Togo	57	39	25	1	18	9	2	1	8	1	24	23	1	..
Uganda	91	149	44	23	18	2	..	3	19	5	29	26	12	..
Zambia	268	906	30	60	91	55	16	10	71	6	69	102	20	..
Zimbabwe	6	166	2	..	..	3	..	1	3	1	1	1	..	..
NORTH AFRICA	142	595	27	17	27	30	40	1	13	0	58	53	2	16
Algeria	..	..	..	..	..	..	..	..	..	..	..	..	..	..
Egypt	54	307	..	5	10	8	31	..	5		34	8	1	6
Libya	..	..	..	..	..	..	..	..	..	..	..	..	..	..
Morocco	52	259	..	12	17	16	6	1	4		10	28	..	10
Tunisia	36	29	27	..	..	6	3	..	4		14	17	1	..
ALL AFRICA	3,529	7,946	1,565	499	453	271	165	83	728	145	1,083	789	323	461

10-2. Divestiture methods employed (to end 1999)

	Sales of shares				Sale of assets			Other methods							
	Com-petitive sale	Direct Sale	Pre-emption rights	Public flotation	Liqui-dation	Compet-itive sale	Direct sale	Debt/ Equity swaps	Leases	Joint ventures	Mgmt./ employee buyouts	Mgmt. con-tracts	Trustees	Resti-tution	Other
SUB-SAHARAN AFRICA	937	83	177	103	631	535	40	13	142	37	35	56	19	51	528
excluding South Africa	928	83	177	102	631	535	40	13	142	37	35	56	19	51	526
excl. S. Africa & Nigeria	923	83	177	65	631	535	40	13	142	37	35	56	19	51	528
Angola	..	..	..	..	..	57	..	..	..	..	..	..	..	..	274
Benin	1	2	..	..	23	12	3	..	2	..	..	2	..	1	..
Botswana	..	..	..	..	..	..	..	..	..	..	..	..	..	..	..
Burkina Faso	15	3	..	..	14	..	..	..	1	..	..	1	1	1	4
Burundi	11	3	..	..	13	5	..	..	..	..	1	9	..	..	..
Cameroon	20	..	..	..	18	..	..	..	..	..	..	..	..	..	10
Cape Verde	20	2	5	..	10	1	1	..	..	..	6	1	..	..	..
Central African Republic	..	..	..	..	26	..	..	..	1	1	..	1	..	..	6
Chad	12	2	..	..	11	..	..	..	..	..	..	5	..	..	1
Comoros	..	..	..	..	..	..	..	..	..	..	..	..	..	..	4
Congo, Dem. Rep. of	1	..	..	..	15	..	..	..	..	..	..	5	..	..	..
Congo, Rep. of	1	..	..	..	53	..	..	..	..	..	..	2	..	..	5
Côte d'Ivoire	15	2	23	22	2	25	8	..	3	1	..	..	..	..	4
Djibouti	..	..	..	..	..	..	..	..	..	..	..	..	..	..	..
Equatorial Guinea	..	..	..	..	..	..	..	..	..	..	..	..	..	..	3
Eritrea	..	..	..	..	..	..	..	..	..	..	..	..	..	..	..
Ethiopia	..	..	..	..	..	10	..	..	..	..	..	..	..	..	115
Gabon	..	..	..	..	..	..	..	..	..	..	..	..	..	..	26
Gambia, The	13	7	..	..	3	1	..	..	5	1	1	1	..	..	2
Ghana	8	11	19	13	56	76	12	2	5	13	..	1	..	..	5
Guinea	42	1	..	..	67	1	..	..	4	..	..	2	..	..	..
Guinea-Bissau	7	2	..	..	8	2	..	..	2	1	..	7	..	12	..
Kenya	13	..	96	16	36	17	4	1	..	..	1	1	..	..	3
Lesotho	5	3	..	..	7	2	..	..	1	..	..	..	..	..	3
Liberia	..	..	..	..	..	..	..	..	..	..	..	..	..	..	..
Madagascar	6	14	..	..	29	15	6	..	1	1	..	3	..	8	3
Malawi	22	5	..	2	..	13	..	1	..	..	..	..	3	..	22
Mali	14	1	..	..	30	11	..	..	1	..	..	1	3	..	4
Mauritania	25	..	..	..	17	3	..	..	..	..	..	1	3	..	7
Mauritius	..	..	..	..	..	..	..	..	..	..	..	..	..	..	..
Mozambique	509	..	..	..	..	22	..	..	37	10	..	1	..	..	..
Namibia	..	..	..	..	..	..	..	..	..	..	..	..	..	..	..
Niger	13	..	..	..	17	..	..	..	..	..	..	2	..	..	2
Nigeria	5	5	..	37	2	29	..	..	..	..	1	..	2	..	..
Rwanda	..	..	..	..	..	..	..	..	..	..	..	..	..	..	2
São Tomé and Principe	..	1	..	..	6	..	..	..	..	..	1	1	..	..	..
Senegal	26	1	1	2	23	1	..	1	3	1	..	1	2	..	1
Seychelles	..	..	..	..	..	..	..	..	..	..	..	..	..	..	..
Sierra Leone	..	..	..	..	1	..	..	..	5	..	..	3	..	..	1
Somalia	..	..	..	..	..	..	..	..	..	..	..	..	..	..	..
South Africa	9	..	..	1	..	1	..	..	..	..	..	..	..	..	2
Sudan	7	..	..	..	..	15	..	5	1	..	..	..	..	..	4
Swaziland	..	..	..	..	..	..	..	..	..	..	..	..	..	..	..
Tanzania	61	4	13	1	84	70	3	1	25	3	6	3	..	2	5
Togo	8	7	..	..	20	13	1	..	6	..	..	2	..	..	..
Uganda	10	..	6	1	18	24	..	2	1	4	1	..	5	11	8
Zambia	37	6	14	4	22	109	2	..	38	1	17	..	..	16	2
Zimbabwe	1	1	..	4	..	..	..	..	..	..	..	..	..	..	..
NORTH AFRICA	..	..	..	..	..	..	..	..	..	..	..	..	..	..	..
Algeria	..	..	..	..	..	..	..	..	..	..	..	..	..	..	..
Egypt	..	..	..	..	..	..	..	..	..	..	..	..	..	..	..
Libya	..	..	..	..	..	..	..	..	..	..	..	..	..	..	..
Morocco	..	..	..	..	..	..	..	..	..	..	..	..	..	..	..
Tunisia	..	..	..	..	..	..	..	..	..	..	..	..	..	..	..
ALL AFRICA	937	83	177	103	631	535	40	13	142	37	35	56	19	51	528

10-3. Progress in privatization: ownership and control changes*

	Transfer of majority owner-ship to private shareholders	Government retention of majority ownership	Government retention of minority interest	Sales of minority government interest	Total share transactions	Total asset sales and liquidation	Other transactions	Total trans-actions
SUB-SAHARAN AFRICA	2,025	220	294	200	1,300	1,206	881	3,387
excluding South Africa	2,022	214	294	200	1,290	1,205	879	3,374
excl. S. Africa & Nigeria	1,974	213	294	200	1,243	1,174	876	3,293
Angola	56	..	..	..	0	57	274	331
Benin	41	3	1	..	3	38	5	46
Botswana	..	..	..	..	0	0	0	0
Burkina Faso	10	..	7	2	18	14	8	40
Burundi	30	..	11	11	14	18	10	42
Cameroon	46	1	..	..	20	18	10	48
Cape Verde	28	2	6	5	27	12	7	46
Central African Republic	26	2	1	..	0	26	9	35
Chad	14	5	6	4	14	11	6	31
Comoros	..	..	..	..	0	0	4	4
Congo, Dem. Rep. of	16	5	..	..	1	15	5	21
Congo, Rep. of	59	1	..	..	1	53	7	61
Côte d'Ivoire	36	9	42	28	62	35	8	105
Djibouti	..	..	..	..	0	0	0	0
Equatorial Guinea	..	..	..	..	0	0	3	3
Eritrea	..	..	..	..	0	0	0	0
Ethiopia	10	..	..	..	0	10	115	125
Gabon	..	1	..	..	0	0	26	26
Gambia, The	16	7	6	6	20	4	10	34
Ghana	161	12	27	24	51	144	26	221
Guinea	90	9	..	..	43	68	6	117
Guinea-Bissau	20	9	..	..	9	10	22	41
Kenya	67	3	104	56	125	57	6	188
Lesotho	11	4	1	1	8	9	4	21
Liberia	..	..	..	..	0	0	0	0
Madagascar	65	4	..	..	20	50	16	86
Malawi	33	..	6	5	29	13	26	68
Mali	52	1	3	3	15	41	9	65
Mauritania	23	3	19	16	25	20	11	56
Mauritius	..	..	..	..	0	0	0	0
Mozambique	460	43	..	..	509	22	48	579
Namibia	..	..	..	..	0	0	0	0
Niger	26	2	2	2	13	17	4	34
Nigeria	48	1	24	17	47	31	3	81
Rwanda	..	..	..	..	0	0	2	2
São Tomé and Principe	8	1	..	..	1	6	2	9
Senegal	30	8	7	4	30	24	9	63
Seychelles	..	..	..	..	0	0	0	0
Sierra Leone	..	9	..	..	0	1	9	10
Somalia	..	..	..	..	0	0	0	0
South Africa	3	6	..	..	10	1	2	13
Sudan	28	1	..	..	7	15	10	32
Swaziland	..	..	..	..	0	0	0	0
Tanzania	202	29	3	3	79	157	45	281
Togo	38	8	9	9	15	34	8	57
Uganda	68	1	3	..	17	42	32	91
Zambia	203	30	6	4	61	133	74	268
Zimbabwe	1	..	..	..	6	0	0	6
NORTH AFRICA	..	..	..	..	..	..	..	..
Algeria	..	..	..	..	..	..	..	..
Egypt	..	..	..	..	..	..	..	..
Libya	..	..	..	..	..	..	..	..
Morocco	..	..	..	..	..	..	..	..
Tunisia	..	..	..	..	..	..	..	..
ALL AFRICA	..	..	..	..	..	..	..	..

*reflect data to end 1999

Technical notes

Tables

Table 10-1. Summary of privatization activity. For purposes of monitoring and reporting on privatization activity, all reported transactions involving a sale of assets or shares (however small) or the formal yielding of management control (as through a management contract) are included in the World Bank's Africa Privatization Database. Hence, in the table, "privatization" is used generically to include: the sale or disposal of some or all of the assets of public enterprises, the sale of government-owned shares in enterprises, the reduction in equity percentage held by a government through share dilutions or through transfer of enterprise assets to a new joint venture, liquidations, leases, and management contracts. Sometimes, the process of privatizing an enterprise involves several consecutive transactions (for example, a sale of a block of shares to a core investor and a subsequent initial public offering). The table summarizes the data contained in the Africa Privatization Database which originate from national privatization agencies and other sources. The data are frequently updated and changes to previous entries occur as more information becomes available. There are a few instances where previously reported privatizations are removed from the database because a transaction has been nullified due to non-fulfillment of contractual conditions on the part of one of the parties. For financial data, the term "sale value" is preferred since the use of the term "proceeds" might imply the value of amounts actually paid. In practice, some deals are structured so that new investors may acquire assets or shares on deferred terms. Also, it should be noted that: (i) in the cases of some subsidiary companies, the cash proceeds are not paid to government but instead go to the parent company; and (ii) for official liquidations, the proceeds are paid to the liquidator who first applies them toward settling enterprise debts.

Table 10-2. Divestiture methods employed (to end 1999). The table shows the various privatization methods employed in each country. The methods employed could not be confirmed for all transactions. "Direct sales" refers to transactions which were negotiated directly with one party and which were not the outcome of a competitive bidding process. However, in some cases a direct sale was concluded (on a non-competitive basis) as a result of a failure of an earlier competitive bidding process. "Preemptive rights" refers to transactions whereby a government has sold shares to an existing private shareholder (or shareholders) who exercised preemptive rights to acquire those shares in accordance with specific provisions of the company's charter (Articles of Association). In some cases, the charter specified the amount to be paid per share or the formula for calculating that amount; otherwise it has been the subject of negotiation. "Joint ventures" refer to the type of transaction whereby a government concluded a deal (usually with a foreign investor) involving the formation of a new company in which the government's equity contribution was in the form of the major or all assets of a public enterprise. The remaining shell company would then be maintained only as a book company or be liquidated; if it were liquidated it is not included as a liquidation since this would be double counting.

Transactions described as "Trustees" refer to privatizations achieved by transference of shares of a public enterprise to a trustee for onward sale, at a later date or over a period, to the public or to selected segments of the public. "Restitutions" are those transactions whereby a company has been handed back to a previous owner from whom the company had been expropriated. "Other sales" includes sundry methods, such as enterprises donated by governments to local communities, but principally comprises transactions where the method of privatization was not reported.

Table 10-3. Progress in privatization: ownership and control changes (to end 1999). This table presents the inferred outcome of privatization transactions on the ownership and control of enterprises or their assets. Ownership changes are important in indicating the effect that privatization transactions may or may not have on the enterprises and in indicating the extent of a government's willingness and/or ability to exit from equity participation in commercial activity. Although a government's influence is not necessarily restricted by its equity participation, it is generally assumed that once a government owns less than 50 percent of the voting shares of a company, that company is "private" and the private shareholders (except in the instance of exercise of golden share rights) have management control of the company. Ownership control is usually unaffected when government continues to be a majority shareholder or sells a minority interest. Concessions, leases, and management contracts are assumed not to have affected ownership rights but to have transferred management control to the private sector for a defined period. The table shows the number of reported transactions where governments have: fully sold wholly- or majority-owned enterprises, sold shares and transferred ownership control but retained a minority equity interest, sold shares but retained ownership control, sold a proportion of a minority stake, and other transactions where management control has been ceded.

Methodology used for regional aggregations and period averages in chapter 10

Table	Aggregations[a]		Period averages[b]
	(1)	(2)	(1)
10-1	x		
10-2	x		
10-3	x		

Note: Regional aggregations are shown in the rows for Sub-Saharan Africa, North Africa, and All Africa. Period averages are shown in the last three columns. This table shows only the methodologies used in this chapter.

a. Regional aggregations: (1) simple total; (2) simple total of the first indicator divided by the simple total of the second indicator (same country coverage); (3) simple total of the gap-filled indicator; (4) simple total of the gap-filled main indicator divided by the simple total of the gap-filled secondary indicator; (5) simple total of the first gap-filled main indicator less the simple total of the second gap-filled main indicator, all divided by the simple total of the secondary indicator; (6) weighted total (by population); (7) median; (8) no aggregation; (9) simple arithmetic mean.

b. Period averages: (i) arithmetic mean (using the same series as shown in the table i.e., ratio if the rest of the table is shown as ratio, level if the rest of the table is shown as level, growth rate if the rest is shown as growth rate); (2) least-squares growth rate (using main indicator); (3) least-squares growth rate (using main indicator in constant terms, with the rest of the table in current terms).

11

Labor Force and Employment

This chapter presents data on the level and structure of the labor force. The distribution of the labor force into various industrial activities is also given, as well as the participation rates of the population in economic activities. Information is also presented on average wages in different sectors.

The treatment of statistics on public sector employment is not consistent among countries. The scope covered often varies. While some countries include education and health sectors, others leave them out. Staff of local, regional, and state or provincial governments are likewise treated differently.

The stipulations on wages take different forms among the countries where such practice exists. While some countries have a minimum wage per hour worked, others stipulate a minimum monthly wage for a worker. To permit some measure of comparability, we have computed and reported the monthly average earnings per wage earner. These earnings are further converted to U.S. dollars at the Atlas exchange rate. These data should be used with caution since some countries have more than one minimum wage rate based on the industry and the occupation within the industry as well as on the region of the country concerned.

The definition of labor force or economically active population is that used by the International Labor Organization (ILO), which follows the UN system of national accounts (SNA). The labor force is measured by dividing economically active persons into two categories: employed and unemployed. Caution in the use of the data is necessary because, as pointed out in the ILO's *World Labor Report 1* (1987), there are many persons who do not clearly come within one of these categories or the other. Many are visibly underemployed in that they work less than full time. Others work full time but earn less than a subsistence income. Some of the unemployed may even be voluntarily idle.

The comparability of the data is further hampered by the fact that practices vary among countries as regards the treatment of such groups as armed forces, inmates of institutions, persons living on reservations, persons seeking their first job, seasonal workers, and persons engaged in part-time economic activities. In some countries, all or part of these groups are included among the economically active, while in others they are treated as inactive. In addition, the extent to which family workers who assist in family enterprises are included among the enumerated economically active population, particularly females, varies considerably from country to country. Further, in some countries the statistics of the economically active relate only to employed and unemployed persons above a specified age, while in others there is no such age provision.

The reference period is also an important factor of difference, especially when it comes to the classification of the labor force according to industry. In some countries, such classification refers to the actual posi-

tion of each individual on the day of the census or survey date, while in others the data recorded refer to the usual position of each person, generally without reference to any given period of time.

The sources for the tables in this chapter are various issues of the ILO's *Yearbook of Labor Statistics*, and electronic ILO files kept in World Bank SIMA.

11-1. Number and gender structure of the labor force

	Total labor force (thousands)			Percentage of total labor force that is female		
	1970	1980	1998	1970	1980	1998
SUB-SAHARAN AFRICA	132,558	169,972	274,935	42.5	42.3	42.2
excluding South Africa	124,385	159,493	258,788	43.1	42.7	42.5
excl. S. Africa & Nigeria	102,035	130,322	210,461	44.5	44.2	43.9
Angola	2,906	3,439	5,521	47.4	47.0	46.3
Benin	1,355	1,663	2,677	48.4	47.0	48.3
Botswana	287	399	687	53.5	50.1	45.5
Burkina Faso	3,267	3,829	5,365	48.9	47.6	46.6
Burundi	1,968	2,272	3,536	50.5	50.2	48.9
Cameroon	3,042	3,635	5,864	37.3	36.8	37.8
Cape Verde	85	92	166	29.1	34.0	39.0
Central African Republic	..	..	..	..	..	..
Chad	1,826	2,239	3,496	42.5	43.4	44.6
Comoros	..	151	239	..	43.1	42.3
Congo, Democratic Rep. of	9,527	11,884	20,251	45.2	44.5	43.5
Congo, Republic of	543	701	1,141	41.2	42.4	43.4
Côte d'Ivoire	2,316	3,278	5,797	33.0	32.2	33.1
Djibouti	..	..	..	..	..	..
Equatorial Guinea	134	95	181	36.3	35.1	35.5
Eritrea	952	1,215	1,940	47.5	47.4	47.4
Ethiopia	13,311	16,973	26,344	42.4	42.3	40.9
Gabon	282	359	543	45.7	45.0	44.5
Gambia, The	246	327	620	44.9	44.8	45.0
Ghana	4,048	5,048	8,676	50.6	51.0	50.6
Guinea	2,067	2,275	3,400	47.7	47.1	47.2
Guinea-Bissau	273	398	546	39.7	39.9	40.4
Kenya	5,634	7,817	14,940	45.2	46.0	46.1
Lesotho	468	565	844	39.4	37.9	36.8
Liberia	609	788	1,214	38.0	38.4	39.5
Madagascar	3,430	4,348	6,858	45.5	45.2	44.7
Malawi	2,349	3,092	5,056	50.6	50.6	48.8
Mali	2,828	3,361	5,192	46.5	46.7	46.3
Mauritania	623	744	1,163	46.7	45.0	43.8
Mauritius	248	348	499	19.9	25.7	32.2
Mozambique	5,261	6,652	8,812	49.2	49.0	48.4
Namibia	356	443	682	39.7	40.1	40.8
Niger	2,124	2,793	4,767	45.1	44.6	44.3
Nigeria	22,350	29,171	48,327	36.8	36.2	36.3
Rwanda	1,976	2,633	4,377	49.4	49.1	48.9
São Tomé and Principe	..	..	..	..	..	..
Senegal	1,996	2,547	4,067	41.6	42.2	42.6
Seychelles	..	..	..	..	..	..
Sierra Leone	1,062	1,262	1,796	35.6	35.5	36.6
Somalia	1,728	2,692	3,903	43.9	43.4	43.4
South Africa	8,172	10,479	16,147	32.7	35.1	37.6
Sudan	5,128	6,912	11,055	26.7	26.9	29.0
Swaziland	159	203	356	33.5	33.5	37.6
Tanzania	7,258	9,476	16,386	50.6	49.8	49.2
Togo	909	1,151	1,828	39.0	39.3	40.0
Uganda	5,200	6,660	10,240	48.2	47.9	47.6
Zambia	1,885	2,410	4,060	44.6	45.4	45.0
Zimbabwe	2,367	3,154	5,377	44.4	44.4	44.5
NORTH AFRICA	22,349	29,252	48,603	25.8	27.2	30.0
Algeria	3,574	4,854	9,874	20.3	21.4	26.4
Egypt, Arab Republic	11,569	14,306	22,718	25.9	26.5	29.7
Libya	616	943	1,538	16.3	18.6	22.1
Morocco	5,052	6,978	10,832	31.4	33.5	34.7
Tunisia	1,538	2,171	3,641	23.7	28.9	31.2
ALL AFRICA	154,906	199,223	323,538	40.1	40.1	40.4

11-2. Children under 14 working in the labor force

	As percentage of population age 10 to 14			
	1970	1980	1990	1998
SUB-SAHARAN AFRICA	36.3	34.7	32.2	29.9
excluding South Africa	39.1	37.2	34.5	31.8
excl. S.Africa & Nigeria	41.1	39.3	36.2	33.5
Angola	31.4	29.7	28.1	26.5
Benin	34.4	30.3	28.6	26.9
Botswana	32.3	25.9	19.4	15.4
Burkina Faso	75.1	70.9	58.7	46.5
Burundi	50.8	50.0	49.4	48.7
Cameroon	38.9	33.9	27.5	23.9
Cape Verde	17.3	16.0	14.7	13.8
Central African Republic	45.0	39.4	33.8	30.1
Chad	41.9	41.6	40.0	37.3
Comoros	45.8	44.7	40.9	38.2
Congo, Democratic Rep. of	36.5	33.2	30.5	29.0
Congo, Republic of	28.3	27.5	26.6	25.7
Côte d'Ivoire	34.6	28.4	22.3	19.4
Djibouti	..	..	..	
Equatorial Guinea	42.7	40.4	35.8	32.8
Eritrea	46.1	43.8	40.8	38.9
Ethiopia	48.5	46.3	43.5	41.6
Gabon	35.6	29.1	22.7	15.8
Gambia, The	45.9	44.4	40.2	35.1
Ghana	16.3	16.2	14.6	12.5
Guinea	43.3	41.2	37.0	32.3
Guinea-Bissau	45.2	43.4	40.4	37.5
Kenya	45.0	45.0	43.4	40.0
Lesotho	30.9	27.7	23.5	21.3
Liberia	31.1	25.7	21.8	16.7
Madagascar	41.7	40.2	37.6	34.8
Malawi	50.7	45.2	38.9	33.0
Mali	62.5	61.2	57.9	52.5
Mauritania	33.3	29.6	25.8	22.8
Mauritius	5.8	4.8	4.0	2.4
Mozambique	40.7	39.5	35.2	33.0
Namibia	40.2	33.6	26.0	19.1
Niger	48.8	47.8	46.8	44.2
Nigeria	30.8	29.2	27.6	24.6
Rwanda	43.3	42.5	42.1	41.5
São Tomé and Principe	..	..	..	
Senegal	46.9	42.9	35.4	28.9
Seychelles	..	..	..	..
Sierra Leone	21.7	19.4	17.1	14.5
Somalia	39.9	37.7	34.5	31.9
South Africa	2.7	0.9	0.0	0.0
Sudan	34.1	33.3	31.4	28.2
Swaziland	19.1	17.2	15.3	12.8
Tanzania	45.6	42.8	42.1	37.9
Togo	40.4	36.1	30.4	27.5
Uganda	50.4	48.8	46.8	44.4
Zambia	21.1	19.0	16.9	15.9
Zimbabwe	41.1	36.7	31.8	28.0
NORTH AFRICA	12.7	15.1	8.8	5.8
Algeria	11.4	7.1	3.3	0.6
Egypt, Arab Republic	23.6	18.3	13.2	10.0
Libya	12.8	8.7	0.5	0.1
Morocco	21.5	20.9	10.6	2.6
Tunisia	12.2	5.8	0.0	0.0
ALL AFRICA	31.4	30.9	28.0	25.8

11-3. Unpaid family workers as share of active workers

	Percentage of unpaid family workers in economically active workers (most recent year available between 1980-97)		
	Female	*Male*	*Total*
SUB-SAHARAN AFRICA	..	..	..
excluding South Africa	..	..	..
excl. S.Africa & Nigeria	..	..	..
Angola	..	..	..
Benin	..	..	
Botswana	41.8	36.0	77.7
Burkina Faso	..	..	..
Burundi	..	..	..
Cameroon	32.7	9.2	41.9
Cape Verde	..	..	..
Central African Republic	..	..	..
Chad	..	..	..
Comoros	..	..	..
Congo, Democratic Rep. of	..	..	..
Congo, Republic of	..	..	..
Côte d'Ivoire	..	..	..
Djibouti	..	..	..
Equatorial Guinea	..	..	..
Eritrea	..	..	..
Ethiopia	..	..	..
Gabon	..	..	..
Gambia, The	..	..	..
Ghana	..	0.0	0.0
Guinea	..	..	..
Guinea-Bissau	..	..	..
Kenya	..	..	..
Lesotho	..	..	..
Liberia	..	..	..
Madagascar	..	..	..
Malawi	..	..	..
Mali	..	..	..
Mauritania	..	..	..
Mauritius	..	..	..
Mozambique	..	..	..
Namibia	..	..	..
Niger	..	..	..
Nigeria	14.9	8.6	23.5
Rwanda	..	..	..
São Tomé and Principe	..	..	..
Senegal	..	..	..
Seychelles	0.4	0.2	0.6
Sierra Leone	..	..	..
Somalia	..	..	..
South Africa	..	..	..
Sudan	..	..	..
Swaziland	..	..	..
Tanzania	..	..	..
Togo	..	..	..
Uganda	..	..	..
Zambia	..	..	..
Zimbabwe	..	..	..
NORTH AFRICA	..	6.9	13.5
Algeria	..	5.6	6.2
Egypt, Arab Republic	1.9	15.0	16.9
Libya	..	..	..
Morocco	..	..	..
Tunisia	18.5	5.1	23.6
ALL AFRICA	..	..	..

11-4. Industrial structure of the labor force

| | Percentage of labor force working in | | | | | | | | |
| | Agriculture | | | Industry | | | Services | | |
	1970	1980	1990	1970	1980	1990	1970	1980	1990
SUB-SAHARAN AFRICA	78	72	68	8	9	9	14	20	24
excluding South Africa	82	76	71	6	7	7	12	18	22
excl. S.Africa & Nigeria	84	80	77	6	7	7	11	13	16
Angola	78	76	75	7	8	8	15	16	17
Benin	81	67	64	5	7	8	14	26	28
Botswana	82	64	46	5	10	20	13	26	33
Burkina Faso	92	92	92	3	3	2	5	5	6
Burundi	94	93	92	2	2	3	4	5	6
Cameroon	85	73	70	5	8	9	10	19	21
Cape Verde	47	37	31	27	31	30	27	33	40
Central African Republic	89	85	80	2	3	3	8	12	16
Chad	92	88	83	2	3	4	5	9	13
Comoros	83	81	77	7	8	9	10	11	13
Congo, Democratic Rep. of	75	72	68	11	12	13	14	16	19
Congo, Republic of	66	58	49	11	13	15	23	29	37
Côte d'Ivoire	76	65	60	6	8	10	19	27	30
Djibouti	..	..	..	..	..	..	..	..	..
Equatorial Guinea	82	78	75	5	5	5	14	17	20
Eritrea	86	83	80	4	5	5	10	12	15
Ethiopia	91	89	86	2	2	2	7	9	12
Gabon	79	65	52	9	12	16	12	22	33
Gambia, The	87	84	82	5	7	8	8	9	11
Ghana	60	61	59	15	13	13	25	25	28
Guinea	92	91	87	1	1	2	7	8	11
Guinea-Bissau	89	87	85	1	2	2	9	11	13
Kenya	86	82	80	5	6	7	9	11	13
Lesotho	43	40	40	36	34	28	21	26	32
Liberia	81	76	72	7	6	6	12	17	22
Madagascar	84	82	78	5	6	7	11	13	15
Malawi	91	87	87	4	5	5	5	7	8
Mali	93	89	86	1	2	2	6	9	12
Mauritania	84	72	55	3	7	10	12	22	34
Mauritius	34	27	17	25	28	43	41	45	40
Mozambique	86	84	83	6	7	8	8	8	9
Namibia	64	56	49	15	15	15	21	29	36
Niger	93	91	90	2	3	4	5	5	6
Nigeria	71	54	43	11	8	7	19	38	50
Rwanda	94	93	92	3	3	3	4	4	5
São Tomé and Principe	..	..	..	..	..	..	..	..	..
Senegal	83	81	77	6	6	8	12	13	16
Seychelles	..	..	..	..	..	..	..	..	..
Sierra Leone	76	70	67	12	14	15	12	16	17
Somalia	81	78	75	6	7	8	13	14	16
South Africa	31	17	14	30	35	32	39	48	54
Sudan	77	72	69	6	8	8	17	20	22
Swaziland	65	50	39	13	19	22	22	31	38
Tanzania	90	86	84	3	4	5	7	10	11
Togo	74	69	66	9	10	10	17	22	24
Uganda	90	87	85	3	4	5	7	9	11
Zambia	79	76	75	7	8	8	14	16	17
Zimbabwe	77	72	68	11	12	8	12	15	24
NORTH AFRICA	51	51	37	18	20	25	31	29	38
Algeria	47	36	26	21	27	31	31	37	43
Egypt, Arab Republic	52	57	40	16	16	22	32	27	38
Libya	29	25	11	25	24	23	46	51	66
Morocco	58	56	45	17	20	25	25	24	31
Tunisia	42	39	28	26	30	33	33	31	39
ALL AFRICA	75	69	63	9	10	11	16	21	26

Note: Figures may not add up to 100 because of rounding.

11-5. Industrial structure of economically active population

| | Agriculture | | | | Industry | | | | Services | | | |
| | Male | | Female | | Male | | Female | | Male | | Female | |
	1980	1995*	1980	1995*	1980	1995*	1980	1995*	1980	1995*	1980	1995*
SUB-SAHARAN AFRICA	62	58	74	68	14	14	5	5	24	29	17	21
excluding South Africa	65	61	77	72	12	12	4	4	23	28	14	18
excl. S.Africa & Nigeria	69	65	80	77	12	12	4	4	19	22	10	12
Angola	67	65	87	86	13	14	1	2	20	21	11	13
Benin	66	62	69	65	10	12	4	4	24	27	27	30
Botswana	53	39	74	55	41	30	8	20	53	50	24	36
Burkina Faso	92	91	93	94	3	2	2	2	5	7	5	5
Burundi	88	86	98	98	4	4	1	1	9	10	1	1
Cameroon	65	62	87	83	11	12	2	3	24	26	11	14
Cape Verde	34	30	39	33	38	38	18	16	28	33	41	51
Central African Republic	79	74	90	87	5	6	1	0	15	20	9	13
Chad	82	77	95	91	6	7	0	1	12	16	4	8
Comoros	70	68	93	90	12	13	3	5	17	20	3	5
Congo, Democratic Rep. of	62	58	84	81	18	20	4	5	20	23	12	14
Congo, Republic of	42	33	81	69	20	23	2	4	38	44	17	27
Côte d'Ivoire	60	54	75	72	10	12	5	6	30	34	20	22
Djibouti	..	..	..	..	..	..	..	..	..	..	..	..
Equatorial Guinea	71	66	91	91	7	7	3	2	23	27	7	8
Eritrea	79	77	88	85	7	8	2	2	14	16	11	13
Ethiopia	90	89	89	88	2	2	2	2	8	9	10	12
Gabon	59	46	74	59	18	21	6	10	24	33	21	32
Gambia, The	78	74	93	92	10	12	3	2	13	14	5	6
Ghana	66	64	57	55	12	12	14	14	22	25	29	31
Guinea	86	83	97	92	2	3	1	1	12	15	3	7
Guinea-Bissau	81	78	98	96	3	3	0	1	17	19	2	3
Kenya	23	19	25	20	24	23	9	9	53	58	10	12
Lesotho	26	29	64	59	52	41	5	5	22	30	31	36
Liberia	69	65	89	84	9	9	1	1	22	26	10	16
Madagascar	73	70	93	88	9	10	2	3	19	20	5	9
Malawi	78	50	96	73	10	25	1	7	12	25	3	3
Mali	86	83	92	89	2	2	1	2	12	15	7	9
Mauritania	65	49	79	63	11	16	2	4	24	35	19	34
Mauritius	29	15	30	13	19	39	40	43	47	46	46	36
Mozambique	72	70	97	96	14	15	1	1	14	15	2	3
Namibia	52	46	42	67	22	21	10	12	27	33	31	39
Niger	86	84	98	97	69	51	29	24	25	41	1	1
Nigeria	52	43	57	44	10	9	5	3	38	49	38	53
Rwanda	88	86	98	98	5	6	1	1	7	8	1	2
São Tomé and Principe	..	..	..	..	..	..	..	..	..	..	..	..
Senegal	74	70	90	86	9	10	2	4	17	20	8	11
Seychelles	..	..	..	..	..	..	..	..	..	..	..	..
Sierra Leone	63	60	82	81	20	22	4	4	17	18	14	16
Somalia	69	66	90	87	12	13	2	2	19	21	8	11
South Africa	18	16	16	10	45	42	16	15	37	42	68	76
Sudan	66	64	88	84	9	10	4	5	24	26	8	11
Swaziland	40	..	38	26	29	..	14	27	30	..	31	39
Tanzania	80	78	92	91	7	8	2	2	13	14	7	7
Togo	70	66	67	65	12	12	7	7	19	22	26	29
Uganda	84	81	91	88	6	7	2	2	10	12	8	10
Zambia	69	68	85	83	13	13	3	3	19	19	13	14
Zimbabwe	29	23	50	38	31	32	8	10	40	46	12	17
NORTH AFRICA	40	25	40	33	24	27	14	24	35	48	36	28
Algeria	27	18	69	57	33	38	6	7	40	45	25	36
Egypt, Arab Republic	45	32	10	43	21	25	13	9	33	43	56	31
Libya	16	7	63	28	29	27	3	5	55	66	34	68
Morocco	48	4	72	3	23	33	14	46	29	63	14	18
Tunisia	33	22	53	20	30	32	32	40	37	44	16	27
ALL AFRICA	58	53	70	67	16	16	6	5	26	31	19	22

Percentage of population economically active

*or most recent available data.

11-6. Wages in agriculture

| | *Monthly earnings in current US dollars* | | | | | | | | | | | |
	1980	*1987*	*1988*	*1989*	*1990*	*1991*	*1992*	*1993*	*1994*	*1995*	*1996*	*1997*
SUB-SAHARAN AFRICA	..	..	..	..	..	..	..	..	..	..	..	..
excluding South Africa	..	..	..	..	..	..	..	..	..	..	..	..
excl. S.Africa & Nigeria	..	..	..	..	..	..	..	..	..	..	..	..
Angola	..	..	..	..	..	..	..	..	..	..	..	..
Benin	..	..	..	..	..	..	..	..	..	..	..	..
Botswana	..	55	54	71	80	97	97	90	90	90	80	80
Burkina Faso	..	..	..	..	..	..	..	..	..	..	..	..
Burundi	..	..	..	..	..	..	..	..	..	..	..	..
Cameroon	..	..	..	..	..	..	..	..	..	..	..	..
Cape Verde	..	..	..	..	..	..	..	..	..	..	..	..
Central African Republic	..	..	..	..	..	..	..	..	..	..	..	..
Chad	..	..	..	..	..	..	..	..	..	..	..	..
Comoros	..	..	..	..	..	..	..	..	..	..	..	..
Congo, Democratic Rep. of	..	..	..	..	..	..	..	..	..	..	..	..
Congo, Republic of	..	..	..	..	..	..	..	..	..	..	..	..
Côte d'Ivoire	..	..	..	..	..	..	..	..	..	..	..	..
Djibouti	..	..	..	..	..	..	..	..	..	..	..	..
Equatorial Guinea	..	..	..	..	..	..	..	..	..	..	..	..
Eritrea	..	..	..	..	..	..	..	..	..	..	..	..
Ethiopia	..	..	..	..	..	..	..	..	..	..	..	..
Gabon	..	..	..	..	..	..	..	..	..	..	..	..
Gambia, The	..	..	..	..	..	..	..	..	..	..	..	..
Ghana	34	52	52	73	64	104	..	..	..	..	..	..
Guinea	..	..	..	..	..	..	..	..	..	..	..	..
Guinea-Bissau	..	..	..	..	..	..	..	..	..	..	..	..
Kenya	59	48	53	48	47	45	..	..	..	..	..	39
Lesotho	..	..	..	..	..	..	..	..	..	..	..	..
Liberia	..	..	..	..	..	..	..	..	..	..	..	..
Madagascar	..	..	..	..	..	..	..	..	..	..	..	..
Malawi	20	13	12	13	15	16	..	..	..	..	..	..
Mali	..	..	..	..	..	..	..	..	..	..	..	..
Mauritania	..	..	..	..	..	..	..	..	..	..	..	..
Mauritius	..	..	..	..	..	..	..	..	..	..	..	..
Mozambique	..	..	..	..	..	..	..	..	..	..	..	..
Namibia	..	..	..	..	..	..	..	..	..	..	..	..
Niger	..	..	..	..	..	..	..	..	..	..	..	..
Nigeria	..	..	..	..	..	..	..	..	..	..	..	..
Rwanda	..	..	..	..	..	..	..	..	..	..	..	..
São Tomé and Principe	..	..	..	..	..	..	..	..	..	..	..	..
Senegal	..	..	..	..	..	..	..	..	..	..	..	..
Seychelles	139	305	304	305	348	366	434	442	456	513	..	..
Sierra Leone	..	..	..	..	..	..	..	..	..	..	..	..
Somalia	..	..	..	..	..	..	..	..	..	..	..	..
South Africa	..	..	..	..	..	..	..	..	..	..	..	..
Sudan	..	..	..	..	..	..	..	..	..	..	..	..
Swaziland	..	310	..	437	423	496	533	512	550	483	..	..
Tanzania	..	..	..	..	..	..	..	..	..	..	..	..
Togo	..	..	..	..	..	..	..	..	..	..	..	..
Uganda	..	..	..	..	..	..	..	..	..	..	..	..
Zambia	112	..	..	..	..	..	..	..	..	..	..	..
Zimbabwe	..	74	76	71	75	56	34	38	35	34	..	..
NORTH AFRICA	..	..	..	..	..	..	..	..	..	..	..	..
Algeria	..	..	..	..	..	..	..	..	..	..	..	..
Egypt, Arab Republic	..	154	154	144	94	53	53	65	69	75	..	..
Libya	..	..	..	..	..	..	..	..	..	..	..	..
Morocco	..	..	..	..	..	..	..	..	..	..	..	..
Tunisia	..	80	82	77	92	89	101	..	..	..	..	..
ALL AFRICA	..	..	..	..	..	..	..	..	..	..	..	..

11-7. Wages in manufacturing

	Monthly earnings in current US dollars											
	1980	*1987*	*1988*	*1989*	*1990*	*1991*	*1992*	*1993*	*1994*	*1995*	*1996*	*1997*
SUB-SAHARAN AFRICA	..	..	..	..	..	..	..	..	..	..	..	..
excluding South Africa	..	..	..	..	..	..	..	..	..	..	..	..
excl. S.Africa & Nigeria	..	..	..	..	..	..	..	..	..	..	..	..
Angola	..	..	..	..	..	..	..	..	..	..	..	..
Benin	..	..	..	..	..	..	..	..	..	..	..	..
Botswana	..	166	181	171	206	199	242	250	200	210	186	173
Burkina Faso	..	..	..	..	..	..	..	..	..	..	..	..
Burundi	..	..	..	..	..	..	..	..	..	..	..	..
Cameroon	..	..	..	..	..	..	..	..	..	..	..	..
Cape Verde	..	..	..	..	..	..	..	..	..	..	..	..
Central African Republic	..	..	..	..	..	..	..	..	..	..	..	..
Chad	..	..	..	..	..	..	..	..	..	..	..	..
Comoros	..	..	..	..	..	..	..	..	..	..	..	..
Congo, Democratic Rep. of	..	..	..	..	..	..	..	..	..	..	..	..
Congo, Republic of	..	..	..	..	..	..	..	..	..	..	..	..
Côte d'Ivoire	..	..	..	..	..	..	..	..	..	..	..	..
Djibouti	..	..	..	..	..	..	..	..	..	..	..	..
Equatorial Guinea	..	..	..	..	..	..	..	..	..	..	..	..
Eritrea	..	..	..	..	..	..	..	..	..	..	..	..
Ethiopia	..	..	..	..	..	..	..	..	..	..	..	..
Gabon	..	..	..	..	..	..	..	..	..	..	..	..
Gambia, The	..	..	..	..	..	..	..	..	..	..	..	..
Ghana	57	99	106	136	138	93	..	..	..	..	..	..
Guinea	..	58	..	..	121	113	122	115	133	131	152	..
Guinea-Bissau	..	..	..	..	..	..	..	..	..	..	..	..
Kenya	169	139	139	136	134	121	..	..	..	..	..	94
Lesotho	..	..	..	..	..	..	..	..	..	..	..	..
Liberia	..	..	..	..	..	..	..	..	..	..	..	..
Madagascar	..	..	..	..	..	..	..	..	..	..	..	..
Malawi	75	57	53	53	65	55	47	40	21	13	..	..
Mali	..	..	..	..	..	..	..	..	..	..	..	..
Mauritania	..	..	..	..	..	..	..	..	..	..	..	..
Mauritius	..	160	181	184	209	235	258	250	287	326	333	306
Mozambique	..	..	..	..	..	..	..	..	..	..	..	..
Namibia	..	..	..	..	..	..	..	..	..	..	..	..
Niger	..	..	..	..	..	..	..	..	..	..	..	..
Nigeria	..	..	..	..	..	..	..	..	..	..	..	..
Rwanda	..	..	..	..	..	..	..	..	..	..	..	..
São Tomé and Principe	..	..	..	..	..	..	..	..	..	..	..	..
Senegal	..	..	..	..	..	..	..	..	..	..	..	..
Seychelles	212	371	346	350	410	427	459	474	479	528	..	..
Sierra Leone	..	..	..	..	..	..	..	..	..	..	..	..
Somalia	..	..	..	..	..	..	..	..	..	..	..	..
South Africa	475	513	535	548	642	685	770	749	..	..	..	..
Sudan	..	..	55	..	83	..	12	..	..	..	..	..
Swaziland	571	507	414	397	533	513	521	351	524	588	556	..
Tanzania	..	..	..	..	..	..	..	..	..	..	..	..
Togo	..	..	..	..	..	..	..	..	..	..	..	..
Uganda	..	..	..	..	..	..	..	..	..	..	..	..
Zambia	..	..	..	..	..	..	..	..	..	..	..	..
Zimbabwe	..	318	327	314	325	256	220	192	191	221	230	..
NORTH AFRICA	..	..	..	..	..	..	..	..	..	..	..	..
Algeria	..	..	..	..	..	..	..	..	..	..	..	..
Egypt, Arab Republic	..	233	252	228	150	75	80	90	98	107	..	..
Libya	..	..	..	..	..	..	..	..	..	..	..	..
Morocco	..	..	..	..	..	..	..	..	..	..	..	..
Tunisia	..	..	..	..	..	..	..	..	..	..	..	..
ALL AFRICA	..	..	..	..	..	..	..	..	..	..	..	..

11-8. Wages in mining and quarrying

| | \textit{Monthly earnings in current US dollars} | | | | | | | | | | |
	1980	1987	1988	1989	1990	1991	1992	1993	1994	1995	1996	1997
SUB-SAHARAN AFRICA	..	..	..	..	..	..	..	..	..	..	..	..
excluding South Africa	..	..	..	..	..	..	..	..	..	..	..	..
excl. S.Africa & Nigeria	..	..	..	..	..	..	..	..	..	..	..	..
Angola	..	..	..	..	..	..	..	..	..	..	..	..
Benin	..	..	..	..	..	..	..	..	..	..	..	..
Botswana	..	291	287	319	450	424	436	496	430	428	372	371
Burkina Faso	..	..	..	..	..	..	..	..	..	..	..	..
Burundi	..	..	..	..	..	..	..	..	..	..	..	..
Cameroon	..	..	..	..	..	..	..	..	..	..	..	..
Cape Verde	..	..	..	..	..	..	..	..	..	..	..	..
Central African Republic	..	..	..	..	..	..	..	..	..	..	..	..
Chad	..	..	..	..	..	..	..	..	..	..	..	..
Comoros	..	..	..	..	..	..	..	..	..	..	..	..
Congo, Democratic Rep. of	..	..	..	..	..	..	..	..	..	..	..	..
Congo, Republic of	..	..	..	..	..	..	..	..	..	..	..	..
Côte d'Ivoire	..	..	..	..	..	..	..	..	..	..	..	..
Djibouti	..	..	..	..	..	..	..	..	..	..	..	..
Equatorial Guinea	..	..	..	..	..	..	..	..	..	..	..	..
Eritrea	..	..	..	..	..	..	..	..	..	..	..	..
Ethiopia	..	..	..	..	..	..	..	..	..	..	..	..
Gabon	..	..	..	..	..	..	..	..	..	..	..	..
Gambia, The	..	..	..	..	..	..	..	..	..	..	..	..
Ghana	64	111	57	64	117	75	..	..	..	..	..	..
Guinea	..	..	..	..	..	..	..	..	..	..	..	..
Guinea-Bissau	..	..	..	..	..	..	..	..	..	..	..	..
Kenya	157	110	104	106	101	93	..	..	..	..	..	96
Lesotho	..	..	..	..	..	..	..	..	..	..	..	..
Liberia	..	..	..	..	..	..	..	..	..	..	..	..
Madagascar	..	..	..	..	..	..	..	..	..	..	..	..
Malawi	36	20	17	17	20	30	23	59	30	18	..	..
Mali	..	..	..	..	..	..	..	..	..	..	..	..
Mauritania	..	..	..	..	..	..	..	..	..	..	..	..
Mauritius	..	202	245	231	256	272	302	280	374	436	457	415
Mozambique	..	..	..	..	..	..	..	..	..	..	..	..
Namibia	..	..	..	..	..	..	..	..	..	..	..	..
Niger	..	..	..	..	..	..	..	..	..	..	..	..
Nigeria	..	..	..	..	..	..	..	..	..	..	..	..
Rwanda	..	..	..	..	..	..	..	..	..	..	..	..
São Tomé and Principe	..	..	..	..	..	..	..	..	..	..	..	..
Senegal	..	..	..	..	..	..	..	..	..	..	..	..
Seychelles	212	327	334	317	348	378	444	455	477	523	..	..
Sierra Leone	..	..	..	..	..	..	..	..	..	..	..	..
Somalia	..	..	..	..	..	..	..	..	..	..	..	..
South Africa	330	371	397	403	477	514	561	541	..	..	..	..
Sudan	..	..	53	..	99	..	..	..	..	..	..	..
Swaziland	822	560	483	309	395	367	395	379	387	523	485	..
Tanzania	..	..	..	..	..	..	..	..	..	..	..	..
Togo	..	..	..	..	..	..	..	..	..	..	..	..
Uganda	..	..	..	..	..	..	..	..	..	..	..	..
Zambia	358		..	..	..	..	..	..	..	..	..	..
Zimbabwe	..	240	254	242	254	204	180	153	153	187	204	..
NORTH AFRICA	..	..	..	..	..	..	..	..	..	..	..	..
Algeria	..	..	..	..	..	..	..	..	..	..	..	..
Egypt, Arab Republic	..	362	375	427	316	174	167	208	210	203	..	..
Libya	..	..	..	..	..	..	..	..	..	..	..	..
Morocco	..	..	..	..	..	..	..	..	..	..	..	..
Tunisia	..	..	..	..	..	..	..	..	..	..	..	..
ALL AFRICA	..	..	..	..	..	..	..	..	..	..	..	..

11-9. Wages in construction

	Monthly earnings in current US dollars											
	1980	1987	1988	1989	1990	1991	1992	1993	1994	1995	1996	1997
SUB-SAHARAN AFRICA	..	..	..	..	..	..	..	..	..	..	..	..
excluding South Africa	..	..	..	..	..	..	..	..	..	..	..	..
excl. S.Africa & Nigeria	..	..	..	..	..	..	..	..	..	..	..	..
Angola	..	..	..	..	..	..	..	..	..	..	..	..
Benin	..	..	..	..	..	..	..	..	..	..	..	..
Botswana	..	149	148	159	182	196	211	220	214	228	197	218
Burkina Faso	..	..	..	..	..	..	..	..	..	..	..	..
Burundi	..	..	..	..	..	..	..	..	..	..	..	..
Cameroon	..	..	..	..	..	..	..	..	..	..	..	..
Cape Verde	..	..	..	..	..	..	..	..	..	..	..	..
Central African Republic	..	..	..	..	..	..	..	..	..	..	..	..
Chad	..	..	..	..	..	..	..	..	..	..	..	..
Comoros	..	..	..	..	..	..	..	..	..	..	..	..
Congo, Democratic Rep. of	..	..	..	..	..	..	..	..	..	..	..	..
Congo, Republic of	..	..	..	..	..	..	..	..	..	..	..	..
Côte d'Ivoire	..	..	..	..	..	..	..	..	..	..	..	..
Djibouti	..	..	..	..	..	..	..	..	..	..	..	..
Equatorial Guinea	..	..	..	..	..	..	..	..	..	..	..	..
Eritrea	..	..	..	..	..	..	..	..	..	..	..	..
Ethiopia	..	..	..	..	..	..	..	..	..	..	..	..
Gabon	..	..	..	..	..	..	..	..	..	..	..	..
Gambia, The	..	..	..	..	..	..	..	..	..	..	..	..
Ghana	37	45	43	51	59	71	..	..	..	..	..	..
Guinea	..	..	84	115	173	159	..	135	132	177	174	..
Guinea-Bissau	..	..	..	..	..	..	..	..	..	..	..	..
Kenya	133	97	98	96	99	95	..	..	..	..	..	80
Lesotho	..	..	..	..	..	..	..	..	..	..	..	..
Liberia	..	..	..	..	..	..	..	..	..	..	..	..
Madagascar	..	..	..	..	..	..	..	..	..	..	..	..
Malawi	60	29	29	29	30	31	34	33	22	17	..	..
Mali	..	..	..	..	..	..	..	..	..	..	..	..
Mauritania	..	..	..	..	..	..	..	..	..	..	..	..
Mauritius	..	170	220	245	255	297	364	324	368	481	507	488
Mozambique	..	..	..	..	..	..	..	..	..	..	..	..
Namibia	..	..	..	..	..	..	..	..	..	..	..	..
Niger	..	..	..	..	..	..	..	..	..	..	..	..
Nigeria	..	..	..	..	..	..	..	..	..	..	..	..
Rwanda	..	..	..	..	..	..	..	..	..	..	..	..
São Tomé and Principe	..	..	..	..	..	..	..	..	..	..	..	..
Senegal	..	..	..	..	..	..	..	..	..	..	..	..
Seychelles	..	..	..	..	..	..	..	..	..	..	..	..
Sierra Leone	..	..	..	..	..	..	..	..	..	..	..	..
Somalia	..	..	..	..	..	..	..	..	..	..	..	..
South Africa	371	347	367	348	394	437	475	424	..	..	..	..
Sudan	..	..	56	..	180	..	13	..	..	..	..	..
Swaziland	525	335	267	192	247	283	470	211	333	227	246	..
Tanzania	..	..	..	..	..	..	..	..	..	..	..	..
Togo	..	..	..	..	..	..	..	..	..	..	..	..
Uganda	..	..	..	..	..	..	..	..	..	..	..	..
Zambia	172	..	..	..	..	..	..	..	..	..	..	..
Zimbabwe	..	209	200	182	179	144	110	102	88	114	124	..
NORTH AFRICA	..	..	..	..	..	..	..	..	..	..	..	..
Algeria	..	..	..	..	..	..	..	..	..	..	..	..
Egypt, Arab Republic	..	246	276	253	153	84	80	96	112	115	..	..
Libya	..	..	..	..	..	..	..	..	..	..	..	..
Morocco	..	..	..	..	..	..	..	..	..	..	..	..
Tunisia	..	..	..	..	..	..	..	..	..	..	..	..
ALL AFRICA	..	..	..	..	..	..	..	..	..	..	..	..

11-10. Wages in transport, storage, and communication

	Monthly earnings in current US dollars											
	1980	*1987*	*1988*	*1989*	*1990*	*1991*	*1992*	*1993*	*1994*	*1995*	*1996*	*1997*
SUB-SAHARAN AFRICA	..	..	..	..	..	..	..	..	..	..	..	..
excluding South Africa	..	..	..	..	..	..	..	..	..	..	..	..
excl. S.Africa & Nigeria	..	..	..	..	..	..	..	..	..	..	..	..
Angola	..	..	..	..	..	..	..	..	..	..	..	..
Benin	..	..	..	..	..	..	..	..	..	..	..	..
Botswana	..	192	239	296	346	417	457	434	468	435	376	344
Burkina Faso	..	..	..	..	..	..	..	..	..	..	..	..
Burundi	..	..	..	..	..	..	..	..	..	..	..	..
Cameroon	..	..	..	..	..	..	..	..	..	..	..	..
Cape Verde	..	..	..	..	..	..	..	..	..	..	..	..
Central African Republic	..	..	..	..	..	..	..	..	..	..	..	..
Chad	..	..	..	..	..	..	..	..	..	..	..	..
Comoros	..	..	..	..	..	..	..	..	..	..	..	..
Congo, Democratic Rep. of	..	..	..	..	..	..	..	..	..	..	..	..
Congo, Republic of	..	..	..	..	..	..	..	..	..	..	..	..
Côte d'Ivoire	..	..	..	..	..	..	..	..	..	..	..	..
Djibouti	..	..	..	..	..	..	..	..	..	..	..	..
Equatorial Guinea	..	..	..	..	..	..	..	..	..	..	..	..
Eritrea	..	..	..	..	..	..	..	..	..	..	..	..
Ethiopia	..	..	..	..	..	..	..	..	..	..	..	..
Gabon	..	..	..	..	..	..	..	..	..	..	..	..
Gambia, The	..	..	..	..	..	..	..	..	..	..	..	..
Ghana	55	36	89	96	100	106	..	..	..	..	..	..
Guinea	..	..	..	..	..	..	..	..	119	121	125	..
Guinea-Bissau	..	..	..	..	..	..	..	..	..	..	..	..
Kenya	237	195	207	193	187	171	..	..	..	..	..	131
Lesotho	..	..	..	..	..	..	..	..	..	..	..	..
Liberia	..	..	..	..	..	..	..	..	..	..	..	..
Madagascar	..	..	..	..	..	..	..	..	..	..	..	..
Malawi	99	47	49	62	63	70	66	63	37	25	..	..
Mali	..	..	..	..	..	..	..	..	..	..	..	..
Mauritania	..	..	..	..	..	..	..	..	..	..	..	..
Mauritius	..	231	290	289	307	339	380	353	376	422	453	426
Mozambique	..	..	..	..	..	..	..	..	..	..	..	..
Namibia	..	..	..	..	..	..	..	..	..	..	..	..
Niger	..	..	..	..	..	..	..	..	..	..	..	..
Nigeria	..	..	..	..	..	..	..	..	..	..	..	..
Rwanda	..	..	..	..	..	..	..	..	..	..	..	..
São Tomé and Principe	..	..	..	..	..	..	..	..	..	..	..	..
Senegal	..	..	..	..	..	..	..	..	..	..	..	..
Seychelles	299	..	..	..	..	..	..	..	..	..	..	..
Sierra Leone	..	..	..	..	..	..	..	..	..	..	..	..
Somalia	..	..	..	..	..	..	..	..	..	..	..	..
South Africa	..	571	583	577	702	794	1,110	1,075	..	..	..	..
Sudan	..	..	48	..	79	..	14	..	..	..	..	..
Swaziland	520	243	242	192	364	442	357	393	480	539	455	..
Tanzania	..	..	..	..	..	..	..	..	..	..	..	..
Togo	..	..	..	..	..	..	..	..	..	..	..	..
Uganda	..	..	..	..	..	..	..	..	..	..	..	..
Zambia	153	..	..	..	..	..	..	..	..	..	..	..
Zimbabwe	..	400	425	429	465	334	289	284	258	275	289	..
NORTH AFRICA	..	..	..	..	..	..	..	..	..	..	..	..
Algeria	..	..	..	..	..	..	..	..	..	..	..	..
Egypt, Arab Republic	..	221	283	248	147	78	84	121	112	117	..	..
Libya	..	..	..	..	..	..	..	..	..	..	..	..
Morocco	..	..	..	..	..	..	..	..	..	..	..	..
Tunisia	..	..	..	..	..	..	..	..	..	..	..	..
ALL AFRICA	..	..	..	..	..	..	..	..	..	..	..	..

11-11. Wages in community, social, and personal services

	1986	1987	1988	1989	1990	1991	1992	1993	1994	1995	1996	1997
SUB-SAHARAN AFRICA	..	..	..	..	..	..	..	..	..	..	..	..
excluding South Africa	..	..	..	..	..	..	..	..	..	..	..	..
excl. S.Africa & Nigeria	..	..	..	..	..	..	..	..	..	..	..	..
Angola	..	..	..	..	..	..	..	..	..	..	..	..
Benin	..	..	..	..	..	..	..	..	..	..	..	..
Botswana	167	186	195	189	231	239	249	265	254	280	243	250
Burkina Faso	..	..	..	..	..	..	..	..	..	..	..	..
Burundi	..	..	..	..	..	..	..	..	..	..	..	..
Cameroon	..	..	..	..	..	..	..	..	..	..	..	..
Cape Verde	..	..	..	..	..	..	..	..	..	..	..	..
Central African Republic	..	..	..	..	..	..	..	..	..	..	..	..
Chad	..	..	..	..	..	..	..	..	..	..	..	..
Comoros	..	..	..	..	..	..	..	..	..	..	..	..
Congo, Democratic Rep. of	..	..	..	..	..	..	..	..	..	..	..	..
Congo, Republic of	..	..	..	..	..	..	..	..	..	..	..	..
Côte d'Ivoire	..	..	..	..	..	..	..	..	..	..	..	..
Djibouti	..	..	..	..	..	..	..	..	..	..	..	..
Equatorial Guinea	..	..	..	..	..	..	..	..	..	..	..	..
Eritrea	..	..	..	..	..	..	..	..	..	..	..	..
Ethiopia	..	..	..	..	..	..	..	..	..	..	..	..
Gabon	..	..	..	..	..	..	..	..	..	..	..	..
Gambia, The	..	..	..	..	..	..	..	..	..	..	..	..
Ghana	76	55	59	81	68	98	..	..	..	..	..	..
Guinea	..	..	..	..	..	..	..	..	..	..	..	..
Guinea-Bissau	..	..	..	..	..	..	..	..	..	..	..	..
Kenya	118	121	128	118	114	104	..	..	..	..	..	75
Lesotho	..	..	..	..	..	..	..	..	..	..	..	..
Liberia	..	..	..	..	..	..	..	..	..	..	..	..
Madagascar	..	..	..	..	..	..	..	..	..	..	..	..
Malawi	..	..	..	..	..	59	50	43	24	12	..	..
Mali	..	..	..	..	..	..	..	..	..	..	..	..
Mauritania	..	..	..	..	..	..	..	..	..	..	..	..
Mauritius	166	183	235	245	262	278	307	278	357	392	394	404
Mozambique	..	..	..	..	..	..	..	..	..	..	..	..
Namibia	..	..	..	..	..	..	..	..	..	..	..	..
Niger	..	..	..	..	..	..	..	..	..	..	..	..
Nigeria	..	..	..	..	..	..	..	..	..	..	..	..
Rwanda	..	..	..	..	..	..	..	..	..	..	..	..
São Tomé and Principe	..	..	..	..	..	..	..	..	..	..	..	..
Senegal	..	..	..	..	..	..	..	..	..	..	..	..
Seychelles	..	..	..	..	..	..	..	..	..	..	..	..
Sierra Leone	..	..	..	..	..	..	..	..	..	..	..	..
Somalia	..	..	..	..	..	..	..	..	..	..	..	..
South Africa	427	537	532	563	679	735	937	..	..	..	..	..
Sudan	..	..	..	..	..	..	..	..	..	..	..	..
Swaziland	..	..	..	223	446	276	412	238	455	352	352	..
Tanzania	..	..	..	..	..	..	..	..	..	..	..	..
Togo	..	..	..	..	..	..	..	..	..	..	..	..
Uganda	..	..	..	..	..	..	..	..	..	..	..	..
Zambia	..	..	..	..	..	..	..	..	..	..	..	..
Zimbabwe	218	246	255	240	259	206	161	139	128	143	192	..
NORTH AFRICA	..	..	..	..	..	..	..	..	..	..	..	..
Algeria	..	..	..	..	..	..	..	..	..	..	..	..
Egypt, Arab Republic	178	203	203	179	128	64	65	67	80	112	..	..
Libya	..	..	..	..	..	..	..	..	..	..	..	..
Morocco	..	..	..	..	..	..	..	..	..	..	..	..
Tunisia	..	..	..	..	..	..	..	..	..	..	..	..
ALL AFRICA	..	..	..	..	..	..	..	..	..	..	..	..

Technical notes

Tables

Table 11-1. Number and gender structure of the labor force. This table (ILO data) provides the total number of persons in the labor force and the percentage that is female. Labor force refers to "economically active" persons, including the armed forces and the unemployed but excluding housewives and students. The "economically active" population comprises all persons of either gender who furnish the labor to produce economic goods and services, as defined by the SNA, during a specified period. The production of economic goods and services should include all production and processing of primary products, whether for the market, for barter, or for own consumption; the production of all other goods and services for the market; and, for households that produce such goods and services for the markets, the corresponding production for own consumption.

Table 11-2. Children under 14 working in the labor force. This table (ILO data) shows the percentage of children between the ages of 10 to 14 that participate in the labor force.

Table 11-3. Unpaid family workers as share of active workers. This table (ILO data) shows the percentage of family members—male and female—that are active workers but receive no compensation for their services.

Table 11-4. Industrial structure of the labor force. The industrial structure of the labor force can often indicate the relative level of development of the economy. This table (ILO data) shows the distribution of the labor force among the various sectors of economic activities. The agriculture sector includes farming, animal husbandry, hunting, forestry, and fishing. The industry sector includes mining and quarrying, manufacturing, construction and public works, electricity, water, and gas. All other branches of activity are included in services.

Table 11-5. Industrial structure of economically active population. This is the percentage of the economically active population working in agriculture, industry, or services. Data are shown for males and females (ILO data).

Table 11-6. Wages in agriculture. Data are from ILO, *Yearbook of Labor Statistics* (1988, 1993, 1994, 1995, and 1998) and show the monthly earnings at the average wage converted to U.S. dollars at the *Atlas* exchange rates in the countries concerned. Earnings here are limited to wages and salaries of employees only unless otherwise specified. They include remuneration for time not worked, such as for annual vacation, other paid leave or holidays, bonuses and gratuities, and housing and family allowances paid by the employer to the employee. They exclude employers' contributions to social security and pension schemes and the benefits received by employees under these schemes, as well as severance and termination pay.

It should be remembered that these earnings do not reflect worker's disposable or net earnings since they include gross wages before deductions, such as taxes or social security contributions.

International comparisons of wages in agriculture should be interpreted with caution because they entail wide coverage variations mainly as a result of the form of remuneration, the nature of the work, and the length of the working day.

For the following countries wages are paid entirely in cash: Botswana, Burundi, Egypt, Malawi, Mauritius, Seychelles, Swaziland, Tanzania, Tunisia, and Zambia.

For the following countries, wages shown are cash portion only, although the workers receive other payments in kind in addition: Ghana, Kenya, and Zimbabwe. Wages for these three countries include the value of food and lodging allowances.

Data for Burundi include family allowances. Data for Egypt are for establishments with 10 or more persons employed. Data for Ghana include forestry and fishing. Data for Kenya include the value of payments in kind. Data for Malawi include forestry and fishing. Data for Mauritius include sugar and tea factories. Data for Seychelles exclude hunting. Data for Swaziland include forestry and refer to skilled male workers only. Data for Zimbabwe include forestry and refer to all persons engaged.

Figures for Egypt were converted from weekly to monthly earnings using a rate of 4.3 weeks per month. Figures for Mauritius and Tunisia were converted from daily to monthly earnings using a rate of 22 days per month.

Table 11-7. Wages in manufacturing. Data are from ILO, *Yearbook of Labor Statistics* (1988, 1993, 1994, 1995, and 1998). Refer to the definitions in Table 11-6.

Data for Burundi include family allowances. Data for Egypt are for establishments with 10 or more persons employed. Data for the Gambia are for establishments with five or more persons employed. Data for Mauritius exclude sugar and tea factories. Data for Seychelles include electricity and water before 1992, and beginning in 1988 earnings are exempted from income tax. Data for Swaziland refer to skilled male workers only. Data for Zimbabwe include the value of payments in kind and refer to all persons engaged.

Figures for Egypt and Sierra Leone were converted from weekly to monthly earnings using a rate of 4.3 weeks per month. Figures for The Gambia were converted from daily to monthly earnings using a rate of 22 days per month.

Table 11-8. Wages in mining and quarrying. Data are from ILO, *Yearbook of Labor Statistics* (1988, 1993, 1994, 1995, and 1998). Refer to the definitions in Table 11-6.

Data for Burundi include family allowances. Data for Egypt are for establishments with 10 or more persons employed. Data for Kenya include the value of payments in kind. Data for Swaziland refer to skilled male workers only. Data for Seychelles include construction, and beginning in 1988 earnings are exempted from income tax. Data for South Africa exclude salt and iron works. Data for Swaziland refer to skilled male workers only. Data for Zimbabwe include the value of payments in kind and refer to all persons engaged.

Figures for Egypt and Sierra Leone were converted from weekly to monthly earnings using a rate of 4.3 weeks per month.

Table 11-9. Wages in construction. Data are from ILO, Yearbook of Labor Statistics (1988, 1993, 1994, 1995, and 1998). Refer to the definitions in Table 11-6.

Data for Burundi include family allowances. Data for Egypt are for establishments with 10 or more persons employed. Data for the Gambia are for establishments with five or more persons employed. Data for Kenya include the value of payments in kind. Data for Swaziland refer to skilled male workers only. Data for South Africa include private construction. Data for Swaziland refer to skilled male workers only. Data for Zimbabwe include the value of payments in kind and refer to all persons engaged.

Figures for Egypt and Sierra Leone were converted from weekly to monthly earnings using a rate of 4.3 weeks per month. Figures for the Gambia were converted from daily to monthly earnings using a rate of 22 days per month.

Table 11-10. Wages in transport, storage, and communications. Data are from ILO, *Yearbook of Labor Statistics* (1988, 1993, 1994, 1995, and 1998). Refer to the definitions in Table 11-6.

Data for Burundi include family allowances. Data for Egypt are for establishments with 10 or more persons employed. Data for the Gambia are for establishments with five or more persons employed. Data for Kenya include the value of payments in kind. Data for Swaziland refer to skilled male workers only. Data for Zimbabwe include the value of payments in kind and refer to all persons engaged.

Figures for Egypt and Sierra Leone were converted from weekly to monthly earnings using a rate of 4.3 weeks per month. Figures for the Gambia were converted from daily to monthly earnings using a rate of 22 days per month.

Table 11-11. Wages in community, social, and personal services. Data are from ILO Yearbook of Labor Statistics (1998). Refer to the definitions in Table 11-6. This sector comprises public administration and defense; sanitary and similar services; educational services; research and scientific institutes; medical, dental, and other health services; welfare institutions; business, professional, and labor associations; and other social and community services. Data for Egypt refer to wage earners. Figures for Egypt were converted from weekly to monthly earnings using a rate of 4.3 weeks per month.

Methodology used for regional aggregations and period averages in chapter 11

Table	Aggregations[a]		
	(1)	(6)	(8)
11-1			
Columns 1-3	x		
Columns 4-6		x	
11-2		x	
11-3			x
11-4		x	
11-5		x	
11-6			x
11-7			x
11-8			x
11-9			x
11-10			x
11-11			x

Note: Regional aggregations are shown in the rows for Sub-Saharan Africa, North Africa, and All Africa. Period averages are shown in the last three columns. This table shows only the methodologies used in this chapter.

a. Regional aggregations: (1) simple total; (2) simple total of the first indicator divided by the simple total of the second indicator (same country coverage); (3) simple total of the gap-filled indicator; (4) simple total of the gap-filled main indicator divided by the simple total of the gap-filled secondary indicator; (5) simple total of the first gap-filled main indicator less the simple total of the second gap-filled main indicator, all divided by the simple total of the secondary indicator; (6) weighted total (by population); (7) median; (8) no aggregation; (9) simple arithmetic mean.

12

Aid Flows

Official development assistance (ODA) consists of concessional financial flows that aim to promote economic development and welfare. ODA disbursements from bilateral and multilateral sources became increasingly important to Africa in the second half of the 1980s. For many countries, the foreign savings made available through ODA flows are equivalent to a sizable share of GDP and to the bulk of their domestic investment. Thus, monitoring aid flows is of special importance because of their significance to the economic performance of the region.

The tables in this chapter show data on net ODA flows and their relative importance to key economic and demographic indicators in recipient countries, real growth in net ODA flows to Sub-Saharan Africa in the 1980s and early 1990s from major donors or donor groups, and the share of each donor's worldwide aid portfolio allocated to Sub-Saharan Africa.

These flows are concessional in character and contain a grant element of at least 25 percent (based on a standard 10 percent discount rate). Net ODA disbursements equal gross ODA disbursements less principal repayments (amortization) of previous ODA loans.

ODA includes both grants (inflows of unrequited transfers from official sources) for current and capital expenditures and disbursements of concessional loans. However, because of different sources and definitions of data, the ODA flows shown in this chapter will not necessarily equal those that could be calculated by adding net disbursements of official concessional long-term loans (Table 6-1 less Table 6-4) and net official transfers (Tables 5-6 and 5-9). For example, one of the reasons for differences is that the flows shown here include "off-shore" disbursements of grants, primarily for technical cooperation, which are generally excluded from transfers as recorded in the balance of payments (Tables 5-6 and 5-9). Other reasons include possible differences in the timing of the recording of disbursements and in the recording of multilateral ODA.

The data on net ODA disbursements are taken from the most recent electronic version of OECD, *Geographical Distribution of Financial Flows to Developing Countries*. The tables include only those flows for which the recipient is specified in creditor reports.

Growth rates (based on constant price series) presented in this chapter may differ from those presented in *ADI 1992* because import price deflators (from World Bank) have been used to deflate the current price series, regardless of the type of donor, to indicate the volume of imports that aid can finance over time. In *ADI 1992*, donor country GNP deflators were used to deflate each DAC donor's aid flows (with the GNP deflators for DAC countries taken from the 1988 DAC chairman's report) thereby indicating the real resource transfer from individual donors, and the ODA flows from multilateral agencies and non-DAC donors were deflated by the average import price deflator for Sub-Saharan countries.

12-1. Net ODA from all donors, nominal

	Millions of U.S. dollars (current prices)											*Annual average*		
	1980	*1990*	*1991*	*1992*	*1993*	*1994*	*1995*	*1996*	*1997*	*1998*	*1999*	*75-84*	*85-89*	*90-MR*
SUB-SAHARAN AFRICA	7,395	17,199	16,917	18,185	16,735	18,065	17,848	15,045	13,354	13,033	11,554	5,836	11,868	15,793
excluding South Africa	7,395	17,199	16,917	18,185	16,459	17,770	17,462	14,686	12,859	12,521	11,015	5,836	11,868	15,507
excl. S.Africa & Nigeria	7,360	16,950	16,655	17,927	16,181	17,580	17,249	14,495	12,658	12,317	10,863	5,792	11,742	15,288
Angola	53	269	279	346	291	450	418	473	355	335	388	51	138	360
Benin	90	268	266	269	288	256	280	288	221	210	211	72	158	256
Botswana	106	147	132	112	130	86	90	75	122	106	61	83	133	106
Burkina Faso	212	331	420	434	467	433	489	415	368	397	398	165	264	415
Burundi	117	264	258	310	217	312	288	111	56	77	74	96	188	197
Cameroon	265	446	517	715	545	730	444	411	498	424	434	187	261	516
Cape Verde	64	108	105	119	117	121	117	117	111	130	136	42	89	118
Central African Republic	111	250	174	176	171	165	166	167	91	120	117	80	163	160
Chad	35	314	264	239	225	213	236	296	228	167	188	79	214	237
Comoros	43	45	64	48	49	39	42	39	27	35	21	30	49	41
Congo, Democratic Rep. of	428	897	476	269	178	245	196	166	157	126	132	317	537	284
Congo, Republic of	92	218	134	114	123	362	125	429	269	65	140	82	101	198
Côte d'Ivoire	210	688	631	757	764	1,594	1,212	964	446	799	447	136	271	830
Djibouti	73	194	107	113	133	129	105	97	85	81	75	60	94	112
Equatorial Guinea	9	61	62	62	53	30	34	31	24	25	20	7	39	40
Eritrea	..	..	..	..	67	157	149	159	123	167	148	..	..	139
Ethiopia	212	1,016	1,095	1,177	1,089	1,071	883	817	572	648	633	208	736	900
Gabon	56	132	143	69	101	181	144	127	39	45	48	50	92	103
Gambia, The	55	99	101	111	85	70	47	37	38	38	33	38	88	66
Ghana	192	563	881	612	617	546	651	649	489	701	607	137	453	632
Guinea	90	293	379	448	408	359	417	299	381	359	238	68	226	358
Guinea-Bissau	59	129	115	104	92	172	116	178	124	96	52	49	92	118
Kenya	397	1,186	920	886	909	675	731	591	445	475	308	319	667	712
Lesotho	94	142	125	143	142	116	114	104	92	66	31	72	107	107
Liberia	98	112	158	119	121	63	122	171	75	73	94	77	78	111
Madagascar	230	398	456	363	363	289	301	357	833	495	358	148	295	421
Malawi	143	503	523	572	495	467	432	492	345	434	446	115	279	471
Mali	267	482	452	432	363	441	541	491	428	346	354	194	398	433
Mauritania	176	237	218	200	325	267	230	272	238	172	219	177	214	238
Mauritius	33	89	67	46	26	14	23	19	42	40	42	36	52	41
Mozambique	169	1,002	1,069	1,463	1,179	1,200	1,064	888	947	1,039	118	141	625	997
Namibia	..	121	182	142	154	137	192	188	165	180	178	0	24	164
Niger	170	396	373	365	344	377	274	254	333	291	187	165	333	319
Nigeria	36	249	262	259	279	190	212	191	201	204	152	44	125	220
Rwanda	155	291	361	351	356	714	702	467	230	350	373	131	222	419
São Tomé and Principe	4	55	51	56	47	50	84	47	33	28	28	7	22	48
Senegal	263	818	635	670	500	640	666	579	422	500	534	254	569	596
Seychelles	22	36	23	19	20	13	13	19	17	24	13	16	23	20
Sierra Leone	91	61	104	133	208	275	206	184	119	106	74	51	85	147
Somalia	433	494	186	653	889	537	189	88	81	80	115	283	462	331
South Africa	..	..	..	..	275	295	386	358	495	512	539	..	..	409
Sudan	625	822	874	541	453	410	239	219	138	209	243	541	936	415
Swaziland	50	54	53	53	52	56	55	30	27	30	29	33	34	44
Tanzania	679	1,173	1,080	1,338	950	965	877	877	944	1,000	990	513	797	1,019
Togo	91	260	200	223	97	125	192	157	125	128	71	81	162	158
Uganda	114	668	665	725	610	750	830	676	813	471	590	85	304	680
Zambia	318	480	883	1,035	872	718	2,034	610	610	349	623	204	411	821
Zimbabwe	164	340	393	792	498	560	491	371	335	280	244	114	259	431
NORTH AFRICA	2,709	7,161	6,975	5,350	3,686	3,851	2,898	3,285	2,893	3,027	2,598	2,680	2,572	4,172
Algeria	176	262	338	406	348	419	312	304	248	393	89	137	177	312
Egypt, Arab Republic	1,387	5,437	5,024	3,602	2,395	2,690	2,014	2,199	1,981	1,951	1,579	1,775	1,640	2,887
Libya	17	19	25	6	4	4	6	8	7	7	7	9	9	9
Morocco	898	1,049	1,231	946	712	631	495	650	463	529	678	536	494	738
Tunisia	232	393	357	390	227	106	71	124	193	147	244	223	252	225
ALL AFRICA	10,105	24,360	23,892	23,535	20,421	21,915	20,746	18,329	16,247	16,060	14,152	8,516	14,440	19,966

Note: In 1995, Zambia completed a 3 year Rights Arrangement Program permitting disbursement of 833.4 M SDR under a new SAF/ESAF arrangement.

12-2. Net ODA from DAC donors, nominal

	Millions of U.S. dollars (current prices)											*Annual average*		
	1980	*1990*	*1991*	*1992*	*1993*	*1994*	*1995*	*1996*	*1997*	*1998*	*1999*	*75-84*	*85-89*	*90-MR*
SUB-SAHARAN AFRICA	4,351	10,815	10,264	10,769	10,158	10,326	9,908	9,088	8,123	8,176	7,624	3,429	7,516	9,525
excluding South Africa	4,351	10,815	10,264	10,769	9,975	10,112	9,590	8,776	7,708	7,755	7,238	3,429	7,516	9,300
excl. S.Africa & Nigeria	4,334	10,642	10,092	10,632	9,904	10,065	9,517	8,729	7,656	7,721	7,185	3,402	7,414	9,214
Angola	36	164	159	194	151	224	242	294	227	214	252	30	94	212
Benin	36	126	160	171	148	142	177	165	148	144	119	36	88	150
Botswana	83	121	104	93	80	57	54	68	56	73	41	63	102	75
Burkina Faso	151	239	270	268	255	265	252	269	218	227	232	112	182	249
Burundi	60	158	123	149	126	108	108	68	38	44	52	50	85	97
Cameroon	171	339	377	579	528	397	346	280	330	303	254	130	205	373
Cape Verde	39	76	79	80	81	82	77	77	68	85	89	28	61	79
Central African Republic	75	100	98	107	117	94	122	121	61	57	59	52	92	94
Chad	20	183	138	148	146	104	127	122	96	75	64	44	119	120
Comoros	13	31	31	23	29	18	22	22	15	19	13	11	28	22
Congo, Democratic Rep. of	317	633	343	163	99	97	118	106	105	80	87	221	336	183
Congo, Republic of	55	202	118	102	116	253	105	395	260	60	121	49	88	173
Côte d'Ivoire	152	531	435	527	708	820	727	449	233	490	366	105	191	529
Djibouti	32	88	83	92	94	94	80	71	62	62	55	35	61	78
Equatorial Guinea	1	44	35	36	28	17	22	23	18	18	15	4	22	25
Eritrea	..	..	..	..	48	96	95	128	81	98	80	..	..	89
Ethiopia	91	510	464	457	417	567	526	448	374	365	325	86	413	445
Gabon	49	127	140	65	97	161	136	113	30	37	34	42	80	94
Gambia, The	17	57	55	50	50	38	25	17	17	13	13	16	50	34
Ghana	107	265	449	333	312	332	359	349	292	375	356	75	187	342
Guinea	33	139	173	233	185	186	220	135	126	148	111	20	126	166
Guinea-Bissau	34	75	62	57	56	124	77	125	59	65	32	29	46	73
Kenya	277	735	608	520	426	401	459	346	301	276	254	244	477	433
Lesotho	64	85	74	69	74	45	62	49	45	33	26	44	63	56
Liberia	60	42	57	26	25	35	31	112	31	31	45	53	54	44
Madagascar	91	268	274	216	228	190	195	230	549	334	192	77	169	268
Malawi	76	216	209	208	159	251	221	264	174	204	228	63	134	213
Mali	131	312	280	239	221	243	285	298	257	236	237	104	248	261
Mauritania	54	106	110	116	196	128	126	99	97	64	89	45	116	113
Mauritius	25	76	62	35	27	8	11	1	3	20	5	23	43	25
Mozambique	115	750	769	1,007	813	733	698	552	622	713	593	104	476	725
Namibia	..	39	95	98	123	113	148	136	123	129	117	0	16	112
Niger	105	255	264	262	254	261	194	163	181	145	120	97	209	210
Nigeria	17	173	172	138	71	47	73	47	52	34	53	27	103	86
Rwanda	97	183	233	187	201	487	339	252	179	209	181	83	127	245
São Tomé and Principe	1	31	24	26	28	26	62	29	21	18	19	2	9	28
Senegal	182	589	421	454	364	475	399	392	292	289	416	157	355	409
Seychelles	18	33	17	15	7	7	11	8	6	17	5	14	17	13
Sierra Leone	57	40	68	74	106	54	60	67	41	53	60	28	50	62
Somalia	139	270	116	497	688	438	119	40	46	42	76	93	299	233
South Africa	..	..	..	..	183	214	319	312	415	421	386	..	..	321
Sudan	272	420	369	188	164	174	131	118	86	150	159	211	499	196
Swaziland	33	36	31	27	33	27	38	21	16	17	15	22	21	26
Tanzania	524	844	764	816	650	570	587	605	569	769	613	383	617	679
Togo	52	155	124	135	77	63	118	97	76	66	47	46	93	96
Uganda	42	244	285	255	348	344	423	370	439	384	357	31	112	345
Zambia	234	409	583	699	511	434	439	354	367	257	340	156	326	439
Zimbabwe	112	296	359	536	310	280	348	281	222	216	219	86	226	307
NORTH AFRICA	1,660	4,221	5,342	4,405	2,640	3,077	2,382	2,631	1,976	1,951	1,774	1,427	2,192	3,040
Algeria	118	232	307	376	265	373	290	263	193	122	37	116	123	246
Egypt, Arab Republic	1,187	3,172	4,157	2,996	1,824	2,311	1,690	1,933	1,497	1,472	1,298	959	1,533	2,235
Libya	10	8	3	1	2	2	3	2	2	4	3	4	5	3
Morocco	188	595	611	734	422	318	347	391	215	251	333	189	354	422
Tunisia	158	214	264	298	127	73	52	42	70	102	102	160	178	134
ALL AFRICA	6,011	15,036	15,605	15,174	12,797	13,403	12,290	11,719	10,099	10,127	9,398	4,856	9,709	12,565

12-3. Net ODA from non-DAC bilateral donors, nominal

	Millions of U.S. dollars (current prices)											Annual average		
	1980	1990	1991	1992	1993	1994	1995	1996	1997	1998	1999	75-84	85-89	90-MR
SUB-SAHARAN AFRICA	685	456	131	42	34	14	11	35	91'	48	-842	560	317	2
excluding South Africa	685	456	131	42	34	14	11	35	91	48	-842	560	317	2
excl. S.Africa & Nigeria	685	456	131	42	34	14	11	35	91	48	-845	560	317	2
Angola	1	2	2	1	3	0	0	0	0	0	0	0	1	1
Benin	2	0	-2	0	0	3	7	6	0	-2	-2	1	2	1
Botswana	0	-2	2	-2	7	1	0	-2	-3	-3	-1	2	0	0
Burkina Faso	0	11	10	2	0	0	6	2	3	3	9	2	5	5
Burundi	4	0	-3	-2	-2	-3	-3	-1	0	-1	0	4	7	-1
Cameroon	23	-3	-2	-1	0	0	1	-2	-2	-2	-4	7	0	-1
Cape Verde	2	0	0	0	1	0	0	3	0	0	0	1	1	0
Central African Republic	2	2	3	0	0	-1	0	1	0	0	0	1	3	1
Chad	0	2	2	0	3	1	1	3	5	5	7	3	0	3
Comoros	16	0	0	0	0	0	0	0	0	0	0	6	1	0
Congo, Democratic Rep. of	5	77	0	2	0	0	0	2	8	2	0	3	0	9
Congo, Republic of	15	0	0	0	0	0	0	0	0	0	0	10	0	0
Côte d'Ivoire	0	0	0	0	0	0	0	0	0	0	1	0	0	0
Djibouti	33	88	3	-1	10	12	3	5	5	2	1	17	14	13
Equatorial Guinea	0	0	6	0	0	0	0	0	0	0	0	0	0	1
Eritrea	..	..	..	..	1	12	5	3	16	31	18	..	..	12
Ethiopia	0	68	1	0	1	0	0	0	0	1	5	11	1	8
Gabon	0	0	0	0	0	0	-1	-2	-3	-1	0	3	3	-1
Gambia, The	7	0	2	-2	-2	-2	-2	-2	-2	0	1	5	-1	-1
Ghana	25	1	9	-4	-4	-6	-6	-2	9	2	4	7	2	0
Guinea	0	4	-1	-2	-4	-2	6	20	34	24	18	11	10	10
Guinea-Bissau	1	0	1	3	1	0	0	1	0	0	0	3	5	1
Kenya	0	5	3	-4	-4	-5	2	-3	-1	-2	1	4	7	-1
Lesotho	0	0	-1	1	1	0	0	4	7	-1	-1	1	0	1
Liberia	9	0	0	0	0	0	0	0	0	0	0	3	0	0
Madagascar	48	-1	0	0	0	0	0	0	0	0	0	12	-2	0
Malawi	0	0	0	0	0	0	0	1	0	0	4	0	0	1
Mali	33	15	4	4	-4	-11	-14	-8	-6	-6	0	17	16	-2
Mauritania	86	25	1	-7	-6	-10	-16	-12	-13	-7	5	83	26	-4
Mauritius	0	1	-2	-1	-2	-1	-2	-4	10	-1	0	1	2	0
Mozambique	20	0	0	2	3	2	2	3	-2	-2	-947	3	4	-94
Namibia	..	0	0	0	0	0	0	0	0	0	0	0	0	0
Niger	2	4	4	0	2	5	0	0	10	1	1	17	5	3
Nigeria	0	0	0	0	0	0	0	0	0	0	2	0	0	0
Rwanda	1	10	3	0	2	1	0	1	1	0	0	2	5	2
São Tomé and Principe	0	0	0	0	0	0	0	0	0	0	0	0	0	0
Senegal	2	2	22	16	14	1	12	10	9	0	3	19	27	9
Seychelles	0	0	0	0	1	0	-1	3	5	1	2	0	1	1
Sierra Leone	4	0	0	0	0	0	1	4	1	3	0	2	4	1
Somalia	128	82	0	10	9	0	0	0	1	0	0	81	7	10
South Africa	..	..	..	..	0	0	0	0	0	0	1	..	..	0
Sudan	160	8	16	20	2	0	1	0	0	0	26	183	148	7
Swaziland	0	0	0	0	0	0	0	0	0	0	0	0	0	0
Tanzania	27	3	-2	-3	-1	6	4	-3	2	2	0	12	3	1
Togo	0	-1	-1	-2	0	0	0	-2	-1	1	3	1	3	0
Uganda	1	43	51	15	1	11	7	8	3	0	1	6	7	14
Zambia	23	0	0	0	0	0	0	0	0	-1	0	11	0	0
Zimbabwe	5	9	-1	-3	-1	-3	-4	-3	-3	-1	-1	6	-2	-1
NORTH AFRICA	739	2,655	985	455	389	110	101'	47	119	228	112	794	176	520
Algeria	41	8	2	4	1	2	-12	.7	12	19	31	7	28	7
Egypt, Arab Republic	4	2,186	510	409	379	· 94	117	54	97	211	71	453	14	413
Libya	0	0	0	0	0	0	0	0	0	0	0	0	0	0
Morocco	644	361	470	52	18	29	19	26	31	29	29	299	111	106
Tunisia	49	100	3	-10	-9	-15	-23	-38	-20	-32	-18	35	23	-6
ALL AFRICA	1,424	3,111	1,116	498	423	124	113	83	210	276	-730	1,354	493	522

12-4. Net ODA from multilateral donors, nominal

	\multicolumn{11}{c}{Millions of U.S. dollars (current prices)}										\multicolumn{3}{c}{Annual average}		
	1980	1990	1991	1992	1993	1994	1995	1996	1997	1998	1999	75-84	85-89	90-MR
SUB-SAHARAN AFRICA	2,359	5,928	6,522	7,373	6,542	7,724	7,928	5,921	5,139	4,809	4,772	1,847	4,035	6,266
excluding South Africa	2,359	5,928	6,522	7,373	6,450	7,644	7,860	5,875	5,059	4,717	4,619	1,847	4,035	6,205
excl. S.Africa & Nigeria	2,340	5,852	6,432	7,253	6,243	7,501	7,721	5,731	4,910	4,548	4,523	1,830	4,012	6,071
Angola	16	103	119	152	137	226	176	179	128	121	136	20	42	147
Benin	53	143	109	98	140	111	96	118	73	68	93	34	68	105
Botswana	23	27	26	21	43	28	35	8	69	36	21	17	31	31
Burkina Faso	61	81	140	164	212	168	231	144	147	167	157	52	77	161
Burundi	54	106	138	163	94	207	182	44	18	33	22	42	95	101
Cameroon	71	109	142	137	16	334	97	134	171	123	183	51	56	145
Cape Verde	23	32	25	39	36	40	40	36	43	45	48	13	27	38
Central African Republic	34	148	73	70	54	72	43	45	30	63	58	27	68	66
Chad	15	128	124	91	76	109	109	171	126	88	116	33	95	114
Comoros	13	15	33	25	20	21	20	17	12	17	8	12	20	19
Congo, Democratic Rep. of	106	187	134	105	79	148	78	57	44	44	45	93	201	92
Congo, Republic of	22	16	16	12	7	109	20	35	9	5	19	23	13	25
Côte d'Ivoire	58	157	196	229	55	773	486	515	213	309	80	31	80	301
Djibouti	9	17	22	22	29	23	22	21	19	17	19	9	19	21
Equatorial Guinea	8	17	21	26	25	13	12	8	6	6	6	4	17	14
Eritrea	..	..	..	..	18	49	49	29	26	38	50	..	..	37
Ethiopia	120	438	630	720	671	504	357	369	198	282	303	111	322	447
Gabon	7	6	3	4	4	20	9	15	11	9	13	5	9	9
Gambia, The	31	42	44	62	37	34	23	22	23	25	19	17	39	33
Ghana	59	297	424	284	309	220	298	303	189	324	248	55	264	289
Guinea	57	150	206	217	228	174	191	143	222	187	109	36	90	183
Guinea-Bissau	24	53	51	45	34	48	39	52	66	31	20	18	41	44
Kenya	120	446	309	370	487	280	270	248	145	201	53	71	183	281
Lesotho	31	57	51	73	68	70	52	51	40	35	7	27	44	50
Liberia	29	70	101	93	97	28	91	58	44	41	49	21	24	67
Madagascar	91	131	182	147	135	99	106	127	284	161	166	59	128	154
Malawi	68	287	314	365	336	216	211	228	171	230	214	52	144	257
Mali	103	154	168	189	146	209	270	201	178	116	117	73	134	175
Mauritania	36	106	107	91	135	150	120	185	154	115	125	49	72	129
Mauritius	8	12	7	11	1	7	14	22	29	21	36	12	7	16
Mozambique	34	252	300	454	363	464	364	333	327	329	473	34	145	366
Namibia	..	82	86	45	31	25	44	51	42	51	60	..	8	52
Niger	64	138	104	103	88	111	80	91	141	146	66	50	118	107
Nigeria	18	77	90	121	208	143	140	143	149	170	96	17	23	134
Rwanda	57	98	125	164	152	226	363	213	50	141	192	46	90	172
São Tomé and Principe	3	24	27	30	18	24	23	19	12	10	8	5	13	20
Senegal	79	227	192	200	122	164	254	177	122	211	115	78	187	178
Seychelles	3	3	6	4	12	6	2	8	6	6	6	2	5	6
Sierra Leone	30	21	36	59	102	222	146	113	76	51	13	21	31	84
Somalia	166	142	70	146	191	99	70	49	34	38	39	109	157	88
South Africa	..	..	..	..	92	80	67	46	80	92	152	..	..	87
Sudan	192	394	489	333	287	235	108	101	52	59	58	147	289	212
Swaziland	17	18	22	26	19	28	18	10	10	14	14	12	12	18
Tanzania	128	326	318	525	300	389	286	274	373	228	376	118	177	340
Togo	39	106	76	89	19	62	74	62	51	61	21	34	65	62
Uganda	70	381	329	455	261	394	400	297	371	87	232	49	186	321
Zambia	62	71	300	336	361	284	1,594	255	243	93	283	37	85	382
Zimbabwe	47	35	35	259	189	283	147	93	116	65	25	28	34	125
NORTH AFRICA	311	284	649	490	658	664	415	606	798	849	712	459	204	613
Algeria	17	22	29	26	82	44	34	35	44	253	21	15	26	59
Egypt, Arab Republic	196	80	357	198	192	285	208	212	388	267	210	363	93	240
Libya	7	12	22	4	2	2	3	6	5	3	4	6	4	6
Morocco	66	92	150	160	273	285	128	233	217	249	316	48	30	210
Tunisia	25	79	91	102	109	49	41	121	144	76	161	28	51	97
ALL AFRICA	2,669	6,213	7,171	7,863	7,200	8,388	8,343	6,527	5,938	5,658	5,483	2,306	4,239	6,878

Note: In 1995, Zambia completed a 3 year Rights Arrangement Program permitting disbursement of 833.4 M SDR under a new SAF/ESAF arrangement.

id Flows

12-5. Net ODA from all donors, real

	Millions of U.S. dollars (constant 1995 prices)										Average annual percentage growth		
	1980	1990	1991	1992	1993	1994	1995	1996	1997	1998	75-84	85-89	90-MR
SUB-SAHARAN AFRICA	9,685	18,911	18,895	19,468	18,473	19,751	17,848	14,989	14,029	14,566	6.7	10.0	-15.7
excluding South Africa	9,685	18,911	18,895	19,468	18,169	19,429	17,462	14,632	13,508	13,993	6.7	10.0	-15.9
excl. S.Africa & Nigeria	9,638	18,637	18,603	19,191	17,861	19,221	17,249	14,442	13,297	13,765	6.9	9.7	-15.8
Angola	69	296	312	371	322	492	418	471	373	375	39.7	9.4	6.3
Benin	118	295	298	288	318	280	280	287	232	235	2.3	19.9	-2.9
Botswana	139	161	147	120	143	94	90	74	128	119	5.4	7.4	-6.2
Burkina Faso	278	364	469	464	515	473	489	414	387	444	4.0	4.5	1.7
Burundi	154	290	288	332	240	341	288	111	59	86	9.5	4.7	-14.3
Cameroon	347	490	577	766	601	798	444	410	524	474	1.5	14.5	-2.2
Cape Verde	84	119	117	127	130	132	117	116	117	145	13.4	1.8	1.6
Central African Republic	145	275	194	189	188	181	166	166	96	134	6.5	7.8	-7.7
Chad	46	345	295	256	248	233	236	295	239	187	-4.4	11.8	-4.3
Comoros	57	50	71	51	54	42	42	39	29	39	2.9	-1.8	-6.1
Congo, Democratic Rep. of	560	986	532	288	197	268	196	165	165	140	0.8	15.9	-19.4
Congo, Republic of	121	240	150	122	136	396	125	428	282	72	2.6	-2.1	2.4
Côte d'Ivoire	275	756	705	810	844	1,742	1,212	961	468	892	-0.6	27.6	3.7
Djibouti	96	213	120	120	147	141	105	96	90	90	4.8	-7.4	-4.4
Equatorial Guinea	12	67	70	66	58	33	34	31	26	28	17.9	30.0	-12.2
Eritrea	..	..	..	..	74	172	149	159	129	187	..	..	11.6
Ethiopia	277	1,117	1,223	1,260	1,203	1,171	883	814	600	724	5.5	9.2	-5.5
Gabon	73	146	160	74	112	198	144	126	41	50	2.3	9.1	-10.3
Gambia, The	71	109	113	118	94	76	47	36	40	42	15.3	10.0	-14.0
Ghana	251	619	984	655	681	597	651	647	514	783	5.5	25.4	-2.6
Guinea	117	322	423	480	451	392	417	298	401	401	16.8	21.1	-0.9
Guinea-Bissau	78	141	128	112	101	188	116	177	131	107	16.5	13.6	-0.3
Kenya	519	1,304	1,028	948	1,004	738	731	588	467	530	9.8	17.2	-10.8
Lesotho	124	156	140	153	157	127	114	104	96	74	12.1	2.3	-7.6
Liberia	128	123	176	128	134	69	122	170	78	81	18.3	-17.4	-1.6
Madagascar	301	438	509	388	400	316	301	355	875	553	8.4	12.7	2.9
Malawi	188	553	584	613	546	510	432	491	362	485	6.5	21.5	-3.2
Mali	350	530	505	462	401	482	541	489	450	387	4.5	1.9	-2.1
Mauritania	230	261	244	214	359	292	230	271	250	192	0.4	-0.3	-2.3
Mauritius	43	97	75	49	29	16	23	19	44	45	1.1	11.7	-11.1
Mozambique	222	1,102	1,194	1,566	1,301	1,312	1,064	885	995	1,162	40.7	26.0	-1.1
Namibia	..	133	203	152	170	150	192	187	173	201	..	55.3	7.2
Niger	223	436	417	391	379	412	274	253	349	326	-1.0	7.6	-3.6
Nigeria	47	274	292	277	308	208	212	190	211	228	-11.8	50.7	-6.1
Rwanda	204	320	404	376	393	781	702	465	241	391	4.8	3.8	2.8
São Tomé and Principe	5	60	57	60	51	55	84	47	35	32	14.0	24.9	-5.0
Senegal	344	900	709	718	552	700	666	577	444	559	6.6	12.7	-5.7
Seychelles	28	40	26	21	22	14	13	19	18	27	3.2	-1.5	-4.7
Sierra Leone	119	67	116	143	229	301	206	183	125	119	14.6	6.6	5.0
Somalia	567	543	208	699	981	587	189	88	85	90	10.4	0.8	-20.2
South Africa	..	..	..	..	304	322	386	357	520	573	..	..	13.8
Sudan	818	904	976	579	500	448	239	218	145	234	10.4	-2.8	-19.3
Swaziland	66	59	59	57	57	61	55	30	28	34	2.0	-0.7	-5.0
Tanzania	889	1,290	1,206	1,433	1,048	1,055	877	873	992	1,117	6.9	10.7	-2.8
Togo	119	286	223	238	107	137	192	156	131	144	4.1	9.2	-7.1
Uganda	149	735	743	776	673	819	830	673	854	526	19.6	20.2	0.1
Zambia	417	528	986	1,108	962	785	2,034	607	641	390	11.0	5.5	-0.4
Zimbabwe	215	373	439	848	550	613	491	370	352	313	66.6	-3.9	-1.7
NORTH AFRICA	3,548	7,873	7,791	5,728	4,069	4,210	2,898	3,273	3,040	3,383	-5.3	-5.0	-6.8
Algeria	230	288	378	434	384	459	312	303	261	440	-6.8	0.2	3.1
Egypt, Arab Republic	1,816	5,979	5,612	3,857	2,644	2,941	2,014	2,191	2,082	2,180	-7.8	-7.2	-7.2
Libya	22	21	28	6	4	4	6	8	7	8	-8.4	12.8	-12.4
Morocco	1,175	1,153	1,375	1,013	786	690	495	647	487	591	6.6	-4.3	-6.5
Tunisia	304	432	399	418	251	116	71	123	203	164	-5.2	9.1	-13.4
ALL AFRICA	13,233	26,784	26,686	25,196	22,542	23,962	20,746	18,262	17,068	17,949	2.4	6.9	-17.2

Note: In 1995, Zambia completed a 3 year Rights Arrangement Program permitting disbursement of 833.4 M SDR under a new SAF/ESAF arrangement.

12-6. Net ODA from DAC donors, real

	Millions of U.S. dollars (constant 1995 prices)									Average annual percentage growth		
	1980	1990	1991	1992	1993	1994	1995	1996	1997	1998	75-84	85-89	90-MR
SUB-SAHARAN AFRICA	5,698	11,891	11,464	11,529	11,213	11,291	9,908	9,054	8,534	9,137	7.2	10.7	-15.8
excluding South Africa	5,698	11,891	11,464	11,529	11,011	11,056	9,590	8,744	8,098	8,667	7.2	10.7	-16.2
excl. S.Africa & Nigeria	5,676	11,701	11,272	11,382	10,932	11,004	9,517	8,696	8,043	8,629	7.6	10.1	-16.0
Angola	47	181	177	208	167	245	242	293	238	240	41.1	10.1	6.7
Benin	47	138	179	183	163	155	177	164	155	161	1.2	22.9	-0.4
Botswana	109	133	116	100	88	62	54	68	59	82	3.9	12.9	-9.0
Burkina Faso	198	262	302	287	281	289	252	268	229	253	6.0	8.4	-0.8
Burundi	78	173	137	159	139	119	108	68	40	50	9.0	-0.2	-12.4
Cameroon	224	373	421	620	583	434	346	279	347	339	3.7	11.4	-3.0
Cape Verde	51	83	88	86	90	89	77	77	71	95	25.2	5.1	0.2
Central African Republic	98	110	110	114	129	103	122	121	64	63	8.1	6.8	-5.2
Chad	26	202	154	159	161	113	127	121	101	83	-4.0	11.9	-7.3
Comoros	18	34	34	25	32	19	22	22	16	21	-0.6	11.2	-7.9
Congo, Democratic Rep. of	415	696	383	174	109	106	118	106	110	89	-0.7	12.9	-19.8
Congo, Republic of	73	222	131	109	128	277	105	393	273	67	2.3	3.6	2.6
Côte d'Ivoire	199	583	486	565	782	897	727	448	245	547	2.1	16.2	-0.3
Djibouti	42	97	93	98	104	103	80	71	65	70	-1.0	3.2	-3.3
Equatorial Guinea	2	48	39	38	31	18	22	23	19	20	118.6	36.9	-10.3
Eritrea	..	..	..	..	53	105	95	127	85	109	..	..	9.8
Ethiopia	120	560	519	489	460	620	526	447	393	408	0.1	8.0	-2.1
Gabon	64	139	157	69	108	176	136	113	32	42	3.6	10.7	-11.7
Gambia, The	22	63	61	54	55	42	25	17	18	15	16.8	8.4	-17.1
Ghana	140	291	501	356	345	363	359	348	307	419	1.6	25.1	-0.8
Guinea	43	153	194	250	204	204	220	134	132	166	19.4	30.2	-3.6
Guinea-Bissau	45	83	70	61	62	135	77	124	61	72	37.9	14.7	1.0
Kenya	363	808	679	556	471	438	459	344	316	308	8.6	12.9	-10.6
Lesotho	83	94	83	74	81	50	62	49	47	36	13.9	0.3	-9.4
Liberia	79	46	63	28	27	39	31	112	33	35	23.9	-19.9	-0.8
Madagascar	119	295	306	231	251	208	195	229	577	373	11.9	11.4	4.8
Malawi	99	238	233	223	175	275	221	263	183	228	-0.7	30.0	-0.2
Mali	172	344	312	256	244	266	285	296	270	264	5.8	0.5	-2.5
Mauritania	70	117	123	125	216	140	126	98	101	71	11.1	9.3	-6.7
Mauritius	33	83	69	37	30	8	11	1	3	22	4.0	13.6	-29.7
Mozambique	150	825	859	1,078	897	801	698	550	653	796	42.9	26.6	-2.3
Namibia	..	43	106	105	136	123	148	136	129	144	..	73.9	13.4
Niger	137	280	295	280	280	286	194	163	190	162	-0.9	7.4	-6.0
Nigeria	23	190	192	147	78	52	73	47	55	38	-17.2	74.4	-20.8
Rwanda	127	201	260	201	222	533	339	251	188	234	4.1	3.1	3.3
São Tomé and Príncipe	2	34	27	28	31	29	62	29	22	20	33.3	32.2	-1.6
Senegal	238	648	471	486	402	519	399	391	307	323	8.5	13.5	-7.3
Seychelles	24	36	19	17	8	8	11	8	7	19	1.5	0.2	-9.6
Sierra Leone	74	44	76	79	117	59	60	67	44	59	16.2	18.1	-3.3
Somalia	182	296	130	532	759	478	119	39	48	47	28.9	6.5	-21.9
South Africa	..	..	..	..	202	234	319	311	436	470	..	..	18.9
Sudan	356	462	412	201	181	191	131	118	90	168	22.9	-1.7	-16.1
Swaziland	43	40	35	29	37	30	38	21	17	19	1.5	-7.5	-3.0
Tanzania	686	928	853	874	718	624	587	603	598	860	5.3	11.2	-3.4
Togo	68	170	139	144	85	69	118	97	80	74	2.8	14.2	-7.5
Uganda	55	269	319	273	384	377	423	368	461	429	25.8	30.5	6.9
Zambia	307	450	651	748	564	475	439	353	386	287	8.7	9.4	-4.9
Zimbabwe	147	325	401	574	342	306	348	280	234	242	61.0	-3.5	-4.0
NORTH AFRICA	2,174	4,641	5,966	4,716	2,914	3,364	2,382	2,622	2,076	2,180	8.4	-4.6	-7.5
Algeria	154	255	343	402	293	408	290	262	202	136	-5.3	-7.2	-1.2
Egypt, Arab Republic	1,554	3,487	4,643	3,208	2,013	2,526	1,690	1,926	1,572	1,645	18.4	-7.5	-6.9
Libya	13	8	3	2	2	2	3	2	2	4	-10.3	4.0	-9.9
Morocco	246	655	682	785	466	348	347	390	226	280	1.5	5.4	-10.2
Tunisia	207	236	295	319	140	79	52	41	73	114	-4.3	6.1	-16.4
ALL AFRICA	7,872	16,532	17,430	16,245	14,127	14,654	12,290	11,676	10,610	11,317	7.5	6.7	-17.6

12-7. Net ODA from non-DAC bilateral donors, real

	Millions of U.S. dollars (constant 1995 prices)										Average annual percentage growth		
	1980	1990	1991	1992	1993	1994	1995	1996	1997	1998	75-84	85-89	90-MR
SUB-SAHARAN AFRICA	898	502	147	45	38	15	11	35	96	54	2.0	-28.4	-29.5
excluding South Africa	898	502	147	45	38	15	11	35	96	54	2.0	-28.4	-29.5
excl. S.Africa & Nigeria	898	502	147	45	38	15	11	35	96	54	2.0	-28.4	-29.5
Angola	1	2	2	1	4	0	0	0	0	0	..	17.6	..
Benin	2	0	-3	0	0	4	7	6	0	-2	1.9	-3.4	..
Botswana	0	-2	2	-2	8	1	0	-2	-4	-3	..	..	..
Burkina Faso	0	12	12	3	0	1	6	2	3	4	8.9	-52.2	8.8
Burundi	5	0	-3	-2	-3	-3	-3	-1	0	-1	28.0	-21.4	..
Cameroon	30	-3	-2	-1	0	0	1	-2	-3	-3	4.6	-72.8	..
Cape Verde	3	0	0	0	1	0	0	3	0	0	-3.2	-21.2	10.4
Central African Republic	3	3	3	0	0	-1	0	1	0	0	-17.0	106.7	..
Chad	0	2	3	0	3	1	1	3	5	5	-27.6	..	27.9
Comoros	22	0	0	0	0	0	0	0	0	0	6.9	-62.7	-13.7
Congo, Democratic Rep. of	7	85	0	2	0	0	0	2	9	3	-63.9	..	12.9
Congo, Republic of	20	0	0	0	0	0	0	0	0	0	11.0	..	..
Côte d'Ivoire	0	0	0	0	0	0	0	0	0	0	..	-99.8	..
Djibouti	43	97	3	-1	11	13	3	5	5	2	-13.1	-47.8	-9.9
Equatorial Guinea	0	0	7	0	0	0	0	0	0	0	..	43.8	..
Eritrea	..	..	..	..	1	13	5	3	17	35	..	..	74.3
Ethiopia	0	74	1	0	1	0	0	0	0	1	7.3	..	-38.2
Gabon	0	0	0	0	0	0	-1	-2	-3	-2	-21.6	..	..
Gambia, The	9	1	2	-2	-2	-2	-2	-2	-3	0	-2.9	..	..
Ghana	33	1	10	-5	-5	-6	-6	-2	9	3	117.9	..	..
Guinea	0	5	-1	-2	-4	-2	6	20	36	26	10.4	7.8	11.3
Guinea-Bissau	2	0	1	3	1	0	0	1	0	0	-6.7	4.6	-27.5
Kenya	0	5	3	-4	-4	-6	2	-3	-1	-2	166.1	-47.8	..
Lesotho	0	0	-1	1	1	0	0	4	7	-1	81.9	..	..
Liberia	12	0	0	0	0	0	0	0	0	0	-69.9	-10.1	..
Madagascar	63	-1	0	0	0	0	0	0	0	0	54.7	..	..
Malawi	0	0	0	0	0	0	0	1	0	0	..	..	..
Mali	43	17	5	4	-5	-12	-14	-8	-6	-6	3.5	-33.1	..
Mauritania	113	27	1	-8	-6	-11	-16	-12	-14	-8	-5.9	-33.2	..
Mauritius	0	1	-2	-1	-2	-1	-2	-4	10	-1	..	1.5	..
Mozambique	27	0	0	2	4	3	2	3	-2	-3	51.0	-10.6	23.8
Namibia	..	0	0	0	0	0	0	0	0	0	..	..	..
Niger	2	4	5	0	2	5	0	0	11	1	16.3	-8.5	-18.5
Nigeria	0	0	0	0	0	0	0	0	0	0	..	-13.5	..
Rwanda	2	11	4	0	3	1	0	1	1	0	-3.9	-9.3	-24.1
São Tomé and Principe	0	0	0	0	0	0	0	0	0	0	..	..	..
Senegal	3	3	24	18	16	2	12	10	9	0	18.1	-27.0	-17.6
Seychelles	0	0	0	0	1	0	-1	3	5	1	..	-39.0	..
Sierra Leone	6	0	0	0	0	0	1	4	1	3	3.5	-24.0	48.5
Somalia	167	90	0	11	10	0	0	0	1	0	-12.3	-44.0	-39.0
South Africa	..	..	..	..	0	0	0	0	0	0	..	..	..
Sudan	210	8	18	21	2	0	1	0	0	0	0.7	-27.5	-42.3
Swaziland	0	0	0	0	0	0	0	0	0	0	..	..	..
Tanzania	36	4	-3	-3	-1	6	4	-3	2	2	45.4	-48.3	3.4
Togo	0	-1	-1	-2	0	0	0	-2	-1	1	-7.2	2.2	..
Uganda	2	47	57	16	1	12	7	8	3	0	-19.5	205.0	-31.9
Zambia	29	0	0	0	0	0	0	0	0	-1	19.3	..	..
Zimbabwe	7	10	-1	-3	-1	-3	-4	-3	-3	-1	15.6	..	..
NORTH AFRICA	967	2,919	1,100	487	429	120	101	47	125	254	-28.4	-24.0	-16.7
Algeria	54	9	2	5	1	3	-12	7	12	21	..	222.2	5.1
Egypt, Arab Republic	5	2,403	570	437	419	103	117	53	102	236	-58.6	..	-28.3
Libya	0	0	0	0	0	0	0	0	0	0	..	..	..
Morocco	843	397	525	56	19	31	19	26	32	33	16.7	-38.7	-28.2
Tunisia	64	110	3	-11	-10	-17	-23	-38	-22	-36	-9.3	14.7	..
ALL AFRICA	1,865	3,420	1,247	533	467	135	113	83	221	308	-14.1	-28.2	-35.7

12-8. Net ODA from multilateral donors, real

	Millions of U.S. dollars (constant 1995 prices)										Average annual percentage growth		
	1980	1990	1991	1992	1993	1994	1995	1996	1997	1998	75-84	85-89	90-MR
SUB-SAHARAN AFRICA	3,089	6,518	7,285	7,894	7,222	8,446	7,928	5,899	5,399	5,374	7.0	12.4	-15.2
excluding South Africa	3,089	6,518	7,285	7,894	7,120	8,358	7,860	5,853	5,315	5,272	7.0	12.4	-15.3
excl. S.Africa & Nigeria	3,065	6,434	7,184	7,764	6,891	8,202	7,721	5,710	5,159	5,082	7.1	12.4	-15.4
Angola	21	114	133	162	151	247	176	178	134	135	42.6	7.3	5.9
Benin	69	157	122	105	154	121	96	117	76	76	3.2	16.2	-6.4
Botswana	30	30	29	22	47	31	35	8	73	40	6.1	0.1	-0.7
Burkina Faso	80	89	156	175	234	183	231	143	154	187	0.6	-0.4	7.1
Burundi	71	117	154	175	104	226	182	44	19	37	9.2	12.8	-16.4
Cameroon	93	120	158	147	18	365	97	133	179	138	-4.0	31.2	0.8
Cape Verde	31	35	28	42	39	43	40	36	45	50	2.8	-3.3	4.4
Central African Republic	44	163	82	75	59	79	43	44	31	71	3.9	9.1	-11.3
Chad	20	141	139	97	84	119	109	170	133	99	-2.6	11.9	-1.4
Comoros	18	16	37	27	22	23	20	17	13	19	23.5	-12.2	-2.6
Congo, Democratic Rep. of	138	206	149	112	87	162	78	57	47	49	5.2	20.8	-18.4
Congo, Republic of	28	18	18	13	8	119	20	35	9	6	-2.2	-16.9	-2.4
Côte d'Ivoire	77	173	219	245	61	845	486	513	224	345	-11.4	84.0	11.3
Djibouti	11	19	24	23	32	25	22	21	20	19	37.3	-14.5	1.9
Equatorial Guinea	11	19	23	28	28	15	12	7	7	7	28.5	22.5	-15.2
Eritrea	..	..	..	..	20	54	49	29	27	43	..	..	3.5
Ethiopia	158	482	703	771	741	551	357	368	208	315	9.0	11.1	-8.5
Gabon	9	6	3	4	4	21	9	15	12	10	3.7	7.2	7.9
Gambia, The	40	46	49	67	41	37	23	22	24	28	13.9	14.3	-10.2
Ghana	78	326	473	304	341	241	298	302	198	362	12.4	23.8	-4.6
Guinea	75	165	231	232	251	191	191	143	233	209	29.0	18.3	0.2
Guinea-Bissau	31	59	57	48	37	53	39	52	69	35	19.4	13.1	-2.5
Kenya	157	490	345	396	537	306	270	247	152	224	11.5	36.1	-11.0
Lesotho	40	63	57	78	75	77	52	51	42	39	9.0	7.9	-6.2
Liberia	38	77	113	100	107	30	91	58	46	46	7.6	-9.9	-1.5
Madagascar	120	144	203	158	149	108	106	126	299	180	3.6	11.2	-0.1
Malawi	89	315	351	390	371	236	211	227	179	257	16.4	16.3	-5.7
Mali	135	169	188	202	161	228	270	201	187	130	2.2	8.7	-0.3
Mauritania	47	117	119	98	149	163	120	184	162	129	1.8	8.7	3.9
Mauritius	10	14	8	12	1	8	14	22	30	24	-6.8	16.3	12.7
Mozambique	45	277	335	486	400	508	364	332	343	368	37.7	25.1	2.0
Namibia	..	90	97	48	34	27	44	51	44	57	..	33.4	-1.1
Niger	83	152	117	111	97	121	80	90	148	163	-4.9	9.4	0.2
Nigeria	24	84	101	129	229	156	140	143	156	190	-1.0	8.3	12.5
Rwanda	75	107	140	175	168	247	363	213	53	157	6.7	5.7	1.8
São Tomé and Principe	4	26	30	33	20	26	23	19	13	11	11.6	20.8	-9.3
Senegal	104	249	214	214	135	179	254	176	128	236	1.8	24.4	-1.8
Seychelles	4	4	7	4	13	6	2	8	6	6	24.9	0.5	1.8
Sierra Leone	39	23	40	63	113	242	146	112	80	56	10.1	-1.8	14.4
Somalia	218	156	78	156	211	109	70	48	36	43	12.2	-5.1	-16.2
South Africa	..	..	..	..	102	88	67	46	84	102	..	..	-1.3
Sudan	252	434	546	357	317	257	108	100	55	65	8.4	4.2	-22.6
Swaziland	23	20	24	28	21	31	18	10	11	15	3.7	9.0	-7.0
Tanzania	167	358	356	562	331	426	286	273	392	255	11.6	11.0	-1.7
Togo	51	116	85	96	21	67	74	62	53	68	6.1	5.7	-6.4
Uganda	92	419	368	487	288	431	400	296	390	98	24.3	13.3	-6.3
Zambia	81	78	335	360	399	311	1,594	254	255	104	18.8	-7.5	9.2
Zimbabwe	61	38	39	277	209	309	147	93	121	72	127.5	-4.8	9.5
NORTH AFRICA	407	313	725	525	726	726	415	604	839	949	-4.4	2.4	8.7
Algeria	22	24	33	28	91	48	34	35	46	282	-11.3	19.8	13.4
Egypt, Arab Republic	256	88	399	212	212	311	208	211	408	299	-3.2	-5.3	7.9
Libya	9	13	25	4	2	2	3	6	5	4	-4.0	22.2	-13.6
Morocco	86	102	167	171	301	311	128	232	228	278	6.7	4.0	13.2
Tunisia	33	86	101	109	121	53	41	120	151	85	-4.5	14.6	1.6
ALL AFRICA	3,496	6,831	8,009	8,418	7,948	9,172	8,343	6,503	6,238	6,323	4.6	11.7	-14.9

Note: In 1995, Zambia completed a 3 year Rights Arrangement Program permitting disbursement of 833.4 M SDR under a new SAF/ESAF arrangement.

12-9. Net ODA from all donors as share of recipient GDP

	Percentage of GDP									Annual average		
	1980	1990	1991	1992	1993	1994	1995	1996	1997	75-84	85-89	90-MR
SUB-SAHARAN AFRICA	2.5	5.9	5.7	6.0	5.8	6.6	5.9	5.0	4.3	2.6	4.9	5.7
excluding South Africa	3.8	9.4	9.3	10.2	10.0	12.1	10.5	8.2	6.9	3.9	7.2	9.6
excl. S.Africa & Nigeria	6.5	11.0	10.8	12.4	11.4	14.3	12.5	10.0	8.6	6.1	8.4	11.4
Angola	..	2.6	2.3	6.1	5.6	11.1	8.3	7.1	5.8	..	1.8	6.1
Benin	6.4	14.6	14.3	16.6	13.7	17.2	14.0	13.3	10.4	7.0	11.1	14.3
Botswana	9.6	4.1	3.3	2.7	2.9	1.9	1.9	1.5	2.4	9.8	6.4	2.6
Burkina Faso	12.4	12.1	15.2	22.0	22.9	23.5	20.7	16.5	14.7	12.4	13.1	18.5
Burundi	12.8	23.4	22.2	28.7	22.4	33.9	28.8	22.6	13.3	11.9	16.6	24.4
Cameroon	3.9	4.0	4.2	6.3	4.6	9.3	5.6	4.5	5.1	3.6	2.4	5.4
Cape Verde	..	36.2	33.1	34.1	35.6	35.0	26.8	28.3	25.8	..	34.6	31.9
Central African Republic	13.9	16.9	12.4	12.4	13.3	19.5	14.9	15.6	9.5	12.8	14.0	14.3
Chad	3.4	19.7	15.0	13.5	16.4	18.2	16.6	18.6	13.4	8.7	18.2	16.4
Comoros	35.1	18.5	26.3	18.3	19.0	21.5	20.2	18.8	14.6	36.9	29.0	19.7
Congo, Democratic Rep. of	..	9.6	5.2	3.3	2.0	3.4	3.1	2.9	2.6	3.8	6.5	4.0
Congo, Republic of	5.4	7.8	4.9	3.9	6.4	20.5	5.9	17.0	11.6	6.4	4.6	9.8
Côte d'Ivoire	2.1	6.4	6.0	6.8	7.4	20.8	12.1	9.0	4.3	1.9	2.8	9.1
Djibouti	..	45.8	23.8	24.1	28.4	26.5	21.6	20.1	16.4	..	25.1	25.8
Equatorial Guinea	..	46.8	48.3	40.3	34.9	24.1	20.6	12.0	5.5	1.1	35.1	29.1
Eritrea	..	..	..	0.0	16.7	31.0	26.1	24.9	16.9	..	..	19.3
Ethiopia	..	14.9	20.6	21.2	17.5	22.0	15.4	14.1	10.0	5.1	10.0	17.0
Gabon	1.3	2.2	2.7	1.2	2.3	4.3	2.9	2.2	0.8	1.6	2.5	2.3
Gambia, The	22.6	31.6	32.4	32.5	23.6	19.5	12.5	9.8	12.1	19.6	38.4	21.8
Ghana	4.3	9.6	13.4	9.6	10.4	10.0	10.1	9.4	8.8	3.6	8.7	10.2
Guinea	..	10.5	12.7	13.7	12.5	10.5	11.3	7.5	8.3	..	11.2	10.9
Guinea-Bissau	53.7	53.2	44.9	46.5	40.4	74.5	45.9	66.5	44.8	37.3	55.4	52.1
Kenya	5.5	13.9	11.5	11.1	18.3	9.5	8.1	6.6	5.0	5.5	8.6	10.5
Lesotho	25.6	22.9	21.6	21.9	20.4	15.4	13.5	12.5	9.5	24.7	29.9	17.2
Liberia	8.8	..	..	..	..	..	..	..	..	7.4	6.9	..
Madagascar	5.7	13.0	17.0	12.1	10.8	9.7	9.6	9.1	23.6	4.6	11.0	13.1
Malawi	11.6	28.0	23.8	31.9	24.0	40.0	29.6	22.1	14.2	11.1	21.4	26.7
Mali	15.0	20.1	18.9	15.3	13.7	23.9	22.1	19.0	17.4	15.0	22.8	18.8
Mauritania	21.6	21.1	19.5	17.0	34.8	26.2	21.6	25.0	22.6	24.2	22.3	23.5
Mauritius	2.9	3.4	2.4	1.4	0.8	0.4	0.6	0.5	0.8	3.6	3.0	1.3
Mozambique	4.8	40.1	42.9	75.1	56.3	54.3	46.0	32.5	27.5	5.8	24.5	46.8
Namibia	0.0	5.0	7.2	4.9	5.7	4.5	5.7	5.9	5.1	0.0	1.2	5.5
Niger	6.8	16.1	16.2	15.8	21.6	24.1	14.4	13.0	16.9	9.9	16.9	17.3
Nigeria	0.1	0.9	1.0	0.8	1.3	0.8	0.8	0.5	0.5	0.1	0.5	0.8
Rwanda	13.4	11.3	19.0	17.4	18.2	95.2	53.6	48.5	31.9	12.5	10.5	36.9
São Tomé and Principe	9.1	109.8	90.8	125.2	98.5	101.1	185.2	104.7	76.8	20.7	46.9	111.5
Senegal	8.8	14.4	11.6	11.2	9.3	17.7	14.9	12.1	9.1	10.5	13.7	12.5
Seychelles	14.7	9.8	6.1	4.4	4.1	2.7	2.6	3.7	2.3	14.5	10.1	4.5
Sierra Leone	7.6	7.0	13.0	19.5	27.1	29.8	23.9	20.8	14.8	4.6	8.0	19.5
Somalia	71.8	53.9	..	..	..	..	..	..	..	42.1	46.8	53.9
South Africa	0.0	0.0	0.0	0.0	0.2	0.2	0.3	0.3	0.4	0.0	0.0	0.2
Sudan	8.2	6.3	7.7	8.6	5.8	5.1	3.3	3.2	1.9	6.6	6.1	5.2
Swaziland	8.6	6.4	6.1	5.5	5.4	5.3	4.4	2.5	2.1	7.9	6.2	4.7
Tanzania	..	27.8	22.8	27.4	20.9	23.0	17.8	15.3	12.8	..	21.8	21.0
Togo	8.0	16.0	12.6	13.2	7.9	12.8	14.7	11.3	8.1	10.0	14.0	12.1
Uganda	9.1	15.6	20.1	25.5	19.0	18.8	14.4	11.3	13.3	7.2	5.9	17.2
Zambia	8.2	14.6	26.2	32.5	26.6	21.5	58.6	18.7	15.4	6.3	16.5	26.8
Zimbabwe	2.5	3.9	4.6	11.7	7.6	8.2	6.9	4.4	3.9	1.6	3.8	6.4
NORTH AFRICA	2.1	5.0	5.6	4.0	2.7	2.8	1.9	1.9	1.6	3.0	1.7	3.2
Algeria	0.4	0.4	0.7	0.8	0.7	1.0	0.8	0.7	0.5	0.5	0.3	0.7
Egypt, Arab Republic	6.1	12.6	13.6	8.6	5.1	5.2	3.4	3.3	2.5	10.3	4.4	6.8
Libya	0.0	..	..	..	..	..	..	..	..	0.0	0.0	..
Morocco	4.8	4.1	4.4	3.3	2.7	2.1	1.5	1.8	1.3	3.8	2.9	2.6
Tunisia	2.7	3.2	2.7	2.5	1.6	0.7	0.4	0.6	1.1	3.5	2.6	1.6
ALL AFRICA	2.4	5.6	5.7	5.4	4.7	5.3	4.6	3.9	3.3	2.7	3.7	4.8

Note: Nigeria's ratios are distorted for 1994-95 because of official exchange rate over-valuation affecting oil exports and oil value added (see chapter 3).

12-10. Net ODA from DAC donors as share of recipient GDP

					Percentage of GDP							*Annual average*		
	1980	*1990*	*1991*	*1992*	*1993*	*1994*	*1995*	*1996*	*1997*	*1998*	*1999*	*75-84*	*85-89*	*90-MR*
SUB-SAHARAN AFRICA	2.2	5.9	5.6	6.0	3.3	3.5	3.1	2.7	2.4	2.5	2.3	2.3	4.6	3.7
excluding South Africa	2.2	5.9	5.6	6.0	6.0	6.7	5.7	4.7	4.0	4.1	3.7	2.3	4.6	5.2
excl. S.Africa & Nigeria	3.6	6.9	6.5	7.3	6.9	8.0	6.9	5.8	4.9	4.9	4.5	3.3	5.4	6.3
Angola	..	1.6	1.3	3.4	2.9	5.5	4.7	3.9	3.0	3.3	2.9	..	1.2	3.2
Benin	2.5	6.8	8.5	10.5	7.0	9.5	8.8	7.5	6.9	6.2	4.9	3.6	6.1	7.7
Botswana	7.4	3.2	2.7	2.3	1.9	1.3	1.1	1.4	1.1	1.5	0.7	7.8	5.0	1.7
Burkina Faso	8.8	8.6	9.7	13.4	12.4	14.3	10.7	10.6	9.2	8.8	9.0	8.3	8.9	10.7
Burundi	6.5	13.9	10.5	13.7	13.4	11.7	10.8	7.5	4.0	5.1	7.3	6.3	7.5	9.8
Cameroon	2.5	3.0	3.0	5.1	4.4	5.1	4.3	3.1	3.6	3.5	2.8	2.5	1.9	3.8
Cape Verde	36.5	22.4	22.5	20.3	22.4	19.8	15.7	15.4	13.4	15.8	15.3	30.6	28.0	18.3
Central African Republic	9.4	6.7	7.0	7.4	9.0	11.0	10.9	11.3	6.1	5.4	5.6	8.2	8.0	8.1
Chad	2.0	10.5	7.3	7.9	10.0	8.8	8.8	7.6	6.4	4.4	4.2	4.7	9.6	7.6
Comoros	10.9	12.2	12.4	8.7	10.9	9.6	10.1	10.3	7.9	9.4	6.8	14.0	15.6	9.8
Congo, Democratic Rep. of	2.2	6.8	3.8	2.0	1.1	1.4	1.9	1.8	1.7	1.1	1.1	1.8	4.1	2.3
Congo, Republic of	3.2	7.2	4.3	3.5	6.1	14.3	4.2	15.5	11.2	3.1	5.5	3.8	4.0	7.5
Côte d'Ivoire	1.5	4.9	4.1	4.7	6.8	10.7	7.3	4.2	2.2	4.4	3.3	1.5	2.0	5.3
Djibouti	..	20.8	18.2	19.6	19.9	19.3	16.2	14.6	12.4	12.0	..	..	16.2	17.0
Equatorial Guinea	..	33.0	27.0	23.3	18.2	13.1	13.2	9.0	3.6	4.0	2.1	..	19.7	14.6
Eritrea	..	..	..	..	11.8	18.8	16.5	20.2	12.4	14.4	12.5	..	..	15.2
Ethiopia	..	7.5	8.7	8.2	6.7	11.6	9.1	7.5	5.9	5.6	5.0	1.9	5.6	7.6
Gabon	1.1	2.1	2.6	1.2	2.2	3.8	2.7	2.0	0.6	0.8	0.8	1.3	2.2	1.9
Gambia, The	6.8	18.0	17.4	14.5	13.6	10.5	6.6	4.4	4.2	3.2	3.4	8.7	21.8	9.6
Ghana	2.4	4.5	6.8	5.2	5.2	6.1	5.6	5.0	4.2	5.0	4.6	2.0	3.6	5.2
Guinea	..	4.9	5.7	7.1	5.6	5.4	5.9	3.4	3.2	3.9	3.0	..	6.3	4.8
Guinea-Bissau	31.1	30.9	24.2	25.1	23.8	52.4	30.3	46.1	21.8	31.5	14.7	21.9	27.6	30.1
Kenya	3.8	8.6	7.6	6.5	8.6	5.6	5.1	3.8	2.8	2.4	2.4	4.3	6.2	5.3
Lesotho	14.8	13.7	10.9	8.4	9.0	5.4	6.6	5.2	4.4	3.7	2.9	12.8	15.5	7.0
Liberia	5.4	..	..	..	..	..	..	..	..	..	..	5.1	4.8	..
Madagascar	2.2	8.7	10.2	7.2	6.8	6.4	6.2	5.8	15.5	8.9	5.2	2.4	6.3	8.1
Malawi	6.1	12.0	9.5	11.6	7.7	21.2	15.5	10.9	6.9	11.7	12.6	6.3	10.4	11.9
Mali	7.3	12.9	11.5	8.4	8.3	13.8	11.6	11.4	10.4	9.0	9.1	8.0	14.2	10.6
Mauritania	7.6	10.4	9.8	9.8	20.8	12.5	11.8	8.9	8.8	6.4	9.2	6.7	13.4	10.8
Mauritius	2.2	2.9	2.2	1.1	0.8	0.2	0.3	0.0	0.1	0.5	0.1	2.3	2.5	0.8
Mozambique	3.3	29.9	30.8	51.5	38.7	32.3	29.2	19.0	17.7	18.2	14.3	4.3	18.7	28.2
Namibia	..	1.7	3.8	3.5	4.7	3.8	4.6	4.4	3.8	4.2	3.8	0.0	0.8	3.8
Niger	4.2	10.3	11.4	11.2	15.8	16.7	10.3	8.2	9.8	7.0	6.0	5.9	10.7	10.7
Nigeria	0.0	0.6	0.6	0.4	0.3	0.2	0.3	0.1	0.1	0.1	0.2	0.1	0.4	0.3
Rwanda	8.3	7.1	12.2	9.2	10.3	64.7	26.4	17.9	9.6	10.3	9.2	7.9	6.0	17.7
São Tomé and Principe	2.8	62.0	42.4	57.3	59.5	53.2	135.2	64.3	48.2	44.4	40.7	6.1	18.7	60.7
Senegal	6.1	10.3	7.7	7.5	6.7	13.0	8.9	8.4	6.7	6.2	8.7	6.5	8.6	8.4
Seychelles	12.4	8.9	4.5	3.6	1.4	1.5	2.2	1.5	1.2	3.2	0.9	13.0	7.2	2.9
Sierra Leone	4.9	4.4	8.4	10.7	13.7	5.8	6.9	7.1	4.9	7.9	8.9	2.5	4.7	7.9
Somalia	23.1	29.4	..	..	..	..	..	..	..	..	..	13.4	30.1	29.4
South Africa	..	..	..	..	0.1	0.2	0.2	0.2	0.3	0.3	0.3	..	..	0.2
Sudan	3.6	3.2	3.2	2.9	2.1	2.1	1.8	1.6	0.8	1.5	1.6	2.5	3.3	2.1
Swaziland	5.6	4.2	3.5	2.7	3.4	2.6	3.0	1.7	1.2	1.4	1.2	5.1	4.1	2.5
Tanzania	..	19.8	15.4	17.7	15.3	12.6	11.2	9.3	7.4	9.0	7.0	8.1	14.6	12.5
Togo	4.6	9.5	7.8	8.0	6.3	6.5	9.0	6.6	5.0	4.7	3.3	5.7	8.0	6.7
Uganda	3.4	5.7	8.6	8.9	10.8	8.6	7.4	6.1	7.0	5.7	5.6	1.6	2.1	7.4
Zambia	6.0	12.4	17.3	22.0	15.6	13.0	12.7	10.8	9.4	7.9	10.8	4.8	12.9	13.2
Zimbabwe	1.7	3.4	4.2	7.9	4.7	4.1	4.9	3.3	2.6	3.2	3.9	1.2	3.3	4.2
NORTH AFRICA	1.3	2.9	4.3	3.3	1.9	2.2	1.6	1.5	1.1	1.0	0.9	1.4	1.5	2.1
Algeria	0.3	0.4	0.7	0.8	0.5	0.9	0.7	0.6	0.4	0.3	0.1	0.4	0.2	0.5
Egypt, Arab Republic	5.2	7.4	11.2	7.2	3.9	4.5	2.8	2.9	2.0	1.8	1.5	4.6	4.1	4.5
Libya	0.0	..	..	..	..	..	..	..	..	..	..	0.0	0.0	..
Morocco	1.0	2.3	2.2	2.6	1.6	1.0	1.1	1.1	0.6	0.7	1.0	1.4	1.9	1.4
Tunisia	1.8	1.7	2.0	1.9	0.9	0.5	0.3	0.2	0.4	0.5	0.5	2.5	1.9	0.9
ALL AFRICA	1.8	4.6	5.1	4.8	2.9	3.1	2.6	2.3	1.9	2.0	1.8	1.9	3.1	3.1

Note: Nigeria's ratios are distorted for 1994-95 because of official exchange rate over-valuation affecting oil exports and oil value added (see chapter 3).

12-11. Net ODA from multilateral donors as share of recipient GDP

	Percentage of GDP											Annual average		
	1980	1990	1991	1992	1993	1994	1995	1996	1997	1998	1999	75-84	85-89	90-MR
SUB-SAHARAN AFRICA	1.2	3.2	3.5	4.2	2.2	2.7	2.5	1.8	1.5	1.5	1.4	1.2	2.5	2.4
excluding South Africa	1.2	3.2	3.5	4.2	4.0	5.2	4.7	3.1	2.6	2.5	2.4	1.2	2.5	3.5
excl. S.Africa & Nigeria	2.0	3.7	4.1	5.1	4.5	6.2	5.5	3.8	3.1	2.9	2.8	1.8	2.9	4.2
Angola	..	1.0	1.0	2.6	2.6	5.6	3.4	2.4	1.7	1.9	1.6	..	0.6	2.4
Benin	3.8	7.7	5.8	6.1	6.6	7.4	4.8	5.3	3.4	2.9	3.9	3.3	4.8	5.4
Botswana	2.0	0.7	0.7	0.5	1.0	0.6	0.7	0.2	1.4	0.7	0.3	2.1	1.6	0.7
Burkina Faso	3.6	2.9	5.0	8.2	10.3	9.0	9.8	5.7	6.2	6.5	6.1	3.9	3.9	7.0
Burundi	5.9	9.4	11.8	15.1	10.0	22.3	18.2	4.9	1.9	3.7	3.1	5.2	8.4	10.0
Cameroon	1.1	1.0	1.1	1.2	0.1	4.2	1.2	1.5	1.9	1.4	2.0	1.0	0.5	1.6
Cape Verde	22.0	9.3	7.3	10.0	9.8	9.6	8.2	7.3	8.5	8.3	8.3	15.6	13.5	8.7
Central African Republic	4.2	10.0	5.2	4.9	4.1	8.4	3.8	4.2	3.0	6.0	5.5	4.4	5.8	5.5
Chad	1.5	7.4	6.6	4.8	5.2	9.2	7.6	10.7	8.4	5.2	7.6	3.6	7.6	7.3
Comoros	10.8	5.8	13.4	9.4	7.5	11.3	9.3	8.1	6.2	8.4	4.3	14.1	12.4	8.4
Congo, Democratic Rep. of	0.7	2.0	1.5	1.3	0.9	2.1	1.2	1.0	0.7	0.6	0.6	0.8	2.5	1.2
Congo, Republic of	1.3	0.6	0.6	0.4	0.4	6.2	0.8	1.4	0.4	0.3	0.9	1.9	0.6	1.2
Côte d'Ivoire	0.6	1.5	1.9	2.1	0.5	10.1	4.9	4.8	2.0	2.7	0.7	0.5	0.8	3.1
Djibouti	..	4.1	4.7	4.6	6.2	4.7	4.5	4.4	3.7	3.3	..	..	5.1	4.5
Equatorial Guinea	..	12.9	16.0	16.8	16.5	10.6	7.3	2.9	1.3	1.4	0.8	0.7	15.3	8.7
Eritrea	..	..	..	4.4	9.7	8.6	4.5	3.9	5.6	7.7	..	..	6.3	
Ethiopia	..	6.4	11.8	12.9	10.7	10.3	6.2	6.1	3.1	4.3	4.7	2.8	4.4	7.7
Gabon	0.2	0.1	0.1	0.1	0.1	0.5	0.2	0.3	0.2	0.2	0.3	0.2	0.2	0.2
Gambia, The	12.8	13.2	13.8	17.9	10.1	9.2	6.0	5.6	5.6	5.9	4.8	8.5	16.9	9.2
Ghana	1.3	5.0	6.4	4.4	5.2	4.0	4.6	4.3	2.7	4.3	3.2	1.4	5.1	4.4
Guinea	..	5.3	6.8	6.6	6.9	5.1	5.1	3.6	5.7	4.9	2.9	..	4.4	5.3
Guinea-Bissau	21.4	21.8	20.0	19.7	14.3	20.5	15.2	19.1	24.4	15.1	9.3	13.1	24.8	17.9
Kenya	1.6	5.2	3.8	4.6	9.8	3.9	3.0	2.7	1.4	1.8	0.5	1.2	2.3	3.7
Lesotho	7.1	9.1	7.6	8.8	8.3	8.4	5.6	5.4	3.9	4.0	0.8	8.0	10.7	6.2
Liberia	2.6	..	..	..	..	..	..	..	..	..	..	2.1	2.1	
Madagascar	2.3	4.3	6.8	4.9	4.0	3.3	3.4	3.2	8.0	4.3	4.5	1.9	4.8	4.7
Malawi	5.5	15.9	14.3	20.3	16.2	18.2	14.8	9.4	6.7	13.2	11.8	4.8	11.0	14.1
Mali	5.8	6.4	6.9	6.6	5.5	11.8	10.9	7.7	7.2	4.4	4.5	5.6	7.5	7.2
Mauritania	5.1	10.4	9.5	7.7	14.3	14.6	11.3	16.6	14.1	11.5	13.0	7.6	8.2	12.3
Mauritius	0.7	0.5	0.3	0.4	0.0	0.2	0.3	0.5	0.7	0.5	0.9	1.2	0.4	0.4
Mozambique	1.0	10.0	12.0	23.2	17.2	20.5	15.2	11.5	9.3	8.4	11.4	1.3	5.6	13.9
Namibia	..	3.5	3.5	1.6	1.2	0.8	1.4	1.6	1.3	1.7	2.0	..	0.4	1.9
Niger	2.5	5.6	4.5	4.4	5.5	7.1	4.2	4.6	7.7	7.0	3.3	3.1	6.0	5.4
Nigeria	0.0	0.3	0.3	0.4	1.0	0.6	0.5	0.4	0.4	0.5	0.3	0.0	0.1	0.5
Rwanda	4.9	3.8	6.5	8.0	7.8	29.9	28.2	15.2	2.7	7.0	9.8	4.3	4.2	11.9
São Tomé and Principe	6.3	47.3	47.8	66.7	38.5	47.8	49.9	41.4	27.7	24.8	17.9	14.6	28.3	41.0
Senegal	2.6	4.0	3.5	3.3	2.2	4.5	5.7	3.8	2.8	4.5	2.4	3.2	4.4	3.7
Seychelles	2.3	0.9	1.6	1.0	2.6	1.2	0.5	1.6	1.1	1.1	1.1	1.3	2.5	1.3
Sierra Leone	2.6	2.3	4.5	8.6	13.2	23.9	16.9	12.0	9.0	7.5	2.0	2.0	2.9	10.0
Somalia	27.5	15.5	..	..	..	..	..	..	..	..	..	15.9	16.0	15.5
South Africa	..	..	..	..	0.1	0.1	0.0	0.0	0.1	0.1	0.1	..	..	0.1
Sudan	2.5	3.0	4.3	5.2	3.6	2.9	1.5	1.4	0.5	0.6	0.6	1.8	1.9	2.4
Swaziland	3.0	2.1	2.5	2.7	1.9	2.7	1.4	0.8	0.8	1.1	1.1	2.7	2.1	1.7
Tanzania	..	7.7	6.4	11.4	7.0	8.6	5.4	4.2	4.9	2.7	4.3	2.9	4.1	6.3
Togo	3.4	6.5	4.8	5.3	1.6	6.3	5.7	4.2	3.4	4.3	1.5	4.2	5.7	4.3
Uganda	5.6	8.9	9.9	15.9	8.1	9.9	7.0	4.9	5.9	1.3	3.6	2.2	3.7	7.5
Zambia	1.6	2.2	8.9	10.6	11.0	8.5	45.9	7.8	6.2	2.9	9.0	1.1	3.6	11.3
Zimbabwe	0.7	0.4	0.4	3.8	2.9	4.1	2.1	1.1	1.3	1.0	0.5	0.4	0.5	1.7
NORTH AFRICA	0.2	0.2	0.5	0.4	0.5	0.5	0.3	0.4	0.5	0.5	0.4	0.5	0.1	0.4
Algeria	0.0	0.0	0.1	0.1	0.2	0.1	0.1	0.1	0.1	0.5	0.0	0.1	0.0	0.1
Egypt, Arab Republic	0.9	0.2	1.0	0.5	0.4	0.5	0.3	0.3	0.5	0.3	0.2	2.2	0.2	0.4
Libya	0.0	..	..	..	..	..	..	..	..	..	..	0.0	0.0	..
Morocco	0.4	0.4	0.5	0.6	1.0	0.9	0.4	0.6	0.6	0.7	0.9	0.3	0.2	0.7
Tunisia	0.3	0.6	0.7	0.7	0.7	0.3	0.2	0.6	0.8	0.4	0.8	0.4	0.5	0.6
ALL AFRICA	0.8	1.9	2.3	2.5	1.6	2.0	1.7	1.3	1.1	1.1	1.0	0.9	1.4	1.7

Note: Nigeria's ratios are distorted for 1994-95 because of official exchange rate over-valuation affecting oil exports and oil value added (see chapter 3).

12-12. Net ODA from all donors as share of recipient GDI

	1980	1990	1991	1992	1993	1994	1995	1996	1997	1998	1999	75-84	85-89	90-MR
					Percentage of GDI								*Annual average*	
SUB-SAHARAN AFRICA	19.5	58.5	54.2	61.4	35.2	36.0	31.2	26.8	22.4	21.3	19.0	20.3	44.9	36.6
excluding South Africa	19.5	58.5	54.2	61.4	59.6	64.0	60.5	47.5	36.1	31.9	27.8	20.3	44.9	50.1
excl. S.Africa & Nigeria	33.7	67.9	68.4	81.7	72.9	76.9	71.5	56.2	43.2	41.1	35.1	30.5	51.9	61.5
Angola	..	22.4	17.7	165.5	49.2	66.7	198.6	..	18.2	21.6	14.0	..	12.7	63.8
Benin	42.4	102.2	97.9	120.5	88.9	108.5	71.2	76.3	55.7	53.4	49.0	40.9	91.4	82.3
Botswana	25.5	12.3	11.1	9.4	11.7	7.2	6.8	5.9	10.5	10.6	5.2	31.0	28.0	9.1
Burkina Faso	72.9	58.2	73.1	103.0	110.2	113.4	86.9	61.2	56.5	52.1	55.4	64.1	60.5	77.0
Burundi	91.9	160.5	153.3	191.2	141.8	319.3	300.0	102.3	72.8	99.5	114.0	89.3	108.0	165.5
Cameroon	18.7	22.4	24.9	43.9	27.7	60.6	38.4	29.4	33.8	26.5	24.3	15.0	11.3	33.2
Cape Verde	116.9	139.1	113.8	87.7	81.4	68.0	56.3	61.2	58.6	65.1	62.6	95.0	131.5	79.4
Central African Republic	198.7	136.7	99.9	101.1	129.1	165.6	109.3	357.4	101.4	84.7	77.9	129.1	115.2	136.3
Chad	..	113.2	215.0	170.1	157.3	108.5	159.4	123.7	102.0	62.1	118.7	159.7	219.0	133.0
Comoros	105.7	92.1	127.0	81.3	89.9	99.5	110.5	136.8	90.7	107.8	76.3	114.1	120.1	101.2
Congo, Democratic Rep. of	29.8	106.0	94.0	47.5	112.7	43.4	32.9	39.6	36.2	22.3	16.1	23.1	47.1	55.1
Congo, Republic of	15.1	49.0	24.0	17.9	21.8	37.6	16.2	28.1	51.7	12.5	28.4	19.5	22.2	28.7
Côte d'Ivoire	7.8	95.2	81.7	98.0	88.5	165.7	89.7	67.1	26.3	39.0	24.5	8.9	25.3	77.6
Djibouti	..	..	164.1	125.7	163.7	225.5	250.3	216.1	180.2	..	..	..	..	189.4
Equatorial Guinea	..	264.5	94.3	165.7	158.2	32.0	26.8	10.5	7.4	6.0	7.0	7.8	..	77.2
Eritrea	..	..	..	..	108.2	173.5	134.8	86.2	45.9	52.0	48.6	..	..	92.7
Ethiopia	..	125.5	207.6	230.0	122.6	144.4	92.9	80.6	52.7	57.4	54.4	37.2	70.3	116.8
Gabon	4.7	10.3	10.0	5.5	10.3	19.8	12.3	9.4	2.4	2.6	3.9	4.1	7.7	8.6
Gambia, The	84.7	140.0	145.4	143.6	110.4	105.9	60.5	43.2	53.8	49.3	47.3	100.5	225.0	89.9
Ghana	76.7	66.2	84.1	74.6	46.5	41.9	50.3	41.9	28.4	39.8	33.7	60.8	78.5	50.7
Guinea	..	59.3	69.5	78.3	69.8	67.9	68.2	44.6	57.1	55.7	37.4	..	69.1	60.8
Guinea-Bissau	190.7	176.2	143.8	95.1	125.2	335.5	203.9	285.4	213.3	410.7	147.1	158.2	161.6	213.6
Kenya	22.3	70.5	63.9	80.8	103.2	57.5	46.1	38.0	27.3	28.4	21.4	27.3	42.0	53.7
Lesotho	59.0	42.8	28.3	26.0	31.7	24.9	20.1	19.0	16.7	16.0	4.5	72.0	61.0	23.0
Liberia	32.1	..	..	..	..	..	..	..	..	..	..	44.5	94.0	..
Madagascar	38.1	76.2	208.4	107.0	94.0	89.1	87.1	76.7	198.3	106.0	74.6	47.1	101.1	111.7
Malawi	46.8	141.4	117.3	159.6	157.5	135.7	177.9	175.1	111.7	185.6	166.2	49.5	125.0	152.8
Mali	96.7	86.6	82.0	69.4	62.2	91.5	95.8	81.9	84.0	62.9	64.0	103.7	117.1	78.0
Mauritania	94.3	116.5	107.8	87.1	166.8	125.5	111.8	131.2	123.4	90.5	128.1	106.9	97.3	118.9
Mauritius	14.1	10.9	8.3	4.9	2.6	1.3	2.3	1.8	3.6	4.0	3.5	15.1	11.6	4.3
Mozambique	80.8	256.0	267.0	479.5	440.2	267.2	194.7	146.5	147.1	113.4	9.1	99.7	215.3	232.1
Namibia	..	15.3	38.9	23.0	35.0	19.3	28.0	26.4	28.5	29.8	28.7	0.0	8.8	27.3
Niger	24.1	197.3	214.3	224.8	334.2	231.9	198.9	132.3	165.9	124.6	90.7	84.2	127.1	191.5
Nigeria	0.3	5.9	4.1	3.6	5.6	4.1	4.6	3.8	3.2	2.2	1.8	0.6	3.2	3.9
Rwanda	82.8	76.9	134.8	120.2	125.1	809.8	363.9	214.1	82.6	110.2	133.8	85.9	68.5	217.1
São Tomé and Principe	26.6	303.2	243.8	318.5	248.9	268.5	485.9	239.1	194.2	154.6	146.6	66.1	148.7	260.3
Senegal	75.1	104.0	89.7	74.9	65.4	94.7	89.0	67.4	53.5	57.8	59.1	81.6	116.5	75.5
Seychelles	38.5	39.7	27.5	20.9	14.5	10.2	8.4	7.3	8.6	11.9	6.3	43.6	43.9	15.5
Sierra Leone	44.0	72.0	122.2	234.4	348.7	348.6	425.0	177.1	..	297.7	3,751.0	38.4	86.9	641.9
Somalia	169.3	347.2	..	..	..	..	..	..	..	..	..	156.0	166.2	347.2
South Africa	..	..	..	..	1.5	1.4	1.4	1.5	2.1	2.4	2.6	..	..	1.8
Sudan	55.9	..	..	..	..	..	..	..	8.1	11.9	15.0	44.3	52.5	11.7
Swaziland	28.4	32.0	29.2	20.9	19.8	16.4	12.8	8.2	6.0	20.2	18.3	25.1	30.8	18.4
Tanzania	..	105.5	82.7	106.8	88.8	86.8	84.3	83.0	82.5	70.5	66.4	..	122.0	85.7
Togo	28.1	60.1	73.0	83.7	104.9	84.7	91.0	64.9	55.7	66.7	37.8	39.6	82.3	72.3
Uganda	148.3	122.2	132.0	159.2	124.2	127.7	87.8	69.5	80.4	46.3	56.1	58.4	59.9	100.5
Zambia	35.2	84.5	237.4	273.5	177.0	260.4	367.5	145.1	107.0	65.9	113.3	34.1	112.2	183.2
Zimbabwe	14.5	22.3	23.8	58.0	42.1	27.9	29.3	22.5	20.4	20.9	38.0	9.3	22.6	30.5
NORTH AFRICA	7.2	17.4	21.3	15.6	11.3	11.9	8.3	9.3	7.9	7.0	5.5	9.4	7.2	11.5
Algeria	1.1	1.4	2.4	2.8	2.4	3.1	2.4	2.6	2.2	3.0	0.7	1.1	1.0	2.3
Egypt, Arab Republic	22.0	43.8	64.2	47.3	31.3	31.3	19.5	19.6	14.8	11.5	7.8	33.9	15.9	29.1
Libya	0.2	..	..	..	..	..	..	..	..	..	..	0.2	..	..
Morocco	19.7	16.1	19.5	14.3	11.8	9.7	7.2	9.1	6.7	6.6	8.0	14.4	12.1	10.9
Tunisia	9.1	9.8	8.5	7.3	5.3	2.8	1.6	2.5	3.9	2.7	4.4	11.3	10.9	4.9
ALL AFRICA	12.8	33.9	36.7	36.0	25.0	26.3	22.3	20.0	16.8	15.3	13.0	13.6	22.7	24.5

Note: Nigeria's ratios are distorted for 1994-95 because of official exchange rate over-valuation affecting oil exports and oil value added (see chapter 3).

12-13. Net ODA from DAC donors as share of recipient GDI

	Percentage of GDI											Annual average		
	1980	1990	1991	1992	1993	1994	1995	1996	1997	1998	1999	75-84	85-89	90-MR
SUB-SAHARAN AFRICA	11.3	37.3	33.6	36.6	21.4	20.5	17.3	16.3	13.6	13.4	12.6	11.7	28.2	22.3
excluding South Africa	11.3	37.3	33.6	36.6	36.1	36.1	33.3	28.4	21.7	19.8	18.3	11.7	28.2	30.1
excl. S.Africa & Nigeria	19.5	43.3	42.3	48.8	44.7	43.7	39.5	33.9	26.2	25.8	23.2	17.6	32.5	37.2
Angola	..	13.7	10.1	92.8	25.6	33.2	114.9	-69.7	11.7	13.8	9.1	..	8.7	25.5
Benin	16.8	48.0	58.8	76.6	45.6	60.2	45.0	43.6	37.4	36.5	27.7	21.0	50.1	47.9
Botswana	20.1	10.1	8.7	7.9	7.2	4.8	4.1	5.4	4.8	7.3	3.5	23.9	20.9	6.4
Burkina Faso	51.9	42.0	47.0	63.5	60.1	69.4	44.9	39.6	33.5	29.7	32.3	43.3	41.5	46.2
Burundi	46.8	95.8	73.0	91.6	82.1	111.0	113.1	62.5	49.5	57.7	79.9	48.1	49.4	81.6
Cameroon	12.1	17.1	18.2	35.5	26.9	33.0	29.9	20.0	22.4	18.9	14.2	10.1	8.7	23.6
Cape Verde	70.7	97.9	85.9	58.9	56.4	45.8	36.9	40.6	35.9	42.7	40.7	58.6	89.1	54.2
Central African Republic	134.5	54.5	56.3	61.2	88.4	94.4	80.8	258.9	68.3	39.9	39.3	84.4	65.2	84.2
Chad	..	66.1	112.0	105.6	102.0	52.7	85.7	50.9	43.2	27.6	40.8	86.5	122.1	68.7
Comoros	32.8	62.2	60.9	39.0	53.1	45.6	57.5	76.4	50.9	56.9	46.9	43.0	67.4	54.9
Congo, Democratic Rep. of	22.1	74.8	67.6	28.7	62.6	17.2	19.8	25.4	24.1	14.2	10.6	16.1	29.5	34.5
Congo, Republic of	9.1	45.4	21.0	16.1	20.5	26.2	13.6	25.8	50.0	11.5	24.5	11.8	19.5	25.5
Côte d'Ivoire	5.6	73.5	56.3	68.3	82.0	85.3	53.7	31.3	13.8	23.9	20.0	7.0	18.0	50.8
Djibouti	..	..	126.7	102.7	115.6	164.6	189.5	157.9	131.2	..	..	..	..	141.2
Equatorial Guinea	..	189.8	53.2	96.1	83.0	17.7	17.3	7.9	5.5	4.4	5.1	..	..	48.0
Eritrea	..	..	..	..	78.0	105.6	85.6	69.1	30.2	30.4	26.3	..	..	60.8
Ethiopia	..	63.0	88.1	89.3	46.9	76.4	55.3	44.2	34.4	32.3	27.9	13.6	39.5	55.8
Gabon	4.2	9.8	9.8	5.2	9.9	17.6	11.6	8.5	1.9	2.2	2.8	3.4	6.7	7.9
Gambia, The	25.6	80.4	79.3	65.5	64.9	58.1	32.6	20.3	24.7	17.6	18.9	46.6	128.1	46.2
Ghana	42.8	31.2	42.8	40.5	23.6	25.5	27.7	22.5	16.9	21.3	19.7	32.8	32.1	27.2
Guinea	..	28.1	31.8	40.8	31.6	35.2	36.0	20.1	18.8	23.0	17.5	..	38.8	28.3
Guinea-Bissau	110.3	103.2	78.2	51.9	77.3	240.8	135.7	200.1	100.5	277.7	90.2	92.8	81.4	135.6
Kenya	15.6	43.7	42.2	47.4	48.4	34.1	28.9	22.3	18.5	16.5	17.6	21.1	30.4	32.0
Lesotho	39.9	25.8	16.7	12.5	16.4	9.8	10.9	9.0	8.1	7.9	3.7	43.0	36.0	12.1
Liberia	19.7	..	..	..	..	..	..	..	..	..	..	32.5	66.7	..
Madagascar	15.0	51.3	125.3	63.6	59.0	58.5	56.4	49.4	130.6	71.5	40.1	25.0	57.7	70.6
Malawi	24.7	60.8	46.8	58.0	50.5	73.0	90.9	93.9	56.4	87.1	84.9	26.2	61.3	70.2
Mali	47.5	56.2	50.7	34.8	37.8	50.4	50.5	49.6	50.3	42.9	42.9	55.7	73.4	47.0
Mauritania	28.7	52.3	54.5	50.6	100.6	60.1	61.2	47.6	50.1	33.5	52.0	25.5	53.1	56.3
Mauritius	10.8	9.3	7.6	3.7	2.7	0.7	1.1	0.1	0.2	2.0	0.4	9.8	9.7	2.8
Mozambique	54.8	191.6	192.1	330.0	303.5	163.3	127.8	91.1	96.6	77.7	45.8	74.1	164.0	162.0
Namibia	..	5.0	20.3	15.8	27.9	15.8	21.6	19.1	21.3	21.3	19.0	0.0	5.4	18.7
Niger	14.9	126.7	151.9	161.3	247.0	160.9	140.9	85.0	90.4	61.8	58.3	51.1	80.2	128.4
Nigeria	0.1	4.1	2.7	1.9	1.4	1.0	1.6	0.9	0.8	0.4	0.6	0.4	2.6	1.6
Rwanda	51.5	48.4	86.9	64.2	70.7	552.7	175.9	115.6	64.3	65.8	64.8	54.3	39.2	130.9
São Tomé and Principe	8.2	171.9	114.6	147.1	151.1	141.4	354.9	145.5	123.4	99.2	101.7	17.6	59.0	155.1
Senegal	51.9	74.9	59.5	50.8	47.5	70.3	53.4	45.6	37.0	33.4	46.0	50.5	73.0	51.8
Seychelles	32.4	36.1	20.1	16.8	5.1	5.8	7.1	3.0	3.3	8.6	2.4	38.5	31.2	10.8
Sierra Leone	27.5	47.2	79.8	130.3	177.4	68.1	122.8	64.4	-201.0	149.0	3,054.3	21.7	51.5	369.2
Somalia	54.4	189.7	..	..	..	..	..	..	..	..	..	49.5	107.6	189.7
South Africa	..	..	..	..	1.0	1.0	1.2	1.3	1.8	1.9	1.9	..	..	1.4
Sudan	24.4	..	..	..	..	..	..	..	5.1	8.5	9.8	17.0	28.3	7.8
Swaziland	18.5	21.4	17.2	10.5	12.7	8.0	8.7	5.6	3.7	11.1	9.4	16.1	20.4	10.8
Tanzania	..	75.9	58.5	65.1	60.8	51.3	56.4	57.3	49.7	54.3	41.2	..	93.3	57.0
Togo	16.1	35.8	45.4	50.7	83.7	42.9	55.8	40.2	33.7	34.3	24.9	21.5	46.6	44.8
Uganda	55.2	44.7	56.6	56.0	70.8	58.7	44.8	38.1	43.4	37.8	34.0	24.1	21.2	48.5
Zambia	25.9	72.0	156.7	184.7	103.7	157.4	79.4	84.3	64.4	48.4	61.8	26.1	88.8	101.3
Zimbabwe	9.9	19.4	21.8	39.2	26.2	14.0	20.7	17.0	13.5	16.1	34.1	7.2	19.8	22.2
NORTH AFRICA	4.4	10.3	16.3	12.8	8.1	9.5	6.8	7.5	5.4	4.5	3.7	4.5	6.2	8.5
Algeria	0.7	1.3	2.1	2.5	1.8	2.8	2.2	2.2	1.7	0.9	0.3	0.9	0.7	1.8
Egypt, Arab Republic	18.8	25.5	53.1	39.4	23.8	26.9	16.3	17.2	11.2	8.7	6.4	15.3	14.9	22.8
Libya	0.1	..	..	..	..	..	..	..	..	..	..	0.1	..	..
Morocco	4.1	9.1	9.7	11.1	7.0	4.9	5.1	5.5	3.1	3.1	3.9	5.5	8.3	6.3
Tunisia	6.1	5.4	6.3	5.6	3.0	1.9	1.2	0.8	1.4	1.9	1.8	8.0	7.7	2.9
ALL AFRICA	7.5	21.1	24.4	23.4	15.7	16.0	13.3	12.8	10.5	9.6	8.6	7.5	15.2	15.6

Note: Nigeria's ratios are distorted for 1994-95 because of official exchange rate over-valuation affecting oil exports and oil value added (see chapter 3).

12-14. Net ODA from multilateral donors as share of recipient GDI

	Percentage of GDI										Annual average		
	1980	*1990*	*1991*	*1992*	*1993*	*1994*	*1995*	*1996*	*1997*	*1998*	*1999*	*75-84*	*85-89*	*90-MR*
SUB-SAHARAN AFRICA	6.2	19.8	20.2	24.8	13.8	15.6	13.8	10.5	8.6	7.8	7.9	6.5	15.5	14.3
excluding South Africa	6.2	19.8	20.2	24.8	23.3	27.8	27.2	18.9	14.1	12.0	11.7	6.5	15.5	20.0
excl. S.Africa & Nigeria	10.8	23.1	25.6	32.9	28.1	33.1	31.9	22.1	16.7	15.1	14.6	9.8	18.0	24.3
Angola	..	8.6	7.5	72.5	23.1	33.5	83.7	-42.3	6.6	7.8	4.9	..	3.9	20.6
Benin	24.8	54.4	40.0	44.0	43.2	46.8	24.5	31.1	18.4	17.3	21.6	19.5	39.7	34.1
Botswana	5.4	2.3	2.2	1.8	3.8	2.4	2.7	0.7	5.9	3.6	1.7	6.4	7.0	2.7
Burkina Faso	21.0	14.2	24.3	38.9	50.0	43.9	41.1	22.5	21.9	21.8	21.8	20.1	17.9	30.0
Burundi	42.2	64.6	81.8	100.6	61.2	211.4	189.9	41.0	23.8	42.6	34.1	39.0	54.8	85.1
Cameroon	5.0	5.5	6.8	8.4	0.8	27.7	8.4	9.6	11.6	7.7	10.3	4.3	2.6	9.7
Cape Verde	42.5	40.8	27.7	29.1	24.6	22.2	19.3	19.1	22.8	22.4	22.0	34.3	40.5	25.0
Central African Republic	60.5	80.9	42.1	39.9	40.7	72.1	28.2	95.3	33.1	44.8	38.6	42.9	48.1	51.6
Chad	..	46.3	101.1	64.5	53.4	55.3	73.4	71.5	56.6	32.7	73.6	69.7	96.9	62.8
Comoros	32.7	29.5	66.0	42.2	36.6	53.9	52.9	60.2	39.8	50.7	29.4	43.1	49.0	46.1
Congo, Democratic Rep. of	7.4	22.1	26.4	18.5	50.0	26.2	13.1	13.6	10.2	7.7	5.5	6.8	17.7	19.3
Congo, Republic of	3.6	3.6	2.9	1.9	1.2	11.3	2.6	2.3	1.7	1.0	3.8	5.7	2.8	3.2
Côte d'Ivoire	2.2	21.8	25.4	29.7	6.4	80.4	35.9	35.8	12.6	15.1	4.4	1.9	7.3	26.8
Djibouti	..	..	33.1	24.0	36.1	40.0	53.1	47.3	39.3	..	..	..	..	39.0
Equatorial Guinea	..	74.3	31.7	69.6	75.2	14.3	9.5	2.6	2.0	1.5	1.9	5.3	..	28.2
Eritrea	..	..	..	..	29.1	54.4	44.5	15.5	9.6	11.9	16.3	..	..	25.9
Ethiopia	..	54.1	119.4	140.7	75.5	67.9	37.6	36.4	18.2	25.0	26.0	20.4	30.6	60.1
Gabon	0.6	0.4	0.2	0.3	0.4	2.1	0.8	1.1	0.7	0.5	1.1	0.5	0.7	0.8
Gambia, The	48.0	59.0	63.0	80.8	48.3	50.9	29.9	25.8	32.6	32.2	27.2	43.2	98.4	45.0
Ghana	23.7	34.9	40.4	34.6	23.3	16.9	23.1	19.5	10.9	18.4	13.7	24.9	46.2	23.6
Guinea	..	30.3	37.9	37.8	38.9	33.0	31.2	21.4	33.2	29.0	17.1	..	27.1	31.0
Guinea-Bissau	75.9	72.9	64.5	40.8	46.4	94.0	68.1	83.0	112.5	133.0	57.0	54.6	71.6	77.2
Kenya	6.7	26.5	21.4	33.7	55.2	23.8	17.0	15.9	8.9	12.0	3.7	5.8	11.2	21.8
Lesotho	19.1	17.2	11.6	13.3	15.0	15.0	9.2	9.4	7.3	8.5	1.0	28.5	24.7	10.7
Liberia	9.4	..	..	..	..	..	..	..	..	..	..	10.9	27.3	..
Madagascar	15.1	25.1	83.2	43.4	35.0	30.6	30.7	27.3	67.9	34.5	34.5	19.9	44.3	41.2
Malawi	22.1	80.6	70.5	101.6	107.0	62.7	87.0	81.1	55.3	98.4	79.8	23.3	63.7	82.4
Mali	37.4	27.7	30.4	30.4	25.0	43.3	47.8	33.6	34.8	21.1	21.2	38.7	38.1	31.5
Mauritania	19.3	52.2	52.9	39.7	69.1	70.2	58.4	89.1	80.1	60.7	73.2	30.4	32.4	64.5
Mauritius	3.4	1.5	0.9	1.2	0.1	0.7	1.3	2.1	2.5	2.1	3.1	4.9	1.4	1.6
Mozambique	16.3	64.4	74.8	148.7	135.4	103.4	66.6	55.0	50.8	35.9	36.5	22.5	49.6	77.2
Namibia	..	10.3	18.5	7.2	7.1	3.5	6.4	7.2	7.2	8.5	9.8	..	3.4	8.6
Niger	9.0	68.8	60.0	63.6	85.4	68.1	57.8	47.3	70.5	62.4	32.2	26.4	45.2	61.6
Nigeria	0.1	1.8	1.4	1.7	4.2	3.1	3.0	2.9	2.4	1.9	1.1	0.2	0.6	2.3
Rwanda	30.6	25.8	46.7	56.1	53.5	255.9	188.2	97.9	18.1	44.4	69.0	29.7	27.7	85.6
São Tomé and Principe	18.4	131.3	129.3	171.4	97.8	127.0	131.0	93.6	70.8	55.4	44.9	48.5	89.7	105.3
Senegal	22.6	28.8	27.1	22.4	15.9	24.2	33.9	20.6	15.4	24.4	12.7	25.0	36.9	22.5
Seychelles	6.1	3.7	7.4	4.5	9.0	4.5	1.6	3.2	3.0	2.9	3.0	4.4	10.9	4.3
Sierra Leone	14.4	24.7	42.4	104.0	171.3	280.5	301.1	108.6	-369.6	141.5	680.4	14.6	31.0	148.5
Somalia	65.0	99.9	..	..	..	..	..	..	..	..	..	58.5	56.2	99.9
South Africa	..	..	..	..	0.5	0.4	0.2	0.2	0.3	0.4	0.7	..	..	0.4
Sudan	17.2	..	..	..	..	..	..	..	3.1	3.3	3.6	12.0	14.7	3.3
Swaziland	9.9	10.6	12.1	10.4	7.1	8.3	4.1	2.6	2.3	9.1	8.9	9.0	10.4	7.5
Tanzania	..	29.3	24.4	41.9	28.1	35.0	27.5	26.0	32.6	16.1	25.2	..	28.7	28.6
Togo	12.0	24.4	27.8	33.6	21.0	41.7	35.1	25.6	22.6	31.8	11.2	17.2	33.4	27.5
Uganda	91.3	69.7	65.3	100.0	53.1	67.2	42.3	30.6	36.7	8.6	22.0	32.2	37.4	49.6
Zambia	6.8	12.5	80.7	88.8	73.3	103.0	288.1	60.8	42.6	17.6	51.5	6.2	23.4	81.9
Zimbabwe	4.2	2.3	2.1	18.9	16.0	14.1	8.8	5.7	7.0	4.8	4.0	2.1	2.9	8.4
NORTH AFRICA	0.8	0.7	1.9	1.4	2.0	2.1	1.2	1.7	2.2	1.9	1.5	1.6	0.6	1.7
Algeria	0.1	0.1	0.2	0.2	0.6	0.3	0.3	0.3	0.4	1.9	0.2	0.1	0.1	0.4
Egypt, Arab Republic	3.1	0.6	4.6	2.6	2.5	3.3	2.0	1.9	2.9	1.6	1.0	7.2	0.9	2.3
Libya	0.1	..	..	..	..	..	..	..	..	..	..	0.1	..	..
Morocco	1.4	1.4	2.4	2.4	4.5	4.4	1.9	3.2	3.1	3.1	3.7	1.3	0.7	3.0
Tunisia	1.0	2.0	2.2	1.9	2.6	1.3	0.9	2.5	2.9	1.4	2.9	1.4	2.2	2.0
ALL AFRICA	3.3	8.3	10.5	11.8	8.7	10.1	8.9	7.1	6.1	5.4	5.0	3.6	6.7	8.2

Note: Nigeria's ratios are distorted for 1994-95 because of official exchange rate over-valuation affecting oil exports and oil value added (see chapter 3).

12-15. Net ODA per capita from all donors

	U.S. dollars (current prices)											Annual average		
	1980	1990	1991	1992	1993	1994	1995	1996	1997	1998	1999	75-84	85-89	90-MR
SUB-SAHARAN AFRICA	21	37	35	37	30	32	31	25	22	21	18	17	27	29
excluding South Africa	21	37	35	37	32	34	32	26	23	21	18	17	27	30
excl. S.Africa & Nigeria	26	45	43	45	40	42	40	33	28	26	23	21	34	37
Angola	7	29	29	35	28	42	38	42	30	28	31	7	16	33
Benin	26	57	55	54	56	48	51	51	38	35	34	21	36	48
Botswana	117	115	100	83	93	60	62	50	79	68	38	91	114	75
Burkina Faso	30	37	46	47	49	44	49	41	35	37	36	24	32	42
Burundi	28	48	46	54	37	52	47	18	9	12	11	23	37	33
Cameroon	31	39	44	59	44	57	34	30	36	30	30	22	24	40
Cape Verde	223	316	302	336	324	326	307	297	275	312	318	144	276	311
Central African Republic	48	85	58	57	54	51	50	50	27	34	33	34	59	50
Chad	8	55	45	39	36	33	35	43	32	23	25	18	40	37
Comoros	129	105	143	106	105	81	85	78	53	67	39	119	123	86
Congo, Democratic Rep. of	16	24	12	7	4	6	4	4	3	3	3	12	16	7
Congo, Republic of	55	98	59	48	51	145	49	163	99	23	49	49	49	79
Côte d'Ivoire	26	59	53	61	60	121	90	69	31	55	30	17	25	63
Djibouti	260	375	201	205	235	221	175	158	137	127	116	212	215	195
Equatorial Guinea	43	173	173	167	139	77	84	75	58	58	46	27	116	105
Eritrea	..	..	..	..	20	45	42	43	33	43	37	..	..	38
Ethiopia	6	20	21	21	20	20	16	14	10	11	10	5	16	16
Gabon	81	138	145	67	97	169	131	112	34	38	39	73	105	97
Gambia, The	85	108	105	110	82	65	42	32	32	31	26	58	109	63
Ghana	18	38	58	39	38	33	38	37	27	38	32	13	33	38
Guinea	20	51	64	74	65	56	63	44	55	51	33	15	42	56
Guinea-Bissau	75	132	116	103	88	162	106	160	109	82	44	64	100	110
Kenya	24	50	38	35	35	26	27	21	16	16	10	19	31	28
Lesotho	70	82	71	80	77	62	59	53	46	32	15	53	66	58
Liberia	52	46	63	47	47	24	45	61	26	25	31	40	34	41
Madagascar	26	34	38	30	29	22	23	26	59	34	24	16	27	32
Malawi	23	59	60	64	54	49	44	49	34	41	41	19	36	49
Mali	41	57	52	48	39	47	56	49	42	33	32	29	51	45
Mauritania	113	117	105	93	148	118	99	114	97	68	84	115	115	104
Mauritius	34	84	63	42	24	13	21	17	36	34	35	37	51	37
Mozambique	14	71	74	100	79	78	67	55	57	61	7	11	45	65
Namibia	..	90	131	100	105	91	124	119	101	108	104	0	19	107
Niger	30	51	47	44	40	43	30	27	34	29	18	30	47	36
Nigeria	1	3	3	3	3	2	2	2	2	2	1	1	1	2
Rwanda	30	42	51	48	47	115	110	69	29	43	45	26	34	60
São Tomé and Principe	44	475	434	464	372	389	638	351	241	200	190	72	208	375
Senegal	47	112	85	87	63	79	80	68	48	55	58	45	84	73
Seychelles	337	513	325	268	269	174	171	247	215	304	162	242	338	265
Sierra Leone	28	15	25	32	48	63	46	40	25	22	15	16	23	33
Somalia	74	63	23	78	105	64	23	10	9	9	12	50	68	40
South Africa	..	..	..	..	7	8	10	9	12	12	13	..	..	10
Sudan	33	34	36	22	18	16	9	8	5	7	8	29	42	16
Swaziland	89	70	67	65	61	64	62	33	28	31	28	60	48	51
Tanzania	37	46	41	49	34	34	30	29	30	31	30	28	34	35
Togo	35	74	55	59	25	31	47	37	29	29	16	31	50	40
Uganda	9	41	39	42	34	40	43	34	40	23	27	7	20	36
Zambia	55	62	110	125	103	82	226	66	65	36	63	35	58	94
Zimbabwe	23	35	39	77	47	52	45	33	29	24	21	15	29	40
NORTH AFRICA	31	63	60	45	30	31	23	25	22	23	19	31	24	34
Algeria	9	10	13	15	13	15	11	11	9	13	3	8	8	11
Egypt, Arab Republic	34	104	94	66	43	47	35	37	33	32	25	44	34	51
Libya	5	4	6	1	1	1	1	2	1	1	1	3	2	2
Morocco	46	44	50	38	28	24	19	24	17	19	24	28	22	29
Tunisia	36	48	43	46	26	12	8	14	21	16	26	36	33	26
ALL AFRICA	23	42	40	38	30	32	29	25	22	21	18	19	27	30

12-16. Net ODA per capita from DAC donors

	U.S. dollars (current prices)											Annual average		
	1980	*1990*	*1991*	*1992*	*1993*	*1994*	*1995*	*1996*	*1997*	*1998*	*1999*	*75-84*	*85-89*	*90-MR*
SUB-SAHARAN AFRICA	12	23	21	22	18	18	17	15	13	13	12	10	17	17
excluding South Africa	12	23	21	22	19	19	18	16	14	13	12	10	17	18
excl. S.Africa & Nigeria	16	28	26	27	24	24	22	20	17	17	15	12	22	22
Angola	5	18	17	20	15	21	22	26	19	18	20	4	11	20
Benin	10	27	33	34	29	27	32	29	26	24	20	11	20	28
Botswana	92	95	79	69	58	40	37	45	36	47	26	69	87	53
Burkina Faso	22	27	30	29	27	27	25	26	21	21	21	16	22	25
Burundi	14	29	22	26	21	18	18	11	6	7	8	12	17	16
Cameroon	20	30	32	48	42	31	26	21	24	21	17	15	19	29
Cape Verde	135	222	228	226	225	219	201	197	168	205	207	95	188	210
Central African Republic	32	34	33	35	37	29	37	36	18	16	17	22	34	29
Chad	5	32	23	25	23	16	19	18	14	10	9	10	22	19
Comoros	40	71	69	51	62	37	44	44	30	35	24	45	69	47
Congo, Democratic Rep. of	12	17	9	4	2	2	3	2	2	2	2	8	10	5
Congo, Republic of	33	91	51	43	48	102	41	150	96	21	42	30	43	69
Côte d'Ivoire	19	46	36	43	56	62	54	32	16	34	25	13	18	40
Djibouti	114	171	156	167	166	161	132	116	100	98	86	125	138	135
Equatorial Guinea	5	124	98	97	73	42	54	57	42	42	33	14	66	66
Eritrea	..	..	..	..	14	27	26	35	21	25	20	..	..	24
Ethiopia	2	10	9	8	8	10	9	8	6	6	5	2	9	8
Gabon	71	132	142	64	93	151	124	101	26	32	29	61	91	89
Gambia, The	26	62	57	50	48	36	23	15	15	11	11	25	62	33
Ghana	10	18	29	21	19	20	21	20	16	20	19	7	14	20
Guinea	7	24	29	38	29	29	33	20	18	21	15	4	23	26
Guinea-Bissau	43	77	63	56	55	117	71	112	51	56	27	37	50	68
Kenya	17	31	25	21	17	15	17	13	11	10	9	15	22	17
Lesotho	47	50	42	38	40	24	32	25	22	16	12	32	39	30
Liberia	32	17	23	10	9	13	11	40	11	11	15	27	24	16
Madagascar	10	23	23	18	18	15	15	17	39	23	13	8	16	20
Malawi	12	25	24	23	17	26	23	26	17	19	21	10	17	22
Mali	20	37	32	27	24	26	29	30	25	22	22	16	32	27
Mauritania	35	53	53	54	89	57	54	41	39	25	34	29	62	50
Mauritius	26	72	58	32	24	7	10	1	2	17	4	24	42	23
Mozambique	9	53	53	69	54	48	44	34	37	42	34	8	34	47
Namibia	..	29	69	69	84	75	96	86	76	77	69	0	12	73
Niger	19	33	33	32	30	30	21	17	18	14	11	18	30	24
Nigeria	0	2	2	1	1	0	1	0	0	0	0	0	1	1
Rwanda	19	26	33	26	27	78	53	37	23	26	22	16	20	35
São Tomé and Principe	14	270	204	214	226	205	466	213	153	128	132	22	84	221
Senegal	33	80	56	59	46	59	48	46	33	32	45	28	52	50
Seychelles	284	468	237	215	94	98	145	102	81	219	61	213	247	172
Sierra Leone	18	10	17	18	25	12	13	14	9	11	12	8	13	14
Somalia	24	35	14	59	81	52	15	5	5	5	8	16	44	28
South Africa	..	..	..	..	5	6	8	8	10	10	9	..	..	8
Sudan	15	17	15	7	6	7	5	4	3	5	5	11	22	8
Swaziland	58	47	39	33	39	31	42	22	17	17	15	39	31	30
Tanzania	28	33	29	30	23	20	20	20	18	24	19	21	26	24
Togo	20	44	34	36	20	16	29	23	17	15	10	18	29	24
Uganda	3	15	17	15	19	19	22	19	22	18	17	2	7	18
Zambia	41	53	73	85	60	50	49	38	39	27	34	27	46	51
Zimbabwe	16	30	36	52	29	26	32	25	19	19	18	11	25	29
NORTH AFRICA	19	37	46	37	22	25	19	20	15	15	13	16	21	25
Algeria	6	9	12	14	10	14	10	9	7	4	1	6	5	9
Egypt, Arab Republic	29	60	78	55	33	40	29	33	25	24	21	23	31	40
Libya	3	2	1	0	0	0	1	0	0	1	1	1	1	1
Morocco	10	25	25	29	17	12	13	15	8	9	12	10	16	16
Tunisia	25	26	32	35	15	8	6	5	8	11	11	25	23	16
ALL AFRICA	14	26	26	25	19	19	17	16	14	13	12	11	18	19

12-17. Net ODA per capita from multilateral donors

	U.S. dollars (current prices)											Annual average		
	1980	1990	1991	1992	1993	1994	1995	1996	1997	1998	1999	75-84	85-89	90-MR
SUB-SAHARAN AFRICA	7	13	13	15	12	14	14	10	8	8	7	5	9	11
excluding South Africa	7	13	13	15	13	15	15	11	9	8	8	5	9	12
excl. S.Africa & Nigeria	8	16	17	18	15	18	18	13	11	10	9	7	12	15
Angola	2	11	12	15	13	21	16	16	11	10	11	3	5	14
Benin	15	30	22	20	27	21	18	21	13	11	15	10	16	20
Botswana	25	21	20	15	31	20	24	6	45	23	13	19	27	22
Burkina Faso	9	9	15	18	22	17	23	14	14	16	14	7	9	16
Burundi	13	19	25	28	16	34	30	7	3	5	3	10	19	17
Cameroon	8	10	12	11	1	26	7	10	12	9	12	6	5	11
Cape Verde	81	93	74	111	98	106	105	93	107	108	112	46	84	101
Central African Republic	15	50	24	23	17	22	13	13	9	18	16	12	25	21
Chad	3	22	21	15	12	17	16	25	18	12	16	7	18	17
Comoros	40	34	75	55	43	44	41	34	23	31	15	45	50	39
Congo, Democratic Rep. of	4	5	3	3	2	3	2	1	1	1	1	3	6	2
Congo, Republic of	13	7	7	5	3	44	8	13	3	2	7	14	7	10
Côte d'Ivoire	7	14	16	19	4	59	36	37	15	21	5	4	7	23
Djibouti	31	34	41	39	52	39	37	35	30	27	29	30	44	36
Equatorial Guinea	37	48	58	70	66	34	30	18	15	15	13	17	50	37
Eritrea	..	..	..	..	5	14	14	8	7	10	12	..	..	10
Ethiopia	3	9	12	13	13	9	6	6	3	5	5	3	7	8
Gabon	10	6	3	4	3	18	8	13	10	7	11	8	10	8
Gambia, The	48	45	45	62	36	31	21	19	19	20	15	26	48	31
Ghana	6	20	28	18	19	13	17	17	10	18	13	5	19	17
Guinea	13	26	35	36	36	27	29	21	32	26	15	8	17	28
Guinea-Bissau	30	55	52	44	33	45	36	47	58	27	17	23	45	41
Kenya	7	19	13	15	19	11	10	9	5	7	2	4	8	11
Lesotho	23	33	29	41	37	37	27	26	20	17	3	20	27	27
Liberia	15	29	41	37	37	10	33	21	15	14	16	11	10	25
Madagascar	10	11	15	12	11	8	8	9	20	11	11	7	12	12
Malawi	11	34	36	41	36	23	22	23	17	22	20	8	18	27
Mali	16	18	19	21	16	22	28	20	17	11	11	11	17	18
Mauritania	23	52	51	43	61	66	52	77	63	45	48	32	38	56
Mauritius	8	12	7	11	1	7	12	20	25	18	31	12	7	14
Mozambique	3	18	21	31	24	30	23	21	20	19	27	3	10	23
Namibia	..	61	62	31	21	16	28	32	26	31	36	..	6	34
Niger	11	18	13	13	10	13	9	10	14	14	6	9	17	12
Nigeria	0	1	1	1	2	1	1	1	1	1	1	0	0	1
Rwanda	11	14	18	22	20	36	57	32	6	17	23	9	14	25
São Tomé and Principe	30	206	230	250	146	184	172	137	88	72	58	50	125	154
Senegal	14	31	26	26	15	20	30	21	14	23	12	14	28	22
Seychelles	53	48	87	58	166	78	33	106	74	73	76	25	79	80
Sierra Leone	9	5	9	14	24	50	32	24	16	10	3	7	8	19
Somalia	28	18	9	17	23	12	8	6	4	4	4	19	23	11
South Africa	..	..	..	..	2	2	2	1	2	2	4	..	..	2
Sudan	10	16	20	13	11	9	4	4	2	2	2	8	13	8
Swaziland	31	23	28	32	22	33	20	11	11	14	14	21	17	21
Tanzania	7	13	12	19	11	14	10	9	12	7	11	6	8	12
Togo	15	30	21	24	5	15	18	15	12	14	5	13	20	16
Uganda	5	23	19	26	14	21	21	15	18	4	11	4	12	17
Zambia	11	9	37	41	42	32	178	28	26	10	29	6	12	43
Zimbabwe	7	4	3	25	18	26	13	8	10	6	2	4	4	12
NORTH AFRICA	4	2	6	4	5	5	3	5	6	6	5	5	2	5
Algeria	1	1	1	1	3	2	1	1	2	9	1	1	1	2
Egypt, Arab Republic	5	2	7	4	3	5	4	4	6	4	3	9	2	4
Libya	2	3	5	1	0	0	1	1	1	1	1	2	1	1
Morocco	3	4	6	6	11	11	5	9	8	9	11	2	1	8
Tunisia	4	10	11	12	13	6	5	13	16	8	17	4	7	11
ALL AFRICA	6	11	12	13	11	12	12	9	8	7	7	5	8	10

Figure 12-1. Total net ODA as a share of recipient GDP, 1997*

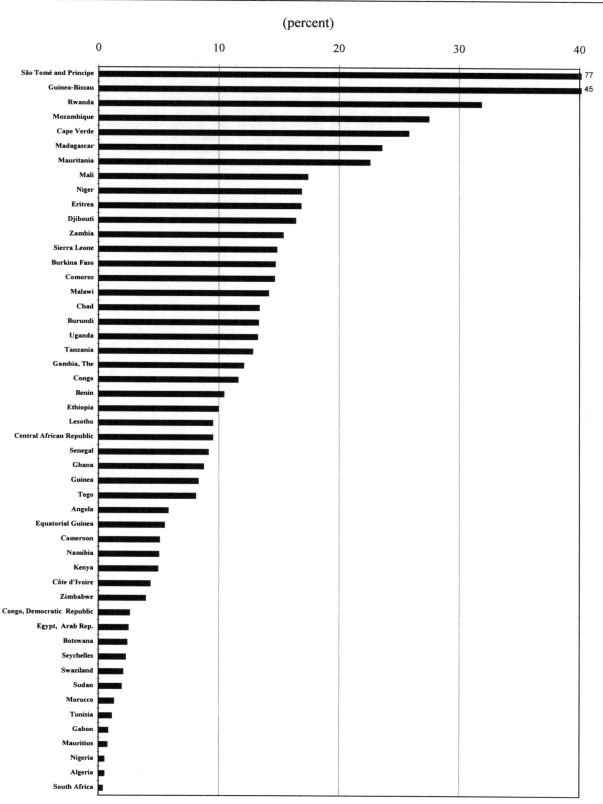

(percent)

* Or most recent year available.

Figure 12-2. Total net ODA per capita, 1999*

(U.S. dollars)

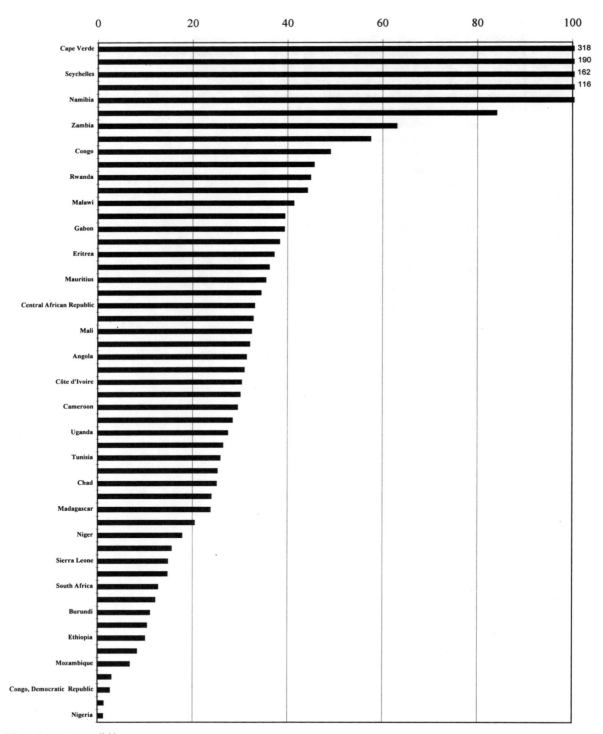

* Or most recent year available.

Technical notes

Tables

Table 12-1. Net ODA from all donors, nominal.
This table represents the total of Tables 12-2 through 12-4.

Table 12-2. Net ODA from DAC donors, nominal.
This table (OECD data) includes net ODA from Australia, Austria, Belgium, Canada, Denmark, Finland, France, the Federal Republic of Germany before reunification, Italy, Japan, the Netherlands, Norway, Sweden, Switzerland, the United Kingdom, and the United States (OECD data). (Ireland and New Zealand have been excluded in compilation because their ODA to Africa is negligible.)

Table 12-3. Net ODA from non-DAC bilateral donors, nominal. This is net ODA from Organization of Petroleum Exporting Countries (OPEC), the former Council for Mutual Economic Assistance (CMEA) countries, and China (OECD data). OPEC countries are Algeria, Iran, Iraq, Kuwait, Libya, Nigeria, Qatar, Saudi Arabia, the United Arab Emirates, and Venezuela. The former CMEA countries are Bulgaria, Czechoslovakia, the former German Democratic Republic, Hungary, Poland, Romania, and the former Soviet Union.

Table 12-4. Net ODA from multilateral donors, nominal. This includes net ODA (OECD data), most notably from the African Development Fund, the European Development Fund for the Commission of the European Communities, the International Development Association (IDA), the International Fund for

Agricultural Development, Arab/OPEC-financed multilateral agencies, and UN programs and agencies (OECD data). The UN programs and agencies include mainly the UN regular program of Technical Assistance, the UN Development Programme (UNDP), the UN High Commissioner for Refugees, the UN Children's Fund (UNICEF), and the World Food Programme. Arab/OPEC-financed multilateral agencies include the Arab Bank for Economic Development in Africa, the Arab Fund for Economic and Social Development (AFESD), the Islamic Development Bank, the OPEC Fund for International Development, the Arab Authority for Agricultural Investment and Development, the Arab Fund for Technical Assistance to African and Arab Countries, and the Islamic Solidarity Fund. ODA flows from the IMF Trust Fund and Structural Adjustment Facility (SAF) are also included.

Tables 12-5, 12-6, 12-7, and 12-8. Net ODA from all donors, from DAC donors, from non-DAC bilateral donors, and from multilateral donors, real. These tables are obtained by deflating data in Tables 12-1 through 12-4 by the World Bank LIMIC import price deflator.

Tables 12-9, 12-10, and 12-11. Net ODA from all donors, from DAC donors, and from multilateral donors as a share of recipient's GDP. These tables show the relative importance of these aid flows to recipients' economies. They are obtained by dividing figures in Tables 12-1, 12-2, and 12-4 by GDP data from Table 2-5, which reflect current prices and exchange rates. For a given level of aid flows, devaluation of a recipient's currency may inflate the ratios shown in the table. Thus, trends for a given country and comparisons across countries that have implemented different exchange rate policies should be interpreted carefully.

Tables 12-12, 12-13, and 12-14. Net ODA from all donors, from DAC donors, and from multilateral donors as a share of recipient GDI. These tables are obtained by dividing figures in Tables 12-1, 12-2, and 12-4 by GDI (World Bank country desks). These tables highlight the relative importance of the indicated aid flows in maintaining and increasing investment in these economies. The same caveats mentioned above apply to their interpretation. Furthermore, aid flows do not exclusively finance investment (for example, food aid finances consumption), and the share of ODA going to investment varies across countries.

Tables 12-15, 12-16, and 12-17. Net ODA per capita from all donors, from DAC donors, and from multilateral donors. These are calculated by dividing figures in Tables 12-1, 12-2, and 12-4 by midyear population (Table 1-2). These ratios offer some indication of the importance of aid flows in sustaining per capita income and consumption levels (shown in Tables 2-19 and 2-20, respectively), although comparisons must be done carefully because exchange rate fluctuations, the actual rise of ODA flows, and other factors vary across countries and over time.

Figures

The following indicators have been used to derive the figures in this chapter.

Figure 12-1. Total net ODA as a share of recipient's GDP (Table 12-9).

Figure 12-2. Total net ODA per capita (Table 12-15).

Methodology used for regional aggregations and period averages in chapter 12

Table	Aggregations[a]		Period averages[b]	
	(1)	*(2)*	*(1)*	*(2)*
12-1	x		x	
12-2	x		x	
12-3	x		x	
12-4	x		x	
12-5	x			x
12-6	x			x
12-7	x			x
12-8	x			x
12-9		x	x	
12-10		x	x	
12-11		x	x	
12-12		x	x	
12-13		x	x	
12-14		x	x	
12-15		x	x	
12-16		x	x	
12-17		x	x	

Note: Regional aggregations are shown in the rows for Sub-Saharan Africa, North Africa, and All Africa. Period averages are shown in the last three columns. This table shows only the methodologies used in this chapter.

a. Regional aggregations: (1) simple total; (2) simple total of the first indicator divided by the simple total of the second indicator (same country coverage); (3) simple total of the gap-filled indicator; (4) simple total of the gap-filled main indicator divided by the simple total of the gap-filled secondary indicator; (5) simple total of the first gap-filled main indicator less the simple total of the second gap-filled main indicator, all divided by the simple total of the secondary indicator; (6) weighted total (by population); (7) median; (8) no aggregation; (9) simple arithmetic mean.

b. Period averages: (i) arithmetic mean (using the same series as shown in the table i.e., ratio if the rest of the table is shown as ratio, level if the rest of the table is shown as level, growth rate if the rest is shown as growth rate); (2) least-squares growth rate (using main indicator); (3) least-squares growth rate (using main indicator in constant terms, with the rest of the table in current terms).

13

Social Indicators

This chapter provides indicators in the areas of demography, health, education, and gender issues in development. These indicators can be useful in evaluating and monitoring the social impact of development progress, aid flows, and structural adjustment policies.

The chapter presents such indicators as dependency ratio, urbanization, crude death rate, life expectancy at birth, infant mortality rate, child mortality rate, immunization rates for children, maternal death rate, and number of population per physician. These indicators are an indirect measure of the physical well being of the population. In the same vein, such indicators as literacy rate among adults, school enrollment ratios by gender, and pupil-teacher ratio give some picture of the progress being made in education and training. Social indicators refer to phenomena that are inherently more qualitative than macroeconomic variables and thus need to be interpreted cautiously. Further caution is called for because of the particular limitations of the data. One of these limitations is the paucity—or even nonexistence—of data on certain indicators in many of the countries covered. This is especially true of indicators dealing with gender issues. Many countries have no data showing the gender breakdown of several social indicators.

Even when data are available, comparison among countries is limited due to varied practices in data gathering and reporting. Often the countries report survey data that cover different portions of the nation. Sometimes surveys are limited to just the urban areas to cover only the largest cities or the capital city alone. This is especially true of the health indicators. Such indicators as immunization rates for children under one year of age, percentage of births attended by health personnel, infant mortality rate, child mortality rate, and maternal death rate are often based on surveys of a handful of hospitals in the urban areas.

Another source of limitation is the definition of terms, which may differ from country to country. Some countries, for example, consider an institution as a "private school" only if it receives no form of financial support from the government, while others classify as "private" all schools not run by the government, whether or not they receive financial support from the government. In like manner, some countries include personnel other than doctors and trained nurses in the term "medical personnel."

Cultural norms may also affect the reported data. This is especially true for gender issues. In some countries, it is assumed that no woman can be the head of any household that also contains an adult male. In population censuses, therefore, enumerators and respondents simply take such assumptions for granted, reporting a male rather than a female as head of the household or family (see United Nations, The World's Women, 1970–90). This distorts the true picture of the percentage of households headed by women.

The main source for this chapter is the *World Development Indicators* in the World Bank Statistical Information Management Analysis Database (SIMA), which contains electronic information as reported by a number of institutions and agencies in the socioeconomic field, such as the United Nations, UNICEF, UNESCO, World Health Organization (WHO), the UNDP, and the ECA. Other sources of data also include reports and publications on children, health, human development, education, and population from various agencies including the World Bank.

In this chapter, columns headed by a period (for example, 1992–97) show data for the latest available year within the period.

13-1. Age and gender structure of the population

	Females as percentage of total population		Age groups as percentage of total population						Age dependency ratio	
			1980			1998				
	1980	1997	0-14	15-64	65+	0-14	15-64	65+	1980	1998
SUB-SAHARAN AFRICA	50.2	50.5	45.1	51.3	2.9	44.5	52.7	2.9	0.9	0.9
excluding South Africa	50.2	50.4	45.6	50.9	2.8	45.3	52.0	2.7	1.0	0.9
excl. S.Africa & Nigeria	50.1	50.4	45.4	50.8	2.9	45.5	51.8	2.8	1.0	0.9
Angola	50.9	50.6	44.6	52.4	3.0	47.6	49.6	2.9	0.9	1.0
Benin	50.7	50.7	45.1	50.8	4.1	46.6	50.6	2.9	1.0	1.0
Botswana	52.2	51.0	48.7	49.8	2.0	42.9	54.9	2.3	1.0	0.8
Burkina Faso	50.5	50.6	47.4	49.8	2.8	47.0	50.2	2.8	1.0	1.0
Burundi	51.9	51.0	44.7	51.8	3.5	45.8	51.6	2.6	0.9	0.9
Cameroon	50.6	50.3	44.3	52.0	3.6	44.1	52.4	3.5	0.9	0.9
Cape Verde	54.0	53.3	45.5	47.2	6.2	40.8	55.4	4.4	1.1	0.8
Central African Republic	..	51.4	41.7	54.4	4.0	42.8	53.6	3.6	0.8	0.9
Chad	50.8	50.5	41.9	54.5	3.6	50.9	46.0	3.1	0.8	1.2
Comoros	49.9	50.2	48.2	49.2	2.6	44.9	52.2	2.6	1.0	0.9
Congo, Democratic Rep. of	51.1	50.6	46.0	51.1	2.8	47.4	49.8	2.7	1.0	1.0
Congo, Republic of	51.2	51.1	45.0	51.5	3.4	46.1	50.8	3.1	0.9	1.0
Côte d'Ivoire	48.9	49.0	46.6	51.0	2.5	43.9	53.4	2.7	1.0	0.9
Djibouti	50.5	50.7	44.1	54.1	2.5	40.4	56.3	3.2	0.9	0.8
Equatorial Guinea	51.2	51.2	40.6	53.9	4.1	43.0	53.6	3.9	0.8	0.9
Eritrea	50.4	50.4	0.0	0.0	0.0	45.0	52.4	2.7	..	0.9
Ethiopia	50.6	49.8	44.6	52.5	2.9	46.4	51.0	2.7	0.9	1.0
Gabon	50.9	50.7	34.1	59.5	6.4	39.2	55.0	5.7	0.7	0.8
Gambia, The	50.7	50.6	42.6	54.4	3.0	42.3	54.6	3.0	0.8	0.8
Ghana	50.4	50.3	45.0	52.2	2.8	43.6	53.3	3.1	0.9	0.9
Guinea	50.1	49.7	45.8	51.6	2.6	45.4	52.0	2.6	0.9	0.9
Guinea-Bissau	50.9	50.8	39.0	57.2	4.0	42.8	53.1	4.0	0.8	0.9
Kenya	50.0	49.9	50.1	46.5	3.4	45.3	53.6	2.9	1.1	0.9
Lesotho	51.8	50.8	41.9	53.9	4.2	40.1	55.9	4.1	0.9	0.8
Liberia	49.5	49.6	44.3	52.0	3.6	44.9	52.5	2.7	0.9	0.9
Madagascar	50.7	50.2	44.4	51.7	4.0	45.3	51.7	3.0	0.9	0.9
Malawi	51.6	50.7	47.5	50.3	2.3	46.3	51.2	2.5	1.0	1.0
Mali	51.2	50.7	46.8	50.7	2.6	47.0	49.7	3.3	1.0	1.0
Mauritania	50.7	50.4	43.7	53.1	3.0	43.8	53.1	3.1	0.9	0.9
Mauritius	50.7	50.1	35.7	60.9	3.7	25.9	67.7	6.1	0.6	0.5
Mozambique	50.8	51.6	43.4	53.4	3.1	44.6	51.4	3.9	0.9	0.9
Namibia	50.6	50.2	43.2	53.4	3.7	41.8	54.4	3.7	0.9	0.8
Niger	50.8	50.6	46.8	50.8	2.5	48.7	48.8	2.4	1.0	1.0
Nigeria	50.6	50.7	46.1	51.2	2.6	44.5	53.0	2.5	1.0	0.9
Rwanda	50.6	50.6	48.7	48.8	2.4	45.0	53.0	2.0	1.0	0.9
São Tomé and Principe	..	50.0	0.0	0.0	0.0	38.7	55.1	6.5	..	0.8
Senegal	50.0	50.1	45.3	51.8	2.8	45.0	52.4	2.6	0.9	0.9
Seychelles	..	48.7	0.0	0.0	0.0	30.6	64.5	3.8	..	..
Sierra Leone	51.0	51.0	43.0	53.9	3.1	45.7	51.8	2.6	0.9	0.9
Somalia	50.6	50.4	46.7	50.3	2.9	47.8	49.8	2.4	1.0	1.0
South Africa	50.2	51.9	39.5	57.2	3.4	33.4	61.8	4.8	0.7	0.6
Sudan	49.9	49.8	44.9	52.4	2.7	39.7	57.2	3.1	0.9	0.7
Swaziland	50.9	52.1	45.9	51.3	2.9	42.6	54.8	2.7	1.0	0.8
Tanzania	50.8	50.5	47.6	50.1	2.3	45.8	51.8	2.4	1.0	0.9
Togo	50.7	50.5	44.6	52.4	3.2	45.8	51.2	3.0	0.9	1.0
Uganda	50.5	50.2	47.8	49.7	2.5	48.9	49.0	2.1	1.0	1.0
Zambia	51.1	50.4	49.4	48.2	2.4	46.0	51.8	2.2	1.1	0.9
Zimbabwe	50.4	50.4	47.9	49.5	2.6	41.7	55.5	2.8	1.0	0.8
NORTH AFRICA	49.5	49.4	42.2	53.9	3.9	35.7	60.3	4.3	0.9	0.7
Algeria	50.4	49.4	46.5	49.6	3.9	37.9	59.7	3.8	1.0	0.7
Egypt, Arab Republic	49.2	49.1	39.5	56.5	4.0	35.9	59.7	4.4	0.8	0.7
Libya	47.1	48.1	46.6	51.2	2.2	39.2	57.8	3.0	1.0	0.7
Morocco	49.9	50.0	43.2	52.7	4.1	33.5	62.2	4.3	0.9	0.6
Tunisia	49.3	49.5	41.6	54.6	3.8	32.2	62.2	5.6	0.8	0.6
ALL AFRICA	50.1	50.3	44.6	51.8	3.1	43.0	54.0	3.1	0.9	0.9

Note: Some age groups may not add up to 100 due to rounding up error.

13-2. Poverty

	GDP per capita, based on PPP, 1998	Percentage of population living under US$ 1 a day, 1984-1997	National poverty headcount as % of population, 1984-1997	% of the population below 2/3 of national mean per capita income, 1991-97		Gini coefficients, 1991-96		Percentage of household income spent on food, 1991-97
				Urban	Rural	Urban	Rural	
SUB-SAHARAN AFRICA	1,532	..	..	22	37	..	..	64
excluding South Africa	1,118			22	37			64
excl. S. Africa & Nigeria	1,172	..	..	22	37	..	..	64
Angola	1,334	..	..	..	..	..	..	..
Benin	1,276	..	33	..	..	..	..	..
Botswana	8,547	33	..	..	..	..	..	..
Burkina Faso	1,035	..	..	13	65	38	46	57
Burundi	636	..	36	..	..	..	..	..
Cameroon	1,929	..	40	..	..	..	..	55
Cape Verde	2,999	..	..	..	..	..	..	..
Central African Republic	1,320	..	..	33	77	51	63	60
Chad	..	..	64	..	..	..	..	..
Comoros	1,488	..	..	..	..	..	..	..
Congo, Democratic Rep. of	847	..	..	..	..	..	..	..
Congo, Republic of	1,641	..	..	..	..	..	..	..
Côte d'Ivoire	1,881	18	..	29	51	39	33	48
Djibouti	..	..	..	38	84	38	39	43
Equatorial Guinea	..	..	..	..	..	..	..	..
Eritrea	813	..	..	..	..	..	..	..
Ethiopia	517	..	..	21	50	56	40	72
Gabon	7,556	..	..	..	..	..	..	..
Gambia, The	1,459	..	64	21	73	43	35	60
Ghana	1,661	..	31	22	37	34	36	39
Guinea	1,838	26	40	18	57	..	..	56
Guinea-Bissau	810	88	49	30	65	55	56	..
Kenya	1,168	50	42	14	53	51	52	71
Lesotho	1,827	49	49	..	..	..	..	..
Liberia	..	..	..	..	..	..	..	..
Madagascar	927	72	70	21	57	..	..	70
Malawi	695	..	54	..	..	..	57	..
Mali	739	..	..	8	64	53	55	75
Mauritania	1,746	31	57	18	56	34	33	70
Mauritius	9,629	..	11	..	..	..	..	..
Mozambique	913	..	..	..	..	..	..	..
Namibia	4,932	..	..	..	..	..	..	..
Niger	842	62	63	14	55	39	31	60
Nigeria	922	31	34	32	52	44	46	67
Rwanda	696	46	51	..	..	..	..	..
São Tomé and Principe	1,536	..	..	..	..	..	..	..
Senegal	1,768	54	33	14	66	..	..	61
Seychelles	11,188	..	..	..	..	..	..	..
Sierra Leone	401	..	68	..	..	..	50	..
Somalia	..	..	..	..	..	..	..	..
South Africa	7,187	24	..	40	86	..	..	56
Sudan	1,640	..	..	..	..	..	..	..
Swaziland	3,313	..	..	36	70	..	..	65
Tanzania	513	11	51	20	51	..	..	70
Togo	1,421	..	32	..	..	..	..	..
Uganda	1,183	69	55	16	46	35	44	63
Zambia	910	85	86	28	70	40	46	64
Zimbabwe	2,325	41	26	..	..	..	..	..
NORTH AFRICA	3,669	..	..	..	..	..	..	..
Algeria	4,540	2	23	..	..	..	..	..
Egypt, Arab Republic	3,120	8	23	..	..	..	..	..
Libya	..	..	..	..	..	..	..	..
Morocco	3,357	1	13	..	..	..	..	..
Tunisia	5,453	4	14	..	..	..	..	..
ALL AFRICA	1,905	..	..	22	37	..	..	64

13-3. Income distribution

	Share of income held by population groups			
	Richest 10%	Richest 20%	Poorest 10%	Poorest 20%
	1986-97	1986-97	1986-97	1986-97
SUB-SAHARAN AFRICA	..	..	..	..
excluding South Africa	..	..	..	..
excl. S. Africa & Nigeria	..	..	..	..
Angola	..	..	..	..
Benin	..	..	..	..
Botswana	..	..	..	..
Burkina Faso	39.5	55.0	2.2	5.5
Burundi	26.6	41.6	3.4	7.9
Cameroon	..	..	..	..
Cape Verde	..	..	..	..
Central African Republic	47.7	65.0	0.7	2.0
Chad	..	..	..	..
Comoros	..	..	..	..
Congo, Democratic Rep. of	..	..	..	..
Congo, Republic of	..	..	..	..
Côte d'Ivoire	28.8	44.3	3.1	7.1
Djibouti	29.9	45.4	2.3	6.3
Equatorial Guinea	..	..	..	..
Eritrea	..	..	..	..
Ethiopia	33.7	47.7	3.0	7.1
Gabon	..	..	..	..
Gambia, The	37.6	52.8	1.5	4.3
Ghana	26.1	41.7	3.6	8.4
Guinea	32.0	47.2	2.6	6.4
Guinea-Bissau	42.3	58.9	0.5	2.1
Kenya	34.9	50.2	1.8	5.0
Lesotho	43.4	60.1	0.9	2.8
Liberia	..	..	..	..
Madagascar	36.7	52.1	1.9	5.1
Malawi	..	..	..	..
Mali	40.4	56.2	1.8	4.6
Mauritania	29.9	45.6	2.3	6.2
Mauritius	..	..	..	..
Mozambique	31.7	46.5	2.5	6.5
Namibia	..	..	..	..
Niger	35.4	53.3	0.8	2.6
Nigeria	40.8	55.7	1.6	4.4
Rwanda	..	..	..	..
São Tomé and Principe	..	..	..	..
Senegal	33.5	48.2	2.6	6.4
Seychelles	..	..	..	..
Sierra Leone	43.6	63.4	0.5	1.1
Somalia	..	..	..	..
South Africa	45.9	64.8	1.1	2.9
Sudan	..	..	..	..
Swaziland	50.2	64.4	1.0	2.7
Tanzania	30.0	45.5	2.9	6.8
Togo	..	..	..	..
Uganda	31.2	46.1	2.6	6.6
Zambia	39.2	54.8	1.6	4.2
Zimbabwe	46.9	62.3	1.8	4.0
NORTH AFRICA	..	..	..	..
Algeria	26.8	42.6	2.8	7.0
Egypt, Arab Republic	25.0	39.0	4.4	9.8
Libya	..	..	..	..
Morocco	30.5	46.3	2.8	6.6
Tunisia	30.7	46.3	2.3	5.9
ALL AFRICA	..	..	..	..

13-4. Urbanization

	Total population (millions)			Average annual percentage growth of total population			Urban population as percentage of total population			Average annual percentage growth of urban population		
	1980	1990	1998	1975-79	1980-90	1990-98	1980	1990	1998	1975-79	1980-90	1990-98
SUB-SAHARAN AFRICA	380.7	508.3	627.3	2.9	2.9	2.7	23.0	28.1	33.4	5.0	5.0	5.0
excluding South Africa	353.2	473.1	585.9	2.9	3.0	2.7	21.1	26.5	32.0	5.5	5.4	5.2
excl. S. Africa & Nigeria	282.0	376.9	465.0	2.9	2.9	2.7	19.6	24.4	29.4	5.4	5.2	5.1
Angola	7.0	9.2	12.0	2.7	2.7	3.3	20.9	27.6	32.9	6.1	5.7	5.7
Benin	3.5	4.7	5.9	2.7	3.2	2.9	27.3	34.5	40.7	7.5	5.7	5.1
Botswana	0.9	1.3	1.6	3.6	3.5	2.6	15.1	41.5	49.3	8.8	14.3	5.3
Burkina Faso	7.0	8.9	10.7	2.3	2.5	2.4	8.5	13.6	17.5	8.2	7.5	5.6
Burundi	4.1	5.5	6.5	2.1	2.8	2.4	4.3	6.3	8.4	8.4	6.9	6.1
Cameroon	8.7	11.5	14.3	2.8	2.9	2.8	31.4	40.3	47.2	6.4	5.5	4.9
Cape Verde	0.3	0.3	0.4	0.7	1.6	2.5	23.5	44.2	59.0	2.6	8.1	6.4
Central African Republic	2.3	2.9	3.5	2.3	2.4	2.2	35.1	37.5	40.4	3.4	3.1	3.1
Chad	4.5	5.7	7.3	2.0	2.6	3.0	18.8	21.1	23.2	6.2	3.8	4.2
Comoros	0.3	0.4	0.5	..	..	2.6	23.2	27.9	32.1	..	..	4.4
Congo, Democratic Rep. of	27.0	37.4	48.2	3.0	3.3	3.2	28.7	27.9	29.7	2.4	3.0	4.0
Congo, Republic of	1.7	2.2	2.8	2.9	2.9	2.9	41.0	53.4	60.9	6.1	5.7	4.6
Côte d'Ivoire	8.2	11.6	14.5	4.0	3.6	2.9	34.7	40.3	45.2	5.8	5.2	4.4
Djibouti	0.3	0.5	0.6	6.5	6.4	2.8	73.6	80.2	82.8	8.1	7.4	3.3
Equatorial Guinea	0.2	0.4	0.4	-2.7	5.3	2.5	27.4	35.7	45.8	-2.5	8.0	5.8
Eritrea	2.4	3.1	3.9	2.7	2.8	2.7	13.5	15.8	18.1	4.8	4.5	4.4
Ethiopia	37.7	51.2	61.3	2.7	3.0	2.2	10.5	13.4	16.7	4.8	5.5	5.1
Gabon	0.7	1.0	1.2	3.1	3.4	2.6	49.6	68.1	79.2	7.8	6.7	4.7
Gambia, The	0.6	0.9	1.2	3.3	3.6	3.6	19.6	25.7	31.1	6.2	6.4	6.2
Ghana	10.7	14.9	18.5	1.7	3.3	2.8	31.2	33.9	37.4	2.5	4.2	4.0
Guinea	4.5	5.8	7.1	1.3	2.5	2.7	19.1	25.7	31.4	4.7	5.6	5.3
Guinea-Bissau	0.8	1.0	1.2	5.1	2.1	2.2	16.9	20.0	22.9	6.4	3.9	4.0
Kenya	16.6	23.6	28.8	3.8	3.6	2.6	16.1	24.1	31.3	8.6	7.9	6.3
Lesotho	1.3	1.7	2.1	2.5	2.5	2.3	13.4	20.1	26.4	7.1	6.8	5.8
Liberia	1.9	2.4	3.0	3.1	2.7	2.4	35.0	42.0	43.7	6.1	4.7	2.9
Madagascar	8.9	11.6	14.6	2.6	2.7	2.9	18.3	23.5	28.4	5.3	5.3	5.3
Malawi	6.2	8.5	10.5	3.3	3.2	2.8	9.1	13.3	22.3	7.1	7.1	9.5
Mali	6.6	8.5	10.6	2.2	2.5	2.8	18.5	23.8	28.7	4.9	5.1	5.3
Mauritania	1.6	2.0	2.5	2.5	2.7	2.8	27.4	43.5	55.1	9.1	7.6	6.0
Mauritius	1.0	1.1	1.2	1.6	0.9	1.2	42.4	40.5	41.0	1.3	0.5	1.3
Mozambique	12.1	14.2	16.9	2.8	1.7	2.2	13.1	26.6	37.6	12.1	9.2	6.9
Namibia	1.0	1.4	1.7	2.7	2.7	2.7	22.8	26.6	30.0	4.8	4.4	4.2
Niger	5.6	7.7	10.1	3.1	3.3	3.4	12.6	16.1	19.6	6.9	5.9	6.0
Nigeria	71.1	96.2	120.8	3.0	3.1	2.9	26.9	35.0	42.2	6.0	5.8	5.4
Rwanda	5.2	7.0	8.1	3.3	3.1	1.0	4.7	5.3	6.0	6.9	4.4	2.5
São Tomé and Principe	0.1	0.1	0.1	1.2	2.5	2.7	30.7	38.9	45.2	4.0	5.0	4.7
Senegal	5.5	7.3	9.0	2.9	2.8	2.7	35.7	40.0	46.0	3.7	4.0	4.5
Seychelles	0.1	0.1	0.1	1.7	0.8	1.5	40.8	53.5	61.9	6.1	3.7	3.4
Sierra Leone	3.2	4.0	4.9	2.0	2.1	2.5	24.1	30.0	35.3	4.7	4.4	4.6
Somalia	5.9	7.8	9.1	7.5	2.5	1.8	22.2	24.2	26.7	8.4	3.4	3.0
South Africa	27.6	35.2	41.4	2.2	2.5	2.1	48.1	48.8	52.9	2.2	2.7	3.4
Sudan	18.7	24.1	28.3	3.1	2.6	2.1	20.0	26.6	34.2	4.6	5.4	5.3
Swaziland	0.6	0.8	1.0	3.2	3.1	3.2	17.8	23.8	25.8	8.7	6.3	4.3
Tanzania	18.6	25.5	32.1	3.1	3.2	3.0	14.8	20.8	30.5	11.6	6.9	8.0
Togo	2.6	3.5	4.5	2.7	3.0	3.1	22.9	28.5	32.3	9.7	5.5	4.6
Uganda	12.8	16.3	20.9	2.8	2.3	3.2	8.8	11.2	13.5	3.9	4.8	5.6
Zambia	5.7	7.8	9.7	3.4	3.1	2.8	39.8	39.4	39.4	6.3	3.1	2.8
Zimbabwe	7.0	9.7	11.7	2.8	3.4	2.4	22.3	28.4	33.9	5.6	5.9	4.7
NORTH AFRICA	88.4	114.1	133.3	2.6	2.6	2.0	44.6	49.2	53.0	3.5	3.6	3.0
Algeria	18.7	25.0	29.5	3.1	3.0	2.2	43.5	52.4	58.8	4.5	4.9	3.8
Egypt, Arab Republic	40.9	52.4	61.4	2.3	2.5	2.0	43.8	44.1	44.9	2.5	2.6	2.2
Libya	3.0	4.4	5.3	4.4	3.9	2.3	69.3	81.8	86.7	7.6	5.7	3.1
Morocco	19.4	24.0	27.8	2.3	2.2	1.8	41.1	48.2	54.5	4.1	3.8	3.4
Tunisia	6.4	8.2	9.3	2.5	2.5	1.8	51.5	57.9	64.1	3.4	3.7	3.1
ALL AFRICA	469.1	622.4	760.6	2.8	2.9	2.5	27.1	32.0	36.8	4.5	4.6	4.4

Note: Minus sign indicates population outflow.

13-5. Components of population change

	Total fertility rate			Crude birth rate			Crude death rate		
	1982	*1992*	*1998*	*1982*	*1992*	*1998*	*1982*	*1992*	*1998*
SUB-SAHARAN AFRICA	6.6	5.9	5.4	46.5	43.0	40.3	17.0	15.4	14.9
excluding South Africa	6.9	6.1	5.6	47.4	43.9	41.4	17.4	15.9	15.4
excl. S. Africa & Nigeria	6.8	6.2	5.7	46.8	44.1	41.7	17.5	16.3	16.2
Angola	7.0	7.2	6.7	50.8	50.8	48.1	22.8	19.2	18.7
Benin	7.0	6.5	5.7	49.3	43.9	40.5	18.1	15.3	13.0
Botswana	6.0	4.8	4.2	44.1	36.8	33.3	9.5	8.0	16.3
Burkina Faso	7.5	6.9	6.7	46.9	47.3	44.3	19.9	18.3	19.1
Burundi	6.8	6.8	6.2	46.2	46.2	42.1	17.9	21.5	20.2
Cameroon	6.4	5.7	5.0	43.9	40.6	38.4	15.7	12.8	12.4
Cape Verde	6.3	5.3	3.9	38.4	36.0	37.1	11.3	7.6	6.3
Central African Republic	5.7	5.3	4.8	42.4	39.6	36.6	18.6	17.4	19.3
Chad	7.1	6.9	6.4	44.2	47.0	44.8	21.4	18.2	16.4
Comoros	7.2	5.2	4.5	45.5	37.0	34.3	16.8	10.2	8.8
Congo, Democratic Rep. of	6.7	6.7	6.3	47.9	46.2	46.0	15.2	14.7	14.7
Congo, Republic of	6.3	6.3	6.0	43.9	44.7	43.4	15.7	16.1	16.3
Côte d'Ivoire	7.4	5.7	5.0	50.1	38.9	37.0	16.0	14.9	16.7
Djibouti	6.6	5.8	5.2	44.2	39.0	37.3	19.1	16.2	15.3
Equatorial Guinea	5.8	5.9	5.4	43.3	43.5	40.5	21.1	18.0	16.1
Eritrea	7.5	6.5	5.7	..	42.4	39.8	..	16.4	12.1
Ethiopia	7.0	6.6	6.4	48.0	49.0	45.2	22.1	20.2	20.2
Gabon	4.5	5.2	5.1	33.1	36.6	36.2	18.1	16.1	15.8
Gambia, The	6.5	6.0	5.6	48.2	43.5	41.8	23.1	19.2	13.3
Ghana	6.5	5.5	4.8	45.0	38.4	35.0	13.1	10.6	9.3
Guinea	6.2	5.7	5.4	46.8	45.0	40.5	23.5	19.0	17.2
Guinea-Bissau	6.0	6.0	5.6	44.7	43.3	41.5	25.1	21.4	20.8
Kenya	7.7	5.2	4.6	49.7	36.1	34.7	12.1	9.4	11.9
Lesotho	5.3	5.0	4.6	38.9	36.4	34.6	13.8	11.3	12.6
Liberia	6.8	6.8	6.2	47.0	48.2	45.1	16.7	24.8	17.3
Madagascar	6.6	6.0	5.7	46.5	45.9	41.4	15.5	12.6	11.1
Malawi	7.6	6.7	6.4	53.5	50.2	46.9	21.6	22.1	23.0
Mali	7.1	..	6.5	49.0	51.1	46.6	21.6	17.5	15.9
Mauritania	6.1	5.9	5.4	42.3	42.6	39.9	18.5	14.7	13.2
Mauritius	2.5	2.3	2.0	22.2	20.4	16.8	6.0	6.7	6.8
Mozambique	6.5	6.3	5.2	45.7	44.9	40.6	20.1	18.6	19.5
Namibia	5.8	5.3	4.8	40.3	38.5	35.3	13.5	11.8	12.6
Niger	7.5	7.4	7.3	51.7	52.1	51.8	22.2	19.2	18.3
Nigeria	6.9	5.9	5.3	49.6	43.3	40.1	17.1	14.2	12.3
Rwanda	8.1	6.6	6.1	50.4	40.0	45.5	18.6	26.6	21.1
São Tomé and Principe	..	4.9	4.6	38.7	43.0	32.1	10.2	9.0	9.4
Senegal	6.7	6.0	5.5	45.5	40.0	39.1	17.7	13.0	12.7
Seychelles	3.5	2.7	2.1	24.1	22.9	20.5	7.4	7.2	6.5
Sierra Leone	6.5	6.5	6.0	48.9	49.1	45.4	28.5	29.8	25.3
Somalia	7.3	7.3	7.2	51.8	52.1	51.8	22.0	25.1	18.1
South Africa	4.2	3.2	2.8	35.5	31.2	24.7	11.1	8.8	8.8
Sudan	6.4	5.0	4.6	43.5	34.9	33.2	15.8	13.9	11.5
Swaziland	6.0	5.1	4.6	43.1	40.2	36.8	13.7	10.7	11.0
Tanzania	6.7	6.0	5.4	46.5	42.8	40.6	14.8	13.5	16.0
Togo	6.9	6.6	5.1	45.0	41.6	39.7	15.8	15.5	15.7
Uganda	7.3	6.9	6.5	49.1	50.2	47.1	17.6	18.2	20.2
Zambia	6.9	6.2	5.5	49.0	44.6	41.7	14.8	15.1	19.3
Zimbabwe	6.2	4.3	3.7	43.0	35.5	30.9	11.8	10.9	13.3
NORTH AFRICA	5.4	3.8	3.2	38.9	28.2	24.5	11.6	7.5	6.5
Algeria	6.3	4.0	3.5	40.6	28.2	25.9	10.7	6.0	5.9
Egypt, Arab Republic	5.1	3.8	3.2	39.1	28.5	24.2	12.7	8.6	6.9
Libya	7.2	4.2	3.7	45.6	28.8	28.8	10.9	5.2	4.5
Morocco	5.1	3.8	3.0	37.3	28.2	25.1	11.4	7.5	6.7
Tunisia	4.9	3.2	2.2	33.7	25.7	17.9	8.4	6.3	5.6
ALL AFRICA	6.4	5.5	5.0	45.1	40.3	37.5	16.0	14.0	13.4

13-6. Survival prospects

	Life expectancy at birth (years)		Infant mortality (per thousand)		Mortality of children under 5 years (per thousand)	Maternal mortality (per 100,000 live births)	Adult HIV-1 seroprevalence (per 100 adults)
	1982	1998	1982	1998	1998	1998 or MR available	end 1999
SUB-SAHARAN AFRICA	48	50	112	92	151	..	8.6
excluding South Africa	48	49	114	94	154	..	7.3
excl. S. Africa & Nigeria	48	48	119	98	163	..	7.8
Angola	42	47	149	124	204	1,500	2.8
Benin	49	53	115	87	140	500	2.5
Botswana	59	46	67	62	105	330	36.1
Burkina Faso	45	44	117	104	210	930	6.5
Burundi	47	42	118	118	196	1,300	11.3
Cameroon	51	54	103	77	150	430	7.7
Cape Verde	62	68	84	55	67	55	..
Central African Republic	47	44	114	98	162	1,100	13.9
Chad	43	48	120	99	172	830	2.7
Comoros	50	60	106	63	88	500	0.1
Congo, Democratic Rep. of	50	51	109	90	141	..	5.1
Congo, Republic of	50	48	88	90	143	890	6.4
Côte d'Ivoire	50	46	105	88	143	600	10.8
Djibouti	45	50	132	106	176	570	11.7
Equatorial Guinea	44	50	138	106	171	820	0.5
Eritrea	44	51	91	61	90	1,000	2.9
Ethiopia	42	43	159	107	173	1,400	10.8
Gabon	49	53	112	86	132	..	4.2
Gambia, The	41	53	154	76	..	1,000	1.9
Ghana	54	60	90	65	96	..	3.6
Guinea	40	47	177	118	184	..	1.5
Guinea-Bissau	39	44	164	128	205	910	2.4
Kenya	56	51	66	76	124	590	14.1
Lesotho	54	55	117	93	144	610	24.0
Liberia	51	47	144	114	187	560	2.8
Madagascar	51	58	112	92	146	490	0.1
Malawi	45	42	163	134	229	620	16.1
Mali	43	50	180	117	218	580	2.0
Mauritania	47	54	117	90	140	..	0.5
Mauritius	67	71	28	19	22	50	0.1
Mozambique	44	45	133	134	213	1,500	12.8
Namibia	54	54	84	67	112	230	19.0
Niger	42	46	136	118	250	590	1.3
Nigeria	46	53	96	76	119	1,000	5.1
Rwanda	46	41	124	123	205	1,300	11.1
São Tomé and Principe	..	64	80	49	64	..	..
Senegal	46	52	112	69	121	560	1.8
Seychelles	69	72	19	15	17	..	..
Sierra Leone	35	37	189	169	283	1,800	3.0
Somalia	43	48	143	121	199	1,600	..
South Africa	58	63	63	51	83	230	19.9
Sudan	49	55	92	69	105	..	1.0
Swaziland	53	56	94	69	117	230	25.0
Tanzania	51	47	104	85	136	530	8.0
Togo	50	49	97	78	144	480	6.0
Uganda	48	42	116	101	170	510	8.3
Zambia	51	43	88	114	192	650	20.1
Zimbabwe	56	51	76	73	125	400	24.3
NORTH AFRICA	59	68	97	44	52	..	0.0
Algeria	60	71	88	35	40	..	0.1
Egypt, Arab Republic	57	67	112	49	59	170	0.0
Libya	62	70	60	23	27	75	0.1
Morocco	60	67	92	49	61	230	0.0
Tunisia	64	72	59	28	32	70	0.0
ALL AFRICA	50	54	109	86	140	..	6.8

13-7. Immunization and ORT use

	Percentage of children (0-1 years) immunized against						ORT use among the under five (percent)
	DPT			Measles			
	1986	1994	1998	1986	1994	1998	1992-93
SUB-SAHARAN AFRICA	32	51	48	36	53	50	..
excluding South Africa	30	51	47	35	53	48	50
excl. S. Africa & Nigeria	34	53	54	40	53	54	..
Angola	10	31	45	60	44	80	48
Benin	17	86	81	20	78	82	28
Botswana	65	78	82	64	71	80	64
Burkina Faso	34	41	40	64	45	45	15
Burundi	65	47	50	41	43	44	49
Cameroon	..	31	48	..	31	47	84
Cape Verde	54	..	80	59	..	66	5
Central African Republic	19	40	45	24	37	39	24
Chad	10	18	23	..	24	30	15
Comoros	24	58	75	26	..	67	70
Congo, Democratic Rep. of	39	29	18	39	33	20	46
Congo, Republic of	68	..	23	86	..	18	67
Côte d'Ivoire	30	41	64	..	47	66	16
Djibouti	26	57	23	19	59	21	56
Equatorial Guinea	3	..	81	17	..	82	40
Eritrea	..	36	60	..	..	52	..
Ethiopia	7	37	57	10	28	45	68
Gabon	48	48	54	58	50	32	25
Gambia, The	73	78	96	62	68	91	51
Ghana	15	48	68	31	49	67	44
Guinea	2	73	56	9	69	58	82
Guinea-Bissau	29	74	63	..	68	51	26
Kenya	72	50	64	65	47	61	69
Lesotho	73	58	57	72	82	53	78
Liberia	15	..	19	39	..	31	15
Madagascar	22	66	68	18	55	65	26
Malawi	70	98	96	65	99	90	50
Mali	3	39	53	5	46	58	41
Mauritania	11	50	28	40	53	20	54
Mauritius	86	89	90	75	85	85	..
Mozambique	32	55	77	39	65	87	60
Namibia	..	80	74	..	68	63	75
Niger	5	..	25	..	..	85	17
Nigeria	16	44	21	17	50	26	80
Rwanda	77	..	77	63	..	66	36
São Tomé and Principe	65	..	73	58	..	59	50
Senegal	..	57	65	..	50	65	27
Seychelles	94	96	99	95	92	93	..
Sierra Leone	..	41	56	..	44	68	60
Somalia	17	..	24	25	..	47	78
South Africa	70	..	76	64	..	82	..
Sudan	14	77	67	11	86	63	47
Swaziland	73	74	76	66	62	62	85
Tanzania	74	83	74	97	79	72	83
Togo	..	71	36	..	59	34	33
Uganda	21	79	46	32	79	30	45
Zambia	66	86	70	36	89	69	90
Zimbabwe	75	80	70	74	79	65	..
NORTH AFRICA	71	87	92	68	85	91	24
Algeria	..	75	80	..	69	75	27
Egypt, Arab Republic	80	92	96	78	92	98	34
Libya	53	..	97	52	..	93	80
Morocco	54	87	93	48	87	91	14
Tunisia	72	91	96	67	87	94	22
ALL AFRICA	38	57	54	41	57	55	48

Notes: ORT = Oral re-hydration therapy; DPT = diphtheria, pertussis (whopping cough), and tetanus.

13-8. Child malnutrition

	Percentage of children (1990-97)			Percentage of infants with low birth weight		Percentage of under-five (1990-97) suffering from moderate to severe		
	Exclusively breastfed, (0-3 months)	Breastfed, plus other food, (6-9 months)	Still breastfeading, (20-23 months)	1988	1993-97	Underweight	Wasting	Stunting
SUB-SAHARAN AFRICA	30	63	47	..	..	..	..	..
excluding South Africa	30	63	47	..	..	..	..	..
excl. S. Africa & Nigeria	37	67	49	..	..	..	..	..
Angola	12	70	49	21	..	41	6	53
Benin	15	97	65	8	..	29	14	25
Botswana	39	82	23	8	8	17	11	29
Burkina Faso	12	44	81	..	21	33	13	29
Burundi	89	66	73	..	16	..	9	43
Cameroon	7	77	35	10	13	22	6	29
Cape Verde	18	..	..	..	..	14	6	16
Central African Republic	23	93	52	15	..	23	7	34
Chad	2	81	62	..	..	39	..	40
Comoros	5	87	45	7	..	26	8	34
Congo, Democratic Rep. of	32	40	64	10	..	34	10	45
Congo, Republic of	43	95	27	..	16	..	..	..
Côte d'Ivoire	3	65	45	15	14	24	8	24
Djibouti	..	..	..	11	..	18	13	26
Equatorial Guinea	..	..	..	..	..	..	..	..
Eritrea	66	45	60	..	..	44	16	38
Ethiopia	74	..	35	..	16	48	8	64
Gabon	57	..	..	10	10	..	..	..
Gambia, The	..	8	58	..	..	26	6	14
Ghana	19	63	48	17	17	27	11	26
Guinea	52	..	15	25	13	..	12	29
Guinea-Bissau	..	..	..	13	20	..	5	..
Kenya	17	90	54	15	16	22	6	34
Lesotho	54	47	52	10	..	16	5	44
Liberia	15	17	25	..	..	..	..	..
Madagascar	61	93	49	10	15	40	7	48
Malawi	11	78	68	20	..	30	7	48
Mali	13	33	60	17	17	27	23	30
Mauritania	90	64	59	..	9	23	7	44
Mauritius	16	29	..	9	..	15	14	10
Mozambique	37	..	..	20	20	26	8	36
Namibia	22	65	23	..	..	26	9	29
Niger	1	67	52	..	15	50	21	41
Nigeria	2	52	43	20	16	39	9	43
Rwanda	90	68	85	..	17	27	4	42
São Tomé and Principe	..	..	..	7	3	..	..	26
Senegal	16	69	50	..	..	22	7	23
Seychelles	..	..	..	10	9	6	..	..
Sierra Leone	..	94	41	13	..	29	9	35
Somalia	..	..	..	..	16	..	..	30
South Africa	..	..	..	..	..	9	3	23
Sudan	14	45	44	15	15	34	17	34
Swaziland	37	51	20	..	..	..	..	..
Tanzania	41	93	53	13	14	31	7	43
Togo	15	25	99	20	20	25	..	34
Uganda	70	64	40	..	..	26	5	38
Zambia	27	88	43	..	13	24	4	42
Zimbabwe	16	93	26	5	14	16	6	21
NORTH AFRICA	45	34	..	..	..	14	..	..
Algeria	48	29	21	9	9	13	9	18
Egypt, Arab Republic	53	37	..	12	12	11	5	30
Libya	..	..	..	5	5	5	3	15
Morocco	31	33	20	..	4	10	2	24
Tunisia	12	53	16	8	16	9	4	23
ALL AFRICA	32	59	45	..	..	..	..	..

13-9. Access to sanitation facilities

	Percentage of population with access to sanitation facilities					
	1990*			1993-97		
	Total	Urban	Rural	Total	Urban	Rural
SUB-SAHARAN AFRICA	..	..	..	..	..	..
excluding South Africa	..	..	..	..	..	..
excl. S. Africa & Nigeria	..	..	..	..	..	..
Angola	18	27	16	16	34	8
Benin	10	45	4	20	54	6
Botswana	36	85	35	55	91	41
Burkina Faso	9	38	5	18	78	11
Burundi	..	..	..	..	..	..
Cameroon	36	..	..	40	73	21
Cape Verde	10	36	9	..	..	..
Central African Republic	19	36	9	..	..	..
Chad	14	..	..	21	74	7
Comoros	..	..	..	23	40	16
Congo, Democratic Rep. of	..	..	..	..	..	..
Congo, Republic of	..	..	..	9	15	4
Côte d'Ivoire	50	..	..	54	59	51
Djibouti	84	94	50	..	..	..
Equatorial Guinea	..	..	..	54	61	48
Eritrea	..	..	..	..	12	0
Ethiopia	..	..	5	8	..	..
Gabon	50	..	..	76	79	67
Gambia, The	..	..	..	37	83	23
Ghana	26	47	17	42	53	36
Guinea	..	..	..	14	24	10
Guinea-Bissau	..	..	..	20	32	17
Kenya	44	75	39	77	69	81
Lesotho	..	..	..	8	..	7
Liberia	21	24	20	18	38	2
Madagascar	..	12	..	15	50	3
Malawi	60	88	56	53	70	51
Mali	21	90	5	31	58	21
Mauritania	35	67	18	32	44	19
Mauritius	100	100	100	..	..	..
Mozambique	..	..	..	21	53	12
Namibia	..	..	..	..	..	..
Niger	9	36	3	17	79	5
Nigeria	..	30	..	36	61	21
Rwanda	55	60	60	..	..	..
São Tomé and Principe	15	39	7	19	..	..
Senegal	..	..	..	58	83	40
Seychelles	99	..	..	98	..	99
Sierra Leone	..	..	..	11	17	8
Somalia	15	60	5	18	..	..
South Africa	..	..	..	46	79	12
Sudan	5	20	1	22	79	4
Swaziland	..	..	..	36	36	37
Tanzania	..	..	..	86	97	83
Togo	14	34	8	..	..	..
Uganda	13	40	10	57	75	55
Zambia	47	56	41	23	40	10
Zimbabwe	56	100	41	66	99	48
NORTH AFRICA	..	..	..	20	37	9
Algeria	59	..	..	..	..	..
Egypt, Arab Republic	..	..	..	11	20	5
Libya	..	..	..	86	90	75
Morocco	..	..	..	40	69	18
Tunisia	52	84	16	..	..	..
ALL AFRICA	..	..	..	..	..	..

*or most recent available data.

13-10. Access to safe water

	Percentage of population with access to safe water					
	1990*			1993-97		
	Total	Urban	Rural	Total	Urban	Rural
SUB-SAHARAN AFRICA	..	60	26	..	..	..
excluding South Africa	..	60	26	..	..	..
excl. S. Africa & Nigeria	..	..	..	..	..	..
Angola	28	80	15	32	69	15
Benin	14	65	45	50	41	53
Botswana	56	100	33	70	100	53
Burkina Faso	35	50	26	..	..	..
Burundi	45	92	27	..	..	..
Cameroon	36	46	30	41	71	24
Cape Verde	31	99	21	..	..	..
Central African Republic	..	..	..	..	..	..
Chad	..	27	30	24	48	17
Comoros	46	99	52	48	74	41
Congo, Democratic Rep. of	36	62	16	..	..	..
Congo, Republic of	47	42	7	..	50	8
Côte d'Ivoire	20	30	10	72	59	81
Djibouti	24	27	14	..	..	..
Equatorial Guinea	..	47	..	95	88	100
Eritrea	..	..	..	7	..	..
Ethiopia	..	..	..	27	90	20
Gabon	52	75	34	67	80	30
Gambia, The	64	92	56	76	..	..
Ghana	..	57	40	56	70	49
Guinea	27	62	15	62	61	62
Guinea-Bissau	31	21	37	53	38	57
Kenya	27	61	21	53	67	49
Lesotho	18	37	14	52	14	64
Liberia	37	50	25	30	58	8
Madagascar	31	81	17	29	83	10
Malawi	32	70	27	45	52	44
Mali	..	..	..	37	36	38
Mauritania	37	80	16	64	87	41
Mauritius	98	95	100	..	..	..
Mozambique	19	50	12	32	17	40
Namibia	..	..	..	..	..	..
Niger	37	48	34	53	46	55
Nigeria	36	60	30	39	63	26
Rwanda	70	55	60	..	..	44
São Tomé and Principe	52	100	61	60	..	..
Senegal	44	63	27	50	82	28
Seychelles	90	..	..	97	99	80
Sierra Leone	24	58	8	34	58	21
Somalia	31	60	20	37	..	..
South Africa	..	..	..	70	90	33
Sudan	..	49	45	50	66	45
Swaziland	33	..	..	43	41	44
Tanzania	52	85	47	49	65	45
Togo	35	68	54	..	..	..
Uganda	16	45	12	34	47	32
Zambia	48	70	32	43	64	27
Zimbabwe	65	100	14	77	99	64
NORTH AFRICA	72	85	41	60	87	40
Algeria	77	86	55	..	..	..
Egypt, Arab Republic	90	93	61	64	82	50
Libya	90	92	75	90	90	91
Morocco	47	74	17	52	98	14
Tunisia	89	98	79	..	..	..
ALL AFRICA	..	..	..	..	..	..

*or most recent available data.

13-11. Health expenditure

	Public expenditure as % of GDP, 1990-97	Private expenditure as % of GDP, 1990-97	Total expenditure		
			as % of GDP, 1990-97	per capita, US$, 1990-97	per capita PPP, international $, 1990-97
SUB-SAHARAN AFRICA	1.2	2.7	..	..	..
excluding South Africa	1.2	..	..	..	..
excl. S.Africa & Nigeria	1.6	..	..	..	..
Angola	3.9	..	..	..	..
Benin	1.6	0.4	2.0	7	19
Botswana	2.4	1.6	4.0	130	288
Burkina Faso	1.2	2.7	3.9	9	34
Burundi	1.5	2.6	4.0	6	23
Cameroon	1.0	4.0	5.0	31	83
Cape Verde	2.8	0.4	3.3	36	96
Central African Republic	1.9	0.9	2.8	8	31
Chad	2.4	0.6	3.1	7	26
Comoros	3.1	1.4	4.6	17	67
Congo, Democratic Rep. of	1.2	1.3	2.5	..	..
Congo, Republic of	1.8	3.2	5.0	42	62
Côte d'Ivoire	1.4	2.3	3.7	27	66
Djibouti	..	..	..	..	..
Equatorial Guinea	3.0	1.6	4.7	55	65
Eritrea	2.9	0.9	2.0	..	15
Ethiopia	1.4	2.4	3.8	4	23
Gabon	0.6	..	..	..	..
Gambia, The	1.4	1.7	3.1	11	46
Ghana	1.4	1.6	3.0	12	53
Guinea	1.2	1.0	2.2	13	43
Guinea-Bissau	1.1	..	..	..	..
Kenya	2.2	1.0	1.0	3	10
Lesotho	3.7	2.4	..	..	..
Liberia	..	..	..	..	..
Madagascar	1.1	1.0	2.1	5	..
Malawi	3.3	..	..	..	..
Mali	2.1	1.5	2.7	8	17
Mauritania	1.8	4.1	5.2	28	68
Mauritius	2.2	1.7	4.0	116	330
Mozambique	2.1	..	..	..	..
Namibia	3.8	3.6	7.4	150	399
Niger	1.3	..	..	..	..
Nigeria	0.2	0.5	0.7	9	6
Rwanda	2.1	..	..	..	..
São Tomé and Principe	6.1	..	..	..	..
Senegal	2.6	2.1	4.7	23	66
Seychelles	4.2	..	..	..	..
Sierra Leone	1.7	6.2	7.9	14	39
Somalia	..	..	..	..	..
South Africa	3.2	3.5	7.1	246	571
Sudan	..	1.9	0.2	4	..
Swaziland	2.5	0.9	3.4	47	141
Tanzania	1.1	..	..	..	..
Togo	1.1	2.1	3.2	11	46
Uganda	1.8	2.9	4.7	14	50
Zambia	2.9	0.7	3.3	16	27
Zimbabwe	1.9	3.1	4.7	38	131
NORTH AFRICA	1.6	2.2	3.9	48	129
Algeria	3.3	1.3	4.6	68	217
Egypt, Arab Republic	1.8	2.0	3.8	48	124
Libya	..	..	..	..	..
Morocco	1.3	2.7	4.0	49	140
Tunisia	3.0	2.9	5.9	118	320
ALL AFRICA	1.4	2.6	..	..	..

13-12. Health care

	Population per physician		Population per hospital bed		Percentage of births attended by trained health personnel	Percentage of population with access to health services
	1981	1990-96	1981	1990-96	1990-95	1990-94
SUB-SAHARAN AFRICA	..	..	..	1,410	..	..
excluding South Africa	..	..	..	1,410	..	..
excl. S.Africa & Nigeria	..	..	..	1,665	..	..
Angola	..	25,014	..	769	17	24.0
Benin	16,989	16,641	886	5,000	34	42.0
Botswana	7,451	5,264	..	625	..	..
Burkina Faso	55,744	25,000	..	714	41	..
Burundi	..	16,682	..	1,428	24	80.0
Cameroon	..	14,286	..	385	58	..
Cape Verde	..	4,367	..	625	49	..
Central African Republic	22,777	16,674	..	1,111	46	..
Chad	..	50,108	..	1,428	..	26.0
Comoros	..	7,716	..	357	..	..
Congo, Democratic Rep. of	..	14,288	..	714	..	59.0
Congo, Republic of	..	3,706	..	294	..	..
Côte d'Ivoire	..	11,113	..	1,250	45	..
Djibouti	4,291	5,272	266	400	..	..
Equatorial Guinea	..	4,750	..	..	5	..
Eritrea	..	49,900	..	..	21	..
Ethiopia	88,119	33,327	..	5,000	..	55.0
Gabon	2,189	4,354	..	313	80	..
Gambia, The	..	49,502	..	1,667	..	..
Ghana	..	..	..	667	..	25.0
Guinea	45,463	6,666	..	1,667	..	45.0
Guinea-Bissau	..	5,546	528	666	50	..
Kenya	10,095	7,108	..	625	45	..
Lesotho	..	20,047	..	..	50	..
Liberia	9,454	..	..	..	..	..
Madagascar	10,060	3,704	..	1,111	71	..
Malawi	53,913	33,344	..	625	57	..
Mali	25,992	16,656	..	..	46	..
Mauritania	..	16,687	..	1,429	..	..
Mauritius	1,813	1,163	..	323	91	99.0
Mozambique	36,970	..	..	1,111	29	..
Namibia	..	4,344	..	..	71	..
Niger	..	50,101	..	8,335	21	30.0
Nigeria	..	5,263	..	588	31	67.0
Rwanda	32,318	24,967	677	588	28	..
São Tomé and Principe	2,388	3,044	..	213	63	..
Senegal	12,687	11,113	..	2,500	47	40.0
Seychelles	..	969	..	..	99	99.0
Sierra Leone	18,975	..	..	..	..	..
Somalia	22,103	24,999	..	1,250	2	..
South Africa	..	1,613	..	..	82	..
Sudan	9,581	10,002	1,110	909	86	70.0
Swaziland	..	9,059	..	..	67	55.0
Tanzania	..	24,994	..	1,111	44	93.0
Togo	21,355	16,695	..	667	..	..
Uganda	21,405	25,007	661	1,111	38	..
Zambia	7,913	11,104	287	..	51	..
Zimbabwe	7,074	6,665	..	2,000	49	..
NORTH AFRICA	5,936	1,291	570	516	..	88.2
Algeria	..	1,220	..	476	77	..
Egypt, Arab Republic	733	625	483	476	46	99.0
Libya	611	694	207	238	68	100.0
Morocco	18,558	2,778	814	909	31	62.4
Tunisia	3,642	1,515	..	500	50	90.0
ALL AFRICA	..	..	..	1,214	..	..

13-13. Illiteracy rate

| | Percentage of population 15 years of age and above that is illiterate | | | | | | | | |
| | 1985 | | | 1990 | | | 1998 | | |
	Total	Male	Female	Total	Male	Female	Total	Male	Female
SUB-SAHARAN AFRICA	56	45	66	50	40	60	41	32	49
excluding South Africa	59	48	70	53	42	63	43	34	52
excl. S. Africa & Nigeria	59	48	70	53	43	64	44	35	53
Angola	..	..	..	..	..	..	..	..	..
Benin	77	66	87	72	59	84	62	46	77
Botswana	37	38	35	32	34	30	24	27	22
Burkina Faso	87	79	94	84	75	92	78	68	87
Burundi	66	53	78	62	50	73	54	45	63
Cameroon	45	34	56	37	28	46	26	20	33
Cape Verde	43	29	53	36	24	46	27	16	35
Central African Republic	72	58	85	67	53	79	56	43	68
Chad	78	69	87	72	63	81	61	51	69
Comoros	49	41	57	46	39	54	42	35	48
Congo, Democratic Rep. of	59	45	73	52	38	66	41	29	53
Congo, Republic of	41	29	52	33	23	42	22	14	29
Côte d'Ivoire	72	62	82	66	56	77	56	47	64
Djibouti	53	38	68	47	33	60	38	26	49
Equatorial Guinea	33	18	48	27	14	39	19	9	29
Eritrea	62	46	77	57	42	72	48	34	62
Ethiopia	76	68	85	72	64	80	64	58	70
Gabon	..	..	..	..	..	..	..	..	..
Gambia, The	80	74	85	74	68	80	65	58	73
Ghana	49	36	61	42	30	53	31	22	40
Guinea	..	..	..	..	..	..	..	..	..
Guinea-Bissau	76	61	91	72	54	89	63	43	83
Kenya	36	24	48	29	19	39	20	12	27
Lesotho	25	39	13	22	35	11	18	29	7
Liberia	67	51	82	61	45	77	49	33	66
Madagascar	47	38	56	42	34	50	35	28	42
Malawi	52	34	68	48	31	64	42	27	56
Mali	81	74	87	74	67	81	62	54	69
Mauritania	66	56	76	64	53	74	59	48	69
Mauritius	23	17	29	20	15	25	16	13	20
Mozambique	71	56	86	67	51	82	58	42	73
Namibia	29	26	33	25	23	28	19	18	20
Niger	90	84	96	89	82	95	85	78	93
Nigeria	59	48	70	51	41	62	39	30	48
Rwanda	53	43	64	47	37	56	36	29	43
São Tomé and Principe	..	..	..	..	..	..	..	..	..
Senegal	76	66	85	72	62	81	65	55	74
Seychelles	..	..	..	..	..	..	..	..	..
Sierra Leone	..	..	..	..	..	..	..	..	..
Somalia	..	..	..	..	..	..	..	..	..
South Africa	21	20	22	19	18	20	15	15	16
Sudan	60	44	75	54	39	68	44	32	57
Swaziland	34	32	36	28	26	30	22	21	23
Tanzania	43	28	57	36	23	49	26	17	36
Togo	59	42	76	54	36	71	45	28	62
Uganda	49	35	63	44	31	57	35	24	46
Zambia	37	25	48	32	22	41	24	16	31
Zimbabwe	24	17	31	19	13	25	13	8	17
NORTH AFRICA	57	43	71	52	38	65	43	31	55
Algeria	53	39	68	46	32	59	35	24	46
Egypt, Arab Republic	57	43	71	53	40	66	46	35	58
Libya	39	22	59	32	17	49	22	10	35
Morocco	67	53	80	61	47	75	53	40	66
Tunisia	47	34	61	41	28	54	31	21	42
ALL AFRICA	56	45	67	50	40	61	41	32	50

13-14. Primary school gross enrollment ratio

	Total			Males			Females		
	1980	*1990*	*1994-97*	*1980*	*1990*	*1994-97*	*1980*	*1990*	*1994-97*
SUB-SAHARAN AFRICA	81	76	78	88	83	85	67	68	71
excluding South Africa	80	72	74	88	80	81	67	64	66
excl. S. Africa & Nigeria	72	67	67	79	73	72	60	59	59
Angola	175	92	..	..	96	..	..	88	..
Benin	67	58	78	91	78	98	43	39	57
Botswana	91	113	108	83	109	107	100	117	108
Burkina Faso	18	33	40	22	41	48	13	26	31
Burundi	26	73	51	32	79	55	21	66	46
Cameroon	98	101	85	107	109	93	90	93	84
Cape Verde	114	121	148	119	..	150	110	..	147
Central African Republic	71	65	..	92	80	..	51	51	..
Chad	..	54	58	..	75	76	..	34	39
Comoros	86	75	75	100	87	..	72	63	..
Congo, Democratic Rep. of	92	70	72	108	81	86	77	60	59
Congo, Republic of	141	133	114	148	141	120	135	124	109
Côte d'Ivoire	75	67	71	90	79	82	60	56	61
Djibouti	37	38	39	..	45	45	..	32	33
Equatorial Guinea	160		..	..	..	..	..	..	..
Eritrea	..	..	53	..	..	59	..	..	48
Ethiopia	37	33	43	48	39	55	27	26	31
Gabon	174	..	162	178	..	163	171	..	161
Gambia, The	53	64	77	70	76	87	36	52	67
Ghana	79	75	79	88	82	84	71	68	74
Guinea	36	37	54	48	50	68	25	24	41
Guinea-Bissau	68	..	62	94	..	79	43	..	45
Kenya	115	95	85	120	97	85	110	93	85
Lesotho	104	112	108	85	100	102	122	123	114
Liberia	48	..	..	61	..	..	35	..	..
Madagascar	130	103	92	131	103	92	129	103	91
Malawi	60	68	134	72	74	140	49	62	127
Mali	26	27	49	34	34	58	19	19	40
Mauritania	37	49	79	48	56	84	26	41	75
Mauritius	93	109	106	94	109	106	91	110	106
Mozambique	99	67	60	115	77	70	84	57	50
Namibia	..	129	131	..	123	129	..	135	132
Niger	25	29	29	33	37	36	18	21	23
Nigeria	109	91	98	123	104	109	95	79	87
Rwanda	63	70	..	66	70	..	60	69	..
São Tomé and Principe	..	..	..	..	..	..	..	..	..
Senegal	46	59	71	56	68	78	37	50	65
Seychelles	..	..	..	..	..	..	..	..	..
Sierra Leone	52	50	..	61	60	..	43	41	..
Somalia	22	..	..	28	..	..	15	..	..
South Africa	90	122	133	..	123	135	..	121	131
Sudan	50	53	51	59	60	55	41	45	47
Swaziland	103	111	117	104	114	120	102	109	114
Tanzania	93	70	67	99	70	67	86	69	66
Togo	118	109	120	144	132	140	93	87	99
Uganda	50	75	74	56	83	81	43	66	68
Zambia	90	99	89	98	..	91	83	..	86
Zimbabwe	85	116	112	..	117	115	..	115	111
NORTH AFRICA	84	91	100	97	100	107	69	83	93
Algeria	95	100	108	108	108	113	81	92	102
Egypt, Arab Republic	73	94	101	84	101	108	61	86	94
Libya	125	105	..	129	109	..	121	102	..
Morocco	83	67	86	102	79	97	63	54	74
Tunisia	102	113	118	117	120	122	87	107	114
ALL AFRICA	81	79	80	90	86	86	68	71	73

Social Indicators

13-15. Pupil progression

	Pecentage of cohort reaching grade 5 (1992-96)			Progression to secondary school 1993		
	Total	Male	Female	Total	Male	Female
SUB-SAHARAN AFRICA	..	..	..	..	..	..
excluding South Africa	..	..	..	..	..	..
excl. S. Africa & Nigeria	..	..	..	..	..	..
Angola	..	..	..	..	..	..
Benin	61	64	57	..	..	..
Botswana	90	87	93	84	84	85
Burkina Faso	75	74	77	27	27	27
Burundi	..	..	..	11	12	11
Cameroon	..	..	..	..	..	..
Cape Verde	..	..	..	..	..	..
Central African Republic	..	..	..	..	..	..
Chad	59	62	53	47	..	..
Comoros	79	..	..	39	..	..
Congo, Democratic Rep. of	64	73	54	27	25	30
Congo, Republic of	55	40	78	..	..	..
Côte d'Ivoire	75	77	71	33	..	..
Djibouti	79	..	..	38	..	..
Equatorial Guinea	..	..	..	..	..	..
Eritrea	70	73	67	80	85	74
Ethiopia	51	51	50	80	82	77
Gabon	59	58	61	..	..	..
Gambia, The	80	78	83	..	..	..
Ghana	..	..	..	..	..	..
Guinea	54	85	68	50	51	47
Guinea-Bissau	..	..	..	..	..	..
Kenya	..	..	..	41	..	..
Lesotho	63	55	71	71	..	..
Liberia	..	..	..	..	..	..
Madagascar	40	49	33	35	35	35
Malawi	34	36	32	15	..	..
Mali	84	92	70	63	64	60
Mauritania	64	61	68	32	34	28
Mauritius	99	98	99	51	49	54
Mozambique	46	52	39	39	39	39
Namibia	86	80	84	74	76	72
Niger	73	72	73	..	..	..
Nigeria	..	..	..	52	..	..
Rwanda	..	..	..	15	..	..
São Tomé and Principe	..	..	..	..	..	..
Senegal	87	89	85	..	..	..
Seychelles	100	98	99	100	..	..
Sierra Leone	..	..	..	..	..	..
Somalia	..	..	..	..	..	..
South Africa	..	..	..	90	87	91
Sudan	74	75	73	61	..	..
Swaziland	76	73	79	79	79	79
Tanzania	81	78	84	12	..	..
Togo	71	79	60	38	40	35
Uganda	..	..	..	32	..	..
Zambia	..	..	..	..	..	..
Zimbabwe	79	78	79	66	..	..
NORTH AFRICA	..	..	..	79	77	81
Algeria	94	93	95	80	77	82
Egypt, Arab Republic	..	..	..	83	82	85
Libya	..	..	..	..	..	..
Morocco	75	76	74	81	79	84
Tunisia	91	90	92	62	62	63
ALL AFRICA	..	..	..	..	..	..

Notes: In Seychelles a policy of automatic promotion is practiced at the primary level of education. Tanzanian figures refer to mainland only.

13-16. Net primary enrollment ratio

	Total			Males			Females		
	1980	*1990*	*1994-99*	*1980*	*1990*	*1994-99*	*1980*	*1990*	*1994-99*
SUB-SAHARAN AFRICA	..	..	..	..	..	..	..	..	..
excluding South Africa	..	..	..	..	..	..	..	..	..
excl. S. Africa & Nigeria	..	..	..	..	..	..	..	..	..
Angola	..	..	..	87	46	..	80	45	..
Benin	..	..	63	72	61	80	34	31	47
Botswana	76	93	81	69	90	79	83	98	83
Burkina Faso	15	27	31	18	33	37	11	21	24
Burundi	20	..	..	23	57	..	16	51	..
Cameroon	..	..	..	77	80	..	66	70	..
Cape Verde	90	..	..	93	100	..	88	99	..
Central African Republic	56	53	..	73	64	..	41	42	..
Chad	..	..	46	38	55	59	15	27	33
Comoros	..	..	..	77	61	..	56	45	..
Congo, Democratic Rep. of	..	54	61	82	61	72	59	48	50
Congo, Republic of	96	..	..	100	95	..	94	87	..
Côte d'Ivoire	..	47	55	65	55	63	45	41	47
Djibouti	..	32	32	37	37	36	22	27	27
Equatorial Guinea	..	..	..	97	92	..	81	89	..
Eritrea	..	..	30	..	..	32	..	..	29
Ethiopia	..	..	32	35	29	40	22	22	25
Gabon	..	..	..	..	..	..	..	..	..
Gambia, The	50	..	65	70	63	72	36	42	57
Ghana	..	..	..	..	..	..	..	..	..
Guinea	..	..	42	39	38	50	20	19	33
Guinea-Bissau	47	..	..	63	55	..	31	31	..
Kenya	91	..	..	92	74	..	89	75	..
Lesotho	67	73	70	55	65	64	80	82	76
Liberia	..	..	..	..	..	..	..	..	..
Madagascar	..	..	61	..	..	60	..	..	62
Malawi	43	50	103	48	52	102	38	48	104
Mali	20	21	31	26	27	38	15	15	25
Mauritania	..	..	57	..	..	61	..	..	53
Mauritius	79	95	98	80	95	98	79	95	98
Mozambique	36	47	40	37	52	45	32	42	34
Namibia	..	..	91	81	81	..	92	93	..
Niger	21	25	25	28	32	30	15	18	19
Nigeria	..	..	..	..	..	..	..	..	..
Rwanda	59	66	..	62	66	..	57	66	..
São Tomé and Principe	..	..	..	..	..	..	..	..	..
Senegal	37	..	60	45	56	65	30	42	55
Seychelles	..	..	..	..	..	..	..	..	..
Sierra Leone	..	..	..	..	..	..	..	..	..
Somalia	16	..	..	20	..	..	12	..	..
South Africa	..	..	..	67	100	..	68	100	..
Sudan	..	..	..	..	..	..	..	..	..
Swaziland	80	88	91	79	88	90	82	89	91
Tanzania	68	51	48	..	51	48	..	52	49
Togo	..	75	81	95	88	93	64	62	69
Uganda	..	..	..	..	..	..	..	..	..
Zambia	77	..	75	81	85	76	73	83	74
Zimbabwe	..	..	..	..	..	..	..	..	..
NORTH AFRICA	..	..	89	84	91	95	62	77	84
Algeria	81	93	94	92	100	97	71	88	91
Egypt, Arab Republic	..	..	93	83	96	98	61	82	88
Libya	..	..	..	100	98	..	100	94	..
Morocco	62	58	74	76	69	86	48	48	67
Tunisia	82	94	98	93	99	99	72	91	96
ALL AFRICA	..	..	..	65	67	..	51	58	..

13-17. Number of school teachers

	Primary						Secondary					
	Total teaching staff			Percentage females			Total teaching staff			Percentage females		
	1980	1990	1994-98	1980	1990	1994-98	1980	1990	1994-98	1980	1990	1994-98
SUB-SAHARAN AFRICA	..	..	..	30	35	40	..	..	..	..	..	..
excluding South Africa	..	..	..	30	35	40	..	..	..	..	..	..
excl. S. Africa & Nigeria	..	..	..	28	32	34	..	..	..	..	..	..
Angola	..	31,062	31,878	..	..	..	..	..	..	..	..	..
Benin	7,994	13,556	16,043	23	25	23	..	..	..	..	..	..
Botswana	5,316	8,956	11,454	72	80	77	1,137	3,716	6,670	37	40	43
Burkina Faso	3,700	8,903	16,724	20	27	24	..	..	..	..	..	..
Burundi	4,805	9,465	11,597	47	46	52	..	2,026	..	..	21	..
Cameroon	26,763	38,430	39,084	20	30	34	8,926	19,820	..	..	..	..
Cape Verde	1,436	..	3,219	..	..	62	184	..	..	..	..	..
Central African Republic	4,130	4,004	..	25	25	..	724	..	..	16	..	..
Chad	..	7,980	11,641	..	6	9	..	..	3,238	..	..	5
Comoros	1,292	1,995	1,508	7	..	..	449	..	..	20	..	..
Congo, Democratic Rep. of	..	114,000	121,054	..	24	22	..	..	..	..	..	..
Congo, Republic of	7,186	7,578	7,060	25	32	36	5,117	6,851	7,173	..	..	16
Côte d'Ivoire	26,460	39,002	40,529	15	19	21	..	..	..	..	..	..
Djibouti	419	742	1,096	..	37	30	278	..	628	..	..	..
Equatorial Guinea	647	..	1,381	..	..	27	..	..	..	..	..	..
Eritrea	..	2,895	5,476	..	45	36	..	..	2,071	..	..	14
Ethiopia	33,322	68,370	109,487	22	24	27	..	23,319	13,109	..	10	8
Gabon	3,441	..	4,605	27	..	41	1,587	..	3,094	24	..	18
Gambia, The	1,932	2,757	4,118	32	31	29	620	756	1,547	25	..	17
Ghana	47,921	66,946	71,340	42	36	36	31,636	..	..	21	..	..
Guinea	7,165	8,699	13,883	14	22	25	..	5,976	6,063	..	12	11
Guinea-Bissau	3,257	..	..	24	..	..	462	..	..	21	..	..
Kenya	102,489	172,117	192,306	..	37	42	17,081	..	..	..	..	..
Lesotho	5,097	6,448	8,089	75	80	79	1,299	..	3,158	..	..	52
Liberia	..	..	..	..	..	..	..	..	..	..	..	..
Madagascar	39,474	38,933	40,591	..	..	47	..	..	21,670	..	..	43
Malawi	12,540	22,942	49,138	..	31	39	953	..	3,172	..	..	1
Mali	6,862	8,156	10,853	20	23	23	..	5,748	..	..	14	..
Mauritania	2,183	3,741	7,064	9	18	24	..	..	2,067	..	..	8
Mauritius	6,379	6,507	5,065	43	44	53	..	..	5,090	..	..	46
Mozambique	17,030	23,107	24,575	22	..	23	..	4,657	5,615	..	..	17
Namibia	..	..	..	..	..	..	..	..	..	..	..	..
Niger	5,518	8,835	11,545	30	33	32	1,284	2,775	3,521	21	18	20
Nigeria	343,551	331,915	416,745	34	43	48	41,581	141,377	152,596	29	33	36
Rwanda	11,912	19,183	..	38	46	..	1,454	2,802	..	16	20	..
São Tomé and Principe	588	..	..	..	..	..	..	..	..	..	..	..
Senegal	9,175	13,394	18,373	24	..	25	4,302	..	..	..	..	..
Seychelles	658	..	577	80	..	88	127	328	689	37	..	50
Sierra Leone	9,528	10,850	..	..	..	..	..	5,969	..	..	18	..
Somalia	8,122	..	..	29	..	..	2,089	..	..	7	..	..
South Africa	160,286	..	181,668	..	..	73	..	..	..	..	..	..
Sudan	43,451	60,047	102,987	31	51	62	18,831	33,628	15,504	..	35	45
Swaziland	3,278	5,083	6,195	79	79	75	..	..	3,173	..	..	44
Tanzania	81,386	96,850	110,186	37	41	44	3,837	7,944	12,751	..	24	26
Togo	9,201	11,105	19,512	21	19	12	..	4,492	5,389	..	12	12
Uganda	38,422	84,149	82,745	30	30	32	3,833	..	..	..	..	..
Zambia	21,455	33,200	38,528	40	..	43	4,882	..	..	..	..	..
Zimbabwe	28,118	59,154	64,538	..	39	44	3,782	24,547	28,254	..	29	36
NORTH AFRICA	..	..	..	..	45	48	..	..	..	..	..	39
Algeria	88,481	151,262	170,956	37	39	45	41,137	127,024	151,948	..	39	45
Egypt, Arab Republic	..	279,315	310,116	..	52	52	121,999	286,797	424,586	31	..	39
Libya	36,591	85,537	..	47	..	..	24,323	..	..	24	..	..
Morocco	56,908	91,680	117,481	30	37	38	36,526	79,657	84,202	..	29	32
Tunisia	27,375	50,609	60,220	29	45	49	14,328	33,058	41,328	29	32	34
ALL AFRICA	..	..	..	30	37	42	..	..	..	..	..	..

Note: Figures include both part-time and full-time teachers.

13-18. Pupil/teacher ratio

	Number of pupils per teacher					
	Primary			Secondary		
	1980	1985	1994-98	1980	1990	1994-98
SUB-SAHARAN AFRICA	..	..	..	..	..	..
excluding South Africa	..	..	..	..	..	..
excl. S. Africa & Nigeria	..	..	..	..	..	..
Angola	..	33	29	..	..	..
Benin	48	31	53	..	..	..
Botswana	32	32	28	18	17	17
Burkina Faso	54	55	47	..	..	..
Burundi	37	66	48	..	22	..
Cameroon	52	51	52	26	25	..
Cape Verde	40	33	29	..	..	..
Central African Republic	60	90	..	..	..	..
Chad	..	67	68	..	..	35
Comoros	46	35	52	..	..	..
Congo, Democratic Rep. of	..	37	45	..	..	..
Congo, Republic of	54	64	70	..	27	30
Côte d'Ivoire	39	36	41	..	..	..
Djibouti	40	44	34	..	..	19
Equatorial Guinea	..	..	55	..	..	..
Eritrea	..	38	44	..	..	43
Ethiopia	64	41	47	..	37	36
Gabon	45	48	56	..	..	26
Gambia, The	24	28	30	..	27	21
Ghana	30	26	33	..	..	..
Guinea	36	38	49	..	14	26
Guinea-Bissau	23	25	..	10	..	..
Kenya	38	31	31	..	..	..
Lesotho	48	55	46	19	..	23
Liberia	..	..	..	..	..	..
Madagascar	38	40	47	..	..	16
Malawi	65	64	59	..	..	45
Mali	42	45	80	..	15	..
Mauritania	41	44	47	..	..	25
Mauritius	20	21	26	..	..	19
Mozambique	..	55	58	..	34	33
Namibia	..	..	..	..	..	..
Niger	41	41	42	30	28	28
Nigeria	..	41	34	..	21	29
Rwanda	59	57	..	..	25	..
São Tomé and Principe	28	35	..	..	..	..
Senegal	46	58	56	..	..	..
Seychelles	22	19	17	..	13	13
Sierra Leone	..	..	..	..	17	..
Somalia	33	19	..	21	..	..
South Africa	..	..	45	..	..	..
Sudan	34	35	29	..	22	26
Swaziland	34	33	34	..	..	19
Tanzania	41	35	37	..	21	17
Togo	55	56	46	..	28	31
Uganda	..	29	35	..	..	..
Zambia	49	44	39	..	..	..
Zimbabwe	44	36	39	..	27	27
NORTH AFRICA	..	..	..	..	..	..
Algeria	35	28	27	25	17	17
Egypt, Arab Republic	..	20	24	..	19	16
Libya	18	16	..	12	..	..
Morocco	38	25	28	22	15	17
Tunisia	39	30	25	20	17	19
ALL AFRICA	..	·..	..	..	..	..

Note: Figures include both part-time and full-time teachers.

13-19. Secondary school gross enrollment ratio

	Total			Males			Females		
	1980	1990	1994-97	1980	1990	1994-97	1980	1990	1994-97
SUB-SAHARAN AFRICA	15	23	27	20	26	29	10	21	24
excluding South Africa	15	19	21	20	22	25	10	16	18
excl. S. Africa & Nigeria	14	17	17	19	21	19	10	14	14
Angola	21	12	..	..	..	..	..	..	..
Benin	16	12	17	24	17	26	8	7	11
Botswana	19	43	65	17	41	62	21	45	68
Burkina Faso	3	7	..	4	9	..	2	5	..
Burundi	3	6	7	4	7	..	2	4	..
Cameroon	18	28	27	24	33	32	13	23	22
Cape Verde	8	21	..	9	..	54	7	..	56
Central African Republic	14	12	..	21	17	..	7	7	..
Chad	..	8	10	..	13	15	..	3	4
Comoros	22	18	21	30	21	24	15	14	19
Congo, Democratic Rep. of	24	..	26	35	..	32	13	..	19
Congo, Republic of	74	53	53	89	63	62	60	44	45
Côte d'Ivoire	19	22	24	26	30	34	11	14	16
Djibouti	12	12	14	15	14	17	9	9	12
Equatorial Guinea	..	..	..	..	..	..	..	..	..
Eritrea	..	..	20	..	..	24	..	..	17
Ethiopia	9	14	12	12	16	14	7	13	10
Gabon	..	..	..	41	..	59	27	..	53
Gambia, The	11	19	25	16	25	30	7	12	19
Ghana	41	36	..	50	45	..	31	28	..
Guinea	17	10	12	24	15	20	10	5	7
Guinea-Bissau	6	..	..	10	..	..	2	..	..
Kenya	20	24	24	23	28	26	16	21	22
Lesotho	18	25	31	14	20	25	21	30	37
Liberia	22	..	..	31	..	..	13	..	..
Madagascar	..	18	16	..	18	16	..	18	16
Malawi	5	8	17	7	11	21	3	5	12
Mali	8	7	10	12	9	17	5	5	8
Mauritania	11	14	16	18	19	21	4	9	11
Mauritius	50	53	65	51	53	63	49	53	66
Mozambique	5	8	7	8	10	9	3	6	6
Namibia	..	44	61	..	39	58	..	49	67
Niger	5	7	7	7	9	9	3	4	5
Nigeria	18	25	33	24	29	36	12	21	30
Rwanda	3	8	..	4	9	..	3	7	..
São Tomé and Principe	..	..	..	..	..	..	..	..	..
Senegal	11	16	16	15	21	20	8	11	12
Seychelles	..	..	..	..	..	..	..	..	..
Sierra Leone	14	17	..	20	22	..	8	13	..
Somalia	9	..	..	13	..	..	5	..	..
South Africa	..	74	94	..	69	88	..	80	103
Sudan	16	24	21	20	27	23	12	21	20
Swaziland	38	44	54	39	44	55	37	43	54
Tanzania	3	5	5	4	6	6	2	4	5
Togo	33	24	27	50	35	40	16	12	15
Uganda	5	13	12	7	17	15	3	10	9
Zambia	16	24	27	22	..	34	11	..	21
Zimbabwe	8	50	49	9	53	52	7	46	45
NORTH AFRICA	41	62	64	49	68	68	31	54	60
Algeria	33	61	63	40	67	65	26	54	62
Egypt, Arab Republic	51	76	75	61	84	83	39	68	73
Libya	76	86	..	89	..	..	63	..	..
Morocco	26	35	39	32	41	44	20	30	34
Tunisia	27	45	65	34	50	66	20	40	63
ALL AFRICA	20	31	34	26	35	37	15	28	31

Note: "Secondary" refers to secondary general education.

13-20. Public expenditure on education

	As percentage of Total public expenditure			As percentage of GDP		
	1980	*1990*	*1993-96*	*1980*	*1990*	*1993-96*
SUB-SAHARAN AFRICA	..	..	..	..	..	..
excluding South Africa	..	..	..	..	..	..
excl. S. Africa & Nigeria	..	..	..	..	..	..
Angola	..	..	..	..	..	..
Benin	..	..	..	..	..	2.6
Botswana	22.2	19.3	26.3	..	..	..
Burkina Faso	15.5	18.3	17.9	1.8	..	..
Burundi	..	..	4.5	..	3.2	3.7
Cameroon	12.4	15.6	14.6	..	..	..
Cape Verde	..	..	..	..	..	..
Central African Republic	..	..	..	3.5	1.9	1.5
Chad	..	..	..	..	..	1.1
Comoros	..	..	..	..	3.4	3.7
Congo, Democratic Rep. of	18.9	..	0.8	..	..	..
Congo, Republic of	..	..	..	5.3	..	5.3
Côte d'Ivoire	..	29.7	..	5.7	..	4.2
Djibouti	..	..	..	..	3.2	..
Equatorial Guinea	..	..	..	..	..	..
Eritrea	..	..	..	..	..	..
Ethiopia	10.2	10.3	14.0	..	2.6	3.6
Gabon	..	..	..	..	..	..
Gambia, The	12.3	..	14.5	2.3	2.4	3.2
Ghana	..	..	..	..	..	..
Guinea	..	..	..	..	..	1.5
Guinea-Bissau	..	..	..	..	..	..
Kenya	22.9	23.3	21.4	5.2	5.4	6.1
Lesotho	..	9.5	19.4	6.5	..	8.8
Liberia	11.9	..	..	..	..	..
Madagascar	..	15.0	9.1	3.5	..	..
Malawi	9.0	..	..	2.0	1.9	3.8
Mali	15.7	..	..	..	..	1.8
Mauritania	..	..	..	4.1	3.7	3.4
Mauritius	17.6	15.0	17.7	4.1	3.0	2.8
Mozambique	..	..	..	..	1.5	..
Namibia	..	..	..	..	..	7.0
Niger	18.0	..	..	..	..	..
Nigeria	..	..	..	..	..	..
Rwanda	..	..	..	2.2	..	..
São Tomé and Principe	..	..	..	..	..	..
Senegal	23.0	..	..	4.1	3.6	3.6
Seychelles	..	..	12.2	..	6.1	4.7
Sierra Leone	..	13.3	..	..	..	..
Somalia	..	..	..	..	..	..
South Africa	..	..	..	..	..	6.3
Sudan	9.8	..	..	3.8	..	0.8
Swaziland	24.6	..	..	3.9	3.9	4.9
Tanzania	13.3	..	..	..	..	..
Togo	..	..	..	4.7	4.4	4.0
Uganda	14.9	..	..	..	..	..
Zambia	11.4	8.2	11.0	3.5	..	1.6
Zimbabwe	15.5	..	..	4.8	7.3	6.8
NORTH AFRICA	15.0	16.9	15.5	..	..	..
Algeria	..	..	..	..	..	..
Egypt, Arab Republic	8.1	14.0	13.8	..	..	..
Libya	..	..	..	..	..	..
Morocco	17.3	18.2	16.6	4.8	4.8	4.7
Tunisia	17.0	17.0	18.7	4.5	5.0	5.3
ALL AFRICA	..	..	..	..	..	..

13-21. Economic opportunities of women

	Female / male ratio of participation in economic activity 1995	Female as percentage of male in occupational group, 1990*			
		Administrative and managerial	Professional and technical	Clerical and sales	Services
SUB-SAHARAN AFRICA	73	11	42	..	..
excluding South Africa	74	10	37	..	..
excl. S.Africa & Nigeria	79	..	..	..	..
Angola	87	..	..	..	..
Benin	93	..	..	..	..
Botswana	85	57	159	151	238
Burkina Faso	87	16	35	168	28
Burundi	97	16	44	..	..
Cameroon	60	11	32	59	46
Cape Verde	64	30	94	170	134
Central African Republic	88	10	23	146	13
Chad	80	..	..	..	..
Comoros	74	..	29	..	..
Congo, Democratic Rep. of	77	10	20	..	..
Congo, Republic of	77	7	40	..	..
Côte d'Ivoire	49	..	..	..	..
Djibouti	..	2	25	..	..
Equatorial Guinea	55	2	37	..	..
Eritrea	90	..	..	..	..
Ethiopia	69	13	31	..	..
Gabon	80	..	..	..	..
Gambia, The	81	18	31	..	..
Ghana	103	10	56	..	..
Guinea	90	..	..	..	..
Guinea-Bissau	67	..	..	..	..
Kenya	85	..	..	..	..
Lesotho	58	50	130	144	209
Liberia	66	..	..	..	..
Madagascar	81	..	..	..	..
Malawi	96	5	53	58	39
Mali	87	25	23	130	71
Mauritania	77	8	26	33	81
Mauritius	46	17	71	44	70
Mozambique	94	13	26	..	..
Namibia	68	26	69	..	..
Niger	79	9	..	..	..
Nigeria	56	6	35	140	13
Rwanda	93	9	47	48	35
São Tomé and Principe	..	..	..	..	..
Senegal	74	..	..	..	..
Seychelles	..	40	139	143	141
Sierra Leone	57	9	47	191	18
Somalia	75	..	..	..	..
South Africa	60	21	88	..	196
Sudan	40	3	40	..	..
Swaziland	60	17	119	116	82
Tanzania	98	..	..	..	..
Togo	67	9	27	..	..
Uganda	91	..	..	..	..
Zambia	83	6	47	136	29
Zimbabwe	80	18	67	52	42
NORTH AFRICA	41	19	39	31	14
Algeria	32	6	38	13	23
Egypt, Arab Republic	40	19	40	40	9
Libya	26	..	..	..	..
Morocco	53	34	46	..	..
Tunisia	44	8	21	..	..
ALL AFRICA	67	13	41	..	..

*or most recent available data.

13-22. Household and economic participation of women

	Percentage of households headed by women (latest available between 1991-98)	Percentage of women in occupational group 1991-98					
		Agriculture	Mining	Utilities & manufacturing	Construction, transport, storage & communications	Service industries	Community, social & personal services
SUB-SAHARAN AFRICA	..	..	..	..	..	..	..
excluding South Africa	..	..	..	..	..	..	..
excl. S.Africa & Nigeria	..	..	..	..	..	..	..
Angola	..	..	..	..	..	..	..
Benin	..	..	..	..	..	..	..
Botswana	..	2	1	12	9	35	41
Burkina Faso	6	..	..	..	..	..	..
Burundi	..	..	..	..	..	..	..
Cameroon	18	..	..	..	..	..	..
Cape Verde	..	..	..	..	..	..	..
Central African Republic	16	..	..	..	..	..	..
Chad	..	14	0	14	14	14	43
Comoros	..	..	..	..	..	..	..
Congo, Democratic Rep. of	..	..	..	..	..	..	..
Congo, Republic of	..	..	..	..	..	..	..
Côte d'Ivoire	12	..	..	..	..	..	..
Djibouti	17	..	..	..	..	..	..
Equatorial Guinea	..	..	..	..	..	..	..
Eritrea	..	..	..	..	..	..	..
Ethiopia	18	10	0	24	6	10	50
Gabon	..	..	..	..	..	..	..
Gambia, The	1	..	..	..	..	..	..
Ghana	14	..	..	..	..	..	..
Guinea	8	..	..	..	..	..	..
Guinea-Bissau	10	..	..	..	..	..	..
Kenya	15	20	0	8	5	11	57
Lesotho	..	..	..	..	..	..	..
Liberia	..	..	..	..	..	..	..
Madagascar	18	..	..	..	..	..	..
Malawi	..	73	0	7	2	4	14
Mali	6	..	..	..	..	..	..
Mauritania	24	..	..	..	..	..	..
Mauritius	..	12	0	64	2	7	15
Mozambique	..	..	..	..	..	..	..
Namibia	..	..	..	..	..	..	..
Niger	6	5	5	20	25	25	25
Nigeria	13	..	..	..	..	..	..
Rwanda	..	..	..	..	..	..	..
São Tomé and Principe	..	..	..	..	..	..	..
Senegal	8	..	..	..	..	..	..
Seychelles	..	..	..	..	..	..	..
Sierra Leone	..	..	..	..	..	..	..
Somalia	..	..	..	..	..	..	..
South Africa	27	..	..	..	..	..	..
Sudan	..	..	..	..	..	..	..
Swaziland	26	23	1	16	4	20	36
Tanzania	11	..	..	..	..	..	..
Togo	..	..	..	..	..	..	..
Uganda	2	..	..	..	..	..	..
Zambia	19	..	..	..	..	..	..
Zimbabwe	..	38	1	6	3	10	..
NORTH AFRICA	..	36	0	21	2	8	32
Algeria	..	..	..	..	..	..	..
Egypt, Arab Republic	..	52	0	10	2	7	29
Libya	..	..	..	..	..	..	..
Morocco	..	3	0	45	2	11	39
Tunisia	..	..	..	..	..	..	..
ALL AFRICA	..	..	..	..	..	..	..

13-23. Relative prices of consumption and investment in PPP terms, 1993

	International price level	*Relative price level (price level of GDP=100)*								*Government consumption*	*Gross Fixed capital formation*
		Private consumption									
	Ratio of PPP rate to $ exchange rate	*Total*	*All food*	*Bread and cereals*	*Clothing and footware*	*Fuel and power*	*Health care*	*Education*	*Transport and communications*		
SUB-SAHARAN AFRICA	..	..	..	..	..	..	..	..	..	..	..
excluding South Africa	..	..	..	..	..	..	..	..	..	..	..
excl. South Africa & Nigeria	..	..	..	..	..	..	..	..	..	..	..
Angola	..	..	..	..	..	..	..	..	..	..	..
Benin	..	..	..	..	..	..	..	..	..	..	..
Botswana	37	125	103	113	157	256	105	98	65	113	108
Burkina Faso	..	..	..	..	..	..	..	..	..	..	..
Burundi	..	..	..	..	..	..	..	..	..	..	..
Cameroon	50	93	87	98	102	173	88	60	97	123	141
Cape Verde	..	..	..	..	..	..	..	..	..	..	..
Central African Republic	..	..	..	..	..	..	..	..	..	..	..
Chad	..	..	..	..	..	..	..	..	..	..	..
Comoros	..	..	..	..	..	..	..	..	..	..	..
Congo, Democratic Rep. of	..	..	..	..	..	..	..	..	..	..	..
Congo, Republic of	64	98	115	105	109	288	58	55	67	78	193
Côte d'Ivoire	52	98	101	112	97	..	89	60	78	116	151
Djibouti	..	..	..	..	..	..	..	..	..	..	..
Equatorial Guinea	..	..	..	..	..	..	..	..	..	..	..
Eritrea	..	..	..	..	..	..	..	..	..	..	..
Ethiopia	..	..	..	..	..	..	..	..	..	..	..
Gabon	80	126	147	95	131	284	90	119	79	152	91
Gambia, The	..	..	..	..	..	..	..	..	..	..	..
Ghana	..	..	..	..	..	..	..	..	..	..	..
Guinea	33	97	106	118	75	173	37	68	94	80	127
Guinea-Bissau	..	..	..	..	..	..	..	..	..	..	..
Kenya	21	90	91	123	85	140	45	41	71	72	196
Lesotho	..	..	..	..	..	..	..	..	..	..	..
Liberia	..	..	..	..	..	..	..	..	..	..	..
Madagascar	..	..	..	..	..	..	..	..	..	..	..
Malawi	34	87	98	109	54	148	31	50	73	79	279
Mali	38	90	92	131	86	..	59	31	90	63	179
Mauritania	..	..	..	..	..	..	..	..	..	..	..
Mauritius	39	93	81	65	72	111	59	87	67	108	134
Mozambique	..	..	..	..	..	..	..	..	..	..	..
Namibia	..	..	..	..	..	..	..	..	..	..	..
Niger	..	..	..	..	..	..	..	..	..	..	..
Nigeria	36	101	150	171	58	56	46	40	47	61	115
Rwanda	..	..	..	..	..	..	..	..	..	..	..
São Tomé and Principe	..	..	..	..	..	..	..	..	..	..	..
Senegal	48	90	87	119	74	227	75	45	79	81	237
Seychelles	..	..	..	..	..	..	..	..	..	..	..
Sierra Leone	29	115	141	192	107	185	34	39	76	37	147
Somalia	..	..	..	..	..	..	..	..	..	..	..
South Africa	..	..	..	..	..	..	..	..	..	..	..
Sudan	..	..	..	..	..	..	..	..	..	..	..
Swaziland	35	92	84	100	138	187	53	66	54	91	..
Tanzania	..	..	..	..	..	..	..	..	..	..	..
Togo	..	..	..	..	..	..	..	..	..	..	..
Uganda	..	..	..	..	..	..	..	..	..	..	..
Zambia	43	113	126	185	98	282	29	46	89	34	213
Zimbabwe	26	105	81	97	91	221	51	77	62	89	..
NORTH AFRICA	..	..	..	..	..	..	..	..	..	..	..
Algeria											
Egypt, Arab Republic	35	90	88	97	124	80	54	49	92	92	106
Libya	..	..	..	..	..	..	..	..	..	..	..
Morocco	37	93	83	77	68	282	81	81	77	106	182
Tunisia	39	92	81	62	142	105	80	109	79	124	159
ALL AFRICA	..	..	..	..	..	..	..	..	..	..	..

13-24. Structure of household consumption in PPP terms, 1997

	Ratio of PPP rate to $ exchange rate	Household consumption per capita PPP	Food		Clothing and footware	Fuel and power	Health care	Education	Transport and communications	Other consumption
			All food	Bread and cereals						
SUB-SAHARAN AFRICA	..	..	..	..	..	..	..	..	..	..
excluding South Africa	..	..	..	..	..	..	..	..	..	..
excluding South Africa & Nigeria	..	..	..	..	..	..	..	..	..	..
Angola	..	..	..	..	..	..	..	..	..	..
Benin	..	1,100	45	13	8	3	3	8	14	17
Botswana	43	3,084	25	9	4	1	7	22	21	19
Burkina Faso	..	..	..	..	..	..	..	..	..	..
Burundi	..	..	..	..	..	..	..	..	..	..
Cameroon	34	1,277	38	7	14	2	6	9	8	24
Cape Verde	..	..	..	..	..	..	..	..	..	..
Central African Republic	..	..	..	..	..	..	..	..	..	..
Chad	..	..	..	..	..	..	..	..	..	..
Comoros	..	..	..	..	..	..	..	..	..	..
Congo, Democratic Rep. of	..	..	..	..	..	..	..	..	..	..
Congo, Republic of	52	791	36	5	3	.1	10	15	18	17
Côte d'Ivoire	39	1,393	35	8	9	..	8	26	11	11
Djibouti	..	..	..	..	..	..	..	..	..	..
Equatorial Guinea	..	..	..	..	..	..	..	..	..	..
Eritrea	..	..	..	..	..	..	..	..	..	..
Ethiopia	..	..	..	..	..	..	..	..	..	..
Gabon	59	2,468	37	7	3	2	8	8	20	23
Gambia, The	..	..	..	..	..	..	..	..	..	..
Ghana	..	..	..	..	..	..	..	..	..	..
Guinea	30	1,456	32	6	19	2	14	9	9	15
Guinea-Bissau	..	..	..	..	..	..	..	..	..	..
Kenya	30	872	38	11	8	2	5	22	10	16
Lesotho	..	..	..	..	..	..	..	..	..	..
Liberia	..	..	..	..	..	..	..	..	..	..
Madagascar	..	..	..	..	..	..	..	..	..	..
Malawi	34	607	45	17	18	2	8	9	8	10
Mali	33	655	48	13	13	..	2	7	14	15
Mauritania	..	..	..	..	..	..	..	..	..	..
Mauritius	41	6,533	24	4	8	3	10	5	19	30
Mozambique	..	..	..	..	..	..	..	..	..	..
Namibia	..	..	..	..	..	..	..	..	..	..
Niger	..	..	..	..	..	..	..	..	..	..
Nigeria	37	692	48	15	8	6	3	4	5	27
Rwanda	..	..	..	..	..	..	..	..	..	..
São Tomé and Principe	..	..	..	..	..	..	..	..	..	..
Senegal	30	1,536	52	11	14	2	2	11	6	13
Seychelles	..	..	..	..	..	..	..	..	..	..
Sierra Leone	42	267	48	13	12	3	13	14	8	2
Somalia	..	..	..	..	..	..	..	..	..	..
South Africa	..	..	..	..	..	..	..	..	..	..
Sudan	..	..	..	..	..	..	..	..	..	..
Swaziland	41	2,579	27	6	6	4	10	17	18	19
Tanzania	..	..	..	..	..	..	..	..	..	..
Togo	..	..	..	..	..	..	..	..	..	..
Uganda	..	..	..	..	..	..	..	..	..	..
Zambia	42	625	47	7	8	1	3	12	10	19
Zimbabwe	33	1,572	28	7	11	2	9	23	14	12
NORTH AFRICA	..	..	..	..	..	..	..	..	..	..
Algeria	..	..	..	..	..	..	..	..	..	..
Egypt, Arab Republic	41	1,962	44	11	7	3	8	8	5	26
Libya	..	..	..	..	..	..	..	..	..	..
Morocco	37	2,360	45	11	9	2	5	10	10	18
Tunisia	38	3,687	35	7	6	2	6	7	15	29
ALL AFRICA	..	..	..	..	..	..	..	..	..	..

Figure 13-1. Life expectancy, 1998

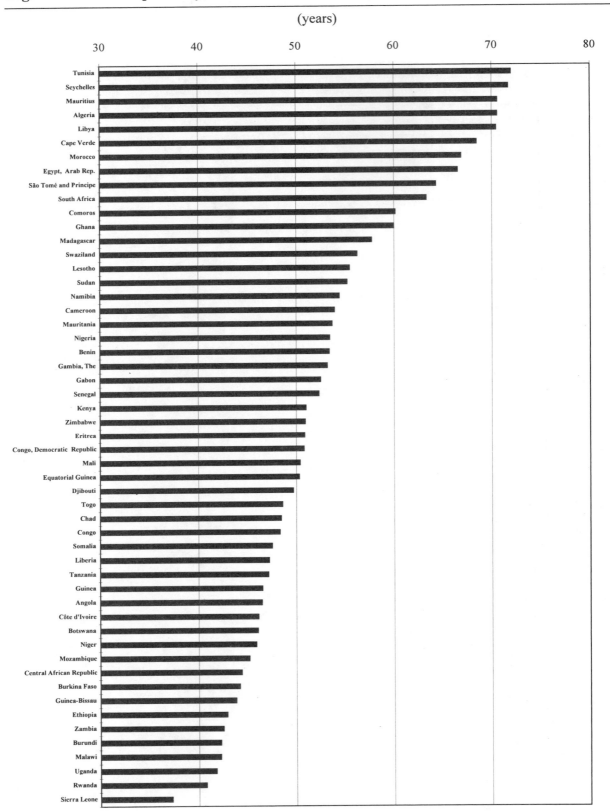

Figure 13-2. GDP per capita based on PPP, 1998

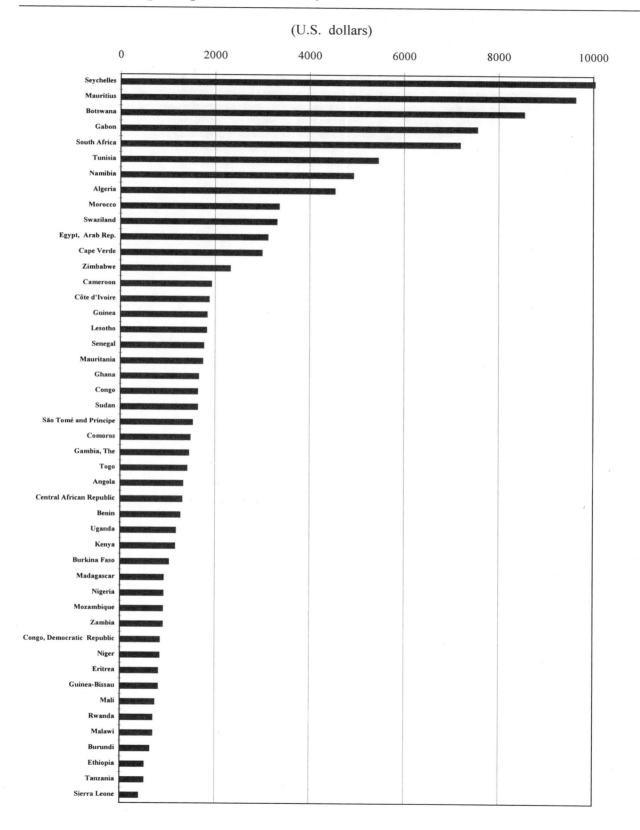

Figure 13-3. Urban population as a percentage of total population, 1998*

(percent)

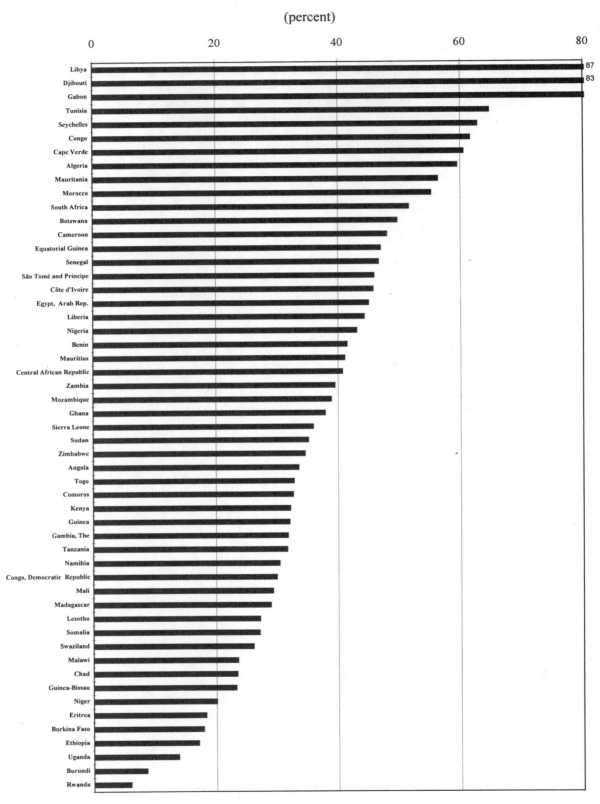

* Or most recent year available.

Figure 13-4. Primary school gross enrollment ratio, 1997*

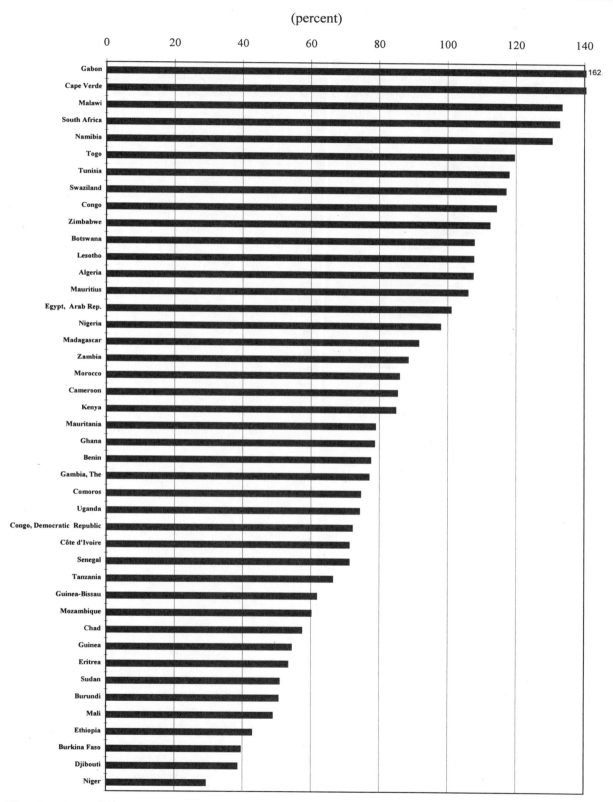

* Or most recent year available.

336

Figure 13-5. Maternal mortality, 1997*

(per 1,000,000 live births)

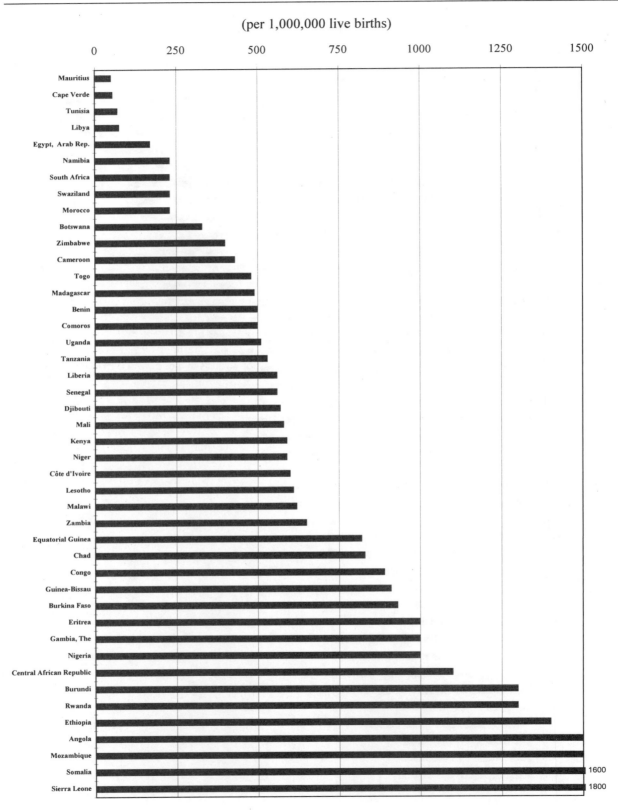

* Or most recent year available.

Technical notes

Tables

Table 13-1. Age and gender structure of the population. Age and gender structure of the population (UN and World Bank data) is the distribution of the total population according to age and gender. Only the female composition of the population is presented, as the male composition can easily be figured as the residual. Figures relate to midyear populations as estimated from the latest censuses. Age dependency ratio is calculated as the ratio of dependents—population under age 15 and above age 65—to the working age population—those aged 15 to 64.

Table 13-2. Poverty. This table presents selected indicators for comparing the incidence and extent of urban and rural poverty. The first indicator uses purchasing power parities rather than official exchange rates to calculate GDP per capita: a measure of the overall mean level of poverty at the national level. The next indicator is the national poverty headcount, which shows the percentage of the population living below the poverty line deemed appropriate for the country by its authorities. The poverty line is defined as the below which adequate standards of nutrition, shelter, and personal amenities cannot be assured. Since these levels are country specific, cross-country comparisons cannot be made. The next indicator, however, uses a relative concept of poverty, which does allow such comparisons. It shows the percentage of the urban and rural populations living on less than two-thirds of the mean national per capita income. Associated with these indicators are the urban and rural

Gini coefficients, which describe the level of inequality in urban and rural income distributions. The last indicator shows the percentage of household income spent on food (UNDP, World Bank, Penn World Tables, and National Household Surveys).

Table 13-3. Income distribution. This table presents the share of income held by the richest and poorest population groups in a country (World Bank data and national household surveys).

Table 13-4. Urbanization. This table presents the number of persons living in urban areas as a percentage of the total population. Average annual percentage growth rates are shown separately for the urban population and the total population. The urban population percentages are based on the number of persons living in areas defined as "urban" according to national definitions of this concept. Since national definitions differ, cross-country comparisons should be made with caution (World Bank data).

Table 13-5. Components of population change. This table presents three determinants of population change: total fertility rate, crude birth rate, and crude death rate. Crude birth rate is the number of births per 1,000 population in a given year. Crude death rate is the number of deaths per 1,000 population in a given year. Total fertility rate is the average number of children that would be born alive to a woman during her lifetime, if she were to bear children at each age in accordance with prevailing age-specific fertility rates (World Bank data).

Table 13-6. Survival prospects. This table shows five health-related indicators: life expectancy at birth, infant mortality rate, child mortality rate, maternal mortality rate, and adult HIVs sero prevalence.

Life expectancy at birth is the number of years a newborn infant would live if prevailing patterns of mortality at the time of its birth were to stay the same throughout its life. Infant mortality rate is the number of deaths of infants under one year of age per 1,000 live births in a given year. Child mortality rate is the number of deaths of children under five years of age per 1,000 live births in a given year. Maternal mortality rate is the annual number of deaths of women from pregnancy-related causes per 100,000 live births. Adult HIV-1 sero prevalence reflects the estimated rate of infection in each country's adult population (aged 15 to 49) (UNAIDS).

Table 13-7. Immunization and ORT use. This is the percentage of children under one year of age immunized against tuberculosis, DPT, polio, and measles. It also gives the use rate of oral rehydration therapy (ORT) among children under five years of age. DPT refers to diphtheria, pertussis (whooping cough), and tetanus. ORT use is the percentage of all cases of diarrhea in children under five years of age treated with oral rehydration salts or an appropriate household solution (WHO data).

Table 13-8. Child malnutrition. Data reported on this table give the percentage of children and babies suffering from nutrition-related problems of low birthweight, underweight, wasting, and stunting. Figures are also given on the extent of breastfeeding among nursing mothers.

Low birthweight refers to babies born weighing less than 2,500 grams. Underweight refers to children under the age of five weighing two standard deviations below the median weight for age of the reference population. Wasting refers to children of ages 12 through 23 months weighing two standard deviations below the median weight for height of the reference population. Stunting refers to children of ages 24 through 59 months standing two standard deviations below the median height-for-age of the reference population (UNDP various years, WHO and World Bank data).

Table 13-9. Access to sanitation facilities. Table 13-9 shows the percentage of the population with access to sanitation facilities (WHO data). Urban areas with access to sanitation facilities are defined as urban populations served by connections to public sewers or household systems, such as pit privies, pour-flush latrines, septic tanks, communal toilets, and other such facilities. Rural populations with access were defined as those with adequate disposal, such as pit privies and pour-flush latrines. Application of these definitions may vary, and comparisons can therefore be misleading.

Table 13-10. Access to safe water. This table refers to the percentage of the population with reasonable access to safe water supply, which includes treated surface waters or untreated, but uncontaminated water, such as that from springs, sanitary wells, and protected boreholes. In an urban area, this may be a public fountain or standpost located not more than 200 meters away. In rural areas, it implies that members of the household do not have to spend a disproportionate part of the day fetching water. Data are presented separately for total, urban and rural population (WHO data).

Table 13-11. Health expenditure. This table shows total health expenditure as percentage of GDP and on a per capita basis—both in current $ and PPP terms. The ratio to GDP is also shown for public and private expenditure. *Total health expenditure* is the sum of public and private health expenditures. It covers the provision of health services (preventive and curative), family planning activities, nutrition activities, and emergency aid designated for health but does not include provision of water and sanitation. *Public health expenditure* consists of recurrent and capital spending from government (central and local) budgets, external borrowings and grants (including donations from international agencies and nongovernmental organizations, and social (or compulsory) health insurance funds. *Private health expenditure* includes direct household (out-of-pocket) spending, private insurance, charitable donations, and direct service payments by private corporations (WHO, IMF, and World Bank data).

Table 13-12. Health care. Indicators presented here are population per physician, population per hospital bed, the percentage of births attended by trained health personnel, and access to health services. The figure for physicians includes, in addition to the total number of registered practitioners in the country, medical assistants whose medical training is less than that of qualified physicians, but who nevertheless dispense similar medical services, including simple surgical operations. The definition of recognized medical practitioners differs among countries. Hospital beds include inpatient beds available in public, private, general, and specialized hospitals and in rehabilitation centers. In most cases acute and chronic care are included. Births attended refers to births attended by physicians, nurses, midwives, trained primary healthcare workers, or trained traditional birth attendants. Access to health services refers to the percentage of the population that can reach appropriate local health services by the local transport in no more than one hour (WHO and World Bank data).

Table 13-13. Illiteracy rate. This table shows the share of illiterate adults in total adult population aged 15 years and over. Literacy is defined as the ability to read and write. A person who can, with understanding, both read and write a short, simple statement about his everyday life is literate. Persons who can read, but cannot write, are included with illiterates. Figures are shown separately for males, females, and both genders combined (UNESCO data).

Tables 13-14. Primary school gross enrollment ratio. This is the total number of pupils enrolled at the primary level of education, regardless of age, expressed as a percentage of the population corresponding to the official school age of primary education in a given country. Data are given separately for males, females, and both genders combined. Figures shown may be more than 100 percent since total enrollment includes pupils above and pupils below the primary school age, as well as repeaters (UNESCO data).

Tables 13-15. Pupil progression. This table provides two education indicators. *Percentage of cohort reaching grade 5 of primary school* shows the percentage of children starting primary school, who eventually attain grade 4. The estimate is based on the Reconstructed Cohort Method, which uses data on enrollment and repeaters for two consecutive years. Progression to secondary school (general) is the number of new children in the first grade of secondary school (general) divided by the number of children enrolled in the final grade of primary school in the previous year (according to the country's duration of primary education (UNESCO and World Bank data).

Table 13-16. Net primary enrollment ratio. This is the ratio of the number of children of official school age enrolled in school to the number of children of official school age in the population (UNESCO data).

Table 13-17. Number of schoolteachers. Teachers in both public and private schools are covered in this table. Data refer to both full-time and part-time teachers, excluding other instructional personnel without teaching functions. Figures are shown here separately for primary and secondary schools. Percentage females means the number of female teachers expressed as a percentage of total teaching staff (UNESCO data).

Table 13-18. Pupil/teacher ratio. This ratio gives the average number of pupils per teacher. Figures are given separately for primary and secondary schools. As teaching staff includes both full-time and part-time teachers, comparability of this ratio between countries may be affected as the proportion of part-time teachers varies greatly from one country to another (UNESCO data).

Table 13-19. Secondary school gross enrollment ratio. This is the secondary school equivalent of the data presented in Table 13-14. It gives the total number of students enrolled at the secondary level of education, regardless of age, expressed as a percentage of the population corresponding to the official school age of secondary education. Data are presented separately for males, females, and both genders combined. Second level, general refers to education in secondary schools that provides general or specialized instruction based upon at least four years of previous instruction at the first or primary level, which do not specifically aim at preparing the pupils directly for a given trade or occupation. Such schools may be called high schools, middle schools, or lyceums and offer courses of study whose completion is a minimum condition for admission into universities. In some countries, some of these schools provide both academic and vocational training. These composite secondary schools are considered as equivalent to the academic type of secondary school and are thus classified as second level, general (UNESCO data).

Table 13-20. Public expenditure on education. This table presents the public expenditure on education (UNESCO) first as a percentage of total public expenditure (IMF/GFS) and then as a percentage of current GDP (Table 2-5).

Table 13-21. Economic opportunities of women. This table shows two indicators. Female/male ratio of participation in economic activity shows the number of female workers in relation to the number of male workers. Females as percentage of males in occupational group show the breakdown of the first indicator for occupational categories (UNDP data).

Table 13-22. Household and economic participation of women. This table presents indicators on gender issues in development. Households headed by women (World Bank data) refers to families in which a woman is acknowledged as the head by the other members. The occupational statistics are based on UN, *Statistical Yearbook 1992–93.*

Table 13-23. Relative prices of consumption and investment in PPP terms, 1993. This table shows 1993 relative prices of consumption and investment using purchasing power parity (PPP). PPP measures the cost of goods in one country relative to a numeraire country, in this case the United States. An international price level above 100 means that the general price level in the country is higher than that in the United States. For example, Kenya's price level of 21 means that a bundle of goods and services purchased for $100 in the United States costs only $21 in Kenya.

The relative prices of components of GDP shown in the table are calculated from their international prices measured relative to each country's price level of GDP. A figure above 100 indicates that the price of that component is higher than the average price level of GDP. This is not the same as saying that the component is more expensive in that country than in the United States. It indicates only that the price for that component is higher than the general price level prevailing in the country.

International price level is the ratio of a country's PPP rate to its official exchange rate for U.S. dollars. Private consumption includes the consumption expenditures of individuals, households, and nongovernmental organizations. *All food* includes all food purchased for household consumption. *Bread and cereals* comprise the main staple products: rice, flour, bread, all other cereals; and cereal preparations. *Clothing and footwear* include purchases of new and used clothing and footwear and repair services. *Fuel and power* exclude energy used for transport (rarely reported to be more than 1 percent of total consumption in low- and middle-income economies). *Health care and education* include government as well as private expenditures. *Transport and communications* cover all personal costs of transport, telephones, and the like. *Government consumption* includes spending on goods and services for collective consumption less spending on recreational and other related cultural services, education, health, and housing. Expenditure on governmental final consumption consists of compensation of employees, consumption of intermediate goods and services, and consumption of fixed capital and indirect taxes paid less proceeds from sales of goods and services to other sectors such as fees charged by municipalities and other government agencies, school fees, fees for medical and hospital treatment and drug sales, and sales of maps and charts. *Gross fixed capital formation* comprises expenditures on construction, producer durables, and changes in stocks. Construction includes residential and nonresidential buildings and roads, bridges, and other civil engineering activities. Producer durables include machinery and nonelectrical equipment, electrical machinery and appliances, and transport equipment. Changes in stocks cover increases in the value of materials and supplies, works in progress, and livestock (including breeding stock and dairy cattle) (ICP and World Bank data).

Table 13-24. Structure of household consumption in PPP terms, 1997. This table reflects shares based on real values of items that make up household consumption. Because the goods and services that make up consumption are valued at uniform prices, PPP-based expenditure shares also provide a consistent view of differences in the real structure of consumption between countries. The shares shown in the table reflect the relative quantities of goods and services consumed rather than their nominal cost.

Although PPPs are more useful than official exchange rates in comparing consumption patterns, caution should be used in interpreting PPP results. PPP estimates are based on price comparisons of comparable items, but not all items can be matched perfectly in quality across countries and over time. Services are particularly difficult to compare, in part because of differences in productivity. Many services, such as government services, are not sold on the open market in all countries, so they are compared using input prices (mostly wages). Because this approach ignores productivity differences, it may inflate estimates of real quantities in lower-income countries (ICP and World Bank data).

Figures

The following indicators have been used to derive the figures in this chapter.

Figure 13-1. Life expectancy (Table 13-6).

Figure 13-2. GDP per capita, based on PPP, 1997 (Table 13-2).

Figure 13-3. Percentage of urban population in total population (Table 13-4).

Figure 13-4. Primary school enrollment ratio (Table 13-14).

Figure 13-5. Maternal mortality (Table 13-6).

Methodology used for regional aggregations and period averages in chapter 13

Table	Aggregations[a]					Period averages[b]	
	(1)	*(2)*	*(6)*	*(7)*	*(8)*	*(1)*	*(2)*
13-1							
Columns 1-8		x					
Columns 9-10			x				
13-2							
Columns 1, 3			x				
Columns 4, 5, 8				x			
Columns 2, 6-7					x		
13-3					x		
13-4							
Columns 1-3	x						
Columns 4-6							x
Columns 7-9			x				
Columns 10-12							x
13-5							
Columns 1-3			x				
Columns 4-6		x					
Columns 7-9		x					
13-6			x				
13-7			x				
13-8			x				
13-9			x				
13-10			x				
13-11							
Columns 1-4			x				
Column 5					x		
13-12			x				
13-13			x				
13-14			x				
13-15			x				
13-16			x				
13-17							
Columns 1-3, 7-9					x		
Columns 4-6, 10-12			x				
13-18			x				
13-19			x				
13-20			x				
13-21			x				
13-22					x		
13-23					x		
13-24					x		

Note: Regional aggregations are shown in the rows for Sub-Saharan Africa, North Africa, and All Africa. Period averages are shown in the last three columns. This table shows only the methodologies used in this chapter.

a. Regional aggregations: (1) simple total; (2) simple total of the first indicator divided by the simple total of the second indicator (same country coverage); (3) simple total of the gap-filled indicator; (4) simple total of the gap-filled main indicator divided by the simple total of the gap-filled secondary indicator; (5) simple total of the first gap-filled main indicator less the simple total of the second gap-filled main indicator, all divided by the simple total of the secondary indicator; (6) weighted total (by population); (7) median; (8) no aggregation; (9) simple arithmetic mean.

b. Period averages: (i) arithmetic mean (using the same series as shown in the table i.e., ratio if the rest of the table is shown as ratio, level if the rest of the table is shown as level, growth rate if the rest is shown as growth rate); (2) least-squares growth rate (using main indicator); (3) least-squares growth rate (using main indicator in constant terms, with the rest of the table in current terms).

14

Environmental Indicators

This chapter was drawn entirely from the World Resources Institute and reflects tables published in their *World Resources 2000*. It includes data on natural resources—their use by sector and the trends in their use—protected resources and those in danger of extinction, commercial energy production and its components, globally threatened species and protection and management programs.

Until the early 1970s, environmental issues were mainly focused on problems of industrial countries and on such issues as water and air pollution, acid rain, and greenhouse gas emissions. Since the publication of the Club of Rome's *The Limit to Growth* in 1972, however, issues of natural resource depletion and degradation have received considerable attention in assessing environmental factors and their impacts on the development prospects of developing nations. At the national level, environmental concerns revolve around population expansion, desertification, deforestation, and the by-products of energy consumption.

Environmental destruction is not, however, confined by geographic borders. For instance, global warming, said to be caused by greenhouse gas emissions, has become a major global environmental concern. The issue of the greenhouse effect may be subject to controversy at the theoretical level and difficult to prove at the practical level. The fact that industrial wastes generated in one country cross-frontiers and cause

environmental damage to other nations is, however, widely acknowledged. Common interests, therefore, compel the international community to jointly work toward a common goal of preserving the environment.

Increasing emphasis on the links between the environment and development, both at the national and international levels, is reflected in the growing number of scientific and analytical studies. Challenging the hegemony of the SNA national income accounting convention, numerous scholarly endeavors are under way to internalize environmental consequences in national income calculations. The argument is made that the SNA methodology overstates national income levels for two reasons. First, it does not account for both the direct and indirect costs of drawing down natural resources. Second, it counts expenditure on resources for environmental protection activities as income. The changes both in methodology and emphasis have created an urgent demand for physical data. The information in this chapter aims to meet this growing demand, notwithstanding the limitations in data coverage and reliability.

The rate of deforestation is of particular concern because the cost of deforestation goes far beyond the loses of forest products, such as timber and fuelwood. There are equally significant indirect costs, including soil erosion; the substitution of animal and agricultural residues for cooking, which would otherwise be used for fertilizer; and climate changes. Deforestation is caused by many factors, including increased demand for settlement area, cultivation, fuelwood, or a combination thereof. The information in this chapter provides an empirical framework for assessing policy alternatives in reversing the continuing depletion of natural resources.

Data on roundwood production and consumption are important in monitoring the causes of deforestation. In addition, since roundwood is a primary source of energy in developing nations, data on roundwood consumption is essential in analyzing air pollution. For instance, for 1985–87, Africa used close to 88 percent of its roundwood production for fuel and charcoal production, while approximately 12 percent of the roundwood production went to industrial uses. To put these figures in perspective, the corresponding figures for Europe are 16 and 84 percent.

Information on fresh water resources available and on the extent and the methods of their uses can provide a partial basis for analyzing Africa's agricultural performance, its potential hydroelectric power, and its populations' health conditions. Almost all Sub-Saharan African countries use a very small fraction of their internal renewable water resources. For instance, Ethiopia, a nation that has suffered from repeated droughts, uses only 2 percent of its water resources. The major problem rests in the uneven geographic distribution of water resources with respect to population density and the state of freshwater drawing technology. The quality of water is as important as the quantity of water available. Water-related disease accounts for 80 percent of all sicknesses and for 90 percent of the 15 million deaths in developing countries each year.

Data on energy production are shown because of related environmental consequences. Biomass fuel, comprising woodfuel and animal and agricultural residues, accounts for 40 to 90 percent of total energy used in Sub-Saharan Africa.

Data on protected areas and endangered species indicate the intentions of countries to safeguard the environment and protect the use of natural resources for future generations.

14-1. Forest resources, 1990-95

	Forest area								
	Total forest			Natural forest			Plantation		
	Extent (000 ha)		Annual % change	Extent (000 ha)		Annual % change	Extent (000 ha)		Annual % change
	1990	1995	1990-95	1990	1995	1990-95	1990	1995	1990-95
SUB-SAHARAN AFRICA	..	..	..	..	..	..	..	..	..
excluding South Africa	..	..	..	..	..	..	..	..	..
excl. S. Africa & Nigeria	..	..	..	..	..	..	..	..	..
Angola	23,285	22,200	-1.0	23,265	22,080	-1.0	120	160	5.8
Benin	4,923	4,625	-1.2	4,909	4,611	-1.3	14	30	15.2
Botswana	14,271	13,917	-0.5	14,270	13,916	-0.5	1	..	..
Burkina Faso	4,431	4,271	-0.7	4,411	4,251	-0.7	20	28	6.7
Burundi	324	317	-0.4	232	225	-0.6	92	120	5.3
Cameroon	20,244	19,598	-0.6	20,228	19,582	-0.6	16	23	7.3
Cape Verde	..	..	..	..	..	..	..	..	..
Central African Republic	30,571	29,930	-0.4	30,565	29,924	-0.4	6	..	..
Chad	11,496	11,025	-0.8	11,492	11,021	-0.8	4	8	13.9
Comoros	..	..	..	..	..	..	..	..	..
Congo, Dem. Rep. of	112,946	109,245	-0.7	112,904	109,203	-0.7	42	60	7.1
Congo, Rep. of	19,745	19,537	-0.2	19,708	19,500	-0.2	37	64	11.0
Côte d'Ivoire	5,623	5,469	-0.6	5,560	5,403	-0.6	63	98	8.8
Djibouti	..	..	..	..	..	..	..	..	..
Equatorial Guinea	1,829	1,781	-0.5	1,826	1,778	-0.5	3	..	..
Eritrea	282	282	0.0	233	233	0.0	..	..	..
Ethiopia	13,891	13,579	-0.5	13,751	13,439	-0.5	189	220	3.0
Gabon	18,314	17,859	-0.5	18,293	17,838	-0.5	21	30	7.1
Gambia, The	95	91	-0.9	94	90	-0.9	1	2	8.1
Ghana	9,608	9,022	-1.3	9,555	8,969	-1.3	53	19	-20.5
Guinea	6,741	6,367	-1.1	6,737	6,363	-1.1	4	11	19.5
Guinea-Bissau	2,361	2,309	-0.4	2,360	2,308	-0.4	1	..	..
Kenya	1,309	1,292	-0.3	1,191	1,174	-0.3	118	240	14.2
Lesotho	6	6	0.0	0	0	0.0	7	6	0.0
Liberia	4,641	4,507	-0.6	4,635	4,501	-0.6	6	8	5.8
Madagascar	15,756	15,106	-0.8	15,539	14,889	-0.9	217	335	8.7
Malawi	3,612	3,339	-1.6	3,486	3,213	-1.6	126	122	-0.6
Mali	12,154	11,585	-1.0	12,140	11,571	-1.0	14	40	21.0
Mauritania	556	556	0.0	554	554	0.0	2	8	27.7
Mauritius	..	..	..	..	..	..	..	..	..
Mozambique	17,443	16,862	-0.7	17,415	16,834	-0.7	28	45	9.5
Namibia	12,584	12,374	-0.3	12,584	12,374	-0.3	0	1	..
Niger	2,562	2,562	0.0	2,550	2,550	0.0	12	60	32.2
Nigeria	14,387	13,780	-0.9	14,236	13,629	-0.9	151	250	10.1
Rwanda	252	250	-0.2	164	162	-0.2	88	247	20.6
São Tomé and Principe	..	..	..	..	..	..	..	..	..
Senegal	7,629	7,381	-0.7	7,517	7,269	-0.7	112	216	13.1
Seychelles	..	..	..	..	..	..	..	..	..
Sierra Leone	1,522	1,309	-3.0	1,516	1,303	-3.0	6	8	5.8
Somalia	760	754	-0.2	756	750	-0.2	4	6	8.1
South Africa	8,574	8,499	-0.2	7,279	7,204	-0.2	965	1,429	7.8
Sudan	43,376	41,613	-0.8	43,173	41,410	-0.8	203	425	14.8
Swaziland	..	..	..	..	..	..	..	..	..
Tanzania	34,123	32,510	-1.0	33,969	32,356	-1.0	154	200	5.2
Togo	1,338	1,245	-1.4	1,317	1,224	-1.5	17	34	14.0
Uganda	6,400	6,104	-0.9	6,380	6,084	-1.0	20	26	5.2
Zambia	32,720	31,398	-0.8	32,677	31,355	-0.8	48	44	-1.9
Zimbabwe	8,960	8,710	-0.6	8,876	8,626	-0.6	84	110	5.4
NORTH AFRICA	..	..	..	..	..	..	..	..	..
Algeria	1,978	1,861	-1.2	1,493	1,376	-1.6	485	972	13.9
Egypt	34	34	0.0	0	0	0	34	..	..
Libya	1,686	1,544	-1.8	1,607	1,465	-2	79	..	..
Morocco	400	400	0.0	190	190	0.0	210	..	..
Tunisia	3,894	3,835	-0.3	3,573	3,514	-0.3	321	565	11.3
ALL AFRICA	538,978	520,237	-0.7	534,226	515,455	-0.7	4,416	..	4.4

Sources: Food and Agriculture Organization of the United Nations and the United Nations Economic Commission for Europe.

Notes: 0 = zero or less than half the unit of measure; negative numbers indicate reduction in forest area; .. = not available.

14-2. Forest ecosystems, 1996

	Land area (000 hectares)	Original Forest as a % of land area a/	Closed forests — Forests as a % of original forest — Current forests b/ 1996	Frontier forests c/ 1996	Percent frontier forests c/ threatened 1996	Forest ecosystems (1996) — Mangroves Area (000 ha)	Mangroves Percent protected	Tropical forests Area (000 ha)	Tropical forests Percent protected	Nontropical forests Area (000 ha)	Nontropical forests Percent protected	Sparse trees and parkland Area (000 ha)	Sparse trees and parkland Percent protected
SUB-SAHARAN AFRICA	..	..	..	..	..	..	..	..	..	..	..	..	..
excluding South Africa	..	..	..	..	..	..	..	..	..	..	..	..	..
excl. S. Africa & Nigeria	..	..	..	..	..	..	..	..	..	..	..	..	..
Angola	124,670	20	15	0	111	0	0	37,564	3	0	0	0	0
Benin	11,062	16	4	0	0	0	0	1,516	18	0	0	585	2
Botswana	56,673	2	100	0	0	0	0	12,123	2	0	0	0	0
Burkina Faso	27,360	0	0	0	0	0	0	0	0	0	0	5,667	16
Burundi	2,568	46	3	0	0	0	0	219	18	0	0	139	3
Cameroon	46,540	80	42	8	97	227	2	20,009	6	0	0	2,416	22
Cape Verde	..	..	..	..	..	..	..	..	..	..	..	..	..
Central African Republic	62,298	52	16	4	100	0	0	17,101	20	0	0	1,451	48
Chad	125,920	0	0	0	0	0	0	3,516	4	0	0	2,857	1
Comoros	..	..	..	..	..	..	..	..	..	..	..	..	..
Congo, Dem. Rep. of	226,705	83	60	16	70	22	0	135,071	7	0	0	172	40
Congo, Rep. of	34,150	100	68	29	65	19	76	24,321	4	0	0	0	0
Côte d'Ivoire	31,800	75	10	2	100	0	0	2,702	23	0	0	625	18
Djibouti	..	..	..	..	..	..	..	..	..	..	..	..	..
Equatorial Guinea	2,805	96	38	0	0	25	0	1,749	0	0	0	0	0
Eritrea	..	..	..	..	..	0	0	1	0	0	0	0	0
Ethiopia	110,000	25	17	0	0	0	0	11,937	19	0	0	4,804	21
Gabon	25,767	100	90	32	100	147	3	21,481	4	0	0	0	0
Gambia, The	1,000	39	62	0	0	51	5	188	5	0	0	244	2
Ghana	22,754	66	9	0	0	0	0	1,694	7	0	0	336	17
Guinea	24,572	76	5	0	0	316	0	3,073	1	0	0	2,723	1
Guinea-Bissau	2,812	100	34	0	0	317	0	1,141	0	0	0	550	0
Kenya	56,914	17	19	0	0	0	0	3,423	8	0	0	2,754	3
Lesotho	3,035	2	0	0	0	0	0	89	9	0	0	0	0
Liberia	9,632	100	44	0	0	0	0	3,149	3	0	0	1	0
Madagascar	58,154	93	13	0	0	310	0	6,940	6	0	0	0	0
Malawi	9,408	12	0	0	0	0	0	3,830	9	0	0	0	0
Mali	122,019	0	0	0	0	0	0	6,132	2	0	0	336	0
Mauritania	102,522	0	0	0	0	..	..	..	..	..	..	..	..
Mauritius	203	..	..	..	..	..	..	..	..	..	..	..	..
Mozambique	78,409	33	14	0	0	565	4	20,863	7	0	0	14,414	7
Namibia	82,329	0	95	0	0	0	0	3,436	11	0	0	0	0
Niger	126,670	0	0	0	0	0	0	27	16	0	0	0	0
Nigeria	91,077	45	11	1	100	1,145	0	11,634	7	0	0	10,588	4
Rwanda	2,467	36	16	0	0	0	0	291	77	0	0	162	2
São Tomé and Principe	..	..	..	..	..	..	..	..	..	..	..	..	..
Senegal	19,253	14	16	0	0	158	3	2,076	7	0	0	8,816	13
Seychelles	..	..	..	..	..	..	..	..	..	..	..	..	..
Sierra Leone	7,162	100	10	0	0	176	1	260	20	0	0	104	0
Somalia	62,734	4	0	0	0	0	0	11,800	1	0	0	1,530	1
South Africa	122,104	13	0	0	0	0	0	10,333	5	52	26	0	0
Sudan	237,600	1	0	0	0	0	0	12,288	12	0	0	5,870	9
Swaziland	1,720	22	0	0	0	0	0	286	3	0	0	0	0
Tanzania	88,359	22	9	0	0	323	0	14,356	16	0	0	583	3
Togo	5,439	33	7	0	0	0	0	224	3	0	0	91	9
Uganda	19,965	70	4	0	0	0	0	3,772	17	0	0	1,850	65
Zambia	74,339	7	70	0	0	0	0	21,989	32	0	0	39	14
Zimbabwe	38,685	7	67	0	0	0	0	15,397	12	0	0	0	0
NORTH AFRICA	..	..	..	..	..	..	..	..	..	..	..	..	..
Algeria	238,174	5	12	0	0	0	0	0	0	2,694	4	1	83
Egypt	99,545	1	0	0	0	0	0	134	0	4	0	0	0
Libya	175,954	1	0	0	0	0	0	0	0	53	0	0	0
Morocco	44,630	22	7	0	0	0	0	0	0	1,862	3	0	0
Tunisia	15,536	18	5	0	0	0	0	0	0	300	2	0	0
ALL AFRICA	2,963,468	23	34	8	77	3,801	1	448,197	9	8,249	2	69,710	11

Source:　Food and Agriculture Organization of the United Nations.

Notes:　a.　Original forest is that estimated to have covered the planet 8000 years ago given current climate conditions.
　　　　b.　Includes frontier and nonfrontier forests.
　　　　c.　Frontier forests are large, relatively undisturbed forest ecosystems.
　　　　0 = zero or less than half of the unit of measure; .. = not available.

14-3. Wood production and trade, 1986-98

| | Average annual roundwood production | | | | | | Average annual forest products production | | | | Trade in forest products | | |
| | Total roundwood | | Wood fuel | | Industrial roundwood | | Wood-based panels | | Paper and paperboard | | Import | Export | |
	Cubic meters (000) 1996-98	Percent change since 1986-88	Cubic meters (000) 1996-98	Percent change since 1986-88	Cubic meters (000) 1996-98	Percent change since 1986-88	Cubic meters (000) 1996-98	Percent change since 1986-88	Metric tons (000) 1996-98	Percent change since 1986-88	Value (million US$) 1996-98	Value (million US$) 1996-98	Percent of total exports 1998
SUB-SAHARAN AFRICA	..	..	..	..	..	..	..	..	..	..	..	..	..
excluding South Africa	..	..	..	..	..	..	..	..	..	..	..	..	..
excl. S. Africa & Nigeria	..	..	..	..	..	..	..	..	..	..	..	..	..
Angola	6,272	37	5,220	38	1,052	32	11	-55	0	0	5	1	0
Benin	5,839	32	5,507	32	332	36	0	0	0	0	2	2	0
Botswana	1,641	33	1,540	33	101	33	0	0	0	0	0	0	..
Burkina Faso	10,506	32	10,022	32	484	32	0	0	0	0	2	0	0
Burundi	1,669	37	1,487	27	182	287	0	0	0	0	3	0	0
Cameroon	15,191	29	11,869	32	3,323	20	124	42	2	-67	22	427	17
Cape Verde	..	..	..	..	..	..	..	..	..	..	..	..	..
Central African Republic	3,388	-1	2,660	-12	728	80	1	-67	0	0	0	27	13
Chad	1,871	37	1,147	36	724	38	0	0	0	0	2	0	0
Comoros	..	..	..	..	..	..	..	..	..	..	..	..	..
Congo, Dem. Rep. of	3,985	30	2,456	33	1,529	25	54	-5	0	0	1	147	8
Congo, Rep. of	48,372	41	44,814	42	3,557	28	21	-47	3	13	6	63	4
Côte d'Ivoire	12,983	21	9,970	33	3,013	-6	306	42	0	0	37	280	6
Djibouti	..	..	..	..	..	..	..	..	..	..	..	..	..
Equatorial Guinea	811	27	447	0	364	92	9	13	0	0	1	57	13
Eritrea	..	..	2,110	..	..	..	0	0	0	0	9	0	0
Ethiopia	48,990	..	46,522	..	2,468	..	13	..	9	..	16	0	0
Gabon	5,144	62	2,491	33	2,653	104	36	-80	0	0	4	288	9
Gambia, The	813	29	700	18	113	208	0	0	0	0	1	0	0
Ghana	21,931	61	20,678	64	1,253	23	136	112	0	0	16	145	9
Guinea	8,643	138	7,977	154	666	32	0	0	0	0	6	9	1
Guinea-Bissau	586	4	422	0	164	18	0	0	0	0	0	3	6
Kenya	28,813	33	26,879	34	1,934	19	52	26	129	41	30	1	0
Lesotho	1,556	27	1,556	27	0	0	0	0	0	0	0	0	0
Liberia	2,936	-19	2,700	0	236	-75	45	644	0	0	1	12	..
Madagascar	9,254	20	8,878	28	376	-53	5	20	4	-62	9	6	1
Malawi	9,449	25	8,950	24	499	45	18	213	0	0	4	2	0
Mali	6,284	24	5,890	24	394	21	0	0	0	0	5	1	0
Mauritania	15	29	9	29	6	29	0	0	0	0	2	0	0
Mauritius	..	..	..	..	..	..	..	..	..	..	..	..	..
Mozambique	17,973	18	16,724	17	1,249	37	3	-64	0	-100	1	10	2
Namibia	..	..	..	..	..	..	..	..	..	..	..	..	0
Niger	6,260	39	5,873	39	386	39	0	0	0	0	2	0	0
Nigeria	95,993	18	87,001	18	8,992	14	38	-80	59	-28	80	30	0
Rwanda	3,020	-48	3,000	-46	20	-92	0	-100	0	0	2	0	0
São Tomé and Principe	..	..	..	..	..	..	..	..	..	..	..	..	..
Senegal	4,785	30	4,029	30	756	28	0	0	0	0	24	0	0
Seychelles	..	..	..	..	..	..	..	..	..	..	..	..	..
Sierra Leone	3,215	16	3,092	18	124	-12	0	0	0	0	2	1	1
Somalia	7,616	8	7,513	8	102	5	0	-100	0	0	0	0	..
South Africa	32,906	46	14,467	36	18,439	55	653	64	1988	19	482	1025	3
Sudan	9,289	23	7,207	23	2,082	23	2	0	3	-69	34	0	0
Swaziland	..	..	..	..	..	..	..	..	..	..	..	..	..
Tanzania	38,193	35	35,947	35	2,246	28	4	-67	25	32	6	5	0
Togo	1,156	41	872	33	284	73	0	0	0	0	3	2	0
Uganda	15,236	30	13,080	30	2,156	33	5	47	3	50	3	0	0
Zambia	8,051	31	7,219	29	832	58	18	-20	3	-2	5	1	0
Zimbabwe	8,192	8	6,260	2	1,932	34	68	148	74	-7	29	22	1
NORTH AFRICA	..	..	..	..	..	..	..	..	..	..	..	..	..
Algeria	2,676	34	2,239	27	437	79	50	0	62	-48	337	0	0
Egypt	2,776	24	2,647	24	129	23	81	27	263	70	949	8	0
Libya	650	2	536	0	114	11	0	0	6	0	46	0	..
Morocco	1,324	-7	539	-31	785	21	35	-75	108	2	336	60	1
Tunisia	2,770	23	2,559	20	211	65	104	16	97	58	203	17	0
ALL AFRICA	..	..	..	..	..	..	..	..	..	..	..	..	..

Source: Food and Agriculture Organization of the United Nations.

Notes: 0 = zero or less than half of the unit of measure; .. = not available.

14-4. Freshwater resources and withdrawals, 1970-2000

	Annual internal renewable water resources		Annual river flows			Annual withdrawals			Sectoral withdrawals (percent)		
	Total (cubic km)	Per capita 2000 (cubic meters)	From other countries (cubic km)	To other countries (cubic km)	Year of data	Total (cubic km)	Percentage of water resources	Per capita (cubic meters)	Domestic	Industrial	Agricultural
SUB-SAHARAN AFRICA	..	..	..	..	..	..	..	..	..	..	..
excluding South Africa	..	..	..	..	..	..	..	..	..	..	..
excl. S. Africa & Nigeria	..	..	..	..	..	..	..	..	..	..	..
Angola	184	14,288	..	..	1987	0.48	0.3	57	14	10	76
Benin	10	1,689	15.5	..	1994	0.15	1.4	28	23	10	67
Botswana	3	1,788	11.8	..	1992	0.11	3.8	81	32	20	48
Burkina Faso	18	1,466	..	..	1992	0.38	2.1	39	19	0	81
Burundi	4	538	..	..	1987	0.10	2.8	20	36	0	64
Cameroon	268	17,766	0.0	0.0	1987	0.40	0.1	38	46	19	35
Cape Verde	..	..	..	..	..	..	..	..	..	..	..
Central African Republic	141	39,001	..	..	1987	0.07	0.0	26	21	6	73
Chad	15	1,961	28.0	..	1990	0.19	1.3	33	16	2	82
Comoros	..	..	..	..	..	..	..	..	..	..	..
Congo, Dem. Rep. of	935	18,101	84.0	..	1994	0.36	0.0	8	61	16	23
Congo, Rep. of	222	75,387	610.0	..	1987	0.04	0.0	20	62	27	11
Côte d'Ivoire	77	5,187	1.0	..	1987	0.70	0.9	66	22	11	67
Djibouti	..	..	..	..	..	..	..	..	..	..	..
Equatorial Guinea	30	66,275	0.0	..	1987	0.01	0.0	30	81	13	6
Eritrea	3	727	6.0	..	..	..	..	..	..	..	..
Ethiopia	110	1,758	0.0	..	1987	2.20	2.0	50	11	3	86
Gabon	164	133,754	0.0	..	1987	0.06	0.0	70	72	22	6
Gambia, The	3	2,298	5.0	..	1990	0.03	1.0	33	7	2	91
Ghana	30	1,499	22.9	..	1970	0.30	1.0	35	35	13	52
Guinea	226	30,416	0.0	..	1987	0.74	0.3	141	10	3	87
Guinea-Bissau	16	13,189	11.0	..	1991	0.02	0.1	17	60	4	36
Kenya	20	672	10.0	..	1990	2.05	10.1	87	20	4	76
Lesotho	5	2,430	0.0	..	1987	0.05	1.0	31	22	22	56
Liberia	200	63,412	32.0	..	1987	0.13	0.1	54	27	13	60
Madagascar	337	21,139	0.0	..	1990	19.70	5.8	1694	1	0	99
Malawi	18	1,605	1.1	..	1994	0.94	5.4	98	10	3	86
Mali	60	5,341	40.0	..	1987	1.36	2.3	164	2	1	97
Mauritania	0	150	11.0	..	1990	16.30	4,075.0	8046	6	2	92
Mauritius	..	..	..	..	..	..	..	..	..	..	..
Mozambique	100	5,081	116.0	..	1992	0.61	0.6	40	9	2	89
Namibia	6	3,592	39.3	..	1990	0.25	4.0	185	29	3	68
Niger	4	326	29.0	..	1990	0.50	14.3	65	16	2	82
Nigeria	221	1,982	59.0	..	1990	4.00	1.8	46	31	15	54
Rwanda	6	815	..	..	1993	0.77	12.2	134	5	1	94
São Tomé and Principe	..	..	..	..	..	..	..	..	..	..	..
Senegal	26	2,784	13.0	..	1990	1.50	5.7	205	5	3	92
Seychelles	..	..	..	..	..	..	..	..	..	..	..
Sierra Leone	160	32,960	0.0	..	1987	0.37	0.2	98	7	4	89
Somalia	6	594	9.7	..	1987	0.81	13.5	115	3	0	97
South Africa	45	1,110	5.2	..	1990	13.30	29.7	391	17	11	72
Sudan	35	1,187	119.0	..	1995	17.80	50.9	669	5	1	94
Swaziland	..	..	..	..	..	..	..	..	..	..	..
Tanzania	80	2,387	9.0	..	1994	1.17	1.5	40	9	2	89
Togo	12	2,484	0.5	..	1987	0.09	0.8	28	62	13	25
Uganda	39	1,791	27.0	..	1970	0.20	0.5	20	32	8	60
Zambia	80	8,747	35.8	..	1994	1.71	2.1	214	16	7	77
Zimbabwe	14	1,208	5.9	..	1987	1.22	8.7	136	14	7	79
NORTH AFRICA	..	..	..	..	..	..	..	..	..	..	..
Algeria	14	442	0.4	0.4	1990	4.50	32.4	180	25	15	60
Egypt	2	34	56.0	0.0	1993	55.10	2,395.7	920	6	8	86
Libya	1	143	0.0	0.0	1995	3.89	486.3	783	9	4	87
Morocco	30	1,058	0.0	0.2	1991	11.05	36.8	454	5	3	92
Tunisia	4	367	0.6	0.0	1996	2.83	80.4	312	13	2	86
ALL AFRICA	..	..	..	..	..	..	..	..	..	..	..

Source: Food and Agriculture Organization of the United Nations.

Notes: 0 = zero or less than half of the unit of measure;   .. = not available.

14-5. Marine and freshwater catches, aquaculture, balance of trade, and fish consumption

	Average annual marine catch a/		Average annual freshwater catch a/		Average annual aquaculture production 1995-97 (metric tons)				Average annual balance of trade b/ 1995-97 (million US$)			Per capita annual food supply from fish and seafood
	(000 metric tons) 1995-97	% change since 1985-87	(000 metric tons) 1995-97	% change since 1985-87	Marine fish	Dia-dromous fish	Fresh-water fish	Molluscs & Crus-taceans	Fish	Molluscs & crustaceans	Fish meal	Total 1997 (kg)
SUB-SAHARAN AFRICA	..	..	..	..	..	..	..	..	..	..	..	..
excluding South Africa	..	..	..	..	..	..	..	..	..	..	..	..
excl. S. Africa & Nigeria	..	..	..	..	..	..	..	..	..	..	..	..
Angola	73	15	6.0	-23	..	..	..	..	-7.9	3.1	..	6.6
Benin	9	2	25.0	-6	..	..	..	..	-5.3	1.8	..	9.4
Botswana	..	..	2.0	20	..	..	..	..	-4.9	-0.3	-0.1	5.7
Burkina Faso	..	..	8.0	5	..	..	25	..	-3.1	0.0	..	1.2
Burundi	..	..	14.8	26	..	..	23	..	-0.1	0.0	..	3.2
Cameroon	64	24	23.0	15	..	..	55	..	-22.3	1.8	-0.3	9.2
Cape Verde	..	..	..	..	..	..	..	..	..	..	..	..
Central African Republic	..	..	12.7	-2	..	..	370	..	..	..	..	3.9
Chad	..	..	91.7	49	..	..	..	..	..	0.0	..	6.8
Comoros									..	..	..	
Congo, Dem. Rep. of	4	93	157.4	3	..	..	750	..	-26.6	7.0	..	25.3
Congo, Rep. of	19	-1	23.9	67	..	..	115	..	-50.4	..	..	5.7
Côte d'Ivoire	56	-28	11.3	-54	..	..	655	..	35.4	4.5	0.1	11.1
Djibouti	..	..	..	..	..	..	..	..	..	..	..	..
Equatorial Guinea	3	9	0.7	76	..	..	..	..	0.2	0.1	..	22.6
Eritrea	3	..	0.0	..	..	..	..	..	0.1	0.0	..	0.3
Ethiopia	0	..	8.5	..	..	..	46	..	-0.1	..	..	0.2
Gabon	33	89	8.8	365	..	..	53	..	-8.9	6.5	..	44.6
Gambia, The	26	211	2.5	-7	..	..	3	..	0.9	2.6	..	23.7
Ghana	352	29	67.9	35	..	..	500	..	64.4	2.1	..	22.5
Guinea	77	154	3.2	26	..	..	3	..	8.4	4.7	0.0	16.0
Guinea-Bissau	5	94	0.3	188	..	..	..	..	5.7	2.9	..	2.7
Kenya	4	-20	172.1	53	..	71	506	0	33.2	5.1	-0.5	4.8
Lesotho	..	..	0.0	..	..	4	10	..	..	..	..	..
Liberia	4	-62	4.0	0	..	..	0	..	-1.9	-0.1	..	4.9
Madagascar	71	101	30.0	-21	..	0	4,153	2,146	13.4	76.8	0.4	7.6
Malawi	..	..	57.9	-22	..	..	227	2	0.0	0.1	-0.4	5.7
Mali	..	..	114.8	102	..	..	73	..	-0.6	..	..	9.5
Mauritania	52	14	5.8	-3	..	..	..	..	22.1	104.6	..	14.2
Mauritius	..	..	..	..	..	..	..	..	..	..	..	..
Mozambique	13	-47	8.0	129	..	..	14	..	-5.4	73.5	..	2.0
Namibia	282	1,466	1.3	51	..	..	5	43	..	..	..	12.4
Niger	..	..	4.7	112	..	..	20	..	-0.9	0.0	..	0.8
Nigeria	224	46	106.0	14	..	24	17,014	..	-208.4	19.6	..	5.8
Rwanda	..	..	3.1	134	..	..	47	..	..	..	..	0.6
São Tomé and Principe	..	..	..	..	..	..	..	..	..	..	..	..
Senegal	352	66	54.4	262	..	..	49	22	205.9	73.2	3.4	36.3
Seychelles	..	..	..	..	..	..	..	..	..	..	..	..
Sierra Leone	48	38	14.7	-9	..	..	28	..	13.1	9.9	..	13.4
Somalia	15	-9	0.3	-26	..	..	..	..	4.1	..	..	1.3
South Africa	497	-50	0.8	4	3	870	101	2,616	101.8	42.7	-37.1	7.8
Sudan	5	382	40.8	64	..	..	1,000	24	0.0	0.0	..	1.7
Swaziland	..	..	..	..	..	..	..	..	..	..	..	..
Tanzania	43	5	310.7	13	..	..	217	..	51.7	8.9	0.0	10.3
Togo	9	-24	5.0	43	..	..	21	..	-22.5	4.8	..	17.3
Uganda	..	..	207.3	11	..	..	205	..	38.5	..	..	9.8
Zambia	..	..	64.6	-2	..	..	4,550	1	-0.3	0.1	-0.2	8.2
Zimbabwe	..	..	16.9	-8	..	100	63	15	-14.7	-1.2	-0.9	3.3
NORTH AFRICA	..	..	..	..	..	..	..	..	..	..	..	..
Algeria	99	42	0.0	-100	37	18	256	27	-7.2	2.1	..	3.5
Egypt	82	99	215.1	67	19,799	..	50,569	..	-108.4	-0.5	..	10.0
Libya	34	108	0.0	0	..	..	100	..	21.4	-0.1	..	6.0
Morocco	663	39	1.7	30	972	155	767	229	269.6	437.0	2.2	7.8
Tunisia	70	-10	0.7	..	886	138	380	111	7.5	76.9	-0.1	9.1
ALL AFRICA	..	..	..	..	..	..	..	..	..	..	..	..

Source: Food and Agriculture Organization of the United Nations.
Notes: a. Aquaculture production is included in country totals.
　　　 b. Exports minus imports.
　　　 0 = zero or less than half of the unit of measure; .. = not available.

14-6. Energy production by source

	Energy production								Total electricity generated	
	From all sources			From non-renewable energy sources						
	(000 metric toe) (a) 1997	% change since 1987	Per capita (kg oil equivalent) 1997	Solid fuels (000 metric toe) (a) 1997	Liquid fuels (000 metric toe) (a) 1997	Gaseous fuels (000 metric toe) (a) 1997	Nuclear fuels (000 metric toe) (a) 1997	Other sources (000 metric toe) (a) 1997	(000 metric toe) (a) 1997	% change since 1987
SUB-SAHARAN AFRICA	..	..	..	..	..	..	..	..	..	..
excluding South Africa	..	..	..	..	..	..	..	..	..	..
excl. S. Africa & Nigeria	..	..	..	..	..	..	..	..	..	..
Angola	41,430	89	3,537	0	35,700	465	0	0	95	37
Benin	1,897	8	337	0	67	0	0	0	4	92
Botswana	..	..	..	..	..	..	..	..	..	..
Burkina Faso	..	..	..	..	..	..	..	..	..	..
Burundi	..	..	..	..	..	..	..	..	..	..
Cameroon	11,250	-7	808	0	6,357	0	0	0	269	25
Cape Verde	..	..	..	..	..	..	..	..	..	..
Central African Republic	..	..	..	..	..	..	..	..	..	..
Chad	..	..	..	..	..	..	..	..	..	..
Comoros	..	..	..	..	..	..	..	..	..	..
Congo, Dem. Rep. of	14,364	29	299	56	1,315	0	0	0	517	11
Congo, Rep. of	13,540	89	4,998	0	12,638	3	0	0	37	53
Côte d'Ivoire	4,908	31	349	0	803	0	0	0	276	55
Djibouti	..	..	..	..	..	..	..	..	..	..
Equatorial Guinea	..	..	..	..	..	..	..	..	..	..
Eritrea	..	..	..	..	..	..	..	..	..	..
Ethiopia	16,316	27	280	0	0	0	0	0	115	50
Gabon	19,786	129	17,403	0	18,794	68	0	0	87	13
Gambia, The	..	..	..	..	..	..	..	..	..	..
Ghana	5,843	48	313	0	361	0	0	0	529	26
Guinea	..	..	..	..	..	..	..	..	..	..
Guinea-Bissau	..	..	..	..	..	..	..	..	..	..
Kenya	11,651	20	410	0	0	0	0	0	364	60
Lesotho	..	..	..	..	..	..	..	..	..	..
Liberia	..	..	..	..	..	..	..	..	..	..
Madagascar	..	..	..	..	..	..	..	..	..	..
Malawi	..	..	..	..	..	..	..	..	..	..
Mali	..	..	..	..	..	..	..	..	..	..
Mauritania	..	..	..	..	..	..	..	..	..	..
Mauritius	..	..	..	..	..	..	..	..	..	..
Mozambique	6,994	-1	379	0	0	0	0	0	86	199
Namibia	..	..	..	..	..	..	..	..	..	..
Niger	..	..	..	..	..	..	..	..	..	..
Nigeria	191,034	55	1,839	86	117,249	4,429	0	0	1,305	35
Rwanda	..	..	..	..	..	..	..	..	..	..
São Tomé and Principe	..	..	..	..	..	..	..	..	..	..
Senegal	1,654	32	189	0	0	20	0	0	108	52
Seychelles	..	..	..	..	..	..	..	..	..	..
Sierra Leone	..	..	..	..	..	..	..	..	..	..
Somalia	..	..	..	..	..	..	..	..	..	..
South Africa (a)	142,139	27	3,667	124,678	401	1,543	3,296	0	17,866	38
Sudan	9,881	18	356	0	259	0	0	0	169	43
Swaziland	..	..	..	..	..	..	..	..	..	..
Tanzania	13,529	23	431	3	0	0	0	0	166	52
Togo	..	..	..	..	..	..	..	..	..	..
Uganda	..	..	..	..	..	..	..	..	..	..
Zambia	5,556	16	647	106	0	0	0	0	689	-8
Zimbabwe	8,152	9	727	2,712	0	0	0	0	628	15
NORTH AFRICA	..	..	..	..	..	..	..	..	..	..
Algeria	125,576	37	4,272	0	61,670	63,381	0	0	1,865	70
Egypt	57,997	9	896	0	44,640	11,070	0	0	4,958	52
Libya	78,942	43	15,151	0	73,067	5,750	0	0	1,563	17
Morocco	836	3	31	211	242	23	0	231	1,129	64
Tunisia	6,655	2	723	0	4,013	1,466	0	0	686	75
ALL AFRICA	..	..	..	..	..	..	..	..	..	..

Source: International Energy Agency (IEA)
Notes: a. Tons of oil equivalent. See technical notes for more information on to
          0 = zero or less than half of the unit of measure; .. = not available or indeterminate.

14-7. Energy consumption by economic sector

	Energy Consumption by Economic Sector (% of total consumption)														
	Industry				Transportation						Agriculture		Commercial and public services		Residential	
	All industries		Iron and steel		Total		Air		Road							
	1987	1997	1987	1997	1987	1997	1987	1997	1987	1997	1987	1997	1987	1997	1987	1997
SUB-SAHARAN AFRICA	..	..	..	..	..	..	..	..	..	..	..	..	..	..	..	..
excluding South Africa	..	..	..	..	..	..	..	..	..	..	..	..	..	..	..	..
excl. S. Africa & Nigeria	..	..	..	..	..	..	..	..	..	..	..	..	..	..	..	..
Angola	..	11.6	..	0.0	..	12.3	..	6.1	..	6.2	..	..	..	0.0	..	75.6
Benin	..	17.1	..	0.0	..	12.6	..	2.4	..	10.1	..	..	..	0.0	..	70.3
Botswana	..	..	..	..	..	..	..	..	..	..	..	..	..	..	..	..
Burkina Faso	..	..	..	..	..	..	..	..	..	..	..	..	..	..	..	..
Burundi	..	..	..	..	..	..	..	..	..	..	..	..	..	..	..	..
Cameroon	..	17.0	..	0.0	..	11.6	..	1.0	..	10.6	..	..	..	0.5	..	69.7
Cape Verde	..	..	..	..	..	..	..	..	..	..	..	..	..	..	..	..
Central African Republic	..	..	..	..	..	..	..	..	..	..	..	..	..	..	..	..
Chad	..	..	..	..	..	..	..	..	..	..	..	..	..	..	..	..
Comoros	..	..	..	..	..	..	..	..	..	..	..	..	..	..	..	..
Congo, Dem. Rep. of	..	21.8	..	0.1	..	5.4	..	1.2	..	4.2	..	..	..	0.0	..	70.9
Congo, Rep. of	..	14.2	..	0.0	..	18.4	..	6.3	..	12.1	..	..	..	0.0	..	65.7
Côte d'Ivoire	..	7.0	..	0.0	..	16.0	..	3.1	..	12.5	..	1.2	..	12.1	..	62.0
Djibouti	..	..	..	..	..	..	..	..	..	..	..	..	..	..	..	..
Equatorial Guinea	..	..	..	..	..	..	..	..	..	..	..	..	..	..	..	..
Eritrea	..	..	..	..	..	..	..	..	..	..	..	..	..	..	..	..
Ethiopia	..	..	..	..	..	..	..	..	..	..	..	..	..	..	..	..
Gabon	..	23.2	..	0.0	..	19.6	..	6.7	..	11.0	..	..	..	0.9	..	51.5
Gambia, The	..	..	..	..	..	..	..	..	..	..	..	..	..	..	..	..
Ghana	16.0	14.1	0.0	0.0	11.0	13.2	1.4	1.2	9.0	11.4	0.7	1.0	0.5	0.7	69.8	69.9
Guinea	..	..	..	..	..	..	..	..	..	..	..	..	..	..	..	..
Guinea-Bissau	..	..	..	..	..	..	..	..	..	..	..	..	..	..	..	..
Kenya	..	11.4	..	0.0	..	12.6	..	4.5	..	7.7	..	6.5	..	0.7	..	67.7
Lesotho	..	..	..	..	..	..	..	..	..	..	..	..	..	..	..	..
Liberia	..	..	..	..	..	..	..	..	..	..	..	..	..	..	..	..
Madagascar	..	..	..	..	..	..	..	..	..	..	..	..	..	..	..	..
Malawi	..	..	..	..	..	..	..	..	..	..	..	..	..	..	..	..
Mali	..	..	..	..	..	..	..	..	..	..	..	..	..	..	..	..
Mauritania	..	..	..	..	..	..	..	..	..	..	..	..	..	..	..	..
Mauritius	..	..	..	..	..	..	..	..	..	..	..	..	..	..	..	..
Mozambique	..	7.8	..	0.0	..	1.5	..	0.4	..	1.1	..	0.6	..	3.4	..	85.0
Namibia	..	..	..	..	..	..	..	..	..	..	..	..	..	..	..	..
Niger	..	..	..	..	..	..	..	..	..	..	..	..	..	..	..	..
Nigeria	..	10.9	..	0.1	..	6.7	..	0.7	..	5.9	..	..	..	0.3	..	79.7
Rwanda	..	..	..	..	..	..	..	..	..	..	..	..	..	..	..	..
São Tomé and Principe	..	..	..	..	..	..	..	..	..	..	..	..	..	..	..	..
Senegal	..	17.0	..	0.0	..	24.0	..	10.0	..	12.6	..	2.3	..	0.6	..	55.3
Seychelles																
Sierra Leone	..	..	..	..	..	..	..	..	..	..	..	..	..	..	..	..
Somalia	..	..	..	..	..	..	..	..	..	..	..	..	..	..	..	..
South Africa	48.4	36.6	17.6	7.8	21.0	23.5	1.3	2.5	17.9	19.2	2.6	3.4	4.1	5.2	19.3	21.3
Sudan	..	7.4	..	0.0	..	17.8	..	1.0	..	16.9	..	0.1	..	2.0	..	70.9
Swaziland	..	..	..	..	..	..	..	..	..	..	..	..	..	..	..	..
Tanzania	..	11.7	..	0.0	..	1.7	..	0.3	..	1.4	..	3.2	..	0.3	..	79.1
Togo	..	..	..	..	..	..	..	..	..	..	..	..	..	..	..	..
Uganda	..	..	..	..	..	..	..	..	..	..	..	..	..	..	..	..
Zambia	..	23.6	..	0.1	..	5.1	..	0.9	..	4.2	..	0.7	..	2.0	..	66.6
Zimbabwe	..	12.2	..	2.0	..	10.0	..	1.5	..	8.3	..	9.2	..	3.6	..	61.8
NORTH AFRICA	..	..	..	..	..	..	..	..	..	..	..	..	..	..	..	..
Algeria	21.2	20.6	4.3	2.3	39.1	18.7	3.3	2.2	34.9	12.2	0.3	0.0	1.5	0.0	23.0	29.2
Egypt	49.6	47.8	0.7	0.5	19.8	20.6	2.9	3.6	16.9	16.9	0.5	0.6	0.0	0.0	23.2	22.9
Libya	32.5	33.8	0.0	0.0	36.8	38.0	6.1	3.4	30.7	34.6	0.0	0.0	0.0	0.0	7.2	9.5
Morocco	31.4	23.7	0.1	0.0	28.0	11.8	5.2	3.7	19.7	5.7	4.9	0.7	6.5	2.4	25.7	24.7
Tunisia	31.7	22.7	1.2	0.6	33.1	28.0	5.8	5.7	21.9	21.9	5.5	6.2	7.5	7.7	22.0	32.9
ALL AFRICA	..	..	..	..	..	..	..	..	..	..	..	..	..	..	..	..

Source: International Energy Agency (IEA)

Notes: 0 = zero or less than half of the unit of measure; .. = not available or indeterminate.

Environmental Indicators

14-8. CO₂ emissions from industrial processes, 1996

	Carbon dioxide (CO₂) emissions (000 metric tons)								Per capita carbon emissions (kilograms) 1996
	Solid fuels 1996	Liquid fuels 1996	Gaseous fuels 1996	Gas flaring 1996	Cement manufact- uring 1996	Total 1990	Total 1996	Total contribution Since 1950	
SUB-SAHARAN AFRICA	..	..	..	..	..	..	..	..	..
excluding South Africa	..	..	..	..	..	..	..	..	..
excl. S. Africa & Nigeria	..	..	..	..	..	..	..	..	..
Angola	0	2,151	344	2,465	149	4,650	5,108	145,552	450
Benin	0	465	0	0	189	564	656	14,762	120
Botswana	6,383	12,579	4	9	691	2,415	19,665	51,505	13,035
Burkina Faso	0	967	0	0	0	1,008	967	14,682	90
Burundi	18	202	0	0	0	194	220	3,975	35
Cameroon	4	3,213	0	0	299	1,488	3,517	86,507	260
Cape Verde	..	..	..	..	..	..	..	..	..
Central African Republic	0	234	0	0	0	198	234	5,866	70
Chad	0	99	0	0	0	143	99	5,027	14
Comoros	..	..	..	..	..	..	..	..	..
Congo, Dem. Rep. of	854	1,436	0	0	5	4,096	2,294	142,475	49
Congo, Rep. of	0	4,741	7	167	50	2,037	4,961	40,161	1,884
Côte d'Ivoire	0	12,817	0	0	249	9,907	13,066	185,109	946
Djibouti	..	..	..	..	..	..	..	..	..
Equatorial Guinea	0	143	0	0	0	117	143	2,862	349
Eritrea	..	..	..	..	..	..	..	..	..
Ethiopia	0	3,048	0	0	320	2,964	3,367	66,509	59
Gabon	0	2,041	1,587	0	65	6,112	3,690	135,432	3,333
Gambia, The	0	216	0	0	0	191	216	4,481	188
Ghana	7	3,342	0	0	698	3,539	4,045	109,271	223
Guinea	0	1,092	0	0	0	1,011	1,092	32,445	150
Guinea-Bissau	0	231	0	0	0	209	231	4,477	208
Kenya	267	5,760	0	0	747	5,822	6,775	180,020	243
Lesotho	..	..	..	..	..	..	..	..	..
Liberia	0	326	0	0	0	465	326	33,189	148
Madagascar	44	1,121	0	0	30	945	1,198	37,860	84
Malawi	44	616	0	0	70	601	733	18,184	75
Mali	0	462	0	0	10	421	473	12,025	46
Mauritania	15	2,876	0	0	60	2,634	2,950	40,648	1,232
Mauritius	..	..	..	..	..	..	..	..	..
Mozambique	158	821	0	0	15	997	997	89,149	56
Namibia	..	..	..	..	..	..	..	..	..
Niger	458	649	0	0	15	1,048	1,121	20,863	119
Nigeria	150	21,596	8,596	51,494	1,495	88,665	83,330	1,944,327	822
Rwanda	0	484	0	2	5	528	491	9,167	90
São Tomé and Principe	..	..	..	..	..	..	..	..	..
Senegal	0	2,770	0	0	294	2,895	3,063	76,142	358
Seychelles	..	..	..	..	..	..	..	..	..
Sierra Leone	0	447	0	0	0	333	447	19,844	104
Somalia	0	0	0	0	15	18	15	13,747	2
South Africa (a)	227,707	56,821	3,532	0	4,684	291,108	292,746	8,541,575	7,678
Sudan	0	3,283	0	0	189	3,459	3,473	137,001	128
Swaziland	..	..	..	..	..	..	..	..	..
Tanzania	15	2,030	0	0	399	2,272	2,444	61,694	80
Togo	0	575	0	0	174	689	751	17,023	180
Uganda	0	986	0	0	50	846	1,033	32,837	53
Zambia	773	1,499	0	0	174	2,444	2,444	111,151	291
Zimbabwe	13,623	4,217	0	0	573	16,646	18,412	369,232	1,667
NORTH AFRICA	..	..	..	..	..	..	..	..	..
Algeria	3,188	22,651	50,567	14,400	3,488	80,443	94,297	1,725,913	3,283
Egypt	3,419	57,778	27,707	0	8,969	75,434	97,873	1,856,890	1,541
Libya	15	25,348	9,966	3,482	1,769	37,772	40,579	855,830	7,978
Morocco	6,225	18,426	40	0	3,189	23,486	27,879	558,859	1,055
Tunisia	238	9,167	4,250	254	2,276	13,260	16,184	318,035	1,782
ALL AFRICA	..	..	..	..	..	..	..	..	..

Sources: Carbon Dioxide Information Analysis Center.
Notes: Estimates are of the carbon dioxide emitted, 3.664 times the carbon it contains.
0 = zero or less than half the unit of measure, .. = not available.

14-9. Globally threatened species: mammals, birds, and higher plants, late 1990s

	Mammals				Birds				Higher plants			
	Total number of known species			No. of species	Total number of known species			No. of species	Total number of known species			No. of species
	All species	Endemic species	Threatened species	per 10,000 km² a/	Breeding species	Endemic species	Threatened species	per 10,000 km² a/	All species b/	Endemic species	Threatened species	per 10,000 km² a/
SUB-SAHARAN AFRICA	..	..	..	..	..	..	..	..	..	..	..	..
excluding South Africa	..	..	..	..	..	..	..	..	..	..	..	..
excl. S. Africa & Nigeria	..	..	..	..	..	..	..	..	..	..	..	..
Angola	276	7	17	56	765	12	13	156	5,000	1,260	20	1,055
Benin	188	0	9	85	307	0	1	138	2,000	..	2	990
Botswana	164	0	5	43	386	1	7	101	..	17	0	563
Burkina Faso	147	0	6	49	335	0	1	112	1,100	..	..	369
Burundi	107	0	5	76	451	0	6	322	2,500	..	0	1,783
Cameroon	409	14	32	114	690	8	14	193	8,000	156	67	2,310
Cape Verde	..	..	..	..	..	..	..	..	..	..	..	..
Central African Republic	209	2	11	53	537	1	2	137	3,600	100	1	921
Chad	134	1	14	27	370	0	3	75	1,600	..	5	322
Comoros	..	..	..	..	..	..	..	..	..	..	..	..
Congo, Dem. Rep. of	450	28	38	74	929	24	26	153	2,867	1,100	69	1,818
Congo, Rep. of	200	2	10	62	449	0	3	140	4,350	1,200	2	1,870
Côte d'Ivoire	230	0	16	73	535	2	12	170	3,517	62	42	1,163
Djibouti	..	..	..	..	..	..	..	..	..	..	..	..
Equatorial Guinea	184	1	12	131	273	3	4	194	3,000	66	6	2,312
Eritrea	112	0	6	50	319	0	3	140	..	..	..	..
Ethiopia	255	31	35	54	626	28	20	133	6,500	1,000	125	1,398
Gabon	190	3	12	64	466	1	4	157	6,500	..	78	2,248
Gambia, The	117	0	4	112	280	0	1	269	966	..	0	935
Ghana	222	1	13	78	529	0	10	186	3,600	43	22	1,308
Guinea	190	1	11	66	409	0	12	142	3,000	88	29	1,043
Guinea-Bissau	108	0	4	71	243	0	1	159	1,000	12	..	655
Kenya	359	23	43	94	847	9	24	221	6,000	265	130	1,703
Lesotho	33	0	2	23	58	0	5	40	1,576	2	0	1,103
Liberia	193	0	11	87	372	1	13	168	2,200	103	1	993
Madagascar	141	93	46	37	202	105	28	53	9,000	6,500	255	2,479
Malawi	195	0	7	86	521	0	9	230	3,600	49	46	1,665
Mali	137	0	13	28	397	0	6	81	1,741	11	5	355
Mauritania	61	1	14	13	273	0	3	59	1,100	..	2	239
Mauritius	..	..	..	..	..	..	..	46	..	..	..	..
Mozambique	179	2	13	42	498	0	14	117	5,500	219	57	1,340
Namibia	250	3	11	58	469	3	8	109	3,978	687	14	942
Niger	131	0	11	27	299	0	2	60	1,170	..	..	238
Nigeria	274	4	26	62	681	2	9	153	4,614	205	16	1,059
Rwanda	151	0	9	110	513	0	6	373	2,288	26	0	1,664
São Tomé and Principe	..	..	..	..	..	..	..	..	..	..	..	..
Senegal	192	0	13	72	384	0	6	144	2,062	26	15	780
Seychelles	..	..	..	..	..	..	..	..	..	..	..	..
Sierra Leone	147	0	9	77	466	1	12	243	2,090	74	8	1,091
Somalia	171	12	18	43	422	11	8	107	3,000	500	57	768
South Africa	255	35	33	52	596	8	16	122	23,000	..	1,875	4,797
Sudan	267	11	21	43	680	1	9	110	3,132	50	2	507
Swaziland	..	..	..	..	..	..	..	303	..	..	..	..
Tanzania	316	15	33	70	827	24	30	183	10,000	1,122	326	2,231
Togo	196	0	8	110	391	0	1	220	2,484	..	0	1,739
Uganda	338	6	18	118	830	3	10	290	5,000	..	8	1,891
Zambia	233	3	11	56	605	2	10	145	4,600	211	5	1,141
Zimbabwe	270	0	9	81	532	0	9	159	4,200	95	73	1,325
NORTH AFRICA	..	..	..	..	..	..	..	..	..	..	..	..
Algeria	92	2	15	15	192	1	8	32	3,100	250	125	520
Egypt	98	7	15	21	153	0	11	33	2,066	70	59	454
Libya	76	5	11	14	91	0	2	17	1,800	134	41	331
Morocco	105	4	18	30	210	0	11	60	3,600	625	182	1,049
Tunisia	78	1	11	31	173	0	6	69	2,150	..	6	873
ALL AFRICA	..	..	..	..	..	..	..	..	..	..	..	..

Source: World Conservation Monitoring Centre (WCMC).

Notes: a. Values are standardized using a species-area curve.

b. Flowering plants only.

.. = not available.

14-10. Globally threatened species: reptiles, amphibians, and fish, late 1990s

	Reptiles				Amphibians				Freshwater fish	
	Total number of known species			No. of species	Total number of known species			No. of species	Total number of known species	
	All species	Endemic species	Threatened species	per 10,000 km² a/	All species	Endemic species	Threatened species	per 10,000 km² a/	All species	Threatened species b/
SUB-SAHARAN AFRICA	..	..	..	..	..	..	..	..	..	..
excluding South Africa	..	..	..	..	..	..	..	..	..	..
excl. S. Africa & Nigeria	..	..	..	..	..	..	..	..	..	..
Angola	..	19	5	..	..	22	0	..	..	0
Benin	..	1	2	..	..	0	0	..	150	0
Botswana	157	2	0	41	38	0	0	10	92	0
Burkina Faso	..	3	1	..	..	0	0	..	..	0
Burundi	..	0	0	..	..	2	0	..	..	0
Cameroon	183	21	3	51	190	66	1	53	354	26
Cape Verde	..	..	..	..	..	..	..	..	..	..
Central African Republic	129	0	1	33	47	0	0	12	..	0
Chad	5	1	1	1	..	0	0	..	..	0
Comoros	..	..	..	..	..	..	..	..	..	..
Congo, Dem. Rep. of	377	35	3	62	80	53	0	13	..	1
Congo, Rep. of	..	1	2	..	..	1	0	..	..	0
Côte d'Ivoire	..	3	4	..	..	3	1	..	..	0
Djibouti	..	..	..	..	..	..	..	..	..	..
Equatorial Guinea	..	4	2	..	..	2	1	..	..	0
Eritrea	85	1	3	38	19	2	0	8	..	0
Ethiopia	188	9	1	40	62	24	0	13	150	0
Gabon	..	3	3	..	..	4	0	..	..	0
Gambia, The	47	1	1	45	30	0	0	29	79	0
Ghana	..	1	4	..	..	4	0	..	..	0
Guinea	..	3	3	..	..	3	1	..	..	0
Guinea-Bissau	..	2	3	..	..	1	0	..	..	0
Kenya	190	18	5	50	88	10	0	23	..	20
Lesotho	..	2	0	..	..	0	0	..	8	1
Liberia	62	2	3	28	38	4	1	17	..	0
Madagascar	363	259	17	95	179	155	2	47	121	13
Malawi	124	7	0	55	69	3	0	31	..	0
Mali	16	4	1	3	..	1	0	..	..	0
Mauritania	..	1	3	..	..	0	0	..	..	0
Mauritius	..	..	..	..	..	..	..	..	..	..
Mozambique	167	5	5	39	62	1	0	15	..	2
Namibia	250	25	3	58	51	2	1	12	114	3
Niger	..	0	1	..	..	0	0	..	..	0
Nigeria	135	7	4	30	109	1	0	24	260	0
Rwanda	..	1	0	..	..	1	0	..	..	0
São Tomé and Principe	..	..	..	..	..	..	..	..	..	..
Senegal	100	1	7	37	2	1	0	1	79	0
Seychelles	..	..	..	..	..	..	..	..	..	..
Sierra Leone	..	1	3	..	..	2	0	..	..	0
Somalia	193	49	2	49	27	3	0	7	..	3
South Africa	315	97	19	65	108	49	9	22	94	27
Sudan	..	8	3	..	..	1	0	..	..	0
Swaziland	..	..	..	..	..	..	..	..	..	..
Tanzania	289	61	4	64	133	49	0	30	..	19
Togo	..	1	3	..	..	3	0	..	..	0
Uganda	149	2	1	52	50	1	0	17	291	28
Zambia	145	3	0	35	65	1	0	16	106	0
Zimbabwe	153	2	0	46	120	3	0	36	112	0
NORTH AFRICA	..	..	..	..	..	..	..	..	..	..
Algeria	81	4	1	13	10	0	0	2	..	1
Egypt	83	0	6	18	6	0	0	1	70	0
Libya	56	1	3	10	3	0	0	1	..	0
Morocco	90	11	2	26	11	1	0	3	..	1
Tunisia	62	1	2	25	7	0	0	3	..	0
ALL AFRICA	..	..	..	..	..	..	..	..	..	..

Source: World Conservation Monitoring Centre (WCMC).

Notes:　　a. Values are standardized using a species-area curve.

　　　　　b. Threatened species include a few marine species.

　　　　　.. = not available.

14-11. National protection of natural areas, 1999

		All protected areas (IUCN categories I-V)				Number of Marine Protected Areas (a) (IUCN Categories I-VI)		
	Number	Area (000 ha)	Percent of land area	No. of Areas at least: 100,000 ha in Size	1 million ha in Size	Total	Littoral	Marine
SUB-SAHARAN AFRICA	..	..	..	..	..	..	..	..
excluding South Africa	..	..	..	..	..	..	..	..
excl. S. Africa & Nigeria	..	..	..	..	..	..	..	..
Angola	13	8,181	6.6	9	2	4	4	3
Benin	2	778	6.9	2	0	..	..	..
Botswana	12	10,499	18.0	7	3	..	..	..
Burkina Faso	12	2,855	10.4	6	1	..	..	..
Burundi	13	146	5.3	0	0	1	1	1
Cameroon	18	2,098	4.4	8	0	2	1	2
Cape Verde	..	..	..	..	..	..	..	..
Central African Republic	13	5,110	8.2	11	2	..	..	..
Chad	9	11,494	9.0	9	2	..	..	..
Comoros	..	..	..	..	..	..	..	..
Congo, Dem. Rep. of	15	10,191	4.3	9	4	1	1	0
Congo, Rep. of	9	1,545	4.5	5	0	1	1	1
Côte d'Ivoire	11	1,986	6.2	4	1	3	3	1
Djibouti	..	..	..	..	..	..	..	..
Equatorial Guinea	0	0	0.0	0	0	4	4	0
Eritrea	3	501	4.3	2	0	..	..	..
Ethiopia	21	5,518	5.0	14	0	..	..	..
Gabon	5	723	2.7	1	0	4	4	1
Gambia, The	6	23	2.0	0	0	5	5	3
Ghana	10	1,104	4.6	3	0	..	..	..
Guinea	3	164	0.7	1	0	1	0	1
Guinea-Bissau	0	0	0.0	0	0	2	2	1
Kenya	50	3,507	6.0	7	1	14	13	10
Lesotho	1	7	0.2	0	0	..	..	..
Liberia	1	129	1.2	1	0	..	..	..
Madagascar	40	1,121	1.9	1	0	3	3	1
Malawi	9	1,059	8.9	3	0	..	..	..
Mali	13	4,532	3.7	8	2	..	..	..
Mauritania	9	1,746	1.7	3	1	5	5	2
Mauritius	..	..	..	..	..	..	..	..
Mozambique	11	4,779	6.0	7	1	7	7	6
Namibia	20	10,616	12.9	7	3	4	4	0
Niger	6	9,694	7.7	4	2	..	..	..
Nigeria	27	3,021	3.3	9	0	..	..	..
Rwanda	6	362	13.8	1	0	..	..	..
São Tomé and Principe	..	..	..	..	..	..	..	..
Senegal	12	2,181	11.1	3	0	7	6	6
Seychelles	..	..	..	..	..	..	..	..
Sierra Leone	2	82	1.1	0	0	..	..	..
Somalia	2	180	0.3	1	0	2	2	2
South Africa	390	6,619	5.4	6	1	20	17	8
Sudan	11	8,642	3.4	6	2	2	0	2
Swaziland	..	..	..	..	..	..	..	..
Tanzania	39	13,817	14.6	19	3	9	8	8
Togo	9	429	7.6	2	0	1	0	1
Uganda	37	1,913	7.9	6	0	..	..	..
Zambia	35	6,366	8.5	11	1	..	..	..
Zimbabwe	48	3,071	7.9	6	1	..	..	..
NORTH AFRICA	..	..	..	..	..	..	..	..
Algeria	18	5,891	2.5	2	2	8	6	3
Egypt	16	794	0.8	1	0	18	16	6
Libya	8	173	0.1	1	0	5	2	3
Morocco	12	317	0.7	1	0	10	9	3
Tunisia	7	45	0.3	0	0	7	5	4
ALL AFRICA	..	..	..	..	..	..	..	..

Source: World Conservation Monitoring Centre (WCMC).

Notes: a. Includes areas with substantial terrestrial components that reach the shore. An area can be both, marine and littoral (see technical notes).

0 = zero or less than half the unit of measure.   .. = not available or indeterminate.

14-12. International protected areas, 1999

	Biosphere reserves		World heritage sites		Wetlands of international importance	
	Number	Area (000 ha)	Number	Area (000 ha)	Number	Area (000 ha)
SUB-SAHARAN AFRICA	..	..	..	..	..	..
excluding South Africa	..	..	..	..	..	..
excl. S. Africa & Nigeria	..	..	..	..	..	..
Angola	0	..	0	0	0	..
Benin	1	880	0	0	0	..
Botswana	0	..	0	0	1	6,864
Burkina Faso	1	16	0	0	3	299
Burundi	0	..	0	0	0	..
Cameroon	3	850	1	526	0	..
Cape Verde	..	..	..	..	..	..
Central African Republic	2	1,640	1	1,740	0	..
Chad	0	..	0	0	1	195
Comoros	..	..	..	..	..	..
Congo, Dem. Rep. of	3	298	5	6,855	2	866
Congo, Rep. of	2	172	0	0	0	..
Côte d'Ivoire	2	1,480	3	1,484	1	19
Djibouti	..	..	..	..	..	..
Equatorial Guinea	0	..	0	0	0	..
Eritrea	0	..	0	0	0	..
Ethiopia	0	..	1	22	0	..
Gabon	1	15	0	0	3	1,080
Gambia, The	0	..	0	0	1	20
Ghana	1	8	0	0	6	178
Guinea	2	133	1	13	6	225
Guinea-Bissau	1	110	0	0	1	39
Kenya	5	1,335	0	0	2	49
Lesotho	0	..	0	0	0	..
Liberia	0	..	0	0	0	..
Madagascar	1	140	1	152	0	..
Malawi	0	..	1	9	1	225
Mali	1	771	1	400	3	162
Mauritania	0	..	1	1,200	2	1,189
Mauritius	1	4	0	0	0	..
Mozambique	0	..	0	0	0	..
Namibia	0	..	0	0	4	630
Niger	1	728	2	7,956	1	220
Nigeria	1	0	0	0	0	..
Rwanda	1	15	0	0	0	..
São Tomé and Principe	..	..	..	..	..	..
Senegal	3	1,094	2	929	4	100
Seychelles	..	..	..	..	..	..
Sierra Leone	0	..	0	0	0	..
Somalia	0	..	0	0	0	..
South Africa	0	..	0	0	15	486
Sudan	2	1,901	0	0	0	..
Swaziland	0	..	0	0	0	..
Tanzania	2	2,338	4	7,380	0	..
Togo	0	..	0	0	2	194
Uganda	1	220	2	132	1	15
Zambia	0	..	1	4	2	333
Zimbabwe	0	..	2	1,095	0	..
NORTH AFRICA	..	..	..	..	..	..
Algeria	2	7,276	1	..	2	5
Egypt	2	2,577	0	0	2	106
Libya	0	..	0	0	0	..
Morocco	0	..	0	0	4	11
Tunisia	4	32	1	13	1	13
ALL AFRICA	46	24,033	30	29,910	72	13,522

Source: World Conservation Monitoring Centre (WCMC), United Nations Educational, Scientific, and Cultural Organization (UNESCO), and Ramsar Convention Bureau, Switzerland

Notes: 0 = zero or less than half the unit of measure.   .. = not available or indeterminate.

Technical notes

Tables

These notes are based on technical notes for each table as presented in WRI 2000. They have been edited and shortened for this volume. Readers are urged to consult the original source for details.

Table 14-1. Forest resources, 1990–95. Total forest consists of all forest area for temperate countries and the sum of natural forest and plantation area categories.

FAO defines a *natural forest* as a forest composed primarily of indigenous (native) tree species. Natural forests include closed forest, where trees cover a high proportion of the ground and where grass does not form a continuous layer on the forest floor (e.g., broad-leaved forests, coniferous forests, and bamboo forests), and open forest, which FAO defines as mixed forest/grasslands with at least 10 percent tree cover and a continuous grass layer on the forest floor. Natural forests encompass all stands except plantations and include stands that have been degraded to some degree by agriculture, fire, logging, and other factors.

Plantations refer to forest stands established artificially by afforestation and reforestation for industrial and nonindustrial usage. Reforestation does not include regeneration of old tree crops (through either natural regeneration or forest management), although some countries may report regeneration as reforestation. Many trees are also planted for nonindustrial uses, such as village wood lots. Reforestation data often exclude this component. The data presented here reflect plantation survival rates as estimated by FAO.

Average annual percent change is shown as a percentage of the exponential growth rate. If negative (in parentheses), these figures reflect net deforestation, which is defined as the clearing of forest lands for all forms of agricultural uses (shifting cultivation, permanent agriculture, and ranching) and for other land uses such as settlements, other infrastructure, and mining. In tropical countries, this entails clearing that reduces tree crown cover to less than 10 percent. Deforestation, as defined here, does not reflect changes within the forest stand or site, such as selective logging (unless the forest cover is permanently reduced to less than 10 percent).

Table 14-2. Forest ecosystems, 1996. *Closed forests* exclude some woodlands and wooded savanna.

Original forest as a percentage of land area refers to the estimate of the percentage of land that would have been covered by closed forest about 8,000 years ago, assuming current climatic conditions, before large-scale disturbance by human society began.

Current forests refer to estimated closed forest cover within the past 10 years or so (this varies by country). Only closed moist forests are given for Africa.

Frontier forests are large, relatively intact forest ecosystems. They represent undisturbed forest areas that are large enough to maintain all of their biodiversity, including viable populations of wide-ranging species associated with each forest type.

Percentage of frontier forests threatened refers to frontier forests where ongoing or planned human activities such as logging, mining, and other large-scale disturbances will eventually degrade the ecosystem through species decline or extinction, drastic changes in the forest's age structure, etc., and would result, if continued, in the violation of one of the above-mentioned criteria.

Tropical forests include all forests located between the Tropics of Cancer and Capricorn. All other forests are put into the *nontropical* category.

Percentage protected includes forest areas that fall within the protected areas in the world that are listed as the World Conservation Union's (IUCN) management categories I-V.

Table 14-3. Wood production and trade, 1986–98.

Total roundwood production refers to all wood in the rough, whether destined for industrial or fuelwood uses.

Industrial roundwood production comprises all roundwood products other than fuelwood and charcoal.

Processed wood production includes sawnwood and panels.

Paper and paper board includes newsprint, printing and writing paper, and other paper and paperboard.

Trade in forest products is the balance of imports minus exports.

Table 14-4. Freshwater resources and withdrawals, 1970–2000.

Annual internal renewable water resources refer to the average annual flow of rivers and groundwater generated from endogenous precipitation. Caution should be used when comparing different countries because these estimates are based on differing sources and dates. These annual averages also disguise large seasonal, inter-annual, and long-term variations. When data for annual river flows from and to other countries are not shown, the internal renewable water resources figure may include these flows. Per capita annual internal renewable water resource data were calculated using 1999 population estimates.

Annual withdrawals as a percentage of water resources refer to total water withdrawals, not counting evaporative losses from storage basins, as a percentage of internal renewable water resources and river flows from other countries. Water withdrawals also include water from desalination plants in countries where that source is a significant part of all water withdrawals.

Per capita annual withdrawals were calculated using national population data for the year of data shown for withdrawals.

Sectoral withdrawals are classified as domestic (drinking water, homes, commercial establishments, public services [for example, hospitals], and municipal use or provision); industry (including water withdrawn to cool thermoelectric plants); and agriculture (irrigation and livestock).

Table 14-5. Marine and freshwater catches, aquaculture, balance of trade, and fish consumption.

Marine and freshwater catch data refer to marine and freshwater fish, killed, caught, trapped, collected, bred, or cultivated for commercial, industrial, and subsistence use (catches from recreational activities are included where available). Crustaceans and mollusks are included. Statistics for mariculture, aquaculture, and other kinds of fish farming are included in the country totals. Figures are the national totals averaged over a 3-year period; they include fish caught by a country's fleet anywhere in the world. Catches of freshwater species caught in low-salinity seas are included in the statistics of the appropriate marine area. Marine catch includes catches of diadromous (migratory between saltwater and freshwater) species.

Data are represented as nominal catches, which are the landings converted to a live-weight basis, that is, the weight when caught.

Landings for some countries are identical to catches.

Aquaculture is defined by FAO as "the farming of aquatic organisms, including fish, mollusks, crustaceans, and aquatic plants. Farming implies some form of intervention in the rearing process to enhance production, such as regular stocking, feeding, and protection from predators, etc. [It] also implies ownership of the stock being cultivated. . . ." Aquatic organisms that are exploitable by the public as a common property resource are included in the harvest of fisheries.

Marine fish include a variety of species groups such as mullets, sea basses, groupers, snappers, tunas, mackerels, etc. *Diadromus fish* include surgeons, river eels, salmons, trouts, etc. *Freshwater fish* include carps, perches, catfish, and tilapias, among others. Mollusks include freshwater molluscs, oysters, mussels, scallops, clams, abalones, and cephalopods. *Crustaceans* include, among others, freshwater crustaceans, crabs, lobsters, shrimps, and prawns. Data on whales and other marine mammals are excluded from this table.

Balance of trade is defined as exports minus imports. Figures are the national totals averaged over a 3-year period in millions of U.S. dollars. Imports are usually on a cost, insurance, and freight basis (c.i.f.) (i.e., insurance and freight costs added in). Exports are generally on a free-on-board basis (FOB) (i.e., not including insurance or freight costs). A surplus of imports over exports is shown in parentheses. Trade in *fish* includes fish that is fresh, frozen, chilled, salted, or smoked as well as fish products and preparations. Trade in *mollusks and crustaceans* includes molluscs and crustaceans that are fresh, chilled, smoked, derived products, etc. Trade in *fish meal* includes meals, solubles, etc.

Per capita annual food supply from fish and seafood is the quantity of both freshwater and marine fish, seafood, and derived products available for human consumption. Data on aquatic plants and whale meat are excluded from the totals. The amount of fish and seafood actually consumed may be lower than the figures provided, depending on how much is lost during storage, preparation, and cooking, and on how much is discarded. Data are presented in kilograms per capita. Years shown are 3-year averages.

Table 14-6. Energy production by source. All energy data in a common unit of 1,000 metric tons of oil equivalent (toe) to facilitate comparisons of energy sourcing, consumption, substitution, and conservation. A toe is defined as 41.868 gigajoules.

Energy production from all sources is the amount of energy from all sources produced by each country in the year specified. In addition to solid, liquid, and gaseous fuels and nuclear electricity, the total also includes hydropower, geothermal, solar, wind, tidal, wave, combustible renewables and waste, and indigenous heat production from heat pumps. *Per capita* shows the amount produced per person for that country.

Energy production from *solid fuels* is the energy produced from all types of primary coal (i.e., hard coal or lignite). Peat is also included in the category.

Energy production from *liquid fuels* is energy produced from liquid fuels such as crude oil or natural gas liquids.

Energy production from *gaseous fuels* is the amount of energy produced from natural gas.

Energy production from *nuclear fuels* shows the primary heat equivalent of the electricity produced by nuclear power plants. Heat-to-electricity conversion efficiency is assumed to be 33 percent.

Total electricity generated is the toe equivalent of the electrical energy produced by thermal, nuclear, geothermal, hydropower (excluding pumped storage production), and other power plants. Electricity generated is not a primary energy source and should not be mistakenly added to the energy production from primary sources presented in this table. These data were converted from gigawatt-hours to toe using a conversion rate of 1Gwh = 86 toe.

Table 14-7. Energy consumption by economic sector. *Industry* sector includes energy consumption by the iron and steel industry, chemical industry, nonferrous metals basic industries, nonmetallic mineral products (glass, ceramic, cement, etc.), transport equipment, machinery, mining and quarrying, food and tobacco, paper, pulp and print, wood and wood products, construction, textile and leather, and any nonspecified industry.

Iron and steel consumption is the energy consumed by the iron and steel industry as a percentage of the total energy consumed by the country.

Transportation sector includes all fuel for air, road, and water transport except fuel used for international marine bunkers and for ocean, coastal, and inland fishing. *Air* transportation includes both international and domestic civil aviation. *Road* transportation includes all human and cargo transport along national road networks.

Agriculture refers to all agricultural and forestry activity, including ocean, coastal, and inland fishing.

Commercial and public services refer to service sectors such as stores, repair shops, and restaurants.

Residential sector includes household energy use.

The IEA reports that it can be difficult to distinguish accurately between the agriculture, commercial, and public services sectors and that a figure for "total energy use" is more accurate than totals for the individual sectors.

Table 14-8. Carbon dioxide emissions from industrial processes, 1996. This table includes data on industrial additions to the carbon dioxide flux from solid fuels, liquid fuels, gas fuels, gas flaring, and cement manufacture. The Carbon Dioxide Information Analysis Center (CDIAC) annually calculates emissions of CO_2 from the burning of fossil fuels and the manufacture of cement for most of the countries of the world. Estimates of total and per capita national emissions do not include bunker fuels used in international transport because of the difficulty of apportioning these fuels among countries benefiting from that transport. Emissions from bunker fuels are shown separately for the country where the fuel was delivered.

Emissions of CO_2 are often calculated and reported in terms of their content of elemental carbon. CDIAC reports them that way. For this table, CDIAC's figures were converted to the actual mass by 3.664 (the ratio of the mass of carbon to that of CO_2).

Solid, liquid, and gas fuels are primarily, but not exclusively, coals, petroleum products, and natural gas. Gas flaring is the practice of burning off gas released in the process of petroleum extraction, a practice that is declining. During cement manufacture, cement is calcined to produce calcium oxide. In the process, 0.498 metric ton of CO_2 is released for each metric ton of cement produced. Total emissions consist of the sum of the CO_2 produced during the consumption of solid, liquid, and gas fuels, and from gas flaring and the manufacture of cement.

Combustion of different fossil fuels releases CO_2 at different rates for the same level of energy production. Burning oil releases about 1.5 times the amount of CO_2 released from burning natural gas; burning coal releases about twice as much CO_2 as natural gas.

Table 14-9. Globally threatened species: mammals, birds, and higher plants, late 1990s. The total number of known species may include introductions in some instances. Data on mammals exclude cetaceans (whales and porpoises), except where otherwise indicated. Threatened bird species are listed for countries included within their breeding or wintering ranges. Higher plants refer to numbers of native vascular plant species, as totals are of full species only, rather than of species and subspecies. The number of endemic species refers to those species known to be found only within the countries listed. Figures are not necessarily comparable among countries because taxonomic concepts and the extent of knowledge vary (for the latter reason, country totals of species and endemics may be underestimates). In general, numbers of mammals and birds are fairly well known, while plants have not been as well inventoried.

The World Conservation Union classifies threatened and endangered species in six categories.

Endangered. "Taxa in danger of extinction and whose survival is unlikely if the causal factors continue operating."

Vulnerable. "Taxa believed likely to move into the endangered category in the near future if the causal factors continue operating."

Rare. "Taxa with world populations that are not at present endangered or vulnerable, but are at risk."

Indeterminate. "Taxa known to be endangered, vulnerable, or rare but where there is not enough information to say which of the three categories is appropriate."

Out of danger. "Taxa formerly included in one of the above categories, but which are now considered relatively secure because effective conservation measures have been taken or the previous threat to their survival has been removed."

Insufficiently known. "Taxa that are suspected but not definitely known to belong to any of the above categories."

The number of threatened species listed for all countries includes full species that are endangered, vulnerable, rare, indeterminate, and insufficiently known, but excludes introduced species or those known to be extinct.

Number of species per 10,000 square kilometers provides a relative estimate for comparing numbers of species among countries of differing size. Because the relationship between area and species number is nonlinear (that is, as the area sampled increases, the number of new species located decreases), a species-area curve has been used to standardize these species numbers.

Table 14-10. Globally threatened species: reptiles, amphibians, and fish, late 1990s. Threatened marine turtles and marine fish are excluded from country totals. Endangered fish species numbers do not include approximately 250 haplochromine and 2 tilapiine species of Lake Victoria cichlids, since the ranges of these species are undetermined.

The number of species per 10,000 square kilometers provides a relative estimate for comparing numbers of species among countries of differing size.

Table 14-11. National protection of natural areas, 1999. All protected areas combine natural areas in five World Conservation Union (formerly the International Union for Conservation of Nature and Natural Resources, IUCN), management categories (areas at least 1,000 hectares).

Totally protected areas are maintained in a natural state and are closed to extractive uses. They encompass the following three management categories: *category I,* scientific reserves and strict nature reserves; *category II,* national parks and provincial parks; and *category III,* natural monuments and natural landmarks.

Partially protected areas are areas that may be managed for specific uses, such as recreation or tourism, or areas that provide optimum conditions for certain species or communities of wildlife. Some extractive use within these areas is allowed. They encompass two management categories: *category IV,* managed nature reserves wildlife sanctuaries; and *category V,* protected landscapes and seascapes.

Protected areas between at least 100,000 hectares and 1 million hectares in size refer to all IUCN category I–V protected areas that fall within these two classifications.

IUCN has an additional management category, category VI, which includes areas "managed mainly for the sustainable use of natural ecosystems." These areas contain predominantly unmodified natural systems, managed to ensure long-term protection and maintenance of biological diversity, while also pro-

viding a sustainable flow of natural products and services to meet community needs.

Marine protected areas include protected areas in any of the IUCN categories (I–VI) that are marine or have a marine component IUCN defines a "marine protected area" as "any area of intertidal or subtidal terrain, together with its overlying water and associated flora and fauna, historical and cultural features, which has been reserved by law or other effective means to protect part or all of the enclosed environment." Marine protected areas (MPAs) include areas that are fully marine as well as arreas that have only a small area of intertidal land. Many of these MPAs have large terrestrial areas. The extent of the marine portion of most protected areas is rarely documented. The degree of protection varies from one country to another, and it may bear little relationship to the legal status of any site. The categories of *marine* and *littoral* are not exclusive. One protected area can be littoral and marine, therefore adding numbers under these two different categories may produce a higher number than the total for MPAs. Littoral is defined as any site that is known to incorporate at least some intertidal area. Such sites can also include marine and/or terrestrial elements. All sites with mangrove and saltmarsh communities are recorded as littoral. Marine is defined as any site that is known to incorporate at least some subtidal area permanently submerged under the ocean. Such sites can also include littoral and terrestrial elements. All sites with coral reefs and seagrasses are recorded as marine.

The values in this table do not include locally or provincially protected sites, or privately owned areas.

Table 14-12. International protected areas, 1999. Internationally protected areas usually include sites that are listed under national protection systems.

Biosphere reserves are representative of terrestrial and coastal environments that have been internationally recognized under the Man and the Biosphere Programme of UNESCO.

World heritage sites represent areas of "outstanding universal value" for their natural features, their cultural value, or for both natural and cultural values. The table includes only natural and mixed natural and cultural sites.

Any party to the Convention on Wetlands of International Importance, Especially as Waterfowl Habitat that agrees to respect the site's integrity and to establish wetland reserves can designate wetlands of international importance.

Marine and coastal protected areas refer to all protected areas greater than 1,000 hectares with littoral, coral, island, marine, or estuarine components. The area given is the whole protected area.

Bibliography

Association for the Development of African Education. 1995. *A Statistical Profile of Education in Sub-Saharan Africa, 1990–93*. Paris.

Candoy-Sekse, Rebecca. 1988. *Techniques of Privatization of State-Owned Enterprises. Volume III. Inventory of Country Experience and Reference Materials*. World Bank Technical Paper 90. Washington, D.C.

Central African Republic, Division of Statistics and Economic Studies. 1994. "Enquete prioritaire sur les conditions de vie des menages." Bangui.

Club of Rome. 1972. The Limit to Growth. Rome.

Côte d'Ivoire, Institut National de Statistique. 1994. "Enquete prioritaire." Abidjan.

Currency Data & Intelligence Inc. Monthly. *Global Currency Report*. New York.

Floyd, Robert, Clive Gray, and R. P. Short. 1984. *Public Enterprise in Mixed Economies: Some Macro-economic Aspects*. Washington, D.C.: International Monetary Fund.

Food and Agriculture Organization (FAO). 1987. *Agrostat Code Book*. Rome.

___. annual. *Fertilizer Yearbook*. Rome.

___. annual. *Food and Agriculture Organization Production Yearbook*. Rome.

___. annual. *Food Aid in Figures*. Rome.

___. annual. *Trade Yearbook*. Rome.

___. annual. *Yearbook of Forest Products*. Rome.

Galal, Ahmed. 1990. "Public Enterprise Reform: A Challenge for the World Bank." PRE Working Paper 407. World Bank, Country Economics Department, Washington, D.C. Processed

___. 1991. Public Enterprise Reform: Lessons from the Past and Issues for the Future. World Bank Discussion Paper 119. Washington, D.C.

The Gambia, Ministry of Finance. 1993. "Report on the 1992 Priority Survey." Banjul.

Grootaert, Christian, and Timothy Marchant. 1991. *The Social Dimensions of Adjustment Priority Survey: An Instrument for the Rapid Identification and Monitoring of Policy Targeting Groups.* SDA Working Paper 12. Washington, D.C.: World Bank.

Guinea, Ministry of Planning and Finance. 1991. "Rapport Final: Enquete sur les informations prioritaire: Dimensions Sociales de l'Adjustment Structurel." Conakry.

Guinea-Bissau, National Institute of Statistics and Census. 1992. "Relatorio Final: Inquerito Ligeiro Junto as Familias." Bissau.

Hemming, Richard, and Ali M. Mansoor. 1988. *Privatization and Public Enterprises.* IMF Occasional Paper 56. Washington, D.C.

International Energy Agency (IEA). 1996. *Energy Statistics and Balances of Non-OECD Countries, 1993–94.* Paris.

International Labour Organization (ILO). annual. *Yearbook of Labor Statistics.* Geneva.

____. 1968. *International Standard Classification of Occupations.* Geneva.

____. 1987. *World Labor Report* 1. Oxford: Oxford University Press.

International Monetary Fund (IMF). 1986. Manual on Government Finance Statistics. Washington, D.C.

____. 1993. *Balance of Payments Manual,* Fifth ed. Washington, D.C.

____. annual. *Balance of Payments Yearbook.* Washington, D.C.

____. annual. *Government Finance Statistics Yearbook.* Washington, D.C.

____. monthly. *International Financial Statistics.* Washington, D.C.

____. various issues. *Recent Economic Development.* Washington, D.C.

International Road Federation. 1995. *World Road Statistics, 1990–94.* Geneva.

International Telecommunication Union (ITU). 1995. *World Telecommunication Development Report.* Geneva.

Jager, William, and Charles Humphreys. 1988. "The Effect of Policy Reforms on Africa." *American Journal of Agricultural Economics* 70 (50): 1036–43.

Kenya, Central Bureau of Statistics. 1993. "Welfare Monitoring Survey." Nairobi.

Metallgesellschaft AG. annual. *Metallstatistik.* Frankfurt am Main.

Mukui, John Thinguri. 1994. "Kenya: Poverty Profiles, 1982–92." Prepared for the Office of the Vice-President and Ministry of Planning and National Development, Nairobi, Kenya.

Nair, Govindan, and Anastosios Filppides. 1988. "How Much Do State-Owned Enterprises Contribute to Public Sector Deficits in Developing Countries?" PPR Working Paper 45. World Bank, Development Economics Vice Presidency, Washington, D.C. Processed.

Organisation for Economic Cooperation and Development (OECD). Various issues. Geographical Distribution of Financial Flows to Developing Countries. Paris.

Republic of South Africa. 1990. *South Africa Statistics.* Pretoria: Government Printer.

Swanson, Daniel, and Teferra Wolde-Semait. 1989. *Africa's Public Enterprise Sector and Evidence of Reforms.* World Bank Technical Paper 95. Washington, D.C.

Uganda, Ministry of Finance and Economic Planning. 1993. "Report on the Uganda National Integrated Household Survey 1992–93." Entebbe.

United Nations. 1950. *Index Numbers of Industrial Production*. New York.

___. 1989. *Compendium of Statistics and Indicators on the Situation of Women*. New York.

___. 1992. *The World's Women, 1970–90*. New York.

___. annual. *Population and Vital Statistics Report*. New York.

___. annual. *Yearbook. G., International Trade Statistics*. New York.

United Nations Children's Fund (UNICEF). annual. *The State of the World's Children*. New York.

United Nations Development Programme (UNDP). 1994. Human Development Report 1994. New York.

United Nations Development Programme and the World Bank. 1989. *African Economic and Financial Data*. Washington, D.C.

___. 1992. *African Development Indicators*. Washington, D.C.

United Nations Program on HIV/AIDS (UNAIDS). 1998. "Report on the Global HIV/AIDS Epidemic." Geneva.

United Nations Statistical Office (UNSO). 1975, 1986. "United National Standard International Trade Classification," revisions 2 and 3 (SITC, rev. 2 and 3). Statistical Papers, series M. no. 34, rev. 2 and 3. New York.
___. *United Nations International Standard Classification of All Economic Activities*, revision 2 (ISIC, rev. 2). New York.

___. annual. *Energy Statistics Yearbook*. New York.

United Nations Educational, Scientific, and Cultural Organization (UNESCO). 1982. Conferences of Ministers of Education and Those Responsible for Economic Planning in African Member States. Paris.

___. 1986. *Regional Bulletin of Education Statistics BREDA – STAT*. Regional Office for Education in Africa. Paris.

___. 1989. *Trends and Projections of Enrollment by Level of Education and by Age, 1960–2025 (as assessed in 1989)*. Division of Statistics on Education. Paris.

___. 1990. *Basic Education and Literacy: World Statistical Indicators*. Paris.

___. annual. *Statistical Yearbook*. Paris.

Wadda, Rohey, and Russel Craig. 1993. "Report on the 1992 Priority Survey." Central Statistics, Ministry of Finance and Economic Affairs, Banjul, The Gambia.

World Bank. 1988. *Education in Sub-Saharan Africa: Policies for Adjustment, Revitalization, and Expansion*. Washington, D.C.

___. 1993a. "Africa Adjustment Study P.E. Sector Reform: Case Studies." Washington, D.C. Processed.

___. 1993b. "Public Enterprise Reform and Privatization in Africa." Washington, D.C. Processed.

___. 1994a. "Kenya Poverty Assessment." Eastern Africa Department, Africa Region. Washington, D.C.

___. 1994b. "A Statistical Profile of Education in Sub-Saharan Africa in the 1980s." Africa Technical Department. Washington, D.C. Processed.

___. 1994c. *World Population Projections, 1994-95*. Washington, D.C.

___. 1994d. "Zambia Poverty Assessment." Southern Africa Department. Washington D.C.

___. 1995. *Bureaucrats in Business*. New York: Oxford University Press.

___. annual. *Commodity Trade and Price Trends.* Washington, D.C.

___. annual. *Global Development Finance* (was *World Debt Tables* up to 1996).

___. annual. *World Bank Atlas.* Washington, D.C.

___. annual. World Debt Tables (until 1996; now Global Development Finance). Washington, D.C.

___. annual. *World Development Indicators.* Washington, D.C.

___. annual. *World Development Report.* New York: Oxford University Press.

World Resources Institute. 2000. *World Resources 2000.* Washington, D.C.

World Resources Institute. 1998. *World Resources, 1998–99.* Washington, D.C.

___. 1996. *World Resources 1996–97.* Washington, D.C.

World Bureau of Metal Statistics. monthly. *World Metal Statistics.* London.

World Health Organization (WHO). annual. *World Health Statistics Annual.* Geneva.

___. various issues. *World Health Statistics Quarterly.* Geneva.

Zambia, Central Statistical Office. 1993. "Social Dimensions of Adjustment: Priority Survey I, 1991." Lusaka.